THE
HOLLYWOOD MUSICAL

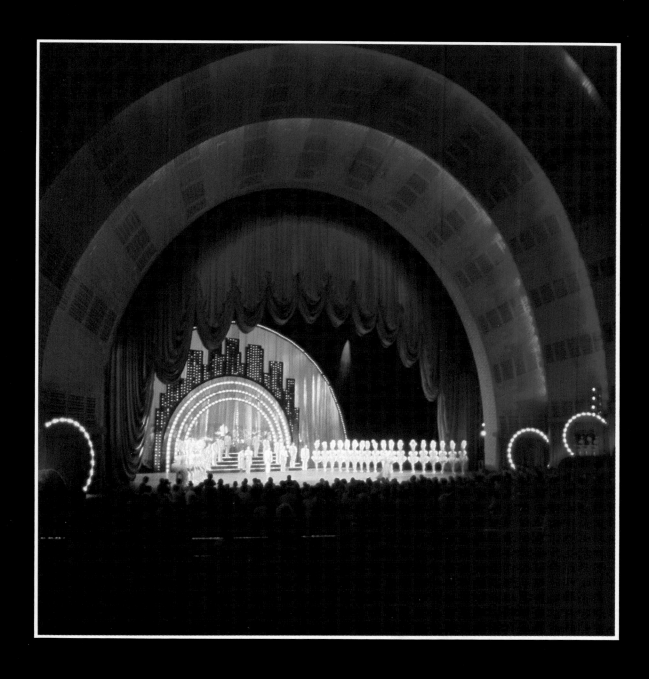

THE
HOLLYWOOD MUSICAL

CLIVE HIRSCHHORN

PORTLAND HOUSE
New York

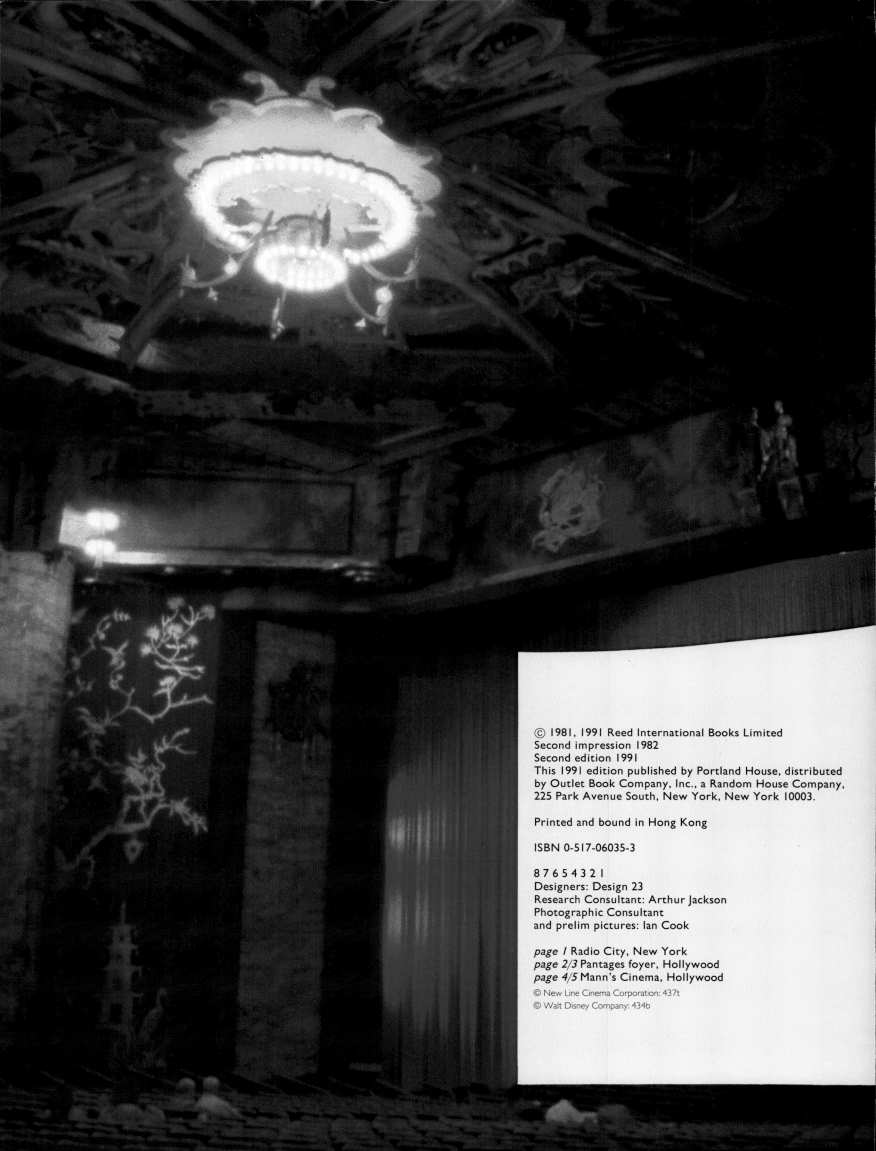

© 1981, 1991 Reed International Books Limited
Second impression 1982
Second edition 1991
This 1991 edition published by Portland House, distributed
by Outlet Book Company, Inc., a Random House Company,
225 Park Avenue South, New York, New York 10003.

Printed and bound in Hong Kong

ISBN 0-517-06035-3

8 7 6 5 4 3 2 1
Designers: Design 23
Research Consultant: Arthur Jackson
Photographic Consultant
and prelim pictures: Ian Cook

page 1 Radio City, New York
page 2/3 Pantages foyer, Hollywood
page 4/5 Mann's Cinema, Hollywood

CONTENTS

FOREWORD

A book such as this surely deserves to be credited with that most wonderful cliché – 'an idea whose time has come', and those of us who have worked hard and long in the field of music and dance will welcome it warmly. True, many good books have been written before, but as far as I know none is as all-embracing as this one. I know it will prove indispensable to the thousands of young people who are studying film seriously in colleges and universities throughout the world, as well as being a source of great joy to every film buff. Like *The Guinness Book of Records* and the Wallace family's *Book of Lists*, I can see it now, being thumbed through to settle bets made in bars, classrooms, or even after academic lectures. Just thinking of all the fights it may stop stamps it as worthwhile.

Then, too, there will be the fanatics like myself who will just love to pick it up and browse through titles, credits and the years the films were produced, saying to themselves 'Was it that long ago?', or 'Why, I must have seen that when I was eighteen – that was *our* song'. How many of us remember old loves, school days, even war-time, through the songs and dances of the musicals of the periods involved. Perhaps nothing else does more to revive memories of faces and places – and for me they are very pleasant memories.

The members of the group who worked at MGM during my tenure there were very serious about musicals. That is not to say that we didn't make them to entertain and uplift the spirit, but we thought that to do this effectively they had to be superbly crafted; and that meant the closest kind of collaboration among the choreographers, directors, producers, musicians, conductors, musical arrangers, designers, costumiers – the list is endless. There were probably more assembled talents in this field at Metro than anywhere else at any other time. Yet we mustn't forget that, overwhelming as MGM was in numbers, other studios possessed a great share of entertainers and creators, and also contributed immensely to the world of musical pictures.

Again, each studio contributed much to the historical changes in the field, starting with **The Jazz Singer**, progressing into European-style operetta, lavish extravaganzas, then more and more into shows that integrated story, song and dance with ever-developing skills.

An all-encompassing reference book of this kind does one other important thing – it illuminates the source from which many of the finished works sprang. This has been, I think, one of the major gaps in many previous publications. If one adds up all the people who worked in this field since the beginning of sound pictures the total is much more, I believe, than the average film-goer realizes. And now this same film-goer, through this book, will be able to comprehend more fully the contribution of all those people who are often forgotten.

So here it is at last – a complete source book; one that will not only serve as the ultimate in reference guides but will rectify and remedy many of the things that have been overlooked in the past.

Gene Kelly

This book
is dedicated to

the many talented men and women whose particular skills behind
the scenes have enhanced the good name of the Hollywood musical. To
most of them you will not be able to attach a face but their contributions to the
genre were incalculable. First and foremost were the musical men themselves:
arrangers, conductors and orchestrators who took the tunes provided by the composers and embellished them with a 'sound' unique to their own studio. At MGM Herbert
Stothart, Conrad Salinger, Skip Martin, Adolph Deutsch, Saul Chaplin, Georgie Stoll, vocal
arranger Ken Darby (who later went to 20th Century-Fox), Kay Thompson, Johnny Green,
Leo Arnaud, Lennie Hayton and André Previn helped many a song to achieve immortality; while
doing the same at 20th Century-Fox were Alfred Newman, Herbert Spencer, Charles Henderson,
Earl Hagen, Emil Newman, Louis Silver, Edward B. Powell and Arthur Lange. Paramount had
Robert Emmett Dolan, Victor Young, Joseph J. Lilley and Van Cleave; and Warner Bros. had Leo
Forbstein, Max Steiner, Heinz Roemheld and Ray Heindorf. Helping to set the fashions of the day
were the studios' brilliant and versatile costume designers, the best of them being Irene Sharaff,
Adrian, Helen Rose, Walter Plunkett (all of whom worked for MGM, Plunkett joining the studio in
1947 after eleven years at RKO), Orry-Kelly (Warner Bros. and 20th Century-Fox), Royer, Yvonne
Wood, Travis Banton, William Travilla and Gwen Wakeling (20th Century-Fox), Edith Head
(Universal) and Jean Louis at Columbia. Cedric Gibbons was the name on almost every MGM
film for decades as art director; Richard Day and Lyle Wheeler were responsible for the way
many of the musicals at 20th Century-Fox looked; and Van Nest Polglase and Carroll Clarke for
the art deco sheen of the Astaire/Rogers offerings at RKO. Anton Grot and Carl Jules Weyl
were the two heavyweight art directors at Warner Bros. in the thirties and forties, and
Paramount's top man was Hans Dreier. Finally, as in the last moments of **Singin' In
The Rain** (MGM, 1952), I'd like to pull back the curtain and pay tribute to those
unseen heroes and heroines who dubbed the voices for so many of the stars, who
would not otherwise have made names for themselves in the musical cinema.
They include Nan Wynn, Martha Mears, Jo Ann Greer, Anita Ellis (all
of whom dubbed for Rita Hayworth – Miss Ellis also vocalizing for
Vera-Ellen), Betty Wand, Trudy Erwin, Carole Richards, Marni
Nixon, Lisa Kirk, Bill Lee and Bill Shirley. Without
them, and all the other 'behind the camera' talents,
the Hollywood musical would simply not
have been possible.

AUTHOR'S ACKNOWLEDGEMENTS

This book has been made possible by the invaluable assistance of many people who have given unstintingly of their
time and expertise.

First and foremost I should like to acknowledge the efforts
of Robyn Karney who, in an editorial capacity, supervised
every stage from inception to completion with a sharp and
critical eye.

I am also greatly indebted to Tom Vallance who gave so
generously of his own extensive knowledge – and his
enthusiasm – in helping to make the book as complete a
record as possible. To George Baxt in New York my heartfelt
thanks for bringing his specialized knowledge of musicals to
bear on both the text and the illustrations; and to Arthur
Jackson in Cornwall my gratitude for putting his extensive list
of credits and song titles at my disposal. The efforts of my
researcher, Corin Moore, who spent literally hundreds of
hours ferreting out obscure information, cannot be over-
estimated either. In this regard my thanks also to Karen
Press. Gilbert Adair and Ronald Bergan both contributed
substantially to the book, and other much appreciated
assistance was given by Tony Slide, Lucy Saroyan and Sam

Gill of the Academy of Motion Picture Arts and Sciences in
Beverly Hills; Monty Arnold, Paul Myers, Dorothy Swerd-
love, David Bartholomew, Donald Fowle, Dr Roderick Bladel,
Dan Patrie and Max Silverman of the Library of Performing
Arts, Lincoln Centre, New York; Peter Seward, Susan Julian-
Huxley, Linda Wood, Brenda Davies, Gillian Hartnoll, Pat
Terilli, Janice Headland and Sandra Archer of the British
Film Institute; The American Film Institute; Mary Corliss of
the Museum of Modern Art, New York; the Stills Archive of
the British Film Institute. My thanks also to Gene Kelly, Lois
McClelland, Ray Block, Eddie Brandt's Saturday Matinee,
Movie Star News, Erik Spilker, Jim Simpson, Madeleine
Harmsworth, Barbara Roett, Dick Vosburgh, Frank Lazarus,
Maxine Andrews, Bill Bast, Tony Sloman, Bernard Hrusa-
Marlow, Reginald Wright, Neil Stevens, Miles Kreuger, Chris
Hahn, Lois Butlin, Susan Wallis, David Watkinson, Bob
Grimes, Rodger Hambleton, Ken Sephton, Howard Mandel-
baum, Vyvyan Cole, Allen L. Salyers and Peter McKriel. I am
indebted too, to the following publications: The New York
Times, The Motion Picture Herald, Kine Weekly, The
Monthly Film Bulletin and Variety.

AUTHOR'S NOTE

Despite my lifelong love and experience of the Hollywood musical I really did not appreciate just how mammoth a number of films over the past 50 years could have a strong case made for their inclusion when I began writing this book. *The Hollywood Musical* aims to be as complete a record of the genre as possible, but clearly it was essential, very early on, to establish workable guidelines as to what constitutes a 'musical'. The decision was a difficult one to make and, necessarily, had to be subjective.

There are no problems with films like **Top Hat** (RKO, 1935), **Coney Island** (20th Century-Fox, 1943), **Singin' In The Rain** (MGM, 1952) or **The Band Wagon** (MGM, 1953). They are quintessential Hollywood musicals whose inclusion in such a book is both automatic and obvious. But what of a film like **Rhapsody** (MGM, 1954)? To many it might be considered a romantic drama with music, rather than a musical. The point is debatable. I believe its inclusion to be justified because its musical content is sufficiently important to the story. On the other hand, a film such as Robert Altman's **A Perfect Couple** (20th Century-Fox, 1979) is not listed as a main entry despite the many songs featured in it. In my opinion the music is not central to the plot, and the film's fundamental concern would in no way be altered had the female protagonist been a model or an actress rather than a pop singer.

Yet, despite exercising all possible care, grey areas still remain. I have attempted to clarify these by including a section at the back of the book which lists films, like **A Perfect Couple**, whose musical content cannot, in all fairness, be overlooked but which, in my personal judgement, can hardly be labelled as a musical. Into this category (which I have called 'fringe' musicals) I have also placed Republic's **Magic Fire** (1956) – a biopic of Richard Wagner—whereas Columbia's **A Song To Remember** (1945) and **Song Without End** (1960) – biopics of Chopin and Liszt—appear as fully-fledged entries. My reason for this is that the excerpts in the first film are too abbreviated to do justice to their composer and are unsatisfying, whereas in the Chopin and Liszt biopics the musical content is altogether more representative of the two composers.

Certain films whose musical programme is fairly substantial do not feature in the book at all: films such as **The Roaring Twenties** (Warner Bros, 1939), **Road House** (20th Century-Fox, 1948), and Paramount's **Dark City** (1950) which has a total of five songs in it. None of these films can be considered a musical. The songs in them exist merely as interludes and are in no way integral to the plot.

The same, I realize, might be said of films such as **You'll Find Out** (RKO, 1940), which *does* appear in the main text. The reason for its inclusion is that its star, Kay Kyser, was a popular band leader whose music-making, together with Ginny Simms, Ish Kabibble, Harry Babbit and Sully Mason, were what the audiences of 1943 paid to see.

Musicals such as **Happy-Go-Lovely** (1950), **A Hard Day's Night** (1964), **Help!** (1965), **The Yellow Submarine** (1968), **Oliver!** (1968), **Chitty Chitty Bang Bang** (1969), **Tommy** (1970), **Scrooge** (1970) and **The Slipper And The Rose** (1976) are not listed in the book at all; for although in some instances they involved American finance, or, in others, American creative talent, they were essentially British,

having been made by British technicians at British studios. At the same time, I have made four exceptions to the rule: **I Could Go On Singing** (United Artists, 1963), **Half A Sixpence** (Paramount, 1971), **The Boy Friend** (MGM, 1971) and **The Rocky Horror Picture Show** (20th Century-Fox, 1975). All four, strictly speaking, do not belong in a book such as this. Yet how could I omit Judy Garland's last film, which also happened to be a musical? **Half A Sixpence** appears solely because it was directed by George Sidney, another of the genre's heavyweights; while **The Boy Friend** justifies its inclusion because it paid homage to the Hollywood musical in general and to Busby Berkeley in particular. Similarly, my decision to include **The Rocky Horror Picture Show** was based on the fact that it too drew its inspiration from Hollywood – in this instance from the vintage Universal horror movie. That it has also become something of a cult film in the United States further influenced my decision.

Films such as **A Funny Thing Happened On The Way To The Forum** (United Artists, 1966), **Dr Dolittle** (20th Century-Fox, 1967), **Goodbye Mr Chips** (MGM, 1969), **Song Of Norway** (ABC, 1970), **Willie Wonka And The Chocolate Factory** (David Wolper Productions, 1971), **Fiddler On The Roof** (United Artists, 1971), **The Little Prince** (Paramount, 1972), **Man of La Mancha** (United Artists, 1972), **Jesus Christ Superstar** (Universal, 1973) etc. are included, as they are all American projects filmed on location outside the USA.

Because of their limited release I have completely omitted the dozens of all-black low-budget musicals made throughout the forties – films such as Herald's **Miracle In Harlem** (1948), **Boy What A Girl** (1947), Famous Films' **Hi-De-Ho** (1947) with Cab Calloway, and Astor Pictures' **Look Out Sister** (1948). Nor are featurettes (such as Walt Disney's **Saludos Amigos**, RKO, 1943) included, nor the plethora of Western musicals starring singing cowboys Gene Autry, Dick Foran, Roy Rogers and Tex Ritter.

Apart from the previously mentioned 'fringe' musicals, the book contains two further appendices: a catalogue of American International and other low-budget rock 'n' roll, twist and 'beach party' musicals of the fifties and sixties; and a list of important documentaries, such as **Woodstock** (Warner Bros, 1970) and **Gimme Shelter** (Cinema V, 1970).

Academy Award winners and nominations are not, as a rule, specifically mentioned in the text, but a special panel containing the lists of Academy Awards (and nominations), the New York Film Critics' Awards, the New York Times Annual 'Ten Best' Awards and the top moneymaking films, all pertaining to musicals mentioned in the main body of the book, appears at the beginning of each year. The first Academy Awards were presented on 16th May 1929 for the years 1927 and 1928. This practice continued until 1934 when the awards were no longer presented on a split year basis; hence those in 1935 covered the year 1934 only.

Despite my efforts to make careful and sensible distinctions as to what should be included in the various sections of the book, I remain painfully aware that there will always be room for disagreement. To those readers who may sometimes be disappointed by the choices I have opted for, I can only repeat that choices had to be made, and I crave their indulgence accordingly.

Clive Hirschhorn London, 1980

INTRODUCTION

The musical was the only new cinematic genre to be born with the coming of the 'talkers' (as the first sound pictures were initially called) and, like many an infant, among the first words it uttered was 'Mammy'. Though there were better films in 1927 than **The Jazz Singer** (Warner Bros.), it was Samson Raphaelson's shamelessly sentimental story, and Al Jolson in blackface singing that famous song, that brought the Hollywood musical into being. If we are still touched by **The Jazz Singer** today, it is largely because of its pioneering aspect.

Though initially dependent on its parents – operetta and musical comedy – for inspiration, the screen musical was soon recognized as a vital art form in its own right, and the many changes of public taste, which more than once threatened its survival, have never managed to kill it off completely. In the 50 years or so since its birth, the musical has proved itself to be the phoenix of the film industry. Unlike perennials such as Westerns and war and crime films, it is the musical alone that periodically disappears, only to rise again from the ashes to prove that reports of its demise are greatly exaggerated. Thanks to some creative genius who has always been there to impart the kiss of life when it was most needed, Hollywood has produced at least one excellent musical every year up until the sixties. Among the greatest of these *auteurs* were Ernst Lubitsch, Rouben Mamoulian, Busby Berkeley, Arthur Freed, Vincente Minnelli, Gene Kelly and Stanley Donen. And even in the seventies, a decade characterized by radical upheavals in taste and form, there have been produced several felicities such as **Cabaret** (Allied Artists, 1972), the second remake of **A Star Is Born** (Warner Bros., 1976), **New York, New York** (United Artists, 1977), **The Rose** (20th Century-Fox, 1979) – a brilliant recreation of the sixties rock scene, and **All That Jazz** (Columbia, 1980). Along with these movies came another wave of names and personalities to revitalize respect for the genre: Bob Fosse, Barbra Streisand, Liza Minnelli and Bette Midler.

IN THE BEGINNING

Most film musicals of the late twenties and early thirties were stagy and static, and the novelty of sound, even with two-colour Technicolor, was not enough to hold the public. As in the fifties when Hollywood thought that new technical advances would coax people out of the comfort of their homes, so it was with the arrival of sound in the twenties. The major studios believed in the talisman of the new toy but they neglected to learn how to use it properly. It was Irving Thalberg, the 'boy wonder' at MGM, who foresaw the possibilities inherent in the film musical – possibilities undreamed of in the philosophy of those who were indiscriminately flooding the screen with mindless 'all talking, all singing, all dancing' attractions. Thalberg asked composer Nacio Herb Brown and lyricist Arthur Freed to create new songs especially for **The Broadway Melody**, thereby starting a tradition that would spawn not only some of the best musicals ever made but also an impressive number of skilled songwriting teams. It was not long before the giants of popular music – George and Ira Gershwin, Irving Berlin, Cole Porter, Jerome Kern, Richard Rodgers and Lorenz Hart – were writing screen originals.

Thalberg's thinking bore other important fruit: in 1929, when the screen musical was a mere two years old, **The Broadway Melody** won the first Oscar for a sound movie and, with it, the brash *parvenu* had arrived to stay. **The Broadway Melody** was significant in several ways, not least for the approval it won from the Academy of Motion Picture Arts and Sciences. It was also MGM's first venture into sound and the first of what was to become the most durable stand-by of the entire genre, the 'backstage musical'.

Because there were so many obstacles to overcome in the industry's conversion to sound, it was an exciting period for anyone willing to accept the challenge. Among the major problems were the cumbersome and stationary camera, and the poor quality of the sound recording. Before the camera became more mobile, dancing could not really be conceived spatially and most dance routines seemed flat and lifeless. Singers had fewer problems in that they could just stand still and sing.

As well as the technical difficulties, there were contextual problems. What worked on the musical stage would not work in the musical film, so new aesthetics had to be conceived. The realistic eye of the camera, through which the subjective eye of the director stared, demanded more than simply filmed theatre. Musical numbers, if they were to break from their stage conventions, had to be structured in the cutting-room. Dance directors now needed to be more than choreographers: they had to possess an understanding of the visual demands of film, while directors needed a definite musical sensibility. Filmed theatre was quickly rejected and stories and screenplays were sought which were created specifically with the screen in mind, and whose music was integral to the plot.

Few film makers, however, realized that the musical numbers, no matter how good, ought to grow naturally out of the texture of the work. It was Rouben Mamoulian and Ernst Lubitsch who first recognized that the film musical could have a freedom and a flexibility unacceptable in most other, more 'realistic' genres. Their European backgrounds helped bring a much needed sophistication to Hollywood and, being well-versed in the tradition of operetta, they knew that characters did not need a naturalistic excuse to burst into song. Lubitsch's **The Love Parade** (Paramount, 1929) pointed the way forward, and two more excellent examples of the technique followed: Mamoulian's **Love Me Tonight** (Paramount, 1932) and Lubitsch's **The Merry Widow** (MGM, 1934). Most film makers, however, felt that the only way to introduce song and dance numbers into the narrative was in the context of a show – a belief which led to the popularity and proliferation of the backstage musical and the 'show-within-a-show' format. Nonetheless, there *were* other attempts at originality. King Vidor filmed much of **Hallelujah** (MGM, 1929) on location, proving that sound – which he dubbed in afterwards – and visual poetry need not be contradictory; while David Butler in **Sunnyside Up** (Fox, 1929) imparted a refreshing spontaneity to the story of a Manhattan slum girl's romance with a handsome millionaire.

Broadway, vaudeville, and even opera stars were lured west by the 'talkers'. But it soon became apparent that stars in one medium did not necessarily shine in another, even though they were musical or dramatic artists. Among those from the musical stage who did achieve screen stardom were Helen Morgan, Eddie Cantor, Jeanette MacDonald, Maurice Chevalier and the Marx Brothers, while some notable casualties included George Jessel, Ann Pennington and Irene Bordoni. But whether they succeeded or not, there were so many performers in Hollywood hoping to immortalize themselves on celluloid between 1929 and 1930 that the studios tried to squeeze as many of them at a time into one film. Thus the film revue was born, consisting usually of a string of unrelated numbers and serving as little more than a showcase for its stars. The revue, which from time to time appeared disguised as another popular musical stand-by, the biographical picture (biopic), was never very satisfactory as it tended to lack artistic unity. The very first movie revue was **Hollywood Revue of 1929** (MGM), and it introduced the Nacio Herb Brown/Arthur Freed hit 'Singin' In The Rain', which was to feature in three more movies before finally giving its name to one of the greatest screen musicals ever made. Two of the best examples of the film revue were **Paramount On Parade** (1930), in which Lubitsch directed Chevalier in three sequences, and the extraordinary **King Of Jazz** (Universal, 1930). John Murray Anderson's innovative direction of the latter proved a forerunner to Busby Berkeley's remarkable inventiveness, and the film, shot in beautiful two-colour Technicolor.

THE EARLY THIRTIES
By 1930, four distinct types of movie musical were emerging: the backstage musical, the film revue, the operetta, and the campus musical. The latter genre was typified by **Good News** (MGM, 1930), whose cast of college kids needed little excuse to go into their dance, and in which the hero scored the winning touchdown in the last few seconds of the Big Match (a climax which was to become a regular feature of such movies for the next twenty-odd years).

Songs, however, were not confined to musicals alone, and as soon as the movies found a voice, even non-musicals felt obliged to include a song or two: Marlene Dietrich sang Leo Robin and Karl Hajos's 'Give Me The Man' and 'What Am I Bid?' in Von Sternberg's *Morocco* (Paramount, 1930) – and undeniably enhanced the inherent eroticism of the film.

It was the independent producer Samuel Goldwyn who gave Busby Berkeley his first chance in movies, appointing him as dance director on **Whoopee** (Goldwyn-United Artists, 1930). By so doing, Goldwyn also gave the cinema one of its few undisputed geniuses. Berkeley immediately began to experiment with space and movement and overhead shots, and almost single-handedly liberated the musical from its stagy confines. **Whoopee** was notable, too, in that its leading man, Eddie Cantor, became one of Hollywood's top stars in the early thirties. It also introduced Betty Grable to the screen.

Because so many all-talking, all-dancing, all-singing pictures had been rushed into production in 1929 and 1930, it was inevitable that saturation point would soon be reached, and it was. The public, choking on a surfeit of mindless musicals, turned apathetic, and the major studios declared a moratorium on the genre. By 1931, with the Depression affecting the film industry, there simply wasn't the money to spend on lavish productions, and many projects, such as Jerome Kern's **Men Of The Sky** (Warner Bros., 1931), were abandoned, or shorn of

most of their musical numbers.

All the same, Paramount – the honey-pot which attracted many European directors – found itself in quixotic mood and took a chance in presenting the scintillating **Love Me Tonight** (1932), directed by Rouben Mamoulian with a score by Richard Rodgers and Lorenz Hart. Maurice Chevalier increased his popularity in this, and in two of Lubitsch's most sophisticated *boudoir* operettas, **The Smiling Lieutenant** (1931) and **One Hour With You** (1932), both also for Paramount. Busby Berkeley staged the numbers in two more Eddie Cantor vehicles, **Palmy Days** (Goldwyn-United Artists, 1931) and **The Kid From Spain** (Goldwyn-United Artists 1932) – both calculated to cheer up the most depressed of the Depression-hit people of America.

But despite its occasional felicities, 1931 and 1932 were two lean years for the musical. Then, just as the genre seemed to be *passé*, Darryl F. Zanuck, head of production at Warner Bros., gave the nod to screenwriters Rian James and James Seymour, dance director Busby Berkeley, director Lloyd Bacon and composers Al Dubin and Harry Warren to go ahead with a song and dance show that would be sufficiently different to attract audiences all over again. The result was **42nd Street** (1933) whose great success led the studio to follow it up with two more backstage extravaganzas in the same year: **Gold Diggers Of 1933** and **Footlight Parade**. Though it was Berkeley's kaleidoscopic production numbers that were the really revolutionary aspect of these musicals – making the parts infinitely greater than the whole – the plots nonetheless moved at a brisk pace, the performances were full of verve, and the screenplays abrasive and witty. Nor was the Depression ignored, and the effective 'My Forgotten Man' number from **Gold Diggers Of 1933** – which owed much to German expressionism – was one of the rare social comment numbers to emerge from a musical, balanced by the same film's optimistic opening – 'We're In The Money'. The only musical to use the Depression as its central subject matter and not merely as background was **Hallelujah I'm A Bum** (United Artists, 1933) which starred Al Jolson in his first film for over two years. A box-office failure, it consolidated the opinion expressed in the well known Hollywood aphorism that Western Union, not the movies, was for sending messages.

In 1933, RKO, having faced bankruptcy the previous year, found prosperity with two magnificent pairings – Fay Wray and King Kong; and Fred Astaire and Ginger Rogers, the latter dancing together for the first time in **Flying Down To Rio**. This was the first musical in which the immaculate dancing of the performers took precedence over the actual staging of the numbers. And, although the nine films they made together for RKO contained several elaborate set pieces, it was not the spectacle, but the Astaire-Rogers magic the customers paid to see. Knowing they were on to a good thing, RKO hired the best composers, designers and supporting actors to back up their money-making team, and with 'The Continental' by Con Conrad and Herb Magidson (from **The Gay Divorcee**, 1934) made history by winning the first Oscar to be awarded to a song.

Along with Ginger Rogers, two blondes emerged to dominate the screen: Mae West, seen at her outrageous best in **I'm No Angel** and **She Done Him Wrong** (both Paramount, 1933) until the interfering Hays Code threw a wet blanket over her innuendos and quenched her fire;

and Shirley Temple who, at the age of seven, was as old as the musical itself. Four of her films were released in 1934, making her not only a top box-office draw, but an institution.

The marriage of Ernst Lubitsch to **The Merry Widow** (MGM, 1934) was, indeed, an occasion for rejoicing for, despite the lavish production values provided by the studio, it nonetheless managed to retain that delicate and insouciant 'Lubitsch touch' which characterized his best work both before and after the coming of sound. **The Merry Widow** also marked the end of what many consider to be the most interesting part of Jeanette MacDonald's career, when she was the only singer in pictures who could sing with her tongue in her cheek. And although she still retained a certain amount of sauce, albeit diluted with sugar, her profitable eight-operetta partnership with Nelson Eddy (beginning in 1935 with MGM's **Naughty Marietta**) was no longer characterized by sexual innuendo but by sentimentality.

Over at RKO Irving Berlin provided some top drawer songs for Astaire and Rogers's **Top Hat**; at Paramount Rodgers and Hart were doing the same for Bing Crosby in **Mississippi** (1935), while at Warner Bros. the prolific team of Al Dubin and Harry Warren wrote for Al Jolson and his wife Ruby Keeler in **Go Into Your Dance** (1935). Dubin and Warren, two of the greatest of all Hollywood composers, had previously written the score for **Dames** (Warner Bros. 1934), and for **Gold Diggers Of 1935** (Warner Bros. 1935) they supplied the perennial 'Lullaby of Broadway' which, in turn, inspired Busby Berkeley to new heights of invention and creativity in one of the greatest production numbers in the history of the genre. It was Hollywood's golden era as far as the songs written especially for movies were concerned, many of them becoming part of the folklore of popular American music.

RUN-UP TO THE FORTIES
In 1936 MGM offered the world **The Great Ziegfeld**, a sumptuous, no-expense-spared biopic of the legendary showman in which Luise Rainer became the first actress to win an Oscar for a musical. In the same year MGM scored a second time with the joyous **Born to Dance**, which made a star of the stylish Eleanor Powell.

At Warner Bros. Berkeley continued to create illusions of space and multiple resources with his intricate and fantastical dance routines, but MGM was fast establishing itself as *the* studio for the musical spectacular, and Jack Warner began to lose interest in the genre, concentrating instead on melodramas and non-musical biopics. The last major Warner Bros. musical of the decade was **Gold Diggers Of 1937** (1936), the feeblest of the series, and it was no accident that Berkeley terminated his contract with the studio in 1939 and headed straight for MGM.

A new genre – the animated musical – was created in 1937 with Walt Disney's **Snow White And The Seven Dwarfs** (RKO). Apart from that, there was little that was new or exciting in the Hollywood musical, and its lack of creative energy cued in its second fall from grace. Except for **Snow White**, the only other innovative musical in 1937 was Mamoulian's **High, Wide And Handsome** (Paramount), a musical western with a Jerome Kern/Oscar Hammerstein II score, which successfully fused the naturalistic with the theatrical.

At MGM Jeanette MacDonald and the doggedly unanimated Nelson Eddy continued their series of operettas with **Maytime** (1937), their most lavish movie yet; and the studio continued along the giant's causeway

with **Rosalie** (1937). For RKO, Astaire and Rogers asked the rhetorical question, **Shall We Dance?** (1937) and were answered with a resounding affirmative from their adoring public. But after seven films together, Fred and Ginger developed the seven-film itch and went separate ways for a while. He made **A Damsel In Distress** (RKO, 1937) with the non-dancing, non-singing Joan Fontaine, while she appeared in three straight films.

1937 was also the year in which Universal was rescued from the economic doldrums by a new star, Deanna Durbin who, in her debut in **Three Smart Girls**, sang in an appealingly plummy soprano and became everybody's favourite teenage daughter. There had, of course, been child stars before: Shirley Temple, Jane Withers, and boy soprano Bobby Breen. But Miss Durbin was no tiny tot and, with the emergence of Judy Garland, Mickey Rooney and Donald O'Connor, a new phenomenon was born— the teenage star.

Despite the popularity of the movies, radio was the great mass medium in the thirties and forties, and instead of fighting off this heavyweight competitor, Hollywood wisely used it to let the fans see as well as hear their air wave favourites on the screen. Among the most popular entertainers of the late thirties were Jack Benny, Fred Allen, Kenny Baker, Eddie (Rochester) Anderson, Ben Bernie, George Burns and Gracie Allen, Kate Smith, Frances Langford, and ventriloquist Edgar Bergen with his talking doll Charlie McCarthy. These, and many, many others appeared in a multitude of musicals with a radio background, most notably Paramount's successful *Big Broadcast* series, the 1938 edition giving the world Ralph Rainger and Leo Robin's 'Thanks For The Memory' sung by Bob Hope and Shirley Ross. It became Hope's theme song and the title of a non-musical film.

In 1938 Busby Berkeley, with only one year left to go on his contract at Warner Bros., turned **Hollywood Hotel**, based on the popular radio programme of the same name, into a modest but successful musical entertainment that traversed no new territory, but which gave Hollywood its unofficial theme song in the Johnny Mercer/Richard Whiting number, 'Hooray For Hollywood'. Not one radio-inspired musical turned out to be a world-beater, but several of them did contain incidental pleasures.

1938 saw the emergence of the 20th Century-Fox big-budget black and white musical with **Alexander's Ragtime Band**, starring Alice Faye and Tyrone Power; while the two major musicals of the year at MGM were **The Great Waltz**, a luxurious biopic of Johann Strauss II, and **Sweethearts**, the first Jeanette MacDonald/Nelson Eddy vehicle in Technicolor. Though all three were box-office successes, it wasn't until **The Wizard Of Oz** (MGM) the following year, that the musical received its much-needed shot in the arm. The first musical masterpiece in Technicolor, it brilliantly integrated sets, costumes, screenplay and score (by Harold Arlen and E.Y. Harburg), featured one of the most popular songs ever to emerge from Hollywood ('Over The Rainbow') and turned 17-year-old Judy Garland into a major star. The same year, songwriter Arthur Freed, who was the assistant producer to Mervyn LeRoy on **Oz**, was given his first assignment as a fully-fledged producer with **Babes In Arms** (MGM), a move which resulted, a few years later, in his becoming the greatest producer of musicals in Hollywood's history.

At 20th Century-Fox, Al Jolson, now at the end of his career, trundled out his old routines for **Rose Of**

Washington Square (1939) and for the same year's Stephen Foster biopic, **Swanee River**, in which he played minstrel impresario E.P. Christy. Astaire and Rogers starred in **The Story Of Vernon And Irene Castle** (RKO) then called the whole thing off, giving audiences a ten-year wait for their one-off return in MGM's **The Barkleys Of Broadway** (1949). As the new decade began, that other famous Hollywood pair, Jeanette MacDonald and Nelson Eddy were still singing cheek by jowl in the sweet-sweet **Bitter Sweet** (MGM, 1940) and the old **New Moon** (MGM, 1940); while a brand new team was setting off on the first of several roads – all of which led directly to the bank. Bob Hope, Bing Crosby and sarong girl Dorothy Lamour starred in **Road To Singapore** (Paramount, 1940) and, for the remainder of the decade, continued to convulse audiences from Rio to Morocco. America's 'good neighbour' policy with Latin America found strong support at 20th Century-Fox, who introduced the beguilingly original Carmen Miranda to American audiences in **Down Argentine Way** (1940), and then starred her in **That Night In Rio** (1941) and **Weekend In Havana** (1941).

Busby Berkeley made what turned out to be the best film of his new career at MGM with **Babes On Broadway** (1941) – his third with Judy Garland and Mickey Rooney, and the one in which Garland movingly sang 'Chin Up, Cheerio, Carry On' to a group of refugee British kids, indicating that at last the Hollywood musical was becoming less isolationist and was beginning to face up to the fact that there was a war on in Europe.

MUSICALS AT WAR

The bombing of Pearl Harbor in 1941 changed everything. From then on, throughout the rest of the war, musicals were not merely decorative, but functioned as an integral part of the war effort. In **Yankee Doodle Dandy** (Warner Bros. 1942) James Cagney whipped up patriotic fervour with George M. Cohan's 'You're A Grand Old Flag', and won an Oscar for his efforts; Bing Crosby sang a tribute to the same banner in **Star-Spangled Rhythm** (Paramount, 1942) and delivered a patriotic oration atop a studio-built Mount Rushmore; while in MGM's **For Me And My Gal** (1942), Gene Kelly became a soldier in World War I and learned to sacrifice his egotism to his country's needs. Most of the major studios helped to boost morale during the war by mustering all the available talent under contract in all-star revues such as **Stage Door Canteen** (United Artists, 1943), **Thank Your Lucky Stars** (Warner Bros. 1943) and **Hollywood Canteen** (Warner Bros. 1944).

Irving Berlin's **This Is The Army** (Warner Bros. 1943) featured real servicemen in its cast; while **Thousands Cheer** (MGM, 1943), with its pin-prick of a plot, staged a grand finale featuring such guest stars as Mickey Rooney, Judy Garland, Lena Horne, Lucille Ball, Eleanor Powell, Red Skelton and Margaret O'Brien. The war years also produced several B-musicals set in munitions factories – which may account for the popularity of such belters as Betty Hutton, Martha Raye and Cass Daley.

As the guns and tanks came off the assembly lines, so musicals slid off the conveyor belts of Hollywood's dream factories in an attempt to satisfy the public's insatiable demand for more and more escapist entertainment. Helping in no small way to alleviate some of the gloom of those war-torn years were The Andrews Sisters, as well as America's big bands. Some of the most popular of these (Tommy Dorsey, Kay Kyser, Harry James, Glenn Miller, Benny Goodman, Jimmy Dorsey, Xavier Cugat) found their way into eight out of ten musicals. America in the forties had caught swing fever and Hollywood was quick to exploit it, despite the generally colourless personalities of the bandleaders themselves.

In 1943, Vincente Minnelli made his debut as a film director (thanks to the talent-spotting of Arthur Freed) in MGM's all-black **Cabin In The Sky**. Another all-black offering in the same year was 20th Century-Fox's **Stormy Weather**. Though both were criticized for propagating the negro stereotype, they at least allowed black artists to express themselves more than they would otherwise have been permitted to do in the segregation-conscious movies of the time, and left their mark with such memorable numbers as 'Happiness Is A Thing Called Joe' (by Harold Arlen and E.Y. Harburg) sung by Ethel Waters in **Cabin In The Sky**, and the title number of **Stormy Weather** (by Arlen and Ted Koehler), sung by Lena Horne. In 1944, Minnelli established himself as a major director with **Meet Me In St Louis** (MGM), and the film's leading lady, Judy Garland, graduated from star to superstar.

Original songs were still being written by all the top composers, among the best being Jerome Kern's 'Long Ago And Far Away' from **Cover Girl** (Columbia, 1944), the film that marked Gene Kelly's promotion from hoofer to dancer, and which saw the beginning of the innovative work he would soon be doing at MGM.

In the forties Broadway shows were frequently manhandled by Hollywood. Storylines were changed and the original Broadway scores were ditched in favour of inferior but more 'popular' material. Cole Porter (**Panama Hattie**, MGM, 1942; **Dubarry Was A Lady**, MGM, 1943; **Mexican Hayride**, Universal, 1949), and Kurt Weill (**Knickerbocker Holiday**, United Artists, 1944; **Lady In The Dark**, Paramount, 1944; **One Touch Of Venus**, Universal, 1948) were the hardest-hit victims of the system. Danny Kaye, who had appeared in *Lady in the Dark* on Broadway, and caused a minor sensation in it, made his screen debut for Sam Goldwyn in **Up In Arms** (1944) and achieved instant movie stardom. Betty Grable, who had replaced Alice Faye at 20th Century-Fox, remained the forces' favourite even when the troops were on their way home, appearing in feather-light Technicolor frolics such as **Pin-Up Girl** (1944) and **The Dolly Sisters** (1945). At MGM, producer Arthur Freed, and his celebrated Freed unit – as his talented production team came to be known – overreached themselves in attempting to explore new frontiers of the musical with a fantasy called **Yolanda And The Thief** (1945). Though the film was a box-office failure, its heart was in the right place and, if nothing else, it pointed the way to the more adventurous MGM musicals to come.

POST-WAR PRODUCTIONS

By 1946 Al Jolson was considered a has-been. But he came to the rescue of an ailing studio in the shape of Larry Parks, who himself became a major star, albeit a short-lived one – thanks to Senator McCarthy – after the release of Columbia's **The Jolson Story** – one of the most popular of all biopics. Nineteen years after Jolson's first words on the screen were the last words in modernity, his voice was again heard by a whole new generation for, though Parks acted the role, the musical soundtrack was dubbed entirely by Jolson.

Biopics of composers or musical performers continued to proliferate in the forties and, in most cases, were little more than a feeble excuse for a series of song and dance numbers which often lacked an appropriate sense of period; and although the music was generally distinguished, the lives depicted were almost interchangeable, most of them adopting a clichéd, rags-to-riches format, and often mercilessly bending or distorting the facts. After Gershwin in **Rhapsody In Blue** (Warner Bros. 1945), other major composers to receive the biopic treatment were Cole Porter in the lamentable **Night And Day** (Warner Bros. 1946), Jerome Kern in the lavish **Till The Clouds Roll By** (MGM, 1946) and Richard Rodgers and Lorenz Hart in the ludicrous **Words And Music** (MGM, 1948). Porter was able to see himself portrayed by Cary Grant but Kern had died the previous year shortly after completing his score for 20th Century-Fox's **Centennial Summer**.

In **Holiday In Mexico** (MGM, 1946), another contribution to Hollywood's 'good neighbour' policy, producer Joseph Pasternak – who had master-minded the career of Deanna Durbin at Universal in the thirties – starred his latest nightingale, Jane Powell. Most of Pasternak's musicals for MGM were sweet, naive and thoroughly conventional, usually featuring nubile young sopranos such as Powell, Ann Blyth and Kathryn Grayson. He also seemed to have a penchant for films with numbers in their titles and came up with no fewer than twelve of them, including **One Hundred Men And A Girl** (Universal, 1937), **Thousands Cheer** (MGM, 1943), **Music For Millions** (MGM, 1944) and **Ten Thousand Bedrooms** (MGM 1957).

In 1947, as the spectre of television began to loom large over film production, the musical once again suffered a decline – both in quality and quantity. There was no news in 1947, except **Good News** (MGM), a remake of the 1930 campus musical, and the only song and dance show of any consequence. It starred June Allyson and Peter Lawford and marked the directorial debut of Charles Walters, who hitherto had functioned only as a choreographer. An integral member of the Arthur Freed unit, Walters, like Stanley Donen, Vincente Minnelli, George Sidney, Robert Alton, Roger Edens and Gene Kelly, helped impart to the MGM musical its distinctive style and 'look'.

The major new face of 1948 was the all-American girl next door, Doris Day, a band singer who rocketed to stardom after her first movie, **Romance On The High Seas** (Warner Bros.). But it was Rouben Mamoulian with **Summer Holiday** (MGM), a musical version of Eugene O'Neill's *Ah Wilderness!*, and Vincente Minnelli with **The Pirate** (MGM), adapted from the Broadway play by S.N. Behrman, who created the most interesting work of the year. Neither film was a commercial success, and both were artistically flawed. But at least they took risks.

In 1948, Gene Kelly, who had partnered Judy Garland in **The Pirate** and danced through the non-musical **The Three Musketeers** (MGM, 1948), broke an ankle playing volley ball and persuaded Fred Astaire to take over his role in **Easter Parade** (MGM). It was like asking a tenor to replace a baritone, yet, despite the stylistic disparity between the two dancers, director Charles Walters and choreographer Robert Alton made it work.

As the decade drew to an end, TV's continuing grip on audiences resulted in a sharp decline in cinema attendances. The situation was aggravated by the McCarthy communist witch-hunts which did nothing to help the prestige of an industry already humiliated by TV, and battered about the ears by numerous economic

upheavals within the movie colony itself. In looking back to a less turbulent period of its past, a wave of nostalgic musicals inundated the screen: **Look For The Silver Lining** (Warner Bros. 1949), **Oh You Beautiful Doll** (20th Century-Fox, 1949), **In The Good Old Summertime** (MGM, 1949), and **Take Me Out To The Ball Game** (MGM, 1949), to name a few. As a final bow to remembrance of things past, Astaire and Rogers danced for the last time together in **The Barkleys Of Broadway** (MGM, 1949). A notable exception to this nostalgic trend, and one of the epoch-making Hollywood musicals, was **On The Town** (MGM, 1949) directed – partially on location in New York – by Gene Kelly and Stanley Donen.

INTO THE FIFTIES

The musicals of 1950 weren't exactly characterized by originality. 20th Century-Fox churned out the same old fluff for Betty Grable (**Wabash Avenue**, a remake of the same studio's **Coney Island**, 1943, that had also starred Grable; and **My Blue Heaven**), and June Haver (**I'll Get By**); while Warner Bros. continued with their series of nostalgic sweet nothings whose titles were borrowed from popular songs (Universal had done the same thing throughout the forties), and whose stars were that rhyming couple, Doris Day and Gordon MacRae. Their films included **Tea For Two** (1950), **On Moonlight Bay** (1951), **Lullaby Of Broadway** (1951) and **By The Light Of The Silvery Moon** (1953). In 1950 Betty Hutton, on loan to MGM from Paramount, stepped in to play the title role in **Annie Get Your Gun** after Judy Garland was fired from the production, and gave it everything she had. But for most people, Hutton, like The Andrews Sisters, will mainly be remembered as a typical product of the forties.

Summer Stock (1950) – a 'let's put on a show' anachronism – turned out to be Judy Garland's last film for MGM. Charles Walters directed it, and although it was beset with production problems, it contained one of the best numbers Garland ever committed to film – Harold Arlen and Ted Koehler's 'Get Happy'. Though Gene Kelly had one excellent solo in **Summer Stock**, it was a retrograde step for him, coming so soon after his more innovative work. The other great male dancer, Fred Astaire, was still on top in 1950, and after accepting an Oscar in 1949 for 'raising the standard of screen musicals' co-starred with Red Skelton and Vera-Ellen in the delightful **Three Little Words** (MGM), a biopic based on the lives of songwriters Burt Kalmar and Harry Ruby, in which he played Kalmar.

In 1950, MGM began to reap the benefits of their latest discovery, Mario Lanza, whose teaming with Kathryn Grayson in **That Midnight Kiss** (1949) and **The Toast Of New Orleans** (1950) spelled box-office dynamite. And if the public believed Lanza to be a great opera singer, that didn't worry MGM one bit. On the contrary, they encouraged this belief by casting him in and as **The Great Caruso** (1951).

Despite the colourful George Sidney remake of **Showboat** (1951), and Astaire's dancing on the ceiling in Stanley Donen's solo directorial debut, **Royal Wedding** (MGM), the best musical of 1951 was Vincente Minnelli's **An American In Paris** (MGM), which was itself overtaken the following year by **Singin' In The Rain** (MGM), another Kelly-Donen collaboration and the pinnacle of the genre. After that, the musical went into another decline. Warner Bros. went back to square one with their impoverished remake of **The Jazz Singer** (1952). MGM, in turn, remade a not-so-merry **Merry Widow** (1952) as well as the RKO 1934 release **Roberta**, this time calling it **Lovely To Look At** (1952). The hey-day was over, and while **Singin' In The Rain** miraculously managed to fuse the past with the present, most of the other attempts to recapture the musical's first early rapture were anaemic failures. Yet, though there were to be fewer and fewer musicals over the next twenty years, some masterpieces were still to come. Minnelli's **The Band Wagon** (MGM, 1953) was one of them, giving Fred Astaire the most challenging role of his long and distinguished career. In **Gentlemen Prefer Blondes** (20th Century-Fox, 1953) directed by Howard Hawks, Marilyn Monroe became a major musical star and forever immortalized the dictum that 'Diamonds Are A Girl's Best Friend'. The latest in a long line of Fox blondes, her quality was incandescent and this film brought out the best in her. Its success, as well as that of **Kiss Me Kate** (MGM, 1953) and **Call Me Madam** (20th Century-Fox), sounded the death knell for the original screen musical and helped clear a path for the arrival of one Broadway import after another. But the shape of things to come was also a large rectangle. CinemaScope made its appearance in 1953 and swallowed up anything approaching taste and charm. At first the giant screen was filled with Demetrius and thousands of gladiators, as well as with Richard and his Crusaders and King Arthur and his Knights. But the musical did not escape for long, and it suffered in the new process in much the same way that a play conceived for a proscenium arch suffers on an open stage. A remake of **Rose Marie** (MGM, 1954) was the first victim of the distorting lens, whose wide-open spaces not even Busby Berkeley could adequately fill. Sigmund Romberg's **The Student Prince**, (MGM, 1954), directed by Richard Thorpe and with an oversized Mario Lanza lending his oversized voice to the mini-talented Edmund Purdom (as the Prince) fared marginally better than Friml's heroine, but **Jupiter's Darling** (MGM, 1954) with Esther Williams and Howard Keel, and **Lucky Me** (Warner Bros. 1954) were disasters.

Paramount had its own wide-screen technique – the less obtrusive Vistavision – and it was seen to good advantage in Irving Berlin's **White Christmas** (1954), a sort of **Holiday Inn** (Paramount, 1942) revisited.

Two directors, however, managed to make a positive virtue out of the long, narrow strip in which they were forced to operate: Stanley Donen in the exuberant **Seven Brides For Seven Brothers** (1954), choreographed by Michael Kidd; and George Cukor in the first remake of **A Star Is Born** (Warner Bros. 1954) – which, with **Singin' In The Rain**, must rank as one of the supreme achievements of the genre. Judy Garland was its star and, like the lady in the Stephen Sondheim song from 'Follies' she could, after its successful release, triumphantly proclaim, 'I'm Still Here!'

1954 saw two more musical biopics: Stanley Donen's entertaining but inaccurate **Deep In My Heart** (MGM, 1954) in which most of the musical stars still under contract to the studio were trotted out in the service of the show's subject, Sigmund Romberg (played by Jose Ferrer); and the altogether more impressive **The Glenn Miller Story** (Paramount), Anthony Mann's moving tribute to one of America's best-loved band leaders. James Stewart and June Allyson starred.

The year ended with Irving Berlin's **There's No Business Like Show Business** (20th Century-Fox), a quintessential backstage story which filled the

CinemaScope screen with the starry presences of Ethel Merman, Dan Dailey, Marilyn Monroe, Johnnie Ray, Donald O'Connor and Mitzi Gaynor.

Broadway shows began to infiltrate Hollywood in earnest in 1955 with **Brigadoon** (MGM), **Kismet** (MGM), **Guys And Dolls** (A Sam Goldwyn Production released by MGM), **Hit The Deck** (MGM) and **Oklahoma!** (20th Century-Fox). But, as usual, it was an original that emerged as the best musical of the year: Gene Kelly and Stanley Donen's **It's Always Fair Weather** (MGM), with a sparkling screenplay by Betty Comden and Adolph Green (who also wrote the lyrics) and a score to match by André Previn. The film took a few satirical swipes at television, but today television gets its revenge by lopping off a third of the wide-screen image. The following year several more Broadway shows reached the screen, the best being Rodgers and Hammerstein's **Carousel** and **The King And I** (20th Century-Fox), and Cole Porter's **Silk Stockings** (MGM) in which Cyd Charisse again proved she was Fred Astaire's best partner since Ginger Rogers. The stylish direction was by Rouben Mamoulian.

1956 was also the year in which the movies and the world of popular music was revolutionized by the advent of rock 'n' roll – the first being Columbia's **Rock Around The Clock** which starred Bill Haley and His Comets. Elvis Presley – Hollywood's latest money-making acquisition – launched his career in 1956 with **Love Me Tender** (20th Century-Fox), his contribution to the rock scene the following year being the popular and profitable **Jailhouse Rock** (MGM). Only Frank Tashlin's **The Girl Can't Help It** (20th Century-Fox) starring the studio's latest blonde, Jayne Mansfield, demonstrated that rock and a sense of humour could co-exist in the same frame.

It was, however, another Broadway import, **The Pajama Game** (Warner Bros.) directed by Stanley Donen and with Doris Day heading the cast, that saved 1957 from hitting rock bottom with its musicals.

1958 saw even fewer musicals than 1957 – but among them was one of the best of the decade – Vincente Minnelli's enchanting **Gigi** (MGM), based on the play by Colette, and with book and lyrics by Alan Jay Lerner and a rapturous score by Frederick Loewe. Leslie Caron, Louis Jourdan, Maurice Chevalier and Hermione Gingold starred – and, at a stroke, one's flagging faith in the screen musical was revived. The year's other major musical was Rodgers and Hammerstein's **South Pacific** (20th Century-Fox), directed with altogether too heavy a hand by Joshua Logan.

SIXTIES, SEVENTIES AND SO ON
In 1961, **West Side Story** reached Hollywood via United Artists, and despite a clash of intentions between directors Jerome Robbins and Robert Wise, was one of the most effective of all Broadway imports, and far superior to the previous year's leaden **Can-Can** (20th Century-Fox), or Vincente Minnelli's pleasant, but not particularly resourceful handling of the Judy Holliday showcase **Bells Are Ringing** (MGM, 1960).

By 1962 rock 'n' roll was *passé*, the current craze being the twist, and we were now invited to **Twist Around The Clock** (Columbia).

But 1962 offered some weightier musicals as well, with Broadway's **Gypsy** and **The Music Man** reaching the screen via Warner Bros. and with admirable fidelity to the original shows. All the same, the Hollywood musical had now become something it had never been before (except, possibly, for a brief moment in its infancy. It had become a Broadway parasite.

Billy Rose's **Jumbo** (MGM, 1962), a stage hit from 1935, saw the end of Busby Berkeley's movie career. He was the second unit director, but his personal imprint on the sequences he directed was unmistakeable. 1962 also saw the end of the Crosby/Hope 'road' shows with **Road To Hong Kong** released, not by Paramount, but by United Artists, and with Joan Collins in the role usually played by Dorothy Lamour, though Lamour was also in it. It was a lamentable experience, as was the undistinguished end to Judy Garland's exciting up-and-down career in the British-made, and optimistically titled, **I Could Go On Singing** (United Artists, 1963).

The next few years offered very little to sing about. Elvis Presley swivelled his hips through a cycle of innocuous vehicles – some better than others – and there were the usual Broadway imports, the best being the Warner Bros. production of Lerner and Loewe's **My Fair Lady** (1964) directed by George Cukor. Twist gave way to a series of equally inane 'beach party' musicals from American International, aimed largely at the teenage market, teenagers having become a viable economic force.

In 1964, Julie Andrews became the second woman to win a Best Actress Oscar in a musical for her work in Walt Disney's **Mary Poppins** (Buena Vista) and, overnight, became the new superstar Hollywood had been waiting for. The following year she scaled ever greater heights of stardom with her appealing performance in the saccharine but extremely successful screen adaptation of Rodgers and Hammerstein's long-running Broadway hit, **The Sound Of Music** (20th Century-Fox), one of the most profitable films in Hollywood's history.

As a direct result of the monumental box-office returns of **The Sound Of Music**, 20th Century-Fox invested heavily in two more big-budget musicals: **Dr. Dolittle** (1967) with Rex Harrison; and **Star!** (1968), a biopic of the late Gertrude Lawrence and another starring vehicle for Julie Andrews. Both lost millions.

In 1967 Julie Andrews appeared for Universal in **Thoroughly Modern Millie**, a lavishly produced twenties romp which more than recouped its costs. But it was the failure of **Star!** coupled with the disastrous **Darling Lili** (Paramount, 1970) which she made for her director husband Blake Edwards, that exacerbated her decline in popularity; a decline which coincided with the spectacular rise of Barbra Streisand.

After her award-winning debut as Fanny Brice in William Wyler's **Funny Girl** (Columbia, 1968)—first seen as a Broadway musical in 1964, also starring Streisand—Hollywood's latest superstar was soon being directed by two giants of the genre: Gene Kelly in **Hello Dolly!** (20th Century-Fox, 1969) and Vincente Minnelli in **On A Clear Day You Can See Forever** (Paramount, 1969) – both via Broadway.

The only other star to equal Streisand, if not quite in popularity, then certainly in talent, was Liza Minnelli, the daughter of Vincente Minnelli and Judy Garland, whose Oscar-winning performance in Bob Fosse's stunningly directed screen translation of the Broadway hit **Cabaret** was the quintessence of star quality.

In 1970, **Woodstock** (Warner Bros.) ushered in a decade of documentary musicals and filmed pop concerts such as **Elvis, That's The Way It Is** (MGM, 1970), **Gimme Shelter** (Cinema V), **The Song Remains The Same** (Warner Bros. 1972) and **Medicine Ball Caravan** (Warner

Bros. 1974) to name only a handful. Broadway blockbusters such as **Fiddler On The Roof** (United Artists, 1971), **Man Of La Mancha** (United Artists, 1972), **1776** (Columbia, 1972), **Jesus Christ Superstar** (Universal, 1973), **Mame** (Warner Bros. 1974) and **The Wiz** (Paramount, 1979) also dominated the scene, though on balance it was not a great decade for musicals. It was, however, a significant one. For, with such shows as Bob Fosse's **Cabaret** (Allied Artists, 1972) and his indulgent, though visually stunning **All That Jazz** (Columbia, 1979) – the first musical to deal directly, and unflinchingly, with the subject of death – a new genre was born: the adult musical.

Mark Rydell's **The Rose** (20th Century-Fox, 1979) also eschewed escapism for gritty reality; while in 1981 Herbert Ross in **Pennies From Heaven** (MGM) attempted, unsuccessfully, to have his cake and eat it by combining a grim, Depression-based story with the mindless extravagance and fantasy of the Hollywood musical of the thirties. Audiences, alas, found the combination unpalatable and the show flopped. So did **Yes, Giorgio,** (1982), another attempt by MGM to recreate the musical of the past: this time, though, its sights were on the all-singing Mario Lanza-type confection so beloved of producer Joe Pasternak in the fifties.

With the failure, in 1982, of Francis Coppola's **One From The Heart** (American Zoetrope), yet another attempt to recreate an old-style, studio-bound musical, and **Annie** (Columbia), John Huston's disastrous account of the Broadway smash, the message was clear: for the musical of the eighties to succeed the accent had to be on youth. All the signs were there in **Saturday Night Fever** (Paramount, 1977), **Grease** (Paramount, 1978) and **Fame** (MGM, 1980) and would continue well into the decade with such dance-orientated hits as **Staying Alive** (Paramount, 1983), **Flashdance** (Paramount, 1983), **Breakin'** (MGM/UA, 1984), **Footloose** (Paramount, 1984) and **Dirty Dancing** (Vestron, 1987), most of which went back several decades for their story-lines.

Another all-dance show, **White Nights** (Columbia, 1985) with Mikhail Baryshnikov and hoofer Gregory Hines also found favour, though such retrograde offerings as **Tap** and **Sing** (Columbia-Tri-Star, 1989) were failures and proved conclusively, as if proof were necessary, that nostalgia was box-office poison. Failures, too, were: Bertrand Tavernier's excellent **Round Midnight** (Warner Bros. 1986) and Clint Eastwood's biopic **Bird** (Warner Bros. 1988) – two further examples of audience indifference to jazz-orientated subjects.

At the beginning of the nineties there was no obviously discernible musical trend emerging, and the future is uncertain. But whatever happens, one thing is sure: the shape of the Hollywood musical has irrevocably changed. Gone are the innocence and the *fun*, the escapism and the expertise. Sadly, all attempts to recapture it have largely been doomed to failure. In the high-tech nineties with its state-of-the-art emphasis on special effects, few protagonists burst spontaneously into song, and when they do, there is usually an orchestra or record player nearby.

The only consolation, of course, is that the Hollywood Musical wasn't always that way – as the following pages abundantly illustrate. So sit back and enjoy – for as Frank Sinatra so accurately observed in **That's Entertainment** (MGM, 1974) as Fred Astaire and Eleanor Powell took to the screen in *Begin The Beguine* from **Broadway Melody Of 1940** (MGM, 1940), you'll never see its like again. . . .

1927/8

Academy Awards

Writing (Adaptation)
NOMINATIONS INCLUDED: *The Jazz Singer* (WB)
Alfred Cohn

Engineering Effects
(Award not given after this year)
The Jazz Singer Nugent Slaughter

Special Awards
Warner Bros. for producing *The Jazz Singer*,
the outstanding pioneer talking picture
which revolutionised the industry.
(statuette)

Following the success of their *Don Juan* on 6 August 1926 – which starred John Barrymore and was the first feature film to use the Vitaphone sound-on-disc system – Warner Bros. decided to take a gamble on a feature in which the characters actually spoke and sang. In reality it was a calculated risk for, despite the success of *Don Juan* (which had a specially commissioned score by William Axt, appropriate sound effects, but no dialogue), the studio was on the verge of bankruptcy anyway; and without a blockbuster to help turn the tide of their declining fortunes, the four Warners – Sam, Jack, Harry and Albert – fully realized that the last reel of their careers as movie moguls was fast unspooling, and that it would only be a matter of time before The End appeared. So they sank everything they had into a property called **The Jazz Singer** whose author, Samson Raphaelson, had first written it as a short story called *The Day of Atonement*, then turned it into a successful stage vehicle for George Jessel. The story of Jakie Rabinowitz, a cantor's son torn between a life in the theatre and a life in the synagogue, it struck the Warners as the perfect subject with which to launch the first 'talker', as it was to become known in the industry. Its star would be George Jessel, who had already appeared for the brothers in a silent called *Private Izzy Murphy* (1926), and whose impact as Jakie Rabinowitz was the talk of Broadway. But when Jessel realized that songs were to be added, he doubled his initial fee and was turned down flat. In an attempt to salvage the situation, Jack Warner offered the role to Eddie Cantor but, fearing the adverse effect on his career should the 'experiment' fail, Cantor refused it. Rather than return to Jessel and pay what he had asked, the brothers decided to approach the man they considered to be the greatest entertainer in the world: Al Jolson. Jolson accepted, and the salary negotiated was $75,000, a third to be paid in cash, the rest in weekly instalments of $6,250, a proportion of which would be reinvested in the picture in order to earn Jolson a percentage of the profits. It was a brilliant piece of casting, endorsed by the wildly enthusiastic cheers of everyone present at the film's historic premiere on 6 October 1927. Though the narrative of **The Jazz Singer** was undiluted *schmaltz* from start to finish, director Alan Crosland, by taking his cameras on location into the predominantly Jewish areas of New York's lower East Side, managed to convey an accurate picture of ghetto life and, ethnically, offered a fascinating glimpse of a community of aliens desperately trying to assimilate themselves into a new society while, at the same time, clinging fervently to their Middle-European traditions. The contrast between life on Hester and Orchard streets, and life on Broadway, was equally marked. As Jakie Jolson was tremendous, and his singing of 'Toot Toot Tootsie Goodbye' by Gus Kahn, Ernie Erdman and Dan Russo, and of 'Mammy' by Sam Lewis, Joe Young and Walter Donaldson, which he performed in blackface (left), allowed audiences hitherto denied the chance to see for themselves, why Jolson was considered to be the greatest performer in the world. His tremendous personality was also evident in the one major dialogue scene: an ad-libbed conversation with his mother (Eugenie Besserer, right) as he sits at the piano in their humble home demonstrating (to Irving Berlin's 'Blue Skies') what 'jazz' is all about. The scene is interrupted by the sudden appearance of Cantor Rabinowitz (Warner Oland) with just one word: 'Stop!' After that the film becomes silent again until Jolson's next song. May McAvoy was cast as Mary Dale, the showgirl in Jakie's life, with other roles going to Otto Lederer, Bobby Gordon (Jakie at 13), Richard Tucker, Nat Carr, William Demarest, Anders Randolf, Will Walling, Roscoe Karns, Myrna Loy (as a chorus girl), and Cantor Joseff Rosenblatt who, as himself, sang the Jewish 'Yahrzeit'. The holy 'Kol Nidre', sung in synagogues on the eve of The Day of Atonement,

was featured twice, 'sung' once by Jolson and once by Oland but, on both occasions, with the voices dubbed. Alfred A. Cohn adapted Raphaelson's play for the screen, and the titles ('God made her a woman and love made her a mother!') were by Jack Jarmuth. The film grossed $3,500,000. Other songs: *My Gal Sal* (Bobby Gordon) Paul Dresser; *Waiting For The Robert E. Lee* L. Wolfe Gilbert, Lewis E. Muir; *Dirty Hands, Dirty Face* (Jolson) Edgar Leslie, Grant Clarke, Jolson, James V. Monaco; *Mother, I Still Have You* (Jolson) Jolson, Louis Silvers. By some terrible irony of fate, none of the four Warner brothers was able to attend the New York premiere of **The Jazz Singer**. Sam Warner, the brother most instrumental in pioneering sound, died of a sinus infection (the result of a broken nose suffered years earlier), on 5 October 1927 – one day before the premiere, and after six operations undertaken in an attempt to save his life. Harry, Albert and Jack Warner immediately took a train to Los Angeles to be in time for the funeral on 9 October.

Fanny Brice made her movie debut in **My Man** (1928), a part-talkie, and the only film she made for Warner Bros. She played a Broadway hopeful who, *en route* to the Great White Way, has an unfulfilling love affair with Guinn Williams (an elastic exerciser in a shop window). The romance might have worked had her selfish sister (Edna Murphy) not wooed him away from her just as the couple were about to be married. Andre De Segurola appeared as the Broadway producer responsible for removing Miss Brice (illustrated) from her unhappy private life and introducing her into the world of the footlights, with other roles under Archie Mayo's tentative direction going to Richard Tucker, Billy Seay, Arthur Hoyt, Ann Brody and Clarissa Selwynne. They, however, were all overshadowed by Miss Brice, whose way with a song (such as 'My Man', an English adaptation by Channing Pollock from Maurice Yvain's French ballad 'Mon Homme'), or a funny sketch (such as 'Mrs Cohen At The Beach') was the only
▽

reason for putting up with a rather novelettish story by Mark Canfield (alias Darryl F. Zanuck), which Robert Lord adapted and Joe Jackson scripted. Other songs: *Second Hand Rose* Grant Clarke, James Hanley; *If You Want A Rainbow (You Must Have The Rain)* Billy Rose, Mort Dixon, Oscar Levant; *I'm An Indian* Blanche Merrill, Leo Edwards; *I Was A Florodora Baby* Ballard MacDonald, Harry Carroll; *I'd Rather Be Blue* Billy Rose, Fred Fisher.

△
Until the arrival in 1939 of *Gone With The Wind* (Selznick International), the most financially successful sound picture in Hollywood's history was **The Singing Fool** (1928), Al Jolson's second part-talkie for Warner Bros. Even more sentimental in its story than *The Jazz Singer*, Jolson, in an extremely self-congratulatory piece of acting, starred as a singer-composer who not only loses his wife (a singularly unanimated performance from Josephine Dunn), but also his adored little Sonny Boy (Davey Lee, seen here on Jolson's lap). He is comforted in his grief and misery by cigarette girl Betty Bronson, whose genuine concern for his well-being helps him to face life afresh. The team of Buddy De Sylva, Lew Brown and Ray Henderson supplied their star with three enormous song hits including 'Sonny Boy', a lachrymose little item which Jolson sang at his ailing son's deathbed and which, allegedly, was written in jest by the composers who simply could not take such a blatant attack on the tear ducts seriously. Whatever the circumstances surrounding the song's creation might have been, its recording sold over three million copies, making it the number one pop song of its time. Jolson received $150,000 for his work on the film, and the three Warner brothers reaped profits in excess of $4,000,000. C. Graham Baker's scenario (from a story by Leslie S. Barrows) allowed Jolson to appear at times in blackface, and also gave parts to Reed Howes, Edward Martindel, Arthur Housman and Robert Emmett O'Connor. The tear-jerking direction was by Lloyd Bacon. Other songs: *It All Depends On You; I'm Sittin' On Top Of The World* Sam Lewis, Joe Young, Henderson; *There's A Rainbow Round My Shoulder* Billy Rose, Jolson, Dave Dreyer; *Keep Smiling At Trouble* De Sylva, Lewis Gensler; *Golden Gate* Maurice Rubens, Nat and Max Lief; *The Spaniard Who Blighted My Life* Billy Merson (all sung by Jolson).

1929

Academy Awards

Best Picture
The Broadway Melody (MGM) produced by
Harry Rapf
NOMINATIONS INCLUDED: *The Hollywood Revue*
(MGM) produced by Harry Rapf

Direction
NOMINATIONS INCLUDED: Harry Beaumont
The Broadway Melody

Art Direction
NOMINATIONS INCLUDED: *The Hollywood Revue*
Cedric Gibbons

The New York Times Annual 'Ten Best'
1st *The Love Parade* (Paramount). 3rd
Hallelujah (MGM). 10th *Sally* (First National).

With **The Broadway Melody** (MGM), produced by Lawrence Weingarten and premiered at Grauman's Chinese Theatre in Hollywood on 1 February 1929, the movie musical was spectacularly launched. The first of the all-talking, all-singing, all-dancing entertainments to revolutionize the industry (and which, for the next two years, would proliferate until, by the end of 1930, they had sung and danced their way out of favour), it was an impressive achievement for MGM, whose skilled technicians showed the rest of Hollywood that with a bit of ingenuity and imagination, the cumbersome sound equipment so restricting to directors weaned on the manoeuverability of the silent camera, need not be the millstone to creativity which it was generally considered to be. Originally conceived by director Harry Beaumont and scenarist Edmund

Goulding as a loosely disguised biopic of the Duncan Sisters, the storyline of **The Broadway Melody** changed direction as it was developed (Norman Houston and James Gleason wrote the dialogue), and became the backstage saga – a springboard which would be used for the stories of countless musicals to come – of a vaudeville sister act and the romantic entanglements that beset it. The movie starred Anita Page (right) and Bessie Love (left), with Miss Love delivering a brave, highly-charged performance as the sister who loses her stage partner as well as the man she loves. Miss Love's emoting re-instated her as a star, but she never again did anything as impressive in her career. Charles King (centre) was the man she loses to her sister, with Jed Prouty. Kenneth Thomson, Edward Dillon, Mary Doran and singer James Burroughs excellent in support. Arthur Freed (later to make such an indelible mark on MGM as their top producer of musicals) and Nacio Herb Brown, a pair of West Coast songwriters, were signed to compose the score – the first ever to be conceived and written especially for the screen – and they came up with a forty-carat stunner which included, of course, the catchy title song which they themselves appeared on screen to demonstrate, and which the studio would reprise several more times in its history, and which would lend its name to a popular series of musical extravaganzas starring Eleanor Powell in the following decade. Charles King was fortunate enough to get the best of the score, including the title song which he warbled on three different occasions, and the melodious 'You Were Meant For Me', while the Misses Page and Love were seen at their best in 'Harmony Babies'. Other songs included *The Wedding Of The Painted Doll*, used in a Technicolor production number; a second number for the two leading ladies called *The Boy Friend*; *Love Boat* (Burroughs and chorus); *Truthful Parson Brown* by Willard Robinson, performed by The Biltmore Trio and Orchestra, and George M. Cohan's famous *Give My Regards To Broadway*, also heard on screen for the first time (in a fragment over the credits).

Though black actor Stepin Fetchit (illustrated) was outstanding in **Hearts In Dixie** (Fox) playing a lazy, work-shy layabout in a poor Negro cotton community shortly after the Civil War, there was a lot else to admire in producer-director Paul Sloane's technically proficient, dramatically touching tale of the sacrifice a father (Clarence Muse) makes to ensure the education of his son (Eugene Jackson). The naturalness of the performances – especially as the majority of the cast (all black except for Richard Carlyle as a physician) had never before appeared in a talkie – as well as the expressiveness of the direction and skilful manipulation of the camera, were striking. Sloane's use of music, mainly traditional Negro spirituals, revealed a genuinely creative feeling for the medium in general and musicals in particular, and he never allowed the music to impose on the narrative unless it made a specific point. The result was a prestigious triumph for William Fox and his team, and a delightful and touching contribution to the art of the Hollywood musical. It was photographed by Glen Williams, written by Walter Weems and choreographed by Fanchon and Marco. Also cast: Bernice Pilot, Clifford Ingram, Mildred Washington, Zack Williams and Gertrude Howard. There was an original title song by Howard Jackson, who also did the scoring for the film.

Lucky In Love (Pathe), a vapid comedy with songs, was particularly deficient in the leading man department. For, as played by Morton Downey (left), the hero of Gene Markey's screenplay – an American stable boy in love with the granddaughter of an Irish earl – was a monumental bore, unworthy of his sweetheart's affections or of the audience's concern. Betty Lawford was the object of Downey's desires; and the villain of the piece, complete with *East Lynne* moustache, was Colin Keith-Johnston. Also cast were Halliwell Hobbes as the Earl, J.M. Kerrigan, Edward McNamara, Richard Taber and Edward O'Connor. It was directed by Kenneth Webb and supervised by Robert Kane. Songs: *Love Is A Dreamer*; *For The Likes O' You And Me*; *When They Sing 'The Wearing Of The Green' In Syncopated Blues* Bud Green, Sammy Stept.

Giving a performance that fell mid-way between George M. Cohan and Al Jolson, in a film that had more than a passing similarity to *The Jazz Singer* (Warner Bros. 1927), George Jessel (left), star of **Lucky Boy** (Tiffany-Stahl) was unable to impart to this Norman Taurog-Charles C. Wilson directed comedy the kiss of life that it so desperately needed. Lacking a freshness of approach both in execution and content, the story (by Viola Brothers Shore, dialogue by Jessel) of a Jewish jeweler's son's attempts to become a Broadway star against the wishes of his family, just refused to play. The fact that it was basically a silent film with dialogue and music sequences added to it, didn't help matters either, although there was a generous helping of songs. Rosa Rosanova (right) and William Strauss were Jessel's parents; Margaret Quimby and Mary Doran the women in his life. Songs: *Lucky Boy*; *My Mother's Eyes* L. Wolfe Gilbert, Abel Baer; *Old Man Sunshine*; *My Real Sweetheart*; *In My Bouquet Of Memories* Sam M. Lewis, Joe Young, Harry Akst; *My Blackbirds Are Bluebirds Now* Irving Caesar, Cliff Friend; *California Here I Come* Al Jolson, B.G. De Sylva, Joseph Meyer.

Whether or not it was due to the unsympathetic nature of the role he played (a composer who shamelessly uses his friends and lovers to further his career), leading man Charles Kaley (centre) made a hasty exit from feature films after **Lord Byron of Broadway** (MGM) was released. Another casualty was his leading lady, Ethelind Terry, whose complete misuse of the medium, both vocally and physically, resulted in an equally hasty departure back to Broadway whence she had come. With the central roles so unappealingly cast, and a story (from the novel by Nell Martin, dialogue by Crane Wilbur and Willard Mack) of only minimal interest, **Lord Byron of Broadway** didn't stand a chance at the box office despite an Arthur Freed-Nacio Herb Brown score which included 'A Bundle Of Old Love Letters' and 'Should I'. Technicolor was used in two sequences: Dimitri Tiomkin's 'Blue Daughter Of Heaven', sung off-screen by James Burroughs, and complete with overhead shots a year before Busby Berkeley's *Whoopee*; and for a fantasy item called 'The Woman In The Shoe'. Sammy Lee was the dance director, with Albertina Rasch in charge of the Tiomkin ballet sequence; and the film was directed by William Nigh and Harry Beaumont. Also cast were Marion Shilling (left), Cliff Edwards (right), Gwen Lee, Benny Rubin, Drew Demarest and John Byron. Other songs: *Only Love Is Real*; *When I Met You*; *You're The Bride And I'm The Groom* Freed, Brown; *Love Ain't Nothing But The Blues* Joe Goodwin, Louis Alter.

△

Syncopation (RKO) was very much in step with the current vogue of backstage musicals, and traversed no new territory in the recounting of its oh-so-familiar tale of a husband and wife vaudeville act that breaks up because one partner is dissatisfied with something or other. In this instance it was the wife who outgrows her unsophisticated husband – but only temporarily. By the final fade they're together again, both privately and professionally. Barbara Bennett (left) and Bobby Watson were top-starred, with Ian Hunter (as the man Miss B. almost leaves Bobby for), Morton Downey (right), Osgood Perkins (father of Anthony), Mackenzie Ward, Verree Teasdale, Dorothy Lee and, best of all, Fred Waring and His Pennsylvanians – whose 'Tin Pan Parade' was a high spot in a film not endowed with an abundance of them – completing the cast. Robert Kane produced, Bert Glennon directed and the screenplay was an adaptation by Frances Agnew of Gene Markey's novel *Stepping High*. Songs: *Jericho* Leo Robin, Richard Myers; *Mine Alone* Herman Ruby, Myers; *Do Something*; *I'll Always Be In Love With You* Bud Green, Sammy Stept, Ruby.

▷

◁

△

Another backstage story, **Close Harmony** (Paramount) starred a versatile Charles 'Buddy' Rogers as a warehouse clerk-cum-bandleader who, through the determined conniving of chorus girl Nancy Carroll (making her musical debut), is given the opportunity to hit the big time with his band. The plot had little going for it, but with Rogers doing all that could humanly be expected of a musical comedy star, and then some, it didn't seem to matter at all. John V.A. Weaver and Percy Heath's screenplay (story by Elsie Janis and Gene Markey) propped up the narrative's carbon-copy situations with a fair quota of gags; and with Jack Oakie (right) and Richard 'Skeets' Gallagher (left) on hand as a singing team called Barney and Bay, audiences went home happy. Also featured were Jesse Stafford and His Orchestra, Matty Roubert, Ricca Allen, Wade Boteler, Baby Mack, Oscar Smith, Greta Granstedt, Harry Green, and Gus Partos. It was directed by John Cromwell and Edward Sutherland. Songs: *She's So I Dunno*; *I Want To Go Places And Do Things*; *I'm All A-Twitter, I'm All A-Twirl* Richard A. Whiting, Leo Robin; *Twelfth Street Rag* Euday L. Bowman, Spencer Williams.

Coincidence took pride of place in the screenplay which Frances Agnew, Eddie Dowling and George J. Crone fashioned for **The Rainbow Man** (Sono Art/Paramount), a vehicle for Eddie Dowling which was heavily reminiscent of Al Jolson's *The Singing Fool* (Warner Bros., 1928), but not nearly as financially successful. Dowling (centre) played a minstrel man called Rainbow Riley who, after the death of an acrobat friend, adopts his son Billy, then falls in love with Mary, a hotel keeper's daughter, only to discover that Mary's dead sister was none other than little Billy's late mother! Too maudlin by half, this overtly sentimental *ragôut* was just about made palatable by the engaging presence of Marian Nixon who, as Mary, was alone in bringing a patina of credibility to the screenplay that the rest of the cast, including Dowling, were quite unable to manage. Both lovely to look at and delightful to hear (her speaking voice was among the best to grace a talking picture in 1929), Miss Nixon's rescuing presence went some distance to counteract the cloying effect of little Frankie Darro as the orphan. Dowling broke into song when you least expected him to, further reducing the credibility of an already far-fetched scenario. Also involved in the tearjerker were Sam Hardy as a minstrel manager, Lloyd Ingraham and Billy Hayes. George W. Weeks and O.E. Goebel produced, and the director was Fred Newmayer. Songs: *Little Pal*; *Rainbow Man* Dowling, James Hanley; *Sleepy Valley* Andrew B. Sterling, Hanley.

TWENTIES MUSICALS

The saga of Margot, a French girl who is ▷
unaware that her somewhat unprepossessing
boyfriend and The Red Shadow, mysterious
leader of the Riffs, are one and the same man,
The Desert Song (Warner Bros.) was the first all-
talking, all-singing operetta to come to the
screen. The story – by Otto Harbach, Laurence
Schwab, Frank Mandel and Oscar Hammerstein
II – suffered from an underlying improbability,
and Harvey Gates's screenplay unintentionally provoked mirth. Nonetheless, Sigmund
Romberg's romantically tuneful score (lyrics by
Hammerstein II) overcame these disadvantages,
and John Boles (left) was a sufficiently dashing
Red Shadow to keep audiences' minds off the
banality of the plot. Carlotta King (right) played
the gullible Margot, with brave support on offer
from Louise Fazenda, John Miljan, Johnny
Arthur, Marie Wells, Edward Martindel, Jack
Pratt, Otto Hoffman, Robert E. Guzman and
Myrna Loy. Directed by Roy Del Ruth and
photographed by Barney McGill partly in two-
colour Technicolor, the movie proved a success
and was remade in 1943 with Dennis Morgan
and in 1953 with Gordon MacRae. Songs: *Riff
Song* (Boles); *French Marching Song* (King); *Then
You Will Know* (Boles, King); *Desert Song* (King,
Boles); *Song Of The Brass Key* (Wells, Pratt); *Sabre
Song* (King, Boles); *Romance* (King); *One Alone*
(Boles); *One Flower* (Guzman, Pratt); *My Little
Castagnette* (Wells).

△
Though saddled with a trite and cumbersome
script by Ernest Vajda, C.E. Andrews and Ethel
Doherty, and working in a language that was
not his own (in a medium still teething where
sound was concerned), Maurice Chevalier's success in his first full-length American feature,
Innocents of Paris (Paramount), was a resounding example of style triumphing over content.
The story of a junk merchant (Chevalier, right)
who rescues a child from drowning in the Seine,
then falls in love with the child's Aunt Louise,
the plot ultimately forced the hero to choose
between romance and a career in the theatre. He
chooses love – but not before singing three
Richard A. Whiting–Leo Robin songs including
the famous 'Louise'. He also sang 'It's A Habit Of
Mine' which opened with a short routine for
chorus girls, then developed into the quintessential Chevalier number, performed by the star with
a straw hat and a cocky demeanour, oozing his
characteristic sexual confidence and legendary
Gallic charm. Sylvia Beecher (left) as his inamorata was nowhere as convincing as her
leading man in a performance that owed more to
the art of elocution than it did to acting.
Completing the cast were Russell Simpson, Mr
and Mrs George Fawcett, John Miljan, Margaret
Livingston, David Durand, Jack Luden and Johnnie Morris. The director was Richard Wallace.
Other songs: *Wait Till You See 'Ma Cherie'*; *On Top
Of The World Alone* Whiting, Robin; *Valentine*
Henri Christine, Herbert Reynolds; *Les Ananas* (a
French version of *Yes, We Have No Bananas*);
Dites-Moi Ma Mere (from Chevalier's Paris
repertoire).

Minnie's Boys, better known to Broadway audiences as the Marx Brothers – Groucho (centre
left), Chico (centre right), Harpo (right) and
Zeppo (left) – made their all-talking, all-singing,
and all-dancing debut with **Cocoanuts** (in 1921
they had appeared in a silent comedy called
Humor Risk, prints of which no longer exist), and
were as enthusiastically welcomed on the screen
as they had been on stage. Virtually a filmed
version of the Sam Harris Broadway presentation, the Paramount film bore several of the
hallmarks (or scars) of the early talkies. The
sound reproduction left much to be desired and
the camera work was static. All the same, the
refreshing zaniness of the quartet helped to
override these technical liabilities, and in their
'Viaduct' sketch gave the movies one of its classic
▽

comedy scenes. Mary Eaton and Oscar Shaw
co-starred as the obligatory young lovers, the
formidable Margaret Dumont was on hand as
Mrs Potter, a haughty guest at the *Hotel de
Cocoanut*, with Kay Francis (her debut), Cyril
Ring, Basil Ruysdael and Sylvan Lee completing
the cast. It was adapted from the George S.
Kaufman–Morris Ryskind–Irving Berlin play by
Ryskind, photographed by George Folsey, super-
vised by Monta Bell for producer Walter
Wanger, and directed by Joseph Santley and
Robert Florey. The score was by Irving Berlin and
included *When My Dreams Come True* (not in the
original production), *Florida By The Sea*, *Monkey-
Doodle-Doo*, and *The Tale Of A Shirt*, which was
ingeniously set to the famous *Toreador Song* from
Bizet's *Carmen*.

△

Minstrel headliner Eddie Leonard (centre) made his talkie debut with **Melody Lane** (Universal), a rather lachrymose musical about a vaudeville dancer and his partner (Leonard, and Josephine Dunn, right) and the travails that overtake them. As was generally the way with such plots, the team – who also happen to be married to each other – split when the lady of the act is offered a role in a stock company, and three years pass before they are reunited in New York. He has become a down-and-out prop man, she a successful dramatic star. Their young daughter Jane La Verne inadvertently effects a happy ending for them, in spite of their differences, when she hurts herself in a fall and is sung (literally) back to health by her pa. Huntley Gordon (left) was also in it. The paying customers avoided it in droves – despite the inclusion of one of Leonard's famous 'trademark' numbers, 'Roly Boly Eyes' (his own composition). It was written by J.G. Hawks and Robert F. Hill from a play by Jo Swerling, with Hill also directing. Songs: *The Song Of The Islands* Charles King; *Here I Am*; *There's Sugar Cane Round My Door*; *The Boogy Man Is Here* Eddie Leonard, Grace Stern, Jack Stern.

Will pretty Lois Moran (centre) agree to ▷ appear in student impresario David Percy's (centre right) musical numbers in the forthcoming college revue? Or will she decide, instead, to appear in the numbers being created for her by Percy's rival, Duke Morrison (later to be known as John Wayne)? That was the basic idea on which **Words and Music** (Fox) hung, and if ever there was a tenuous excuse for a series of songs and dances, this was it. In fact, the reason it happened at all was to use Lois Moran's numbers which had been cut from William Fox's *Movietone Follies of 1929* to bring that film down to manageable length! Helen Twelvetrees, William Orlamond, Elizabeth Patterson, Ward Bond, Richard Keene, Frank Albertson, Tom Patricola, the dancing Collier Sisters, plus adagio dancers Vina Gale, Arthur Springer, Harriet and John Griffith, and Helen and Charles Huff also appeared; the musical numbers were staged by Frank Merlin and Edward Royce, it was presented by William Fox, and directed by James Tinling from a screenplay by Andrew Bennison (story by Frederick Hazlitt Brennan and Jack McEdwards). Songs included: *Stepping Along* William Kernell; *Too Wonderful For Words* Kernell, Dave Stamper, Edmund Joseph, Paul Gerard Smith; *Shadows* Con Conrad, Sidney Mitchell, Archie Gottler.

A typical case, prevalent at the time, of songs ▷ in search of a good storyline, **William Fox Movietone Follies of 1929** (GB: **Movietone Follies of 1929**), concerned itself with the slim-line tale of a southerner from Virginia (John Breeden) who travels to New York in order to buy up a show which is still in rehearsal just so that he can fire his girlfriend Lila (Lola Lane) from the cast because he disapproves of the stage as a career. It doesn't quite work out that way and, pre-dating *42nd Street* (Warner Bros., 1933) by four years, young Lila finds herself catapulted to stardom when the leading lady indulges in a spot of temperament and refuses to go on. With the show an established hit, Breeden sells his interest in it at a profit, and persuades Lila to return to Virginia and marry him. Sue Carol (right), who led the striking 'Breakaway' number, was featured; so were Dixie Lee and David Rollins (left), and the rest of the cast included De Witt Jennings, Sharon Lynn, Arthur Stone, adagio dancers Harriet and John Griffith, and Stepin Fetchit. It was written and directed for producer William Fox by David Butler (dialogue by William K. Wells), the musical numbers were staged by Marcel Silver

and Fanchon, the score was by Con Conrad, Sidney Mitchell and Archie Gottler (who played a stage manager in it), and the musical director, Arthur Kay, did the on-screen conducting. Songs and musical numbers: *Walking With Susie*; *Why Can't I Be Like You?*; *Legs*; *That's You, Baby*; *Look What You've Done To Me*; *Big City Blues*; *Pearl Of Old Japan*. Interesting sideline: As well as normal photography, the film was made in Fox's 70mm Grandeur System which was well received at a preview. The soundtrack was three times as wide as on 35mm film, resulting in superior sound quality, but movie managements, already in debt through conversion to sound, were not receptive since it required new projectors and screens with ground glass surfaces.

In bringing Phillip Dunning and George Abbott's 1927 stage hit **Broadway** to the screen, director Paul Fejos devised a camera crane (at a cost of $75,000) capable of travelling at every conceivable angle and at a speed of six hundred feet a minute. His object? To impart a greater fluidity to the tale of an innocent Broadway hoofer who finds himself involved in a bootlegging murder. Producer Carl Laemmle Jr's $1,000,000 production for Universal contained an elaborate cabaret setting (the film's visual *pièce de resistance*) which was a trifle out of kilter with the sleazy, hard-hitting atmosphere purveyed in the Broadway original; while the addition of several musical numbers gave the material even further gloss – but not enough to diminish the undeniable impact of the tense backstage melodrama being played out among the protagonists. Glenn Tryon (illustrated centre) was excellent as the innocent hoofer, Merna Kennedy somewhat less so as the girl he loves. Repeating the roles they had created on stage were Thomas E. Jackson as sleuth Dan McCorn, and Paul Porcasi as the owner of *The Paradise Night Club* where much of the action takes place. Robert Ellis was the bad guy of the piece, with Evelyn Brent effective as Pearl, the vengeful showgirl who, with a bullet aimed at point-blank range, puts an end to Ellis's criminal activities. Others in the cast were Otis Harlan, Marion Lord, Fritz Feld, Leslie Fenton, and Gus Arnheim and His Cocoanut Grove Ambassadors. The screenplay was by Edward T. Lower Jr and Charles Furthman, and the splashy but routine dance numbers the work of Maurice L. Kusell. Hal Mohr was the cameraman, and the nightclub sequences were in 'natural' colour. The film was remade in 1942. Songs and musical numbers: *Broadway; The Chicken Or The Egg; Hot Footin' It; Hittin' The Ceiling; Sing A Little Love Song* Con Conrad, Sidney Mitchell, Archie Gottler.

◁ **Smiling Irish Eyes** (First National) starred James Hall as a fiddle-playing songwriter who deserts the Irish mist to pursue the bright lights of Broadway, leaving behind him the girl with whom he has written the film's well-known title song (actual composers Ray Perkins and Herman Ruby). The neglected lass who follows her love to America, only to suffer disillusionment before living happily ever after, was played by Colleen Moore in her first all-singing, all-dancing picture, produced by her husband John McCormick. Heavy handed and prosaic, the screenplay was by Tom Geraghty and the direction by William A. Seiter with choreography by Larry Ceballos (see illustration). Also in it were Claude Gillingwater, Robert Homans, Aggie Herring and Betty Francisco. Songs included *A Wee Bit Of Love; Then I'll Ride Home With You; Old Killarney Fair* Norman Spencer, Herman Ruby.

Honky Tonk (Warner Bros.) was memorable mainly for the central performance of Sophie Tucker – 'the last of the red-hot mommas' – with songs by Jack Yellen (who also wrote the dialogue) and Milton Ager, as well as 'Some Of These Days' by Shelton Brooks, the number now indivisible from the star who made it famous. Tucker (illustrated) starred as a nightclub singer who sacrifices her all to educate her daughter. But the ungrateful girl, on learning of her mother's profession, denounces her, thus giving Miss Tucker ample opportunity to tug at the audience's heartstrings, which she did to great effect. The film, adapted by C. Graham Baker from a story by Leslie S. Barrows, offered something for everyone, and everyone was duly enthusiastic. Lila Lee was featured as the daughter, and the supporting cast included Audrey Ferris, George Duryea, Mahlon Hamilton and John T. Murray. The dances were directed by Larry Ceballos, and the film by Lloyd Bacon who did full justice to the aggressive talent of his star. Songs: *I'm The Last Of The Red Hot Mommas; I'm Doin' What I'm Doin' For Love; He's A Good Man To Have Around; I'm Feathering A Nest (For A Little Bluebird); I Don't Want to Get Thin*. Remade as *Lullaby Of Broadway* (Warner Bros., 1951).
▽

First National's **Broadway Babies** was another runner from the popular backstage stable. Although fairly predictable, it had enough twists and turns to sustain interest, and leading lady Alice White (illustrated) emerged with credit. Not hitherto renowned as a musical comedy star, Miss White displayed a surprisingly good voice, and convinced both as a dancer and as an actress in this tale of a pure-hearted chorus girl in love with her stage manager (Charles Delaney). Their romance is disrupted by the arrival of a Detroit rum-runner (Fred Kohler) who almost succeeds in winning Alice's heart. Her love for her stage-manager prevails, however, the situation being assisted by Kohler's convenient demise at the hands of a trigger-happy gangster. The sprightly direction was by Mervyn LeRoy, whose cast was completed by Sally Eilers and Marion Byron (doing well as Miss White's co-chorines), Tom Dugan, Bodil Rosing, Louis Natheaux, Jocelyn Lee and Maurice Black. It was written by Monte Katterjohn and Humphrey Pearson from a story by Jay Gelzer, and the songs included: *Wishing And Waiting For Love; Jig Jigaloo* Grant Clarke, Harry Akst; *Broadway Baby Doll* Al Bryan, George W. Meyer.

The Time, The Place And The Girl (Warner Bros.), a lively campus musical, followed the career of a college football hero (Grant Withers) whose inflated ego takes a knock after his graduation when he becomes a less than successful bond salesman. Withers (right) however, has a way with the ladies – which his boss capitalizes on by getting him to offload bad bonds on to naive females, one of whom turns out to be the boss's wife! Written by Robert Lord from the W.M. Hough-Joseph E. Howard-Frank R. Adams play, it was directed by Howard Bretherton with a cast that featured Betty Compson (left), James R. Kirkwood, Vivian Oakland, Gretchen Hartman and Irene Haisman. The Vitaphone sound-on-disc system employed the roar of football crowds to good effect. Songs: *I Wonder Who's Kissing Her Now* Frank Adams, Harold Orlob, Will Hough, Joe Howard; *Collegiate* Mo Jaffe, Nat Bonx; *Doin' The Racoon* Raymond Klages, J. Fred Coots, herb Magidson; *Fashionette* Robert King, Jack Glogau; *Jack And Jill* Larry Spier, Sam Coslow; *How Many Times* Irving Berlin; *Everything I Do I Do For You* Al Sherman; *If You Could Care* E. Ray Goetz, Arthur Wimperis, Herman Darewski.
▽

Silent star Betty Compson, whose numerous accomplishments also included playing the violin, got a chance to do just that in **Street Girl** (Radio Pictures). And to prove that she could also act, she lumbered herself with a Hungarian accent – or what passed for one – and never faltered. She played a destitute violinist called Freddie Joyzelle who improves the fortunes of a quartet of jazz musicians. As the boys scratch, bang, thump and blow nightly at a run-down East Side restaurant, Freddie is scheming to change their venue to a smart Hungarian restaurant and to up their salary from a lousy hundred bucks a week to an impressive three thousand. Needless to say, she has a romantic involvement with one of the boys in the band but, after a few obligatory complications, Jane Murfin's serviceable screenplay ended happily ever after. Miss Compson was delightful and there was good work from Ned Sparks (right) who had all the best lines as the most pessimistic member of the group. John Harron (centre) played Betty's beau, with Jack Oakie (2nd left) and Guy Buccola (left) completing the combo. Joseph Cawthorn (2nd right) and Ivan Lebedeff (as Prince Nicolas of Aragon) were also in it; so were Doris Eaton and the Radio Pictures Beauty Chorus, Raymond Maurel and the Cimini Male Chorus, and Gus Arnheim and His Cocoanut Grove Ambassadors. William Le Baron produced, and the director was the talented Wesley Ruggles. Pearl Eaton staged the dances, and Oscar Levant and Sidney Clare wrote the songs which included: *Huggable And Sweet*; *My Dream Memory*; *Broken Up Tune*.

▽

Carl Laemmle's part-talking production of the Jerome Kern–Oscar Hammerstein II Broadway success **Show Boat** (Universal) was something of a curiosity, and it failed to find a responsive public. Originally filmed as a silent picture – with songs and dialogue being added for the sound version – it also contained an 18-minute prologue, introduced by Laemmle and Florenz Ziegfeld, featuring (for no reason that made any sense) three extracts from the original stage production with the original stage cast. Tess Gardella and the Jubilee Singers sang 'C'Mon Folks' and 'Hey Feller'; Helen Morgan sang 'Bill' and 'Can't Help Lovin' Dat Man' and Jules Bledsoe, with the same chorus that accompanied him on Broadway, performed 'Ol Man River'. The film version of the show that followed these extracts suffered by comparison. Laura La Plante (centre), whose singing voice was dubbed by Eva Olivetti, starred as an excessively lachrymose Magnolia; Joseph Schildkraut (left), speaking with more than just a trace of an accent, played Gaylord Ravenal, looking better than he sounded, and overacting shamelessly; Otis Harlan as Cap'n Andy was totally defeated by the comedy in the role and in no way matched up to Charles Winninger's already legendary Broadway performance, while Emily Fitzroy as the Cap'n's martinet wife,

△

For their production of **Dance of Life**, based on a play by George Manker Watters and Arthur Hopkins called *Burlesque*, Paramount recruited Hal Skelly (centre) from Broadway to recreate the role of Ralph 'Skid' Johnson, a burlesque entertainer who takes to drink when he allows success on Broadway to go to his head, and his pretty dancer wife Bonny (Nancy Carroll, centre right, in the role played on stage by Barbara Stanwyck), to divorce him after he resumes an affair with a former flame (Dorothy Revier). But it all comes right in the end when Miss Carroll, who has remarried, decides that her old husband needs her more than her wealthy new one and unselfishly returns to him. As in the original play, audiences were given a no-punches-pulled glimpse at backstage life, and a graphic – even

Parthenia Hawks, was generally considered to ▷ be wildly eccentric. The best and most consistent performance was given by Alma Rubens as the tragic Julie. (A tragic figure in real life too, Miss Rubens, a drug addict, died in 1931 at the age of 33 after being committed to the California Institute for the Insane.) **Show Boat's** screenplay – a rambling and diffuse effort by Charles Kenyon – was one of the chief reasons for the film's disappointing critical reception; so were Harry Pollard's over-earnest direction and Edward J. Montaigne's sloppy editing. Others in the cast were Elise Bartlett, Jack McDonald Stepin Fetchit, Neely Edwards, Theodore Lorch and Jane La Verne (right) plus the combined voices of the Billbrew Chorus, Silvertone Quartet, The Four Emperors of Harmony, Claude Collins, and Jules Bledsoe singing a series of Negro spirituals off-screen. Other songs: *Ol' Man River*; *Can't Help Lovin' Dat Man* Kern, Hammerstein II; *The Lonesome Road* Gene Austin, Nathaniel Shilkret; *Here Comes That Show Boat* Maceo Pinkard, Billy Rose; *Love Sings A Song In My Heart* Joseph Cherniavsky, Clarence J. Marks; *Coon, Coon, Coon* Gene Jefferson, Leo Friedmann; *Down South* Sigmund Spaeth, William H. Myddleton; *I've Got Shoes*; *Deep River* (traditional). **Show Boat** was remade by Universal (1936) and MGM (1951).

painful – account of a performer on the skids. Skelly was first rate throughout; so were his two leading ladies. The associate producer was David O. Selznick, it was directed by John Cromwell and Edward Sutherland (from a screenplay by Benjamin Glazer, dialogue by George Manker Watters), and the cast included Ralph Theodore, Charles D. Brown, Al St John, May Boley and Oscar Levant. A scene in The Ziegfeld Follies was photographed in two-colour Technicolor. Songs: *True Blue Lou*; *King of Jazzmania*; *Cuddlesome Baby*; *Flippity Flop*; *Ladies Of The Dance* Sam Coslow, Richard A. Whiting, Leo Robin. The source play *Burlesque* was later filmed again as *Swing High, Swing Low* (Paramount, 1937), and as *When My Baby Smiles At Me* (20th Century-Fox, 1948).

The first of the no-plot, all-star movie revues, **The Hollywood Revue of 1929** came to the screen with all MGM's manifold resources lavished upon it. The result was an over-produced (by Harry Rapf) extravaganza that attempted to out-Ziegfeld Ziegfeld in the sheer scope of its presentation. Though uneven in quality, it had its moments – notably Cliff Edwards introducing Arthur Freed and Nacio Herb Brown's 'Singin' In The Rain' (illustrated), Marion Davies doing 'Tommy Atkins On Parade' (also Freed and Brown), and the Gus Edwards–Joe Goodwin number called 'While Strolling Through The Park One Day' which featured Cliff Edwards, Gus Edwards, Polly Moran, Marie Dressler and Bessie Love. The movie also offered audiences a chance to see John Gilbert, Norma Shearer and Lionel Barrymore in an extract from *Romeo and Juliet*. The show was compered by Conrad Nagel and Jack Benny, included two Technicolor sequences, and called on Buster Keaton and Laurel and Hardy to provide the bulk of the laughs. It was directed by Charles F. Riesner, with Sammy Lee and George Cunningham in charge of the dance direction. Al Boasberg and Robert Hopkins wrote it; Cedric Gibbons and Richard Day dreamed up the sets. The very full musical programme also featured the following songs and musical numbers: *You Were Meant For Me* (Conrad Nagel dubbed by Charles King) Freed, Brown; *Low-Down Rhythm* (Jane Purcell, dancers) Raymond Klages, Jesse Greer; *For I'm The Queen* (Marie Dressler) Andy Rice, Martin Broones; *Gotta Feelin' For You* (Joan Crawford, Paul Gibbons, Biltmore Trio) Jo Trent, Louis Alter; *Bones And Tambourines* (Ensemble); *Strike Up the Band* (Brox Sisters, dancers); *Tableau Of Jewels* (James Burroughs, girls) Fred Fisher; *Lon Chaney Will Get You If You Don't Watch Out* (Gus Edwards, dancers); *Your Mother And Mine* (illustrated left, Jack Benny, Karl Dane, George K. Arthur); *Orange Blossom Time* (Charles King, Albertina Rasch Ballet, Belcher Child Dancers); *Minstrel Days* (Gus Edwards, chorus); *Nobody But*

You (Cliff Edwards); *I Never Knew I Could Do A Thing Like That* (Bessie Love, Boys); *Marie, Polly And Bess* (Dressler, Moran, Love) Gus Edwards, Joe Goodwin.

TWENTIES MUSICALS

'Rough and profane' was how one reviewer described **The Cock-Eyed World** (Fox) – a sequel to Laurence Stallings and Maxwell Anderson's *What Price Glory* (Fox, 1926) which again starred Victor McLaglen (left) and Edmund Lowe (right), with Raoul Walsh directing, as he had the first time round. Lacking the irony of the earlier film, or its deep involvement with the subject of war, **The Cock-Eyed World** was a moderately entertaining comedy with several songs scattered throughout the narrative. The screenplay, by Walsh and William K. Wells, was based on an unpublished play by Stallings and Anderson, and focused mainly on the friendly rivalry that existed between Sergeant Flagg (McLaglen) and Quirt (Lowe), particularly where women were concerned. And the women concerned were a Russian minx (Jeanette Dagna), a Brooklyn flapper (Jean Bary) and a Spanish spitfire named Elenita (Lily Damita, centre). Also in the cast were El Brendel, Bob Burns, Joe Brown and Stuart Erwin. The film was a moderate success. Songs: *Semper Fidelis* John Philip Sousa; *Over There* George M. Cohan; *Rose Of No Man's Land* James Caddigan, James Brennan; *Ka-Ka-Katy* Geoffrey O'Hara; *What Has Become Of Hinky Dinky Parlay Voo* Al Dubin, Irving Mills, Jimmy McHugh, Irwin Dash; *You're The Cream In My Coffee* Buddy De Sylva, Lew Brown, Ray Henderson; *Glorianna* Sidney Clare, Lew Pollack; *So Long; So Dear To Me* Con Conrad, Sidney Mitchell, Archie Gottler.

Apart from the usual suspension of disbelief without which the musical as a genre could not exist, **Broadway Scandals** (Columbia) asked audiences to accept Carmel Myers (left), an actress of average ability, as Valeska, a Broadway superstar whose incandescence alone could light up the Great White Way. The plot has Myers coming between a young song-and-dance man (Jack Egan, right) and his sweetheart (Sally O'Neil) when she asks the former, who is in the process of devising a new act with the latter, to become her leading man. Egan at first refuses, but accepts when girlfriend Sally agrees to join the chorus of the show. Through Egan's influence Sally scores a personal triumph when given a spot of her own, as a result of which Miss Myers throws a jealous tantrum and has the talented young upstart fired. Predictably Egan packs his bags and temporarily exits the big-time, until he and Sally can, quite literally, get their act together. Harry Cohn produced, George Archainbaud directed, Gladys Lehman wrote the scenario, and Norman Huston and Howard J. Green the dialogue (from a story by Green). Others in the cast were Tom O'Brien, J. Barney Sherry, John Hyams and Charles Wilson. Songs included: *What Is Life Without Love?* Fred Thompson, David Franklin, Jack Stone; *Does An Elephant Love Peanuts?* James Hanley; *Can You Read In My Eyes* Sam Coslow; *Love's The Cause Of All My Blues* Jo Trent, Charles Daniels; *Would I Love To Love You* Dave Dreyer, Sidney Clare; *Rhythm Of The Tambourine; Kickin' The Blues Away* David Franklin.

◁ Warner Bros. attempted to repeat the success of *The Jazz Singer* and *The Singing Fool* by drawing on the same ingredients for **Say It With Songs**. This time Al Jolson (foreground) starred as a radio singer who is jailed for having accidentally killed a man who flirted with his (Jolson's) wife. Jolson was paid the astronomical sum of half a million dollars to appear in what turned out to be an unmitigated disaster – with the songwriting team of Buddy De Sylva, Lew Brown and Ray Henderson providing yet another funereal air *à la* 'Sonny Boy', this time called 'Little Pal', which completely failed to repeat the success of the earlier song. Darryl F. Zanuck and Harvey Gates were responsible for the story, with Joseph Jackson receiving credit for adaptation and dialogue. The director was Lloyd Bacon. Jolson's wife was played by Marian Nixon, and Davey Lee (Little Pal) appeared in a featured role, with other parts going to Holmes Herbert, Fred Kohler, John Bowers and Kenneth Thomson. Songs included: *Why Can't You; Used To You; I'm In Seventh Heaven; One Sweet Kiss* De Sylva, Brown, Henderson; *Back In Your Own Backyard; I'm Ka-razy About You* Dave Dreyer, Al Jolson, Billy Rose.

◁ A hit for Warner Bros. and a personal triumph for Winnie Lightner (whose career had started in vaudeville), **Gold Diggers of Broadway** was adapted from Avery Hopwood's stage play *Gold Diggers*, first filmed by Warner Bros. in 1923. Robert Lord's scenario provided some genuine love interest and a fair amount of comedy in the familiar story of three girls and the wealthy trio of chumps who fall for their charms; and under Roy Del Ruth's direction, it zinged along, substantially enhanced by the imaginative use it made of Technicolor, and by a clutch of Al Dubin–Joe Burke songs. These included two hit numbers (crooned by Nick Lucas), 'Tiptoe Through The Tulips', and 'Painting The Clouds With Sunshine', the latter lending its name to the 1951 remake of the movie starring Virginia Mayo. Larry Ceballos staged the musical numbers (illustrated) with the accent on tap; Nancy Welford and Ann Pennington played Miss Lightner's fellow 'gold diggers'; with other featured roles going to Conway Tearle, Lilyan Tashman, William Bakewell, Helen Foster and Albert Gran. Other songs included: *In A Kitchenette; Go To Bed; And Still They Fall In Love; What Will I Do Without You?; Mechanical Man; Song Of The Gold Diggers*.

Marianne is the only musical in the history of the genre in which the leading lady and a pig attempt to upstage one another. In this instance, the leading lady was Marion Davies (left) with the pig the main fulcrum of Dale Van Every's silly World War I comedy (dialogue by Gladys Unger and Laurence Stallings). For without the animal – whom Miss Davies befriends and attempts to save from the slaughterhouse – she would never have met Private Lawrence Gray (right) and fallen in love. Actually, in a rather desperate attempt to keep the movie buoyant, Miss Davies did a lot else besides fall in love – she sang, she danced, she emoted and, for her *pièce de resistance*, impersonated Sarah Bernhardt and Maurice Chevalier! She even encumbered herself with a French accent throughout the film's seven reels, but to little avail. With **Marianne**, Cosmopolitan Productions and MGM failed to bring home the bacon and the film's luke-warm reception was not entirely surprising. Cliff Edwards (Ukelele Ike) and Benny Rubin provided some boisterous comedy, with Scott Kolk, Robert Edeson, George Baxter and Emile Chautard in support. A silent version of the film was also shot, with Oscar Shaw and Robert Castle featured in the roles played in the sound version by Lawrence Gray and George Baxter. Robert Z. Leonard directed. Songs: *When I See My Sugar*; *Marianne*; *Oo-La-La* Roy Turk, Fred Ahlert; *Hang On To Me*; *Just You, Just Me* Raymond Klages, Jesse Greer; *Blondy* Arthur Freed, Nacio Herb Brown.

Adapted by Hugh Herbert from a story by Ben Hecht, **The Great Gabbo** (James Cruze Productions) gave the celebrated Austrian actor-director Erich von Stroheim (illustrated) a heaven-sent opportunity to chew up the scenery – which he did to stunning effect. He played Gabbo, a ventriloquist whose unbridled egotism results in his losing the one girl he loves (Betty Compson), his sanity and, finally, his dummy and soulmate Otto, whom he smashes up in an outburst of jealous rage. Dramatic stuff, directed a trifle crudely by James Cruze (real-life husband of Miss Compson), and vigorously performed by a cast that included Donald Douglas and Marjorie 'Babe' Kane. The choreography was by Maurice Kusell, and the songs by Paul Titsworth, Lynn Cowan, Donald McNamee and King Zany. These were: *The New Step*; *I'm In Love With You*; *I'm Laughing*; *Ickey*; *Every Now And Then*; *The Web Of Love*; *The Ga-Ga Bird*.

Because of the huge risk factor involved in an all-black presentation, Nicholas Schenck, the President of MGM, refused to allow **Hallelujah** to proceed until its producer/director King Vidor agreed to invest his salary in the production itself. The result was an impressive music drama about a poor cotton-picking family in the South, and one of the year's best films. It starred Daniel L. Haynes as Zeke (centre) and Nina Mae McKinney as Chick, the harlot whose link with a disreputable bunch of craps shooters brings about Zeke's downfall and his ultimate search for religion. Victoria Spivey played the good girl Haynes really loves, William Fountaine was Chick's conniving lover and Everett McGarrity the younger brother Haynes accidentally shoots after being cheated out of his money in a rigged game of craps. The first full-length, all-black, all-talking feature, **Hallelujah** made stunning use of negro spirituals in the telling of its somewhat melodramatic story (by Vidor, dialogue by Ransom Rideout) and, against Vidor's wish, also

The first Viennese operetta to be filmed as an all-talking, all-singing, all-dancing extravaganza, **Married in Hollywood** (Fox) by Oscar Straus, with additional music by Dave Stamper and Arthur Kay and lyrics by Harlan Thompson, was a well-recorded effort in which its leading players, Norma Terris (right) and J. Harold Murray – both Broadway recruits from Ziegfeld shows – sang better than they acted. Considering the paucity of plot (American girl vocalist, while on a European tour, falls in love with a Balkan prince much to the chagrin of his parents), this was no liability at all. It was the music that mattered and audiences did not go home disappointed. The final sequences were filmed in 'natural' colour and showed the prince and his showgirl united in Hollywood where she has become a star of motion pictures, and where he has fled following a palace revolution, about to live happily ever after. If vocally the film belonged to its two Broadway visitors, the acting honours went to Walter Catlett in the role of a film producer whose talent spotting results in Miss Terris's Hollywood contract. Also cast were Irene Palasty (left), Lennox Pawle, Tom Patricola, Evelyn Hall and Herman Bing. It was produced by William Fox, written by Harlan Thompson, choreographed by Edward Royce and directed by Marcel Silver with a pleasing sense of rhythm and pace. The songs included: *Dance Away The Night*; *Peasant Love Song*; *A Man, A Maid*; *Deep In Love*; *Bridal Chorus*; *National Anthem*; *Once Upon A Time*.

had a couple of Irving Berlin songs tacked on to the completed picture. The first, called 'Waiting At The End Of The Road', was sung by the Dixie Jubilee Singers at a market place while waiting for the cotton they have just picked to be weighed; while the second, 'Swanee Shuffle', provided Nina Mae McKinney with a jazzy come-hither dance as part of her plan to entice Haynes. Though Vidor disapproved acutely of the studio's interference with his work, his film remains an honest depiction of the kind of life lived by the American negro in a particular period of history and, fifty years later, retains its power to move audiences profoundly. The innovative camera set-ups (especially evident in a chase through a swamp), the subtlety of the direction, the exemplary deployment of sound, and the conviction of all the central performances combined to make **Hallelujah** a watershed in the development of the screen musical. The film was shot 'silent' on location, the sound being dubbed in in Hollywood.

△

William Fox's **Sunnyside Up** (Fox), one of the most inventive and original musicals of the year, successfully attempted to break away from the familiar backstage musical to tell the simple, uncluttered (and, it must be said, unoriginal) story of a poor girl from Yorkville, Manhattan, and her romance with a handsome young millionaire from Long Island. Janet Gaynor (illustrated in background) was the girl, Charles Farrell (foreground left) the beau, and it mattered not a jot that neither performer was particularly talented as a musical comedy star nor, if you closed your eyes, that their singing voices sounded identical. What they did have was charm and appeal, plus a first-rate score by De Sylva, Brown and Henderson behind which to hide their conspicuous lack of ability. Two-colour 'Multicolor' also came to their rescue in an entertainment sequence staged, for charity, in Farrell's Long Island retreat; so did a rather remarkable (for its time) production number called 'Turn On The Heat' sung by Sharon Lynn, in which a bevy of girls, clad in Eskimo furs, slowly shed their winter garments as their igloos melt, and the freezing Arctic setting changes to a tropical paradise complete with palm trees that miraculously materialize, fully grown, from little holes in the ground. The heat intensifies, everything in sight catches fire, and the girls make a spectacular exit by diving into a surrounding ornamental

pool. The scene ends with a sheet of water sprouting upwards in place of the more traditional curtain. The film's other production number, while more modest in scale, featured the hit song 'If I Had A Talking Picture Of You' rendered first by Gaynor and Farrell, then by an entire kindergarten of tots. The score produced two further hits, 'I'm A Dreamer', sung by Gaynor to her own accompaniment on a zither, and the rousing title song, which climaxed a neighbourhood party in a poor section of New York's East Side. The slender sub-plot was provided by Marjorie White and Frank Richardson as a couple of ordinary tenement dwellers, who also got a crack at the title song, as well as one of their own, a ditty called 'You've Got Me Pickin' Petals Off O' Daisies'. The score contained two more songs, 'You Find The Time, I'll Find The Place' sung by Sharon Lynn, and 'It's Great To Be Necked', sung by Marjorie White as 'It's Great To Be Necht (on a braw brecht moonlicht nicht)', the sequence being an unacknowledged parody of Sir Harry Lauder's songs. The story and dialogue were by De Sylva, Brown and Henderson, and the dance numbers the brainchild of Seymor Felix. The director was David Butler, and his supporting cast included El Brendel, Mary Forbes, Joe Brown, Peter Cawthorne and Jackie Cooper. **Sunnyside Up**, without doubt, was one of the formative musicals of the early talkies.

The Love Parade (Paramount), with music and lyrics by Victor Schertzinger and Clifford Grey, was Ernst Lubitsch's first sound film and Jeanette MacDonald's (centre) screen debut. It was also the first of four films Chevalier and MacDonald were to make together, and the first full-scale musical conceived by a director of genius. The story concerns Queen Louise of Sylvania (MacDonald) who, while waiting for her dream lover to come along, learns of the sexual proclivities of her foreign emissary, Count Alfred (Chevalier), in Paris. Titillated, she calls for him in order to prove his prowess on home ground. She is satisfied and marries him. But the count doesn't really enjoy playing the role of Prince Consort, for not only does MacDonald wear the crown, but also the trousers. In the end, however, male chauvinism wins the day, and the queen agrees to make him her king. Although the film lacked the fluidity of movement Lubitsch was to achieve in later musicals such as *Monte Carlo* (Paramount, 1930) and *The Merry Widow* (MGM, 1934), there was sufficient imagination in the handling of the scenario and the score was integrated into the action to breathtaking effect. It was written by Ernest Vajda and Guy Bolton from a play by Leon Xanrof and Jules Chancel, and produced by

As was typical of most campus musical comedies, the students on view in **So This Is College** (MGM) didn't so much as open a book throughout the eleven reels it took to unspool – study clearly being the least important item on scenarists Al Boasberg, Delmer Daves and Joe Farnham's agenda. They were far more concerned with the friendship between two football-playing buddies and the romance each is having with a scheming college girl whose duplicity is revealed at the big USC–Stanford match. Elliott Nugent (left, sitting), Robert Montgomery (foreground right) and Sally Starr (centre) were recruited from Broadway by producer-director Sam Wood to breathe freshness into the workaday plot, but despite the inclusion of some exciting stock footage of an actual football match between the two universities (filmed in 1928) and the addition of four songs, the movie – like Miss Starr – came and went. Cliff Edwards (foreground, 2nd right), Polly Moran, Phyllis Crane, Dorothy Dehn, Max Davidson and Ann Brody were also cast. Songs: *Sophomore Prom* Jesse Greer; *College Days*; *Campus Capers* Martin Broones; *I Don't Want Your Kisses* Fred Fisher, Martin Broones.
▽

Lubitsch with a supporting cast that included Lupino Lane, Lillian Roth, Edgar Norton, Lionel Belmore and Eugene Pallette. Songs: *Nobody's Using It Now* (Chevalier – the first musical soliloquy in a talking picture); *Paris, Stay The Same* (Chevalier, Lupino Lane); *Dream Lover* (MacDonald, chorus); *Anything To Please The Queen* (MacDonald, Chevalier); *Wedding March* (chorus); *Let's Be Common* (Lane, Lillian Roth); *March Of The Grenadiers* (Macdonald, men); *Champagne* (Lane); *My Love Parade* (MacDonald, Chevalier); *Sylvania's Queen* (chorus); *The Queen Is Always Right* (Roth, Lane, chorus); *Valse Tatjana* (ballet music by O. Potoker).
▽

△

Paramount should have found a stronger vehicle for Gertrude Lawrence's talkie debut than **The Battle of Paris**, a woebegone effort in which the star fought valiantly against the inanities of the plot (story and screenplay by Gene Markey) – and lost. She played a street singing Parisienne who, after teaming up with a pickpocket called Zizi (Charles Ruggles), falls in love with Walter Petrie (left) an American artist whose pocket Zizi has picked, and decides to become his model. Miss Lawrence (right) demonstrated her unique way with a couple of undistinguished Cole Porter songs (his movie debut), but the film as a whole found no takers and was a dismal flop. Gladys Du Bois, Arthur Treacher and Joe King were also cast and the director was Robert Florey. Songs: *They All Fall In Love*; *Here Comes The Bandwagon* Porter; *What Makes My Baby Blue*; *Housekeeping For You* Howard Dietz, Jay Gorney.

With **Applause** (Paramount), filmed at the Astoria Studios in New York, 29-year-old torch singer Helen Morgan was given the finest screen role of her career, and director Rouben Mamoulian a chance to turn his considerable talents to talking pictures. The result was an unqualified artistic success for both of them. The story of an ageing Broadway burlesque queen called Kitty Darling, it showed Morgan sharing a squalid, drunken existence with Hitch, an unscrupulous comedian, and the effect her 17-year-old daughter, April, has on her when she arrives from a convent to take up residence in the big city. April's appearance results in Morgan (right) marrying the no-good Hitch out of a sense of propriety, but the marriage is a disaster and in no time at all Hitch is making passes at April who rejects them and, instead, becomes engaged to a sailor. Distressed, however, at her mother's rapid decline, April decides to give up the sailor in order to look after her. But Morgan takes poison rather than allow her daughter to ruin her happiness by becoming her 'meal ticket'. Showing tremendous cinematic flair, Mamoulian contrasted the relentlessly sordid aspects of his story (from the novel by Beth Brown) with lengthy passages depicting a more serene existence at the convent and, in both milieus, allowed his camera to move with more fluidity than was customary for early talking pictures. His use of sound was equally innovative, and instead of using only one mic-

△ A lavish, if somewhat uncinematic screen transplant of Ziegfeld's 1927 stage hit, **Rio Rita** (RKO), directed (in 24 days) by Luther Reed for producer William Le Baron, retained the spirit and spectacle of the Broadway production and was the most successful movie adaptation of a musical comedy – and one of the most remunerative – to date. Like the stage show, in which a basically flimsy plot chased a pleasing score without ever catching up with it, the film's narrative line was hardly its trump card, and the story, which mainly concerned itself with the mysterious identity of a bandit known as Kinkajou – and the distinct possibility that he may even be Rio Rita's brother – took third billing to the opulence of the production (the latter half being filmed in Technicolor) and the attractive presence of John Boles (right) and Bebe Daniels (centre) for whom Harry Tierney and Joseph McCarthy's melodious score presented no problems at all. Bert Wheeler and Robert Woolsey (making their talking picture debuts) were the obligatory comic relief, with other roles going to Don Alvarado (left), Dorothy Lee, George Renevant (who turns out to be the dreaded Kinkajou), Helen Kaiser, Fred Burns and Tiny Sandford. The dance director was Pearl Eaton. The songs included *You're Always In My Arms* (*But Only In My Dreams*); *Sweetheart We Need Each Other*; *Following The Sun Around*; *Rio Rita*; *If You're In Love You'll Waltz*; *The Kinkajou*; *The Ranger's Song* Tierney, McCarthy. Remade by MGM in 1942 as an Abbott and Costello vehicle.

rophone insisted, for certain scenes, on two, the sound from both being mixed together later. Because of the uncompromisingly unglamorous view it took of its subject, **Applause** was not the box-office success Mamoulian and his producers Jesse L. Lasky and Walter Wanger had hoped for, yet it remains one of the most striking of all the early talkies – and the apogee of its star's up-and-down career. Certainly she did nothing finer, and the four songs she sings in the film are superbly rendered. Joan Peers co-starred as her daughter, and was splendid; but Fuller Mellish Jr's performance as Hitch (left) was unfortunately not up to their high standard. being melodramatic and over-stated. The scenario and dialogue were by Garrett Fort and the cameraman was George Folsey. The rest of the cast included Henry Wadsworth. Jack Cameron and Dorothy Cumming. Songs: *What Wouldn't I Do For That Man* E.Y. Harburg, Jay Gorney; *Yaka Hula Hickey Dula* E. Ray Goetz, Joe Young. Pete Wendling; *Give Your Little Baby Lots Of Lovin'* Dolly Morse, Joe Burke; *I've Got A Feelin' I'm Fallin'* Billy Rose. Harry Link. Fats Waller (all sung by Helen Morgan); *Pretty Baby* Gus Kahn. Egbert Van Alstyne. Tony Jackson; *Turkey Trot* Robin Hood Bowers. Edgar Smith; *Waiting For The Robert E. Lee* Lewis F. Muir. L. Wofe Gilbert; *Doin' The New Raccoon* Dolly Morse, Joe Burke; *Smiles* J. Will Callahan. Lee Roberts; *Sweetheart Of All My Dreams* Art and Kay Fitch. Bert Lowe; *That's My Weakness Now* Bud Green, Sammy Stept.

Burnt-cork comedians George Moran and Charles Mack (illustrated left and right) known to their fans as The Black Crows. made their talkie debut in **Why Bring That Up?** (Paramount). a well-crafted comedy by George Abbott, who directed and wrote the dialogue from a story by Octavus Roy Cohen, which gave Messrs M and M several opportunities to reprise some of their better-known sketches – including the one about the early bird and the worm. The story itself wasn't much (the duo find themselves involved with a minx who, in cahoots with her shady lover, attempts to fleece Moran of all he owns), but it served its purpose as a comic springboard for its two popular stars. The denouement, however, in which Mack, after being knocked unconscious by the minx's lover, is nursed back to health by Moran, who in desperation goes through some of their act together, was mawkish in the extreme and derivative of at least two other films in 1929 employing a similar device. Evelyn Brent starred as the minx, with Freeman S. Wood as her accomplice, and Harry Green, Bert Swor, Lawrence Leslie and Henry Lynch completed the cast. Songs included: *Do I Know What I'm Doing While In Love* Richard A. Whiting, Leo Robin; *Shoo Shoo Boogie Boo* Whiting, Sam Coslow.

Vaudevillian Belle Baker (centre) scored a personal success in **The Song of Love** (Columbia), a mawkish backstage story by Howard Green. Henry McCarthy and Dorothy Howell which reunites her with her husband (and former stage partner) after she retires from the business, and he fools around with a flirtatious blonde called Maizie. Actually, it is their young son (David Durand, right) who is responsible for the reconciliation, and were he not so unpalatably cute one might almost have been happy for him. Ralph Graves (left) played the philandering father, Eunice Quedens (to become better known as Eve Arden) was Maizie. Harry Cohn supervised the production, Erle C. Kenton directed, and the supporting cast included Arthur Housman and Charles Wilson. Songs: *I'm Somebody's Baby Now* Mack Gordon, Max Rich; *I'm Walking With The Moonbeams* (*Talking To The Stars*) Gordon, Rich, Maurice Abrahams; *I'll Still Go On Wanting You* Bernie Grossman; *White Way Blues* Gordon, Rich, George Weist.

Of all the studios introducing colour in 1929, Warner Bros. took the initiative in risking full use of it and, under Darryl F. Zanuck's supervision, made the first all-colour, all-talking, all-singing **On With The Show** (illustrated). Directed by Alan Crosland from a screenplay by Robert Lord (based on Humphrey Pearson's play *Shoestring*), it was both ambitious and unsuccessful. The story was one of backstage intrigue (a genre which was to proliferate to excess and finally find its best expression in Warner Bros's epoch-making *42nd Street* four years later) surrounding the out-of-town tryout of a show destined to be a huge hit once it has opened, but dogged in the interim with financial problems for everybody, particularly the producer who can't pay his cast or meet any other expenses. What distinguished this offering was a story structure in which the musical numbers – composed by Grant Clarke and Harry Akst, and choreographed by Larry Ceballos – were part of the show-within-a-show, whose plot the audience was able to follow simultaneously with the backstage intrigues. That aside, it was a catalogue of misjudgements. Zanuck perversely cast Betty Compson in the lead role of a temperamental musical comedy star, although Miss Compson was unacceptable both as a singer and as a dancer. This resulted in a professional dancer having to sub for her in the long shots, and in Josephine Houston dubbing her vocals. The movie was disadvantageously photographed through the claustrophobic camera booths of the time, and recounted its tale with little concession to the needs of film: not untypically, the full-stage ensemble numbers, photographed by a static head-on camera placed at a necessarily large distance from the stage, reduced the dancers to little specks; and, on this occasion, simultaneous sound-recording was achieved by concealing 38 microphones – also at quite some distance from the performers – which led to the music being drowned by the noise of dancing feet. The general clumsiness of the production was underlined by an irritating performance from Joe E. Brown (making his debut for Warners), and an astoundingly inadequate contribution from Sally O'Neil, whose one vocal number also required the services of Josephine Houston. The only player to emerge unscarred was Ethel Waters with her singing of 'Am I Blue' and 'Birmingham Bertha'. Also featured: Louise Fazenda, William Bakewell, Lee Moran, Harry Gribbon, The Fairbanks Twins and The Harmony Emperors' Quartet. Other songs included: *In The Land Of Let's Pretend*; *Let Me Have My Dream*; *Welcome Home*; *Don't It Mean A Thing To You?*; *Lift The Juleps To My Two Lips*; *On With The Show*.

Just as Mr Leonard crooned his ailing daughter back to life in *Melody Lane*, so Morton Downey (illustrated) nursed his ailing mother back to health in **Mother's Boy** (Pathe) – doing so at the cost of his Broadway debut. At the very moment that he is about to step onto the stage and wow 'em, his sweetheart (Helen Chandler) rushes backstage to inform him of the grim tidings, whereupon he deserts the show for his mother's bedside, and is rewarded for his filial devotion by making front page news the next morning and becoming a star! Unable to cope with Gene Markey's syrupy scenario, Downey floundered in the waves of its excessive sentimentality and sank without trace – taking with him Beryl Mercer (right, as his mother), John T. Doyle (his dad), Brian Donlevy and Osgood Perkins. Robert T. Kane produced, Bradley Barker directed – or so the credits would have us believe – and Sammy Stept and Bud Green composed the songs, which included: *There'll Be You And Me*; *Come To Me*; *I'll Always Be Mother's Boy*; *The World Is Yours And Mine*.

▽

The Show of Shows (Warner Bros.) was an extraordinary omnibus of individual revue items, and one which, with its bizarre combinations of acts and performers, certainly lived up to the studio's publicity claim that it was '. . . a connoisseur's collection of the supreme examples of almost every form of stage and screen entertainment'. Directed, partly in Technicolor, by John Adolfi, and with both Larry Ceballos and Jack Haskell staging dance routines, audiences were treated to a series of sketches performed by Beatrice Lillie, Louise Fazenda and Lloyd Hamilton, an introduction by Rin-Tin-Tin to an ornate 'Chinese Fantasy', Nick Lucas crooning to an oriental princess (Myrna Loy, who else!) and a rotund Winnie Lightner warbling 'Singing In The Bathtub'. And that was just for starters!

▽

One production number grouped eight sets of sisters (including Loretta Young who was to go on to talkie stardom), each group wearing the national dress of a different country, singing 'Meet My Sister', with Richard Barthelmess as MC, while Douglas Fairbanks Jr led a bunch of well-known stars in a satire set in 1900. An item called 'The Execution Number', with the Mexican badlands for background, featured Monte Blue with some of the screen's leading 'heavies' headed by Noah Beery. The finale starred Betty Compson and Alexander Gray together with 15 individual acts, the whole thing coming to a climax with each of the film's stars singing 'Lady Luck'. The most unexpected item to emerge somewhere in the midst of all this, was a scene from Shakespeare's *Henry VI, Part*

Three played by John Barrymore with support from Anthony Bushell and E.J. Radcliffe. Also in it: Alice White, George Carpentier, Irene Bordoni, Ted Lewis and His Orchestra, Dolores Costello, Grant Withers (left, with Myrna Loy), Harriette Lake (soon to be better known as Ann Sothern), Ben Turpin, Lupino Lane, Jack Mulhall, Chester Morris, Chester Conklin, The Williams Adagio Dancers and, as overall Master of Ceremonies, Frank Fay who, unfortunately, was self-congratulatory and not very amusing. Songs and musical numbers: *Lady Luck* (Ted Lewis and Orchestra);*What's Become Of The Florodora Boys?* Ray Perkins; *Motion Picture Pirates* M.K. Jerome; *If I Could Learn To Love* (Georges Carpentier, Alice White, Patsy Ruth Miller) Herman Ruby, Jerome; *Pingo Pongo* (Winnie Lightner); *If Your Best*

Friends Won't Tell You Al Dubin, Joe Burke; *The Only Song I Know* (Nick Lucas); *Meet My Sister, Dear Little Pup* (Frank Fay, Winnie Lightner) J. Keirn Brennan, Perkins; *Your Mother And Mine* Joe Goodwin, Gus Edwards; *Just An Hour Of Love* (Irene Bordoni); *Li-Po-Li* (Nick Lucas, Myrna Loy); *Military March* Al Bryan, Ed Ward; *Rock-A-Bye Your Baby With A Dixie Melody* Joe Young, Sam Lewis, Jean Schwartz; *Your Love Is All I Crave* (Frank Fay, Harry Akst at the piano) Al Dubin, Perry Bradford, Jimmy Johnson; *Singing In The Bathtub* Herb Magidson, Ned Washington, Michael Cleary; *You Were Meant For Me* (Bull Montana, Winnie Lightner) Arthur Freed, Nacio Herb Brown; *Jumping Jack* (Louise Fazenda, Frank Fay) Bernie Seaman, Herman Ruby, Marvin Smolev, Rube Bloom.

TWENTIES MUSICALS

Pert June Clyde (left) spent most of her time in **Tanned Legs** (RKO) trying to straighten out other people's lives – including her mother's, her father's, and her sister's. A pity she couldn't have had a go at Tom Geraghty's screenplay (story by George Hull), or Marshall Neilan's plodding, couldn't-care-less direction. Arthur Lake (right) was cast as Little Miss Fixit's boyfriend, Sally Blane (in real life Loretta Young's sister) was her sister, Albert Gran her father and Nella Walker her mother. Shapely Ann Pennington was in it too – as Tootie a flapper. Also: Dorothy Revier, Allen Kearns. It was produced by Louis Sarecky. Songs included: *You're Responsible; With You, With Me; How Lovely Everything Could Be* Oscar Levant, Sidney Clare. Interesting sideline: Arthur Lake later spent 12 years playing Dagwood Bumstead in the *Blondie* films.
▽

Another musical comedy with a college setting, **Sweetie** (Paramount) was amiable nonsense that benefitted greatly from the eccentric presence of 'boop-a-doop' girl Helen Kane (left) as a student at 'Miss Twill's School For Girls'. The main joke in the George Marion Jr–Lloyd Corrigan screenplay was that Miss Twill's school was situated next to the all-male Pelham college, and as much comic mileage was drawn from this geographical proximity as the writers could devise. The usual romantic entanglements germane to such plots surfaced and were eventually unravelled. Pelham beat Oglethorpe in the big game – and Helen Kane got to sing a couple of numbers in her much imitated but actually inimitable way. Most notable of these was 'He's So Unusual' (by Al Lewis, Abner Silver and Al Sherman), a heartfelt lament that 'sweetie' would much rather play football than spend time with her. Also on hand were Nancy Carroll, as a chorus girl, and, more conspicuously, Jack Oakie as Miss Kane's sweetie, whose rendering of the 'Alma Mammy' college song (by Richard A. Whiting and George Marion Jr) was one of the best things in a so-so film. Stanley Smith, William Austin, Stuart Erwin, Wallace Mac-Donald and Charles Sellon completed the cast, the dance numbers were staged by Earl Lindsey and the director was Frank Tuttle. Other songs: *My Sweeter Than Sweet; The Prep Step; I Think You'll Like It; Bear Down Pelham* Richard A. Whiting, George Marion Jr.

Colleen Moore (right), always a sincere and ▷ versatile performer, played what amounted, almost, to dual roles in **Footlights and Fools** (Warner Bros./First National). The story by Katherine Brush (screen adaptation by Miss Brush with Tom Geraghty and Carey Wilson) was one of tears and heartache and furnished the movie with its unpopular down-beat ending. Miss Moore, as plain Betty Murphy, is packed off to Paris by a Broadway producer (Edward Martindel) to acquire a French image, whereupon he brings her back as an 'imported' musical comedy star known as Fifi d'Auray. Fifi–Betty is courted by two men – a worthless ne'er-do-well and an eligible millionaire – and mistakenly chooses to marry the former. When she sees him in his true light and sends him away, the millionaire has gone out of her life for ever and she is left with only the pathetic trappings of stardom for company. In spite of a slight tendency to 'cuteness', Colleen Moore, who featured in three out of the film's five Technicolored production numbers, triumphed in her dual characterizations, and audiences adored her. John McCormick produced and William A. Seiter directed with pedestrian efficiency, drawing adequate performances from Raymond Hackett and Fredric March (on loan from Paramount) as Fifi's suitors, and Virginia Lee Corbin (left) as a dumb chorine, Max Scheck, formerly of the Folies Bergères, Paris, directed the dances. Songs and musical numbers included: *If I Can't Have You; You Can't Believe My Naughty Eyes; Ophelia Will Fool You; Pilly Pom Pom Plee* Al Bryan, George Meyer.

In spite of its several song and dance numbers, **Is ▷ Everybody Happy?** (Warner Bros.) which starred the clarinet-playing Ted Lewis, was, on the whole, a miserable musical. The plot had Lewis (foreground) subjected to a series of unhappy situations such as being disowned by his parents and rejected by his girlfriend, none of which prevented him from springing up again to inquire buoyantly 'Is everybody happy?' – an unfortunate question in the circumstances! Joseph Jackson and James A. Starr were responsible for the overtly sentimental dialogue, Larry Ceballos staged the musical numbers, and Archie Mayo was given the unenviable task of directing it. Also featured in the cast were Alice Day, Ann Pennington, Lawrence Grant, Julia Swayne Gordon and Otto Hoffman. Songs and musical numbers: *Wouldn't It Be Wonderful?*; *I'm The Medicine Man For The Blues*; *Samoa*; *New Orleans* Grant Clarke, Harry Akst; *In The Land Of Jazz*; *Start Up The Band* Ted Lewis; *St Louis Blues* W.C. Handy; *Tiger Rag* attributed to both Jelly Roll Morton and to Nick La Rocca and the Original Dixieland Jazz Band; *Is Everybody Happy Now?* Maurice Rubens, Jack Osterman, Ted Lewis.

Irene Bordoni (left), recreating the role she had played so successfully on stage, made her talkie debut in **Paris** (First National), as did her English co-star, the debonair musical comedy star Jack Buchanan (right). Though the original show on which the movie was based was written by Cole Porter, Martin Brown and E. Ray Goetz (Miss Bordoni's real-life husband at the time), the film, unaccountably, did not use Porter's score, thus depriving itself of the one element that might have guaranteed its success. Louise Closser Hale starred as a mother whose determination to protect her son (Jason Robards) from marrying a chorus girl (Miss Bordoni) takes her from Massa- ▽

chusetts to Paris; with other roles going to Margaret Fielding and ZaSu Pitts. Although primarily made in black and white (and Vitaphone) Technicolor sequences were featured, and the emphasis of the entertainment was on spectacle. Adaptation and dialogue was by Hope Loring, the songs were composed by Al Bryan and Ed Ward and the choreography was by Larry Ceballos. The film was both produced and directed by Clarence Badger. Songs and musical numbers included: *Crystal Girl*; *Miss Wonderful*; *Paris*; *I Wonder What Is Really On His Mind*; *I'm A Little Negative*; *Somebody Mighty Like You*; *My Lover* (*Master Of My Heart*).

As Rudy Vallee's ability to infuse life into the roles he played was limited to a fixed facial expression, it was just as well that in his debut effort, **The Vagabond Lover** (Radio Pictures), few demands were made of him. All that he was called on to do was sing a handful of ballads pleasantly and, of course, play the saxophone. On both counts he acquitted himself adequately. Or, as one contemporary scribe noted at the time, his voice made you think 'of moonlight and roses' and the public agreed. What the plot made you think of was better left unsaid (it had Vallee, centre, invading a Long Island mansion, then impersonating the man who, through a correspondence course, taught him how to play the saxophone). The film also featured Sally Blane as the love interest, Charles Sellon, Norman Peck, Danny O'Shea, Nella Walker, Malcolm Waite and the Connecticut Yankees. They were all outflanked, however, by Marie Dressler who, as a *nouveau riche* society matron, was the best thing in a pretty mundane effort, written and produced by James Ashmore Creelman with Marshall Neilan directing. Songs included: *If You Were The Only Girl In The World* Clifford Grey, Nat D. Ayer; *A Little Kiss Each Morning*; *Georgie Porgie* sung by a quartet of little girls; *I Love You, Believe Me I Love You* Ruby Cowan, Philip Bartholomae, Phil Boutelje; *I'll Be Reminded Of You* Ken Smith, Edward Heyman; *I'm Just A Vagabond Lover* Leon Zimmerman, Rudy Vallee. ▽

TWENTIES MUSICALS

Released late in a season which had seen several ▷ other campus musicals, **The Forward Pass** (First National) was a pleasant, romantic college caper, and nothing more. Douglas Fairbanks Jr starred as the college quarterback who, after resigning from the team before a big match as a result of a romantic misunderstanding, resolves his emotional problems in time to make the crucial winning pass. Loretta Young (revealing a pleasant contralto voice) co-starred as the misunderstanding, with solid support on hand from Allan Lane as the undergraduate heavy, and from Guinn Williams (left) who provided the comedy interest. Edward Cline directed on location at the University of Southern California: the story was by Harvey Gates with dialogue by Howard Emmett Rogers; and the serviceable songs were by Ned Washington, Herb Magidson and Michael Cleary. Also in it were Bert Rome, Lane Chandler, Marion Byron (right), Floyd Shackleford, and The University of Southern California Football Team. Songs included: *One Minute Of Heaven*; *I Gotta Have You*; *Hello Baby*; *Huddlin'*.

△

Adapted by Adelaide Heilbron from George M. Cohan's play of the same name, **Little Johnny Jones** (Warner Bros./First National) starred Eddie Buzzell as an American jockey who journeys to England and wins the Derby. Directed without distinction by Mervyn LeRoy, but with Buzzell's (centre) comedic flair and his appealing way with a song (in this case two songs: 'Yankee Doodle Boy' and 'Give My Regards To Broadway', both by Cohan) lending Herculean support to a shaky structure, it cantered to the finishing post coming in for a place rather than a win. Completing the field were Alice Day, Robert Edeson and Edna Murphy. Other songs and musical numbers included: *Painting The Clouds With Sunshine* Al Dubin, Joe Burke; *Straight, Place and Show* Herman Ruby, M.K. Jerome; *Go Find Somebody To Love* Herb Magidson Michael Cleary; *My Paradise* Magidson, James Cavanaugh.

Sally, the 1920 stage musical by Guy Bolton and Jerome Kern, was adapted for the screen by Waldemar Young for Warner Bros./First National, who lavished a fortune on its celluloid incarnation in the hope of repeating on the screen the success it had enjoyed on Broadway. The lovely Marilyn Miller (centre) who had appeared in it on stage, again played the Broadway-bound waitress and, according to the studio's publicity blurb, was helped on her way by '150 beauties in the largest indoor scene ever photographed in color... 36 Albertina Rasch girls who dance more perfectly than other choruses can clog... an orchestra of 110 to play ▽ the song hits that Sally made famous, and many new numbers added for the screen production'. John Francis Dillon was the director with Larry Ceballos responsible for the musical numbers. Also cast were Alexander Gray, Joe E. Brown, T. Roy Barnes, Pert Kelton, Ford Sterling and Maude Turner Gordon. Jerome Kern's score included *Look For The Silver Lining* (lyrics by Buddy De Sylva) and *Sally* (lyrics by Clifford Grey). Other songs: *Walking Off Those Balkan Blues*; *After Business Hours (That Certain Business Begins)*; *All I Want To Do, Do, Do Is Dance*; *If I'm Dreaming Don't Wake Me Up Too Soon*; *What Will I Do Without You?* Al Dubin, Joe Burke.

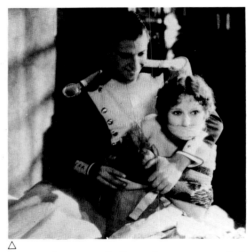

△ Although **The Painted Angel** (Warner Bros.) provided Billie Dove (illustrated) with a poor vehicle for her talents, the former Ziegfeld girl nonetheless managed to bring more than a touch of class to this story of a singer from New Orleans who becomes the queen of the New York nightclub circuit, and tangles with two men – one of whom she loves and one of whom she doesn't. Forrest Halsey's rather ordinary screenplay, based on a story by Fannie Hurst, took second place to the elaborately staged musical numbers, with director Millard Webb doing his best to give the property a high surface gloss in lieu of its indifferent content. Reliable support came from Edmund Lowe and George MacFarlane as the men in Miss Dove's life, with Cissy Fitzgerald, J. Farrell MacDonald and Norman Selby in it too. The songs were written by Herman Ruby and M.K. Jerome, and they included: *Help Yourself To My Love*; *Bride Without A Groom*; *Only The Girl*; *Everybody's Darling*; *That Thing*.

△

A piece of romantic fluff, **Devil May Care** (MGM) was the perfect vehicle for screen idol Ramon Novarro (left), whom cinema audiences had heard only once before in MGM's *The Pagán*, singing 'The Pagan Love Song'. For his dashing all-talkie debut, however, he was cast as Armand, a devotee of Napoleon who, following the Emperor's banishment to Elba, escapes death from Royalist soldiers, meets a beauty called Leonie (Dorothy Jordan, right), learns that she has no time for Bonapartists, narrowly avoids arrest, disguises himself as a footman and – for a second time – encounters the tempting Leonie. This time he falls in love with her. And this time she requites it. Novarro, doing all the things audiences had come to expect of him – such as proving his prowess with a horse and a sword – also established himself as a light tenor of immense charm, making the most of Herbert Stothart's 'The Shepherd's Serenade'. The first of the many operettas MGM would film throughout the thirties, **Devil May Care** also featured Marion Harris (a Broadway star making her only screen appearance), John Miljan, William Humphrey (as Napoleon), George Davis, Clifford Bruce and, in a Technicolor sequence depicting the gardens at Versailles, the Albertina Rasch Ballet (with music by Dimitri Tiomkin). It was adapted by Richard Schayer, with a scenario by Hans Kraly and dialogue by Zelda Sears, and directed by Sidney Franklin, and the score was by Herbert Stothart and Clifford Grey. Songs: *Bon Jour*; *Louie*; *March Of The Old Guard*; *Why Waste Your Charms*; *The Gang Song*; *Madame Pompadour*; *Charming*; *If He Cared*.

△

Considered by many at the time to be too bawdy for the more refined members of the audience, **Hot For Paris** (Fox) starred Victor McLaglen (right) as a rather uncouth sailor who wins a million dollars in a lottery as well as the heart of Miss Fifi D'Orsay. Unrestrainedly directed by Raoul Walsh, and with performances to match by Ed Brendel (left), Polly Moran, Lennox Pawle, Charles Judels and, especially, leading man McLaglen, it was a high-spirited romp whose lack of pretension was equalled only by its lack of subtlety. It was written by Charles J. McGuirk and William K. Wells from a story by Walsh, and presented by William Fox. Songs: *I'm The Duke Of Kakiyak*; *Sweet Nothings Of Love*; *If You Want To See Paree*; *Sing Your Little Folk Song* Walter Donaldson, Edgar Leslie.

William Powell (centre), fresh from his success as detective Philo Vance, was officially elevated to star status in **Pointed Heels** (Paramount), a backstage musical in which he played a wealthy theatrical producer. The plot, however, pivoted on the travails of a young composer (the excellent Phillips Holmes, left) whose parents stop his allowance after he defies them by marrying a chorus girl (Fay Wray, right) and, as such, it offered cinemagoers – already satiated with this type of yarn – naught for their comfort. A ballet sequence in Technicolor was easy on the eye, but the ear was punished by pert and perky Helen Kane whose incessant baby-talk was, by now, outstaying its welcome. Skeets Gallagher, Adrienne Dore and Eugene Pallette were also cast; it was written by Florence Ryerson and John V.A. Weaver (from a story by Charles Brackett), and directed by Edward Sutherland. Songs included: *I Have To Have You* Richard A. Whiting, Leo Robin; *Ain't Cha* Mack Gordon, Max Rich.

▽

1930

Academic Awards

Best Picture
NOMINATIONS INCLUDED: *The Love Parade* (Paramount) produced by Ernst Lubitsch

Best Actor
NOMINATIONS INCLUDED: Maurice Chevalier *The Love Parade & The Big Pond* (Paramount). Lawrence Tibbett *The Rogue Song* (MGM).

Direction
NOMINATIONS INCLUDED: Ernst Lubitsch *The Love Parade*. King Vidor *Hallelujah* (MGM).

Cinematography
NOMINATIONS INCLUDED: *The Love Parade* Victor Milner

Art Direction
King Of Jazz Herman Rosse
NOMINATIONS INCLUDED: *The Love Parade* Hans Dreier. *Sally* (First National) Jack Okey. *The Vagabond King* (Paramount) Hans Dreier.

Best Sound Recording (New category)
NOMINATIONS INCLUDED: *The Love Parade* Franklin Hansen. *Song Of The Flame* (First National) George Groves.

△

For **The Rogue Song**, an all-Technicolor feature, MGM recruited baritone Lawrence Tibbett from the Metropolitan Opera for the occasion, giving him his screen debut. He played the part of Yegor, the tribal chief of a group of mountain bandits in southern Russia, and it was a felicitous piece of casting which thrilled cinema audiences who had never heard such a powerful voice emanating from the screen before. Tibbett's acting wasn't bad either, and the sheer bravado of his performance bulldozed its way through the Francis Marion–John Colton screenplay (from the Franz Lehar–A.M. Willner–Robert Bodansky operetta *Gypsy Love*) without anyone noticing just how silly it all was. Catherine Dale Owen played Princess Vera, who flogs Yegor for kidnapping her (he sings more passionately with each stroke of the lash!), with other roles going to Judith Vosselli, Ullrich Haupt, Nance O'Neil, Lionel Belmore, Stan Laurel and Oliver Hardy, Florence Lake and Kate Price. Actor Lionel Barrymore, temporarily changing mantles, directed, with Albertina Rasch in charge of the choreography (the Rasch Ballet illustrated). The ballet music was by Dimitri Tiomkin, and the songs included: *When I'm Looking At You*; *Song Of The Shirt*; *Rogue Song* Herbert Stothart, Clifford Grey; *The White Dove* Franz Lehar, Grey.

Glorifying the American Girl (Paramount), the ▷ only film ever to be supervised by Florenz Ziegfeld in person, hardly glorified the American backstage film musical and, once again, was little more than an excuse to present a clutch of musical numbers (some of them photographed in Technicolor) in lieu of an intelligent storyline. J.P. McEvoy and Millard Webb (who also directed) came up with a scenario that had a dedicated Mary Eaton (as a Ziegfeld hopeful) eschewing domestic bliss with Edward Crandall by opting, instead, for the love of her audience. But it did at least serve as a showcase for the talented Helen Morgan who, in her accustomed pose on a white piano, sang 'What Wouldn't I Do For That Man' by E.Y. Harburg and Jay Gorney, which she had first introduced, amid many dialogue interruptions, in Paramount's *Applause*; and Eddie Cantor, doing his celebrated 'Cheap Charlie' tailor skit, as well as Rudy Vallee and His Orchestra. Appearing as themselves in the audience of a 'first night' sequence were Mr and Mrs Florenz Ziegfeld, Mayor and Mrs James Walker, Ring Lardner, Noah Beery, Texas Guinan, Johnny Weissmuller, Irving Berlin, Adolph Zukor and Charles Dillingham, all identified in voice-over narration by Norman Brokenshire. The musical numbers (see illustration) were staged by Frank Tours, and the ballet ensembles by Ted Shawn. Songs: *Blue Skies* Irving Berlin; *I'm Just A Vagabond Lover* Leon Zimmerman, Rudy Vallee; *At Sundown*; *Beautiful Changes*; *Sam The Old Accordion Man*; *There Must Be Someone Waiting For Me* Walter Donaldson; *Baby Face* Harry Akst, Benny Davis. Interesting sideline: The film had been planned by Ziegfeld as the first all-talking, all-singing movie immediately after he saw *The Jazz Singer* in October 1927, but the project was subjected to 18 months of delay by Jesse Lasky and Walter Wanger, partly because of initial uncertainty about sound, and partly because of Ziegfeld's notoriety concerning money matters. For a musical, it suffered especially from inferior sound quality through being shot at Paramount's Astoria Studios on Long Island, rather than on the West Coast where all efforts at improving sound techniques were focused.

A married man who manufactures Bibles for a living gives some perfectly innocent assistance to three girls from three different cities, but the inevitable complications ensue when they all arrive together at his Atlantic City cottage. Such was the slender but enduring thread on which **No, No, Nanette** (First National) hung. As it turned out, it was a very successful screen transfer of the Broadway musical by Otto Harbach and Frank Mandel. The screenplay, by Howard Emmett Rogers with dialogue by Beatrice Van, was generous with its laughs, and the show's irresistible good spirits were well communicated by director Clarence Badger, and choreographer Larry Ceballos. The Technicolor sequences were exceptionally striking and the songs good enough to eat. Bernice Claire (left) played Nanette, heading an adequate if not glittering cast which also featured Alexander Gray (right), Lilyan Tashman, Bert Roach, ZaSu Pitts, Louise Fazenda and Lucien Littlefield. Songs and musical numbers: *Dance Of The Wooden Shoes* Ned Washington, Herb Magidson, Michael Cleary; *As Long As I'm With You* Grant Clarke, Harry Akst; *King Of The Air*; *Dancing To Heaven* Al Bryan, Ed Ward; *Tea For Two*; *No, No, Nanette*; *I Want To Be Happy* Vincent Youmans, Irving Caesar. ▷

Vincent Youmans's slight but tuneful musical comedy **Hit the Deck**, which opened on Broadway on 25 April 1927 for a successful run of 352 performances, came to the screen via Radio Productions and, despite some attractive two-colour Technicolor camerawork, was a lustreless rendition of the original. Polly Walker played Looloo, the owner of a coffee shop; Jack Oakie (centre) was Bilge, the gob she loves. Others in the cast included Roger Gray, Franker Woods, Harry Sweet, Marguerita Padula, June Clyde, Wallace MacDonald and Ethel Clayton. It was adapted (from a story by Herbert Fields) and directed by Luther Reed, with Pearl Eaton in charge of the dance direction. Songs: *Sometimes I'm Happy*; *Hallelujah*; *Why, Oh Why* Vincent Youmans, Clifford Grey, Leo Robin; *Keeping Myself For You* Youmans, Sidney Clare; *More Than You Know* Youmans, Edward Eliscu, Billy Rose; *I Know That You Know* Youmans, Anne Caldwell. Remade in 1955 by MGM. ▽

Rum-running in Chicago provided the colourful backdrop to **Roadhouse Nights** (Paramount), a melodrama with songs which starred Helen Morgan (right), fresh from her triumph in *Applause*, as a singer working in the roadhouse hide-out of a gang of bootleggers. The stand-out performance in a uniformly excellent cast, though, was that of Charles Ruggles playing a reporter who discovers the gang's whereabouts and, as coincidence would have it, turns out to be Miss Morgan's childhood sweetheart. Jimmy Durante made an auspicious debut as Daffy, a singer-comedian also working at the road-house, with Fred Kohler (left, as the heavy), Fuller Mellish Jr, Leo Donnelly, Joe King and Tammany Young in support. Originally called *The River Inn*, its febrile plot was the brainchild of the celebrated Ben Hecht, with Garrett Fort contributing the scenario and dialogue. The slick, no-nonsense direction was by Hobart Henley. Songs: *Everything Is On The Up and Up*; *Hello, Everybody, Folks* Eddie Jackson, Lou Clayton, Jimmy Durante; *It Can't Go On Like This* E.Y. Harburg, Jay Gorney.

Bessie Love's (left) tendency to martyr herself in almost every film she made bordered on the perverse. She did it again in **They Learned About Women** (MGM), this time offering herself to a vaudevillian-cum-baseball player although it is his partner she *really* loves. A sort of trial run for MGM's 1949 hit *Take Me Out To The Ball-Game*, it featured rhythm and harmony boys Joe Schenk (right) and Gus Van (centre) in their first talkie and Mary Doran as a foxy lady, with comedian Benny Rubin, J.C. Nugent, Tom Dugan, Eddie Gribbon and Francis X. Bushman. It was written by Sarah Y. Mason and Arthur 'Bugs' Naer from a story by A.P. Younger, Sammy Lee was in charge of the rigorous dance routines, and Jack Conway and Sam Wood directed it. Apart from 'Dougherty Is The Name' by Van and Schenk, Jack Yellen and Milton Ager wrote the songs, which included: *Harlem Madness*; *He's That Kind Of A Pal*; *Aint You Baby?*; *A Man Of My Own*; *Does My Baby Love*; *There'll Never Be Another Mary*; *Ten Sweet Mamas*.

Hoping to impress her husband's wealthy but cantankerous uncle, and inherit his fortune, Charlotte Greenwood (centre), repeating her stage success in Warner Bros.' screen version of **So Long Letty**, allows her place to be temporarily taken by a more conventional woman. Bert Roach co-starred as her husband and together they brought joy and merriment to Arthur Caesar and Robert Lord's well-turned screen-play. Director Lloyd Bacon was in good form too, and brought a lightness of touch to the proceed-ings that spelled box-office success. Claude Gillingwater, Patsy Ruth Miller, Marion Byron (left), Helen Foster (right) and Grant Withers were also featured. Apart from the title number, by Earl Carroll, the stage score was scrapped in favour of new songs by Grant Clarke and Harry Akst. These included: *One Sweet Little Yes*; *Clowning*; *Beauty Shop*; *Am I Blue?*; *Let Me Have My Dreams*; *My Strongest Weakness Is You* and, by Clarke and Charles Tobias, *Sugar Cane*.

Harry Richman (left), made his talking debut in **Puttin' on the Ritz** (United Artists) and, although he was hardly an actor of quality or the possessor of matinée idol good looks, his singing was attractive enough – which was all that mattered, considering that the oft-reprised title song was by Irving Berlin. As for the plot (by John W. Considine Jr, dialogue by William K. Wells), it was the familiar backstage yarn in which a washed-up vaudevillian finds success on Broadway, allows it to go to his head, sees the error of his ways, reforms – and gets the girl. From a purely visual point of view, the musical highspot was the 'Alice In Wonderland' sequence, photographed in eye-catching two-colour Technicolor, which made stunning use of the film's lovely and talented leading lady, Joan Bennett (right). James Gleason and Lilyan Tashman were also in it as a couple of actors in search of a job, with other parts going to Aileen Pringle (as a madcap socialite), Purnell Pratt and Richard Tucker. John Considine Jr produced it, it was choreographed by Maurice

The static, unimaginative *mise-en-scène* imposed on **The Vagabond King** (Paramount) by its German director Ludwig Berger, making his first sound picture, was at noticeable variance with the melodic sweep of Rudolf Friml's famous 1925 score, so that – apart from the music, and the beautiful two-colour Technicolor in which the film was photographed – there was little to recommend it. Dennis King (left), repeating the central role of the 15th-century poet Villon which he had created on stage, contributed to the theatricality by refusing to accept that the camera and the upper balcony actually had very little in common; while Jeanette MacDonald (right) appearing as Katherine, the royal niece of Louis XI (O.P. Heggie) and Villon's mistress, was mannered to the point of embarrassment. Only Lillian Roth (as Huguette) seemed unfettered by it all and, both vocally and dramatically, gave a performance of conviction and depth, especially in her rendering of the haunting 'Huguette Waltz'. The operetta was adapted for the screen by Herman J. Mankiewicz and, in supporting roles, featured Warner Oland (even more villain-ous than usual) as the evil Thibault, Lawford Davidson, Arthur Stone and Thomas Ricketts. Songs and musical numbers included: *Love For Sale*; *Love Me Tonight*; *Only A Rose*; *Some Day*; *Song Of The Vagabonds* Friml, Brian Hooker; *If I Were King*; *King Louis*; *Mary, Queen Of Heaven* Sam Coslow, Leo Robin, Newell Chase.

Kusell, and the director was Edward Sloman. Other songs: *With You* Irving Berlin; *There's Danger In Your Eyes Cherie* Harry Richman, Jack Meskill, Pete Wendling; *I'll Get By* Fred Ahlert, Roy Turk; *Singing A Vagabond Song* Sam Messenheimer, Harry Richman, Val Burton.

Song of the West (Warner Bros.) was the screen version of Oscar Hammerstein II and Laurence Stallings's stage musical *Rainbow*, but barely survived its journey to celluloid. Not at their best on this occasion, its stars, John Boles and Vivienne Segal were further hindered by poor sound recording and by a screenplay by Harvey Thew which allowed them very few opportunities for solid characterization. In fact, apart from the visually satisfying Technicolor photography by Dev Jennings, this romantic operetta with its Wild West backdrops held little allure. Its nebulous screenplay also drew uninspired direction from Ray Enright. Joe E. Brown (right), who dies in the service of the plot, Edward Martindel, Eddie Gribbon, Marion Byron (left) and Sam Hardy were also cast. Songs: *The Bride Was Dressed In White*; *Hay Straw*; *West Wind*; *The One Girl* Vincent Youmans, Oscar Hammerstein II; *Come Back To Me* Grant Clarke, Harry Akst.

Though not much plot attached itself to **It's A Great Life** (MGM), it was nonetheless an excellent showcase for the Duncan Sisters (Rosetta and Vivian, foreground) who, in the Al Boasberg–Willard Mack screenplay (story by Byron Morgan and Alfred Block), played a couple of sisters working in the sheet-music section of a large department store. They're fired, enter vaudeville, split up when one of them falls in love with a piano player (Lawrence Gray), become re-united and, finally, return to the stage. Comedy and songs featured in more or less equal proportions but the girls unfortunately couldn't quite pull off either to the patrons' satisfaction, and the film bombed. Jed Prouty and Benny Rubin were in it too, and it was produced and directed by Sam Wood. Songs: *Smile, Smile, Smile*; *Lady Love*; *I'm The Son Of A-*; *I'm Following You*; *It Must Be An Old Spanish Custom*; *Hoosier Hop*; *I'm Sailing On A Sunbeam* Dave Dreyer, Ballard MacDonald; *Let A Smile Be Your Umbrella* (*On A Rainy Day*) Irving Kahal, Francis Wheeler, Sammy Fain.

Mistaken identity loomed large in **Let's Go Places** (Fox), which featured Joseph Wagstaff (centre) as a young and ambitious singer who, *en route* to Hollywood, takes on the identity of a famous operatic tenor only to discover, in the last reel, that the man whom he's impersonating is none other than his uncle! It was pretty inconsequential stuff (inconsequentially directed by Frank Strayer for producer William Fox), and featured Lola Lane (left foreground) as the girl in Wagstaff's life, Charles Judels and Eddie Kane as a couple of comic-book Frenchmen, Walter Catlett (left) as a Hollywood film director and, to complete the cast, Frank Richardson (centre left), Larry Steers (right), Sharon Lynn (right foreground), Dixie Lee and Ilka Chase. William K. Wells fashioned the scenario and dialogue from a story by Andrew Bennison. The substantial number of songs featured included: *Parade Of The Blues*; *Hollywood Nights*; *Reach For A Rainbow*; *Out In The Cold*; *Um, Um In The Moonlight* Con Conrad, Sidney Mitchell, Archie Gottler; *Snowball Man* James Hanley, James Brockman; *The Boop-Boop-A-Doopa-Doo Trot* George A. Little, John Burke; *Fascinatin' Devil* Joseph McCarthy, James V. Monaco; *Let's Go Places* Cliff Friend, James V. Monaco.

She Couldn't Say No (Warner Bros.) was a rather boring Lloyd Bacon-directed effort which told the story of a nightclub entertainer promoted to stardom through the efforts of a former gangster. The gangster, however, loves another, more classy woman – a situation which provided Arthur Caesar and Robert Lord's screenplay (from a play by Benjamin M. Kaye) with what little dramatic momentum it had. Winnie Lightner (at piano) in the lead was fine when she was called upon to sing and be herself; it was the heavy emoting that eventually defeated her. Others cast were Tully Marshall, Johnny Arthur and Louise Beavers, and the songs were by Al Dubin and Joe Burke. These included: *Darn Fool Woman Like Me*; *Watching My Dreams Go By*; *Bouncing The Baby Around*. The movie was remade in 1940.

Originally shown at New York's Roxy Theatre in a 70mm Grandeur System print, **Happy Days** (Fox) was a mammoth all-star extravaganza of varying quality whose plot (by Sidney Lanfield) was little more than an excuse to assemble all Fox's players in one massive musical entertainment. The story, such as it was, concerned the efforts of a Mississippi riverboat soubrette (Marjorie White) to persuade all the performers who had ever served their apprenticeship on the boat to pool their collective talents and stage a benefit minstrel show in Memphis to save the riverboat from closure through lack of funds. She succeeds, and the results of her efforts formed the basis of this Benjamin Stoloff-directed showcase. Apart from the principal roles which went to Miss White, Charles E. Evans, Richard Keene, Stuart Erwin and Martha Lee Sparks, the film also utilized the talents of Janet Gaynor (right), Charles Farrell (left), Victor McLaglen, El Brendel, William Collier Sr, Tom Patricola, George Jessel, Dixie Lee, Nick Stuart, Rex Bell, Frank Albertson, Sharon Lynn, 'Whispering' Jack Smith, Lew Brice, J. Farrell MacDonald, Will Rogers, Edmund Lowe, Walter Catlett (who also staged the musical numbers), Frank Richardson, Ann Pennington, David Rollins, Warner Baxter, J. Harold Murray, The Slate Brothers, James J. Corbett and George MacFarlane (as the interlocutors), and George Olden and His Orchestra. Songs and musical numbers: *Mona*; *Snake Hips*; *Crazy Feet* (Dixie Lee) Con Conrad, Sidney Mitchell, Archie Gottler; *Minstrel Memories*; *I'm On A Diet Of Love* L. Wolfe Gilbert, Abel Baer; *We'll Build A Little World Of Our Own* (Gaynor, Farrell); *A Toast To The Girl I Love*; *Dream On A Piece Of Wedding Cake* James Hanley, James Brockman; *Vic and Eddie* Harry Stoddard, Marcy Klauber.

◁ After the phenomenal success of *The Broadway Melody* (1929), MGM sought out a follow-up property for Bessie Love and Charles King and came up with **Chasing Rainbows** – originally, and more appropriately, titled *Road Show*. Another backstage story – but this time one which dealt with a group of show-folk travelling on the road, it was, if anything, even better than its illustrious predecessor, with stronger characterizations and altogether more subtle and convincing dialogue (by Charles F. Riesner, Kenyon Nicholson, Robert Hopkins, and Al Boasberg). The story, though (by Bess Meredyth), adapted by Wells Root, was not all that dissimilar to *The Broadway Melody* and, in purely narrative terms, again involved Bessie Love (left) in a traumatic love-relationship with Charles King (2nd left) who, once again, loves another (Nita Martan). But in this case, Bessie finally gets him when Nita (right) paves the way for a happy ending by walking out on Charles. Yet audiences, by now satiated with musicals, simply refused to come, and not even the fact that the final section of the film was in Technicolor proved sufficient inducement for them to see it. Two years later, however, the same audience who had largely ignored the film on its release, were whistling and singing its one hit song 'Happy Days Are Here Again' (by Milton Ager and Jack Yellen) – the theme of Roosevelt's election campaign and just the right kind of rampant optimism the country needed at the time. **Chasing Rainbows** was directed by Charles F. Riesner, with Sammy Lee in charge of the musical numbers, and the cast included Jack Benny (going serious for once as a jaundiced stage manager), Marie Dressler, Polly Moran, Gwen Lee, Eddie Phillips and the Baltimore Trio. Other songs: *Lucky Me, Lovable You*; *Do I Know What I'm Doing*; *Everybody Tap* Ager, Yellen; *Love Ain't Nothin' But The Blues* Joe Goodwin, Louis Alter; *Dynamic Personality* Fred Fisher, Ed Ward, Reggie Montgomery; *Poor But Honest* Gus Edwards; *Gotta Feeling For You* Jo Trent, Louis Alter.

A successful John Gilbert silent, **Cameo Kirby** (Fox) was refurbished for the talkies with J. Harold Murray in the Gilbert role, and Norma Terris as his leading lady. Its setting was New Orleans in 1850, and its melodramatic story (from a 1909 play by Booth Tarkington and Harry Leon) told of the romance that blossomed between a planter's daughter (Terris) and a Mississippi riverboat gambler (Murray, left) after the latter rescues the former from a gang of local thugs. Too familiar in content to make much impact, its chief virtues were Murray's pleasant personality and agreeable voice, both of which ▽

were seen and heard at their best in the songs 'Romance', 'After A Million Dreams', and 'Tankard And Bowl', by Walter Donaldson and Edgar Leslie. The film, which was written by Marion Orth and directed by Irving Cummings, also featured Douglas Gilmore (centre), Robert Edeson, Myrna Loy (right), Charles Morton and Stepin Fetchit (in Fred Strauss and Ed Brady's 'I'm A Peaceful Man'). There was one further song, 'Drink To My Broken Dreams', by L. Wolfe Gilbert and Abel Baer, and George MacFarlane and Beulah Hall Jones completed the cast. Remade as *Mississippi* (Paramount, 1935).

△
A handful of enjoyable performances from Nancy Carroll, Stanley Smith, Skeets Gallagher, Lillian Roth (on couch), Mitzi Green and Jobyna Howland (standing) – plus a bracing screenplay by Herman J. Mankiewicz (from the 1921 play *Come Out Of The Kitchen* by Alice Duer Miller and A.E. Thomas), imparted to **Honey** (Paramount) the sweet taste of success. All about a proud but impecunious young woman (Carroll) who finds true love when she is forced to lease the family manse to a wealthy widow from New York, it adapted well to the screen, and, with the addition of a pleasant score by W. Franke Harling and Sam Coslow, emerged as one of the year's more agreeable albeit modest entertainments. Wesley Ruggles directed. Songs: *In My Little Hope Chest*; *Sing You Sinners*; *I Don't Need Atmosphere*; *Let's Be Domestic*; *What Is This Power I Have?*

THIRTIES MUSICALS

Saddled with the type of plot on which the golden silents had thrived, but which looked distinctly second-hand in 1930, there was little that Dixie Lee could do to raise the temperature of **The Big Party** (Fox). She played a singing sales clerk in the music section of a department store who, after being fired for insulting a customer, finds employment in an exclusive dressmaking emporium. It soon becomes clear to her that, for certain services rendered to the establishment's married owners, Mr Goldfarb and Mr Dupuy, she can enjoy a life of unbridled luxury. Being a good girl at heart, though, she decides that the price is too high, and returns to the boy she loves and a more modest, but honest life. Harlan Thompson wrote it, with roles for Sue Carol, Frank Albertson (left), Walter Catlett (Mr Goldfarb), Richard Keene, 'Whispering' Jack Smith (right), Charles Judels (Mr Dupuy), and Ilka Chase; it was produced by William Fox and directed by John Blystone. Songs: *Nobody Knows But Rosie* James Hanley, Joseph McCarthy; *I'm Climbing Up A Rainbow* Edward G. Nelson, Harry Pease; *Bluer Than Blue Over You; Good For Nothing But Love* William Kernell, Harlan Thompson.
▽

In **Be Yourself** (United Artists), a starring vehicle for Fanny Brice, the great vaudevillian sang one of her best songs ever, 'Cookin' Breakfast For The One I Love' (by Billy Rose and Henry Tobias). For the rest it was a routine *My Man*-inspired melodrama in which the rather plain-looking Fanny (Mrs Billy Rose in real life) worked hard to keep her pugilist sweetheart (Robert Armstrong, right) out of the arms of the more alluring Gertrude Astor (left). Produced by Joseph M. Schenck and directed by Thornton Freeland (screenplay by Freeland and Max Marcin) it made little impact on the public and was soon forgotten. Also cast: Budd Fine, Marjorie 'Babe' Kane, Rita Flynn and Jimmy Tolson. Other songs: *When A Woman Loves A Man* Billy Rose, Ralph Rainger; *Kicking A Hole In The Sky; Sasha, The Passion Of The Pasha* Billy Rose, Ballard MacDonald, Jesse Greer.
▽

△

Jazz baby Joan Crawford's camel hair coat and her jodhpur riding outfit got the best notices for **Montana Moon** (MGM), a musical with a Western setting which top-starred Crawford as a big city girl who marries a cowpoke (John Mack Brown), makes him jealous on their wedding night by dancing torridly with Ricardo Cortez (illustrated), decides to return to New York, but changes her mind when Brown, masquerading as a bandit, pretends to hold up her getaway train, and carries her off with him. With songs by Arthur Freed, Nacio Herb Brown, Herbert Stothart and Clifford Grey to keep the Sylvia Thalberg–Frank Butler–Joe Farnham screenplay lilting along, and the popularity of its leading lady to provide marquee interest, MGM hoped for big things from this one. But the public's increasing apathy towards musicals was in no way assuaged by it (inferior sound recording didn't help either) and they stayed away. The director was Mal St Clair. Songs: *The Moon Is Low; Happy Cowboy* Freed, Brown; *Montana Call; Let Me Give You Love; Trailin' In Old Montana* Stothart, Grey.

△

John McCormack made an auspicious film debut in **Song O' My Heart** (Fox), stealing all the notices – and everyone's hearts – in the process. Set in Ireland, it was filmed on location in Erin and told the four-hanky story of a singer (McCormack, centre) who gives up a promising career when the woman he loves is forced to marry someone else. Years later, after she and her two children have been deserted by her husband, McCormack continues to show his undying love by helping the family as best he can. Unashamedly sentimental in its approach to its rather weepie subject, it relied on McCormack's voice, rather than on his limited acting ability, to render the necessary emotion, and in eleven out of eleven songs he delivered the goods to the tearful delight of audiences everywhere. Though solidly directed by Frank Borzage, who made stunning use of the surrounding scenery in the telling of this homely little tale, the film's supporting cast, with the exception of an ingratiating youngster called Tommy Clifford, was less than impressive. It included Ireland's own Maureen O'Sullivan (really inadequate as the daughter, right) and Alice Joyce, not much better as the mother. Also: John Garrick (left), J.M. Kerrigan, J. Farrell MacDonald and Effie Ellsler. It was written by Sonya Levien and Tom Barry, presented by William Fox and photographed in 70mm. Songs included: *Little Boy Blue* Ethelbert Nevin; *Paddy Me Lad* Albert Malotte; *A Fair Story By The Fireside; Just For A Day; Kitty My Love; The Rose Of Tralee* Charles Glover, C. Mordaunt Spencer; *I Hear You Calling Me* Harold Herford, Charles Marshall; *A Pair Of Blue Eyes; I Feel You Near Me; Song O' My Heart* Charles Glover, William Kernell, James Hanley; *Then You'll Remember Me* Alfred Burns, William Michael Balfe.

◁ **High Society Blues** (Fox) was a cloying experience which brought out the very worst in its two stars, Janet Gaynor (right) and Charles Farrell. They played star-crossed lovers whose combined mental age appeared to be about 9¼. Far more interesting was the behaviour of their parents. Farrell's folks (Louise Fazenda and Lucien Littlefield) are *nouveau riche* upstarts; Gaynor's (William Collier Sr, and Hedda Hopper, left) founder members of the genuine *haut monde*. The conflict that results when the two families find that they are neighbours provided the red meat of Dana Burnet's story (screenplay by Howard J. Green). However, by projecting the two young stars into the foreground of events, director David Butler allowed the potentially interesting social aspects of the situation to go for nothing, which was a pity as it left audiences no choice but to endure the pair's icky warblings for much of the film's running time. Songs: *I'm In The Market For You; High Society Blues; Just Like In A Story Book; Eleanor (The Song I Sing In My Dreams); I Don't Know You Well Enough For That* Joseph McCarthy, James Hanley.

As romantic musical comedies go, **The Golden Calf** (Fox) was nothing to worship. A really witless story of a lovelorn secretary who fools her boss (a commercial illustrator and the object of her affections) by undergoing a Cinderella-like transformation, posing as a Southern belle and gaining employment as his model, it starred Jack Mulhall (centre) as the deceived employer (and a man clearly in need of an optometrist's attention), and Sue Carol (right) as the schemer. Miss Carol had her moments; the film, on the other hand, was a write-off. It was written by Harold Atteridge from a story by Aaron Davis, was directed by Millard Webb, and also featured comedian El Brendel (left), Marjorie White, Richard Keene, Paul Page, Walter Catlett and Ilka Chase. William Fox presented it, and his associate producer was Ned Marin. Songs: *You Gotta Be Modernistic*; *Maybe Someday*; *Can I Help It If I'm In Love With You?*; *Telling The World About You*; *A Picture No Artist Can Paint* Cliff Friend, James V. Monaco.

Lawrence Gray (right) played a songwriting heel in **Children of Pleasure** (MGM), completely oblivious of the love being bestowed on him by pretty Helen Johnson. He only has eyes for heiress Wynne Gibson (left) who has agreed to marry him but, after overhearing her telling a friend that she regards their impending marriage as nothing more than an experiment, he changes his mind and – you guessed it – abandons her for patient little Helen. Kenneth Thomson, Lee Kohlmar, May Boley and Benny Rubin completed the cast; it was written by Richard Schayer and Crane Wilbur (from Wilbur's play *The Songwriter*), choreographed by Sammy Lee and directed by Harry Beaumont. Songs: *Leave It That Way*; *Dust*; *Girl Trouble* Andy Rice, Fred Fisher; *A Couple Of Birds With The Same Thought In Mind* Howard Johnson, Edward Ward, Reggie Montgomery; *The Whole Darned Thing's For You* Roy Turk, Fred Ahlert.

An ambitious (in scope) but facile attempt to ▷ reconstruct the events leading up to the French Revolution and the composition of the stirring 'La Marseillaise', **Captain of the Guard** (Universal) suffered, primarily, from a screenplay that most of the cast found unspeakable. Laura La Plante played an innkeeper's daughter fired by the spirit of revolution; John Boles (centre) was her Royalist music master, and captain of the guard. The couple fall in love but, predictably, their political differences make life difficult for them. Sam de Grasse played the scheming Bazin, Stuart Holmes was the pleasure-seeking Louis XVI, Evelyn Hall Marie Antoinette, Lionel Belmore the Colonel of Hussars, Richard Cramer was Danton and George Hackathorne Robespierre. The songs, by William Francis Dugan and Heinz Roemheld, scored by Charles Wakefield Cadman, were the film's saving grace, and La Plante and Boles greedily clung to their every note. It was written by George Manker Watters and Arthur Ripley from a story by Houston Branch (a credit at the beginning of the film apologized for its historical

True to its title, **The Cuckoos** (Radio Pictures), originally written for the stage by Guy Bolton, Harry Ruby and Bert Kalmar (and called *The Ramblers*) starred Bert Wheeler (right) and Robert Woolsey (left) whose anything-goes personalities combined with a yarn of such towering nonsense that the finished result was a thoroughly irrational *mélange* of spirited hi-jinx involving the kidnapping of a wealthy girl by a nobleman and the consequences thereof. Messrs W. and W. played a couple of impecunious fortune tellers but, for all the sense the plot made, they might just as well have been undertakers. The lunatic farrago (partly filmed in Technicolor) also engaged the talents of June Clyde, Hugh Trevor, Dorothy Lee (2nd right), Ivan Lebedeff, Mitchell Lewis (centre), Marguerita Padula and Jobyna Howland. It was adapted by Chris Wood, produced by Louis Sarecky and irreverently directed by Paul Sloane, whose work on *Hearts in Dixie* had been much admired the previous year. Songs: *I Love You So Much*; *Knock Knees*; *Looking For The Limelight In Your Eyes*; *All Alone Monday* Bert Kalmar, Harry Ruby; *Dancing The Devil Away* Kalmar, Otto Harbach, Ruby; *Wherever You Are* Charles Tobias, Cliff Friend; *If I Were A Travelling Salesman* Al Dubin, Joe Burke.

inaccuracies), and directed by Paul Fejos and John S. Robertson – the former beginning the film (under the title of 'La Marseillaise'), the latter completing it. Songs: *Song Of The Guard*; *For You*; *Maids On Parade*; *You, You Alone*; *Can It Be?*; *It's A Sword*; *La Marseillaise*.

Silent comic Buster Keaton made a bright and breezy talking-picture debut in **Free and Easy** (MGM) as the manager of a beauty contest winner from Kansas (Anita Page) whom he takes, together with her oversized mother (Trixie Friganza, right), to Hollywood – where he is convinced a career in the movies awaits her. It's Buster (centre, with Estelle Moran, left) however, who, after gatecrashing his way into the studio (and being chased in, out, and around its sound stages) finishes up in front of the cameras – with Miss Page having to settle for true love in the arms of heart-throb Robert Montgomery. Funny in parts with some fascinating behind-the-scenes glimpses of MGM at work (plus guest appearances by Fred Niblo, Gwen Lee, John Miljan, Lionel Barrymore, William Collier Sr, Dorothy Sebastian, Karl Dane, Jackie Coogan and Cecil B. de Mille), **Free and Easy** was an uneven entertainment which gave no indication that its talented star's days were sadly numbered as a major box-office attraction. It was adapted by Paul Dickey and the screenplay was by Richard Schayer with dialogue by Al Boasberg, and choreography by Sammy Lee. It was produced and directed by Edward Sedgwick, and simultaneously shot in French and Spanish for the European market – a common Hollywood practice until the 1940s. Songs included: *Free And Easy*; *It Must Be You* Roy Turk, Fred Ahlert; *Penitentiary Blues*; *Cubanita*; *You've Got Me That Way* William Kernell.
▽

Another all-star revue, but one which concentrated more on the personalities of the numerous performers involved than on spectacle, **Paramount on Parade** was an entertaining showcase for the studio's remarkable roster of talents, both in front of and behind the camera. After its Technicolored opening title number featuring Virginia Bruce and the Paramount Publix Ushers (danced by Mitzi Mayfair), Jack Oakie, Leon Errol and Skeets Gallagher introduced themselves as the occasion's masters of ceremony, and then introduced, in turn, practically every star under contract to Paramount at the time including (in alphabetical order) Iris Adrian, Richard Arlen, Jean Arthur, Mischa Auer, William Austin, George Bancroft, Clara Bow, Evelyn Brent, Mary Brian, Clive Brook, Nancy Carroll, Ruth Chatterton, Maurice Chevalier, Gary Cooper, Cecil Cunningham, Stuart Erwin, Henry Fink, Kay Francis, Mitzi Green, Phillips Holmes, Helen Kane, Dennis King, Abe Lyman and His Band, Fredric March, Nino Martini, Mitzi Mayfair, the Marion Morgan Dancers, David Newell, Warner Oland, Zelma O'Neal, Eugene Pallette, Joan Peers, Jack Pennick, William Powell, Charles 'Buddy' Rogers, Lillian Roth, Rolfe Sedan and Stanley Smith. Though eleven directors had a hand in steering the film to its success – Dorothy Arzner, Otto Brower, Edmund Goulding, Victor Heerman, Edwin H. Knopf, Rowland V. Lee, Lothar Mendes, Victor Schertzinger, Edward Sutherland, Frank Tuttle, and Ernst Lubitsch who was responsible for the three Chevalier sequences ('Sweeping The Clouds Away', illustrated) including the Technicolor finale – the overall production supervisor was Elsie Janis, with Albert S. Kaufman credited as producer. David Bennett was the dance director. Needless to say, the songs and musical numbers were numerous, and included: *Anytime's The Time To Fall In Love* (Charles 'Buddy' Rogers, Lillian Roth, chorus); *What Did Cleopatra Say?* (Helen Kane); *I'm True To The Navy Now* (Clara Bow, men) Elsie Janis, Jack King; *We're The Masters Of Ceremony* (Jack Oakie, Leon Errol, Skeets Gallagher) Ballard MacDonald, Dave Dreyer; *Come Back To Sorrento* (Nino Martini) Ernesto de Curtis, Leo Robin; *I'm In Training For You* (Jack Oakie, Zelma O'Neal; danced by Mitzi Mayfair and girls); *Dancing To Save Your Sole* (Nancy Carroll, Abe Lyman's Band, chorus; danced by Al Norman); *Let Us Drink To The Girl Of My Dreams* (Richard Arlen, Jean Arthur, Virginia Bruce, Mary Brian, Gary Cooper, James Hall, Phillips Holmes, David Newell, Joan Peers, Fay Wray) L. Wolfe Gilbert, Abel Baer; *My Marine* (Ruth Chatterton) Richard A. Whiting, Ray Egan; *All I Want Is Just One Girl* (Maurice Chevalier) Richard A. Whiting, Leo Robin; *I'm Isadore The Toreador* (Harry Green, Kay Francis) David Franklin; *Sweeping The Clouds Away* (Maurice Chevalier, girls) Sam Coslow; *Nichavo* (Dennis King) Mme Mana-Zucca, Helen Jerome. Inset right: Charles 'Buddy' Rogers, Lillian Roth. Inset Below: Helen Kane.

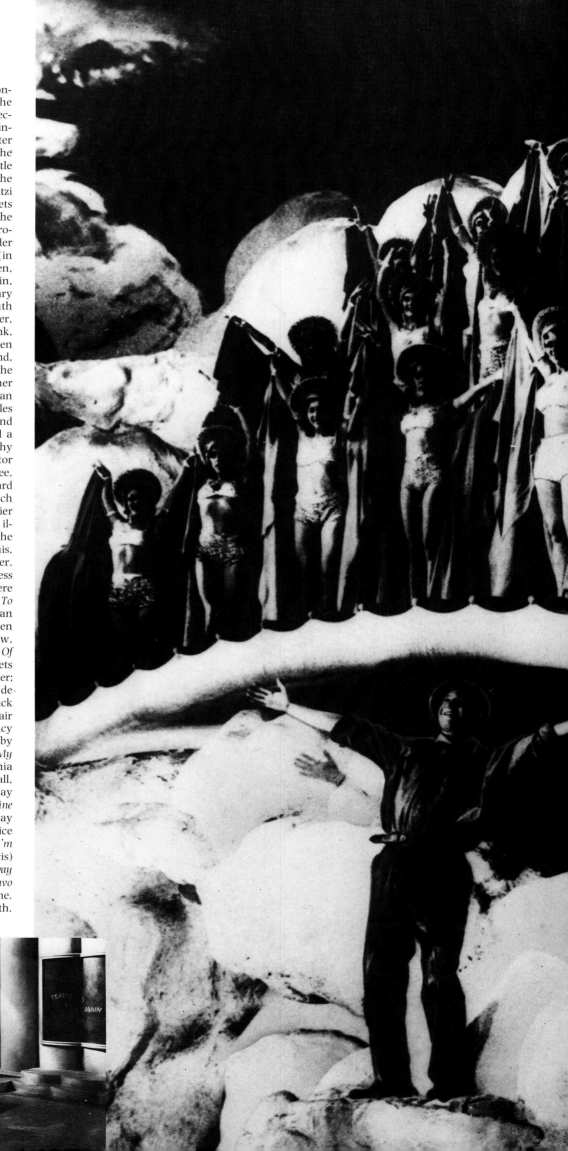

THIRTIES MUSICALS

The screen version of the 1925 operetta by Oscar Hammerstein II, Otto Harbach, Herbert Stothart and George Gershwin, **Song of the Flame** (First National) was given an elaborate Technicolor production which even went into wide screen at one point. But its story of a peasant (Bernice Claire, left) known as 'The Flame', who incites the mob to revolution in Russia with her 'Song of the Flame', was a tedious exercise. Gordon Rigby's rather flat adaptation of the material – which involved 'The Flame' in a love affair with a Russian prince (Alexander Gray, right) whose life she saves by agreeing to sacrifice her virginity to an evil fellow-conspirator (a singing Noah Beery), only had vitality in the musical numbers felicitously staged by Jack Haskell. Alan Crosland's direction was, on the other hand, unremarkable. The songs, which included some extra new numbers composed for the movie, were: *The Cossack Love Song*; *Song Of The Flame* Hammerstein II, Stothart, Gershwin, Harbach; *Petrograd*; *Liberty Song*; *The Goose Hangs High*; *Passing Fancy*; *One Little Drink* Grant Clarke, Harry Akst, Ed Ward; *When Love Calls* Ed Ward.

Probably the worst of all the early campus musicals, **Sunny Skies** (Tiffany Productions) gave top billing to comedian Benny Rubin (centre) who, as a college student called upon to undergo a blood transfusion, gave an unpalatable performance that veered uneasily between farce and pathos. The finale had the hero (Rex Lease) redeeming a bout of drunkenness by making a winning touchdown in the last minutes of an all-important game. Ho-hum . . . Marceline Day (right), Marjorie 'Babe' Kane (left), Greta Granstedt, Wesley Barry and Robert Randall lent support. It was written by Erle Snell and George Cleveland (story by A.P. Younger), and the director was Norman Taurog. Songs included: *Wanna Find A Boy*; *Must Be Love*; *You For Me*; *Sunny Days*.

Showgirl in Hollywood (First National), based on J.P. McEvoy's novel *Hollywood Girl*, was an attempt to satirize the movie industry, but the satire went badly off-course in this Harvey Thew-James A. Starr adaptation. Nevertheless, in taking a behind-the-scenes look at the mechanics of movie-making, the film did provide an accurate view of how early sound films were made. The plot, such as it was, concerned a comedy performer's rise to Hollywood stardom after being spotted by a film producer in a New York nightclub. Alice White (left) was top cast, with support from Jack Mulhall (right), John Miljan, Ford Sterling, Virginia Sale, Herman Bing and, notably, Blanche Sweet. The director was Mervyn LeRoy, the songsmiths Bud Green and Sammy Stept, the dance director Jack Haskell, and it was photographed (by Sol Polito) in black and white with Technicolor sequences. Robert Lord produced. Songs included: *Hang On To The Rainbow*; *I've Got My Eye On You* (not to be confused with the later Cole Porter standard from *Broadway Melody of 1940*); *There's A Tear For Every Smile In Hollywood* Green, Stept; *My Sin* Buddy De Sylva, Lew Brown, Ray Henderson.

For almost half of its running time, a farcical plot involving a butler (El Brendel) who pretends to be a lumberman, and a wealthy blade (William Collier Jr) who fancies himself as the Casanova of the showgirl circuit, all but sabotaged the efforts of **Movietone Follies of 1930** (Fox) to entertain. Fortunately, the situation improved in the second half, with music coming to the rescue via Marjorie White, Frank Richardson, and erstwhile Ziegfeld girl Noel Francis, whose singing of a Con Conrad–Jack Meskill ditty called 'Cheer Up And Smile' was the vocal highlight of the film. A blackface routine called 'Here Comes Emily Brown', also by Conrad and Meskill, performed by Frank Richardson and Marjorie White (both illustrated), ran it a close second. It was written by William K. Wells, directed by Benjamin Stoloff, choreographed by Danny Dare and Maurice Kusell, and also featured Miriam Seegar, Huntly Gordon, Paul Nicholson, and Yola d'Avril as a French maid much given to tantrums. Other songs included: *You'll Give In* Joseph McCarthy, James Hanley; *I Wanna Be A Talking Picture Queen* McCarthy, Hanley, James Brockman; *Doin' The Derby* Conrad, Meskill; *I Feel A Certain Feeling Coming On*; *Bashful* Cliff Friend, James V. Monaco.

One of the previous year's stage shows by Richard Rodgers, Lorenz Hart and Owen Davis, **Spring is Here** (First National) was rewritten for the screen by James A. Starr with a reasonable ration of witty dialogue. Which was just as well, considering the unconvincing plot: father (Ford Sterling) of a pretty young thing (Bernice Claire, illustrated) disapproves of her romantic attachment to Lawrence Gray, favouring Alexander Gray instead. Dad banishes Lawrence from the family manse, but he returns to elope with Bernice. Alexander, however, intervenes, and finally carries her off. There was support from Louise Fazenda, Inez Courtney, Frank Albertson (illustrated) and Natalie Moorhead, and the direction was by John Francis Dillon. Songs: *Spring Is Here In Person* – not to be confused with the more famous *Spring Is Here (Why Doesn't My Heart Go Dancing?)* which Rodgers and Hart later wrote for the film *I Married An Angel*; *Yours Sincerely*; *Rich Man, Poor Man*; *Baby's Awake Now*; *With A Song In My Heart* Rodgers and Hart; *Cryin' For The Carolines*; *Have A Little Faith In Me*; *Bad Baby*; *How Shall I Tell?* Sam Lewis, Joe Young, Harry Warren.

Bride of the Regiment (First National) was another filmed operetta and, like so many of its predecessors, was characterized by a tediousness which no amount of Technicolor and spectacle could relieve. Its nonsensical plot told of a countess who saves her husband from the firing squad by flirting with a lecherous Austrian colonel. The colonel passes out from too much champagne, dreams that the countess has willingly submitted to him, and sets her husband free. John Francis Dillon directed, Ray Harris and Humphrey Pearson wrote the screenplay, Jack Haskell staged the musical numbers and the songs were by Al Dubin, Al Bryan and Ed Ward. The protagonists were Vivienne Segal, Walter Pidgeon (as the colonel, centre), and Allen Prior, with support from Louise Fazenda, Ford Sterling, Lupino Lane, Claude Fleming (right) and Myrna Loy (left). Songs included: *Brokenhearted Lover*; *Cook's Song*; *Dream Away*; *Heart Of Heaven*; *I'd Like To Be A Happy Bride*; *One Kiss And Then Goodbye Sweetheart*. Remade as *That Lady in Ermine* (20th Century-Fox, 1948).

Hold Everything was yet another Broadway original – by Buddy De Sylva, Ray Henderson, Lew Brown and John McGowan – that came to the screen via Warner Bros. in an adaptation by Robert Lord with a score by Al Dubin and Joe Burke. A vehicle for Joe E. Brown, top-cast as Gink Schiner, an indolent and mediocre prizefighter, it was the comedy rather than the music that won on points, and which kept the comedian's fans happy as he went about upsetting his sweetheart (Winnie Lightner, foreground) by flirting with all the pretty girls, busybodying himself around a fighter's training camp where Georges La Verne (real-life champ Georges Carpentier) is preparing for a heavyweight title bout, and astounding everyone by making a success of his own fight at the tournament. There were various threads of sub-plot, one of which involved Carpentier with a pushy society girl (Dorothy Revier); and another which had a crooked promoter trying to 'fix' a fight only to be foiled by Brown. It was photographed in Technicolor, zippily directed by Roy Del Ruth, and had a cast that also featured Sally O'Neil, Bert Roach, Edmund Breese, Tony Stabeneau and Jimmie Quinn. Songs: *Take It On The Chin*; *When Little Red Roses Get The Blues For You*; *Sing A Little Theme Song*; *Physically Fit*; *Girls We Remember*; *All Alone Together*; *Isn't This A Cockeyed World*.

◁ After the sheen and sophistication which Ernst Lubitsch imparted to *The Love Parade*, **The Big Pond** (Paramount), produced by Monta Bell and directed by Hobart Henley, which also starred Maurice Chevalier, was a disappointingly pedestrian effort that not even the four songs imposed onto Robert Presnell and Garrett Fort's narrative (dialogue by Preston Sturges) could redeem. Based on the play by George Middleton and A.E. Thomas, it had Chevalier (right) working as a guide in Venice and falling in love with an American tourist (Claudette Colbert, left) whose father, believing Chevalier to be nothing more than an opportunist, offers him a job in his New York chewing gum factory. Complications arise and Chevalier is fired, but saves the day by inadvertently inventing rum-flavoured gum. So much for the plot. The star's perky personality was an undoubted plus in a film littered with minuses, and his singing of 'You Brought A New Kind Of Love To Me' by Irving Kahal, Pierre Norman and Sammy Fain, offered cinemagoers three minutes of magic out of the movie's total 85-minute running time. George Barbier and Marion Ballou played Miss Colbert's parents, with Andrée Corday, Frank Lyons, Nat Pendleton and Elaine Koch completing the cast. It was filmed at Paramount's Astoria Studios on Long Island, in both English and French. Other songs: *Livin' In The Sunlight, Lovin' In The Moonlight* Al Lewis, Al Sherman; *This Is My Lucky Day* Buddy De Sylva, Lew Brown, Ray Henderson; *Mia Cara* Kahal, Norman, Fain.

△ Director Harry Beaumont attempted to infuse MGM's **The Florodora Girl** (GB: **The Gay Nineties**) with as much period atmosphere and detail as possible, and succeeded. He succeeded, too, in drawing from its star Marion Davies (right) a genuinely funny performance as Daisy, a man-shy Florodora girl who, after being taken in hand by her colleagues, finds love in the arms of a millionaire (Lawrence Gray, left). Gene Markey's screenplay (additional dialogue by Ralph Spence, Al Boasberg and Robert Hopkins) was affectionately satirical about the milieu it set out to recreate, and provided good roles for Walter Catlett, Claud Allister and Sam Hardy. Ilka Chase, Jed Prouty, Louis John Bartels and Nance O'Neil were also cast. A stage sequence (*Tell Me Pretty Maiden* by Owen Hall and Leslie Stuart) was filmed in Technicolor, and the songs included: *My Kind Of Man*; *Pass The Beer And Pretzels*; *Swingin' In The Lane* Herbert Stothart, Clifford Grey.

△ Charles 'Buddy' Rogers fans had a field day with their idol in **Safety in Numbers** (Paramount), a witless little musical which left non-admirers groaning at the antics of both the hero (centre), and the three Follies girls who are ordered by the lad's guardian uncle to educate him in the ways of the world – prior to his inheriting $25,000,000. Kathryn Crawford (right), Josephine Dunn (left) and Carole Lombard (centre right) comprised the trio, with Miss Crawford eventually hooking Rogers for herself. Geneva Mitchell, Roscoe Karns, Francis McDonald and Virginia Bruce (centre left) had parts in it as well; it was written by Marion Dix (from a story by George Marion Jr and Percy Heath), and directed by Victor Schertzinger with David Bennett in charge of the dances. Songs: *My Future Just Passed*; *The Pick-Up*; *Do You Play, Madame?*; *I'd Like To Be A Bee In Your Boudoir*; *You Appeal To Me*; *Business Girl*; *Pepola* George Marion Jr, Richard A. Whiting.

The undisputed hero of Universal's lavish Technicolor revue **King of Jazz** was its director John Murray Anderson who, in an astonishing motion picture debut, revealed a creative imagination that was as refreshing as it was rare. And although the film's quality varies, its best moments are bold and unforgettable. Watching the film today, one is struck by the sheer originality of Anderson's concepts and the way in which subsequent musicals have borrowed from them (see illustrations). For example, the 'A Bench In The Park' number (by Jack Yellen and Milton Ager), performed by The Brox Sisters, The Rhythm Boys, George Chiles, and Paul Whiteman and His Orchestra, predated Busby Berkeley's 'Pettin' In The Park' (from *Gold Diggers Of 1933*) by a couple of years, yet the similarities between the two sequences are striking. In Yellen and Ager's 'Happy Feet', performed by The Sisters G, there is a moment that recalls Berkeley's '42nd Street' routine in the use it makes of cut-out New York skyscrapers. And there can be no mistaking the resemblance between the final tableau of 'The Melting Pot Of Jazz' and the final tableau of MGM's *Till The Clouds Roll By* (1946); or the finale of the 'Bridal Veil' sequence (music by Yellen and Ager) with the moment in MGM's *The Great Ziegfeld* (1941) when a garment of equal proportions is shown to breathtaking effect. Anderson's staging of Gershwin's 'Rhapsody In Blue' vies in originality with 'The Melting Pot Of Jazz' (in which the music of various nationalities is mixed in one giant cauldron to produce a new sound called Jazz), and is perhaps the most dazzlingly inventive sequence in the entire film. To contemporary audiences used to the garishness of many of the current colour processes, the two-colour Technicolor used in **King of Jazz** makes a welcome change and is one of the chief assets of an extraordinary entertainment. Other musical numbers: *So The Bluebirds And The Blackbirds Got Together*, by Harry Barris and Billy Moll, performed by Bing Crosby and The Rhythm Boys, Al Rinker, and Harry Barris; *It Happened In Monterey* by Mabel Wayne and Billy Rose, sung by John Boles; *Ragamuffin Romeo* by Mabel Wayne and Harry De Costa, performed by Jeannie Lang, George Chiles, Don Rose and Marian Statler; Yellen and Ager's *The Song Of The Dawn* also sung by John Boles; *Mississippi Mud* by Harry Barris and James Cavanaugh, performed by Crosby and The Rhythm Boys; *Music Hath Charms* by Yellen and Ager, performed by Crosby; *When Day Is Done* by Buddy De Sylva and Robert Katscher (used by Ferde Grofé as part of his arrangement for the *A Bench In The Park* sequence). Also of note is the fact that Paul Whiteman's band at that time included such great jazz musicians as guitarist Eddie Lang and violinist Joe Venuti, and in addition to his arrangements for the principal numbers, orchestrator Ferde Grofé's scoring involved several medleys designed to give solo specialty spots to members of the band. In these, segments were heard from Kreisler's *Caprice Viennoise, Nola* by Felix Arndt and James Burns, *Linger Awhile* by Harry Owens and Vincent Rose, and *Aba Daba Honeymoon* by Arthur Fields and Walter Donovan. There were several folk, classical, and light classical pieces: *A-Hunting We Will Go*; Luigini's *Ballet Egyptien*; *Rule Britannia*; *D'Ye Ken John Peel*; *Santa Lucia*; *Funiculi-Funicula*; *Comin' Through The Rye*; *Wiener Blut*; *Fair Killarney*; *The Irish Washerwoman*; *Ay-yi Ay-yi-yi*; *Song Of The Volga Boatmen*; *Otchichornya*; some Sousa marches, and a couple of parodies called *Has Anybody Seen Our Nelly?* and *Oh, How I'd Like To Own A Fishstore*. Carl Laemmle produced, Frederick T. Lowe Jr wrote it, with sketches by Harry Ruskin, and Hal Mohr, Jerome Ash and Ray Rennahan photographed it.

THIRTIES MUSICALS

Director Leo McCarey, still a novice where sound was concerned, came a cropper with **Let's Go Native** (Paramount), a punchdrunk comedy that dissipated a potentially amusing idea in a welter of trite dialogue, triter lyrics, soporific choreography and undistinguished photography. What it *did* have going for it though, was a fairly pleasant score by Richard A. Whiting (lyrics by George Marion Jr who, incidentally, was an erstwhile writer of silent-screen titles) and a pleasing performance from Jack Oakie as a taxi-driver. Jeanette MacDonald (centre) received second billing to Oakie and was passable in the role of a modiste who, in order to escape her creditors, sets sail for South America. She never gets there, for the ship founders during a storm and, together with several other members of the *dramatis personae*, she finds herself marooned on a tropical island. What happens on the island formed the kernel of George Marion Jr and Percy Heath's screenplay, and it should have been far more diverting than it was. James Hall (centre foreground) played Miss MacDonald's boyfriend, with Kay Francis (left foreground), Charles Sellon, David Newell, Eugene Pallette, Skeets Gallagher and The King's Men in it too. Songs: *Let's Go Native*; *My Mad Moment*; *It Seems To Be Spring*; *Joe Jazz*; *I've Gotta Yen For You*.

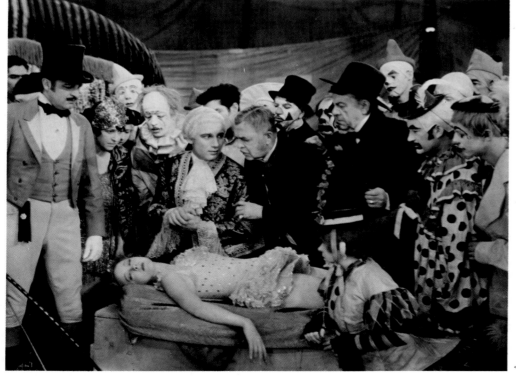

Grant Withers and Sue Carol brought more conviction to **Dancing Sweeties** (Warner Bros.) than this tepid romance, boringly directed by Ray Enright, deserved. Written by Gordon Rigby and Joseph Jackson (from a story by Harry Fried) it concerned a young couple who meet during a dance contest, fall in love and marry. The husband is ambitious and they part when the wife is unable to learn complicated new dance routines, but they get together again and settle for a life of domestic bliss. Also featured in this

pitifully thin plot were Edna Murphy, Tully Marshall, Eddie Phillips, Kate Price and Ada Mae Vaughan. Songs: *Wishing And Waiting For Love* Grant Clarke, Harry Akst; *Hullabaloo* Bobby Dolan, Walter O'Keefe; *I Love You, I Hate You* Al Bryan, Joseph Meyer; *The Kiss Waltz* Al Dubin, Joe Burke. *Dancing With Tears In My Eyes*, also by Dubin and Burke, was removed from the final print because the front office didn't think it good enough. It later became an enduring hit for Rudy Vallee on radio.

Apart from singing a few songs, Clara Bow did quite a bit of heavy-duty emoting in **Love Among The Millionaires** (Paramount). She played a waitress in a railroad cafe who finds herself in the midst of a romance with a brakeman called Jerry (Stanley Smith). Except that Jerry isn't a brakeman at all – he's a junior executive out to learn the business, as his father happens to be president of the railroad company. At a Palm Beach gathering Miss Bow, believing herself to be too common for the likes of him, attempts to sabotage the romance by deliberately singing in a manner likely to offend the guests. She almost succeeds, but true love wins through and Clara's martyrdom is short-lived. So was the film. It was adapted by Grover Jones and William Conselman from a story by Keene Thompson, with dialogue by Herman J. Mankiewicz, was directed by Frank Tuttle, and also featured 9-year-old Mitzi Green (right) whose impersonation of Clara Bow (centre), her elder sister in the story, was the film's high-spot. Also cast were Skeets Gallagher, Stuart Erwin, Charles Sellon (left) and Theodore Von Eltz. Songs included: *Believe It Or Not I've Found My Man*; *That's Worth Waiting For*; *Love Among The Millionaires*; *Rarin' To Go*; *Don't Be A Meanie* L. Wolfe Gilbert, Abel Baer.

A circus melodrama with songs, **Swing High** (Pathe) didn't. Its leaden, convoluted, intrigue-filled tale of circus life and love remained moribund while the heroine (Helen Twelvetrees, foreground) of James Seymour and Ray B. McCarey's screenplay – story by Seymour, and Joseph Santley who also directed – manages to save her sweetie (Fred Scott, centre, holding her hand) from the local siren (Dorothy Burgess) but not, alas, the film. Also on hand: John Sheehan, Daphne Pollard, Stepin Fetchit, Chester Conklin and Ben Turpin. E.B. Derr produced. Songs: *Do You Think I Could Grow On You?*; *It Must Be Love*; *With My Guitar And You*; *Shoo The Hoodoo Away*; *There's Happiness Over The Hill* Mack Gordon, Abner Silver, Ted Snyder.

Another campus musical, but this time set in
Spain, **In Gay Madrid** (MGM) starred heart-
throb Ramon Novarro (left) whose amorous
exploits result in his being sent from Madrid to
Santiago where his father hopes he will settle
down and study. But there are pretty girls in
Santiago too – especially Carmina (Dorothy
Jordan, right), and in no time at all lover boy is
wooing her with half a dozen romantic ballads.
Competent performances from a cast that in-
cluded Lottice Howell, Claude King, Eugenie
Besserer, William V. Mong and Beryl Mercer,
with a screenplay (Bess Meredyth, Salisbury
Field and Edwin Justus Mayer, story by
Alejandro Perez Lugin) and direction (by Robert
Z. Leonard) to match, all added up to a pleasing,
lightweight entertainment. Songs included: *Dark
Night* Herbert Stothart, Clifford Grey, Xavier
Cugat; *Santiago*; *Smile While We May* Roy Turk,
Grey; *Into Your Heart* Turk, Fred Ahlert.

Golden Dawn, an operetta by Otto Harbach,
Oscar Hammerstein II, Emmerich Kalman and
Herbert Stothart, was first seen on the stage in
1927. Warner Bros. brought it to the screen,
complete with East African setting and
Technicolor photography, neither of which was
able to blur the absurdities of the subject matter.
An incredible story about a native uprising
against the British and the Germans in World
War I, it seemed to defeat the judgement of both
scenarist Walter Anthony and director Ray
Enright, and the best that can be said of Larry
Ceballos's musical numbers is that, nowadays,
they can be regarded as a piece of camp.
Vivienne Segal (illustrated) and Walter Woolf
King were inoffensive in the leads, but the same
cannot be said of a blacked-up Noah Beery
Muddling along between these extremes were
Alice Gentle, Lupino Lane, Dick Henderson, Otto
Matiesen and Marion Byron. Most of the dialogue
was accompanied by music, a device the critics
found tiresome. Harbach, Hammerstein and
Kalman contributed four songs – *Whip Song*;
Dawn; *My Bwana* and *We Too* – and the Grant
Clarke–Harry Akst combo wrote *My Heart's Love
Call*; *Africa Smiles No More*; *Mooda's Song*; *In A
Jungle Bungalow*.
▽

Boop-a-doop girl Helen Kane (centre) and Victor ▷
Moore starred as the star and owner of a
medicine show in **Dangerous Nan McGrew**
(Paramount), a feeble musical which flickered
into life only when Miss Kane gurgled out her
songs. For the rest it was a tedious non-starter
which squandered the talents of James Hall,
Stuart Erwin, Frank Morgan and Louise Closser
Hale. It was written by Paul Gerard Smith and
Pierre Collings (from a story by Charles Beahan
and Garrett Fort) and incohesively directed by
Malcolm St Clair – who was clearly more at
home with Rin-Tin-Tin at Warner Bros. Songs:
Dangerous Nan McGrew; *I Owe You* Don
Hartman, Al Goodhart; *Aw! C'mon, Whatta Ya
Got To Lose?* Richard A. Whiting, Leo Robin; *Once
A Gypsy Told Me* (*You Were Mine*) Irving Kahal,
Sammy Fain, Pierre Norman.

As part of his fraternity initiation, Eddie Fripp
(Arthur Lake, left) had to kick the first man he
met, and kiss the first girl. This led to all sorts of
complications – mainly romantic – in **Cheer Up
and Smile** (Fox), a youth-orientated romp in
which the hero, amidst several other improbable
occurrences, becomes a singing sensation after
taking the place of 'Whispering' Jack Smith
(centre) who has been knocked unconscious in a
New York nightspot! The female lead, and the
girl of Lake's dreams, was Dixie Lee (right), with
Howard J. Green's screenplay (from a story by
Richard Connell) giving roles to Johnny Arthur,
Charles Judels, John Darrow, Sumner Getchell
and Franklin Pangborn. William Fox produced
and the director was Sidney Lanfield. Songs: *The
Shindig*; *Where Can You Be?*; *The Scamp Of The
Campus*; *When You Look In My Eyes*; *You May
Not Like It But Its A Great Idea* Raymond Klages,
Jesse Greer.
▽

One Mad Kiss (Fox) was one bad musical. All
about a Spanish Robin Hood who single-
handedly does battle with corrupt government
officials in the interest of the oppressed, it starred
Jose Mojica (left) as the outlaw, Mona Maris
(centre) as a dancehall girl, and Antonio Moreno
(centre right) as the hissable dictator Don Es-
trada. It was written by Dudley Nichols from a
play by Adolph Paul, presented by William Fox
and directed by Marcel Silver and James Tinling.
It was also made in Spanish and, if nothing else,
offered an abundance of songs. These were: *Oh,
Where Are You*; *One Mad Kiss* Jose Mojica, Troy
Saunders; *Behind The Mask*; *Monkey On A String*;
Oh! Have I A Way With The Girls! James Hanley,
Joseph McCarthy; *Only One*; *The Gay Heart* Dave
Stamper, Clare Kummer; *Once In A While* Stam-
per, Kummer, Cecil Arnold; *In My Arms*; *I Am
Free* William Kernell; *Lament* Dudley Nichols,
Jose Mojica.
▽

THIRTIES MUSICALS

Ernst Lubitsch's astonishing mastery of every ▷ aspect of the cinema was in generous evidence in **Monte Carlo**, a sophisticated melding of music, romance and comedy. All about a beautiful countess (Jeanette MacDonald, left) who abandons her would-be husband on the day of their wedding, takes the famous *Blue Express* to Monte Carlo, and falls in love with a count disguised as a barber (Jack Buchanan, right), it was another supremely effective demonstration of the efficacy of the integrated musical (Paramount's *The Love Parade* and *Love Me Tonight* being earlier examples) compared to the boring predictability of the many photoplays passing for musicals at the time. Not as overtly carnal in atmosphere as *The Love Parade*, the film substituted romance for sex and charm for passion – due largely to the casting of Jack Buchanan who, unlike Maurice Chevalier, exuded, in everything he did, a sense of propriety. The result was utterly delightful and caused one critic to remark that with *The Love Parade* and **Monte Carlo** safely preserved on celluloid, the rest of the year's musicals could be burned without anyone noticing the loss. Musically, the sequence that received most recognition (and rightly so) was the one aboard the *Blue Express*, in which MacDonald, in perfect counterpoint to the jets of steam emanating from under the speeding wheels of the train and the rhythmic movement of the pistons, sings 'Beyond The Blue Horizon' to a landscape of peasants who momentarily abandon their labours on the land and join her in the second chorus. Another musical highlight was an operatic sequence in which the opera's plot closely paralleled the one being played out between the protagonists. Entitled *Monsieur Beaucaire*, it was especially written by Whiting, Harling and Robin who based it on a story of the same name by Booth Tarkington and Eleanor G. Sutherland. Other highlights: a love duet sung over a telephone (called 'Give Me A Moment Please'), and the melodious 'Always In All Ways' beautifully sung by MacDonald and Buchanan. The music was by Richard A. Whiting and W. Franke Harling and the lyrics by Lubitsch's favourite lyricist, the talented and innovative Leo Robin. Ernest Vajda wrote the screenplay (from the play *The Blue Coast* by Hans Mueller), with additional dialogue by Vincent Lawrence. The cast was completed by Claud Allister, ZaSu Pitts, Tyler Brooke, John Roche, Lionel Belmore, Albert Conti and Helen Garden, and the appropriately attractive settings were by Hans Dreier. Other songs: *Day Of Days* (chorus); *She'll Love Me And Like It* (Allister, MacDonald); *Trimmin' The Women* (Buchanan, Roche, Brooke); *Whatever It Is, It's Grand* (Buchanan, MacDonald).

The famous comedy team of Ole Olsen and Chic ▷ Johnson (left) made their Warner Bros. debut in **Oh! Sailor Behave!** as a couple of American sailors on the Bay of Naples (a convincing reconstruction on the studio backlot) who, among other things, are searching for a man with a wooden leg guilty of robbing a Navy storehouse. Typical of their particular brand of comedy was aiming a pea-shooter at the legs of possible suspects, then clearing from suspicion anyone who jumps on being hit. The screenplay, by Joseph Jackson with dialogue by Jackson and Sid Silvers, was adapted from an unsuccessful Broadway comedy by Elmer Rice, and the movie itself chalked up only moderate returns at the box office. This may well have been because the prevailing decline in interest in musicals led Warner Bros. to delay the release of this one. It was directed by Archie Mayo, with Charles King (right) and Irene Delroy providing the love interest; and the supporting cast included Lotti Loder, Noah Beery, Lowell Sherman, Vivien Oakland and Charles Judels. Olsen and Johnson wrote a song of their own for it ('The Laughing Song') with Al Dubin and Joe Burke on hand to provide the others. They included: *Love Comes In The Moonlight*; *Leave A Little Smile*; *Tell Us Which One Do You Love*; *Highway To Heaven*.

Nothing of any consequence happened in **Sweethearts On Parade** (Columbia). As Photoplay succinctly put it: 'Another nice little girl from the country goes to the big city. Another suave millionaire, with more money than morals, lures the little girl to his yacht. Another poor but honest hero saves her. And another movie is born.' And dies, they might have added. Alice White (right) was the 'nice girl', Kenneth Thomson the millionaire, and Lloyd Hughes the poor but honest hero. Marie Prevost was in it too – so were Ray Cooke (left), Wilbur Mack, Ernest Wood and Max Asher. Al Cohn and James Starr provided the story, Colin Clements wrote the screenplay; it was produced by Al Christie and directed by Marshall Neilan. Songs: *Sweethearts On Parade* Charles Newman, Carmen Lombardo; *Dream Of Me* Henry Cohen, Irving Bibo; *Yearning Just For You* Benny Davis, ◁ Joe Burke; *Misstep* Irving Bibo.

◁ The plot devised by George S. Kaufman and Morrie Ryskind for the Marx Brothers (Harpo, left, Chico, centre left) in **Animal Crackers** (Paramount) was, as usual, of little importance compared to the distinctly surreal antics of the team, and in their second talkie the quartet firmly established themselves as the screen's most outrageous purveyors of mirth. Set on a large estate belonging to the redoubtable Margaret Dumont (centre), and pivoting on the theft of a valuable painting, Ryskind's scenario allowed Groucho (right) to run riot as Captain Jeffrey Spaulding, an African explorer who makes his entrance sitting in a bamboo and tiger-skin hammock carried by four strapping Nubian warriors. Director Victor Heerman's cast included Lillian Roth and Hal Thompson as the young lovers, Louis Sorin as an art connoisseur, as well as Kathryn Reece, Richard Greig, Edward Metcalf and The Music Masters (as six footmen). Several songs were imposed upon the unorthodox proceedings and they included: *Why Am I So Romantic?*; *Hooray For Captain Spaulding* Bert Kalmar, Harry Ruby; *Collegiate* Mo Jaffe, Nat Bonx; *Some Of These Days* Shelton Brooks.

◁ Paramount took no gambles with their production of **Queen High**, and played it safe by casting Frank Morgan and Charles Ruggles as business partners who manufacture garters but are always at loggerheads with one another. Their particular brand of comedy and skilful handling of dialogue kept Frank Mandel's undemanding screenplay (from a 1917 play by Edward Henry Peple, and the Laurence Schwab–Buddy De Sylva–Lewis Gensler 1926 musical reworking of it) simmering with laughs, and made the musical interpolations seem almost superfluous. Ginger Rogers (left) and Stanley Smith (right) provided the love interest and sang several of the songs with gusto, with Helen Carrington, Theresa Maxwell Canover, Nina Olivette, Tom Brown and Betty Garde in support. Mandel and Schwab produced and the director was Fred Newmeyer. Songs: *I Love The Girls In My Own Peculiar Way* E.Y. Harburg, Henry Souvaine; *It Seems To Me*; *I'm Afraid Of You* Edward Eliscu, Arthur Schwartz, Ralph Rainger; *Everything Will Happen For The Best* B.G. De Sylva, Lewis Gensler.

Based on James Gleason's play *Mr Bones*, **Mammy** (Warner Bros.) starred Al Jolson as an end-man in a travelling minstrel show and was a smash hit. Gordon Rigby's screenplay (dialogue by Joseph Jackson) didn't exactly sparkle, but with an Irving Berlin score to go with it, who cared? As it was, the story was a slightly melodramatic hodge-podge dealing with the desperate financial straits of the minstrel show, Al's love for Lois Moran which provokes the jealousy of her current beau (Lowell Sherman), and a card game which leads to Sherman being wounded for which Al is blamed and arrested. But all comes right in the end and, apart from Jolson himself (left), the film was memorable mainly for recreating the world of the minstrel show in all its aspects: from the blacking-up procedure in the dressing rooms to the street parades before the big event. The musical high point was an extended minstrel revue featuring about 60 performers and filmed in good-looking Technicolor (the rest of the film was black and white). It was directed by Michael Curtiz for producer Walter Morosco, and the cast, who did their best to make their presences felt in the overwhelming scene-hogging company of Jolson, included Louise Dresser (right), Mitchell Lewis, Hobart Bosworth and Tully Marshall. The Berlin songs were: *To My Mammy*; *Across The Breakfast Table Looking At You*; *Let Me Sing And I'm Happy*; *Knights Of The Road*; *Yes, We Have No Bananas* by Frank Silver and Irving Cohn sung to
◁ the tunes of several well-known operatic arias.

◁ **Top Speed** (First National), from the play by Bert Kalmar, Harry Ruby and Guy Bolton, and written for the screen by Humphrey Pearson and Henry McCarty, was a real gas for Joe E. Brown fans and even quite tolerable to those who couldn't stand him. A musical comedy, with the emphasis on the comedy, it featured Brown as a lowly clerk who pretends to be a millionaire and wins a boat race in a craft owned by his girlfriend's father. There was a villain thrown in for good measure (and who, thanks to Brown's intervention, gets his come-uppance), plus some well-staged dance numbers by Larry Ceballos. It was directed by the relative newcomer Mervyn LeRoy, whose efficiency and sense of comic timing was nowhere better demonstrated than in his inventive handling of the climactic boat race. LeRoy's attractive and talented cast included Bernice Claire (right), Jack Whiting (left), Laura Lee, Rita Flynn, Edmund Breese and, making his debut for Warner Bros., Frank McHugh, one of the studio's most durable character actors. Songs: *As Long As I Have You And You Have Me*; *Looking For The Lovelight In The Dark* Al Dubin, Joe Burke; *Knock Knees*.

THIRTIES MUSICALS

Sweet Kitty Bellairs (Warner Bros.) was, on the face of it, just another operetta-style romp, set this time in 18th-century England, and not immediately noticeable for the drawing power of its stars or a score of obvious hit tunes. On examination, though, it revealed several virtues not characteristic of Hollywood musicals of the time. While the story, centring on the romance of a coquette and a highwayman during one summer in fashionable Bath, was slight, the telling of it was done in an authentic period style and played by actors who were clearly cast for their understanding of high comedy. Very much a traditional ballad opera in musical flavour, the package was a seductive and undisguisedly romantic one, whose origins dated back to a novel, *The Bath Comedy* by Agnes and Egerton Castle, which became a stage play by David Belasco in 1903, from which it was adapted for the silent screen as a vehicle for Mae Murray. This Technicolor musical version had a screenplay by J. Grubb Alexander, and a rich crop of salty and clever songs by Bobby Dolan and Walter O'Keefe (who later became famous for his updating of the 1868 song 'The Man On The Flying Trapeze'). Alfred E. Green directed, capturing the intended flavour of the piece to charming perfection, with an excellent cast that included Claudia Dell (centre right) as the warm-hearted, flirtatious heroine, Perry Askam (right) as a fop, Ernest Torrence as an elderly and irascible cuckold and Walter Pidgeon (centre left), June Collyer, Lionel Belmore (left) and Arthur Edmund Carewe lending first class support. The Dolan–O'Keefe musical numbers were *Tally Ho; Highwayman Song; Song Of The City Of Bath; Drunk Song; Pump Song; Duelling Song; My Love; You-oo, I Love But You; Peggy's Leg.*

◁ An operetta, with sequences in Technicolor. **Dixiana** (RKO) starred Bebe Daniels (right) as a circus performer in the New Orleans of the 1840s, and Everett Marshall (left, from the Metropolitan Opera) as the wealthy Southerner she falls for. Marshall's mother (Jobyna Howland) disapproves of her prospective daughter-in-law's background and prolongs the plot by separating the couple. But after some treacherous goings-on perpetrated by a gambler sporting the name of Royal Montague (Ralf Harolde, centre) it all came right in the end. Some broad-comedy was supplied by the irrepressible team of Bert Wheeler and Robert Woolsey and, in one of the film's more genuinely spontaneous moments, Bill Robinson tap-danced. For the rest, it was a pleasant, well-sung, attractively directed (by Luther Reed who also adapted it from a short story by Anne Caldwell) piece of romantic fiction that whiled away the time painlessly enough. William Le Baron produced, the cast including Joseph Cawthorn, Dorothy Lee, Edward Chandler, Raymond Maurel and George Herman. Songs: *Dixiana* Benny Davis, Harry Tierney; *Here's To The Old Days; A Tear, A Kiss, A Smile; My One Ambition Is You; A Lady Loved A Soldier; Mr and Mrs Sippi; Guiding Star* Anne Caldwell, Harry Tierney.

Based on a 1925 play by Vincent Lawrence, and ▷ a remake of the 1927 comedy *Spring Fever* (MGM), **Love in the Rough** (MGM) was an amiable enough musical which gave Robert Montgomery and his co-star Dorothy Jordan (right-hand couple) a chance to prove how pleasantly they sang – especially in the Dorothy Fields–Jimmy McHugh number 'Go Home And Tell Your Mother'. Montgomery played a golfer who helps his sweetheart (Miss Jordan) to win a wager of $3,000 by beating an opponent in a climactic golf tournament. There wasn't a great deal more to it than that, but the songs, all by Fields and McHugh, were pleasant enough, and for those who liked Benny Rubin's particular brand of comedy, he was on hand to provide it, together with a cast that also included J.C. Nugent, Dorothy McNulty and Tyrrell Davis (left-hand couple), Harry Burns and Allan Lane. It was adapted by Sarah Y. Mason and scripted by Joe Farnham and Robert E. Hopkins, and the director was Charles F. Riesner. Other songs: *I'm Doing That Thing; I'm Learning A Lot From You; Like Kelly Can; One More Waltz.*

By the time the 1927 Laurence Schwab–Lew ▷ Brown–Frank Mandel–Buddy De Sylva musical **Good News** came to the screen via MGM, it was old news, and its tired story (football hero threatens the chances of his college team by neglecting his studies, but is successfully coached by an ugly duckling astronomy student who blossoms – *mirabile dictu* – into a beauty) certainly needed all the help it could get from the score by De Sylva, Brown and Henderson, and the other first-league composers, which went with it. Stanley Smith and an insipid Mary Lawlor starred as the footballer and the girl who helps him improve his grades, with Bessie Love (illustrated), Cliff Edwards, Lola Lane, Dorothy McNulty (she would become known as Penny Singleton), Thomas Jackson, specialty dancer Al (Rubberlegs) Norman and Delmer Daves also on hand to lend stalwart support to this rah-rah musical. It was adapted for the screen by Frances Marion, and directed by Nick Grinde with some assistance from Edgar McGregor, the show's original Broadway director. Due to the moratorium being imposed on musicals towards the end of 1930, the release print of **Good News** had several numbers excised from it, notably the duets of 'The Best Things In Life Are Free' and 'Lucky In Love'; and a Lola Lane number called 'That's How You Know We're Co-Eds'. The standout number was the ever-popular 'Varsity Drag'. Other songs: *He's A Lady's Man; Good News; Tait Song; Students Are We* De Sylva, Lew Brown, Henderson; *If You're Not Kissing Me; Football* Arthur Freed, Nacio Herb Brown; *I Feel Pessimistic* J. Russell Robinson, George Waggner; *Gee But I'd Like To Make You Happy* Reggie Montgomery. Remade in 1947.

Another unashamed dollop of romance for Ramon Novarro fans, **Call of the Flesh** (MGM), also known as *The Singer From Seville*, again placed the Mexican idol (illustrated) in a Spanish setting – this time as a would-be opera singer who captures the heart of convent girl Dorothy Jordan (illustrated). Novarro's singing, and a sequence in Technicolor, were the highlights of John Colton's rather workaday screenplay (story by Dorothy Farnum) though Renée Adorée, whose last film this was to be, was delightful as a Spanish dancer in love with Novarro. Less happily cast was Russell Hopton as Enrique, Miss Jordan's brother, whose big moment, when he tries to persuade Novarro not to marry his sister, went for nothing. Also in it were Ernest Torrence, Nance O'Neil, and Mathilde Comont. The competent direction was by Charles Brabin, with dance direction from Eduardo Cansino. Songs: *Just For Today*; *Not Quite Good Enough For Me* Herbert Stothart, Clifford Grey; *Lonely* Stothart, Grey, Novarro. Operatic excerpts, all sung by Novarro, included 'Vesti la Giubba' *Pagliacci* Leoncavallo; 'Cavatina' *L'Elisir d'Amore* Donizetti; 'Questa o quella' *Rigoletto* Verdi.
▽

△

With the bulk of its original score removed, RKO's **Leathernecking** (G.B.: **Present Arms**), partly filmed in colour, was the celluloid transposition of a Rodgers and Hart–Herbert Fields stage musical, *Present Arms*, the musical numbers of which had been directed on Broadway in 1928 by Busby Berkeley. The hackneyed story was of an army private (Ken Murray, 2nd left) who decides to impress society in general and his sweetheart (Irene Dunne) in particular by pretending to be a captain. Sprightly performances from Murray, Benny Rubin (right), Lilyan Tashman, Eddie Foy Jr (2nd right), Ned Sparks, Fred Santley (left) and Louise Fazenda kept it bearable: ditto director Edward Cline's pleasing lightness of touch. Pearl Eaton was responsible for the dance routines, the associate producer was Louis Sarecky, and the screenplay by Jane Murfin from an adaptation by Alfred Jackson. Songs: *You Took Advantage Of Me*; *A Kiss For Cinderella* Rodgers and Hart; *All My Life*; *Careless Kisses*; *Evening Star*; *Nice And So Peculiar* Benny Davis, Harry Akst; *Shake It Off And Smile* Sidney Clare, Oscar Levant.

Al Jolson (illustrated) starred in the movie version of his 1925 stage success, **Big Boy** (Warner Bros.), again playing the part of a negro jockey who triumphs over adversity and eventually wins the Kentucky Derby. Although there wasn't a great deal of mileage left in William K. Wells, Perry Vekroff and Rex Taylor's screenplay (from a play by Harold Atteridge), it was larded with wise-cracks, making up in humour what it lacked in originality. Alan Crosland directed with a refreshing lightness of touch after his *sturm-und-drang* approach to *The Jazz Singer* (Warner Bros. 1927) and, in supporting roles cast Claudia Dell, Louise Closser Hale, Lloyd Hughes, Eddie Phillips, John Harron and Noah Beery. But it was Jolson the customers wanted – and it was Jolson they got. With a vengeance! Songs: *What Will I Do Without You?* Al Dubin, Joe Burke; *Tomorrow Is Another Day*; *Liza Lee* Bud Green, Sammy Stept; *Down South* Sigmund Spaeth, William H. Myddleton; *The Handicap March* Dave Reed Jr, George Rosey; *Sonny Boy* Buddy De Sylva, Lew Brown, Ray Henderson.
▽

◁ An all-Technicolor musical with a golfing background, **Follow Thru** (Paramount) featured Jack Haley in the role he created the previous year on Broadway – though top billing went to Nancy Carroll as a golf pro's daughter out to beat her rival in love in a golfing tournament, and Charles 'Buddy' Rogers as the golf instructor who coaches her to victory. Haley played a girl-shy millionaire and in this, his first screen appearance, holed in one with both audiences and critics and launched his movie career. Zelma O'Neal (illustrated), Eugene Pallette, Thelma Todd, Claude King and Kathryn Givney were also in it; it was written and directed by Laurence Schwab and Lloyd Corrigan (from the stage show by Schwab, Buddy De Sylva, Lew Brown and Ray Henderson) and produced by Schwab and Frank Mandel. Songs: *A Peach Of A Pair* George Marion Jr, Richard A. Whiting; *It Must Be You* Edward Eliscu, Manning Sherwin; *Button Up Your Overcoat*; *Then I'll Have Time For You*; *I Want To Be Bad* De Sylva, Brown, Henderson.

THIRTIES MUSICALS

△

▽

Heads Up (Paramount) was a routine musical starring Charles 'Buddy' Rogers as an officer with the Coast Guards who goes through no end of bother to win the love of pretty Margaret Breen (against her mother's wishes), and to expose his rival as a fugitive bootlegger. Originally seen as a 1929 Broadway musical with music and lyrics by Richard Rodgers and Lorenz Hart, it was adapted for the screen by John McGowan and Jack Kirkland, directed by Victor Schertzinger with uneasy shifts of emphasis between comedy and melodrama, and featured Victor Moore and Helen Kane (foreground) as the comic support, with Helen Carrington, Gene Cowing, Harry Shannon, Preston Foster and Billy Taylor also cast. The dances were staged by George Hale. Songs included: *My Man Is On The Make*; *A Ship Without A Sail* Rodgers, Hart; *If I Knew You Better* Victor Schertzinger.

Like the Broadway hit on which it was based, **Whoopee** (Goldwyn) starred Eddie Cantor who, having previously made two unsuccessful films, became a Hollywood star with this one. It also introduced Busby Berkeley to screen audiences, and was one of the first musicals to use two-colour Technicolor really effectively. Based on a story by E.J. Ruth, a play by Owen Davis called *The Nervous Wreck*, and on the stage musical by William Anthony McGuire, Walter Donaldson and Gus Kahn (and written for the screen by William Conselman), it concerned itself with a hypochondriac (Cantor) who finds himself on an Arizona ranch peopled with cowboys, Indians, and a multitude of Broadway chorus girls. It provided plenty of scope for Cantor's comic persona, as well as giving him four Donaldson–Kahn numbers to sing, most notably 'Making Whoopee', the one song to have survived the transition from Broadway, and Cantor's biggest-ever hit. Berkeley, who staged the dances for **Whoopee**, cut his teeth on the numbers, all of which bore his unmistakable imprint (see illustration), and made quite a debut for himself. Believing that the film musical was 'terribly static and restricted', Berkeley came to Hollywood at the behest of Sam Goldwyn, who promised him complete artistic freedom. Taking advantage of this promise, and with the confidence of youth on his side, he immediately eliminated three of the four camera crews usually employed in the filming of production numbers and concentrated on only one camera – a practice he continued throughout

his career. In **Whoopee**'s opening sequence, 'Cowboy Number', a young Betty Grable leads the chorus and becomes the centre of Berkeley's first abstract pattern of dancers. For the first time ever the chorus girls were filmed in close-up, the camera becoming the surrogate for the average male out front in the stalls. As Berkeley commented to Goldwyn, 'We've got these beautiful girls, why not let the public see them?' In addition, the girls provided the perfect counterpoint to Berkeley's abstract forms and, as such, would in future humanize all his choreographic flights of fantasy. **Whoopee** was produced by Samuel Goldwyn and Florenz Ziegfeld, directed by Thornton Freeland, and also starred Eleanor Hunt. Its supporting cast included Paul Gregory, John Rutherford, Ethel Shutta, Spencer Charters, Chief Caupolican, Albert Hackett and William H. Philbrick – all from the original stage production. Other songs: *Mission Number*; *A Girlfriend Of A Boyfriend Of Mine*; *Makin' Waffles*; *My Baby Just Cares For Me*; *Stetson*; *The Song Of The Setting Sun* Donaldson, Kahn; *I'll Still Belong To You* Nacio Herb Brown, Edward Eliscu.
Interesting sideline: Florenz Ziegfeld's participation in the production was, for the most part, nominal. Following the 1929 crash, Ziegfeld and Goldwyn formed a joint corporation to film **Whoopee** and *Kid Boots*, but Ziegfeld alienated Goldwyn by insisting that his name be first in the corporation, with the result that Goldwyn restricted his access to the sound stages, and *Kid Boots* did not get made (except for the silent version, with Cantor, in 1926).

△

Thankfully the only musical to be attempted by the epic-orientated Cecil B. De Mille, **Madam Satan** (MGM) was a curious entertainment that cost a great deal of money to make and laid a brick at the box office. Set aboad a giant dirigible, its acorn of a plot (by Jeanie MacPherson, Gladys Unger and Elsie Janis) had a wealthy socialite (Kay Johnson, right) attempting to win back the love of her husband (Reginald Denny, left) by assuming the identity of a mysterious 'Madam Satan'. The climax of this hodge-podge was a spectacular costume party given aboard the dirigible, the floor show being an electrical ballet (staged by LeRoy Prinz and composed by Herbert Stothart) in which the participants, among other things, pretend to be spark plugs. A bolt of lightning, doubtless offended by the bad taste of it all, wrathfully strikes the floating airship, forcing its occupants to descend via the relative safety of New York via parachute. Husband and wife, by the way, were blissfully reunited. No less than forty-six players were credited, and they included Lillian Roth as the wild showgirl Denny temporarily leaves his wife for, Roland Young, Elsa Peterson, Irwin Boyd, Tyler Brooke, Wilfred Lucas, Albert Conti and, in a small part, composer Jack King. Cedric Gibbons and Mitchell Leisen dreamed up the sets, the gowns were by Adrian, and it was photographed by Robert Rosson. Songs and musical numbers included: *We're Going Somewhere*; *The Cat Walk*; *This Is Love* Herbert Stothart, Clifford Grey; *All I Know Is You Are In My Arms*; *Low Down*; *Auction Number*; *Satan's Song*; *Live And Love Today* Elsie Janis, Jack King.

One of the worst musicals of the year, **The Lottery Bride** (United Artists) – about a Norwegian lass who becomes the lottery bride of a miner only to discover that her husband is the older brother of the man she *really* loves – starred Jeanette MacDonald (right), had a score especially written for the occasion by Rudolf Friml, and settings by the great William Cameron Menzies. To no avail, alas. The film, hastily and carelessly directed by Germany's Paul L. Stein, only fuelled the flames of the public's fast-growing antipathy to musicals and it was a monumental failure, bringing naught but embarrassment to its participants. They included the British John Garrick (left), Broadway's Robert Chisholm (whose fine voice was the film's one redeeming feature), ZaSu Pitts and Joe E. Brown. It was adapted by Horace Jackson from a story by Herbert Stothart called *Bride 66* and scripted by Howard Emmett Rogers. Songs: *You're An Angel*; *My Northern Light*; *Yubla*; *Round She Whirls*; *High And Low*; *Shoulder To Shoulder*; *Napoli*; *I'll Follow The Trail*; *Come Drink To The Girl That You Love* Friml, J. Keirn Brennan.

A highly romantic and greatly fictionalized account of the life of Jenny Lind ('the Swedish nightingale') reached the screen in an MGM musical drama called *A Lady's Morals* (GB: *Jenny Lind*). It also marked the successful debut in pictures of the Metropolitan Opera's Grace Moore. Intent on giving the facts of Miss Lind's life a novelettish veneer, screenwriters Hans Kraly, Claudine West, John Meehan and Arthur Richman (story by Dorothy Farnum) partnered the Swedish soprano with a cocky young composer called Paul Brandt (Reginald Denny), who, in the course of the narrative, is hurt in a riot and goes blind. But none of this mattered very much (except possibly to the fictional Mr Brandt), since the film's *raison d'être* was the glowing presence of Miss Moore (illustrated, with Gilbert Emery) – and the arias and songs she sang throughout. They included a selection from Donizetti's *The Daughter Of The Regiment*, the 'Casta Diva' from Bellini's *Norma*, 'Is It Destiny?', 'The Student's Song' and 'I Hear Your Voice' by Clifford Grey and Oscar Straus, 'Oh Why' by Arthur Freed, Herbert Stothart and Henry M. Woods, 'Lovely Hour' by Carrie Jacobs Bond, and 'Swedish Pastorale' by Howard Johnson and Herbert Stothart. Wallace Beery played P.T. Barnum, with other parts going to Jobyna Howland as Miss Lind's companion, Gus Shy, George F. Marion, Paul Porcasi and Judith Vosselli. Sidney Franklin directed.

◁

△

Maurice Chevalier's fourth film for Paramount – excluding *Paramount on Parade* – was **Playboy of Paris**, and it desperately needed the magic touch of Ernst Lubitsch to bring it to life. What it got, instead, was the leaden one of Ludwig Berger, who also produced. (A French version, called *Le Petit Café*, starring Chevalier, Françoise Rosay and an all-French cast fared better and was generally considered to be the superior of the two.) The story had Chevalier being a waiter by day (illustrated) and a playboy by night, much to the distress of his employer (O.P. Heggie) and his employer's daughter (Frances Dee), who is in love with him. Complications abound and, in the end, Chevalier finds himself being challenged to a duel. Vincent Lawrence's screenplay (adapted by Percy Heath from Tristan Bernard's play *Le Petit Café*) made quite sure that it all ended happily, without, alas, being able to guarantee the same good fortune at the box office. One sequence, however, which became a classic, featured Chevalier tasting and appraising the heady contents of several barrels of wine. It was the best thing in a film that always promised more than it delivered. Others in the cast were Stuart Erwin, Eugene Pallette, Dorothy Christy, Cecil Cunningham, and Tyler Brooke. Songs: *My Ideal*; *It's A Great Life If You Don't Weaken*; *In The Heart Of Old Paree*; *Yvonne's Song* Richard A. Whiting, Newell Chase, Leo Robin.

THIRTIES MUSICALS

◁ Warner Bros.' predilection for operettas, more often than not taken from established stage successes, often resulted in catastrophe. With **Viennese Nights**, however, they acquired something specially written for the screen by Oscar Hammerstein II and Sigmund Romberg, and it turned out just fine. Filmed entirely in two-colour Technicolor, the story spanned 40 years, telling of a young composer (Alexander Gray, 2nd right) and the attractive woman (Vivienne Segal, centre right) who ought to have married him, but who weds a philanderer (Walter Pidgeon, centre left) instead. It had its over-*schmaltzy* moments and a profusion of plot but, nonetheless, made for a melodious and pleasing entertainment rich in Romberg waltzes. Alan Crosland directed a cast which included Bert Roach (right), Milton Douglas, Jean Hersholt, June Purcell and Louise Fazenda, and Jack Haskell directed the dances. Songs included: *I Bring A Love Song; I'm Lonely; You Will Remember Vienna; Here We Are; Regimental March; Yes, Yes, Yes; Goodbye My Love; Viennese Nights.*

Jeanette MacDonald, on loan to Fox from Paramount who didn't quite know what to do with her in the face of the negative reaction to musicals, sang opera for the first time in **Oh, For a Man!** beginning, no less, with the 'Liebestod' from Wagner's *Tristan and Isolde*. A slender but enjoyable trifle about an opera star (MacDonald, right) whose apartment is invaded by a burglar with a penchant for singing, it had MacDonald not only arranging for the rogue (Reginald Denny, left) to have his voice professionally trained, but falling in love with him as well! All very improbable, but adequately scripted (by Philip Klein and Lynn Starling), and delightfully performed by Miss MacDonald who was on top of the flimsy material all the way. Director Hamilton MacFadden made quite sure that his star always looked good and, in addition, drew enjoyable performances from vivacious Marjorie White and haughty Alison Skipworth. Completing the cast were Bela Lugosi, Albert Conti, Andre Cheron and William Davidson. Songs: *Believe Me If All Those Endearing Young Charms* (Matthew Locke, lyrics by Thomas Moore); *On A Summer Night; I'm Just Nuts About You* William Kernell; and a German art song (composer uncertain).

▽

△

Two of the best voices to grace the screen in 1930 – those of Lawrence Tibbett (left) and Grace Moore (centre) – brought glory to the Sigmund Romberg–Oscar Hammerstein II operetta **New Moon** which MGM presented in a no-expense-spared production, and which was a heartening box-office success. Transposed from its original French setting to Russia, its typical operetta-type plot (by Frank Mandel and Laurence Schwab) had the Princess Tanya (Moore) falling for a dashing lieutenant (Tibbett) despite the fact that she is already engaged to a Russian governor called Brusiloff (Adolphe Menjou, right). Roland Young, Guy Shy and Emily Fitzroy were in it too; adapted by Sylvia Thalberg and Frank Butler (dialogue by Cyril Hume), with Jack Conway directing. Songs: *Lover Come Back To Me; One Kiss; Stout-Hearted Men; Wanting You; Marianne; Funny Little Sailor Men; Farmer's Daughter; What Is Your Price Madame.*

The talkies helped to establish a lot more stars than they ruined – comedian Ed Wynn (illustrated) being a prime example. His distinctive, if somewhat squeaky, voice responded excellently to the machinations of the movie microphone, as audiences discovered in **Follow the Leader** (Paramount), a screen adaptation by Gertrude Purcell and Sid Silvers of a William K. Wells–George White–Buddy De Sylva–Lew Brown–Ray Henderson musical comedy called *Manhattan Mary*. In it, Wynn played a former acrobat turned waiter who, through a series of mishaps, finds himself elected the leader of a notorious gang called 'The Hudson Dusters'. Ginger Rogers was cast opposite him as a singer aching for a crack at Broadway, with Stanley Smith as the man she loves. Also cast were Lou Holtz, Lida Kane and newcomer Ethel Merman, who was brought in as a last-minute replacement for Ruth Etting, and got to sing the Sammy Fain–Irving Kahal number 'Satan's Holiday'. The director was Norman Taurog. Other songs included De Sylva, Brown and Henderson's *Broadway, The Heart Of The World*, retained from the original stage show; and *Brother, Just Laugh It Off* by E.Y. Harburg, Arthur Schwartz and Ralph
◁ Rainger.

Another casualty of the cinema-going public's ▷ declining interest in musicals was **Are You There?** (Fox), a vehicle for Canadian comedienne Beatrice Lillie (centre), which had four of its songs dropped after completion. Initial press reaction was not favourable and so the film never went out on full general release. A pity, as its rediscovery a few years ago revealed it to be the perfect showcase for its irrepressible star's outrageously zany sense of fun. She played a private eye who is hired by the son of a duke to prevent his father from marrying the Countess Helenka. Disguised as Lady Diana, a big game hunter, Miss Lillie gets to work on the case and exposes the duke's intended as a fraud – winning in the process the love of the old boy for herself. Harlan Thompson wrote it, Hamilton Mac-Fadden directed it and an excellent cast included John Garrick as the duke's son, George Grossmith as the duke, and Olga Baclanova as the phoney countess. Surviving songs: *Lady Detective*; *Queen Of The Hunt Am I*; *Baghdad Daddies* Grace Henry, Morris Hamilton.

△

Melville Crossman's (a pseudonym for Darryl F. Zanuck) story about two shopgirls who embark on a gold-digging search for a rich old man benefitted from an excellent screenplay by Arthur Caesar, and reached the screen as **The Life of the Party** (Warner Bros.) with Winnie Lightner as the star. Filmed in Technicolor and crisply directed by Roy Del Ruth, the movie's appearance unfortunately coincided with the current wave of unpopularity that was affecting screen musicals, so that what had been conceived as a full-scale musical lost all but one of its numbers to the cutting-room floor. Nevertheless, Miss Lightner (left) together with Irene Delroy as her friend, were backed up by a collection of effectively amusing performances from Charles Butterworth (right), Jack Whiting, Arthur Hoyt and, notably, Charles Judels as a hot-tempered couturier. The song that remained was *Can It Be Possible?* Sidney Mitchell, Archie Gottler, Joseph Mayer. Casualties were *One Robin Doesn't Make A Spring*; *Somehow* Frederick Loewe, Earle Crooker.

Sunny, the Otto Harbach–Oscar Hammerstein II–Jerome Kern stage success in which the effervescent Marilyn Miller (illustrated, below left, with Jerome Kern) had so delighted audiences on Broadway, was picked up for the movies, complete with its star and its Harbach–Hammerstein–Kern melodies, by First National. The plot was quite nonsensical: English circus bareback rider dresses up as a boy, stows away on board a New York-bound ship, is discovered, and, after being taken care of by some sympathetic passengers, marries one of them. But the story, adapted by Humphrey Pearson and Henry McCarty, was secondary to the gaiety of Miss Miller's singing and dancing. Joe Donahue played the man whom Sunny marries; and others featured in the cast were Lawrence Gray, O.P. Heggie, Inez Courtney, Barbara Bedford, Judith Vosselli and Clyde Cook. William A. Seiter made a good job of the direction, and the movie was embellished by ballet sequences directed by Theodore Kosloff. The songs incuded: *Sunny*; *Who?*; *Two Little Love Birds*; *D'ya Love Me?*; *I Was Alone*.

▽

Kiss Me Again (First National), originally known as *The Toast Of The Legion*, was a Technicolor screen adaptation of Victor Herbert's famous operetta *Mademoiselle Modiste*. Julian Josephson and Paul Perez reworked the original book by Henry Blossom and provided star parts for Walter Pidgeon (right) and Bernice Claire (left) in a story which led the pair of them, as a French lieutenant and his inamorata Mademoiselle Fifi, along the rocky road to love, encountering a number of Victor Herbert melodies (lyrics by Henry Blossom) on their way. William A. Seiter directed with a cast that also included Edward Everett Horton, Claude Gillingwater, Frank McHugh, Judith Vosselli, June Collyer and Albert Gran. Songs: *Kiss Me Again*; *The Time, The Place And The Girl*; *When The Cat's Away*; *I Want What I Want When I Want It*; *Mascot Of The Troop*; *If I Were On The Stage*; ◁ *Love Me, Love My Dog*.

Buddy De Sylva, Lew Brown and Ray Henderson followed their 1929 hit *Sunnyside Up* with **Just Imagine** (Fox), the first science fiction musical which, though fascinating in the way it predicted such things as automatic doors, space exploration, test-tube babies, food-substitute pills, televisual telephones and, most alarmingly, names replaced by numbers, suffered from an inferior screenplay, some pedestrian direction (by David Butler), and a score that in no way matched *Sunnyside Up* or the same team's *Good News*. The performances by El Brendel (centre right, as Single O), Maureen O'Sullivan (as LN-18), John Garrick (centre left, as J-21), Marjorie White (right, as D-6), Frank Albertson (left, as RT-42), Hobart Bosworth (as Z-4) and Mischa Auer (as B-36) were serviceable enough, but as the boldness of the concept was never reflected in anything they had to do or say, none of them was able to make much impact. The dance director was Seymour Felix and the imaginative settings the work of Stephen Goosson and Ralph Hammeras. Songs: *The Drinking Song*; *The Romance Of Elmer Stremmingway*; *Never Never Wed*; *There's Something About An Old-Fashioned Girl*; *Mothers Ought To Tell Their Daughters*; *I Am The Words, You Are The Melody*; *Dance Of Victory*; *Never Swat A Fly*.

▽

1931

Academy Awards

Art Direction
NOMINATIONS INCLUDED: *Just Imagine* (Fox) Stephen Goosson & Ralph Hammeras. *Whoopee* (Goldwyn, UA) Richard Day.

The New York Times Annual 'Ten Best'
3rd *The Smiling Lieutenant* (Paramount)

The Annual Top Moneymaking Films
INCLUDING (In alphabetical order): *Animal Crackers* (Paramount). *Check And Double Check* (RKO).

The Hot Heiress (First National) was a totally negative contribution to the screen musical. The public failed entirely to respond to the story of a riveter (Ben Lyon, left) who is taken up by a society woman from Port Chester (Ona Munson, right) and passed off as an architect; and even some original songs by Richard Rodgers and Lorenz Hart didn't help – a particular pity since the tunes themselves were well received, and critics remarked that a few more wouldn't have been amiss. The story and screenplay were by Herbert Fields, and the cast included Walter Pidgeon, Thelma Todd, Tom Dugan, Inez Courtney and Holmes Herbert, all of whom remained obstinately inert under the direction of Clarence 'Badger, whose limited acquaintance with musicals was all too evident. As a result of the film's artistic as well as commercial failure, the composers withdrew from their next two assignments for the studio. Songs included: *You're The Cats*; *Nobody Loves A Riveter*; *Like Ordinary People Do*; *Too Good To Be True* (deleted before the film's release). Remade in 1934 as *Happiness Ahead*, and again in 1941.
▽

Though the critics were respectful about MGM's ▷ **The Prodigal** (originally called *The Southerner*), this Lawrence Tibbett vehicle – in which the booming baritone played a self-imposed hobo who, after traversing the highways and byways of life for five years in the company of two other self-made tramps, returns to the bosom of his genteel Southern family and falls in love with his brother's wife – was not a success. In it, Tibbett (left) sang the famous 'Without A Song' by Vincent Youmans, Edward Eliscu and Billy Rose (the one thing he was never without!). But as the film was without an audience, it was of no consequence to anyone that it was the best moment in this Harry Pollard-directed curiosity. Bess Meredyth and Wells Root wrote it, with parts for Roland Young and Cliff Edwards as Tibbett's hobo buddies, and Esther Ralston as the sister-in-law he falls for. Also: Purnell Pratt, Emma Dunn. Hedda Hopper (right), Stepin Fetchit, and Theodore von Eltz. Other songs included: *Life Is A Dream* Arthur Freed, Oscar Straus; *Home Sweet Home* John Howard Payne, Sir Henry Bishop.

A remake of Ludwig Berger's *Ein Walzertraum* (*A Waltz Dream*), **The Smiling Lieutenant** (Paramount) reunited Maurice Chevalier with director Ernst Lubitsch, and gave the ailing screen musical a temporary respite that was hailed by critics and public alike as a welcome watering-hole in a desert of mediocrity. The story of an officer of the guards who, due to circumstances entirely out of his control, finds himself married to the rather plain-looking Princess Anna, it featured Chevalier (left) as the officer, Miriam Hopkins as his wife, and Claudette Colbert (right) as Nikki, the beautiful woman he really loves. Ironically, it is Nikki who, taking pity on the princess, teaches her how to improve her appearance, with the result that overnight she becomes a ravishing beauty whose good looks more than satisfy the man she has married. A wry and enchanting fairy-tale, its screenplay (by Ernest Vajda and Samson Raphaelson) frothed along, bringing out the best in its director and his three principal players. Enhanced by a melodious Oscar Straus score (lyrics by Clifford Grey), it simply couldn't miss – and didn't. Also cast were Charles Ruggles, George Barbier, Hugh O'Connell, Robert Strange and Con MacSunday. Songs: *Toujours L'Amour In The Army* (Chevalier); *Breakfast Table Love*; *Jazz Up Your Lingerie* (Colbert, Hopkins); *Live For Today*; *While Hearts Are Singing* (introduced by Colbert); *One More Hour Of Love* (Chevalier).

△

Beguiled by the British musical comedy star Evelyn Laye, Sam Goldwyn prevailed upon two Pulitzer Prize-winning writers, Louis Bromfield and Sidney Howard, to fashion a story that would do justice to her American screen debut. What they actually came up with was a rather mindless operetta called **One Heavenly Night** (United Artists) which, as it turned out, was anything but. Miss Laye (right) played a flower girl from Budapest who spends most of the time masquerading as a cabaret star. She falls in love with the dashing if somewhat roguish Count Mirko Tabor (John Boles, left) and, after a few elementary complications, marries him. Goldwyn's faith in his leading lady was justified. She scored a personal success and emerged from the venture unscathed. So did comedian Leon Errol who, in the course of the film's 82-minute running time, managed to air his entire repertoire of comic *shtick*. The film itself, directed by George Fitzmaurice, was dismissed as old-fashioned hogwash, and Goldwyn never again turned his hand to operetta. Miss Laye made only one more film in America before returning to Britain where she continued to charm London West End audiences for several decades. Others in the cast were Lilyan Tashman, Hugh Cameron, Marion Lord, Luis Alberni and Lionel Belmore. Songs: *I Belong To Everybody*; *Along The Road of Dreams*; *My Heart Is Beating*; *Goodnight Serenade*; *Heavenly Night* Nacio Herb Brown, Bruno Granichstaedten, Edward Eliscu, Clifford Grey.

Bright Lights (Warner Bros./First National) was another backstage musical filmed in Technicolor in which its star, Dorothy Mackaill (right), was at her best as a Hula dancer. Unfortunately, there was nothing else to be said in favour of this story about an actress who gives up her career for marriage, only to find a series of obstacles obstructing her path to happiness. Humphrey Pearson wrote the banal screenplay for producer Robert North and director Michael Curtiz, and Larry Ceballos staged the musical numbers. Noah Beery, Frank Fay (left), Inez Courtney, Eddie Nugent, Edmund Breese, Daphne Pollard and Frank McHugh were also featured and the songs included: *I'm Crazy For Cannibal Love* Al Bryan, Ed Ward; *Chinatown, My Chinatown* William Jerome, Jean Schwartz; *Song Of The Congo* Ned Washington, Benny Rubens.

THIRTIES MUSICALS

Delicious (Fox) did not quite live up to its title, but it gave immense pleasure to Janet Gaynor–Charles Farrell fans, and boasted a clutch of songs by George and Ira Gershwin. The story (by Guy Bolton, adapted by Bolton and Sonya Levien) focused squarely on the attempts of a Scottish immigrant (Gaynor, left) to give an Ellis Island official (Lawrence O'Sullivan) the slip, in the course of which she finds herself pursued by an adoring Russian composer (played by the Brazilian Raul Roulien), and a wealthy American playboy (Farrell, right). El Brendel continued to fracture the English language by pretending to be Swedish, with other parts going to Manya Roberti, Virginia Cherrill, Olive Tell and Mischa Auer. The director was David Butler. Songs: *Somebody From Somewhere* (Gaynor); *Delishious* (Roulien); *Blah-Blah-Blah* (Brendel); *We're From The Journal, The Wahrheit, The Telegram, The Times* (Dream sequence); *Katinkitschka* (Gaynor, Brendel, chorus); *The New York Rhapsody* (subsequently expanded into a concert work called *Second Rhapsody*).

W.C. Fields, playing the boorish father of a poor barmaid, introduced his famous juggling act at a formal dinner party in **Her Majesty Love** (Warner Bros./First National). It was a great success and the highlight of a musical that was otherwise distinguished only by its astounding ineptitude. Directed with a clenched Teutonic fist by William Dieterle, it wasted Marilyn Miller (left) in the starring role of the barmaid, and didn't do much better by Leon Errol as her unsuitable suitor, Ben Lyon (right) as the man she really loves, and a supporting cast which included Chester Conklin, Virginia Sale, Ford Sterling, Harry Stubbs, Maude Eburne, Harry Holman and Ruth Hall. It took six writers to think it up: R. Bernauer and R. Oesterreicher were responsible for the story, Robert Lord and Arthur Caesar adapted it, and Henry Blanke (later to become one of Warner Bros.' major producers) and Joseph Jackson wrote the script. Songs: *You're Baby-Minded Now*; *Because Of You*; *Don't Ever Be Blue*; *Though You're Not The First Wine* Al Dubin, Walter Jurmann.

'A surging Niagara of entertainment with more girls, more fun, more story and more Cantor than you've ever seen before!' was how a Goldwyn publicity blurb sold **Palmy Days**, and although the production values in this successful follow-up to *Whoopee* (Goldwyn, 1930) weren't quite as lavish as those of its predecessors, it was pretty entertaining hokum just the same, with Cantor in fine form throughout. The plot, which Cantor (illustrated) devised together with Morrie Ryskind and David Freeman, was no world beater (it had Cantor inadvertently helping a gang of phoney spiritualists to rob their unsuspecting client of $24,000), but it put him through a number of comic situations, all of which he played to the hilt. It even allowed him his obligatory blackface routine, a Keystone Kops-like chase, and a chance to appear in drag with the Goldwyn Girls. Much of the action took place in a bakery staffed with beautiful females, with leggy Charlotte Greenwood as the bakery's resident physical culturist on hand to improve Cantor's physique. The heavy of the piece was George Raft, and the cast was completed by Spencer Charters, Barbara Weeks, Charles B. Middleton, Paul Page, Harry Woods and Betty Grable. Busby Berkeley staged the dances with an originality rarely encountered in early screen musicals. Gregg Toland photographed it, and the director was Edward Sutherland. Songs: *Bend Down Sister*; *Goose Pimples*; *Dunk Dunk Dunk* Ballard MacDonald, Con Conrad; *There's Nothing Too Good For My Baby* Cantor, Bennie Davis, Harry Akst; *My Honey Said Yes, Yes* (performed by Cantor in blackface and the show's one durable hit) Cliff Friend.

Another victim of the moratorium the public continued to impose on musicals was baritone Lawrence Tibbett who ended his association with MGM after he completed **The Cuban Love Song**, and returned to the Metropolitan Opera. And although his swan song for the studio did no business, it was probably his most accomplished film. In a story that was more than coincidentally similar to Puccini's *Madame Butterfly*, it had opera star Tibbett (left) cast as an American marine who fathers a son by a beautiful Cuban peanut vendor, in spite of the fact that he has a socialite girlfriend in San Francisco. Beautifully photographed by Robert Rosson and with direction by W.S. Van Dyke that skilfully helped camouflage the fissures in the screenplay (by C. Gardner Sullivan, Bess Meredyth, John Lynch, John Colton, Gilbert Emery, Robert E. Hopkins and Paul Hervey Fox), **The Cuban Love Song** was one of the year's better musicals, and it was no fault of the artists involved that the public didn't want to know. Its score yielded the ever popular 'Peanut Vendor' song by Marion Sunshine, L. Wolfe Gilbert and Moisés Simons – though the song which gave the show its title and which Tibbett sang as both a baritone and (thanks to some fancy dubbing) a tenor, was musically more interesting. Lupe Velez (right), in one of the best parts of her chequered career, played Tibbett's exotic Cuban mistress Nenita; Karen Morley was his American sweetheart. Jimmy Durante scored a personal success as one of Tibbett's marine buddies, with other roles going to Ernest Torrence, Louise Fazenda, Hale Hamilton, Mathilde Comont and Phillip Cooper. Other songs included: *The Marine Hymn*; *Tramps At Sea*; *You're In The Army Now*; *Nobody's Sweetheart* Gus Kahn, Ernie Erdman, Billy Meyers, Elmer Schoebel.
▽

△

MGM wasted no time in purchasing the Buddy De Sylva–Lew Brown–Ray Henderson hit **Flying High** when it opened on Broadway in 1930. But by the time it reached the screen, under the same title (GB: **Happy Landing**), the following year, it was decidedly *de trop*. Bert Lahr (left), who appeared in the stage version, made his movie debut by repeating the same role on the screen, the female lead going to the unique Charlotte Greenwood (right), in a role Kate Smith played on Broadway. Lahr played an intrepid aviator who, due to no skill of his own but because of a fault in the landing gear, inadvertently breaks the world record for high flying. Also cast were Pat O'Brien, Kathryn Crawford, Charles Winninger, Hedda Hopper and Guy Kibbee. The musical routines were staged by Busby Berkeley, who, as he had done in *Whoopee* (Goldwyn, 1930), again revealed his penchant for a pretty girl and an eye-catching formation. The screenplay was by A.P. Younger (additional dialogue Robert E. Hopkins) from an adaptation by Charles F. Riesner, who also directed the film. Only the title song was retained from the original De Sylva, Brown and Henderson score – with Dorothy Fields and Jimmy McHugh supplying new songs and musical numbers. These included: *Happy Landing* and *We'll Dance Till Dawn*.

◁ A generous crop of songs by Oscar Hammerstein II and Sigmund Romberg was not enough to rescue **Children of Dreams** (Warner Bros.), yet another example of the kind of idiotic plot which, by the middle of 1931, was helping to hammer the nails into the coffin of the screen musical. This particular effort centred on a pair of humble itinerant fruit pickers who become romantically involved, with the girl, in order to save her father from being sent to jail, taking up a career as an opera singer. Paul Gregory (left) and Margaret Schilling (right) in the lead roles brought an agreeable quality to the otherwise sorry circumstances, and Alan Crosland directed a cast which also featured Tom Patricola, Bruce Winston, Charles Winninger and Marion Byron. The film was written by Romberg and Hammerstein, whose score included: *Fruit Picker's Song*; *Oh, Couldn't I Love That Girl*; *Her Professor*; *Children Of Dreams*; *Sleeping Beauty*; *If I Had A Girl Like You*; *Seek Love*; *Yes Sir*.

1932

Academic Awards
Best Picture
NOMINATIONS INCLUDED: *The Smiling Lieutenant*
(Paramount) produced by Ernst Lubitsch.
One Hour With You (Paramount) produced
by Ernst Lubitsch.

The New York Times Annual 'Ten Best'
7th *One Hour With You*

The Annual Top Moneymaking Films
INCLUDING: *Delicious* (Fox). *One Hour With
You.*

A scintillating cast plus a cracking good screenplay (by Frances Marion) worked its alchemy on **Blondie of the Follies** (MGM), a backstage yarn about a chorus girl's romance with a debonair playboy. Marion Davies (centre, with The Rocky Twins) was the chorine, Robert Montgomery the man-about-town, and Billie Dove a longstanding chum of Miss Davies's who, to further the plot, also happens to be in love with Montgomery. The standout moment in the show had Jimmy Durante and Miss Davies impersonating John Barrymore and Greta Garbo in MGM's then current hit, *Grand Hotel*, with entertaining performances on offer too from James Gleason (as Davies's father), ZaSu Pitts, Sidney Toler and Douglass Dumbrille. The resourceful direction was by Edmund Goulding. Songs and musical numbers: *Goodnight My Love* Harry Tobias, Gus Arnheim, Jules Lemare; *Tell Me While We're Dancing* Harry Link, Nick Kenny; *Why Don't You Take Me?* Edmund Goulding; *Three On A Match* Ray Egan, Ted Fiorito; *Goin' Fishin'* Walter Samuels, Leonard Whitcup; *It Was So Beautiful* Arthur Freed, Harry Barris; *Don't Take Your Girl To The Grand Hotel* Dave Snell.
▽

The first screen version of George and Ira Gershwin's stage hit **Girl Crazy** (RKO), in an adaptation by Herman Mankiewicz, starred Bert Wheeler (third from right) as a taxicab driver who, in a $400 ride, transports Robert Woolsey (with glasses) to the one-horse town of Custerville, Arizona where, after a few adventures *en route*, Wheeler finds himself elected as Sheriff. A classic Gershwin score, augmented by a song the brothers wrote especially for the film called 'You've Got What Gets Me', the take-it-or-leave-it humour of its stars, and young Mitzi Green (left foreground) interrupting the narrative to do some spot-on impersonations of George Arliss and Edna May Oliver, added up to a musical romp that was never dull, but wasn't inspired either. Eddie Quillan (right), Stanley Fields (centre, as the villain), Dorothy Lee (centre foreground, as Woolsey's contralto-voiced wife), Kitty Kelly (left), Arline Judge and Chris Pin Martin were also in it, and the director was William A. Seiter. Remade by MGM in 1943 for Mickey Rooney and Judy Garland, and again in 1967 as *When The Boys Meet The Girls*. Songs: *Could You Use Me?; But Not For Me; Embraceable You; Sam and Delilah; I Got Rhythm.*
▽

△

Crooner (Warner Bros./First National), starred David Manners (left) as a college saxophone player whose agent (Ken Murray) turns him into an overnight singing sensation (his vocals were dubbed by Brick Holton). Once at the top, however, the crooner's newly inflated ego gets the better of him, causing his downfall and a return to the obscurity from whence he came. Charles Kenyon wrote the screenplay from a story by Rian James which was just as violent an exposé of the instant success syndrome as Bud Schulberg's *A Face In The Crowd* (Warner Bros./New Productions) was to be 25 years later. It was directed with skill and polish by Lloyd Bacon, with Ann Dvorak, Sheila Terry, Teddy Joyce, William Janney, Eddie Nugent, J. Carrol Naish, Betty Gillette and Guy Kibbee (right) also cast. Songs included: *I Send My Love With The Roses* Al Dubin, Joe Burke; *Three's A Crowd* Al Dubin, Irving Kahal, Harry Warren; *Sweethearts Forever* Cliff Friend, Irving Caesar; *Now You've Got Me Worrying For You* Irving Kahal, Sammy Fain; *Banking On The Weather* Joe Young, Fain; *In A Shanty In Old Shanty Town* Young, John Siras.

George M. Cohan, 'Mr Broadway' himself, made his talking picture debut in **The Phantom President** (Paramount). Although the film – in which Cohan played dual roles: a presidential candidate and a medicine man who is his physical double – received favourable notices, its underlying theme of political skulduggery (with the medicine man pretending to be the candidate) didn't attract audiences, and it flopped. Or, as Richard Rodgers who, with Lorenz Hart, composed the unmemorable score for it remarked: 'Even Hoover was more popular than the film.' Cohan's manic behaviour during shooting was widely publicized: he wanted to write, produce and direct it as, indeed, he had done with his stage shows, and his generally surly behaviour and unwillingness to grant interviews, or to co-operate with any other form of publicity, certainly damaged the chances of the finished product. Though Cohan (right) did well enough with the role, he was up against stiff competition from Jimmy Durante (left, as the medicine man's partner), whose performance divided the critics as to which of the two players was the more effective. Claudette Colbert was cast as a prospective presidential wife, serving little purpose other than to look pretty – which she did. George Barbier, Sidney Toler, Louise Mackintosh and Jameson Thomas were also in it, the screenplay (from a novel by George F. Worts) was by Walter DeLeon and Harlan Thompson, and it was admirably directed by Norman Taurog. Songs: *Give Her A Kiss; The Country Needs A Man; Somebody Ought To Wave A Flag; The Convention.*
◁

The well-known and popular comedy team of Joe Smith and Charles Dale made their feature film debut in **Manhattan Parade** (Warner Bros.), a Technicolor backstage musical with the accent on slapstick. Based on a play by Sam Shipman, the screenplay by Robert Lord and Houston Branch offered a golden opportunity to satirize the New York musical theatre, with Smith and Dale playing a couple of Broadway producers who also happen to be brothers. But any resemblance to the Shuberts was both minimal and accidental in this overweight treatment of a story which had the producers trying to cope with the exaggerated demands of a Russian director (spiritedly played by Luis Alberni). Winnie Lightner (left) was also in it with child star Dickie Moore – they shared a scene together and it was the best thing in the show. Charles Butterworth, Walter Miller, Greta Granstedt (right) and Bobby Watson completed the cast for director Lloyd Bacon, and the songs included: *I Love A Parade; Temporarily Blue* Ted Koehler, Harold Arlen; *I'm Happy When You're Jealous* Bert Kalmar, Harry Ruby.
▽

Clearly inspired by the visual styles of René Clair and Ernst Lubitsch, director Frank Tuttle set out to make a romantic comedy in a similar vein. The result was **This is the Night** (Paramount), a slick and engagingly performed version of Avery Hopwood's play *Naughty Cinderella* (screenplay by George Marion Jr and Benjamin Glazer). Once again marital infidelity was the subject involving, among others, attractive Thelma Todd who, while her husband (Cary Grant), an Olympic Games athlete, is hurling javelins in Los Angeles, is having a romantic dalliance in Paris with a wealthy Parisian bachelor (Roland Young). The plot thickens with the unexpected arrival of Grant (left), necessitating Young to find a temporary wife – which he does in the shape of the attractive and charming Lily Damita (right). The four saunter off to Venice where a wild time is had by all, including Charles Ruggles as a playboy friend of Young's who goes along for the ride and ends up in the welcoming arms of La Damita. Completing the cast were Irving Bacon, Claire Dodd and Davison Clark. Songs included: *This Is The Night* Sam Coslow, Ralph Rainger; *Madame Has Lost Her Dress*; *Tonight Is All A Dream* George Marion Jr, Rainger.
▽

Though Ernst Lubitsch is generally credited with the direction of **One Hour With You** (a remake of his 1924 comedy *The Marriage Circle* for Warner Bros.), at least half of the film was directed by George Cukor who was assigned to it shortly after Lubitsch was appointed overall production supervisor at Paramount. Lubitsch's continued involvement with the film, however, resulted in Cukor eventually relinquishing his control while, at the same time, fighting Paramount to credit him officially with the work he had already done on it. After taking the matter to arbitration, Cukor won, and on some ads is credited as being the film's sole director with the production 'under the supervision of Ernst Lubitsch'. Yet, as most of the film's pre-production work was handled by Lubitsch, the film – despite Cukor's involvement – has the master's unmistakable touch welded to it, and although not quite in the same league as *The Love Parade*, was a delightfully sophisticated musical just the same. It reunited Maurice Chevalier and Jeanette MacDonald (Kay Francis was originally pencilled in for the role) as a husband and wife (illustrated) who indulge in a spot of marital infidelity, with Genevieve Tobin (in a role which Lubitsch had intended to go to Carole Lombard) encouraging it all. Charles Ruggles was also cast (as a police commissioner), so were Donald Novis, Roland Young, George Barbier, Josephine Dunn, Richard Carle, Charles Judels and Barbara Leonard. A special French version was simultaneously shot with Ernst Ferny, Andre Cheron, and Pierre Etchepare replacing Young, Barbier and Ruggles, and Lily Damita replacing Miss Tobin. It was written by Samson Raphaelson from a play by Lothar Schmidt and had a score by Oscar Straus and Richard A. Whiting, with lyrics by Leo Robin. Songs: *One Hour With You* (MacDonald, Chevalier, Tobin, Ruggles, Novis); *Three Times A Day*; *Now I Ask You What Would You Do* (Chevalier) Whiting, Robin; *We Will Always Be Sweethearts* (MacDonald, Chevalier); *What A Little Thing Like A Wedding Ring Can Do*; *Oh That Mitzi* (Chevalier); *It Was Only A Dream Kiss*; *Mitzi-Colette Talk Song* Straus, Robin; *Police Station Talk Song* John Leipold.
▷

◁ Capitalizing on the enormous popularity of radio – the cheapest entertainment available to a nation financially crippled by the Depression – Paramount produced **The Big Broadcast**, giving radio fans from coast to coast not only a chance to hear their particular favourites, but to see them as well. And it started a vogue that would last until the arrival of television. In paying homage to a rival medium, director Frank Tuttle (consciously or unconsciously) stressed the motion picture's supremacy over the 'air lanes' by indulging in some weird and wonderful trick photography (a cat liquefies and slides under a door; a clarinet melts; a clock comes to life etc. etc.). These devices also served to jazz up a rather routine narrative about a singer (Bing Crosby, left) and a Texas millionaire (Stuart Erwin, right) who are both in love with the same girl (Leila Hyams). Based on the play *Wild Waves* by William Ford Manley, it was written by George Marion Jr and featured Sharon Lynn, George Burns and Gracie Allen, George Barbier, Ralph Robertson, Major, Sharp and Minor, Spec O'Donnell, Alex Melesh, Kate Smith, The Boswell Sisters, Cab Calloway and His Orchestra, The Mills Brothers, Arthur Tracy, Vincent Lopez and His Orchestra, Donald Novis, Don Ball, James Wallington, Norman Brokenshire, William Brenton and Eddie Lang. The songs – and their performers – included: *Where The Blue Of The Night Meets The Gold Of The Day* (Bing Crosby – it became his theme song) Roy Turk, Crosby, Fred Ahlert; *When The Moon Comes Over The Mountain* (Kate Smith – it became her theme song) Kate Smith, Harry Woods, Howard Johnson; *Shout, Sister, Shout* (The Boswell Sisters) Clarence Williams; *Minnie The Moocher* (Cab Calloway and His Orchestra) Calloway, Irving Mills, Clarence Gaskill; *Goodbye Blues* (The Mills Brothers) Arnold Johnson, Jimmy McHugh; *Marta* (Arthur Tracy) L. Wolfe Gilbert, Moisés Simons; *Nola* (Vincent Lopez and His Orchestra) James F. Burns, Felix Arndt; *Hot Toddy* (Calloway and His Orchestra) Benny Carter; *Dinah* (Crosby) Sam M. Lewis, Joe Young, Harry Akst; *The Boswell Weeps* (Boswell Sisters, George Burns, Grace Allen, Leila Hyams); *Here Lies Love* (Tracy, Crosby, Lopez and Orchestra); *Please* (Crosby with Eddie Lang on guitar) Ralph Rainger, Leo Robin; *Tiger Rag* (Mills Brothers) attributed variously to Jelly Roll Morton, and to Nick La Rocca and the Original Dixieland Jazz Band; *Trees* (Donald Novis) Joyce Kilner, Oscar Rasbach; *Crazy People* (Boswell Sisters) Edgar Leslie, James V. Monaco; *It Was So Beautiful* (Kate Smith) Arthur Freed, Harry Barris; *Kicking The Gong Around* (Calloway and Orchestra) Ted Koehler, Harold Arlen; and, for the finale, a reprise of *Please* (Crosby, Eddie Lang, Stuart Erwin).

From its brilliantly original opening depicting a dawn chorus of the sounds and noises that herald the awakening of Paris each morning, to the final moments in which Jeanette MacDonald chases a train on horseback in order to stop Maurice Chevalier from leaving her, **Love Me Tonight** (Paramount) remains one of the most enchanting and cohesive musicals in the history of the genre. Despite the opening scene which roots it firmly in reality, the plot soon spirals off into fantasy, switching from the streets of Paris to a mediaeval château. Maurice Courtelin (Maurice Chevalier), 'the best tailor in all France', pursues the Vicomte de Vareze (Charles Ruggles) to his château because the vicomte owes him a vast sum of money. Afraid that the appearance of the tailor might put him out of favour with his uncle, the duke (C. Aubrey Smith), the vicomte introduces Chevalier as a baron. Chevalier's charm works its spell on all the members of the household except, of course, the proud Princess Jeanette (Jeanette MacDonald) who realizes only at the end of the film that she loves him – even though 'the son of a gun is nothing but a tailor'. Clearly influenced by Ernst Lubitsch, director Rouben Mamoulian, who went on to make only four more musicals, was never again able to integrate plot and songs as successfully as in **Love Me Tonight**. One of Mamoulian's strengths was the ability to visualize an entire film in musical

terms, and the unity of style he strove for was nowhere better illustrated than in **Love Me Tonight**'s opening number, 'Isn't It Romantic?'. The song emerges from rhyming dialogue between Chevalier and Bert Roach. Chevalier starts it and Roach continues 'the very catchy strain'. A taxi-driver begins whistling it and his passenger, who happens to be a composer, writes it down. He puts words to the music in a train and it is overheard by soldiers, who are then themselves heard singing it as they march across the countryside. A gypsy hears it, plays it on his violin, and it is heard by Jeanette MacDonald in her château. Thus, by this musical chain, she is already linked with Chevalier before they have even met. This cutting from one scene to another during a number, though commonplace today, was extremely innovative, and gave the songwriting team of Richard Rodgers and Lorenz Hart a freedom they had never had on the stage, and which they exploited triumphantly. The music score was recorded before shooting began, thus allowing Mamoulian to choreograph the movements of his actors to the music, as when Chevalier bounds up the steps of the château or, in the hunt scene, where horses and stags 'dance' to the rhythms on the soundtrack. This unity of action and melody is continued right to the end when the song 'The Son Of A Gun Is Nothing But A Tailor' makes a plot point more concisely and effectively than any dialogue could do. One of the great films of the decade, it was written by Samuel Hoffenstein, Waldemar Young and George Marion Jr from a play by Leopold Marchand and Paul Armont, and produced by Mamoulian with a supporting cast that also included Charles Butterworth, Myrna Loy, Elizabeth Patterson, Ethel Griffies, Blanche Frederici, Marion Byron, George 'Gabby' Hayes and Joseph Cawthorn. Other songs and musical numbers: *Mimi* (a brilliant Chevalier music-hall pastiche); *Lover* (MacDonald); *A Woman Needs Something Like That* (MacDonald, Cawthorn); *The Poor Apache* (Chevalier); *Love Me Tonight* (MacDonald, Chevalier); *Song Of Paree* (Chevalier, Byron, Hayes, others); *How Are You?*; *A Hot Time In The Old Town Tonight* (used satirically in 'Dead March' tempo to comment on the aristocratic fogies playing bridge in the castle and written, not by Rodgers and Hart, but by Theodore Metz). Illustrations show: (top) Chevalier; (left) L to R, Loy, Chevalier, MacDonald; (below) Chevalier and MacDonald.

△

Eddie Cantor's third musical for Samuel Goldwyn was **The Kid From Spain**, and although it cost a mammoth $1,400,000 to make, it cleaned up at the box office (tickets at its Rivoli Theatre engagement in New York were an exorbitant two dollars and twenty cents each), and was the most popular and financially successful musical of 1932. Directed by Leo McCarey (whose work in it so impressed the Marx Brothers that they engaged him to steer them through *Duck Soup* at Paramount the following year), and with Busby Berkeley again staging the musical numbers, it was pure escapist nonsense that managed to smash through the country's apathy towards musicals. The story opened with Cantor and his buddy (Robert Young) being expelled from college. In no time at all they're implicated in a bank robbery and flee to Mexico where Cantor (illustrated), posing as a Mexican in order to pass the border guard, is mistakenly thought to be Don Sebastian, a celebrated matador. As the complications proliferated, so did Cantor's numerous routines and set-pieces, the best being a scene in a bullring where he had to prove his non-existent prowess as a matador. The musical highlight had Cantor performing (in blackface and with The Goldwyn Girls) the Bert Kalmar–Harry Ruby–Irving Caesar–Harry Akst hit 'What A Perfect Combination', which soon became another Cantor standard. Love interest was supplied by the Polish-born comedienne and singer Lyda Roberti, with other roles going to Ruth Hall, John Miljan, Noah Beery, J. Carrol Naish, Robert Emmett O'Connor, Stanley Fields and Paul Porcasi. In the ranks of The Goldwyn Girls were Betty Grable, Paulette Goddard, Lucille Ball and Virginia Bruce. Berkeley's dance routines were by now only a step or two away from greatness, and they contributed immeasurably to the overall success of the film. The screenplay was by Kalmar, Ruby, and William Anthony McGuire. Other songs and musical numbers: *The College Song* (Betty Grable and The Goldwyn Girls); *In The Moonlight* (Cantor and The Goldwyn Girls); *Look What You've Done* (Cantor and Lyda Roberti) Kalmar, Ruby; *Untitled Dance* (Specialty number) Grace Poggi.

1933

Academy Awards

Best Picture
NOMINATIONS INCLUDED: *42nd Street* (WB) produced by Darryl F. Zanuck. *She Done Him Wrong* (Paramount) produced by William Le Baron.

Sound Recording
NOMINATIONS INCLUDED: *42nd Street* Nathan Levinson. *Gold Diggers Of 1933* (WB) Nathan Levinson.

The Annual Top Moneymaking Films
INCLUDING: *42nd Street*. *Gold Diggers Of 1933*. *I'm No Angel* (Paramount). *The Kid From Spain* (Goldwyn, UA).

After a small role in Paramount's *Night After Night* (1932), Mae West, who'd been a professional performer for over thirty years, received the full star treatment in **She Done Him Wrong** (Paramount). Though somewhat sanitized for the movies, this reworking of her 1928 stage success *Diamond Lil* was pretty outspoken for its time, with its star's particular talent for drenching the most innocent line in sexual innuendo more than compensating for the dialogue and lyrics that had to go. It was the film in which Miss West (right) first delivered her invitation to 'Come up and see me . . .' (on this occasion to Cary Grant, left), and it was the film in which she first demonstrated to the cinema-going world that all you needed to become a sex goddess was a suggestive strut and nasal twang. It was also the film that saved Paramount's bacon, the healthy box-office receipts staving off the studio's impending bankruptcy. West played Lady Lou (Diamond Lil), a gay nineties Bowery belle whose sentimental streak turns out to be her downfall. There was nothing sentimental, however, about her performance, or about Harvey Thew and John Bright's screenplay, or about Lowell Sherman's first-rate direction. And although Mae occupied stage centre for most of the time, fine performances were also registered by her co-star Cary Grant (as a police agent masquerading as a Salvation Army recruit), Gilbert Roland, Noah Beery Sr, Rafaela Ottiano, David Landau and Rochelle Hudson. Songs: *A Guy What Takes His Time* Ralph Rainger, Leo Robin; *I Wonder Where My Easy Rider's Gone* Shelton Brooks; *Silver Threads Among The Gold* Eben E. Rexford, Hart Pease Danks; *Pretty Baby* Egbert Van Alstyne, Tony Jackson, Gus Kahn; *Frankie And Johnny* (traditional).

Having taken a successful gamble by experimenting with sound in *The Jazz Singer* (Warner Bros. 1927), Al Jolson took another chance six years later for United Artists with **Hallelujah I'm a Bum** (GB: **Hallelujah I'm a Tramp**) – and flopped. A pity, as it was certainly the best, most adventurous film he had ever made. With its hints of John Gay's *The Beggar's Opera*, René Clair's *A Nous La Liberté* (1931) and Charlie Chaplin's much-loved tramp permeating S.N. Behrman's rhyming-couplet screenplay from a story by Ben Hecht, what emerged was the only musical in Hollywood's history that was about, and dealt directly with, the Depression. And as such, audiences found the modest little tale of Bumper (Jolson, left), a Central Park hobo and self-styled 'mayor' of hobos anonymous, too near the knuckle for comfort. What they wanted in 1933 was Busby Berkeley and his escapist meanderings rather than entertainment that underlined the problems of the day. The film cost $1,250,000 to make (an exorbitant amount considering its modest setting and lack of production numbers), much of it going to Jolson whose contract with United Artists involved him in a three-picture deal at $25,000 a week for forty weeks. (The other two pictures were never made.) Roland Young was originally cast as Hastings, the Mayor of New York, but fell ill after shooting commenced, making it necessary to re-shoot his scenes with his replacement, Frank Morgan. This also added to the cost. Finally, two separate versions of the title song were filmed, the word 'bum' (unacceptable to British audiences at the time) being changed to 'tramp'. Richard Rodgers and Lorenz Hart wrote the score, expanding on the style they'd adopted for *Love Me Tonight* (Paramount, 1932) and *The Phantom President* (Paramount, 1932). In purely musical terms, it was an interesting experiment for its two songwriters who used rhymed conversation with musical accompaniment to create what Rodgers has referred to as 'musical dialogue'. It was not, however, to the public's taste. The film was lovingly and carefully directed by Lewis Milestone who, in other featured roles, cast the great silent comedian Harry Langdon (right) as well as Madge Evans, Bert Roach, Tyler Brooke and Chester Conklin. Songs included: *What Do You Want With Money?*; *You Are Too Beautiful* (one of the loveliest ballads Jolson ever sang); *I'll Do It Again*; *I've Got To Get Back To New York*.

Plot definitely came second in **Melody Cruise** (RKO), a musical farce which had its director, Mark Sandrich, disguising its Lilliputian story (by himself and Ben Holmes) with so much trick photography that he might almost have been auditioning for entry into the exclusive magic circle. Charles Ruggles and Phil Harris (right) starred as a couple of well-to-do buddies journeying by steamship from New York to California, with Greta Niesen (left), Helen Mack, June Brewster and Shirley Chambers as the women who complicate their lives. Chick Chandler, Florence Roberts and Marjorie Gateson were also in it and the screenplay was by Sandrich and Holmes, with additional dialogue by Alan Rivkin and P.J. Wolfson. Songs: *I Met Her At A Party*; *He's Not The Marrying Kind*; *Isn't This A Night For Love*; *This Is The Hour* Val Burton, Will Jason.

Radio star Kate Smith (left) who, with her outsized proportions, was hardly ideal film material, starred in Paramount's **Hello Everybody** in which she was called on to do no more than play herself. Based on a story by Fannie Hurst (screenplay by Dorothy Yost and Lawrence Hazard), it featured Miss Smith as a quiet country girl who, between her radio engagements, is content to stay at home and tend the farm. Romance intrudes in the shape of Randolph Scott and, although she falls hopelessly in love with him, he only has eyes for her sister, pretty Sally Blane. Forever philosophical about such matters, cheerful Kate resigns herself to her loveless existence by revelling contentedly in the happiness of others. William A. Seiter directed it, and his cast included Julia Swayne Gordon, Jerry Tucker, George Barbier and Charles Grapewin (right). Songs: *Moon Song*; *Out In The Great Open Spaces*; *Queen Of Lullaby Land*; *Twenty Million People*; *Pickaninnies' Heaven* Arthur Johnston, Sam Coslow.

▽

△

Having made *Delicious* (Fox) a couple of years back, Janet Gaynor (centre right) now appeared in **Adorable** (Fox) as a manicurist who falls for a delicatessen dealer. Except that she isn't a manicurist at all, but the princess of a mythical kingdom called Hipsburgy-Legstadt; and he, it turns out, is not a delicatessen dealer, but an officer. Their romance blossomed and a good time was had by all – except, possibly, the handful of paying customers who found Miss Gaynor's thick overlay of winsomeness a mite too cloying for comfort. The French actor Henry Garat (centre left), making his American debut, played the officer, with C. Aubrey Smith as Hipsburgy-Legstadt's Prime Minister. Herbert Mundin, Blanche Frederici and Hans von Twardowski completed the cast. It was adapted from a Paul Frank–Billy Wilder story by George Marion Jr and Jane Storm, and had a score by Werner Richard Heymann, George Marion Jr and Richard A. Whiting. The director was William Dieterle, whose skill managed to keep a potentially indigestible story, if not exactly adorable, relatively free of whimsy. Songs: *My First Love To Last*; *My Heart's Desire*; *I Loved You Wednesday*; *It's All For The Best*; *Adorable*.

△

W.C. Fields (centre) of the boozy mien, silk hat, bulbous nose and unlit cigar featured hilariously in **International House** (Paramount), a roisterous comedy in which Edmund Breese as a certain Dr Wong gathers together several prominent funsters in order to unveil an invention of his which, he assures them, resembles a cross between a radio and that new thing called television. Representing Russia at the demonstration is Bela Lugosi; while America's ambassador is Stuart Erwin, whose penchant for contracting childhood diseases is demonstrated when he falls prey to a bout of the measles and has to be quarantined. Exactly how Fields happened to fetch up at International House was anyone's guess, including the scriptwriters' Walter DeLeon and Francis Martin (story by Lou Heifetz and Neil Brent). But no one complained, and the mirth he provoked guaranteed another much needed box-office success for Paramount. Also contributing to the laughter were Burns and Allen, as the establishment's resident doctor and nurse, Lumsden Hare, Franklin Pangborn and Peggy Hopkins Joyce whose boudoir the great W.C. took a clandestine delight in visiting. Rudy Vallee, Cab Calloway and Baby Rose Marie were seen and heard in guest spots (as part of Dr Wong's demonstration), and it was directed by Edward Sutherland. Songs included: *Thank Heaven For You*; *My Bluebird's Singing The Blues*; *She Was A China Tea-Cup And He Was Just A Mug*; Ralph Rainger, Leo Robin; *Reefer Man* (played and sung by Cab Calloway and His Orchestra) Andy Razaf, J. Russell Robinson.

The indisputable hit of **A Bedtime Story** (Paramount) was six-month-old Baby LeRoy Winebrenner, better known as Baby LeRoy. And there was nothing its star, Maurice Chevalier, could do about it other than accept defeat gracefully. Chevalier (left) played a big game hunter who, after returning to Paris (and his fiancée) from Africa, finds an abandoned Master LeRoy (illustrated), decides to adopt him, hires a maid called Sally (Helen Twelvetrees) and marries her after his fiancée (Gertrude Michael) walks out on him. Though lacking the sheen and sophistication of Chevalier's earlier efforts with Lubitsch and Mamoulian, Waldemar Young's conventional screenplay (from a novel by Roy Horniman) was certainly entertaining enough and, as directed by Norman Taurog for producer Emanuel Cohen, kept the soft-hearted in the audience agreeably enthralled. Edward Everett Horton (right) co-starred, with other parts going to Adrienne Ames, Earle Foxe, Betty Lorraine, Ernest Wood, Reginald Mason and Henry Kolker. Baby LeRoy's success in **A Bedtime Story** led to a contract with Paramount which lasted for just over three years, at which point, aged four, the infant retired. The songs, by Ralph Rainger and Leo Robin, were *M'sieu Baby*; *In A Park In Paree*; *Look What I've Got*; *Home-Made Heaven*.

▽

◁ A baby also featured in **Broadway Bad** (Fox), as the offspring of chorus girl Joan Blondell, and the focal point of a custody trial. That wasn't the only cliché in Arthur Kober and Maude Fulton's screenplay (story by William R. Lipman, and A.W. Pezet). Miss Blondell (right), after rejecting the advances of a lecherous playboy (Ricardo Cortez) marries wealthy Allen Vincent. Her past association with Cortez niggles at her husband, however, and they are soon divorced. Undefeated, Miss B. goes on to make a name for herself in the theatre and, of course, wins the custody of her baby (from a former marriage). The so-what? direction was by Sidney Lanfield, whose cast included Ginger Rogers (as a chorus girl with a heart of spun sugar), Adrienne Ames, Victor Jory, Frederick Burton (left), Spencer Charters (centre), Margaret Seddon and Donald Crisp. Songs: *Forget The Past*; *Forbidden Melody*; *The Islands Are Calling Me*; *Till The End of Time*; *Derelict Song* Sidney Mitchell, Harry Akst; *Little Man* L. Wolfe Gilbert, James Hanley.

Just as *The Broadway Melody* (MGM 1929) created a vogue for the backstage musical before familiarity with the genre began to breed contempt, so **42nd Street** (Warner Bros.) – another behind-the-scenes saga – singlehandedly revitalized a dying, if not already dead, institution. The movie offered Depression-weary audiences, via its dance director, Busby Berkeley, an entertainment that managed to be simultaneously hard-hitting and escapist. Freshness was the keynote to **42nd Street**, and it was apparent in every aspect of Darryl F. Zanuck's production, from his casting of newcomers Dick Powell and Ruby Keeler as the young hero and heroine, to his choice of composers Al Dubin and Harry Warren. His most far-reaching decision of all, however, was to sign Berkeley (on Mervyn LeRoy's advice) to breathe life into the production numbers. 'Young And Healthy', for example, apart from Sol Polito's brilliant black and white photography (soon to become a feature of Berkeley's musicals in the same way that Van Nest Polglase's white sets were a fixture of the Astaire–Rogers musicals at RKO), offered viewers a kaleidoscope of pulchritude as its participants grouped themselves into interesting formations, and demonstrated just how effective a few lengths of ribbon could be when imaginatively deployed. More innovative was 'Shuffle Off To Buffalo', set on a Pullman carriage that jack-knifed open to reveal a trainload of women preparing for bed as Ginger Rogers and Una Merkel cynically warn a honeymoon couple (Keeler and Clarence Nordstrom) to be wary of marriage ('When she knows as much as we know. She'll be on her way to Reno' runs one of the couplets). The number showed Berkeley at his inventive best, and proved that he did not have to rely on spectacle alone to achieve some of his most memorable effects. Spectacle, however, dominated the grand **42nd Street** finale, a rousing, gloriously costumed, stunning paean to Broadway and its denizens. The fact that Ruby Keeler (illustrated), in this her first of nine films for the studio, couldn't sing, and wasn't a particularly good dancer, somehow didn't seem to matter. On the contrary, if she was able to become a star, so could every other kid like her in America – and audiences, pummelled into despair by the Depression, went home with hope in their hearts. A milestone in Hollywood's history, **42nd Street** was scripted by Rian James and James Seymour (from a story by Bradford Ropes), and contained the immortal line – uttered by a desperate Warner Baxter to an unflappable Ruby Keeler as she is about to go on stage in place of the show's ailing leading lady – 'Sawyer, you're going out a youngster, but you've got to come back a star!' Dick Powell played Ruby's sweetheart, Bebe Daniels the leading lady she replaces. Other well-known Warner regulars in the cast were: George Brent, Guy Kibbee, Ned Sparks, Allen Jenkins and, briefly, Al Dubin and Harry Warren who, apart from the numbers already mentioned, wrote two other songs for the show: 'It Must Be June', and the durable 'You're Getting To Be A Habit With Me'. Composer Harry Akst also had a small part, and the movie was directed by Lloyd Bacon.

THIRTIES MUSICALS

A one-joke musical, **It's Great to be Alive** (Fox) starred Brazilian tenor Raul Roulien who, as a result of being forced to land on an island when his plane develops engine trouble, narrowly escapes contracting masuclitis, a dreaded disease which wipes out the entire male population of the world – except, of course, him. Six years later Roulien (right) is discovered by some women, and after being auctioned to the highest bidder, becomes the subject of an international congress run by top scientist Edna May Oliver. Unfortunately screenwriters Paul Perez and Arthur Kober (story by John D. Swain) were unable to think up enough funny lines to cover the film's 69-minute running time, with the result that, once the initial situation was established, little else was left other than the star's pleasant singing to keep audiences in the theatre. Also cast: Gloria Stuart (left), Dorothy Burgess, Joan Marsh, Herbert Mundin and Emma Dunn. The director was Alfred Werker. Songs: *Goodbye Ladies*; *I'll Build a Nest*; *Women*; *It's Great To Be The Only Man Alive* William Kernell.
▽

Bing Crosby (illustrated) followed *The Big Broadcast* with a minor campus musical called **College Humor** (Paramount). He played a professor of drama in a small mid-western university who, much to the jealous disapproval of the campus Casanova (Richard Arlen), is being wooed by Mary Carlisle (right). It was all over in 68 minutes, yet Claude Binyon and Frank Butler's screenplay (from a story by Dean Fales) found time to accommodate a handful of songs – and even the traditional last reel football match, without which no self-respecting campus caper could consider itself complete. George Burns and Gracie Allen were on hand as a couple of caterers, and it was directed by Wesley Ruggles. Songs: *Down The Old Ox Road*; *Learn To Croon*; *Moon Struck*; *Play Ball*; *Alma Mater*; *Colleen of Killarney*; *I'm a Bachelor Of The Art Of Ha-Cha-Cha* Arthur Johnston, Sam Coslow.
▽

The diminutive Lilian Harvey, whose popularity ▷ in Germany resulted in a contract with William Fox, made her American debut in **My Weakness**, a musical fantasy which, despite a rather banal Cinderella-like story proved to be an excellent showcase for its charming, ebullient star. The delightful aura Miss Harvey's (left) presence imparted to the simple tale of a servant girl's romance with a handsome young man (Lew Ayres, centre) made one almost overlook some of the more excruciating attempts at humour in David Butler, Bert Hanlon, and Ben Ryan's screenplay (story by Buddy De Sylva), and her singing was entrancing. Charles Butterworth played a stamp collector who, in one of the film's more memorable moments, enquires of Miss H. whether she, too, is an 'ardent philatelist'; other parts went to Harry Langdon (as an ageing cupid in charge of steering Miss Harvey's romance with Mr Ayres to success), Sid Silvers, Dixie Frances (right), Irene Bentley and Henry Travers. David Butler directed it and the songs were by De Sylva, Leo Robin and Richard A. Whiting. They included: *How Do I Look?*; *Gather Lip Rouge While You May*; *You Can Be Had So Be Careful*.

There was too much harmony in Paramount's **Too Much Harmony** (see illustration) and not nearly enough plot. A backstage musical with a fair number of wisecracks to keep it intermittently buoyant, it starred Bing Crosby as a Broadway star who, after being stranded in Ohio, discovers a 'local' act which he transfers to Broadway; Judith Allen and Lilyan Tashman as rivals for his love (he chooses Miss Allen) and, best of all, Jack Oakie and Skeets Gallagher as the act he discovers. Also: Harry Green (as a volatile Jewish producer), Ned Sparks (as a confirmed thespian hater), Kitty Kelly, Grace Bradley and Evelyn Oakie (Jackie's real-life mother). The original story was by Joseph L. Mankiewicz who, in time, would think up better plots than this; the screenplay was by Harry Ruskin, and it was directed by Edward Sutherland. Songs: *Thanks*; *The Day You Came Along*; *Black Moonlight*; *Boo Boo Boo*; *Buckin' The Wind*; *Two Aristocrats*; *Cradle Me With a Ha-Cha Lullaby* Arthur Johnston, Sam Coslow.
▽

Evalyn Knapp (left) made no impression at all (except, possibly, a bad one) as a musical comedy star in **Dance Girl, Dance** (Invincible). More invisible than invincible, it was a backstage story of negligible dimensions which starred the usually roguish Alan Dinehart (right) as a kindly impresario and Edward Nugent as the complacent father of Miss Knapp's child. The story and screenplay were by Robert Ellis and the director was Frank Strayer. Songs: *It Takes A Lot of Jack* J. Keirn Brennan, George Grandee; *Seeing Is Believing* James Morley, Lee Zahler; *Peanut Vendor's Little Missus* Eugene Conrad, Harry Carroll.
▽

Warner Bros. continued its successful series of spectacular musicals with **Footlight Parade** – an abrasive, no-punches-pulled backstage yarn which starred a dynamic James Cagney (left) making his fourteenth appearance in three years for Warner Bros. as Chester Kent, a show-biz obsessed producer of 'prologues' (musical interludes that preceded feature films in the early days of talkies). The first hour of the film concerned itself with the mechanics behind the prologues and painted a realistic picture of the cut-throat milieu in which show folk work. The latter third of the film was devoted to the unveiling of the prologues themselves, each one a masterpiece of cinematic invention for which dance director Busby Berkeley must take all the credit. The first, 'Honeymoon Hotel' by Al Dubin and Harry Warren, was similar in mood and content to 'Shuffle Off To Buffalo' from *42nd Street*, and was a rather *risqué* little item showing newlyweds Dick Powell and Ruby Keeler cosily ensconced in a hotel full of other newlyweds; 'By A Waterfall' was fifteen minutes of unbridled spectacle as a hundred or so girls splashed about in a giant aquacade and, to an insidious melody by Irving Kahal and Sammy Fain, grouped themselves into a series of abstract patterns and shapes, each more breathtakingly inventive than the last. The finale, 'Shanghai Lil' (by Dubin and Warren) had a definite narrative to it, and was the story of a sailor (Cagney) who, after looking high and low for his Shanghai Lil finds her in a waterfront dive, does a tap dance with her, then, in answer to a bugle call, returns to his ship – but not before hundreds of sailors, marines and civilians go through a variety of Berkeleyesque formations, including forming themselves into the American eagle. There were two other songs in the film, 'Ah, The Moon Is Here' and 'Sitting On A Backyard Fence', both by Kahal and Fain. It was written by Manuel Seff and James Seymour, directed by Lloyd Bacon, and also featured Joan Blondell (centre), Guy Kibbee, Ruth Donnelly, Claire Dodd, Hugh Herbert, Frank McHugh, Arthur Hohl, Gordon Westcott (right) and Paul Porcasi.

Al Jolson punched columnist Walter Winchell on the nose for writing **Broadway Thru a Keyhole** (20th Century/United Artists), which Jolson claimed was a snide attack on his wife, Ruby Keeler, chronicling as it did, the involvement a cabaret star has with a gangster and a crooner. It was also the last film in which Texas Guinan (playing the owner of a nightspot) got to utter her immortal catch phrase 'C'mon suckers. Give this little girl a big hand!' for she died shortly after its completion. A rather hackneyed return to the backstage yarn and its clichéd trappings, it starred Constance Cummings as the cabaret star, Russ Columbo as the crooner and Paul Kelly as the gangster. Gregory Ratoff was in it too, giving the only really convincing performance as an illiterate cabaret impresario, and others included Frances Williams (illustrated). Eddie Foy Jr and Blossom Seeley. The several musical numbers were lavishly staged, but without much originality. Gene Towne and Graham Baker wrote the screenplay, and the director was Lowell Sherman. Songs: *Doing The Uptown Lowdown*; *I Love You Pizzicato*; *You're My Past, Present And Future*; *When You Were A Girl On A Scooter And I Was A Boy On A Bike* Mack Gordon, Harry Revel.
▽

Claudette Colbert (right) sang with her own voice in **Torch Singer** (Paramount) and brought a certain amount of credibility to a role that didn't really deserve it. She played the torch singer of the title who, after signing her baby away, rues her decision, becomes the host of a children's hour on radio, and spends the rest of the film searching for her lost infant. As he turns out to be that delightful little scene-thief Baby LeRoy, one could understand her predicament. Ricardo Cortez was also in it and, for comic relief, so was Lyda Roberti (left), with David Manners, Florence Roberts, Cora Sue Collins, Helen Jerome Eddy and Charles Grapewin completing the cast. It was adapted from a story by Grace Perkins by Lenore Coffee and Lynn Starling, and directed by Alexander Hall and George Somnes for producer Albert Lewis. Songs: *Don't Be A Cry Baby*; *Give Me Liberty Or Give Me Love*; *It's A Long Dark Night*; *The Torch Singer* Ralph Rainger, Leo Robin.
▽

To paraphrase W.C. Fields, no show called **Moonlight and Pretzels** (GB: **Moonlight and Melody**) could be all bad – and indeed, most of it was very good. Though it was presented by Universal, its plot was pure Warner Bros. (song-plugger stranded in small town is helped by local beauty to put on a Broadway show proving that you can't keep a good formula down. Stage star Roger Pryor (front centre, making his movie debut) played the song-plugger, Mary Brian (centre left) the girl who comes to his rescue. A heavily-accented Leo Carillo (right front) was top-cast as a Broadway gambler who puts money into the show, though the standout performance was given by Lillian Miles (2nd right front), whose rendition of 'Are You Makin' Any Money Baby?' (by Herman Hupfeld) was the best thing in the show. It was directed by Karl Freund from a screenplay by Monte Brice and Sig Herzig (story by Brice and Arthur Jarrett) and, in support, featured Bobby Watson and William Frawley with unbilled guest appearances by Jack Denny and His Orchestra, Bernice Claire, Alexander Gray, Richard Keene and Mary Lang. Other songs: *Ah But Is It Love?*; *Moonlight and Pretzels*; *Dusty Shoes*; *Let's Make Love Like The Crocodiles* E.Y. Harburg, Jay Gorney; *There's A Little Bit Of You In Every Love Song* Harburg, Sammy Fain; *Gotta Get Up And Go To Work* Herman Hupfeld.
▽

After the runaway success of *42nd Street*, Warner Bros. wasted not a single moment in following it up, returning to one of their earliest properties for inspiration – Avery Hopwood's *Gold Diggers of Broadway* which they retitled **Gold Diggers of 1933**. Dick Powell was cast as a songwriter whose wealthy family disapproves of his profession and threatens to disinherit him if he goes ahead with his plan to marry a chorus-girl (Ruby Keeler). In the end, of course, via a number of plot complications (some of them tedious), all ends well. Also cast were Joan Blondell, Warren William, Aline MacMahon, Guy Kibbee, Ned Sparks and Ginger Rogers. Busby Berkeley was again called on to stage the dance numbers and did so magnificently, proving, for those who still needed proof, that when it

came to interpreting a song in visual terms, he was peerless. Al Dubin and Harry Warren wrote the entire score, and Ginger Rogers, clad from head to toe in silver dollars, opened the show with their ironic 'We're In The Money'. The *risqué* 'Pettin' In The Park' was a literal trans-lation of its title in which a parkful of amorous young lovers are interrupted by a thunderstorm. The girls scurry off to change their wet clothes behind drawn shades and reveal – in silhouette – the outlines of bodies that are clearly nude. Then came 'The Shadow Waltz' (illustrated) in which sixty violin-playing chorines formed themselves into patterns, the visual climax of the number being an overhead shot of them grouped into one enormous neon-lit violin, complete with neon bow! Best of all, though, was the 'My

Forgotten Man' finale, a powerful piece of social comment, stirringly sung by Etta Moten, which eloquently and movingly pleaded the case for World War I ex-servicemen who found them-selves unemployed as a result of the Depression. Over 150 extras appeared in the sequence, playing soldiers who had just returned from the front, or ex-servicemen queueing in breadlines 15 years later. A dubbed Joan Blondell took up the moving refrain, sang of their sad plight, and brought the film to its memorable close. Mervyn LeRoy directed from a screenplay by Erwin Gelsey and James Seymour; Sol Polito photographed it and the splendid art direction was by Anton Grot. The film featured one more Dubin–Warren number, 'I've Got To Sing A Torch Song', sung by Dick Powell.

Mae West (illustrated) followed *She Done Him* ▷
Wrong with **I'm No Angel** (Paramount) and the
sexual innuendo that permeated both films and
brought hot flushes to the meeker members of
her sex were almost certainly responsible for the
introduction of the Hays Code the following
year. Mae played the voluptuous Tira – a
sideshow vamp who falls for suave socialite Cary
Grant, hoping at the same time that their
romantic liaison will improve her status in
society. When he refuses to marry her she sues
him for breach of promise and a million dollars.
Always on top of the occasion Miss West
eventually got her man and, at least until the
next guy she fancied came along, lived happily
ever after. With its proliferation of wisecracks,
the overt sexuality of its star, the matinee-idol
good looks of Cary Grant, and the general
excellence of its supporting cast – Edward
Arnold, Ralf Harolde, Dennis O'Keefe, Russell
Hopton, Gertrude Michael, Kent Taylor, Dorothy Peterson, Gregory Ratoff and Gertrude
Howard as Beulah, the maid – **I'm No Angel**
again struck it rich at the box office, consolidat-
ing its leading lady's already formidable reputation as the hottest gal in town. Harvey Brooks,
Gladys DuBois and Ben Ellison wrote the songs;
Miss West wrote the screenplay (with some help
from Harlan Thompson and Lowell Brentano)
and the solid, capably supportive direction was
by Wesley Ruggles. Songs: *No One Loves Me Like
That Dallas Man of Mine*; *They Call Me Sister
Honky Tonk*; *I Want You, I Need You*; *I'm No
Angel*.

△
Originally a Broadway revue in which Ethel
Merman scored a hit with her rendition of 'Eadie
Was A Lady', **Take A Chance** (Paramount) came
to the screen without Miss Merman, but with
several of the show's songs intact, and with
Lilian Roth (right) in the Merman role. Its hodge-
podge of a story didn't help it to win a large
audience, but those prepared to take a chance on
it were at least rewarded with some enjoyable
musical numbers and some spirited playing from
a cast that included James Dunn (left), Cliff
Edwards (centre right), June Knight (centre left),
Charles 'Buddy' Rogers and Lilian Bond. It was
adapted from the Lawrence Schwab stage show
by Schwab, Buddy De Sylva and Monte Brice, and
directed by Schwab and Brice. Songs: *Turn Out
The Light* Buddy De Sylva, Richard A. Whiting,
Nacio Herb Brown; *Should I Be Sweet*; *Rise 'n Shine*
De Sylva, Vincent Youmans; *It's Only A Paper
Moon* Billy Rose, E.Y. Harburg. Harold Arlen;
Come Up And See Me Sometime Arthur Swan-
strom, Louis Alter; *Night Owl* Herman Hupfeld;
New Deal Rhythm Roger Edens, E.Y. Harburg.

Heart-throb Buster Crabbe (right) starred opposite Mary Carlisle (centre) in a small-scale
campus musical from Monogram called **The
Sweetheart of Sigma Chi**. Though a flirt, Miss
Carlisle stops collecting fraternity pins from her
many male admirers when handsome Buster
enters her life. From then on it's smooth rowing
most of the way, with Crabbe working wonders
to see that his boat team wins the big race.
Charles Starrett was his rival in love, with other
parts going to Florence Lake (left), Eddie Tamblyn, Sally Starr and Mary Blackford. It was based
on a story by George Waggner, who wrote the
screenplay with Luther Reed and Albert De
Mond, and Edward L. Marin directed. Songs
included: *Fraternity Walk*; *It's Spring Again*
George Waggner, Ed Ward; *Sweetheart Of Sigma
Chi* Byron D. Stokes, F. Dudleigh Vernor. Remade
by Monogram in 1946.
▽

△
A backstage musical spanning almost fifty years
and three generations, telling of the life and hard
times of a vaudeville family called Hackett,
Broadway to Hollywood (MGM) married an almost documentary-like look at a now-forgotten
era of entertainment with a hearts-and-flowers
story which culminated in the youngest member of the Hackett household, Ted the Third
(Eddie Quillan) finding fame and fortune in
Tinsel City. 10-year-old Mickey Rooney (who'd
been in pictures since the age of three and who
would later be number one at the box office for
three years in a row) played Ted the Third as
a child, with Alice Brady (centre) and Frank
Morgan (right) top-cast as the Hacketts who,
way back in 1886, started it all. Jimmy Durante
made an appearance; so did Jackie Cooper
(left). Nelson Eddy (debuting with a song
called 'In The Garden Of My Heart' by Ernest
R. Ball and Caro Roma), Fay Templeton (also
making her movie debut) and Una Merkel,
Tad Alexander, Edward Brophy, Ruth Chan-

ning, Jean Howard and the omni present Albertina Rasch dancers completed the cast. It was
written and directed by Willard Mack (from a
story by Mack and Edgar Allan Woolf) and
produced by Harry Rapf. Songs: *We Are The
Hacketts* Al Goodhart; *When Old New York Was
Young* Howard Johnson, Gus Edwards; *Ma Blu-
shin' Rosie* Edgar Smith, John Stromberg; *Come
Down Ma Evenin' Star* Robert B. Smith, John
Stromberg; *The Honeysuckle And The Bee* Albert
H. Fitz, William H. Penn. The film contained
several sequences in colour from *The March Of
Time*, a revue which MGM commenced shooting
in 1930, but abandoned mid-way. The sequen-
ces from *The March Of Time* – dance direction by
Sammy Lee – were Dimitri Tiomkin's *Snow
Ballet*; *Hansom Cab Drivers* Jean Schwartz; *The
March Of Time* Louis Alter, Howard Johnson;
Bedelia Schwartz, William Jerome; *There'll Be A
Hot Time In The Old Town Tonight* Theodore Metz,
Joe Hayden; *Poor Little G String* Fred Ahlert, Roy
Turk; *Melody In F* Anton Rubinstein.

It all began when Dorothy Jordan, deciding that marriage to executive producer Merian C. Cooper was preferable to dancing the Carioca atop seven white pianos with a relative unknown called Fred Astaire, opted out of her commitment to RKO, and was replaced by Ginger Rogers. It took only one number – the aforementioned Carioca (illustrated) – to make the world realize that in Astaire and Rogers, the musical had found a dance team of incomparable dazzle, and it was no accident that the last shot of **Flying Down to Rio** is not of its two stars – Dolores Del Rio and Gene Raymond – but of Astaire and Rogers. Clearly the studio knew a good thing when it saw one. The film itself – despite a threadbare plot (exotic Brazilian beauty cannot decide whom she loves more: an American aviator-cum-songwriter, or her fiancé back home in Brazil) – contained a wonderful Vincent Youmans score (his last before retiring to Denver with tuberculosis) and a spectacular finale (staged by Dave Gould) featuring dozens of girls in Rockette-like formation, dancing on the wings of aeroplanes, thousands of feet above the city of Rio de Janeiro. Van Nest Polglase designed the sets, and would continue to do so for all the Astaire–Rogers musicals at RKO. Hermes Pan (uncredited) was the assistant dance director, and the screenplay was by Cyril Hume, H.W. Haneman and Erwin Gelsey, from a play by Anne Caldwell based, in turn, on a story by Lou Brock, the associate producer. Raul Roulien, Blanche Frederici, Walter Walker, Etta Moten, Paul Porcasi, Franklin Pangborn, Eric Blore and Luis Alberni were also in it, and the director was Thornton Freeland.
Songs: *Music Makes Me* (Rogers); *The Carioca* (Moten); *Orchids in The Moonlight* (Roulien, Astaire, Del Rio); *Flying Down To Rio* (Astaire, chorus) lyrics by Edward Eliscu and Gus Kahn.

A screenplay (by Gene Fowler and Benjamin Glazer with additional dialogue by Claude Binyon and Frank Butler) composed largely of rhyming couplets did little to help Maurice Chevalier in **The Way To Love**, the last film he made for Paramount before accepting an offer from Irving Thalberg at MGM. In the feeblest of his American efforts so far, Chevalier (right) was cast as a Parisian sidewalk hawker whose one ambition in life is to become a tourist guide. He succeeds, and after rejecting the advances of Nydia Westman, finds true happiness with Ann Dvorak (left). Miss Dvorak, on loan from Warner Bros., replaced Sylvia Sidney who walked out of the picture mid-way through shooting, citing ill-health as the reason. The role was then offered to Carole Lombard who, after reading the script, turned it down, doubtless resorting to some of the foul language for which she was notorious, as she did so. Less fortunate were Edward Everett Horton, Arthur Pierson, Minna Gombell, Blanche Frederici, Douglass Dumbrille, John Miljan, Sidney Toler and a dog called Mutt, who were in it to the bitter end. Benjamin Glazer produced, and the director was Norman Taurog.
Songs: *Lover of Paree*; *In A One-Room Flat*; *Lucky Guy*; *The Way To Love*; *Its Oh, It's Ah, It's Wonderful* Ralph Rainger, Leo Robin.

Wholesome James Dunn (left) who specialized in playing Mr Average – from humble soda jerks to jobbing clerks – found himself thinking up slogans for a meat-packing outfit in **Jimmy and Sally** (Fox), a likeable romantic comedy with songs which co-starred Claire Trevor as the girl who provides him with his best ideas but gets no credit for it. Romantic problems intruded but they were all worked out to everyone's satisfaction. Paul Schofield and Marguerite Roberts wrote it; James Tinling directed, and his cast included Harvey Stephens, Lya Lys (right), Jed Prouty, Gloria Roy, Alma Lloyd and John Arledge. Songs included: *You're My Thrill*; *Eat Marlowe's Meat*; *It's The Irish In Me* Sidney Clare, Jay Gorney.

A romantic musical comedy that was a three-time loser – being neither romantic, musical, nor comic – **My Lips Betray** (Fox) betrayed all concerned with its predictably coy plot and, as a vehicle for Lilian Harvey (illustrated), was less good even than her first Hollywood effort, *My Weakness* (Fox). Written by the usually sophisticated S.N. Behrman (from a play by Attila Orbok), its operetta-like plot rooted the action in the mythical country of Ruthania, and concerned the amorous cavortings of an impoverished working girl (Harvey) and the King of Ruthania (John Boles) who, disguised as a songwriting captain, falls in love with her. It was all too much to bear, and under John Blystone's soggy direction, collapsed in a heap – leaving its stars with icing sugar all over their attractive faces. El Brendel was in it too and his continued assault on the English language elicited groans all round. Nor was there much joy to be derived from the performances of Irene Browne (as the Queen Mother), Maude Eburne (mildly amusing as the heroine's guardian), Henry Stephenson and Herman Bing. Songs: *His Majesty's Car*; *To Romance*; *Why Am I Happy?*; *The Band Is Gaily Playing* William Kernell.

Modest but enjoyable, **Going Hollywood** was Bing Crosby's first film for MGM (and his last until *High Society* in 1956), and provided him with one of his biggest hit songs to date – 'Temptation'. It was composed by Arthur Freed and Nacio Herb Brown, who furnished the film with its six other new songs as well. It also starred Marion Davies (left), in one of her best roles, as a French teacher in a girls' school who follows Crosby (right) to Hollywood and, in the best fairy-tale fashion finds herself replacing Fifi D'Orsay as the object of his affections as well as the leading lady in his next film. It could only happen in Hollywood and did – many times. Broadway's Patsy Kelly, making her feature film debut, was in it too, so were Ned Sparks (excellent as a cynical film director), and Stuart Erwin as a show backer. Lennie Hayton appeared as conductor and pianist. It was written by Donald Ogden Stewart from a story by Frances Marion, and was directed by Raoul Walsh with a lightness of touch absent in his tough-guy assignments at Warner Bros. a decade later. Other songs: *We'll Make Hay While The Sun Shines*; *Our Big Love Scene*; *Going Hollywood*; *Cinderella's Fella*; *After Sundown*; *Beautiful Girl* Freed, Brown; *Just An Echo In The Valley* Reginald Connelly, Jimmy Campbell, Harry Woods.

Duck Soup was the last film the Marx Brothers made at Paramount before moving to MGM, the last to include Zeppo as part of the team, and their least successful at the box office in spite of the superior quality of its timeless humour and penetrating wit. Furthermore, it was banned in Italy by Mussolini – a fact which filled the brothers with immense pride. The only Marx Brothers comedy to be set in a mythological kingdom (Freedonia) it featured Groucho (right) as Rufus T. Firefly who, possessing the statesmanship of Gladstone, the humility of Lincoln and the wisdom of Pericles, is made dictator of the place. It was written by Bert Kalmar and Harry Ruby (who also supplied the songs) with additional dialogue by Nat Perrin and Arthur Sheekman. Leo McCarey directed it and at least one sequence in which Harpo and Chico, while decked out to look like Groucho, pretend to be his reflection in a mirror, was visually superb. Margaret Dumont (left) was in there pitching again, with Raquel Torres, Louis Calhern and Edgar Kennedy also cast. Songs: *Freedonia Hymn*; *His Excellency Is Due*; *The Country's Going To War*; *When The Clock On The Wall Strikes Ten*; *The Laws Of My Administration*.

THIRTIES MUSICALS

Another campus musical, **College Coach** (GB: **Football Coach**) starred Dick Powell (right), who sang well, but whose performance as a footballer required a super-human feat of imagination to render it believable. Written by Niven Busch and Manuel Seff, the movie took a somewhat cynical, gently satirical look at the world in which football coaches operate, and gave opportunities (all well taken) to Pat O'Brien (centre) as an aggressive coach, Ann Dvorak as his wife, and Arthur Byron as the college president. The contours of the story blurred somewhat towards the end, It was directed by William A. Wellman with steady performances from Lyle Talbot (left), Hugh Herbert, Arthur Hohl, Guinn Williams, Nat Pendleton and Donald Meek, with Robert Lord producing for Warner Bros. Songs included: *Lonely Lane*; *Men Of Calvert* Irving Kahal, Sammy Fain; *Just One More Chance* Sam Coslow, Arthur Johnston; *Meet Me In The Gloaming* Arthur Freed, Al Hoffman, Al Goodhart; *What Will I Do Without You* Johnny Mercer, Hilda Gottlieb.

Determined to cash in on the success of *42nd Street* (Warner Bros.), MGM surfaced with a backstage story which they called **Dancing Lady.** All about a highly moral burlesque hoofer and her struggles to make it – honestly and legitimately – to Broadway, it starred Joan Crawford (right) as the dancing lady of the title, Franchot Tone as the wealthy playboy who wants to marry her, and Clark Gable (left) as the dance director who puts up his own money to save the show when its backer withdraws after being bribed by Tone to do so. Needless to say, Gable is rewarded for his services to the theatre by getting the girl, while audiences were rewarded for their patience in putting up with such familiar goings-on by several well-staged musical numbers, and by being in on the first screen appearance of a newcomer called Fred Astaire who featured in the best of them. Playing himself, Astaire – in top hat and tails – partnered Joan Crawford in 'Heigh Ho, The Gang's All Here' and, with a change of costume, in 'Let's Go Bavarian', both by Burton Lane and Harold Adamson. Nelson Eddy appeared in the finale, giving his all to a song called 'That's The Rhythm Of The Day' by Rodgers and Hart, a production number which was particularly Busby Berkeley-influenced (Eddie Prinz and Sammy Lee staged the dances) with its crowded city streets, and its elderly women transformed into youthful beauties in a beauty salon. Winnie Lightner was featured in an Arthur Freed–Nacio Herb Brown number called 'Hold Your Man', but the real hit song was Lane and Adamson's 'Everything I Have Is Yours', sung by Art Jarrett with Miss Crawford. May Robson, Robert Benchley, Eunice Quedens, Ted Healy, and The Three Stooges were in it too. It was written by Allen Rivkin and P.J. Wolfson from the novel by James Warner Bellah, and directed by Robert Z. Leonard. Other Songs: *Hey Young Fella, Close Your Old Umbrella*; *My Dancing Lady* Dorothy Fields, Jimmy McHugh.

Mack Gordon and Harry Revel wrote a clutch of good songs for Paramount's **Sitting Pretty**, the best and most durable being 'Did You Ever See A Dream Walking'. The film itself hasn't passed the test of time quite so well, but was nonetheless a well-directed (by Harry Joe Brown), entertainingly plotted (by Jack McGowan, S.J. Perelman and Lou Breslow; story by Nina Wilcox Putnam) musical which starred Jack Oakie and Jack Haley (right) as a couple of tin-pan alley songwriters who find fame and fortune (and Ginger Rogers, left) in Hollywood. Lively, amiable, undemanding and unpretentious, it also featured Thelma Todd, Gregory Ratoff, Lew Cody and, playing a pianist and a song publisher respectively, Harry Revel and Mack Gordon. Other songs: *I Wanna Meander With Miranda*; *Good Morning Glory*; *Ballad Of The South*; *You're Such A Comfort To Me*; *Many Moons Ago*; *And Then We Wrote*; *Lucky Little Extra*; *There's A Bluebird At My Window*; *Lights, Action, Camera, Love.*

Girl Without a Room (Paramount) was a film without a plot. Well, almost. Charles Farrell (right) played a young artist from Tennessee who wins a scholarship to study in Paris and, once there, discovers that his style of painting is considered *passe*. Undaunted, he attempts to be futuristic and less representational in his approach, and is rewarded by winning a prize. His painting, however, is only deemed a success if viewed upside down. Alas, it didn't matter from what angle you viewed **Girl Without a Room**, it still didn't look good. Charles Ruggles (left), Marguerite Churchill, Gregory Ratoff, Walter Woolf King, Grace Bradley, Mischa Auer and Leonid Kinskey were also cast; it was written for the screen by Claude Binyon and Frank Butler (story by Jack Lait), with Ralph Murphy directing. Songs included: *You Alone*; *Roof-Top Serenade*; *The Whistle Has To Blow* Val Burton, Will Jason.

△
Samuel Goldwyn abandoned the idea of adapting Bernard Shaw's play *Androcles and The Lion* as a vehicle for Eddie Cantor and turned, instead, to Broadway's George S. Kaufman and Robert E. Sherwood for a script that would suit his money-making star's unique qualities. The association was not a happy one, however, and ended in court after Goldwyn refused to pay the two writers, claiming that they had supplied him with no more than an unworkable first draft. Three gag-writers (Arthur Sheekman, George Oppenheimer and Nat Perrin) were then engaged to pep up the original Kaufman–Sherwood story, after which William Anthony McGuire was called in to structure it all into a workable motion-picture. The result was **Roman Scandals**, a quintessential Cantor musical. In it, Cantor, an eccentric delivery boy in a midwestern town, who is involved in local politics,

dreams that he is a food-tasting slave to the evil Emperor Valerius in Ancient Rome, where most of the film is then set. How Cantor (centre), in this extended dream sequence, proves Valerius guilty of fraud, formed the basis of what passed as the plot – and gave its star ample opportunity to do all the things he did best. The film was climaxed with the obligatory chase (this time by chariot) and even contrived a scene which allowed Cantor to go into blackface. It took place in a Roman bath-house, with Cantor exhorting (in song) a hundred or so girls, to 'keep young and beautiful, if you want to be loved'. The number – an elaborate affair complete with revolving mirrored doors, was the film's musical highspot – and, although the philosophy it expressed, as well as the degrading use it made of the black women in it, may strike contemporary viewers as singularly distasteful, there can be

no denying the brilliance of Busby Berkeley's staging. Less successful was the rather disorganized slave-market sequence in which Berkeley's chorines were nude except for long blonde wigs. The number was shot at night, and on a closed set. Though the film was primarily a vehicle for its star, it also gave torch singer Ruth Etting a chance to sing a Dubin–Warren ballad called 'No More Love'; which she did most touchingly. Gloria Stuart and David Manners were the young lovers whose romance Cantor helps promote. Verree Teasdale the Empress Agrippa, and Edward Arnold the spouse she is constantly trying to poison. Greg Toland photographed it, and the director was Frank Tuttle. There was another Dubin–Warren song, 'Build A Little Home', and 'Put A Tax On Love' by L. Wolfe Gilbert and Harry Warren; both were sung by Cantor.

1934

△

Hips Hips Hooray (RKO) was a formula farce in which Wheeler and Woolsey (illustrated) were cast as a pair of lipstick salesmen who find themselves pursued by a couple of detectives after they inadvertently steal some valuable securities; and again, by chance, find themselves involved in a cross-country car race. As neither the two comedians nor director Mark Sandrich (who brought much more panache to the films he directed with Fred Astaire and Ginger Rogers) could think up any variations on these well-worn situations, the film plodded along from one bad gag to the next – temporary relief coming in the shape of Ruth Etting, whose singing of 'Just Keep On Doing What You're Doing' (by Bert Kalmar and Harry Ruby) was as welcome as a breath of warm wind in the Arctic. Kalmar and Ruby also provided the storyline which, with Edward Kaufman, they fashioned into a screenplay with parts for Thelma Todd, Dorothy Lee and George Meeker. It was all over in 69 minutes. Other songs, also by Kalmar and Ruby: *Tired Of It All*; *Keep Romance Alive*.

Nunnally Johnson's story for **Moulin Rouge** (20th Century Films – released by United Artists) was mildly reminiscent of Ferenc Molnar's *The Guardsman*, except that in the Johnson work it is the husband (Franchot Tone, centre) who cannot recognize his wife, when, posing as her twin sister, she indulges in a flirtation with him. Constance Bennett (right) played both the wife and her sister, changing only her accent and the colour of her hair. A backstage tale in which the twin sisters played entertainers, it was brightly scripted by Johnson and Henry Lehrman, featured three pleasant songs by Al Dubin and Harry Warren (one of which, 'The Boulevard of Broken Dreams' provided the inspiration for a production number), and utilized the talents of Tullio Carminati (left), Helen Westley (her motion picture debut), Andrew Tombes, Russ Brown and Ivan Lebedeff; as well as the voices of The Boswell Sisters and Russ Columbo. The musical numbers were staged by Russell Markert, and the director was Sidney Lanfield. Other songs: *Coffee In The Morning And Kisses At Night*; *Song of Surrender*.

▽

Based on the operetta by Jerome Kern and Otto Harbach. which opened on Broadway in 1931 and ran for 395 performances, **The Cat and the Fiddle** reached the screen in a modified version by Samuel and Bella Spewack, and although it was Jeanette MacDonald's first musical for MGM, its star was Ramon Novarro (right). He and Jeanette (left) played composers who meet in Brussels and fall in love. She is a success, he isn't and reluctantly decides to leave her. But the couple are reunited in the end, with Miss MacDonald coming to his rescue when, on the eve of his first operetta's premiere, the prima donna walks out on the show. Guess who takes her place! Producer Bernie Hyman hoped that the 'living in sin' aspect of the storyline would not fall foul of the Hays code or upset the studio hierarchy who were being pressured, as a result of the moralistic climate of the times, to concentrate on wholesome family entertainment. He need not have worried – directed by William K. Howard, it came and went without ruffling anyone's composure. With its copper-toned soprano now ensconced at MGM, it would only be a matter of months before her talent would be exploited to its full and given the sort of production values that Louis B. Mayer (whose favourite star she was to become) deemed worthy of her. Ramon Novarro, on the other hand, was fast declining in popularity and would only make two more films for the studio under his present contract. **The Cat and the Fiddle**, whose finale was photographed in 3-colour Technicolor, also featured Frank Morgan as the womanizing Alphonse Daudet and Charles Butterworth as a harpist whom nobody asks to play, with Jean Hersholt, Vivienne Segal, Frank Conroy and Henry Armetta in other roles. Songs: *The Night Was Made For Love*; *The Breeze Kissed Your Hair*; *One Moment Alone*; *Impressions In A Harlem Flat*; *Poor Pierrot*; *She Didn't Say 'Yes'*; *Don't Tell Us Not To Sing*; *I Watch The Love Parade*; *A New Love Is Old*; *The Crystal Candelabra*; *Ha! Cha Cha*; *Try To Forget*.
▽

It was all over in 65 minutes. but while it lasted ▷ Universal's **Myrt and Marge** (GB: **Laughter in the Air**) seemed twice as long. The backstage adventures and misadventures of radio stars Myrt (Myrtle Vail) and her real-life daughter Marge (Donna Damerel, right), it was mindless even by Universal's B-picture standards. Clearly Myrt and Marge were better heard than seen, for, on this sorry occasion, seeing was simply not believing. Also cast: Eddie Foy Jr (left), Ted Healy, Thomas Jackson, Trixie Friganza, J. Farrell MacDonald and The Three Stooges. Al Boasberg directed from a script by Beatrice Banyard. Songs included: *Draggin' My Heels Around*; *Isle Of Blues*; *What Is Sweeter?* Joan Jasmin, M.K. Jerome.

Gregory Ratoff purloined all the acting honours in **Let's Fall in Love** (Columbia), a romantic comedy with music and lyrics by Harold Arlen and Ted Koehler. His co-stars (illustrated) were Edmund Lowe and newcomer Ann Sothern, and the story Herbert Fields thought up for them (screenplay also by Fields) was an unassuming little trifle about a harrassed film producer (Ratoff) and his director (Lowe) who, at the last minute, have to find a replacement for a temperamental Swedish star (Tala Birell) after she walks out on them. In desperation, Lowe takes a chance on a Brooklyn sideshow performer (Sothern) and, out-Higginsing Professor Higgins, manages to deceive the whole of Hollywood when, six weeks later, he presents her as his latest Swedish discovery. The usual romantic complications arise after Miss Sothern falls besottedly in love with her handsome director, a situation with which his fiancée (Miriam Jordan) shows her acute displeasure, by blowing the gaff on the deception. A satisfying blend of music, romance and comedy, it also featured Arthur Jarrett, Majorie Gateson and Betty Furness, and was directed by David Burton with a sense of fun that never deserted him. Songs included: *Let's Fall In Love*; *Breakfast Ball*; *This Is Only The Beginning*; *Love Is Love Anywhere*.

Though Lilian Harvey was top-cast in **I Am Suzanne** (Fox) as a dancer in love with a puppeteer (Gene Raymond), the real stars of the film were Pordrecca's Piccoli marionettes who were featured in several key scenes. One of these was an elaborate dream sequence set in Puppet Land, where Miss Harvey (illustrated) finds herself standing trial for taking a pot-shot at a puppet which her lover has fashioned after her own image. It was written by Rowland V. Lee and Edwin Justus Mayer, directed by Mr Lee and, in supporting roles, featured Leslie Banks, Georgia Caine, Geneva Mitchell, Halliwell Hobbes and Lionel Belmore. But they were all upstaged by the marionettes. Songs: *Just A Little Garret*; *Oh How I've Sinned*; *One Word*; *San Moritz*; *Wooden Woman*; *Oski-O-Lay-Li-O-Mo* Frederick Hollander.

George Raft, who didn't quite possess the necessary dramatic weight as an actor to endow **Bolero** (Paramount) with anything more than an attractive surface gloss, played an egotistical dancer who, tired of tacky dance halls, longs to open a night club of his own in Paris. But a weak heart, and his disdain of it, thwarts his ambitions and he dies in his dressing room just as his great dream is about to become a reality. Carole Lombard was co-starred as Raft's partner, and their dance sequences (see illustration), directed by LeRoy Prinz, despite the use of doubles in certain shots, were thrilling, the climactic sequence taking place, not unsurprisingly to the strains of Ravel's 'Bolero'. It was adapted by Carey Wilson and Kubec Glasmon from an idea by Ruth Ridenour, and the screenplay was by Horace Jackson. William Frawley, Frances Drake, Sally Rand and Raymond (Ray) Milland were also featured, and it was directed by Wesley Ruggles. There were no songs.

Palooka (GB: **The Great Schnozzle**) offered Jimmy Durante his first starring role in a movie, playing a manager to Stuart Erwin's dim-witted pugilist. Based on the Ham Fisher comic-strip of the same name, this United Artists film also featured William Cagney, brother of James, as an inebriated prize fighter whose drunkenness in the ring allows the useless Palooka to take the championship from him. Mr Cagney's physical resemblance to his more famous brother was remarkable; his talent, alas, less so. Lupe Velez (illustrated) was cast as a sulphurous beauty called Nina Madero – and the object of Palooka's affections; pretty Mary Carlisle was his long-suffering girl back home, and Marjorie Rambeau his mother. Also in it were Robert Armstrong, Thelma Todd, Guinn Williams and Franklyn Ardell. It was directed by Benjamin Stoloff from a screenplay by Gertrude Purcell, Jack Jevne, Arthur Kober, Ben Ryan and Murray Roth – a somewhat excessive line-up of writers, considering its insubstantial plot. Songs: *Like Me A Little Bit Less (Love Me A Little Bit More)* Harold Adamson, Burton Lane; *Palooka*; *It's A Grand Old Name* Ann Ronell, Joe Burke; *Count Your Blessings* Irving Caesar, Ferde Grofé, Edgar A. Guest; *Inka Dinka Doo* Ben Ryan, Jimmy Durante.

THIRTIES MUSICALS

△

Alice Faye (right), hitherto a vocalist with Rudy Vallee and His Orchestra, struck it lucky in her first film **George White's Scandals** (Fox), replacing Lilian Harvey who was originally scheduled to star but who quit the production just before shooting commenced. A backstage story whose rumour of a plot was designed to keep audiences guessing whether or not leading man Rudy Vallee and Miss Faye would get together for the final clinch (they did), it took its capable cast through several well-staged production numbers (including one in which a chorus girl dives off the rim of a champagne glass and into the drink) and gave fans of the great Jimmy Durante (left) a chance to see what the comedian looked like in blackface – not much different, as it turned out. Gregory Ratoff, Cliff Edwards, Dixie Dunbar, Gertrude Michael and Richard Carle were also in it, three men had a hand in its direction (George White, Thornton Freeland and Harry Lachman), and it was written by Jack Yellen from a story by Mr White. George Hale staged the musical numbers which, while unashamedly derivative of Busby Berkeley, especially in 'Hold My Hand' (by Ray Henderson, Jack Yellen and Irving Caesar), lacked the master's touch. No complaints, however, about Alice Faye, whose debut effort revealed her to have all the qualities audiences would respond to in her later, more successful musicals. Other songs: *Oh, You Nasty Man; So Nice; My Dog Loves Your Dog; Sweet And Simple; Six Women; Following In Mother's Footsteps; Every Day Is Father's Day With Baby* Henderson, Yellen, Caesar; *Picking Cotton* De Sylva, Brown, Henderson; *The Man On The Flying Trapeze* revised by Walter O'Keefe.

△

Wonder Bar (Warner Bros./First National) supervised by Robert Lord and directed by Lloyd Bacon, was a paradigm of the Warner Bros. recipe for thirties musicals – nightclub cabaret, band singers, hostesses, complicated semi-romantic, semi-humorous sub-plots, an Al Dubin–Harry Warren score and the talents of Al Jolson, Dick Powell and Busby Berkeley. The Earl Baldwin screenplay, from the Geza Herczeg-Karl Farkas-Robert Katscher Broadway flop, had the owner of a Paris niterie (Jolson) and a band singer (Powell) both in love with a cabaret star (Dolores Del Rio) who, in turn, is only interested in romance with her dance partner (Ricardo Cortez) the intended 'victim' of a wealthy socialite (Kay Francis). Audiences were also expected to follow the exploits of Guy Kibbee and Hugh Herbert who, although married to Louise Fazenda and Ruth Donnelly, were conducting flirtations with two of the club's hostesses (Fifi D'Orsay and Merna Kennedy)! To complete the feeling that one was definitely on familiar Warner Bros. territory, Henry O'Neill had a supporting role. Also: Hal LeRoy (his debut). Berkeley, on this occasion, was not at his best, and a production number (illustrated) executed in excruciatingly poor taste and in which Jolson, in blackface, sang 'Going To Heaven On A Mule' to 200 children done up as black angels, was the one blemish on an otherwise immaculate career. But he redeemed himself in the spectacular 'Don't Say Goodnight' number in which he presented an infinity of chorus boys and girls by the clever deployment of mirrors. Other songs: *Wonder Bar; Why Do I Dream These Dreams?; Vive La France; Tango Del Rio.*

A musical with a Hollywood background, **Bottoms Up** (Fox) traversed familiar territory, but was agreeable enough and attractively cast. Spencer Tracy (illustrated), Herbert Mundin and Sid Silvers played a trio of likeable vagabonds who decide to take a young Canadian beauty queen under their wing and help her attain stardom in the movies. Pat Paterson, an English actress making her American debut, played the beauty queen, John Boles was cast opposite her as the vain and arrogant leading man she falls for, with Harry Green as the producer who makes it all possible. Completing the cast were Thelma Todd, Robert Emmett O'Connor, Dell Henderson, Suzanne Kaaren and Douglas Wood. It was written by Buddy De Sylva, David Butler and Sid Silvers, and was directed by Butler. Songs: *Waiting At The Gate For Katie* Richard A. Whiting, Gus Kahn; *Turn On The Moon; Little Did I Dream; I'm Throwin' My Love Away* Burton Lane, Harold Adamson.

▽

◁ There was very little to like in **I Like It That Way** (Universal), a mercifully short (67 minutes) programmer with a nightclub background starring Gloria Stuart as a nightclub star, Roger Pryor as an insurance agent in love with Miss Stuart, and Marian Marsh as his switchboard operator sister who hangs up her telephone and joins the chorus instead. Also cast: Shirley Grey, Lucille Gleason, Noel Madison, Gloria Shea (centre), Mae Busch, Merna Kennedy and, in a bit part, Mickey Rooney. It was written by Chandler Sprague and Joseph Santley (story by Harry Sauber) and directed by Harry Lachman. Songs: *Blue Sky Avenue* Herb Magidson, Con Conrad; *Let's Put Two And Two Together; I Like It That Way; Goin' To Town* Sidney Mitchell, Archie Gottler.

△
A variation on J.M. Barrie's *The Admirable Crichton* but with the addition of several first-rate songs, **We're Not Dressing** (Paramount) gave Bing Crosby (centre) one of his best screen roles to date – as a sailor ship-wrecked on a desert island. A lively cast that included Carole Lombard (left, as an aloof millionairess who at first resists, then succumbs to Crosby's charms), George Burns and Gracie Allen, Leon Errol, Ray Milland and Ethel Merman (right), responded well to Norman Taurog's equally lively direction; it was produced by Benjamin Glazer (who also supplied the story – courtesy of Sir James) and written by Horace Jackson, George Marion Jr, and Francis Martin. Songs: *Once In A Blue Moon*; *Love Thy Neighbor*; *Goodnight Lovely Little Lady*; *It's Just a New Spanish Custom*; *May I?*; *She Reminds Me Of You*; *I'll Sing About The Birds And The Bees*; *Let's Play House* Mack Gordon, Harry Revel.

Though **Melody in Spring** (Paramount) was ▷ clearly designed as a showcase for Lanny Ross's pleasing tenor voice, grand larceny was committed by Charles Ruggles (right) who stole the show – and the reviews. He played an eccentric manufacturer of puppy pretzels, whose hobby is collecting bed-post knobs, and whose obsession is keeping Mr Ross as far away as possible even if it means rushing off to the Swiss Alps. The amiable nonsense was well directed by Norman McLeod, whose cast included Mary Boland, George Meeker, Herman Bing, Norma Mitchell, Wade Boteler and William J. Irving. Frank Leon Smith wrote the story, and the screenplay was by Benn W. Levy. Songs: *Melody In Spring*; *The Open Road*; *It's Psychological*; *Ending With A Kiss* Harlan Thompson, Lewis Gensler.

△
Harold Teen (GB: **The Dancing Fool**) was a Warner Bros. remake of a 1928 First National picture, which had been directed by Mervyn LeRoy with Arthur Lake, Mary Brian and Alice White in the leads. What attracted the studio to the material is uncertain – it surely couldn't have been the paper-thin plot and screenplay (by Paul Gerard Smith and Al Cohn from the comic strip by Carl Ed) which told of the love of a slow-witted small-town journalist for a high school graduate, and how his social gaffes impede the progress of the romance. There were the obligatory complications which were resolved in a musical finale staged by a Broadway producer for the town's younger set. Hal Le Roy (right) starred as Harold the dumb newsman, showing himself to be a very proficient dancer, and Rochelle Hudson played Lillums, the object of his affections. Patricia Ellis (as the leader of the 'younger set'), Guy Kibbee (centre), Hobart Cavanaugh, Chick Chandler, Eddie Tamblyn, Douglass Dumbrille (left) and Mayo Methot were also in it for director Murray Roth (who captured the small-town atmosphere very well), and supervisor Robert Lord. Irving Kahal and Sammy Fain provided the numbers which were: *How Do You Know It's Sunday?*; *Simple And Sweet*; *Two Little Flies On A Lump of Sugar*; *Collegiate Wedding*.

◁ Another movie musical to capitalize on the popularity of radio was the tuneful **Twenty Million Sweethearts** (First National), which starred Dick Powell (right) as a singing waiter whose way with a song leads to radio stardom. His mentor was played by Pat O'Brien (left) who, the following year, was to go through the same routine with a singing hotel porter in the person of James Melton. A modest production, which yielded the mammoth Al Dubin–Harry Warren hit 'I'll String Along With You', it was a gentle, often charming satire on the air waves which gave Ginger Rogers (centre) her first important role, and also featured The Mills Brothers, Ted Fiorito and His Band, Allen Jenkins, Henry O'Neill and Joseph Cawthorn. Powell, however, was very much at the centre of things and cemented his boyish, clean-cut image with a boyish, clean-cut performance that doubtless won him twenty million sweethearts more. Sam Bischoff supervised the production, Ray Enright directed from a screenplay by Warren Duff and Harry Sauber (story by Paul Finder Moss and Jerry Wald). It was remade in 1949 as *My Dream Is Yours*. Other songs: *Fair And Warmer*; *Out For No Good*; *What Are Your Intentions?* Al Dubin, Harry Warren; *How'm I Doin'?* Lem Fowler, Don Redman; *The Man On The Flying Trapeze* Walter O'Keefe.

THIRTIES MUSICALS

Stand Up And Cheer (Fox) had audiences doing ▷
just that for a jaunty anti-Depression musical
whose manifesto was simply to entertain. It
seems as though the fictitious President of the
United States who featured (unseen) as part of
Will Rogers and Phillip Klein's plot, had the
same idea – for he summons to Washington a
Broadway producer (Warner Baxter) and offers
him the newly created job of Secretary of
Entertainment. Baxter accepts, and henceforth
the film is little more than an excuse (and a good
excuse, as it turns out) for a series of musical
items performed by the talented likes of John
Boles, Sylvia Froos, James Dunn (left), Nick
(later Dick) Foran, Stepin Fetchit and a small girl
of uncommon appeal called Shirley Temple
(centre right). It even called upon a performing
penguin to convince a crestfallen Mr Fetchit that
he isn't a penguin at all, but Jimmy Durante. The
screenplay was by Ralph Spence, it was directed
by Hamilton McFadden, produced by Winfield
Sheehan, co-starred Madge Evans and, in supporting roles, featured Arthur Byron, Ralph
Morgan, Jimmy Dallas, 'Aunt Jemima' (Tess
Gardella), Mitchell and Durant (as a couple of
senators) and Nigel Bruce. Songs: *I'm Laughin'*;
We're Out Of The Red; *Broadway's Gone Hill-Billy*;
Baby Take A Bow (sung by Shirley Temple); *This Is
Our Last Night Together* Jay Gorney, Lew Brown;
She's Way Up Thar Brown; *Stand Up And Cheer*
Brown, Harry Akst.

Jimmy Durante, playing a character called
Schnarzan, had a fairly amusing scene in **Hollywood Party** (MGM) doing battle with a lion;
and Walt Disney supplied a Mickey Mouse
cartoon (in colour) which helped take one's
mind off the 'entertainment' on offer. But the
story thought up by publicity man Howard Dietz
and Arthur Kober (who also scripted it) about an
elaborate Hollywood party thrown by Durante,
just wouldn't play. Party guests included Stan
Laurel (centre) and Oliver Hardy (left), Mrs Jean
Durante, Lupe Velez (right), The Three Stooges,
Ted Healy and His Orchestra, Frances Williams,
Shirley Ross, Polly Moran, Eddie Quillan, June
Clyde and Harry Barris. Harry Rapf and Howard
Dietz produced it and, although uncredited,
Richard Boleslawski, Allan Dwan and Roy Row-
land directed it. The dances were staged by
Seymour Felix, George Hale and Dave Gould. No
gate-crashers for this one. Songs: *I've Had My
Moments* Gus Kahn, Walter Donaldson; *Feelin'
High* Dietz, Donaldson; *Hollywood Party*; *Hello*;
Reincarnation Rodgers and Hart (Amazingly,
eleven other Rodgers and Hart numbers, includ-
ing the hit 'Blue Moon', were cut before the print
was released!).
▽

△
'Wouldn't it be funny to go to your own
wedding and find you hadn't shown up'
was typical of the kind of lines J.P. McEvoy,
Claude Binyon, Keene Thompson and Ray
Harris wrote for Gracie Allen (right) in their
musical farce **Many Happy Returns**. The sort of
scenario (story by Lady Mary Cameron) where
anything could happen and usually did, its
central idea, which was worked over until
exhaustion rendered it inert, was a promise
made by Miss Allen's long-suffering father
(George Barbier) to George Burns (left) that, if he
marries his daughter, he will willingly pay him
ten dollars for every mile he (Burns) travels with
her. The more miles, the better. Guy Lombardo
co-starred as Guy Lombardo, with other roles
going to Joan Marsh, Franklin Pangborn, Ray
Milland, Egon Brecher and William Demarest.
The director was Norman McLeod. Songs: *Fare
Thee Well*; *I Don't Wanna Play*; *Bogey Man* Arthur
Johnston, Sam Coslow; *The Sweetest Music This
Side Of Heaven* Carmen Lombardo, Cliff Friend.

After her performance in *Stand Up And Cheer*,
Paramount paid Fox a thousand dollars a
week to acquire the services of Shirley Temple
(then four years old) for their film of Damon
Runyon's **Little Miss Marker** (GB: **Girl in Pawn**),
and it was cheap at the price. Although Little
Miss Talent (left) received fourth billing to
Adolphe Menjou (right), Dorothy Dell and Charles Bickford, no one doubted that she was the
star of the show. Having previously had only bit
parts in feature films she was now cast in the
more substantial role of a marker for her
gambler father, who, after putting her up as
security for a 20-dollar loan, loses his bet and
commits suicide. The 'marker' automatically ◁
becomes the legal property of Sorrowful Jones
(Menjou) a bookmaker, who henceforth devotes
his attention to the upkeep and well-being of his
adorable little charge. The fact that Menjou,
despite the unfair competition, managed to turn
in one of his best performances was evidence
enough of his own extraordinary talent. Less
lucky were Warren Hymer (centre), Lynne
Overman, Frank McGlynn Sr, Jack Sheehan,
Garry Owen, Willie Best, Puggy White, Tammany Young and Sam Hardy – who, as typically
colourful bits of Runyonesque embroidery –
barely managed a look in. The engaging screenplay was by William R. Lipman, Sam Hellman
and Gladys Lehman, and the director, who knew
just how far to go with his *wunderkind* star, was
Alexander Hall. It was remade in 1949 as
Sorrowful Jones, in 1963 as *40 Pounds Of Trouble*,
and in 1980 as *Little Miss Marker*. Songs: *Low-
Down Lullaby*; *I'm A Black Sheep Who's Blue*; *Laugh
You Son-of-a-Gun* Ralph Rainger, Leo Robin.

Producer Pandro S. Berman borrowed Jimmy
Durante (left) and Lupe Velez (right) from MGM
to star in RKO's **Strictly Dynamite**, a comedy
which, unfortunately, was more of a damp
squib. As protracted as its star's famous nose, it
unsuccessfully attempted to spread out, over 71
minutes, a feeble story involving the travails of a
radio comedian (Durante) desperately in search
of some new gags. Clearly afflicted with the same
problem were scenarists Maurine Watkins,
Ralph Spence, Milton Raison and Jack Harvey
(working from a play by Robert T. Colwell and
Robert A. Simon) who, relying on Durante's
penchant for mispronunciation, broke up the
English language but not, alas, the audience.
Also cast: Norman Foster and Marian Nixon (as
purveyors of an equally tedious sub-plot), Wil-
liam Gargan, Eugene Pallette, Minna Gombell,
Sterling Holloway, Franklin Pangborn, The
Mills Brothers. Elliott Nugent was the director.
Songs: *Money In My Clothes* Irving Kahal,
Sammy Fain; *Swing It Sister*; *Oh Me, Oh My, Oh
You* Harold Adamson, Burton Lane; *Hot Patatta*
Jimmy Durante.
▽

It all came right in the end. but oh! the romantic entanglements that befell Alice Faye (left) and Lew Ayres (right) in **She Learned About Sailors** (Fox). All about what happens to a waterfront singer (Faye) in Shanghai after the resistible comedy team of Jack Durant and Frank Mitchell intercept a letter in which her inamorata (Ayres) suggests that, due to his impecunious situation, they should discontinue seeing each other, it was a pretty tedious piece of musical flotsam that did very little to win its female star a new crop of fans. William Conselman and Henry Johnson wrote it from a story by Randall H. Faye, it was produced by John Stone, and directed by George Marshall. Also cast: Wilma Cox, Paul McVey and Harry Green. It was remade in 1940 as *Sailors' Lady* (20th Century-Fox). Songs: *Here's The Key To My Heart*; *She Learned About Sailors* Sidney Clare. Richard A. Whiting; *If I Were Adam And You Were Eve* James Hanley.

Earl Carroll's **Murder at the Vanities** (Paramount) was only half a success, the musical half (see illustration) taking precedence over its plot. All about the sinister backstage activities of a murderer – its thrills and chills were of the synthetic kind and served no purpose other than to interrupt the songs. Carl Brisson was the Vanities' personable leading man (although evincing minimal acting ability on this occasion); Kitty Carlisle his sweet-voiced leading lady. Jack Oakie appeared as a press agent. Victor McLaglen as a police lieutenant. with Dorothy Stickney, Gertrude Michael, Jessie Ralph, Gail Patrick, Donald Meek, Barbara Fritchie and Clara Lou (later Ann) Sheridan in support. It was adapted from the Earl Carroll-Rufus King stage show by Carey Wilson, Joseph Gollomb and Sam Hellman and slickly directed by Mitchell Leisen. Songs: *Lovely One*; *Where Do They Come From Now?*; *Marijuana*; *Live And Love Tonight*; *Cocktails For Two*; *Ebony Rhapsody* (introduced by Duke Ellington and His Orchestra) Arthur Johnston, Sam Coslow.

Based on a play by Gene Fowler and Ben Hecht, and borrowing the title from a Heywood Broun revue. **Shoot the Works** (Paramount) invaded the milieu of side-shows and flea circuses. Starring Jack Oakie – as an ingratiating no-goodnik whose sweetheart (Dorothy Dell, right) realizes his intrinsic worth just as she is about to say 'I do' to someone else – it boasted several good tunes, but little else. Arline Judge (centre right) played the wife of a flagpole sitter, with other parts going to Alison Skipworth, Ben 'Yowsah' Bernie (left), Roscoe Karns (centre left), William Frawley, Paul Cavanagh, and Lew Cody, who died shortly after the film was completed. Sadly, so did Dorothy Dell. The screenplay was by Howard J. Green and Claude Binyon, and the director was Wesley Ruggles. Songs: *Do I Love You?*; *Take A Lesson From The Larks* Ralph Rainger, Leo Robin; *Were Your Ears Burning?*; *With My Eyes Wide Open I'm Dreaming*; *In The Good Old Wintertime* Mack Gordon, Harry Revel; *A Bowl Of Chop Suey and You-ey* Al Goering, Ben Bernie.

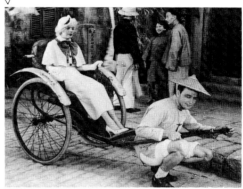

Though the storyline devised by Robert Lord and Delmer Daves (screenplay by Daves) for **Dames** was no *War And Peace* – chorus-girl Joan Blondell wheedles money out of Guy Kibbee so that songwriter Dick Powell can get his show on – its production numbers (see illustrations) by Busby Berkeley were once again mind-bogglingly effective. The best of these was the title number (by Al Dubin and Harry Warren), a paean to feminine pulchritude or, as one of the lyrics puts it, 'What do you go for, go see a show for, tell the truth you go to see those beautiful dames.' Clad in frilly white blouses, headgear to match and black tights, dozens of girls configurated into intricate geometric patterns, with Berkeley's innovative trick photography helping to create an overall sense of wonderment and spectacle that none of his contemporaries was able to emulate. With 'The Girl At The Ironing Board', another Dubin–Warren number, Joan Blondell as a laundress serenades a pile of pyjamas and men's underwear which suddenly jerks into life and becomes part of the routine. Though far less elaborate in scale than the 'Dames' sequence, it was visually as inventive as anything Berkeley had done so far, with Miss Blondell's pleasing handling of the vocal providing an added bonus. The film's most popular sequence, however, was

Berkeley's staging of Dubin and Warren's 'I Only Have Eyes For You'. A brilliant song in its own right, it was a literal visualization of Dubin's lyrics, and featured scores of Ruby Keelers as part of a dream Dick Powell is having on a New York subway; a dream in which even the faces in the advertisements turn into his sweetheart. Highspot of the number is the jigsaw made by the girls as each, equipped with a board on her back, bends over so that the boards interlock to form a giant-size picture of Ruby. It was Berkeley at his imaginative best, and the sort of work that helped to rescue the musical once more, and keep it alive and kicking for the rest of the decade. Two other songs were featured: 'When You Were A Smile On Your Mother's Lips' by Irving Kahal and Sammy Fain, and 'Try To See It My Way' by Mort Dixon and Allie Wrubel, and while they were pleasant enough, they never achieved the popularity of the three Dubin–Warren contributions. The director was Ray Enright, whose cast included ZaSu Pitts, Hugh Herbert, Phil Regan, Arthur Vinton, and songwriter Sammy Fain making an appearance as – a songwriter. Top left illustration shows L to R: Keeler, Pitts and Kibbee.

THIRTIES MUSICALS

△

Gift of Gab (Universal) was a shapeless and cumbersome liability about an arrogant radio announcer (Edmund Lowe, right) who redeems himself in the eyes of his girl (Gloria Stuart, centre) when he risks his life to inform his listeners of the whereabouts of a missing plane. Over thirty big name performers tried to salvage it with their respective skills but to no avail, proving, once and for all, that if you're saddled with a stinker, you're saddled with a stinker. For the record, the stars included Ruth Etting, Phil Baker, Ethel Waters, Alice White, Alexander Woollcott, Victor Moore (left), Helen Vinson, Gene Austin, Andy Devine, Wini Shaw, Sterling Holloway, Boris Karloff, Bela Lugosi, Paul Lukas, and Gus Arnheim and His Orchestra. It was directed by Karl Freund from a screenplay by Rian James and Lou Breslow, and a story by Jerry Wald and Philip G. Epstein. Songs: *Talking To Myself*; *I Ain't Gonna Sin No More*; *Gift of Gab* Herb Magidson, Con Conrad; *Somebody Looks Good* George Whiting, Albert von Tilzer; *Don't Let This Waltz Mean Goodbye*; *Walkin' On Air* Jack Meskill, von Tilzer; *What A Wonderful Day* Harry Tobias, Al Sherman; *Tomorrow – Who Cares* Murray Mencher, Charles Tobias.

◁ Though censor Will Hays imposed all sorts of strictures on Mae West's **Belle of the Nineties** (Paramount), he was unable to censor the lady's libidinous personality or the walk that launched a thousand female impersonators' hips across the length and breadth of the country. As she had been in her previous two films, Mae (illustrated) was a smash and although her performance as Ruby Carter, the chief attraction at the Sensation House, New Orleans, was fundamentally no different from Lady Lou or Tira, it was once again an object lesson in innuendo. There was a plot of sorts (story and screenplay by Miss West) involving a pair of rivals for her affection ('I prefer two kinds of men – domestic and foreign'), some stolen jewels, and a prize fight, but what mattered were the wisecracks it spawned ('It's better to be looked over than overlooked') rather than the story it told, and its screenplay became the most widely quoted of the year. Roger Pryor played Tiger Kid, the good man Mae falls for, John Miljan was the Sensation House's villainous owner ('His mother should have thrown him away and kept the stork') with Katherine De Mille as his jealous mistress. John Mack Brown was also in it, so were James Donlan (father of Yolande), Tom Herbert, Stuart Holmes, Harry Woods and Edward Gargan. Duke Ellington and His Band accompanied Miss West and, keeping a firm control on it all, was director Leo McCarey. Songs: *My Old Flame*; *Troubled Waters*; *My American Beauty*; *When A St Louis Woman Comes Down To New Orleans* Arthur Johnston, Sam Coslow; *The Memphis Blues* George A. Norton, W.C. Handy.

△

Jimmy Durante starred in **Student Tour** (MGM) and once again was the victim of a haven't-we-been-here-before plot. Seems his celebrated proboscis just had no talent for smelling out an original idea. He played the trainer of a college rowing team that found itself in serious danger of jeopardising an around-the-world tour to England – and a chance to compete in an important rowing event while over there – because all its members have flunked a philosophy exam. To alleviate the situation, professor Charles Butterworth (left, with Durante) generously offers to accompany them on the cruise and help them with their studies. His plain-Jane niece (Maxine Doyle) comes along for the ride as well – and proves Dorothy Parker right by removing her glasses and instantly finding true love in the hefty arms of the team's personable captain (Phil Regan). A few good Arthur Freed–Nacio Herb Brown songs momentarily helped inject some momentum into Ralph Spence and Philip Dunne's screenplay (story by George Seaton, Arthur Bloch and Samuel Marx) but not enough to make it anything more than the B-picture it was. The cast also included, Florine McKinney, Douglas Fowley, Monte Blue, Betty Grable, Herman Brix (Bruce Bennet) and, in a flashy guest appearance (his last before star-status was accorded him in *Naughty Marietta*, MGM 1935), Nelson Eddy. The director was Charles Riesner. Songs: *A New Moon Is Over My Shoulder*; *From Now On*; *By The Taj Mahal*; *The Snake Dance*; *The Carlo*; *Fight 'Em* Freed, Brown; *I Just Say It With Music* Jimmy Durante.

Having lured Maurice Chevalier, Jeanette Mac-Donald and Ernst Lubitsch from Paramount, and with a complicated legal situation regarding the rights now satisfactorily settled, MGM's Irving Thalberg mounted the third and best version of **The Merry Widow**, Lehar's enduring masterpiece. The result was one of the great screen musicals of all time, an enchantingly intoxicating mixture of music and romance, sparklingly directed, and performed with style and grace by its two leading players. In as near perfect an adaptation of an operetta as the screen had yet seen, writers Ernest Vajda and Samson Raphaelson took certain liberties with the spirit of the piece. What they helped to create was a musical fairy-tale of incomparable sophistication whose nearest rival in excellence to date was *Love Me Tonight* (Paramount, 1932). Mac-Donald, of course, played the widow (illustrated); Chevalier (who had wanted Grace Moore for the widow) was the irresistably charming and handsome reprobate Count Danilo. Edward Everett Horton played Ambassador Popoff, Una Merkel Queen Dolores, George Barbier King Achmed, with other parts going to Minna Gombell, Ruth Channing, Sterling Holloway, Donald Meek, Akim Tamiroff and Herman Bing. (A French version called *La Veuve Joyeuse*

was simultaneously shot with several cast changes among the supporting performers.) Though Lehar's melodies underscored most of the action throughout the film, the musical and visual highlight was undoubtedly the Grand Ball. As the lilting 'Merry Widow Waltz' (lyrics by Lorenz Hart) reached its climax, the dancers, effectively costumed in sharply contrasting black and white, whirled their way down a large mirrored passageway while an overhead shot charted their melodious progress. The moment was a *tour de force* for its brilliant director and one of breathtaking beauty for the spectator. The brilliant and prolific Lorenz Hart also supplied new lyrics for 'Girls Girls Girls', as well as for the rapturous 'Vilia', 'Maxims', 'Melody Of Laughter', and 'If Widows Are Rich'; with Gus Kahn contributing a lyric of his own to 'Tonight Will Teach Me To Forget'. Despite the high critical praise with which this best of all Merry Widows was received, it is astonishing to note that it failed to find a large audience. And although it took Jeanette MacDonald one step closer to the superstardom she was to enjoy after *Naughty Marietta* (MGM) the following year, it ended Chevalier's brief association with the studio until his triumphant return to it over 20 years later in *Gigi* (1957). Remade in 1952.

Grace Moore made opera respectable in **One Night Of Love** (Columbia) – at least as far as the movies were concerned. Cunningly calculated to appeal to audiences who had hitherto regarded opera as a five-letter word of repellent aspect, and a form of entertainment strictly for eggheads, its simple story – of a young soprano's rise to eminence and the faith and patience lavished on her by a celebrated Italian music maestro – captured the imaginations of audiences everywhere and overnight turned Miss Moore (right) into a superstar. Tullio Carminati (left) played her devoted but long-suffering teacher, Lyle Talbot the handsome American she meets, and for whom she almost jettisons her career. Completing the cast were Mona Barrie, Jessie Ralph, Luis Alberni and Andres de Segurola. It was directed by Victor Schertzinger (a composer whose hobby was making movies; or a movie-maker whose hobby was writing songs) who combined his twin interests by providing the film with its appealing title number (lyrics by Gus Kahn). The screenplay was by S.K. Lauren, James Gow and Edmund North from a story by Dorothy Speare and Charles Beahan. Miss Moore sang the famous *Ciri-Biri-Bin* by A. Pestalozza and Rudolf Thaler, and other operatic music included extracts from Donizetti's *Lucia di Lammermoor*, Puccini's *Madame Butterfly* and Bizet's *Carmen*.

Bing Crosby was joined by Miriam Hopkins no less, in **She Loves Me Not** (Paramount), one of the few vehicles so far to come 'the groaner's' way in which the plot was as good as the songs. Aided and abetted by fellow Princeton student Edward Nugent, Crosby takes pity on attractive Curly Flagg (Hopkins), a cabaret dancer who, after witnessing a murder, flees the scene of the crime for fear of being implicated. He gives her sanctuary and, in a reversal of what was expected of Brandon Thomas's Charley's Aunt, insists that she dress up in male attire to avoid detection (see illustration). All the predictable complications ensued – but thanks to the ingenuity of producer Benjamin Glazer's screenplay (from the play by Howard Lindsay and the novel by Edward Hope), some nifty direction by Elliott Nugent, and a clutch of first rate performances – especially from Kitty Carlisle as Crosby's fiancée, and Henry Stephenson as a college Dean – it was an entertaining romp. Remade in 1942 as *True To The Army* (Paramount). Also cast: Lynne Overman, Warren Hymer, Judith Allen, George Barbier and Henry Kolker. Songs: *Love In Bloom* Ralph Rainger, Leo Robin; *After All, You're All I'm After* Edward Heyman, Arthur Schwartz; *Straight From The Shoulder (Right From The Heart)*; *I'm Hummin' (I'm Whistlin', I'm Singin')*; *Put A Little Rhythm In Everything You Do* Mack Gordon, Harry Revel; *Cocktails For Two* Arthur Johnston, Sam Coslow.

THIRTIES MUSICALS

Wake Up and Dream (Universal) put audiences to sleep with a plot about a vaudeville trio, their struggle to reach the big time, and the romantic sacrifice made by one of the members when he realizes that his best girl loves his best friend. It starred popular crooner Russ Columbo (right, whose last film this was before his untimely death) and Roger Pryor (centre) as the buddies, with June Knight (left) as the girl they both love. Also: Catharine Doucet, Henry Armetta, Andy Devine, Spencer Charters, Wini Shaw and Paul Porcasi. The story and screenplay were by John Meehan Jr (who probably filched it from some mediaeval strolling player); it was produced by B.F. Ziedman, and directed with his mind understandably not on the job by Kurt Neumann. Songs: *Too Beautiful For Words* Bernie Grossman, Russ Columbo, Jack Stern; *When You're In Love*; *Wake Up And Dream*; *Let's Pretend There's A Moon* Grossman, Stern, Grace Hamilton. Macabre sideline: Russ Columbo died in a bizarre shooting accident at a friend's house. The friend struck a match against one of a pair of duelling pistols being used as paperweights on a desk, and believed to be unloaded. The gun fired, and the bullet ricocheted off the desk, striking Columbo on the head. Or so the story went.

▽

Happiness Ahead (First National) was a musical with a window-cleaning background, in which Josephine Hutchinson made her screen debut as a bored heiress who pretends to join the proletariat. Harry Sauber and Brian Marlow's screenplay lacked sparkle, but its shortcomings mattered not a jot thanks to Mervyn LeRoy's resourceful direction, as well as a handful of excellent songs and the bouncy presence of Dick Powell (illustrated) as the manager of a window-cleaning company. The production was supervised by Sam Bischoff whose cast included John Halliday, Frank McHugh, Allen Jenkins, Ruth Donnelly, Dorothy Dare, Marjorie Gateson and Jane Darwell. Songs: *Beauty Must Be Loved* Irving Kahal, Sammy Fain; *There Must Be Happiness Ahead*; *Pop Goes Your Heart*; *All On Account Of A Strawberry Sundae* Mort Dixon, Allie Wrubel; *Massaging Window Panes* Bert Kalmar, Harry Ruby.

▽

Arguing that a divorce could never be 'gay', but accepting the fact that it was possible for a divorcée to be gay (the term being used, of course, in its dictionary-definition sense!) the Hays office forbade the use of the title *The Gay Divorce* but allowed **The Gay Divorcée** (RKO), by which name Cole Porter's Broadway and West End hit was introduced to movie audiences everywhere. Except that by the time it reached the screen, little of what Cole Porter actually wrote was in evidence, 'Night and Day' being the only number its 29-year-old producer, Pandro S. Berman, saw fit to include. Instead, it had Fred Astaire and Ginger Rogers (illustrated) co-starring for the first time, and although the couple spent only about ten minutes of the film's 107 minutes dancing, they were ten minutes of heaven which reinforced the studio's belief that it had stumbled on the greatest dance duo since Vernon and Irene Castle. Just as MGM had shown concern over the slightly *risqué* content of *The Cat And The Fiddle*, so RKO initially agonized over **The Gay Divorcée**, whose slender plot demanded that Rogers be caught *in flagrante* in order to facilitate her divorce. (Astaire is mistakenly thought to be the co-respondent hired for the job.) But no-one complained. On

▽

the contrary, the film was an outsized smash that instantly turned the dancing duo into household names. Though nothing else in the film measured up to the incomparable 'Night And Day', in which muted strings effectively alternate with full brass as Fred successfully seduces Ginger across a ballroom floor, audiences were introduced to 'The Continental' composed by Con Conrad and Herb Magidson, the first song ever to receive an Academy Award, in a 17-minute production number whose most striking feature was its Art Deco setting; and got a chance to see Betty Grable's knees in action in 'Let's K-nock K-nees' (by Mack Gordon and Harry Revel). Erik Rhodes and Eric Blore repeated the roles they created on Broadway, Rhodes playing the *real* co-respondent, Blore a waiter; with Alice Brady, Edward Everett Horton, William Austin and Paul Porcasi completing the cast. It was written by George Marion Jr, Dorothy Yost and Edward Kaufman; Dave Gould was credited as dance director (though Astaire, assisted by Hermes Pan, choreographed his own numbers), and Mark Sandrich directed. Other songs: *Needle In A Haystack* (Astaire) Con Conrad, Herb Magidson; *Don't Let It Bother You* (Astaire) Mack Gordon, Harry Revel.

◁ It seemed that Herbert Fields and Lew Brown, the authors of RKO's **Down To Their Last Yacht** (GB: **Hawaiian Nights**), were down to their last desperate idea when they penned the storyline for this sorry excuse of a musical (screenplay by Marion Dix and Lynn Starling) about a once wealthy family who, felled by the Depression, charter out their yacht as a means of earning a living. Mary Boland played the Queen of Malakamokalu, whose island (see illustration) the yacht has the misfortune to happen upon, with Polly Moran, Ned Sparks, Sidney Fox, Sidney Blackmer, Sterling Holloway and Marjorie Gateson other victims of the plot and of Paul Sloan's couldn't-care-less direction. Songs: *Tiny Little Finger On Your Hand* Val Burton, Will Jason; *There's Nothing Else To Do In Ma-La-Ka-Mo-Ka-Lu But Love* Sidney Mitchell, Cliff Friend; *Beach Boy*; *Funny Little World*; *Queen March*; *Beach Boy Bolero* Ann Ronell, Max Steiner.

Big, beautiful and boring – that was **Caravan** (Fox), a technically proficient operetta, opulently produced by Erik Charell (author of *White Horse Inn*), and starring Charles Boyer in his first English lead. Boyer's leading lady was Loretta Young (both illustrated, seated), and the paper-thin plot had Miss Young, as the Countess Wilma, arriving at the Hungarian village of Tokay on the eve of her 21st birthday to take over her inheritance – a vast estate hitherto owned by her father. Trouble is that the estate only really becomes hers when she marries. The wily Baron von Tokay (C. Aubrey Smith) attempts to exploit her situation by suggesting that she marries his son, an army lieutenant (Phillips Holmes, miscast in the role). The countess, who has never laid eyes on the lieutenant, refuses and, out of pique, marries Lazi (Boyer), the leader of a group of gypsy musicians, who has arrived in Tokay for the grape harvest. After

the wedding, however, the countess and the lieutenant, neither knowing who the other is, meet and fall in love. Lazi is uncommonly understanding about the situation, and releases his new bride so that she may embrace happiness with the man she really loves. Scripted by Samson Raphaelson from a novel by Melchior Lengyel, and with music and lyrics by Werner Richard Heymann and Gus Kahn, **Caravan** mixed spectacle and music in equal proportions, but with so tenuous a storyline on which to hang it all, that it found the paying customers (in the aftermath of the new-style musicals at Warner Bros.) not at all receptive to its old-fashioned, operetta-like quality. Louise Fazenda, Eugene Pallette, Charles Grapewin, Noah Beery, Dudley Digges, Jean Parker and Lionel Belmore were also cast. Songs and musical numbers included: *Ha-Cha-Cha*; *Wine Song*; *Happy, I Am Happy*.

△
Distinctly patriotic in flavour, **Flirtation Walk** (Warner Bros./First National) was a military musical whose major attraction was its stars, Dick Powell (right) and Ruby Keeler (left). It gave the impression of being a better movie than it actually was, thanks largely to the Mort Dixon–Allie Wrubel score and the dance routines which were rollickingly staged by Bobby Connolly, and it turned out a winner at the box office. Written by Delmer Daves from a story by himself and Lou Edelman, it was set mainly in West Point Academy (to which it was dedicated) and though it purported to give audiences a 'behind the scenes' peek at life in such an institution, its particular focus was on the tentative, naive romance between Powell and Keeler. Also in the cast for director Frank Borzage and supervisor Robert Lord were Pat O'Brien, Ross Alexander, Glen Boles, John Eldredge, Henry O'Neill, Guinn Williams and Frederick Burton. The Dixon–Wrubel songs included: *Flirtation Walk*; *Mr and Mrs Is The Name*; *When Do We Eat?*.

THIRTIES MUSICALS

Jerome Kern and Oscar Hammerstein II's tuneful stage success **Music In The Air** (Fox), though coming uncomfortably close to Viennese operetta in content, managed to avoid the more unpalatable excesses of that genre thanks to a robust screenplay (by Howard I. Young and Billy Wilder) that never took more than one lump of sugar at a time in the telling of its potentially cloying story. Gloria Swanson (left) was given top billing as a temperamental German prima donna who, after quarrelling with the lyricist of her new operetta, punishes him by seducing an innocent young Bavarian schoolmaster (Douglass Montgomery, vocals dubbed by James O'Brien) while the lyricist (John Boles, right), to annoy the prima donna, promises the teacher's sweetheart (June Lang, vocals dubbed by Betty Hiestand) that he will write a show for her, It ends with the two youngsters returning to their little village of Ebendorf, grateful to be free of the selfish connivances of show-folk. A uniformly excellent cast which also included Al Shean (repeating the role he played on Broadway), Reginald Owen, Joseph Cawthorn, Hobart Bosworth and Marjorie Main, garnered uniformly favourable reviews and was generally well received. Joe May directed, and the excellent score included: *I've Told Every Little Star*; *One More Dance*; *The Song Is You*; *We Belong Together*; *There's A Hill Beyond A Hill*; *I'm So Eager*.

▽

Alice Faye (centre left) teamed up with James Dunn (centre) in **365 Nights in Hollywood** (Fox) as a Hollywood hopeful from Peoria who joins a bogus film school but who, through the devotion of a has-been movie director, finds fame, fortune and, of course, romance. Two large-scale production numbers *en route* to the happy ending helped take the curse off William Conselman and Henry Johnson's singularly trite screenplay (story by James Starr), though funnymen Frank Mitchell and Jack Durant as a couple of icemen put the curse straight back on it. John Qualen, John Bradford and Frank Melton were in it too, it was produced by Sol Wurtzel and the director was George Marshall. Songs included: *You're My Future Star*; *Yes To You* Sidney Clare, Richard A. Whiting.

▽

△

Another tailor-made Eddie Cantor vehicle. **Kid Millions**, about a simple-minded 'nebbish' (Cantor, centre) who inherits $77,000,000 from his archaeologist father, cost millions, and made millions. Set for much of its time in Egypt, and with a plot that had various characters contriving to separate Eddie from his fortune, it was a zippy musical with all the usual Cantor ingredients, plus a spectacular Technicolor finale set in an ice-cream factory in Brooklyn, and featuring Broadway's Ethel Merman who, in her third film, almost tucked the show under her ample arms and ran away with it. Merman also featured in the opening number – a ditty called 'An Earful Of Music' (by Gus Kahn and Walter Donaldson) and gave audiences precisely that. Ann Sothern and George Murphy as the obligatory young lovers got to sing the film's big romantic ballad ('Your Head On My Shoulder'

by Harold Adamson and Burton Lane) while Cantor, in his traditional blackface sequence (a minstrel show set on board a ship) and playing end man to George Murphy's interlocutor, offered a vigorous rendition of Irving Berlin's 'Mandy'. The musical numbers were the responsibility of Seymour Felix who seemed to rely on the hefty budget for staging them. Arthur Sheekman, Nat Perrin and Nunnally Johnson wrote the original screenplay and Roy Del Ruth called the shots. The extremely serviceable supporting cast included Jesse Block, Eve Sully, Berton Churchill, Warren Hymer, Paul Harvey and Edgar Kennedy. Other songs: *When My Ship Comes In* (Cantor); *Okay Toots* (Cantor, Goldwyn Girls); *Ice Cream Fantasy* (Merman, Goldwyn Girls Cantor, Hymer) Kahn, Donaldson; *I Want To Be A Minstrel Man* (Nicholas, Goldwyn Girls) Adamson, Lane.

△

Little Mitzi Green did her celebrated impersonation of George Arliss, and Nancy Carroll (left) took the mickey out of Garbo *à la Grand Hotel* (MGM 1932) in **Transatlantic Merry Go Round** (United Artists), an 'anything goes' musical into which everything went. A combination thriller, melodrama, farce and revue, it was set, as its title suggested, on board a transatlantic ocean liner, and involved the somewhat bizarre activities of (among others) a pair of shady gamblers, a thief, an unfaithful wife who has no idea her husband has come along for the ride as well, and an escaped convict. It really made no sense at all

but was rich in incident, full of good tunes, and had a talented cast that also included Gene Raymond, Jack Benny (right), Sydney Howard, Sid Silvers, Sidney Blackmer, Ralph Morgan, William Boyd, Shirley Grey, and Jimmy Grier and His Orchestra. The screenplay was by Joseph Moncure March and Harry W. Conn from an original story by Leon Gordon. Edward Small produced, and the director was Benjamin Stoloff. Songs: *It Was Sweet Of You*; *Rock and Roll*; *Moon Over Monte Carlo* Sidney Clare, Richard A. Whiting; *If I Had A Million Dollars* Johnny Mercer, Matt Malneck.

One of the few musicals intentionally aimed at children. **Babes in Toyland** (MGM) produced by Hal Roach, was a 79-minute delight. It starred Stan Laurel and Oliver Hardy (as Stannie Dum and Ollie Dee) who, accompanied by a tuneful Victor Herbert score, invaded nurseryland to the merriment of children (and their parents) the world over. Stan and Ollie (illustrated) played a couple of toymakers who, due to Stannie's characteristic ineptitude (instead of making 600 toy soldiers one foot high, he makes 100 soldiers six foot high) inadvertently become the heroes of Toyland when the city's ramparts are stormed by the dreaded Bogeymen. Grateful inhabitants included Little Bo-Peep (Charlotte Henry), Tom-Tom (Felix Knight), Little Boy Blue (Johnny Downs) Curly Locks (Jean Darling), Mother Goose (Virginia Karns), Widow Peep (Florence Roberts) and Little Miss Muffet (Alice Dahl). It was entrancingly directed by Charles Rogers and Gus Meins from a screenplay by Nick Grinde and Frank Butler. Songs included: *Toyland*; *Don't Cry Bo-Peep*; *A Castle In Spain*; *I Can't Do That Sum*; *Go To Sleep, Slumber Deep* Victor Herbert, Glen MacDonough; *Who's Afraid Of The Big Bad Woolf* Ann Ronell, Frank Churchill; *March Of The Toys* Victor Herbert.
▽

△

Radio star Joe ('You nasty man') Penner (foreground) made a cheerful movie debut in **College Rhythm** (Paramount) and, together with his famous duck, served, amongst other things, as a mascot when two department stores go collegiate and compete for the honours in a climactic football game. Such was the nonsensical aspect of George Marion Jr's plot (screenplay by Walter DeLeon, John McDermott and Francis Martin). And if the story didn't actually help the undertaking, it didn't hinder it either, credit having to go to the above-mentioned Mr Penner for being the personable comedian he was, to tenor Lanny Ross for singing so sweetly, to Lyda Roberti (centre) for her inimitable rendition of the title song which Mack Gordon and Harry Revel wrote as part of their bouncy score, to Jack Oakie (right) for the usual purveyance of his humour, to Norman Taurog for his energetic, well-paced direction, and to Helen Mack, Mary Brian, George Barbier and Franklin Pangborn for their stalwart support. Other songs: *Stay As Sweet As You Are*; *Goo-goo I'm Ga-Ga Over You*; *Let's Give Three Cheers For Love*; *Take A Number From One To Ten*.

With each new film, Bing Crosby (right) seemed to enjoy an increasingly comfortable relationship with the camera, and **Here Is My Heart** (Paramount) revealed him to be a light comedian with an enviable sense of timing. He played a millionaire crooner who, bored with what life has been offering him, journeys to Monte Carlo where he falls in love with a disdainful princess. He succeeds in entering her hotel suite by posing as a waiter, and in no time at all (75 minutes to be precise) claims her for his own. Kitty Carlisle (left) was suitably glacial as the princess, but once thawed, proved a most sympathetic partner especially in the duets. It was written by Edwin Justus Mayer and Harlan Thompson from a play by Alfred Savoir and efficiently directed by Frank Tuttle, with Roland Young, Alison Skipworth and Reginald Owen excellent in other roles. Songs: *Love Is Just Around The Corner* Lewis Gensler, Leo Robin; *June In January*; *With Every Breath I Take*; *You Can't Make A Monkey Of The Moon* Ralph Rainger, Leo
◁ Robin.

1935

Mae West (left), in modern-dress and with the old *avoirdupois* very much in evidence on those parts of her body hitherto occupied by curves, didn't generate quite the same enthusiasm in **Goin' To Town** (Paramount) as she had in her previous pictures. The potentially amusing story of a cattle queen who inherits an oilfield from a fellow who, in turn, has won her in a dice game (but stops a bullet for cattle rustling), its chief concern was with Miss West's attempts to crash high society and become part of the Newport aristocracy. And although Mae fashioned a screenplay for herself (story by Marion Morgan and George B. Dowell) that, predictably, had its fair quota of wisecracks, the film lacked a sense of fun. West's attack on the *haut monde* seemed too heartfelt for genuine enjoyment and it imparted to the film a decided feeling of unease. It was directed by Alexander Hall for producer William Le Baron, and co-starred Paul Cavanagh (right, as a social asset Miss West sets her sights on, then pursues to South America) and Ivan Lebedeff, with Tito Coral, Marjorie Gateson and Fred Kohler Sr in support. Apart from an amusing sequence in which Mae was seen and heard as Delilah in a performance of Saint-Saens' *Samson and Delilah* (singing 'Softly Awakes My Heart', an English version of the aria *Mon Coeur S'ouvre A Ta Voix*), she also sang three other songs: *Love Is Love In Any Woman's Heart*; *He's A Bad, Bad Man But He's Good Enough For Me* Sammy Fain, Irving Kahal; *Now I'm A Lady* Fain, Kahal, Sam Coslow.

Lottery Lover (20th Century) chronicled the escapades of a handful of naval cadets in Paris who happen to find a garter belonging to sexy revue star Gaby Aimee (Peggy Fears, right). The sailors draw lots to see who will be the lucky guy to return it to her, and the winner turns out to be a love-shy greenhorn named Frank (Lew Ayres, left). How he coped formed the basis of a patchy screenplay by Franz Schultz and Billy Wilder (story by Sig Herzig and Maurice Hanline) whose entertainment value was minimal. Pat Paterson, Sterling Holloway and Reginald Denny co-starred, with Alan Dinehart, Walter King and Eddie Nugent in support. The director was William Thiele. Songs: *There's A Bit Of Paree In You*; *Ting-A-Ling-A-Ling*; *Close Your Eyes And See*; *All For The Love Of A Girl* Don Hartman, Jay Gorney.

If there was one thing George Raft (right) could do better than anyone else it was the **Rumba** (Paramount). In fact, apart from a slight plot involvement with some gangsters who have reasons for not wanting Mr Raft to dance, Raft occupied most of the film's running time rumba-ing with partners Iris Adrian, the exotic Margo, and the lovely Carole Lombard (left), who, to Raft's consternation, falls in love with someone else. It was adapted from a story by Guy Endore and Seena Owen by Howard J. Green, with additional dialogue by Harry Ruskin and Frank Partos; was choreographed by LeRoy Prinz, featured a specialty dance by Veloz and Yolanda, was produced by William Le Baron, and directed by Marion Gering with Monroe Owsley, Samuel S. Hinds, Virginia Hammond and Gail Patrick completing the cast. Songs: *I'm Yours For Tonight*; *The Magic Of You*; *The Rhythm Of The Rumba*; *Your Eyes Have Said*; *If I Knew* Ralph Rainger, Leo Robin.

The sweet music in **Sweet Music** (Warner Bros.) included the title number by Al Dubin and Harry Warren; *I See Two Lovers*; *Fare Thee Well Annabelle* and *The Snake Charmer* by Mort Dixon and Allie Wrubel; *Good Green Acres of Home*; *Ev'ry Day*; *Don't Go On A Diet*; *Winter Overnight*; *There's A Different You In Your Heart*, and *Seltzer Theme Song* by Irving Kahal and Sammy Fain. Indeed, the songs were far better than the plot – by Jerry Wald – that they accompanied, or the film's two leads, Rudy Vallee (right) and Ann Dvorak (left). Miss Dvorak couldn't sing, Mr Vallee couldn't act; a fact which somewhat incapacitated the screenplay (by Wald, Carl Erickson and Warren Duff), and rendered the Beatrice-and-Benedick romance between the two stars totally ineffectual. Far more convincing were the contributions of Ned Sparks, Helen Morgan, Alice White, Allen Jenkins, Joseph Cawthorn and Robert Armstrong. Another plus factor was Bobby Connolly's staging of the dance numbers. Alfred E. Green directed, and the production supervisor was Sam Bischoff.

MGM's irresponsibility in not issuing a health warning to diabetics when it released **The Night Is Young** cannot be over-estimated. For the sugar content of this Sigmund Romberg–Oscar Hammerstein II operetta (book by Vicki Baum, screenplay by Edgar Allan Woolf and Frank Schulz) was lethal. The oh-so-familiar story of an archduke (Ramon Novarro, left) who spurns the love of a princess for that of a common-or-garden ballet dancer (Evelyn Laye, right), it did the movie careers of its two stars no good whatsoever, Miss Laye permanently returning to Britain after its completion, and Novarro deserting Hollywood for the next 14 years. It didn't do audiences much good either, and the wise ones (of whom there were many) stayed away. One song, however, managed to survive both the critics' venom and the ravages of time: 'When I Grow Too Old To Dream'. For the rest, the score was no more inspired than the plot it accompanied, and was soon forgotten. Also cast: Charles Butterworth, Edward Everett Horton, Herman Bing, Una Merkel, Donald Cook, Henry Stephenson, Charles Judels, Albert Conti and, as the Countess Rafay (whoever she was), Rosalind Russell. Harry Rapf produced and the director was Donald Murphy. Other songs: *My Old Mare*; *The Night Is Young*; *The Noble Duchess*; *Lift Your Glass*; *There's A Riot In Havana*.

Sweet Adeline (Warner Bros.) was a pretty dull affair which nevertheless served as an excuse for some heavenly numbers by Jerome Kern and Oscar Hammerstein II. It also starred Irene Dunne as a gay-nineties Hoboken lass whose affections are craved by all the male customers of her father's popular *biergarten*, but whose heart, in the end, is won by a handsome young songwriter (Donald Woods, 2nd right). Erwin S. Gelsey wrote it, Bobby Connolly staged the musical numbers, Edward Chodorov supervised the production, and Mervyn LeRoy directed with a supporting cast that included Phil Regan, Hugh Herbert (centre), Ned Sparks (right), Joseph Cawthorn, Louis Calhern, Nydia Westman, Dorothy Dare and Winifred Shaw (left). Songs included: *Here Am I*; *Why Was I Born?*; *Don't Ever Leave Me*; *'Twas Not Long Ago*; *We Were So Very Young*; *Lonely Feet*.

Part gangster melodrama and part musical, **Stolen Harmony** (Paramount) was a George Raft offering in which the tough guy with the nimble feet even played the saxophone. But he was basically a dancin' man and, after being released from prison, joins up with maestro Ben 'Yowsah' Bernie and His Band and embarks on a cross-country bus tour, eventually helping to perk up the Leon Gordon, Harry Ruskin, Claude Binyon and Lewis Foster screenplay (story by Leon Gordon) by helping the police catch a gang of gunmen led by Lloyd Nolan. Grace Bradley (illustrated with Raft) played his dancing partner, with other roles going to Iris Adrian, Goodee Montgomery, Paul Gerrits, Ralf Harolde, William Cagney, William Pawley and Charlie Arnt. It was produced by Albert Lewis, and the director was Alfred Werker. Songs: *Would There Be Love*; *Let's Spill The Beans*; *I Never Had A Man To Cry Over*; *Fagin Youse A Viper* Mack Gordon, Harry Revel.

Flushed with the critical and financial success of *The Gay Divorcée* (1934), RKO, in between frequent visits to the bank, lost no time in securing yet another hit Broadway property for Fred Astaire (foreground centre) and Ginger Rogers. This time it was Jerome Kern and Otto Harbach's **Roberta** which, despite a ridiculous plot by Alice Duer Miller (all-American football hero inherits his aunt's chic dress salon in Paris) managed, somehow, to inspire Kern to write his most ravishing score since *Show Boat*. The melodies even impressed producer Pandro S. Berman who, treating Kern in a slightly less cavalier manner than he had done Cole Porter in *The Gay Divorcée*, retained four of the show's original numbers ('Let's Begin', 'Smoke Gets In Your Eyes', 'Yesterdays', and 'I'll Be Hard To Handle' with new lyrics by Bernard Dougall), used three more as background music ('You're Devastating', 'The Touch Of Your Hand', and 'Don't Ask Me Not To Sing') and commissioned a further two from Kern and lyricist Dorothy Fields – the haunting 'Lovely To Look At' (prominently featured in the show's fashion parade finale) and the lively 'I Won't Dance', originally written by Kern and Hammerstein II for a London show called *Three Sisters*, now given new lyrics by Fields. Ballard MacDonald and James Hanley's 'Indiana' was interpolated into the score. Four people had a hand in the screenplay (Jane Murfin, Sam Mintz, Glenn Tryon and Allan Scott) providing evidence that four heads were definitely not better than one. They did, however, manage to give Fred and Ginger the best moments in the show, a fact which could not have pleased the aristocratic Irene Dunne, who was billed above Astaire and Rogers but who, unfortunately, had to shoulder the burden of the cumbersome plot. Miss Dunne's musical highspot came with her wistful rendition of the incomparable 'Smoke Gets In Your Eyes' – but it was Fred and Ginger the public came to see. No accident therefore, that they, rather than Miss Dunne, featured in the last shot of the film – just as they had done in *Flying Down To Rio*. Of the five numbers they were given, the best was 'I'll Be Hard To Handle' – and the most interesting in that it was the first time in a dance routine they were able to bait each other competitively. Miss Rogers's handling of the lyric – à la Lyda Roberti who had played the role in the original stage production – also happened to be the funniest thing in the show. Randolph Scott was cast as the footballer who unexpectedly finds himself involved in the world of *haute couture* (and the man with whom Miss Dunne falls hopelessly in love), and Helen Westley played his aunt Roberta, with Claire Dodd, Victor Varconi, Luis Alberni and Ferdinand Munier completing the cast. The director was William A. Seiter. It was remade by MGM as *Lovely To Look At* in 1952.

THIRTIES MUSICALS

△

Lanny Ross, originally cast as the leading man in **Mississippi** (Paramount) was replaced after a newly-appointed studio head took a look at the lack-lustre rushes. His replacement, at the suggestion of producer Arthur Hornblow Jr, was Bing Crosby (right). Adapted from Booth Tarkington's novel *Magnolia* by Herbert Fields and Claude Binyon, **Mississippi** was the story of a young pacifist who, after refusing on principle to defend his sweetheart's honour and being banished in disgrace, joins a riverboat troupe as a singer, acquires a reputation as a crackshot after a saloon brawl in which the villain of the piece accidentally kills himself with his own gun, falls in love with his former fiancée's sister (Joan Bennett, left), and finally bullies her apprehensive family into accepting him. Though the burden of the plot rested squarely on Crosby's capable shoulders, it was his co-star W.C. Fields as Commodore Jackson, owner of the riverboat, who hogged the limelight. His comic routines – most notably the one in which, to the glaring disapproval of his opponents in a poker game, he deals himself five aces and has somehow to rectify the situation – were vintage Fields and deservedly attracted most of the critical kudos. The screenplay was by Francis Martin and Jack Cunningham, the score, which yielded three hits all sung by Crosby – 'Down By The River', 'Soon', and 'Easy To Remember' – was by Richard Rodgers and Lorenz Hart, although Stephen Foster's 'Swanee River' was also interpolated for Crosby to sing, with a Negro choral accompaniment. Completing the cast were Queenie Smith, Gail Patrick, Claude Gillingwater, John Miljan, Ed Pawley, Fred Kohler Sr and John Larkin. Directed by Edward Sutherland. A remake of *Cameo Kirby* (Fox, 1930).

Darryl F. Zanuck – the man who helped revitalize the musical with *42nd Street* (Warner Bros. 1933) – anxious that 20th Century should not, in any way, be considered inferior to Warner Bros., wasted no time in preparing a musical he hoped would be even more spectacular in scope and achievement than *42nd Street*. The result was **Folies Bergère**, in the event hardly an innovative world-beater but a diverting enough *bon-bon* with two big production numbers – one of which used leading man Maurice Chevalier's boater as its visual motif; the great entertainer's trademark was scaled up to fill the entire set. The other number relied on copious rain, several dozen girls and an equal number of umbrellas. Though the routines were briskly enough staged by Dave Gould (see illustration) they failed to compare with the work Berkeley was pioneering at Warner Bros. and at best were moderately eye-catching. The story itself concerned a Parisian millionaire who, finding it necessary to be in two places at once (a secret business meeting and a ball), engages the professional services of a Folies Bergère comedian to impersonate him at the ball. The role was perfect for Chevalier (though Zanuck's first choice was Charles Boyer), who played both the business man and the artist, and he sailed through it, picking up excellent reviews. (A more *risqué* French version featuring topless girls at the Folies was made at the same time, and was equally well received.) Merle Oberon co-starred as the businessman's wife and Ann Sothern was his show-girl mistress, with other roles assigned to Walter Byron, Lumsden Hare, Robert Greig, Eric Blore, Halliwell Hobbes and Phillip Dare. William Goetz and Raymond Griffith were the associate producers, it was written by Bess Meredyth and Hal Long from a play by Rudolph Lothar and Hans Adler, and the director was Roy Del Ruth. It was remade as *That Night in Rio* (1941) and again in 1952 as a vehicle for Danny Kaye called *On The Riviera*, both by 20th Century-Fox. Songs: *Singing A Happy Song*; *Rhythm Of The Rain* Jack Meskill, Jack Stern; *You Took The Words Right Out Of My Mouth* Harold Adamson, Burton Lane; *Valentine* Henri Christine, Herbert Reynolds (English lyrics), Albert Willemetz (French lyrics).

Carl Brisson played two parts in **All The King's Horses** (Paramount): a Ruritanian monarch and his film-star double. The double doubles as king – both on the throne and in the royal bedroom, thus leaving His Majesty free to take a little jaunt to Vienna. Frank Tuttle and Frederick Stephani's adaptation of the play and the musical on which it was based (the first by Lawrence Clark and Max Giersberg; the second by Frederick Herendeen and Edward Horan) was drenched in tedium, making life especially difficult for Mr Brisson and his co-star Mary Ellis, both of whom, however, sang pleasantly. Edward Everett Horton, Katherine De Mille, Eugene Pallette, Arnold Korff and Marina Schubert were also in it, it was produced by William Le Baron, and directed by Frank Tuttle (production number illustrated). Songs: *A Little White Gardenia*; *Be Careful Young Lady*; *Dancing The Viennese*; *A King Can Do No Wrong*; *When My Prince Charming Comes Along* Sam Coslow.

◁

△
Busby Berkeley not only directed the musical sequences in **Gold Diggers Of 1935** (Warner Bros.), but was given a crack at the entire film. Unfortunately, the story Robert Lord and Peter Milne devised for it (screenplay by Manuel Seff and Peter Milne), and which they set in a New England summer resort hotel (involving the romantic pairings of several guests), was weak even by musical comedy standards. But the two major production numbers (which formed part of a charity show being staged at the hotel) were something else – particularly 'Lullaby Of Broadway' (illustrated), arguably the acme of Berkeley's remarkable career and his own favourite among all the numbers he created. The sad little tale of a 'Broadway baby' who lives by night and sleeps by day, it chronicled the last twenty-four hours in her life prior to her being pushed accidentally, out of a window in a Manhattan nightspot and plunging to her death. The number – by Al Dubin and Harry Warren – begins

with Wini Shaw's face as a white speck (on an otherwise black screen) becoming larger and larger until she is seen in full close-up. After finishing the song Miss Shaw turns her head away from the camera and puts a cigarette in her mouth, whereupon the contours of her face become the contours of the Manhattan skyline as seen from the air. The number's climax, set in a massive nightclub and featuring some of the best precision dancing ever filmed, involved over a hundred men and women who, photographed from every conceivable angle, abandoned themselves to the music in a frenzy of movement that had audiences gasping in awe for its entire duration. The sequence ended as it began, with Miss Shaw's face now receding into the background until all that was left was a black screen. The other full-scale production number, 'The Words Are In My Heart' (also by Dubin and Warren) made use of fifty-six miniature pianos and fifty-six girls. Another example of Berkeley's

imagination working at full pitch, it necessitated fifty-six men concealing themselves under the pianos as a means of moving them about – and although careful examination of the sequence reveals their exact whereabouts, the effect is nonetheless remarkable – particularly the moment (photographed backwards) in which the pianos group themselves into a perfect oblong, in much the same way that Berkeley's girls formed a jigsaw of Ruby Keeler's face in *Dames* (Warner Bros. 1934). Dubin and Warren wrote one other number for the film, 'I'm Going Shopping With You', first presented in the opening sequence, then later sung by Dick Powell (playing a medical student-cum-hotel clerk) as he accompanies his co-star Gloria Stuart on an expensive shopping expedition. The cast was completed by Frank McHugh, Joseph Cawthorn, Adolphe Menjou, Hugh Herbert, Alice Brady, Glenda Farrell, Grant Mitchell, Dorothy Dare and Thomas Jackson.

THIRTIES MUSICALS

Originally bought as a vehicle for Marion Davies, ▷ but shelved when the cinema-going world imposed its moratorium on musicals at the beginning of the decade, Louis B. Mayer blew the dust off his favourite operetta and offered it to his favourite star, Jeanette MacDonald (right). The piece in question was Victor Herbert's **Naughty Marietta** (MGM) the success of which single-handedly restored the good name of operetta and ensured the genre's continued popularity for the remainder of the thirties, and even into the forties and fifties. Not altogether sure of its chances of success, Mayer chose the fast-working W.S. Van Dyke II ('one-take Woody' as he was known to his associates) to direct, confident, that with his characteristic efficiency and sound economic sense, Van Dyke would bring the film in on time and at a reasonable cost. For Jeanette's leading man he chose Nelson Eddy (left) who had already been under contract to the studio for two years, but whose combined screen appearances totalled no more than seven minutes. It was another gamble, but worth the taking because of his undeniably strong baritone voice. The gamble paid off and the combination of Victor Herbert's soaring melodies (new lyrics by Gus Kahn), John Lee Mahin, Frances Goodrich and Albert Hackett's sweepingly romantic screenplay, the unlikely but successful chemistry created by its two stars (plus, of course their gloriously ringing voices) as well as Van Dyke's crisp, no-nonsense handling of the narrative – was a winning one, guaranteeing long lines and happy faces wherever the film was shown. MacDonald played Marietta, a French princess who, rather than marry a Spanish grandee she despises, escapes to the Colonies on a Louisiana-bound cargo ship. Nelson Eddy was the dashing mercenary, Warrington, who comes to the ship's rescue when it is attacked by pirates. Just as you didn't have to be a mathematician to know that two and two made four, so it required no special psychic skill to realize that the couple would soon be plighting their troth – though not before the requisite complications threatened, momentarily, to stand in the way of their happiness. Frank Morgan was cast as the befuddled Governor of New Orleans, with other parts going to Elsa Lanchester, Douglass Dumbrille, Joseph Cawthorn, Walter Kingsford, Harold Huber, Edward Brophy and Akim Tamiroff. The producer was Hunt Stromberg. Songs: *Chansonette; Antoinette And Anatola; Prayer; Tramp, Tramp, Tramp; The Owl And The Bob Cat; 'Neath The Southern Moon; Mon Ami Pierrot* (traditional French); *Italian Street Song; I'm Falling In Love With Someone;* and the ecstatic *Ah Sweet Mystery Of Life* (the last three with the original lyrics by Rida Johnson Young).

Columbia followed the enormous success of *One Night of Love* (1934) with **Love Me Forever**, another Grace Moore (illustrated) vehicle again directed by Victor Schertzinger, who again composed the title song (with Gus Kahn), and demonstrated that grand opera need not be boring to a mass audience, though it may be necessary to take certain liberties with the likes of Verdi – such as expanding his quartet from *Rigoletto* into a full-blown chorus number (which is exactly what happened in **Love Me Forever** – though in fairness it must be said that this crass interference was accounted for in the plot). By and large though, the operatic excerpts were convincingly presented and contributed hugely to the overall popularity of the film. Leo Carillo starred opposite Miss Moore as a wealthy nightclub proprietor who falls prey to the soprano's looks, charm and voice and who demonstrates his undying devotion by building a café which he names after her. And as he was also instrumental in arranging her Metropolitan debut, he could be forgiven for not taking too kindly to the news that his protégée was in love with a good-looking young man from Boston (Michael Bartlett). But injustice wasn't what the film was all about and screenwriters Jo Swerling and Sidney Buchman (story by Schertzinger) skilfully softened the blow in the interests of a happy ending. The associate producer was Max Winslow, whose cast included Robert Allen, Spring Byington, Thurston Hall, Douglass Dumbrille and Luis Alberni. Apart from the title song and a number called 'Whoa' (also by Schertzinger and Kahn), Miss Moore's musical programme included extracts from Puccini's *La Bohème* and from *Rigoletto*, as well as the songs 'Il Bacio' by Luigi Arditi and 'Funiculi-Funicula' ◁ by Luigi Denza.

Fox's favourite chanteuse, Alice Faye, headed the cast of **George White's 1935 Scandals** (Fox) and although coping admirably with the musical side of things, she was unable to salvage much of its seen-it-once-too-often plot. Though the screenplay was credited to Jack Yellen and Patterson McNutt, the story, presumably, was the brainchild of the great Mr White himself, for the entire production was not only produced and directed by him, but conceived by him as well. He also featured prominently in the cast, playing an impresario called George White who, while on location in Florida, happens to see an act featuring singers Alice Faye and James Dunn (both illustrated centre), which he books for his next Scandals. The ups-and-downs of backstage life take their toll on the two young people – particularly where romance is concerned – but after the obligatory complications, it all ends happily. Faye's big production number was 'Oh, I Didn't Know' (by Jack Yellen, Herb Magidson and Joseph Meyer), an untidy effort staged by George White, and she also sang 'You Belong To Me' by Yellen and Cliff Friend as well as 'It's An Old Southern Custom' by Yellen and Meyer. Lyda Roberti, Cliff Edwards, Arline Judge, Emma Dunn and Benny Rubin were in it too, but it was newcomer Eleanor Powell who, in her screen debut, made the critics sit up and take note of her extraordinary terpsichorean skills. MGM also sat up and took note and a few months later turned her into a major star with *The Broadway Melody of 1936*. Other songs: *According To The Moonlight* Yellen, Magidson, Meyer; *I Was Born Too Late* Yellen, Meyer; *I Got Shoes, You Got Shoesies; Hunkadola* Yellen, Friend, Meyer; *It's Time To Say Goodnight* Friend, Meyer.

The best thing about **Love in Bloom** (Paramount) was the score by Mack Gordon and Harry Revel. For the rest it was a bottom-drawer effort which had the nerve, in 1935, to re-heat for the umpteenth time, that soggy old chestnut about the carnival girl (Dixie Lee, right) who, in trying to escape her past, almost sacrifices her personal happiness when she rejects the love of a poor young songwriter (Joe Morrison, left) on the grounds that she's worthless and will do him no good at all. What did nobody any good was the screenplay by J.P. McEvoy and Keene Thompson, whose inability to dredge up a single good idea put paid to the stalwart efforts of its hard-working cast – including George Burns and Gracie Allen (top-billed), J.C. Nugent, Lee Kohlmar, Richard Carle and Mary Foy, Elliott Nugent directed; and the producer was Benjamin Glazer. Songs: *My Heart Is An Open Book; Here Comes Cookie; Got Me Doing Things; Let Me Sing You To Sleep With A Love Song.*
▽

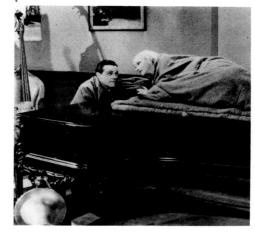

Al Jolson's magnetic personality ramrodded its ▷
way through Warner Bros./First National's **Go
Into Your Dance** (GB: **Casino de Paree**), another
backstage musical with the usual attendant
clichés. He starred opposite his wife, Ruby Keeler
(left), and so successful was their team effort
that Jolson (right) – who in a fit of uncharacteris-
tic generosity publicly proclaimed Ruby to be 'the
ten best women in pictures all rolled into one' –
refused to repeat the exercise for fear of unfavourable comparisons with her. He played
an arrogant, couldn't-care-less Broadway star
whose bad behaviour renders him unem-
ployable, but who, thanks to the love, devotion
and help of an understanding nightclub dancer
(Keeler), successfully opens a casino in New
York. Complication occurs in the guise of a
racketeer backer who, on hearing that he has
been double-crossed, sets out to eliminate
Jolson. But it was, after all, a musical and not
one of Warner Bros.' famous crime-orientated
melodramas and it ended happily. Apart from
Jolson's dynamic performance, the film also
boasted seven songs by Al Dubin and Harry
Warren, including two production numbers –
'About A Quarter To Nine' and 'A Latin
From Manhattan' – the first of which gave
Jolson a chance to appear in blackface to the
accompaniment of one of Dubin and Warren's
catchiest melodies. In the second, which takes
place in a nightclub, Jolson gleefully exposes the
'Latin From Manhattan' as a hoofer from Tenth
Avenue ('she was in a Broadway chorus, known
as Susie Donahue' runs one of the lyrics). The
number opens out, becomes a showcase for Miss
Keeler's rather limited talents, goes Spanish and
ends with her and Jolson atop an enormous
globe of the world. Both sequences were staged
by Bobby Connolly without any of Berkeley's
flair, but with the actual quality of the songs
more than compensating for the deficiency of
visual inventiveness. Helen Morgan was co-
starred together with Glenda Farrell, Barton
MacLane and Patsy Kelly, with Miss Morgan
sitting characteristically on a piano, singing
a characteristic torch song called 'The Little
Things You Used To Do'. The film was scripted
by Earl Baldwin from a novel by Bradford Ropes,
and directed by Archie Mayo. Other songs: *Cielito
Lindo* Neil Wilson, Carlo Fernandez, Sebastian
Yradier; *Go Into Your Dance; Mammy, I'll Sing
About You; A Good Old-Fashioned Cocktail With A
Good Old-Fashioned Girl; Casino De Paree*.

Metro-Goldwyn-Mayer attempted, unsuccessfully, to turn sexy Jean Harlow (left) into a
musical comedy star in **Reckless**, a rather lurid
tale inspired by a real-life scandal in which
Broadway actress Libby Holman was accused of
killing her husband (and with more than a hint
in it of Harlow's own marriage with Paul
Bern). As written for the screen by P.J. Wolfson
(story by David O. Selznick alias Oliver Jeffries)
Harlow, a Broadway musical comedy star, marries a drunken playboy (Franchot Tone), and
although she genuinely attempts to show just
how good a wife she can be, is rejected by his
ultra-posh family as being not good enough.
When, a short while after their marriage, the
playboy blows his brains out, Harlow is blamed
and, after facing a hostile audience at her
come-back performance, passionately implores
them to believe that she is innocent, and requests that she at least be allowed to finish her
song. Moved by her sincerity, they relent, and
her come-back ends in triumph – with William
Powell literally waiting in the wings to make an
honest woman of her. Harlow's singing was
dubbed by Virginia Verrill, and she was clearly
unable to cope with the dances, her lack of
ability in this direction necessitating some skilful
editing and the use of doubles in some of the
scenes. May Robson, Ted Healy, Nat Pendleton,
Carl Randall (right), Rosalind Russell, Henry
Stephenson, Nina Mae McKinney, Allan Jones
(making his debut), and young Mickey Rooney
were also in it; David O. Selznick produced, and
the director was Victor Fleming. The film's title
number was written by Jerome Kern and Oscar
Hammerstein II, providing the inspiration for a
rather meandering production number (staged
by Carl Randall and Chester Hale) and was
reprised several times. Other songs: *Everything's
Been Done Before* Harold Adamson, Edwin H.
Knopf, Jack King; *Hear What My Heart Is Saying*
◁ Adamson, Burton Lane.

Under the Pampas Moon (Fox) was a cinematic
Tower of Babel with such a conglomeration of
phoney accents that it practically needed sub-
titles to render it intelligible. Not that Ernest
Pascal and Bradley King's screenplay (from a
story by Gordon Morris) made much sense
anyway. But at least it gave the ravishingly lovely
dancer Rita Cansino (later to be better known as
Hayworth) a chance to do something called the
Zamba; and specialty dancers Veloz and Yolanda
a crack at the Tango. For the rest it was a dreary-
beyond-belief tale of an Argentinian gaucho
(Warner Baxter, left, repeating the role he tried
six years earlier in Fox's *In Old Arizona*) who
couldn't make up his mind which he preferred:
his horses or his lady (Ketti Gallian, right). John
Miljan (centre), J. Carrol Naish, Soledad Jiminez,
Jack La Rue, Armida, Ann Codee and Paul
Porcasi were also in it; it was produced by Buddy
De Sylva, Jack Donohue directed the dances, and
the director was James Tinling. Songs: *The
Gaucho* Buddy De Sylva, Walter Samuels;
Querida Mia Paul Francis Webster, Lew Pollack;
Zamba Arthur Wynter-Smith; *Love Song Of The
Pampas; Veredita; Je T'Adore* Miguel de Zarraga,
Cyril J. Mockridge.
▽

THIRTIES MUSICALS

A totally indifferent effort from First ▷ National/Warner Bros., **In Caliente** offered an anaemic plot in which a magazine editor gives an unfavourable review to a torrid Mexican dancer, then falls in love with her. Pat O'Brien and Dolores Del Rio (foreground) starred in the Jerry Wald–Julius J. Epstein screenplay (from a story by Ralph Block and Warren Duff) and Lloyd Bacon directed; but it was left to Busby Berkeley to salvage what he could with his staging of 'The Lady In Red' (by Mort Dixon and Allie Wrubel) sung with pazazz by Winifred Shaw and again, in her distinctive hayseed style by Judy Canova, and the 'Muchacha' (by Al Dubin and Harry Warren), in which he transformed a hotel patio into a bandit's hideaway, complete with swirling Mexicans, their dancing sweethearts, and eight magnificent horses. Also cast were Leo Carrillo, Edward Everett Horton, Glenda Farrell, The De Marcos, The Canova Family, Phil Regan, and Herman Bing. Other songs: *To Call You My Own*; *In Caliente* Mort Dixon, Allie Wrubel.

△

What happens when a man and a woman, both married to other people, decide not to commit suicide by jumping off the Eiffel Tower, but, by pretending to have an affair with each other, to make their respective spouses jealous instead – was what producer Benjamin Glazer expected audiences to pay good money to find out in **Paris in Spring** (Paramount). The answer, as it happened, was nothing very much. At least nothing that hadn't been seen in dozens of romantic comedies since pictures first began to flicker. For the record, it starred Mary Ellis, Tullio Carminati (right), Ida Lupino (left), Lynne Overman, Jessie Ralph and James Blakely, was adapted by Keene Thompson from a play by Dwight Taylor and written for the screen by Samuel Hoffenstein and Franz Shultz. The director was the celebrated Lewis Milestone. Songs: *Paris In The Spring*; *Bon Jour Mamselle*; *Why Do They Call It Gay Paree?*; *Jealousy* Mack Gordon, Harry Revel.

△

Though Alice Faye, on loan-out from her *alma mater* 20th Century-Fox, received top billing with George Raft in **Every Night At Eight** (Paramount), it was Frances Langford (centre right), billed below the title, who finished up with Raft (right) at the final fade. Miss Langford, together with Faye (centre) and a well-groomed (for once!) Patsy Kelly (left) played a trio of would-be singers who, after being fired from their jobs in a mint-julep factory, are engaged by orchestra leader Raft and led to stardom. It was a pleasant enough diversion for Depression-weary audiences, and had an excellent set of songs to help keep its screenplay (by Gene Towne, Graham Baker, and Bert Hanlon; story by Stanley Garvey) buoyant. Best of the bunch were 'I Feel A Song Comin' On' (by Dorothy Fields, Jimmy McHugh and George Oppenheimer), a full-scale production number for Alice Faye who sounded like Mae West and looked like Jean Harlow, and 'I'm In The Mood For Love' (by Dorothy Fields and Jimmy McHugh) sung by Frances Langford. It was produced by Walter Wanger and directed by Raoul Walsh, whose cast also included Jimmie Hollywood, Henry Taylor, Eddie Bartel, Harry Barris (illustrated, at piano), Walter Catlett, Herman Bing and Bud Flanagan (later known as Dennis O'Keefe). Other songs: *Take It Easy*; *Speaking Confidentially*; *Every Night At Eight* Fields, McHugh; *Then You've Never Been Blue* Ted Fiorito, Joe Young, Sam Lewis, Frances Langford.

The best thing about **Two For Tonight** (Paramount) was that it didn't run more than 61 minutes. The second best thing was the score provided by Mack Gordon and Harry Revel. Otherwise it was a disappointing effort whose screenplay (by George Marion Jr and Jane Storm with additional dialogue by Harry Riskin from a play by Max Lief and J.O. Lief), was an albatross round its tuneful neck. All about a songsmith who undertakes to write a complete Broadway musical in seven days, it starred Bing Crosby (centre right) as the optimistic composer and Joan Bennett as the female interest, with Lynne Overman, Mary Boland (right), Thelma Todd, ▽

James Blakely (left), Douglas Fowley (at piano), Charles E. Arnt (far right) and Charles Lane in support. There was nothing wrong with the film's basic idea, but a tighter plot would have helped, and one was left with the impression that **Two For Tonight** was exactly the kind of show Crosby might have come up with in the seven days he was given to write his musical. The director was Frank Tuttle, and the producer Douglas MacLean. Songs: *I Wish I Were Aladdin*; *Without A Word Of Warning*; *From The Top Of Your Head To The Tip Of Your Toes*; *Takes Two To Make A Bargain*; *You're Beautiful*; *Two For Tonight*.

Coming four years before 20th Century-Fox's Technicolor version of the same subject, **Harmony Lane** (Mascot) was one of the first of the large number of musical biopics produced in Hollywood. It starred Douglass Montgomery (illustrated) as the celebrated composer Stephen Foster, Evelyn Venable as the girl he loves (but who settles for another), and Adrienne Ames as the girl he marries on the rebound. The story of Foster's fatal dissipation and drunkenness was sketchily told by scenarist Joseph Santley (who also directed) from a story by Milton Krims. William Frawley was prominently featured as minstrel man E.P. Christy, with Joseph Cawthorn, Clarence Muse (as Old Joe), Gilbert Emery, Florence Roberts, James Bush, Cora Sue Collins, David Torrence, and Victor DeCamp also in the cast. There were lots of missed opportunities, especially in the insipid handling of the well known music. The producer was Nat Levene. Songs included: *Oh Susanna!*; *My Old Kentucky Home*; *Old Black Joe*; *Weep No More My Lady*; *Swanee River* Foster.
▽

Broadway Gondolier (Warner Bros.) was another in a long list of musicals that owed their inspiration to radio, the story this time revolving around a taxi driver whose one ambition in life is to succeed as a radio singer. A complicated scheme cooked up by two girls takes the cabby to Venice, and finally turns his dream into a reality. Functioning as little more than a showcase for its star, Dick Powell (right), it was a tedious effort momentarily enlivened by Al Dubin and Harry Warren's tuneful score – most notably 'Lulu's Back In Town' – and a supporting cast that featured Joan Blondell and Louise Fazenda as Powell's allies, as well as Adolphe Menjou, Bob Murphy (left), The Mills Brothers, The Canova Family and Ted Fiorito and His Band. It was directed by Lloyd Bacon from a Warren Duff-Sig Herzig screenplay (story by Herzig, E.Y. Harburg and Hans Kraly). Other songs: *The Rose In Her Hair*; *Lonely Gondolier*; *Outside Of You*; *You Can Be Kissed*; *The Pig And The Cow*.
▽

Though Fred Astaire admitted in his autobiography that he disliked top hat, white tie and tails, you'd never have known it from his classic title-song tribute to all three (illustrated) in **Top Hat** (RKO) – the first Astaire–Rogers musical in which the team received top billing, and generally regarded as the most satisfying of the entire series. In fact **Top Hat**, with its cunningly contrived, soufflé-light plot and a score by Irving Berlin that must surely rank as one of the finest ever written for a film, comes as near to perfection as could decently be expected. Plot-wise, the movie takes the mistaken identity theme to the -nth degree, Astaire being the chief victim of the farcical situations that occur when Miss Rogers, with whom he has fallen in love, believes him to be the husband of a friend of hers. The deception persists throughout most of the film's 101-minute running time, but in such skilful counterpoint to the score, and with its numerous variations on its single theme spiralling off into the realms of the sublimely absurd, that it is impossible not to surrender completely to the delightful idiocy of it all. Added to which, it was played by a cast whose particular stock-in-trade was to bring conviction to such improbable japes. Thus, even if the story didn't grab the audience, the performances did. But what people lined up at the box office in their hordes to see was the dancing of Fred and
▽

Ginger, and they were not disappointed. Astaire demonstrated again that he was simply incapable of a graceless movement or gesture – whether as the sartorially elegant man about town in the title song, or the incurable romantic in 'Cheek to Cheek'. And Rogers, who was in three out of the five routines, again proved herself to be, if not quite the equal of her miraculous partner, an excellent dancing co-star just the same. Her slightly common quality humanized the duo and, artistically as well as temperamentally, the combination proved infallible. The cast was completed by Edward Everett Horton (as Fred's manager), Helen Broderick (as Horton's wife, whom Rogers believes has married Astaire), Erik Rhodes, Eric Blore, Leonard Mudie, Lucille Ball (as a clerk in a flower shop), Edgar Norton and Gino Corrado. It was written by Dwight Taylor and Allan Scott and adapted from a play by Alexander Farago and Aladar Laszlo by Karl Noti. Hermes Pan was the dance director, Pandro S. Berman the producer, and it was directed, once again, by Mark Sandrich. Other musical numbers: *No Strings* (Astaire); *Isn't This A Lovely Day* (Astaire, Rogers); *Top Hat, White Tie And Tails* (Astaire); *The Piccolino*, the latter providing the film with its 'big finish' but in which the dancing sequence for Fred and Ginger needed, perhaps, to be a little longer than it was.

The trials and tribulations of putting on a show, ▷ at least as experienced by Gene Raymond (right) in **Hooray for Love** (RKO), hardly made for good entertainment, and despite an attractive score by Dorothy Fields and Jimmy McHugh, and the welcome participation of Ann Sothern (left foreground), Bill Robinson, Jeni Le Gon, Maria Gambarelli and Pert Kelton – who performed the film's musical numbers as part of an intimate revue – there was little else to shout hooray for. Thurston Hall, Lionel Stander, Georgia Kane, Etienne Girardot and Fats Waller were also in it; it was written by Lawrence Hazard and Ray Harris from a story by Marc Lachmann; the associate producer was Felix Young and it was directed by Walter Lang. Songs: *Hooray For Love*; *I'm In Love All Over Again*; *I'm Living In A Great Big Way*; *You're An Angel*; *Palsie Walsie*; *Got A Snap In My Fingers*.

THIRTIES MUSICALS

Taking their cue from scenarists Walter DeLeon, Francis Martin and Ralph Spence, audiences put the mish-mash of what passed for plot in **The Big Broadcast of 1936** to one side, and enjoyed the special brand of lunatic humour purveyed by Jack Oakie as radio's number one singing heart-throb (except that he employs a double to do his vocalizing), by Lyda Roberti as an improbable countess who is in love with his voice (and consequently finds herself having to spirit two men off to her mythical kingdom), and by George Burns and Gracie Allen whose latest invention – a contraption they call the Seeing Eye – allows you to hear *and* see whatever is coming out of the radio. Variety was the spice of many a musical motion picture, and there was a fair share of it on offer on this occasion, with a team called Willy West and McGinty knocking themselves out to generate a laugh or two as they attempted to build a house. Bing Crosby (illustrated) also appeared, and delivered a song called 'I Wished On The Moon' by Dorothy Parker and Ralph Rainger. Ethel Merman belted out 'It's The Animal In Me' by Mack Gordon and Harry Revel (originally filmed for *We're Not Dressing*), and there were guest appearances too, by The Vienna Boys' Choir, Ray Noble and His Band, Amos 'n' Andy, Bill Robinson and the Nicholas Brothers. The featured players included Wendy Barrie, Henry Wadsworth, C. Henry Gordon, Benny Baker and a larger-than-life Akim Tamiroff. Benjamin Glazer produced, and the director was Norman Taurog. Other songs: *Cheating Machita (Armagura); Through The Doorway Of Dreams I Saw You* Richard A. Whiting, Leo Robin; *Double Trouble; Miss Brown To You; Why Dream?* Whiting, Robin, Ralph Rainger; *Why Stars Come Out At Night* Ray Noble; *Goodnight Sweetheart* Noble, James Campbell, Reg Connelly.

Ann Sothern (right) received billing above Jack Haley in **The Girl Friend** (Columbia), a minor effort directed by Edward Buzzell from a screenplay by Gertrude Purcell and Benny Rubin, and a story by Gene Towne and Graham Baker. Concerned with the rather far-fetched circumstances which lead to Mr Haley's hitherto unproduced play about Napoleon triumphing as a Broadway musical, it was amiable nonsense that also featured Roger Pryor (left), Victor Kilian and Thurston Hall (as composers posing as producers) Ray Walker, Margaret Seddon and Inez Courtney. Songs included: *What Is This Power?; Two Together; Welcome To Napoleon* Gus Kahn, Arthur Johnston.

Dick Powell starred in six musical films in 1935. **Shipmates Forever** (Warner Bros./Cosmopolitan/First National), the fourth of these, was well directed by Frank Borzage from a slim-line story and screenplay by Delmer Daves which had Powell playing an admiral's son who is expected to distinguish himself in the Navy. The lad prefers to sing rather than swab the decks but finally gives in to family pressure and the advice of Ruby Keeler (illustrated with Powell). Lou Edelman supervised the production which had an excellent supporting cast in Lewis Stone (as Powell's father), Ross Alexander, Eddie Acuff, Dick Foran, John Arledge and Robert Light, and an unmemorable Al Dubin–Harry Warren score. Songs: *Don't Give Up The Ship; I'd Rather Listen To Your Eyes; All Aboard The Navy; I'd Love To Take Orders From You; Do I Love My Teacher.*

Broadway Melody Of 1936 (MGM) was in no way a sequel to the epoch-making *The Broadway Melody* (MGM 1929), and, apart from its similarity of title and milieu, the only other points it had in common with the earlier film were a marvellous Arthur Freed–Nacio Herb Brown score, its overwhelming entertainment value, and its enormous potency at the box office. For the rest, it boasted a completely different storyline and a whole new set of characters – such as Jack Benny, top-cast as an odious gossip columnist and scourge of handsome producer Robert Taylor, whose relationship with a society girl (as well as the backer of his show) Benny keeps threatening to expose. Then there was leggy tap-dancer Eleanor Powell whose second screen appearance (as a childhood sweetheart of Mr Taylor's) vaulted her to stardom within weeks of the film's release. Buddy Ebsen and his sister Vilma were in it too as a couple of Broadway hopefuls; so were Una Merkel, June Knight, Sid Silvers, Nick Long Jr and Frances Langford, Dave Gould staged the production numbers, the best being the elaborate 'I've Got A Feeling You're Fooling' routine (illustrated, Powell centre), although the more modest 'Sing Before Breakfast' – performed by Powell and the Ebsens on the roof of a tenement building during a slump in the trio's fortunes – was remarkable for the sheer *joie de vivre* it exuded. Writing credits belonged to Moss Hart (story), Jack McGowan and Sid Silvers (screenplay) and Harry Conn (additional dialogue); the big budget production was in the hands of John W. Considine Jr, and the director was Roy Del Ruth. Other songs: *You Are My Lucky Star* (Powell, Langford); *Broadway Rhythm* (Powell, Langford); *On A Sunday Afternoon* (Ebsens).

Lawrence Tibbett (centre) made an auspicious ▷
comeback in **Metropolitan**, a marvellously entertaining satire on the exclusive and élitist
world of grand opera in general and the Metropolitan in particular, and the first film made by
the newly formed 20th Century-Fox. Basically
about the seemingly insuperable difficulties experienced by American singers in their attempts
to graduate from sword-carrying in the chorus
to major roles, the story (by Bess Meredyth,
screenplay by Meredyth and George Marion Jr)
centred on the attempts of a temperamental
coloratura (Alice Brady in fine form) to establish
a rival opera company in Philadelphia. Virginia
Bruce co-starred as an ambitious soprano, with
other roles going to Cesar Romero (as a tenor),
Luis Alberni (right), Thurston Hall, George
Marion Sr (left), and Ruth Donnelly. Darryl F.
Zanuck produced, and the excellent direction
was by Richard Boleslawski. The music featured
the negro spiritual 'De Glory Road' by Clement
Wood and J. Russell Bodley and 'On The Road To
Mandalay' by Rudyard Kipling and Oley Speaks,
as well as the operatic sequences which included
arias from Gounod's *Faust* (Tibbett, Bruce); arias
from Rossini's *The Barber of Seville* (Tibbett); The
Prologue to Leoncavallo's *Pagliacci* (Tibbett);
The Toreador Song from Bizet's *Carmen* (Tibbett); The Gypsy Song from *Carmen* (Alice Brady)
and Micaela's Aria from *Carmen* (Bruce). Interesting sideline: This film saw the beginning of
the ill-fated career of Harold Arlen and E.Y.
Harburg's composition 'Last Night When We
Were Young'. It was cut from the film except as
background music, and cut again from later
movies in versions by Judy Garland and Frank
Sinatra on the grounds that it was too sad.

Warner Bros.' **I Live For Love** (GB: **I Live For
You**) was a 64-minute musical programmer
which had little to distinguish it from other 64-
minute programmers. Jerry Wald, Julius J.
Epstein and Robert Andrews wrote the screenplay about a volatile South American actress's
romance with a glamorous street singer, the
roles going to Dolores Del Rio (right) and Everett
Marshall (left), the latter singularly lacking
the charms and/or attractiveness the story
called for. Surprisingly enough, however, the
movie turned in satisfactory box-office returns,
thanks entirely to director Busby Berkeley who,
when called on to do so, was always able to make
the most with the least. The production was
by Bryan Foy, and had a cast that included
Guy Kibbee, Allen Jenkins, Berton Churchill,
Don Alvarado (centre), Hobart Cavanaugh and
Mary Treen. Orry-Kelly designed the gowns,
and the five songs, mainly ballads for Marshall,
were by Mort Dixon and Allie Wrubel. Best of the
bunch was 'Mine Alone'. The others were: *Silver
Wings*; *I Wanna Play House*; *I Live For Love*; *A Man
Must Shave*.
▽

Thanks a Million (20th Century-Fox) was a racy
musical with a political background and, no
doubt, the phrase uttered by legions of satisfied
customers on leaving the cinema. Intelligently
written by Nunnally Johnson, and with a
genuine sense of humour coursing through it, it
starred Dick Powell (centre, with The Yacht
Club Boys) on loan from Warner Bros., as a
candidate for the Governorship of Pennsylvania,
and Fred Allen as the manager of a musical
comedy troupe who fervently believes that what
politics needs is a lot more entertainment. In a
brilliant debut performance, he sets out to prove
it. Ann Dvorak provided the romance and, after
walking out of Powell's life when he is successfully elected, walks right back into it after he
proves his love for her by resigning. His voters,
however, refuse to let the dictates of his heart
louse up their whole campaign, and insist that
he return to office; which, with Miss Dvorak's
approval and support, he does. Also cast: Patsy
Kelly, Raymond Walburn, Benny Baker,
Andrew Tombes, Alan Dinehart and Paul
Harvey. Darryl F. Zanuck produced, and the
director was Roy Del Ruth. The film was remade
by 20th Century-Fox in 1946 as *If I'm Lucky*.
Songs: *Thanks A Million*; *I'm Sitting High On a
Hilltop*; *Sugar Plum*; *New O'leans*; *Sing Brother*;
I've Got A Pocketful Of Sunshine; *The Square Deal
Party* Gus Kahn, Arthur Johnston; *Happy Days
Are Here Again* Jack Yellen, Milton Ager.
▽

Nino Martini possessed a strong tenor voice but
very little acting ability, as was evident in **Here's
to Romance** (Fox) – a plodding tale about a
singer's struggles *en route* to the Metropolitan
Opera House. Genevieve Tobin played a wealthy
society matron who fancies Signor Martini's
chances of success almost as much as she fancies
Signor Martini; Anita Louise was the tenor's
sweetheart, and Reginald Denny Miss Tobin's
husband, and Maria Gambarelli (illustrated)
were also featured. The great soprano Ernestine
Schumann–Heink played Martini's singing
teacher and, in one of the film's better moments,
sang Brahms' *Lullaby*. It was written by Ernest
Pascal and Arthur Rickman from a story by
Pascal and Sonya Levien, produced by Jesse
Lasky, and directed by Alfred E. Green. Songs:
Midnight in Paris; *Here's To Romance*; *I Carry You
In My Pocket* Ralph L. Grosvenor; as well as
operatic extracts from Mascagni's *Cavalleria
Rusticana*, Leoncavallo's *Pagliacci*, Puccini's
Tosca and Massenet's *Manon*.
▽

THIRTIES MUSICALS

△

Dizzy Dames (Liberty) found Marjorie Rambeau all in a tizz. Unbeknown to her daughter, she has been running a theatrical boarding house. And, although the place is perfectly respectable, a telegram announcing the daughter's imminent arrival at the establishment causes something of an uproar, with the residents having to promise to behave like proper ladies and gentlemen. It was pretty nonsensical stuff (suggested by a P.G. Wodehouse short story and scripted by George Waggner), but a production number called 'Martinique' by Arthur Swanstrom, George Waggner and Louis Alter and sung by Lillian Miles, had its moments. The rest of the score was routine. The director was veteran William Nigh, and his cast included Florine McKinney (as the daughter, right), Lawrence Gray (who got to sing most of the songs), Inez Courtney, John Warburton (left), Berton Churchill, Fuzzy Knight and Kitty Kelly. M.H. Hoffman produced. Other songs included: Love Is The Thing Harry Tobias, Neil Moret; I Was Taken By Storm Edward Heyman, Louis Alter; Let's Be Frivolous Howard Jackson, George Waggner.

If Grace Moore could heap prestige and, more importantly, box-office returns, on Columbia, then Lily Pons could do the same for RKO. Or so reasoned producer Pandro S. Berman, still flushed with the success of his Astaire–Rogers films. With this belief firmly in mind, he commissioned a screenplay that would suit the vocal and dramatic qualities of the diminutive Metropolitan Opera star. The result was I Dream Too Much (screenplay by James Gow and Edmund North from a story by Elsie Finn and David G. Wittels), about a provincial lass who is alerted by a French impresario to the fact that she has an excellent voice, and should become a singer. It also starred Henry Fonda as the young operatic composer Miss Pons marries, and to whose own career she then devotes all her energies until success eventually comes to him after the opera he has been working on for years is rewritten as a musical comedy, starring his wife. Directed by John Cromwell, with good performances from both Miss Pons (left) and Fonda (right), and a supporting cast that included Eric Blore (as a seal trainer), Osgood Perkins (as the impresario), Lucien Littlefield, Esther Dale, Scotty Beckett and Lucille Ball. several new songs by Jerome Kern and Dorothy Fields, and extracts from Verdi's Rigoletto ('Caro Nome') and Delibes's Lakme ('Bell Song') it couldn't miss – and didn't. The orchestra was conducted by Andre Kostelanetz, Pons's real-life husband. Songs: I Dream Too Much; Jockey On The Carousel (with Jimmy McHugh); I Got Love; I'm The Echo, You're The Song.

△

Ginger Rogers (left) took time off from her full-scale musicals with Fred Astaire to appear in a minor effort called In Person (RKO), for which she received top billing. But in 1935, Rogers without Astaire was like Amos without Andy, as producer Pandro S. Berman discovered to the studio's cost in his silly tale about a film star whose fear of being recognized in public results in her donning a wig, glasses and false teeth as part of her obsessional quest for anonymity. Like its heroine, scenarist Allan Scott (story by Samuel Hopkins Adams) should have done something to disguise the plot from being recognized as the twaddle it was. Instead it was left to a cast that included George Brent (right), Alan Mowbray, Grant Mitchell and Samuel S. Hinds to make something of it – which none of them was able to do. The director was William A. Seiter with Hermes Pan in charge of the dances. Songs included: Don't Mention Love To Me; Got A New Lease On Life; Out Of Sight Out Of Mind Dorothy Fields, Oscar Levant.

A really inept entertainment about a wealthy young man and the poor, seaside resort singer he falls for (but from whom he keeps his healthy financial situation a secret), Coronado (Paramount) starred Johnny Downs (left) and Betty Burgess as the young lovers, as well as the victims of a screenplay (by Don Hartman and Frank Butler; story by Hartman and Brian Hooker) so polluted with clichés, that it was a miracle they survived the ordeal at all. The film was less fortunate than they and suffered a painful and humiliating demise at the box office. Also cast: Jack Haley (right), Leon Errol, Alice White, Jameson Thomas, Berton Churchill, Nella Walker, and Eddy Duchin and His Orchestra. William Le Baron was the producer, and it was directed by Norman McLeod. Songs: All's Well In Coronado By The Sea; You Took My Breath Away; How Do I Rate With You?; Keep Your Fingers Crossed; Midsummer Madness; Down On The Beach At Oomph; Mashed Potatoes Sam Coslow, Richard A. Whiting; I've Got Some New Shoes Coslow, Walter Bullock, Whiting; Which Is Which Sidney Clare, Troy Sanders.

The oft-told tale of a showgirl's rise to stardom turned up yet again in **Broadway Hostess** (Warner Bros./First National), starring Winifred Shaw. It didn't make any impact though, with its colourless screenplay by George Bricker failing to ignite Frank McDonald's mundane direction. Bobby Connolly staged the dances, Bryan Foy supervised the production, and other unfortunate accessories to the fact were Genevieve Tobin (centre right), Lyle Talbot (centre), Allen Jenkins (right), Phil Regan, Marie Wilson and Spring Byington. Songs: *He Was Her Man*; *Let It Be Me*; *Weary*; *Who But You*; *Playboy Of Paris* Mort Dixon, Allie Wrubel; *Only The Girl* Herman Ruby, M.K. Jerome.

A really inexcusable effort from the studio that gave the world *Top Hat*, **To Beat The Band** (RKO) starred Hugh Herbert who, in order to gain custody of a large estate has, according to a clause in his aunt's will, to marry a widow. As Mr Herbert already has a fiancée, he finds himself in something of a quandary. So what he does is to prevail upon a potential suicide to marry his girl as soon as possible in the hope that it won't be too long before she is duly widowed. It was written by Rian James from a story by George Marion Jr, produced by Zion Myers, and directed by Ben Stoloff with a cast that included Helen Broderick (right), Roger Pryor, Eric Blore (left), Phyllis Brooks and Evelyn Poe. Also in it were Johnny Mercer and The California Collegians, and Fred Keating and His Orchestra. Songs: *Eeny-Meeny-Miney-Mo*; *I Saw Her At Eight O'Clock*; *If You Were Mine*; *Meet Miss America*; *Santa Claus Came In The Spring* Johnny Mercer, Matt Malneck.

Little more than an excuse for a series of musical items mainly featuring Ted Lewis (left foreground) and His Orchestra, **Here Comes The Band** (MGM) was a modest effort, skilfully directed by Paul Sloane from his own story, and a screenplay by Victor Mansfield and Ralph Spence. The plot line concerned the efforts of an impoverished young song writer (aren't they all?) to see that justice is done when a crooked music publisher (aren't they all?) steals his song. He is helped by a wealthy young girl and the finale takes place in a courtroom where the composer has gathered together several ethnic groups from across the country who, at a given moment, start singing to the judge in an attempt to prove that the song in question wasn't only written by the composer in question – but was inspired by American folk music. Harry Stockwell, father of the more famous Dean, made his debut as the composer ('he looks like Franchot Tone and sounds like Nelson Eddy' was how the publicity blurb described him); Virginia Bruce was his girlfriend, with Ted Healy and Nat Pendleton as a couple of taxi drivers. Also: Billy Gilbert (hilarious in a sneezing routine), Herman Bing (as a yodeller), Donald Cook, Spanky MacFarland and Bert Roach. The producer was Lucien Hubbard. Songs: *Heading Home* Ned Washington, Herbert Stothart; *Roll Along Prairie Moon* Ted Fiorito, Cecil Mack, Albert von Tilzer; *Tender is The Night* Harold Adamson, Walter Donaldson; *You're My Thrill* Washington, Burton Lane; *I'm Bound For Heaven*; *The Army Band* Adamson, Lane.

A skilful retread of *Daddy Longlegs* (First National, 1919, and Fox, 1931), **Curly Top** was another unashamed Shirley Temple vehicle which again revealed this phenomenally talented little institution to be one of the screen's great success stories. Rescuing the kind of screenplay (by Patterson McNutt and Arthur Beckhard; story by Jean Webster) that usually drives sane men and women to dipsomania, Shirley single-handedly notched up a box-office triumph for 20th Century-Fox, and, in the process, introduced the world to 'Animal Crackers' (by Ted Koehler, Irving Caesar and Ray Henderson). She also danced a hula (illustrated) in the film and did a classy tap routine on top of a grand piano while co-star John Boles who, in the course of the story, adopts little Shirley but marries Rochelle Hudson, her older sister, sang the film's title song. Also cast were Jane Darwell, Esther Dale, Rafaela Ottiano and, as Boles's butler, Arthur Treacher. Its *schmaltz*-laden direction was by Irving Cummings (the film's opening shot held the dimpled Miss Temple in close-up for an inordinately long time) and the producer was Winfield Sheehan. It was remade in 1955 as *Daddy Long Legs* (20th Century-Fox), a vehicle for Fred Astaire and Leslie Caron. Other songs: *It's All So New To Me* Koehler, Caesar, Henderson; *Curly Top* Koehler, Henderson; *The Simple Things In Life*; *When I Grow Up* Edward Heyman, Henderson.

Stars Over Broadway (Warner Bros.) marked the screen debuts of popular singer Jane Froman and operatic tenor James Melton, whose movie careers entirely failed to happen for them. The world of radio, in which the film was set, provided an unoriginal background for an unoriginal story about an agent (Pat O'Brien, left) who turns a hotel porter (Melton) into a radio star. Trouble is, when Melton makes it to the top of the pop air-waves, he decides he really wants to be an opera singer. O'Brien objects, which sends Melton to the bottle, so O'Brien reluctantly gives in. All ends happily with Melton going off to Italy for operatic training. Somewhere in the middle of all this Jane Froman warbled away – to rather better advantage than her spoken moments which were pitiful. Supervisor Sam Bischoff showed great perception when, doubting the drawing power of his stars, he scaled down his budget accordingly. This pleased the studio accountants, but diminished the contributions of dance directors Busby Berkeley and Bobby Connolly, necessitating the complete elimination of a major Berkeley item showing a forest of silver trees that swayed prettily to Al Dubin and Harry Warren's 'September In The Rain'. Jerry Wald and Julius J. Epstein wrote the screenplay from a story by Mildred Cram; and William Keighley directed a cast that also featured Jean Muir (right), Frank McHugh, Phil Regan, Frank Fay and E.E. Clive. The Al Dubin–Harry Warren songs included *Broadway Cinderella*; *Where Am I?*; *At Your Service Madam*; *You Let Me Down*; *Over Yonder Moon*; *September In The Rain* (background music only). There were also operatic excerpts from Verdi's *Aida* and Flotow's *Martha*, and a number by Carson J. Robison called *Carry Me Back To The Lone Prairie*.

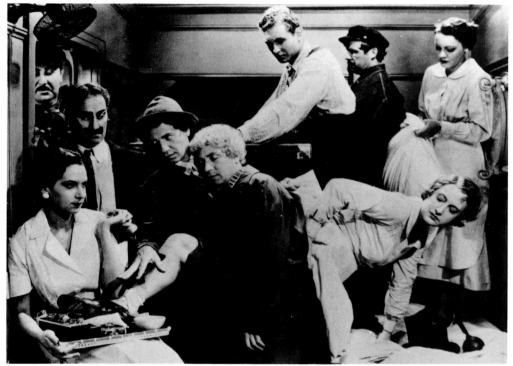

Irving Thalberg continued to siphon off Paramount's top stars by signing the Marx Brothers, minus Zeppo (who preferred to dissociate himself from heavy filming commitments, being happier with a commercial enterprise in which he was involved), to a long-term contract at MGM with the promise of more money and stronger production values as bait. The brothers bit, and their first effort for the studio was **A Night At The Opera** – one of the best films they made at MGM and a classic screen comedy that has never lost its zest, familiarity with its jokes and its routines breeding content. Written by George S. Kaufman and Morrie Ryskind (from a story by James Kevin McGuiness) many of whose gags were, at Thalberg's insistence, first 'tried out' on the road by the brothers as proof of their efficacy (or otherwise), its manic plot had Groucho posing as an opera impresario in the hope of coming between Margaret Dumont and her considerable fortune (a portion of which he wishes to relieve her of), and Chico managing the non-existent operatic career of an ambitious tenor. What Harpo was up to was anyone's guess – apart from making life hazardous for those unfortunate enough to cross his path. The comic business invented by the writers and the brothers under the guidance of director Sam Wood reached a climax in a performance of Verdi's *Il Trovatore* with Harpo doing his level

best to cause a one-man revolution backstage. ('A battleship in 'Il Trovatore' the haughty Miss Dumont exclaims as Harpo gleefully lowers a backdrop of one during Azucena's scene at the gypsy encampment.) But there were lots of other things to laugh at as well, such as the stateroom scene (illustrated), in which a battalion of people sardine their way into a cabin not much bigger than the trunk that's in it already; or the sequence in which the brothers (who are stowaways) attend a mayoral gathering in New York disguised as Russian aviators as a means of avoiding detection. Allan Jones (centre) in a role that would originally have been played by Zeppo, was cast as the tenor whom Chico manages, with Kitty Carlisle as his love interest. Sig Rumann, Edward Keane and Robert Emmett O'Connor completed the cast. Apart from the operatic sequence that climaxed the film, and the obligatory piano and harp solos by you-know-who (Chico played Nacio Herb Brown's 'All I Do Is Dream Of You'; Harpo reprised 'Alone' by Nacio Herb Brown and Arthur Freed). **A Night At The Opera** contained two additional songs: the aforesaid 'Alone' which, sung by Jones and Miss Carlisle, was the most successful standard to emerge from a Marx Brothers film to date. Also: 'Cosi Cosa' by Ned Washington, Bronislau Kaper and Walter Jurmann.

◁
A stewpot of a musical whose indigestible ingredients included anti-war propaganda, pacifism, gangsterism and a touch of the old mistaken-identity ruse, **Sweet Surrender** (Universal) asked audiences to do just that where its plot was concerned, but failed to provide the wherewithal for doing so. Set largely on board a Europe-bound ocean liner, and involving a crooner (Frank Parker, left), his dancer sweetheart (Tamara, making her screen debut), and the dancer's double (also played by Tamara), it lacked conviction in every department but primarily in the performances of its leading man and most of the supporting players (including comedians Helen Lynd, right, and Russ Brown, and Arthur Pearson as the heavy). Only Tamara in her dual role evinced anything that remotely resembled talent, and her dancing, especially in the 'Appassionata' finale, performed at the Paris Opera House no less, was the highspot of a pretty dire show. It was written by John V.A. Weaver from an original story by Herbert Fields, and adapted by Charles Beahan. It was presented by Carl Laemmle, and the director was Monte Brice. Songs: *Love Makes The World Go Round; Take This Ring; I'm So Happy I Could Cry; The Day You Were Born; Twenty Four Hours A Day* Edward Heyman, Dana Suesse, James Hanley, Arthur Swanstrom.

Though Alice Faye was top billed in **Music Is Magic**, it was Bebe Daniels (given third billing) who had the showier part; just as the fourth-billed Frances Langford in *Every Night At Eight* (Fox) was the real star of that one despite Faye's above-the-title status. Miss Daniels, whose last American film this was to be, played an ageing actress who, after passing off her daughter as her sister in a futile attempt to keep the years at bay, finally accepts the fact that she is no longer a youngster, and graciously allows Faye (left), hitherto relegated to the chorus, to go on in her place. One of the first musicals to be made by the newly formed 20th Century-Fox company, it eschewed opulence, concentrating instead on the intrinsic talent of its stars. The result was a modest musical programmer that ran a mere 66 minutes, featured several passable songs, the resistible participation of comedians Frank Mitchell and Jack Durant (illustrated – mercifully their last appearance in a Faye musical), as well as Ray Walker, Rosina Lawrence, Thomas Beck, Luis Alberni, Lynn Bari and the always welcome Hattie McDaniel – also called Hattie in the film, but Amanda in the credits. It was written by Edward Eliscu and Lou Breslow from a play by Gladys Unger and Jesse Lasky Jr, the dances were staged by Jack Donohue, the associate producer was John Stone and the director George Marshall. Songs: *Honey Chile; Love Is Smiling At Me* Oscar Levant, Sidney Clare; *Music Is Magic* Arthur Johnston, Clare; *La Locumba* Raul Roulien, Clare.

▽

The storyline of **Old Man Rhythm** (RKO) strayed from the usual campus formula (but only slightly) in having a father (George Barbier) enrol as a freshman at his son's college in order to keep a watchful eye on the lad's extra-mural activities. Charles 'Buddy' Rogers was the son, Grace Bradley the gold-digger he falls for, but who walks out on him after she hears that his family have been ruined financially in a business deal. Also cast: Barbara Kent, Betty Grable, Eric Blore, Eric Rhodes, John Arledge (left), Donald Meek, Johnny Mercer (right), Erich Von Stroheim Jr, Claude Gillingwater Jr, Douglas Fowley (2nd left), and as a coed, Lucille Ball. It was written by Sig Herzig and Ernest Pagano (story by Lewis Gensler, Herzig and Don Hartman). Hermes Pan staged the dance numbers and the director was Edward Ludwig. Songs: *Old Man Rhythm*; *I Never Saw A Better Night*; *There's Nothing Like A College Education*; *Boys Will Be Boys*; *When You Are In My Arms*; *Come The Revolution Baby* Johnny Mercer, Lewis Gensler.

Dixie Lee's (centre) problem in **Redheads on Parade** (Fox) was how to vamp the amorous elderly backer of her show (who would otherwise withdraw his financial support) without incurring the jealousy of her lover and co-star John Boles. Scenarists Rian James and Don Hartman's problem (story by Hartman, Gertrude Purcell and Jay Gorney) was how to make it all meaningful to an audience tired of the machinations of show-folk. They partially succeeded thanks to the yeoman support of a cast that also included Alan Dinehart and Jack Haley and a handful of okay songs. The director was Norman McLeod. Songs and musical numbers: *I Found A Dream*; *Good Night Kiss*; *I Like Myself For Liking You*; *Redheads On Parade*; *I've Got Your Future All Planned*; *Tinsel Town*; *You Beautiful Thing* Don Hartman, Jay Gorney.

Very little money was spent on **The Old Homestead** (Liberty), a programmer (lobby card illustrated) which chronicled the big-city adventures of a country band who attract the attention of a radio talent scout in New York. Mary Carlisle, Lawrence Gray and Fuzzy Knight starred, and the director was William Nigh. Songs: *Moonlight In Heaven* Jack Scholl, Louis Alter; *Somehow I Know* Harry Tobias, Neil Moret, Charles Rosoff; *The Plowboy* J. Keirn Brennan, Ted Snyder; *When The Old Age Pension Check Comes To Our Door* Manny Stone.

Radio's amateur hour provided the inspiration for **Millions in the Air** (Paramount), which could just as easily have been called 'Son Of The Big Broadcast of 1936'. A flimsy story (sponsor's daughter conceals her true identity in order to appear on her father's show with a singing ice-cream salesman) provided the merest of excuses for a series of musical and comedy items. Among those helping to turn the Paramount lot into a broadcasting studio were John Howard (left, ice-cream salesman), Wendy Barrie (right, sponsor's daughter), George Barbier (the Sponsor), plus Robert Cummings, Inez Courtney, Dave Chasen, Benny Baker, Bennie Bartlett, Eleanore Whitney, Alden Chase and Joan Davis. It was written by Sig Herzig and Jane Storm, produced by Harold Hurley and directed by Ray McCarey. Songs included: *Laughing At The Weather Man*; *A Penny In My Pocket* Ralph Rainger, Leo Robin; *You Tell Her – I Stutter* Billy Rose, Cliff Friend; *Love Is Just Around The Corner* Leo Robin, Lewis Gensler.

In **Ship Café** (Universal) Carl Brisson played a ship's stoker who discovers that he can get the boat going in more ways than one – he can sing. Cue for a few songs, and some rather tepid romance as supplied by an adventurous, self-seeking society vamp (Mady Christians) and the more genuine Arline Judge. A programme musical (it was all over in 65 minutes), it also featured Eddie Davis (illustrated) and William Frawley, had a screenplay by Harlan Thompson and Herbert Fields, and was directed by Robert Florey. Songs: *Fatal Fascination*; *I Won't Take No For An Answer*; *It's A Great Life*; *I Lost My Heart*; *Change Your Mind* Ray Noble.

1936

Academy Awards

Best Picture
The Great Ziegfeld (MGM) produced by Hunt Stromberg
NOMINATIONS INCLUDED: *San Francisco* (MGM) produced by John Emerson and Bernard H. Hyman

Best Actor
NOMINATIONS INCLUDED: Spencer Tracy *San Francisco*

Best Actress
Luise Rainer *The Great Ziegfeld*

Best Supporting Actor
(New category)
NOMINATIONS INCLUDED: Stuart Erwin *Pigskin Parade* (20th Century-Fox)

Direction
NOMINATIONS INCLUDED: Robert Z. Leonard *The Great Ziegfeld*. W.S. Van Dyke *San Francisco*.

Writing (Original story)
NOMINATIONS INCLUDED: *The Great Ziegfeld* William Anthony McGuire. *San Francisco* Robert Hopkins. *Three Smart Girls* (Universal) Adele Commandini.

Art Direction
NOMINATIONS INCLUDED: *The Great Ziegfeld* Cedric Gibbons, Eddie Imazu & Edwin B. Willis

Sound Recording
San Francisco Douglas Shearer
NOMINATIONS INCLUDED: *Banjo On My Knee* (20th Century-Fox) E.H. Hansen. *That Girl From Paris* (RKO) Franklin Hansen. *Three Smart Girls* Homer G. Tasker.

Film Editing
NOMINATIONS INCLUDED: *The Great Ziegfeld* William S. Gray

Song
'The Way You Look Tonight' *Swing Time* (RKO) Jerome Kern *cm*; Dorothy Fields *lyr*.
NOMINATIONS INCLUDED: 'I've Got You Under My Skin' *Born To Dance* (MGM) Cole Porter. 'Pennies Heaven' from *Pennies from Heaven* (Columbia) Arthur Johnston *cm*; Johnny Burke *lyr*. 'When Did You Leave Heaven' *Sing Baby Sing* (20th Century-Fox) Richard A. Whiting *cm*; Walter Bullock *lyr*.

Assistant Director
NOMINATIONS INCLUDED: Joseph Newman for *San Francisco*

Dance Direction
Seymour Felix for 'A Pretty Girl Is Like A Melody' number from *The Great Ziegfeld*.
NOMINATIONS INCLUDED: Busby Berkeley for 'Love And War' number from *Gold Diggers Of 1937* (WB). Bobby Connolly for '1000 Love Songs' number from *Cain and Mabel* (WB). Dave Gould for 'Swingin' The Jinx' number from *Born To Dance*. Jack Haskell for 'Skating Ensemble' number from *One In A Million* (20th Century-Fox). Russell Lewis for 'The Finale' number from *Dancing Pirate* (RKO). Hermes Pan for 'Bo Jangles' number from *Swing Time*.

The New York Times Film Critic Awards
Best Actress
Luise Rainer *The Great Ziegfeld*

The New York Times Annual 'Ten Best'
(eleven films this year)
11th *The Great Ziegfeld*

The Annual Top Moneymaking Films
INCLUDING: *Broadway Melody Of 1936* (MGM). *Follow The Fleet* (RKO). *The Great Ziegfeld*. *The King Steps Out* (Columbia). *A Night At The Opera* (MGM). *Rhythm On The Range* (Paramount). *Rose Marie* (MGM). *San Francisco*. *Show Boat* (Universal). *Thanks a Million* (Fox).

△ Paramount's **Collegiate** (GB: **The Charm School**) was the sort of programmer that made the other half of a double bill thoroughly embarrassed at the company it was keeping. Though Joe Penner (left) received top billing, the story (by Alice Duer Miller, screenplay by Walter DeLeon and Frances Martin) revolved around co-star Jack Oakie whose man-about-Broadway life-style is somewhat disrupted when he learns that, thanks to a clause in his aunt's will, he has become the dean of a girl's college. Adding one more 'r' to the three r's – Oakie introduces a course in rhythm, appointing Betty Jane Cooper as dance instructress and tunesmiths Mack Gordon and Harry Revel as song coaches. Cue for several musical numbers (by Gordon and Revel) and not much else. Penner played an amnesiac who finds himself in possession of a large bankroll, with other parts going to Ned Sparks, Lynne Overman (as Oakie's Man Friday), Frances Langford, Betty Grable (right), Henry Kolker and Donald Gallagher. Louis Lighton produced and the director was Ralph Murphy. 'I Feel Like A Feather In The Breeze' and 'You Hit The Spot' were the best two numbers in a score which included 'Rhythmatic' and 'My Grandfather's Clock In The Hallway'.

Strike Me Pink was the sixth and last film Eddie Cantor (left) made for Samuel Goldwyn and, as usual, it contained all the familiar Cantoresque ingredients. Fourteen writers, legend has it, worked on the screenplay (though only three were credited: Frank Butler, Francis Martin and Philip Rapp; story by Clarence Budington Kelland) and what they eventually came up with was the tale of a timid little tailor who, after purchasing a book called: *Man Or Mouse: What Are You?*, becomes (with the help of girlfriend Sally Eilers) king pin on the campus by agreeing to run an amusement park, unaware that several notorious gangsters are more than just slightly interested in the slot-machine concession. How, in a breathless, knockabout finale, he manages to help the police apprehend the heavies, provided the film with its main comic set-piece. For the rest it was the music that counted – with co-star Ethel Merman (right) prominently featured in three of the four numbers written especially for the film by Harold Arlen and Lew Brown (and staged by Robert Alton). Norman Taurog directed it all for the whacky nonsense it was, and his cast was completed by William Frawley, Parkyakarkus (Harry Parke), Helen Lovell, Gordon Jones, Brian Donlevy, Jack La Rue, Sunnie O'Dea, Rita Rio (later Dona Drake), Edward Brophy and the 1936 Goldwyn Girls. Songs: *First You Have Me High, Then You Have Me Low* (Merman); *The Lady Dances* (Cantor, Rio, Goldwyn Girls); *Calabash Pipe* (Cantor, Merman); *Shake It Off With Rhythm* (Merman, Goldwyn Girls).

Darryl F. Zanuck relied on Alice Faye to sell **King of Burlesque** (20th Century-Fox) rather than on costly production numbers, and instructed dance director Sammy Lee to avoid overhead shots and feather boas like the plague. The result was a backstage musical efficiently directed by Sidney Lanfield, fairly modest in scale, but generous in entertainment value. It also benefitted from a first-class screenplay by Harry Tugend (based on a story by Vina Delmar, and adapted by James Seymour), the main business of which concerned the rise, fall and resurrection of a small-time burlesque entrepreneur who, after graduating to Broadway and presenting a string of popular hit shows, marries above his station, produces an ultra-sophisticated flop, divorces his wife, returns to Broadway after a down-and-out period, and, with the help of Miss Faye (left), as well as an elevator operator, a boot-black, telephonist and

an office boy (all with show-business in their ▷ blood) puts on a revue that turns out to be a smash. It was spiritedly performed by a strong cast that included Warner Baxter (centre, as the producer), Jack Oakie (right, as Baxter's right-hand man), Mona Barrie (as the society broad Baxter marries), Arline Judge (as Oakie's intended), Gregory Ratoff (as an impecunious show backer) – as well as Fats Waller, Nick Long Jr, Kenny Baker and Charles Quigley. An excellent score provided Alice Faye with several hits ('I'm Shooting High', 'Whose Big Baby Are You', 'I've Got My Fingers Crossed' and 'Spreading Rhythm Around') by Jimmy McHugh and Ted Koehler. Other songs: *Lovely Lady* (by McHugh and Koehler) and *I Love To Ride The Horses* (by Jack Yellen and Lew Pollack). It was remade in 1943 as *Hello, Frisco, Hello* (20th Century-Fox), with Alice Faye again providing the glamour in the same role as before.

John Boles starred in **Rose of the Rancho** (Paramount) as a government agent out to track down a mysterious character by the name of Don Carlos, whose nocturnal activities involve him in leading a group of Spanish vigilantes against a posse of land-grabbers. Except that Don Carlos isn't a man at all, but lovely Gladys Swarthout (illustrated – her debut) whose daytime activities, as the daughter of Don Pascual – give no indication of the grit of which the girl is made. A sort of distaff *Desert Song* but without, alas, a score to match (although one song, 'If I Should Lose You' by Ralph Rainger and Leo Robin, has stood the test of time) – **Rose of the Rancho** – based on a play by Richard Walton Tully and David Belasco, and written for the screen by Frank P. Partos, Charles Brackett, Arthur Sheekman and Nat Perrin (adaptation by Harlan Thompson and Brian Hooker), was an uneasy mixture of operetta and low-comedy (the latter in the capable hands of Willie Howard, essaying the role of a Jewish cowboy called Pancho Spiegelgass and Herb Williams as an insurance broker) that never knew in what direction it wished to go. Charles Bickford, Grace Bradley, H.B. Warner, Charlotte Granville and Don Alvarado were also in it, William Le Baron produced, and Marion Gering directed. Songs: *If I Should Lose You*; *Thunder Over The Prairie*; *Little Rose Of The Rancho*; *Got A Girl In Cal-i-for-ni-ay*; *There's Gold In Monterey*; *Where Is My Love*; *The Padre And The Bride* Rainger, Robin.
▽

Paramount acquired the rights to Cole Porter's 1934 smash hit musical **Anything Goes** (with a book by Guy Bolton and P.G. Wodehouse which Howard Lindsay and Russel Crouse revised) and brought it to the screen with several of the original Porter songs intact, and with Ethel Merman (centre) repeating the role she created on the stage. Victor Moore and William Gaxton, however, were not on hand to impart to the film version some of the qualities that made the show such a success on Broadway – their roles being played instead by Charles Ruggles and Bing Crosby. All of which meant that the aptly titled **Anything Goes**, while it had quite a lot going for it, did not, alas, have everything. Mr Moore's absence was a grievous body blow to the undertaking, which nothing Ruggles did as the Rev. D. Moon – Public Enemy Number 13 – could disguise. What basically the film lacked, was sparkle – the one ingredient its rather silly

book cried out for if it was to make any kind of musical comedy sense at all. But it *did* have Ethel Merman singing 'You're The Top' and 'I Get A Kick Out Of You' plus two more Porter standards, as well as a few new songs by several other accomplished writers, so all was not lost. The story, which concerned Crosby's shipboard romance with an English heiress (Ida Lupino), the furtherance of which required him to pose as a gangster, was re-worked for the screen by Walter DeLeon, Sidney Salkow, John C. Moffit and Francis Martin. Benjamin Glazer produced it, and the director was Lewis Milestone. Also cast: Arthur Treacher and Margaret Dumont. Other songs included: *Anything Goes*; *All Through The Night* (background only); *There'll Always Be A Lady Fair* Porter; *Sailor Beware* Richard A. Whiting, Leo Robin; *Shanghi-de Ho*; *My Heart and I* Frederick Hollander, Robin; *Moonburn* Edward Heyman, Hoagy Carmichael. Remade 1956.

△

Colleen was Ruby Keeler's penultimate film for Warner Bros. and the sixth and last time she would co-star with Dick Powell. However, the hitherto popular twosome, with Miss Keeler (left) at her least animated, were unable to rescue Peter Milne, Sig Herzig and F. Hugh Herbert's paltry screenplay (from a story by Robert Lord) and the film failed to find many takers. All about an eccentric millionaire (Hugh Herbert) who, after hiring a gold-digging floozie (Joan Blondell) to run his dress shop for him, finds himself having to contend with nephew Powell's scheme to replace Blondell with honest, sincere Miss Keeler, it featured Jack Oakie, Louise Fazenda, Paul Draper (right), Marie Wilson, Luis Alberni and Hobart Cavanaugh. Alfred E. Green directed, and the dance numbers were staged without much zest or imagination by Bobby Connolly. The score, by Al Dubin and Harry Warren, was one of the least distinguished of their career. Songs: *I Don't Have To Dream Again*; *You've Gotta Know How To Dance*; *An Evening With You*; *A Boulevardier From The Bronx*.

Though Mae West (illustrated) took to religion ▷ in **Klondike Annie** (Paramount), she still had to mind her p's and q's as far as the censor was concerned, with the result that the quips in her latest offering were decidedly short of innuendo. ('I can always tell a lady,' remarks co-star Victor McLaglen, to which comes the reply, 'Yeah? What do you tell 'em?') But Mae West functioning at only 60° proof was better than nothing, and there was enough of her intrinsic personality to keep her fans contented in this tale of a Barbary Coast broad (West) who, after murdering her Chinese lover (Harold Huber), hops on a freighter for the Klondike, takes the place of a recently deceased Salvation Army sister, and, once in the Klondike, gives a decided shot in the arm to the religious services at which she officiates. And whatever one might have said about her material, no one complained when she declared, in words and music by Gene Austin, that she was just an 'Occidental Woman In An Oriental Mood For Love'. Philip Reed, Soo Yong, Lucille Webster Gleason, Helen Jerome Eddy, Tetsu Komai, Harry Beresford and Conway Tearle were in it too, it was written by Miss West from her play of the same name (story by Marian Morgan and George B. Dowell) with additional material suggested by Frank Mitchell Dazey. William Le Baron produced and the director was Raoul Walsh. Other songs: *Mister Deep Blue Sea*; *Cheer Up Little Sister*; *I Hear You Knockin' But You Can't Come In*; *It's Never Too Late To Say No*; *This May Not Be Love But It's Wonderful*; *It's Better To Give Than To Receive*; *Open Up Your Heart And Let The Sunshine In* Gene Austin, James Johnson; *My Medicine Man* Sam Coslow.

◁ Originally intended as a vehicle for the increasingly popular Grace Moore, and rewritten to accommodate the soprano's operatic talents, Rudolf Friml's **Rose Marie** (MGM) underwent a change of plans when Miss Moore's commitments clashed with the film's shooting schedule. As it was imperative that the film be shot in summer (much of it on location in Lake Tahoe), Jeanette MacDonald (illustrated) was given the starring role. As she would again be teamed with Nelson Eddy, the studio was justifiably confident that the same people who paid to see *Naughty Marietta* would pay to see **Rose Marie**. Not that much of the original stage version's plot (first seen in 1924) survived the surgery performed on it by screenwriters Frances Goodrich, Albert Hackett and Alice Duer Miller. Instead of the backwoods singer originally intended by librettists Otto Harbach and Oscar Hammerstein II, Rose Marie La Flamme now became Marie de Flor, a Canadian opera singer of renown; and instead of the Mountie existing as a subsidiary character whose function was merely to assist in bringing the lovers together, he now became the hero who gets his woman. A virtual newcomer called James Stewart, in his second screen appearance, was cast as the soprano's errant brother who escapes from a penitentiary and, badly wounded, hides out in the north woods. The question is: who will find him first? His sister, or the Mountie with whom she eventually falls in love? With so much beautiful music and scenery on offer – plus the romantic appeal of the two stars – it didn't really matter much, happy endings being obligatory to plots of this sort anyway. *The* quintessential operetta, and probably the one most closely associated with MacDonald and Eddy, **Rose Marie** was, as MGM's hierarchy had hoped,

Based on the play by George M. Cohan, **Song and Dance Man** (20th Century-Fox) with a screenplay by Maude Fulton, was a platitudinous backstage story of a song and dance partnership. Claire Trevor (right) and Paul Kelly (left) were the performing duo, with Michael Whalen cast as the man Miss Trevor loves. What little plot there was concerned the unselfish sacrifices Kelly makes in order to ensure his partner's happiness with her handsome beau. Ruth Donnelly, James Burke, Helen Troy, Lester Matthews, Ralf Harolde, Gloria Roy and Margaret Dumont were in it too. Sol M. Wurtzel produced, and the director was Allan Dwan. Songs: *You're My Favourite One*; *On Holiday In My Playroom*; *Join The Party*; *Let's Get Going*; *Ain't He Good Looking?*; *Dancing In The Open* Sidney Clare, Lew Pollack.

▽

another box-office hit, collecting rave reviews and legions of new fans for its singing love-birds wherever it was shown. Apart from its stars, the film also featured Reginald Owen, Allan Jones (one of the studio's fastest-rising new talents), George Regas, Robert Greig, Una O'Connor, Lucien Littlefield, Alan Mowbray, Herman Bing, Gilda Gray and a young Englishman named David Nivens (later to become Niven). Hunt Stromberg produced and the director was again W.S. Van Dyke. Songs and musical numbers: *Rose Marie*; *Indian Love Call* Friml, Harbach, Hammerstein II; *The Mounties*; *Totem Tom Tom* Friml, Harbach, Stothart, Hammerstein II (staged by Chester Hale); *Just For You* (adapted from the original score's 'Finaletto' by Stothart, new lyrics by Gus Kahn); *Pardon Me Madame* Stothart, Gus Kahn; *Dinah* Harry Akst, Sam Lewis, Joe Young; *Some Of These Days* Shelton Brooks; *Tes Yeux* Rene Alphonse Rabey; scenes from Gounod's *Romeo and Juliet* and Puccini's *Tosca*. Remade in 1954.

After *Top Hat* (RKO, 1935) came **Follow the Fleet** ▷
(RKO) and it was apparent to all the world that
the fabulous team of Fred Astaire, Ginger Rogers
and Irving Berlin could do no wrong. Re-
furbished from a 1922 play by Hubert Osborne
called *Shore Leave* which, in turn, provided the
inspiration for the 1927 Broadway musical *Hit
The Deck* (filmed by RKO in 1930), its adapters
Dwight Taylor and Allan Scott concentrated the
serious love interest (as was the case in RKO's
Roberta, 1934) on its two co-stars, leaving
Astaire and Rogers free to entertain the customers. Which they did stupendously. He played
an ex-dancer turned sailor; she was a former
partner of his, now singing for her supper in a
San Francisco dance-hall. They meet up at a
dance contest and join forces to put on a fund-
raising show for the restoration of a schooner.
Heaven knows the plot was no masterpiece, but
at least it was innovative in that it dispensed
with the hitherto obligatory comedians (Blore,
Pangborn, Everett Horton *et al*) who usually
tagged along on such occasions. It allowed
Ginger Rogers to do a solo tap dance (her first
and last in an Astaire–Rogers musical), and, for
the first time in six movies took Astaire out of
formal attire and put him into something more
relaxed than top hat, white tie and tails – except
for one extremely formal number, the famous
'Let's Face The Music And Dance' (illustrated)
first sung by Astaire, then danced by him and
Rogers as the finale to their fund-raising effort.
The rest of the numbers showed the team in a
much more casual mood than audiences had
become used to, and the results were enchanting. Then, of course, there was Berlin's seductive
score. By alternating his more zingy numbers –
such as 'Let Yourself Go', first sung by Ginger,
then danced by her and Fred, and 'I'm Putting
All My Eggs In One Basket', introduced by
Astaire at the piano, then danced by both of
them in another of their 'competitive' routines –
with such sombre ballads as 'Get Thee Behind
Me Satan' and 'But Where Are You' both sung
by a lovelorn Harriet Hilliard, Berlin created a
perfectly balanced musical programme, every
one of whose songs have since become part of
America's rich musical heritage. Randolph Scott
appeared as Miss Hilliard's love interest, and the
man for whom the schooner is being salvaged;
with Astrid Allwyn, Ray Mayer, Harry Beresford, Addison Randall and Russell Hicks in
support. And if you look closely you'll catch
glimpses of Betty Grable, Lucille Ball and Tony
Martin. The film was produced by Pandro S.
Berman, choreographed by Hermes Pan, and
directed by Mark Sandrich. Other songs: *We Saw
The Sea; I'd Rather Lead A Band.*

Any resemblance between Hal Roach's **The
Bohemian Girl** (MGM) and Michael W. Balfe's
renowned operetta of the same name was pure
luck. But fidelity in this instance didn't matter at
all. What did were the comic antics of Laurel and
Hardy (left) who were given plenty of scope to
indulge themselves as a pair of Gypsy rogues
who adopt a little girl unaware that the child
(Darla Hood) is a princess. A fair share of
laughter and a fair share of the original score
guaranteed success at the box office – the slight
tremor audiences experienced on leaving the
cinema after each performance being Balfe
turning in his grave. It was directed by James W.
Horne and Charles Rogers, featured Jacqueline
Wells, Joy Hodges, James Finlayson, Mae Busch
(2nd right), Antonio Moreno (right), Harry
Bowers and Thelma Todd (who died tragically

shortly after the film was completed); with
additional music by Nathaniel Shilkret and
Robert Shayon. No screenwriter was credited
but the screenplay utilized the original book by
Alfred Bunn, written in 1843. Songs included: *I
Dreamt That I Dwelt In Marble Halls; Then You'll
Remember Me; The Heart Bowed Down; But
Memory Is The Only Friend That Grief Can Call It's
Own* Balfe, Bunn; *Heart Of A Gipsy* Shilkret,
Shayon.
▽

◁ The only other child star of the period even
remotely comparable to Shirley Temple in popularity was Jane Withers (right) whose starring
role in **Paddy O'Day** (20th Century-Fox) was a
jaunty showcase for her engaging talents. She
played an Irish immigrant who, after experienc-
ing problems with the immigration authorities,
escapes deportation by running away to the
house where she believes her mother is employed as a cook – only to discover that her
mother is dead. Pinky Tomlin, however, is
conveniently on hand to take care of her and, by
marrying a Russian dancer who was on the
same ship as young Paddy, is able to adopt her
against the wishes of his spinsterish aunts. The
dancer was played by Rita Cansino (left), soon to
become Rita Hayworth. On the evidence of her
nondescript performance here, anyone betting
on her chances of superstardom would have
been on the receiving end of extremely
favourable odds. It was written by Lou Breslow
and Edward Eliscu, produced by Sol Wurtzel and
directed by Lewis Seiler. The cast was completed
by Jane Darwell, George Givot, Francis Ford,
Vera Lewis, Louise Carter, Russell Simpson and
Michael and Nina Visaroff. Songs: *Keep That
Twinkle In Your Eye; I Like A Balalaika* Sidney
Clare, Edward Eliscu, Harry Akst; *Changing My
Ambition* Pinky Tomlin.

THIRTIES MUSICALS

△

Grace Moore (right) stepped out of Grand Opera and into the champagne world of operetta in **The King Steps Out** (Columbia) – a delightful Viennese romance in which, after rescuing her sister (Frieda Inescort) from an unwanted marriage with Emperor Francis Joseph of Austria (a bewigged Franchot Tone, left), she pretends to be a dress maker, then marries the man herself. Based on the operetta *Cissy* by Gustav Holm, Ernest Decsey and Hulbert and Ernst Marischka, with music by Fritz Kreisler, it came to the screen in a screenplay by Sidney Buchman, with Dorothy Fields reworking some of the original lyrics and with several of the tunes borrowed from Kreisler's *Apple Blossoms*. Walter Connolly co-starred (marvellously) as the King of Bavaria (or, as his wife remarks of him, 'a grease spot on the pages of history'), with Herman Bing type-cast to perfection as Pretzelberger, the owner of an establishment called *The Golden Ox*. Raymond Walburn, Victor Jory, Elisabeth Risdon, Nana Bryant and Thurston Hall were also on hand to keep the plot alive between songs, and the director was the imposing Josef von Sternberg who brought just the right featherweight touch the material required. Albertina Rasch staged a ballet sequence. Songs included: *The Old Refrain*; *Learn How To Lose*; *Stars In My Eyes*; *Madly In Love*; *Soldier's March*; *What Shall Remain?*; *Call To Arms*.

Phil Regan (left) starred in **Laughing Irish Eyes** (Republic) and took to the blarney with consummate ease and conviction. He played an Irish crooner who is signed up by fight promotor Walter C. Kelly in the mistaken belief that he is a prizefighter, and whisked off to America to prove his worth in the ring. He succeeds and, if the film made any point at all, it was that every Irish tenor is basically a pugilist at heart. Or the other way round. Evalyn Knapp played the fight promotor's daughter who wins the tenor after he wins the middleweight title; with Ray Walker, Mary Gordon, Warren Hymer, Betty Compson, J.M. Kerrigan, Oscar O'Shea (right). Herman Bing and Raymond Hatton in support. Clive Cooper, Ben Ryan and Stanley Rauh wrote the screenplay from a story by Sidney Sutherland and Wallace Sullivan, and it was directed by Joseph Santley. Songs included: *All My Life*; *Bless You Darling Mother*; *Laughing Irish Eyes* Sidney Mitchell, Sammy Stept.

▽

△

The Music Goes Round (Columbia) told the story of musical comedy star who, while on holiday, comes across a troupe of wildly untalented showboat players, takes them back to New York with him, and, without letting them in on the joke, features them as the mirthmakers of his new revue. Apart from the brief appearances of Mike Riley and Ed Farley (demonstrating the mysteries of a three-valve sax horn), Herman Bing and Michael Bartlett, the film had precious little to offer in the way of entertainment. The score by Lew Brown, Harry Akst, Harry Richman and Victor Schertzinger – who also directed – was moderately pleasant, and a couple of the dance routines were passable. It was Jo Swerling's flaccid screenplay (from a story by Sidney Buchman) that was basically at fault, and there was nothing its stars, Harry Richman (left), Rochelle Hudson (right) and Walter Connolly, could do to prevent the tedium it engendered. Also cast: Douglass Dumbrille, Lionel Stander, Henry Mollison and Etienne Girardot. Songs: *Rolling Along*; *This Is Love*; *Susannah*; *There'll Be No South* Brown, Akst; *I'm Betting On You* Brown, Akst, Richman; *Life Begins When You're In Love* Schertzinger, Brown, Richman; *The Music Goes Round and Around* Red Hodgson, Ed Farley, Mike Riley.

◁ Shirley Temple's talents and range were seemingly inexhaustible, and in **Captain January** (20th Century-Fox) she even sang the sextet from Donizetti's *Lucia di Lammermoor* – except that, appropriate to her size, it wasn't a sextet in this particular version, but a scaled-down trio with co-stars Guy Kibbee (centre) and his cribbage-playing crony Slim Summerville (right). She also belted out a few lines of 'Asleep In The Deep' (by Arthur Lamb and H.W. Petrie), in imitation *basso profundo*. Furthermore, she matched Buddy Ebsen step for step in a dance routine they had together – and indulged in a spot of high dramatics in the service of the rather hoary screenplay fashioned especially for her by Sam Hellman, Gladys Lehman and Harry Tugend (from a novel by Laura E. Richards). In it she played the victim of a shipwreck who, after being rescued and raised by kindly Cap'n Kibbee, finds herself in danger of being separated from him when an unfriendly sheriff arrives on the scene with orders to send her to an institution. Though basically little more than a melodrama of silent screen vintage, audiences flocked to see it, turning it into one of the studio's biggest money-makers of the year. June Lang, Sara Haden, Jane Darwell and Jerry Tucker were also cast, it was produced by Darryl F. Zanuck and directed by David Butler, with Jack Donohue staging the dances. Songs included: *Early Bird*; *At The Codfish Ball* Sidney Mitchell, Lew Pollack; *The Right Somebody To Love* Jack Yellen, Pollack.

△

Though Alice Faye received second billing to Shirley Temple in **Poor Little Rich Girl** (20th Century-Fox), it wasn't until the film was half over that she made her first appearance in it. But by then Shirley (illustrated) had the whole thing sewn up and there was little anyone else could do to get a look in. A reworking of a 1917 vehicle for Mary Pickford, the Sam Hellman–Gladys Lehman–Harry Tugend screenplay (suggested by the stories of Eleanor Gates and Ralph Spence) was a typical Temple concoction in which the money-making young 'un, neglected by her wealthy soap-manufacturing father (Michael Whalen), joins up with two vaudeville performers (Faye and Jack Haley), becomes a successful radio star working for a rival soap manufacturer, and is ultimately reunited with her repentant old man. Miss Temple's remarkable versatility was more than somewhat catered for by composers Mack Gordon and Harry Revel, whose 'When I'm With You', 'But Definitely' (pronounced 'definally' by the young star) and 'You've Gotta Eat Your Spinach, Baby', gave her ample scope to demonstrate all over again just what a little trouper she was. Gloria Stuart, Sara Haden, Jane Darwell, Claude Gillingwater, Paul Stanton, Henry Armetta and Charles Coleman were also in it; Tony Martin (in what was to be the first of his four film appearances with Alice Faye) had an 80-second unbilled spot as a radio vocalist singing 'When I'm With You'; Jack Haskell and Ralph Cooper staged the musical numbers, the associate producer was Buddy De Sylva and it was directed by Irving Cummings. Other numbers: *Oh My Goodness*; *Buy A Bar Of Barry's*; *Wash Your Necks With A Cake Of Peck's*; *Military Man* Gordon, Revel.

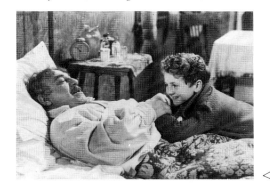

Hi Gaucho! (RKO), with a story and direction by Thomas Atkins, was probably the gauchest musical of the year. John Carroll, wearing a Spanish accent as thick as Adele Buffington's scenario, played the hero, with Steffi Duna (centre) as the heroine he saves from Rod La Rocque (right), a bandit who turns out to be none other than the elderly Don to whom she has been promised, against her wishes, in marriage. The cast was completed by Montague Love, Ann Codee (left), Tom Ricketts and Paul Porcasi, and Albert Hay Malotte wrote the songs. These were: *Song Of The Open Road*; *Bandit Song*; *My Little White Rose*; *Panchita*.

Eight-year-old Bobby Breen (right), discovered by Eddie Cantor on one of his radio shows, made his screen debut in **Let's Sing Again** (RKO), a synthetic weepie in which, after being abandoned by his Neapolitan mother, young Bobby is sent to an orphanage, runs away to join a travelling show, is adopted by kindly Henry Armetta (left) and finally, while hitch-hiking to New York with Signor Armetta, stumbles across his long-lost father. Breen demonstrated his precocity by singing 'La Donna e Mobile' from Verdi's *Rigoletto*, and pleased the women in the audience hugely. His father was played by George Houston, with Vivienne Osborne, Grant Withers, Inez Courtney, Richard Carle, Lucien Littlefield, Ann Doran and Clay Clement completing the cast. It was written by Don Swift and Dan Jarratt, produced by Sol Lesser, and directed by Kurt Neumann. Songs included: *Let's Sing Again* Gus Kahn, Jimmy McHugh; *Sleep My Little One* Selma Hautzig, Hugo Riesenfeld.

Purnell Pratt, playing a dyspeptic millionaire grandfather, heaved a sigh of relief when Eddie Nugent (right) replaced Ben Lyon in grand-daughter Joan Marsh's (left) heart; and audiences everywhere heaved an even bigger sigh of relief when **Dancing Feet** (Republic) was over. The kind of mindless yarn in which a tap routine goes over big with radio audiences at home, it also featured Isabel Jewell, James Burke, Vince Barnett and Nick Condos. It was written (from a novel by Rob Eden) by Jerome Chodorov, Olive Cooper and Wellyn Totman, and directed by Joseph Santley. Songs: *Every Time I Look At You*; *Dancing Feet*; *In And Out*; *Land Of Dreams*; *And Then*; *Get In Step*; *Here I Am Again*; *Here Comes Love*; *Water Wheel*; *I'm Glad It's Me*; *Dreaming Of You*; *Never Give Up*; *Recollections Of Love* Sidney Mitchell, Sammy Stept.

Al Jolson (illustrated) starred in **The Singing Kid** (Warner Bros./First National) as a musical comedy star who, after losing his voice, takes a countryside sabbatical which not only results in the return to normal of his vocal chords, but in his acquiring a sweetheart. A few trivial complications temporarily beset his career but, in the end, he's back treading the boards on Broadway where he belongs. Warren Duff and Pat C. Flick's screenplay (story by Robert Lord) creaked (or, in this instance, croaked) and not even Jolson's supreme showmanship could rescue it from the brink of mediocrity on which it remained perched throughout its 85-minute running time. William Keighley directed, Bobby Connolly took charge of the musical numbers, Robert Lord supervised the production, and Sybil Jason, Edward Everett Horton, Cab Calloway, Lyle Talbot, Allen Jenkins, Beverly Roberts and Claire Dodd were in it too. Songs: *My How This Country Has Changed*; *Save Me Sister*; *You're The Cure For What Ails Me*; *Here's Looking At You*; *I Love To Sing-a* E.Y. Harburg, Harold Arlen; *You Gotta Have That Hi-Di-Ho In Your Soul* Irving Mills, Cab Calloway.

▽

THIRTIES MUSICALS

Apart from its superb colour photography by William V. Skall, and Robert Edmond Jones's striking set designs, everything else about **The Dancing Pirate** (Pioneer Pictures, released by RKO) walked the plank – including the two songs specially written for it by Richard Rodgers and Lorenz Hart. All about a Bostonian dance teacher (Charles Collins, illustrated) who, after being shanghaied by pirates, escapes somewhere along the Mexican coast and, in the noblest Fairbanks or Barrymore tradition, wins the hand of the local Alcalde's daughter, it featured Frank Morgan as the Alcalde and Steffi Duna as his daughter with Luis Alberni, Victor Varconi, Jack La Rue and William V. Mong lending atmosphere rather than dramatic support. Rita Hayworth's family, The Royal Cansinos, featured in one of the sequences, with Mitchell Lewis, Cy Kendall, Julian Rivero, Harold Waldridge, Vera Lewis and Nora Cecil completing the cast. It was adapted by Jack Wagner and Boris Ingster from a story by Emma Lindsay Squier, written by Ray Harris and Francis Faragoh, produced by John Speaks and directed by Lloyd Corrigan. Songs included: *Are You My Love?*; *When You're Dancing The Waltz*.
▽

Metro Goldwyn Mayer's cinematic glorification of Broadway's legendary Florenz Ziegfeld began four years after the impresario's death at the age of 65 with **The Great Ziegfeld**, and continued with *Ziegfeld Girl* (1941) and *Ziegfeld Follies* (1944). Though all three films traded in spectacle, the first was the best, the longest (180 minutes) and the most opulent. With a budget of over a million and a half dollars, and a cast that included William Powell as the great showman himself, Luise Rainer as his first wife Anna Held, and Myrna Loy as his second wife Billie Burke, it was the classiest biopic ever to emerge from Hollywood, and one of the most successful in its recreation of the period in which Ziegfeld flourished. Its money-no-object approach mirrored Ziegfeld's own attitude towards show business entirely; and although for legal reasons, fiction melded with fact in scenarist William Anthony McGuire's efficient account of both Ziegfeld's private and professional life, what was never distorted was the essence of his subject's reach-for-the-stars approach to his work. Nor did the screenplay put a foot wrong in conveying the sheer daring of the man's creative imagination or his infallible eye for talent. Best of all, though, by utilizing the full resources of a major motion picture studio, the film was able to offer audiences a breathtakingly effective cinematic equivalent of a night out at the Follies. If Ziegfeld had had the resources of a film studio at his command, this, you were made to feel, was just the sort of movie he himself would have produced to honour his forty years in the business. For, as convincing as most of the performances were (and for a Hollywood biopic they were exceptionally convincing), it was the musical numbers staged by Seymour Felix, in settings devised

△

Hearts Divided (Warner Bros./Cosmopolitan/First National) was a misguided remake of *Glorious Betsy* (1928), from Rida Johnson Young's play about a romance between Betsy, a Baltimore beauty, and Napoleon Bonaparte's younger brother. The roles went to Marion Davies (right) and, at her insistence, Dick Powell (left), neither of whom could cope with Laird Doyle and Casey Robinson's screenplay. Matters were made worse for Powell who, decked out in coiffured wig and pantaloons, looked absurd. Neither the highly competent director, Frank Borzage, nor his accomplished cast – Claude Rains (centre), Charles Ruggles, Edward Everett Horton, Arthur Treacher and Henry Stephenson – could make any headway in this miserable production (supervised by Harry Joe Brown). Songs included: *My Kingdom For A Kiss*; *Two Hearts Divided* Al Dubin, Harry Warren; *Nobody Knows The Trouble I Seen*; *Rise Up Children And Shine* (Negro spirituals sung by the Hall Johnson Choir).

for them by Cedric Gibbons, that quite understandably attracted the crowds. And although none of the numbers could rival, in originality and ingenuity, the work being done by Busby Berkeley at Warner Bros., the sheer overwhelming size of them set a new standard in opulence that has never been surpassed. Most spectacular of all was the wedding-cake setting used for Irving Berlin's 'A Pretty Girl Is Like A Melody' (vocal by Dennis Morgan – billed as Stanley Morner – but with Allan Jones's voice on the sound track) in which scores of extras, in what is now a collector's item of super-opulent kitsch, sang and danced snippets from the classics as the camera worked its way round the mighty edifice until it reached Virginia Bruce at the top (illustrated). The basic structure of the set was used again with certain variations for the title number of the Jeanette MacDonald–Nelson Eddy vehicle *Sweethearts* (MGM 1938) and the finale of *Till The Clouds Roll By* (MGM 1946). It made stunning use of an all-enveloping curtain, which appeared again in *Sweethearts*. In fact, imaginatively deployed curtains would soon become a feature of MGM's more elaborate production numbers, most effectively in the finales of *The Broadway Melody Of 1940*, *Lady Be Good* (1941) and *Babes On Broadway* (1942). Though nothing else in **The Great Ziegfeld** was quite as eye-catching as the Berlin number, Seymour Felix's staging of 'You Gotta Pull Strings', 'She's A Ziegfeld Follies Girl', 'You', and 'You Never Looked So Beautiful' (by Walter Donaldson and Harold Adamson) in a continuous sequence had as much pazazz as the camera could comfortably contain; as did 'A Circus Must Be Different In A Ziegfeld Show', devised by Harriet Hoctor, with music by Con Conrad and

A very dispiriting business indeed, **Three Cheers For Love** (Paramount) was the story of a film producer's daughter (Eleanore Whitney, centre) who discovers that the finishing school to which she has been sent is under the management of a stranded theatrical troupe. The 'students' are all ladies of the chorus; while the faculty members are hoofers to a man. In no time at all Miss Whitney becomes an accomplished 'gypsy', and at the annual school show which is attended by her important father, the entire cast land themselves contracts at Miracle Studios – whose slogan is 'If It's A Good Picture It's A Miracle'. Barry Trivers's screenplay (from a story by George Marion Jr) had Robert Cummings (left), William Frawley, Roscoe Karns, John Halliday (right), Elizabeth Patterson, Grace Bradley, Olympe Bradna, Louis Da Pron and Veda Ann Borg wilting under the burden of their lines and – apart from some moderately effective tap-dancing from Miss Whitney and Mr Da Pron – it was a case of full marks for mediocrity. A.M. Botsford produced and Ray McCarey directed. Songs: *Where Is My Heart?*; *The Swing Tap*; *Tap Your Feet*; *Long Ago And Far Away* (not to be confused with the later, more famous Kern–Gershwin number from Columbia's *Cover-Girl*, 1944) Ralph Rainger, Leo Robin.
▽

lyrics by Herb Magidson. On a more modest ▷ scale there was Fanny Brice singing 'Yiddle On Your Fiddle' (by Irving Berlin), 'Queen Of The Jungle' (by Walter Donaldson and Harold Adamson), and part of 'My Man' (by Channing Pollock and Maurice Yvain). Luise Rainer, more at home in her dramatic moments, such as the famous telephone call to Ziegfeld after reading that he has remarried, was nevertheless quite charming in 'Won't You Come And Play With Me' and 'It's Delightful To Be Married' (adapted by Anna Held and Vincent Scotto from 'La Petite Tonkinoise' by Scotto and Henri Christine), the latter song cropping up again as part of George Pal's animated sequence in *Ziegfeld Follies*. There was a fairly good impression by Buddy Doyle of Eddie Cantor (in long shot) singing 'If You Knew Susie' (by Buddy De Sylva and Joseph Meyer) and a fair to middling one of Will Rogers by A.A. Trimble. Ray Bolger featured prominently in one of the star turns on the New Amsterdam Roof; Frank Morgan was delightfully (and predictably) vague as a friendly rival of Ziegfeld's, and Nat Pendleton perfect casting as strong-man Sandow, Ziegfeld's first major show-biz attraction. Completing the cast were Ernest Cossart, Joseph Cawthorn, Paul Irving, Herman Bing, Charles Judels and Raymond Walburn. It was produced by Hunt Stromberg and directed with workmanlike efficiency by Robert Z. Leonard. The classical music interpolated in the 'A Pretty Girl Is Like A Melody' number included snippets from Dvorak's Humoresque No. 7 in G flat; 'One Fine Day' from Puccini's *Madame Butterfly*; Liszt's *Liebestraum*; Johann Strauss II's *The Blue Danube Waltz*; 'On With The Motley' from Leoncavallo's *Pagliacci*; and *Rhapsody In Blue* by George Gershwin.

THIRTIES MUSICALS

Apart from Helen Westley (as Parthenia Hawks) and Queenie Smith (as Ellie) all the principal performers in director James Whale's memorable screen version of Edna Ferber, Jerome Kern and Oscar Hammerstein II's **Show Boat** (Universal) had appeared in various stage productions of the classic musical, and their total familiarity with (and commitment to) their roles was very much in evidence throughout. Irene Dunne (right) played Magnolia Hawks, Allan Jones (left) was her Ravenal, and Charles Winninger Cap'n Andy, with Paul Robeson quite magnificent as Joe, and Helen Morgan ditto as the mulatto Julie. Donald Cook played Morgan's husband Steve, with other roles going to Hattie McDaniel as Joe's wife Queenie, Francis X. Mahoney as Rubberface and Charles Middleton as Sheriff Mahoney. An extremely faithful adaptation (by Hammerstein himself) of the original 1927 Broadway presentation, plus the addition of three new Kern–Hammerstein songs – 'I Have The Room Above Her' (sung by Jones and Miss Dunne); 'Ah Still Suits Me' (Robeson ▽

and McDaniel), and 'Gallivantin' Around' (sung by Miss Dunne in blackface) – the film only falters in its modern section towards the end in which several plot points were arbitrarily and unconvincingly resolved. The loss of 'Why Do I Love You' (relegated in the final release print to the background) was also to be regretted. For the rest, however, Whale's **Show Boat** with its brilliant camerawork by John J. Mescall, the vigorous staging of its musical numbers by LeRoy Prinz, and the visual splendour of its art direction (by Charles D. Hall) offered audiences a most satisfactory version of an undisputed musical comedy masterpiece. The producer was Carl Laemmle Jr. It was remade by MGM in 1951. Other songs: *Cotton Blossom*; *Cap'n Andy's Ballyhoo*; *Where's The Mate For Me?*; *Make Believe*; *Ol' Man River*; *Can't Help Lovin' Dat Man*; *Mis'ry's Comin' Around*; *You Are Love*; *Bill*; as well as *Goodbye Ma Lady Love* Joe Howard; *At A Georgia Camp Meeting* Kerry Mills; *After The Ball* Charles K. Harris; *Washington Post March* John Philip Sousa.

An unusual offering from Warner Bros., and one which brought the studio a great deal of prestige but no money, was Marc Connelly's **The Green Pastures**. The music, which contributed immeasurably to the atmosphere of the film, was comprised of negro spirituals arranged and conducted by Hall Johnson, and impressively sung by his Choir. Connelly saw his story as a fable which would demonstrate 'certain aspects of a living religion in the terms of its believers', and he constructed it as a re-telling of the Bible as seen through the eyes of negro children at a Sunday school in a Southern backwater. Rex Ingram was cast in the central role of 'De Lawd' and delivered a performance of dignity and towering strength. Just before his entrance, the memorable line 'Gangway for de Lawd God Jehovah' was uttered – an example of the tone and flavour of the film's approach to religion. Today **The Green Pastures** would be thought somewhat racist in its depiction of blacks as humble and ingenuous simpletons, but in 1936 it represented a worthy attempt to break new ground in the cinema (see illustration). Henry Blanke supervised the production and William Keighley (with Marc Connelly) directed a cast of excellent players including Eddie 'Rochester' Anderson (as Noah), Oscar Polk, Frank Wilson, George Reed, Abraham Gleaves and Myrtle Anderson. The spirituals sung were: *Joshua Fit De Battle Of Jericho And De Walls Came Tumblin' Down*; *De Old Ark's A-moverin'*; *Let My People Go*; *Run, Sinner, Run*; *Death's Gwinter Lay His Cold Hands On Me*; *When The Saints Come Marchin' In.* ▽

Sitting on the Moon was an innocuous, pleasant little programmer about a couple of songwriters (Roger Pryor and William Newell), who fall for an ex-film star (Grace Bradley, illustrated), and for her comical pal (Pert Kelton). There wasn't much more in it than that, but it was neatly packaged by director Ralph Staub whose cast also included Joyce Compton as a professional blackmailer (claiming that Pryor married her in one of his drunken moments), Henry Kolker, Henry Wadsworth, Pierre Watkin and The Theodores – a dance team who featured prominently in one of the specialty dances. The associate producer was Albert E. Levoy, it was written by Raymond L. Schrock from a story by Julian Field, and adapted by Rex Taylor and Sidney Sutherland. Songs included: *Sitting On The Moon*; *Lost In My Dreams*; *How Am I Doin' With You?* Sidney Mitchell, Sammy Stept. ▽

△
Though Bing Crosby was the official star of **Rhythm on the Range** (Paramount), the first of two Westerns he would appear in during his lengthy career (the other was the 1969 remake of 20th Century-Fox's *Stagecoach*), the real attraction and 'find' of the show was an eccentric newcomer with a voice as big as her mouth called Martha Raye. She played a cowboy's sister (making her entrance on Grand Central Station!) who, although only part of the sub-plot, lit up the screen whenever she was on – particularly in her vigorous, full-throated rendition of a Sam Coslow number called 'Mr Paganini'. Audiences (and critics) loved her, and with her first film her career was triumphantly launched. For the rest – well, it was a pleasing enough musical, low on plot, high on songs (including the popular 'Empty Saddles' by Billy Hill, from a poem by J. Keirn Brennan, and 'I'm An Old Cowhand' by Johnny Mercer, with which Bing scored a huge hit) – with Crosby (illustrated) as a singing cowboy (he even sings a lullaby to a 2000-pound Hereford bull!) who meets a runaway heiress (Frances Farmer) on a freight train, and marries her. Bob Burns, Samuel S. Hinds, Warren Hymer, Lucille Webster Gleason and George E. Stone were also featured, the little pinprick of a screenplay employed the services of Walter DeLeon, Francis Martin, John C. Moffitt and Sidney Salkow (story by Mervin J. Houser), it was breezily directed by Norman Taurog, and the happy producer was Benjamin Glazer – for it was one of Paramount's top money-making films of the year. Other songs: *I Can't Escape From You* Leo Robin, Richard A. Whiting; *Drink It Down* Ralph Rainger, Robin; *Hang Up My Saddle*; *Rhythm On The Range* Walter Bullock, Whiting; *Memories* Whiting, Frederick Hollander; *Round-up Lullaby* Bager Clark, Gertrude Rose.

◁ An enjoyable programmer, **Walking on Air** (RKO) was the story of an impetuous young woman (Ann Sothern) who, to annoy her father, persuades a personable young college student (Gene Raymond, centre, with blond hair) to pretend to fall madly in love with her in the guise of an aristocratic but irritating Frenchman. This way she hopes her stubborn father will finally allow her to marry the man she *really* loves (Alan Curtis). But the inevitable happens and Miss Sothern finds herself walking on air when she realizes that it isn't Mr Curtis she wants, but handsome Mr Raymond. Such was the stuff of romantic musical comedy, and in the capable hands of its attractive cast, it worked well enough. Jessie Ralph and Henry Stephenson played Miss Sothern's parents, with other roles going to Gordon Jones, George Meeker, Maxine Jennings, Anita Colby and Charles Coleman. It was written by Bert Kalmar, Harry Ruby, Viola Brothers Shore and Rian James from a story by Francis M. Cockrell, and directed by Joseph Santley. Songs included: *Cabin On A Hilltop*; *Let's Make A Wish*; *My Heart Wants to Dance* Kalmar, Ruby.

△
Just before the release of **Stage Struck** (First National), its stars Joan Blondell and Dick Powell were married. Which was just as well, for the event generated some interest in the movie which might otherwise have passed unnoticed by their fans. Although directed by Busby Berkeley, and with songs by E.Y. Harburg and Harold Arlen, it was a modest effort resting, yet again, on a backstage story which, this time, had Blondell in the (unlikely) guise of an untalented performer who finances her own show for Broadway and hires Powell to direct it. Disagreements spring up between them, but their reconciliation is effected by the ever-smooth Warren William. So much for the plot, enclosed in a disappointing screenplay by Tom Buckingham and Pat C. Flick (from a story by supervisor Robert Lord) which the cast – Frank McHugh, Jeanne Madden (illustrated), Carol Hughes, Hobart Cavanaugh and Spring Byington – were unable to improve. Songs and musical numbers included: *In Your Own Quiet Way*; *Fancy Meeting You*; *You're Kinda Grandish*; *The New Parade*.

△
A disaster musical (as opposed to a musical disaster), **San Francisco** was an artistic, technical and financial triumph for its studio, MGM, as well as a personal one for its three stars: Clark Gable (left), Jeanette MacDonald (right) and Spencer Tracy (centre right). Relying on such sure-fire ingredients as romance, nostalgia, sex, religion, music and spectacle (all expertly tied with a ribbon of moral retribution to keep the more sinful elements of the package in a neat, and thoroughly acceptable, perspective), it told the story of a midwestern opera singer (Mac-Donald) who, in 1906, is offered a job along the rough-and-ready Barbary Coast by cabaret owner Blackie Norton (Gable). But it is not long before the *diva*, who has fallen in love with her boss, is discovered by Nob Hill's aristocracy, and deserts Norton's cabaret for a career as an opera star on 'the other side of the tracks'. Norton subbornly refuses to alter his life-style in accordance with the soprano's loftier ambitions; she is equally determined to safeguard her new-found position in society. It is an impossible situation for both of them, and it takes an earthquake – literally – to reconcile them. Spencer Tracy played Father Mullin, the tough but compassionate chaplain of a Barbary Coast mission, with other roles in Anita Loos's stunningly professional, all-purpose screenplay (story by Robert Hopkins and additional dialogue by Erich von Stroheim) going to such vintage performers as Jack Holt (centre left), Edgar Kennedy and Al Shean, as well as Jessie Ralph, Shirley Ross, Ted Healy, Margaret Irving and Harold Huber. Val Raset staged the dances, the impressive musical direction was by Herbert Stothart, and the superb special effects were the work of James Basevi, who was also responsible for the locust plague in MGM's *The Good Earth* (1936), and the hurricane in United Artists' *The Hurricane* (1937). It was produced by John Emerson and Bernard H. Hyman, and directed with the precision and detail of a successful military manoeuvre, by W.S. Van Dyke, with D.W. Griffith in charge of the crowd scenes. It was no surprise to anyone that **San Francisco** was one of the biggest money-makers of the year. Songs: *Happy New Year*; *San Francisco* Bronislau Kaper, Walter Jurmann, Gus Kahn; *Noontime* Ted Healy; *Love Me And The World Is Mine* Ernest R. Ball, David Reed Jr; *A Heart That's Free* A.J. Robyn, T. Railey; *The Holy City* Stephen Adams, F.E. Weatherley; *Would You?* Arthur Freed, Nacio Herb Brown; *Nearer My God To Thee* Lowell Mason, Sarah F. Adams; *The Battle Hymn Of The Republic* William Steffe, Julia Ward Howe; *At A Georgia Camp Meeting* Kerry Mills; *The Philippine Dance* Bob Carleton; *A Hot Time In The Old Town Tonight* Joe Hayden, Theodore Metz, and 'The Jewel Song', 'Soldiers' Chorus;' 'Il Se Fait Tard' and 'Anges Purs' from Gounod's *Faust*; 'Sempre Libera' from Verdi's *La Traviata*.

THIRTIES MUSICALS

Frank Morgan (left) did not let little Shirley Temple have it all her own way for an instant in **Dimples** (20th Century-Fox) and, as her lovable reprobate of a grandfather, made the kid work twice as hard as was her wont to justify her top-star billing. Which she did – going somewhat over the top as little Eva in a performance of *Uncle Tom's Cabin*. Through a series of typical Temple-like plot contrivances (one of which involved wealthy dowager Helen Westley offering Morgan $5,000 if he will allow her to adopt his granddaughter), Arthur Sheekman and Nat Perrin's screenplay transformed the film's diminutive leading lady from a street waif to a Broadway star and, as was the way with such Cinderella stories, was another solid gold winner. Shirley again demonstrated her skill as a tap-dancer (dance direction by Bill Robinson), as well as her way with a song, reducing, on several occasions, the less stony-hearted members of her audience to appreciative tears. Robert Kent, Stepin Fetchit, Astrid Allwyn, Berton Churchill, Delma Byron, Paul Stanton, John Carradine, Herman Bing and The Hall Johnson Choir were also in it; Nunnally Johnson produced, and the director was William A. Seiter. Songs: *Hey, What Did The Bluebird Say?*; *He Was A Dandy*; *Picture Me Without You*; *Oh Mister Man Up In The Moon*; *Dixie-Anna* Ted Koehler, Jimmy McHugh; *Get On Board*; *Swing Low Sweet Chariot* (Negro spiritual).

▽

A new-look Alice Faye starred in **Sing, Baby, Sing** (20th Century-Fox) with fuller, more attractive eyebrows taking the place of the plucked, pencilled-in job which audiences had been subjected to in her previous films; and with a softer hairstyle far more in keeping with her warm personality than the vampish Harlow look the studio had hitherto been encouraging her to emulate. She was also given one of her best scores to date – and turned 'You Turned The Tables On Me' into a solid hit for its composers Sidney Mitchell and Louis Alter. And, in the brief role of an unknown singer who is given his big chance in a radio broadcast, Tony Martin did well by composers Walter Bullock and Richard A. Whiting with 'When Did You Leave Heaven?'. Loosely based on (or inspired by) John Barrymore's then topical and much publicized romance with Elaine Barrie, the screenplay – by Milton Sperling, Jack Yellen and Harry Tugend, story by Sperling and Yellen – was a trifling titbit about a temperamental Hollywood star (Adolphe Menjou in brilliant comic form) who, one drunken night during a New York holiday, develops a Romeo fixation on a nightclub singer called Joan (Faye, right). In the cold, sober light of the next morning, however, he profoundly regrets his declarations of love the night before, and boards the next train for Hollywood. But his Juliet is literally one jump ahead of him having already hopped on a plane. Amiable balderdash, but with its stars and supporting cast – Gregory Ratoff (centre left), Ted Healy, Patsy Kelly (centre), Michael Whalen (left) and The Ritz Brothers – all giving of their best, it was perfect entertainment for the masses, and the masses agreed. The associate producer was Buddy De Sylva, with Sidney Lanfield directing. Other songs: *Love Will Tell*; *Sing, Baby, Sing* Jack Yellen, Lew Pollack; *The Music Goes 'Round and Around* (Ritz Brothers) Red Hodgson, Ed Farley, Mike Riley; *When My Baby Smiles At Me* (Ritz Brothers) Andrew B. Sterling, Ted Lewis, Bill Munro; *Singing A Vagabond Song* (Ritz Brothers) Sam Messenheimer, Val Burton, Harry Richman.

▷

Fred and Ginger's sixth film together was originally called *I Won't Dance* but underwent a title change to *Never Gonna Dance*. Still not happy with the negative aspect of the second title, the studio finally settled for **Swing Time** (RKO). But it hardly mattered. An Astaire–Rogers musical by any name reeked of class and this one was no exception, but for its box-office returns which, while certainly healthy enough, were no improvement on *Top Hat* (RKO 1935) or the recent *Follow The Fleet*. The blame must fall squarely at the typewriters of scenarists Howard Lindsay and Allan Scott, whose screenplay was as tedious and, at times, as asinine as Erwin Gelsey's story. Astaire played a hoofer with a chronic predilection for gambling who, after arriving late for his wedding, is packed off by his fiancée's incensed father (Lander Stevens) and ordered not to darken the family doorstep again until he manages to find $25,000 as an antidote to his irresponsible behaviour. What he finds instead is Ginger Rogers and with miraculous sleight of foot, the pair of them (illustrated) danced rings around the plot, almost succeeding in making one forget the banalities of what they had to do and say whenever the music stopped. Melodically **Swing Time**, with a score by *Roberta's* Jerome Kern and Dorothy Fields, was musical comedy's answer to the crown jewels, with each number a dazzler. From the delightfully tongue-in-cheek 'Pick Yourself Up' to the ecstatic 'Waltz In Swing Time' with its familiar alternations of volume and tempo, Kern's sureness of touch never for an instant faltered. He was as much at home with the uncharacteristic (for him) rhythmic patterns of 'Bojangles Of Harlem' (brilliantly choreographed by Hermes Pan, and the only number Astaire ever performed in blackface) as he was with the hauntingly beautiful 'The Way You Look Tonight' which Astaire tenderly sang to a vulnerable Ginger while her hair was covered in shampoo. Though there were no more than seven musical interludes in **Swing Time** (the remaining three being 'It's Not In The Cards', a brief dance by Astaire which opens the film, the delectable 'A Fine Romance' sung by Rogers to Astaire during a steady fall of snow, in which she laments his lack of romantic ardour and to which he sings an 'answer' version, and the miraculous 'Never Gonna Dance'), the impact they made was sufficient to help audiences suspend disbelief and enjoy the plot for the twaddle it was. Having had time off for good behaviour in *Follow The Fleet*, those inevitable buttresses of the sub-plot, the comedians, were back – this time in the guise of Helen Broderick (as Rogers's Tobasco-tongued best friend), the unpleasantly unctuous Eric Blore (as a dance-school proprietor) and, making his debut in an Astaire–Rogers film, Victor Moore as Astaire's Man Friday. Betty Furness played the hapless fiancée who loses Fred, with other roles going to Georges Metaxa, John Harrington, Pierre Watkin and Abe Reynolds. It was produced by Pandro S. Berman ◁ and directed by George Stevens.

Completed in 1934 but delayed two years by Hays code censorship problems, **Frankie and Johnny** (Republic) finally reached the screen in a dehydrated 66-minute version whose plot was little more than a translation of the famous song from which it took its title. Helen Morgan, in what was positively her worst screen role, played Frankie, a singer in a St Louis casino; Chester Morris (illustrated with Morgan) was Johnny, a gambler; with Lilyan Tashman (who, sadly, died before the film's release) giving the best performance in the film as Nellie Bly, the girl Johnny falls for after he and Frankie have married. Moss Hart wrote the screenplay from a story by Jack Kirkland; Chester Erskine directed, and the cast included Florence Reed, Walter Kingsford, William Harrigan, John Larkin and Cora Witherspoon. Songs: *Give Me A Heart To Sing To* Victor Young, Ned Washington; *Get Rhythm In Your Feet*; *If You Want My Heart* J. Russell Robinson, William Livingstone (all sung by Morgan); *Frankie And Johnny* (anonymous).
▽

Following in the tradition of Lawrence Tibbett, Grace Moore, Gladys Swarthout, Jan Kiepura, Nino Martini, Lily Pons, Jeanette MacDonald and Nelson Eddy, opera stars Marion Talley and Michael Bartlett lent their voices to the movies for **Follow Your Heart** (Republic), a rather vapid story (about a home-loving Kentucky lass who discovers the joys of music when a stranded opera company comes to roost at the old family plantation) that needed all the help it could get. Though nothing could successfully disguise the inherent silliness of Lester Cole, Nathanael West and Samuel Ornitz's screenplay (based on an idea by Dana Burnett), it had more than its fair share of musical interludes, both classical (see illustration) and popular, and at least one deliciously eccentric performance – that of Luis Alberni, giving his well-worn but always watchable characterization of an impresario. Nigel Bruce, Vivienne Osborne, Henrietta Crosman, Walter Catlett, John Eldredge, Mickey Rentschler, Ben Blue and The Hall Johnson Choir were in it too, it was produced by Nat Levene, and directed without flair by Aubrey Scotto. There were operatic excerpts from Donizetti's *Lucia Di Lammermoor*, Meyerbeer's *Les Huguenots* (the 'Page Song', sung by Miss Talley) and Thomas's *Mignon*; as well as *Magnolias in the Moonlight*; *Who Minds About Me?* Walter Bullock, Victor Schertzinger; and *Follow Your Heart* Sidney Mitchell, Schertzinger.

In **Give Us This Night** (Paramount) it was the Metropolitan Opera's Jan Keipura who could be seen and heard singing his lungs out to Gladys Swarthout, herself a recruit from the Met, but one who on this occasion (as indeed was the case in Paramount's *Rose of The Rancho*) didn't get a great deal of singing done herself. Philip Merivale was third-billed as an operatic impresario with a problem. And, according to the screenplay by Edwin Justus Mayer and Lynn Starling, story by Jacques Bacharach, his problem was finding a new tenor as a replacement for the past-it Forcellini (Alan Mowbray). Enter Kiepura (a singing fisherman from Sorrento), and exit plot. Musically, composer Erich Wolfgang Korngold broke new ground by writing the first original operatic sequence for a motion picture – the climactic *Romeo and Juliet* (see illustration) – but apart from that, the obscurely titled **Give Us This Night** was a mediocre entertainment directed by Alexander Hall, who either couldn't, or wouldn't, lift a megaphone to Kiepura, whose hammy and generally operatic performance almost singlehandedly sunk the show. William Le Baron produced, and his cast included Benny Baker, Michelette Burani, William Collier Sr, Sidney Toler and Mattie Edwards. Songs: *Sweet Melody Of Night*; *I Mean To Say I Love You*; *My Love And I*; *Music In The Night*; *Give Us This Night*; *Was There Ever A Voice* Korngold, Oscar Hammerstein II.
▽

△
Though primarily designed as a showcase for Metropolitan Opera star Nino Martini, **The Gay Desperado** (Pickford/Lasky, released by United Artists), expertly directed by Rouben Mamoulian, came into its own when Wallace Smith's ingenious screenplay was allowed to get on with its story (by Leo Birinski) of a music-loving Mexican bandit (Leo Carillo, centre) who kidnaps a singing caballero as well as a spoiled heiress (Ida Lupino). What made the film so entertaining was the satiric swipe it took at contemporary American gangster films through the character of Carillo, whose every mannerism had clearly been inspired by the likes of Cagney, Robinson, and Raft. Harold Huber (unhatted, left) and Mischa Auer were cast as a pair of the unlikeliest bandits ever to hit the screen, with James Blakely, Stanley Fields, Adrian Rosley, Paul Hurst, Alan Garcia and Frank Puglia completing the cast. Songs: *The World Is Mine Tonight* Holt Marvell (a pseudonym of Eric Maschwitz), George Posford; *Cielito Lindo* Neil Wilson, Carlo Fernandez, Sebastian Yradier; *Estralita* Frank LaForge, Manuel Ponce; *Adios Mi Terra* Miguel Sandoval; *Lamento Gitano* Walter Samuels, Leonard Whitcup; *Mamacita Mia* (composer unknown); 'Celeste Aida' from Verdi's *Aida*.

Cain and Mabel (Warner Bros.) was hand-picked for Marion Davies, whose failing career William Randolph Hearst, her lover, was determined to revitalize by persuading Jack Warner to hire Clark Gable from MGM as her co-star. Al Dubin and Harry Warren supplied the score, Bobby Connolly was engaged as dance director, with Lloyd Bacon calling the shots to a cast that included Allen Jenkins, Walter Catlett, David Carlyle (later Robert Paige), Hobart Cavanaugh, Ruth Donnelly and Pert Kelton. Laird Doyle's screenplay, from a story by H.C. Witwer, concerned a waitress (Miss Davies, right) turned musical comedy star and a boxer (Gable, left), who agree to a publicity romance concocted by a newspaperman (Roscoe Karns) only to find (predictably) that they really *have* fallen in love, and are happy to sacrifice their public images for a private life of romantic bliss. Miss Davies didn't do too badly in her acting scenes, but couldn't quite cut it in the musical numbers; and despite everything the film had going for it, it wasn't a success. The production was supervised by Sam Bischoff. Songs: *Coney Island*; *Here Comes Chiquita*; *I'll Sing You A Thousand Love Songs* which interpolated *The Shadow Waltz*; *The Rose In Her Hair*; *L'Amour, Toujours L'Amour* (by Catherine Chisholm Cushing and Rudolf Friml); *Believe Me If All Those Endearing Young Charms* by Thomas Moore and Anon (possibly Matthew Locke).
▽

Another excuse for a selection of songs, dances, sketches and general madcap merriment, **The Big Broadcast of 1937** (Paramount) loosely attached itself to an expendable story which involved a small town radio announcer (Shirley Ross) and the gleeful delight she takes in berating a popular network tenor (Frank Forest) over the air. It was typical of the radio-inspired musical, so popular at the time. As improbable as snow in July – but just as refreshing – it relied on its talented cast rather than on Walter DeLeon and Francis Martin's who-would-have-believed-it screenplay (which had Martha Raye belting out a swing version of 'Here Comes The Bride' at a wedding) to sock it to 'em; Jack Benny as the director of a radio station, and George Burns and Gracie Allen as the sponsors of the Platt Golf Ball Hour, dispensing comic largesse every time they opened their mouths. If the story was improbable, so was the mixture of talent assembled by director Mitchell Leisen. Incongruously rubbing shoulders, but with harmonious results, were Leopold Stokowski, Benny Goodman and Benny Fields, with Eleanore Whitney and Louis Da Pron (illustrated), and Ray Milland as the man Miss Ross finally marries. It was beautifully photographed by Theodor Sparkuhl, produced by Lewis E. Gensler and based on a story by Erwin Gelsey, Arthur Kober and Barry Trivers. Songs: *Hi-Ho The Radio*; *La Bomba*; *You Came To My Rescue*; *There's Love In Your Eyes*; *I'm Talking Through My Heart*; *Vote For Mr Rhythm* Ralph Rainger, Leo Robin. ▷

△

Frances Langford (left) made another bid for stardom in **Palm Springs** (GB: **Palm Springs Affair**) for Paramount but, apart from her appealing singing voice, she lacked that elusive something that made audiences care, and elicited only indifference from press and public alike. She was hardly helped by Myles Connolly's story, which Humphrey Pearson adapted and Joseph Fields scripted. All about an aristocratic but impecunious gambler (Sir Guy Standing) whose daughter (Langford) almost marries a millionaire (David Niven, right) as a means of helping her father out of his financial troubles (she changes her mind and marries Smith Ballew, a poor but handsome cowboy instead), it offered an amusing performance from Standing, a handful of pleasant songs and very little else. Spring Byington (centre), E.E. Clive, Sterling Holloway, Grady Sutton and Sarah Edwards completed the predominantly English cast, and the director was Aubrey Scotto. Songs: *The Hills Of Old Wyoming*; *I Don't Want To Make History (I Just Want To Make Love)*; *Palm Springs*; *Dreaming Out Loud* Ralph Rainger, Leo Robin; *Will I Ever Know?* Mack Gordon, Harry Revel; *I'm In The Mood For Love* Dorothy Fields, Jimmy McHugh.

The highwater mark of **Hats Off** (Grand National) was a production number towards the end of the film featuring several young ladies dressed in white flowing robes, who execute a dance step or two while floating about in billowy cloud formations on a revolving merry-go-round. For the rest it was a tedious romance between two rival press agents (John Payne and Mae Clarke) and, in the service of Sam Fuller and Edmund Joseph's screenplay (additional dialogue by Lawrence Thiele), also featured Luis Alberni (in his familiar guise of a Broadway impresario), Skeets Gallagher, funny girl Helen Lynd (centre), Franklin Pangborn, Robert Middlemass and George Irving. Also: Two Stooges, Three Radio Rogues and 75 'Grand National Gorgeous Girlies' (illustrated). Arthur Dreifuss and Victor Petroff staged the dance numbers, and it was produced and directed by Boris Petroff. Songs: *Where Have You Been All My Life?*; *Little Old Rhythm*; *Twinkle, Twinkle Little Star*; *Let's Have Another*; *Zilch's Hats*; *Hats Off* Herb Magidson, Ben Oakland.

Our good friend the mistaken identity plot rushed headlong into view in **Happy-Go-Lucky** (Republic), skidded along the many incomprehensible meanderings of Raymond Schrock and Olive Cooper's screenplay (from an original story by Eric Taylor, Wellyn Totman and Endre Bohem) and finally knocked itself out in a futile attempt to pull itself together. Basically the story of a young woman who, after believing her fiancé to be lost in the Pacific, assumes that the tap-dancer she sees in a Shanghai theatre, and whose looks are strikingly similar to her missing beau, is none-other than her sweetheart himself but suffering from loss of memory, it involved murder and kidnapping, and anything else you might care to think of. It also involved Evelyn Venable (illustrated right) and Phil Regan (left) in the leading roles of the hapless protagonists in the muddle, as well as Jed Prouty, William Newell and Jonathan Hale. The director was Aubrey Scotto. Songs included: *Right Or Wrong* Ted Koehler, Sammy Stept; *A Treat For The Eyes* Stept, Cliff Friend; *Happy-Go-Lucky*.
▽

Go West Young Man (Paramount) had nothing whatsoever to do with Horace Greeley's famous remark of over a century ago; nor was it the advice given by a theatrical agent to an up and coming young female impersonator. It was the title of Mae West's adaptation of Lawrence Riley's stage play *Personal Appearance*, all about a famous movie idol (West, right) who, after signing a contract not to marry for five years, is scrupulously watched by her press agent to see that she does not violate that contract. It was by no means vintage Mae, but entertaining just the same, and terrifically performed by a supporting cast that included Randolph Scott (left), Lyle Talbot, Alice Brady, Isabel Jewell and, best of all, as the press agent, Warren William. It was produced by Emanuel Cohen and directed by Henry Hathaway. Songs included: *I Was Saying To The Moon; On A Typical Tropic Night; Go West Young Man* Johnny Burke, Arthur Johnston.
▽

△

Absurdity begat absurdity in **Can This Be Dixie?** (20th Century-Fox), a ludicrous programmer which served no purpose other than to cast aspersions on the sanity of the creative talents involved. Pivoting on whether or not Slim Summerville can make good the phoney cheque for five hundred dollars he signed in payment of a debt owed by crusty old Claude Gillingwater (if he cannot, then a scheming Yankee banker gets to marry a pretty Southern belle who will be forced into wedlock in order to save her grandfather's plantation), it was an unequivocal stinker that not even the precocious talent of its young star, Jane Withers (illustrated), could begin to redeem. It was written by Lamar Trotti from a story by Trotti and George Marshall, directed by Marshall and produced by Sol M. Wurtzel, with Sammy Lee in charge of the choreography. The rest of the cast included Helen Wood, Thomas Beck, Sara Haden, Donald Cook, James Burke, Jed Prouty and Hattie McDaniel. Songs: *Pick Pick Pickaninny; Does You Wanna Go To Hebben?; Uncle Tom's Cabin Is A Cabaret Now; It's Julep Time In Dixieland* Sidney Clare; Harry Akst.

Lawrence Tibbett (illustrated) found himself on the lower half of a double bill in **Under Your Spell** (20th Century-Fox), a shamefully flimsy vehicle for one of the screen's most commanding voices. He played an overworked singer (but not on this occasion) who, with the help of his butler (Arthur Treacher) temporarily manages to escape the hurly-burly of show business only to be lured back into it by a society heiress called Cynthia Drexel (Wendy Barrie). Gregory Ratoff played Tibbett's manager called Petroff, with Berton Churchill as a judge, Jed Prouty and Claudia Coleman (as a Mr and Mrs Twerp), and Charles Richman completing the cast. It was written (feebly) by Frances Hyland and Saul Elkins (based on stories by Bernice Mason and Sy Bartlett) and directed by Otto (Ludwig) Preminger (making his American debut). Songs included: *Amigo; My Little Mule Wagon; Under Your Spell* Arthur Schwartz, Howard Dietz.
▽

Unsure what to do with a young artist on their books by the name of Judy Garland (illustrated) MGM loaned her out to 20th Century-Fox for **Pigskin Parade**. It was her first feature film and in it she received ninth billing below Dixie Dunbar, Arline Judge, Betty Grable, Johnny Downs, Stuart Erwin, The Yacht Club Boys, Jack Haley and Patsy Kelly. Though she made no major impact, she had three songs by Sidney Mitchell and Lew Pollack ('Balboa', 'The Texas Tornado' and 'It's Love I'm After') which she delivered charmingly, and as a freckle-faced, pig-tailed hillbilly by the name of Sairy Dodd – adequately satisfied the demands of an un-demanding screenplay by Harry Tugend, Jack Yellen and William Conselman. The story was by Arthur Sheekman, Nat Perrin and Mark Kelly and, in a nutshell, concerned a hillbilly football team from Texas who, by mistake, are invited to play against Yale in New Haven. Stuart Erwin was the team's country bumpkin quarterback (whose penchant for sending watermelons sailing over the field had made him a local celebrity); Garland was his kid sister, Jack Haley was the team's coach, Patsy Kelly his enthusiastic wife. A delightful campus musical with the accent on horseplay rather than on ball play, **Pigskin Parade** also featured Tony Martin, Fred Kohler Jr, Grady Sutton, Elisha Cook Jr, Alan Ladd and Eddie Nugent, Darryl F. Zanuck produced and the direction was by David Butler. Other songs: *You Do The Darndest Things, Baby; T.S.U. Alma Mater; Hold That Bulldog; You're Slightly Terrific* Mitchell, Pollack; *Woo Woo; We'd Rather Be In College* The Yacht Club Boys.
▷

They could have called it 'The Broadway Melody
of 1937' but in deference to Eleanor Powell. each
one of whose taps was worth its weight in
silver dollars, they named it **Born to Dance**
(MGM). And it mattered not one iota that Miss
Powell found herself understudying Virginia
Bruce (who played an impossibly difficult musical comedy star) because, just like little Ruby
Keeler in *42nd Street* (Warner Bros. 1933) she
stepped in at the last moment and, well, you
know the rest. Nor did it matter a jot that Miss
Bruce featured in Sid Silvers and Jack
McGowan's screenplay (story by McGowan,
Silvers and Buddy De Sylva) as a singer, while
there could be no mistaking the fact that Miss
Powell's talents lay in other directions. What
counted in **Born to Dance** wasn't its thimbleful
of plot (which also involved sailors on shore
leave) but the splendour of Cole Porter's tip-top
score and the razz-a-matazz of its staging (by
Dave Gould). Particularly splashy was the all-
out 'Swingin' The Jinx Away' finale, set on
board a typical musical comedy battleship and
involving the services of literally scores of dance
extras as well as Buddy Ebsen, Frances Langford
and, of course, Miss Powell (centre), whose
spectacular entrance down a long spiral stairway left no one in any doubt as to who was the
star of the show. Other musical highlights in this
nautical farrago were Miss Bruce's rendering
of 'I've Got You Under My Skin', Powell tapping
her way through the sound barrier with 'Rap-
Rap-Tap on Wood'; Reginald Gardiner conducting an invisible orchestra in Central Park in a
version of Ponchielli's 'Dance of The Hours'
which miraculously turns into 'Easy to Love';
and a deliciously camp item called 'Love Me, Love
My Pekinese' sung by Miss Bruce to a ship-load of
admiring sailors. Completing the score were the
opening number 'Rolling Home', 'Hey Babe,
Hey', and 'Entrance of Lucy James'. James
Stewart received second billing to Miss Powell
and though clearly no asset to musical comedy,
got by on his charm and appealing good looks.
Completing the cast were Alan Dinehart, Una
Merkel, Raymond Walburn, Juanita Quigley
and the dance team of Georges and Jaina. It was
zestfully directed by Roy Del Ruth and the
producer was Jack Cummings.

College Holiday (Paramount), which starred
Jack Benny, George Burns, Gracie Allen and
Martha Raye was a musical comedy seeped in
vaudeville 'shtick' that generated an appeal of its
own by the sheer nothingness of its piffling plot
(Ancient Greece freak converts bankrupt hotel
into a love laboratory for the mating of perfect
physical specimens of both sexes). Jack Benny's
role in all this was to recruit suitable candidates,
but he decides, instead, to gather together a
group of college entertainers who, rather than
take part in the aforementioned experiment, put
on a minstrel show. Result? The hotel makes
enough money to get back on its feet. Benny's
unique interpretation of 'Love in Bloom' by
Ralph Rainger and Leo Robin, a few duets by co-
stars Marsha Hunt and Leif Erickson, plus the
terpsichorean skills of Johnny Downs (left) and
Eleanore Whitney (right) momentarily helped
keep the mindlessness of it all at bay; and there
was good support, too, from Mary Boland,
Olympe Bradna. Louis Da Pron, Ben Blue and
Etienne Girardot. It was written by J.P. McEvoy,
Harlan Ware, Henry Myers and Jay Gorney,
produced by Harlan Thompson and directed by
Frank Tuttle. Songs: *I Adore You*; *A Rhyme For
Love*; *So What?* Rainger, Robin; *Who's That
Knocking At My Heart?*; *The Sweetheart Waltz*
Burton Lane, Ralph Freed.

There was very little difference in content between Bobby Breen's sentimental weepie **Rainbow on the River** (RKO) and a typical Shirley
Temple vehicle. In **Rainbow**. Breen played a
post-war Southern lad who is forced to leave the
care and protection of a loving black mammy
(Louise Beavers) for a miserable existence in New
York with his Yankee grandmother (May Robson) and an assortment of uninviting relatives
(Benita Hume, Marilyn Knowlden (left), Alan
Mowbray). But just as Miss Temple would have
done, young Master Breen (right) soon brings a
smile to his grandmother's face and, with the
inevitable dispossession of his hateful relatives,
not to mention the timely arrival of his faithful
mammy to help put a smile on *his* face – Earl
Snell and William Hurlburt's screenplay (from a
novel by Mrs C.V. Jamison) was assured of its
happy ending. The Hall Johnson Choir were
there to provide some musical support (as they
usually were with stories that involved the
South); it was directed by Kurt Neumann in a
manner that indicated he had a sideline business
manufacturing paper handkerchiefs, and the
producer was Sol Lesser. As well as the durable
'Rainbow On The River' by Paul Francis Webster
and Louis Alter the score also included 'Waiting
For The Sun To Rise' by Arthur Swanstrom and
Karl Hajos.

James Melton (centre right), whose first screen musical hadn't exactly turned him into a star, fared no better in his second attempt for Warner Bros./First National, a feeble programmer called **Sing Me a Love Song** (GB: **Come Up Smiling**), whose lack of production values clearly reflected the studio's own lack of faith in their leading man. A silly screenplay by Sig Herzig and Jerry Wald, from a story by Harry Sauber, had Melton as a playboy who takes up incognito employment in his own store, and who, in no time at all, falls in love with one of his staff (Patricia Ellis, right). Directed by Ray Enright for supervisor Sam Bischoff, the movie also featured Hugh Herbert, Allen Jenkins, ZaSu Pitts (centre left), Dennis Moore, Nat Pendleton, Walter Catlett (left), and Ann Sheridan, with Bobby Connolly in charge of the musical numbers. Songs: *Summer Night*; *The Little House That Love Built*; *That's The Least You Can Do For A Lady* Al Dubin, Harry Warren; *Your Eyes Have Told Me So* Gus Khan, Walter Blaufuss, Egbert Van Alstyne.
▽

Though the plot Sam Engel dreamed up for Shirley Temple's latest offering **Stowaway** (20th Century-Fox) was very much in keeping with all her other plots – orphaned daughter of murdered Chinese missionaries stows away on board wealthy Robert Young's (centre) luxury cruise ship, is adopted by him, and, in return, sees to it that he and his wife Alice Faye (centre left) live happily ever after – it benefitted greatly from a better-than-usual screenplay (by William Conselman, Arthur Sheekman and Nat Perrin) and from a really strong cast who, under William A. Seiter's attentive direction, were actually allowed to give performances in their own right. The result was one of the best, most entertaining Temple musicals to date and, apart from its tacked-on seasonal ending (in which Shirley sang 'That's What I Want For Christmas' by Irving Caesar and Gerald Marks), the least sentimental. With its young star conversing in Chinese as well as doing impersonations of Eddie Cantor, Ginger Rogers (with a Fred Astaire doll!), and Al Jolson (singing 'Mammy'); and Alice Faye singing two really excellent Mack Gordon and Harry Revel songs – 'Goodnight My Love' (one of her biggest hits) and 'One Never Knows Does One' – the film was a box-office smash and one of the studio's most profitable films in 1936. Eugene Pallette, Helen Westley, Arthur Treacher, J. Edward Bromberg, Allan Lane (right) and Astrid Allwyn were also cast; and it was produced by Buddy De Sylva, with Earl Carroll and Harold Wilson as associate producers. Other songs: *You Gotta S-M-I-L-E If You Want To Be H-A-P-P-Y*; *I Wanna Go To The Zoo*; Gordon, Revel.
▽

Deanna Durbin (centre) made her feature film debut in **Three Smart Girls** (Universal) with Nan Grey (right) and Barbara Read (left) completing the trio. Miss Durbin's limited acting abilities were in no way stretched in Adele Commandini and Austin Parker's entertaining screenplay (story by Miss Commandini), but what she had to do (which was to reunite her divorced parents) she did ably and charmingly enough. Her screen sisters – the Misses Grey and Read – were also part of the reconciliation plot and went about their business equally well. Daddy was played by Charles Winninger, Binnie Barnes was a gold-digger who sets her sights on him, and Nella Walker was his ex-wife. Also cast: Ray Milland, Alice Brady, Mischa Auer, Ernest Cossart, Hobart Cavanaugh, Dennis O'Keefe and Franklin Pangborn. It was produced and directed by Joseph Pasternak and Henry Koster (whom studio head Carl Laemmle imported from Germany when Universal's European division closed) with Charles Rogers as executive producer. Gus Kahn, Walter Jurmann and Bronislau Kaper wrote two songs especially for Miss Durbin – 'My Heart Is Singing' and 'Someone To Care For Me' – both of which became instant hits. Miss Durbin also sang 'Il Bacio' by Luigi Arditi. Twelve years later Joe Pasternak repackaged the property at MGM, turned it into a Technicolor vehicle for Jane Powell and Jeanette MacDonald, and called it *Three Daring Daughters*.

△

Music came to the aid of **Banjo On My Knee** (20th Century-Fox), in which the studio tank doubled as the Mississippi River, where the film was set. All about 'pappy' Walter Brennan's attempts to get his son, Joel McCrea (left), to consummate his marriage to Barbara Stanwyck (right) – McCrea, due to some trouble with the police on his wedding night, takes off and only returns nine reels later – it featured Stanwyck in one of her few comedy roles, and singing her own songs. On this occasion, however, the leads were outclassed by the supporting performers, best of whom were Walter Catlett as a put-upon photographer, and Buddy Ebsen, whose eccentric hoofing was one of the film's genuine delights. Also cast: Helen Westley, Tony Martin, The Hall Johnson Choir, Katherine De Mille and Minna Gombell. Associate producer Nunnally Johnson wrote it from a novel by Harry Hamilton; it was produced by Darryl F. Zanuck and directed by John Cromwell. Songs: *Where The Lazy River Goes By* (sung by Stanwyck); *There's Something In The Air*; *With A Banjo On My Knee* Harold Adamson, Jimmy McHugh; *St Louis Blues* W.C. Handy.

Paramount loaned Bing Crosby to Columbia for **Pennies from Heaven**, a convoluted and improbable yarn in which the crooner played a modern-day troubadour whose ambition is to become a lute-strumming gondolier in Venice. But after being falsely accused of smuggling, he finds himself serving a short sentence in prison instead. Prior to his release he is handed a note by a convicted murderer *en route* to the electric chair with the name and address of the murdered man's only living relatives. The convict's last wish is that Crosby (illustrated, centre) should make amends to the family on his behalf. The relatives turn out to be a 10-year-old girl called Patsy (Edith Fellows, centre right) and her imprudent grandfather (Donald Meek). Just how he helps them formed the basis of Joe Swerling's faintly ludicrous screenplay (from a story by William Rankin). Despite a really stalwart attempt on Crosby's behalf to bring a patina of credibility to his characterization, as well as an engaging performance from little Miss Fellows, **Pennies from Heaven** was a so-so musical which, apart from its catchy title song and two Arthur Johnston–Johnny Burke numbers, a number called 'Skeleton In The Closet' (performed by Crosby and Louis Armstrong) and 'One, Two, Button Your Shoe' (Crosby), didn't have a great deal going for it. Madge Evans, John Gallaudet, Tom Dugan, Nana Bryant, Harry Tyler, William Stack, Tom Ricketts and Charles Wilson were also featured, the producer was Emanuel Cohen and it was directed by Norman McLeod. Other songs: *So Do I*; *Let's Call A Heart A Heart* Johnston, Burke.
▽

1937

Academy Awards

Best Picture
NOMINATIONS INCLUDED: *In Old Chicago* (20th Century-Fox) produced by Darryl F. Zanuck with Kenneth MacGowan. *100 Men And A Girl* (Universal) Produced by Charles R. Rogers with Joe Pasternak

Supporting Actress
Alice Brady *In Old Chicago*

Writing (Original Story)
NOMINATIONS INCLUDED: *A Damsel In Distress* (RKO) Carroll Clark. *Every Day's A Holiday* (Major Productions, Paramount) Wiard Ihnen *Manhattan Merry-Go-Round* (Republic) John Victor Mackay. *Vogues Of 1938* (Wanger, UA) Alexander Toluboff. *You're A Sweetheart* (Universal) Jack Otterson.

Sound Recording
NOMINATIONS INCLUDED: *Hitting A New High* (RKO) John O. Aalberg. *In Old Chicago* E.H. Hansen. *Maytime* Douglas Shearer. *100 Men And A Girl* Homer Tasker.

Film Editing
NOMINATIONS INCLUDED: *100 Men And A Girl* Bernard W. Burton

Assistant Director
(Award not given after this year.) Robert Webb *In Old Chicago*

Music
Song
'Sweet Leilani' *Waikiki Wedding* (Paramount) Harry Owens
NOMINATIONS INCLUDED: 'Remember Me' *Mr Dodd Takes The Air* (WB) Harry Warren *cm*; Al Dubin *lyr*. 'That Old Feeling' *Vogues Of 1938* Sammy Fain *cm*; Lew Brown *lyr*. 'They Can't Take That Away From Me' *Shall We Dance* (RKO) George Gershwin *cm*; Ira Gershwin *lyr*. 'Whispers In The Dark' *Artists And Models* (Paramount) Frederick Hollander *cm*; Leo Robin *lyr*.

Score
(Throughout 1937, Best Score was considered a music department achievement and the award was presented to the department head instead of to the composer.) *100 Men And A Girl* Universal Studio Music Dept.; Charles Previn, head. (No composer credit.)
NOMINATIONS INCLUDED: *In Old Chicago* 20th Century-Fox Studio Music Dept.; Louis Silvers, head. (No composer credit.) *Make A Wish* (Lesser, RKO) Dr Hugo Riesenfeld, musical director. Score by Dr Hugo Riesenfeld. *Maytime* (MGM) M-G-M Studio Music Dept.; Nat W. Finston, head. Score by Herbert Stothart. *Snow White And The Seven Dwarfs* (Disney, RKO) Walt Disney Studio Music Dept.; Leigh Harline, head. Score by Frank Churchill, Leigh Harline and Paul J. Smith. *Something To Sing About* (Grand National) Grand National Studio Music Dept.; C. Bakaleinikoff, musical director. Score by Victor Schertzinger.

Dance Direction
(Award not given after this year.) Hermes Pan for 'Fun House' number from *A Damsel In Distress*
NOMINATIONS INCLUDED: Busby Berkeley for 'The Finale' number from *Varsity Show* (WB). Bobby Connolly for 'Too Marvelous For Words' number from *Ready, Willing And Able* (WB). Dave Gould for 'All God's Chillun Got Rhythm' number from *A Day At The Races* (MGM). Sammy Lee for 'Swing Is Here To Stay' number from *Ali Baba Goes To Town* (20th Century-Fox). Harry Losee for 'Prince Igor Suite' number from *Thin Ice* (20th Century-Fox). LeRoy Prinz for 'Luau' number from *Waikiki Wedding*.

The Annual Top Moneymaking Films
INCLUDED: *Artists And Models. The Big Broadcast Of 1937* (Paramount). *Born to Dance* (MGM). *College Holiday* (Paramount). *Maytime. Mountain Music* (Paramount). *One In A Million* (20th Century-Fox). *On The Avenue* (20th Century-Fox). *Pigskin Parade* (20th Century-Fox). *Rainbow On The River* (Principal, RKO). *Shall We Dance. Swing Time* (RKO). *Wake Up And Live* (20th Century-Fox). *Waikiki Wedding. You Can't Have Everything* (20th Century-Fox).

Although Martha Raye received top billing for the first time in **Hideaway Girl** (Paramount), Joseph Moncure March's screenplay (story by David Garth) centred on co-star Shirley Ross and her unfortunate marriage to a phoney count (Monroe Owsley) who steals other people's jewels for a living. Miss Raye, in an attempt to repeat the success she had had with a Sam Coslow song called 'Mr Paganini' in *Rhythm On The Range* (Paramount, 1936) belted out a number called 'Beethoven, Mendelssohn and Liszt' (also by Mr Coslow), but the joke wasn't as amusing the second time around, and it was left to Shirley Ross (illustrated) to make something of the movie's only potential hit – 'You're Dancing Into My Heart' by Ralph Freed and Burton Lane. Robert Cummings (illustrated), Louis Da Pron, Wilma Francis and Elizabeth Russell were also in it; it was produced by A.M. Botsford and directed by George Archainbaud. Other songs: *What Is Love?* Ralph Rainger, Leo Robin, Victor Young; *Two Birdies Up A Tree* Ralph Freed, Burton Lane.
▽

Though Lily Pons (right) sang 'Una Voce Poco Fa' from Rossini's *The Barber of Seville* in **That Girl From Paris** (RKO), the goings-on in her latest effort were decidedly low-brow. The story (by Jane Murfin, based on a magazine story by I. Carey Wonderly) required the *diva* to jilt a rather persistent suitor by masquerading as a peasant and joining up with a group of swing musicians collectively known as McLean's Wildcats. In no time at all she falls in love with the Wildcats' leader Windy (Géne Raymond, 2nd left) and – well, that, more or less, was it. As insubstantial as air, it existed only to show off its petite star's vocal prowess in a range of moods and styles, and, accordingly, the varied musical programme featured Johann Strauss II's 'The Blue Danube' in swing-time and Heinrich Panofka's 'Tarantella' – plus a handful of songs by Arthur Schwartz and Edward Heyman. P.J. Wolfson and Dorothy Yost's screenplay gave comic employment to Jack Oakie (centre), Herman Bing, Lucille Ball (left), Mischa Auer (2nd right), and Frank Jenks (3rd right); it was produced by Pandro S. Berman, and briskly directed by Leigh Jason. Andre Kostelanetz conducted the operatic sequences. Songs: *Seal It With A Kiss; My Nephew From Nice; Love and Learn; Moonface; The Call To Arms.* Remake of *Street Girl* (1929). ◁

On The Avenue (20th Century-Fox) was a routine backstage musical, but with enough Irving Berlin numbers in it to lull audiences into forgetting the trivia which claimed their attention. Dick Powell (right) played a Broadway star-cum-producer whose current show contains a lampooning sketch of a society millionairess (Madeleine Carroll), and had Miss Carroll doing her damnedest to make Powell drop the sketch but succeeding only in falling in love with him – much to the chagrin of the show's star, Alice Faye. Although Faye (centre) was third-billed, she dominated the proceedings, singing such Berlin favourites as 'This Year's Kisses', 'I've Got My Love To Keep Me Warm' (with Dick Powell), 'He Ain't Got Rhythm', and 'Slumming On Park Avenue'. The Ritz Brothers, Alan Mowbray, George Barbier, Cora Witherspoon, Stepin Fetchit (left), Joan Davis, Sig Rumann and Billy Gilbert supported, Darryl F. Zanuck produced, Seymour Felix directed the dances and Roy Del Ruth the film, from a screenplay by Gene Markey and William Conselman. Reworked by 20th Century-Fox (1960) as Let's Make Love. Other songs: The Girl On The Police Gazette; You're Laughing At Me. Oddly, the title song was dropped prior to the film's release.

Darryl F. Zanuck paid Olympic ice-skating champion Sonja Henie $75,000 to make her screen debut in One In a Million (20th Century-Fox) and was not in the least bit surprised when, at the final accounting, the film netted a mammoth $2,000,000. Cleverly buttressed by a strong cast that included Adolphe Menjou, Jean Hersholt (right), and Don Ameche (centre), with the Ritz Brothers, Arline Judge and Dixie Dunbar there to supply the laughs – screen newcomer Henie (left) skated her way across a thin-ice plot which had her being trained for a future Olympics by her Swiss innkeeper father (Hersholt). Menjou appeared as the impresario of an all-girl band, with Borrah Minnevitch and his Harmonica Rascals, Leah Ray, Shirley Deane, Montagu Love and Albert Conti completing the cast. Miss Henie's fresh, wholesome personality, coupled with her unquestioned ability to set poetry in motion every time she slapped on her blades, made her an instant star and one of the studio's biggest money-makers. Leonard Praskins and Mark Kelly provided both the story and screenplay; Zanuck produced, and it was directed by Sidney Lanfield. Songs: One In A Million; We're Back In Circulation Again; Who's Afraid Of Love? Lovely Lady In White; The Moonlight Waltz Sidney Mitchell, Lew Pollack.
▽

Little Jane Withers (centre) thwarted a spy plot in The Holy Terror (20th Century-Fox), though her sleuthing activities were not nearly as entertaining as the production's numerous musical and comical embellishments – such as the singing of Tony Martin and Leah Ray, the familiar clowning of El Brendel, ditto Joan Davis, and the rubber-legged antics of Joe Lewis (foreground left). John Eldredge, Andrew Tombes, Gavin Muir and Fred Kohler Jr were also in it, and it was written by Lou Breslow and John Patrick with James Tinling directing. Songs: There I Go Again; Don't Know Myself Since I Know You; Don't Sing; The Call Of The Siren; Everybody Swing Sidney Clare, Harry Akst.
▽

In With Love And Kisses (Melody Pictures) Pinky Tomlin (2nd left, foreground) was a country-bumpkin songwriter who can only write when he is milking cows. Maybe scriptwriter Sherman Lowe (story by Lowe and Al Martin) should have indulged in a spot of milking as well, for there was no sign of inspiration anywhere in this 67-minute programmer. The far-fetched plot had a radio singer (Toby Wing, left) stealing one of Tomlin's songs, then being pursued by a racketeer (Russell Hopton) who has decided to go into the music publishing business hoping to make a mint out of Tomlin's cow-inspired compositions. The below par direction was by Leslie Goodwins whose cast included Arthur Houseman (foreground centre), Fuzzy Knight, and, as themselves, The Peters Sisters, Jerry Bergen and Billy Gray, and Chelito and Gabriel. Songs included: Don't Ever Lose It; I'm Right Back Where I Started Coy Poe, Pinky Tomlin; The Trouble With Me Is You Harry Tobias, Tomlin; Sweet Buddy LeRoux, Tomlin, Al Heath; With Love And Kisses Connie Lee; Sittin' On The Edge Of My Chair Paul Parks, Coy Poe, Tomlin.
▽

What happens when an elegant Viennese waltz-palace loses its three-quarter-time patrons to the more energetic tempi of an American jazz band who have taken up residence next door, was the subject of Champagne Waltz (Paramount), a pleasant but by no means vintage musical that starred Gladys Swarthout (as the daughter of the ousted waltz maestro) and Fred MacMurray (as the jazz band's leader), with Jack Oakie, Veloz and Yolanda (illustrated), Herman Bing, Vivienne Osborne, Frank Forest, Benny Baker, Ernest Cossart and Fritz Leiber rounding off the cast. Basically a contest between 'serious' music and the more popular kind, it was climaxed by an elaborate production number featuring both forms, with neither emerging from the melée particularly well. Don Hartman and Frank Butler wrote it from a story by Billy Wilder and H.S. Kraft, it was produced by Harlan Thompson and directed, with only the occasional lightness of touch it required, by Edward Sutherland. Apart from 'The Blue Danube' by Strauss II and 'Champagne Waltz' by Milton Drake, Ben Oakland and Con Conrad (danced by Veloz and Yolanda), the score included: Could I Be In Love Leo Robin, William Daly; The Merry-Go-Round Ann Ronell; Paradise In Waltz Time Sam Coslow, Frederick Hollander; When Is A Kiss Not A Kiss Ralph Freed, Burton Lane.
▽

THIRTIES MUSICALS

Only one song – 'Will You Remember?' – ▷ remained from Sigmund Romberg's original score in the film version of **Maytime** (MGM) – and it was reprised six times in various forms throughout this sumptuously mounted (by Hunt Stromberg) production for Jeanette Mac-Donald and Nelson Eddy (illustrated). The rest of the music comprised mainly operatic extracts, which was perfectly acceptable since the re-furbished story (by Noel Langley, who also wrote the screenplay) concerned a great opera singer and the tragic love affair she has with a young baritone. In one of his more jocular moods, Eddy sang 'Ham and Eggs', in which he codded several famous arias, but the film's big musical event was a specially composed opera called 'Czaritza', based on themes from Tchaikovsky's Fifth Symphony, during which its two principals (MacDonald and Eddy) realize, as they sing their hearts out to each other, that, after years apart, they are still passionately in love. If **Maytime** was pleasing to the ear, it was also a treat for the eye, being the best photographed (by Oliver T. Marsh) of all the MacDonald-Eddy black and white operettas. Director Robert Z. Leonard kept the proceedings tasteful despite the melodramatic plot, and imbued the film with a melancholy appropriate to the passing of time. The story, told in flashback by the aged soprano Marcia Mornay (MacDonald) to a young would-be singer (Lynne Carver), pointed the moral that a love once found must never be relinquished, no matter what. John Barrymore appeared as Mac-Donald's jealous mentor, dominating the screen in what was to be one of his last decent roles, with Herman Bing, Tom Brown, Sig Rumann, Rafaela Ottiano, Charles Judels, Paul Porcasi, Guy Bates Post and Billy Gilbert prominent in a large supporting cast. Other music included: *Now Is The Month Of Maying* traditional, with lyrics by Thomas Morley; *Summer Is A Cumin In* (trad); *Love's Old Sweet Song* J.L. Molloy, G. Clifton Bingham; *Vive L'Opera* folk song with lyrics by Bob Wright and Chet Forrest; *Le Regiment De Sambre Et Meuse* Robert Planquette; *Plantons La Vigne* (trad); *Carry Me Back To Old Virginny* James Bland; *Santa Lucia* Teodoro Cottrau; *Les Filles De Cadiz* Delibes, de Musset; an aria from *Les Huguenots* Meyerbeer.

Hollywood's exotic idea of Hawaii was splashed ▷ across the screen in **Waikiki Wedding** (Paramount), a hula-hula romance which starred Bing Crosby (centre) as a public relations man for a pineapple concern, and Shirley Ross (right) as a disillusioned Miss Pineapple Girl. The story had the former doing his persuasive best to convince the latter that Hawaii was the most love-kissed spot on earth – and, with some help from composers Ralph Rainger, Leo Robin and Harry Owens, and some hindrance from choreographer LeRoy Prinz, whose grass-skirted dances were enough to put the most ardent Hawaiian chauvinist off the place, he succeeded. Particularly winning was Owens's 'Sweet Leilani', crooned into immortality by Bing. Martha Raye (left) was in it too, so was comedian Bob Burns, as well as George Barbier, Leif Erickson, Grady Sutton, Granville Bates and Anthony Quinn. It was written by Frank Butler, Don Hartman and Walter DeLeon (from a story by Butler and Hartman), produced by Arthur Hornblow, and directed by Frank Tuttle. Other songs: *Sweet Is The Word For You*; *In A Little Hula Heaven*; *Blue Hawaii*; *Okolehao*; *Nani Ona Pua* Rainger, Robin.

Grace Moore (featured centre) played an Australian prima donna in **When You're In Love** (Columbia), with Cary Grant as the man she marries out of convenience in order to gain entrance to the United States from Mexico. The rest of Robert Riskin's screenplay (from an idea by Ethel Hill and Cedric Worth) predictably concerned itself – between songs – with turning the marriage of convenience into a genuine love match. Aline MacMahon played Miss Moore's manager, with Henry Stephenson, Thomas Mitchell, Catharine Doucet, Luis Alberni, Gerald Oliver Smith, Emma Dunn, George Pearce and Frank Puglia completing the cast. Jerome Kern and Dorothy Fields supplied Miss Moore with two new numbers: 'Our Song' and 'The Whistling Boy' – both pleasant enough; Leon Leonidoff (of Radio City Music Hall) staged the production ensembles. It was directed by Robert Riskin, with Everett Riskin as associate producer. Other songs: *Minnie The Moocher* Cab Calloway, Irving Mills, Clarence Gaskill (arranged for Grace Moore by Al Siegal); *In The Gloaming* Meta Orred, Annie F. Harrison; *Siboney* Dolly Morse, Ernest Lecuona; Schubert's *Serenade*; *The Waltz Song* ◁ (from 'Romeo and Juliet') Gounod.

In **Top Of The Town** (Universal) Gertrude Niesen sang four Harold Adamson–Jimmy McHugh songs: 'Blame It On The Rhumba', 'Where Are You?', 'Jamboree', and 'Top Of The Town', and Ella Logan sang three more: 'I Feel That Foolish Feeling Coming On', 'There's No Two Ways About It', and 'Fireman Save My Child'. The Three Sailors (alias Jason, Robson and Blue) did several imitations, including one of a giraffe; Mischa Auer turned his talents to *Hamlet* (for which he deserved no thanks) and a 12-year-old Jacqueline-of-all-trades called Peggy Ryan made her debut. Gregory Ratoff (as an agent) was also in it; so were George Murphy (left), Hugh Herbert, Henry Armetta, Claude Gillingwater, Ernest Cossart, The Californian Collegians and The Four Esquires. As for the plot, it had something to do with an heiress (Doris Nolan, right) who opens a fashionable Manhattan nightclub on top of a skyscraper. Brown Holmes and Charles Grayson wrote it (from a story by Lou Brock, who was also the associate producer) and the director was Ralph Murphy.

The story of **Swing While You're Able** (Melody Pictures) went something like this: Rich gal and her father have motor breakdown in the sticks, discover a hillbilly crooner and sign him to a radio contract. Business manager for the gal's old man sees the newcomer as a rival to romance and has him kidnapped on the eve of his first broadcast. Singer escapes, catches cold, and loses his voice. But he regains it – as well as the girl. End of story. Irredeemable in every way it featured Pinky Tomlin (right) as the hillbilly and Toby Wing (centre) as his girl. Marshall Neilan directed it (badly) from a story by Stanley Lowenstein and Charles Condon (screenplay by Condon and Sherman Lowe), with a cast that included H.C. Bradley, Monte Collins, Bert Roach, Suzanne Kaaren and 'Prince' Michael Romanoff, as well as Jimmy Newell and the Three Brian Sisters. Songs: *I'm Gonna Swing While I'm Able* Paul Parks, Connie Lee; *Swing, Brother, Swing* Al Heath, Buddy LeRoux; *Leave It Up To Uncle Jake* Parks, Lee, Heath, LeRoux; *You're My Strongest Weakness* Coy Poe, Heath, LeRoux; *One Girl In My Arms* Harry Tobias, Roy Ingraham; *I'm Just A Country Boy At Heart* Pinky Tomlin, Parks, Lee.

A lively little entry from Paramount, **Turn Off The Moon** satirized, to the accompaniment of several Sam Coslow songs, the astrology business. It starred Charles Ruggles as the owner of a furniture shop, and featured Marjorie Gateson as a secretary called Myrtle Tweep whom Ruggles has had every intention of marrying. Trouble is, their stars, so far, have never been right. They come right (according to astrologer Andrew Tombes) the night before the store's much trumpeted silver jubilee show (featuring Kenny Baker, several specialty acts, and Phil Harris and His Orchestra). All sorts of plot complications (courtesy of scenarists Marguerite Roberts, Harlan Ware and Paul Gerard Smith; story by Mildred Harrington) occurred – mainly involving Eleanore Whitney (illustrated) and Johnny Downs, a young couple whose own romance (according to the astrologer) has to be settled before Ruggles and Gateson get to say 'I do'. But it all came right in the end and, under Lewis Seiler's direction (choreography by LeRoy Prinz), the show twinkled brightly. It was edited by future director Edward Dmytryk. Also cast: Ben Blue, Romo Vincent – doing an impression of Charles Laughton in *Mutiny On The Bounty* (MGM, 1935) – Constance Bergen and Franklin Pangborn. Songs: *Turn Off The Moon*; *Easy On The Eyes*; *Jammin*; *That's Southern Hospitality*; *Little Wooden Soldier*.

Sing And Be Happy (20th Century-Fox) was the one about the irresponsible young blade who flouts the family business tradition (they run a successful ad. agency) to pursue a carefree existence of his own choosing. Anthony (Tony) Martin (right) finally made it to the top of the bill with this one, but the Ben Markson-Lew Breslow–John Patrick screenplay allowed him little opportunity to shine in anything but the songs (by Sidney Clare and Harry Akst). Leah Ray (left) provided the romantic interest, with other parts in it for stiff-necked Helen Westley, Joan Davis, Allan Lane, Dixie Dunbar (wasted), Chick Chandler and Berton Churchill. Milton H. Feld produced and the director was James Tinling. Songs included: *Sing And Be Happy*; *Travelin' Light*; *What A Beautiful Beginning*.

Nobody's Baby (MGM) was clearly intended to bring out the maternal instincts of the distaff members of the audience in telling the story of a ballroom dancer (Rosina Lawrence) who abandons her husband just as she is about to have a baby. She is cared for by Patsy Kelly (on bed) and Lyda Roberti (illustrated standing), as well as their respective boyfriends, Lynne Overman and Robert Armstrong. So much for the plot (by Harold Law, Hal Yates and Pat C. Flick, who also provided the screenplay). Director Gus Meins managed to chalk up a few hearty laughs, thanks to the comedic abilities of his two leading ladies, but by and large **Nobody's Baby** was nobody's triumph. Don Alvarado, Tom Dugan, Orrin Burke, and Dora Clement were also cast, and the producer was Hal Roach. Songs: *Quien Sabe*; *I Dreamed About This*; *All Dressed Up In Rhythm*; *Nobody's Baby* Walter Bullock, Marvin Hatley.

Another musical which found its inspiration in radio, **Wake Up And Live** (20th Century-Fox) top-billed Walter Winchell and Ben Bernie, capitalizing on the real-life radio 'feud' between them. Alice Faye, in third place as radio's 'wake up and live' advice-dispensing girl, got to sing one of her biggest hits – Mack Gordon and Harry Revel's 'There's A Lull In My Life', and Jack Haley (illustrated with Faye), as a crooner with mike fright, was a successful recipient of Miss Faye's good counselling who, with his microphone phobia finally conquered, becomes known on the air as 'The Phantom Troubadour'. The serviceable screenplay was by Harry Tugend and Jack Yellen (story by Curtis Kenyon from a novel by Dorothea Brande); it was directed by Sidney Lanfield for associate producer Kenneth MacGowan, and the cast included Patsy Kelly, Leah Ray – excellent singing Gordon and Revel's 'I Love You Much Too Much Muchacha', which number Joan Davis followed with a specialty dance – Ned Sparks, Walter Catlett, Grace Bradley and Douglas Fowley, as well as another two specialty acts, The Condos Brothers and The Brewster Twins. Jack Haley's singing voice was provided by the dubbing of Buddy Clark. Other songs: *Wake Up And Live*; *Never In A Million Years*; *Red Seal Malt*; *It's Swell Of You*; *Oh, But I'm Happy*; *I'm Bubbling Over* Mack Gordon, Harry Revel; *De Camptown Races* Stephen Foster.

THIRTIES MUSICALS

After *A Night At The Opera* (MGM, 1935), the Marx Brothers kept their fans waiting two years for **A Day At The Races** while they went on the road to try out, before live audiences, many of the routines used in their second MGM film. The end product revealed their Marxmanship to be slightly off centre – but not disastrously so, and if the irreverent zaniness that dominated most of their work at Paramount was less conspicuous than it had been before, the film still had enough good things in it to keep the front office happy. Musically it was more elaborate than any of its predecessors, the most effective sequence being 'All God's Chillun Got Rhythm' composed, as was the rest of the score, by Gus Kahn, Walter Jurmann and Bronislau Kaper. A musical interlude dominated by negros (including a teenage Dorothy Dandridge), it blended spirituals with jitterbug, and featured Harpo (illustrated) as a really swinging Pied Piper. Less successful was a long and curious ballet sequence ('Blue Venetian Waters') that was pure kitsch and had not a single positive feature. Groucho played Dr Hugo Hackenbush, a horse doctor who takes over a sanitorium at the request of wealthy Mrs Upjohn (Margaret Dumont); Harpo was a jockey, Chico a Tootsie-Frootsie ice-cream vendor. The film's horse-race finale was in the best Marxian tradition and the funniest thing in the film. Sam Wood directed. Also cast: Allan Jones, Maureen O'Sullivan, Douglass Dumbrille, Sig Rumann, Robert Middlemass and The Crinoline Choir. Other songs: *Tomorrow Is Another Day*; *A Message From The Man In The Moon* (fragment).
▽

◁ **High Wide And Handsome** (Paramount), set in Pennsylvania in 1859, was one of the screen's few really worthwhile 'pioneer' musicals. Written by Oscar Hammerstein II, and with a beautiful and beautifully integrated score by Hammerstein and Jerome Kern, it depicted the bitter struggle between poor oil prospectors and the greedy railroad freight tycoons who set out to prevent them from building a pipe-line. A supremely good example of the Hollywood musical in advance of the stage musical (the epoch-making *Oklahoma!* arrived on Broadway six years later), it starred Irene Dunne (illustrated) – who had four songs in all, including the rousing title number and the lyrical 'Folks Who Live On The Hill', Randolph Scott (illustrated) as a farmer, and Dorothy Lamour as a singer, as well as Alan Hale and Akim Tamiroff as a pair of agreeable villains, Elizabeth Patterson, Charles Bickford, William Frawley and Raymond Walburn. Responsible for its striking unity of vision was director Rouben Mamoulian, again making a significant contribution to the evolution of the film musical. The choreographer was LeRoy Prinz. Other songs: *Can I Forget You?*; *The Things I Want*; *Allegheny Al*; *Will You Marry Me Tomorrow, Maria?*

△

Described at the time as 'an amateur show put on by professionals', **The Hit Parade** (Republic) made an assiduous attempt to follow in the more illustrious footsteps of the *Big Broadcast* series, but lost its way round about reel two. Added to which, its roster of stars, including The Gentle Maniacs, The Toc Toc Girls, Eddy Duchin, Duke Ellington and Carl Hoff's Orchestras, Pick and Pat, Al Pearce (the Voice of Experience), Oscar and Elmer, ventriloquist Max Terhune (whose specialty was imitating trains) and Ed Thorgersen were no match for Bing Crosby, Kate Smith, Jack Oakie, Burns and Allen, Ethel Merman, Bill Robinson, Lyda Roberti, Cab Calloway and The Mills Brothers – all of them distinguished alumni of the Paramount series. The story (by Bradford Ropes, screenplay by Ropes and Samuel Ornitz), which would barely fill an eye-glass, concerned Phil Regan's attempts to find a new singing star for his radio show. He does, in the shape of Frances Langford (illustrated, with Phil Regan) who fits the bill on every count, except that she's being pursued by a parole officer – a fact that only comes to light on the eve of her big broadcast . . . Louise Henry, Pert Kelton, Edward Brophy, Inez Courtney, Monroe Owsley and William Demarest were in it too; it was produced by Nat Levine and directed by Gus Meins. Songs: *Sweet Heartache* Ned Washington, Sammy Stept; *Hail Alma Mater* Sammy Stept; *Last Night I Dreamed Of You*; *You'd Like It*; *I'll Reach For A Star*; *The Lady Wants To Dance*; *Was It Rain*; *Love Is Good For Anything That Ails You* Lou Handman, Walter Hirsch; *I've Got To Be A Rug Cutter* Duke Ellington.

△

Though called **New Faces Of 1937** (RKO), there weren't many of them about in this top-heavy revue into which everything, except flair, was thrown. It starred Joe Penner, Milton Berle, Parkyakarkas (radio comedian Harry Parks) and Harriet Hilliard, with Jerome Cowan, Thelma Leeds, Lorraine Krueger, Tommy Mack, Bert Gordon. The Three Chocolateers (illustrated), Patricia Wilder and, making her debut in a small way, Ann Miller. A backstage excuse for a series of songs, dances (staged by Sammy Lee) and sketches, it had very little to recommend it with the exception of several Sammy Fain–Lew Brown songs, the best of them being 'Our Penthouse On Third Avenue', 'Love Is Never Out Of Season', 'It Goes To Your Feet', and 'I Didn't Have You'. No fewer than six people had a hand in the screenplay (Nat Perrin, Philip G. Epstein, Irving Brecher, Harold Kussell, Harry Clork and Howard J. Green) which, in turn, was derived from a story by George Bradshaw appropriately called *Shoestring*. Edward Small produced, and the director was Leigh Jason. Other songs included: *Take The World Off Your Shoulders* Fain, Brown; *Widow In Lace* Walter Bullock, Harold Spina; *New Faces* Charles Henderson; *Peckin'* Ben Pollack, Harry James.

James Melton's three-picture contract with Warner Bros. was completed with **Melody For Two**. Unfortunately, it was not a case of third time lucky, and Melton (illustrated) left the movie business forever but for a brief appearance in the 'La Traviata' sequence in MGM's *Ziegfeld Follies* (1946), having signally failed to achieve anything resembling stardom. Granted, he hadn't exactly been helped by his material which, in this instance was no better than his first two attempts. This time, Richard Macaulay's story (screenplay by George Bricker, Luci Ward and Joe K. Watson) cast him as an unsympathetic, self-indulgent and querulous bandleader who is eventually taken out of his ill humour by Patricia Ellis, but alas, too late for audiences to care. Marie Wilson (illustrated), Eddie Anderson, Charles Foy, Fred Keating, Dick Purcell, Winifred Shaw, Craig Reynolds and Donald O'Connor were also in it for director Louis King and supervisor Brian Foy; and the musical numbers were staged by Bobby Connolly and Richard Vreeland. Songs included the Al Dubin-Harry Warren classic, 'September In The Rain', which had first been heard as background music in *Stars Over Broadway* (Warner Bros. 1935). Dubin and Warren also composed the title number. Other songs: *A Flat In Manhattan*; *An Excuse For Dancing*; *Jose O'Neill The Cuban Heel*; *Dangerous Rhythm* M.K. Jerome, Jack Scholl.
▽

There was feudin', fightin', fussin' and fun a-plenty in **Mountain Music** (Paramount), a raucous romp through hillbilly territory, that starred Bob Burns and zippy Martha Raye as two of the dog-garndest sweethearts yew ever did see. Trouble is, he's suffering from bouts of schizophrenia, and only loves Miss Raye when he's aberrating. As it only takes a bucket of cold water poured over his head to bring him back to his senses, a determined Martha spends most of her time preventing him from being sluiced. Musical highlights to emerge from this good-natured nonsense were Raye's energetic handling of 'Good Morning', and Rufe Davis's one-man-band interpretation of 'Mama Don't 'Low No Bull Fiddle Playin' In Heah' – both by Sam Coslow, who supplied the entire score. John C. Moffitt, Duke Atterbury, Russel Crouse and Charles Lederer wrote it from a story by MacKinlay Kantor; it was produced by Benjamin Glazer, directed by Robert Florey and had a cast that also included John Howard, Terry Walker (left), George 'Gabby' Hayes (centre), Jan Duggan and Fuzzy Knight (right). Other songs: *If I Put My Heart In A Song*; *Can't you Hear That Mountain Music?*; *Thar She Comes*; *Hillbilly Wedding*.

For his first musical since Warner Bros. 'Footlight Parade' (1933), James Cagney (2nd right) moved to Grand National and, under Victor Schertzinger's direction, danced and sang his way through several numbers in **Something To Sing About**. He played a band leader who, after fame and fortune beckons in the shape of a Hollywood contract, marries his former band singer (Evelyn Daw, right) only to find the terms of his contract require his bachelorhood, which he then has to fake. William Frawley (left), Kathleen Lockhart (2nd left), James Newill, Mona Barrie and Harry Barris were also cast. Austin Parker wrote the lively screenplay, Harland Dixon staged the dance numbers, and the producer was Zion Myers. Songs: *Right Or Wrong*; *Any Old Love*; *Something To Sing About*; *Loving You*; *Out Of The Blue* Victor Schertzinger.

First seen as a Paramount silent in 1919, **23½ Hours Leave**, a World War I comedy, resurfaced from Grand National with its story more or less intact (a rookie takes a bet that he will breakfast with his general – and wins), but with the addition of four sprightly songs by Ted Koehler and Sammy Stept. It was produced by Douglas MacLean who had played the lead in the first version; directed by John G. Blystone, and this time featured James Ellison (right), Terry Walker, Morgan Hill, Arthur Lake (centre) Paul Harvey, Pat Gleason (left), Wally Maher Andy, and Ward Bond. The screenplay was by Harry Ruskin and Henry McCarty (additional dialogue by Samuel J. Warshawsky) from a story by Mary Roberts Rinehart. Whatever significance its story, with its special emphasis on life in a training camp, may have had in 1919, had evaporated by 1937 and the film made no impression whatever. Songs: *Good Night My Lucky Day*; *Now You're Talking My Language*; *It Must Be Love*; *We Happen To Be In The Army*.

Fred Astaire and Ginger Rogers's seventh feature in four years was **Shall We Dance** (RKO) in which Astaire was cast as a ballet dancer with a phoney Russian name (Petroff) and accent, and Rogers as an equally phoney broad who wishes to marry into society. They soon catch each other out and, after the inevitable complications and misunderstandings provided by Allan Scott and Ernest Pagano's screenplay (adapted by P.J. Wolfson from a story by Lee Loeb and Harold Buchman), end up as a dancing team. It was, alas, all rather infantile, with Edward Everett Horton and Eric Blore contributing to the general tedium of the plot. But who cared about plot when there were so many glorious George and Ira Gershwin numbers (eg 'Slap That Bass', 'They All Laughed', 'Let's Call The Whole Thing Off') to take one's mind off it? For 'Slap That Bass' (choreography by Hermes Pan and Harry Losee), Van Nest Polglase created a highly stylized ship's engine room in which Astaire (illustrated) imitated the movement of the machines to a jivey arrangement of the number accompanied by the ship's black engineers; while 'Let's Call The Whole Thing Off' was a sensational rollerskate routine and a sparkling highlight; as was the ironic and wistful presentation (by Astaire) of the classic 'They Can't Take That Away From Me'. Yet, in spite of the marvellous moments, the film remained curiously unsatisfying. Mark Sandrich again directed, with Pandro S. Berman producing. Completing the cast were Jerome Cowan, Ketti Gallian, William Brisbane, Frank Moran and Harriet Hoctor. Other numbers: *Beginner's Luck*; *Shall We Dance*; *Walking The Dog*.

THIRTIES MUSICALS

Artists And Models (Paramount) was the very model of a major musical. With a cast that included Jack Benny (left), Ida Lupino (right), Richard Arlen (centre), Gail Patrick, Ben Blue, Judy Canova, Hedda Hopper and Donald Meek, as well as Louis Armstrong, Martha Raye, Andre Kostelanetz and His Orchestra, The Yacht Club Boys, Connee Boswell, Russell Patterson's 'Personettes' and the Water Waltzers – it was a most appealing lucky-dip of a show that also happened to benefit greatly from a first-class screenplay by Walter DeLeon and Francis Martin (story and adaptation by Sig Herzig, Gene Thackrey, Eve Greene and Harlan Ware). Not that the story was any great shakes, mind you. On the contrary, there was very little to it (Jack Benny as president of an advertising agency has to see that the 'queen' is crowned at the 'Artists and Models' Ball). But it moved at a terrific pace, the dialogue was sharp and snappy, and the musical numbers – especially a sequence featuring the puppet Personettes in a typical Busby Berkeley-ish routine (called 'Mr Esquire', by Ted Koehler and Victor Young) – were bright and tuneful. LeRoy Prinz was the choreographer, it was produced by Lewis E. Gensler, and expertly directed by Raoul Walsh. Songs: *Pop Goes The Bubble*; *Stop, You're Breaking My Heart* Ted Koehler, Burton Lane; *Whispers In The Dark* Leo Robin, Frederick Hollander; *I Have Eyes* Ralph Rainger, Leo Robin; *Public Melody Number One* Ted Koehler, Harold Arlen (staged by Vincente Minnelli on his first abortive Hollywood trip).

A variation of sorts on their *If I Had A Million* (1932), Paramount's **Double Or Nothing** again teamed Bing Crosby and Martha Raye in a featherweight musical in which Crosby, Raye, Andy Devine and William Frawley are given the chance to make a million dollars by an eccentric philanthropist who wants to prove to his sceptical brother that most people are honest and enterprising. Though Crosby sang five songs, the standout number 'It's On, It's Off' (Al Siegel, Sam Coslow) which satirized the art of the strip-tease, was given to Martha Raye. Charles Lederer, Erwin Gelsey, Duke Atterbury and John C. Moffitt wrote it from a story by M. Coates Webster; it was produced by Benjamin Glazer and directed by Theodore Reed. Also cast: Mary Carlisle (illustrated centre, with Bing, as his love interest), Benny Baker, Sam Hinds, Fay Holden and the talented and greatly underused Frances Faye, in an unbilled screen debut. Other songs: *Double Or Nothing* Johnny Burke, Victor Young; *Listen My Children*; *Smarty* Ralph Freed, Burton Lane; *All You Want To Do Is Dance*; *The Moon Got In My Eyes*; *It's The Natural Thing To Do* Johnny Burke, Arthur Johnston; *After You* Al Siegel, Sam Coslow.

In **You Can't Have Everything** (20th Century-Fox), Alice Faye played a fictitious grand-daughter of Edgar Allan Poe with ambitions to become a playwright. But unlike her illustrious grandad, her talents pointed in a completely different direction: Broadway. Impresario Don Ameche (in the first of six films he and Miss Faye would make together) falls in love with her, buys the rights to her play 'North Winds' – a howling stinker – and turns it into a successful musical comedy. The story by Gregory Ratoff (screenplay by Harry Tugend, Jack Yellen and Karl Tunberg) wasn't much better than 'North Winds', but likewise made a successful musical film, thanks partly to Mack Gordon and Harry Revel's excellent score. Particularly catchy was the title

song, as well as 'Please Pardon Us We're In Love', sung by Miss Faye, and 'The Loveliness Of You' sung by eighth-billed Tony Martin. Also included in the cast: The Ritz Brothers (illustrated foreground), Charles Winninger, Louise (Gypsy Rose Lee) Hovick, Arthur Treacher, Wally Vernon and Louis Prima, with specialty dancers Tip, Tap and Toe, George Humbert, Jed Prouty, Dorothy Christy and Clara Blandick. Norman Taurog was the capable director, and the associate producer was Laurence Schwab. Other songs: *Afraid To Dream*; *Danger, Love At Work*; *Long Underwear* Mack Gordon, Harry Revel; *It's A Southern Holiday* Louis Prima, Jack Loman, Dave Franklin; *Rhythm On The Radio* Louis Prima.

The Singing Marine (Warner Bros.) starred Dick Powell (centre) as – would you believe? – a singing marine, who sang five of the show's six songs. The slender plot (screenplay by Delmer Daves) had Powell rocketing to overnight fame by winning a radio talent contest, becoming unbearably overbearing, and losing his girlfriend as a consequence. In time, however, he is made to see the error of his ways and returns to being the pleasant, modest guy we all knew he really was. And that, apart from two musical sequences put together by Busby Berkeley from the Al Dubin– Harry Warren songbook (the better of the two being 'Night Over Shanghai' with lyrics by Johnny Mercer, was all it had to offer. It was directed by Ray Enright whose cast also included Doris Weston (as Powell's girl), Lee Dixon (far left), Hugh Herbert, Eddie Acuff (centre left), Jane Darwell, Allen Jenkins (far right), harmonica player Larry Adler as himself, Guinn Williams (centre right), Veda Ann Borg and Jane Wyman. Other songs: *I Know Now*; *'Cause My Baby Says It's So*; *The Lady Who Couldn't Be Kissed*; *You Can't Run Away From Love*; *The Song Of The Marines* (later adopted as the Marine Corps official anthem).

The screenplay (by Jack McGowan, story by McGowan and Sid Silvers) for **Broadway Melody Of 1938** (MGM) had already been completed when Judy Garland, that 'new hot little singing sensation' as she was billed, was thrust into the production. McGowan reshaped his scenario to accommodate her talents, and found a spot in the narrative for her to sing – to a photograph of Clark Gable – 'Dear Mr Gable', Roger Edens's special adaptation of the old James V. Monaco–Joseph McCarthy song 'You Made Me Love You', which Judy had introduced at the MGM studio birthday party for 'The King'. The scene lasted only a few minutes, but it was without doubt, the highlight of the show. Robert Taylor, Eleanor Powell, George Murphy, Buddy Ebsen and Sophie Tucker were the stars – the latter playing the owner of a theatrical boarding house in New York. Judy was her talented daughter. Plot-wise it didn't amount to very much, and its climax, which pivoted on a race-horse being scared into victory through a booming, over-amplified voice, was a straight lift from the Marx Brothers' recent *A Day At The Races* (MGM). But the musical numbers – staged by Dave Gould – were in the opulent MGM tradition (see illustration) and, although not as inventive as they had been for *The Broadway Melody Of 1936*, were breezy enough to help one overlook the deficien-

cies in the script. Also on hand to bolster the material were Willie Howard, The Robert Mitchell Boys' Choir, Robert Wildhack, Robert Benchley, Charles Igor Gorin, and Raymond Walburn. It was produced by Jack Cummings and directed by Roy Del Ruth. Songs: *I'm Feeling Like A Million* (Powell, Murphy): *Yours And Mine* (Powell, Garland, Robert Mitchell Boys' Choir); *Everybody Sing* (Garland); *Follow In My Footsteps* (Powell, Murphy, Ebsen); *Your Broadway And My Broadway* (Tucker); *Broadway Rhythm* (Powell); *Sun Showers* (Powell) Arthur Freed, Nacio Herb Brown; *Some Of These Days* (Tucker) Shelton Brooks.

Vogues Of 1938 (United Artists) – produced by Walter Wanger in magnificent Technicolor – was an opulent, no-expense-spared fashion show (see illustration) that used a mildly diverting screenplay by Sam and Bella Spewack as a peg on which to hang its endless parade of gorgeous gowns. Warner Baxter starred as the owner of a chic Fifth Avenue salon, Helen Vinson was his stage-struck wife, and Joan Bennett his assistant who, to Baxter's relief, woos him away from his wife, with other parts in the capable, if familiar, hands of Mischa Auer, Jerome Cowan, and Marjorie Gateson as well as the not-so-well-known Virginia Verrill who introduced 'That Old Feeling', the Lew Brown–Sammy Fain classic hit. The film gave some of the country's top models a chance to move off a magazine cover and onto celluloid, and featured such national favourites as Miss Chesterfield, Miss Lucky Strike, Miss Lux Soap, and Miss Pepsodent. It was splashily directed by Irving Cummings whose stunning use of Technicolor was, apart from the fashions on view, the show's most saleable asset. Songs: *Lovely One* Frank Loesser, Manning Sherwin; *Turn On The Red Hot Heat (Burn The Blues Away)* Paul Francis Webster, Louis Alter; *King Of Jam* Louis Alter.

left to right: Gorin, Tucker, Murphy, Powell, Taylor, Garland, Ebsen.

THIRTIES MUSICALS

Photographed in a sepia tint midway between rose and brown, MGM's **The Firefly** ran 138 minutes and was a lavishly produced bore, redeemed only by its Rudolf Friml score and by some splendid singing from its stars Jeanette MacDonald and Allan Jones (illustrated). Bearing absolutely no relation to its stage counterpart (in which a lady street singer from New York, disguised as a cabin boy follows her sweetheart to Bermuda on a yacht belonging to his fiancée), the screen version relocated itself in Spain at the time of the Napoleonic invasion and became the protracted story of a spy called Nina Maria (MacDonald) who charms information out of French officers. Jones played Don Diego, a counter-spy for the French and together he and Jeanette made beautiful music – most notably with 'The Donkey Serenade', which was specially arranged for the film by Herbert Stothart from Friml's 1920 solo piano piece 'Chanson', with lyrics by Bob Wright and Chet Forrest. Otto Harbach's original book was adapted by Ogden Nash, with Frances Goodrich and Albert Hackett responsible for the rather waterlogged screenplay. The musical numbers were staged by the ubiquitous Albertina Rasch, Hunt Stromberg produced and Robert Z. Leonard directed. Also in it were Warren William, Henry Daniell, Douglass Dumbrille, Leonard Penn, Tom Rutherford and George Zucco. Songs: *Giannina Mia* lyrics by Otto Harbach; *Love Is Like A Firefly*; *English March*; *A Woman's Kiss* new lyrics by Bob Wright, Chet Forrest; *He Who Loves And Runs Away* lyrics by Gus Kahn; *Sympathy* lyrics by Kahn, Otto Harbach; *When A Maid Comes Knocking At Your Heart* lyrics by Harbach, Wright, Forrest; *Danse Jeanette* Herbert Stothart; *Para La Salud* arranged by Stothart; *Ojos Rojos* Argentine folk song, arranged and played by Manuel Alvarez Maciste.

Bobby Breen's third feature, **Make A Wish** (Principal/RKO) was his best to date, thanks to its sugar-free screenplay by Gertrude Berg – who also provided the story – Bernard Schubert and Earle Snell (additional dialogue by William Hurlburt). A simple, uncluttered yarn in which young master Breen (right) helps to inspire Basil Rathbone (left), a composer suffering from composer's block, to finish his operetta, it also featured newcomer Marion Claire as Breen's widowed mother, a singer who soon finds herself romantically involved with the struggling Mr Rathbone. A pleasant Oscar Straus–Paul Francis Webster–Louis Alter score, including 'Music In My Heart' and 'My Campfire Dreams', both appealingly sung by Breen, kept audiences whistling for months. Henry Armetta, Ralph Forbes, Billy Lee, Donald Meek, Herbert Rawlinson and Leonid Kinskey completed the cast. It was produced by Sol Lesser and directed – extremely well – by Kurt Neumann. Other songs: *Make A Wish*; *Birch Lake Forever* Straus, Webster, Alter; *Old Man Rip* Webster, Alter; *Polly Wolly Doodle* (traditional).

In **The Life Of The Party** (RKO) Joe Penner (left) starred as the wealthy suitor chosen by Ann Shoemaker to wed her singing daughter Harriet Hilliard. But Miss Hilliard has other ideas – the best one being Gene Raymond, with whom she falls in love, and after a few rather tedious complications, marries. A cast that also included Parkyakarkus, Victor Moore (as a private detective hired specifically to see that Raymond remains free of woman trouble), Helen Broderick (as Miss Hilliard's agent), Billy Gilbert, Ann Miller, Franklin Pangborn and Margaret Dumont (right) promised more than they delivered: it was written by Bert Kalmar, Harry Ruby and Viola Brothers Shore (story by Joseph Santley), produced by Edward Kaufman and directed by William A. Seiter. The film's one production number – 'Yankee Doodle Band' (by Herb Magidson and Allie Wrubel) featured Ann Miller in a shameless emulation of Eleanor Powell (the vocal by Miss Hilliard), with choreography by Sammy Lee that was, at best, serviceable; while Hilliard and Raymond were handed the show's best tune, 'Let's Have Another Cigarette' by Magidson and Wrubel. Other songs: *The Life Of The Party*; *So You Won't Sing*; *Chirp A Little Ditty* Magidson, Wrubel; *Roses In December* George Jessel, Ben Oakland.

Talent Scout (GB: Studio Romance) was a Warner Bros./First National concoction which intended to glorify the scouts who went up and down the country seeking out new talent. The idea, apparently, had been inspired by the studio's own promotion campaign for *Gold Diggers Of 1937* which sent a bevy of chorus beauties across the continent by air. In the event, the movie had a young girl singer (Jeanne Madden centre) discovered and catapulted to fame, not by a Hollywood talent scout, but by a Hollywood matinée idol (Donald Woods right) who falls in love with her. The flaccid screenplay was by George Bilson and William Jacobs, William Clemens directed, and Bryan Foy supervised the production. Fred Lawrence, Rosalind Marquis, Joseph Crehan and Charles Halton (left) were also in it. Songs: *In The Silent Picture Days*; *I Am The Singer, You Are My Song*; *Born To Love*; *I Was Wrong* M.K. Jerome, Jack Scholl.

Sonja Henie's (illustrated) second feature, **Thin** ▷ **Ice** (20th Century-Fox), had a more substantial screenplay (by Boris Ingster and Milton Sperling, from a play by Attila Orbok) and was marginally better than its predecessor. All about a skating instructress in a large Swiss hotel and the romance she has with a newspaper correspondent who, to Miss H.'s surprise, turns out not to be a newspaperman at all, but Prince Rudolph, it co-starred Tyrone Power as the Prince, with Arthur Treacher, Raymond Walburn, Joan Davis (who got to sing a marvellous Mack Gordon–Harry Revel number called 'I'm Olga From The Volga'), Sig Rumann, Alan Hale, Leah Ray and Melville Cooper, excellent in support. Harry Losee staged the eye catching ballet and dance sequences; Raymond Griffith produced and the director was Sidney Lanfield. Other songs: *My Secret Love Affair*; *Over Night*; *My Swiss Hillbilly* Sidney Mitchell, Lew Pollack.

One Hundred Men And A Girl (Universal) was a resounding hit for its young star Deanna Durbin, whose spontaneous charm and refreshing light soprano voice were more than adequate compensation for her lack of acting ability. Not that a strong dramatic performance would, in any way, have enhanced this delightful fairy-tale about a young girl's determination to form a symphony orchestra in order to give work to a hundred unemployed musicians; and, once having formed her orchestra, to beg, borrow, or steal the services of Leopold Stokowski (illustrated, with Durbin, orchestra) to help launch it on the public. Energetic enthusiasm was what was called for, and that, precisely, was what Miss Durbin delivered, leaving the acting to co-star Adolphe Menjou (as her father), Eugene Pallette, Mischa Auer, and Alice Brady. The unsophisticated screenplay by Bruce Manning, Charles Kenyon, Hans Kraly and James Mulhauser was just the job for the occasion, and its climax in which the musicians, having inveigled themselves into Stokowski's residence, embark on Liszt's *Hungarian Rhapsody No. 2*, triggered off a chain reaction of excited delight in audiences everywhere. It was produced by Charles Rogers and Joe Pasternak (the latter returning again and again to this sort of subject, both at Universal and later at MGM), and directed with a beguiling ingenuousness by Henry Koster. Songs: *It's Raining Sunbeams* Sam Coslow, Frederick Hollander; *A Heart That's Free* Alfred G. Robyn, Thomas T. Railey; *Alleluia* Mozart (from Exultate, Jubilate K165); excerpts from *Lohengrin* Wagner; *La Traviata* Verdi; Tchai- ◁ kovsky's *Fifth Symphony*.

◁ Four talented writers – Jerry Wald, Richard Macaulay, Sig Herzig and Warren Duff – dreamed up **Varsity Show** which, at 120 minutes, proved to be one of Warner Bros.' longest musicals, but, where plot was concerned, one of its shortest. Supervised by Lou Edelman and directed by William Keighley, the movie starred Dick Powell as a Broadway impresario and former Winfield College alumnus who steps in to save the day when the annual Winfield show is about to flounder for want of a producer. The show-within-the-show's finale was staged by Busby Berkeley who, working on a staircase fifty feet high and sixty feet wide, designed it as a tribute to halls of learning everywhere with a series of overhead shots in which a chorus of several hundred men and women (see illustration) spelled out the initals of several colleges across the country. Also featured were Fred Waring and His Pennsylvanians, Priscilla and Rosemary Lane (debut for all three), Walter Catlett and Ted Healy. Songs: *Love Is On The Air Tonight*; *Moonlight On The Campus*; *Old King Cole*; *Have You Got Any Castles, Baby?*; *We're Working Our Way Through College*; *On With The Dance*; *You've Got Something There*; *When Your College Days Are Gone* Johnny Mercer, R.A. Whiting. Remade in 1950 as *Fine And Dandy*.

Though **Music For Madame** (RKO) was Jesse L. Lasky's third attempt to turn singer Nino Martini into a star (and his third failure to do so), its only point of interest lay in the fact that actress Joan Burfield appeared as Joan Fontaine (right). For the rest it told a rather melodramatic tale about a young Italian tenor (Martini, singing, left) who, after arriving in Hollywood in search of screen stardom, falls in with a bunch of thieves who use him as a front man. Thus, while Signor M. is singing his soul out in an impassioned interpretation of Leoncavallo's 'Vesti la Giubba' (from *Pagliacci*) at a wedding, the crooks are looting the gifts. Robert Harari and Gertrude Purcell's screenplay took advantage of its Hollywood background to make some satirical comments on the movie capital, but the film was basically too lightweight an affair to sustain this element which evaporated without trace. Alan Mowbray, Billy Gilbert, Alan Hale (centre right), Grant Mitchell, Erik Rhodes (centre), Lee Patrick, and Jack Carson in a brief appearance as an assistant director, were also in the cast, John Blystone directed. Songs: *Music For Madame* Herb Magidson, Allie Wrubel; *My Sweet Bambino*; *I Want The World To Know* Rudolf Friml, Gus Kahn; *King Of The Road* Nathaniel Shilkret, Eddie Cherkose. ▽

THIRTIES MUSICALS

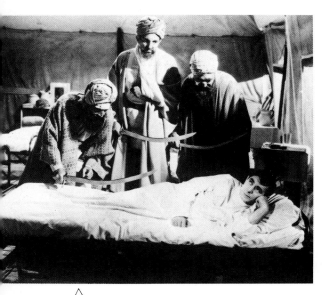

Betty Grable (right), slowly working her way up in the world, received second billing in **This Way Please** (Paramount), playing an usherette who falls for a visiting movie star (Charles 'Buddy' Rogers, left), with reliable Ned Sparks, Jim and Marian Jordon (radio's Fibber McGee and Molly) and Wally Vernon providing the laughs. They were all outdone, however, by Rufe Davis, whose uncanny series of way-out imitations gave the film its one and only taste of originality. Porter Hall, Lee Bowman, Mary Livingstone and Akim Tamiroff offered more conventional support. It was written by Grant Garrett, Seena Owen and Howard J. Green (story by Maxwell Shane and Bill Thomas), produced by Mel Shauer and directed by Robert Florey. Songs: *Is It Love Or Is It Infatuation?* Sam Coslow, Frederick Hollander; *This Way Please*; *Delighted To Meet You*; *What This Country Needs Is Voom Voom* Al Siegel, Sam Coslow; *I'm The Sound-Effects Man 'Jock'*, George Gray.

Having found himself a citizen of ancient Rome in *Roman Scandals* (Goldwyn, 1933), Eddie Cantor, as a movie-freak called Aloysius Babson, takes an overdose of pain-killer and in **Ali Baba Goes To Town** (20th Century-Fox) wakes up in Baghdad circa 937. In no time at all he is running the place on contemporary American lines – building filling stations for camels, etc; and even persuading the Sultan to stand for president. It was amiable balderdash in the truest Cantor sense, with the star (illustrated, on bed) in fine form as the hero. A pleasing score by Mack Gordon, Harry Revel and Raymond Scott didn't hurt it one bit; and Harry Tugend and Jack Yellen's screenplay (from a story by Gene Towne, C. Graham Baker and Gene Fowler) allowed Cantor and his supporting cast to indulge in much merriment throughout. The up and coming Tony Martin was second-billed, with other roles going to Roland Young as the Sultan, Louise (Gypsy Rose Lee) Hovick as one of the Sultan's 865 wives, John Carradine, Douglass Dumbrille, Virginia Field, Alan Dinehart, Maurice Cass and Ferdinand Gottschalk. Also in it were The Peters Sisters, Jeni Le Gon, The Raymond Scott Quintet and The Pearl Twins. David Butler directed, and the producer was Laurence Schwab. Songs: *Laugh Your Way Through Life*; *Swing Is Here To Stay*; *I've Got My Heart Set On You*; *Vote For Honest Abe*; *Arabania* Mack Gordon, Harry Revel; *Twilight In Turkey* Raymond Scott.

Blossoms On Broadway (Paramount), written by Theodore Reeves, centred on the con-man activities of Edward Arnold who, after reading about the arrival of a lady gold-mine owner called 'Death Valley Cora' Keene (Kitty Kelly), kidnaps her, and substitutes accomplice Shirley Ross (left). As there was clearly not enough plot to spread out over the film's running time, director Richard Wallace recruited the services of Weber and Fields, Rufe Davis, William Frawley and The Radio Rogues to provide some added diversion. He need not have bothered, for nothing, except a new script, could have saved this one from being the stinker it was. Also cast were John Trent (right), Frank Craven, John Arthur and Edward Brophy. B.P. Schulberg produced. Songs included: *Blossoms On Broadway* Ralph Rainger, Leo Robin; *No Ring On Her Finger*; *You Can't Tell A Man By His Hat* Frank Loesser, Manning Sherwin.

The Ritz Brothers (illustrated) were given the full star treatment in **Life Begins In College** (20th Century-Fox), and practically winded themselves in an attempt to justify their top billing. But for audiences, who dogmatically believed that a little of the Ritz boys went quite far enough, the occasion was one of unmitigated torture. Hardly ever off the screen, they played the joint proprietors of Klassy Kampus Klothes and, in the film's climactic final moments, found themselves involved in a football match against a rival college. Karl Tunberg and Don Ettlinger's screenplay (from a series of stories by Darrell Ware) was so full of sub-plots that it wasn't always apparent exactly who was doing what to whom, or why – but if you looked carefully it was just possible to detect, in the midst of all the self-conscious jollity, a romance between the coach's daughter (Gloria Stuart) and a strapping football captain (Dick Baldwin). Co-star Joan Davis spent half the time pursuing Nat Pendleton (as a Red Indian) and the other half singing, dancing and clowning. Tony Martin was also in it; so were Fred Stone, Joan Marsh, Dixie Dunbar, Elisha Cook Jr, and, as the radio announcer commentating on the big match, Ed Thorgersen. Nick Castle and Geneva Sawyer staged the dances, Harold Wilson produced, and William A. Seiter directed. Songs: *Big Chief Swing It*; *Our Team Is On The Warpath*; *Fair Lombardy*; *Why Talk About Love?*; *The Rhumba Goes Collegiate* Sidney Mitchell, Lew Pollack; *Sweet Varsity Sue* Al Lewis, Charles Tobias, ◁ Murray Mencher.

52nd Street (United Artists) was the story of 52nd Street, New York – and some of its inhabitants – from 1912 to 1937. It was also an over-ambitious musical, produced by Walter Wanger and directed by Harold Young, that allowed itself to be led up too many blind alleys. Peopling it were Ian Hunter as Rufus Rondell, a man ostracized for marrying into showbusiness; Pat Paterson (left), ZaSu Pitts and Dorothy Peterson as his snobbish sisters, Leo Carillo as an accordion-playing street musician, Sid Silvers and Jack White as a pair of hoofers, as well as Al Shean (at piano), Ella Logan, Collette Lyons, Kenny Baker, Rocco and Saulter, Cook and Brown, Jerry Colonna, Georgie Taps and Al Norman. It was written by Grover Jones with additional dialogue by Sid Silvers, and choreographed by Danny Dare. Songs: *I Still Love To Kiss You Goodnight*; *Nothing Can Stop Me Now*; *I'd Like To See Some Mo' Of Samoa*; *Don't Save Your Love For A Rainy Day*; *Fifty-Second Street*; *23-Skidoo*; *Let Down Your Hair And Sing*; *We Love The South* Walter Bullock, Harold Spina. ▽

Following the sensational audience reaction to Judy Garland in *Broadway Melody of 1938*, the young hopeful, who had been kicking her heels at MGM was rushed into shooting two films back to back: **Thoroughbreds Don't Cry**, and the musically more elaborate *Everybody Sing*, which was held for later release. Although **Thoroughbreds** was a racing story with songs, rather than a fully-fledged musical, it teamed Mickey Rooney and Judy (illustrated) for the first time, doing for them what *Flying Down To Rio* had done for Fred and Ginger. The plot hinged on the efforts of an English lad to win an important race with his horse, The Pookah. How he goes about it after his jockey is 'set down' by the stewards, provided the real meat of Lawrence Hazard's entertaining, if predictable screenplay (story by Eleanore Griffin and J. Walter Rubin). Ronald Sinclair was the young horse-owner (the role was originally intended for Freddie Bartholomew), Mickey Rooney played the 'put down' jockey. The film also starred Sophie Tucker as the owner of a boarding house for jockeys – and Judy's caring aunt; with C. Aubrey Smith (as Sinclair's grandfather), Forrester Harvey, Charles D. Brown, Frankie Darro, Henry Kolker and Helen Troy rounding out the cast. The capable direction was by Alfred E. Green, and Harry Rapf produced. Songs: *Sun Showers*; *Got A Pair Of New Shoes* (Garland) Arthur Freed, Nacio Herb Brown.

Jam-packed with songs by Johnny Mercer and Richard A. Whiting, four production numbers and several dances staged by Bobby Connolly, and a plot of mind-bending complications and contrivances, **Ready, Willing And Able** (Warner Bros.) delivered a lot – of nonsense as it unfortunately turned out. The main fault (as was often the case) was with the screenplay by Jerry Wald, Sig Herzig and Warren Duff which was too slow and laboured by half in its recounting of the ups and downs which beset two penniless Broadway aspirants – a songwriter (Lee Dixon) and a writer-actor and embryo producer (Ross Alexander) – who find a backer with a condition attached to the cheque: that they import a certain famous English star (Wini Shaw) for their intended show. So far so good, but the boys are duped into signing up an American college girl (Ruby Keeler, illustrated, foreground) of the

Fred Astaire without Ginger Rogers was like Laurel without Hardy, and the omission badly damaged **A Damsel In Distress** (RKO), an otherwise delightful musical. After seven movies together, Rogers wanted a break, so the studio, having unsuccessfully tried to acquire the services of British musical comedy star Jessie Matthews, cast Joan Fontaine as Fred's partner – although it was patently clear that dancing was not one of her accomplishments. To further underline the fact that this was not a typical Astaire-Rogers vehicle, they borrowed George Burns and Gracie Allen (illustrated, with Astaire centre) from Paramount, and signed Reginald Gardiner (rather than Eric Blore or Edward Everett Horton) to play the butler. But despite the subterfuge, they were unable to conceal that what they had on their hands was an Astaire-Rogers musical with one half of the partnership missing, or that her demure substitute was disappointing. The screenplay (by P.G. Wodehouse, Ernest Pagano and S.K. Lauren from a novel by Wodehouse and a play by Wodehouse and Ian Hay) concerned an American dancer in England who attempts to woo and wed Lady Alyce (Fontaine), a virtual prisoner of her aristocratic

same name as the English star in the belief that she's the genuine article. There was a deal of skulduggery and a plethora of song to be got through before the final happy fade, and although the cast, which featured Allen Jenkins (excellent as the former owner of a performing seal show turned unscrupulous agent), Louise Fazenda, Carol Hughes, Hugh O'Connell and Addison Richards were ready and willing, they weren't able to rescue the whole silly undertaking. Ross Alexander acted and sang notably well, and Ruby Keeler was Ruby Keeler (her final film for Warner Bros.). Ray Enright directed for production supervisor Sam Bischoff. Songs and musical numbers: *Too Marvellous For Words*; *Just A Quiet Evening*; *Sentimental And Melancholy*; *Gasoline Gypsies*; *The World Is My Apple*; *Handy With Your Feet*; *There's A Little Old House*; *Ready, Willing And Able*.

family in Totleigh Castle. After the requisite amount of misunderstandings, all ended happily with a jolly Anglo-American marriage. George Stevens directed with the refinement he had brought to *Swingtime* (RKO, 1936), and George and Ira Gershwin, who provided the score, had massive hits with the atmospheric 'A Foggy Day', and 'Nice Work If You Can Get It' (in which Astaire pounded away on a multitude of percussion instruments), and a lot of fun sending up the English in 'The Jolly Tar And Milkmaid'. But the most imaginative number of all was 'Stiff Upper Lip' in which Astaire, Burns and Allen abandoned themselves to Hermes Pan's witty and visually delightful choreography in a fair-ground sequence which, amongst other things, featured heavily distorting mirrors. The film was produced by Pandro S. Berman who, in supporting roles, cast Ray Noble, Constance Collier, Montagu Love and Harry Watson. Mr Gardiner's singing voice was dubbed by Mario Berini. Other songs: *I Can't Be Bothered Now*; *Put Me To The Test* (instrumental only, danced by Astaire, Burns, Allen); *Sing Of Spring*; *Things Are Looking Up*; *Ah Che A Voi Perdoni Iddio* (from Flotow's 'Marta').

THIRTIES MUSICALS

△

Grace Moore starred in **I'll Take Romance** (Columbia) and, apart from the tuneful title song by Oscar Hammerstein II and Ben Oakland, as well as a number by Milton Drake and Marie Costa called 'A Frangesa', she also sang the gavotte from Massenet's *Manon*, the drinking song from Verdi's *La Traviata* and the title role in a duet from Puccini's *Madame Butterfly*. But audiences who expected a plot to accompany the vocalizing were in for a disappointment. Based on a story by Stephen Morehouse Avery (screenplay by George Oppenheimer and Jane Murfin), the hair-line narrative concerned co-star Melvyn Douglas's attempts, against opposition from Moore's (centre) aunt (Helen Westley), to persuade the soprano to journey to Buenos Aires in order to open a new opera season there. The operatic sequences were adequately staged by Wilhelm von Wymetal Jr but there simply wasn't enough substance in the film as a whole for it to approximate the success of some of its star's earlier, more full-bodied vehicles. Everett Riskin produced, it was directed by Edward H. Griffith, and, in supporting roles, featured Stuart Erwin, Margaret Hamilton, Walter Kingford, Richard Carle and Ferdinand Gottschalk.

Alice Faye's (foreground centre) only film for Universal was **You're A Sweetheart**, and it wasn't up to much. Largely responsible for its failure was the convoluted yarn fashioned for it by Warren Wilson, Maxwell Shane and William Thomas (screenplay by Monte Brice and Charles Grayson) which, when it finally unravelled itself, concerned the efforts of publicity seeking producer George Murphy to get his latest show to open on Broadway. Faye's singing of 'So It's Love' by Mickey Bloom, Arthur Quenzer and Lou Bring, was pleasant enough; so was the title number by Harold Adamson and Jimmy McHugh, choreographed by Carl Randall and featuring Faye and Murphy who danced together

▽

surprisingly well. But the rest was a flattish brew of *shtick* and nonsense that had about as much freshness to it as a stuffy backstage dressing-room. Charles Winninger, Andy Devine, William Gargan, Frank Jenks and Donald Meek were also featured, and there were specialty items by The Four Playboys, Malda and Ray, and The Noville Brothers. It was produced by Buddy De Sylva and directed by David Butler. The movie was remade in 1943 as *Cowboy From Manhattan*. Other songs: *Broadway Jamboree*; *My Fine Feathered Friend*; *Who Killed Maggie*; *Oh, Oh, Oklahoma* Adamson, McHugh; *Scraping The Toast* Murray Mencher, Charles Tobias.

Manhattan Merry-Go-Round (Republic) chased its own tail on a one-way ride to oblivion. Based on a musical revue by Frank Hummert and written for the screen by Harry Sauber, it chronicled the unlikely escapades of a bunch of hoods who, led by Leo Carillo, take over a recording company. Phil Regan, James Gleason, Ann Dvorak, Henry Armetta, Luis Alberni, Smiley Burnette and Moroni Olsen were also cast, but the film's real interest and its *raison d'être* were in the special appearances of Ted Lewis (right), Cab Calloway and Louis Prima (with their orchestras), Gene Autry, Kay Thompson and her radio choir, Jack Benny, The Lathrops, and Rosalean and Seville (illustrated). Harry Sauber produced, and the director was Charles F. Riesner. Songs included: *Mamma I Wanna Make Rhythm* Jerome Jerome, Richard Byron, Walter Kent; *Manhattan Merry-Go-Round* Pinky Herman, Gustave Haenschen; *Heaven?*; *I Owe You* Jack Lawrence, Peter Tinturin; *It's Round-up Time In Reno* Gene Autry.

◁ **Thrill Of A Lifetime** (Paramount) was the spill of a lifetime for Betty Grable (illustrated) who, together with The Yacht Club Boys, Judy Canova, Ben Blue, Eleanore Whitney, Johnny Downs, Leif Erickson (illustrated), Larry Crabbe and Franklin Pangborn, was up to her pretty neck in Seena Owen and Grant Garrett's silly screenplay (additional dialogue by Paul Gerard Smith). Grable played a plain-Jane secretary mooningly in love with her playwright boss, but getting nowhere fast until she removes her specs and changes her hairstyle, when – *mirabile dictu!* Miss Canova livened up the proceedings slightly by flinging herself head-first into a hillbilly number; and there was temporary respite from tedium, too, when sultry Dorothy Lamour sang the title song. The rest, metaphorically speaking, was silence. George Archainbaud directed. Songs: *Keeno, Screeno And You; I'll Follow My Baby; Thrill Of A Lifetime; Paris In Swing; Sweetheart Time* Sam Coslow, Frederick Hollander; *It's Been A Whole Year; If We Could Run The Country For A Day* The Yacht Club Boys.

△
Hitting A New High (RKO) did no such thing. A really lamentable vehicle for little Lily Pons (illustrated centre), its storyline (by Robert Harari and Maxwell Shane) found the admirable coloratura masquerading as Oogahunga the Bird-Girl, somewhere in the wilds of Africa. Her real name, however, is Suzette and she's not a bird girl at all, but a nightclub singer who longs for a crack at opera. It's her press agent (Jack Oakie) who has come up with the 'bird-girl' gimmick, and who sends her to Africa in the hope that she will be discovered by an influential opera lover (Edward Everett Horton) while he is on safari there. She is – and *voilà*, The Met! Gertrude Purcell and John Twist's screenplay only compounded the lunacy of the basic plot, with Raoul Walsh's direction also failing to overcome the sheer crassness of it all. Eric Blore, John Howard, Eduardo Ciannelli and Luis Alberni were in it too, and the producer was Jesse L. Lasky. Songs: *You're Like A Song; I Hit A New High; Let's Give Love Another Chance; This Never Happened Before* Harold Adamson, Jimmy McHugh. Operatic excerpts: *Lucia Di Lammermoor (The Mad Scene)* Donizetti; *Mignon (Je Suis Titania)* Thomas; *Le Rossignol Et La Rose (The Nightingale Song)* Saint-Saëns' incidental music for Dieulafoy's play *Parysatis*.

Another merry-go-round that got absolutely nowhere, was the one on offer from Universal called **Merry-Go-Round Of 1938.** But at least this one had Bert Lahr (right) delivering himself of 'The Woodman's Song' (by E.Y. Harburg and Harold Arlen), and comedian Jimmy Savo (left) revelling in 'River Stay 'Way From My Door' (by Mort Dixon and Harry Woods). Otherwise it was an unappealingly frenetic account of Messrs Lahr and Savo's farcical antics in Hollywood. Mischa Auer (centre), Billy House (2nd left), Alice Brady, Joy Hodges, Louise Fazenda and Dave Apollon and His Orchestra were also involved; it was written by Monte Brice and A. Dorian Otvos from a story by Brice and Harry Myers, and directed for producer Charles R. Rogers by Irving Cummings. Other songs: *I'm In My Glory; More Power To You; You're My Dish* Harold Adamson, Jimmy McHugh.
▽

Swing It Professor (GB: Swing It Buddy) from Conn-Ambassador, which ran just over an hour, was the one about the college music professor who, after much resistance, discovers swing. That was all there was to it. Yet it was surprisingly proficient considering its lack of star names both in front of and behind the camera, although Pinky Tomlin (right) did have a following from radio. Tomlin was the professor, with other parts for tap-dancer Paula Stone (left), Mary Kornman, Milburn Stone, Pat Gleason and Gordon Elliott. Also in it: The Three Gentle Maniacs and The Four Squires. It was written and adapted (from a story by Connie Lee) by Nicholas Barrows and Robert St Clair, and directed by old-timer Marshall Neilan. Songs included: *I'm Sorta Kinda Glad I Met You; An Old-Fashioned Melody; Richer Than A Millionaire* Al Heath, Connie Lee, Buddy LeRoux.
▽

△

Rosalie (MGM) teamed Nelson Eddy with Eleanor Powell in a preposterous cross between operetta and campus musical, with Powell (centre) as the Princess Rosalie of Romanza, and a miscast Eddy as the football hero she meets while attending college in America. They fall in love, of course, even though she is engaged to a prince (Tom Rutherford). The resolution had Eddy saving Romanza from political upheaval and becoming the ruler of the country by marrying Rosalie. Nothing, however, could save the film which, despite its plethora of production numbers (music by Cole Porter no less), even managed to squeeze in a tiresome sub-plot involving Ray Bolger and Virginia Grey. Miss Powell had two good numbers – 'I've A Strange New Rhythm In My Heart', which she tapped out in the college dorm, and the awesomely elaborate title number (also sung by Eddy) which must surely have given employment to every out-of-work extra in Hollywood. Eddy was also handed one of Porter's most lyrical ever ballads, 'In The Still Of The Night'. Ilona Massey, Edna May Oliver, Billy Gilbert, Reginald Owen, George Zucco, Jerry Colonna and William Demarest were in it too; it was based on a musical play by William Anthony McGuire and Guy Bolton (which had been presented on Broadway

by Florenz Ziegfeld with a score by Sigmund Romberg and George Gershwin), and McGuire also contributed the screenplay and produced the movie. The Albertina Rasch dancers were featured, with Miss Rasch herself in charge of the musical numbers. W.S. Van Dyke directed, and incorporated footage from the unreleased *Rosalie* (1930) which had starred Marion Davies. In spite of anything one might say about it, **Rosalie** was one of the top money-makers of the year. Other songs: *Who Knows? Spring Love Is In The Air; Why Should I Care? It's All Over But The Shouting; To Love Or Not To Love; M'Appari* from Flotow's 'Marta'; also, medleys which incorporated snatches from the following: *On Brave Old Army Team* Philip Equer; *The Caissons Go Rolling Along* Edmund L. Gruber; *Anchors Aweigh* Alfred H. Miles, Royal Lovell, Charles A. Zimmerman; *Addio (Goodbye Forever)* Paolo Tosti (lyrics G.J. Whyte-Melville); *Polovtsian Dances* from Borodin's 'Prince Igor'; Tchaikovsky's *Swan Lake*; a medley of Sousa marches (danced by Powell) which included *Washington Post March; Stars And Stripes Forever; Semper Fidelis* and *El Capitain; The Wedding March* from Mendelssohn's 'A Midsummer Night's Dream'; *Gaudeamus Igitur* (traditional) and *Oh Promise Me* Reginald DeKoven, Scott Clement.

△

Warren Hull and Patricia Ellis (centre), on loan from Warner Bros., starred in Republic's **Rhythm In The Clouds**, a 64-minute quickie in which Miss Ellis played an impoverished songwriter who, in desperation, fakes a letter which gains her admittance to a wealthy songwriter's apartment while he is out of town, and then uses his name to draw attention to herself. A passable programmer (which most cinemagoers *did* pass), it was written by Olive Cooper from a story by George Mence and Ray Bond, in an adaptation by Nathanael West, and directed by John H. Auer. Also cast: William Newell, Richard Carle, Zeffie Tilbury and Charles Judels. Songs: *Don't Ever Change; Hawaiian Hospitality; Two Hearts Are Dancing* Lou Handman, Walter Hirsch, Harry Owens, Ray Kinney.

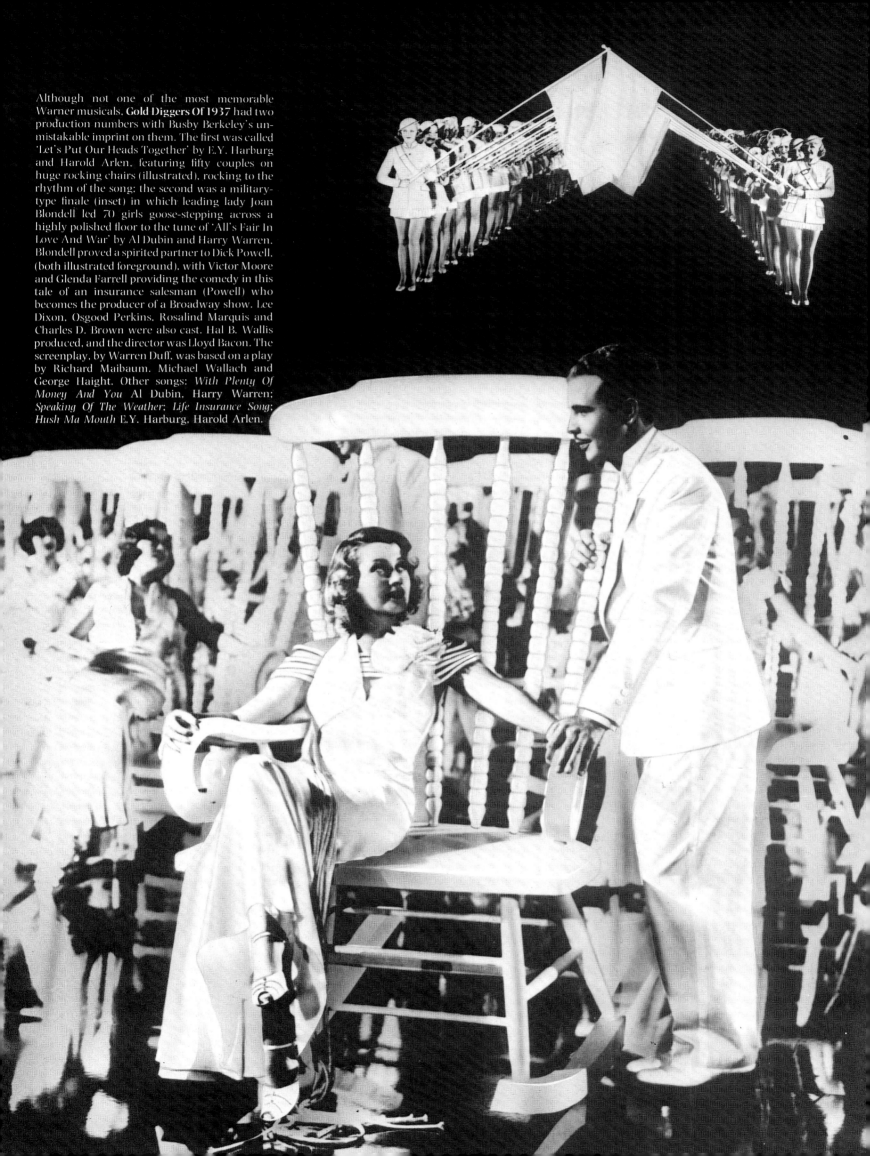

Although not one of the most memorable Warner musicals, **Gold Diggers Of 1937** had two production numbers with Busby Berkeley's unmistakable imprint on them. The first was called 'Let's Put Our Heads Together' by E.Y. Harburg and Harold Arlen, featuring fifty couples on huge rocking chairs (illustrated), rocking to the rhythm of the song; the second was a military-type finale (inset) in which leading lady Joan Blondell led 70 girls goose-stepping across a highly polished floor to the tune of 'All's Fair In Love And War' by Al Dubin and Harry Warren. Blondell proved a spirited partner to Dick Powell, (both illustrated foreground), with Victor Moore and Glenda Farrell providing the comedy in this tale of an insurance salesman (Powell) who becomes the producer of a Broadway show. Lee Dixon, Osgood Perkins, Rosalind Marquis and Charles D. Brown were also cast. Hal B. Wallis produced, and the director was Lloyd Bacon. The screenplay, by Warren Duff, was based on a play by Richard Maibaum, Michael Wallach and George Haight. Other songs: *With Plenty Of Money And You* Al Dubin, Harry Warren; *Speaking Of The Weather*; *Life Insurance Song*; *Hush Ma Mouth* E.Y. Harburg, Harold Arlen.

1938

The Great Chicago Fire of 1871 provided the climax to **In Old Chicago** (20th Century-Fox), a disaster musical whose roisterous tale of political chicanery was interspersed with seven songs and a jig. Alice Faye (right) was a music-hall singer torn between two brothers: bad guy Tyrone Power (centre), and good guy Don Ameche (left). Fate supplied the denouement and, as Chicago burned spectacularly in the background, all matters of the heart were satisfactorily resolved. The period detail was well attended to by director Henry King, with Faye's musical numbers helping to evoke the appropriate atmosphere of the era in which it all took place. Alice Brady, Andy Devine, Brian Donlevy and Berton Churchill offered reliable support; it was written by Lamar Trotti and Sonya Levien from an original story by Niven Busch, and produced by Darryl F. Zanuck with Kenneth MacGowan as his associate. Songs: *In Old Chicago* Mack Gordon, Harry Revel; *I'll Never Let You Cry*; *Take A Dip In The Sea* Sidney Mitchell, Lew Pollack; *Carry Me Back To Old Virginny* James A. Bland; *Sweet Genevieve* George Cooper, Henry Tucker; *How Many Miles To Dublin Town* (traditional); *The Irish Washerwoman* (traditional jig).
▽

Columnist Walter Winchell and orchestra leader Ben Bernie (left) found themselves locked in comic combat in **Love And Hisses** (20th Century-Fox), a snappily written (by Curtis Kenyon and Art Arthur, story by Arthur) entertainment with a better-than-average plot and several specialty numbers. The storyline had Winchell publicly panning Bernie's latest singing discovery (Simone Simon). Determined not to let Mrs Winchell's little boy get away with it, Bernie makes his singer change her name to Yvette – the idea being to re-present her to Winchell, whom he feels sure will fall for the deception, and then expose him. Joan Davis and Bert Lahr (centre) provided musical as well as comic support. Also in it: Robert Kellard (right), and The Raymond Scott Quintet, specialty performers Ruth Terry, Chilton and Thomas, The Peters Sisters and The Brewster Twins. Sidney Lanfield directed for producer Kenneth MacGowan. Songs: *Sweet Someone; Broadway Gone Hawaiian; I Want To Be In Winchell's Column; Be A Good Sport; Lost In Your Eyes* Mack Gordon, Harry Revel; *Power House* Raymond Scott; *The Wolf Song* Norman Zeno; *Darling, Je Vous Aime Beaucoup* Anna Sosenko.
◁

Humphrey Bogart, of all people, turned up in a musical for Warner Bros. and, clearly, wasn't at all happy about it. Hardly surprising, for the idiotic subject matter of **Swing Your Lady** was no more than a protracted, ill-conceived jape. The screenplay, by Joseph Schrank and Maurice Leo from the play by Kenyon Nicholson and Charles Robinson, had Bogey starring as an unsuccessful wrestling promoter who conceives the lunatic idea of matching a hulking thick-head against a lady blacksmith of Amazonian proportions. The two unfortunates called on to make something of these undignified roles were Nat Pendleton and Louise Fazenda, with Penny Singleton, Sammy White (illustrated), Frank McHugh, Allen Jenkins, Ronald Reagan, Leon Frank and Elviry Weaver also in it for director Ray Enright. The musical numbers, written by M.K. Jerome and Jack Scholl and staged by Bobby Connolly, comprised: *Mountain Swingaroo*; *Hillbilly From Tenth Avenue*; *The Old Apple Tree*; *Swing Your Lady*; *Dig Me A Grave In Missouri*.

Sonja Henie's third – and at 102 minutes, longest – feature, was also her sprightliest to date. Called **Happy Landing** (20th Century-Fox), it was a tasty casserole of a musical whose several and varied ingredients were kept nicely simmering under chef Darryl F. Zanuck's watchful and expert eye. Don Ameche (illustrated right) co-starred, and the original screenplay, devised by Milton Sperling and Boris Ingster, with parts as well for Cesar Romero (illustrated centre, as an orchestra leader who is managed by Mr Ameche) and Ethel Merman, had Miss Henie (illustrated) being conquered in love by the dashing Cesar. But when she realizes that underneath his smooth exterior beats the heart of a heel, she changes her romantic allegiance to the likeable Don. Several ballet-on-ice sequences, an energetic tap routine by the Condos Brothers (danced to Raymond Scott's 'War Dance of the Wooden Indians'), a clutch of songs from Merman, plus the comic contributions of funnymen Billy Gilbert, Wally Vernon and El Brendel, all contributed to a superior musical entertainment, expertly directed by Roy Del Ruth. Songs: *Hot And Happy*; *Yonny And His Oompah*; *You Are The Music To The Words In My Heart*; *A Gypsy Told Me* Jack Yellen, Samuel Pokrass; *You Appeal To Me* Walter Bullock, Harold Spina.

Mae West (right) wrote and starred in **Every Day's A Holiday** (her last film for Paramount), a turn-of-the-century tale that found its formidable star well below form. She played Peaches O'Day, a game gal who thinks nothing of selling Brooklyn bridge to any 'schnook' who's stupid enough to believe it's hers to sell; and who, to escape the police, pretends to be Mademoiselle Fifi, a Parisian musical comedy star. A trite story, with trite, laboured dialogue, **Every Day's A Holiday** disappointed West fans everywhere and was in no way comparable to her previous efforts. Edmund Lowe co-starred, with other roles going to Charles Butterworth (left), Walter Catlett, Lloyd Nolan, Roger Imhof, Charles Winninger, Herman Bing and Chester Conklin. Emanuel Cohen produced, and it was directed by Edward Sutherland. Songs: *Jubilee* Stanley Adams, Hoagy Carmichael; *Fifi*; *Flutter By, Little Butterfly* Sam Coslow; *Every Day's A Holiday*; *Along The Broadway Trail* Coslow, Barry Trivers.

The Goldwyn Follies (United Artists) was Sam Goldwyn's first all-Technicolor production and it cost him a couple of million dollars. A two-hour extravaganza with music and lyrics by George and Ira Gershwin, with Vernon Duke supplying the music for the ballet sequences – and utilizing the talents of George Balanchine and The American Ballet in a bid to bring culture to the masses – it was basically a variety show with a tenuous plot that unsuccessfully attempted to recreate, cinematically, some of the magic of the Ziegfeld Follies. The musical programme consisted of a 'Romeo and Juliet' ballet and a 'Water Nymph' ballet with Vera Zorina (illustrated centre), making her screen debut, 'Here, Pussy, Pussy' (by Ray Golden and Sid Kuller), 'Serenade To A Fish' performed by The Ritz Brothers, and Kenny Baker singing 'Love Walked In', 'Love Is Here To Stay' (by the Gershwins), and 'Spring Again' (by Vernon Duke and Ira Gershwin). In addition, Charles Kullman and Helen Jepson sang arias from Verdi's *La Traviata*, Ella Logan presented 'I Was Doing Alright' (the Gershwins), Jepson returned with 'La Serenata' (by Alfred Silvestri and Enrico Toselli), and 'I Love To Rhyme' (the Gershwins) featured Phil Baker, and Edgar Bergen and Charlie McCarthy (also making their screen debut). The mish-mash, while well-intentioned, demonstrated the maxim that one bad turn deserved another, and was directed by George Marshall with H.C. Potter (uncredited) from a screenplay credited to Ben Hecht (although, apparently, 10 other writers had been involved along the way). Also cast: Adolphe Menjou, Andrea Leeds (singing voice dubbed by Virginia Verrill), Jerome Cowan, Nydia Westman, and The Goldwyn Girls. On 11 July 1937, George Gershwin died, leaving Vernon Duke – with Oscar Levant's help – to polish up the final construction of his last four songs for the film. ▷

It took four years to make **Snow White And The Seven Dwarfs** (RKO), the first full-length animated film (illustrated), and despite the gloomy prognostications of the industry, the risk paid off and marked the beginning of the fabulous Walt Disney empire. It also established animation as a new and vital art form, although some of the film's detractors found many of the images too horrifying for children, while others thought much of it too twee for adults. Neither observation was entirely spurious, but it cannot be denied that its overall conception, and the superb invention in the animation itself, was breathtaking. Music played an important part in its success, and many of the show's songs became instant hits – most notably 'Some Day My Prince Will Come', 'Whistle While You Work' and 'Heigh-Ho' by Frank Churchill and Larry Morey, scored and arranged by Paul J. Smith and Leigh Harline. The latter two skilfully helped to characterize each of the seven dwarfs. The voices on the sound track belonged to Adriana Caselotti, Harry Stockwell, Lucille La Verne, Scotty Matraw, Roy Atwell, Pinto Colvig, Billy Gilbert, Moroni Olsen and Stuart Buchanan, and the supervising director was David Hand. Other songs: *I'm Wishing*; *With A Smile And A Song*; *The Washing Song*; *Isn't This A Silly Song?*; *One Song*; *Buddle-Uddle-Um-Dum*; *Music In Your Soup*; *You're Never Too Old To Be Young.*

THIRTIES MUSICALS

The best way to enjoy **Rascals** (20th Century-Fox) was to leave one's mind in the hat-check room with one's hat – and simply to abandon oneself to the arrant nonsense being perpetrated in the name of entertainment. Into a gypsy camp lorded over by little Jane Withers (left) comes Rochelle Hudson – who has also left her mind in the hat-check room (or somewhere) – for she cannot remember who she is or how she got there. Undaunted, she becomes a camp fixture, specializing in palm reading, and before you can say Ziegeuner, is having an affair with Robert Wilcox, an erstwhile Yale man and another resident of the encampment. A surgeon, however, restores Miss Hudson's memory to her, after which she forgets her strange interlude among the gypsies and returns to civilization and the gold-digging baron (Joss Crespo) who intends to marry her for her money. But Crespo hasn't reckoned with little Miss Withers, whose ingenuity saves Miss Hudson's skin, if not the film. Borrah Minnevitch and the Minnevitch Gang provided harmonica support whenever it was needed (and sometimes when it wasn't); with other parts going to Steffi Duna (right), Katharine Alexander and Paul Stanton. The original screenplay was by Robert Ellis and Helen Logan, it was produced by John Stone and directed by H. Bruce Humberstone. Songs: *Blue Is The Evening*; *Take A Tip From A Gypsy*; *What A Gay Occasion*; *Song Of The Gypsy Band* Sidney Clare, Harry Akst.

△

Start Cheering (Columbia), an entertaining *mélange* of comedy and music, was a campus caper with a difference: there was no winning touchdown just as the last few yards of film were unspooling. Although Charles Starrett was the hero (he played a Hollywood star who, after appearing in several campus movies, decides to give the real thing a try), top-billing went to the irrepressible Jimmy Durante (left) as Willie Gumbatz, side-kick to the star's harrassed manager (Walter Connolly, second-billed). Joan Perry, Raymond Walburn, Broderick Crawford, Hal LeRoy and Ernest Truex were featured in support. There were several specialties as well, including The Three Stooges, Dr Craig E. Earle (Professor Quiz), Gertrude Niesen (right), Arthur Hoyt (centre), Louis Prima and His Band, Johnny Green and His Orchestra, and Chaz Chase, a performer who made a healthy living eating cigarettes, cigarette boxes, burning matches, wrapping paper and practically anything else most normal people would find unappetizing. The screenplay was by Eugene Solow and Richard E. Wormser (story by Corey Ford), and the director was Albert S. Rogell. Songs: *My Heaven On Earth* Charles Tobias, Phil Baker, Samuel Pokrass; *You Walked Into My Life*; *Start Cheering* Milton Drake, Ben Oakland; *Rockin' The Town*; *Hail Sigma PSI* Ted Koehler, Jimmy Green; *When I Strut Away In My Cutaway* Jimmy Durante.

Despite the incorporated talents of Milton Berle, Jack Oakie, Bob Burns, Kenny Baker, Ann Miller, Victor Moore, Helen Broderick, Jane Froman, Buster West and the Hal Kemp Orchestra, **Radio City Revels** (RKO) was a dispiriting non-starter. Oakie and Berle played a pair of written-out songwriters who stumble across a tin-pan-alley goldmine in the shape of out-of-town songwriter (Burns) who, unbeknown to himself, sings all his best songs in his sleep. Not being a particularly honest duo, Messrs Oakie and Berle filch the songs, and spend a great deal of the film's running time trying to keep their unsuspecting benefactor asleep. They had fewer problems doing the same thing to their audiences. A prolific but languid score by Allie Wrubel and Herb Magidson (which they probably also wrote while asleep) was of no service to the show (production number illustrated) at all. Four grown men (Matt Brooks, Anthony Veiller, Eddie Davis and Mortimer Offner, story by Brooks) wrote it; Edward Kaufman was the producer, and it was directed by Ben Stoloff. Songs: *Goodnight Angel*; *Love, Honour And Oh Baby*; *Speak To Your Heart*; *Why Must I Love You*; *Take A Tip From The Tulip*; *Morning Glories In The Moonlight*; *I'm Taking A Shine To You*; *You're the Apple Of My Eye*; *Swinging In The Corn*; *There's A New Moon Over The Old Mill*.

▽

A race between two ocean liners – *The Gigantic* ▷ and *The Colossal* – was the narrative excuse for **The Big Broadcast Of 1938** (Paramount), a musical tombola with not all the prizes on offer worth the having. It did, however, introduce the Ralph Rainger-Leo Robin hit 'Thanks For The Memory', sung by Bob Hope (his feature film debut) and Shirley Ross, and, as such, cannot entirely be dismissed. Martha Raye (illustrated centre) was on hand to render 'Mama, that Moon Is Here Again', also by Rainger and Robin; Dorothy Lamour sang another of their numbers called 'You Took The Words Right Out Of My Heart' while, for no apparent reason other than to provide a touch of variety, the great Wagnerian soprano Kirsten Flagstad gave out with some high C's on the high seas in Brunnhilde's War Cry 'Ho-jo-to-ho' from Wagner's *Die Walküre*. W.C. Fields received top billing, but his material on this occasion hardly did him justice. Ben Blue, Grace Bradley, Leif Erickson, Lynne Overman, Tito Guizar, and Shep Fields and His Orchestra were in it too; it was adapted by Howard Lindsay and Russel Crouse from a story by Frederick Hazlitt Brennan, and the screenplay was by Walter DeLeon, Francis Martin and Ken Englund. Harlan Thompson produced, and it was directed by Mitchell Leisen. Other songs: *Don't Tell A Secret To A Rose*; *This Little Ripple Had Rhythm* (a cartoon sequence played by Shep Fields and Orchestra); *The Waltz Lives On* Rainger, Robin; *Zuni Zuni* Tito Guizar; *Sawing A Woman In Half* Jack Rock.

Hollywood Hotel (Warner Bros.) marked the end of an era. It was the last of the spectacular musicals created by the Warner Bros.–Busby Berkeley partnership which began with *42nd Street* in 1933. Public taste was changing and Berkeley was to adapt to this change in his last years at Warner's and, more auspiciously, at MGM during the forties. Gone were the spectacular sets, the intricate overhead shots and the battalions of extras. Instead Berkeley (who directed the entire film) now relied on his unfailing ability to create interest through inventive camera set-ups and through the sheer brilliance of his editing – best illustrated on this occasion in the humorous 'Let That Be A Lesson To You' by Johnny Mercer and Richard A. Whiting – who wrote all the new songs – set in a drive-in diner, in which Dick Powell (centre right) and almost the entire cast (including Benny Goodman, left, and His Orchestra) were involved in a marvellous routine that made stunning use of the cars and the customers. The film's most celebrated song, however, was 'Hooray for Hollywood' which almost overnight became the movie capital's rousing theme song. The screenplay was by Jerry Wald, Maurice Leo and Richard Macaulay, and it featured Powell as a singing saxophonist who wins a talent contest and goes to Hollywood. In a comedy-of-errors situation, he believes he has been asked to escort the famous film star Mona Marshall (Lola Lane) to a première when, in fact, it is her stand-in (Rosemary Lane) he's been lumbered with. A plot point, which would be used more effectively fourteen years later in MGM's *Singin' In The Rain*, also had Powell dubbing the singing of ham actor Alan Mowbray. By the final fade, the singer-cum-saxophonist and the stand-in get their big break and, needless to say, are romantically united. Also featured were Ted Healy (right), Frances Langford (centre left), Hugh Herbert, Johnnie Davis (centre), Glenda Farrell, Allyn Joslyn, Edgar Kennedy, Mabel Todd, and the movie gossip columnist Louella Parsons. Other songs: *Sing You Son Of A Gun*; *I'm Like A Fish Out Of Water*; *I've Hitched My Wagon To A Star*; *Silhouetted In The Moonlight* Mercer, Whiting; *I'm A Ding Dong Daddy From Dumas* (Benny Goodman Orchestra) Phil Baxter; *Blue Moon* Rodgers and Hart; *Otchichornya* (trad).

In 20th Century-Fox's **Rebecca Of Sunnybrook Farm** (first filmed by Mary Pickford for Artcraft, 1917, then by Fox with Marian Nixon, 1932), Shirley Temple fared better than Miss Withers, her closest rival, had done in *Rascals*. The Temple version of Kate Douglas Wiggin's durable story bore about as much relation to the original novel as Hollywood musicals did to reality, but it was a thoroughly beguiling effort just the same, drenched in professional expertise and, on balance, one of the best films its junior power-house ever made. With her hair pulled back (a sign of advancing years, no doubt!), Shirley took in her familiar stride Karl Tunberg and Don Ettlinger's screenplay which, in a nutshell, made her a pawn in a battle to exploit her precocious talents on radio. In one of the film's cheekiest moments, Shirley (illustrated) sat at a piano and delivered a medley of past Temple hits ('On The Good Ship Lollipop', 'When I'm With You', 'Animal Crackers' etc) just as a trouper like Ethel Merman or Mary Martin might have done. That the exercise wasn't in the least squirm-making was testament enough to a remarkable talent. Completing the cast were Randolph Scott, Jack Haley, Phyllis Brooks, Helen Westley, Slim Summerville, Alan Dinehart, The Raymond Scott Quintet, and Bill Robinson, with whom Temple danced 'The Parade Of The Wooden Soldiers' by Sidney Mitchell, Lew Pollack and Raymond Scott. The film was directed by Allan Dwan. Songs: *Crackly Corn Flakes*; *Alone With You*; *Happy Ending*; *Au Revoir* Sidney Mitchell, Lew Pollack; *An Old Straw Hat* Mack Gordon, Harry Revel; *Come And Get Your Happiness* Jack Yellen, Samuel Pokrass.

Phil Regan (right) starred in **Outside Of Paradise**, a pleasant offering from Republic, written and produced by Harry Sauber, about an Irish band leader-cum-singer who inherits a half-interest in a castle in Ireland and opens a niterie in it – much to the chagrin of co-owner Penny Singleton (left). It took 68 minutes for the couple to work out their differences, which was just the right amount of time needed by director John H. Auer to wrap it all up before it outstayed its welcome. Bert Gordon, Leonid Kinskey, Ruth Coleman, Mary Forbes and Lionel Pape supported. A brief comic ballet featured Renie Riano. Songs: *All For One*; *Outside Of Paradise*; *Doing Shenanigans*; *A Little Bit Of Everything*; *A Sweet Irish Sweetheart Of Mine* Peter Tinturin, Jack Lawrence.

Alice Faye (right) and husband Tony Martin (centre) starred, with Fred Allen, Joan Davis (left) and Jimmy Durante, in **Sally, Irene, And Mary** (20th Century-Fox), a *divertissement* whose strength lay not in Karl Tunberg and Don Ettlinger's plot (screenplay by Harry Tugend and Jack Yellen) about a trio of singing manicurists (Faye, Davis and Marjorie Weaver, centre right) and the tribulations that blight their Broadway-bound paths – but in its attractive score and performances. Making the most of the least, the talented company, augmented by Gregory Ratoff, Louise Hovick, Barnett Parker and Mary Treen, sold it all for more than it was worth, with top-of-the-bill Miss Faye in fine vocal form throughout, her golden moment being Walter Bullock and Harold Spina's 'This Is Where I Came In'. Nick Castle staged the dances, most notably Raymond Scott's 'Minuet in Jazz', and it was slickly directed by William A. Seiter for associate producer Gene Markey. **Sally, Irene, And Mary**, originally filmed as a silent by MGM in 1925, was, in turn, based on a play by Eddie Dowling and Cyrus Wood. Any similarity between the two versions was purely coincidental. Other songs: *Got My Mind On Music*; *Sweet As A Song* Mack Gordon, Harry Revel; *Half Moon On The Hudson*; *I Could Use A Dream*; *Who Stole The Jam?*; *Help Wanted* Walter Bullock, Harold Spina; *Hot Patatta* Jimmy Durante.

THIRTIES MUSICALS

Dorothy Lamour (left), without her sarong, starred in **Tropic Holiday** (Paramount), together with Ray Milland (right) who, as a scriptwriter, journeys to Mexico for local colour and/or inspiration. What he finds, of course, is Miss Lamour – and in between some comic interruptions from Bob Burns (who does a take-off of Fredric March's suicide scene from Selznick's 1937 *A Star Is Born*) and Martha Raye (who impersonates a toreador), plus some Mexican-type dance routines from LeRoy Prinz – woos her incessantly. Though Dottie warbled several numbers by the Mexican composer Augustin Lara (lyrics Ned Washington), she was outsung by the genuine article, a Mexican called Elvira Rios – who provided the film with its one undisputed stroke of ethnic authenticity. It took four men to write it (Don Hartman, Frank Butler, John C. Moffitt and Duke Atterbury, story by Messrs Hartman and Butler), Arthur Hornblow produced, and the director was Theodore Reed. The cast included Binnie Barnes, Tito Guizar, Pepito, Chris Pin Martin, The Dominguez Brothers, and The San Cristobal Marimba Band. Songs: *The Lamp On The Corner*; *Tonight We Live*; *My First Love*; *Tropic Night* Lara, Washington; *Havin' Myself A Time* Ralph Rainger, Leo Robin.

▽

There wasn't much joy in **Joy Of Living** (RKO), ▷ an irritating musical which starred Irene Dunne (left) as a successful Broadway star whose parasitic family and their impossible demands on her, prevent her from enjoying life to the full. Then along comes Douglas Fairbanks Jr (right), the son of a wealthy banking family from Boston, whose *joie de vivre* and infuriating habit of imitating Donald Duck initially do nothing to ingratiate him with the staid and proper Miss Dunne. But underneath that prim exterior of hers is a pent-up spirit just waiting to be unleashed and, in no time (one hour and forty minutes), Fairbanks is the man who unleashes it. A pleasant, but not particularly memorable, score by Jerome Kern and Dorothy Fields helped take some of the strain off the performers – but it was tough going just the same, with Alice Brady, Guy Kibbee, Jean Dixon, Eric Blore and Lucille Ball practically knocking themselves out in an attempt to inject humour into Gene Towne, Graham Baker and Allan Scott's humourless screenplay (story by Dorothy and Herbert Fields). Warren Hymer, Franklin Pangborn, Billy Gilbert and Frank Milan were in it too, Felix Young produced, and it was directed by Tay Garnett. Songs: *Just Let Me Look At You*; *You Couldn't Be Cuter*; *What's Good About Good Night?*; *A Heavenly Party*.

David Belasco's play, **The Girl Of The Golden West**, served for three films and a Puccini opera before surfacing as one of MGM's vehicles for Jeanette MacDonald and Nelson Eddy (illustrated). The miscasting of Miss MacDonald, aligned to an indifferent Sigmund Romberg–Gus Kahn score, hardly made for scintillating entertainment, and the oft-told story – of a tomboyish saloon owner who undergoes a process of refinement after encountering the bandit Ramirez (Eddy) – seemed pretty stale by 1938. Walter Pidgeon and an ill-used Buddy Ebsen were featured in William Anthony McGuire's glossy production; so were Leo Carillo, H.B. Warner, Cliff Edwards, Monty Woolley, Priscilla Lawson, Billy Bevan, Charles Grapewin and Noah Beery Sr. Musically, the 'Mariache' sequence (staged by Albertina Rasch) was the most exciting, and the liveliest few minutes in a rather heavy-going couple of hours. It was directed without flair by Robert Z. Leonard from a screenplay by Isabel Dawn and Boyce DeGaw. Other songs: *Sun-Up To Sun-Down*; *Shadows On The Moon*; *Soldiers Of Fortune*; *The Wind In The Trees*; *Senorita*; *The West Ain't Wild Anymore*; *Who Are We To Say*; plus Bach/Gounod's *Ave Maria* and Liszt's *Liebestraum* (*Dream Of Love*) with a Gus Kahn lyric added to it.

▽

△

Though Judy Garland sang five numbers in **Everybody Sing** (MGM) – a title the rest of its cast took literally – and received second billing to Allan Jones, it was still not sufficient a showcase to turn her into a major box-office attraction. She would have to wait one more year for *The Wizard Of Oz* (MGM) for real stardom to be accorded her. Meantime, she did very nicely, thank you, as attractive Lynne Carver's plain-Jane younger sister, living in a household full of theatre folk whose respective fortunes are on the wane, but who, thanks to Judy, are given a chance to shine again. Fanny Brice was third billed as Olga Chekaloff, a Russian servant, and although Florence Ryerson and Edgar Allan Woolf's screenplay (additional dialogue by James Green) found room for her to do her famous 'Baby Snooks' routine (illustrated right, with Garland, left), her inimitable talents were far from satisfactorily exploited. Reginald Owen and Billie Burke played Miss Garland and Miss Carver's parents (and Miss Brice's employers), with Reginald Gardiner, Helen Troy, Monty Woolley, Adia Kuznetzoff and Henry Armetta completing the cast. It was produced by Harry Rapf and directed by Edwin L. Marin, with Roger Edens in charge of the attractively scored vocal arrangements. Songs: *Swing, Mr Mendelssohn, Swing*; *The One I Love*; *Down On Melody Farm* (also sung as a specialty number to the melody of the Quartet from Verdi's *Rigoletto*); *The Show Must Go On*; *I Wanna Swing*; *Never Was There Such A Perfect Day* Gus Kahn, Bronislau Kaper, Walter Jurmann; *Quainty Dainty Me*; *Why? Because* Bert Kalmar, Harry Ruby; *Cosi Cosa* Ned Washington, Kaper, Jurmann; *Swing Low, Sweet Chariot* (traditional, arranged by Edens).

◁ Ten-year-old Bobby Breen's fourth film was **Hawaii Calls** (Principal/RKO) and it found him stowing away on a Hawaii-bound ship with little Pua Lani and not so little Ned Sparks. Once in Hawaii, Master Bobby (illustrated) turns super-spy and apprehends a bunch of villains who have stolen some secret plans concerning an Hawaiian fortification. In between all this, the *wunderkind* raised his voice in song – and out came 'Macushla' (by Dermot McMurrough and Josephine V. Rowe), 'Down Where The Trade Winds Blow' and 'Hawaii Calls' (both by Harry Owens) and, for his big finish, 'Aloha Oe' (by Queen Liliukalani of Hawaii, 1878). The shamelessly predictable screenplay was by Wanda Tuchock (from a novel by Don Blanding), and it was directed by Edward F. Cline whose cast included Irvin S. Cobb, Warren Hull, Gloria Holden, Juanita Quigley and Mamo Clark.

Based on a play by Paul Frank and Georg Fraser, **Josette** (20th Century-Fox) was a mistaken identity affair with Simone Simon (illustrated) as chanteuse Josette, the girl whose identity is mistaken.Brothers Don Ameche and Robert Young are convinced that she's out to seduce their old man (William Collier Sr) when, in fact, she isn't a seductress at all. She isn't even Josette and, to judge from her vocalizing, she's no singer either. Seems she's just pretending to be all these things in order to save Bert Lahr's nightclub from destruction. It was all part of a rather far-fetched screenplay (by James Edward Grant, from a story by Laszlo Vadnay) that needed all the help it could get from Mack Gordon and Harry Revel's score, which on this occasion was about as inspired as the material it accompanied and therefore not very helpful after all. The associate producer was Gene Markey and the director was Allan Dwan. Songs included: *Where In The World*; *In Any Language*; *May I Drop A Petal In Your Glass Of Wine?*

Cocoanut Grove (Paramount) was a musical account of a band leader's (Fred MacMurray) journey from Chicago to Los Angeles where he and his band hope to audition for a spot at the famous Cocoanut Grove niterie. That was it plotwise, but it was enough on which to hang a series of serviceable songs, and to allow such performers as Harriet Hilliard (as a singer who pretends to be a school teacher), The Yacht Club Boys (illustrated, with MacMurray), Ben Blue, Rufe Davis, Billy Lee, Eve Arden and Harry Owens to do their thing. Sy Bartlett and Olive Cooper wrote it, George Arthur produced and the director was Alfred Santell. Songs: *You Leave Me Breathless* Ralph Freed, Frederick Hollander; *Says My Heart* Frank Loesser, Burton Lane; *Dreamy Hawaiian Moon*; *Cocoanut Grove* Harry Owens; *Ten Easy Lessons* 'Jock', Loesser, Lane; *Swami Song* Alfred Santell, Lane; *The Musketeers Song* Bert Kalmar, Harry Ruby, The Yacht Club Boys; *The Four Of Us Went To Sea* The Yacht Club Boys.

Loosely based on a short story by O. Henry called *The Badge Of Policeman O'Roon*, **Doctor Rhythm** (Paramount) owed more to Beatrice Lillie than it did to the celebrated author who inspired it. For the yarn originally spun by O. Henry was nowhere in evidence. Miss Lillie (centre), happily, was, and – although the salvage operation she was called on to perform was too much for even her formidable comic talents – she did at least provide the film with a few cherished moments of genuine clowning. The rest was a pretty risible effort which starred Bing Crosby as a medico who agrees to replace officer Andy Devine as Mary Carlisle's protector. Dr Crosby crooned his head off in several Johnny Burke–James V. Monaco ballads, but to little purpose. The screenplay adaptation was by Jo Swerling and Richard Connell, it was produced by Emanuel Cohen and directed by Frank Tuttle with a cast that also included Rufe Davis, Laura Hope Crews, Fred Keating, John Hamilton, Sterling Holloway, Henry Wadsworth, Franklin Pangborn, and a special appearance by Louis Armstrong. Songs: *My Heart Is Taking Lessons*; *This Is My Night To Dream*; *On The Sentimental Side*; *Doctor Rhythm*; *Only A Gipsy Knows*; *Trumpet Player's Lament*; *P.S. 43* Burke, Monaco; *Rhythm* Rodgers, Hart.

Three Ritz Brothers for the price of one was about the best item on offer in 20th Century-Fox's **Kentucky Moonshine (GB: Three Men And A Girl)**, a frenetic musical farce which featured the over-the-top trio as impecunious entertainers who, in a desperate bid for survival, purchase some false whiskers, and make for them thar Kentucky Hills where they hope to be discovered as authentic performing hillbillies (illustrated). The screenplay was caused by M.M. Musselman and Art Arthur (story by Musselman and Jack Lait Jr), with additional material and comedy songs by Sid Kuller and Ray Golden; it was directed by David Butler for producer Kenneth MacGowan, and also featured Tony Martin, Marjorie Weaver, Slim Summerville, John Carradine, Wally Vernon and Berton Churchill. Songs: *Moonshine Over Kentucky*; *Isn't It Wonderful, Isn't It Swell?*; *Sing A Song Of Harvest*; *Reuben Reuben*; *I've Been Swingin'* Sidney Mitchell, Lew Pollack; *Kentucky Opera* Sidney Clare, Jule Styne.

What happens after Gracie Allen turns the small-town college she has inherited into a watering hole for vaudevillians could be seen in **College Swing** (Paramount), a plotless – and, frankly, mindless – variety show which used (or perhaps ill-used), the variegated talents of the aforementioned Miss Allen, her husband George Burns, Martha Raye (right), Bob Hope (left), Edward Everett Horton, Florence George, Ben Blue, Betty Grable, Jackie Coogan, John Payne, Cecil Cunningham, Robert Cummings, Skinnay Ennis, The Slate Brothers and Jerry Colonna. Walter DeLeon and Francis Martin scripted it from a story by Frederick Hazlitt Brennan who, in turn, got the idea from Ted Lesser. Producer Lewis Gensler was responsible for the assemblage of talent on view, and Raoul Walsh, who could do far, far better work than this, directed. Songs: *I Fall In Love With You Every Day* Frank Loesser, Manning Sherwin; *What A Rumba Does To Romance*; *You're A Natural*; *The Old School Bell* Loesser, Sherwin; *Moments Like This*; *How 'Dja Like To Love Me?*; *What Did Romeo Say To Juliet?* Loesser, Burton Lane; *College Swing* Loesser, Hoagy Carmichael.

Cowboy From Brooklyn (Warner Bros.) was yet another musical vehicle for Dick Powell (illustrated), but one with a slightly different flavour. Earl Baldwin's screenplay (from a play by Louis Pelletier and Robert Sloane) had the star playing a singing drifter who takes a job on a ranch and is discovered by a talent scout who turns him – surprise, surprise – into a big radio star. Supposedly a light comedy, the film was feeble to a degree, and even the casting of the talent scout (Pat O'Brien) reflected a singular lack of inspiration. A low-spot for crooning Dick and his fans, it also featured Priscilla Lane, Dick Foran, Ann Sheridan and Ronald Reagan for director Lloyd Bacon and associate producer Lou Edelman. Songs included: *I've Got A Heartful Of Music*; *I'll Dream Tonight*; *Ride, Tenderfoot, Ride* Johnny Mercer, Richard A. Whiting; *Cowboy From Brooklyn* Mercer, Harry Warren.

THIRTIES MUSICALS

When Warner Bros. made **Gold Diggers In Paris** they were in the midst of an economy drive which precluded the musical numbers from being as lavishly and elaborately staged as they had been in the past. This, however, didn't stop Busby Berkeley's inventiveness, and his work was the best thing in a show intended as another star vehicle for radio crooner Rudy Vallee (right, with Rosemary Lane). As the boss of a troupe of nightclub dancers who find themselves unintentionally taking part in a dance festival in Paris where they've been mistaken for the American Ballet Company, Vallee made no impact at all; but Berkeley used his dancing girls to good effect, and there was some lively comedy from co-star Curt Bois. Ray Enright directed from a screenplay by Earl Baldwin and Warren Duff; Sam Bischoff was associate producer, and Hugh Herbert, Allen Jenkins, Gloria Dickson, Melville Cooper, Ed Brophy, Eddie Anderson and the Schnickelfritz Band were also cast. Songs: *The Latin Quarter; I Wanna Go Back To Bali; Put That Down In Writing; A Stranger In Paree* Al Dubin, Harry Warren; *Day Dreaming All Night Long; Waltz Of The Flowers; My Adventure* Warren, Johnny Mercer.

Contrary to what his fans were used to, there ▷ was a little more depth (but not that much more) to Bing Crosby's role in **Sing You Sinners** (Paramount), a prepossessing little item in which the Bingle (centre) played a crooner with a love of horse-racing (or a punter with a yen to croon). Either way it didn't matter much, for each of his passions was given equal screen-time – the former being shared by his brothers Fred MacMurray (left) and Donald O'Connor (right). No one in the family, however, shared his love of gambling and therein lay the gist of Claude Binyon's original screenplay. Two of Bing's songs became standards: 'I've Got A Pocketful Of Dreams' and 'Don't Let That Moon Get Away' (by Johnny Burke and James V. Monaco); and another – Frank Loesser and Hoagy Carmichael's 'Small Fry' – became a big, and durable, hit. Also cast: Elizabeth Patterson as the boys' mother, Ellen Drew, John Gallaudet, William Haade and Irving Bacon. It was produced and directed by Wesley Ruggles. Other songs: *Laugh And Call It Love; Where Is Central Park* Burke, Monaco.

Judy Garland's (centre) fifth feature, **Love Finds Andy Hardy** (MGM), again cast her as the girl no one falls in love with, but who's everybody's favourite confidante. Mickey Rooney (illustrated), alias Andrew Hardy, in his eternal quest for romance, befriends her, but has his head romantically turned by Ann Rutherford (left) and sexy Lana Turner (right) – a Mervyn LeRoy discovery who followed the celebrated producer-director from Warner Bros. to MGM. The plot, from the stories by Vivien R. Bretherton from characters created by Aurania Rouveral in her 1928 play *Skidding* (screenplay by William Ludwig), involved the Hardy family in a catalogue of domestic crises, some serious, such as grandma's stroke, some trivial, such as where Andy is to find the eight dollars he still owes on his car. Under George B. Seitz's engagingly warm-hearted direction it worked like a charm, with grown-ups Lewis Stone and Fay Holden as Ma and Pa Hardy. The cast was completed by Cecilia Parker, Betty Ross Clarke, Marie Blake, Don Castle and Gene Reynolds. Songs: *What Do You Know About Love?; Meet The Beat Of My Heart* Mack Gordon, Harry Revel; *In Between* Roger Edens.

While good old reliable Judy Garland went from one film to another, lending adequate support and bolstering plots with her vibrant singing, Deanna Durbin went from strength to strength playing leading roles and, in **Mad About Music** (Universal), her third feature, received top billing as well as a bouquet of good reviews which must have been the envy of her plain-Jane rival at MGM. Deanna's latest told the slight but endearing story of a lass (Durbin, centre) whose vain actress mother (Gail Patrick) has kept her sequestered in a Swiss school in order to prolong her own youthful glamour-girl reputation in Hollywood. With no parents to call her own, Deanna invents a father, boasting to the other girls at the school that he is an intrepid hunter etc. etc. Her white lies, however, catch up with her when her chums demand to meet him and, were it not for the timely intervention of Herbert Marshall (left) – well, who knows what might have happened? Excellent performances from all the aforementioned, plus good work too from Arthur Treacher (right), William Frawley, Young Jackie Moran (as Miss Durbin's first romantic conquest), Helen Parrish and Marcia Mae Jones, helped contribute to the film's success, as did Cappy Barra's Harmonica Band with whom Durbin sang 'I Love To Whistle' (by Harold Adamson and Jimmy McHugh); and The Vienna Boys' Choir, with whom she sang Gounod's 'Ave Maria'. It was written by Bruce Manning and Felix Jackson from a story by Marcella Burke and Frederick Kohner, produced by Joe Pasternak and directed by Norman Taurog. Remade in 1963 as *The Toy Tiger* with Tim Hovey in the Durbin role. Other songs included: *Chapel Bells; Serenade To The Stars* Adamson, McHugh.

Martha Raye's larger than life personality was at its most effective when used sparingly and with care. In **Give Me A Sailor** (Paramount), for which she received top billing, it was dragged bodily through scene after scene of heavy-handed merry-making, and came to a slap-sticky end. The film also starred Bob Hope, Betty Grable and Jack Whiting, but you'd hardly have known it. In fact, screenwriters Doris Anderson and Frank Butler even had a scene in which Miss Raye (illustrated centre) wins a beauty contest for possessing the loveliest of legs – the *chutzpah* of which, considering *La* Grable's presence – was nothing short of monumental! A romantic farce in which Hope and Whiting, much to Miss Raye's chagrin, are both in love with Grable, it had the two couples going through all sorts of romantic permutations before the final fade. J.C. Nugent, Clarence Kolb, Nana Bryant, Emerson Treacy and Bonnie Jean Churchill were also in it; it was based on a play by Anne Nichols, produced by Jeff Lazarus and directed by Elliott Nugent. Songs: *What Goes On Here In My Heart?*; *The US And You*; *A Little Kiss At Twilight*; *It Don't Make Sense* Ralph Rainger, Leo Robin.

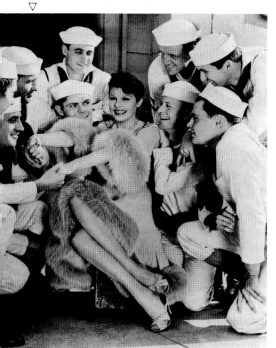

Another typical Shirley Temple offering, **Little Miss Broadway** (20th Century-Fox), written by Harry Tugend and Jack Yellen and directed by Irving Cummings, once again found Shirley cast as an orphan – this time living in a hotel for ageing vaudevillians which is under threat of closure by wealthy Edna May Oliver. Miss Oliver (right), however, reckons without the charms of little Miss T. who, apart from ensuring the film its obligatory happy ending, sang and danced two imperishable numbers with co-stars George Murphy (left) and Jimmy Durante: 'We Should Be Together' and 'Swing Me An Old-Fashioned Song' by Walter Bullock and Harold Spina. Darryl F. Zanuck produced, and his cast included Jane Darwell, Phyllis Brooks, George Barbier, Claude Gillingwater, Donald Meek, El Brendel and Patricia Wilder. Other Songs: *Be Optimistic*; *How Can I Thank You*; *I'll Build A Broadway For You*; *Little Miss Broadway*; *If All The World Were Paper*; *Thank You For The Use Of The Hall* Bullock, Spina; *When You Were Sweet Sixteen* James Thornton; *Happy Birthday To You* Patty Smith Hill, Mildred J. Hill; *Auld Lang Syne* (traditional melody, words by Robert Burns).

Straight, Place And Show (GB: **They're Off**), from 20th Century-Fox, was originally intended as a starring vehicle for Ethel Merman but somehow finished up as a typical Ritz Brothers (illustrated) caper, also featuring horses in its narrative. Or, more specifically, one particular horse, which the brothers, who sell pony rides for ten cents a time, inherit. They discover the creature to be a magnificent jumper and plan to enter him in a profitable steeplechase. Trouble is, they don't have the requisite thousand dollars entrance fee . . . Miss Merman, who sang several songs in what might best be described as the vocal equivalent of the Ritz Brothers' knock-'em-in-the-aisles approach to comedy, finished in third place behind Richard Arlen, with other parts going to Phyllis Brooks, George Barbier, Sidney Blackmer and Will Stanton. It was written by M.M. Musselman and Allan Rivkin (additional dialogue by Lew Brown) from an unproduced play by Damon Runyon and Irving Caesar, produced by Darryl F. Zanuck, and directed by David Butler. Songs: *With You On My Mind*; *Why Not String Along With Me?* Lew Brown, Lew Pollack; *International Cowboys* Ray Golden, Sid Kuller, Jule Styne.

A screenplay by Jerry Wald and Richard Macaulay furnished the last musical film which Busby Berkeley directed for Warner Bros./First National. Small and lightweight in scale, but enjoyable just the same, **Garden Of The Moon** was set in a nightclub of that name whose irritable owner is in a state of war with his band leader over a lady both of them want. Dick Powell was chalked in as the band leader but John Payne finally played it; and Margaret Lindsay (illustrated with Payne) was the girl (Bette Davis was originally offered the role, but declined without thanks). The trio was completed by Pat O'Brien, and the rest of the cast, for associate producer Lou Edelman, also featured Johnnie Davis, Melville Cooper, Isabel Jeans and Penny Singleton. The pleasing score was by Al Dubin and Harry Warren with Johnny Mercer, but there was clearly little in it to inspire Berkeley, whose work on the film was no more than adequate. Songs included: *Garden Of The Moon*; *The Girlfriend Of The Whirling Dervish*; *Love Is Where You Find It* (not to be confused with the well known number from MGM's *The Kissing Bandit*, 1948); *The Lady On The Two Cent Stamp*; *Confidentially*.

THIRTIES MUSICALS

Listen Darling (MGM) was the kind of bright, light and touching little family film at which MGM excelled. It combined the talents of Judy Garland (right) with the seasoned 14-year-old Freddie Bartholomew (left), and a tiny Scotty Beckett, to relate how all three of them succeed in bringing Mary Astor (Judy and Scotty's widowed mother) and personable Walter Pidgeon together. Edwin L. Marin directed, Jack Cummings produced, it was written by Elaine Ryan and Ann Morrison Chapin (story by Katherine Brush), and also featured Gene Lockhart, Charles Grapewin and Alan Hale. James Hanley's 'Zing Went The Strings Of My Heart' (sung by Garland) was the show's big hit, but the score also included 'Ten Pins In The Sky' by Joseph McCarthy and Milton Ager, and 'On The Bumpy Road To Love' by Al Lewis, Al Hoffmann and Murray Mencher.

A slight but not unamusing screenplay by Karl Tunberg, Don Ettlinger and Jack Yellen (story by Tunberg and Ettlinger) helped turn **Hold That Co-Ed (GB: Hold That Girl)** into respectable, tuneful, light entertainment from 20th Century-Fox, with heavyweight John Barrymore (illustrated) top-cast as a Governor running for Senator who has a passionate interest in college education and football. His opponent, both in the political arena and on the playing field was George Barbier (both men have their own football teams), with other parts in this well-cast offering going to George Murphy, Marjorie Weaver (illustrated), Joan Davis, Jack Haley, Ruth Terry, Donald Meek, Johnny Downs, Guinn Williams and The Brewster Twins. Darryl F. Zanuck produced, and the director was George Marshall. Songs: *Here Am I Doing It*; *Hold That Co-Ed* Mack Gordon, Harry Revel; *Limpy Dimp* Sidney Clare, Nick Castle, Jule Styne; *Heads High* Lew Brown, Lew Pollack.

Alexander's Ragtime Band was a magnificent musical cavalcade whose catalogue of 23 Irving Berlin compositions made it one of the best and most durable musicals produced by 20th Century-Fox in the thirties. With such evergreens as 'Now It Can Be Told', 'Blue Skies', 'A Pretty Girl Is Like A Melody', 'Say It With Music' and 'Heat Wave', thrillingly sung in contrasting styles by leading lady Alice Faye and co-star Ethel Merman – the sheer range and variety of Berlin's prodigious output was amply demonstrated. Though plot-wise it was little more than an on-off-and-on-again love affair between a band leader (Tyrone Power, right) and a singer (Faye, left), the film effectively reflected the changes in popular music between 1915 and 1938, even though the protagonists hardly aged a day in 23 years! Kathryn Scola and Lamar Trotti's screenplay, with its numerous cues for songs, found employment for Don Ameche (who loves Miss Faye but – as was the case in *In Old*

Chicago, 20th Century-Fox – loses her to the good-looking Mr Power), as well as Jack Haley, Jean Hersholt, Dixie Dunbar, Chick Chandler, Helen Westley, John Carradine, Wally Vernon, Ruth Terry, and Douglas Fowley. It was produced by Darryl F. Zanuck, with Harry Joe Brown as his associate, and directed efficiently but with little sense of period, by Henry King. Other songs: *Alexander's Rag-Time Band* (Faye); *Rag-Time Violin*; *Everybody's Doing It* (Faye, Dunbar, Vernon); *This Is The Life* (Vernon); *Oh How I Hate To Get Up In The Morning* (Haley); *We're On Our Way To France*; *Pack Up Your Sins And Go To The Devil* (Merman); *What'll I Do*; *Remember* (Faye); *Everybody Step* (Merman); *All Alone* (Faye); *Gypsy In Me*; *Easter Parade* (Ameche); *My Walking Stick* (Merman); *International Rag* (Faye, Chandler, Vernon); *When The Midnight Choo-Choo Leaves For Alabam* (Faye); *For Your Country And My Country*; *I Can Always Find A Little Sunshine At The YMCA*.

A modest programmer with a modest running time of 65 minutes, **Freshman Year** (Universal) returned to the campus but not, mercifully, to the football field. William Lundigan starred as an undergraduate who hits on an original money-making scheme: selling 'flunk' insurance. Policies cost fifty cents a piece and the payout, should one flunk, is ten dollars. Unfortunately, professor Ernest Truex decides to flunk practically every policy holder, a gesture which results in overnight bankruptcy for Lundigan. But the annual college show (see illustration) Lundigan is promoting clicks, and its profits help clear his debts. Dixie Dunbar, Constance Moore, Stanley Hughes and Frank Melton were also cast; so were The Three Diamond Brothers, The Three Murtah Sisters The Lucky Seven Choir and, in a bit part as a student, Alan Ladd. What they all added up to was only moderately entertaining. It was written by Charles Grayson from a story by Thomas Ahearn and F. Murray Grossman, produced by George Bilson and directed by Frank McDonald. Songs included: *Chasin' You Around* Frank Loesser, Irving Actman; *Ain't That Marvellous?*; *Swing That Cheer* Joe McCarthy, Harry Barris.

A more mature Deanna Durbin (illustrated left) than the schoolgirl last witnessed in Universal's *Mad About Music* surfaced in **That Certain Age** (Universal), and although the boy she finally settles for is Jackie Cooper, a great deal of the film saw its charming leading lady in the thrall of Melvyn Douglas (as a journalist on her father's newspaper). Irene Rich and John Halliday played Deanna's parents, with Nancy Carroll, Juanita Quigley, Jackie Searl (illustrated right), Charles Coleman and Peggy Stewart completing the cast for producer Joseph Pasternak and director Edward Ludwig. The score was by Harold Adamson and Jimmy McHugh, and included a big hit for the young star with 'My Own'. The screenplay, from an original story by F. Hugh Herbert, was by Bruce Manning, Charles Brackett and Billy Wilder, and was hardly what the paying customers came to see. Other songs: *That Certain Age*; *You're As Pretty As A Picture*; *Be A Good Scout* Adamson, McHugh; *Juliet's Waltz Song* (*Je Veux Vivre Dans Ce Rêve*) from Gounod's 'Romeo and Juliet'; *Les Filles de Cadiz* Alfred de Musset, Léo Delibes.

After making a few pictures apart, Fred Astaire and Ginger Rogers were teamed again in **Carefree** (RKO) which had a memorable score by Irving Berlin – but the great period was over. The studio was in financial difficulties, Astaire and Rogers (illustrated) didn't really want to continue the partnership, director Mark Sandrich was to leave RKO for Paramount after a dispute, and the number 'I Used To Be Colour Blind', which was intended as a colour sequence for **Carefree** proved to be too expensive and was filmed in black and white. Astaire played a psychiatrist (not very convincingly), and Ginger Rogers a patient sent to him by her boyfriend (Ralph Bellamy) because she cannot make up her mind whether or not to marry him. True to the cliché, the patient fell for her analyst. Using anaesthetics and hypnosis to control Ginger's mind, Astaire painted a rather simplistic view of

Like *Vogues of 1938* (United Artists, 1937), **Artists And Models Abroad** (Paramount) was an excuse for a fashion show-cum-revue but not as good – or as good-looking – an excuse as the earlier effort. Jack Benny (right) was top billed, and the plot (by Howard Lindsay and Russel Crouse, from an idea by J.P. McEvoy) had him romancing a Texas oil millionaire's daughter (Joan Bennett, left) as well as giving a stranded theatrical troupe a grand tour of Paris. The screenplay (by Lindsay, Crouse and Ken Englund) failed to come to grips with the material, and the result of so much nonsense parading as entertainment was, to use Benny's own summation of the film, 'lousy'. Others involved were Mary Boland, Charles Grapewin, Fritz Feld, Joyce Compton and The Yacht Club Boys. Arthur Hornblow Jr produced and the director was Mitchell Leisen, with LeRoy Prinz directing the dances. Songs: *What Have You Got That Gets Me?*; *You're Lovely Madame*; *Do The Buckaroo* Ralph Rainger, Leo Robin; *You're Broke You Dope* Jack Rock and The Yacht Club Boys.

psychiatry; but the screenplay by Allan Scott and Ernest Pagano (story and adaptation by Dudley Nichols and Hagar Wilde) was in no way meant to be taken seriously and served to give Ginger Rogers one of her finest comic roles. Despite Astaire's extraordinary golf number ('Since They Turned Loch Lomond Into Swing') and the usual carefree elegance that informed everything he did, it was his partner's film all the way, and she was seen at her delightful best in 'The Yam', another of those invented dance crazes that had begun five years earlier with 'The Carioca' in *Flying Down To Rio* (RKO). Hermes Pan was the choreographer, it was produced by Pandro S. Berman, and the cast included Luella Gear, Jack Carson, Clarence Kolb, Franklin Pangborn and Hattie McDaniel. The fourth (and best) of the Berlin songs was the superb 'Change Partners'.

Bobby Breen (left) was at it again in **Breaking The Ice** (RKO) – this time as a put-upon youngster who finds care and affection from a Philadelphia tinker after running away from his Dutch uncle in another part of Pennsylvania. He lands a job singing at an ice-skating rink where he meets, not Sonja Henie, but a six-year-old who skates almost as well, called Irene Dare. Bobby Breen fans didn't complain, but those less kindly disposed to the precocious youngster's knowing way with a song stayed away in droves. Charles Ruggles (centre) was the tinker, with other parts going to Dolores Costello, Robert Barrat, Dorothy Peterson, John King, Billy Gilbert and Margaret Hamilton. It was written by Mary McCall Jr, Manuel Seff and Bernard Schubert (from a story by Fritz Falkenstein and N. Brewster Morse), produced by Sol Lesser and directed by Edward F. Cline. Songs: *Happy As A Lark*; *Put Your Heart In A Song*; *The Sunny Side Of Things* Frank Churchill; *Telling My Troubles To A Mule*; *Goodbye, My Dreams, Goodbye* Webster, Victor Young.

Like a bird flying through the Vienna woods, the ▷
music of Johann Strauss II soared, hovered and
sang through MGM's **The Great Waltz** – and as
arranged and adapted by Dimitri Tiomkin, with
lyrics by Oscar Hammerstein II and sung mostly
by Miliza Korjus, there was little need for
anything else. It was directed by Frenchman
Julien Duvivier who, in his first Hollywood film,
allowed his cameraman to move freely in three-
four time. The result was a visual as well as an
aural delight, and a brilliant, if at times
schmaltzy, evocation of waltz-mad Vienna with
its opulent ballrooms and song-filled *biergartens*.
Fernand Gravet (illustrated) played Strauss,
Luise Rainer was his neglected wife, and Miliza
Korjus (right) the reason for her neglect. Best
sequence in the film: Strauss composing 'Tales
From The Vienna Woods', using the woods
themselves, and the magical sounds that escape
from them, as inspiration. It was written by
Samuel Hoffenstein and Walter Reisch (story
by Gottfried Reinhardt) and lavishly produced
by Bernard Hyman. Also cast: Hugh Herbert,
Lionel Atwill, Herman Bing and Sig Rumann.
Songs: *Voices Of Spring*; *Du Und Du*; *The Bat*; *I'm In
Love With Vienna*; *One Day When We Were Young*;
Revolutionary March; *There'll Come A Time*.

◁ Sonja Henie (illustrated centre) was again
teamed with Cesar Romero in **My Lucky Star**
(20th Century-Fox) whose screenplay, by Harry
Tugend and Jack Yellen (story by Karl Tunberg
and Don Ettlinger), was an ingenious contrivance that once again managed to accommodate
the limited talents of its Norwegian skating star.
This time she was a salesgirl in a department
store who, after being discovered by the boss's
son (Romero) to be something of an enchantress
on skates, is sent to a sports-minded college
where she soon establishes herself as queen of
the campus and persuades the powers-that-be to
stage their annual winter ice show in her boss's
department store. It was silly to a degree, but
hugely entertaining. The musical highlights
were the 'Alice In Wonderland Ice Ballet' staged
by Harry Losee, and the Mack Gordon–Harry
Revel hit, 'I've Got A Date With A Dream'. Comic
support came in the shape of the unstoppable
Joan Davis and Arthur Treacher, with Richard
Greene, Buddy Ebsen, George Barbier, Louise
(Gypsy Rose Lee) Hovick, Billy Gilbert, Paul Hurst
and Elisha Cook Jr also in it. Darryl F. Zanuck
produced and his director was the reliable Roy
Del Ruth. Other songs: *Could You Pass In Love*;
This May Be The Night; *The All-American Swing*;
Plymouth University Song Gordon, Revel.

◁ Adolphe Menjou (centre left), Jack Oakie (centre
right), Jack Haley, Arleen Whelan, Tony Martin
(centre), Binnie Barnes (right), George Barbier,
Warren Hymer, Gregory Gaye and Andrew
Tombes lent their motley talents to an unassuming and really rather jolly entry called **Thanks
For Everything** (20th Century-Fox). Written
with a buoyant touch by Harry Tugend (story by
Gilbert Wright, adaptation by Curtis Kenyon
and Art Arthur), its simple story had advertizing
executive Menjou, together with his public
relations man Oakie, conducting a coast-to-
coast search for Mister Average Man, who turns
out to be Jack Haley from Plainville, Mo. An
attractive score by Mack Gordon and Harry
Revel, allied with some nifty direction by William A. Seiter, made this Darryl F. Zanuck
production a delight. Songs: *You're The World's
Fairest*; *Three Cheers For Henry Smith*; *Puff-A-
Puff*; *Thanks For Everything*.

△

Romance In The Dark (Paramount) arrived on
the scene about eight years too late for it to find a
willing audience for its old-fashioned operetta-
ish plot. Gladys Swarthout starred as a Hungarian peasant girl who, after arriving in Budapest, becomes a pawn in a contest between
tenor John Boles and his manager John Barrymore (illustrated) both of whom fancy themselves as the nation's number one Don Juan. For
the purposes of his little game, Boles transforms
her into a Persian enchantress called Princess
Zilona and shamefully uses her to bait his rival.
Barrymore's performance was a total caricature
of his former self – though it was never made
clear from H.C. Potter's direction whether or not
this was deliberately intended. Miss Swarthout
and Mr Boles sang a great deal better than they
acted, though considering how little there was
to get one's teeth into in the Frank Partos–Ann
Morrison Chapin screenplay (from a play by
Hermann Bahr) this was not surprising. Claire
Dodd, Fritz Feld, Curt Bois and Ferdinand Gott-
schalk were also in it, and it was produced by
Harlan Thompson. Songs: *Tonight We Love*
Ralph Rainger, Leo Robin; *Blue Dawn* Ned
Washington, Phil Boutelje; *Bewitched By The
Night* Jay Gorney; *Romance In The Dark* Sam
Coslow, Gertrude Niesen; *The Nearness Of You*
Ned Washington, Hoagy Carmichael.

Going Places (Warner Bros./First National), a fourth remake of William Collier's play *The Hottentot*, went no place at all and gave Dick Powell (right) his third dud in a row (coming, after *Cowboy From Brooklyn* and *Hard To Get*, both from Warners) with its unconvincing story about a sports goods salesman who, to improve business, poses as a jockey and gets involved with a set of horse-loving socialites. In this way he meets and falls in love with pretty Miss Anita Louise, whose horse he rides to success in a race. Jerry Wald, Sig Herzig and Maurice Leo wrote it, Ray Enright directed for producer Hal B. Wallis, and although the film had a mammoth hit in 'Jeepers Creepers' (by Johnny Mercer and Harry Warren) it was Louis Armstrong who sang it with Maxine Sullivan, not Powell the star. Also in it: Allen Jenkins (left), Ronald Reagan, Walter Catlett (centre right), Thurston Hall and Harold Huber (centre left), and other songs included: *Say It With A Kiss*; *Oh, What A Horse Was Charley* Mercer, Warren; *Mutiny In The Nursery* Mercer.
▽

△

Despite a score by Oscar Hammerstein II and Ben Oakland, **The Lady Objects** (Columbia), directed by Erle C. Kenton never overcame the melodramatics at the heart of Gladys Lehman and Charles Kenyon's mediocre screenplay. All about a halfback (Lanny Ross) who marries his college sweetheart (Gloria Stuart, at mirror), and the repercussions that follow when she becomes a highly successful criminal lawyer and he just a workaday architect, it also involved a murder, with Joan Marsh as the victim. Other victims (not of murder, just the plot) were Roy Benson, Pierre Watkin, Robert Paige and Arthur Loft. Ross's singing was better than his acting, and one number, 'A Mist Over The Moon', had quality. Other songs: *That Week In Paris*; *Home In Your Arms*; *When You're In The Room*; *Sky High*; *Naughty, Naughty*; *Victory Song* (lyric by Milton Drake).

Sweethearts was the first three-colour Technicolor picture made by MGM – and ravishing it was too, thanks largely to the art direction of Cedric Gibbons and the costumes by Adrian. A glorious wedding cake of a musical, its hard centre was provided by Dorothy Parker and Alan Campbell's screenplay which put Nelson Eddy (right) and Jeanette MacDonald (centre) into a contemporary setting and gave them some decent lines to speak for a change. They played a musical comedy team in the sixth year of their hit Broadway show *Sweethearts*, who, to the dismay of the show's producer (Frank Morgan), its writer (Mischa Auer) and its composer (Herman Bing) are coaxed to Hollywood by an unscrupulous agent (Reginald Gardiner, left). But Hollywood plays havoc with their private lives and, after a temporary separation, they return to Broadway in triumph. It was produced by Hunt Stromberg, directed by W.S. Van Dyke, and although skilfully avoiding the original plot of *Sweethearts* (as written for the stage by Victor Herbert with book and lyrics by Fred DeGresac, Harry B. Smith and Robert B. Smith), utilized several of the show's original songs – 'Wooden Shoes', 'Every Lover Must Meet His Fate' and the title number (similar in its staging to 'A Pretty Girl Is Like A Melody' from *The Great Ziegfeld*, MGM, 1936) – by including them in a show-within-a-show format. All had new lyrics by Bob Wright and Chet Forrest, and Albertina Rasch was in charge of their staging. Also in the cast were Florence Rice, Douglas MacPhail, Allyn Joslyn, Raymond Walburn, Gene Lockhart, Berton Churchill and Olin Howland. Other Songs: *Summer Serenade*; *Pretty As A Picture*; *On Parade*; *Game Of Love* (lyrics by Wright and Forrest); *The Message To The Violet*; *Keep It Dark* Gustav Luders, Frank Pixley; *Little Gray Home In The West* Hermann Lohr, D. Eardley-Wilmot; *In The Convent They Never Taught Me That* Victor Herbert, Robert B. Smith; *Happy Day* Herbert Stothart, Wright, Forrest.
▽

THIRTIES MUSICALS

△

Fisherman's Wharf (RKO) was another vehicle for Bobby Breen (illustrated), once again cast as an orphan who, after running away from home, is befriended by a group of San Franciscan fishermen. It was the formula as before with sentimentality and song its chief selling points. Sol Lesser produced, it was written by Bernard Schubert, Ian Hunter and Herbert Clyde Lewis, and directed by Bernard Vorhaus. Leo Carillo and Lee Patrick were also featured; so was a trained seal. Songs: *Fisherman's Chantey* William Howe, Harlan Myers; *Sell Your Cares For A Song* Charles Newman, Victor Young; *Blue Italian Waters* Paul Francis Webster, Frank Churchill.
▽

Just Around The Corner (20th Century-Fox) was the writing on the wall as far as its star Shirley Temple was concerned. The first of her films not to find overwhelming favour at the box office, its sentimental story, written with treacle-flavoured ink by Ethel Hill, J.P. McEvoy and Darrell Ware (from a novel by Paul Gerard Smith), proved too much even for Temple addicts to swallow. In this one, 10-year-old Shirley helps her down-and-out widowed architect father (Charles Farrell) to improve his lot and to find a wife (Amanda Duff). Plot-wise it was par-for-the-course for a Temple movie; what audiences found harder to take were the blatantly manipulative scenes in which Shirley indulged in a spot of soapbox oratory praising the efforts of Uncle Sam (whom she believes to be Claude Gillingwater) in keeping the country on its feet. She even stages a benefit show at a nickel a head to help keep this Uncle Sam solvent! On the plus side, however, there were Joan Davis and Bert Lahr as the sort of chauffeur and maid everybody ought to have, who accompanied Shirley in a happy little ditty called 'This Is A Happy Little Ditty' (by Walter Bullock and Harold Spina, who wrote the score); Shirley's singing of the delightful 'I Love To Walk In The Rain', and some neat, if by now familiar tap dancing from Bill Robinson (illustrated with Temple). Franklin Pangborn, Cora Witherspoon, Bennie Bartlett and Hal K. Dawson were in it too; Nick Castle and Geneva Sawyer staged the musical numbers; Darryl F. Zanuck produced, and the syrupy direction was by Irving Cummings. Other songs: *Brass Buttons And Epaulets*; *I'm Not Myself Today*; *I'll Always Be Lucky With You*; *Just Around The Corner*.

20th Century-Fox were puttin' on the Ritz again with **The Three Musketeers**, which starred Don Ameche as a dashing D'Artagnan and the Ritz frères as his dashing-about lackeys. Dumas' familiar story involving, as it usually did, some business about the Queen's emerald brooch and the thwarting of wicked Cardinal Richelieu – was knocked sideways and upside down in this slapstick incarnation of it – with its trio of comedians (masquerading as The Three Musketeers, illustrated, in hats) all but winding themselves in search of an easy laugh. Had Dumas been alive he'd doubtless have served Ritz on all of them. Lionel Atwill (de Rochefort), Gloria Stuart (the Queen), Pauline Moore (Lady Constance), Joseph Schildkraut (the King),
▽

John Carradine (Naveau), Douglass Dumbrille (Athos), John King (Aramis), Russell Hicks (Porthos), Binnie Barnes (Milady de Winter) and Miles Mander (Cardinal Richelieu) took it far more seriously than the occasion merited, their stylish performances being very much out of kilter with the contents of M.M. Musselman, William A. Drake and Sam Hellman's free-wheeling, over-the-top adaptation (special material by Sid Kuller and Ray Golden). Its saving grace was the Samuel Pokrass–Walter Bullock score that accompanied the knockabout horseplay. Raymond Griffith produced, and the director was Allan Dwan. Songs included: *My Lady*; *Song Of the Musketeers*; *Chicken Soup* (Ritz Brothers speciality); *Voilà*.

Made for no purpose other than to fill in time on ▷ a double bill, **Swing, Sister, Swing** (Universal) cashed in on the jitterbug craze – as reflected in its story (by Burt Kelly, screenplay by Charles Grayson) of a group of small-town jitterers (see illustration) who find overnight fame on Broadway, but who are just as suddenly plummeted back into their small-town oblivion. Ken Murray was top-starred as a high-powered agent, with Johnny Downs and Kathryn Kane (both illustrated centre) introducing the 'Baltimore Bubble' to New York. The duo were accompanied by trombonist Eddie Quillan with other parts going to Ernest Truex, Edna Sedgwick and Nana Bryant. Ted Weems and His Orchestra were in it too. Matty Kelly staged the routine dance routines, the associate producer was Burt Kelly, and it was directed by Joseph Santley. Other songs: *Gingham Gown; Just A Bore; Wasn't It You?; Kaneski Waltz* Frank Skinner, Charles Henderson.

In **St Louis Blues** (Paramount), Dorothy Lamour starred as a Broadway star who, to escape the sarong-girl image her manager (Jerome Cowan) has helped create for her, leaves New York for Missouri where she encounters show-boat owner Lloyd Nolan (a role originally offered to, and rejected by, George Raft). Nolan gives her a job in his new revue and all goes well until rival carnival owner William Frawley discovers that Dottie has violated her stage contract, and capitalizes on the fact by preventing Nolan from opening his revue. Adapted by Frederick Hazlitt Brennan from a story by Eleanore Griffin and William Rankin (screenplay by John C. Moffitt and Malcolm Stuart Boylan), its parts were better than its whole – with the black singer Maxine Sullivan giving her all to 'Otchichornya' and 'Loch Lomond' – and proving to be the hit of the show. Lamour languished her way through 'Junior' and the title song (by W.C. Handy), 'Blue Nightfall' by Frank Loesser and Burton Lane, 'I Go For That' by Loesser and Matt Malneck, and 'Let's Dream In The Moonlight' by Raoul Walsh and Malneck; and there was additional vocal support from Tito Guizar. Also cast: Jessie Ralph, William Frawley, Mary Parker (at centre with Nolan), composer Matt Malneck and His Boys, and The King's Men. Jeff Lazarus produced, the choreography was by LeRoy Prinz, and it was directed by Raoul Walsh. Other songs: *The Song In My Heart Is A Rhumba* Loesser, Lane; *Kinda Lonesome* Leo Robin, Sam Coslow, Hoagy Carmichael.

▽

A jolly little sequel to *Three Smart Girls* (Universal, 1936), **Three Smart Girls Grow Up** (Universal) starred daisy-fresh Deanna Durbin (left), this time as a little Miss Fixit who, in the nicest possible way, sets about marrying off her sisters (Nan Grey, centre, and Helen Parrish, right) to Robert Cummings and William Lundigan. Miss Durbin sang 'Because' (by Edward Teschemacher and Guy D'Hardelot) which became one of her biggest hits ever, and radiated sweetness and light – again in the nicest possible way. A most agreeable entertainment, it was written by Bruce Manning and Felix Jackson, produced by Joe Pasternak, and directed with an infallible instinct for his young star's limitations and strengths, by Henry Koster. Other songs included *The Last Rose Of Summer* Thomas Moore, Richard Alfred Milliken.

▽

Paris Honeymoon (Paramount) was a pleasant ▷ enough diversion which contained a few good Ralph Rainger–Leo Robin songs for Bing Crosby and a witty screenplay by Frank Butler and Don Hartman (from a story by Angela Sherwood). What it really needed was the Lubitsch touch to do it justice; what it got, however, was the Frank Tuttle touch. Bing (right), as a Texas millionaire, goes to Europe to be near wealthy countess Shirley Ross. However, while spending time in an impressively eerie castle, he meets a beautiful peasant girl (Franciska Gaal, left) and decides he prefers innocence to sophistication. The film catered mainly for an audience with a similar preference. Also cast were Edward Everett Horton, Akim Tamiroff, Ben Blue and Gregory Gaye. The producer was Harlan Thompson. Songs: *I Have Eyes; Sweet Little Headache; Funny Old Hills; Joobalai; The Maiden By The Brook; Work While You May* Rainger, Robin; *I Ain't Got Nobody* Roger Graham, Dave Peyton, Spencer Williams.

Let Freedom Ring (MGM) was a patriotic Western with songs, starring Nelson Eddy and Virginia Bruce (illustrated). Its main theme was anti-discrimination, and the best thing that could be said for it was that its heart was in the right place. Whether director Jack Conway or singer Nelson Eddy were in the right place was another matter. All about the 'people's' fight against political corruption and land monopoly (as personified by Edward Arnold, left), it featured Eddy in several popular classics and ended with him leading a group of workers in a rousing chorus of 'America' (by Henry Carey and the Rev. Samuel Francis Smith). A long list of worthwhile supporting actors included Victor McLaglen, Lionel Barrymore, Charles Butterworth, Guy Kibbee, Raymond Walburn, H.B. Warner and George 'Gabby' Hayes. Harry Rapf produced, and it was written by Ben Hecht. Songs: *Home Sweet Home* Henry Bishop, John Howard Payne; *Love Serenade* Riccardo Drigo, new lyrics by Bob Wright and Chet Forrest; *Ten Thousand Cattle Straying* Owen Wister; *When Irish Eyes Are Smiling* Ernest R. Ball, Chauncey Olcott, George Graff Jr; *Pat-Sez He* Phil Ohman, Foster Carling; *The Dusty Road* Otis and Leon Rene; *Where Else But Here* Sigmund Romberg, Edward Heyman; *Funiculi Funicula* Luigi Denza; *I've Been Working On The Railroad* (traditional).

▽

1939

Best Picture
NOMINATIONS INCLUDED: *The Wizard Of Oz* (MGM) produced by Mervyn LeRoy

Best Actor
NOMINATIONS INCLUDED: Mickey Rooney *Babes In Arms* (MGM)

Art Direction
NOMINATIONS INCLUDED: *First Love* (Universal) Jack Otterson and Martin Obzina. *The Wizard Of Oz* Cedric Gibbons and William A. Horning.

Sound Recording
NOMINATIONS INCLUDED: *Balalaika* (MGM) Douglas Shearer. *The Great Victor Herbert* (Paramount) Loren Ryder.

Special Effects (New Category)
NOMINATIONS INCLUDED: *The Wizard Of Oz* A. Arnold Gillespie and Douglas Shearer

Music
Song
'Over The Rainbow' *The Wizard Of Oz* Harold Arlen *cm*; E.Y. Harburg *lyr*.
NOMINATIONS INCLUDED: 'Faithful Forever' *Gulliver's Travels* (Paramount) Ralph Rainger *cm*; Leo Robin *lyr*. 'I Poured My Heart Into A Song' *Second Fiddle* (20th Century-Fox) Irving Berlin

Scoring
NOMINATIONS INCLUDED: *Babes In Arms* Roger Edens and George Stoll. *First Love* Charles Previn. *The Great Victor Herbert* Phil Boutelje and Arthur Lange. *Swanee River* (20th Century-Fox) Louis Silvers. *Way Down South* (Lesser, RKO) Victor Young.

Original Score
The Wizard Of Oz Herbert Stothart
NOMINATIONS INCLUDED: *Gulliver's Travels* Victor Young

Special Award
To Judy Garland for her outstanding performance as a screen juvenile during the past year. (miniature statuette)

The Annual Top Moneymaking Films
INCLUDED: *Sweethearts* (MGM). *That Certain Age* (Universal). *Three Smart Girls Grow Up* (Universal).

Ice Follies of 1939 (MGM) introduced audiences to the celebrated International Ice Follies, with the latter half of producer Harry Rapf's extravaganza comprising a series of lavishly mounted skating sequences (in Technicolor) which certainly dazzled the eye. There was very little nourishment for the mind, however, and the film's workaday first half was clearly the springboard for the second. All about a small-time skater (James Stewart, left) who, in time, becomes a motion picture producer, and the romance he has with an actress (Joan Crawford, centre), it traversed *A Star Is Born* (Selznick, United Artists, 1937) territory inasmuch as its conflict derived from a relationship in which the wife, initially, becomes more famous than her spouse. The screenplay by Florence Ryerson and Edgar Allan Woolf (story by Leonard Praskins) completely lacked the dazzle of the skating numbers, and it was an uphill battle for its stars to bring even a patina of credibility to it all. Lewis Stone appeared as a movie mogul, with other roles going to Lew Ayres (right, Stewart's partner in the early days of his skating act), Bess Ehrhardt, Lionel Stander, Charles D. Brown, Roy and Eddie Shipstad, and Oscar Johnson. The director was Reinhold Schunzel. Songs *Loveland In The Wintertime* Cliff Friend, Dave Franklin; *Something's Gotta Happen Soon* Arthur Freed, Nacio Herb Brown; *It's All So New To Me* Bernice Petkere, Marty Symes; *Cinderella Reel*; *Blackbirds* Roger Edens, Franz Waxman.
▽

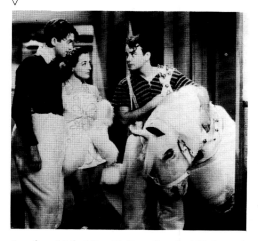

Another Little Miss Fixit surfaced at Universal, this time in the shape of ten-year-old Gloria Jean (featured centre), a cross between Shirley Temple and Deanna Durbin, but a cut-price version of both. In **The Underpup** she played a slum girl who is given the opportunity to spend a holiday in an exclusive girls' camp and, in no time at all, is offering good counsel to sundry characters, including the cliché rich kid whose parents are about to be divorced. Robert Cummings, Nan Grey, C. Aubrey Smith, Beulah Bondi, Virginia Weidler (2nd left), Margaret Lindsay, Raymond Walburn, Ann Gillis (right foreground), Pat Cavanagh and Billy Gilbert were also in it; it was written by Grover Jones from a story by I.A.R. Wylie, produced by Joe Pasternak (whose strength seemed to lie in uncovering new young talent) and directed by Richard Wallace. It set no new standards in youth-orientated entertainment, but it was no disgrace to the genre either. Songs: *March Of The Penguins (High School Cadets March)* John Philip Sousa; *Annie Laurie* Lady John Douglas Scott; *Lo! Here The Gentle Lark* Sir Henry Bishop's musical setting of stanza 143 of Shakespeare's *Venus and ◁ Adonis*; *I'm Like A Bird* (composer unknown).

△

Broadway Serenade (GB: **Serenade**) was a misguided attempt from MGM to show that Jeanette MacDonald could do without Nelson Eddy; and although few doubted that the Iron Butterfly (as she was nicknamed) was more talented than the Singing Capon (Eddy's soubriquet), her career was hardly furthered by this cumbersome effort. Its main interest lay not in its star, but in the finale staged by Busby Berkeley – in his first assignment at MGM. Unfortunately even that proved a disappointment, and the sequence, which had MacDonald standing on a 30-foot pedestal singing 'Broadway Serenade For Every Lonely Heart' – an arrangement by Herbert Stothart and Edward Ward, with lyrics by Gus Kahn, of Tchaikovsky's 'None But The Lonely Heart' – while surrounded by dancing couples and men in masks representing the great classical composers, was a top-heavy catastrophe. The film also made a brave attempt to change Jeanette's image by giving her a few swing numbers. They didn't work either. Nor did the time-worn plot about a successful wife and an unsuccessful husband (Lew Ayres, illustrated, with MacDonald). In fact, one way and another **Broadway Serenade** had very little to recommend it. It was produced and directed by Robert Z. Leonard from a screenplay by Charles Lederer (story by Lew Lipton, John Trainor and Hans Kraly), and also featured Ian Hunter, Frank Morgan, Rita Johnson, Virginia Grey and Franklin Pangborn. Songs included: *High Flyin'*; *One Look At You* Herbert Stothart, Edward Ward, Bob Wright, Chet Forrest; *Time Changes Everything* Gus Kahn, Walter Donaldson; *Un Bel Di (One Fine Day)* from Puccini's 'Madame Butterfly'; *No Time To Argue* Sigmund Romberg, Kahn; *Italian Street Song* Victor Herbert, Rida Johnson Young; *Les Filles de Cadiz* Delibes, De Musset; *Quando M'En Vo (Musetta's Waltz)* from Puccini's 'La Boheme'; *Musical Contract* Stothart, Ward; *Gay Nineties Medley*; *Nursery Medley* (composers various).

There were more juvenile escapades in **Way Down South** (RKO), a Bobby Breen starrer and a shameless piece of emotional manipulation in which the young singer, having been orphaned, finds that his late father's sugar plantation has fallen into the hands of executor Alan Mowbray, a man whose capacity for cruelty made Simon Legree look like St Francis of Assisi. Undaunted, Bobby (right) single-handedly undertakes the humanitarian task of saving the plantation's faithful slaves in general, and kindly old Uncle Caton (Clarence Muse, left) in particular. Platitudinous from start to finish, it was written by actor Muse and Langston Hughes, directed for producer Sol Lesser by Bernard Vorhaus, and featured Ralph Morgan (as Bobby's unfortunate father, centre), Steffi Duna, Sally Blane, Stymie Beard (upper right), Edwin Maxwell, Charles Middleton and The Hall Johnson Choir, who contributed some spirituals including *Nobody Know De Trouble I Seen*; *Sometimes I Feel Like A Motherless Child*; *Lord If You Can't Come Send One Angel Down*. Other songs: *Good Ground*; *Louisiana* Muse, Hughes.

▽

Though Jack Benny co-starred with Dorothy Lamour in **Man About Town** (Paramount), it was his master-servant relationship with Eddie (Rochester) Anderson that hit the box-office jackpot in this engaging and totally disarming effort, wittily scripted by Morrie Ryskind from a story he wrote with Allan Scott. The joke at its core lay in how Benny (right), with his singular lack of sex appeal, sets out to make Miss Lamour (his inamorata) jealous. His scheme involved setting up a phoney romance with a couple of women (Binnie Barnes, left, and Isabel Jeans) who, in turn, are out to make their own husbands jealous; and were it not for the heaven-sent intervention of Anderson, it might all have ended in tears. Anderson's mirthful dancing to 'Fidgety Joe' (by Frank Loesser and Matt Malneck) was a joy, and from Miss Lamour it was a case of Lamour *toujour l'amour* with her dreamy rendition of 'Strange Enchantment' by Loesser and Frederick Hollander. 'That Sentimental Sandwich', another Loesser-Hollander number, also featured the dulcet tones of the sarong girl, this time in concert with Phil Harris. Betty Grable (who was originally cast opposite Mr Benny but had to be replaced by Lamour due to an appendectomy operation) recovered sufficiently to appear in the aforementioned 'Fidgety Joe', which she sang *con brio*. Edward Arnold, Monty Woolley, E.E. Clive and Leonard Mudie were also cast, the dance sequences were staged by LeRoy Prinz, it was produced by Arthur Hornblow, and directed, most energetically, by Mark Sandrich. There was one other song, 'Bluebirds In The Moonlight' by Ralph Rainger and Leo Robin.

▽

△

The only original thing about **East Side of Heaven** (Universal) was that it featured a baby whose presence, for once, *postponed* a wedding. Bing Crosby (right) starred as a singing cab driver who, through a series of unlikely plot contrivances, finds himself playing father to a ten-month-old infant, Sandy, much to the disapproval of the babe's wealthy family. Joan Blondell co-starred as a switch-board operator whose wedding plans are delayed by the unexpected appearance of Master Sandy, with Mischa Auer (left) prominently on hand as Crosby's best friend and accomplice. The songs were by Johnny Burke and James V. Monaco, and apart from the lively 'Hang Your Heart On A Hickory Limb' sung in a café by Crosby, Jane Jones (as Mrs Kelly, the café's owner), two lady chefs, and a group of waitresses collectively known as The Music Maids, most of the numbers were ballads. C. Aubrey Smith, Jerome Cowan, Robert Kent, Mary Travers, Irene Hervey and Arthur Hoyt were also cast; it was written by William Conselman from a story by David Butler and Herbert Polesie, with Butler also in charge of the direction. Other songs: *Sing A Song Of Sunbeams*; *That Sly Old Gentleman*; *East Side Of Heaven* Burke, Monaco; *My Melancholy Baby* (instrumental only) Ernie Burnett.

Second Fiddle (20th Century-Fox) began as an ▷ amusing satire on the much-publicized, much delayed casting of Scarlet O'Hara in you-know-what, with Sonja Henie (illustrated), a skating school-teacher from Minneapolis, being selected (as candidate number 436) to star as Violet Jansen in Hollywood's epic production of 'Girl Of The North'. After that the film deteriorated dramatically into a routine romance between Miss Henie and the studio's handsome publicity man (Tyrone Power), with satire playing second fiddle to Harry Tugend's predictable screenplay (story by George Bradshaw). Even Irving Berlin's songs failed to strike the right note despite the valiant efforts of co-stars Rudy Vallee and Mary Healy to sing life into them. Edna May Oliver (as Miss Henie's aunt), Lyle Talbot, The Brian Sisters, Alan Dinehart, Minna Gombell, Stewart Reburn (right) and Spencer Charters completed the cast, it was produced by Darryl F. Zanuck, and directed by Sidney Lanfield. Songs: *I Poured My Heart Into A Song*; *Back To Back*; *An Old-Fashioned Tune Always Is New*, *The Song Of The Metronome*; *When Winter Comes*; *I'm Sorry For Myself*.

THIRTIES MUSICALS

As Vernon and Irene Castle were the Fred Astaire and Ginger Rogers of their day, it seemed natural that Fred and Ginger (illustrated) should star in **The Story of Vernon and Irene Castle**, the last film they made for RKO. Financially, it was the least successful of their movies together and, artistically, it was very uneven, although their ballroom dancing was undeniably captivating and effortless, and there were some good individual moments – a montage depicting a whirlwind tour of the States by the Castles, with the couple dancing across a giant map of America was particularly effective. There was an infectious joy, too, in their routines to 'Waiting For The Robert E. Lee' (by L. Wolfe Gilbert and Abel Baer) and 'Too Much Mustard' (by Cecil Macklin). But, after eight light-hearted and jubilant musicals together, the public simply could not, and would not, accept the death of Fred (alias Vernon) in the last reel, and withdrew their support. The overweening presence of the real Irene Castle on the set had not helped matters, understandably causing both

Astaire and Rogers to feel somewhat restricted in approaching their roles. The film was produced by George Haight and Pandro S. Berman, directed by H.C. Potter and choreographed by Hermes Pan. The screenplay, based on the books *My Husband* and *My Memories of Vernon Castle* by Irene Castle, was by Richard Sherman, Oscar Hammerstein II and Dorothy Yost, and the supporting cast included Edna May Oliver (a splendid comic performance), Walter Brennan, Lew Fields, Etienne Girardot, Rolfe Sedan, Leonid Kinskey and Clarence Derwent. Though the only song to be specifically written for the film was 'Only When You're In My Arms' (by Con Conrad, Bert Kalmar and Harry Ruby), a large number of other songs germane to the period were featured. Excluding background tunes, these were: *Oh You Beautiful Doll* A. Seymour Brown, Nat D. Ayer; *Glow Little Glow Worm* Lillia Cayley Robinson, Paul Lincke; *By The Beautiful Sea* Harold Atteridge, Harry Carroll; *Row, Row, Row* William Jerome, James V. Monaco; *The Yama Yama Man* Collin Davis, Karl

Hoschna; *Come, Josephine In My Flying Machine* Alfred Bryan, Fred Fisher; *By The Light Of The Silvery Moon* Edward Madden, Gus Edwards; *Cuddle Up A Little Closer* Otto Harbach, Karl Hoschna; *King Chanticleer (Texas Tommy)* Nat D. Ayer; *While They Were Dancing Around* Joseph McCarthy, James V. Monaco; *The Darktown Strutters' Ball* Shelton Brooks, French lyrics by Elsie Janis; *Rose Room* Harry Williams, Art Hickman; *Très Jolie Waltz* Emil Waldteufel; *Syncopated Walk* Irving Berlin; *Maxixe Dengozo* Ernesto Nazareth; *Little Brown Jug* Joseph E. Winner; *You're Here And I'm Here* Harry B. Smith, Jerome Kern; *Chicago* Fred Fisher; *Hello, Frisco, Hello* Gene Buck, Louis A. Hirsch; *Way Down Yonder In New Orleans* Henry Creamer, Turner Layton; *Take Me Back To New York Town* Andrew B. Sterling, Harry von Tilzer; *It's A Long Way To Tipperary* Jack Judge, Harry Williams; *Hello, Hello, Who's Your Lady Friend* Worton David, Bert Lee, Harry Fragson; *Destiny Waltz* Sidney Baynes; *Nights Of Gladness* Charles Ancliffe; *Missouri Waltz* J.R. Shannon, Frederick Logan, John Eppell.

Children featured prominently in **They Shall Have Music** (GB: **Melody of Youth**), another attempt by producer Samuel Goldwyn (for United Artists) to bring culture to the masses. It was certainly more successful in every respect than the misguided *The Goldwyn Follies* (United Artists, 1938), and it top-billed Jascha Heifetz (illustrated, for whose services Goldwyn paid $120,000) as a violinist who is persuaded by a bunch of quasi-juvenile delinquents, led by Gene Reynolds (now the producer of TV's *M.A.S.H.*), to save their settlement home by giving a fund-raising concert. Heifetz's co-operation ensured a happy ending, but not before scriptwriter John Howard Lawson (story by Irmgard Von Cube) released a veritable Niagara of tears from audiences everywhere. The word 'heartwarming' could have been invented for the sole purpose of describing the feeling director Archie Mayo conveyed in his overtly sentimental approach to the story; but so adroit was his handling of the various elements in Goldwyn's prestigious production, only the flintiest cynic would disagree with that assessment of its quality. Walter Brennan, Andrea Leeds, Joel McCrea, Porter Hall, Terry Kilburn and the Peter Merembum California Junior Symphony Orchestra helped round out an excellent cast. Musical items included Heifetz performing *The Rondo Capriccioso* Saint-Saens; *Souvenir d'un Lieu Cher, opus 42, No 3* Tchaikovsky; *Hora Staccato* Dinicu-Heifetz; *Concerto in E Minor For Violin And Orchestra (3rd Movement)* Mendelssohn; *Waltz in D Flat, Opus 64, No 1 (The Minute Waltz)* Chopin (this last played by Dolly Loehr, later Diana Lynn, making her film debut).

Considered by Bob Hope (centre right) to be the low spot of his career, **Some Like It Hot** (Paramount) – not to be confused with Billy Wilder's 1959 masterpiece – cast the comedian as an amusement park barker who sets out to exploit the talents of Gene Krupa (background centre) as well as his sweetheart Shirley Ross (centre left) in an attempt to keep his dying sideshow alive. Weighing in at 64 minutes, it was a really puerile attempt to blend music with comedy, and buried alive the talents of its stars and supporting players Una Merkel, Rufe Davis, Bernard Nedell, Frank Sully and Bernadene Hayes. It was directed by George Archainbaud, and scripted by Lewis R. Foster and Wilkie C. Mahoney from a play by Ben Hecht and Gene Fowler, with William C. Thomas as associate producer. Songs included: *The Lady's In Love With You* Frank Loesser, Burton Lane; *Some Like It Hot* Loesser, Gene Krupa, Remo Biondi; *Heart And Soul* Loesser, Hoagy Carmichael.

▽

Though Al Jolson, virtually at the end of his screen career, was given third billing in **Rose of Washington Square** (20th Century-Fox), he almost stole the show with his electric interpretation of such golden oldies as 'California, Here I Come' (by B.G. De Sylva, Joseph Meyer and Jolson), 'My Mammy' (by Joe Young, Sam Lewis, Walter Donaldson), 'Pretty Baby' (by Gus Kahn, Tony Jackson and Egbert Van Alstyne), 'Toot Toot Tootsie Goodbye' (by Gus Kahn, Ernie Erdman and Dan Russo) and 'Rock-A-Bye Your Baby With A Dixie Melody' (by Jean Schwartz, Sam Lewis and Joe Young). Unfortunately, there wasn't nearly as much wattage in the plot, which had Alice Faye (illustrated centre) – an excellent performance – falling for no-goodnik Tyrone Power and sticking by him even when he ends up in Sing Sing. And sing sing she did through thick and thin, her big musical moment being 'My Man' by Channing Pollock and Maurice Yvain, a number generally associated with Fanny Brice. In fact, producer Nunnally Johnson's screenplay clung so closely to the facts of Miss Brice's life, that the celebrated comedienne sued the studio and received an out of court settlement. Also cast were William Frawley, Joyce Compton, Hobart Cavanaugh and Louis Prima (left). The dances were staged by Seymour Felix with Gregory Ratoff directing. Other songs: *I Never Knew Heaven Could Speak* Mack Gordon, Harry Revel; *Rose Of Washington Square* James Hanley, Ballard MacDonald, Joseph McCarthy; *The Curse Of An Aching Heart* Al Piantadosi, Henry Fink; *I'm Sorry I Made You Cry* N.J. Clesi; *The Vamp* Byron Gay; *Ja-da* Bob Carleton; *I'm Just Wild About Harry* Noble Sissle, Eubie Blake.
▽

△

Dick Powell (seated) who had served the Warner Bros. musicals so well for so long, ran out of steam as far as the studio was concerned towards the end of the decade, and was relegated to second billing below Ann Sheridan in his last film for the studio called **Naughty But Nice**. Powell played a composer attempting to get his symphony published, in the course of which attempts he gets involved with a bunch of Tin Pan Alley-ites, one of whom is conveniently Miss Sheridan (then at the height of the studio's 'oomph' girl campaign) who got to sing more songs than her leading man. The screenplay, by Richard Macaulay and Jerry Wald, set out to take a few satirical swipes at Tin Pan Alley and its endless 'borrowings' from the classics, but the satire didn't sit and, in spite of music from Johnny Mercer, Harry Warren, Wagner, Liszt, Mozart and Bach, it was a pretty tedious affair. Produced by Sam Bischoff and directed by Ray Enright, it also featured Gale Page (centre), Helen Broderick (centre right), Ronald Reagan (2nd left), William Davidson (left) and ZaSu Pitts (2nd right). Songs: *Corn Pickin'; Hooray For Spinach; I'm Happy About The Whole Thing; In A Moment of Weakness; I Don't Believe In Signs.*
▽

The **Wizard of Oz** (MGM) was an enchanting entertainment that really lived up to the blurb – 'for children of all ages'. Today, it still seems as fresh as it was in 1939, when it became an instant movie classic and made an international star of 17-year-old Judy Garland. Although Mervyn LeRoy's production was beset with problems in every department – not least that of the screenplay which went through numerous versions – the finished product was superb, more than compensating for the many difficulties encountered in its gruelling five-month shooting schedule, and the many months of pre-production preparation. In the end, everything

worked – from the final screenplay adapted from L. Frank Baum's novel and credited to Noel Langley, Florence Ryerson and Edgar Allan Woolf – to the songs, by Harold Arlen and E.Y. Harburg, giving plenty of opportunity for excitement, spectacle, tenderness and comedy. Four noted directors were involved in the production: Richard Thorpe was fired after 12 days and his footage scrapped because it lacked fairy-tale feeling. George Cukor directed three days of tests in which he got rid of Judy's blonde wig and 'cute' doll-face make-up (a hang-over, perhaps, from the studio's unsuccessful attempt to obtain Shirley Temple), which made the point that restoring Dorothy's down-to-earth ingenuousness was the way to enhance the fairy-tale quality of her Technicolored adventure in the Land of Oz. Victor Fleming, who received sole director credit, spent four months getting these sequences on film before having to leave to take over Gone With The Wind. Fleming drew unsurpassed performances from Ray Bolger as the Scarecrow, Bert Lahr as the Cowardly Lion, Jack Haley (replacing Buddy Ebsen who fell ill with aluminium poisoning) as the Tin Man (all three illustrated, with Garland), and Margaret Hamilton as the Wicked Witch. Choreographer Bobby Connolly was in charge of the musical numbers and the daunting task of teaching 150 midget-Munchkins to sing and dance. (In all, 9,200 actors were employed on the film, and there were 3,210 costume designs, 8,428 separate make-ups and 68 sets!) Though it was a

brilliant idea to open the film in black and white for the Kansas scenes, directed by King Vidor in 10 days after Fleming departed, and then going into colour as Dorothy (Garland) enters the Land of Oz, it was not the eye-catching colour photography or Connolly's elaborately staged musical numbers that lingered in the memory, but Vidor's staging of Judy's simple and tender singing of 'Over The Rainbow' in her own backyard. Incredible as it now seems, anti-LeRoy politicking after the first sneak preview nearly succeeded in getting this classic sequence cut out of the picture. Billie Burke (dubbed by Lorraine Bridges) was cast as Glinda the Good Witch, and Frank Morgan played the Wonderful Wizard, with Charles Grapewin as Uncle Henry, Clara Blandick as Auntie Em, and Pat Walshe as Chief of the Wicked Witch's Winged Monkeys. Other songs: *Come Out, Come Out Wherever You Are* (Burke); *It Really Was No Miracle* (Garland); *Ding Dong The Witch Is Dead* (Garland, Burke, Munchkins); *We Welcome You To Munchkinland* (Munchkins); *Follow The Yellow Brick Road* (Garland, Munchkins); *We're Off To See The Wizard* (Garland, Bolger, Lahr, Haley); *If I Only Had A Brain (A Heart, The Nerve)* (Bolger, Lahr, Haley); *Lions And Tigers And Bears* (Lahr); *You're Out Of The Woods* (chorus); *The Merry Old Land Of Oz* (chorus); *If I Were King Of The Forest* (Lahr); *Optimistic Voices* (chorus on soundtrack).

THIRTIES MUSICALS

△

Suggested by the career of showman Gus Edwards – the man who discovered Eddie Cantor and Eleanor Powell – **The Star Maker** (Paramount) was curiously lacking in talent, with Bing Crosby (centre) the only name in its cast. As the singing showman, Crosby sets up a vaudeville act with a group of under-seventeens, until he gets into trouble with the law which rules that children of a certain age cannot work after eight at night. So he enters that sensational new medium – radio. Crosby sailed through it all with his usual charm and rich baritone (and had another hit with 'An Apple For The Teacher' by Johnny Burke and James V. Monaco); the kids were fine, and so were Linda Ware, Louise Campbell, Ned Sparks and Laura Hope Crews in support. Roy Del Ruth directed from a screenplay by Frank Butler, Don Hartman and Arthur Caesar (story by Caesar and William Pierce), and Charles R. Rogers produced. Other songs: *Go Fly A Kite*; *A Man And His Dream*; *Still The Bluebird Sings* Burke, Monaco; *School Days*; *If I Were A Millionaire* Will Cobb, Gus Edwards; *Jimmy Valentine* Edward Madden, Edwards; *Sunbonnet Sue* Robert B. Smith, Edwards.

On Your Toes (Warner Bros./First National) should, on paper, have been a blockbuster of a musical. It was based on a successful George Abbott stage play, had a Rodgers and Hart score, the great Balanchine was its choreographer, James Wong Howe and Sol Polito photographed it and Orry-Kelly designed the clothes. In the event, however, an awful screenplay by Jerry Wald and Richard Macaulay sabotaged the venture, and for a film that could so easily have danced its way to glory, it was, apart from the noteworthy 'Slaughter On Tenth Avenue' sequence, exceptionally dull. All about an American composer/dancer who is mistaken for a traitor by a visiting Russian ballet company, it starred Eddie Albert (left – Ray Bolger created the role on stage) and Vera Zorina (2nd left) with James Gleason, Alan Hale (centre), Frank McHugh (centre left), Leonid Kinskey (2nd right), Donald O'Connor, Gloria Dickson (right) and Queenie Smith in support. Ray Enright directed for associate producer Robert Lord. Songs and musical numbers (all heard as background only) included: *There's A Small Hotel*; *Quiet Night*; *On Your Toes*; *Princess Zenobia Ballet*.

▽

Described by one contemporary critic as 'the Watteau shepherdess of Universal'. Deanna Durbin was given her first screen kiss (amidst much newspaper ballyhooing of the fact) in **First Love**. A modern-day Cinderella story, it had Durbin (right), as an orphan, being rescued from unappreciative relatives by Robert Stack (left), the handsome bestower of that much publicized kiss. Helen Parrish played Deanna's attractive but sour glamour-girl cousin. Eugene Pallette her wealthy uncle (who, with justification hates every member of his family), and Leatrice Joy an astrology-obsessed aunt, with other parts going to Lewis Howard, June Storey and Charles Coleman. The serviceable, if crushingly unoriginal, screenplay was by Bruce Manning and Lionel Houser, Joe Pasternak produced, and the director was that reliable *schmaltz*-monger, Henry Koster. Songs and other musical numbers included: *Spring In My Heart* (from a melody by Johann Strauss adapted by Hans Salter, lyrics Ralph Freed); *Amapola* Albert Gamse, Joseph M. LaCalle; *Home Sweet Home* John Howard Payne, Sir Henry Bishop; *One Fine Day* from Puccini's 'Madame Butterfly'.

▽

△

A routine programmer to demonstrate the skating wizardry of six-year-old Irene Dare (centre foreground), **Everything's On Ice** (RKO) did just that and, in addition, threw in a plot about the kid being financially exploited by uncle Roscoe Karns in Florida. It was written by Adrian Landis and Sherman Lowe, directed by Erle C. Kenton and produced by the man in charge of Bobby Breen's cinematic adventures, Sol Lesser. Also cast: Edgar Kennedy, Lynne Roberts, Eric Linden, Mary Hart and Bobby Watson. Songs included: *Georgie Porgie*; *Everything's On Ice* Milton Drake, Fred Stryker.

Hawaiian Nights (Universal) was a tired programmer, set in the land of hula skirts, that starred Johnny Downs (featured right centre) as a bandleader whose occupation angers his father (Thurston Hall) to such an extent that he banishes the lad to the South Seas – the most inappropriate place imaginable, as Charles Grayson and Lee Loeb's screenplay (story by John Grey) made boringly clear. Mary Carlisle (centre), Constance Moore, Eddie Quillan (left) Etienne Girardot, Samuel S. Hinds and Princess Luana were in it for producer Max H. Golden, and it was directed by Albert S. Rogell. Come back Dorothy Lamour, all is forgiven! Songs: *Hawaii Sang Me To Sleep*; *Hey, Good Lookin!*; *I Found My Love*; *Then I Wrote The Minuet In G* (based on a melody by Beethoven) Frank Loesser, Matt Malneck.

From Hawaii to Honolulu (MGM) where, despite the slight change in geography, the situation continued grim. Robert Young played two parts in it: a film star, and the pineapple farmer with whom he changes places, with Eleanor Powell (illustrated left on walkway) top-starred as a dancing lady Young (the film star) meets on board ship. Miss Powell at least, was given several opportunities to do what she did best, and on one occasion even did it with a skipping rope. Also in tow were George Burns and Gracie Allen (illustrated with Powell), Rita Johnson, Clarence Kolb and Sig Rumann (as a psychiatrist). Because there was so little musical activity at Warner Bros., musicals again having temporarily fallen out of favour by 1939, Harry Warren was loaned to MGM to write the score, which he did with Gus Kahn as lyricist. Best musical moments were 'The Leader Doesn't Like Music' which had Gracie Allen doing a Mae West, and The King's Men, led by Ken Darby spoofing the Marx Brothers. Herbert Fields and Frank Partos wrote the original screenplay, Edward Buzzell directed and the producer was Irving Cummings. Other songs included: *This Night Was Made For Dreaming*; *Honolulu* Warren, Kahn; *Hymn To The Sun* P.G. Wodehouse, Armand Versey.

Not nearly as inventive as Walt Disney's *Snow White And The Seven Dwarfs* (RKO, 1937), nor as well drawn, Gulliver's Travels (Paramount) was another full-length animated cartoon (see illustration) in Technicolor aimed at the pre-teenage market – and with very little in it to appeal to adults. Concentrating on the Lilliputian section of Swift's satire (the satirical tone on this occasion being totally eliminated), it had a screenplay by Edmond Seward, Dan Gordon, Cal Howard, Red Pierce and I. Sparber (Seward was credited with the adaptation), was produced by Max Fleischer (whose crowning artistic achievement was his creation of Betty Boop), and directed by his brother Dave. The voices of Jessica Dragonette and Lanny Ross were used in the musical sequences. Songs: *Bluebirds In The Moonlight*; *All's Well*; *We're All Together Again*; *Forever*; *Faithful*; *Faithful Forever* (the previous two numbers joined); *I Hear A Dream* Ralph Rainger, Leo Robin; *It's A Hap-Hap-Happy Day* Sammy Timberg, Winston Sharples, Al Neiburg.

The Great Victor Herbert (Paramount) was a largely fictionalized account of the life of the great Victor Herbert, with Walter Connolly as the eponymous maestro, and Allan Jones (featured foreground centre) and Mary Martin as a temperamental tenor and an actress who both played a large part in Russel Crouse and Robert Lively's lightweight screenplay (story by Lively and Andrew L. Stone, the latter also serving as producer and director). A quintessential Hollywood biopic, dedicated more to entertaining than enlightening, its *raison d'être* was to present Herbert's impressive catalogue of hits, and this it did unstintingly, with twenty-eight numbers in all being featured. Singing newcomer Susanna Foster (centre right) was also cast; so were Lee Bowman, Judith Barrett, Jerome Cowan, John Garrick (foreground centre left), Pierre Watkin and Richard Tucker. Songs (and their lyricists) included: *Someday* William Le Baron; *Al Fresco*; *Thine Alone*; *Punchinello*; *Kiss Me Again*; *All For You*; *Neapolitan Love Song* Henry Blossom; *Absinthe Frappé*; *Rose Of The World*; *March Of The Toys* Glen Macdonough; *There Once Was An Owl*; *To The Land Of Romance* Harry B. Smith; *Ah, Sweet Mystery Of Life*; *I'm Falling In Love With Someone* Rida Johnson Young; *Sweethearts* Robert B. Smith.

THIRTIES MUSICALS

Kay Kyser and his 'Kollege of Knowledge' – hitherto the exclusive property of radio – made their cinematic bow in **That's Right, You're Wrong** (RKO) whose trumped-up story (by David Butler and William Conselman, screenplay by Conselman and James V. Kern) had Kyser (right) and his mob being signed to do a film that was never made because its scriptwriters could not come up with a workable idea – a case of fiction mirroring fact. It was produced and directed by David Butler with a cast that also included Adolphe Menjou, May Robson, Lucille Ball, Dennis O'Keefe, Edward Everett Horton, Roscoe Karns, and Kyser regulars Ginny Simms (centre), Harry Babbitt (centre left), Sully Mason (left) and Ish Kabibble. Songs: *I'm Fit To Be Tied* Walter Donaldson; *Scatterbrain* Johnny Burke, Frankie Masters, Kahn Keene, Carl Bean; *Little Red Fox* James Kern, Hy Heath, Johnny Lange, Lew Porter; *The Answer Is Love* Charles Newman, Sammy Stept; *Chatterbox* Jerome Brainin, Allan Roberts; *Happy Birthday To Love* Dave Franklin.

A highly romanticized, largely fictitious account of the life, times and music of Stephen Foster, **Swanee River** (20th Century-Fox) in no way did justice to the memory of one of America's great songsmiths. The fact that the real-life Foster married a girl from Pittsburgh, whereas his celluloid counterpart (played by Don Ameche) becomes betrothed to a Southern lass (Andrea Leeds) was of no consequence to scenarists John Taintor Foote and Phillip Dunne who might arguably have been forgiven for twisting history had their fiction, at least, proved entertaining. But it didn't – rendering their unscrupulous manipulations inexcusable. Salvageable from the Technicolored detritus of Darryl F. Zanuck's production were a handful of Foster favourites, galvanically performed in blackface by Al Jolson as minstrel singer E.P. Christy (illustrated centre with Ameche). Felix Bressart, Chick Chandler, Russell Hicks, and George Reed were also cast; so were The Hall Johnson Choir. The musical items were staged by Nick Castle and Geneva Sawyer, and the film was directed by Sidney Lanfield. Songs: *Oh Susanna*; *De Camptown Races*; *My Old Kentucky Home*; *Ring Ring De Banjo*; *Jeannie With The Light Brown Hair*; *Old Black Joe*; *Swanee River*; *Suite For Small Orchestra* Foster; *Curry A Mule* Sidney Lanfield, Louis Silver; *Gwine Down The River* William O. Davis; *Mule Song* Hall Johnson.

There were very few set-pieces in **At the Circus** (MGM) to compare, for example, with the cabin scene in *A Night At The Opera* (MGM, 1935), but Groucho singing 'Lydia The Tattooed Lady' (by E.Y. Harburg and Harold Arlen) in his inimitable off-key voice and then attempting an accompanying dance, was a delight. Of course, any film with The Marx Brothers (illustration: Groucho, left, Chico, centre) was bound to contain comic gems, although in this instance they were as loosely strung together as the plot (circus owner Kenny Baker has to find $10,000 to save his show and gets Groucho, alias lawyer J. Cheever Loophole, to help him). Florence Rice, Eve Arden, Margaret Dumont and Fritz Feld were also cast. Edward Buzzell directed for producer Mervyn LeRoy and the screenplay was by Irving Brecher. Bobby Connolly directed the dances. Other songs: *Two Blind Loves*; *Step Up And Take A Bow*; *Swingali* Harburg, Arlen; *Blue Moon* (Harpo's harp solo) Richard Rodgers and Lorenz Hart.

Based on the 1936 English operetta with music by George Posford and Bernard Grun (book and lyrics by Eric Maschwitz), **Balalaika** (MGM) was about the struggle between the nobility and the revolutionaries in Russia. Reflecting Hollywood's revived interest in a potential ally against the growing Nazi threat, the film didn't really take sides, but made Russia in revolution seem more like Ruritania. In its own way an attempt at *detente*, it would have been about as welcome in the Kremlin as Hitler, but in America it was accepted as a splendid musical entertainment in the opulent MGM tradition. Nelson Eddy (illustrated centre) played Prince Peter Karagin, a Cossack who poses as a poor music student because of his love for Lydia, a revolutionary-minded singer played by Hungarian Ilona Massey in her first starring role and billed as 'the new Dietrich'. Unfortunately, her limited soprano voice and insipid acting proved hindrances throughout her brief career, and this occasion was no exception. Although one song, 'At The Balalaika' (by Posford and Maschwitz, with new lyrics by Bob Wright and Chet Forrest), was retained from the original London production, there were plenty of replacement numbers, all sung by Eddy and, as MGM thought befitting, a fulsome male chorus. Frank Morgan, Dalies Frantz, Lionel Atwill, C. Aubrey Smith (left) and the Russian Cossack Choir gave adequate support to the screenplay by Leon Gordon, Charles Bennett and Jacques Deval. Reinhold Schunzel directed it for producer Lawrence Weingarten. Other songs and musical numbers: *After Service* (traditional Russian religious chant, arranged by Herbert Stothart); *A Life For The Czar* Mikhail Glinka (lyricist uncertain); *Ride, Cossack Ride*; *Tanya*; *Wishing Episode* (*Mirror Mirror*) Stothart, Wright, Forrest; *Gorko* (traditional Russian drinking song, adapted by Stothart); *Polonaise In A Flat, Opus 53* Chopin; *Song Of The Volga Boatman* (traditional, arranged by Chaliapin and Koeneman); *Chanson Boheme*; *Chanson du Toreador*; *Si Tu M'Aimes* (all from 'Carmen') Bizet; *Shadows On The Sand* (from *Scheherazade*) Rimsky-Korsakov, arranged by Wright and Forrest; *God Save The Czar* Alexei Lvov; Vasili Zhukovsky; *Stille Nacht* (*Silent Night*) Franz Gruber, Joseph Mohr; *Otchichornya* (traditional); *Flow, Flow, White Wine* Stothart, Gus Kahn; *The Magic Of Your Love* Franz Lehar, new lyrics Kahn, Clifford Grey.

Babes In Arms (MGM), from the Broadway hit by Richard Rodgers and Lorenz Hart, was the first film Busby Berkeley directed in its entirety at MGM, and the first produced by lyricist Arthur Freed. Both debuts were auspicious: Berkeley redeemed himself from the failure of his kitschy finale for *Broadway Serenade* and began an important second phase in his extraordinary career; and Freed was to become one of Hollywood's greatest producers of musicals. Brilliantly adapting to the MGM house-style, Berkeley was able to bring out the best in his stars Mickey Rooney and Judy Garland (illustrated), both of whom were given ample opportunity to display their multiple talents in a large-scale minstrel show, as well as in several more intimate songs. Rooney even managed to squeeze in excellent impersonations of Clark Gable and Lionel Barrymore. Jack McGowan and Kay Van Riper's screenplay concerned a group of impecunious vaudevillians and their enterprising offspring who, in order to raise funds for their parents, stage a hit revue and, in the process, gave birth to a whole cycle of musicals in which someone or other (usually Rooney) would exclaim exuberantly: 'Hey kids,

let's put on a show!' Charles Winninger, Guy Kibbee (a survivor from Berkeley's Warner Bros. days), June Preisser, Grace Hayes, Betty Jaynes, Ann Shoemaker and Margaret Hamilton were also cast. Of the original Rodgers and Hart score, only 'Babes In Arms' and 'Where Or When' remained. Other songs and musical numbers: *Broadway Rhythm* (Garland); *Good Morning* (Garland and Rooney); *You Are My Lucky Star* (Jaynes) Arthur Freed, Nacio Herb Brown; *I Cried For You* (Garland) Freed, Gus Arnheim, Abe Lyman; *God's Country* (Garland, Rooney, Jaynes and chorus) Harold Arlen, E.Y. Harburg, Roger Edens; *Ja-da* (Winninger) Bob Carleton; *Rock-A-Bye, Baby* (chorus) Effie I. Crockett; *Silent Night* (chorus) Franz Gruber, arranged Edens; *Darktown Strutters' Ball* (chorus) Shelton Brooks; *I Like Opera, I Like Swing* (Garland, Jaynes); *Figaro* (Garland); *My Daddy Was A Minstrel Man* (chorus) Roger Edens; *Oh! Susanna* (chorus) Stephen Foster; *Ida, Sweet As Apple Cider* (chorus) Eddie Leonard, Eddie Munson; *Moonlight Bay* (chorus) Edward Madden, Percy Wenrich; *I'm Just Wild About Harry* (Garland) Noble Sissle, Eubie Blake; *The Stars And Stripes Forever* (chorus) John Philip Sousa.

A 63-minute programmer featuring Cecil Cunningham (centre), Constance Moore, Johnny Downs, Janet Beecher (left), Marjorie Rambeau (centre left), Hedda Hopper (right), Edgar Kennedy, William Demarest, Horace McMahon and Paula Stone, Universal's **Laugh It Off** (GB: **Lady Be Gay**) was the saga of four down-and-out actresses who, in a last desperate attempt to salvage their careers, requisition a down-and-out nightclub to stage a floor show. Taking its title literally was easier said than done, for, as written by Harry Clork and Lee Loeb (from a story by Loeb and Mortimer Braus) and directed by Albert S. Rogell (who also produced), there wasn't much in it to laugh off. Songs: *My Dream And I; Doin' The 1940; Laugh It Off; Who's Gonna Keep Your Wigwam Warm?* Sam Lerner, Ben Oakland.

The Forties The Forties The Fo
The Forties The Fo
The Forties The
The Forties The Fo
The Forties The Fo
The Forties The Fo
The Forties The Fo
The Forties The Fo
The Forties The
The Forties The Fo

Alice FAYE · Carmen MIRANDA
John PAYNE · Cesar ROMERO
in Technicolor
week-end in havana

DAN DAILEY
GIVE MY REGARDS TO BROADWAY
Technicolor
COLOR BY

CHARLES WINNINGER · NANCY GUILD
CHARLIE RUGGLES · FAY BAINTER

1940

Academy Awards

Cinematography (black and white)
NOMINATIONS INCLUDED: *Spring Parade* (Universal) Joseph Valentine
(colour)
NOMINATIONS INCLUDED: *Bitter Sweet* (MGM) Oliver T. Marsh and Allen Davey. *Down Argentine Way* (20th Century-Fox) Leon Shamroy and Ray Rennahan.

Art Direction (New Classifications) (black and white)
NOMINATIONS INCLUDED: *The Boys From Syracuse* (Universal) Jack Otterson *Lillian Russell* (20th Century-Fox) Richard Day, Joseph C. Wright.
(colour)
NOMINATIONS INCLUDED: *Bitter Sweet* Cedric Gibbons and John S. Detlie, *Down Argentine Way* Richard Day and Joseph C. Wright.

Sound Recording
Strike Up The Band (MGM) Douglas Shearer
NOMINATIONS INCLUDED: *Spring Parade* Bernard B. Brown

Special Effects
NOMINATIONS INCLUDED: *The Boys From Syracuse* John P. Fulton, Bernard B. Brown and Joseph Lapis.

Music
Song
'When You Wish Upon A Star' *Pinocchio* (Disney, RKO) Leigh Harline *cm*; Ned Washington *lyr*.
NOMINATIONS INCLUDED: 'Down Argentine Way' *Down Argentine Way* Harry Warren *cm*; Mack Gordon *lyr*. 'I'd Know You Anywhere' *You'll Find Out*. (RKO) Jimmy McHugh *cm*; Johnny Mercer *lyr*. 'It's A Blue World' *Music In My Heart* (Columbia) music and lyrics by Chet Forrest and Bob Wright. 'Love Of My Life' *Second Chorus* (Paramount) Artie Shaw *cm*; Johnny Mercer *lyr*. 'Only Forever' *Rhythm On The River* (Paramount) James V. Monaco *cm*; Johnny Burke *lyr*. 'Our Love Affair' *Strike Up The Band* music and lyrics by Roger Edens and George Stoll. 'Waltzing In The Clouds' *Spring Parade* Robert Stolz *cm*; Gus Kahn *lyr*. 'Who Am I?' *Hit Parade Of 1941* (Republic) Jule Styne *cm*; Walter Bullock *lyr*.

Score
Tin Pan Alley (20th Century-Fox) Alfred Newman
NOMINATIONS INCLUDED: *Hit Parade Of 1941* Cy Feuer. *Irene* (Imperadio, RKO) Anthony Collins. *Second Chorus* Artie Shaw. *Spring Parade* Charles Previn. *Strike Up The Band* George Stoll and Roger Edens.

Original Score
Pinocchio Leigh Harline, Paul J. Smith and Ned Washington

Special Award
To Bob Hope, in recognition of his unselfish services to the motion picture industry. (special silver plaque)

The New York Film Critics Awards
Special Award
Walt Disney *Fantasia*

The New York Times Annual 'Ten Best'
10th *Fantasia*

The Annual Top Moneymaking Films
INCLUDED: *Babes In Arms* (MGM). *Gulliver's Travels* (Paramount). *Lillian Russell* (20th Century-Fox). *Road To Singapore* (Paramount).

Joseph Tierney and Harry McCarthy's 1919 stage musical **Irene** came to the screen via RKO with Herbert Wilcox in charge of the production and direction, and his future wife Anna Neagle (illustrated) as its star. A tuneful, if old-fashioned affair, it featured Miss Neagle as an Irish sales girl who, in the best Cinderella tradition, is introduced into Long Island's *haut monde* with two personable Prince Charmings hovering in the background for her attention. A glossy concoction whose visual highlight was a ball sequence photographed in Technicolor, at which Miss Neagle sang and danced to the durable 'Alice Blue Gown', it also starred Ray Milland and Alan Marshal as the two suitors, Roland Young as a couturier and Billie Burke as Marshall's mother, with May Robson, Arthur Treacher, Marsha Hunt, Isabel Jewell and Doris Nolan completing the cast. The screenplay was by Alice Duer Miller. Pleasant but dated, it was the sort of picture you could take or leave without noticing the difference. Songs: *Irene*; *Castle Of Dreams*; *You've Got Me Out On A Limb*; *There's Something In The Air*; *Worthy Of You*; *Sweet Vermosa Brown* Tierney, McCarthy. ▽

Walt Disney's second full-length animated feature was **Pinocchio** (RKO), a captivating re-telling of the famous Collodi fantasy about a puppet boy (see illustration) who can only become flesh and blood after he acquires the virtues of truth, courage and unselfishness. Considered by many to be superior even to *Snow White And The Seven Dwarfs* (RKO, 1937), it also combined music with animation in a glorious burst of inspiration, and has provided pleasure and wonderment for children of all ages during the forty years it has been on release. Ben Sharpsteen and Hamilton Luske were the supervising directors, it was photographed in Technicolor, and featured the voices of Dickie Jones as Pinocchio, Christian Rub as Gepetto the woodcarver, Cliff Edwards as Jiminy Cricket (Pinocchio's conscience), Evelyn Venable as the Blue Fairy, Walter Catlett as J. Worthington Foulfellow, Frankie Darro as Lampwick, and Charles Judels as Stromboli and the coachman. Songs: *When You Wish Upon A Star*; *Little Woodenhead*; *Hi-Diddle-Dee-Dee (An Actor's Life For Me)*; *I've Got No Strings*; *Give A Little Whistle*; *As I Was Say'n' To The Duchess*; *Pinocchio*; *Three Cheers For Anything*; *Turn On The Old Box*; *Jiminy Cricket* Leigh Harline, Ned Washington.

Universal was at it again, stealing song titles to boost programmer musicals, with **Oh Johnny, How You Can Love!** in which Tom Brown starred as a travelling salesman who picks up a spoiled young heiress (Peggy Moran) after the car in which she is travelling to an elopement rendezvous is involved in a crash. After the usual plot complications, which included an encounter with escaping bank robbers, the salesman and the heiress decide they are made for each other, thus cueing in the end title with the inevitable clinch. A really sophomoronic effort, it was written by Edwin Rutt, produced by Ken Goldsmith, directed by Charles Lamont and featured Betty Jane Rhodes (who sang the catchy title number, by Abe Olman and Ed Rose, at an auto-camp jamboree), Allen Jenkins, Donald Meek (illustrated with Moran), Juanita Quigley and Isabel Jewell. They all deserved better. Other songs included: *Maybe I Like What You Like*; *Swing Chariot Swing*; *Make Up Your Mind* Paul Gerard Smith. Frank Skinner.
▽

Road to Singapore (Paramount) was the first of the long-running 'Road' series, and although one of the year's top-grossing films, wasn't all that good. Bing Crosby (centre) played a carefree millionaire's son who, to escape matrimony and the prospect of becoming actively involved in the family shipping business, takes off for exotic Singapore in tandem with his game-for-anything buddy, Bob Hope (right). There they meet sarong-girl Dorothy Lamour (left) whose idea of making a living is having cigarette ends whipped out of her mouth by mean-looking Anthony Quinn. Messrs Hope and Crosby take her away from all that and – well, you know the rest. Charles Coburn played Crosby's wealthy father, Judith Barrett was the fiancée Crosby deserts, with other parts in Don Hartman and Frank Butler's less-than-scintillating screenplay (story by Harry Hervey) being filled by Jerry Colonna, Pierre Watkin and Gaylord Pendleton. It was produced by Harlan Thompson and the director was Victor Schertzinger. The musical numbers were staged by LeRoy Prinz. Songs: *Sweet Potato Piper*; *Too Romantic*; *Kaigoon* Johnny Burke, James V. Monaco; *Captain Custard*; *The Moon And The Willow Tree* Burke, Victor Schertzinger. Interesting sideline: George Burns and Fred MacMurray were originally offered the male leads, but on reading the script gave it the thumbs down.

It's A Date was the annually prescribed dose of Deanna Durbin (left) from Universal Studios, and although it underwent a change in its customary director – from Henry Koster to William A. Seiter – the ineffable and always very popular Durbin persona remained unchanged in this story of a famous actress's daughter whose rise to fame is in direct proportion to her illustrious mother's decline. Kay Francis co-starred as the mother, with other parts in this entertaining if slightly far-fetched tale going to Walter Pidgeon, Eugene Pallette, Lewis Howard (right), Samuel S. Hinds, S.Z. Sakall, Henry Stephenson, Virginia
▽

Brissac, and Harry Owens and His Royal Hawaiians. It was written by Norman Krasna from a story by Jane Hall, Frederick Kohner and Ralph Block and, musically, offered Miss Durbin a pot-pourri of numbers which included Schubert's 'Ave Maria'. Other songs: *Love Is All* Pinky Tomlin, Harry Tobias; *It Happened In Kaloha* Ralph Freed, Frank Skinner; *Rhythm Of The Islands* Eddie Cherkose, Leon Belasco, Jacques Press; *Hawaiian War Chant* Ralph Freed, Johnny Noble, Prince Leleiohaku of Hawaii; *Quando M'en Vo (Musetta's Waltz)* from Puccini's 'La Boheme'; *Loch Lomond* (traditional).

Forties Musicals

△

A low-budget programmer running a mere 69 minutes, **Music In My Heart** (Columbia) starred Tony Martin (foreground) as a foreign singer who, in order to avoid deportation, appears in a musical comedy with Rita Hayworth (second-billed), a girl of the tenements and the object of newspaper publisher Alan Mowbray's affections. Miss Hayworth looked stunning throughout, and some of the songs by Bob Wright and Chet Forrest were more than serviceable in the flimsy context of James Edward Grant's screenplay. And that, in the final accounting, was that. Also cast: Edith Fellows, Eric Blore, George Tobias, Joseph Crehan, George Humbert and Andre Kostelanetz and His Orchestra (illustrated). Irving Starr produced and the director was Joseph Santley. Songs: *No Other Love*; *Punchinello*; *Oh What A Lovely Dream*; *Prelude To Love*; *I've Got Music In My Heart*; *It's A Blue World* Wright, Forrest.

△

A reworking of their 1929 movie, *The Broadway Melody*, MGM's **Two Girls On Broadway** (GB: **Choose Your Partners**) starred curvaceous Lana Turner (left), and Joan Blondell (right, making her MGM debut), as sisters in the roles originally played by Anita Page and Bessie Love, with George Murphy (centre) as the hoofer they both fall for. The rest of the non-stellar cast included Kent Taylor, Richard Lane, Wallace Ford and Otto Hahn. A production number in which Turner and Murphy demonstrated their terpsichorean skills was the musical highlight in this otherwise modest and moderately entertaining remake. It was written by Joseph Fields and Jerome Chodorov from the story by Edmund Goulding, produced by Jack Cummings and directed by S. Sylvan Simon. Songs: *Rancho Santa Fe*; *True Love* Gus Kahn, Walter Donaldson; *My Wonderful One Let's Dance* Arthur Freed, Nacio Herb Brown, Roger Edens; *Maybe It's The Moon* Bob Wright, Chet Forrest, Donaldson; *Broadway's Still Broadway* Ted Fetter, Jimmy McHugh.

A limp-wristed programmer about a press agent who cultivates a model by pronouncing her Miss Manhattan in order to promote a line of inexpensive clothes, **Ma, He's Making Eyes At Me** (Universal) starred Tom Brown as the press agent and Constance Moore as the model (illustrated with Brown), with Anne Nagel, Richard Carle, Fritz Feld, Jerome Cowan and Elisabeth Risdon in support. Charles Grayson and Edmund L. Hartmann wrote it from a story by Ed Sullivan, and it was directed by Harold Schuster. Songs included: *Ma, He's Making Eyes At Me* Sidney Clare, Con Conrad; *Unfair To Love* Sam Lerner, Frank Skinner; *A Lemon In The Garden Of Love* M.E. Rourke, Richard Carle.

▽

Jack Benny (illustrated) as Buck Benny in **Buck Benny Rides Again** was aided and abetted by his comic sidekick Andy Devine, as well as Eddie (Rochester) Anderson, Phil Harris, Virginia Dale, Lillian Cornell and Kay Linaker as he attempted to convince Ellen Drew, the love interest, that looks deceive and that underneath his unlikely exterior beats the heart of a pure cowboy. Inspired by Benny's radio programme, it was amiable nonsense that attracted the customers and notched up a box-office hit for Paramount. William Morrow and Edmund Beloin wrote it from an adaptation by Zion Myers of a story by Arthur Stringer, and it was produced and directed by Mark Sandrich. Songs: *Drums In The Night*; *My My*; *Say It (Over And Over Again)*; *My Kind Of Country* Frank Loesser, Jimmy McHugh.

▽

Bing Crosby and 12-year-old songstress Gloria Jean (illustrated) were teamed for **If I Had My Way** (Universal) but failed to make box-office music together. Bing played a construction worker who takes charge of Gloria after her father is killed in an accident, and together they journey to New York in search of Gloria's great-uncle (Charles Winninger), an erstwhile vaudevillian. Aided by travelling companion El Brendel, they turn a neighbourhood restaurant into a nightclub, calling on old-time entertainers like Blanche Ring and Eddie Leonard to get the place going with their inimitable renditions of 'Ida, Sweet As Apple Cider' (by Eddie Leonard and Eddie Munson) and 'I've Got Rings On My Fingers' (by Maurice Scott, R.P. Western and F.J. Barnes). It was a fifth carbon copy of a well-worn plot, hacked out by William Conselman and James V. Kern, with David Butler producing and directing a cast that also included Allyn Joslyn, Donald Woods, Claire Dodd, Nana Bryant and Moroni Olsen as well as Trixie Friganza and Julian Eltinge. Other songs: *I Haven't Time To Be A Millionaire*; *Meet The Sun Halfway*; *April Played The Fiddle*; *The Pessimistic Character (With The Crab Apple Face)* Johnny Burke, James V. Monaco; *If I Had My Way* Lew Klein, James Kendis.

▽

The highlight of **Broadway Melody of 1940**
(MGM) was undoubtedly Fred Astaire and
Eleanor Powell dancing to Cole Porter's 'Begin
the Beguine' (see illustration). It was a sequence
so magical that it made one regret that this was
their only film together. The number, photographed in sharply contrasting black and white,
and danced on a glittering mirrored floor against
a starry background, contained two separate
duos by the stars, both routines triumphantly
surviving the rather kitschy stage-dressing provided for the occasion by choreographer Bobby
Connolly. Porter wrote the rest of the score as
well, which included Astaire's 'I've Got My Eyes
On You', and another excellent ship-board production number for Eleanor Powell called 'I Am
The Captain'. Astaire and co-star George Murphy
did a simple but effective vaudeville routine in
'Please Don't Monkey With Broadway', and
Murphy and Powell danced well together in the
lyrical 'Between You And Me'. The only miscalculation was the arty, pierrot-like ballet version of 'I Concentrate On You' for Powell,
Astaire and Douglas MacPhail, which suited
none of their personalities. The film also contained one of the funniest sequences ever committed to celluloid: Charlotte Arren's screwy
version (à la Beatrice Lillie and Fanny Brice) of
the song 'Il Bacio' (by Luigi Arditi). In a terrible
miscarriage of justice, the lady received no
billing at all for her hilarious effort. The screenplay by Leon Gordon and George Oppenheimer
(from a story by Jack McGowan and Dore
Schary, the latter to become the head of MGM in
the fifties), in no way matched the incomparable
dazzle of its two stars, and told the trivial tale of a
pair of hoofers (Astaire and Murphy) who split
when one of them (Murphy) mistakenly gets a
contract to dance on Broadway without the
other. In the interests of the plot Murphy (who
made his reputation as a hoofer) had the ego-
deflating role of being the lesser of the two
dancers – which, of course, he was. Frank
Morgan, Ian Hunter, Florence Rice and Lynne
Carver supported, Jack Cummings produced,
and Norman Taurog directed. There was one
other musical number, 'Juke Box Dance', for
Powell and Astaire.

Forties Musicals

20th Century-Fox's **Lillian Russell** was set in the gay nineties, an era to which studio head Darryl F. Zanuck would return again and again throughout the forties. Though handsomely mounted, with meticulous attention to period detail lavished on Travis Banton's sumptuous costumes and Thomas Little's elegant settings, William Anthony McGuire's screenplay was a slow-moving encumberance which gave movie-goers only the merest whiff of Miss Russell's extraordinary life and career. The fact that McGuire shed two of Russell's four marriages from the scenario didn't prevent it from being a bit of a bore – with performances from Don Ameche as her first husband, and Henry Fonda (a reporter) as her second, that contributed to the all-pervading *ennui*. Alice Faye (illustrated) was top-cast as Lillian Russell and, although she was beautifully photographed throughout and sang some of Miss Russell's golden oldies with deep-throated verve, the few opportunities provided by the screenplay to be anything more than a walking cliché, coupled with her own limited abilities as a dramatic actress, left audiences with very little for their money. The film was far better served by Helen Westley and comedians Weber and Fields, who came out of retirement to lend an air of authenticity to an otherwise synthetic occasion. Others in the cast were Edward Arnold (as Diamond Jim Brady, a role he had played once before, in *Diamond Jim* Universal, 1935), Leo Carillo as Tony Pastor, the first man to give Russell a break in show business, as well as Dorothy Peterson, Ernest Truex, Lynn Bari, Eddie Foy Jr, and Nigel Bruce and Claude Allister as a bickering Gilbert and Sullivan. It was produced by Darryl F. Zanuck and directed by Irving Cummings with Seymour Felix in charge of the musical numbers. Songs: *Blue Lovebird* Gus Kahn, Bronislau Kaper; *Adored One* Mack Gordon, Alfred Newman; *Waltz Is King* Gordon, Charles Henderson; *Back In The Old Days Of Broadway* Henderson, Newman; *Come Down Ma Evenin' Star*; *Ma Blushin' Rosie* John Stromberg, Robert B. Smith; *After The Ball* Charles K. Harris; *The Band Played On* John E. Palmer, Charles B. Ward.

Richard Rodgers and Lorenz Hart's superbly melodic score for their hit **The Boys From Syracuse** (Universal), first presented on Broadway in 1938, received short shrift from producer Jules Levey, whose filmed version of this quintessential tale of mistaken identity (based on Shakespeare's *The Comedy Of Errors*) fell just this side of disaster. Numbers like 'Sing For Your Supper', 'Falling In Love With Love', 'He And She' and 'This Can't Be Love' – classics every one of them – were only included by default, or in truncated versions that failed to do them justice, while new ones (such as 'Who Are You' and 'The Greeks Have No Word For It'), were added. Leonard Spigelgass and Charles Grayson's screenplay (based on the George Abbott stage version) traded in anachronisms at the expense of the satire originally intended, with cigar-smoking Greeks and checkered chariot-cabs typical of the humour on offer. All about two pairs of twins – one pair married, the other not – and the confusion that is wrought when the married pair and the unmarried pair become mixed up, it starred Allan Jones (left) and Joe Penner in the dual roles of the twins with Martha Raye (right), Rosemary Lane (centre), Charles Butterworth, Irene Hervey, Alan Mowbray, Eric Blore and Samuel S. Hinds also cast. Dave Gould choreographed and the director was Edward Sutherland.

Universal continued to borrow titles for programmer musicals from popular tunes with **Margie** – a marginally better effort than *Ma, He's Making Eyes At Me* – about the marital difficulties encountered by would-be songwriter Tom Brown, and his would-be radio scriptwriter wife Nan Grey. The accent was more on comedy than music, with Allen Jenkins, Eddie Quillan (right), Wally Vernon (left), Edgar Kennedy and Mischa Auer providing most of the laughs. It was written by Erna Lazarus, W. Scott Darling and Paul Gerard Smith (story by Lazarus and Darling), produced by Joseph G. Sandford and directed by Otis Garrett and Paul Gerard Smith. Songs included: *Margie* Benny Davis, J. Russell Robinson, Con Conrad; *When Banana Blossoms Bloom* Sam Lerner, Charles Previn; *Oh Fly With Me* Paul Gerard Smith. Previn.

One of Bing Crosby's better musicals, **Rhythm on the River** (Paramount) cast Bing (illustrated) as an easy-going songwriter who'd much rather own a catboat than write music but who, to keep the wolf from the door, becomes a ghost composer for a played-out tunesmith (Basil Rathbone). Working as Rathbone's ghost lyricist is Mary Martin and, after an uneasy courtship and unwitting collaboration, the young couple finally get each other – and the recognition they deserve. Charmingly directed by Victor Schertzinger, with pleasing, relaxed performances from its principal players, the film benefited from a better-than-average screenplay by Dwight Taylor (story by Billy Wilder and Jacques Thery) as well as the supporting performances of Oscar Levant, as Rathbone's deliciously cynical assistant, Charles Grapewin, Lillian Cornell and William Frawley. The producer was William Le Baron. Songs: *Rhythm On The River*; *Only Forever*; *That's For Me*; *Ain't It A Shame About Mame?*; *When The Moon Comes Over Madison Square*; *What Would Shakespeare Have Said?* Johnny Burke, James V. Monaco.

Judy Canova (left) received star billing for **Scatterbrain** (Republic), a musical with a country-and-western flavour to it – especially in the Ozarkian twang perpetrated by its leading lady. A mistaken-identity tale, in which Miss C. finds herself being packed off to Hollywood as the star of a forthcoming movie, it was a modest effort that yielded modest returns, both financially and artistically. Alan Mowbray co-starred as the harassed film director whose unenviable task it is to off-load an unwilling Miss Canova as best he can, with Joseph Cawthorn in support as the producer and Ruth Donnelly as his quick-witted secretary. Also cast: Billy Gilbert (right), Luis Alberni, Eddie Foy Jr and Isabel Jewell. Gus Meins produced and directed; Jack Townley and Val Burton scripted, with additional dialogue by Paul Conlan. The film contained one production number, 'Scatterbrain' (by Johnny Burke, Frankie Masters, Kahn Keene and Carl Bean), and other songs included *Benny The Beaver* by Johnny Lange and Lew Porter.

Bearing in mind that *Naughty Marietta* (1935) was one of MGM's biggest hits, scenarists Jacques Deval and Robert Arthur came up with an almost identical story line for the same studio with **New Moon** (based on the operetta by Oscar Hammerstein II, Laurence Schwab and Frank Mandel). Jeanette MacDonald (right) again played a French aristocrat forced to flee to Louisiana, and Nelson Eddy (left) the pirate chief she falls for. Five years had added a bit to Eddy's girth and, in other ways too, the film was heavier than its predecessor. But it did have some bewitching Sigmund Romberg melodies to recommend it, the MGM sheen germane to such occasions, and stalwart support from Mary Boland, George Zucco, Richard Purcell, H.B. Warner, Grant Mitchell and, in a very small role, Buster Keaton. The musical sequences were staged by Val Raset, with Robert Z. Leonard as both producer and director. Songs: *Lover Come Back To Me*; *Softly As In A Morning Sunrise*; *Stout-Hearted Men*; *Dance Your Cares Away*; *The Way They Do It In Paris*; *Shoes*; *One Kiss*; *Wanting You*; *Marianne*; *Ombra Mai Fu (Handel's Largo)*; *La Marseillaise* Claude Rouget de Lisle.

◁ Shirley Temple's last film for 20th Century-Fox for nine years was **Young People** in which the ageing twelve-year-old (centre) played an orphan who is given a home by old-time vaudevillians Jack Oakie (left) and Charlotte Greenwood (right). A formula Temple movie, utilizing clips from some of her earlier films, its screenplay by Edwin Blum and Don Ettlinger peddled the usual *schmaltz* – but, as she had done on so many previous occasions, Temple somehow managed to make it all quite palatable. Arleen Whelan, George Montgomery, Kathleen Howard, Minor Watson, Mae Marsh and Frank Sully had roles in it too; it was produced by Harry Joe Brown, and directed by Allan Dwan. The score was by Mack Gordon and Harry Warren, the latter having left Warner Bros. after seven brilliantly prolific years as their number one songsmith. Songs: *Tra-la-la*; *Fifth Avenue*; *I Wouldn't Take A Million*; *The Mason-Dixon Line*; *Young People*.

Hugh Herbert (centre) played no fewer than six characters in **La Conga Nights** (Universal), all of them in desperate search of an author. For the story, devised by scenarists Jay Dratler, Harry Clork and Paul Smith, comprised more shadow than substance, involving, as it did, a cab driver-cum-amateur-vaudevillian (Dennis O'Keefe), the small-town singer (Constance Moore, centre right) he meets, and the show they put on in a boarding house. Herbert – playing himself, his four sisters and his mother – turns out to be the owner of the boarding house, and is thus able to quash the eviction order slapped on tenant O'Keefe (far left) for non-payment of rent. Mindless to a degree, it also featured Ferike Boros (2nd right), Armida (who sang the traditional 'La Cucaracha', arranged by Harold Potter), Eddie Quillan and Joe Brown Jr. Ken Goldsmith produced and the direction was by Lew Landers. Songs included: *Carmenita McCoy*; *Havana*; *Chance Of A Lifetime* Frank Skinner, Sam Lerner.

Forties Musicals

Another B-picture musical romance from the ▷ Universal stable, **I'm Nobody's Sweetheart Now** was a simple, moderately entertaining tale about a couple of youngsters, Dennis O'Keefe and Helen Parrish (illustrated), who thwart their politically-minded parents by refusing to marry other people for political expediency and settling, instead, for each other. Lewis Howard and Constance Moore played the rejected pair, with twittery Laura Hope Crews, Samuel S. Hinds, Berton Churchill, Margaret Hamilton, Marjorie Gateson and The Dancing Cansinos also featured in Scott Darling, Erna Lazarus and Hal Block's 64-minute screenplay. Arthur Lubin directed and the associate producer was Joseph Sandford. Songs included: *I'm Nobody's Sweetheart Now* Gus Kahn, Ernie Erdman, Billy Meyers, Elmer Schoebel; *There Goes My Love*; *Got Romance* Everett Carter, Milton Rosen.

A bargain-basement musical, with newcomer Jane Frazee resembling a marked-down Lana Turner and diminutive Mary Lee a junior, cut-price Judy Garland, **Melody and Moonlight** (Republic) was a radio-inspired yarn with Johnny Downs top-cast as a bell-boy with ambitions to become a hoofer; and Miss Frazee a deb whose show-biz aspirations are vetoed by her millionaire father (Jonathan Hale) who, in the final reel, becomes the radio sponsor for his daughter's (and Downs's) tap-dancing radio show. Every bit as silly as it sounds, it was efficiently directed by Joseph Santley from a screenplay by Bradford Ropes (story by David Silverstein) and featured Jerry Colonna (left), Barbara Jo Allen (radio's Vera Vague, right), Mary Lee and Frank Jenks. Robert North produced. Songs: *Rooftop Serenade*; *Tahiti Honey*; *Top O'The Mornin*; *I Close My Eyes*; *Melody And Moonlight* Jule Styne, Sol Meyer, George Brown. ▽

△

The Ritz Brothers, having left 20th Century-Fox for Universal, continued to pilfer scenes that weren't worth stealing in the first place in **Argentine Nights**, a musical whose Latin American background provided the inspiration for a tale about a trio of destitute girl singers who, in cahoots with their managers (the brothers Ritz) flee their creditors by heading for the Argentine. The only good thing that came out of it was The Andrews Sisters (illustrated), though it was a shame that their movie debut couldn't have been more auspicious. Constance Moore, George Reeves, Peggy Moran and Anne Nagel were also cast; it was written by Arthur T. Horman, Ray Golden and Sid Kuller (from a story by J. Robert Bren and Gladys Atwater), produced by Ken Goldsmith, and directed by Albert S. Rogell. Songs included: *Hit The Road*; *Oh, He Loves Me* Don Raye, Hughie Prince, Vic Schoen *Rhumboogie* Raye, Prince; *Brooklynonga*; *The Spirit of 77B* Hal Borne, Sid Kuller, Ray Golden; *Amigo We Go Riding Tonight*; *The Dowry Song* Sammy Cahn, Saul Chaplin.

A backstage musical with a vengeance (as well as with Maureen O'Hara, Louis Hayward, Lucille Ball (illustrated), Ralph Bellamy, Virginia Field and Maria Ouspenskaya), **Dance Girl Dance** (RKO) charted the tribulations that befall chorus girls in their journey from anonymity to stardom, with a mis-cast O'Hara and a bouncing Ball as members of Ouspenskaya's dancing troupe. Maureen has cultural aspirations and wishes to be a ballet dancer; Lucille is more realistic and settles for fame as a stripper. Both fall for attractive Mr Hayward. So much for the plot. Ball, third-billed, ran away with the film (not that there was anywhere special to take it to) as well as the notices, and with her number 'Oh Mother, What Do I Do Now?' (by Bob Wright and Chet Forrest) proved once and for all, that she was no mere chorine. (Several years later she proved her business acumen as well by buying the studio!) Mary Carlisle, Katherine Alexander, Edward Brophy, Walter Abel, Harold Huber and Ernest Truex completed the cast. It was written by Tess Slesinger and Frank Davis from a story by Vicki Baum, produced by Erich Pommer and directed by Dorothy Arzner. Other songs: *Morning Star* Wright, Forrest; *The Jitterbug Bit* Wright, Forrest, Ed Ward; *Urban Ballet* Ward. ▽

◁ Republic paid $500 to *Collier's* magazine for a story they published called **Sing Dance Plenty Hot** (GB: **Melody Girl**) then discarded the content, retaining only the title. The new plot by Vera Caspary and Bradford Ropes (screenplay by Ropes) was an anaemic contrivance about a phoney promoter of charity shows (Lester Matthews) who absconds with the money he is allegedly engaged in raising for clients Barbara Jo Allen, Elisabeth Risdon and Ruth Terry – three prospective purchasers of a children's home. Miss Terry and Johnny Downs were top-cast as the romantic interest, with Billy Gilbert (doing an abbreviated version of his oft-performed sneezing act), Claire Carleton, Mary Lee and Leonard Carey completing the cast. It was produced by Robert North and directed by Lew Landers. Illustration shows a production number. Songs: *Tequila*; *When A Fella's Got A Girl*; *What Fools These Mortals Be*; *I'm just A Weakie* Jule Styne, George Brown, Sol Meyer.

Again using a hit tune as a title; **I Can't Give You Anything But Love** (Universal) offered audiences 61 ludicrous minutes of non-entertainment as Broderick Crawford, a gangster with a passion for lyric writing, kidnaps Johnny Downs (right), a young composer with whom he works in a collaborative effort to get a message in song to a long-lost sweetheart. Peggy Moran (left), Warren Hymer, John Sutton, Gertrude Michael and Jessie Ralph also appeared for director Albert S. Rogell; it was written by Arthur T. Horman (adaptation by Paul Gerard Smith) and produced by Ken Goldsmith. Songs included: *I Can't Give You Anything But Love* Dorothy Fields, Jimmy McHugh; *Sweetheart Of School* 59; *Day By Day* Paul Gerard Smith, Frank Skinner.

▽

△

Another in the 'let's put on a show' mould, **Strike Up the Band** (MGM) was an exuberant paean to youth, with Mickey Rooney, now the nation's number one box-office attraction (as he had been in 1939 and would be again in 1941), on the very top of his form. There was nothing the kid could not do – and under maestro Busby Berkeley's watchful eye, he did it all. Whether singing, dancing, playing the drums, the xylophone, or the hapless hero in a turn-of-the-century melodrama, Mickey reigned supreme. His confidence and energy were positively awesome and although John Monks Jr and Fred Finkelhoffe's scenario (about the attempts of a high-school orchestra to enter a coast-to-coast band contest) landed him with some blush-making sentimental dialogue – particularly to his mother (Ann Shoemaker) Rooney pulled it off magnificently, turning what could, in less capable hands, have been an embarrassment, into a triumph. His perfect foil was Judy Garland whose natural, unassuming performance was in such marked contrast to his own larger-than-life, bull-dozing effort, that it was easy to underestimate her overall contribution to the film. If Rooney (right) had versatility and vitality, Garland (left) had charm, and it was nowhere better demonstrated than in her wistful rendition of Roger Eden's song 'Nobody', sung in the college

library, in which she bemoans the fact that though Romeo has Juliet and Metro-Goldwyn has Mayer, she has nobody at all. The film's finale, to the Gershwins' rousing 'Strike Up The Band' was another military-type extravaganza of which Berkeley was so fond and an excellent example of what could be achieved with imaginative camera set-ups (and superb editing) rather than lavish sets. The film also featured Paul Whiteman (as himself) as well as June Preisser, William Tracy, Larry Nunn, Margaret Early, and Virginia Brissac. The producer, not surprisingly, was Arthur Freed, whose song 'Our Love Affair', written with Roger Edens, and in which a bowl of fruit miraculously turns into a symphony orchestra (thanks to Vincente Minnelli who supplied the idea, and animator George Pal who executed it) was one of the musical highlights of the film. Other songs and musical numbers: *Drummer Boy*; *Do The Conga*; *Nell of New Rochelle* Roger Edens; *Sing, Sing, Sing* Louis Prima; *I Just Can't Make My Eyes Behave* Will Cobb, Gus Edwards; *Heaven Will Protect The Working Girl* Edgar Smith, A. Baldwin Sloane; *The Curse Of An Aching Heart* Henry Fink, Al Piantadosi; *The Sidewalks Of New York* James W. Blake, Charles B. Lawlor; *Light Cavalry Overture* Franz von Suppé; *Over The Waves* Juventino Rosas.

Forties Musicals

While an appendectomy prevented Betty Grable from playing the lead in Paramount's *Man About Town* (1939), ironically, it was an appendectomy that clinched her star-billing in **Down Argentine Way** (20th Century-Fox). This time it was Alice Faye who was rushed to hospital, with Betty being summoned from Broadway by producer Darryl F. Zanuck to take her place. And, although it made a star of her, a Brazilian bombshell called Carmen Miranda (illustrated centre) was the real hit of the show – despite the fact (or maybe because of it) that she had nothing whatsoever to do with the plot. She sang three songs (including the catchy 'South American Way' by Al Dubin and Jimmy McHugh) and took the country by storm. For the rest, it was a brightly Technicolored concoction, all about an American heiress (Grable) who falls in love with an Argentinian horse-breeder (Don Ameche). Betty's legs looked a treat, so did co-star Charlotte Greenwood's. The Nicholas Brothers and Thomas and Catherine Dowling featured as specialty items, with J. Carrol Naish, Henry Stephenson, Katherine Aldridge, Leonid Kinsky, Chris Pin Martin and Robert Conway in support. The musical numbers were staged by Nick Castle and Geneva Sawyer, 'Down Argentine Way' being the choreographic hit of the show. Another was the Greenwood-Kinskey ditty, 'Sing To Your Senorita' (both numbers by Mack Gordon and Harry Warren). The director was Irving Cummings. Other songs: *Two Dreams Met*; *Nenita* Gordon, Warren; *Mama Yo Quiero* Al Stillman, Jaraca and Vincente Paiva; *Doin' The Conga* Gene Rose; *Bambu*.

▽

Spring Parade (Universal) was the cinematic equivalent of a liberal helping of *Sacher torte mit schlag*. A free 'n easy, Viennesey tale of love and romance, it starred Deanna Durbin (illustrated) – prettily perched on the brink of womanhood – as a baker's assistant who falls in love with a dashing young corporal (Robert Cummings, illustrated conducting orchestra) right under Emperor Franz Joseph's (Henry Stephenson) very nose. Insubstantial but delightful was the general consensus of opinion, and with S.Z. Sakall (as the baker), Walter Catlett, Allyn Joslyn, Reginald Denny, Franklin Pangborn and a couple of engaging youngsters called Butch and Buddy in support, producer Joe Pasternak delivered another hit to Universal. Bruce Manning and Felix Jackson wrote it (from a story by Ernst Marischka), and Henry Koster directed. Songs and musical numbers: *Blue Danube Dream* Johann Strauss II, lyrics by Gus Kahn; *Waltzing In The Clouds*; *It's Foolish But It's Fun*; *When April Sings* Kahn, Robert Stolz; *In A Spring Parade* Kahn, Charles Previn.

▽

△

With no other purpose than to provide an opportunity for some of Paramount's younger contract artists to peddle their wares, **Dancing on a Dime** was a routine backstage yarn about a stranded theatrical troupe who, despite insufficient finances, stage a successful show. Robert Paige (3rd right), Grace McDonald, Peter Hayes (right), Eddie Quillan (centre), Frank Jenks (left), Virginia Dale, Carol Adams, Lillian Cornell and William Frawley appeared, it was directed by Joseph Santley from a screenplay by Maurice Rapf, Anne Morrison Chapin, and Allen Rivkin (story by Jean Lustig and Max Kolpe) and was produced by A.M. Botsford. Songs: *I Hear Music*; *Manana*; *Dancing On A Dime* Frank Loesser, Burton Lane; *Lovable Sort Of Person*; *Debutante Of The Year* Loesser, Victor Young.

Originally intended as a follow-up to their successful *Alexander's Ragtime Band* (1938), 20th Century-Fox's **Tin-Pan-Alley** was written for Alice Faye, Tyrone Power and Don Ameche. But it didn't work out that way, and instead John Payne and Jack Oakie were given the male leads. And, while in the process of changing the original conception, Zanuck shrewdly had scenarists Robert Ellis and Helen Logan (story by Pamela Harris) write in a part for Betty Grable, who had recently scored such a success in *Down Argentine Way*. Although Grable (right) received second billing to Faye (left) and played her dancing partner sister, she didn't have a great deal to do with the plot, lending, in the main, a decorative quality to the show's several musical numbers – most notably 'The Sheik Of Araby' (by Harry B. Smith, Francis Wheeler and Ted Snyder). As originally staged by dance director Seymour Felix, the number – which also featured Faye and Billy Gilbert – revealed too much flesh for the Hays Office and had to be trimmed accordingly. All about the frustrating attempts of a pair of songwriters (Payne and Oakie) to establish a music publishing firm, the film spanned 24 years (from 1915 to 1939) but you'd never have known it from the enviable agelessness of the leading players. The score offered only one new number: 'You Say The Sweetest Things, Baby' (by Mack Gordon and Harry Warren), the rest being 'oldies'. Allen Jenkins, Esther Ralston, John Loder and Elisha Cook Jr were also in it, together with The Nicholas Brothers, Princess Vanessa Ammon, The Brian Sisters and The Robert Brothers.

Kenneth MacGowan was the associate producer and the director was Walter Lang. It was remade by 20th Century-Fox in 1950 as *I'll Get By*. Other songs: *America I Love You* Edgar Leslie, Archie Gottler; *Goodbye Broadway, Hello France* Francis Riesner, Benny Davis, Billy Baskette; *K-K-K-Katy* Geoffrey O'Hara; *Moonlight Bay* Edward Madden, Percy Wenrich; *Honeysuckle Rose* Andy Razaf, Thomas 'Fats' Waller; *Moonlight And Roses* Ben Black, Neil Moret, Edwin H. Lemare.

The Trade Descriptions Act was emphatically contravened by the title of **A Little Bit of Heaven** (Universal) which, while not exactly a little bit of the other place either, was certainly no musical paradise. A predictable story about an East Side kid whose singing triumph on radio causes all sorts of domestic upheavals in her suddenly wealthy family, it was another vehicle for 12-year-old Gloria Jean (centre), who brought no particular distinction to Daniel Taradash, Gertrude Purcell, and Harold Goldman's pedestrian screenplay (story by Grover Jones). A strong supporting cast which included Robert Stack, Hugh Herbert, C. Aubrey Smith, Charles Previn (left), Stuart Erwin, Nan Grey, Eugene Pallette, Billy Gilbert, Butch and Buddy, Frank Jenks, Sig Arno (right), Noah Beery Jr and Monte Blue, made no impact whatsoever on Joe Pasternak's production; neither did Andrew Marston's ho-hum direction. Songs: *A Little Bit Of Heaven* J. Keirn Brennan, Ernest Ball; *What Did We Learn At School?* Vivian Ellis; *Dawn Of Love* Ralph Freed, Charles Previn; *After Every Rain Storm* Sam Lerner, Frank Skinner. ▷

Forties Musicals

Any film that boasted the combined talents of Peter Lorre (right), Boris Karloff and Bela Lugosi surely couldn't be all that bad, but **You'll Find Out** (RKO), defying common sense and the law of averages, was a wholesale stinker that top-starred Kay Kyser and his Kollege of Knowledge in a woebegone musical chiller whose plot pivoted on whether or not the aforementioned trio of ghouls will succeed in bumping off a certain person at a house party being given in her honour. Kyser (left) and his team are signed up to provide the party with its entertainment, and although they soon become involved in the strange goings-on, find the time, every fifteen minutes or so, to fulfil their part of the contract. Helen Parrish, Alma Kruger, Joseph Eggenton and Kyser regulars Ish Kabibble, Ginny Simms, Harry Babbit and Sully Mason completed the cast. It was written by James V. Kern from a story by Kern and David Butler, with Butler also producing and directing. Songs: *You've Got Me This Way*; *Like The Fella Once Said*; *The Bad Humour Man*; *I'd Know You Anywhere*; *I've Got A One Track Mind*; *Don't Think It Ain't Been Charming* Johnny Mercer, Jimmy McHugh.

Fantasia (RKO), the third full-length Walt Disney feature, was the most daring cinematic experiment since Warner Bros.' *The Jazz Singer* 13 years earlier. Filmed in dazzling Multiplane Technicolor and 'Fantasound', it was introduced by Deems Taylor with Leopold Stokowski and the Philadelphia Orchestra in charge of the music, and offered a once-in-a-lifetime experience that, if anything, has gained in stature over the last forty years to become one of the cinema's undisputed works of art. Setting out to marry images to three kinds of music (music that tells a story, music that paints a picture, and 'absolute' music for music's sake) the film, which opened with a brilliant abstract realization of Bach's Toccata and Fugue in D Minor, was a miraculous blending of animation and musical sound. The item that perhaps best illustrated Disney's achievement in synchronizing the two, was the sequence to 'The Sorcerer's Apprentice' (Dukas) in which Mickey Mouse was featured as the apprentice (illustrated) who, after his master retires for the night, invokes some magic of his own, The spell, involving a broom which comes to life, goes completely out of control, and it is only after the sorcerer's lair has been flooded that order is finally restored. Less programmatic was 'The Nutcracker Suite' (Tchaikovsky), whose lilting melodies conjured up an enchanted forest, illuminated by fairies of light and inhabited by mushroom Chinamen and dancing flower Cossacks. A feast for eye and ear, it was matched in its invention and graphic detail by Disney's vision of the 'Pastoral Symphony' (Beethoven) set in an idyllic mythological kingdom of nymphs and satyrs, and in whose best moment the Goddess of Night skims across the sky with her cloak of black. **Fantasia**'s comic highspot was a spirited interpretation of 'The Dance Of The Hours' (from Ponchielli's *La Giaconda*), performed by prancing hippopotami, undulating crocodiles, ostriches engaging in *entrechats*, and light-footed elephants. Stravinsky's 'Rite Of Spring' graphically evoked the Creation, with belching craters of fire and warring prehistoric monsters, while the powers of Good and Evil were strikingly contrasted by 'Night On The Bare Mountain' (Mussorgsky) – with grotesque and frightening images of floating skeletons and satanic cauldrons – and Schubert's sublime 'Ave Maria' with its cleansing vision of light-infused landscapes. Joe Grant and Dick Huemer were in charge of the story direction, and the production was supervised by Ben Sharpsteen.

Judy Garland played a dual role in **Little Nellie Kelly** (MGM): grown-up Nellie Kelly who dies in childbirth, then (for the rest of the film's running time) Nellie's daughter. Though Judy (left) sang her way through Jack McGowan's screenplay with her usual charm and sparkle, the 18-year-old George M. Cohan play on which it was based emerged as an over-brogued bit of burdensome blarney in which grandad Charles Winninger, having done his best to put the kibosh on his daughter's romance, is after doin' the very same t'ing to his granddaughter. George Murphy (right) was in it too; so were Douglas MacPhail, Arthur Shields, Rita Page, Forrester Harvey, James Burke and George Watts. Norman Taurog directed, Arthur Freed produced. The songs: *Nellie Kelly I Love You* George M. Cohan; *Nellie Is A Darlin*; *It's A Great Day For The Irish* Roger Edens; *A Pretty Girl Milking Her Cow* (adapted by Edens); *Singin' In The Rain* Arthur Freed, Nacio Herb Brown.

Producer-director George Abbott brought his stage hit **Too Many Girls** (RKO) to the screen, recruiting from Broadway four of its original cast members (Hal LeRoy, Desi Arnaz, Eddie Bracken and Van Johnson), Lucille Ball (top-billed), Richard Carlson, Ann Miller (illustrated centre, with Desi Arnaz) and Frances Langford. The result was one of the best of all campus musicals, part of whose success belonged to its delicious score by Richard Rodgers and Lorenz Hart. All about an heiress (Ball) and the four football-hero bodyguards who accompany her to a small Western college, it was a zany delight with a screenplay by John Twist that happily retained the infectious good humour of the original. Hit songs were 'I Didn't Know What Time It Was' and 'You're Nearer' (the latter written especially for the film), both sung by heroine Ball but dubbed by Trudy Erwin. Desi Arnaz's bongo-tapping to 'Spic and Spanish' was another musical standout. Other songs: *Love Never Went to College*; '*Cause We All Got Cake*; *Heroes In The Fall*; *Pottawatomie*; *Look Out*.
▽

Noel Coward wept when he saw **Bitter Sweet** (MGM) – not because he was so moved, but because he thought it so dreadful. His ironic and tender operetta was, he believed, vulgarized by being turned into just another vehicle for Jeanette MacDonald and Nelson Eddy. And he was right. But then MGM's production team was inclined to make everything in its own ultra-glamorous image, even the modest garret where MacDonald and Eddy were supposedly living in poverty – and it was surely asking too much to expect audiences to believe that Jeanette was an English lass of 18 (she was in fact an attractive 38) and Eddy a starving Viennese singing teacher. Fortunately, several Coward songs were retained from 'The Master's' original stage show, including the 'Zigeuner' finale (illustrated), exquisitely staged in white and sepia by Ernst Matray. George Sanders was the villain of the piece (he kills Eddy in a duel), with Ian Hunter, Felix Bressart, Curt Bois, Edward Ashley, Fay Holden, and Veda Ann Borg in support. It was produced by Victor Saville and directed by W.S. Van Dyke from a screenplay by Lesser Samuels. Other songs: *I'll See You Again*; *If You Could Only Come With Me*; *What Is Love?*; *Tokay*; *Love In Any Language* (new lyrics by Gus Kahn); *Dear Little Café*; *Kiss Me*; *Ladies Of The Town* Coward; *Una Voce Poco Fa* (from Rossini's 'The Barber of Seville').

The corn on offer in Republic's **Barnyard Follies** could have been measured out in hectares, as moppet Mary Lee, together with some other agriculturally-minded youngsters (illustrated), put on a barnyard show with the help of a stranded troupe of performers in order to raise $5,000. Aimed largely at country and western radio fans – and featuring several C and W radio stars, it was directed by Frank McDonald for producer Armand Schaefer, written by Stuart McGowan from an idea by Robert T. Shannon, and featured Rufe Davis (having a field day with his famous barnyard imitations), June Storey, Jed Prouty, Victor Kilian and Joan Woodbury. Songs: *Big Boy Blues*; *Barnyard Holiday*; *Lollipop Lane* Fred Rose, Johnny Marvin; *Mama Don't Allow It* Charles Davenport; *Poppin' The Corn* Sol Meyer, Jule Styne.
▽

Befuddlement was the chief ingredient in **Hulla-baloo** (MGM), and as perpetrated by that ace befuddler, Frank Morgan (illustrated), it had its amusing moments. He played a middle-aged hoofer who attempts to establish himself on radio just as three erstwhile amours in his life (and their resultant offspring) descend on him. Virginia Grey, Billie Burke, Charles Holland, Nydia Westman, Ann Morriss, Donald Meek, Reginald Owen and newcomers Dan Dailey and Virginia O'Brien were also featured; it was written by Nat Perrin from an idea by Bradford Ropes and Val Burton, and directed by Edwin L. Marin for producer Louis K. Sidney. Songs: *Carry Me Back To Old Virginny* James Bland; *We've Come A Long Way Together* Ted Koehler, Sammy Stept; *A Handful Of Stars* Jack Lawrence, Ted Shapiro; *You Were Meant For Me* Arthur Freed, Nacio Herb Brown.

▷

△

Popular radio comedians Bud Abbott (foreground right) and Lou Costello (foreground centre) made their movie debut in a big-budget effort from Universal called **One Night in the Tropics**, whose entertainment value was on a decidedly small scale. Despite its score by Jerome Kern, Oscar Hammerstein II and Dorothy Fields, and a cast that included Allan Jones, Nancy Kelly and Mary Boland, as well as Peggy Moran (left) and Leo Carillo (centre), it failed to jell and was a box-office bomb. About a would-be husband who loses his prospective wife to an insurance broker on his wedding day, its screenplay by Gertrude Purcell and Charles Grayson (adapted by Kathryn Scola and Francis Martin from a novel by Earl Derr Biggers) was a crazy mish-mash in which only Abbott and Costello, as a couple of undercover men, managed to make any impression at all. The director was Edward Sutherland. Songs: *Back In My Shell*; *Remind Me*; *You And Your Kiss* Kern, Fields; *Your Dream Is The Same As My Dream* Kern, Hammerstein II, Otto Harbach.

Even in 1925 when it first appeared on Broadway, the best thing about the Frank Mandel–Otto Harbach–Vincent Youmans musical **No No Nanette** was its music. Strange, therefore, that in its second celluloid airing (the first, by Warner Bros. was in 1930) RKO, and producer-director Herbert Wilcox, chose to relegate its long-life score to the background, favouring, instead, its tedious plot about an ingenuous lass who comes to the aid of her philandering uncle after his amorous escapades land him in trouble. Anna Neagle (illustrated) starred, and it was a case of No No Miss Neagle as she coyly simpered her way through Ken Englund's soft-centred screenplay. She was well supported by Richard Carlson, Victor Mature, Roland Young, Helen Broderick, ZaSu Pitts, Eve Arden, Tamara, and Billy Gilbert. But to no avail. **No No Nanette** with a watered-down score was like a rainbow without its colours. Briefly discernible through the plot were: *Tea For Two*; *I Want To Be Happy*; *Where Has My Hubby Gone?*; *Take A Little One-Step*; *No, No Nanette*.

△

The celebrated Jack Benny–Fred Allen radio 'feud' reached the screen in **Love Thy Neighbour** (Paramount), with Mary Martin co-starring as Allen's singing niece who, after landing a part in producer Benny's up-coming musical show, does her best to effect a truce between the two cantankerous rivals. Strictly for Benny–Allen fans, it was hard going for non-devotees, though to judge from the healthy box-office returns, the latter category were clearly in the minority. It was written by William Morrow, Edmund

▽

The cinema continued its love affair with radio in **Hit Parade of 1941** (Republic) which starred Kenny Baker and Frances Langford (illustrated) as a couple of love birds attached to a two-watt radio station acquired by antique dealer Hugh Herbert. Mary Boland, Phil Silvers and Patsy Kelly joined Herbert as the laugh-mongers of the occasion; Ann Miller was on tap for a couple of dance routines, while Six Hits and A Miss, as well as Borrah Minnevitch and His Harmonica Rascals featured as the specialty items. Also in it: Sterling Holloway, Donald McBride and Franklin Pangborn. A moderately entertaining effort that needed a better screenplay than the one provided by Bradford Ropes, F. Hugh Herbert and Maurice Leo (additional sequences by Sid Kuller and Ray Golden), it was directed by John H. Auer with most of the music and lyrics by Jule Styne and Walter Bullock. Songs included: *Who Am I?*; *Swing Low Sweet Rhythm*; *In The Cool Of The Evening*; *Make Yourself At Home* Styne, Bullock; *Dinah* John Stromberg, Edgar Smith; *Margie* Benny Davis, Con Conrad, J. Russell Robinson; *Mary Lou* Abe Lyman, George Waggner, Robinson.

▽

Beloin, Ernest Pagano and Z. Myers, produced and directed by Mark Sandrich, and in supporting roles featured Verree Teasdale, Eddie Anderson (who, as usual, committed grand larceny with every scene in which he appeared), Virginia Dale, Theresa Harris, The Merry Macs and The Merriel Abbott Dancers (see illustration). Songs included: *Do You Know Why?*; *Isn't That Just Like Love?*; *Dearest Darest I* Johnny Burke, Jimmy Van Heusen; *My Heart Belongs To Daddy* Cole Porter.

△

A musical Western aimed at a more general audience than those usually attracted to horse operas, **Melody Ranch** (Republic) corralled the non-Western talents of Jimmy Durante, Ann Miller (illustrated), Barton MacLane, Barbara Allen and Jerome Cowan, in an attempt to lend showbiz appeal to a sagebrush saga in which Gene Autry, top-cast as a radio singing star, returns to his home town as honorary sheriff just in time to see that three unfortunate lawbreakers get their just desserts. George 'Gabby' Hayes was also in it; so were Mary Lee, Joseph Sawyer, Horace McMahon and Vera Vague. Written by Jack Moffitt and F. Hugh Herbert and directed by Joseph Santley. Songs included: *Torpedo Joe*; *What Are Cowboys Made Of*; *Rodeo Rose*; *Stake Your Dreams On Melody Ranch* Eddie Cherkose, Jule Styne; *We Never Dream The Same Dream Twice* Gene Autry, Fred Rose.

1941

Academy Awards

Writing (Original Screenplay)
NOMINATIONS INCLUDED: *Tall, Dark And Handsome* (20th Century-Fox) Karl Tunberg and Darrell Ware

Cinematography (black and white)
NOMINATIONS INCLUDED: *The Chocolate Soldier* (MGM) Karl Freund. *Sun Valley Serenade* (20th Century-Fox) Edward Cronjager.
(colour)
NOMINATIONS INCLUDED: *Louisiana Purchase* (Paramount) Harry Hallenberger and Ray Rennahan

Art Direction (Interior Decoration)
(For the first time Set Designers are given plaques, while Art Directors continue to receive Oscars)
(colour)
NOMINATIONS INCLUDED: *Louisiana Purchase* Raoul Pene du Bois and Stephen A. Seymour

Sound Recording
NOMINATIONS INCLUDED: *The Chocolate Soldier* Douglas Shearer

Music
Best Song
'The Last Time I Saw Paris' *Lady Be Good* (MGM) Jerome Kern *cm*; Oscar Hammerstein II *lyr*.
NOMINATIONS INCLUDED: 'Baby Mine' *Dumbo* (Disney, RKO) Frank Churchill *cm*; Ned Washington *lyr*. 'Blues In The Night' *Blues In The Night* (WB) Harold Arlen *cm*; Johnny Mercer *lyr*. 'Boogie Woogie Bugle Boy Of Company B' *Buck Privates* (Universal) Hugh Prince *cm*; Don Raye *lyr*. 'Chattanooga Choo Choo' *Sun Valley Serenade* Harry Warren *cm*; Mack Gordon *lyr*. 'Dolores' *Las Vegas Nights* (Paramount) Lou Alter *cm*; Frank Loesser

lyr. 'Out Of The Silence' *All American Co-Ed* (Roach, UA) Lloyd B. Norlind. 'Since I Kissed My Baby Goodbye' *You'll Never Get Rich* (Columbia) Cole Porter.

Scoring of a Musical Picture (New classification)
Dumbo Frank Churchill and Oliver Wallace
NOMINATIONS INCLUDED: *All American Co-Ed* Edward Ward. *Birth Of The Blues* (Paramount) Robert Emmett Dolan. *Buck Privates* Charles Previn. *The Chocolate Soldier* Herbert Stothart and Bronislau Kaper. *Ice Capades* (Republic) Cy Feuer. *Sun Valley Serenade* Emil Newman. *Sunny* (RKO) Anthony Collins. *You'll Never Get Rich* Morris Stolof.

Special Awards
To Leopold Stokowski and his associates for their unique achievement in the creation of a new form of visualized music in Walt Disney's production of *Fantasia*, thereby widening the scope of the motion picture as entertainment and as an art form. (certificate)
To Walt Disney, William Garity, John N.A. Hawkins and the RCA Manufacturing Company for their outstanding contribution to the advancement of the use of sound in motion pictures through the production of *Fantasia*. (certificates)

1941 Irving G. Thalberg Award
Walt Disney

The New York Times Annual 'Ten Best'
8th *Dumbo*

The Annual Top Moneymaking Films
INCLUDED: *Hold That Ghost* (Universal). *Road to Zanzibar* (Paramount) *Ziegfeld Girl* (MGM) *Buck Privates*.

Singer 'Wee' Bonnie Baker and the band leader Orrin Tucker (centre) made indifferent movie debuts in **You're The One** (Paramount), a lower case musical whose narrative centred on agent Edward Everett Horton's attempts to book his client, Baker, as a singer in Tucker's band. After much unfunny horseplay, he succeeded. It was produced by Gene Markey (who also scripted), and featured Albert Dekker, Jerry Colonna (right), Lillian Cornell (left) and Walter Catlett. Ralph Murphy directed, and musical numbers were staged by LeRoy Prinz. Songs: *Strawberry Lane; I Could Kiss You For That; My Resistance Is Low; The Yogi Who Lost His Will Power; Gee I Wish I'd Listened To My Mother* Johnny Mercer, Jimmy McHugh; *Oh, Johnny, Oh* Abe Olman, Ed Rose.

A musical more flat than sharp and rarely natural, **Let's Make Music** (RKO) starred Bob Crosby in a musty old tale about a music teacher (class of students illustrated) who, while on holiday in New York, comes to realize that Bach, Beethoven and Brahms are all very well, but that Boogie hath charms too. It was written by Nathanael West, directed by Leslie Goodwins for producer Howard Benedict, and also featured Jean Rogers (as the teacher), Elisabeth Risdon, Joseph Buloff, Joyce Compton, Bennie Bartlett and Louis Jean Heydt. Songs: *Fight On Newton High* Dave Dreyer; *You Forgot About Me* Dick Robertson, Sammy Mysels, James Hanley; *Big Noise From Winnetka* Gil Rodin, Bob Haggart, Ray Bauduc, Bob Crosby; *Central Park* Johnny Mercer, Matt Malneck.

A Night At Earl Carroll's (Paramount) was precisely that, with showman Carroll relying on the most anaemic of plot excuses to present a nightclub act (chorus number illustrated) of varying quality. The story had a gangster kidnapping Carroll's floor-show principals as part of a feud he (the gangster) is having with a fictitious Hollywood mayor (not to be confused with the factual Hollywood Mayer) thereby forcing the master showman to improvise a scratch entertainment – utilizing the talents of a singing cigarette vendor, the boys and girls of the chorus, and a couple of the paying customers. The film had little marquee value, with Ken Murray, Rose Hobart, Elvia Allman, Blanche Stewart, Russell Hicks (as the mayor) and Mr Carroll himself the prime attractions. It was written by Lynn Starling and directed by Kurt Neumann. Songs: *Li'l Boy Love* Frank Loesser, Frederick Hollander; *I Wanna Make With The Happy Times* Loesser, Gertrude Niesen; *Cali-Con-Ga* Earl Carroll, Dorcas Cochran, Nilo Menendez; *One Look At You* Carroll, Ned Washington, Victor Young.

Both Bud Abbott and Lou Costello, as well as Universal Pictures, struck it lucky with **Buck Privates**. The comedy team found stardom and a place (third) in the nation's popularity polls (Mickey Rooney and Clark Gable were occupying spots one and two); while the studio, who invested a mere $90,000 in the movie's production, recouped its cost 10 times over. **Buck Privates** was a runaway hit, and Universal's top grossing film in 1941. Bud and Lou played street-corner tie salesmen who, while fleeing the police, take cover in a movie theatre. Except that it isn't a movie theatre any longer but an army induction centre. In no time at all they find themselves enlisted, whereupon reality gives way to fantasy, with life in the army revealed as one long laugh from start to finish. The War Office couldn't have wished for a better 84 minutes of recruitment propaganda than this, especially with The Andrews Sisters (illustrated) as a trio of Pied Pipers doing their close-harmony best for the war effort with such numbers as 'Boogie Woogie Bugle Boy From Company B', and 'Bounce Me Brother With A Solid Four' (both by Don Raye and Hughie Prince). Lee Bowman and Alan Curtis (who were billed above Abbott and Costello) also appeared as recruits (Bowman as a wealthy socialite, Curtis as his bodyguard), with Jane Frazee, Nat Pendleton, Samuel S. Hinds, Harry Strang, Nella Walker, Leonard Elliott and Shemp Howard completing the cast. It was written by Arthur T. Horman and directed by Arthur Lubin. Other songs: *When Private Brown Meets A Sergeant*; *Wish You Were Here* Raye, Prince; *You're A Lucky Fellow Mr Smith* Raye, Prince, Sonny Burke; *I'll Be With You In Apple Blossom Time* Neville Fleeson, Albert von Tilzer.

△

Another wad of army propaganda, but not nearly as amusing as *Buck Privates*, **Cadet Girl** (20th Century-Fox) focussed on the dilemma of George Montgomery (left) as to whether to marry Carole Landis (right) and embark on a life of unruffled domesticity; or whether he should enter West Point and study for a commission. It hardly mattered one way or another, for Stanley Rauh and H.W. Hanemann's screenplay, from a story by Jack Andrews and Richard English, was so under-written and under-characterized that it precluded involvement. John Shepperd, William Tracy, Janis Carter, Robert Lowery, Basil Walker, Charles Tannen and Chick Chandler were also featured, and the director was Ray McCarey. Songs: *My Old Man Was An Army Man*; *She's A Good Neighbour*; *I'll Settle For You*; *It Happened, It's Over, Let's Forget It*; *It Won't Be Fun (But It's Got To Be Done)*; *Making A Play For You*; *Uncle Sam Gets Around* Ralph Rainger, Leo Robin.

△

Lupe Velez, as Madame La Zonga (centre), the star of a niterie of the same name, was the only reason for wasting time on **Six Lessons From Madame La Zonga** (Universal). Leon Errol co-starred as a phoney Latin, with other roles in this ineffectual little programmer going to Charles Lang as the leader of an Oklahoma band trying desperately to land a café date in Cuba, Helen Parrish as the girl of his dreams, and Eddie Quillan as his pal. Cast in support were Guinn Williams and Shemp Howard. Its quartet of scenarists were Stanley C. Rubin, Marion Orth, Larry Rhine and Ben Chapman, the director was John Rawlings, and it was produced by Joseph G. Sandford. Songs and musical numbers included: *Six Lessons From Madame La Zonga* Charles Newman, James V. Monaco; *The Matador's Wife*; *Jitterumba* Everett Carter, Milton Rosen.

The eighth film to feature cartoonist Chic Young's Blondie and Dagwood, **Blondie Goes Latin** (GB: **Conga Swing**) from Columbia, relied this time as much on music as it did on comedy. Richard Flournoy and Karen DeWolf's entertaining account of what happened when the Bumsteads joined ailing boss J.C. Dithers on a Latin American cruise again had Penny Singleton (right) and Arthur Lake impersonating Young's immortal Mr and Mrs, with Larry Simms as Baby Dumpling, and other parts shared out between Ruth Terry, Tito Guizar (left), Jonathan Hale, Danny Mummert and Irving Bacon. The original story was by Quinn Martin, it was produced by Robert Sparks and directed by Frank R. Strayer. Songs: *You Don't Play A Drum (You Beat It)*; *I Hate Music Lessons*; *Querida*; *You Can't Cry On My Shoulder*; *Castillian Cotillion* Bob Wright, Chet Forrest.

▽

Forties Musicals

△

One of the glories of the Fox musical was its colour: gaudily bright, unashamedly splashy, and just the job for taking audiences' minds off the similarities of the plots it embellished. **That Night in Rio** was *the* quintessential Fox war-time musical – an over-blown, over-dressed, over-produced and thoroughly irresistible cornucopia of escapist ingredients whose sheer professionalism was as dazzling as the colour, the sets, the costumes and the girls (see illustration) that had been poured into it. A remake of *Folies Bergère* (20th Century/United Artists, 1935) it gave Alice Faye lead billing, though when Carmen Miranda wasn't scene-stealing everytime *she* appeared, the film was very much Don Ameche's. In the role originally played by Maurice Chevalier, Ameche (illustrated, at desk) was called upon to prove he wasn't just a pretty face by playing a dual role: an American singer in a Rio nightclub, and a well-known local banker with a quite uncanny resemblance to the entertainer. George Seaton, Bess Meredyth and Hal Long's screenplay (additional dialogue by Samuel Hoffenstein, based on a play by Rudolph Lothar and Hans Adler, and adapted by Jessie Ernst) stuck very closely to the earlier version, with Miranda in the Ann Sothern role, and Faye in the part originally played by Merle Oberon. Mack Gordon and Harry Warren provided the film with an infectiously bouncy score, and Carmen Miranda with two of her biggest hits – 'Chica Chica Boom Chic' (an exuberantly staged production number by Hermes Pan) and 'I Yi Yi Yi Yi (I Like You Very Much)'. The supporting cast included S.Z. Sakall, J. Carrol Naish, Curt Bois, Leonid Kinskey and Frank Puglia. Miranda's orchestra The Banda Da Lua, were also on hand to make music; so were a specialty trio called The Flores Brothers. Maria Montez also appeared in a bit part. Fred Kohlmar was the associate producer and it was directed by Irving Cummings. Other songs: *Boa Noite* (*Good Night*); *They Met In Rio*; *The Baron Is In Conference* Gordon, Warren; *Cae Cae* (Portuguese) Roberto Martins.

In *That Certain Age* (Universal, 1938), Deanna Durbin had slipped painlessly, and with the minimum amount of fuss, into puberty. Three years later in **Nice Girl?** (seated centre), having at last reached womanhood, she flexed her seductive muscles at Franchot Tone (seated left) who, as a New York representative of a Scientific Foundation on a visit to her professor father, reacts to the flirtation with acute embarrassment. After a few more unsuccessful flirtations Durbin decides to keep her blossoming womanhood in check, and sensibly returns to her long-standing, home-grown sweetheart (Robert Stack, standing left). Richard Connell and Gladys Lehman's screenplay (from a story by Phyllis Duganne) kept it all very proper, indeed, almost innocent, and, as performed by the ingenuous Miss Durbin as well as a first-rate cast including Walter Brennan (as a lovesick postman), Robert Benchley (seated right, as the *paterfamilias*) and Ann Gillis (standing, as Deanna's man-hungry younger sister), as well as Helen Broderick, Anne Gwynne (seated right), Elizabeth Risdon and Nana Bryant, it was as refreshing as a breeze in a heatwave. Joe Pasternak produced, and calling the shots was William A. Seiter. Songs: *Love At Last* Eddie Cherkose, Jacques Press; *Perhaps* Aldo Franchetti, Andreas De Segurola; *Beneath The Lights Of Home*; *Thank You America* Bernie Grossman, Walter Jurmann; *The Old Folks At Home* Stephen Foster.

▽

Leon Errol, Helen Parrish (centre right) and Charles Lang starred in **Where Did You Get That Girl?** an off-the-cuff programmer from Universal in which a struggling singer (Parrish) and songwriter (Lang), after meeting by chance and falling in love, team up with a dance band led by Eddie Quillan (centre left) and, during a rehearsal in a recording studio, are inadvertently involved in a hold-up. The ensuing publicity lands them a recording contract and the film ends with the love-birds about to be married. Jay Dratler, Paul Franklin and Stanley Crea Rubin wrote it (story by Dratler), Arthur Lubin directed a cast that also included Franklin Pangborn, Stanley Fields and Tom Dugan; and the producer was Joseph G. Sandford. Songs included: *Where Did You Get That Girl?* Harry Puck, Bert Kalmar; *Sergeant Swing*; *Rug-Cuttin' Romeo* Milton Rosen, Everett Carter.

▽

△

Nevada's gambling haven was put to no good use at all in **Las Vegas Nights** (Paramount), a musical whose paltry excuse for existing at all was Tommy Dorsey and His Orchestra. Vaguely concerned with a group of impecunious entertainers at loose in the city, it featured Phil Regan, an unfunny Bert Wheeler (foreground centre), without Woolsey, Constance Moore, Lillian Cornell, Virginia Dale, Hank Ladd, and a trio of Mexicans collectively known as Mexican Trio. It was written by Ernest Pagano and Harry Clork with additional dialogue by Eddie Welch, and was directed by Ralph Murphy for producer William Le Baron. The most notable feature of this nothing film was that a young singer called Frank Sinatra made his screen debut, singing 'Dolores' (by Frank Loesser and Louis Alter) with Dorsey's band. Songs: *Song Of India* Rimsky-Korsakov, arranged by 'Red' Bone; *On Miami Shore* William Le Baron, Victor Jacobi; *I'll Never Smile Again* Ruth Lowe; *I've Gotta Ride*; *Mary, Mary, Quite Contrary* Frank Loesser, Burton Lane.

Suffering from the law of diminishing returns, The Marx Brothers's (left) MGM efforts contained fewer laughs with each new film, **Go West** being their least funny to date. It did, however, have a chase sequence on a train that was a comic gem. For the rest, it was a routine tale about three guys from the East who become involved with all sorts of unsavoury characters in the West. Irving Brecher wrote it, it was directed by Edward Buzzell for producer Jack Cummings, and in supporting roles featured John Carroll (far right), Diana Lewis (right), Walter Woolf King and Robert Barrat. Songs: *Ridin' The Range* Gus Kahn, Roger Edens; *You Can't Argue With Love*; *As If I Don't Know* Kahn, Bronislau Kaper; *Land Of The Sky Blue Water* (in a rendition by Harpo) Charles Wakefield Cadman; *Beautiful Dreamer*; *Oh Susanna* Stephen Foster.

After the surprise success of *Road To Singapore* (Paramount, 1940), the studio teamed Bing Crosby (centre right), Dorothy Lamour and Bob Hope (centre) in **Road To Zanzibar** which, in every way, was superior to their first faltering, albeit financially successful effort. This time Bing and Bob played a couple of carnival performers and conmen who, after selling a phoney diamond mine to the kind of murderous heavy it isn't wise to sell phoney diamond mines to, leave the country as fast as they can and make for exotic Zanzibar. There, in a parody of every jungle epic that ever featured a restless native or a throbbing tom-tom, the intrepid duo link up with two con-women – a sarong-free Miss Lamour and her sidekick Una Merkel – and together they set out on a cross-country safari that left audiences limp with laughter. The rib-tickling screenplay (always allowing for the Crosby–Hope ad libs *en route*) was by Frank Butler and Don Hartman (story by Hartman and Sy Bartlett), it was produced by Paul Jones, and directed by Victor Schertzinger. Songs: *You Lucky People, You*; *It's Always You*; *You're Dangerous*; *On The Road To Zanzibar*; *Birds Of A Feather* Johnny Burke, Jimmy Van Heusen.

Flung together in an obvious attempt to capitalize on the success of Universal's *Buck Privates*, Republic's **Rookies On Parade** (GB: **Jamboree**) was a dispiriting effort written by Karl Brown, Jack Townley and Milt Gross from a story by Sammy Cahn and Saul Chaplin. The plot pivoted around the attempts of Bob Crosby and Eddie Foy Jr, two songwriters who are drafted into the army, to put on a show, and it buried them in the hole it made. Ruth Terry, Gertrude Niesen (centre), Marie Wilson (2nd left), Cliff Nazarro, William Demarest and Sidney Blackmer (right) were also in it for producer Albert J. Cohen. Nick Castle staged the dances, and the director was Joseph Santley. Songs: *The Army Builds Men*; *I Love You More*; *Mother Never Told Me Why*; *My Kinda Love*; *You'll Never Get Rich*; *What More Do You Want* Sammy Cahn, Saul Chaplin; *Rookies On Parade* Eddie Cherkose, Jule Styne.

A wacky, slightly demented Adolphe Menjou (left) joined forces with millionaire playboy John Hubbard in **Road Show** (United Artists), an off-beat, off-balance effort which also starred Carole Landis (right) as a beautiful but bankrupt carnival owner. Supporting players Charles Butterworth (centre), Patsy Kelly, George E. Stone, Margaret Roach, Willie Best, and The Charioteers did their best to keep it buoyant, but the dead weight of Arnold Belgard, Harry Langdon and Mickell Novak's screenplay (from a novel by Earl Hatch) was more than mere flesh and blood could carry. It was produced and directed by Hal Roach with a decided air of desperation infiltrating every scene. Songs: *I Should Have Known You Years Ago* Hoagy Carmichael; *Slav Annie*; *Yum Yum*; *Calliope Jane* Carmichael, Stanley Adams.

Pot O' Gold (GB: **The Golden Horn**) was a hit-and-miss affair from United Artists which scored more misses than hits in a radio-orientated tale of a music-hating sponsor's battle with a group of down-and-out entertainers. Charles Winninger was the crusty old sponsor, with personable James Stewart (illustrated) and beautiful Paulette Goddard heading the cast. Mary Gordon, Frank Melton, Jed Prouty, Dick Hogan, James Burke, and Horace Heidt and His Orchestra also appeared; it was written by Walter DeLeon from a story by Andrew Bennison, Monte Brice and Harry Tugend (idea by Haydn Roth Evans and Robert Brilmayer), produced by James Roosevelt (son of the President) and directed by George Marshall. Songs: *Do You Believe In Fairy Tales?* Mack David, Vee Lawnhurst; *When Johnny Toots His Horn* Hy Heath, Fred Rose; *A Knife, A Fork And A Spoon* Dave Franklin; *Broadway Caballero*; *Pete The Piper*; *Hi Cy, What's Cookin?*; *Slap Happy Band* Lou Forbes, Henry Sullivan.

MGM pulled out all the stops for **Ziegfeld Girl**, an eye-filling spectacle that traced the lives and loves of three Ziegfeld girls: vaudeville singer Judy Garland (left), elevator girl Lana Turner (right), and wife of a penniless violinist, Hedy Lamarr (centre). Garland makes it; Turner doesn't; and Lamarr swaps her place in the chorus for married bliss. With Busby Berkeley in charge of the production numbers, Cedric Gibbons the sumptuous sets and Adrian the mind-boggling costumes, the visual aspect of the film was, in every respect, splendiferous. Where it let itself down was in its soap-opera plot (by William Anthony McGuire, screenplay by Marguerite Roberts and Sonya Levien), an endless parade of sob-story clichés that held not a single surprise. Viewed today through the jaundiced eyes of the eighties, the film emerges as a camp wallow from start to finish; a highly-charged dose of forties sentimentality that also happens to be quite preposterously entertaining. All the same, apart from Busby Berkeley's brilliantly inventive staging of a Spanish dance by Antonio and Rosario, where the lighting and the camera movements create an excitement equal to that provided by the performers, the two big set pieces – 'Minnie From Trinidad' by Roger Edens (performed by Garland) and 'You Stepped Out Of A Dream' (sung by Tony Martin) by Gus Kahn and Nacio Herb Brown relied on opulence rather than on invention for their effects. Pandro S. Berman's production borrowed several sequences from *The Great Ziegfeld* (MGM, 1936), including the famous 'wedding cake set' but, instead of Virginia Bruce being the cherry on the top of the giant edifice (as she was in the earlier film), part of the set was reconstructed to allow Judy Garland to take her place which, in a skilful piece of editing, she did most tellingly. The men in **Ziegfeld Girl** were James Stewart (top-billed) as Miss Turner's truckdriver sweetheart, Tony Martin, who has a brief dalliance with the beauteous Hedy Lamarr, together with Jackie Cooper, Ian Hunter, Charles Winninger (as Mr Gallagher), Al Shean (as himself), Edward Everett Horton, Philip Dorn, Paul Kelly and Dan Dailey. The cast was completed by Eve Arden, Felix Bressart and Rose Hobart. It was directed very stylishly by Robert Z. Leonard. Other songs and musical numbers included: *Laugh? I Thought I'd Split My Sides* (Garland, Winninger) Roger Edens; *Caribbean Love Song* (Martin) Edens, Ralph Freed; *I'm Always Chasing Rainbows* (Garland) Joseph McCarthy, Harry Carroll; *Whispering* (unidentified male vocal trio) John Schonberger, Richard Coburn, Vincent Rose; *Mr Gallagher And Mr Shean* (Winninger, Shean) Ed Gallagher and Al Shean; *You Never Looked So Beautiful Before* (Garland, chorus) Walter Donaldson, Harold Adamson.

Too Many Blondes (Universal) was minor
league entertainment that starred Rudy Vallee
(right) and Helen Parrish (centre) as a newlywed radio team. and Iris Adrian as the blonde
siren who comes between them. Sixty minutes
and four songs later, it all ended happily for the
couple. Audiences, however, were less fortunate. Lon Chaney Jr, Jerome Cowan (left),
Shemp Howard, Eddie Quillan and Humberto
Herpera and His Orchestra were also in it; it was
directed by Thornton Freeland from a screenplay by Maxwell Shane and Louis S. Kaye (story
by Shane) and produced by Joseph G. Sandford.
Songs: *Whistle Your Blues To A Bluebird*; *Don't
Mind If I Do*; *Let's Love Again* Everett Carter,
Milton Rosen; *The Man On The Flying Trapeze*
George Leybourne, Alfred Lee, adapted by
Walter O'Keefe.

Hollywood's wooing of Latin America continued
with They Met in Argentina (RKO), though it is
doubtful whether this minor offering did anything to further the cause of hemispheric soli-
darity. Producer Lou Brock was clearly unable
to decide whether the film was primarily for the
USA or the South American market, with the
result that it found favour in neither place –
despite a score by no less a team than Richard
Rodgers and Lorenz Hart. All about a Texas oil
millionaire (Robert Middlemass) – who, after
failing to secure oil lands in Argentina, seeks out
a famous race horse in Buenos Aires and orders
his representative (James Ellison) to buy the nag
at any price – it centred on the love affair Ellison
has with Maureen O'Hara (featured centre), the
beautiful daughter of the prize horse's owner.
One production number, called 'The Chaco',
brightened proceedings momentarily, but it was
76 minutes of tedium just the same, with co-
stars Alberto Vila (featured left) and Buddy
Ebsen, as well as Robert Barrat, Diosa Costello,
Victoria Cordova and Antonio Moreno hopelessly at sea in Jerry Cady's silly screenplay
(story by Lou Brock and Harold Daniels). It was
directed by Leslie Goodwins and Jack Hively
proving, indisputably, that two heads are not
necessarily better than one. Songs: *You've Got
The Best Of Me*; *Amarillo*; *Cutting The Cane*; *Never
Go To Argentina*; *Lolita*; *North America Meets South
America*; *Simpatica*.

Essaying a role that Mabel Normand played twenty-two years earlier, Judy Canova appeared in and as **Sis Hopkins**, a big budget (for Republic) production that cost half a million dollars. And although no one ever expected sophistication from Miss Canova of the 'sawmill voice and hayrick legs', as one notable wag at the time described her, her cavortings at the co-educational college she was placed in by scriptwriters Jack Townley, Milt Gross and Edward Eliscu (story by F. McGrew Willis) were crude even by hinterland standards. Bob Crosby and His Band were also in it; so were Jerry Colonna (giving an embarrassingly over-ripe performance as a professor), Charles Butterworth, Susan Hayward (who would soon graduate to better things), Katharine Alexander and Elvia Allman. Joseph Santley directed (production number illustrated). Songs: *Cracker Barrel County*; *If You're In Love*; *Look At You, Look At Me*; *Well! Well!*; Frank Loesser, Jule Styne; *Sempre Libre* (from 'La Traviata') Verdi.

Ruby Keeler (centre) returned to the screen after a three-year absence in Columbia's **Sweetheart of the Campus** (GB: **Broadway Ahead**), a low-voltage campus musical whose seven musical numbers did little to alleviate the tedium generated by Robert D. Andrews and Edmund Hartmann's screenplay (story by Andrews) about a stranded dance band that attaches itself to a college in order to stimulate enrolment. Ozzie Nelson (right) and His Band were there to make music; so was Harriet Hilliard (centre right), who sang two songs and got the guy. Byron Foulger (2nd left), Gordon Oliver, Don Beddoe (left), Charles Judels, George Lessey (2nd right), Kathleen Howard (centre left) and The Four Spirits of Rhythm completed the cast. Louis Da Pron staged the dances, Jack Fier produced, and the director was Edward Dmytryk. Songs included: *When The Glee Club Swings The Alma Mater* Charles Newman, Walter G. Samuels; *Where* Jacques Krakeur; *Tom, Tom The Elevator Boy* Samuels; *Tap Happy*; *Zig Me Baby With A Gentle Zag*; *Here We Go Again* Eddie Cherkose, Jacques Press.

The Great American Broadcast (20th Century-Fox), the fifth and final radio-orientated musical in which Alice Faye appeared, opened promisingly with cameo appearances by Kate Smith, Jack Benny, Eddie Cantor, Rudy Vallee and Walter Winchell, and fulfilled that promise in an apocryphal but hugely entertaining yarn about the pioneering days of radio *circa* 1919. As was the case in *Alexander's Ragtime Band* (20th Century-Fox, 1936) and *Tin Pan Alley* (20th Century-Fox, 1940), petite Miss Faye found herself the victim of a romantic triangle (male interest being supplied by Jack Oakie and John Payne) but, in the last reel, chooses Mr Payne, as you knew all along she would. Six super Mack Gordon-Harry Warren songs, plus several golden oldies, added zest to Don Ettlinger, Edwin Blum, Robert Ellis and Helen Logan's racy screenplay; so did the casting of The Ink Spots, The Nicholas Brothers and The Wiere Brothers (illustrated) in specialty spots. Cesar Romero was in it too; so were Mary Beth Hughes, Eula Morgan, William Pawley and Lucien Littlefield. Kenneth MacGowan was the associate producer and the director was Archie Mayo. Songs: *I've Got A Bone To Pick With You*; *It's All In A Lifetime*; *I Take To You*; *Long Ago Last Night*; *Where You Are*; *The Great American Broadcast* Gordon, Warren; *Alabamy Bound* Buddy De Sylva, Bud Green, Ray Henderson; *Give My Regards To Broadway* George M. Cohan; *If I Didn't Care* Jack Lawrence; and a largely unrecognizable version of The Sextet from Donizetti's *Lucia Di Lammermoor*.

The National Music Camp for young artists at Interlochen, Michigan was the setting of **There's Magic in Music** (Paramount), a gauche, thoroughly undistinguished tribute to that institution, which starred Allan Jones as its manager and Susanna Foster (background right) as a young burlesque performer whom he brings to the camp, and who, after an initial period of adjustment (and a few impersonations of Marlene Dietrich and singer Bonnie Baker) becomes everybody's sweetheart. Miss Foster's performance, like Frederick Jackson's screenplay (from a story by Andrew Stone and Robert Lively and an idea by Ann Ronell) was woefully inadequate; so was producer Stone's direction. The supporting performances from Margaret Lindsay, Lynne Overman, Grace Bradley and William Collier Sr weren't much better. Dolly Loehr (Diana Lynn) played part of Grieg's Piano Concerto. A song, *Fireflies On Parade*, by Ronell, was also featured.

Having made their mark on the army in *Buck Privates* (Universal), Abbott and Costello put out to sea in **In The Navy** (Universal), but with much less comic feed-back than in their earlier excursion on *terra firma*. Though they supplied the laughs in the Arthur T. Horman-John Grant screenplay (story by Horman), the plot centred on a heart-throb crooner (Dick Powell) who joins the navy to avoid the incessant advances of his adoring lady fans. Powell sang 'Starlight, Starbright' and was joined by Dick Foran in 'A Sailor's Life For Me', with the Andrews Sisters' (illustrated) 'You're Off To See The World', 'Gimme Some Skin' and 'Hula Ba Lua' completing the musical programme. With its fair quota of laughs and a cast that also included Claire Dodd (as a reporter), Billy Lenhart, Kenneth Brown, Shemp Howard and the dancing Condos Brothers, **In The Navy**, competently directed by Arthur Lubin, was another Universal hit. All the songs were by Don Raye and Gene De Paul.

Second Chorus (Paramount) was that rare thing: a Fred Astaire failure. In it he played an undergraduate trumpeter (Bobby Hackett blew for him) who deliberately flunks his exams in order to remain on at college as long as he can. Undergraduate was the word for the whole sorry business – despite Fred's (foreground right) cinematic involvement with the popular Artie Shaw Band (which he conducted in the finale) and leading lady Paulette Goddard, whose undeniable beauty was no substitute for her equally undeniable lack of dancing talent – though she was certainly better equipped in this department than Joan Fontaine in *A Damsel In Distress* (RKO, 1937). Astaire danced on only three occasions, none of them particularly noteworthy except, possibly, for their brevity. Burgess Meredith (foreground left) was in it too (as Astaire's rival in love); so were Charles Butterworth, Frank Melton, Jimmy Conlin, Adia Kuznetzoff and Michael Visaroff. It was written by Frank Cavett, Elaine Ryan and Ian Hunter (story by Cavett), produced by Boris Morros and directed by Henry C. Potter with Hermes Pan in charge of the choreography. Musical numbers: *(I Ain't Hep To That Step) But I'll Dig It* Johnny Mercer, Hal Borne; *The Love Of My Life* Mercer, Artie Shaw; *Poor Mr Chisholm* Mercer, Bernie Hanighen; *Swing Concerto* Shaw; *Sweet Sue* Will Harris, Victor Young (both performed by Artie Shaw and His Orchestra); *I'm Yours* E.Y. Harburg, Johnny Green.

Angels with Broken Wings (Republic) suffered from a really confused and confusing screenplay by George Carleton Brown and Bradford Ropes (story by Brown) which vaguely had something to do with a group of kids, led by Leo Gorcey, trying to arrange a marriage between Katharine Alexander and Sidney Blackmer. Binnie Barnes, Gilbert Roland (seated), Mary Lee (centre left), Billy Gilbert (left) and Jane Frazee (right) were also in it. It was produced by Albert J. Cohen with Bernard Vorhaus in charge of the direction. Songs: *Bye-Lo Baby*; *Has To Be*; *In Buenos Aires*; *Three Little Wishes*; *Where Do We Dream From Here* Jule Styne, Eddie Cherkose.

Husband and wife team Herbert Wilcox and Anna Neagle, having unsuccessfully endeavoured to blow the gathering cobwebs off *Irene* and *No, No Nanette* (both RKO, 1940), now turned their attention to the Jerome Kern-Oscar Hammerstein II-Otto Harbach hit of yesteryear, **Sunny** (first filmed in 1930 by Warner Bros./First National, now by RKO). Miss Neagle, however, was no Marilyn Miller and the attempt hardly seemed worth the effort. Reducing Harbach's original book to the conventional tale of a circus performer who marries a New Orleans aristocrat despite his family's stern disapproval of the match, producer-director Wilcox emerged with a rather faded, old-fashioned entertainment. John Carroll (as the aristocrat) and Ray Bolger (illustrated, with Neagle) co-starred, with other roles going to Edward Everett Horton, Grace and Paul Hartman, Frieda Inescort, Helen Westley, Benny Rubin and Muggins Davies. Bolger's spirited if somewhat eccentric dancing was the second best thing in the show, the best being Kern's immortal score. All the same, by 1941 the enterprise was crippled by a sense of *déjà vu*. The refurbished screenplay was by Sig Herzig. Songs: *Who?*; *Sunny*; *D'Ya Love Me?*; *Two Little Love Birds*.

A 1940 hit song called **San Antonio Rose** gave Universal its inspiration for yet another in their seemingly inexhaustible series of B-musicals whose titles were filched from the hit-parade. All about the rivalry that existed between two road-house operators, it ran 62 minutes, featured no fewer than nine songs (six of them sung by The Merry Macs), with Jane Frazee heading a cast that also included Robert Paige (left foreground with Frazee), Eve Arden (as Frazee's sister and on-stage partner), Lon Chaney Jr, Shemp Howard, Richard Lane, Louis Da Pron, Charles Lang and Luis Alberni. Three of the songs, including the title number (by Bob Willis), 'Hi Neighbour' (by Jack Owens) and the 'Hut Sut Song' (by Leo Killion and Ted McMichael) were hits, but the rest were unmemorable and the film, written by Hugh Wedlock Jr, Howard Snyder and Paul Gerard Smith from an original story by Jack Lait Jr, had little to recommend it. The musical numbers were staged by Nick Castle, with Charles Lamont in charge of the direction for producer Ken Goldsmith. Other songs included: *Once Upon A Summertime* Jack Brooks, Norman Berens; *Mexican Jumping Beat*; *You've Got What It Takes* Don Raye, Gene De Paul; *You're Everything Wonderful*; *Bugle Woogie Boy* Henry Russell; *Sweep It* Frank Skinner.

Announced as the Marx Brothers' swan song to pictures, **The Big Store** was their fifth and last film for MGM, though, as it turned out, not the last they were to make. In it, the brothers (illustrated) played a trio of store detectives out to apprehend Douglass Dumbrille (centre right) the store's crooked owner. Though generally considered by *aficionados* to be far from vintage Marx, it was full of good things, from Groucho dictating a letter to Harpo and not being able to hear himself over the clatter of the latter's ear-splittingly noisy typewriter, to the frenzied department store chase that climaxed the film. The comic highspot, however, was unintentional, and it occurred with co-star Tony Martin's lugubrious rendition of 'The Tenement Symphony' (by Sid Kuller, Ray Golden and Hal Borne), one of MGM's all-time worsts. Virginia Grey, Margaret Dumont, William Tannen, Henry Armetta and Virginia O'Brien (singing 'Rock-A-Bye Baby' by Effie I. Crockett) were also in it. Kuller, Golden and Hal Fimberg wrote it from a story by Nat Perrin. Louis K. Sidney produced and Charles F. Riesner directed. Other songs: *Sing While You Sell* Kuller, Borne, Hal Finberg; *If It's You* Milton Drake, Artie Shaw, Ben Oakland; *Mama Yo Quiero* Al Stillman, Vincente and Jaraca Paiva (played as a piano duet by Chico and Harpo).

A splashy, big-budget Technicolor merry-go-round of a musical, **Moon Over Miami** (20th Century-Fox) starred Betty Grable (illustrated) as a waitress in an open-air hamburger joint who, after coming into a legacy, takes off with her aunt and sister (Carole Landis) for Miami – the millionaires' playground. A remake of *Three Blind Mice* (20th Century-Fox, 1938), which featured Loretta Young in the Grable role, it wrapped up its slender story in several opulently staged production numbers and several more bouncy Ralph Rainger-Leo Robin songs and, one way and another, was a most delightfully packaged assortment of goodies. Don Ameche (top-starred) and Robert Cummings provided the romantic interest, and Charlotte Greenwood and Jack Haley the comedy, with Jack Cole and Company, as well as the dancing Condos Brothers (foreground left) punctuating the narrative with some specialty turns. The cast was completed by Cobina Wright Jr, Lynne Roberts, Robert Conway, George Lessey, Robert Greig and Minor Watson. It was written by Vincent Lawrence and Brown Holmes from a play by Stephen Powys, and adapted by George Seaton and Lynn Starling, Hermes Pan staged the musical numbers and the breezy direction was by Walter Lang. Songs and musical numbers: *What Can I Do For You?*; *You Started Something*; *Kindergarten Conga*; *Oh Me Oh Mi-A-Mi*; *Is That Good*; *Solitary Seminole*; *Loveliness And Love*; *I've Got You All To Myself* Rainger, Robin; *Moon Over Miami* Edgar Leslie, Joe Burke (played behind main titles only). It was remade in 1946 as *Three Little Girls in Blue* (20th Century-Fox).

Melody Lane (Universal) offered an ineffectual hour in which The Merry Macs played a quartet of entertainers from Iowa who are signed to appear in a radio show in New York. But the show is sponsored by a breakfast food magnate whose interference in the radio programme he pays for is a one-way ticket to trouble. Leon Errol (left) was the meddlesome magnate, with other roles going to Anne Gwynne, Robert Paige, Billy Lenhart, Kenneth Brown, Louis Da Pron, Butch and Buddy (illustrated), and Little Sandy. Hugh Wedlock Jr, Howard Snyder and Morton Grant wrote it from a story by Bernard Feins (adaptation by George Rony), and it was directed for producer Ken Goldsmith by Charles Lamont. Songs and musical numbers: *Listen To The Mocking Bird*; *Septimus Winner*; *Peaceful Ends The Day*; *Cherokee Charlie*; *Let's Go To Calicabu*; *Swing-A-Bye My Baby*; *Changeable Heart*; *If It's A Dream Don't Wake Me*; *Since The Farmer In The Dell* Norman Berens, Jack Brooks.

Radio came to the rescue of **Swing It Soldier**, a 'B' from Universal whose cast (Ken Murray, Frances Langford (centre), Don Wilson, Blanche Stewart, Elvia Allman, Susan Miller, Iris Adrian, Hanley Stafford and Thurston Hall) – not to mention its plot about a pregnant soldier's wife and the twin sister who agrees to stand in for her in a radio show – was augmented by such airwave favourites as Skinnay Ennis and His Orchestra, Kenny Stevens, Stop, Look and Listen and Three Cheers. Louis Da Pron appeared in a snappy solo devised by choreographer Reginald Le Borg, Susan Miller scored in a jazzed-up version of 'Annie Laurie'; while Langford's big moment found her singing 'I'm Gonna Swing My Way To Heaven' (Eddie Cherkose, Jacques press). Dorcas Cochran and Arthur V. Jones wrote it, the producer was Joseph G. Sandford, and Harold Young directed. Other songs and musical numbers included: *Rug-Cuttin' Romeo* Everett Carter, Milton Rosen; *My Melancholy Baby* George Norton, Ernie Burnett.

▽

With a cast that included Ann Miller (illustrated). Rudy Vallee, Rosemary Lane and Allen Jenkins, plus several specialty acts such as Six Hits and A Miss, Glen Gray and His Casa Loma Orchestra, Eddie Durant's Rhumba Orchestra, as well as The Three Stooges, **Time Out For Rhythm** (Columbia) promised to deliver the goods. But it was dull, dull, dull, with the unstoppable Miss Miller valiantly tapping away in a hopeless attempt to infuse vitality into a plot about two quarrelling theatrical agents. It was based on a play by Alex Ruben and a story by Bert Granet, with a screenplay by Edmund L. Hartmann and Bert Lawrence. Irving Starr produced and his director was Sidney Salkow. Songs and musical numbers: *Boogie Woogie Man; Time Out For Rhythm; Twiddlin My Thumbs; Obviously The Gentleman Prefers To Dance; As If You Didn't Know; The Rio De Janeiro; Shows How Wrong A Gal Can Be* Sammy Cahn, Saul Chaplin.
▽

As originally written for the stage by Clare ▷ Booth, **Kiss The Boys Goodbye** (Paramount) was a caustic satire on Hollywood and its eternal search for new talent, especially someone to play Scarlett O'Hara in *Gone With The Wind*. The film version, with a score by Frank Loesser and Victor Schertzinger (Schertzinger also directed), removed its sting and watered down its pungent content, substituting, instead, a familiar tale about a Southern chorus girl who makes good. Mary Martin (illustrated) was Cindy Lou, and her singing of 'That's How I Got My Start' was the bright spot in a film sadly lacking in them. Don Ameche, who received top billing, played a movie director unable to resist Miss Martin's charms, with Oscar Levant (illustrated left), tossing around gags and harpsichord toccatas with equal abandon. Connee Boswell (who scored a personal hit singing the film's best song 'Sand In My Shoes', which became an enduring standard), Eddie (Rochester) Anderson, Virginia Dale, Barbara Jo Allen, Raymond Walburn, Elizabeth Patterson and Jerome Cowan rounding off the cast. Harry Tugend and Dwight Taylor scripted it. Other songs: *Find Yourself A Melody; I'll Never Let A Day Pass By; Kiss The Boys Goodbye;* and several negro spirituals.

Jane Frazee (left), Johnny Downs, Iris Adrian and The Peters Bros lent vocal support to a Universal quickie called **Sing Another Chorus,** with Sunnie O'Dea (right) featuring in a dance routine staged by Larry Ceballos. Best musical item, however, was a Spanish specialty by Rosario and Antonio. For the rest, it was formula film-making with a screenplay by Marion Orth, Paul Gerard Smith and Brenda Weisberg (story by Sam Robins) in which a college graduate, after being tricked by a producer into persuading his dress-manufacturing father to put up the coin for a show, finds that the producer has absconded with the money. A happy ending, however, is provided by the manufacturer's employees, who resourcefully stage a fashion show to everyone's satisfaction, turning imminent disaster into triumph. Director Charles Lamont, alas, was unable to do the same for his film, nor could a cast that included Mischa Auer (centre), George Barbier, Joe Brown Jr, Walter Catlett and Charles Lane. Ken Goldsmith produced. Songs: *Boogie Woogie Boogie Man; Dancing On Air; Walk With Me; Two Weeks Vacation With Pay; Mr Yankee Doodle; We Too Can Sing* Everett Carter, Milton Rosen.
▽

△

Four musical numbers, two by Ted Lewis (left) and two by The Andrews Sisters, tended to reduce the lickety-split pace set by director Arthur Lubin in **Hold That Ghost** (Universal), another successful Abbott and Costello (illustrated) vehicle which took place for most of its running time in the allegedly haunted house the duo inherit after the murder of a gangster. Costello, as usual, was the chief victim of the strange goings on that bedevil the manse, and one of the funniest sequences involved an airborne candle that stubbornly refuses to perform when Costello's shrieks bring Abbott racing into the room. Joan Davis played a professional radio screamer whose voice fails her at a crucial moment in Robert Lees and Fred Rinaldo's plot (screenplay by Lees, Rinaldo and John Grant), with Richard Carlson, Mischa Auer, Evelyn Ankers (another well-known screamer), Marc Lawrence, Shemp Howard and Russell Hicks also contributing to the fun. The associate producers were Bert Kelly and Glenn Tryon. Songs: *Sleepy Serenade* Mort Greene, Lou Singer; *Aurora* Harold Adamson, Mario Lago, Roberto Roberti; *When My Baby Smiles At Me* Harry von Tilzer, Andrew B. Sterling; *Me And My Shadow* Billy Rose, Al Jolson, Dave Dreyer.

As World War II continued, audiences looked for escapist entertainment and musical movies continued to abound – or, as in the case of **Navy Blues** (Warner Bros.), to rebound. This particular offering attached some songs by Arthur Schwartz and Johnny Mercer to a really pathetic story which did no more than follow a noisy crew on a frenzied journey to Honolulu. Lloyd Bacon directed a cast that included Ann Sheridan, Jack Oakie (right), Martha Raye, Jack Haley (left), Herbert Anderson, Jack Carson and Jackie Gleason, none of whom could rescue the drivel written by Sam Perrin, Jerry Wald, Richard Macaulay and Arthur T. Horman, and produced by Hal B. Wallis and Jerry Wald, with choreography by Seymour Felix. Songs: *In Waikiki; You're A Natural; Navy Blues; When Are We Going To Land Abroad?*
▽

Forties Musicals

Walt Disney returned to his beloved animal kingdom with **Dumbo** (RKO), a short (64 minutes) but near-perfect feature cartoon whose simple story about a circus elephant who could fly offered Disney's animators many opportunities for invention – all of them brilliantly seized. Less ambitious in concept than either *Snow White And The Seven Dwarfs* (RKO, 1937) or *Pinocchio* (RKO, 1940), it was one of the most heart-warming of all Disney's cartoon features and, in the justly celebrated Pink Elephant sequence, contained some of the finest animation the screen has ever seen. Though it took only a year and a half from conception to completion, and cost under a million dollars to make (compared with *Snow White*'s $1,750,000 four years earlier), **Dumbo** (see illustration) remains one of the most enchanting entertainments of the decade. The voices of Edward Brophy, Herman Bing, Verna Felton, Sterling Holloway and Cliff Edwards were heard on the soundtrack; the story was by Helen Aberson and Harold Pearl, and the supervising director was Ben Sharpsteen. Songs included: *Look Out For Mr Stork*; *Baby Mine*; *All Aboard*; *Pink Elephants On Parade*; *When I See An Elephant Fly* Oliver Wallace, Frank Churchill, Ned Washington.

Producer Hal Roach called **All-American Co-Ed** (United Artists), which ran a mere 48 minutes, a 'streamlined' featurette. A campus programmer in which Johnny Downs (who started in the business as a Roach 'Our Gang' kid) drags up as a blonde *femme fatale* and enters a rival university's beauty contest, it also starred Frances Langford (left) who, together with Downs and a group called The Tanner Sisters, shared the show's four songs. Also cast were Harry Langdon (right) as a press agent, Marjorie Woodworth, Noah Beery Jr, Esther Dale (centre) and impressionist Kent Rogers whose imitation of Gary Cooper was spot on. The screenplay was by Cortland Fitzsimmons from an adaptation (by Kenneth Higgins) of an original story by Hal Roach Jr and the choreographer LeRoy Prinz. Prinz also directed and co-produced. Songs: *I'm A Chap With A Chip On My Shoulder*; *Up At The Crack Of Dawn*; *The Farmer's Daughter* Charles Newman, Walter G. Samuels; *Out Of The Silence* Lloyd B. Norlind.
▽

The first of two films to feature popular band leader Glenn Miller, **Sun Valley Serenade** (20th Century-Fox) also saw a return to the screen, after a two-year absence, of Sonja Henie. Though Mr Miller and Miss Henie had absolutely nothing in common, the combination of their respective talents struck a responsive chord in war-time audiences, and the film was a smash. About the romantic complications that arise when Miller's manager (John Payne) agrees to keep a watchful eye on a pretty Norwegian refugee (Henie), its lightweight plot (by Art Arthur and Robert Harari; screenplay by Robert Ellis and Helen Logan) proved the perfect foundation on which to build several musical numbers, the highlight being a climactic skating ballet choreographed by Hermes Pan and breathtakingly performed by Miss Henie on black ice. The score by Mack Gordon and Harry Warren was a humdinger, with 'Chattanooga-Choo-Choo', danced by The Nicholas Brothers (illustrated) and Dorothy Dandridge, an absolute show-stopper. Also making it into the pop charts were 'It Happened In Sun Valley', 'I Know Why (And So Do You)' and 'The Kiss Polka'. Andy Razaf and Joe Garland's 'In The Mood' was featured too. Milton Berle, Lynn Bari (vocals dubbed by Pat Friday) and Joan Davis were also in it for producer Milton Sperling, and the director was H. Bruce Humberstone. Interesting sideline: Because the film was running over budget, Darryl F. Zanuck specified that the black-ice finale had to be completed in three days. On the third day, just as the sequence was being wrapped up, Henie crashed into one of the male skaters, fell, and covered herself in black dye. Zanuck flatly refused to allow choreographer Hermes Pan an extra day to reshoot, so, just before Miss Henie's fall, the film dissolves to a shot of her and John Payne skiing down one of Sun Valley's slopes in ◁ lieu of the ending originally planned.

A remake of *That Girl From Paris* (RKO, 1936), which was itself a remake of *Street Girl* (Radio Pictures, 1929), **Four Jacks and A Jill** (RKO) was a confusing Irish stew of a musical in which four struggling musicians (Ray Bolger, William Blees, Eddie Foy Jr and Jack Briggs) adopt a hungry girl (Anne Shirley, left) who then poses as a European singer and an intimate of royalty in an attempt to find employment. Desi Arnaz (centre left) appeared as a taxi driver, and June Havoc, sister of Gypsy Rose Lee, made her debut as a nightclub *chanteuse* called Opal. Jack Durant appeared as Ardle McNardle, a gangster, with other parts in producer John Twist's incomprehensible screenplay (story by Monte Brice) going to Fritz Feld (right), Henry Daniell, Robert Smith and Fortunio Bonanova. Apart from some nifty dancing by Ray Bolger (centre right), especially a pantomime routine of a prize-fighter meeting the champ, the film had little, if any entertainment value at all. Jack Hively directed. Songs: *I'm In Good Shape (For The Shape I'm In)*; *Karanina*; *Wherever You Are*; *I Haven't A Thing To Wear*; *Boogie Woogie Conga*; *You Go Your Way (And I'll Go Crazy)* Mort Greene, Harry Revel.
▽

A slapstick cowboy musical, **Go West Young Lady** (Columbia) never quite made it, despite a promising cast that included Penny Singleton (illustrated), Glenn Ford, Ann Miller, Charles Ruggles and Jed Prouty. Largely to blame for its lack of sparkle was its screenplay (by Richard Flournoy and Karen De Wolf; story by De Wolf), a clichéd oater all about a new marshal who rids the town of a menace masquerading under the name of Pecos Pete. The songs were by Saul Chaplin and Sammy Cahn, the best two being 'I Wish I Could Be A Singing Cowboy' and 'Somewhere On The Trail'. Robert Sparks produced, Frank Strayer directed, and the cast included Allen Jenkins, Edith Meiser, The Foursome, and Bob Wills and His Texas Playboys. Other musical numbers: *Go West Young Lady*; *Most Gentlemen Don't Prefer A Lady*; *Doggy Take Your Time*; *Rise To Arms (The Pots And Pans Parade)*.
▽

△

Lady Be Good (MGM) was a curate's egg of a show. It had five excellent songs, a wham-bang finale staged by Busby Berkeley to George and Ira Gershwin's 'Fascinatin' Rhythm', and a cast that included Eleanor Powell, Ann Sothern, Robert Young, Lionel Barrymore, John Carroll, Red Skelton and Dan Dailey. Yet, whenever the music stopped, the movie was quite asphyxiatingly boring. The fault, as was so often the case, lay in the written word and, as written by Jack McGowan, Kay Van Riper and John McClain, the words were stinkers. Bearing absolutely no resemblance to the Gershwin stage hit of the same name, this **Lady Be Good** told an interminable story about a pair of songwriters (Sothern and Young) who split up after composer Young allows success to go to his head. They are re-united, but acrimony will out, and once again they part. But not for long. Remorseful of his behaviour Young begs Sothern to take him back yet again, and, if only to ensure a happy ending, she does. Though Eleanor Powell (illustrated) received top-billing, she hardly impinged on the narrative at all, her main purpose being to pep up proceedings with three tap routines, including the finale for which she was joined by eight grand pianos, a hundred male dancers in white tie and tails as well as canes, a spectacular 65-foot chiffon curtain that zig-zagged across 2000 square feet of sound stage, plus the dancing Berry Brothers and singer Connie Russell. It was Ann Sothern, however, who sang the durable number 'The Last Time I Saw Paris' (by Oscar Hammerstein II and Jerome Kern), an especially poignant moment in view of Paris's recent occupation by the Germans. Norman Z. McLeod directed and the producer was Arthur Freed. Other songs included: *Lady Be Good* George and Ira Gershwin; *You'll Never Know* Roger Edens; *Your Words And My Music* Arthur Freed, Edens.

△

Jane Frazee (left), Leon Errol, Mischa Auer, Johnny Downs (right), Sunnie O'Dea, Maria Montez, Marjorie Gateson, Richard Carle and The Merry Macs tried valiantly to pummel some life into **Moonlight in Hawaii** (Universal), but the Morton Grant-James Gow-Erna Lazarus screenplay (from a story by Eve Greene) just lay there – stubbornly resisting all help. Errol and Carle played a couple of Hawaiian pineapple juice manufacturers, each on the make for wealthy Miss Gateson whose money they covet; while Downs and the Merry Macs spent most of the film's 59-minute running time trying to appear on either Errol or Carle's radio programme. The film's one production number – 'Aloha Low Down' (by Don Raye and Gene De Paul) featured several hula girls and an orchestra conducted by Mischa Auer. Ken Goldsmith produced and his director – who was totally unable to make head or tail of it – was Charles Lamont. Songs: *It's People Like You*; *Poi*; *We'll Have A Lot Of Fun*; *Moonlight In Hawaii* Raye, De Paul; *Hawaiian War Chant* Ralph Freed, Johnny Noble, Prince Leliohaku of Hawaii.

Forties Musicals

Columbia's classiest, most expensive musical to date, **You'll Never Get Rich**, had a score by Cole Porter and starred Fred Astaire and Rita Hayworth (illustrated) – together for the first time. Yet, despite the 'triumphant teaming of beauty and rhythm' as the ads put it, the film came to life only in flashes and hardly lived up to the promise of its attractive ingredients. The story of a Broadway dance director who finds himself drafted into the army, its only surprise lay in Hayworth's extraordinary abilities as a dancer. The equal of her illustrious partner in grace and precision, she danced her way through several numbers – most notably the 'Boogie Barcarolle', and 'So Near And Yet So Far', revealing herself, in the opinion of many, to be one of the best partners Astaire ever had – notwithstanding Ginger Rogers. Certainly she was a better dancer than Rogers, but whether or not she was a better partner, remains open to debate. Other musical highlights included 'The A-stairable Rag' danced by Astaire and backed by the Delta Rhythm Boys (Buddy Colette on clarinet, A. Grant on guitar, Chico Hamilton on drums, Red Mack on trumpet, Joe Comfort on a jug); 'Shootin' The Works For Uncle Sam' (Astaire and a bevy of pretty chorus girls), and the 'Wedding Cake Walk', a production number (staged by Robert Alton) featuring a chorus line of fifty, in a set comprising a giant wedding cake with a tank on top of it. The film also starred Robert Benchley as a producer up to his neck in romantic entanglements, with John Hubbard, Osa Massen, Frieda Inescort, Guinn Williams, Donald MacBride, Cliff Nazarro, Ann Shoemaker and Marjorie Gateson in support. The direction was by Sidney Lanfield for producer Samuel Bischoff. Other songs and musical numbers: *Since I Kissed My Baby Goodbye*; *Dream Dancing*.

In its modest way **Zis Boom Bah** (Monogram), a college caper, was a triumph of professionalism over poor material, with featured performers Grace Hayes, Peter Lind Hayes (her real-life son), Mary Healy (left) and Benny Rubin refusing to be floored by Connie Lee and Harvey Gates's hoary old screenplay, or the conspicuous lack of anything resembling an adequate budget. Miss Hayes played a successful musical comedy star who is reunited with her college-student son after twenty years. Grace buys her boy a café which she then transforms into a fashionable theatre restaurant, and the film ends with a floor show staged by local students – the best of the bunch being a young dancer called Roland Dupree. Skeets Gallagher, Huntz Hall, Jan Wiley (right), Frank Elliott, Eddie Kane and Leonard Sues completed the cast, and the director was veteran William Nigh. Songs: *Annabella*; *It Makes No Difference When You're In The Army* Johnny Lange, Lew Porter; *Put Your Trust In The Moon* June Baldwin, Charles Callender; *Zis Boom Bah* Elaine Cannon; *Good News Tomorrow*; *I've Learned To Smile Again* Neville Fleeson.

Having neatly tucked the army and the navy under their comic belts, Abbott and Costello did the inevitable and, in **Keep 'em Flying** (Universal), their fourth film in 1941, joined the air-force. They, in turn, were joined by Martha Raye (illustrated) playing twin sisters, one of whom adores Costello (illustrated) while the other does not. The usual A. and C. 'shtick' permeated the proceedings, with plot once again taking second place to it. The new songs were by Don Raye and Gene De Paul, best of which was the very popular 'Pig Foot Pete' sung by Miss Raye, and 'You Don't Know What Love Is'. Dick Foran was in it too, as a stunt flyer, and the cast was completed by Carol Bruce, William Gargan, Charles Lang, Truman Bradley, William Davidson and Loring Smith. It was written by True Boardman, Nat Perrin and John Grant from a story by Edmund Hartmann and directed by Arthur Lubin. Other songs included: *Together*; *I'm Looking For The Boy With The Wistful Eyes*; *Let's Keep 'Em Flying* Raye, De Paul; *I'm Getting Sentimental Over You* Ned Washington, George Bassman.

A tribute of sorts to the Original Dixieland Jazz Band, a quintet of musicians who helped introduce jazz to the white folk, **Birth of the Blues** (Paramount) was an entertaining, if somewhat simplistic, account of the rough passage had by jazz when it first infiltrated the consciousness of a generation more at home with the staid rhythms of the waltz. Bing Crosby (in one of his favourite roles) played an itinerant clarinettist who fetches up in New Orleans and, together with a rag-bag collection of musicians, including a hot trumpet player (Brian Donlevy) whose services he acquires after bailing him out of jail, sets up shop in a posh Bourbon Street niterie and, after a couple of initial set-backs, becomes the hottest thing in the Vieux Carré. Mary Martin (illustrated) co-starred as a singer who joins his group and, in a snappy performance of 'Wait Till The Sun Shines Nellie' (by Andrew Sterling and Harry von Tilzer) came as near to movie greatness as she ever would. Other musical highlights included 'The Waiter And The Porter And The Upstairs Maid' (by Johnny Mercer), sung by Crosby, Martin and Jack Teagarden, and an impassioned account of W.C. Handy's classic 'St Louis Blues' by Ruby Elzy. Harry Tugend and Walter DeLeon wrote it (story by Tugend) with parts for Eddie (Rochester) Anderson (illustrated left), Jack Teagarden (and his orchestra), J. Carrol Naish, Warren Hymer, Horace MacMahon, and a monstrous moppet called Carolyn Lee. It was directed by Victor Schertzinger, who died shortly after its completion. Other songs: *Gotta Go To The Jailhouse*

Robert E. Dolan, Harry Tugend; *Memphis Blues* W.C. Handy; *By The Light Of The Silvery Moon* Edward Madden, Gus Edwards; *Tiger Rag* The Original Dixieland Jazz Band; *Waiting At The Church* Henry Pether, F.W. Leigh; *Cuddle Up A Little Closer* Otto Harbach, Karl Hoschna; *Shine* Lew Brown, Cecil Mack, Ford Dabney; *My Melancholy Baby* George Norton, Ernie Burnett; *St James Infirmary* Joe Primrose; *Birth Of The Blues* Buddy De Sylva, Lew Brown, Ray Henderson; *At A Georgia Camp Meeting* Kerry Mills.

Strictly for hinterland audiences, Republic's **Puddin' Head** (GB: **Judy Goes to Town**) was a corny-copia of hayseed gags dispensed, in the main, by Judy Canova (right), who played a country gal (what else?) living on a farm in the middle of Fifth Avenue, New York. Her property is encroached upon by a neighbouring skyscraper, and her privacy by a couple of city slickers (Raymond Walburn and Eddie Foy Jr) who do their best to get her to sell. Slim Summerville was also cast, and so were Francis Lederer (illustrated left), Astrid Allwyn, Alma Kruger, Hugh O'Connell, Chick Chandler, Paul Harvey, and The Sportsmen. Jack Townley and Milton Gross wrote it (original story by Townley), with additional dialogue by Howard Snyder and Hugh Wedlock Jr. Albert J. Cohen produced and the flaccid direction was by Joseph Santley. Songs and musical numbers included: *Hey Junior; You're Telling I; Manhattan Holiday; Puddin' Head* Eddie Cherkose, Sol Meyer, Jule Styne.

Forties Musicals

Having previously been down Argentine Way, and spent a night in Rio, audiences were invited to take time off for a **Week-End in Havana** (20th Century-Fox), another tuneful and colourful excursion into Latin America – Hollywood style – with Alice Faye and Carmen Miranda (illustrated) joined, this time, by John Payne. Story had Faye (as a Macy's shop girl) being given a free weekend in Havana after her cruise ship runs aground in a storm, and falling head over heels for shipping executive Payne. Miranda (now earning $5,000 a week), played a night-club entertainer (her usual role on such occasions) who has a crush on co-star Cesar Romero, and she was a knockout in the climactic 'The Nango' (by Mack Gordon and Harry Warren), excitingly staged by Hermes Pan. Cobina Wright Jr, George Barbier, Sheldon Leonard, Leonid Kinsky and Billy Gilbert also appeared, it was written by Karl Tunberg and Darrell Ware, produced by William Le Baron, and breezily directed for the mindless escapism it was, by Walter Lang. Other songs: *Tropical Magic; A Weekend In Havana; When I Love I Love* Gordon, Warren; *Romance And Rhumba* Gordon, James V. Monaco; *Mama Inez* L. Wolfe Gilbert, Eliseo Grenet; *Rebola A Bola* Oliveira, Almaro.
▽

◁ **The Chocolate Soldier** (MGM) was something of a curiosity. Plot-wise it had nothing whatsoever to do with the Oscar Straus operetta (based on Shaw's *Arms And The Man*) from which it took its title, although it retained several of the score's more popular numbers such as 'My·Hero', 'Sympathy' and 'The Flower Presentation'. It was, in fact, a modest remake of Ferenc Molnar's *The Guardsman*, which first reached the screen via MGM in 1931 as a vehicle for the distinguished husband-and-wife team, Alfred Lunt and Lynn Fontanne. In the remake, Nelson Eddy had the Lunt role, with opera star Rise Stevens as his wife. Instead of their being actors, the new version (with a screenplay by Leonard Leigh and Keith Winter) cast them (illustrated) as opera stars currently appearing in Straus's 'The Chocolate Soldier' and, as was the case with *Sweethearts* (MGM 1938), the operetta extracts heard in the film were featured as part of a show-within-a-show. The story of a husband so jealously in love with his wife that he appears to her in disguise in order to test her fidelity, it gave Eddy his best-ever opportunity to shine. And although his 'straight' moments as the jealous spouse were lamentably unconvincing, his performance while masquerading as a flamboyant Cossack, was a revelation, and the most effective piece of acting he ever committed to film. Nigel Bruce, Florence Bates, Dorothy Gilmore, Nydia Westman, Max Barwyn and Charles Judels completed the cast; it was directed by Roy Del Ruth for producer Victor Saville, with Ernst Matray in charge of the musical staging. Other songs and musical numbers: *Thank The Lord The War Is Over; Ti-ra-la-la; Seek The Spy* Straus, Stanislaus Stange; *While My Lady Sleeps* Bronislau Kaper, Gus Kahn; *Mephistopheles' Song Of The Flea* Mussorgsky; *Mon Coeur S'Ouvre A Ta Voix* (from 'Samson and Delilah') Saint-Saens.

An insubstantial jape, **Rise and Shine** (20th Century-Fox) starred Jack Oakie (illustrated) as Boley Bolenciecwcz, a brainless footballer placed in the charge of a screwy professor (Donald Meek) and his family, and whose well-being is a major concern of a big-time gambler from New York called Jimmy M'Gonigle (Sheldon Leonard). Just why, didn't really matter. What did was Oakie's engaging central performance (one of his best ever), plus the excellent support offered by George Murphy as Leonard's under-cover man, Linda Darnell (illustrated centre) as the love interest, Walter Brennan, Milton Berle, Ruth Donnelly, Raymond Walburn and Donald MacBride. Based on James Thurber's *My Life And Hard Times*, its genuinely wacky screenplay was by Herman J. Mankiewicz and it was produced by Mark Hellinger, with Allan Dwan directing at an exuberant pace. Songs: *I'm Making A Play For You; Central Two Two Oh Oh; I Want To Be The Guy; Hail To Bolenciecwcz; Get Thee Behind Me Clayton; Men Of Clayton* Ralph Rainger, Leo Robin.
▽

Blues in the Night (Warner Bros.) was a compact little musical with a serious flavour that, despite an intermittent tendency to melodrama, made for above average entertainment. A pretty accurate account of the milieu inhabited by itinerant jazz musicians as they drift through a series of one-night engagements and involve themselves with a variety of women, Robert Rossen's screenplay (from a play by Edwin Gilbert) was given strong support by his principal actor, Richard Whorf (later to become a well-known director) with a cast that included Priscilla Lane, Betty Field (centre), Lloyd Nolan (right), Jack Carson (left), Wallace Ford (background) and Billy Halop. Jimmy Lunceford and Will Osborne, with their orchestras, were also featured, and Elia Kazan appeared as a clarinettist. Director Anatole Litvak kept a perceptive grip on the proceedings for producer Henry Blanke, and Johnny Mercer and Harold Arlen wrote the songs, two of which were notable: the great title standard, which was introduced in the film by William Gillespie with the Lunceford orchestra, and 'This Time The Dream's On Me' (sung by Priscilla Lane). Other songs: *Hang On To Your Lids Kids*; *Says Who, Says You, Says I*.

With their filming of Olson and Johnson's **Hellzapoppin'**, Universal were clearly not prepared to emulate the risks taken with the stage version, and their reticence was spelled out at the beginning of the movie when Richard Lane (playing the director) quite categorically told Messrs O. and J. (illustrated centre) that there has to be more to a film than just a rag-bag collection of gags. After all, he exclaims, 'This is Hollywood, we change everything here. We've *got* to.' And they did, adding a routine love triangle between Robert Paige (who is endeavouring to stage a show at his palatial Long Island estate), Jane Frazee, and Lewis Howard. Martha Raye was also in it, her chief contribution to the unorthodox proceedings being to pursue Mischa Auer (as a moneyed count), and to sing the zany 'Watch The Birdie' (by Don Raye and Gene De Paul). A hit and miss affair with lots of good sight gags and an equal amount of laboured ones, **Hellzapoppin'**'s chief fault was that it went only so far when it should have gone further. The result was a curious hybrid that left audiences more baffled than entertained. Hugh Herbert popped in and out of the film as a private detective; Shemp Howard surfaced briefly as a cinema projectionist, and Clarence Kolb, Nella Walker, Katherine Johnson, Elisha Cook Jr, and a specialty act called Slim and Sam were also featured. It was written by Nat Perrin and Warren Wilson (story by Perrin) with H.C. Potter directing for producer Jules Levey. Other songs: *What Kind Of Love Is This?*; *You Were There*; *Heaven For Two*; *Hellzapoppin'*; *Putting On The Dog*; *Congeroo*; *Conga Beso* Raye, De Paul; *Waiting For The Robert E. Lee* L. Wolfe Gilbert, Lewis F. Muir.

Playmates (RKO) offered audiences the sad and sorry spectacle of John Barrymore at the end of his professional tether. Giving a wildly undisciplined performance, he masochistically caricatured and parodied himself, playing a much-married, out-of-work actor who, in order to land a radio contract and rid himself of his creditors, agrees to give Kay Kyser (right) a crash course in Shakespeare. The result? A ghastly finale in which Mr K. and his Kollege of Knowledge put a beat to the bard's iambic pentameters and did some terrible things to *Romeo and Juliet*. Lupe Velez was in it too (as a lady bull-fighter); so were May Robson, Patsy Kelly, Peter Lind Hayes, and Kyser regulars Ginny Simms (centre), Harry Babbitt (left), Ish Kabibble and Sully Mason. James V. Kern wrote it from a story he devised with M.M. Musselman (additional dialogue by Arthur Phillips) and it was produced and directed by David Butler. Songs: *Humpty Dumpty Heart*; *How Long Did I Dream?*; *Que Chica*; *Thank Your Lucky Stars And Stripes*; *Romeo Smith And Juliet Jones* Johnny Burke, Jimmy Van Heusen.

▽

If brevity is the soul of wit, it can also do wonders for a slender story, as demonstrated in **Fiesta** (United Artists), another of producer Hal Roach's 'streamlined' quickies which ran only 43 minutes. Brilliantly photographed in Technicolor and featuring five numbers, it told the simple story of a suitor's successful attempts to win back the love of his fiancée after she switches her affections. Ann Ayars was top-billed as the fickle lass at the heart of the tale, with George Negrete and George Givot (right) as the men in her life. It all took place during a fiesta on a Mexican ranch owned by Antonio Moreno, with Miss Ayars and Negrete, as well as Armida (illustrated centre), Jose Arias and His Mexican Tipica Orchestra and the Guadalajara Trio supplying the music. Courtland Fitzsimmons supplied the dialogue from an adaptation by Kenneth Higgins, and the director was LeRoy Prinz (who also co-produced). Songs: *El Ralajo* Lamberto Layva, Jesus Castillion, Oscar Felix; *I'll Never Forget Fiesta* Bob Wright, Chet Forrest, Nilo Menendez; *Never Trust A Jumping Bean*; *Quien Sabe* Wright, Forrest, Ed Ward; *La Golondrina* Narciso Serradell.

1942

The young 'uns were at it again in **Get Hep to Love** (GB: **It Comes Up Love**) whose faintly ludicrous story (by M.M. Musselman, screenplay by Jay Dratler) was little more than a funnel into which Universal poured all of its teenage talent. It starred Gloria Jean (left) now a ripe old 14, as a talented soprano who, to escape the greedy clutches of an exploiting aunt (Edith Barrett) runs away and gets herself adopted by a young married couple (Jane Frazee and Robert Paige). Miss Jean sang 'Sempre Libera' from Verdi's *La Traviata*, 'Villanelle' (by Eva Dell Acqua and Ralph Freed) and 'Drink To Me Only With Thine Eyes', in a manner that failed to bring the opera houses of the world clamouring to secure her services; and was supported by Donald O'Connor (right), Peggy Ryan, Cora Sue Collins, Nana Bryant, Irving Bacon and The Jivin' Jacks and Jills. The director was Charles Lamont. Other songs: *Siboney* Dolly Morse, Ernesto Lecuona; *Those Endearing Young Charms* Thomas Moore, Matthew Locke; *Let's Hitch A Horsie To The Automobile* Al Hoffman, Mann Curtis, Jerry Livingston; *Heaven For Two* Don Raye, Gene De Paul.
▽

Louisiana Purchase (Paramount), a Broadway musical with music and lyrics by Irving Berlin and a book by Morrie Ryskind from a story by Buddy De Sylva, reached the screen in glorious Technicolor with Bob Hope (illustrated centre) in the role originally created by William Gaxton. A sharp-witted satire on political corruption, the film had Hope being framed by his crooked associates and becoming the target of an investigation by US Senator Oliver P. Loganberry (Victor Moore, in the role he played in the Broadway production). Vera Zorina (also from the Broadway production) was cast as a dancer employed by the grafters to compromise Loganberry, with other roles going to Irene Bordoni (also from Broadway), Dona Drake, Andrew Tombes (2nd left), Donald McBride (left), Raymond Walburn (2nd right), Maxie Rosenbloom and Frank Albertson (right). Hope's big moment comes near the end when 'through courtesy of Jimmy Stewart' (who did the same thing in *Mr Smith Goes To Washington*, Columbia, 1939) he conducts a filibuster on the legislature, reciting *The Face On The Bar-room Floor* and reading from *Gone With The Wind*! The film, written for the screen by Jerome Chodorov and Herbert Fields, featured only four Berlin songs, and a ballet for Zorina. Buddy De Sylva produced, and the director was Irving Cummings. Songs: *Prologue: Take A Letter To Paramount Pictures* and *Before The Picture Starts; You're Lonely And I'm Lonely; Louisiana Purchase; It's A Lovely Day Tomorrow; Dance With Me (At the Mardi Gras)*.
◁

△

△
Those curious enough to find out **What's Cookin'** (Universal) (GB: **Wake Up and Dream**), left the cinema with very little on their plates. Really a jam session by The Andrews Sisters (Patti and Maxene, illustrated), Woody Herman and His Orchestra, Jane Frazee and The Jivin' Jacks and Jills, about a group of youngsters (Grace McDonald, Donald O'Connor, Gloria Jean, Peggy Ryan) determined to make it into show business. Robert Paige was the male lead with other parts going to Leo Carillo (centre right), Charles Butterworth (left), Billie Burke, Franklin Pangborn and little Susan Levine (right). Jerry Cady and Stanley Roberts wrote it and it was adapted by Haworth Bromley from a story by Edgar Allan Woolf. Edward F. Cline directed. Songs and musical numbers included: *What To Do* (Andrews Sisters) Sid Robin; *Blue Flame* (Herman) James Noble; *Woodchopper's Ball* (Herman) Joe Bishop, Herman; *I'll Pray For You* (Frazee, Andrews Sisters, Jean) Arthur Altman, Kim Gannon; *Amen (Yea-Man)* (Herman) Roger Segure, Bill Hardy, Vic Schoen; *You Can't Hold A Memory In Your Arms* (Frazee, Herman and orchestra) Hy Zaret, Arthur Altman; *If; Love Laughs At Anything* Don Raye, Gene De Paul.

Juke Box Jenny (Universal) offered 61 minutes of swing and jitterbug via the orchestras of Charles Barnet (left) and Wingy Manone, as well as The Milt Herth Trio and The King's Men. It had a story – a harebrained effort in which Harriet Hilliard (centre), through some manipulative exploitation by record salesman Ken Murray, becomes the Juke Box Jenny of the title – but it was just a thread on which to hang the musical numbers. Don Douglas, Iris Adrian, Marjorie Gateson, Sig Arno and Joe Brown Jr were also cast. Robert Lees, Fred Rinaldo, Arthur V. Jones and Dorcas Cochran wrote it; the associate producer was Joseph G. Sandford, and the director was Harold Young. Songs included: *Swing It Mother Goose; Give Out; Macumba* Everett Carter, Milton Rosen; *Fifty Million Nickels* Charles Barnet; *Sweet Genevieve* George Cooper, Henry Tucker; *Then You'll Remember Me* Alfred Bunn, Michael Balfe.
▽

If you took your cue from screenwriters Fred Finkelhoffe and Elaine Ryan and paid little attention to the plot of **Babes on Broadway** (MGM), it was possible to have a pretty good time. For the show was generously larded with songs, all of them expertly staged by Busby Berkeley, who also directed for producer Arthur Freed. Its narrative was little more than a formula contrivance (a bunch of kids get together to put on a settlement-house show in order to raise enough money to send some underprivileged children to the country), but its marquee value was enormous, with Mickey Rooney (right, voted the world's most popular star three years in a row) and Judy Garland (left) heading a cast that also included youngsters Ray McDonald, Virginia Weidler and Richard Quine, as well as Fay Bainter, Donald Meek, James Gleason, Luis Alberni and, playing himself, Alexander Woollcott. Though the film ended with a spectacular minstrel show featuring its two young stars in blackface, there were other pleasures along the way, such as the delightful 'How About You' (by Ralph Freed and Burton Lane), sung and danced by Rooney and Garland and staged in a modest living-room by Berkeley at his most resourceful and inventive; and the infectious 'Hoe Down' (by Freed and Roger Edens) performed by the younger members of the cast whose combined energy output was enough to light up Broadway. Also effective was

the shamelessly sentimental 'Chin Up, Cheerio, Carry on' (by E.Y. Harburg and Burton Lane) sung by Garland against a backdrop of the Houses of Parliament and other London landmarks, for English children everywhere; and a lengthy production number set in a derelict theatre, memories of whose past successes are conjured up in Mickey and Judy's imagination, as, in turn, they impersonate Scotland's very well known entertainer, Sir Harry Lauder, Walter Hampden (as Cyrano de Bergerac), Fay Templeton, George M. Cohan, Blanche Ring and Sarah Bernhardt. Mickey also did an impersonation of Carmen Miranda as she appeared in *Down Argentine Way* (20th Century-Fox, 1940) that was quite breathtakingly accurate. Other songs and musical numbers: *Babes On Broadway* Freed, Lane; *Bombshell From Brazil; Blackout Over Broadway* Edens; *Mama, Yo Quiero* Al Stillman, Jaraca and Vincente Paiva; *Franklin D. Roosevelt Jones* Harold Rome; *Anything Can Happen In New York* Harburg, Lane; *By The Light Of The Silvery Moon* Edward Madden, Gus Edwards; *Alabamy Bound* Buddy De Sylva, Bud Green, Ray Henderson; *Old Folks At Home (Swanee River)* Stephen Foster; *Waiting For The Robert E. Lee* L. Wolfe Gilbert, Lewis F. Muir; *Mary's A Grand Old Name; Yankee Doodle Boy* George M. Cohan; *She Is Ma Daisy* Sir Harry Lauder, J.D. Harper; *I've Got Rings On My Fingers* F.J. Barnes, R.P. Weston, Maurice Scott.

Forties Musicals

I Married an Angel (MGM) was the last, and least successful, film made by Jeanette Mac-Donald (illustrated centre) and Nelson Eddy as a team. Originally purchased by the studio in the early thirties as a vehicle for Miss MacDonald, but shelved because of its then slightly *risqué* content, it surfaced as a fairly successful Broadway musical in 1938, with words and music by Lorenz Hart and Richard Rodgers. MGM re-activated the property, but should never have bothered, for, as lumberingly scripted by Anita Loos, with performances by its principals, and direction by W.S. Van Dyke II to match, its rumour of a story became infected with elephantiasis. The charming insouciance of the original – in which a banker from Budapest marries a virginal angel then sets about to clip her wings – was reduced to a flat-footed romp with Eddy, as a middle-aged *roué*, falling asleep at his birthday party and dreaming that he marries a strait-laced angel who deserts him after he becomes bored with her lack of sophistication. The ending's twist was that, on awakening from the dream, he discovers the 'angel' among his guests. Totally bereft of the satirical observations on love and marriage that helped it garner plaudits on Broadway, the show was akin to a suet pudding in consistency, and failed to please even MacDonald and Eddy's less discriminating admirers. Also cast: Edward Everett Horton, Binnie Barnes, Reginald Owen, Douglass Dumbrille, Mona Maris and Janis Carter. The producer was Hunt Stromberg. Songs: *I Married An Angel* (MacDonald); *I'll Tell The Man In The Street* (Eddy); *Spring Is Here* (MacDonald, Eddy) Rodgers, Hart; *Tira Lira La* (children's and girl's ensemble), Rodgers, Bob Wright, Chet Forrest (Broadway's *At The Roxy Music Hall* with new lyrics); *A Twinkle In Your Eye* (MacDonald) Rodgers and Hart, additional lyrics Wright and Forrest; *Caprice Viennoise* (MacDonald) Fritz Kreisler; *Chanson Bohème* (MacDonald, Eddy) from Bizet's 'Carmen', English lyrics by Wright and Forrest; *Anges Purs* (MacDonald) from Gounod's 'Faust'; *Aloha Oe* (MacDonald) Queen Liliukalani of Hawaii; *Hey Butcher* (Eddy); *There Comes A Time* (Horton); *To Count Palaffi* (Horton); *May I Present The Girl* (Horton); *Now You've Met The Angel* (Eddy); *But What Of Truth* (MacDonald) Herbert Stothart, Wright, Forrest.

▽

△

Betty Grable of the legs and Victor Mature of the chest lent their limited talents to **Song of the Islands** (20th Century-Fox), a sun-drenched, Technicolored bit of romantic hokum designed to show off its two stars' physical attributes rather than their acting talents. Betty (foreground centre) played the daughter of an Irish beachcomber (Thomas Mitchell) now resident on a Pacific Island; Victor was the son of a cattle baron (George Barbier). While the two fathers feud over plantation rights and who owns what, their well-shaped offspring fall in love, fall out of love, and fall back into love with boring predictability. Between lovin' and hatin', a grass-skirted Betty took time off to sing 'Blue Shadows And White Gardenias' and 'O'Brien Has Gone Hawaiian' (by Mack Gordon and Harry Owens), and was joined by Hilo Hattie for a Mack Gordon-Harry Owens number called 'Sing Me A Song Of The Islands' and Gordon and Owens's 'Down On Ami Ami Oni Oni Isle'. Billy Gilbert appeared as a reformed cannibal, with other parts going to Jack Oakie, Lillian Porter, Hal K. Dawson, Amu Cordone, and Harry Owens and His Royal Hawaiians. The screenplay was the work of Joseph Schrank, Robert Pirosh, Robert Ellis and Helen Logan; Hermes Pan choreographed, it was produced by William Le Baron and directed by Walter Lang as if it were a brightly coloured travelogue. Which, in a sense, it was. Other songs and musical numbers: *Maluna Malolo Mawaena*; *What's Buzzin' Cousin* Gordon, Owens; *Hawaiian War Chant* Ralph Freed, Johnny Noble, Prince Leleiohaku of Hawaii; *Cockeyed Mayor Of Kaunakakai* R. Alex Anderson, Al Stillman; *Home On The Range* (authorship unknown).

Bud Abbott and Lou Costello found themselves on a dude ranch in **Ride 'em Cowboy** (Universal), the wide open spaces furnishing them with an abundance of sight gags (such as Costello attempting to ride the meanest bucking bronco in captivity). Actually, they're not cowboys at all, but peanut vendors mistaken for cowboys, just as co-star Dick Foran (illustrated, with Anne Gwynne), also masquerading as the real McCoy is nothing but a country-and-western singer-cum-author learning the tricks of his trade. It was unutterable nonsense from fade in to fade out, but Abbott and Costello fans devoured all 82 minutes of it at a gulp, turning it into another top-grossing smash for the studio. The Merry Macs appeared in place of the Andrews Sisters, and had two good Don Raye-Gene De Paul numbers in 'Wake Up Jacob' and 'Beside The Rio Tonto'. They were joined by Ella Fitzgerald in 'Rockin' 'n Reelin' (also by Raye and De Paul) with Ella branching out on her own for 'A Tisket A Tasket' which she adapted together with Al Feldman. The film's biggest hit, however, was Raye and De Paul's 'I'll Remember April' which they wrote with Patricia Johnston and which became an instant and enduring standard. Also cast: Johnny Mack Brown, Samuel S. Hinds, Douglass Dumbrille, Richard Lane, Charles Lane, Morris Ankrum, The Hi-Hatters, The Buckaroos Band and The Ranger Chorus of Forty. It was adapted by Harold Shumate from a story by Edmund L. Hartmann and scripted by True Boardman and John Grant, with Arthur Lubin directing for producer Alex Gottlieb. There was one other song, 'Give Me My Saddle', also by Raye and De Paul.

▽

△

Republic paid five thousand dollars for the rights to Lew Brown's stage musical **Yokel Boy** (GB: **Hitting the Headlines**) as a screen vehicle for Judy Canova who appeared in it on stage. But somewhere along the line the studio changed its plans. Canova was dropped from the project, and with her went the original story as well, only the title being retained. Russell Rouse was contracted to provide a completely different plot – and came up with an idea about a yokel (Eddie Foy Jr) whose only claim to fame is that he has seen more movies than anyone else in his particular part of the backwoods and can predict, with an amazing degree of accuracy, how much any given picture will gross in his home-

town. As a gag, the production assistant (Roscoe Karns) of a rundown Hollywood studio (Republic, perhaps?) hires his services, thereby unleashing a chain of events, none of which made much sense as scripted by Isabel Dawn. Albert Dekker was top-starred as a gangster, with other parts going to Joan Davis (illustrated centre, who sang a couple of numbers quite pleasantly), Alan Mowbray, Mikhail Rasumny, Lynne Carver and Marc Lawrence. Robert North produced and it was directed by Joseph Santley. Songs: *Comes Love*; *It's Me Again*; *Let's Make Memories Tonight*; *I Can't Afford To Dream* Lew Brown, Charles Tobias, Sammy Stept; *Jim* Caesar Petrillo, Nelson Shawn, Edward Ross.

⊲ Betty Grable received top billing for the first time in **Springtime in the Rockies** (20th Century-Fox), an altogether more satisfying musical than *Song Of The Islands*, though its content hardly won plaudits for originality. In fact, it was assembly-line stuff, but assembled by producer William Le Baron with such an astute sense of showmanship that only a few ungrateful customers were churlish enough to complain. The story had Grable and her co-star John Payne playing a couple of Broadway stars who love each other dearly but can't seem to hit it off in each other's company for very long. To boot, Payne has a roving eye for the ladies which offends Betty to such an extent that, in a fit of jealous pique, she pairs off with Cesar Romero (illustrated, with Grable). Equally piqued, Payne begins a liaison with Carmen Miranda. But it all sorts itself out in the end. Mack Gordon and Harry Warren provided a very whistleable score on which to peg the nonsense, the most durable number being 'I Had The Craziest Dream' performed by Harry James and Helen Forrest. Betty and Payne sang 'Run Little Raindrop Run' and, with Cesar Romero, indulged in some nifty terpsichory (courtesy of choreographer Hermes Pan) in 'A Poem Set To Music', as well as in the wham-bang finale 'Pan American Jubilee'. High-kicking Charlotte Greenwood joined the party; so did Edward Everett Horton, Frank Orth, and Jackie Gleason. There were some tantalizing shots of the Canadian rockies, and wrapping it all up in a pretty parcel, was Fox's shimmering Technicolor which, after Grable's legs, was the show's most attractive asset. Irving Cummings directed. A year after the film was made, Grable and Harry James were married. Other musical numbers: *Chattanooga Choo Choo*; *Tic Tac Do Meu Coracao Vermelho*, *Silva* (all performed by Miranda).

Busby Berkeley's contribution to **Born to Sing** (MGM) was a patriotic finale called 'The Ballad For Americans' – a laudatory piece of flag-waving to the land of the bold and the free in which 'Americans of all types' (as Berkeley put it) paraded around a revolving, 40-foot high platform, in rhythm to John Latouche and Earl Robinson's rousing and flagrant American propaganda. For the rest, it was a 'let's put on a show' effort with Virginia Weidler (2nd right) and Ray McDonald (3rd right) subbing for Judy Garland and Mickey Rooney. The results were pretty squirm-making, with Harry Clork and Franz G. Spencer's screenplay being the kind only its authors could love. Miss Weidler played a resourceful youngster whose father, an ex-convict but also a composer in his more ▽

honest moments, is being taken for a ride by an unscrupulous publisher. Angered into activity by the injustice of it all, a group of kids decide to bring the ex-con's music to the attention of the public by putting on a show and kidnapping the city's leading critics who are then forced to cover the opening. Also lending their services to the malarky were Rags Ragland, Douglas McPhail, Sheldon Leonard, Henry O'Neill, Larry Nunn (right), Leo Gorcey (2nd left), Beverly Hudson, Richard Hall and erstwhile Our Gang star, Darla Hood. The producer was Frederick Stephani and it was directed adequately by Edward Ludwig. Songs: *I Hate The Conga* Earl Brent; *Alone*; *You Are My Lucky Star* Arthur Freed, Nacio Herb Brown; *I Love Ya* Lennie Hayton, Earl Brent.

△

An unashamed contrivance designed solely to provide Bert Lahr, its star, with an opportunity to do his inimitable comic thing, **Sing Your Worries Away** (RKO) featured him as a carefree composer whose composure is understandably ruffled when co-star Sam Levene drives him to the brink of suicide in an attempt to lay his hands on his $3,000,000 inheritance. Lahr (centre) gave out with all the expected comic reactions to his unenviable situation, and now and again allowed stripper June Havoc, Dorothy Lovett (as his niece), Buddy Ebsen (right), Patsy Kelly and Margaret Dumont a chance to do their particular thing as well. But it was basically a one-man show which his fans devoured. The King Sisters and Alvino Rey and His Orchestra also appeared; Monte Brice wrote it from a story by Erwin Gelsey and Charles E. Roberts (idea by Charles S. Belden); Cliff Reid produced, Edward Sutherland directed. Songs: *It Just Happened to Happen*; *Sally, My Dear Sally*; *Sing Your Worries Away*; *Cindy Lou McWilliams*; *How Do You Fall In Love?* Mort Greene, Harry Revel.

Director Victor Schertzinger's **The Fleet's In** (Paramount), released posthumously, was brash war-time escapism, whose chief attraction was the appearance of a newcomer from Broadway named Betty Hutton. Recruited to Hollywood by studio chief Buddy De Sylva (who produced Betty's Broadway hit *Panama Hattie*), she sang the show's two best songs, 'Build A Better Mousetrap' and 'Arthur Murray Taught Me Dancing In A Hurry' (by Johnny Mercer and Victor Schertzinger), being joined in the latter by comedian Eddie Bracken of whom a little went a long way. The story, which had been made twice before – as *True To The Navy* with Clara Bow in 1930, and as *Lady be Careful* with Mary Carlisle and Lew Ayres in 1936 – centred on a painfully shy sailor (William Holden, illustrated) who is mistakenly believed to be a ladykiller, and whose buddies take bets as to whether or not he will be able to kiss an attractive but forbiddingly aloof nightclub singer known as The Countess (Dorothy Lamour, illustrated), and then persuade her to attend a party being given by the admiral's daughter (Cass Daley, making her debut). Holden succeeds on all counts, even winning Miss Lamour's affections in the end. Hutton played Lamour's irrepressible roommate and Bracken was the gob she falls for, with other roles going to Gil Lamb, Leif Erickson and Betty Jane Rhodes. The film also featured Tommy Dorsey and His Band, with Helen O'Connell and Bob Eberly. The screenplay was based on a play by Kenyon Nicholson and Charles Robinson, and it was written by Walter DeLeon, Sid Silvers and Ralph Spence (who were responsible for the earlier versions as well). The associate producer was Paul Jones. It was re-made yet again in 1961, by Paramount, as a vehicle for Dean Martin and Jerry Lewis called *Sailor Beware*. Other songs included: *I Remember You*; *When You Hear The Time Signal*; *The Fleet's In*; *Tomorrow You Belong To Uncle Sam*; *Why Doesn't Anything Happen To Me?*; *(It's Somebody Else's Moon) Not Mine*; *Tangerine* Mercer, Schertzinger.

Judy Canova, whose performances were about as subtle as Joe Louis's fists, turned up again in **Sleepytime Gal** (Republic), a mistaken identity effort with Canova (illustrated at piano) being taken for a gambler's singing moll whom several representatives of Chicago's underworld want eliminated. It was minor fare, written by Art Arthur, Albert Duffy and Max Lief from a story by Mauri Grashin and Robert T. Shannon, directed by Albert S. Rogell for associate producer Albert J. Cohen, and featured Tom Brown (left), Billy Gilbert, Ruth Terry, Thurston Hall, Elisha Cook Jr and Skinnay Ennis and His Band. Songs: *I Don't Want Nobody At All*; *Barrelhouse Bessie*; *When The Cat's Away* Jule Styne, Herb Magidson; *Sleepytime Gal* Richard A. Whiting, Ange Lorenzo, Joseph R. Alden, Ray Egan (all sung by Canova).

My Favourite Spy (RKO) proved, irrevocably, that Kay Kyser (illustrated) was no comedian, and his attempts to inject humour into a silly yarn about a bandleader chosen by Army Intelligence to infiltrate a spy ring which hangs out in the very club in which he and his band are appearing, were painfully inept. But then so was the whole sorry enterprise, with Ellen Drew, Jane Wyman (left), Helen Westley, William Demarest, Una O'Connor, Hobart Cavanaugh and Moroni Olsen working in vain to bring credence to Sig Herzig and William Bowers's screenplay (from a story by M. Coates Webster). Harold Lloyd produced and the director was Tay Garnett. Songs included: *Just Plain Lonesome*; *Got The Moon In My Pocket* Johnny Burke, Jimmy Van Heusen.

The distinguished director William Dieterle ▷ came a terrible cropper with **Syncopation** (RKO), a ponderous tribute to the blues which succeeded only in passing on that colour to its audiences. Jackie Cooper appeared as a Chicago lad, Bonita Granville (illustrated) was the New Orleans girl he falls for. They have two things in common: a love of jazz and a passion for the poetry of Walt Whitman. Cooper played the trumpet (dubbed by Rex Stewart), so did co-star Todd Duncan (dubbed by Bunny Berigan), with Harry James, Benny Goodman, Charlie Barnet, Joe Venuti, Gene Krupa, Connee Boswell and the Hall Johnson Choir also going through their paces. Adolphe Menjou (illustrated extreme left) received top billing but didn't have very much to do, and the cast was completed by George Bancroft, Ted North, Frank Jenks and Jessie Grayson. It was written by Philip Yordan and Frank Cavett from a story by Valentine Davies, and produced by Dieterle. The film ran 88 minutes and featured 11 musical numbers. They included: *Goin' Up The River* Dave Torbett, Leith Stevens; *You Made Me Love You* Joseph McCarthy, James V. Monaco; *Only Worry For A Pillow*; *Chicago Ragtime* Stevens; *Under A Falling Star* Rich Hall, Stevens; *Slave Market* Hall Johnson.

Dennis O'Keefe and Jane Frazee (illustrated right) starred in **Moonlight Masquerade** (Republic), a trivial programmer whose trite story concerned an agreement by Jed Prouty (left) and Paul Harvey, owners of an oil company, to marry off their respective son and daughter to each other despite the fact that the young couple have never ever met. Complications, as they say, ensued. Lawrence Kimble wrote it, Nick Castle choreographed, and the cast was completed by Betty Kean, Eddie Foy Jr, Erno Verebes, Franklin Pangborn, Tommye Adams and The Three Chocolateers. John H. Auer thought up the story line, and also produced and directed. It was a decidedly unhappy Auer all round. Songs included: *What Am I Doing Here In Your Arms?* Mort Greene, Harry Revel.

Almost Married (Universal) was another Jane Frazee programmer in which Miss F. (right) as a nightclub singer does Robert Paige (left) a favour by agreeing to a mock marriage in order to help him out of a previous romantic entanglement. Naturally, the couple fall in love and, in the end, marry for real. The pickings on this one were slim, with Eugene Pallette (centre), Elizabeth Patterson, Charles Coleman and Maude Eburne also featured in Hugh Wedlock Jr and Howard Snyder's tenuous screenplay (story by Theodore Reeves). The director was Charles Lamont. Songs: *After All These Years*; *Take Your Place In The Sun*; *The Rhumba* Eddie Cherkose, Jacques Press; *Just To Be Near You*; *Mister Five By Five* Don Raye, Gene De Paul.
▽

James Cagney (illustrated centre) was superb as George M. Cohan in **Yankee Doodle Dandy** (Warner Bros.), the best musical of 1942 and one of the best biopics to come out of Hollywood. In fact, so convincing was Cagney's performance as the arrogant, energetic Cohan that not only did he win an Oscar for it, but he influenced future generations of Cohan mimics who, in their impressions of the pint-sized showman found themselves imitating Cagney's particular Cohan strut rather than the real thing. And who could blame them? For Cagney's performance, both physically and temperamentally, captured to perfection the appearance as well as the essence of the man. Cagney's talent and experience as a hoofer was also very much in evidence throughout, especially in LeRoy Prinz and Seymour Felix's brilliant staging of the big set piece featuring a lengthy extract from Cohan's early hit *Little Johnny Jones* (which Warner Bros. had filmed twice: as a silent in 1923, and again in 1930), and incorporating two of the maestro's biggest hits – 'Yankee Doodle Boy' and 'Give My Regards To Broadway'. Cagney's exuberant singing and dancing in both numbers positively glowed with vitality and it is doubtful whether Cohan himself could have performed them more convincingly or with more vigour. Though Robert Buckner and Edmund Joseph's warm and witty screenplay (story by Buckner based on the life of Cohan)

took certain liberties (Cohan was not, for example, born on July 4th but a day earlier), it was about as faithful a re-telling of the Cohan story as Hollywood was capable of, and although frequently embellishing certain particulars, it rarely deviated from the essentials. Thus we see Cohan in his early years, as part of a family vaudeville act known as The Four Cohans, and witness his big break in *Peck's Bad Boy*. We follow his successful association with producer Sam H. Harris (Richard Whorf), are in the stalls on the first night of the aforementioned *Little Johnny Jones*, and eavesdrop on his relationship with the girl who eventually becomes his wife, Mary (Joan Leslie). The narrative begins in 1937 with Cohan (who, at the time was appearing as President Roosevelt in *I'd Rather Be Right* by George Kaufman and Moss Hart, words and music by Rodgers and Lorenz Hart) paying a call on Roosevelt (Captain Jack Young) and relating his life story to him. The President decorates him for his services to the American Musical Theatre and, by the end of the film, we are left in no doubt as to how well deserved the decoration was. Walter Huston was cast as Cohan's father Jerry, with Rosemary De Camp as his wife and Jeanne Cagney as his sister Josie. Irene Manning played the legendary Fay Templeton, and did well by two more Cohan favourites, 'Mary's A Grand Old Name' and 'So Long Mary', with other roles going to George Barbier (as Erlanger), S.Z.

Sakall, Walter Catlett and Eddie Foy Jr who, as Eddie Foy Sr, shared one of the film's best scenes with Cagney in which the two men meet by chance with each pretending not to know who the other is. Frances Langford was also featured, and sang 'The Love Nest' (by Louis A. Hirsch and Otto Harbach) and 'Little Nellie Kelly' on her own, and was joined by Cagney for the rousing 'Over There'. She also sang 'In A Kingdom Of Our Own', 'The Man Who Owns Broadway', 'Molly Malone' and 'Billie'. All production credits were outstanding, with James Wong Howe's sharp black and white photography a joy throughout; ditto Carl Jules Weyl's art direction and Milo Anderson's costumes. The film was produced by Hal B. Wallis and William Cagney, and directed with awe-inspiring professionalism and considerable flair by versatile Michael Curtiz. Other songs and musical numbers: *45 Minutes From Broadway* (Cagney); *Harrigan* (Cagney, Leslie); *I Was Born In Virginia* (Cagney, Huston, De Camp, Jeanne Cagney); *You're A Grand Old Flag* (Cagney); *You're A Wonderful Girl* (Cagney, Huston, De Camp, Jeanne Cagney); *Off The Record* (from *I'd Rather Be Right* – Cagney); Medley comprising: *Blue Skies, Grey Skies*; *Oh You Wonderful Girl*; *The Barbers' Ball* (Cagney, Huston, De Camp, Jeanne Cagney); *The Warmest Baby In The Bunch* (Leslie) Cohan; *All Aboard For Old Broadway* (Chorus) Jack Scholl, M.K. Jerome.

20th Century-Fox returned to its favourite period, the gay nineties, for **My Gal Sal** on which it lavished all of its considerable resources. Main difference between this and other Fox sallies into musical nostalgia was the casting of Rita Hayworth (illustrated) in place of either Betty Grable or Alice Faye. It was a refreshing change and, as photographed in Technicolor by Ernest Palmer, Miss Hayworth (whose vocals were dubbed by Nan Wynn) never looked lovelier, or, as directed by Irving Cummings, appeared more radiant or more alluring. The story, purported to be based on a book by Theodore Dreiser called *My Brother Paul*, was a fundamentally fictitious account of the life and raucous times of composer Paul Dresser who, in the Gospel according to Saint Zanuck, rose from medicine man's assistant on the Wabash to become a Tin Pan Alley heart-throb turbulently in love with a fiery Broadway star (Hayworth). Victor Mature played the composer in question, and the success of his performance owed more to his beef-cake appearance than to his abilities as an actor. As the film was little more than a beautifully coiffured and costumed excuse to indulge in some period atmosphere and to showcase the talents of its lovely leading lady, there was an abundance of production numbers staged by Val Raset and Hermes Pan (the latter partnering Hayworth on one occasion) the best being 'On The Banks Of The Wabash' (by Dresser), 'On The Gay White Way' (by Ralph Rainger and Leo Robin), and the finale 'My Gal Sal' (also by Dresser). Carole Landis was shamefully wasted in a throw-away bit, and the cast was completed by John Sutton, James Gleason, Phil Silvers, Walter Catlett, Mona Maris, Frank Orth and Stanley Andrews. It was written to formula by Seton I. Miller, Darrell Ware and Karl Tunberg and produced by Robert Bassler. Other songs: *Mr Volunteer*; *The Convict And The Bird*; *Come Tell Me Your Answer Yes Or No*; *I'se Your Honey*; *If You Want Me*; *Liza Jane* Dresser; *Oh! The Pity Of It All*; *Here You Are*; *Midnight At The Masquerade*; *Me And My Fella And A Big Umbrella* Rainger, Robin; *Two Little Girls In Blue* Charles Graham; *Daisy Bell* Harry Dacre.

206

In their remake of the 1929 **Rio Rita** (RKO), MGM cast Bud Abbott (left) and Lou Costello (right) in the roles originally played by Bert Wheeler and Robert Woolsey, and co-starred the Universal money-makers with Kathryn Grayson (illustrated, in her second film; the first was *Andy Hardy's Private Secretary*, MGM), and John Carroll (centre) as the lovers. Being 1942, and with the world at war, scenarists Richard Connell and Gladys Lehman updated the story to include fifth columnists, saboteurs and other such cloak-and-dagger characters, never losing sight of the fact that it was, fundamentally, a vehicle for Abbott and Costello. And just to ensure that the laughs were as forthcoming as they usually were in the team's more modest efforts at Universal, producer Pandro S. Berman hired John Grant to supply them with special comedy material, such as the moment in which Costello finds himself part of the washing in a hotel laundry, or when the boys discuss a Pekinese owned by a Mrs Pike. S. Sylvan Simon directed, and his cast also included Patricia Dane, Tom Conway, Peter Whitney, Barry Nelson and Eros Volusia. Songs and musical numbers: *Ranger's Song*; *Rio Rita* Joseph McCarthy, Harry Tierney; *Long Before You Came Along* E.Y. Harburg, Harold Arlen; *Brazilian Dance* Nilo Barnet; *Ora O Conga* Lacerdo.
▽

◁ In **True to the Army** (Paramount) raucous Judy Canova of the extrovert mien joined the army, not as a girl, but as a fella, in order to escape the clutches of a racket gang. From then on it was uphill most of the way, with predictable routines about medical examinations, etc. etc. cluttering up much of the film's 76-minute running time. The good things came in the shape of shapely Ann Miller, and in the pleasant tenor of Allan Jones (both illustrated) – small but cherishable pleasures amid a welter of slapstick foolery that beset Art Arthur and Bradford Ropes's screenplay from a play by Howard Lindsay and a novel by Edward Hope (adapted by Edmund Hartmann and Val Burton). Jerry Colonna, Clarence Kolb, Edward Pawley, Rod Cameron and John Miljan completed the cast. Sol C. Siegel and Jules Scherman produced, and it was directed by Albert S. Rogell. Songs and musical numbers: *In The Army*; *Need I Speak*; *Jitterbug's Lullaby*; *Spangles On My Tights*; *Wacky For Khaki* Frank Loesser, Harold Spina; *Swing In Line* Loesser, Joseph J. Lilley; *Love In Bloom* Ralph Rainger, Leo Robin; *I Can't Give You Anything But Love* Dorothy Fields, Jimmy McHugh.

Pickle manufacturer Hugh Herbert's well-meaning interference in the lives of a couple of radio stars whose on-air marital spats are misinterpreted by him as being the real thing, formed the basis of **Don't Get Personal** (Universal), an unbelievably silly programmer whose unbelievably silly screenplay (by Hugh Wedlock Jr and Howard Snyder from a story by Bernard Feins) gave employment to Mischa Auer, Jane Frazee (left), Anne Gwynne, Robert Paige (right), Ernest Truex, Richard Davies and Sterling Holloway. Miss Frazee sang three songs (two with Robert Paige) but they hardly compensated for the inanities perpetrated in the narrative. Ken Goldsmith produced and the director was Charles Lamont. Songs: *It Doesn't Make Sense*; *Now What Do We Do?*; *Every Time A Moment Goes By* Jack Brooks, Norman Berens.
▽

Holiday Inn (Paramount) was a bumper musical
package that paired Bing Crosby and Fred
Astaire for the first time. They played a song-
and-dance team which splits up when Crosby
decides to take to the country and lead a life of
moderate relaxation – working only on public
holidays. In fact, he opens a Holiday Inn on New
Year's Eve dedicated to that very proposition –
and for 15 days a year, entertains the public
there. A romantic sub-plot involving Marjorie
Reynolds (whose singing voice was dubbed by
Martha Mears) and Virginia Dale slid easily into
the general scheme of things, without in any
way proving an encumbrance to the generous
musical programme provided by Irving Berlin –
who also thought up the story which Elmer Rice
adapted and Claude Binyon scripted. Each of the
15 public holidays celebrated in the film had
an accompanying song (July 4th had two), the
most famous of all being the staggeringly successful, timelessly popular 'White Christmas',
introduced, of course, by Crosby, whose Decca
recording went on to sell over 25 million copies.
In addition Crosby had nine other songs, and did
a duet with Astaire who, in turn, took the floor no
fewer than six times – most memorably in a
routine involving fire-crackers called 'Let's Say It
With Fire-Crackers'. The rest of the cast included
Walter Abel, Louise Beavers, Marek Windheim,
Irving Bacon, Jacques Vanaire, Harry Barris and
Bob Crosby's Bob Cats. Danny Dare staged the
musical numbers and it was produced and
directed by Mark Sandrich. **Holiday Inn** received
unanimously favourable reviews, grossed a for-
tune and even had a chain of motels named after
it. (Illustration shows Crosby and Marjorie Rey-
nolds, both in blackface, singing 'Abraham,
Abraham' in the 'Lincoln's Birthday' sequence).
Other songs and musical numbers: *I'll Capture
Your Heart Singing* (Crosby, Astaire, Dale); *Lazy*
(Crosby); *You're Easy To Dance With* (Astaire,
Dale, Reynolds); *Happy Holiday* (Crosby, Rey-
nolds); *Holiday Inn* (Crosby, Reynolds); *Let's
Start The New Year Right* (Crosby); *Be Careful, It's
My Heart* (Crosby, Astaire, Reynolds); *I Can't Tell
A Lie* (Astaire, Reynolds, Bob Cats); *Easter Parade*
(Crosby); *Song Of Freedom* (Crosby); *Plenty To Be
Thankful For* (Crosby).

The Mayor of 44th Street (RKO) was a real ▷
stinker. Not only that, but it gave young people
everywhere a bad name, for much of the plot
concerned the mean-minded activities of a
group of youngsters who round up their jit-
terbugging buddies and indoctrinate them into
the ways of delinquency. Chief victim was
hoofer George Murphy (right), whose dance-
band agency is the delinquents' chief target.
Their tactics are to bust up dance sessions in the
hope of receiving a payoff from the band that
happens to be playing at the time. Anne Shirley
(left) co-starred as Murphy's former dance
partner, William Gargan was a tolerant cop and
Richard Barthelmess a paroled hood who involves himself with the hooligans in an attempt
to streamline their operation. All very unsavoury indeed. Freddy Martin's band and vocalist Joan Merrill supplied most of the music.
Lewis R. Foster and Frank Ryan wrote it from a
story by Robert Andrews (suggested in turn
from a magazine article by Luther Davis and
John Cleveland), and it was directed by Alfred E.
Green for producer Cliff Reid. Songs: *Your Face
Looks Familiar; Heavenly, Isn't It?; Let's Forget It;
You're Bad For Me; A Million Miles From Manhattan; When There's A Breeze On Lake Louise* Mort
Greene, Harry Revel.

Based on the Phillip Dunning-George Abbott
play of the same name, **Broadway** (Universal),
first filmed in 1929, was remade for George Raft
who, playing himself, reminisced, in flashback,
about the good-old, bad-old days when he was a
Broadway hopeful whose career was temporarily bucked by various members of the under-
world and bootlegging fraternity, one of whom
even tried to steal his dance partner (Janet Blair)
from him. Raft playing Raft (illustrated, dancing) required no serious acting at all, and none
was forthcoming. Best performances were by
Pat O'Brien as a roving detective (a role he
had once played on stage), and Broderick Crawford as a killer. There was good work, too, from
Marjorie Rambeau (seated at piano), Anne
Gwynne, S.Z. Sakall (standing at piano), and
Edward Brophy. The screenplay was by Felix
Jackson and Don Bright, Bruce Manning
produced, and the director was William A.
Seiter. Songs and musical numbers: *Dinah* Joe
Young, Sam Lewis, Harry Akst; *Sweet Georgia
Brown* Ben Bernie, Kenneth Casey, Maceo Pin-
kard; *I'm Just Wild About Harry* Noble Sissle,
Eubie Blake; *The Darktown Strutters Ball; Some Of
These Days* Shelton Brooks; *Yes, Sir, That's My
Baby* Gus Kahn, Walter Donaldson; *Alabamy
Bound* B. De Sylva, Bud Green, Ray Henderson. ◁

△

△

△

Bambi (RKO) was Walt Disney's most naturalistic film. Based on the famous story by Felix Salten, it was low-keyed and the gentlest of all the Disney animated cartoons, and in its total commitment to its portrayal of the seasons and elements of nature, set a pattern that Disney would follow years later in his True-Life Adventure series. As in all past Disney cartoon features, colour and music played an important part in helping to create mood and atmosphere, the brilliantly detailed 'April Shower' sequence – revealing the forest at its most mysterious and beautiful – exemplifying the superb craftsmanship that went into every frame. In Bambi (illustrated) the world was introduced to the character of Thumper who, along with the seven dwarfs, Dumbo, and Jiminy Cricket, became a favourite with children everywhere. The film's supervising director was David D. Hand; the story was adapted by Larry Morey with Perce Pearce in charge of the story direction. No vocal credits were given. Songs: Love Is A Song; Let's Sing A Gay Little Spring Song; Little April Shower; I Bring You A Song Frank Churchill, Larry Morey.

A backstage musical starring John Payne, Betty Grable and Victor Mature, Footlight Serenade (20th Century-Fox) was the story of an egotistical prizefighter (Mature) who, after finding himself in the cast of a Broadway show, makes a play for chorus girl Grable (illustrated left). Trouble is, Betty's married to Payne, who is not at all amused by the flirtation and who, by the long arm of coincidence, has a scene in the show with Mature in which he spars with him. Now read on . . . Jane Wyman (right), James Gleason, Phil Silvers, Cobina Wright Jr and June Lang were also in it. Robert Ellis, Helen Logan and Lynn Starling wrote the screenplay from a story by Fidel La Barba and Kenneth Earl, it was efficiently directed by Gregory Ratoff, and the producer was William Le Baron. Somewhat surprisingly, the film was shot in black and white. Songs: Are You Kidding?; I'm Still Crazy For You; I Heard The Birdies Sing; Living High; I'll Be Marching To A Love Song; Land On Your Feet Ralph Rainger, Leo Robin; I'm Stepping Out With A Memory Tonight Herb Magidson, Allie Wrubel.

▽

As ridiculous as a zoot suit and just as shapeless, Private Buckaroo (Universal) was a 68-minute contribution (or hindrance) to the war effort that showed what happened when the Andrews Sisters joined forces with Harry James and His Music Makers to stage a show for servicemen. One good song emerged: 'Don't Sit Under The Apple Tree With Anyone Else But Me' by Lew Brown, Sammy Stept and Charles Tobias, splendidly harmonized by the trio. For the rest, it was little more than a jam session which utilized the talents of Dick Foran, Joe E. Lewis, Jennifer Holt, Shemp Howard (illustrated, with the Andrews Sisters), Richard Davies, Mary Wickes, Donald O'Connor, Peggy Ryan, Huntz Hall and The Jivin' Jacks and Jills. It was stencilled by Edmund Kelso and Edward James from a dozen or so previous Universal efforts (story by Paul Gerard Smith) and directed by Edward F. Cline. Songs: Three Little Sisters Irving Taylor, Vic Mizzy; Private Buckaroo Charles Newman, Allie Wrubel; Johnny Get Your Gun Again Don Raye, Gene De Paul; We've Got A Job To Do Vickie Knight; You Made Me Love You Joseph McCarthy, James V. Monaco; Six Jerks In A Jeep Sid Robin; That's The Moon My Son Art Kassel, Sammy Gallop.

△

Another Bud Abbott and Lou Costello caper, Pardon My Sarong (Universal) cast them as Chicago bus drivers whose involvement with a wealthy playboy yacht racer (Robert Paige, illustrated) leads to all sorts of unlikely adventures, including a skirmish with jewel thief Lionel Atwill and a chase through an island volcano and a Tarzan-like jungle. Native islander Nan Wynn (whose major contribution to the film industry was as Rita Hayworth's singing voice) was in charge of the musical side of things, with other parts going to Virginia Bruce as yachtsman Paige's sister, William Demarest, Leif Erickson, Samuel S. Hinds, and The Ink Spots who did a turn in a West Coast nightclub before the frantic events in True Boardman, Nat Perrin and John Grant's screenplay got underway. Also involved: The Sarango Girls, Jack La Rue, Tip, Tap And Toe, The Katherine Dunham Dancers and Charley The Seal. Katherine Dunham staged the dances and the director was Erle C. Kenton. Songs: Island Of The Moon; Lovely Luana; Vingo Jingo Don Raye, Gene De Paul; Do I Worry? Bobby Worth, Stanley Cowan; Shout Brother Shout Clarence Williams.

They should have handed out magnifying glasses to every customer attending Priorities on Parade (Paramount), so hard was it to find its plot. Those with 20-20 vision, however, might barely have discerned a piece of patriotism in the guise of entertainment, as a group of swing musicians took up employment in an aeroplane factory – including shapely Ann Miller (left), who looked a treat in overalls and, together with welder Betty Rhodes (centre), helped convey the message to American womanhood that their services in the war effort would be greatly appreciated. The film also featured Johnnie Johnston (right), Vera Vague (Barbara Allen), Harry Barris, Eddie Quillan, Dave Willock and an act called The Debonairs. A rag-bag of songs, dances, sketches, gags and anything else scriptwriters Art Arthur and Frank Loesser could think up as they went along, comprised the content of the film which Albert S. Rogell directed with as much subtlety as a pratfall. Songs: I'd Love To Know You Better; Here Comes Katrinka; Co-Operate With Your Air-Raid Warden; Concita Marquita Lolita Pepita Rosetta Juanita Lopez; Payday Herb Magidson, Jule Styne; You're In Love With Someone Else But I'm In Love With You Frank Loesser. Styne.

There was plot-a-plenty in Republic's Joan of Ozark (GB: Queen of Spies), a Judy Canova starrer, with Joe E. Brown (centre) and Eddie Foy Jr as the male leads. Canova was an Ozark hillbilly who, while quail-potting one day, lands a pigeon. The pigeon turns out to be a carrier for a bunch of Nazi spies, chief of whom is Jerome Cowan. Canova hands the message to the FBI and becomes 'public patriot number one', while Cowan (left), who runs a night club in New York as a front to his activities, orders Canova's immediate execution. Enter theatrical agent Joe E. Brown. He goes to the Ozarks and signs Canova for Cowan's niterie – with mind-boggling results. Best musical moment was 'The Lady From Lockheed' number (by Mort Greene and Harry Revel) nicely staged by Nick Castle. Alexander Granach, Anne Jeffreys, Otto Reichow, Wolfgang Zilzer and Donald Curtis completed the cast. It was written by Monte Brice and Bradford Ropes from a story by Robert Harari and Eve Greene (additional dialogue by Jack Townley), produced by Harriet Parsons, and directed by Joseph Santley. Other songs: Backwoods Barbecue Greene, Revel; Wabash Blues Dave Ringle, Fred Meinken.

▽

Though the Andrews Sisters received top billing in Universal's 65-minute programmer **Give Out Sisters**, it was co-star Grace McDonald (centre) around whom Paul Gerard Smith and Warren Wilson's screenplay (story by Lee Sands) revolved. McDonald played an heiress whose successful attempts to break into show business as a dancer result, among other things, in the Andrews Sisters having to masquerade as her three elderly, disapproving aunts. It was utter drivel, of course, but directed by Edward F. Cline with enough flair to make it watchable. There were five songs in all, four of them harmonized by the Sisters Andrews; a few dance routines (staged by John Mattison) and a fair amount of comedy by Charles Butterworth, Walter Catlett and William Frawley. Also cast for producer Bernard W. Burton were Dan Dailey (centre with McDonald), Donald O'Connor (centre right), Peggy Ryan (centre left), Edith Barrett, Marie Blake, Fay Helm, Emmett Vogan and The Jivin' Jacks and Jills. Songs and musical numbers: *Pennsylvania Polka* Lester Lee, Zeke Manners; *The New Generation* Walter Donaldson; *Who Do You Think You're Fooling?* Ray Stillwell, Ray Gold; *Jiggers, The Beat* Al Lerner, Sid Robin; *You're Just A Flower From An Old Bouquet.*
▽

Clearly there was something special about Eleanor Powell and ships. At least as far as MGM was concerned. After her battleship finale in *Born To Dance* (1936) they put her to sea in *Honolulu* (1939), gave her a shipboard production number in *Broadway Melody of 1940*, and in **Ship Ahoy** starred her as the unwitting carrier, while on a cruise to Puerto Rico, of a magnetic device coveted by enemy agents. The film was unmitigated nonsense from start to finish, but Powell (illustrated centre) interrupted the narrative doldrums with her dancing – particularly effective in a number called 'I'll Take Tallulah' (by E.Y. Harburg and Burton Lane). On board for a few easy laughs and to complicate the simple-minded plot, were Red Skelton (centre left), Bert Lahr and Virginia O'Brien, with Tommy Dorsey (right foreground) and His Orchestra (plus Frank Sinatra, Connie Haines, The Pied Pipers and Jo Stafford), momentarily blowing life into the proceedings with a ditty called 'Last Call For Love' (by Harburg, Lane and Margery Cummings). Harry Clork, Harry Kurnitz and Irving Brecher wrote it from a story by Matt Brooks, Bradford Ropes and Bert Kalmar; the dance numbers were staged by Bobby Connolly, Jack Cummings produced it, and the director was Edward Buzzell. Other songs and musical numbers: *Poor You* (Skelton, O'Brien, Dorsey, Sinatra) Lane, Harburg; *Tampico* (Powell) Walter Ruick; *On Moonlight Bay* (Dorsey, Sinatra, Pied Pipers) Percy Wenrich, Edward Madden.
▷

Despite a really cockle-brained story, absurd even by musical programmer standards, **Youth on Parade** (Republic), against all the odds and thanks largely to an excellent performance by Ruth Terry, emerged as an entertaining trifle and one of the better campus romps of the year. All about a bunch of students who 'invent' a model pupil then, to avoid expulsion, have to produce her to satisfy their psychology professor, the film starred John Hubbard (right, as the Professor), Martha O'Driscoll (left, vocals dubbed by Margaret Whiting), Tom Brown, Yvonne De Carlo, Charles Smith, Lynn Merrick, Chick Chandler and Nana Bryant. The aforementioned Miss Terry was the model pupil – a New York actress hired by the students to carry off the deception. It was written by George Carleton Brown with additional dialogue by Frank Gill Jr, produced by Albert J. Cohen, and directed by Albert S. Rogell. It was also the first time that the famous songwriting team of Jule Styne and Sammy Cahn were paired, their big hit in this instance being 'I've Heard That Song Before', introduced here by Bob Crosby and His Orchestra, although it was Harry James's recorded version that went on to sell over a million copies. Other songs: *You're So Good To Me*; *If It's Love*; *Man*; *Cotcha Too Ta Mee*; *You Got To Study Buddy.*
▽

Composers Mack Gordon and Harry Warren who provided the score for **Orchestra Wives** (20th Century-Fox) had two more walloping hits with 'I've Got A Gal In Kalamazoo' and 'At Last' and – as performed by Glenn Miller (left) and His Orchestra, with special emphasis on Tex Beneke, Marion Hutton and The Modernaires – captured to perfection America's musical tastes in the early forties. The rest of the film was nowhere as good, with George Montgomery, Ann Rutherford, Lynn Bari (vocals dubbed by Pat Friday), Carole Landis, Cesar Romero, Virginia Gilmore, Mary Beth Hughes, Tamara Geva, Frank Orth, Henry Morgan, Grant Mitchell and The Nicholas Brothers trying valiantly to pep up a story involving the antagonism shown by several orchestra-members' wives to Miss Rutherford, the new spouse of one of the players. It was written with neither wit nor verve by Karl Tunberg and Darrell Ware from a story by James Prindle, and directed for producer William Le Baron by Archie Mayo. Other songs: *Serenade In Blue*; *People Like You and Me*; *That's Sabotage.*

△

That old musical standby, the campus caper, surfaced again in **Sweater Girl** (Paramount) which elevated Eddie Bracken (illustrated) to star status, and co-starred him with June Preisser, whose pretty face and way with a cartwheel were about the sum total of what she had to offer. A tale that any self-respecting professor of creative literature would have jettisoned with an 'F', it involved a group of college kids in the preparation of a musical revue but with a spot of murder (the victim being campus editor Kenneth Howell) thrown in for no good measure at all. Frieda Inescort, Betty Rhodes, Nils Asther, Ella Neal and Johnnie Johnston (another murder victim) were also cast for producer Sol C. Siegel, it was written by Eve Greene (additional dialogue by Robert Blees) from a story by Beulah Marie Dix and Bertram Milhauser; and directed by William Clemens. Songs included: *I Don't Want To Walk Without You*; *I Said No*; *Sweater Girl*; *What Gives Out Now* Frank Loesser, Jule Styne. Interesting sideline: according to Styne, it was 'I Don't Want To Walk Without You' (and the slightly risqué 'I Said No') that made him and Loesser 'hot properties' in the Hollywood composer stakes. Introduced by Johnnie Johnston in the film, it was a huge wartime hit. Remake of *College Scandal* (1935).

For Me And My Gal (MGM) was a World War I story with a vaudeville background that introduced movie audiences to Gene Kelly, a 30-year-old song and dance man who, a couple of years earlier, had electrified Broadway with his performance as Joey Evans in the Richard Rodgers-Lorenz Hart-John O'Hara musical *Pal Joey*. In a perfect piece of casting, the movie had Kelly (right) as a hoofer called Harry Palmer who teams up with Judy Garland (centre) and her boyfriend George Murphy (left) to form an act. But there are complications: Murphy is in love with Garland; Garland is in love with Kelly; and Kelly is in love with Kelly – and with the idea of success. His lifelong ambition, which he finally achieves, is to play the Palace Theatre in New York, but getting there is an uphill battle, particularly with the War intervening in his plans. Producer Arthur Freed originally intended to cast Murphy in the Kelly role but, realizing the similarity between Harry Palmer and 'Pal' Joey, switched them round in the hope that Kelly would bring the same dynamic quality to the screen as he had to the stage. He did, but he was let down by the screenplay which, with its combination of corn and sentimentality, and its characterization of Harry which transformed him from ruthlessly ambitious hoofer to self-effacing war hero, was more contrived and unsubtle than anything in vaudeville itself. Richard Sherman, Fred Finkelhoffe and Sid Silvers wrote it from an original story by Howard Emmett Rogers. The film, however, did give audiences an introduction to Kelly's energetic dancing in a series of routines that, although cornball, perfectly evoked the mood and flavour of the period. Kelly and Garland (who received top billing) worked brilliantly together, establishing a magical *rapport*, and their performance of the title number (by Edgar Leslie, E. Ray Goetz and George W. Meyer) was the undoubted highlight of the movie. The contrast between a vulnerable, hesitant Judy and a confident, punch-packing Kelly was highly effective and, despite the film's somewhat maudlin plot, 1942 audiences were not averse to undiluted patriotism, and they turned it into a box-office smash for MGM making, at the same time, an international star of Gene Kelly. Marta Eggerth (her US debut) appeared briefly, with other parts going to Ben Blue, Horace (later Stephen) McNally, Richard Quine, Lucille Norman and Keenan Wynn. It was directed by Busby Berkeley but, surprisingly, the musical numbers were staged by Bobby Connolly. Songs and musical numbers: *Oh, Johnny, Oh* (danced by Kelly) Ed Rose, Abe Olman; *They Go Wild, Simply Wild Over Me* (Kelly dance) Joseph McCarthy, Fred Fisher; *The Doll Shop* Roger Edens; *Oh You Beautiful Doll* (Kelly, Garland) A. Seymour Brown, Nat D. Ayer; *Don't Leave Me Daddy* Joe Verges; *Sailors' Hornpipe* traditional; *By The Beautiful Sea* Harold Atteridge, Harry Carroll; *When You Wore A Tulip* (Garland, Kelly) Jack Mahoney, Percy Wenrich; *Do I Love You?* (Eggerth) E. Ray Goetz, Henri Christine; *After You've Gone* (Garland) Henry Creamer, Turner Layton; *Tell Me* (Eggerth, male group) Max Kortlander, J. Will Callahan; *Till We Meet Again* (Eggerth) Ray Egan, Richard A. Whiting; *We Don't Want The Bacon* Howard Carr, Harry Russell, Jimmie Havens; *Ballin' The Jack* (Garland, Kelly) Jim Burris, Chris Smith; *What Are You Going To Do To Help The Boys?* Gus Kahn, Egbert Van Alstyne; *Mademoiselle From Armentières* authorship uncertain; *How Ya Gonna Keep 'Em Down On The Farm* (Garland) Sam M.

Lewis, Joe Young, Walter Donaldson; *Where Do We Go From Here* (Garland, chorus) Howard Johnson, Percy Wenrich; *It's A Long Way To Tipperary* (Garland) Jack Judge, Harry Williams; *Goodbye Broadway, Hello France* (male chorus) C. Francis Riesner, Benny Davis, Billy Baskette; *Smiles* (Garland) J. Will Callahan, Lee M. Roberts; *Oh Frenchy* Sam Ehrlich, Con Conrad; *Pack Up Your Troubles* (Garland) George Asaf, Felix Powell; *When Johnny Comes Marching Home* (Garland) Louis Lambert, adapted by Roger Edens.

Sonja Henie's penultimate film for 20th Century-Fox was a wheezy old bore called **Iceland** (GB: **Katina**) which, like Republic's *Ice-Capades Revue*, existed merely to dazzle audiences with some nifty blade work. But unlike *Ice-Capades Revue*, the plot of **Iceland** intruded to the detriment of the skating sequences, leaving audiences limp with indifference. Henie (illustrated) played a Reykjavik lass who throws over her uninspiring local fella (Sterling Holloway) for handsome marine corporal John Payne. But, unlike her performance on the rink, the romance flows anything but smoothly, and it's a case of girl getting boy, girl losing boy, and – well, you know the rest. Sammy Kaye and His Band were around to keep it musically buoyant, and, with a score by Mack Gordon and Harry Warren, they succeeded. The best number was 'There Will Never Be Another You' sung by Joan Merrill, who also sang 'You Can't Say No To A Soldier', while co-star Jack Oakie, Payne and Henie, got acquainted to the accompaniment of the catchy 'It's A Lovers' Knot'. However, two patriotic ditties featuring Miss Henie – 'Let's Bring New Glory To Old Glory' and 'I Like A Military Tune' – were an embarrassment. Also in it were Felix Bressart, Osa Massen, Fritz Feld, Adeline DeWalt Reynolds and Ludwig Stossel. The skating sequences were staged by James Gonzales, it was scripted by Robert Ellis and Helen Logan, and directed for producer William Le Baron by H. Bruce Humberstone.

Forties Musicals

Having paid $130,000 for the screen rights to Cole Porter's Broadway hit **Panama Hattie**, MGM retained its title but precious little else. The results were pretty dire and reduced Porter's galvanic show about a nightclub owner's romance with a blue-nosed divorcée (approval having first to be given by the divorcée's young daughter) to an incohesive blur. On Broadway the role of the nightclub owner was played (definitively) by Ethel Merman; on the screen little Miss Ann Sothern (illustrated left) had a bash at it – and it bashed back, leaving the lady decidedly winded. Sothern sang 'I've Still Got My Health' and, as a duet with Jackie Horner, 'Let's Be Buddies' (both by Porter) who contributed three more songs to the score, including the memorable 'Make It Another Old Fashioned Please' (again sung by Sothern), and 'Just One Of Those Things', arranged by Roger Edens for Lena Horne, who also sang a rhumba with the Bernard Brothers called 'The Sping' (by Phil Moore and J. Le Gon). Deadpan Virginia O'Brien (illustrated right) was in it too, in the role played on stage by Betty Hutton, and sang Porter's 'Fresh As A Daisy', and an item in dubious taste by E.Y. Harburg and Walter Donaldson called 'Did I Get Stinkin' At The Savoy' which was originally intended for Miss Sothern who refused to sing it. The finale, devised by Vincente Minnelli (who was brought in, with Roy Del Ruth, to devise and shoot extra sequences after the disastrous first previews), was staged without much flair by Danny Dare to a patriotic Harburg-Burton Lane number called 'The Son Of A Gun Who Picks On Uncle Sam', and involved the talents of the entire company, including funny men Red Skelton, Rags Ragland and Ben Blue. Also in it were Marsha Hunt, Alan Mowbray, Dan Dailey and Carl Esmond. The screenplay, loosely based on the original Herbert Fields-Buddy De Sylva book, was by Jack McGowan and Wilkie Mahoney, and it was directed by Norman Z. McLeod for producer Arthur Freed. Despite its weaknesses, the film grossed over $4,000,000. Other songs: *Hattie From Panama; Good Neighbours* Roger Edens; *Berry Me Not* Phil Moore; *La Bumba Rhumba* Alex Hyde; *Hail, Hail, The Gang's All Here* lyrics Theodore F. Morse to the melody of Sir Arthur Sullivan's *Come Friends Who Plough The Sea* (from 'The Pirates of Penzance').

Several attractive skating sequences breezily staged by Harry Losee, and performed by a top-notch troupe of show skaters including Vera Hruba (Ralston), Megan Taylor, Lois Dworshak, Donna Atwood, 'Red' McCarthy, Phil Taylor, Joe Jackson Jr, Jackson and Lyman, Robin Lee, Dench and Stewart, The Benoits, Eric Waite and Babs Savage, were the *raison d'etre* for Republic's **Ice-Capades Revue** (GB: **Rhythm Hits The Ice**). It had a routine screenplay by Bradford Ropes and Gertrude Purcell about a New England farm girl (Ellen Drew) who inherits a bankrupt ice show, and runs into difficulties with an unscrupulous rival producer. But that didn't bother audiences in the least. What they came to see was some of the best skating in the world, and they certainly got their money's worth (see illustration). The non-skaters included Richard Denning, Jerry Colonna, Barbara Allen and Harold Huber, and the film was directed by Bernard Vorhaus. Musical numbers: *Tequila* Sol Meyer, George R. Brown, Jule Styne; *The Guy With The Polka-dotted Tie* Meyer, Styne; *Song Of The Islands* Charles E. King; *After All* Meyer, Walter Scharf; *The Caissons Go Rolling Along* Edmund L. Gruber; *Army Air Corps Song* Robert Crawford.

Kathryn Grayson (illustrated), fast establishing herself as MGM's answer to Deanna Durbin, starred in Joseph Pasternak's production of **Seven Sweethearts**, playing the youngest of Dutchman (!) S.Z. Sakall's (right) seven daughters, all of whom live in a Dutch community in Michigan. Plot had reporter Van Heflin (left) covering a tulip festival in the village and, in the process, falling for Miss Grayson. Trouble is, family tradition has it that none of the other daughters may marry before the eldest (a pushy, would-be actress, played by Marsha Hunt), thus leading to all sorts of romantic complications which Walter Reisch and Leo Townsend's original screenplay neatly solved. Cecilia Parker, Peggy Moran, Diana Lewis, Dorothy Morris, Frances Rafferty, Frances Raeburn, Isobel Elsom and Donald Meek were also cast, and it was directed by Frank Borzage. Songs included: *You And The Waltz And I; Little Tingle Tangle Toes* Paul Francis Webster, Walter Jurmann.

With ten musical numbers on offer, there wasn't a great deal of time left for plot in **Behind The Eight Ball** (GB: **Off The Beaten Track**), a 59-minute programmer from Universal which involved The Ritz Brothers (as The Jolly Jesters), Carol Bruce (illustrated), Dick Foran, Grace McDonald, Johnny Downs, William Demarest, and Sonny Dunham and His Orchestra. Set in a backwoods theatre requisitioned by enemy spies who are using the place for short-wave broadcasts, Stanley Roberts and Mel Ronson's screenplay – which also threw in a touch of murder – gave the Ritzes several opportunities to pummel their ridiculous antics to death. Which they did with gleeful, albeit irritating, abandon. Eddie Prinz staged the dances, Howard Benedict produced, and the director was Edward F. Cline. Songs: *Atlas; Keep 'Em Laughing; Bravest Of The Brave; Riverboat Jamboree; You Don't Know What Love Is; Golden Wedding Day; Wasn't It Wonderful? Mr Five By Five; Don't You Think We Ought To Dance?* Don Raye, Gene De Paul; *When My Baby Smiles At Me* Andrew B. Sterling, Harry von Tilzer.

Inane was the word for **Moonlight in Havana** (Universal), a programmer whose convoluted plot by Oscar Brodney featured Allan Jones (seated right) as a singing baseball player who – and here's the catch – can only sing when he's suffering from a cold. Which makes life difficult for nightclub owner William Frawley (right) who has engaged Jones for his floor show. A specialty act called Grace and Nico provided the film with one highspot in a knockabout burlesque ballroom routine, with the score (by Dave Franklin) yielding two passable tunes for Jones and his co-star Jane Frazee: 'Got Music' and 'Isn't It Lovely'. Also involved in the musical programme were The Horton Dance Group and The Jivin' Jacks and Jills. The rest of the cast was completed by Marjorie Lord, Don Terry, Sergio Orta, Wade Boteler, Hugh O'Connell and Jack Norton. Bernard Burton produced and the director was Anthony Mann, with the musical numbers staged by Edward Prinz. Other songs: *I Don't Need Money; Rhythm Of The Tropics; Moonlight In Havana* Franklin; *I Wonder Who's Kissing Her Now* Will M. Hough, Frank R. Adams, Joseph E. Howard, Harold Orlob.

▷ The formula devised by Paramount for the Crosby-Lamour-Hope 'Road' pictures was an obvious winner, and the series continued with **Road to Morocco**, a tuneful, utterly irresistible musical comedy that also happened to be an inspired spoof on Hollywood's endless stream of exotic 'thousand-and-one-nights' epics. With Edith Head in charge of the costumes and some evocative Middle-Eastern settings by Hans Dreier, the film looked as good as it sounded and, like its predecessors, made a fortune. Lamour (centre, with Crosby; Hope 2nd right) played the beautiful Princess Shalmar, Anthony Quinn was a thoroughly unpleasant Arabian chieftain called Mullay Kasim, Vladimir Sokoloff an astrologer called Hyder Kahn, with other roles going to Dona Drake (right), Mikhail Rasumny, George Givot, Andrew Tombes, Leon Belasco and Monte Blue. Johnny Burke and Jimmy Van Heusen wrote the songs, the best one being 'Moonlight Becomes You', which also became Crosby, who had one of his biggest hits with it. It was written by Frank Butler and Don Hartman, produced by Paul Jones, and expertly directed by David Butler with Paul Oscard staging the dances. Other songs: *Road To Morocco; Constantly; Ain't Got A Dime To My Name.*

△

Having enjoyed nine years of stardom as queen of the MGM lot, Jeanette MacDonald's last film for the studio for six years, and her least successful, both artistically and financially, was **Cairo**, a spoof on spy thrillers which, in a war-torn world, failed to find audiences responsive to its little joke. MacDonald played an opera *diva* turned cabaret star, with Robert Young (right) cast opposite her as a newspaperman convinced she's a Nazi spy. A leaden, cumbersome screenplay by John McClain, based on an idea by Ladislaus Fodor, gave the stars no opportunity to twinkle at all. Ethel Waters, as MacDonald's maid, was also in it, plus Reginald Owen (left), Mona Barrie, Lionel Atwill, Dooley Wilson, Eduardo Ciannelli, Harry Worth, and The King's Men. The dances were staged by Sammy Lee, and W.S. Van Dyke directed. Songs: *Buds Won't Bud* Harold Arlen, E.Y. Harburg; *Cairo; Keep The Light Burning Bright* Howard Dietz, Harburg; *The Waltz Is Over* Harburg, Arthur Schwartz; *We Did It Before And We Can Do It Again* Charles Tobias, Cliff Friend; *Les Filles de Cadiz* Leo Delibes, Alfred de Musset; *A Heart That's Free* Alfred G. Robyn, T. Railey; *Il Bacio* Luigi Arditi; *The Sextet* (from 'Lucia di Lammermoor') Donizetti; *To A Wild Rose* Edward MacDowell; *From The Land Of The Sky Blue Waters* Charles Wakefield Cadman, Nelle Richmond Eberhart; *Beautiful Ohio* Mary Earl (pseudonym of Robert A. King), Ballard MacDonald; *Waiting For The Robert E. Lee* L. Wolfe Gilbert, Lewis F. Muir; *Avalon* (from a theme from Puccini's 'Tosca') Al Jolson, Vincent Rose; *Home Sweet Home* John Howard Payne, Sir Henry Bishop.

Strictly in the Groove (Universal) spread sixteen songs over 59 minutes and, as such, was true to its title. But it was decidedly out of the groove where its plot was concerned involving, as it did, the son (Richard Davies) of a resort chain operator (Russell Hicks) who, after flunking college, is sent by his old man to a dude ranch in Arizona where he meets and falls in love with Mary Healy, the owner of a rival hostelry. Leon Errol (seated centre) as a cantankerous cattle baron, Franklin Pangborn and Shemp Howard (left) were in it for laughs, while the musical side of things fell to the aforementioned Miss Healy, The Jimmy Wakely Trio, The Dinning Sisters, Grace McDonald, Ozzie Nelson and His Band, and vocalist Martha Tilton. It was written by Kenneth Higgins and Warren Wilson and directed by Vernon Keays for producer Joseph G.

Sandford. Songs and musical numbers: *Elmer's Tune* Elmer Albrecht, Sammy Gallop, Dick Jurgens; *Be Honest With Me* Gene Autry, Fred Rose; *You Are My Sunshine* Jimmie Davis, Charles Mitchell; *Miss You* Charles, Harry and Henry Tobias; *Somebody Else Is Taking My Place* Dick Howard, Bob Ellsworth, Russ Morgan; *Jersey Jive* Ozzie Nelson; *Happy Cowboy* Bob Nolan; *It Makes No Difference Now* Jimmie Davis, Floyd Tillman; *Sweethearts Or Strangers* Davis, Lou Wayne; *A Pretty Girl Milking Her Cow* (traditional); *Ridin' On* Harold Adamson, Jimmy McHugh; *Dancing On Air* Everett Carter, Milton Rosen; *I Never Knew* Tom Pitts, Ray Egan, Roy J. Marsh; *I'll Remember April* Don Raye, Gene De Paul; *Chisholm Trail* and *Buffalo Gal* (both performed by The Jimmy Wakely Trio, composers unidentified).

Forties Musicals

◁ A patchwork quilt of a show, **Seven Days Leave** (RKO) top-starred beefy Victor Mature (in his last role before joining the Coast Guards for the duration of the War) as an army draftee who stands to inherit $100,000, but only if he can persuade a wealthy society girl (Lucille Ball, illustrated, with Mature) to marry him within seven days. Plot complications arise in the shape of Mapy Cortes who, as Mature's fiancée, does her best to hold on to him. The film offered audiences a *pot-pourri* of ingredients, none of them particularly appetizing, and it did poor business despite the inclusion of two popular radio programmes of the time: *The Court of Missing Heirs*, and Ralph Edwards's *Truth or Consequences*. The score, by Frank Loesser and Jimmy McHugh, had Ginny Simms warbling 'Can't Get Out Of This Mood' and Marcy McGuire introducing the hit number 'I Get The Neck Of The Chicken'. The rest of the cast included Peter Lind Hayes, Walter Reed, Wallace Ford and Arnold Stang, as well as Freddy Martin and Les Brown with their orchestras. The original screenplay was by William Bowers, Ralph Spence, Curtis Kenyon and Kenneth Earl, and it was produced and directed by Tim Whelan. Other songs: *A Touch Of Texas*; *Please Won't You Leave My Girl Alone?*; *Baby*; *You Speak My Language*; *Puerto Rico*; *Soft Hearted*.

△

Oscar-winning choreographer Dave Gould, whose early successes included the aeroplane sequence in RKO's *Flying Down To Rio* (1933) and Maurice Chevalier's two lavish routines in *Folies Bergère* (20th Century-Fox, 1935), found himself on poverty row with **Rhythm Parade**. A modest musical from Monogram, its trickle of a plot about a showgirl, and the misunderstandings that arise when she agrees to look after her sister's eight-month-old son, was, as far as Howard Bretherton (who co-directed with Gould) was concerned, a good enough excuse to present, *in toto*, Los Angeles nightclub owner Nils T. Granlund's Florentine Gardens Revue. The talent on offer included Ted Fiorito (illustrated right) and His Orchestra, The Mills Brothers and Candy Candido, plus four production numbers, the best of which were 'Tootin' My Own Horn' (by Edward Kay and Eddie Cherkose) and 'Petticoat Army' (by Dave Oppenheim and Roy Ingraham). Chick Chandler, as an agent, and Cliff Nazarro, as a producer, provided the comedy, with Granlund, as Master of Ceremonies, contributing a few gags of his own. Romance came via Gale Storm (illustrated left) as the showgirl and Robert Lowery. Also in it were Margaret Dumont, Julie Milton and Sugar Geise. The screenplay was by Carl Foreman and Charles R. Marion, and the producer was Sydney M. Williams. Other songs and musical numbers: *'Neath The Yellow Moon In Old Tahiti* Kay, Cherkose; *Mimi From Tahiti*; *You're Drafted* Oppenheim, Ingraham; *Wait Till The Sun Shines Nellie* Andrew B. Sterling, Harry von Tilzer; *Sweet Sue* Will J. Harris, Victor Young.

Star-Spangled Rhythm was Paramount's contribution to the war effort in 1942. A bumper bonanza of unlimited talent, its chief purpose was to unleash on servicemen everywhere an hour and a half of unbridled entertainment as a 'thank you' for the good work they were doing at the Front. And although they wrapped their package of goodies in a story of star-spangled banality (Victor Moore, right, as Paramount's gatekeeper, pretends to be a studio executive for the benefit of his son, Eddie Bracken, 2nd right, and finds himself arranging a massive stage show for the boys in blue, utilizing all of the studio's available talent), what mattered were the sketches and musical numbers. Offering their services in this connection were Betty Hutton (centre), Johnny Johnston, Dick Powell, Vera Zorina, Eddie (Rochester) Anderson, Mary Martin, The Golden Gate Four, Paulette Goddard, Veronica Lake (dubbed by Martha Mears), Dorothy Lamour, Cass Daley, Betty Jane Rhodes, Bob Hope, William Bendix, Jerry Colonna, Alan Ladd, Fred MacMurray, Marjorie Reynolds and, topping it all off with a patriotic finale set against a backdrop of Mount Rushmore and glorifying America's past, Bing Crosby singing 'Old Glory' by Johnny Mercer and Harold Arlen, who wrote all the songs. The film also featured Walter Abel, Anne Revere, Gil Lamb (2nd left), Edward Fielding and Edgar Dearing. Harry Tugend wrote it, it was choreographed in a mixture of styles by Danny Dare and George Balanchine, produced by Joseph Sistrom, and directed by George Marshall. Other songs and musical numbers included: *That Old Black Magic*; *Hit The Road To Dreamland*; *A Sweater, A Sarong And A Peek-A-Boo Bang*; *I'm Doing It For Defence*; *Sharp As A Tack*; *On The Swing Shift*.

▽

Fred Astaire and Rita Hayworth (illustrated) ▷
were paired again in **You Were Never Lovelier**
(Columbia), a romantic musical with the currently fashionable Latin-American background
(though it could have been anywhere) which, in
all respects, was superior to their previous effort,
You'll Never Get Rich (Columbia 1941). With a
sparkling score by Jerome Kern and Johnny
Mercer, and a pussywillow of a plot that engagingly brought Astaire, as a horse-playing
nightclub dancer from New York, and an aloof
Hayworth, as the second of four daughters of
hotel owner Adolphe Menjou, together in an on-
off-on again relationship, the film wafted effort-
lessly on wings of song and dance to its happy
ending, again revealing Hayworth – particularly in the 'Shorty George' routine and the
lyrical 'I'm Old Fashioned' – to be a really
stunning dancer. The latter number, marvellously orchestrated by Conrad Salinger, was a
long duet for the two stars set in a moonlit
terrace and garden, and proved not only the
highlight of the film, but one of the really great
numbers in the history of the film musical.
Musical backing was provided by Xavier Cugat
and His Orchestra, giving the film its only
authentic Latin-American flavour; while the
rest of the cast included Leslie Brooks, Adele
Mara, Larry Parks, Isobel Elsom, Gus Schilling
and Barbara Brown. It was written by Michael
Fessier, Ernest Pagano and Delmer Daves from a
story by Carlos Oliveri and Sixto Pondal Rios,
Val Raset staged the musical numbers, the
director was William A. Seiter and Louis F.
Edelman produced. Other songs and musical
numbers: *Audition Dance* (Astaire, Cugat and
Orchestra); *Dearly Beloved* (Hayworth, dubbed
by Nan Wynn; danced by Hayworth, Astaire);
Wedding In The Spring (Lina Romay, Cugat and
Orchestra); *You Were Never Lovelier* (Astaire;
danced Astaire, Hayworth); *These Orchids* (The
Delivery Boys) Kern, Mercer; *Chiu Chiu* (Romay,
Cugat and Orchestra) Alan Surgal, Nicanor
Molinare.

△
Running under an hour, **Flying With Music** was
an inconsequential programmer from United
Artists about a detective dodger (George Givot,
centre) who escapes to Florida in the guise of a
tour leader to a bevy of beauties. Marjorie
Woodworth, William Marshall, Ed Gargan, Jerry
Bergen and Norma Varden were also in it, it was
produced by Hal Roach, written by M. Coates
Webster and Louis S. Kaye, and directed by
George Archainbaud. The music was by Edward
Ward, and the lyrics by Bob Wright and Chet
Forrest. Songs: *If It's Love*; *Rotana*; *Pennies For
Peppino*; *Caribbean Magic*; *Song Of The Lagoon*.

△

1943

Academy Awards

Cinematography (colour)
The Phantom Of The Opera (Universal) Hal Mohr and W. Howard Greene.
NOMINATIONS INCLUDED: *Hello, Frisco Hello* (20th Century-Fox) Charles G. Clarke and Allen Davey. *Thousands Cheer* (MGM) George Folsey.

Art Direction (Interior Decoration) (colour)
The Phantom Of The Opera Alexander Golitzen and John B. Goodman; Russell A. Gausman and Ira S. Webb.
NOMINATIONS INCLUDED: *The Gang's All Here* (20th Century-Fox) James Basevi and Joseph C. Wright; Thomas Little. *This Is The Army* (WB) John Hughes and Lt. John Koenig; George J. Hopkins. *Thousands Cheer* Cedric Gibbons and Daniel Cathcart; Edwin B. Willis and Jacques Mersereau.

Sound Recording
NOMINATIONS INCLUDED: *Riding High* (Paramount) Loren Ryder. *This Is The Army* Nathan Levinson. *The Phantom Of The Opera* Bernard B. Brown.

Music
Song
'You'll Never Know' *Hello, Frisco Hello* Harry Warren *cm*; Mack Gordon *lyr*.
NOMINATIONS INCLUDED: 'Change Of Heart' *Hit Parade Of 1943* (Republic) Jule Styne *cm*; Harold Adamson *lyr*. 'Happiness Is A Thing Called Joe' *Cabin In The Sky* (MGM) Harold Arlen *cm*; E.Y. Harburg *lyr*. 'My Shining Hour' *The Sky's The Limit* (RKO) Harold Arlen *cm*; Johnny Mercer *lyr*. 'Say A Pray'r For The Boys Over There' *Hers To Hold* (Universal) Jimmy McHugh *cm*; Herb Magidson *lyr*. 'That Old Black Magic' *Star Spangled Rhythm* (Paramount) Harold Arlen *cm*; Johnny Mercer *lyr*. 'They're Either Too Young Or Too Old' *Thank Your Lucky Stars* (WB) Arthur Schwartz *cm*; Frank Loesser *lyr*. 'We Mustn't Say Goodbye' *Stage Door Canteen* (Lesser, UA) James V. Monaco *cm*; Al Dubin *lyr*. 'You'd Be So Nice To Come Home To' *Something To Shout About* (Columbia) Cole Porter.

Scoring Of A Musical Picture
This Is The Army Ray Heindorf
NOMINATIONS INCLUDED: *Coney Island* (20th Century-Fox) Alfred Newman. *Hit Parade Of 1943* Walter Scharf. *The Sky's The Limit* Leigh Harline. *Something To Shout About* Morris Stoloff. *Stage Door Canteen* Frederick E. Rich. *Star Spangled Rhythm* Robert Emmett Dolan *Thousands Cheer* Herbert Stothart.

The Phantom Of The Opera Edward Ward.
The Annual Top Moneymaking Films
INCLUDED: *Coney Island. Dixie* (Paramount). *Hello, Frisco Hello. Hers To Hold. The Road To Morocco. Stage Door Canteen. Star Spangled Rhythm. This Is The Army.*

Kenny Baker, Patricia Morison and Belita starred in **Silver Skates**, an adequate ice revue from Monogram, with a routine screenplay by Jerry Cady that accommodated the talents of Irene Dare (illustrated centre), Frick and Frack, Eugene Turner, and Ted Fiorito and His Orchestra. Also in it: Danny Shaw, Joyce Compton, Frank Faylen, Paul McVey and Henry Wadsworth. The static direction was by Leslie Goodwins, and Lindsley Parsons produced. Songs and musical numbers: *Love Is A Beautiful Song; Dancing On Top Of The World; Lovely Lady; Can't You Hear Me Calling From The Mountain; Cowboy Joe; A Boy Like You And A Girl Like Me* Roy Ingraham, Dave Oppenheim; *Sing A Song Of The Sea* Oppenheim, Archie Gottler.

After a two-year absence in which she took time off to have her baby Alice Faye (centre left) returned to the Fox lot for **Hello, Frisco, Hello**, another period musical (in Technicolor) set on the Barbary Coast, which co-starred John Payne (centre right), Jack Oakie (right) and June Havoc (left). The film charted Faye's rise from saloon entertainer to West End star sensation, and the abortive romance she has with Payne, a social-climbing loser who marries into the Nob Hill élite via Lynn Bari. Very trivial, but very entertaining in the characteristically opulent Fox style, the film's 98-minute running time crammed as many musical numbers as it could comfortably contain without shredding the narrative too drastically, with the only new song being the lilting 'You'll Never Know' by Mack Gordon and Harry Warren. Val Raset staged the production numbers, the magnificent gay nineties costumes were by Helen Rose, and the evocative settings by James Basevi and Boris Leven. The cast included Laird Cregar, Ward Bond, John Archer, George Barbier and Esther Dale, and the screenplay was by Robert Ellis, Helen Logan and Richard Macaulay. Bruce Humberstone directed with super-efficiency, and the producer was Milton Sperling. Songs and musical numbers: *Ragtime Cowboy Joe* (Faye, Oakie, Havoc) Grant Clarke, Maurice Abrahams, Lewis F. Muir; *San Francisco* (chorus) Bronislau Kaper, Walter Jurmann, Gus Kahn; *Has Anybody Here Seen Kelly* (Faye, Oakie) Will Letters, C.W. Murphy, William J. McKenna; *Sweet Cider Time* (Faye, chorus) Percy Wenrich, Joseph McCarthy; *Hello, Frisco, Hello* (Faye, Payne, Oakie, Havoc) Louis A. Hirsch, Gene Buck; *Why Do They Always Pick On Me?* (Faye) Harry von Tilzer, Stanley Murphy; *Bedelia* (chorus) Jean Schwartz, William Jerome; *Doin' The Grizzly Bear* (Faye, Oakie, Havoc) George Botsford, Irving Berlin; *By The Light Of The Silvery Moon* (Faye, chorus) Gus Edwards, Edward Madden; *Gee, But It's Great To Meet A Friend From Your Own Home Town* (Oakie, Havoc) James McGavisk, William G. Tracey; *It's Tulip Time In Holland* (Roller Skating specialty) Richard A. Whiting, Dave Radford; *I've Got A Girl In Every Port* (Oakie) composer unknown; *When You Wore A Tulip* Jack Mahoney, Percy Wenrich; *Strike Up The Band, Here Comes A Sailor* Andrew B. Sterling, Charles B. Ward; *King Chanticleer (Texas Tommy)* Nat D. Ayer.

◁

Two production numbers, 'Clickety-Clack Jack' and 'I'd Love To Make Love To You' (by Mort Greene and Karl Hajos), momentarily enlivened **The Sultan's Daughter** (Monogram), but for most of its 63 minutes, it was a creaky, poor man's *Road* film, which starred ex-stripper and one time extra Ann Corio (illustrated left) as the titular heroine who finds her curvaceous body being sought after by a couple of American vaudevillians, and her valuable oil fields by a pair of German agents. Charles Butterworth (illustrated right) was the Sultan, and the cast was completed by Tim and Irene Ryan (Mr Ryan having collaborated on the screenplay with M.M. Raison), Edward Norris, Fortunio Bona-nova, Jack La Rue, Chris Pin Martin, and Freddie Fisher and His Orchestra. Philip S. Krasne and James S. Burkett produced, and the director was Arthur Dreifuss. Other songs and musical numbers: *I'm Always The Girl*; *The Sultan's Daughter* Greene, Hajos.

The Ritz Brothers dominated (and were the ruin of) Universal's **Hi Ya Chum** (GB: **Everything Happens To Us**) whose 61-minute running time seemed interminable. The trio, *en route* to Holly-wood, found themselves stranded in a Califor-nian boom town where they open a restaurant. They fell over backwards, forwards, sideways, but ultimately always flat on their faces, in an attempt to milk merriment out of Edmund L. Hartmann's knockabout screenplay. Jane Frazee (featured centre left) and Robert Paige co-starred, with June Clyde (centre right) Paul Hurst, Edmund McDonald, Lou Lubin, Andrew Tombes and Ray Walker completing the cast. Harold Young directed, Howard Benedict pro-duced. Songs: *He's My Guy*; *You Gotta Have Personality*; *Two On A Bike*; *Doo Dat*; *I'm Hitting A High Spot* Don Raye, Gene De Paul.

Dick Foran starred in **Hi Buddy** (Universal), a tune-filled programmer in which, thanks to his stalwart fund-raising efforts in putting on a servicemen's benefit show, a boys' club is saved from closure. The thin skein of plot was all that was needed on which to hang a series of military-flavoured song and dance specialties performed by The King's Men, The Step Broth-ers, The Four Sweethearts, Lorraine Krueger, Marilyn Kay, Dick Humphreys and Dolores Diane. There were songs too, from co-stars Harriet Hilliard and Robert Paige (right). It was written by Warren Wilson with parts in it for Marjorie Lord, Bobs Watson, Tommy Cook, Jennifer Holt, Gus Schilling and Wade Boteler, the producer was Paul Malvern, and it was directed by Harold Young. Songs and musical numbers included: *Hi Buddy*; *We're In The Marines*; *Mr Yankee Doodle* Everett Carter, Milton Rosen; *We're In The Navy* Don Raye, Gene De Paul; *Here's To Tomorrow* Charles Newman, Lew Pollack; *Take Me In Your Arms* Mitchell Parish, Fritz Rotter, Fred Markush; *Stardust* Hoagy Carmichael, Parish, *Old Folks At Home*; *De Camptown Races* Stephen Foster.

The world of modelling provided the back-ground for United Artists' **The Powers Girl** (GB: **Hello Beautiful**), whose threadbare plot pirouet-ted on the passion two sisters – Carole Landis and Anne Shirley – have for George Murphy (left). E. Edwin Moran and Harry Segall supplied the dialogue (from a story by William A. Pierce and Malvin Wald); and Benny Goodman and His Orchestra, plus Dennis Day, the music (new songs by Jule Styne and Kim Gannon). The supporting cast included Alan Mowbray (right), Jean Ames, Mary Treen and Rafael Storm; it was produced by Charles R. Rogers, and directed by Norman Z. McLeod. Songs: *Three Dreams*; *Out Of This World*; *The Lady Who Didn't Believe In Love*; *Partners*; *We're Looking For The Big Bad Wolf* Styne, Gannon; *A Pretty Girl Is Like A Melody* Irving Berlin; *I Know That You Know* Vincent Youmans, Anne Caldwell; *One O'Clock Jump* Count Basie, Harry James; *Roll 'Em* Mary Lou Williams.

If the plot of **When Johnny Comes Marching Home** (Universal), about a soldier-cum-singer who returns to his old theatrical boarding house while on leave, and finds love and romance, sent confirmed insomniacs to sleep, the music pro-vided by Phil Spitalny and his radio 'Hour of Charm' all-girl orchestra (illustrated), woke them up again. As there was much more music than plot, a quiet nap was therefore out of the question. Allan Jones starred as the soldier, Jane Frazee was the girl he falls for – with other parts in Oscar Brodney and Dorothy Bennett's work-manlike screenplay going to Gloria Jean, Donald O'Connor, Peggy Ryan, Richard Davies, Clyde Fillmore, Olin Howlin and Emma Dunn. Also featured were the Four Step Brothers. Charles Lamont directed, and the dances were staged by Louis Da Pron. Songs and musical numbers included: *This Is It*; *Say It With Dancing* Don Raye, Gene De Paul; *This Is Worth Fighting For* Edgar De Lange, Sammy Stept; *When Johnny Comes Marching Home* Louis Lambert, adapted by Buddy Kaye; *One Of Us Has Gotta Go* Inez James, Buddy Pepper; *We Must Be Vigilant* Edgar Leslie, Joe Burke (based on E.H. Meacham's 'American Patrol').

A quickie with a South Sea Island setting, **Rhythm Of The Islands** (Universal) offered an hour of 'dual support' entertainment in which Allan Jones, posing as a native chief, and Andy Devine (centre) as a beachcomber, sell their island paradise to millionaire Ernest Truex (right). Jones falls in love with Truex's daughter, Jane Frazee (left), and there are a few un-welcome interruptions by some hostile natives from a neighbouring island. But Jones's singing charms the tribe's chief, and, as the sun slowly set in the Golden West, everyone lived happily ever after. Marjorie Gateson, Mary Wickes, Acquanetta, Nestor Paiva, John Maxwell, The Step Brothers and The Horton Dancers were also in it; Oscar Brodney and M.M. Musselman wrote it; the director was Roy William Neill, and his producer Bernard W. Burton. It came and went in 59 minutes. Songs: *Savage Serenade*; *Tropic Lullaby*; *Blue Mist*; *Chant Of The Tom Tom*; *Manhattan Isle*; *Isle Of Romance*; *I've Set My Mind On You* Inez James, Buddy Pepper.

Forties Musicals

For bobby-soxers and hepcats only, **Reveille with Beverly** (Columbia) tacked a mere mirage of a plot (all about a girl who runs an early morning wake-up programme for soldiers at a nearby camp) on to several indifferent musical numbers, and wasted the talents of Ann Miller (illustrated in 'Thumbs Up And V For Victory') as the rise-and-shine disc jockey, Frank Sinatra (who sang only one song, Cole Porter's 'Night and Day'), Bob Crosby, Freddie Slack, and Duke Ellington and Count Basie and their bands. The Mills Brothers and The Radio Rogues were featured as part of an army show, with other roles going to William Wright, Dick Purcell, Franklin Pangborn, Tim Ryan, Larry Parks, Barbara Brown, Douglas Leavitt, Wally Vernon and Adele Mara. It was written by Howard J. Green, Jack Henley and Albert Duffy, produced by Sam White, and clumsily flung together by director Charles Barton. Other musical numbers included: *Big Noise From Winnetka* Gil Rodin, Bob Crosby, Ray Bauduc, Bob Haggart; *Take The A Train* Billy Strayhorn; *One O'Clock Jump* Count Basie, Harry James; *Cow-Cow Boogie* Don Raye, Gene De Paul, Benny Carter.

▽

△

A remake of *You're A Sweetheart* (Universal, 1937), **Cowboy In Manhattan** took 54 minutes to relate the story of a songwriter (Robert Paige) who pretends to be a millionaire in order to win the love of a Broadway star (Frances Langford, centre). It was about 50 minutes too long. Leon Errol, Walter Catlett, Joe Sawyer, Jennifer Holt, and George Cleveland completed the cast for director Frank Woodruff, and it was written by Warren Wilson from the story he originally wrote with William Thomas and Maxwell Shane. Songs: *A Cowboy Is Happy*; *Whistle Your Blues To A Bluebird*; *Mr Moon*; *Private Cowboy Jones*; *Need I Say More*; *Dancing On Air*; *Got Love* Everett Carter, Milton Rosen.

▽

Close on the heels of *Hi Ya Chum*, came **Hi Ya Sailor** (Universal), which ran two minutes longer than the previous film in the telling of a yawnsome yarn about a merchant seaman-cum-songwriter's adventures in New York. Donald Woods (right) was the songwriter, Elyse Knox a lady cab driver he befriends, and Phyllis Brooks the songstress who gets to sing one of his creations. It was produced and directed by Jean Yarbrough from a screenplay by Stanley Roberts (story by Fanya Lawrence). Also cast: Eddie Quillan (centre left), Jerome Cowan, Frank Jenks (left), Matt Willis (centre right), Ray Eberle and His Orchestra, Leo Diamond Quintet, The Delta Rhythm Boys, The Hacker Duo, The Nilsson Sisters, Wingy Manone and His Orchestra, and Mayris Chaney and her Dance Trio. Songs included: *A Dream Ago*; *Babies Ball*; *Spell Of The Moon*; *Hi Ya Sailor*; *So Goodnight*; *Just A Step Away From Heaven* Everett Carter, Milton Rosen; *The More I Go Out With Somebody Else* Billy Post, Don Pierce, Pierre Norman; *Oh Brother* Maxine Manners, Jean Miller; *One O'Clock Jump* Count Basie, Harry James.

Though **Happy Go Lucky** (Paramount) starred Mary Martin and Dick Powell, it was the dynamic Betty Hutton (right, again in pursuit of Eddie Bracken) who stole the show, and whose infectious singing of 'Murder He Says' (by Frank Loesser and Jimmy McHugh) was the best thing in it. The story concerned an ex-cigarette girl (Martin, centre) who blows her life's savings on a cruise to the Caribbean where, aided by a singing beachcomber (Powell, left) she sets her sights for millionaire Rudy Vallee. What she finishes up with is Mr Powell, and what audiences finished up with was a formula musical, in Technicolor, that was lovely to look at, and passed 83 minutes with the minimum amount of discomfort. Mabel Paige, Clem Bevans and Frances Raymond also had parts in the Walter DeLeon-Norman Panama-Melvin Frank screenplay (story by Michael Uris, adaptation by John Jacoby), with Curtis Bernhardt directing for associate producer Harold Wilson. The dance numbers were staged by Paul Oscard. Other songs: *Let's Get Lost*; *Happy Go Lucky*; *Fuddy Duddy Watchmaker*; *Sing A Tropical Song*; *Ugly Woman* Loesser, McHugh; *Ta-Ra-Ra-Boom-De-Ay* Henry J. Sayers (special material by Loesser). ▷

△

Hit Parade of 1943 (Republic) pleasingly divided its 86-minute running time between the plot and the musical numbers that underlined it. About a played-out songwriter (John Carroll) and his relationship with a Midwestern tune-smith (Susan Hayward, right) who provides him with his inspiration (i.e. 'ghosts' his songs for him), the film also featured Gail Patrick, Eve Arden (left), Melville Cooper, Walter Catlett and Mary Treen, plus a host of specialty performers, including Jack Williams, Dorothy Dandridge, Pops and Louie, The Music Maids, The Three Cheers, Chinita, The Golden Gate Quartet, and the orchestras of Count Basie, Freddy Martin and Ray McKinley. The score, with the exception of two numbers, was by Harold Adamson and Jule Styne, with 'Take A Chance', 'A Change Of Heart', and 'Who Took Me Home Last Night' topping the popularity poll. Frank Gill wrote it with additional dialogue by Frances Hyland, and it was directed by Albert S. Rogell, with Nick Castle in charge of the choreography for producer Herbert J. Yates and associate producer Albert J. Cohen. Other songs and musical numbers included: *Tam Boom Bah*; *That's How To Write A Song*; *Harlem Sandman*; *Do These Old Eyes Deceive Me* Adamson, Styne; *Yankee Doodle Tank* Andy Razaf, J.C. Johnson; *Nobody's Sweetheart* Elmer Schoebel, Ernie Erdman, Gus Kahn, Billy Meyers. Note: reissued for television, retitled **Change Of Heart**.

With the exception of an oldie called 'What Do You Want To Make Those Eyes At Me For' (by Joseph McCarthy, Howard Johnson and James V. Monaco), the nine other songs featured in **Follow the Band** (Universal), an hour-long programmer, all took place in a nightclub in New York where, according to the storyline by Richard English (screenplay by Warren Wilson and Dorothy Bennett), a young farmer, in town to obtain membership to the National Dairy Association, finds himself playing the trombone. It must have been quite a floor show, for the talent on offer included Frances Langford (illustrated), The King's Men, Alvino Rey, Skinnay Ennis, The King Sisters, The Groove Boys, Ray Eberle, Hilo Hattie, and The Bombardiers. Eddie Quillan was the trombone-playing farmer, and the two women in his life were Mary Beth Hughes and Anne Rooney, with parts in it also for Leon Errol (standing centre) and Samuel S. Hinds. Louis Da Pron staged the musical numbers, it was directed by Jean Yarbrough, and the associate producer was Paul Malvern. Other songs and musical numbers: *My Melancholy Baby* (Langford) George A. Norton, Ernie Burnett; *My Devotion* (Rey, King Sisters) Roc Hillman, Johnny Napton; *Ain't Misbehavin'* (Hughes) Fats Waller, Harry Brooks, Andy Razaf; *Swingin' The Blues* (Hughes) Everett Carter, Milton Rosen; *Spellbound* (Eberle) Carter, Rosen; *Hilo Hattie* (Hattie) Harold Adamson, Johnny Noble; *The Army Air Corps* (Bombardiers) Robert Crawford; *Rosie The Riveter* (King Sisters, Alvino Rey) Redd Evans, John Jacob Loeb; *Don't Tread On The Tail Of Me Coat* (The King's Men) composer unknown.

A moribund programmer, **Tahiti Honey** (Republic) starred Simone Simon (right), whose role in Lawrence Kimble, H.W. Haneman and Frederick Kohner's screenplay (story by Kohner) was to play Florence Nightingale to a rather decrepit band and, in the process, to woo its attractive leader (Dennis O'Keefe, left). Locales included Miami, San Francisco, New Orleans and, of course, Tahiti – but one way and another, they all looked pretty much the same. Michael Whalen, Lionel Stander, Wally Vernon, Dan Seymour, Tommye Adams and Tom Seidel completed the cast. John H. Auer produced and directed. Songs and musical numbers included: *Tahiti Honey* Jule Styne, George H. Brown, Sol Meyer; *You Could Hear A Pin Drop*; *Any Old Port In A Storm*; *This Gets Better Every Minute*; *Koni Plenty Hu-Hu*; *Of Course I'm A Cossack* Charles Newman, Lew Pollack.

Twenty-one-year-old Judy Garland (illustrated left) starred in **Presenting Lily Mars** (MGM), a cosy homespun tale of an ambitious young singer's rise from small-town anonymity to fame on Broadway, and the romance she has with a Broadway producer *en route*. Van Heflin (illustrated), the studio's workmanlike actor-for-all-occasions, played the producer, with other roles going to Fay Bainter, Richard Carlson, Spring Byington, Marta Eggerth, Connie Gilchrist, Leonid Kinskey, Ray McDonald, Annabelle Logan (later Annie Ross), Bob Crosby and His Bob Cats and, in a small part as a chorus girl, Marilyn Maxwell. It was produced by Joe Pasternak who had left Universal for the greater freedom offered by MGM, yet so budget conscious was he in his debut effort at the studio, that Louis B. Mayer prevailed upon him to re-shoot the film's finale in a more typically opulent MGM fashion. Pasternak complied, and the sequence was restaged by Charles Walters who brought a class and sophistication to it that seemed at variance with what had preceded it, and which also featured Tommy Dorsey and His Orchestra. Norman Taurog directed from a screenplay by Richard Connell and Gladys Lehman and the novel by Booth Tarkington. Songs: *Kulebiaka*; *When I Look At You*; *Is It Love (Or The Gypsy In Me?)* Paul Francis Webster, Walter Jurmann; *Sweethearts Of America* Ralph Freed, Burton Lane; *Every Little Movement Has A Meaning Of Its Own* Otto Harbach, Karl Hoschna; *Where There's Music* Roger Edens; *Three O'Clock In The Morning* Dorothy Terriss, Julian Robledo; *Broadway Rhythm* Arthur Freed, Nacio Herb Brown; *Tom, Tom The Piper's Song*.

Despite a couple of excellent Cole Porter tunes ('You'd Be So Nice To Come Home To', 'I Always Knew'), **Something to Shout About** (Columbia) was nothing of the sort, with routine backstage shenanigans and generally unexciting performances anchoring it in mediocrity. Janet Blair (fresh from her triumph in Columbia's *My Sister Eileen*) played an ingenuous singer from Altoona who becomes embroiled in a behind-the-scenes intrigue surrounding a Broadway musical, with Don Ameche (left), Jack Oakie, William Gaxton, and Cobina Wright Jr (right), as the untalented 'star' and backer of the show whom Miss Blair replaces at the eleventh hour, also prominently featured in Lou Breslow and Edward Eliscu's collection of clichés (adapted by George Owen from a story by Fred Schiller) that masqueraded as a script. Dancer Lily Norwood (real name Tula Finklea) made her debut in the film, shortly afterwards changing her name to Cyd Charisse. Livening up the proceedings was a nifty dog act called The Bricklayers and, in two spots, pianist Hazel Scott. David Lichine choreographed, his most effective contribution being the 'Hasta Luego' sequence. Teddy Wilson and His Band were also featured, and it was produced and directed by Gregory Ratoff. Other songs and musical numbers: *Lotus Bloom*; *Something To Shout About*; *Through Thick And Thin* Porter.

Johnny Doughboy (Republic) was an unsuccessful attempt to give child star Jane Withers (centre right) the glamour girl treatment. She played a 16-year-old film star who, weary of all the kids' roles she's continually asked to play, runs away and finds romance – and disappointment – with a middle-aged playwright (Henry Wilcoxon). She then joins a juvenile edition of The Hollywood Caravan, called 'Junior Victory Caravan', where, together with a group of other teenage performers (all members of a 20-minus club), she goes on a tour of several army camps. Bobby Breen was also in it, but played a non-singing role as his boy soprano had finally broken. Baby Sandy, Alfalfa Switzer, 'Spanky' McFarland, Butch and Buddy, Cora Sue Collins, Robert Coogan, Grace Costello and The Falkner Orchestra were all part of the 20-minus brigade, with other roles going to Patrick Brook, William Demarest, Ruth Donnelly and Etta McDaniel. It was written by Lawrence Kimble from a story by Frederick Kohner and produced and directed by John H. Auer. Songs and musical numbers included: *Baby's A Big Girl Now*; *All Done All Through*; *It Takes A Guy Like I*; *Victory Caravan* Sammy Cahn, Jule Styne; *All My Life* Sidney Mitchell, Sammy Stept; *Johnny Doughboy Found A Rose In Ireland*; *Better Not Roll Those Big Blue Eyes At Somebody Else* Kay Twomey, Al Goodhart.

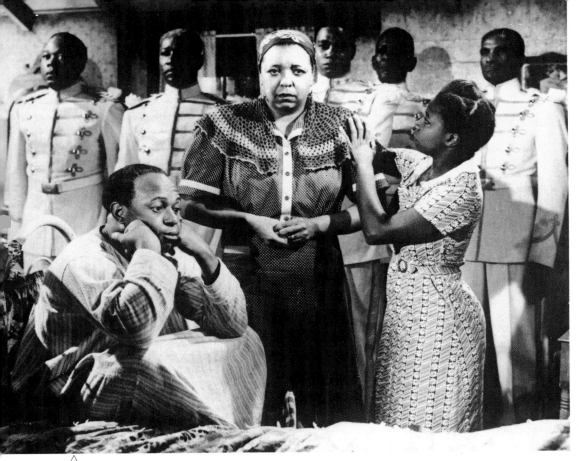

△
Lupe Velez (illustrated centre) played a dual role in **Redhead From Manhattan** (Columbia) – that of a Broadway star, and the star's cousin. They switch identities when Lupe the star is about to have a baby, and the resultant confusion was merely irritating. Michael Duane, Tim Ryan, Gerald Mohr, Lewis Wilson, Lillian Yarbo, and Arthur Loft supported; it was written by Joseph Hoffman from a story by Rex Taylor, with Lew Landers directing for producer Wallace Mac-Donald. Songs and musical numbers: *Why Be Down-hearted? An Ounce Of Bounce*; *The Fiestingo*; *Let's Fall In Line*; *I'm Undecided* Walter G. Samuels, Saul Chaplin; *Twiddlin' My Thumbs* Sammy Cahn, Chaplin.

△
Vincente Minnelli made an auspicious directorial debut with **Cabin in the Sky** (MGM), an all-black musical first seen on Broadway in 1940 where it was an artistic rather than a financial success. Like *The Green Pastures* (Warner Bros., 1936), most of the characters in **Cabin** were simplistic negro stereotypes whose homespun philosophies were pickled in a kind of whimsical folk-lore totally offensive to the more enlightened black. But having accepted that, there was much in it to enjoy, not least the wonderful score by John Latouche, Vernon Duke, Harold Arlen and E.Y. Harburg. Ethel Waters (centre) repeated her vibrant stage performance as Petunia Jackson, with Eddie (Rochester) Anderson (seated left) as her husband (the role originally created by Dooley Wilson), a likeable gambler named Little Joe who cannot resist the temptations of the flesh. And since the flesh that tempted him belonged to Lena Horne, who could blame him! The whimsy intruded when, after a *fracas* in a nightclub in which Little Joe is almost killed, representatives from Heaven (Kenneth Spencer) and Hell (Rex Ingram) fight for possession of his soul. But as handled by Minnelli and his attractive cast, it was never unpalatable. Musical highlights were Waters's singing of the title song (by Latouche and Duke), the sublime 'Happiness Is A Thing Called Joe' (by Arlen and Harburg) – written especially for the film – as well as 'Taking A Chance On Love' (by Latouche, Duke and Ted Fetter), and a lively version of 'Honey In The Honeycomb' (Latouche and Duke) sung by Lena Horne. It was written by Joseph Schrank and produced by Arthur Freed, and the cast included Louis Armstrong, 'Bubbles' Bublett, Oscar Polk, Mantan Moreland, Willie Best, Bill Bailey, Butterfly McQueen (right), Ernest Whitman, Duke Ellington and His Orchestra, and The Hall Johnson Choir. Other songs: *Life's Full Of Consequences* (Anderson, Horne); *Li'l Black Sheep* (Hall Johnson Choir) Arlen, Harburg; *In My Old Virginia Home* (Ellington) Latouche, Duke; *Going Up* composed and performed by Duke Ellington; *Things Ain't What They Used To Be* (Ellington) Ted Persons, Mercer Ellington; *Shine* (Bublett) Lew Brown, Ford Dabney, Cecil Mack.

△
The vivacious and talented Vivian Blaine made her movie debut in **Jitterbugs** (20th Century-Fox) singing three songs in a riverboat nightclub. For the rest it was a mediocre Laurel and Hardy vehicle whose plot line (screenplay and story by Scott Darling) featured them as the willing, if not always able, confederates of a man who attempts to return to Miss Blaine the family fortune out of which she has been cheated by a ring of con-men. To facilitate the plan, Hardy (illustrated with Virginia de Luce) pretends to be a philandering Texan, while Laurel gets into drag as a Bostonian dowager called Aunt Emily. Mal St Clair, who started his career directing Rin-Tin-Tin movies, was the director, and the producer was Sol M. Wurtzel. The dances were staged by Geneva Sawyer, and the cast was completed by Bob Barley, Douglas Fowley, Noel Madison, Lee Patrick, Robert Emmett Keane and Charles Halton. Songs and musical numbers: *The Moon Kissed The Mississippi*; *If The Shoe Fits, Wear It*; *I've Got To See For Myself* Charles Newman, Lew Pollack.

Unless you count her participation in the finale ensemble, Dorothy Lamour (left) didn't do any singing in **Dixie** (Paramount), leaving the vocalizing to Bing Crosby (right) who, as Daniel Decatur Emmett of the 'Virginia Minstrels', lubricated his vocal chords to pleasant effect with such numbers as 'Sunday, Monday Or Always', 'If You Please', 'She's From Missouri', and 'Kinda Peculiar Brown', by Jimmy Van Heusen and Johnny Burke. A largely fictitious account of how Emmett's most popular song, 'Dixie', underwent a tempo change from a slow ballad to a rousing Southern anthem (there was a fire backstage, and Emmett speeded up the song so as to finish it before the fire finished the theatre!), the film also featured Marjorie Reynolds whom Emmett marries out of sympathy when she is stricken with polio (his real love is Lamour), as well as Billy De Wolfe (centre), Lynne Overman, and Eddie Foy Jr, with whom Emmett forms a minstrel troupe in New Orleans. Louis Da Pron appeared as a minstrel dancer, and the cast was completed by Raymond Walburn and Grant Mitchell. It was beautifully photographed in Technicolor (Crosby's first colour film, apart from Universal's *King of Jazz* in 1930), and lavishly costumed by Raoul Pene Du Bois. The dances were staged by Seymour Felix, it was written by Darrell Ware and Karl Tunberg from a story by William Rankin and an adaptation by Claude Binyon, and directed by Edward Sutherland with a pleasing sense of period atmosphere. The associate producer was Paul Jones. Other songs: *A Horse That Knows His Way Back Home*; *Miss Jemima Walks By* Burke, Van Heusen.
▽

Serving no purpose other than to fill the lower half of a double bill, **She Has What It Takes** (Columbia) flaunted a title that was simply asking for trouble. The 'She' in question was Jinx Falkenburg (illustrated right), whose shapely legs were no substitute for her lack of ability in other areas. Miss F. played a small-time singer masquerading as the daughter of a recently deceased stage star, in which guise she persuades a powerful newspaper columnist to sweet-talk a Broadway producer (Joe King) into starring her in a show by way of a tribute to her supposed mother. All goes smoothly until rival columnist Constance Worth discovers the deception . . . The Radio Rogues and The Vagabonds were cast, together with Douglas Leavitt, Matt Willis, Daniel Ocko and George McKay, with Tom Neal (illustrated) co-starring. Paul Yawitz contrived the screenplay (from a story by himself and Robert Lee Johnson), it was produced by Colbert Clark, and the director was Charles Barton. Songs and musical numbers included: *Let's March Together* Saul Chaplin; *I Bumped My Head On A Star* Cindy Walker; *Honk Honk* Roy Jacobs, Gene De Paul; *Timber Timber* Don Reid, Henry Tobias; *Moon On My Pillow* Charles, Henry and Elliott Tobias.

When press agent Marty May is unsuccessful in securing a singing spot on a well-known radio show for his attractive young client Betty Rhodes (right), he conceives the idea of publicizing a romance between her and MacDonald Carey (centre), a recently returned war hero. And that was all there was to **Salute for Three** (Paramount), a rather tasteless trifle that couldn't make up its mind whether it wanted to be a musical, a farce or a drama. The musical numbers were staged in the show's Manhattan canteen, a recreation centre for servicemen, and featured Dona Drake (left) and Her All-Girl Band, Cliff Edwards in a number called 'My Wife's A WAAC' by Jule Styne and Kim Gannon (whose score was better than the film deserved), and comedy ballroom duo Lorraine and Rognan. The screenplay was by Doris Anderson, Curtis Kenyon, Hugh Wedlock Jr and Howard Snyder (story by Art Arthur), and Ralph Murphy directed. Other songs: *Don't Worry*; *What Do You Do When It Rains?*; *I'd Do It For You* Styne, Gannon; *Left, Right* Styne, Gannon, Sol Meyer; *Valse Continental* Victor Young.

A 66-minute filler from Republic, **My Best Gal** starred Jane Withers (foreground right) as a drugstore assistant who, despite an excellent voice, wants no part of show biz. But what she did want – and what she eventually got – were two different things, as those audiences who remained in the cinema after the main feature was over, discovered. Very much the second half of a double bill, it also featured Jimmy Lydon as an embryo composer of musicals and Frank Craven as Miss Withers's ex-hoofer grandfather, as well as George Cleveland (foreground left), Fortunio Bonanova, Franklin Pangborn, Mary Newton and Jack Boyle. Dave Gould staged the musical numbers, it was written by Olive Cooper and Earl Felton from an original story by Richard Brooks, with Anthony Mann directing for associate producer Harry Grey. Songs and musical numbers included: *Where There's Love*; *I've Got The Flyin'est Feelin'*; *Upsy Downsy* Kim Gannon, Walter Kent.

A group of youngsters headed by Gloria Jean, Donald O'Connor (centre) and Peggy Ryan, (right), starred in a quickie from Universal called **Mr Big**. Nothing big about the story (some kids get together to turn a drama school's annual show into a swinging revue), but with Eddie Miller and His Bobcats, tap dancer Bobby Scheerer, The Ben Carter Choir and The Jivin' Jacks and Jills to lend musical support, plus some bouncy dance routines from choreographer Louis Da Pron, it was a pleasant enough way to spend 64 minutes. Robert Paige, Elyse Knox, Samuel S. Hinds, Elinor Donahue, Florence Bates and Ray Eberle were also cast; it was written by Dorothy Bennett and Jack Pollexfen from a story by Virginia Rocks, and directed for producer Ken Goldsmith by Charles Lamont. Songs and musical numbers: *This Must Be A Dream*; *Kittens With Their Mittens Laced*; *Things I Want To Say*; *Spirit Is In Me*; *Rude, Crude And Unattractive*; *Thee And Me*; *We're Not Obvious* Inez James, Buddy Pepper; *Moonlight And Roses* Ben Black, Neil Moret.

Though **Stage Door Canteen** (United Artists) offered a *soupçon* of a plot involving a tender little war-time romance between a soldier (William Terry) and a canteen hostess (Cheryl Walker), it was basically a tribute to the American Theatre Wing who sponsored the enterprise, offering laymen a glimpse of the sort of entertainment servicemen might, if they were lucky, expect to see on any given night of the week at the celebrated Stage Door Canteen in New York. In one bumper round-up of talent, producer Sol Lesser managed to persuade Alfred Lunt to wash a few dishes, Katharine Cornell (her only film appearance) to distribute oranges, and, in other capacities, marshalled the talents of Judith Anderson, Henry Armetta, Benny Baker, Tallulah Bankhead, Ralph Bellamy, Edgar Bergen and Charlie McCarthy, Helen Broderick, Ray Bolger, Lloyd Corrigan, Ina Claire, Jane Darwell, William Demarest, Virginia Field, Dorothy Fields, Gracie Fields, Lynn Fontanne, Arlene Francis, Vinton Freedley, Helen Hayes, Katharine Hepburn, Hugh Herbert, Jean Hersholt, Sam Jaffe, Allen Jenkins, George Jessel, Roscoe Karns, Gypsy Rose Lee, Harpo Marx, Aline MacMahon, Elsa Maxwell, Yehudi Menuhin, Ethel Merman, Paul Muni, Merle Oberon, Franklin Pangborn, George Raft, Lanny Ross, Selena Royle, Martha Scott, Cornelia Otis Skinner, Ethel Waters, Johnny Weissmuller, Dame May Whitty, Ed Wynn, and the bands of Count Basie, Xavier Cugat (illustrated), Benny Goodman (with vocalist Peggy Lee), Kay Kyser, Guy Lombardo, and Freddy Martin. The screenplay was by Delmer Daves and it was directed by Frank Borzage. Ninety per cent of the box-office take went to the American Theatre Wing. Songs and musical numbers: *We Mustn't Say Goodbye*; *The Machine Gun Song*; *Sleep, Baby, Sleep*; *You're Pretty Terrific Yourself*; *Don't Worry Island*; *Quick Sands*; *We Meet In The Funniest Places*; *American Boy*; *A Rookie And His Rhythm* Al Dubin, James V. Monaco; *She's A Bombshell From Brooklyn* Sol Lesser, Dubin, Monaco; *The Girl I Love To Leave Behind* Richard Rodgers, Lorenz Hart; *Why Don't You Do Right?* Joe McCoy; *Bugle Call Rag* Jack Pettis, Billy Meyers, Elmer Schoebel; *Marching Through Berlin* (adaptation of *Deutschland Uber Alles* by Belford Hendricks); *The Lord's Prayer* Albert Hay Malotte.

If *Stage Door Canteen* utilized some of the world's most talented white performers, **Stormy Weather** (20th Century-Fox) rounded up the country's top black artists in a non-stop explosion of song and dance items – loosely threaded together by the merest wisp of a plot involving a tenuous romance between Lena Horne and Bill Robinson. The film spanned a quarter of a century (from 1911 to 1936) in the evolution of black music, and used a revue format to present a series of songs, dances and sketches characteristic of the periods touched upon. Apart from Miss Horne and Mr Robinson, the all-black cast included Cab Calloway and His Orchestra, Fats Waller, The Nicholas Brothers, Katherine Dunham and her dancers, Dooley Wilson (who, unfortunately, wasn't given a song), Ernest Whitman, The Tramp Band, The Shadracks, Ada Brown, and Babe Wallace. The musical numbers were staged by Clarence Robinson, the most elaborate being the title number (by Harold Arlen and Ted Koehler), thrillingly sung by Miss Horne (illustrated) and danced by Katherine Dunham and her troupe. The screenplay was by Frederick Jackson and Ted Koehler, adapted by H.S. Kraft from a story by Jerry Horwin and Seymour B. Robinson. It was directed by Andrew Stone and produced by William Le Baron. Other songs and musical numbers included: *There's No Two Ways About Love* (Robinson, Horne, Calloway) Ted Koehler, James P. Johnson, Irving Mills; *Ain't Misbehavin'* (Waller) Andy Razaf, Fats Waller, Harry Brooks; *Dat, Dot, Dah* (Wallace, The Tramp Band) Cyril J. Mockridge; *I Can't Give You Anything But Love Baby* (Horne, Robinson) Dorothy Fields, Jimmy McHugh; *That Ain't Right* (Brown, Waller) Nat King Cole, Irving Mills; *Diga, Diga, Doo* (Horne, chorus) Fields, McHugh; *I Lost My Sugar In Salt Lake City* (Mae E. Johnson) Johnny Lange, Leon René; *Geechy Joe* (Calloway) Jack Palmer, Andy Gibson, Calloway; *Jumpin' Jive* (Nicholas Brothers) Calloway, Frank Froeba, Palmer; *My, My, Ain't That Something* (Robinson; Finale; Nicholas Brothers, Horne, Calloway) Pinky Tomlin, Harry Tobias; *Rang Tang Tang* (Robinson, children) Cyril J. Mockridge; *At A Georgia Camp Meeting* Kerry Mills; *De Camptown Races* Stephen Foster; *Linda Brown* Al Cowans; *Nobody's Sweetheart* (Whitman) Gus Kahn, Ernie Erdman, Elmer Schoebel, Billy Meyers; *Rhythm Cocktail* (Robinson, Calloway) Calloway.

Singer Ginny Simms was given star status in **Hit The Ice** (Universal), a lively Abbott and Costello (illustrated, with Cornelia Campbell) vehicle in which the comedians starred as a couple of press photographers, who, in Robert Lees, Frederic Rinaldo and John Grant's tailor-made screenplay (from a story by True Boardman) are mistaken for a pair of bank robbers. Four Harry Revel-Paul Francis Webster songs – including a spectacular (for Universal) sequence on ice – interrupted the frantic plot complications in which Patric Knowles, Elyse Knox, Joseph Sawyer, Marc Lawrence, Sheldon Leonard and Johnny Long and His Orchestra were featured. Charles Lamont's direction was precisely what Abbott and Costello fans had come to expect, and the producer was Alex Gottlieb. Songs: *I'm Like A Fish Out Of Water; Happiness Bound; I'd Like To Set You to Music; Slap Polka.*

Written by Charles R. Marion, Albert Beich and Frank Tarloff from a story by Ewart Adamson and Jack White, **Campus Rhythm** (Monogram) was a routine campus programmer about a radio singer (Gale Storm) who runs away from her sponsor and guardian, enrols at a college under an assumed name, and returns to the world of radio in the last reel, bringing a college band with her. Her co-star was Johnny Downs, with Candy Candido (left), Robert Lowery (centre), Ge-Ge Pearson and Doug Leavitt in support. Lindsley Parsons produced, Arthur Dreifuss directed. Songs and musical numbers included: *Walking The Chalk Line* Jules Loman, Louis Herscher; *Swing Your Way Through College* Andy Iona Long, Herscher; *It's Great To Be A College Girl; College Sweetheart* Herscher.

Harvest Melody (PRC) found attractive Rosemary Lane as a famous film star doing her bit for the war effort by pitching hay on the farm – and pitching woo in the direction of Johnny Downs (right). It was all a publicity stunt dreamed up by her agent (Sheldon Leonard), but after a spell in the country Miss Lane decides she *likes* the cool fresh wind in her hair, life without care etc., and gives up a lucrative contract that would have taken her back to Hollywood. Or to paraphrase the well-known song, 'How you gonna keep her down in Hollywood, Now that she's seen the farm'! Charlotte Wynters, Luis Alberni, Claire Rochelle and Syd Saylor were also cast; so were Eddie Le Baron (left) and His Orchestra, and that bunch of impersonators called The Radio Rogues. It was written by Allan Gale from an original story by Martin Mooney and Andy Lamb, and directed by Sam Newfield. Songs: *You Could Have Knocked Me Over With A Feather; Put It In Reverse; Let's Drive Out To A Drive-In* Benny Davis, Harry Akst; *Tenderly* Leo Shuken, Walter Colmes.

By 1943 Betty Grable was the favourite pin-up girl of servicemen everywhere, and the world's number one box-office attraction. With a minimum of talent, a great deal of sex appeal (including what was purported to be the best pair of legs in the world), and the good fortune, professionally, to be surrounded by a production team at 20th Century-Fox who knew exactly how to exploit her, she entered the golden years of her career with **Coney Island**, a formula – but splashily produced (by William Perlberg) – antidote to the grim realities at the front. Again set at the turn of the century, it top-starred Grable (illustrated left) as a saloon entertainer whose career is promoted and encouraged by two carnival men – George Montgomery and Cesar Romero (illustrated right) – rivals both in love and professionally. There wasn't much more to it than that, and the musical numbers far outshone George Seaton's screenplay in which Betty sang a few oldies such as 'Cuddle Up A Little Closer' (by Karl Hoschna and Otto Harbach), 'Pretty Baby' (by Gus Kahn, Tony Jackson, and Egbert Van Alstyne), and 'Put Your Arms Around Me Honey' (by Albert von Tilzer and Junie McCree). She also sang a few numbers by the much missed Ralph Rainger who had died in a plane crash in 1942, and Leo Robin – most notably 'Take It From There' and 'Lulu From Louisville'. Charles Winninger and Phil Silvers also appeared, so did Matt Briggs, Paul Hurst, Frank Orth and Carmen D'Antonio. The film ended with an elaborately staged production number called 'There's Danger In A Dance' (Rainger, Robin), choreographed by Hermes Pan. Walter Lang directed. It was remade in 1950 as *Wabash Avenue* with Grable again in the lead. Other songs: *Get The Money; Old Demon Rum; Beautiful Coney Island* Rainger, Robin; *Who Threw The Overalls In Mrs Murphy's Chowder?* George L. Giefer; *Darktown Strutters Ball* Shelton Brooks; Medley: *Deep River* traditional, *Oh Susanna; The Old Folks At Home* Stephen Foster; *Let Me Call You Sweetheart* Beth Slater Whitson, Leo Friedman; *Dengozo (Maxixe)* Ernesto Nazareth.

Freddie Slack, Harry Owens (illustrated with baton), Ted Weems, and their respective orchestras, were given above-the-title billing in **Hat Check Honey**, an indifferent programmer from Universal. The movie also featured Leon Erroll as an old-time vaudevillian, Richard Davies (left) as the son he 'fires' from their stage act in order to give the boy a chance to make it on his own, and Grace McDonald as the glamorous 'hat check honey' Davis falls for. Walter Catlett, Ramsay Ames (2nd left), Jimmy Cash, Milburn Stone and Mary Gordon also appeared, and it was written by Maurice Leo and Stanley Davis from a story by Al Martin. The associate producer was Will Cowan and it was directed by Edward F. Cline. Songs and musical numbers: *Slightly Sentimental; Nice To Know You; A Dream Ago; Rockin' With You; A Small Batch O'Nod; Loose Wig; Drumola; Rhythm Of The Islands; It Happened In Kaloha* Everett Carter, Milton Rosen.

Forties Musicals

George Abbott's smash Broadway musical **Best Foot Forward** came to the screen in Technicolor, compliments of MGM, with most of its youthful exuberance intact, but labouring under a screenplay dogged with *longueurs*. Its tissue paper plot about a fearless lad who invites a famous film star to be his date at a military school dance, was all that was needed to set one's toes a-tapping, and with Lucille Ball as the illustrious star – turning on the glamour as well as all the males, with her sentimental 'You're Lucky' by Hugh Martin and Ralph Blane (who provided the entire score but for two inter-polated instrumentals) – it couldn't miss. Tommy Dix as the hero played the role created on the stage by Gil Stratton. Other recruits from the Broadway cast were those two diminutive lasses Nancy Walker (right), June Allyson (left), Kenny Bowers and Jack Jordan, and the rest of the movie cast was completed by William Gaxton, Virginia Weidler (wasted), Gloria De Haven (centre), Beverly Tyler, Chill Wills, Henry O'Neill, and Harry James and His Music Makers. Charles Walters staged the energetic musical numbers with assistance from Jack Donohue and Stanley Donen; it was written by Irving Brecher and Fred Finkelhoffe from the original book by John Cecil Holm, and directed by Edward Buzzell for producer Arthur Freed. Other songs and musical numbers: *Wish I May; Three Men On A Date; Ev'ry Time; The Three B's; Buckle Down Winsocki; Alive And Kicking* Martin, Blane; *The Flight Of The Bumble Bee* Rimsky-Korsakov; *Two O'Clock Jump* Count Basie, Harry James, Benny Goodman.

Judy Canova (illustrated) found herself standing for 'morality candidate' in an all-feminine reform campaign to restore law and order to boom town **Sleepy Lagoon** (Republic). Backed by Ruth Donnelly, she wins the election and begins her battle against a group of shady politicians headed by the town's mayor (Will Wright). A workaday programmer with little to recommend it other than its brevity (it ran 64 minutes), it also featured Dennis Day (left), Joe Sawyer, Ernest Truex, Douglas Fowley, Jack Raymond (illustrated as clown) and Mike Riley and His Orchestra. It was written by George Carleton Brown and Frank Gill (story by Prescott Chaplin), and directed by Joseph Santley. The producer was Albert J. Cohen. Songs and musical numbers: *If You Are There; You're The Fondest Thing I Am Of; I'm Not Myself Anymore* Ned Washington, Phil Ohman; *Sleepy Lagoon* Jack Lawrence, Eric Coates; *I'm On My Way; I Do* Buddy Pepper, Inez James; *Take It And Git* James T. Marshall, Johnny Green.

In **Spotlight Scandals**, a better than average programmer from Monogram, Frank Fay (left) starred as an actor stranded in a small town who becomes partners with the local barber (Billy Gilbert) in a vaudeville act. They soon become headliners but, in time, Gilbert steps aside to allow Fay to go it alone as a radio celebrity. After a series of business and romantic complications, the team is finally reunited. Bonnie Baker and Iris Adrian (centre) provided the female interest, with Harry Langdon (right), James Bush, Betty Blythe and Jim Hope completing the cast. The film's backstage setting allowed for several production numbers (staged by Jack Boyle), as well as a miscellany of musical interludes as supplied by The Radio Rogues, Henry King and His Orchestra, Herb Miller and His Orchestra, Claudia Dell, and Eddie Parks. It was written by William X. Crowley and Beryl Sachs, produced by Sam Katzman and Jack Dietz, and directed by William Beaudine. Songs and musical numbers included: *The Restless Age* Ed Rose, Abe Olman; *Goodnight Now; The Lilac Tree; Tempo Of The Trail; Oh Johnny*.

It was thumbs down for **Thumbs Up** (Republic), a 67-minute nonentity which found Brenda Joyce (left) as a nightclub chanteuse, falling in love with Douglas Heath of the RAF, but determined, at the same time, to exploit her friendship with theatrical manager Arthur Margetson in a bid for stardom. Elsa Lanchester (centre) co-starred, with J. Pat O'Malley, Queenie Leonard, Molly Lamont (right), Gertrude Niesen, George Byron, Andre Charlot and The Hot Shots completing the cast. Frank Gill Jr wrote it (from an idea by Ray Golden and Henry Moritz), Albert J. Cohen produced, and the director was Joseph Santley. Songs and musical numbers included: *From Here On; Love Is A Corny Thing; Who Are The British* Sammy Cahn, Jule Styne; *Zing Went The Strings Of My Heart* James Hanley.

Radio's Al Pearce played a dual role in **Here Comes Elmer** (Republic): himself, and a low pressure door-to-door salesman. A mistaken identity yarn in which a group of entertainers search for a sponsor, its musical talent was recruited mainly from radio, and included Artie Auerbach, William Comstock, Pinky Tomlin, Wendell Niles, The Sportsmen, The 'King' Cole Trio, and Jan Garber and His Band. The cast was completed by Dale Evans, Frank Albertson, Wally Vernon, Gloria Stuart, Arlene Harris, Nick Cochrane, Will Wright, Thurston Hall and Luis Alberni. It was written by Jack Townley and Stanley Davis, and directed by Joseph Santley for associate producer Armand Schaefer. Songs: *Straighten Up And Fly Right* Nat 'King' Cole, Irving Mills; *Don't Be Afraid To Tell Your Mother* Pinky Tomlin, Coy Poe, Jimmie Greer; *You're So Good To Me* Sammy Cahn, Jule Styne; *Hitch Old Dobbin To The Shay Again* J.C. Lewis Jr, Judd Conlon; *Put On Your Old Grey Bonnet* Stanley Murphy, Percy Wenrich.

No answer was forthcoming in **What's Buzzin' Cousin?** (Columbia), and not much entertainment value either, as Ann Miller (illustrated) – top starred – set out to refurbish a hotel she had inherited in an uninviting ghost town. She was assisted in her endeavours by Eddie (Rochester) Anderson, John Hubbard, Freddy Martin and His Orchestra, Leslie Brooks, Jeff Donnell, Carol Hughes and Theresa Harris, Harry Sauber wrote it from a story by Aben Kandel, with John P. Medbury contributing some additional dialogue, and it was directed by Charles Barton for producer Jack Fier. Songs and musical numbers included: *$18.75* Wally Anderson; *Ain't That Just Like A Man; Short, Fat And 4F* Don Raye, Gene De Paul; *Nevada* Mort Greene, Walter Donaldson; *Knocked Out Nocturne* Jacques Press.

The Andrews Sisters sang an average of one song every twelve minutes in **How's About It?**, an hour-long programmer from Universal in which they played a trio of elevator operators in a music publishing building, who are hoping for a crack at the big time. Robert Paige co-starred as a music publisher accused of plagiarising Grace McDonald's lyrics, but a romantic involvement between the pair of them quashes the impending damages suit he would otherwise have had to face. With the Andrews girls and young hoofer Bobby Scheerer supplying the music, and Paige and McDonald the romance, it was left to Walter Catlett and Shemp Howard (illustrated with two Andrews Sisters – Patty left, Maxene right) to provide the laughs. Which they spasmodically did. Erle C. Kenton directed from a screenplay by Mel Ronson (original story by Jack Goodman and Albert Rice, adapted by John Grey), and the producer was Ken Goldsmith. Songs and musical numbers: *Don't Mind The Rain* Ned Miller, Chester Cohn; *Take It And Git* William and Melville Chapman, James T. Marshall, Johnny Green; *East Of The Rockies* Sid Robin; *Going Up* Irving Gordon, Allen Roth; *Here Comes The Navy* (*Beer Barrel Polka*) Lew Brown, W.A. Timm, J. Vejvoda, Clarence P. Oakes.

Universal, a studio not noted for its extravagance, opened its tight fists and spent one and a half million dollars on a Technicolor remake of **The Phantom of the Opera**, a lavishly costumed (by Vera West), opulently produced (by George Waggner) chiller that singularly failed to chill. Little wonder, since the accent was more on music than on horror, with Nelson Eddy and Susanna Foster top-starred as the Paris Opera's main attraction. Lurking behind the scenes with vengeance on his mind was Claude Rains (illustrated, in the Lon Chaney role), giving the only ineffectual performance of his career as an elderly violinist who believes that his music is being stolen by publisher Miles Mander. But with music predominating to the extent that it did, there wasn't a great deal that he could do in Eric Taylor and Samuel Hoffenstein's screenplay (based on the story by Gaston Leroux and adapted by John Jacoby) *other* than lurk. Arthur Lubin directed without distinction, and his cast included Edgar Barrier, Jane Farrar, Barbara Everest, Steve Geray, Frank Puglia, Hume Cronyn and, as Franz Liszt, Fritz Leiber. The opera sequences were staged by William von Wymetal and Lester Horton, and featured scenes from Flotow's *Martha*, as well as two operas contrived for the film from Tchaikovsky's Symphony No. 4 and the music of Chopin. The other music was 'Lullaby Of The Bells', by Edward Ward and George Waggner, sung by Eddy and Foster, and also heard as both a violin solo and a piano concerto.

Newcomers David Bruce (left) and June Vincent as a couple whose marriage is on the rocks, try, in **Honeymoon Lodge** (Universal), to salvage what's left of their relationship by returning to the scene of their courtship in a mountain resort. What they don't reckon on is the arrival of Harriet Hilliard (right) and Rod Cameron – the latter pursuing Miss Vincent, the former being pursued by Mr Bruce. However, it was all smoothed out – to the accompaniment of several song and dance items delivered by Miss Hilliard and her real-life husband Ozzie Nelson (and orchestra), as well as by Ray Eberle, high tenor Bobby Brooke (singing 'Do I Worry' by Bobby Worth and Stanley Cowan), Tip, Tap and Toe, and Veloz and Yolanda. Franklin Pangborn, Andrew Tombes, Clarence Muse (centre) and Martin Ashe completed the cast for producer Warren Wilson (who also provided the story), it was scripted by Clyde Bruckman, and directed by Edward Lilley. Other songs and musical numbers: *I'm Through With Love* Gus Kahn, Matt Malneck, Fud Livingston; *Why Don't You Fall In Love With Me?* Al Lewis, Mabel Wayne; *I Never Knew* Tom Pitts, Ray Egan, Roy K. Marsh; *Jersey Jive* Minor Hassel, Ozzie Nelson.

Deanna Durbin (illustrated centre right), now a fully grown woman, suffered the pangs of an unhappy love affair in **Hers to Hold** (Universal), a tear-jerker which found her working in an aircraft factory in order to be close to pilot Joseph Cotten (illustrated centre left), the man she loves. But being war time, he is soon parted from her, thus cueing in an unhappy ending and the dabbing of moist eyes throughout the house. Charles Winninger played Deanna's father, with other roles in this competent but unexceptional weepie going to Gus Schilling, Nella Walker, Evelyn Ankers, Ludwig Stossel, William Davidson and Irving Bacon. Lewis R. Foster wrote it from a story by John D. Klorer, Felix Jackson produced, and Frank Ryan directed. There were five songs, all performed by Miss Durbin, including a popular war-time hit, *Say A Pray'r For The Boys Over There* by Herb Magidson and Jimmy McHugh. Other songs: *Begin the Beguine* Cole Porter; *Kashmiri Love Song* Lawrence Hope, Amy Woodforde-Finden; *The Seguidilla* from Bizet's 'Carmen'.

Melody Parade was a Monogram programmer set in a nightclub whose desperate owner, Tim Ryan (right) needs a financial windfall if the spot is to stay open. Enter Irene Ryan, whom Tim erroneously believes has inherited a fortune and will be able to bail him out. Complications begat complications, with time off for several musical interludes by Mary Beth Hughes (2nd left), top-starred as a hat-check girl with show biz aspirations, Ted Fiorito and His Orchestra, The Loumel Morgan Trio, black crooner Jerry Cooper, Armida, and Anson Weeks and His Band. Eddie Quillan (left), Paul Porcasi (centre) and Andre Charlot completed the cast, it was written by Tim Ryan and Charles R. Marion for producer Lindsley Parsons, and directed by Arthur Dreifuss with Jack Boyle in charge of the musical numbers. Songs: *I Don't Know*; *Woman Behind The Man Behind The Gun*; *Amigo*; *Whatever Possessed Me*; *Mr And Mrs Commando*; *Don't Fall In Love*; *Speechless* Eddie Cherkose, Edward Kay.

Even its star, Leon Errol (illustrated), looked unhappy throughout **Gals Incorporated** (Universal). Fortunately, his suffering (and ours) was over in a mere 61 minutes – the time it took director Leslie Goodwins to unfurl Edward Dein's screenplay (from a story by Dave Gould and Charles Marion) about a millionaire (Errol) who plays sugar daddy to a nightclubful of gold diggers, much to the consternation of his sister (Minna Phillips) and his son (David Bacon). Harriet Hilliard, Grace McDonald, Betty Kean, Maureen Cannon and Lillian Cornell completed the cast, with Glen Gray and His Casa Loma Orchestra, plus The Pied Pipers, supplying the music. Songs included: *Here's Your Kiss*; *Hep Hep Hooray*; *All The Time It's You* Everett Carter, Milton Rosen.

Mary Lee (illustrated, centre left foreground) emerged as the star of the Annual Pennington Revue (Pennington being a school for the kids of show folk) in **Nobody's Darling** (Republic), an unassuming 'B' whose whisper of a story was little more than a pedestal on which its young star was prettily perched. Gladys George appeared as Mary's mum, Louis Calhern was her dad, with other roles in Olive Cooper's screenplay (original story by F. Hugh Herbert) going to Jackie Moran (as Mary's youthful inamorata), Lee Patrick, Bennie Bartlett, Marcia Mae Jones and Lloyd Corrigan. Anthony Mann directed and the producer was Harry Grey. Songs and musical numbers included: *It Had To Be You* Gus Kahn, Isham Jones; *Blow, Gabriel, Blow* Cole Porter; *I'm Always Chasing Rainbows* Joseph McCarthy, Harry Carroll; *On The Sunny Side Of The Street* Dorothy Fields, Jimmy McHugh; *Row, Row, Row Your Boat*.

▽

There were lots of topical gags about war-time rationing in **Let's Face It** (Paramount), a musical farce based on the stage show by Cole Porter and Herbert and Dorothy Fields (and a play by Norma Mitchell and Russell G. Medcraft). The film version starred Bob Hope (illustrated centre) in the role created on Broadway by Danny Kaye and, let's face it, with three philandering businessmen, their justifiably suspicious wives, the three soldiers hired by the put-upon wives to make their spouses jealous, as well as the three legitimate girlfriends of the soldiers and the three floozies being dated by the husbands all showing up at the same time, confusion reigned supreme. With fifteen people to juggle around in the finale, director Sidney Lanfield had his hands full, but coped with it all as if it were a military manoeuvre. And just to add to the plot's density, scenarist Harry Tugend had Hope heroically capturing an enemy submarine by holding a mirror to the periscope and sending it aground off Long Island Sound. Betty Hutton (centre left) co-starred as Hope's fiancée – a woman who runs a health farm for overweight ladies – and the trio of aggrieved wives were Eve Arden, ZaSu Pitts and Phyllis Povah. Other roles in Fred Kohlmar's production went to Dave Willock, Cully Richards, Marjorie Weaver, Dona Drake, Raymond Walburn, Andrew Tombes and Arthur Loft. Songs and musical numbers included: *Let's Not Talk About Love* (Hutton); *Let's Face It* (Willock, Richards, chorus) Cole Porter; *Who Did? I Did* (Hope, Hutton) Jule Styne, Sammy Cahn.

◁ **Du Barry was a Lady** (MGM) was, to say the least, a disappointment. Although its basic story was similar to Cole Porter's Broadway original (by Buddy De Sylva and Herbert Fields) in which a nightclub employee wins a sweepstake, drinks a Mickey Finn, and dreams that he is Louis XV, and that his Du Barry is the nightclub's singer with whom he happens to be hopelessly in love, practically everything else that made the Broadway show such a hit was changed or discarded. Though three of Porter's songs survived the transition, the majority of the numbers were written by Ralph Freed and Burton Lane, E.Y. Harburg, Lew Brown and Roger Edens, and although there was nothing fundamentally wrong with them, they weren't as good as the Porter songs, neither were they as *risqué*. Lucille Ball (centre left) and Red Skelton (centre) played the roles created on Broadway by Ethel Merman and Bert Lahr, with Rags Ragland and Zero Mostel in support. Gene Kelly (left) was in it too, as a dancer in love with Miss Ball, and who, in the dream sequence, is re-incarnated as a dashing revolutionary known as The Black Arrow. His best moment came near the beginning in a routine called 'Do I Love You' (by Porter) which choreographer Charles Walters staged with an imaginative and exciting fusion of music and movement. Virginia O'Brien (centre right) appeared in the role created on Broadway by Betty Grable, and devoured a rather sexy number Roger Edens wrote for her called 'No Matter How You Slice It, It's Still Salome'. Tommy Dorsey (right) and his boys (including Dick Haymes, and with female vocalist Jo Stafford) gave a good account of 'Katie Went To Haiti' (Porter), as well as an instrumental rendition of 'I'm Getting Sentimental Over You' (by Ned Washington and George Bassman), and the entire company ended the film with Porter's rousing 'Friendship'. If only the screenplay (by Irving Brecher) had matched the quality of some of the aforementioned musical sequences. Du Barry would indeed have been a lady – as it turned out, she was a bit of a tramp and – worse still – a bit of a bore. Arthur Freed produced in Technicolor, and the director was Roy Del Ruth. Other songs and musical numbers: *Du Barry Was A Lady* Ralph Freed, Burton Lane; *I Love An Esquire Girl* Freed, Roger Edens, Lew Brown; *Ladies Of The Bath* Edens; *Madame, I Love Your Crepes Suzettes* Freed, Lane, Brown.

On learning that her employees can't stand her, Esther Dale, president of Bird Dairies, sets out to discover why, by posing as a labourer, in **Swing Your Partner** (Republic). The screenplay, written by Dorrell and Stuart McGowan provided roles for Lulubelle and Scotty, Richard Lane (centre left), Vera Vague (centre right), Roger Clark and Judy Clark as well as for radio entertainers Ransom Sherman, Harry 'Pappy' Cheshire,

George 'Shug' Fisher and The Tennessee Ramblers. Armand Schaefer produced and it was directed by Frank McDonald. Songs included: *Cheese Cake*; *Swing Your Partner* Charles Henderson; *Cracker Barrel County* Frank Loesser, Jule Styne; *Everybody Kiss Your Pardner* Dick Sanford, John Redmond, Frank Weldon; *Shug Shug Yodel* George 'Shug' Fisher; *In The Cool Of The Evening* Walter Bullock, Jule Styne.

The oft-quoted remark about there being nothing wrong with a bad musical that a new book, new music, new lyrics, new sets and new performances wouldn't improve, applied to **Follies Girl** (PRC), a no-no effort whose marquee value was limited to the very limited Wendy Barrie, Gordon Oliver and Doris Nolan (centre), plus several of radio's currently popular band-

Is Everybody Happy? (Columbia) opened with clarinettist Ted Lewis (illustrated foreground centre) playing an engagement in San Francisco. At an army camp there, he meets the son of an old vaudeville partner of his and learns that the lad (Larry Parks) refuses to marry the girl he loves (Nan Wynn) because he fears returning home from the war an invalid. So Ted tells him a story (in flashback) about a pianist who, in World War I, had his hand blown off in the trenches, but returned home to marry the girl he left behind and, with piano playing no longer possible, took up the trumpet instead. Convinced, the young man decides he'll marry his girl after all, and does so in a military ceremony. And was everybody happy? Not according to the indifferent box-office returns. Michael Duane, Lynn Merrick, Bob Haymes and Dick Winslow were also in it; it was written by Monte Brice and directed by Charles Burton. Musical numbers: *It Had To Be You* Gus Kahn, Isham Jones; *More Than Anyone Else In The World* Charles Kenny, Ruth Lowe; *This Old High Hat of Mine* Ted Lewis; *Cuddle Up A Little Closer* Otto Harbach, Karl Hoschna; *I'm Just Wild About Harry* Eubie Blake, Noble Sissle; *Way Down Yonder In New Orleans* Henry Creamer, Turner Layton; *On The Sunny Side Of The Street* Dorothy Fields, Jimmy McHugh; *St Louis Blues* W.C. Handy; *Pretty Baby* Kahn, Tony Jackson, Egbert Van Alstyne; *Am I Blue?* Grant Clarke, H. Akst.

leaders including Johnny Long, Bobby Byrne, Ray Heatherton and Ernie Holst. Realizing that this line-up might not be enough, producer-director William Rowland hired the services of The Charles Weidman Dance Group, Lazara and Castellanos, The Song Spinners, The Heat Waves, Gil Thompson, and Claire and Arena. The story – a convoluted and highly implausible yarn featuring a burlesque singer, a dress designer, a private in the army, and several whiskery ploys such as mistaken identity, was by Marcy Klauber and Charles Robinson. Songs: *Keep The Flag A-Flying* Mary Schaefer; *No Man In The House* Nick and Charles Kenny, Sonny Burke; *Someone To Love* Robert Warren; *I Told A Lie* Nick Kenny, Kim Gannon, Ken Lane; *Shall We Gather At The Rhythm?* Kenny, Burke, John Murphy; *Fascination*; *I Knew Your Father's Son*; *Thoity Poiple Boids* Fred Wise, Buddy Kaye, Sidney Lippman.

Allan Jones (centre in tuxedo), Kitty Carlisle (centre) and Leo Carrillo starred in **Larceny with Music** (Universal), with Carrillo as the owner of a nightspot who, believing that Jones is about to inherit a fortune, hires the singer for his club. The most striking aspect of the film was the extraordinary number of complications that scenarist Robert Harari managed to work into 64 minutes of screen time. Lee Patrick, William Frawley, Gus Schilling, Samuel S. Hinds and Sig Arno were in it, together with The King Sisters (illustrated, foreground left and right), and Alvino Rey and His Orchestra. Howard Benedict produced and the director was Edward Lilley. Songs and musical numbers included: *When You Wore A Tulip* Jack Mahoney, Percy Wenrich; *For The Want Of You* Jule Styne, Eddie Cherkose; *They Died With Their Boots Laced*; *Do You Hear Music*; *Please Louise* Don Raye, Gene De Paul; *Only In Dreams* Sam Lerner, Charles Previn.

The most distinctive thing about **The Sky's The Limit** (RKO) was that it yielded the Johnny Mercer-Harold Arlen evergreen 'One For My Baby (And One More For The Road)'. For the rest it was a lustreless musical that featured Astaire (illustrated) as a Flying Tiger war hero who, rather than spend time on a coast-to-coast glory tour, assumes a false name, pretends to be a civilian and takes himself to New York where he meets and falls for Joan Leslie, a photographer for a picture magazine who is passionately committed to the war effort. The usual misunderstandings helped pad out Frank Fenton and Lynn Root's flaccid screenplay; so did three so-so dance routines, staged by Astaire. Miss Leslie's singing voice was dubbed by Sally Sweetland (though she did all her own dancing – and not too badly at that), and the cast was completed by Robert Benchley, Robert Ryan, Elizabeth Patterson, Marjorie Gateson, Eric Blore, Clarence Kolb, Richard Davies, Paul Hurst, Ed McNamara, Olin Howlin, and Freddie Slack and His Orchestra. David Hempstead produced and the director was Edward H. Griffith. Other musical numbers: *My Shining Hour* performed by Joan Leslie; *A Lot In Common With You* danced by Astaire and Leslie. Mercer, Arlen.

Sonja Henie's last film for her *alma mater*, 20th ▷
Century-Fox, was **Wintertime**, and it was the
least good of the series: an ice-capade that
melted long before the final fade. Plot with a
small 'p' had Sonja (illustrated centre), as a
Norwegian skating star, saving a run-down
winter resort in Canada simply by being there.
Appearing opposite Miss Henie were Jack Oakie
(as the owner of the resort), S.Z Sakall as her
uncle, and Cornel Wilde as the romantic inter-
est. Also: Cesar Romero, Carole Landis, Helene
Reynolds, Don Douglas, Geary Steffen, Dick
Elliott, and Woody Herman and His Orchestra.
E. Edwin Moran, Jack Jevne and Lynn Starling
wrote it from a story by Arthur Kober, John
Brahm directed, and the producer was William
Le Baron. Musical numbers: *Wintertime*; *Later
Tonight*; *Dancing In The Dawn*; *I'm All A-Twitter
Over You*; *We Always Get Our Girl*; *I Like It Here*;
Ice Ballet (arranged by David Raksin) Nacio Herb
Brown, Leo Robin.

MGM's big-budget contribution to Uncle Sam's
war effort was the roaringly successful
Thousands Cheer, not to be confused with Irving
Berlin's 1933 Broadway revue *As Thousands
Cheer*. What originally started life as a small-
scale romance between a colonel's daughter and
a circus aerialist-turned-soldier, became a full-
scale musical crowned with a jewelled tiara of
guest stars, all of whom appeared in a lengthy
showcase finale. Gene Kelly played the army
private and former aerialist, Kathryn Grayson
(illustrated), was the colonel's daughter, John
Boles the colonel, and Mary Astor his estranged
wife. The finale, set in a servicemen's camp, had
Mickey Rooney as MC, again giving his imitations of Clark Gable and Lionel Barrymore (in
MGM's *Test Pilot*, 1938), just as he had done four
years earlier in *Babes In Arms* (MGM). If the
studio's proud boast was that it had more stars
than there were in heaven, they were all in
Thousands Cheer. Eleanor Powell, no longer as
youthful or as agile as she had been in her
Broadway Melody series, still managed to dance
up a storm; Red Skelton did an item with child
star Margaret O'Brien in which they had a
competition to see who could eat the most ice
cream; Frank Morgan as a phoney medic leer-
ingly examined three WAVES (one of whom was
Lucille Ball); deadpan Virginia O'Brien sang 'In
A Little Spanish Town' (by Sam M. Lewis, Joe
Young, Mabel Wayne) flanked by Gloria De
Haven and June Allyson; Lena Horne gave a
memorable account of 'Honeysuckle Rose' (by
Andy Razaf and Fats Waller); Kay Kyser, Bob
Crosby and Benny Carter appeared with their
respective bands; Maxine Barrett and Don Loper
danced beautifully together to 'Tico Tico' (by
Zequinha Abreu), while Judy Garland – snap-
pily accompanied by Jose Iturbi – belted out a
number called 'The Joint Is Really Jumpin' in
Carnegie Hall' (by Ralph Blane, Hugh Martin
and Roger Edens), Kathryn Grayson sang 'Daybreak' (by Harold Adamson and Ferde Grofé),
'Three Letters In The Mailbox' (by Paul Francis
Webster and Walter Jurmann), 'Let There Be
Music' (by E.Y. Harburg and Earl Brent), 'The
United Nations On The March' (by Dimitri
Shostakovitch, Harburg, Harold Rome and Herbert Stothart), and 'Sempre Libera' from Verdi's
La Traviata. The only chance Gene Kelly got to
dance was when, confined to quarters for in-
subordination and made to clean the local PX,
he did what was called 'The Mop Dance' – the
freshest, most inventive few minutes in the
show, to music comprising 'I Dug A Ditch' (by
Lew Brown, Ralph Freed and Burton Lane) and
'Let Me Call You Sweetheart' (by Beth Slater
Whitson and Leo Friedman). The rest of the cast
was completed by Ben Blue, Frances Rafferty,
Mary Elliott, Frank Jenks, Frank Sully, Dick
Simmons and Ben Lessy, with guest appearances
also from Ann Sothern, Marsha Hunt, Marilyn
Maxwell, John Conte and Sara Haden. The film
was written by Paul Jarrico and Richard Collins,
the director was George Sidney, and it was produced by Joseph L. Pasternak, who, with this
one, presented MGM with one of the top money-
making musical movies of the year. Other songs
and musical numbers: *Should I?* Arthur Freed,
Nacio Herb Brown; Medley: *American Patrol*
E.H. Meacham; *Columbia, The Gem of The
Ocean* (authorship disputed); *Yankee Doodle*
(anonymous).

△

Another star-studded variety show from Warner Bros. tailored to the war-torn times, **This is the Army** was Irving Berlin's glowing musical homage to the American soldier. A film version of the stage success that had raised the astronomical sum of $1,951,045.11 for Army Emergency Relief, it succeeded in earning a great deal more than that for producer Hal B. Wallis who took back only his production costs from the profits. Michael Curtiz directed with a patriotic flavour that was faithful to the original, and which featured the 350 soldiers who had appeared in the Broadway production, as well as Joan Leslie, George Murphy, Ronald Reagan, George Tobias, Alan Hale, Charles Butterworth, Dolores Costello, Frances Langford, Gertrude Niesen, Kate Smith, and Sergeant Joe Louis. The screenplay was by Casey Robinson and Captain Claude Binyon; LeRoy Prinz and Robert Sidney took charge of the musical numbers, and composer-lyricist Berlin appeared in one of them – 'Oh How I Hate To Get Up In The Morning'. Most of the principals contributed their services free, while the soldiers worked for their regular army pay. Other songs and musical numbers: *This Is The Army Mr Jones* (Full company); *The Army's Made A Man Out Of Me* (M/Sgt Ezra Stone, Sgt Julie Oshins, Sgt Philip Truex); *God Bless America* (Kate Smith); *I'm Getting Tired So I Can Sleep* (Sgt James Burell); *What The Well-Dressed Man In Harlem Will Wear* (Pvt James Cross); *I Left My Heart At The Stagedoor Canteen* (Adjt Earl Oxford); *How About A Cheer For The Navy* (Company, illustrated); *Poor Little Me, I'm On K.P.* (Tobias, chorus); *With My Head In The Clouds* (Sgt Robert Shanley); *Your Country And My Country* (Gertrude Niesen); *My Sweetie* (Murphy); *We're On Our Way To France* (Murphy, Tobias, Hale, company); *What Does He Look Like* (Frances Langford); *Mandy* (Cpl Ralph Magelssen, company); *Ladies Of The Chorus* (Hale, company); *This Time Is The Last Time* (Sgt Shanley, company); *American Eagles* (Shanley, company).

Never a Dull Moment (Universal) was The Ritz Brothers' last film, and the best of the three they made for Universal. Running exactly an hour, it was true to its title, with the brothers posing as Chicago mobsters as part of their nightclub act. When, however, they discover that what they've really been hired for is to receive stolen jewels pick-pocketed from the club's patrons by Mary Beth Hughes, they want out. Which was easier said than done. Frances Langford (illustrated seated) co-starred as the club's resident nightingale, with Stuart Crawford, Elisabeth Risdon, George Zucco, Jack La Rue, Ruby Dandridge (standing right) and Franklin Pangborn (left) also featured. Apart from Miss Langford, who sang 'My Blue Heaven' (by George Whiting and Walter Donaldson), and 'Sleepytime Gal' (by Richard Whiting, Joseph Alden, Ray Egan and Ange Lorenzo), there were appearances by The Rogers Dancers, and ballroom dancers Grace and Igor Poggi. Mel Ronson and Stanley Roberts wrote it (story by Roberts), it was produced by Howard Benedict, and directed by Edward Lilley. Other songs and musical numbers included: *Hello*; *Yakimboomba* Eddie Cherkose, David Rose, Jacques Press; *Once You Find Your Guy* Cherkose, Rose.

▽

Thank Your Lucky Stars (Warner Bros.) typified a certain kind of movie musical which only a major studio could afford to turn out during the war: one which presented a bumper pack of stars (not all of them necessarily equipped as musical performers) to bring entertainment into the lives of the soldiers overseas as well as the families they left behind. With a screenplay by Norman Panama, Melvin Frank and James V. Kern (from a flimsy story by Everett Freeman and Arthur Schwartz) about two producers – S.Z. Sakall and Edward Everett Horton – who get involved with an unknown female songwriter (Joan Leslie, centre), a singer (Dennis Morgan, left), and Eddie Cantor (right) in a dual role, **Thank Your Lucky Stars** boasted a line-up of talent which had Dinah Shore, Ann Sheridan, Alexis Smith, Joyce Reynolds, Hattie McDaniel, Willie Best, Spike Jones and His City Slickers, Jack Carson, Alan Hale, Errol Flynn, Olivia De Havilland, Jesse Lee Brooks, and Ida Lupino all appearing in the charity show which formed the movie's grand finale. Even John Garfield turned up – with a really excruciating rendition of 'Blues In The Night', by Johnny Mercer and Harold Arlen – but the cherry on the top was the now legendary appearance of Bette Davis singing the Arthur Schwartz-Frank Loesser war-time lament, 'They're Either Too Young Or Too Old'. LeRoy Prinz choreographed, David Butler directed and Mark Hellinger produced. Other songs and musical numbers: *How Sweet You Are* (Shore); *I'm Riding For A Fall* (Morgan, Leslie); *Goodnight Good Neighbour* (Morgan, chorus, Alexis Smith); *Love Isn't Born, It's Made* (Sheridan, Reynolds); *Thank Your Lucky Stars* (Shore); *We're Staying Home Tonight* (Cantor); *No You, No Me* (Morgan, Leslie); *The Dreamer* (Shore, reprised by De Havilland, Lupino, Tobias); *Ice-Cold Katy* (McDaniel, Best, Brooks, Rita Christina); *I'm Going North* (Carson, Hale); *That's What You Jolly Well Get* (Flynn, chorus) Schwartz, Loesser; *Hotcha Cornia* (Jones), a madcap version of 'Otchichornya'.

▽

Forties Musicals

In **Swingtime Johnny** (Universal), The Andrews Sisters (illustrated standing) did their bit for the war effort by donning overalls in a munitions factory and making shell casings. In a rather depressing 61 minutes, they made more music than munitions, none particularly memorable – unless you included 'Boogie Woogie Bugle Boy' (by Don Raye and Hughie Prince) which they first sang in Universal's *Buck Privates* in 1941. Harriet Hilliard (right), Peter Cookson, Tim Ryan, Matt Willis, Bill Phillips, Tom Dugan, Ray Walker, and Mitchell Ayres and His Orchestra also appeared for producer Warren Wilson (who also provided the story); it was scripted by Clyde Bruckman and directed by Edward Cline. Other songs and musical numbers: *Sweet And Low*; *Poor Nell* Everett Carter, Milton Rosen; *You Better Give Me Lots Of Loving* Kermit Goell, Fred Spielman; *I May Be Wrong But I Think You're Wonderful* Henry Sullivan, Harry Ruskin; *Boogie Woogie Choo Choo* Johnny Murphy, Roy Jordan; *When You And I Were Young Maggie* J.A. Butterfield, George W. Johnson.

More routine programmer fare from Universal with **You're a Lucky Fellow Mr Smith**. Story this time showed how Evelyn Ankers, *en route* to Chicago to marry David Bruce so as to clinch an inheritance, is tricked into marriage with Allan Jones (left) before her arrival in the windy city. Patsy O'Connor (right, cousin to Donald) was responsible for promoting the romance between them, with other parts going to Stanley Clements (centre), Billie Burke, Luis Alberni, Mantan Moreland and Francis Pierlot. The King's Men were in it too, and sang five songs. It was written by Lawrence Riley, Ben Barzman and Louis Lantz (story by Oscar Brodney), with Felix Feist directing for producer Edward Lilley. Songs and musical numbers: *Your Eyes Have Told Me So* Gus Kahn, Walter Blaufuss, Egbert Van Alstyne; *When You're Smiling* Joe Goodwin, Mark Fisher, Larry Shay; *What Is This Thing Called Love?* Cole Porter; *On The Crest Of A Rainbow* Al Sherman, Harry Tobias; *You're A Lucky Fellow Mr Smith* Don Raye, Hughie Prince, Sonny Burke; *Soldier Specialty* Inez James, Buddy Pepper.

Always a Bridesmaid (Universal) was another Andrews Sisters programmer which hardly involved them in the plot at all – a responsibility that fell, instead, to Patric Knowles (centre left) as a detective who joins a lonely hearts club to uncover a swindler who is using the club as a front for his nefarious activities. In the end, Knowles gets his man, and, as it turns out, his woman too, a detective played by Grace McDonald (centre). The Andrews Sisters starred as the club hostesses – three lonely gals who can hold a tune better than they can hold a man. Also cast: Charles Butterworth, Billy Gilbert, Edith Barrett, Addison Richards, Walter Baldwin, and The Jivin' Jacks and Jills. It was written by Mel Ronson from a story by Oscar Brodney, and directed by Erle C. Kenton for producer Ken Goldsmith. Songs included: *Thanks For The Buggy Ride* Jules Buffano; *Yoo-Hoo* Vic Schoen, Ray Jacobs, John Wilforth; *As Long As I Have You* Earl Hanbrich, Al Lewis, Howard Simon; *That's My Affair* Hy Zaret, Irving Weiser; *Mr Five By Five* Don Raye, Gene De Paul; *Ride On* Harold Adamson, Jimmy McHugh.

Around the World (RKO) was a mish-mash thrown together with a little bit of this (Kay Kyser and His Band, illustrated), and a little bit of that (Joan Davis, Mischa Auer) – the former involved in a touring camp show, the latter with Nazi agents. They all worked so hard to be entertaining, you could almost see the perspiration beading their brows. For the record (and the record-buying public), there were seven songs by Harold Adamson and Jimmy McHugh in it, the best being 'Roodle-Ee-Doo', and 'Don't Believe Everything You Dream'. Marcy McGuire, Wally Brown, Alan Carney, and Kyser regulars Georgia Carroll, Harry Babbitt, Ish Kabibble and Sully Mason, completed the cast. Ralph Spence wrote it, and there was special material by Carl Herzinger. It was produced and directed by Allan Dwan. Other songs: *Candlelight And Wine*; *He's Got A Secret Weapon*; *They Chopped Down The Old Apple Tree*; *Great News In The Making*; *A Moke From Shamokin*.

Romance was the key-note of **She's For Me** (Universal), an hour-long filler whose plot (by scenarist Henry Blankfort) centred around the niece (Lois Collier, centre) of an attorney (David Bruce, centre left), her resentment at his continual curbing of her extravagant ways, and her setting out to woo his playboy buddy (George Dolenz, centre right), Bruce disapproves of this situation, so he solicits the help of a singer (Grace McDonald) to break up the romance, but falls in love with her himself. Helen Brown, Mantan Moreland, Charles Dingle, Douglas Wood, Leon Belasco, Frank Faylen, Eddie Le Baron's Rhumba Orchestra and The Rogers Trio were also in it. Frank Gross produced, the dances were staged by Louis Da Pron, and it was directed by Reginald Le Borg. Songs and musical numbers included: *Cae Cae* John Latouche, Pedro Barrios, Roberto Martins; *Do I Know What I'm Doing?*; *Closer And Closer*; *Ain't You Got No Time For Love?*.

The top man in Universal's **Top Man** (GB: **Man Of The Family**) was Donald O'Connor (left) who, in the best Andy Hardy tradition, takes over the running of the Warren household when Papa Warren (Richard Dix, right) is called up for active service. Without wasting a second, energetic O'Connor organizes a morale-boosting show in an airplane factory, and is even commended for his efforts by the Navy Department. O'Connor worked industriously to keep it on the boil, and despite the film's obvious Hardy family derivations, succeeded. Susanna Foster was the romantic interest (the type of role usually played by Judy Garland), with other parts going to Lillian Gish (as Mrs Warren), Peggy Ryan, Anne Gwynne, David Holt, Noah Beery Jr, Marcia Mae Jones, Louise Beavers (centre) and Samuel S. Hinds. Count Basie and His Orchestra were in it; so were Borrah Minnevitch and His Harmonica Rascals. It was written by Zachary Gold from a story by Ken Goldsmith, produced by Milton Schwarzwald, and directed by Charles Lamont. Songs and musical numbers included: *Wrap Your Troubles In Dreams* Ted Koehler, Harry Barris, Billy Moll; *Basie Boogie* Count Basie; *Dark Eyes*.

A remake of Buster Keaton's silent comedy *Spite Marriage* (MGM, 1929), the same studio's **I Dood It** (GB: **By Hook or by Crook**) was slightly reshaped by Sig Herzig and Fred Saidy to suit the antic humour of Red Skelton (illustrated). In his most energy-consuming performance to date, Skelton played a pants presser besotted with an actress (Eleanor Powell) currently appearing in a Civil War melodrama. Powell marries him on the rebound when her sweetheart ups and leaves her for another but, after foiling a saboteurs' plot (the film's only topical war-time reference) and making a hilarious appearance in the Civil War melodrama, Skelton discovers to his delight that his wife really loves him after all. A frantic potboiler, with the star working overtime to keep it buoyant, it wasted Powell in a couple of indifferent Bobby Connolly-staged dance routines, both of which were shot before director Vincente Minnelli began work on the film, and which, contrary to his wishes, were retained by producer Jack Cummings. One of these routines, danced to Cole Porter's 'Swinging The Jinx Away', was first seen in MGM's *Born To Dance* in 1936, and had Miss Powell on a battleship yet again! Lena Horne, playing herself, was in it too, and sang 'Jericho' by Leo Robbins and Richard Myers which also featured Hazel Scott. Ms. Scott also played the Vernon Duke-Ted Fetter-John Latouche standard 'Taking A Chance On Love', Jimmy Dorsey and His Orchestra, plus Helen O'Connell and Bob Eberly, were also featured, Dorsey's big moments being 'Star Eyes' by Don Raye and Gene De Paul, and 'One O'Clock Jump' by Count Basie. The rest of the cast included Richard Ainley, Patricia Dane, Sam Levene, Thurston Hall, John Hodiak, Butterfly McQueen and Andrew Tombes. Other musical numbers: *Hola E Pae* Johnny Noble; *So Long Sarah Jane* Lew Brown, Ralph Freed, Sammy Fain.

Originally intended for Alice Faye but given to Betty Grable when Miss Faye decided to opt for domesticity, **Sweet Rosie O'Grady** was just one more 20th Century-Fox formula musical, set in the 1880s and drenched in sumptuous Technicolor. In this production Grable (illustrated) played Madeleine Marlowe, a Brooklyn-born musical comedy star who, after a triumphant tour of England, returns to America where a reporter (Robert Young) from *The Police Gazette* tarnishes her refined image by exposing her origins. Miss Marlowe is, in fact, Rosie O'Grady, an erstwhile singer at *Flugelman's Beer Garden* in the Bowery. Grable retaliates by exposing Young as a former suitor out to further his own career in the ensuing glare of the publicity his 'revelations' create. Of course, they're both really crazy about each other – even though it takes them 74 minutes to realize it. Meantime, their squabbling was sandwiched between several songs by, among others, Mack Gordon and Harry Warren, of which the most durable was 'My Heart Tells Me', sung by Grable – at her most attractive – in a bath tub. The production numbers were staged by Hermes Pan and included 'Get Your Police Gazette', 'The Wishing Waltz' (in which Pan was featured), and 'Going To The County Fair' (all by Gordon and Warren). Unlike John Payne, Don Ameche or Cesar Romero, Robert Young was no singer and, apart from joining in a couple of choruses of four of the songs, including the title number, left the bulk of the vocalizing to his leading lady. Adolphe Menjou co-starred with characteristic aplomb as the editor of *The Police Gazette*, with other roles in William Perlberg's pleasant (and profitable) production going to Phil Regan, Lilyan Irene, Frank Orth, Virginia Grey, Reginald Gardiner, Sig Rumann, Alan Dinehart, Hobart Cavanaugh, The Leo Diamond Solidaires, and St Brendan's Choir. It was scripted by Ken Englund from a story by William R. Lipman, Frank Stephani and Edward Van Every, and directed by Irving Cummings. Other songs and musical numbers: *Waiting At The Church* (Grable, chorus) Fred W. Leigh, Henry E. Pether; *Battle Cry* (Irene); *Sweet Rosie O'Grady* (Grable, Young, Menjou) Maude Nugent; *Sidewalks Of New York* (orch) Charles Lawlor, James Blake; *Two Little Girls In Blue* (Grable, Young) Charles Graham; *Little Annie Rooney* (Grable, Young, Orth) Michael Nolan; *My Sam* (Grable); *Where, Oh Where Is The Groom?* (Grable, chorus) Gordon, Warren; *Heaven Will Protect The Working Girl* (Grable, Young) Edgar Smith, A. Baldwin Sloane.

Though Deanna Durbin (illustrated) was now over twenty-one, her girlish charms had by no means evaporated, and her role in **His Butler's Sister** (Universal) brought out the same qualities that had made her a star in the mid-thirties. She played an ingenuous young singer who arrives in New York hoping to find fame and fortune as the protégée of composer Franchot Tone (illustrated). It just so happens that Mr Tone has in his employ a butler (Pat O'Brien) who turns out to be none other than Miss Durbin's half-brother and, in no time at all, she is put to work as a maid. But a love affair blossoms between employer and employee and, after several misunderstandings, the situation is satisfactorily resolved. A delightfully inconsequential romance, it provided Deanna with several occasions on which to burst into song, most notably in a number by Bernie Grossman and Walter Jurmann called 'In The Spirit Of The Moment'. She also sang an aria from Puccini's *Turandot*, Victor Herbert's 'When You're Away' (lyrics Henry Blossom Jr), and a medley of popular Russian songs. The original screenplay was by Samuel Hoffenstein and Betty Rheinhardt, with roles in it for Akim Tamiroff, Alan Mowbray, Frank Jenks, Hans Conried and Sig Arno as a quintet of middle-aged suitors. Iris Adrian and Robin Raymond were also in it and sang 'Is It True What They Say About Dixie?' (by Irving Caesar, Sammy Lerner and Gerald Marks). Frank Borzage directed the confection sweetly, and the producer was Felix Jackson.

A prefabricated programmer about a girl (Gloria Jean) who leaves her rural existence in Vermont to attend a drama school in New York, but returns home when she runs out of money, **Moonlight In Vermont** (Universal) was about as low key as they came. It ended with a barnyard revue (production number illustrated) staged by some of Miss Jean's fellow students who arrive in Vermont to help out with the harvest and, apart from focussing on the promising song and dance talents of newcomer Ray Malone, offered very little in the way of solid entertainment. George Dolenz, Fay Helm, Betty McCabe and Sidney Miller were also in it for director Edward Lilley, it was scripted by Eugene Conrad, choreographed by Louis Da Pron, and produced by Bernard Burton. Songs and musical numbers: *In The Middle Of Things*; *Something Tells Me*; *Dobbin And A Wagon Full Of Hay*; *Be A Good Girl*; *After The Beat*; *Pickin' The Beets* Inez James, Sidney Miller; *Lover* Richard Rodgers, Lorenz Hart.

Despite its title, there was no attempt in **Dough-boys in Ireland** (Columbia) to portray the life of Yankee soldiers in Northern Ireland. Most of the characters were American rangers whose only skirmish was a brief raid on an unidentified coast. The film was really a showcase for the pleasant tenor of Kenny Baker (left) who, in the midst of romancing pretty colleen Jeff Donnell (right), sang a clutch of well known Irish ballads. Lynn Merrick appeared as Miss Donnell's romantic competition, with other parts going to Guy Bonham, Wamp Carlson, Buddy Yarus, Dorothy Vaughan, Harry Shannon and The Jesters and, making his tenth screen appearance, Bob (Robert) Mitchum. Howard J. Green scripted it (additional dialogue by Monta Bell), Lew Landers directed, and the producer was Jack Fier. Songs included: *Mother Machree* Rida Johnson Young, Chauncey Olcott, Ernest R. Ball; *When Irish Eyes Are Smiling* Ball, Olcott, George Graff Jr; *My Wild Irish Rose* Olcott; *All Or Nothing At All* Jack Lawrence, Arthur Altman; *I Have Faith; I Knew; Little American Boy; McNamara's Band* Shamus O'Connor, John J. Stanford; *There Must Be An Easier Way To Make A Living.*
▽

The Gang's All Here (GB: **The Girl He Left Behind**) was Alice Faye's last musical before retiring into motherhood, and the first film that Busby Berkeley directed in colour. It was also the only occasion on which star and director worked together. A no-expense-spared production (by William Le Baron for 20th Century-Fox) that took as much as seven months to shoot, it was probably the costliest of Fox's war-time musicals, with Berkeley indulging himself in a couple of large-scale production numbers that echoed his pre-war work at Warner Bros. 'The Lady With The Tutti-Frutti Hat' was one of them, 'The Polka Dot Polka' (both by Leo Robin and Harry Warren) the other. In the first, Carmen Miranda (shown left) – second billed – made an entrance in a golden cart pulled by two gold painted oxen and wearing a mammoth headdress of fruit. The number featured 60 girls carrying giant bananas which they formed into various patterns, and was so suggestive in its phallic overtones that it was banned in Brazil! The film's finale offered audiences another of Berkeley's extravagant flights of fancy, and involved two 50ft high by 15ft wide mirrors brought together in a 'V' shape, the centre of which contained a revolving platform, 18 ft in diameter, on which he placed his dancers, thus enabling them to form an endless variety of characteristic Berkeley patterns. The sequence also featured 60 neon-lit hoops which the girls used to stunning effect throughout the rest of the number. In the film's less flashy moments, Alice Faye sang two enchanting Robin-Warren ballads, 'A Journey To A Star', and 'No Love, No Nothin'', both of which became enormous hits. The plot? A bubble about a soldier (James Elli-son) who has to choose between showgirl Faye (right) and his fiancée, Sheila Ryan (centre). Charlotte Greenwood, Edward Everett Horton, Phil Baker, Eugene Pallette and Dave Willock were also cast; so were Tony De Marco and Benny Goodman, who even shared a vocal with Miranda. June Haver made her debut as a hat-check girl, and Jeanne Crain was seen for the first time too, in a one-line part. It was written by Walter Bullock from a story by Nancy Wintner, George Root Jr and Tom Bridges. Other songs and musical numbers: *Paducah* (Miranda, Goodman); *Minnie's In The Money* (Goodman, orchestra); *You Discover You're In New York* (Miranda, Baker) Robin, Warren; *Brazil* (Miranda, tenor, chorus) Ary Barroso, S.K. Russell; and the rather elaborate finale, *Polka Dot Ballet*, by David Raksin.

Ole Olsen (left) and Chic Johnson's (right) first film since *Hellzapoppin'* (Universal, 1941) was the moderately diverting **Crazy House** (Universal), in which they starred as a pair of zany movie makers. Director Edward Cline kept it going at an appropriately brisk pace, only putting the brakes on in the romantic interludes between Patric Knowles and Martha O'Driscoll, and in the film's two production numbers – 'Pocketful Of Pennies' (by Eddie Cherkose and Franz Steininger), and 'Tropicana' (by Don Raye and Gene De Paul). Cass Daley (centre) who with each new film came to resemble Martha Raye more, played a dual role, with Percy Kilbride, Leighton Noble, Thomas Gomez, Edgar Kennedy and Franklin Pangborn also cast. There were cameo appearances from Alan Curtis, Allan Jones, Billy Gilbert, Hans Conried, Shemp Howard, Lon Chaney Jr, Andy Devine, Robert Paige, The Glenn Miller Singers with Marion Hutton, Count Basie and His Band, Tony and Sally De Marco, The Chandra Kaly Dancers, The Laison Brothers, The Five Hertzogs, The Delta Rhythm Boys, Basil Rathbone and Nigel Bruce as Sherlock Holmes and Dr Watson, The Bobby Brooks Quartet, Andrew Tombes – and Uncle Tom Cobleigh and all. It was written by Robert Lees and Frederick Rinaldo. Other songs and musical numbers included: *Get On Board, Little Children* Raye, De Paul; *Lament Of A Laundry Girl* Jerry Seelen, Lester Lee, Ted Shapiro; *Donkey Serenade* Rudolf Friml, Bob Wright, Chet Forrest; *My Rainbow Song* Mitchell Parish, Matt Malneck, Frank Signorelli; *My Song Without Words* John Latouche, Vernon Duke; *I Ought To Dance* Sammy Cahn, Saul Chaplin; ◁ *Crazy House* Cherkose, Rosen.

△

Girl Crazy (MGM) was one of the year's best musicals and a much more beguiling entertainment than the earlier version of it made in 1932 by RKO. Realizing that there was simply no way in which they could improve upon the George and Ira Gershwin score, the studio wisely decided to retain the numbers, as well as the story (by Guy Bolton and Jack McGowan) in which a young, girl-crazy playboy is sent to an all-male college in Arizona, and discovers that six o'clock in the morning is the time people get up – and not the other way round. He also discovers the dean's granddaughter and, together, they stage a bumper rodeo to raise much needed funds for the college. It was the perfect vehicle for Mickey Rooney (centre) and Judy Garland (right) who, in this, their eighth film together, were perfect in it. Busby Berkeley was originally signed to direct the entire film, but his disagreements with Roger Edens, the show's musical arranger, as well as with Judy Garland (with whom he had not seen eye-to-eye on *For Me And My Gal* at MGM in 1942), led to his dismissal by producer Arthur Freed, though his services were retained for the finale, a typical Berkeley-esque whirlabout to the tune of 'I've Got Rhythm'. The other dance numbers were staged by Charles Walters. Garland sang 'Embraceable You', 'Bidin' My Time' and 'But Not For Me', and, it must be said, Gershwin never had it so good. 'Could You Use Me', her duet with Rooney, was just one more musical highlight in a show full of them. Rooney teamed up with June Allyson for 'Treat Me Rough', and Tommy Dorsey and His Orchestra were featured in 'I Got Rhythm', 'Bronco Busters', 'Fascinatin' Rhythm', and 'Cactus Time In Arizona'. There was one new song, 'Happy Birthday Ginger', by Roger Edens. The cast also included Gil Stratton, Robert E. Strickland, Rags Ragland (left), Nancy Walker, Guy Kibbee and Frances Rafferty. The screenplay was by Fred Finkelhoffe, and the director who replaced Berkeley was Norman Taurog. The film was remade for a third time in 1965 as *When The Boys Meet The Girls* (MGM).

Mae West returned to the screen, after a three year absence, in a luke-warm entertainment from Columbia called **The Heat's On** (GB: *Tropicana*). Apart from a seduction scene involving the hapless Victor Moore which recalled some of her more distinctive moments way back in the thirties, the film – about a musical comedy star (West) and her association with two crooked producers (Moore, and William Gaxton) – failed to pack a knockout punch. By 1943, what was left of the celebrated West innuendo was decidedly *passé*. Xavier Cugat and His Orchestra (illustrated), vocalist Lina Romay, and pianist Hazel Scott helped buttress Fitzroy Davis, George S. George and Fred Schiller's original screenplay; so did a series of production numbers by David Lichine. But whichever way you looked at it, it was West one always came back to and, for once in her life, she failed to deliver the goods. Also cast: Alan Dinehart, Mary Roche, Almira Sessions and Lloyd Bridges. Milton Carter produced and the director was Gregory Ratoff. Songs and musical numbers: *Just A Stranger In Town*; *Hello, Mi Amigo*; *The White Keys And The Black Keys*; *There Goes That Guitar* Henry Meyers, Edward Eliscu, Jay Gorney; *Antonio* Leo Huntley, John Blackburn, Fabian Andre; *The Caissons Go Rolling Along* Edmund L. Gruber; *There Goes My Heart* Benny Davis, Abner Silver; *Thinking About The Wabash* Jule Styne. ◁

Sigmund Romberg's gloriously tuneful operetta, **The Desert Song**, which Warner Bros. had originally filmed in 1929, got new treatment from the same studio – treatment which was in keeping with Warner's dedication to contemporary issues. Thus audiences found the Riffs being oppressed by the Nazis in French Morocco in 1939. The Nazis are attempting to have a railway built between Dakar and the North African coast, but what they don't know is that the downtrodden Riff labourers are in fact led by an American who fought in the Spanish Civil War, and who naturally sees to it that the job is never completed. This genial heroic twaddle was given considerable help by the score, as well as by the star, Dennis Morgan (left) and his leading lady Irene Manning (right), who, between them, sang most of it. Robert Buckner wrote the screenplay from Lawrence Schwab, Frank Mandel, Oscar Hammerstein II and Otto Harbach's original musical play, LeRoy Prinz staged the dance numbers, and Robert Florey directed (in Technicolor). Also cast were Bruce Cabot, Gene Lockhart, Lynne Overman, Faye Emerson, Victor Francen, Curt Bois and Jack La Rue. Songs and musical numbers: *The Riff Song*; *Desert Song*; *One Alone*; *Romance*; *French Military Marching Song*; *One Flower* Harbach, Hammerstein, Romberg; *Fifi's Song* Jack Scholl, Romberg; *Gay Parisienne* Scholl, Serge Walters; *Long Live The Night* Scholl, Mario Silva, Romberg. ◁

Dorothy Lamour (right) wiggled her shapely body to little effect in **Riding High** (GB: **Melody Inn**), an insipid musical from Paramount in which she played an ex-burlesque queen who returns to her Arizona home to find papa Victor Moore's (left) silver mine on the skids. Dick Powell (centre) co-starred as a mining engineer (and Dorothy's male interest), with other parts going to Cass Daley (as the owner of a dude ranch), Gil Lamb, Bill Goodwin, Rod Cameron and Glenn Langan, Milt Britton's Orchestra and dancer Cy Landry supplied the rhythm, while scenarists Walter DeLeon, Arthur Phillips and Art Arthur (working from a play by James Montgomery) supplied the blues. Miss Daley and Mr Lamb, in an attempt to lift some of those blues, worked well beyond the call of duty with a few energetic routines; so did Victor Moore, but in the end they were defeated by the poor material. Danny Dare staged the dances, Fred Kohlmar produced, and the director was George Marshall. Songs and musical numbers: *You're The Rainbow*; *Get Your Man*; *Whistling In The Light* Ralph Rainger, Leo Robin; *I'm The Secretary To The Sultan* Robin; *Injun Gal Heap Hep* Rainger, Robin, Joseph Lilley; *Willie The Wolf Of The West* Johnny Mercer, Lilley; *He Loved Me Till The All-Clear Came* Mercer, Harold Arlen. ▽

1944

Academy Awards

Best Picture
Going My Way (Paramount) produced by
Leo McCarey

Best Actor
Bing Crosby *Going My Way*
NOMINATIONS INCLUDED: Barry Fitzgerald *Going
My Way*

Supporting Actor
Barry Fitzgerald *Going My Way*

Direction
Leo McCarey *Going My Way*

Writing (Original Story)
Going My Way Leo McCarey
(Original Screenplay)
NOMINATIONS INCLUDED: *Two Girls And A Sailor*
(MGM) Richard Connell and Gladys Lehman
(Screenplay)
Going My Way Frank Butler and Frank
Cavett
NOMINATIONS INCLUDED: *Meet Me In St Louis*
(MGM) Irving Brecher and Fred F.
Finklehoffe

Cinematography (black and white)
NOMINATIONS INCLUDED: *Going My Way* Lionel
Lindon
(colour)
NOMINATIONS INCLUDED: *Cover Girl* (Columbia)
Rudy Mate and Allen Davey. *Lady In The
Dark* (Paramount) Ray Rennahan. *Meet Me
In St Louis* George Folsey

Art Direction (Set Decoration)
(black and white)
NOMINATIONS INCLUDED: *Step Lively* (RKO)
Albert S. D'Agostino and Carroll Clark;
Darrell Silvera and Claude Carpenter.
(colour)
NOMINATIONS INCLUDED: *Cover Girl* Lionel
Banks and Cary Odell; Fay Babcock. *The
Desert Song* (WB) Charles Novi; Jack
McConaghy. *Lady In The Dark* Hans Dreier
and Raoul Pene du Bois; Ray Moyer.

Sound Recording
NOMINATIONS INCLUDED: *Brazil* (Republic)
Daniel J. Bloomberg. *Cover Girl* John
Livadary. *His Butler's Sister* (Universal)
Bernard B. Brown. *Hollywood Canteen* (WB)
Nathan Levinson. *Music In Manhattan* (RKO)
Stephen Dunn.

Film Editing
NOMINATIONS INCLUDED: *Going My Way* Leroy
Stone

Music
Song
'Swinging On A Star' *Going My Way* Jimmy
Van Heusen *cm*; Johnny Burke *lyr*.
NOMINATIONS INCLUDED: 'I Couldn't Sleep A
Wink Last Night' *Higher And Higher* (RKO)
Jimmy McHugh *cm*; Harold Adamson *lyr*. 'I'll

Walk Alone' *Follow The Boys* (Feldman,
Universal) Jule Styne *cm*; Sammy Cahn *lyr*.
'I'm Making Believe' *Sweet And Lowdown*
(20th Century-Fox) James V. Monaco *cm*;
Mack Gordon *lyr*. 'Long Ago And Far Away'
Cover Girl Jerome Kern *cm*; Ira Gershwin *lyr*.
'Now I Know' *Up In Arms* (RKO) Harold
Arlen *cm*; Ted Koehler *lyr*. 'Remember Me
To Carolina' *Minstrel Man* (PRC) Harry
Revel *cm*; Paul Webster *lyr*. 'Rio de Janeiro'
Brazil Ary Barroso *cm*; Ned Washington *lyr*.
'Silver Shadows And Golden Dreams' *Lady
Let's Dance* (Monogram) Lew Pollack *cm*;
Charles Newman *lyr*. 'Sweet Dreams
Sweetheart' *Hollywood Canteen* M.K. Jerome
cm; Ted Koehler *lyr*. 'Too Much In Love'
Song Of The Open Road (Rogers, UA) Walter
Kent *cm*; Kim Gannon *lyr*. 'The Trolley
Song' *Meet Me In St Louis* music and lyrics
by Ralph Blane and Hugh Martin.

Scoring Of A Musical Picture
Cover Girl Carmen Dragon and Morris Stoloff
NOMINATIONS INCLUDED: *Brazil* Walter Scharf.
Higher And Higher (RKO) C. Bakaleinikoff.
Hollywood Canteen Ray Heindorf. *Irish Eyes
Are Smiling* (20th Century-Fox) Alfred
Newman. *Knickerbocker Holiday* (RCA, UA)
Werner R. Heymann and Kurt Weill. *Lady
In The Dark* Robert Emmett Dolan. *Lady Let's
Dance* Edward Kay. *Meet Me In St. Louis*
George Stoll. *The Merry Monahans*
(Universal) H.J. Salter. *Minstrel Man* Leo
Erdody and Ferde Grofé. *Sensations Of 1945*
(Stone, UA) Mahlon Merrick. *Song Of The
Open Road* Charles Previn. *Up In Arms*
(Avalon, RKO) Louis Forbes and Ray
Heindorf.

Special Awards
To Margaret O'Brien, outstanding child
actress of 1944. (miniature statuette)
To Bob Hope, for his many services to the
Academy, a Life Membership in the
Academy of Motion Picture Arts and
Sciences.

The New York Film Critics Awards
Best Motion Picture
Going My Way

Best Actor
Barry Fitzgerald *Going My Way*

Best Direction
Leo McCarey *Going My Way*

The New York Times Annual 'Ten Best'
4th *Going My Way*. 9th *Meet Me In St Louis*.

The Annual Top Moneymaking Films
INCLUDED: *Cover Girl*. *The Gang's All Here*
(20th Century-Fox). *Girl Crazy* (MGM). *Going
My Way*. *Lady In The Dark*. *Let's Face It*
(Paramount). *Sweet Rosie O'Grady* (20th
Century-Fox). *Thank Your Lucky Stars* (WB).
Thousands Cheer (MGM).

△
All about a runaway socialite (Martha
O'Driscoll, illustrated left) who yearns to join
the WACS, and the adventures she has with a
shipyard worker (Noah Beery Jr, standing
centre) on a weekend's leave, **Weekend Pass**
(Universal), with a mere tendril of a plot by its
producer Warren Wilson (screenplay by Clyde
Bruckman), needed a stronger cast than the one
working for director Jean Yarbrough to keep it
buoyant. Several specialty acts, including The
Delta Rhythm Boys (singing 'All Or Nothing At
All' by Jack Lawrence and Arthur Altman),
ballroom dancer Mayris Chaney and partner,
Leo Diamond and his harmonica trio, and The
Sportsmen, were roped in for added diversion,
but it was no use. **Weekend Pass** was a per-
functory non-starter whose supporting cast in-
cluded George Barbier, Andrew Tombes, Irving
Bacon and Dennis Moore (seated right). Other
musical numbers included: *I Am, Are You?*; *I Like
To Be Loved*; *She's A Girl A Man Can Dream Of*; *We
Build 'Em, You Sail 'Em* Everett Carter, Milton
Rosen; *We're In The Navy* Don Raye, Gene De
Paul.

Allan Jones's full-throated singing was the chief
attraction of Universal's **Sing a Jingle** (GB: **Lucky
Days**), a 'home-front' B-musical whose tiny plot
concerned the complications that arise when
famous tenor Jones (illustrated) enrols for war
work in a mid-west defence plant. June Vincent
(left) was his attractive romantic foil, with
other parts in John Grey, Eugene Conrad, Lee
Sands and Fred Rath's churned-out screenplay
going to Edward Norris, the comedy team of
Betty Kean and Gus Schilling, Samuel S. Hinds,
Jerome Cowan, and an acrobatic tap dancer
called Dicky Love. It was produced and directed
by Edward C. Lilley. Songs and musical numbers
included: *Sing A Jingle*; *We're The Janes That Make
The Planes*; *Mademoiselle* Inez James, Sidney
Mitchell; *The Night We Called It A Day* Tom
Adair, Matt Dennis; *Beautiful Love* Haven Gilles-
pie, Wayne King, Victor Young, Egbert Van
Alstyne; *Love You Are My Music* Dan Twohig,
Gustave Klemm.
▽

A showcase to display the skating wizardry of Belita (illustrated), **Lady Let's Dance** (Monogram) actually had some money spent on it, and featured five full-scale production numbers staged by Dave Gould. However, it still couldn't actually boast a story, although one was credited to Bradbury Scott and producer Scott R. Dunlap. The screenplay (by Peter Milne and Paul Gerard Smith) also gave employment to James Ellison, Walter Catlett (centre), Lucien Littlefield, Maurice St Clair (left) and ice comedians Frick and Frack. The direction was by Frank Woodruff. Songs and musical numbers: *Dream Of Dreams*; *Rio*; *In The Days Of Beau Brummel*; *Lady Let's Dance*; *Happy Hearts*; *Ten Million Men And A Girl* Dave Oppenheim, Ted Grouya; *Silver Shadows And Golden Dreams* Charles Newman, Lew Pollack.

▽

△

Set in a mythical college called Adams, **You Can't Ration Love** (Paramount) found a group of college girls in a co-ed institution doing just that: rationing dates, due to the war-time unavailability of eligible men. The story showed how one of the non-draftees (Johnnie Johnston), a hitherto insipid chemistry student, suddenly becomes a swoon crooner and the school's very own celebrity. Betty Rhodes (right) played the girl responsible for Johnston's unexpected stardom, with other roles in Val Burton's screenplay (from a story by Muriel Roy Bolton) going to Bill Edwards, Marjorie Weaver, Marie Wilson (left), Johnnie 'Scat' Davis, The Artega All-Girl Orchestra and Mabel Paige. Acrobats Roland Dupree and Christine Forsythe were there too. Walter McEwen produced, and the director was Lester Fuller. Songs and musical numbers: *Love Is This*; *Ooh-A-Oh*; *Look What You Did To Me*; *How Did It Happen?* Jerry Seelen, Lester Lee; *I Don't Want To Walk Without You* Frank Loesser, Jule Styne; *Oodles of Noodles* Jimmy Dorsey; *One O'Clock Jump* Count Basie, Harry James; *Louise* Leo Robin, Richard A. Whiting.

Though **Swing Out The Blues** (Columbia) starred Bob Haymes, the narrative, fashioned by Dorcas Cochran from a story by Doris Malloy, mainly concerned the efforts of a quartet of singing instrumentalists called The Vagabonds (illustrated), to hang on to their professional meal-ticket (Haymes) after he weds socialite Lynn Merrick. Considering the overall slimness of the material and the lack of star names, it was a better than average quickie, adroitly directed by Mal St Clair, whose cast also included Janis Carter, Tim Ryan, Joyce Compton, Arthur Q. Bryan and Kathleen Howard. Sam White produced. Songs included: *Prelude To Love* Chet Forrest, Bob Wright; *Rockabye Baby* Effie I. Crockett; *Dark Eyes* (English version of 'Otchichornya', lyric by A. Salami); *It Can't Be Love*; *We Should Be Ever So Quiet*. ▷

△

In **She's a Sweetheart**, a passable low-budget filler from Columbia, Jane Darwell (left) was featured as the proprietor of a boarding house who turns her establishment into a canteen for servicemen with short-time passes. Jane Frazee (top-billed) played an entertainer with Larry Parks (centre) as her co-star and romantic interest. Nina Foch, Jimmy Lloyd (right), Ross Hunter and Carole Mathews were also in it for producer Ted Richmond. The original screenplay was by Muriel Roy Bolton, and the director was Del Lord. Songs and musical numbers: *Who Said Dreams Don't Come True?* Benny Davis, Al Jolson, Harry Akst; *I've Waited A Lifetime* Edward Brandt; *I Can't Remember When* Robert Schermann, Jack Krakeur; *What The Sergeant Said* Jackie Camp; *My Other Love* Bob Wright, Chet Forrest; *Mom* Saul Chaplin; *American Prayer* Lawrence Stock, Vincent Rose, Al Stillman.

Higher and Higher was a stage musical by Richard Rodgers and Lorenz Hart, with a book by Joshua Logan and Gladys Hurlbut, that had a moderate run on Broadway in 1940 – the star turn of the evening being a performing seal. The property was bought by RKO, underwent several changes, and resurfaced with a new score and a cast that included Michele Morgan, Jack Haley (who appeared in it on Broadway), Frank Sinatra (illustrated centre), Leon Errol (3rd left), Victor Borge, Marcy McGuire, Mary Wickes (2nd right), Elisabeth Risdon, Barbara Hale (centre with Sinatra), Mel Torme (right), Paul and Grace Hartman and Dooley Wilson. About a pretty scullery maid (Morgan) transformed, through the connivance of a group of servants, into a debutante, in which guise she catches the attention of the personable young man next door (Sinatra), it was a variation on the usual Cinderella theme in that Miss Morgan spurns the love of the story's Prince Charming, preferring, instead, butler Jack Haley. Of the eight featured songs by Harold Adamson and Jimmy McHugh, Sinatra sang five, soloing on 'A Lovely Way To Spend An Evening', 'The Music Stopped', and 'I Couldn't Sleep A Wink Last Night'. And although he didn't get the girl in the end, he got the bobby-soxers shrieking hysterically every time he opened his mouth. It was written by Jay Dratler and Ralph Spence (additional dialogue by William Bowers and Howard Harris), choreographed by Ernest Matray and produced and directed by Tim Whelan. Other songs and musical numbers: *Disgustingly Rich* Rodgers, Hart; *I Saw You First*; *Boccherini's Minuet In Boogie*; *It's A Most Important Affair*; *Today I'm A Debutante*; *You're On Your Own*.

▽

Though **Lady in the Dark** (Paramount) lit up box offices throughout the land, it was, despite its glorious Technicolor, only a pale imitation of the Moss Hart-Kurt Weill stage musical on which it was based, with star Ginger Rogers (paid a generous $122,500 for participating in her first colour film) no substitute in the show's more dramatic moments, for Gertrude Lawrence who created the role on Broadway. Rogers (illustrated) played the editor of a chic fashion magazine who, on the verge of a nervous breakdown, consults a psychiatrist (Barry Sullivan) in an attempt to clarify her thoughts on three men (Ray Milland, Warner Baxter, Jon Hall) in her life. In her sessions with analyst Sullivan, she relates her decidedly Freudian dreams to him – the final dream, set in a circus, becoming the film's main production number, and featuring Weill's 'The Saga of Jenny', its renowned lyric by Ira Gershwin. Regrettably, executive producer Buddy De Sylva eliminated much of the show's original score, including the marvellous 'My Ship', only a few bars of which remained, thus rendering nonsensical a major 'psychological' plot point with which the song was concerned. Also gone was the brilliant patter number 'Tchaikovsky', sung on Broadway by Danny Kaye, whose role as a photographer was now played by Mischa Auer. Frances Goodrich and Albert Hackett wrote the rather confused screenplay, it was produced by Dick Blumenthal, stunningly costumed by Raoul Pene Du Bois, and directed as best as he was able to considering the interfering circumstances by Mitchell Leisen. Other songs and musical numbers: *Suddenly It's Spring* Johnny Burke, Jimmy Van Heusen; *Girl of The Moment*; *One Life To Live*; *It Looks Like Liza*; *This is New* Ira Gershwin, Kurt Weill; and *Artist's Waltz* Robert Emmett Dolan. ▷

△

In **Swing Fever** (MGM) Kay Kyser (left) played a somewhat retiring musician with an uncanny gift for hypnosis. He should have used it on screenwriters Nat Perrin and Warren Wilson (story by Matt Brooks and Joseph Hoffman), for the *mélange* of music and comedy they offered (involving Kyser and his 'gift' to help win a prizefight) needed all the outside help it could get. There was nothing at all hypnotic about the show, and director Tim Whelan, and a cast that included Marilyn Maxwell (right), William Gargan, Lena Horne, Nat Pendleton, Curt Bois, Morris Ankrum, Maxie Rosenbloom and the Meriel Abbot Dancers, were powerless to make it appear otherwise. Two 'gag' appearances by Harry James and Tommy Dorsey didn't help much either. Meriel Abbot choreographed, and the producer was Irving Starr. Songs and musical numbers: *Mississippi Dream Boat* Lew Brown, Ralph Freed, Sammy Fain; *I Planted A Rose*; *One Girl And Two Boys* Freed, Brown, Nacio Herb Brown; *You're So Different* Fain; *Sh! Don't Make A Sound* Sunny Skylar.

In **Ghost Catchers** (Universal), a formula musical farce, Messrs Olsen and Johnson (centre and right) play a pair of nightclub owners who find themselves involved with a Southern colonel (Walter Catlett), his two daughters (Gloria Jean, left, and Martha O'Driscoll) and a haunted mansion. Leo Carrillo, Henry Armetta and Lon Chaney were in it too; so were music makers Morton Downey, Ella Mae Morse and Kirby Grant and his orchestra. Louis Da Pron staged the dances, it was written and produced by Edmund T. Hartmann and directed by Edward F. Cline. Songs and other musical numbers included: *Blue Candlelight*; *Three Cheers For The Customer* Paul Francis Webster, Harry Revel; *Quoth The Raven* Webster, Revel, Edward Ward; *I'm Old Enough To Dream* Ward, Everett Carter; *These Foolish Things* Harry Link, Holt Marvell, Jack Strachey; *After You've Gone* Henry Creamer, Turner Layton.
▽

△

Pre-dating *Kiss Me Kate* (MGM) by nine years, **Casanova in Burlesque** took Shakespeare's *The Taming of the Shrew* and, utilizing the okay-for-some talents of comedian Joe E. Brown, as well as his attractive co-star June Havoc, gave it the hepcat works. Brown (featured left) played a college professor, Miss Havoc a burlesque actress with Shakespearian ambitions. A surprisingly lively entry from Republic, it also featured Dale Evans, Marjorie Gateson, Lucien Littlefield, Ian Keith and Roger Imhoff. Albert J. Cohen produced and it was directed from an excellent screenplay by Frank Gill Jr (story by John Wales) by Leslie Goodwins, with choreography by Dave Gould. Songs and musical numbers: *Who Took Me Home Last Night?* Harold Adamson, Jule Styne; *Mess Me Up*; *Casanova Joe*; *Five-A-Day Fatima*; *Willie The Shake*; *Taming Of The Shrew* Walter Kent, Kim Gannon.

When defence worker Una Merkel knocks herself out while demonstrating to her foreman what she thinks is wrong with the particular machine she is working on, she has a dream, and in **Sweethearts of the USA** (GB: **Sweethearts on Parade**) – an inept programmer from Monogram – we share her dream with her. Parkyakarkus featured prominently in it as an addlepated, music-loving detective on the lookout for a bunch of bank robbers, with other figments of Miss Merkel's far-fetched subconscious materializing in the shape of Donald Novis, Lillian Cornell, Judith Gibson, Joel Friend, Cobina Wright Sr, Marion Martin, Vince Barnett and Ralph Sanford. The orchestras of Jan Garber, Henry King and Phil Ohman provided what little entertainment value there was in the film's 63-minute running time. Lester Cutler produced, it was scripted by Arthur St Clare, Jane Keith and Richard Long (story by Keith) and directed by Lew Collins. (Musical number illustrated). Songs and musical numbers: *Sweethearts Of The USA*; *All The Latins Know Is Si Si*; *You Can't Brush Off A Russian*; *We're The Ones*; *Hold On To Your Hat*; *That Reminds Me* Charles Newman, Lew Pollack.

Frances Langford (featured left) sang four songs in **Career Girl** (PRC), none of them very distinguished. She starred as a Kansas City hopeful who arrives in New York, takes up residence (just as others had done before her in Edna Ferber's *Stage Door*) at a theatrical boarding house and, after the usual disappointments, lands a make-or-break job singing in a revue. Audiences were left in suspense as to the outcome of the job, for the film ended while the show was still in rehearsal. A programmer with no redeeming qualities, it was written by Sam Neuman from a story by Dave Silverstein and Stanley Rauh, produced by Jack Schwartz and directed by Walter W. Fox whose cast included Edward Norris, Iris Adrian, Craig Woods, Linda Brent, Ariel Heath and Lorraine Krueger. Songs and musical numbers included: *Blue In Love Again*; *Dream Come True* Tony Romano, Morey Amsterdam; *That's How The Rhumba Began*; *Some Day* Sam Neuman, Michael Brown.

Hammered together with a couple of rusty nails and with little sense of shape, **Beautiful But Broke** (Columbia) was very much in the 'B' league. It starred Joan Davis (left foreground), whose chief function in Monte Brice's screenplay (story by Arthur Housman, adaptation by Manny Seff), apart from pulling funny faces, was to take over a theatrical agency specializing in big bands when the boss goes off to war. The current shortage of male combos forces her to form an all-girl troupe, which she does, but which she then leaves stranded in a Nevada warplant community. In an attempt to give the haphazard narrative even a modicum of entertainment value, producer Irving Briskin called on the talents of Jane Frazee (centre foreground), Bob Haymes, Judy Clark (right foreground), and Willie West and McGinty – but it was no use. As directed by Charles Barton, it stubbornly refused to play. Also cast: John Hubbard, Danny Mummert, Byron Foulger and George McKay. Songs and musical numbers: *Pistol Packin' Mama* Al Dexter; *Just Another Blues* Jimmy Paul, Dick Charles, Larry Marks; *Shoo-Shoo Baby* Phil Moore; *Take The Door To The Left* James Cavanaugh, Walter G. Samuels; *Mama, I Want To Make Rhythm* Walter Kent, Richard Byron, Richard Jerome; *Mr Jive Has Gone To War* L. Wolfe Gilbert, Ben Oakland; *We're Keeping It Private* Mort Greene, Walter Donaldson.

Donald O'Connor (illustrated) without whom no Universal musical would be complete, starred in **Chip Off The Old Block**. He played a naval school cadet who falls in love with the pretty and talented daughter of a musical comedy star, and, needless to say, finds himself in show business. Ann Blyth (her first lead role) was the daughter, with other parts in this juvenile farrago by Eugene Conrad and Leo Townsend (story by Robert Arthur) taken by Peggy Ryan (illustrated), Helen Vinson, Helen Broderick, Arthur Treacher, Patric Knowles, J. Edward Bromberg, Ernest Truex, Minna Gombell, Dean Manning and quiz-kid Joel Kupperman. Bernard W. Burton produced, with Louis Da Pron in charge of the dances, and Charles Lamont the direction. Songs and musical numbers: *Is It Good Or Is It Bad?* Charles Tobias; *Mighty Nice To Have Met You*; *Spelling Prep* Bill Grage, Grace Shannon; *I Gotta Give My Feet A Break* Inez James, Sidney Miller; *Love Is Like Music* Milton Schwarzwald; *My Song* Lew Brown, Ray Henderson, *Sailor Song* Eugene Conrad.

Harriet Hilliard starred in **Hi Good Lookin'** (Universal), a superior programmer in which she played a singer from the midwest who arrives in Hollywood – not to break into pictures, but to make it as a radio vocalist. With a little bit of help from newcomer Kirby Grant, she succeeds. Grant and Hilliard sang several songs, separately and together; Ozzie Nelson's orchestra contributed a few up-tempo arrangements; Jack Teagarden and His Orchestra made one brief appearance; The Delta Rhythm Boys launched into 'Paper Doll' (by Johnny Black) and Tip, Tap and Toe (illustrated) delivered one dance routine. Eddie Quillan co-starred, and was joined in the comedy bits by Betty Kean and Fuzzy Knight. Also in it were Roscoe Karns, Vivian Austin, Marjorie Gateson and Milburn Stone. It was written by Bradford Ropes, Eugene Conrad and Paul Gerard Smith from a story by Smith, produced by Frank Gross and directed by Edward Lilley. Other songs and musical numbers included: *You're Just The Sweetest Thing* Buzz Adlam, Walter Bishop; *Deacon Jones* Johnny Lange, Hy Heath, Richard Loring; *Aunt Hagar's Blues* W.C. Handy; *Just A Stowaway On A Ship Of Dreams* Vic Knight; *A Slight Case Of Love* Buzz Adlam; *By Mistake* Inez James, Sidney Miller; *I Won't Forget The Dawn* Don Raye, Gene De Paul.

Forties Musicals

△

Cover Girl (Columbia), written by Virginia Van Upp, and adapted by Marion Parsonnet and Paul Gangelin from a play by Erwin Gelsey, was the conventional story of a Brooklyn nightclub dancer (Rita Hayworth, left) who deserts her lover (Gene Kelly, right) and becomes a cover girl. But she soon learns that money and fame are no substitute for love, and returns to the simple life and the man she cares for. The story was told against a series of flashbacks, set at the turn of the century, in which Hayworth's grandmother (also played by Hayworth) is shown to have followed exactly the same course. Lee Bowman and Otto Kruger were the two wealthy men who lured Hayworth away from Kelly; Phil Silvers was Kelly's faithful side-kick, while Eve Arden was cast as a wise cracking, high-powered executive on the look-out for the ideal cover girl. Apart from its hackneyed plot, the film groaned under the weight of much that was trite and unoriginal, not least of which was the main production number (staged by Seymour Felix) glorifying the American cover girl through giant 'blow-ups' of the country's most famous magazines. (MGM would do it better in *Easter Parade* 1947, to the accompaniment of Irving Berlin's 'The Girl On The Magazine Cover'). Yet, for all its blemishes, **Cover Girl** was important in that it marked Kelly's transition from hoofer to dancer, his famous 'alter ego' sequence being remarkably advanced for its time. The dance began in a mood of tranquillity, with Kelly walking alone through Brooklyn late one night and suddenly seeing his reflection in a shop window. The reflection turns to flesh and

blood, and steps down from the window into the street. At first Kelly and his 'doppelganger' dance in unison. Then they begin to challenge each other until in the end, the ego image is destroyed and the dance ends quietly – as so many of Kelly's dances tended to do. The rest of the numbers – all but one by Jerome Kern and Ira Gershwin – were far less innovative, the two best staged being the haunting 'Long Ago and Far Away' sung by Kelly and Hayworth (the latter dubbed by Martha Mears) and set in a dingy Brooklyn nightclub against a back-drop of chairs piled on tables (illustrated). **Cover Girl** was important to Gene Kelly's career in that it contained several elements which he would later refine, rework and enlarge in some of his musicals at MGM. Who, for example, would deny that the street setting of the 'alter ego' dance influenced the title number in *Singin' In The Rain* (1952)? Or that the 'Make Way For Tomorrow' (co-lyricist E.Y. Harburg) routine, which he performed together with Phil Silvers and Hayworth, contained exactly the kind of exuberance that permeated the whole of *On The Town* (1949)? **Cover Girl** was produced (in Technicolor) by Arthur Schwartz, choreographed, by Felix, Val Raset and Kelly, and also featured Jinx Falkenburg, Leslie Brooks, Jess Barker, Curt Bois, Ed Brophy, Thurston Hall and The Cover Girls. Other songs and musical numbers: *Put Me To The Test* (Kelly, Hayworth); *Sure Thing* (Hayworth); *That's The Best Of All*; *The Show Must Go On* (Hayworth, chorus); *Who's Complaining* (Silvers) Kern, Gershwin; *Poor John* (Hayworth) Fred W. Leigh, Harry E. Pether.

Pardon My Rhythm (Universal) was formula entertainment which starred Gloria Jean (left), whose adolescent romance with a drummer (Mel Torme, centre) comes in for some rough patches when Bob Crosby, in order to sign Torme to a contract, gets Marjorie Weaver to flirt with him. Gloria, in turn, points her playwright father (Patric Knowles) in Miss Weaver's direction, thus generating sufficient confusion to pad out Val Burton and Eugene Conrad's routine screenplay (story by Hurd Barrett). The Misses Jean and Weaver were each given two songs to sing, while Bob Crosby took time off from the plot to croon the Gus Kahn-Isham Jones standard, 'I'll See You In My Dreams'. Also in it: Walter Catlett, Evelyn Ankers, Patsy O'Connor (right) and Ethel Griffies. Jack Slattery and The Mel Torme Trio also appeared. It was produced by Bernard Burton and directed by Felix Feist. Other songs: *Do You Believe In Dreams?* Don George, Irving Bibo, Al Piantadosi; *Spell Of The Moon*; *Shame On Me*; *Drummer Boy*; *You've Got To Hand It To The Band*.

▽

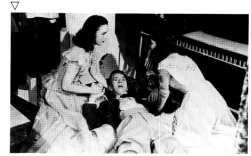

Ann Sheridan and Dennis Morgan (illustrated) made a pleasing star team in **Shine on Harvest Moon** (Warner Bros.), a run-of-the-mill backstage musical with far too weak a script to fill out its long (111 minutes) running time. Though it set out to tell the real life stories of Nora Bayes (Miss Sheridan), a honky-tonk girl in vaudeville, and songwriter Jack Norworth (Morgan) with whom she went into partnership and then married, there were so many fictional embellishments in it that real life gave way to reel-life in an avalanche of clichés. Among the redeeming features were several pleasant songs, particularly the enduring title number attractively photographed in Technicolor (the rest of the film was in black and white) and the splendid singing of co-star Irene Manning. Jack Carson and Marie Wilson were also in it and at their best in a comedy number called 'So Dumb But So Beautiful' by M.K. Jerome and Kim Gannon; and the supporting players included S.Z. Sakall, Robert Shayne, William Davidson and Bob Murphy. It was directed in a pedestrian fashion by David Butler from a pedestrian screenplay by Sam Hellman, Richard Weil, Francis Swann and James V. Kern, choreographed by LeRoy Prinz and produced by William Jacobs. Other songs included: *Shine On Harvest Moon* Jack Norworth, Nora Bayes; *When It's Apple Blossom Time In Normandy* Harry Gifford, Huntley Trevor, Tom Mellor; *What's The Matter With Father?* Harry Williams, Egbert Van Alstyne; *Pretty Baby* Gus Kahn, Tony Jackson, Van Alstyne; *Time Waits For No One* Cliff Friend, Charles Tobias; *I Go For You* M.K. Jerome, Kim Gannon; *Every Little Movement Has A Meaning Of Its Own* Otto Harbach, Karl Hoschna; *Just Like A Gypsy* Seymour B. Simons, Bayes; *Take Me Out To The Ball Game* Norworth, Albert von Tilzer; *Breezin' Along With The Breeze* Haven Gillespie, Seymour B. Simons, Richard A. Whiting.

Meet the People started life as a small-scale revue in Los Angeles in 1940, failed to make the grade on Broadway, and finished its days as an undistinguished musical for MGM starring Lucille Ball (right) and Dick Powell. Ball played a Broadway luminary who accepts a job as a welder in a Delaware shipyard in order to 'meet the people' and to prove to playwright Powell, who has dismissed her from his show as being a snooty bitch, that she isn't too proud to undertake some of life's more menial tasks. Point made and duly taken, she becomes queen of the yard, and wins Powell's undying love. Bert Lahr (left) also appeared, so did Virginia O'Brien (who was in the original show in Los Angeles, and as a result of her work in it was signed by MGM). Miss O'Brien sang 'Say That We're Sweethearts Again' (by Earl Brent) and ran away with the notices. June Allyson had a small part in it too, and the cast was completed by Rags Ragland, Steve Geray, Howard Freeman, Paul Regan and Betty Jaynes. Specialty items included a couple of Oriental dancers called Mata and Hari, Vaughn Monroe and His Orchestra, The King Sisters, and Spike Jones and His City Slickers. It was scripted by S.M. Herzig and Fred Saidy from a story by Sol and Ben Barzman and Louis Lantz, produced by E.Y. Harburg, directed by Charles F. Riesner, and choreographed by Sammy Lee, Charles Walters and Jack Donohue. Other songs and musical numbers included: *Meet The People*; *In Times Like These*; *Schickelgruber* Ralph Freed, Sammy Fain; *I Like To Recognize The Tune* Richard Rodgers, Lorenz Hart; *It's Smart To Be People* E.Y. Harburg, Burton Lane.

Hot Rhythm (Monogram) set out to be a gentle spoof on radio commercials but finished up, 79 minutes later, as a conventional love story between a jingle writer (Robert Lowery) and a singer (Dona Drake, far right). Standard B-picture fare, it also featured Tim Ryan, Irene Ryan (centre), Sidney Miller, Jerry Cooper, Robert Kent, and Harry Langdon (centre left). William Beaudine directed it from a story and screenplay by Tim Ryan and Charles Marion, and the producer was Lindsley Parsons. Songs and musical numbers included: *Where Were You?*; *Talk Me Into It*; *Happiest Girl In Town*; *Right Under My Nose*; *Say It With Your Heart* Edward J. Kay, N. Brown, Virginia Wicks, Lou Herscher.

Not exactly a programmer, but unable to stand up on its own without double-bill support, **Hey Rookie** (Columbia) was a so-so effort which involved Larry Parks – as an enlisted musical comedy producer – in staging a show for his fellow soldiers, despite the hindering antics of comedians Joe Besser (featured centre left) and Jimmy Little. Ann Miller (centre) provided the glamour, with other parts going to Joe Sawyer, Selmer Jackson, Larry Thompson, Barbara Brown, Charles Trowbridge and Charles Wilson, as well as Hi-Lo-Jack and a Dame, The Condos Brothers, Jack Gilford, Bob Evans and his dummy, The Vagabonds, and the Johnson Brothers. Based on a musical staged in Los Angeles' Belasco Theatre where it had a 36-week run, it was written by Henry Myers, Edward Eliscu and Jay Gorney who, together with Sergeant J.C. Lewis also wrote the songs. Val Raset and Stanley Donen choreographed, Irving Briskin produced, Charles Barton directed. Musical numbers included: *There Goes Taps*; *When The Yardbirds Come To Town*; *So What Serenade*; *Hey Rookie*; *Take A Chance*; *You're Good For My Morale*; *It's Great To Be In Uniform*; *Streamlined Sheik*; *It's A Swelluva Life In The Army*.

A romantic musical of no consequence whatsoever, **Moon Over Las Vegas** (Universal) featured Anne Gwynne (right) and David Bruce as a young married couple who cannot make a go of their relationship, and Vera Vague (centre) as a well-meaning relative who advises Miss Gwynne that the only way to salvage the situation is to make her hubby jealous. Most of it took place in Las Vegas, and betting on the happy-ever-after outcome (after a few obligatory complications) was no gamble at all. Vivian Austin, Alan Dinehart (2nd right), Lee Patrick, Joe Sawyer, Milburn Stone (centre right), Addison Richards, Mantan Moreland, Gene Austin and The Sherill Sisters, Connie Haines, Capella and Patricia, Lillian Cornell, Anne Triola, Jimmy Dodd, and The Sportsmen completed the cast. George Jeske and Clyde Bruckman wrote it (original story by Jeske) and it was produced and directed by Jean Yarbrough. Songs and musical numbers: *A Dream Ago*; *Faithful Flo*; *Moon Over Las Vegas*; *So Goodnight* Everett Carter, Milton Rosen; *A Touch Of Texas* Frank Loesser, Jimmy McHugh; *You Marvellous You* Gene Austin; *Oklahoma's One With Me* Jimmy Dodd; *My Blue Heaven* George Whiting, Walter Donaldson.

Forties Musicals

△

Two Girls and a Sailor (MGM), one of the year's better musicals, was about two girls (June Allyson, 2nd left, and Gloria De Haven) and the sailor (Van Johnson, left) they meet in a canteen they run for servicemen. Both are smitten by his charm and good looks. In the end he reveals himself to be a millionaire whose money, unbeknown to the girls, has made their 'canteen' possible; and, after being faced with a choice between Allyson and De Haven, he chooses the former. So much for the plot (story and screenplay by Richard Connell and Gladys Lehman), a sturdy enough chassis on which producer Joe Pasternak, director Richard Thorpe and choreographer Sammy Lee mounted several well-staged numbers and showcased the talents of its stars, as well as those of Lena Horne (singing 'Paper Doll' by Johnny Black), Virginia O'Brien (singing 'Take It Easy' by Albert De Bru, Irving Taylor, Vic Mizzy) and Jose and Amparo Iturbi playing De Falla's 'Ritual Fire Dance'. Jimmy Durante (centre) was also in it, as an old-time vaudevillian, and sang one of his best and most famous songs: 'Inka Dinka Doo' (by Durante and Ben Ryan). The rest of the cast was completed by Tom Drake, Henry Stephenson, Henry O'Neill, Ben Blue (right), Carlos Ramirez, Frank Sully, Donald Meek and Frank Jenks, with guest stars Gracie Allen (performing a 'Concerto for Index Finger,' conducted by Albert Coates, which included scales and 'chopsticks'!), The Wilde Twins, Harry James and His Band (with Helen Forrest) and Xavier Cugat and His Orchestra (with Lina Romay) contributing substantially to the general air of merriment that pervaded it all. Other songs and musical numbers: *My Mother Told Me* (De Haven, reprised Johnson, Drake, Sully) Ralph Freed, Jimmy McHugh; *A Love Like Ours* (Allyson, De Haven) Mann Holiner, Alberta Nichols; *In A Moment Of Madness* (James, Forrest) Freed, McHugh; *Young Man With A Horn* (Allyson, James) Freed, George Stoll; *Sweet And Lovely* (Allyson, De Haven, James) Gus Arnheim, Jules Lemare, Harry Tobias; *Granada* (Ramirez, James) Dorothy Dodd, Augustin Lara; *Estrellita* (James) Manuel Ponce, adapted Frank La Forge; *A-Tisket-A-Tasket* (Allyson, De Haven) Al Feldman, Ella Fitzgerald; *Did You Ever Have The Feeling?* (Durante) Durante; *Flash* (James) James; *Charmaine* (James) Erno Rapee, Lew Pollack; *Babalu* (Cugat) Bob Russell, Marguerita Lecuona; *The Thrill Of A New Romance* (Cugat) Harold Adamson, Xavier Cugat; *You Dear* (James) Freed, Sammy Fain; *Castles In The Air* (James) Freed, Sammy Fain; *Who Will Be With You When I'm Far Away?* (Durante) Durante; *Dardanella* (orchestral) Fred Fisher, Felix Bernard, Johnny S. Black; *My Wonderful One Let's Dance* (orchestral) Roger Edens, Arthur Freed, Nacio Herb Brown.

Kurt Weill and Maxwell Anderson's 1938 Broadway flop **Knickerbocker Holiday** was a heavy-handed anti-fascist tract that also criticized governmental interference from Washington. It came to the screen via the Producers Corporation of America and United Artists, with its political content watered down and with only three of the original Weill-Anderson songs in the score. What emerged in this trite screen reincarnation was a tedious period piece set in New York during the time of Peter Stuyvesant and involving a romance between a printer of subversive literature (Nelson Eddy, right) and the pretty daughter (Constance Dowling, left) of a Dutch councillor. Charles Coburn (in the role created on stage by Walter Huston) played Stuyvesant, and got to sing the show's one undisputed hit. 'September Song' (by Weill and Anderson). Ernest Cossart, Johnnie 'Scat' Davis, Richard Hale, Shelley Winter (later Winters), Glenn Strange, Fritz Feld, Otto Kruger, Chester Conklin, Percival Vivian and Charles Judels were also in it, and David Boehm, Roland Leigh and Harold Goldman, working from an adaptation by Thomas Lennon, wrote the screenplay. It was produced and directed by Harry Joe Brown. Other songs and musical numbers: *The One Indispensable Man* (Coburn, Cossart); *There's Nowhere To Go But Up* (Eddy, male chorus) Weill, Anderson; *Hear Ye* (Conklin, chorus); *Love Has Made This Such A Lovely Day* (Eddy, Dowling, Winters); *Zuyder Zee* (male quartet); *One More Smile* (Eddy, Dowling) Jule Styne, Sammy Cahn; *Holiday* (Davis, chorus) Theodore Paxton, Nelson Eddy; *Jail Song* (Eddy) Weill, Furman Brown, Eddy; *Sing Out* (Eddy, chorus) Franz Steininger, Furman Brown.

▽

A slightly subdued Donald O'Connor (illustrated right) starred with Susanna Foster in **This is the Life**, a better-than-average 'B' from Universal which even managed, at times, to be quite charming. All about the crush young Miss Foster develops for an older army officer, and the efforts of O'Connor (her boyfriend) to keep the two of them apart, it featured Patric Knowles (as the officer), Louise Allbritton, Dorothy Peterson, Peggy Ryan (left), Jonathan Hale, Eddie Quillan and Frank Jenks, as well as Ray Eberle and His Orchestra and the Bobby Brooks Quartet, in a neat little screenplay by Wanda Tuchock (from a play by Sinclair Lewis and Fay Wray). Louis Da Pron choreographed, and it was directed for producer Bernard W. Burton by Felix Feist. Songs and musical numbers: *Gremlin Walk*; *It's The Girl*; *Yippee-I-Vot* Inez James, Sidney Miller; *With A Song In My Heart* Richard Rodgers, Lorenz Hart; *All Or Nothing At All* Jack Lawrence, Arthur Altman; *You're A Lallapalooza* Bill Grage, Grace Shannon; *At Sundown* Walter Donaldson; *L'Amour Toujours L'Amour* Rudolph Friml, Catherine Chisholm Cushing.

Based on an actual USO Camp Tour of England and North Africa, undertaken in 1943 by Kay Francis (left), Carole Landis (centre), Martha Raye (right) and Mitzi Mayfair (2nd right), **Four Jills in a Jeep** (20th Century-Fox) starred the same quartet of travellers in a decidedly tepid entertainment, hastily flung together by producer Irving Starr to capitalize on that much publicized tour. Music and romance were the main items on the girls' agenda (in real life Miss Landis met a pilot on the tour and married him; in the film she does the same), the musical aspect being augmented for the occasion by the guest appearances of Alice Faye, Betty Grable and Carmen Miranda. George Jessel was Master of Ceremonies. Grable sang 'Cuddle Up A Little Closer' (by Karl Hoschna and Otto Harbach from *Coney Island*, 20th Century-Fox, 1943), Faye reprised 'You'll Never Know' (by Mack Gordon and Harry Warren, from *Hello, Frisco, Hello*, 20th Century-Fox, 1943), while Miranda again launched into 'I Yi Yi Yi Yi, I Like You Very Much' (by Gordon and Warren, from *That Night In Rio*, 20th Century-Fox, 1941). John Harvey, Phil Silvers, Dick Haymes, Lester Matthews, Paul Harvey and Miles Mander were also in it, and so were Jimmy Dorsey and His Orchestra. Robert Ellis, Helen Logan, and Snag Werris wrote it from a story by Froma Sand and Fred Niblo Jr, Don Loper staged the dances, and it was directed by William A. Seiter. Other songs and musical numbers: *Crazy Me*; *You Send Me*; *How Blue The Night*; *How Many Times Do I Have To Tell You?* Harold Adamson, Jimmy McHugh; *Mr Paganini* Sam Coslow; *No Love, No Nothing* Leo Robin, Harry Warren; *Over There* George M. Cohan; *When The Caissons Go Rolling Along* Edmund L. Gruber.

▽

▷

△

Rosemary Lane and Johnny Downs (left) starred in **Trocadero** (Republic) as a couple of youngsters who inherit a nightclub, but only make a success of it when they hire a swing band. The rest of the plot was taken care of when romance entered their lives. But the story (by Charles F. Chaplin and Garret Holmes, screenplay by Allen Gale) was secondary to the musical programme, with several big bands (led by Bob Chester, Matt Malneck, Gus Arnheim, Wingy Manone and, the real-life owner of the Trocadero, Eddie Le Baron) contributing strongly to the film's box-office potential. Ida James was also in it (singing Phil Moore's 'Shoo-Shoo Baby'); so were The Radio Rogues, doing a few more of their celebrated imitations. Cartoonist Dave Fleischer did some drawings, and Cliff Nazarro entertained with his double-talk. The cast was completed by Dick Purcell, Ralph Morgan, Sheldon Leonard, Marjorie Manners (right) and Emmett Vogan. It was directed for producer Walter Colmes by old-timer William Nigh. Other songs and musical numbers included: *The Music Goes 'Round And Around* Red Hodgson, Ed Farley, Mike Riley; *Roundabout Way* Sidney Clare, Lew Porter; *Bullfrog Jump*; *How Could You Do That To Me* Porter; *The King Was Doing The Rhumba* Jay Chernis, Porter; *Trying To Forget* Tony Romano; *Can't Take The Place Of You* Walter Colmes, Porter.

Eddie Cantor celebrated thirty-five years in show business by producing and starring in **Show Business** (RKO), an entertaining if familiar backstage yarn in which he played a character called Eddie Martin. The route taken by Joseph Quillan and Dorothy Bennett's screenplay (story by Bert Garnet) ended at the Ziegfeld Follies (by way of Miner's Bowery), and was a conventional rags-to-riches cliché which contained a romantic sub-plot for co-stars George Murphy (left, as a burlesque hoofer) and Constance Moore. Cantor (centre) and Joan Davis supplied the comedy – such as it was – and the cast was completed by attractive Nancy Kelly (right), Don Douglas and Pat Rooney. Nick Castle choreographed and Edwin L. Marin directed. Songs and musical numbers included: *It Had To Be You* (Murphy,

▽

Bob Crosby (illustrated) was worth his weight in prairie dust in **The Singing Sheriff**, a 60-minute Western spoof from Universal in which he appeared as a Broadway star who, through a series of unlikely circumstances, finds himself playing sheriff in a small mid-western town and rounding up a murderous gang of bandits. Crosby's performance (a collection of double and treble takes) was about as convincing as Henry Blankfort and Eugene Conrad's cornball screenplay (story by John Grey), and it was left to Fay McKenzie, Fuzzy Knight, Iris Adrian, Samuel S. Hinds, Edward Norris, Andrew Tombes, Joe Sawyer and the Spade Cooley Orchestra to salvage what they could of Bernard W. Burton's slapdash production. Leslie Goodwins directed. Crosby sang five of the songs, which included: *Beside The Rio Tonto* Don Raye, Gene De Paul; *Reach For The Sky*; *You Look Good To Me* Inez James, Sidney Miller; *Another Night* Don George, Irving Bibo; *Who's Next* Virginia Wicks, Bill Lava; *When A Cowboy Sings* Dave Franklin.
▽

Moore) Gus Kahn, Isham Jones; *I Don't Want To Get Well* (Murphy, Cantor) Howard Johnson, Harry Pease, Harry Jentes; *I Want A Girl* (Murphy, Moore, Cantor, Davis) Harry von Tilzer, William Dillon; *They're Wearing 'Em Higher In Hawaii* (Cantor, Murphy) Joe Goodwin, Halsey K. Mohr; *Alabamy Bound* (Cantor) Buddy De Sylva, Bud Green, Ray Henderson; *The Curse Of An Aching Heart* (Cantor) Harry Fink, Al Piantadosi; *While Strolling Through The Park One Day* (Murphy, Moore, Cantor, Davis) Robert A. King; *Making Whoopee* (Cantor) Walter Donaldson, Gus Kahn; *Dinah* (Murphy, Moore, Cantor, Davis) Sam M. Lewis, Joe Young, Harry Akst; *You May Not Remember* (Kelly) George Jessel, Ben Oakland; *The Daughter Of Rosie O'Grady* (Rooney) Monte Brice, Donaldson.

△

Leon Errol played twin brothers in **Slightly Terrific** (Universal): an impresario who promises a group of youngsters he will stage their show, and the impresario's manufacturer brother. The two men are mistaken for each other, and the ensuing confusion provided scenarists Edward Dein and Stanley Davis (story by Edith Watkins and Florence McEnany) with barely enough material to spread across the film's 61-minute running time. The younger brigade included Anne Rooney (left), Eddie Quillan, Ray Malone (right) and Betty Kean, with Lillian Cornell. The Stardusters, The Maritza Dancers, The Eight Rhythmeers, Donald Novis, Jayne Forrest and Lorraine Krueger also in it for producer Alexis Thurn-Taxis and director Edward F. Cline. Songs and musical numbers included: *Hold That Line*; *Me And My Whistle*; *A Dream Said Hello*; *Rhythm's What You Need*; *The Happy Polka*; *Stars And Violins* Everett Carter, Milton Rosen; *The Blue Danube* Johann Strauss (melody adapted and lyric written by Katherine Bellamann); *Put Your Arms Around Me Honey* Junie McCree, Albert von Tilzer.

What happened to a Merchant Marine crew during their seven days shore leave in San Francisco, was chronicled without much panache or originality in **Seven Days Ashore** (RKO). Wally Brown, Alan Carney, Alan Dinehart, Marcy McGuire (centre), Gordon Oliver, Margaret Dumont, Dooley Wilson, Virginia Mayo, Marjorie Gateson, as well as Freddie Slack and Freddie Fisher and their bands were featured in Edward Verdier, Irving Phillips and Lawrence Kimble's screenplay (story by Jacques Deval); Charles O'Curran was in charge of the dances and it was produced and directed by John H. Auer. Songs and musical numbers included: *Apple Blossoms In The Rain*; *Hail And Farewell*; *Jive Samba*; *Ready, Aim, Kiss*; *Sioux City Sue* Mort Greene, Lew Pollack.
▽

Jam Session (Columbia) was a tuneful miscellany aimed specifically at hepcats and with only one purpose in mind: to unleash on them a set of swinging musical numbers. Hence Charlie Barnet and His Band gave out with 'Cherokee' (by Ray Noble); Louis Armstrong was seen and heard in 'I Can't Give You Anything But Love' (by Dorothy Fields and Jimmy McHugh); Teddy Powell and His Orchestra were on hand for 'Murder He Says' (by Frank Loesser and Jimmy McHugh); Glen Gray and his boys delivered a Gray original called 'No Name Jive'; Jan Garber and Orchestra played 'I Lost My Sugar In Salt Lake City' (by Leon René and Johnny Lange), while Nan Wynn sang 'Brazil' (by S.K. Russell and Ary Barroso) and The Pied Pipers gave out 'It Started All Over Again' (by Bill Carey and Carl Fischer). Ann Miller (illustrated centre), who top-starred, wound up the proceedings with Sammy Cahn and Jule Styne's 'Victory Polka'. Manny Seff's screenplay (story by Harlan Ware and Patterson McNutt) featured Miller as the winner of a dance contest, her prize being a round-trip ticket to Hollywood. The plot, such as it was, involved Miss Miller in a romance with a screenwriter (Jess Barker) whose career she almost ruins through a series of unintentional mishaps. Stanley Donen staged the numbers, Irving Briskin produced, Charles Barton directed and the supporting cast included Charles D. Brown, Eddie Kane, George Eldredge, Renie Riano and Clarence Muse. Other songs and musical numbers: *Teddy Bear Boogie* (Powell and Orch) Teddy Powell; *St Louis Blues* (Armstrong) W.C. Handy; *Jive Bomber* (Powell and Orch) Lyle 'Spud' Murphy; *C-Jam Blues* Duke Ellington.

Considering its total absence of star names, **Stars on Parade** (Columbia) was something of a misnomer, but quite entertaining just the same. Another 'let's-put-on-a-show' effort (this time to demonstrate to the talent-seeking producers of Los Angeles that there is an abundance of saleable young performers in their very own back yard), it featured Larry Parks (left), Lynn Merrick (seated centre), Ray Walker (centre), Jeff Donnell, Judy Clark (2nd right), Robert Williams (right) and Selmer Jackson as well as Frank and Jean Hubert (doing their popular drunk act), The Chords doing their musical instrument imitations, The Ben Carter Choir in a selection of negro spirituals, The King Cole Trio, and tenor Danny O'Neill. Monte Brice wrote it, Wallace MacDonald produced and the director was Lew Landers. Songs and musical numbers included: *My Heart Isn't In It* Jack Lawrence; *It's Love Love Love* Mack David, Joan Whitney, Alex Kramer; *Ezekiel Saw The Wheel* negro spiritual; *When They Ask About You* Sammy Stept; *Jumpin' At The Jubilee* Ben Carter, Mayes Marshall; *Taking Care Of You* Lew Brown, Harry Akst; *Where Am I Without You?* Don Raye, Gene De Paul; *Two Hearts In The Dark* Dave Franklin; *Somewhere This Side of Heaven*.

MGM threw a great deal of talent but not much craftsmanship into **Broadway Rhythm**. Garishly photographed in Technicolor, it was inspired by the Jerome Kern-Oscar Hammerstein II stage show *Very Warm For May*, but retained only the great Kern ballad 'All The Things You Are' sung by Ginny Simms – a Louis B. Mayer favourite who failed to achieve stardom – preceded by a perfunctory medley of 'That Lucky Fellow,' 'In Other Words' 'Seventeen' and 'All In Fun' sung by George Murphy. All about a Broadway producer (Murphy) and the problems that beset his latest show, the film served as a showcase for several talented young people, most notably Lena Horne who, hideously costumed and against a strikingly awful set, did her best with 'Brazilian Boogie' by Hugh Martin and Ralph Blane (see illustration). She was better served in the more simply staged 'Somebody Loves Me' (by Buddy De Sylva, Ballard MacDonald and George Gershwin). Nancy Walker and Ben Blue were terrific in the delightfully eccentric 'Milkman Keep Those Bottles Quiet' (by Don Raye and Gene De Paul), and the three Ross Sisters, contortionists *extraordinaire*, twisted their bodies into some really weird shapes to the tune of 'Solid Potato Salad' (by Raye and De Paul), and 'Manhattan Serenade' (by Louis Alter). Gloria De Haven and Charles Winninger as Murphy's sister and father sang and danced 'Pretty Baby' (by Gus Kahn, Tony Jackson and Egbert Van Alstyne) with Kenny Bowers, and, from Dean Murphy, there were several impersonations – the one of Bette Davis coming off best. The cast was completed by Eddie (Rochester) Anderson, Hazel Scott, and Tommy Dorsey and His Orchestra. Scenarists Dorothy Kingsley and Harry Clork had the unenviable task of concocting a screenplay from a story by Jack McGowan that would accommodate the various talents on hand while still making sense of the narrative, and it was directed (without any visual flair at all) by Roy Del Ruth for producer Jack Cummings. Other songs and musical numbers: *Oh You Beautiful Doll* (Winninger) A. Seymour Brown, Nat D. Ayer; *Amor* (Simms) Sunny Skylar, Gabriel Ruiz, Ricardo Lopez Mendez; *I Love Corny Music* (Winninger, Dorsey); *Irresistible You* (Murphy, Simms, Dorsey); *Who's Who In Your Love Life?* (Ensemble) Raye, De Paul; *National Emblem March* (Dorsey) E.E. Bagley; *What Do You Think I Am?* (De Haven, Bowers) Hugh Martin, Ralph Blane; *Waltz in D Flat, Opus 64, No 1* ('Minute Waltz') (Hazel Scott) Chopin; *Ida, Sweet As Apple Cider* (Bowers) Eddie Leonard, Eddie Munson; *A Frangesa* (orchestral) P.M. Costa.

Bathing Beauty (MGM) covered a peanut of a plot (songwriter enrols as a student at a women's college to be near his swimming-instructress wife) with lashings of Technicolored icing, and the result was a lavish piece of escapist entertainment on a par with 20th Century-Fox's *The Gang's All Here* (1943). It starred Red Skelton as the songwriter and Esther Williams as his instructress wife, with Basil Rathbone, Janis Paige, Bill Goodwin, Jean Porter, Carlos Ramirez, Donald Meek, Margaret Dumont, and Jacqueline Daly also in it for producer Jack Cummings and director George Sidney. Skelton drew attention away from Kenneth Earl, M.M. Musselman and Curtis Kenyon's story (adaptation by Joseph Schrank, screenplay by Dorothy Kingsley, Allen Boretz and Frank Waldman) in a series of comic routines, the best being his participation (complete with tutu) in a ballet class; and there was diversion too, from Harry James and His Orchestra (with Helen Forrest singing 'I Cried For You' by Arthur Freed, Gus Arnheim and Abe Lyman); Xavier Cugat and His Orchestra (with Lina Romay singing 'Bim Bam Boom' by J. Camacho and Noro Morales); and organist Ethel Smith with her electrifying version of 'Tico-Tico' (by Zequinha Abreu). But nothing topped the spectacular water ballet (illustrated) that climaxed the film. Staged by John Murray Anderson, it featured Esther Williams (centre) and several dozen aquatic chorines in a deliciously kitschy rendition of Strauss's 'Blue Danube Waltz' with alternate jets of water and flame bursting out of an Olympic-sized swimming pool to the rhythms of the music. The rest of the show was choreographed by Robert Alton and Jack Donohue. Other songs and musical numbers: *By The Waters of Minnetonka* (Smith) Thurlow Lieurance, J.M. Cavanass; *Hora Staccato* (James) Grigoras Dinicu, Jascha Heifetz; *Te Quiero Dijiste* (*Magic Is The Moonlight*) (Ramirez) Maria Grever, Charles Pasquale; *I'll Take The High Note* (Skelton, James, Porter, Smith, Janis Paige, Ramirez, Forrest, Buddy Moreno) Harold Adamson, Johnny Green; *Trumpet Blues and Cantabile* (James); James, Jack Mathias; *Loch Lomond* (girls' chorus) traditional.

Another war-time parade of talent for the especial delight of the lads at the front, **Follow The Boys** ransacked Universal's list of contract artists (and added several free-lancers) to come up with a star-studded tribute to the many artists who brought entertainment to the troops via the Hollywood Victory Committee. Lou Breslow and Gertrude Purcell's screenplay contained the merest smidgin of a plot (about hoofer George Raft's neglect of his wife Vera Zorina – both illustrated – and his involvement with the effort), but it was nothing more than a shaky clothes line on which to peg the contributions of the guest stars. Using footage of celebrities doing actual wartime entertainment duty, producer Charles K. Feldman concocted a film whose historic interest today far outweighs its achievement as a piece of film-making. Charles Grapewin, Grace McDonald, Charles Butterworth, George Macready, Elizabeth Patterson Theodore von Eltz and Regis Toomey completed the cast, as far as the 'plot' was concerned, though it was the guest artists audiences really came to see. They included Dinah Shore singing 'I'll Get By' (by Roy Turk and Fred Ahlert), 'I'll Walk Alone' (by Jule Styne and Sammy Cahn) and 'Mad About Him, Sad About Him, How Can I Be Glad Without Him Blues' (by Larry Marks and Dick Charles); Sophie Tucker, who sang 'Some Of These Days' (by Shelton Brooks) and 'The Bigger The Army And The Navy' (by Jack Yellen); Jeanette MacDonald reprising 'Beyond The Blue Horizon' (by Richard A. Whiting, W. Franke Harling and Leo Robin), as well as Gus Kahn and Isham Jones's 'I'll See You In My Dreams'; the Andrews Sisters performing a ▷ medley of past and present hits including 'Bei Mir Bist Du Schoen' (by Sammy Cahn, Saul Chaplin, Jacob Jacobs, Sholom Secunda); 'Beer Barrel Polka' (by Lew Brown and Jaromir Vejvoda) and 'Shoo Shoo Baby' (by Phil Moore); Artur Rubinstein playing Chopin's 'Polonaise in A Flat', and – from the sublime to the ridiculous – The Delta Rhythm Boys doing 'The House I Live In' (by Earl Robinson and Lewis Allan). Also featured were Orson Welles and Marlene Dietrich (in a magic act), Donald O'Connor and Peggy Ryan, W.C. Fields, Carmen Amaya, Leo and Gautier's Dog Act, The Bricklayers, Ted Lewis, Freddie Slack, Charlie Spivak and Louis Jordan and their orchestras and, in the Hollywood Victory Committee sequence, Maria Montez, Susanna Foster, Louise Allbritton, Robert Paige, Alan Curtis, Lon Chaney Jr, Gloria Jean, Andy Devine, Turhan Bey, Evelyn Ankers, Noah Beery Jr, Samuel S. Hinds, Louise Beavers, Clarence Muse, Gale Sondergaard, Peter Coe, Nigel Bruce, Thomas Gomez, Martha O'Driscoll, Maxie Rosenbloom, Lois Collier, Elyse Knox, and Randolph Scott. The choreographers were George Hale and Joe Schoenfeld, and the film was directed by Edward Sutherland. Other songs and musical numbers included: *A Better Day Is Coming* Cahn, Styne; *Tonight* Kermit Goell, Walter Donaldson; *Is You Is Or Is You Ain't My Baby?* Billy Austin, Louis Jordan; *I Feel A Song Coming On* Dorothy Fields, Jimmy McHugh, George Oppenheimer; *Kittens With Their Mittens Laced* Inez James, Buddy Pepper; *Liebestraum* Liszt.

△

Jack Haley (illustrated left), the star of **Take It Big** (Paramount), spent much of the film's 76 minutes bemoaning his lot as the rear section of Pansy the horse in an act he shares with Richard Lane (the horse's front), singer Harriet Hilliard, and band leader Ozzie Nelson. Then one day he inherits a dude ranch and believes his troubles are over. But they're just beginning – for the swanky establishment he takes possession of belongs to someone else, *his* ranch being a dilapidated old property on the verge of collapse. The drivel was partially rescued by Miss Hilliard's pleasant vocalizing, the singing of Frank Forest (who, at one point, launched into an aria from Rossini's 'The Barber of Seville') and several good tunes by Jerry Seelen and Lester Lee; but the best tune was 'Sunday, Monday Or Always', an established hit by Johnny Burke and Jimmy Van Heusen, which Crosby had introduced in *Dixie* (Paramount, 1943). The film also featured Arline Judge, Mary Beth Hughes, Fritz Feld, Fuzzy Knight, Lucille Gleason and Nils T. Granlund. It was written by Howard J. Green, with Frank McDonald directing for producers William Pine and William Thomas. Other songs and musical numbers included: *Love And Learn; Life Can Be Beautiful; Take It Big; I'm A Big Success With You.*

With over two million copies of her famous pin-up girl pose (i.e. the one in which she wears a white bathing suit and looks seductively over her shoulder) adorning the lockers of servicemen everywhere, it was only a matter of time before 20th Century-Fox featured their blonde star Betty Grable (illustrated centre) in a musical called, quite simply, **Pin-Up Girl**. The results, however, were far from favourable, due, in the main, to an asinine screenplay by Robert Ellis, Helen Logan and Earl Baldwin (story by Libbie Block) that cast Grable as a stenographer in Washington who, after meeting Navy hero John Harvey, pretends to be a Broadway star. Joe E. Brown and Martha Raye were drafted into the sliver of a plot to provide humour, and for audiences who found it difficult enough taking them on their own, the combination was decidedly deadly. For spectacle there was The Skating Vanities in an interminable number called 'Red Robins, Bob Whites and Blue Birds' ▽

(by Mack Gordon and James V. Monaco, who provided the film with all its music and lyrics); while the energetic Condos Brothers tapped themselves into quite a frenzy on two breathless occasions. Grable and choreographer Hermes Pan danced together in a production number called 'Once Too Often'; and Martha Raye did exactly what was expected of her in 'Yankee Doodle Hayride'. The film ended with a military-style finale (led by Grable) that was a stultifying bore. Eugene Pallette, Dorothea Kent, Dave Willock, Robert Homans, Marcel Dalio, Roger Clark and Charles Spivak and His Orchestra completed the cast. Bruce Humberstone directed, and it was produced (in Technicolor) by William Le Baron. Grable was seven months pregnant when the film was completed. Other songs and musical numbers: *You're My Little Pin-Up Girl; Time Alone Will Tell; Don't Carry Tales Out of School; Story Of The Very Merry Widow.*

Forties Musicals

The cast list of **Sensations of 1945** (United Artists) included Eleanor Powell (as a lady with a penchant for getting her name in the papers), W.C. Fields, Sophie Tucker (doing one of her standards called 'You Can't Sew A Button On A Heart'), Cab Calloway and Woody Herman and their bands, The Lew Paul Trio, The Pallenberg Bears, David Lichine, Gene Rodgers, The Coplands, Mel Hall, 'Uncle Willie', The Johnson Brothers, Hubert Castle, Dorothy Donegan and The Cristianis, as well as Dennis O'Keefe, C. Aubrey Smith, Eugene Pallette, Mimi Forsythe, Lyle Talbot and Bert Roach. That they were quite unable to give producer-director Andrew Stone's casserole a distinctive flavour was due to the anything-goes manner of its presentation and a storyline by Frederick Jackson (screenplay by Dorothy Bennett and Andrew Stone) that was so tenuous – involving, as it did, Miss Powell (illustrated) in a series of promotional stunts, one of which lands her in jail – it might just as easily have been dispensed with altogether. It was choreographed by Lichine and Charles O'Curran. Songs and musical numbers included: *Mister Hepster's Dictionary*; *Wake Up Man You're Slippin'*; *One Love*; *Kiss Serenade*; *No Never*; *Spin Little Pin Ball* Harry Tobias, Al Sherman.

Martha Tilton (left), best known as a swing singer with Benny Goodman's band, starred in **Swing Hostess** (PRC), a really hackneyed effort about a singer's frustrated attempts to find employment with a band. Iris Adrian (centre), Cliff Nazarro, Harry Holman (right), Emmet Lynn, Betty Brodel, and Charles Collins and His Band were also in it; Louise Rousseau and Gail Davenport wrote it and Sam Neufeld produced and directed. Songs and musical numbers included: *I'll Eat My Hat*; *Let's Capture This Moment*; *Say It With Love*; *Music To My Ears*; *Highway Polka*; *Got An Invitation* Ray Evans, Jay Livingston, Lewis Bellin.

Frank Sinatra, at the height of his popularity, received top billing in **Step Lively** (RKO), a musical remake of the Marx Brothers comedy *Room Service* (RKO, 1938). He played a playwright and his co-star was George Murphy as a small-time revue producer holed up in a hotel with a cast of twenty, and no money to pay the bill. Gloria De Haven (in bath) appeared as a curvaceous showgirl who takes Sinatra's fancy, with Adolphe Menjou, Walter Slezak, Eugene Pallette, Wally Brown, Alan Carney, Anne Jeffreys and Grant Mitchell completing the cast. If a singing playwright wasn't exactly true to the frenzied spirit of the John Murray-Allen Boretz play on which it was based, Sinatra's legion of screaming fans certainly didn't complain, and with his vocalizing of such Jule Styne-Sammy Cahn numbers as 'Come Out, Come Out Wherever You Are', 'As Long As There's Music' and 'Some Other Time', he had them swooning in the aisles. The musical numbers were staged by Ernest Matray; Warren Duff and Peter Milne wrote it; Tim Whelan directed with a jolly sense of pace, and the producer was Robert Fellows. Other songs: *Where Does Love Begin*; *Ask The Madame*; *Why Must There Be An Opening Song?* Styne, Cahn.

Betty Hutton (right), now earning $5,000 a week, was again teamed with Dorothy Lamour (centre left) in **And The Angels Sing** (Paramount). They in turn were joined by Diana Lynn (centre right) and Mimi Chandler (left) to form a quartet of sisters (called Angel) whose vocal talents are 'discovered' by Fred MacMurray, a conniving bandleader who fleeces them of $190 but nonetheless finishes up in the arms of Miss Lamour. A rather slapdash affair, knocked together by Melvin Frank and Norman Panama from the fragments of story provided by Claude Binyon, it did at least allow the frenetic Miss Hutton to shine in several Johnny Burke-Jimmy Van Heusen songs, the best being 'Bluebirds In My Belfry' and 'His Rocking Horse Ran Away'. For the rest, it was pretty witless stuff, with Raymond Walburn as the girls' easy-going father, Eddie Foy Jr, Frank Albertson, Mikhail Rasumny and Frank Faylen also cast. Danny Dare choreographed, the producer was E.D. Leshin and it was directed with little sparkle by George Marshall. Other songs and musical numbers: *For The First Hundred Years*; *It Could Happen To You*; *Knocking On Your Own Front Door*; *How Does Your Garden Grow*; *My Heart's Wrapped Up In Gingham*; *When Stanislaus Got Married* Burke, Van Heusen.

Gloria Jean starred in **Reckless Age** (Universal), a 63-minute quickie which found her rebelling against the rules of her home life as laid down by her wealthy grandfather (Henry Stephenson), running away and, unbeknown to Grandpa, joining one of his many dime stores as a clerk. She sang three songs, 'Il Bacio' (by Luigi Arditi), 'The Cradle Song' (by Irving Bibo, based on Brahms's *Wiegenlied*), and 'Santa Lucia' (by Teodoro Cottrau), with other musical numbers going to Harold Nicholas of the pre-war Nicholas Brothers, who did a song-and-dance version of 'Mama Yo Quiero' (by Al Stillman and Jaraca and Vincente Paiva), and The Delta Rhythm Boys. Kathleen Howard was also in it, so were Jane Darwell, Franklin Pangborn (centre foreground), Andrew Tombes, Marshall Thompson (centre), Lloyd Corrigan, and nightclub comedian Jack Gilford, whose contribution to producer-director Felix F. Feist's workaday programmer was a sketch about an employee trying to keep awake during a pep talk from the boss, first introduced by Gilford in the 1940 stage revue *Meet The People*. Gertrude Purcell and Henry Blankfort wrote the screenplay from an original story by Al Martin. Other songs and musical numbers included: *Get On Board Little Children* Don Raye, Gene De Paul; *Very Often On My Face* Bill Grage, Grace Shannon.

An oater with music, starring Jane Frazee and such radio favourites as The Hoosier Hotshots, Cousin Emmy (illustrated centre), Jimmy Wakely and His Oklahoma Cowboys, Red River Dave and, from Harlem, The King Cole Trio, Columbia's **Swing in the Saddle** (GB: **Swing and Sway**) designed for backward (or, at best, backwood) audiences, told the story of a couple of actresses (Frazee and Sally Bliss) in the west who find themselves mistaken for kitchen help. Elizabeth Beecher, Morton Grant and Bradford Ropes's screenplay (from a story by Maurice Leo) had them going along with the idea in order to discover the identity of a 'lonely hearts' correspondent who has proposed marriage to them. Guinn Williams, Slim Summerville, Mary Treen, Carole Mathews and Byron Foulger also appeared for producer Jack Fier, and the director was Lew Landers. Songs and musical numbers included: *Amor* Sunny Skylar, Gabriel Ruiz; *Hey Mabel* Fred Stryker; *By The River Sainte Marie* Edgar Leslie, Harry Warren; *She Broke My Heart In Three Places* Oliver Drake; *When It's Harvest Time In Peaceful Valley* Robert Martin, Raymond McKee; *There'll Be A Jubilee* Phil Moore.

▽

Crooner Benny Fields (illustrated right) was the *raison d'être* for **Minstrel Man** (PRC), a sentimental weepie about a minstrel headliner (Fields) who allows his daughter to be reared by Gladys George and Alan Dinehart after his wife (Molly Lamont) dies in childbirth. Meanwhile Fields continues to pursue his career wherever he can. Years later, with his daughter (Judy Clark, illustrated in blackface) now grown up and a performer herself, he returns in time to catch the opening night of her show, and, in the best Hollywood tradition, joins her on stage in a chorus of his hit song 'Remember Me To Carolina' (by Paul Francis Webster and Harry Revel). Apart from Fields's easy-going personality, the film was notable for its musical arrangements by Ferde Grofé. Roscoe Karns, Jerome Cowan, John Raitt, Eddie Kane and The Ernestos completed the cast for producer Leo Fromkess. Irwin Franklin and Pierre Gendron wrote it from a story by Martin Mooney and Raymond L. Schrock, and the director was Joseph H. Lewis. Other songs: *My Melancholy Baby* George A. Norton, Ernie Burnett; *Cindy*; *I Don't Care If The World Knows About It*; *Shakin' Hands With The Sun*; *The Bamboo Cane* Webster, Revel.

▽

It took 61 minutes for **South Of Dixie** (Universal) ▷ to tell the lightweight, far-fetched tale of a phoney writer of Southern pop tunes (David Bruce, on bed) who, after being promoted as a subject for a film biography, has to go South to whip up a suitable family background for himself. He takes Southerner Anne Gwynne along to tutor him in the proper accent, and also finds himself involved in a romance with the daughter (Ella Mae Morse) of a Southern colonel (Samuel S. Hinds). Jerome Cowan (kneeling), Joe Sawyer, Eddie Acuff, Marie Harmon, Oscar O'Shea and Louise Beavers were also cast; Clyde Bruckman wrote it from a story by Sam Coslow, and it was produced and directed by Jean Yarbrough. Songs and musical numbers included: *Shoo Shoo Baby* Phil Moore; *Never Again*; *I'm A-Headin' South*; *Loo-Loo-Louisiana*; *Cross My Heart* Everett Carter, Milton Rosen; *When It's Darkness On The Delta* Marty Symes, A.J. Neiberg, Jerry Livingston; *Weep No More My Lady* Joan Whitney, Alex Cramer.

One of Bing Crosby's best, and best-loved, films, **Going My Way** was a heart-warming hit from Paramount that revealed the popular crooner (right) to be the possessor of more than just a melting voice. He played Father Chuck O'Malley, a young Catholic priest sent to Saint Dominic's Church to take over the day-to-day running of it from Father Fitzgibbon (Barry Fitzgerald), the last of whose 45 years as pastor has resulted in a general decline (through old age and old-fashioned ideas) in the premises and in the number of people attending services. The film's mainstay was the relationship between the two men, which producer-director Leo McCarey never allowed to topple over into sentimentality, even though he came pretty close to it every now and then. A first-rate screenplay by Frank Butler and Frank Cavett (original story by McCarey) also contributed substantially to the film's overall success; as did its pleasing score, especially the tender 'Too-ra-loo-ra-loo-ra' (by J.R. Shannon) sung by Crosby to Fitzgerald, and 'Swingin' On A Star' (by Johnny Burke and Jimmy Van Heusen) performed by Crosby and a group of kids. Frank McHugh, *diva* Rise Stevens, Gene Lockhart, William Frawley, James Brown (left), Jean Heather (centre), Porter Hall, Fortunio Bonanova and Eily Malyon made up the excellent supporting cast. Also featured were the Robert Mitchell Boys' Choir. Other songs included: *The Day After Forever* (Crosby, Heather); *Going My Way* (Crosby, Stevens) Burke, Van Heusen; *Silent Night* (Crosby, Robert Mitchell Boys' Choir) Franz Gruber, Joseph Mohr; *Habanera* (Stevens) from Bizet's 'Carmen'; *Ave Maria* Schubert.

▽

△

Carmen Miranda (illustrated centre) was top-starred for the first time in **Greenwich Village** (20th Century-Fox), one of the studio's few financially unsuccessful Technicolor musicals of the period, and was unable to carry the entire production (as she was expected to do) on her slender shoulders. Her co-stars, Don Ameche and William Bendix, weren't much help either, their names not being strong enough to light up the marquees of the world with promise and expectation. All about a composer (Ameche) who, in the 1920s arrives in Greenwich Village, falls in love with a singer and finds his concerto turned into a smash hit song thanks to nightclub proprietor Bendix presenting it in a flashy show uptown, it also featured Vivian Blaine (as the singer Ameche falls for), with other roles in scenarists Earl Baldwin and Walter Bullock's fabrication (based on a story by Frederick Hazlitt Brennan, adapted by Michael Fessier and Ernest S. Pagano) going to Felix Bressart, B.S. Pully, Emil Rameau and Frank Orth. Padding out the slender material were dancers Tony and Sally de Marco, a group called The Revuers – Judy Holliday, Betty Comden and Adolph Green (whose act was cut from the release print) and The Four Step Brothers. The surviving specialties were all far more entertaining than the top-billed performers. William Le Baron produced, and the director was Walter Lang. Songs and musical numbers included: *I Like To Be Loved By You* Vermelho, Silva; *I'm Down To My Last Dream*; *It Goes To Your Toes*; *Give Me A Band And A Bandana*; *Oh Brother*; *It's All For Art's Sake*; *I Have To See You Privately*; *This Is Our Lucky Day*; *You Make Me So Mad*; *Never Before*; *I've Been Smiling In My Sleep*; *Tell Me It's You*; *That Thing They Talk About* Leo Robin, Nacio Herb Brown; *Whispering* John Schonberger, Richard Coburn, Vincent Rose; *Swinging' Down The Lane* Gus Kahn, Isham Jones; *When You Wore A Tulip* Jack Mahoney, Percy Wenrich; *I'm Just Wild About Harry* Eubie Blake, Noble Sissle.

A modest, and modestly enjoyable, excursion into nostalgia, **Atlantic City** (Republic) chronicled the attempts of a young impresario (Brad Taylor) to turn Atlantic City into an international playground. The problems he encountered, both in his private and professional life, formed the basis of Doris Gilbert, Frank Gill Jr and George Carleton Brown's screenplay (story by Arthur Caesar), but by the final fade they were resolved to everyone's satisfaction. Constance Moore (kneeling right) was top-cast as the neglected wife who walks out on Taylor (but returns after his amusement pier is reduced to ashes in a fire), with other roles going to Charles Grapewin, Jerry Colonna (centre, appearing in various guises as a general factotum) and Robert E. Castaine, plus Al Shean and Jack Kenny (as Gallagher and Shean), Gus Van and Charles Marsh (as Van and Schenck), Belle Baker, Jose Frisco, Buck and Bubbles, and Paul Whiteman and Louis Armstrong with their orchestras. Seymour Felix choreographed ('Kiddyland Revue' sequence illustrated), Albert J. Cohen produced, and it was directed by Ray McCarey. Songs and musical numbers included: *Nobody's Sweetheart* Gus Kahn, Ernie Erdman, Billy Meyers, Elmer Schoebel; *Mister Gallagher And Mister Shean* Gallagher, Shean; *On A Sunday Afternoon* Andrew B. Sterling, Harry von Tilzer; *Ain't Misbehavin'* Andy Razaf, Fats Waller, Harry Brooks; *After You've Gone* Henry Creamer, Turner Layton; *I Ain't Got Nobody* Roger Graham, Dave Peyton, Spencer Williams; *By The Beautiful Sea* Harry Carroll, Harold Atteridge; *The Bird On Nellie's Hat* Arthur J. Lamb, Alfred Solman; *Darktown Strutters' Ball* Shelton Brooks.

Anne Shirley (2nd right), Dennis Day (centre) and Philip Terry (centre right) proved no draw at all for **Music in Manhattan** (RKO), a rather mindless programmer which found Miss Shirley, much to her discomfort, being pursued by an air force hero (Terry) whom, a short while before, she had pretended she was married to. The story, devised by Maurice Tombragel, Hal Smith and Jack Scholl (screenplay by Lawrence Kimble), made no sense at all, and at best, was an excuse for the film's musical numbers which Charles O'Curran staged without flair, and which featured the orchestras of Charlie Barnet and Nilo Menendez as well as Bob Mascagno and Italia De Nubila. Raymond Walburn (left), Jane Darwell (right) and Patti Brill completed the cast for producer-director John H. Auer. Songs and musical numbers included: *Did You Happen To Find A Heart?*; *One Night In Acapulco*; *When Romance Comes Along*; *Mexico*; *I Can See You Now* Herb Magidson, Lew Pollack.

Very much a *Road To . . .* film at heart, but with Eddie Bracken and Gil Lamb substituting for Crosby and Hope, **Rainbow Island** (Paramount) did at least have Dorothy Lamour (illustrated, top starred) giving audiences a taste of what it might have been had her two regular travellers been on hand to dispense the mirth and the music. All about a trio of sailors (Bracken, Lamb and Barry Sullivan) who find themselves cast away on a Pacific Island, the story (by Seena Owen, screenplay by Walter DeLeon and Arthur Phillips) was mainly concerned with the trio's attempts to keep themselves from being taken as sacrificial victims by the island's resident natives. They succeed, of course, in this case thanks solely to Bracken's resemblance to one of their local gods. A moderately entertaining spoof which had Lamour sending herself up in a sarong (and singing 'Beloved' by Ted Koehler and Burton Lane), it could have done with a slightly more inventive script than the one it had but, on the credit side, it allowed Bracken to give his most effective comic performance to date. Forrest Orr, Anne Revere, Reed Hadley, Marc Lawrence (left), Adia Kuznetzoff, Olga San Juan and Elena Verdugo were also cast; it was produced (in Technicolor) by Sol C. Siegel, choreographed by Danny Dare and directed by Ralph Murphy. Other songs and musical numbers: *What A Day Tomorrow*; *We Have So Little Time*; *The Boogie Woogie Man Will Get You If You Don't Watch Out* Koehler, Lane.

Danny Kaye (centre) made a spectacularly successful bid for screen stardom in his first film, **Up In Arms**, produced in Technicolor by Sam Goldwyn and released by RKO. Arriving in Hollywood via vaudeville, the 'Borscht Circuit', Broadway, and the nightclubs, Kaye's cinematic debut was described by one critic at the time as the most exciting since Garbo's, and watching him work in **Up In Arms** it is not difficult to see why he inspired such extravagant plaudits. As Danny Weems, a hypochondriac employed as an elevator boy in a building full of doctors, his performance offered a whacky blend of inspired clowning and madcap exuberance (as well as some excellent singing) that had the added distinction of being totally original. A drastic reworking of Eddie Cantor's 1930 vehicle *Whoopee* (United Artists), **Up In Arms**'s screenplay (by Don Hartman, Allan Boretz and Robert Pirosh) made good use of Kaye's unique talents, involving him in a plot in which he, his room-mate (Dana Andrews, left) and their respective

Bob Crosby (left) starred in a woebegone filler from Columbia called **Meet Miss Bobby Socks**. He played a war veteran who finds fame as a crooner, as well as romance in the shape of Lynn Merrick (right). All that audiences found was 68 minutes of *ennui*. Ina Ray Hutton co-starred, and the rest of the cast included Louis Jordan, Louise Erickson (2nd left), the Kim Loo Sisters, Pat Parrish, Mary Currier (centre), and Howard Freeman (2nd right). It was written by Muriel Roy Bolton, produced by Ted Richmond, and directed by Glenn Tryon. Songs and musical numbers included: *Fellow On A Furlough* Bobby Worth; *I'm Not Afraid* Kim Gannon, Walter Kent; *Come With Me My Honey* Mack David, Joan Whitney, Alex Kramer; *Two Heavens* Don George, Ted Grouya; *Deacon Jones* Johnny Lange, Hy Heath, Richard Loring.

girlfriends (Dinah Shore, right, and Constance Dowling) find themselves drafted to the Pacific. In between the resultant confusion, there were several well staged (by Danny Dare) production numbers, the most memorable being Kaye's 'Manic-Depressive Pictures Presents' (by Sylvia Fine, soon to become Mrs Kaye, and Max Liebman), a paean to movie credits which took place in the lobby of a cinema. Another Fine and Liebman contribution was 'Melody In 4F' – a typical Kaye scat song first performed by him in Cole Porter's 1941 Broadway hit, *Let's Face It*, Also in the cast for director Elliott Nugent were Louis Calhern, George Mathews, Benny Baker, Elisha Cook Jr, Lyle Talbot, June Lang, Walter Catlett, Donald Dickson, Margaret Dumont and Richard Powers, and The Goldwyn Girls (including Virginia Mayo who would soon be appearing in several more Kaye vehicles as a star in her own right). Other songs and musical numbers: *Now I Know*; *All Out For Freedom*; *Tess's Torch Song*; *Jive Number* Ted Koehler, Harold Arlen.

▵

Twelve musical numbers were spread over 62 minutes in **Twilight on the Prairie** (Universal), leaving very little time for scenarist Clyde Bruckman to develop his plot (from an original story by Warren Wilson) about a buckaroo radio band (illustrated) who, after finding themselves marooned in Texas while on their way to Hollywood to make a picture, are given employment in a ranch owned by Vivian Austin, and run by a dyspeptic Leon Errol. Eddie Quillan received top billing and the rest of the cast included Johnny Downs, Connie Haines, Dennis Moore, and Jack Teagarden and His Band. A routine filler aimed at the lower half of a double bill, it was produced by Warren Wilson and directed by Jean Yarbrough. Songs and musical numbers included: *Let's Love Again; Where The Prairie Meets The Sky; Don't You Ever Be A Cowboy* Everett Carter, Milton Rosen; *Texas Polka* Oakley Haldeman, Vic Knight, Lew Porter; *No Letter Today* Frankie Brown; *I Got Mellow In The Yellow Of The Moon* Jimmy Dodd; *Sip Nip Song* Don George, Brenda Weisberg; *Salt-Water Cowboy* Redd Evans; *The Blues* Jack Teagarden; *Little Brown Jug* Joseph E. Winner; *And Then* Sidney Mitchell, Sammy Stept.

The music publishing business formed the background of **Kansas City Kitty** (Columbia), a programmer in which Joan Davis (illustrated at piano) starred as a song plugger who is tricked into buying a publishing house, only to have a plagiarism suit flung at her by an irate composer claiming that 'Kansas City Kitty', the hit song published by the firm, wasn't written by the cowboy who has put his name to it but by himself. Matt Willis was the outraged songsmith, with other roles in Ted Richmond's indifferent little production going to Jane Frazee (centre left) and Bob Crosby (who had little to do in Manny Seff's trifling screenplay), Erik Rolf, Tim Ryan, Robert Emmett Keane, John Bond, and The Williams Brothers (all four illustrated, Andy right). Stanley Donen staged the dances, Del Lord directed. Songs included: *Kansas City Kitty* Walter Donaldson, Edgar Leslie; *Tico Tico* Zequinha Abreu, Ervin Drake; *Nothing Boogie From Nowhere* Saul Chaplin; *Pretty Kitty Blue Eyes* Mann Curtis, Vic Mizzy.
▽

The backstage trials and tribulations that befall a vaudeville family called the Monahans was the hackneyed subject of Universal's **The Merry Monahans** which – apart from Donald O'Connor, Peggy Ryan and Jack Oakie (featured centre) playing the family in question – offered cinema audiences a nostalgic trip down memory lane to the musical accompaniment of at least twenty old favourites from way back when. Ann Blyth was also among the cast and sang 'Isle d'Amour' by Earl Carroll and Leo Edwards and 'When You Wore A Tulip' by Jack Mahoney and Percy Wenrich, with other parts in Michael Fessier and Ernest Pagano's how-many-times-have-we-seen-it-before? screenplay going to Rosemary De Camp, John Miljan, Gavin Muir, Isabel Jewell, Robert Homans and Marion Martin. Louis Da Pron and Carlos Romero were in charge of the musical staging, Fessier and Pagano produced, and it was directed by Charles Lamont. Songs and musical numbers included: *Lovely; Beautiful To Look At; We're Having A Wonderful Time; Impersonations; Stop Foolin'* Don George, Irving Bibo; *What Do You Want To Make Those Eyes At Me For?* Howard Johnson, Joseph McCarthy, James V. Monaco; *Rock-A-Bye Your Baby With A Dixie Melody* Sam Lewis, Joe Young, Jean Schwartz; *Rose Room* Harry Williams, Art Hickman; *I'm Always Chasing Rainbows* Joseph McCarthy, Harry Carroll; *In My Merry Oldsmobile* Vincent Bryan, Gus Edwards; *I Hate To Lose You* Grant Clarke, Archie Gottler.
▽

Adapted by Edward Dein from a story by Patricia Harper, and scripted by Eugene Conrad, **My Gal Loves Music** (Universal) was an hour-long filler that starred Grace McDonald (left) who, thanks to a brainstorm by medicine-man Walter Catlett, poses as a 14-year-old prodigy and wins a trip to New York with a radio appearance on a show sponsored by a vitamin pill manufacturer (Alan Mowbray). Best song was 'Over and Over' (by Everett Carter and Milton Rosen) attractively sung by Miss McDonald. Producer-director Edward Lilley kept it light and frothy, drawing the best from a cast that also included Bob Crosby (right) as a piano-playing band leader, Betty Kean, a young tenor called Freddie Mercer, Tom Daly, and Chinita and Trixie. Other songs and musical numbers included: *I Need Vitamin U* Clarence Gaskill; *Somebody's Rockin' My Rainbow; Give Out, Pepita;* Carter, Rosen.
▽

▵

The best thing about **Song of the Open Road** (United Artists) was that it introduced screen audiences to a fresh new talent called Jane Powell (left). For the rest it was an adolescent (in every sense) yarn about a juvenile film star (Powell) who runs away to join a youth hostel, every last one of whose members can either sing, dance or play a musical instrument. They included Bonita Granville, Jack Moran, Peggy O'Neill and Bill Christy. Also cast were Reginald Denny, Regis Toomey, Rose Hobart, Sig Arno and, as themselves, Edgar Bergen and Charlie McCarthy, W.C. Fields (right), Pat Starling, The Condos Brothers, The Lipham Four, The Hollywood Canteen Kids, Catron and Popp, and Sammy Kaye and His Orchestra. It was scripted by Albert Mannheimer from a story by Irving Phillips and Edward Verdier, choreographed by George Dobbs and directed by S. Sylvan Simon for producer Charles R. Rogers. Songs and musical numbers included: *Here It Is Monday; Rollin' Down The Road; Too Much In Love* Kim Gannon, Walter Kent; *Marche Militaire* Schubert; *Hawaiian War Chant* Johnny Noble, Ralph Freed, Prince Leleiohaku of Hawaii; *Notre Dame; Carmona.*

▵

Benny Goodman and His Band (illustrated) featured prominently in **Sweet and Low Down**, a pot-boiler from 20th Century-Fox whose narrative (screenplay by Richard English) concerned the romances and overriding ambition of a swollen-headed trombone player (James Caldwell) attached to the Goodman outfit. It was dull, predictable, and indifferently acted by a cast that included Linda Darnell and Lynn Bari (as the girls in Caldwell's life), Jack Oakie as his faithful buddy, as well as Allyn Joslyn, John Campbell, Dickie Moore, Buddy Swan, Beverly Hudson and The Pied Pipers. Archie Mayo directed for producer William Le Baron. Joe Harris played the trombone for Caldwell, and Lynn Bari's vocals were dubbed by Lorraine Elliott. Best sequence: a gig at the senior prom of a boys' military school whose 15-year-old 'generals' all appear to have the aplomb of an Eisenhower. Songs and musical numbers: *I'm Making Believe; Chuch-Chug-Choo-Choo-Chug; Hey Bub, Let's Have A Ball; Ten Days With Baby* Mack Gordon, James V. Monaco; *I Found A New Baby* Jack Palmer, Spencer Williams; *Jersey Bounce* Robert B. Wright, Bobby Plater, Tiny Bradshaw, Edward Johnson; *Let's Dance* Fanny Baldridge, Gregory Stone, Joseph Bonine; *The World Is Waiting For The Sunrise* Gene Lockhart, Ernest Seitz; *Mozart's Clarinet Quintet* (performed by Goodman and strings); *No Love No Nothing* Leo Robin, Harry Warren; *Rachel's Dream* Benny Goodman; *I Yi Yi Yi Yi, I Like You Very Much* Gordon, Warren.

Forties Musicals

Meet Me in St Louis (MGM) was a tender and loving account of a year in the life of a prosperous St Louis family called Smith (see illustration). Nothing earth-shattering actually happened to them between 1902 and 1903 apart from romance entering the lives of two of the four Smith sisters, and father's decision (to the delight of his brood) not to move to New York. But, as lovingly scripted by Irving Brecher and Fred Finkelhoffe from a series of *New Yorker* stories by Sally Benson, the domestic trivia that surrounded the day-to-day activities of the Smith family was the very stuff of life itself. Apart from the fact that the film lacks a knock-out finale, ending as it does, with a shot of the family attending the opening of the St Louis Exposition, but showing practically nothing of the Fair itself, it remains 113 minutes of unalloyed delight. Directed by Vincente Minnelli with a lingering eye for period detail and a marvellous sense of nostalgia for the good old days and the good old sense of values that informed them, its basically sentimental content was never allowed to cloy, thanks to a complete absence of cuteness throughout. Even child star Margaret O'Brien as Tootie, the baby of the family, gave a performance which had a hard centre to it. Falling into four distinct sections, the film not only reflected a way of life (slightly romanticized, to be sure) but also the changing moods in the household as dictated by each season. Technicolor (employed by Minnelli for the first time) was brilliantly used to enhance these seasonal changes and was one of the film's chief sources of pleasure. But then almost everything about **Meet Me in St Louis**

gave pleasure, not least Judy Garland's (centre) glowing performance as Esther, the Smith sister who develops a crush on the boy next door (Tom Drake, 2nd left, standing) and expresses it in two songs: 'The Boy Next Door' and, in five of the most magical minutes ever proffered in a musical, the brilliantly orchestrated (by Conrad Salinger) 'Trolley Song' (both numbers by Hugh Martin and Ralph Blane). Another musical highlight was Garland's singing of 'Under The Bamboo Tree' (by Bob Cole and J. Rosamond Johnson), in which she was joined vocally, and in a brief cake-walk, by Margaret O'Brien. The choreography was by Charles Walters, and the exquisite photography by George Folsey. Lucille Bremer (3rd left, standing) and Joan Carroll (centre right on floor) were the other Smith sisters, Henry Daniels Jr the Smiths' (Leon Ames and Mary Astor) only son (seated with Margaret O'Brien on lap), Harry Davenport grandpa, and Marjorie Main their stentorian maid Katie, as much a part of the family as if she were born into it. The film's meticulous production carried the unmistakable imprint of its producer, Arthur Freed. Other songs and musical numbers: *Have Yourself a Merry Little Christmas* (Garland) Blane, Martin; *Meet Me In St Louis* (Garland, Bremer, Carroll, Davenport) Andrew B. Sterling, Kerry Mills; *Skip To My Lou* (Garland, Bremer, Daniels Jr, Drake) traditional, revised by Martin and Blane; *You And I* (Ames, dubbed by Arthur Freed, and Astor, dubbed by D. Markas) Freed, Nacio Herb Brown; *I Was Drunk Last Night* (O'Brien) traditional; *Over The Bannister* (Drake, Garland) traditional, arranged Salinger.

Kay Kyser starred in **Carolina Blues** (Columbia), as a bandleader out to raise money for a cruiser through a series of war bond rallies featuring himself and his well-known band. Ann Miller co-starred as an entertainer who looks to Mr K for a job; and Victor Moore was in it too, playing six elderly members (both male and female) of a family called Carver. Kyser regulars Georgia Carroll, Harry Babbitt, and the relentlessly unfunny Ish Kabibble were also featured in Joseph Hoffman and Al Martin's silly screenplay (story by M.M. Musselman and Kenneth Earl); so were Harold Nicholas (centre), The Cristianis, The Layson Brothers, and The Four Step Brothers. Sammy Cahn and Jule Styne provided the score. Sam Bischoff produced, Sammy Lee choreographed, and the director was Leigh Jason. Songs and musical numbers included: *Poor Little Rhode Island*; *There Goes That Song Again*; *Thinking About The Wabash*; *You Make Me Dream Too Much*; *Thanks A Lot*; *Mr Beebe*.

Dorothy and Herbert Fields and Cole Porter's successful 1943 Broadway musical, **Something for the Boys**, came to the screen from 20th Century-Fox in glorious Technicolor, but with only one contribution to the film's score by Porter (the title song). All about a trio of fancy-free cousins who inherit a rambling mansion in Kentucky near an army camp, and turn it into a home for soldiers' wives, it top-starred Carmen Miranda (illustrated 2nd left) – now one of the highest paid women in America at a salary in excess of $200,000 a year – featured Vivian Blaine (left) and Phil Silvers as the proprietors, and introduced Perry Como to movie audiences. Also in it were Michael O'Shea, Sheila Ryan (centre right), Glenn Langan (right), Roger Clark, Thurston Hall and, in a small part, Judy Holliday. Humorous, tuneful, and always attractive to look at, it was snappily directed by Lewis Seiler from a screenplay by Robert Ellis, Helen Logan and Frank Gabrielson, vigorously choreographed by Nick Castle, and produced in characteristically splashy Fox style by Irving Starr. The musical numbers were by Harold Adamson and Jimmy McHugh and they included: *I'm In The Middle Of Nowhere* (Como); *Wouldn't It Be Nice* (Blaine, O'Shea); *Samba Boogie* (Miranda); *I Wish We Didn't Have To Say Goodnight* (Blaine, Como); *Boom Brachee* (Miranda).

A follow up to Universal's musical chiller, *The Phantom of the Opera* (1943), **The Climax** starred that vintage ghoul, Boris Karloff, as the resident physician of a European opera house who labours under a chronic disability: madness. Years before, his unrequited passion for a soprano ended in his murdering her and storing her body in his attic. Twenty years later he meets a girl (Susanna Foster, illustrated) with a similar voice to that of his former love, and is determined to see that she, too, goes the way of all flesh . . . Enjoyable hokum and stylishly directed by George Waggner (who produced, and also wrote the film's lyrics to Edward Ward's music), it featured Turhan Bey, Gale Sondergaard, Thomas Gomez, June Vincent, George Dolenz and Ludwig Stossel. It was written by Curt Siodmak and Lynn Starling from a play by Edward Locke, with Siodmak in charge of the adaptation. The operetta sequences were staged by Lester Horton. Songs and musical numbers included: *Now At Last*; *Someday I Know*; *The Magic Voice*; *The Boulevardier* Waggner, Ward; themes from the music of Schubert and Chopin.

Mexico's popular singing star Tito Guizar (illustrated) starred in **Brazil**, a big-budget musical from Republic that utilized middle-of-the-road talents in a small story about a Brazilian composer (Guizar) and his successful efforts to tame an American authoress (Virginia Bruce, illustrated) who has just written an unflattering book called *Why Marry A Latin?* Needless to say, by the end of the film Miss Bruce, with Señor Guizar, is in a far better position to answer her own question. Pleasant but unexceptional entertainment, it also featured Edward Everett Horton, Robert Livingston, Veloz and Yolanda, Fortunio Bonanova, Richard Lane, Frank Puglia and specialty dancer Aurora Miranda (Carmen's sister). Roy Rogers made a guest appearance singing 'Hands Across The Border' (by Ned Washington and Phil Ohman), which he first introduced in Republic's western of the same name the previous year. **Brazil**'s screenplay was by Frank Gill Jr and Laura Kerr (story by Richard English), and it was directed for producer Robert North by Joseph Santley. Other songs and musical numbers included: *Brazil*; *Rio de Janeiro*; *Upa Upa* Ary Barroso, Bob Russell; *Moonlight Fiesta* Harry Tobias, Al Sherman.

Night Club Girl (Universal) was a rags-to-riches yarn about a couple of kids (Vivian Austin, left, and Billy Dunn) who, thanks to the help of columnist Edward Norris, are given a chance to try out their act at a Hollywood niterie run by Maxie Rosenbloom. Unfortunately, they overeat on hot dogs and, when it comes to the crunch, are too sick to do themselves justice. As written by Henry Blankfort and Dick L. Hyland from a story by Adele Commandini, there was no excuse for it at all – except, possibly, as a springboard for the appearances of several well-established nightclub and specialty acts, including The Delta Rhythm Boys, The Mulcays and Paula Drake. Also cast were Judy Clark (right), Leon Belasco, Andrew Tombes, Fred Sanborn, Virginia Brissac, Minna Gombell (centre), and Clem Bevans. Frank Gross produced. Louis Da Pron choreographed and Edward F. Cline directed. Songs and musical numbers included: *Wo-Ho* Jimmy Nolan, Jim Kennedy; *One O'Clock Jump* Count Basie; *The Peanut Song* Nate Wexler, Red Maddock, Al Trace; *Vingo Jingo* Don Raye, Gene De Paul; *I Need Love* Milton Pascal, Edgar Fairchild; *What A Wonderful Day* Harry Tobias, Al Sherman; *Pagan Love Song* Arthur Freed, Nacio Herb Brown.

◁ Just as Betty Grable was once groomed to replace Alice Faye, so June Haver waited in the wings to take over from Betty – and, in **Irish Eyes Are Smiling**, another in 20th Century-Fox's series of turn-of-the-century song *fests*, her bid for stardom finally arrived. Haver played Mary 'Irish' O'Brien, a blonde lass who falls in love with Ernest R. Ball, the real-life composer (with Chauncey Olcott and Rida Johnson Young) of 'Mother Machree' (sung by a boy soprano in the film), 'Dear Little Boy Of Mine' (with J. Keirn Brennan), and 'When Irish Eyes Are Smiling' (with Olcott and George Graff), sung by Dick Haymes. A largely fictitious biopic, with Haymes as Ball, the film top-starred Monty Woolley as a Broadway impresario and, in secondary roles, featured Anthony Quinn, Beverly Whitney, Maxie Rosenbloom, Veda Ann Borg, Clarence Kolb and Chick Chandler. Specialty dancer Kenny Williams also appeared; so did operatic stars Leonard Warren and Blanche Thebom. Familiar to a degree, its backstage intrigues and boy-meets-loses-gets-girl plot (screenplay by Earl Baldwin and John Tucker Battle from a story by E.A. Wellington) were pretty tedious, requiring more personality than Haver and Haymes (both illustrated) possessed to give it the fillip it pitifully lacked. Best song was a 'newie' by Mack Gordon and James V. Monaco called 'Bessie With A Bustle' which was brightly staged by Hermes Pan, and looked good in Technicolor. Damon Runyon produced, and the formula direction was by Gregory Ratoff. Other songs and musical numbers: *Let The Rest Of The World Go By*; *A Little Bit Of Heaven* Ball, J. Keirn Brennan; *Strut Miss Lizzie* Henry Creamer, Turner Layton; *I'll Forget You* Ball, Annalu Burns; *Love Me And The World Is Mine* Ball, Dave Reed Jr; *I Don't Want A Million Dollars* Gordon, Monaco; *Be My Little Baby Bumble Bee* Stanley Murphy, Henry I. Marshall.

▷

▷

Forties Musicals

In **Here Come The Waves** (Paramount), Bing Crosby took a few satirical swipes at the bobby-soxers of the nation whose swooning over crooners like himself and Sinatra (the latter deliciously parodied in a dreamy version of 'That Old Black Magic' by Harold Arlen and Johnny Mercer) was, by the mid-forties, reaching epidemic proportions. He played Johnny Cabot, a singing idol who, together with his buddy Sonny Tufts, meets a singing sister act, both girls being played by the volatile Betty Hutton (illustrated). One of the sisters (Sue) falls for Crosby's charm at first sight; the other (Allison) is totally unimpressed. Needless to say it is in the latter guise that Miss Hutton succeeds in winning her man, but not before a plethora of plot complications (screenplay by Allan Scott, Ken Englund, and Zion Myers) sabotages the progress of their romance. As the story unfurls, Crosby (illustrated) joins the navy hoping to be assigned to destroyer duty, but finds himself instead – thanks to the connivance of Hutton (as Sue) – in charge of the benefit shows being presented by the Waves. An undemanding *mélange* of comedy and music, it was choreographed by Danny Dare, boasted several good numbers by Arlen and Mercer (the best being 'Accentuate The Positive' performed by Crosby and Tufts) and was spiritedly directed by Mark Sandrich, who also produced. The rest of the cast included Ann Doran, Gwen Crawford, Noel Neill, Catherine Craig and Marjorie Henshaw. Other songs and musical numbers: *I Promise You; Let's Take The Long Way Home; There's A Fella Waiting In Poughkeepsie; Here Come The Waves; Join The Navy.*

One of Universal's rare 'A' sized musicals in that it ran over an hour (94 minutes in fact) and had some money spent on it, **Bowery to Broadway** did not, however, rate an 'A' for achievement. A period piece set in an era which seemed to be the exclusive property of 20th Century-Fox, it featured Jack Oakie and Donald Cook as a couple of Irishmen who both run beer gardens under the El railroad tracks of New York. In time, they put their friendly rivalry to one side, join forces, move uptown to bustling 42nd Street, and become the toast of Broadway with a series of no-expense-spared shows. What such familiar material needed was a stronger, more exciting line-up of talent than the one assembled by producer John Grant, and which included Maria Montez (top starred), Susanna Foster, Turhan Bey, Ann Blyth, Louise Allbritton (as Lillian Russell), Frank McHugh, Rosemary De Camp, Leo Carillo, Andy Devine and, doing a specialty called 'He Took Her For A Sleigh Ride', Donald P'Connor and Peggy Ryan (both illustrated in carriage). It was written by Edmund Joseph, Bart Lytton and Arthur T. Horman (story by Joseph and Horman), choreographed by Louis Da Pron, Carlos Romero and Johnny Boyle, and directed by Charles Lamont. Other songs and musical numbers included: *The Love Waltz; There'll Always Be A Moon* Everett Carter, Edward Ward; *Montevideo; Coney Island Waltz* Kim Gannon, Walter Kent; *My Song Of Romance* Don George, Dave Franklin; *Under The Bamboo Tree* Bob Cole, J. Rosamond Johnson; *Daisy Bell* Harry Dacre; *Yip-I-Addy-I-Ay* Will Cobb, John H. Flynn; *Wait Till The Sun Shines Nellie* Andrew B. Sterling, Harry von Tilzer; *Just Because You Made Dem Goo Goo Eyes At Me* Hughie Cannon, John Queen.

One of the most successful of all the war effort musicals was **Hollywood Canteen**, which grossed an absolute fortune for Warner Bros. while serving the purpose of keeping the boys at the front, and the public back home, happy. The screenplay, by Delmer Daves who also directed the film, had even less plot than was usual for entertainments of this nature: Robert Hutton and Dane Clark, two soldiers on sick leave from the South Pacific, spend a couple of memorable nights at the Hollywood Canteen before returning to active duty. Hutton finds himself the lucky winner of the prize for the millionth guest at the Canteen and gets a luxury suite and a car for the weekend, as well as a date with his dream girl, Joan Leslie, who played herself. However, it wasn't its story which brought queues to the box office, but the guest artists who embroidered it. In alphabetical order, they included The Andrews Sisters, Jack Benny (centre), Joe E. Brown, Eddie Cantor, Kitty Carlisle, Jack Carson, Joan Crawford, Helmut Dantine, Bette Davis (right), Faye Emerson, Victor Francen, John Garfield, Sydney Greenstreet, Alan Hale, Paul Henreid, Andrea King, Peter Lorre, Ida Lupino, Irene Manning, Nora Martin, Joan McCracken, Dolores Moran, Dennis Morgan, Eleanor Parker, William Prince, Joyce Reynolds, John Ridgely, Roy Rogers and Trigger, S.Z. Sakall, Alexis Smith, Zachary Scott, Barbara Stanwyck, Craig Stevens, Joseph Szigeti (left), Donald Woods, Jane Wyman, and Efrem Zimbalist, as well as Jimmy Dorsey and Carmen Cavallaro and their orchestras. It was produced by Alex Gottlieb, with choreography by LeRoy Prinz. Songs and musical numbers: *Don't Fence Me In* (Andrews Sisters, Roy Rogers) Cole Porter; *You Can Always Tell A Yank* (Morgan, Brown) E.Y. Harburg, Burton Lane; *What Are You Doing The Rest Of Your Life?* (Wyman, Carson) Ted Koehler, Burton Lane; *We're Having A Baby (My Baby And Me)* (Cantor, Martin) Harold Adamson, Vernon Duke; *Sweet Dreams Sweetheart* (Carlisle, Leslie); *Hollywood Canteen* Ted Koehler, M.K. Jerome, Ray Heindorf; *I'm Gettin' Corns For My Country* (Andrews Sisters) Jean Barry, Dick Charles; *Once To Every Heart* (Carlisle) Dorothy Donnelly, Sigmund Romberg; *Tumbling Tumbleweeds* (Sons of the Pioneers) Bob Nolan; *King Porter Stomp* (Dorsey Band) Jelly Roll Morton; *The General Jumped At Dawn* (Dorsey, Golden Gate Quartet) Larry Neal, Jimmy Mundy; *Ballet In Jive* (McCracken) Ray Heindorf; *Slavonic Dance* (Szigeti) Dvorak; *Voodoo Moon* (Cavallaro, Rosario and Antonio) Marion Sunshine, Julio Blanco, Obdulio Morales.

Bearing a decided resemblance in mood and atmosphere to the Rodgers and Hammerstein Broadway smash, *Oklahoma!*, Universal's **Can't Help Singing** (it even had a song in it called 'Cal-i-for-ni-ay') sashayed onto the screen in abundant Technicolor, and told the outdoor story (set in 1847) of a sprightly young girl who ignores her father's wishes and journeys west in order to marry an army lieutenant. But she changes her mind *en route* when she meets a gentleman who appeals to her more. Deanna Durbin (illustrated), looking enchanting in Technicolor, was the girl. Robert Paige (illustrated) the fellow she settles for, and Ray Collins her disapproving father. With a charming score by Jerome Kern and E.Y. Harburg, some really dazzling outdoor photography (by Woody Bredell and W. Howard Greene), and a spirited performance by its leading lady, Lewis R. Foster and Frank Ryan's screenplay (from a story by John Klorer and Leo Townsend, based, in turn, on *Girl of the Overland Trail* by Samuel J. and Curtis B. Warshawsky) stood up remarkably well considering its operetta-like machinations. Akim Tamiroff and Leonid Kinskey as a pair of Slavic fortune hunters new to the foreign customs of the country, were excellent in comic support, and the rest of producer Felix Jackson's cast included Clara Blandick, David Bruce, Olin Howlin, June Vincent, Thomas Gomez, Andrew Tombes and George Cleveland. The capable direction was by Frank Ryan. Songs and musical numbers: *Can't Help Singing*; *More And More*; *Cal-i-for-ni-ay*; *Elbow Room*; *Swing Your Sweetheart*; *Any Moment Now*.

Babes on Swing Street (Universal) was, as its title suggested, another excuse to allow a group of industrious kids to put on a show. This time they do so in order to raise enough money to further their education at music school. A sub-plot involving the timid uncle (Leon Errol) of one of the youngsters who lives in fear and trembling of his maiden aunt, Errol's sister (Alma Kruger), helped pad out Howard Dimsdale and Eugene Conrad's workaday screenplay (story by Brenda Weisberg). Ann Blyth (left), top-billed, sang 'Peg O'My Heart' (by Alfred Bryan and Fred Fisher); Peggy Ryan (centre) co-starred. Also cast: Andy Devine (right), Anne Gwynne, June Preisser, Kirby Grant, Billy Dunn, Freddie Slack and His Orchestra, The Rubenettes, and Marion Hutton, who sang the catchy 'Take It Easy' (by Albert De Bru, Irving Taylor and Vic Mizzy). Louis Da Pron choreographed, and it was directed by Edward Lilley for associate producer Bernard W. Burton. As programmers go, this one went. Other songs and musical numbers: *Just Being With You*; *Hotcha Sonja*; *I've Got A Way With The Boys*; *Wrong Thing At The Right Time*; *Musical Chairs*; *Music And You* Inez James, Sidney Miller; *Youth Is On The March* Everett Carter, Milton Rosen; *Siboney* Dolly Morse, Ernesto Lecuona; *Loch Lomond* (traditional).

Producer Joe Pasternak and director Henry Koster were united for the first time since their Universal days in **Music for Millions** (MGM), an irresistible weepie that combined a soppy story with dollops of classical music. It told of cellist June Allyson (right) who is about to have a baby, but is suffering because she has had no word from her serviceman husband away on active duty in the Pacific. Margaret O'Brien (left), who received top billing, was cast as Allyson's comforting younger sister, with Jimmy Durante on hand as maestro Jose Iturbi's manager (!) to dispense a couple of characteristic Durante-type ditties in characteristic Durante-type style, most notably 'Umbriago' which he wrote with Irving Caesar. Also from Durante came 'Toscanini, Iturbi and Me' (by Walter Bullock and Harold Spina) and it brought the house down. Marsha Hunt, Hugh Herbert, Harry Davenport, Marie Wilson, Larry Adler, Ben Lessy and Ethel Griffies completed the cast. The screenplay was an original, written by Myles Connolly. Other songs and musical numbers included: *At Sundown* Walter Donaldson; *Summer Holidays* Helen Deutsch, Herbert Stothart; Debussy's *Clair de Lune*, and a selection of various pieces by Tchaikovsky, Dvorak and Grieg.

A boy-meets-girl-on-ice story, **Lake Placid Serenade** (Republic) allowed Czechoslovakian figure-skating star Vera Hruba Ralston (illustrated) to don her blades on several occasions and, in the end, to find herself in the arms of Robert Livingston. There was little more to it than that, with Walter Catlett (a high-pressure producer), Lloyd Corrigan (a genial Czechoslovakian godfather), Eugene Pallette (a paternal American uncle), and Stephanie Bachelor (Miss Ralston's predatory rival in love) doing their best to flesh out Dick Irving Hyland and Doris Gilbert's insubstantial screenplay (story by Frederick Kohner). Also cast, and playing themselves, were Ray Noble and His Orchestra, Harry Owens and His Royal Hawaiians, Roy Rogers, and ice specialty acts McGowan and Mack, Twinkle Watts, and The Merry Messiters. Steve Sekely directed. Musical numbers included: *Deep Purple* Mitchell Parish, Peter De Rose; *My Isle Of Golden Dreams* Gus Kahn, Walter Blaufuss; *National Emblem March* E.E. Bagley; *Winter Wonderland* Dick Smith, Felix Bernard; *Intermezzo* Robert Henning, Heinz Provost; *Waiting For The Robert E. Lee* L. Wolfe Gilbert, Lewis F. Muir; *When Citrus Is In Bloom*; *Drigo's Serenade* Ricardo Drigo; *While Strolling In The Park* Robert A. King.

Patty, Maxene and LaVerne Andrews starred in **Moonlight and Cactus** (Universal), a short (60 minutes) but tuneful programmer whose plot (by scenarists Eugene Conrad and Paul Gerard Smith) told the uncomplicated story of a rancher who returns to his ranch after active service with the merchant marines to find that, in his absence, all the cowhands have been replaced by women. Believing that a woman's place is in the home, and not on his land, he resents their invasion of his property, but soon changes his tune when his lady foreman proves to him that women can be as efficient as men. The Andrews Sisters (illustrated, with Shemp Howard) served little purpose other than to sing, with the main burden of the plot falling on Tom Seidel as the returning rancher and Elyse Knox as his female foreman. Best song was a novelty item performed by the Andrews girls called 'Send Me A Man, Amen' (by Ray Gilbert and Sidney Miller). Leo Carillo played a cattle thief, with other parts going to Eddie Quillan, Murray Alper, Tom Kennedy and Minerva Urecal. Mitchell Ayres and His Orchestra were also featured. Edward F. Cline directed, the dances were staged by Charles O'Curran and the producer was Frank Gross. Other songs and musical numbers: *Wa Hoo* Cliff Friend; *Home* Harry and Jeff Clarkson, Peter Van Steeden; *C'Mere Baby* Lanny Gray, Roy Jordan; *Heave Ho My Lads, Heave Ho* Jack Lawrence; *Down In The Valley* Frank Luther; *Sing* Harold Mooney, Hughie Prince.

1945

Academy Awards

Best Picture
NOMINATIONS INCLUDED: *Anchors Aweigh* (MGM) produced by Joe Pasternak.

Best Actor
NOMINATIONS INCLUDED: Gene Kelly *Anchors Aweigh*. Cornel Wilde *A Song To Remember* (Columbia)

Writing (Original Story)
NOMINATIONS INCLUDED: *A Song To Remember* Ernst Marischka
(Original Screenplay)
NOMINATIONS INCLUDED: *Music For Millions* (MGM) Myles Connolly

Cinematography (colour)
NOMINATIONS INCLUDED: *Anchors Aweigh* Robert Planck and Charles Boyle. *A Song To Remember* Tony Gaudio and Allen Davey.

Sound Recording
NOMINATIONS INCLUDED: *Rhapsody In Blue* (WB) Nathan Levinson. *A Song To Remember* John Livadary. *The Three Caballeros* (Disney, RKO) C.O. Slyfield. *Wonder Man* (Goldwyn, RKO) Gordon Sawyer.

Film Editing
NOMINATIONS INCLUDED: *A Song To Remember* Charles Nelson.

Special Effects
Wonder Man John Fulton and A.W. Johns

Music
Song
'It Might As Well Be Spring' *State Fair* (20th Century-Fox) Richard Rodgers *cm*; Oscar Hammerstein II *lyr*.
NOMINATIONS INCLUDED: 'Accentuate The Positive' *Here Come The Waves* (Paramount) Harold Arlen *cm*; Johnny Mercer *lyr*. 'Anywhere' *Tonight And Every Night* (Columbia) Jule Styne *cm*; Sammy Cahn *lyr*.

'The Cat And The Canary' *Why Girls Leave Home* (PRC) Jay Livingstone *cm*; Ray Evans *lyr*. 'Endlessly' *Earl Carroll Vanities* (Republic) Walter Kent *cm*; Kim Gannon *lyr*. 'I Fall In Love Too Easily' *Anchors Aweigh* Jule Styne *cm*; Sammy Cahn *lyr*. 'I'll Buy That Dream' *Sing Your Way Home* (RKO) Allie Wrubel *cm*; Herb Magidson *lyr*. 'More And More' *Can't Help Singing* (Universal) Jerome Kern *cm*. E.Y. Harburg *lyr*. 'Sleighride In July' *Belle Of The Yukon* (International, RKO) Jimmy Van Heusen *cm*; Johnny Burke *lyr*. 'So In Love' *Wonder Man* David Rose *cm*; Leo Robin *lyr*.

Scoring Of A Dramatic Or Comedy Picture
NOMINATIONS INCLUDED: *A Song To Remember* Miklos Rozsa and Morris Stoloff.

Scoring Of A Musical Picture
Anchors Aweigh George Stoll
NOMINATIONS INCLUDED: *Belle Of The Yukon* Arthur Lange. *Can't Help Singing* Jerome Kern and H.J. Salter. *Hitchhike To Happiness* (Republic) Morton Scott. *Incendiary Blonde* (Paramount) Robert Emmett Dolan. *Rhapsody In Blue* Ray Heindorf and Max Steiner. *State Fair* Charles Henderson and Alfred Newman. *Sunbonnet Sue* (Monogram) Edward J. Kay. *The Three Caballeros* Edward Plumb, Paul J. Smith and Charles Wolcott. *Tonight And Every Night* Marlin Skiles and Morris Stoloff. *Why Girls Leave Home* Walter Greene. *Wonder Man* Lou Forbes and Ray Heindorf.

The New York Times Annual 'Ten Best'
3rd *Anchors Aweigh*

The Annual Top Moneymaking Films
INCLUDED: *Anchors Aweigh*. *Here Come The Waves*. *Hollywood Canteen*. *Incendiary Blonde*. *Irish Eyes Are Smiling* (20th Century-Fox). *Meet Me In St Louis*. *Music For Millions*. *Nob Hill* (20th Century-Fox). *Rhapsody In Blue*. *A Song To Remember*. *Thrill Of A Romance* (MGM). *Wonder Man*.

A well-mounted production did little for **A Song For Miss Julie**, routine programmer fare from Republic about a couple of playwrights (Barton Hepburn and Roger Clark) who have great difficulty in persuading the oldest living relative of the subject of their new operetta to give her permission for the project to go ahead. Shirley Ross received top billing as the fan-dancing wife of playwright Hepburn, with other roles in Rowland Leigh's screenplay (story by Michael Foster) going to Cheryl Walker, Elisabeth Risdon (as the troublesome elderly relative), and Jane Farrar (illustrated left, with Roger Clark), with appearances, too, from the famous ballet dancers Alicia Markova and Anton Dolin. Larry Ceballos choreographed it, the producers were William Rowland and Carley Harriman, with Rowland also in charge of the direction. Songs and musical numbers included: *It All Could Have Happened Before*; *That's What I Like About You*; *The Country Ain't The Country Anymore*; *I Love To Remember*; *Sweet Sunday* Marla Shelton, Louis Herscher.
▽

There was not much fun in **Dixie Jamboree**, a filler from PRC, which was as slow-moving as the Mississippi on which most of the 'action' took place. Story (by Lawrence E. Taylor, screenplay by Sam Neuman) concerned a show boat called the *Ellabella* and all who sailed in her. Guy Kibbee, for example, sells patent medicines to its passengers; Lyle Talbot (2nd right) and Frank Jenks are on board posing as holidaymakers when in fact they're a couple of fugitive con-men; Eddie Quillan (left), as a trumpeter, comes along for the ride in the company of a pair of Indians he's adopted and, providing them all with entertainment, are Frances Langford (right), Fifi D'Orsay (centre) and Charles Butterworth, as well as the Ben Carter Negro Choir. Jack Schwarz produced and the director was Christy Cabanne. Songs and musical numbers included: *Dixie Show Boat*; *No, No, No*; *If It's A Dream*; *You Ain't Right With The Lord*; *Big Stuff* Michael Breen, Sam Neuman.
◁

As a piece of accurate screen biography, **A Song To Remember** (Columbia) was a film to forget. As a solid, if somewhat fanciful, piece of commercial story-telling, embellished by some great music, and lushly packaged in exquisite Technicolor, it was more than acceptable. Purporting to be the life story of the great Polish composer Frederic Chopin, it starred Cornel Wilde (right) as the tubercular young pianist (Jose Iturbi dubbed the actual piano playing) and beautiful Merle Oberon (left) as George Sand (Mademoiselle Dudevant). Paul Muni, however, received billing above them both as Professor Joseph Elsner – and, under Charles Vidor's unrestraining direction, gave one of the wildest, most undisciplined performances of his distinguished career. Stephen Bekassy played Franz Liszt, Nina Foch was Constantia and George Coulouris Louis Pleyel. As scripted by Sidney Buchman (from a story by Ernst Marischka) they emerged as caricatured stereotypes, allowing audiences not a single glimpse into their souls – a criticism applied even more strenuously to Chopin and Sand, the latter being made to appear as the villain of the piece. ('Discontinue that so-called Polonaise jumble you've been playing for days,' she says to Chopin in one of the great bad lines of all time). Still, it looked good, and made an absolute fortune for the studio. Louis F. Edelman produced. Also cast: Sig Arno, Howard Freeman, George Macready, Claire DuBrey and Frank Puglia. The music: *Valse in D Flat (Minute Waltz) Op 64 No 1* (about half was played); *Mazurka in B Flat Op 7 No 1* (complete); *Impromptu No 4 in C Sharp Minor (Fantasie Impromptu) Op 66* (complete); *Etude in A Flat Op 25 No 1* (first ten bars only); *Polonaise in A Flat Op 53* (only half was played); *Scherzo in B Flat Minor Op 31* (complete); *Etude in E Op 10 No 3* (theme of film); *Nocturne in E Flat Op 9 No 2* (almost complete); *Berceuse in D Flat Op 57* (complete); *Waltz in C Sharp Minor Op 64 No 2* (almost complete); *Nocturne in C Minor Op 48 No 1* (almost complete); a montage consisting of *Etude in A Minor Opus 25 No 11*; *Ballade in A Flat Opus 47*; *Valse in A Flat Op 42*; *Valse in A Flat Op 34 No 1*; *Etude in C Minor Op 10 No 12 (Revolutionary Etude)*.

A sort of animated *Hellzapoppin*, **The Three Caballeros** (RKO) was a visual humdinger from Walt Disney that showered the screen with a wealth of shapes, forms, sounds, colour and images. What little structure it had revolved around a birthday package received by Donald Duck. The first gift he opens is a movie projector, and the film accompanying it is all about a penguin who sails for the South Seas because he hasn't been able to acclimatize himself to the Antarctic. After that we are introduced to Little Gauchito, who wins a local donkey race but is disqualified when the spectators realize that the donkey he has entered has wings. The next gift Donald unwraps is a pop-up book on Brazil, inside of which is his old pal Joe Carioca. In no time at all, the two of them insinuate themselves into the pages and embark on a wild musical adventure in the course of which they meet Aurora Miranda (illustrated) with whom Donald falls hopelessly in love. The last gift is Mexico, where Donald and Joe Carioca are joined by a rooster called Panchito for a magic carpet tour of the country, culminating in a fiesta and a bull-fight. Brilliantly inventive throughout, and with some exhilarating live-action sequences combined with animation, **The Three Caballeros** remains one of Disney's most dazzling achievements. The production supervisor and director was Norman Ferguson and, apart from Miss Miranda, the numerous performers seen or heard included Carmen Molina, Dora Luz, Nestor Amarale, Almirante, Trio Calaveras, Ascensio Del Rio Trio, The Padua Hill Players and the voices of Clarence Nash (Donald Duck), Sterling Holloway, Jose Olivera (Joe Carioca), Joaquin Garay (Panchito), Fred Shield, Frank Graham, and Carlos Ramirez. Songs and musical numbers: *The Three Caballeros* Manuel Esperon, Ray Gilbert, Ernesto Cortazar; *Baia* Ary Barroso, Gilbert; *Os Quindins De Yaya (Angel-May-Care)* Barroso, Ervin Drake; *You Belong To My Heart* Augustin Lara, Gilbert; *Mexico* Charles Wolcott, Gilbert.

Designed for the lower half of a double bill, **Blonde Ransom** (Universal) was a par-for-the-course filler that starred Donald Cook (left) as a New York nightclub owner in danger of losing his club through gambling debts, and Virginia Grey (right) as a wealthy socialite who fakes a kidnapping in order to raise the $63,000 Cook needs to save his club from bankruptcy. Pinky Lee and Collette Lyons were also featured, so were George Barbier, Jerome Cowan and George Meeker. M. Coates Webster wrote it from a story by Robert T. Shannon, and William Beaudine directed. Songs: *Musical Wedding*; *The Life Of The Party*; *A Million Dollars Worth Of Dreams*; *Hinky Dinky Pinky* Jack Brooks, Norman Berens, Al Sherman.

Bud Abbott (right) and Lou Costello (left) starred in **Here Come The Co-Eds** (Universal), one of the better of their more recent efforts. They played a pair of caretakers who come to the rescue of a girls' school which is due to close through lack of funds. Also in it was Lon Chaney Jr who, for reasons of his own, *wants* the school to close, and, in the guise of a wrestler called The Masked Marvel, meets dumpy Lou in the ring. Their bout together was the best thing in a film that also included some energetic tapping from Peggy Ryan (2nd left), and some spirited playing from Phil Spitalny and His All-Girl Orchestra featuring Evelyn Kaye (Mrs Spitalny) and Her Magic Violin! Martha O'Driscoll (centre), June Vincent (2nd right), Donald Cook, Charles Dingle, Richard Lane, Joe Kirk and Bill Stern completed the cast. Arthur T. Horman and John Grant wrote it from a story by Edmund L. Hartmann (Grant also producing) and it was directed by Jean Yarbrough. Songs and musical numbers included: *Hooray For Our Side*; *I Don't Care If I Never Dream Again*; *Jumping On Saturday Night*; *Someday We Will Remember*; *Let's Play House* Edgar Fairchild, Jack Brooks.

Forties Musicals

Tonight and Every Night (Columbia) was a wartime musical about war-torn London, which took place in the intimate Music Box Theatre (supposedly the Windmill Theatre) whose proud boast was that it never closed. Its English setting was reflected in the studio's choice of producer-director Victor Saville, but not in its cast, all of whom were American. Rita Hayworth and Janet Blair starred as a couple of dancers who find romance when a pilot (Lee Bowman) enters Rita's life, and a young dancer (Marc Platt) falls for Janet. Drama intrudes when Platt and Blair are killed in an air-raid and the film ends with Hayworth (illustrated centre) reluctantly rejecting marriage to Bowman in order to continue entertaining the troops at the Music Box. Though Saville's skilful handling of Lesser Samuels and Abem Finkel's screenplay (based on the play *Heart Of A City* by Lesley Storm) kept the narrative well clear of bathos, the chief architects of the film's success were choreographers Jack Cole and Val Raset, without whose lusciously staged production numbers, particularly Hayworth's exotic 'You Excite Me' (all the songs were written by Sammy Cahn and Jule Styne), and 'Tonight And Every Night'– an intriguing and imaginative item in which the characters in a newsreel actually step out from the edges of the screen to form part of the number itself – the film would not have been nearly as entertaining as it was. Marc Platt indulged in a rather bizarre dance number which called on him to mime to one of Hitler's speeches; and Janet Blair, apart from her singing of the attractive title number and a pretty ballad called 'Anywhere', was also seen (and heard) to excellent effect in a comic duet with Hayworth called 'The Boy I Left Behind'. Completing the cast were Leslie Brooks, Professor Lamberti, Dusty Anderson, Florence Bates (as the Music Box's owner), Stephen Crane, Jim Bannon, Ernest Cossart, Patrick O'Brien and Gavin Muir. The stunning Technicolor photography was by Rudolph Maté and it was beautifully costumed by Jean Louis and Marcel Vertes. Hayworth's vocals were dubbed by Martha Mears. Other songs and musical numbers: *Cry And You Cry Alone* (Hayworth, Platt) *What Does An English Girl Think Of A Yank?* (Hayworth).

254

A showcase for some of the younger talent under contract to Columbia, **Let's Go Steady** was an hour-long programmer about a group of out-of-town youngsters who, having been conned out of fifty dollars by a phoney New York publisher, decide to promote themselves by persuading bandleaders and radio stations to give their efforts an airing. The film featured crooners Jackie Moran and Mel Torme, singer-dancer June Preisser (left), mimic Jimmy Lloyd, Arnold Stang (right), Pat Parrish, and Skinnay Ennis and His Band. It was written by Erna Lazarus from a story by William R. Sackheim, and directed by Del Lord for producer Ted Richmond. Songs and musical numbers included: *Tantza Babele*; *Sioux Falls S.D.*; *Baby Boogie* Mel Torme.

Though Maxene, Patty and La Verne Andrews received top billing in **Her Lucky Night** (Universal), the undernourished screenplay which Clyde Bruckman badgered out of a story by producer Warren Wilson, revolved around the efforts of Martha O'Driscoll to nab herself a beau after a fortune teller predicts that the man in her life will be found sitting next to her in a movie house. With this in mind, she buys two cinema tickets, tosses one out of the window and hopes for the best. Noah Beery Jr co-starred, with other parts going to George Barbier, Maurice Cass, Olin Howlin and Robert Emmett Keane. The Andrews gals (illustrated) played nightclub entertainers as well as cupids in Miss O'Driscoll's romance, and sang five songs in all, including the popular 'Dance With A Dolly With A Hole In Her Stocking' by Terry Shand, Mickey Leader and Jimmy Eaton. Edward Lilley directed. Other songs and musical numbers: *Sing A Tropical Song* Frank Loesser, Jimmy McHugh; *Is You Is Or Is You Ain't My Baby?* Billy Austin, Louis Jordan; *Straighten Up And Fly Right* Nat King Cole, Irving Mills; *The Polka Polka* Maxine Manners.

Bring on the Girls (Paramount), filmed in Technicolor, was the one about the millionaire who is bugged by the thought that women find his money more attractive than they do him. So he decides to join the navy on the assumption that girls never think of sailors as being wealthy. Eddie Bracken was the man with the problem; Veronica Lake a sexy, gold-digging cigarette girl who, despite Bracken's subterfuge, sets out to nab him. Marjorie Reynolds was the secondary romantic interest and, apart from falling for Bracken's buddy Sonny Tufts, got to sing most of the songs. Alan Mowbray appeared as a butler, with other roles going to dancer Johnny Coy, Grant Mitchell, Peter Whitney, Porter Hall, Thurston Hall, Lloyd Corrigan, Sig Arno, Andrew Tombes and, as a hat-check girl, Yvonne De Carlo. Spike Jones and His Orchestra were also in it, contributing a characteristically unorthodox interpretation of 'Chloe' by Gus Kahn and Neil Moret. Danny Dare choreographed, Sidney Lanfield directed – without making an attempt to give the well-worn material (screenplay by Karl Tunberg and Darrell Ware) anything other than the faintest re-tread – and the producer was Fred Kohlmar. (Production number illustrated). Other songs and musical numbers: *How Would You Like To Take My Picture?*; *Uncle Sammy Hit Miami*; *Bring On The Girls*; *You Moved Right In*; *I'm Gonna Hate Myself In The Morning* Harold Adamson, Jimmy McHugh; *Egyptian Ella* Walter Doyle.

Eadie was a Lady (Columbia) was a lively, if somewhat implausible, concoction about a vivacious student from a strait-laced girls' school who leads a life of impeccable respectability by day, but spends her nights as the chief attraction of a burlesque show. Ann Miller (left) was the lady with a double life, with Joe Besser, her co-star, playing a burlesque comedian turned school teacher. William Wright (centre) was Miss Miller's sweetheart (and manager of the burlesque house at which she is employed), with other parts in Monte Brice's screenplay going to Jeff Donnell, Jimmy Little, Marion Martin (right), Kathleen Howard, Tom Dugan and Douglas Wood. Hal McIntyre and His Orchestra were also in it. Michael Kraike produced, Jack Cole was in charge of the dances, and the director was Arthur Dreifuss. Songs and musical numbers included: *Tabby The Cat* Harold Dickinson, Howard Gibeling; *She's A Gypsy From Brooklyn* L. Wolfe Gilbert, Ben Oakland; *Next Victory Day*; *I'm Gonna See My Baby* Phil Moore; *Eadie Was A Lady* Nacio Herb Brown, Buddy De Sylva, Richard A. Whiting.

Part adventure, part musical, part comedy and wholly unsatisfactory, Song of the Sarong (Universal), made for the bottom half of a twin bill, recounted the escapades of intrepid William Gargan who, in return for $1,000,000, agrees to journey to a remote island in order to seek out a fortune in pearls – the catch being that the gems are heavily guarded by savages. Sarong-clad Nancy Kelly (illustrated) played the white queen of the island, with Eddie Quillan and Fuzzy Knight on hand to give slapstick support to producer-scenarist Gene Lewis's creaking plot. Also in it: George Dolenz, George Cleveland, Mariska Aldrich, Morgan Wallace and Larry Keating. The dances were staged by Charles Romero and the director was Harold Young. Songs and musical numbers included: *Ridin' On The Crest Of A Cloud*; *Pied Pipers From Swingtown* Jack Brooks; *Island Of The Moon*; *Lovely Luana* Don Raye, Gene De Paul; *De Camptown Races* Stephen Foster.

Will pretty Audrey Long, a feature writer for a glossy American magazine, marry photographer Phillip Terry? Or will she marry her fiancée (Marc Cramer), an American businessman in Rio? That was the question posed in Pan-Americana (RKO), as good (or as bad) an excuse as any for an avalanche of Latin-American song and dance numbers provided by such exotic talents as Rosario and Antonio, Miguelito Valdes (foreground left), Harold and Lola, Chinita Marin, Chuy Castillon, The Padilla Sisters, Chuy Reyes and His Orchestra and the Nestor Amaral Samba Band. Eve Arden as the magazine's managing editor and Robert Benchley (its foreign editor) were in it to garner the odd laugh or two, but Lawrence Kimble's screenplay (story by Frederick Kohner and John H. Auer, who also produced and directed) didn't make it easy for them. Ernest Truex and Isabelita (illustrated) completed the cast. The choreographer was Charles O'Curran. Songs and musical numbers included: *Stars In Your Eyes*; *Rhumba Matumba*; *Guadalajara*; *Negra Leona*; *La Morine De Mi Copla*; *Baramba* Mort Green, Gabriel Ruiz; *Ba-Ba-Lu* Bob Russell, Marguerita Lecuona.

Running exactly an hour, Honeymoon Ahead (Universal) was a briskly paced programmer which starred Allan Jones (right) as a crooning convict whose unexpected release from jail causes havoc in the prison choir. So much so, that certain influential members of the choir immediately hatch a plot involving their singing star in a bank robbery in order to get him back. Jones's love interest was Grace McDonald (centre) whose father was Raymond Walburn, with other roles in Ellwood Ullman and Val Burton's screenplay (story by Burton) going to Vivian Austin, Jack Overman, Murray Alper, Eddie Acuff (left) and John Abbott. William Cowan produced and the director was Reginald Le Borg. Songs and musical numbers included: *Time Will Tell*; *Now And Always*; *Round The Bend*; *How Lovely* Everett Carter, Milton Rosen.

The youthful team of Donald O'Connor and Peggy Ryan (both illustrated) lent their considerable energies to Patrick the Great (Universal), a pleasant, but in no way exceptional, show-biz story about the conflict that arises between O'Connor and his actor father (Donald Cook) when the former is offered a part in a Broadway show that the latter wanted for himself. It's partly resolved, though, when Frances Dee accepts Cook's proposal of marriage. Miss Dee wasn't given a chance to be anything other than just personable in the Bertram Milhauser-Dorothy Bennett screenplay (story by Jane Hall, Frederick Kohner and Ralph Block); and Eve Arden, as a wise-cracking secretary, was wasted too. Completing the cast for producer Howard Benedict were Thomas Gomez, Gavin Muir, Andrew Tombes and Irving Bacon. It was directed by Frank Ryan with Louis Da Pron in charge of the dances. The songs and musical numbers were by Charles Tobias, David Kapp, Sidney Miller, Inez James and Charles Previn, and they included: *Song Of Love*; *For The First Time*; *Don't Move*; *Ask Madam Zan*; *The Cubacha*; *When You Bump Into Someone You Know*.

Too familiar in content even to support its one-hour running time, Penthouse Rhythm (Universal) was about three brothers and a sister and the difficulties they encounter in their bid for musical recognition. Jimmy Dodd, Bobby Worth, Louis Da Pron and Judy Clark were the kids on the make, with other roles in Stanley Roberts and Howard Dimsdale's screenplay (from a story by Roberts and Min Selvin) going to Kirby Grant, Lois Collier, Edward Norris, Maxie Rosenbloom, Eric Blore, Minna Gombell, Edward S. Brophy, Marion Martin, Donald MacBride, Velasco and Lenee (illustrated centre) and Harry Barris. Edward Cline directed and the producer was Frank Gross. Songs and musical numbers included: *Society Numbers*; *Let's Go American*; *When I Think Of Heaven*; *Up Comes Love*; *Peter Had A Wife And Couldn't Keep Her*.

Forties Musicals

Prettily dolled up in eye-catching Technicolor, **Belle of the Yukon** (International/RKO) had no place to go but down, due, in the main, to a screenplay that choked on its relentless diet of clichés. All about Randolph Scott's attempt to become a law-abiding citizen of Malamute (whose notorious dance hall is his favourite haunt), it also starred Gypsy Rose Lee (illustrated foreground centre), the Belle of the title with whom Scott is romantically involved, and Dinah Shore as a singer in love with a piano player (William Marshall). Sub-plots abounded, and there were several musical interludes, most notably Dinah Shore's singing of 'Sleigh Ride in July', and 'Like Someone In Love' (by Johnny Burke and Jimmy Van Heusen). But when the screenplay, by James Edward Grant from a story by Houston Branch, wasn't tying itself up into complicated knots, it was traversing territory too familiar for comfort. William Seiter directed, it was choreographed by Don Loper, and also featured Bob Burns, Charles Winninger, William Marshall, Guinn Williams, Robert Armstrong, Florence Bates, Victor Kilian and Edward Fielding. Other songs and musical numbers included: *Every Girl Is Different*; *Belle Of The Yukon* Burke, Van Heusen; *I Can't Tell Why I Love You But I Do, Do, Do* Will Cobb, Gus Edwards.

In **I'll Tell The World** (Universal), a crisply scripted (by Henry Blankfort) quickie, Lee Tracy played an announcer who puts a fair-to-middling radio station on the map by establishing a popular lonely hearts programme. Several specialties – from tap dancers to cowboy crooners – provided the musical accompaniment, with Brenda Joyce, Raymond Walburn (centre), June Preisser (right), Thomas Gomez (left), Howard Freeman and Lorin Raker also cast for producer Frank Gross and director Leslie Goodwins. Songs and musical numbers included: *Slap Polka* Harry Revel, Paul Francis Webster; *Walk A Little Faster* Dave Franklin; *Moonlight Fiesta* Harry Tobias, Al Sherman; *Where The Prairie Meets The Sky* Everett Carter, Milton Rosen.
▽

Swing Out Sister, an adequate hour-long programmer from Universal, followed the romantic complications of a young singer (Frances Raeburn, centre) who is trilling away at a nightclub when she should be pursuing her operatic studies. The two men in her life are the club's proprietor (Milburn Stone) and a symphony conductor with boogie-woogie tendencies (Rod Cameron, right). Both men in turn are accepted and rejected while Little Miss Indecision makes up her mind whether it is the highbrows or the lowbrows to whom she should appeal. Miss Raeburn, incidentally, was Kathryn Grayson's sister in real life. The screenplay by Henry Blankfort was teased out of a story by Eugene Conrad and Edward Dein; Bernard W. Burton produced, and the director was Edward Dein. Others cast were Billie Burke in another of her bird-brained characterizations, and Arthur Treacher (2nd left) as Cameron's British-accented, bass-playing sidekick, as well as Jacqueline De Wit (left), Samuel S. Hinds, Fuzzy Knight, Edgar Dearing and The Leo Diamond Quintet. Songs and musical numbers: *Emperor Waltz* Johann Strauss II; *Only In Dreams*; *Love Is A Bluebird On The Wing*; *All I Want To Do Is Swing*; *Happy-Go-Lucky-Lady*; *Swing It Mr Chumbly*.

The Naughty Nineties (Universal), starring Bud Abbott, and Lou Costello (illustrated), almost went that far back in time for its material. The comedians played a couple of interfering employees on a Mississippi river boat, and repeated in their desperation for a laugh, their oft-performed 'Who's On First?' routine. Alan Curtis, Rita Johnson, Henry Travers, Lois Collier, Joe Sawyer, and Joe Kirk were also involved; it was written by Edmund L. Hartmann (who also produced), John Grant, Edmund Joseph and Hal Fimberg, John Boyles staged the dances, and the director was Jean Yarbrough. Songs and musical numbers: *Rolling Down The River*; *Uncle Tom's Cabin*; *I Can't Get You Out Of My Mind* Jack Brooks, Edgar Fairchild; *On A Sunday Afternoon* Andrew B. Sterling, Harry von Tilzer; *I'd Leave My Happy Home For You* Will Heelan, Von Tilzer; *Nora Malone* Junie McCree, Albert von Tilzer; *Ma Blushin' Rosie* John Stromberg, Edgar Smith.

In their desperation to find a new plot that would encompass all the old backstage clichés, Republic came up with **Earl Carroll Vanities** which told the unlikely tale of a mythological princess (known as Drinia of Turania, and played by Constance Moore) who, while on a fund-raising trip to New York with her mother (Mary Forbes), becomes the leading lady in one of Mr Carroll's Broadway extravaganzas (production number illustrated). Dennis O'Keefe was the romantic interest, Alan Mowbray appeared as a Grand Duke, with other roles in Frank Gill Jr's silly screenplay (from a silly story by Cortland Fitzsimmons) going to Stephanie Bachelor, Eve Arden, Otto Kruger, Pinky Lee, Parkyakarkus and Leon Belasco. Woody Herman and His Orchestra were also in it for producer Albert J. Cohen; Sammy Lee choreographed, and the director was Joseph Santley. Best song: 'Endlessly', by Kim Gannon and Walter Kent, sung by Miss Moore. Other songs and musical numbers: *Apple Honey* Woody Herman; *Who Dat Up Dere?* Gannon, Kent; *Riverside Jive* Alfred Newman; *Rockabye Boogie*; *You Beautiful Thing, You*.
▽

A programmer from Columbia, **Blonde From Brooklyn** was a thoroughly inconsequential entertainment that starred Robert Stanton (illustrated – formerly Bob Haymes, brother of Dick) as a song-and-dance man newly released from the army, and Lynn Merrick (illustrated) as the jukebox singer he meets and with whom he plans a radio career as a musical duo. Erna Lazarus's screenplay made sure that a lot of things went wrong before they finally went right, and gave employment to Thurston Hall (as a rascally pseudo-Southern colonel), Mary Treen, Walter Soderling, Arthur Loft and Regina Wallace. Ted Richmond produced and the director was Del Lord. Songs included: *My Baby Said Yes* Sid Robin, Ted Walters.
▽

Olsen and Johnson made an unhappy exit from movies with **See My Lawyer** (Universal), playing a couple of comedians who attempt to worm their way out of a nightclub contract by insulting the guests when club owner Franklin Pangborn refuses to release them. In the process, they bring several law suits upon themselves, giving much needed employment to three clientless attorneys. Producer Edmund L. Hartmann, and Stanley Davis's screenplay (from a play by Richard Maibaum and Harry Clork) gave employment to a host of specialty acts including Carmen Amaya and her dance company, The King Cole Trio (with Nat King Cole), The Cristianos Troupe, The Rogers Adagio Trio, The Six Willys, The Hudson Wonders and The Four Teens, as well as Alan Curtis, Grace McDonald, Noah Beery Jr, Edward S. Brophy, Richard Benedict, Lee Patrick and Gus Schilling. Which didn't leave much time or room for Messrs O. and J. whose only good scene was the one in which they insulted the guests at Pangborn's niterie by squirting soda in their faces and flinging mud in their eyes. Director Edward Cline bravely attempted to give it some cohesion, but failed (production number illustrated). Songs and musical numbers included: *Fuzzy Wuzzy* Bob Bell, Roy Branker; *Penny Arcade* Dave Franklin; *We're Making A Million*; *Take It Away*; *It's Circus Time* Everett Carter, Milton Rosen; *Man On The Little White Keys* Joe Greene, Nat King Cole.

A Technicolored commercial for showman Billy Rose, **Billy Rose's Diamond Horseshoe** was assembly-line entertainment from 20th Century-Fox. Betty Grable (illustrated centre) starred as a showgirl with a 'mink coat complex', and her co-star was up-and-coming Dick Haymes, playing a young doctor with greasepaint in his veins. It all took place in and around Rose's opulent niterie, and together the two attractive stars made beautiful music, courtesy of Mack Gordon and Harry Warren, particularly in their duets 'I Wish I Knew' and 'The More I See You'. Phil Silvers (as a stage manager) breezed in and out of director George Seaton's conventional screenplay (suggested from a play by John Kenyon Nicholson), making the most of the gags provided for him, with William Gaxton (as Haymes's hoofer father) bringing to his role the authority and experience of a lifetime on the Broadway boards. Beatrice Kay, Margaret Dumont and Roy Benson completed the cast, with Carmen Cavallaro and Willie Solar featured as specialties. Resident choreographer Hermes Pan was given several opportunities to interrupt the narrative with some well-staged dance routines, especially 'Cooking Up A Show'. William Perlberg produced. **Billy Rose's Diamond Horseshoe** was the last score Harry Warren wrote for Fox before moving to MGM. Other songs and musical numbers: *Welcome To The Diamond Horseshoe* (Grable, chorus); *In Acapulco* (Grable, Cavallaro); *You'll Never Know* (Grable); *Play Me An Old-Fashioned Melody* (Grable, Gaxton, Kay); *A Nickle's Worth Of Jive* (Grable) Gordon, Warren; *Carrie Marry Harry* (Kay, Gaxton) Junie McCree, Albert von Tilzer; *Let Me Call You Sweetheart* (Kay) Beth Slater Whitson, Leo Friedman; *Sleep Baby Sleep* (Kay) S.A. Emery; *Shoo Shoo Baby* (Grable) Phil Moore; *Aba Daba Honeymoon* (Solar) Arthur Fields, Walter Donovan; *I'd Climb The Highest Mountain* (Haymes) Lew Brown, Sidney Clare; *My Melancholy Baby* (Haymes) George A. Norton, Ernie Burnett.

That's The Spirit (Universal) was a musical fantasy that starred Jack Oakie (left) as a long-deceased hoofer who returns to earth in order to help his daughter (Peggy Ryan) make a career for herself on the stage – much to the disapproval of her grandfather (Gene Lockhart). Unfortunately, whimsy of this nature needed a more skilful screenplay than the producer-writer team of Michael Fessier and Ernest Pagano provided, and much tighter direction than it got from Charles Lamont. June Vincent (illustrated) played Oakie's widow, with other parts going to tap-dancer Johnny Coy, Andy Devine, Arthur Treacher, Irene Ryan, and Buster Keaton. Songs and musical numbers: *Oh, Oh, Oh*; *Fellow With A Flute* Inez James, Sidney Miller; *Evenin' Star*; *No Matter Where You Are* Jack Brooks, H.J. Salter; *Nola* Felix Arndt; *How Come You Do Me Like You Do?* Roy Bergere, Gene Austin; *Baby, Won't You Please Come Home?* Clarence Williams, Charles Warfield; *Bugle Call Rag* J. Hubert Blake, Carey Morgan; *Ja-Da* Bob Carleton; *Do You Ever Think Of Me?* Earl Burnett, John Cooper, Harry D. Kerr.

Forties Musicals

Sam Goldwyn followed his successful screen
launch of Danny Kaye in *Up In Arms* (RKO,
1944) with **Wonder Man** (RKO), and offered
audiences a package they couldn't and didn't
refuse: two Danny Kayes for the price of one,
with Technicolor, the inevitable Goldwyn
Girls, and the debut of another promising newcomer – Vera-Ellen – thrown in as added
attractions. The result was one of the top
money-making films of the year. Another
musical fantasy, it told the story of two brothers
(both played by Kaye), one of whom is a devil-
may-care nightclub performer, the other a
rather ascetic scholar who spends most of his
time in public libraries because he loves the
smell of leather bindings. The plot pivoted on the
confusion caused when the extrovert brother is
murdered by gangsters, and his soul mischiev-
ously enters the body of the introvert, demanding vengeance. Virginia Mayo (illustrated right),
an ex-Goldwyn Girl now elevated to star status,
co-starred (as a librarian) with Kaye (left) in
what was to be the first of four films they made
together; with Vera-Ellen third-billed as the
murdered brother's fiancée and dance partner.
Donald Woods, Allen Jenkins, Edward S.
Brophy, Steve Cochran (his debut), Otto Kruger,
Richard Lane, Natalie Schafer and Huntz Hall
also appeared. Sylvia Fine provided Kaye with
two specialty songs – 'Orchi Tchornya', in
which he gave a hilarious impression of a
Russian baritone beset by a sneezing fit; and
'Opera Number' – a frenetic opera parody that
also happened to further the plot for, in it, Kaye
was able to sing the whole story of his brother's
murder (and reveal whodunnit) to the district
attorney in the audience. There were two other
numbers: 'Bali Boogie' (by Sylvia Fine), performed by Kaye, Vera-Ellen, Jack Norton and
The Goldwyn Girls, and 'So In Love' by Leo
Robin and David Rose, sung by Vera-Ellen
(whose vocals were dubbed by June Hutton),
with Cecil Cunningham and The Goldwyn Girls.
John Wray choreographed. The screenplay was
by Don Hartman, Melville Shavelson and Phillip
Rapp, based on an adaptation of an Arthur
Sheekman story by Jack Jevne and Eddie Moran;
it was produced by Goldwyn (in Technicolor)
and directed with an appropriate sense of the
ridiculous by Bruce Humberstone.

Hitchhike To Happiness (Republic) featured
radio's Al Pearce (left) as a would-be playwright
who, while waiting for his big break, takes
employment as a waiter in a small New York
restaurant frequented largely by show folk. His
customers, aware of his theatrical yearnings,
decide to perpetrate a hoax on an irritating
Hungarian producer (Willy Trenk) by leading
him to believe that Pearce has written a masterpiece that will make all concerned with it rich.
Complications proliferate, with Dale Evans (as a
famous radio singer), Brad Taylor (as a songwriter), William Frawley (a producer), Irving
Bacon (a playwright), Joyce Compton (centre),
Robert Strong (right) and Jerome Cowan (a faded
star) all contributing to the fun. Jack Townley
wrote it (story by Manny Seff and Jerry Horwin);
Joseph Santley directed for producer Donald H.
Brown. Songs included: *Hitchhike To Happiness*;
For You And Me; *Sentimental*; *My Pushover Heart*
Kim Gannon, Walter Kent.

Jane Powell (left) starred in **Delightfully Dangerous**, a ponderous offering from United Artists in
which she appeared as a charming Miss Fixit
who, after learning that her big sister (Constance
Moore, right) isn't a famous Broadway star at
all, but a burlesque queen, sets out to rectify
matters – in the course of which she also
manages to marry her off to a good-looking
Broadway producer (Ralph Bellamy). Fifteen-
year-old Miss Powell warbled a collection of old
and new songs in her pretty coloratura, providing Walter DeLeon and Arthur Phillips's screenplay, from a story by Irving Phillips, Edward
Verdier and Frank Tashlin, with its only genuine
freshness. Arthur Treacher played a butler
(that's how original it all was!), with Louise
Beavers, Ruth Tobey, Ruth Robinson, Andre
Charlot, Shirley Hunter Williams, and Morton
Gould and His Orchestra completing the cast for
producer Charles R. Rogers and director Arthur
Lubin. Songs and musical numbers included: *In
A Shower Of Stars*; *Mynah Bird*; *I'm Only Teasin'*;
Through Your Eyes To Your Heart; *Once Upon A
Song* John Jacob Loeb, Redd Evans; and, to
showcase Miss Powell's range of vocal abilities, a
medley of songs by Johann Strauss.

Charles Coburn played a professional card sharp
in the moderately entertaining **Shady Lady**
(Universal), with Ginny Simms (illustrated) as
his nightclub singer niece and Robert Paige as
the deputy State Attorney in charge of gambling. Alan Curtis was cast as Simms's racketeer
boss, with other roles going to Martha O'Driscoll, Kathleen Howard, James Burke, John Gallaudet, Joe Frisco and Thomas E. Jackson. It was
produced and directed by George Waggner,
scripted by Curt Siodmak, Gerald Geraghty and
M.M. Musselman (additional dialogue by Monty
Collins) and choreographed by Lester Horton.
Songs and musical numbers: *In Love With Love*;
Mam'selle Is On Her Way George Waggner,
Milton Rosen; *Tango* Edgar Fairchild; *Cuddle Up A
Little Closer* Karl Hoschna, Otto Harbach.

Where Do We Go From Here? (20th Century-Fox), which had a pleasing score by Kurt Weill and Ira Gershwin, was an ambitious musical fantasy that starred Fred MacMurray (right) as a disappointed 4-F yearning to get into the army. Instead he is confined to a salvage depot where, while polishing an old lamp one day, he releases a genie (Gene Sheldon) who gratefully grants him three wishes. Naturally, MacMurray says he wants to be drafted – and, indeed he is. Except that genie Sheldon's magic is as rusty as the lamp from which he sprang – and MacMurray finds himself spirited off to Valley Forge in the days of Washington. His trip through history continues when he finds himself aboard Columbus's *Santa Maria*, (the best sequence in the film, staged as an opera) and, on yet another occasion, purchases Manhattan Island from a Red Indian for twenty-four dollars. The two women he meets in the course of his travels are Joan Leslie and June Haver (left), with other parts in Morrie Ryskind's original screenplay (based on a story by himself and Sig Herzig) going to Anthony Quinn (centre, as an Indian chief), Alan Mowbray (as Washington) and Fortunio Bonanova (as Columbus) as well as Herman Bing, Howard Freeman and John Davidson. In general Gregory Ratoff's direction lacked the requisite lightness of touch the material demanded, but it had its moments. The dances were staged by Fanchon, and the producer was William Perlberg. Songs and musical numbers: *All At Once*; *Song Of The Rhineland*; *The Nina, The Pinta and The Santa Maria*; *Christopher Columbus*; *If Love Remains*; *Morale*.

George Gershwin's rise to fame from his humble East-side origins provided scenarists Howard Koch and Elliot Paul (story by Sonya Levien) with a springboard from which to launch their platitudinous and overworked screenplay for **Rhapsody in Blue**, Warner Bros.' largely fictitious account of the great composer's life and times. With no more than a passing nod at verisimilitude, producer Jesse L. Lasky cast Robert Alda (at piano) as Gershwin, and allowed his team of writers to put words into his subject's mouth that were, at times, frankly embarrassing. But with the complete Gershwin catalogue at the studio's disposal, music spoke louder than words – especially the performances (by Oscar Levant) of the celebrated 'Rhapsody In Blue', first heard by movie audiences in Universal's 1930 Technicolor revue *King of Jazz*, and the Concerto in F. Joan Leslie played ingenue Julie Adams, with Alexis Smith cast as the moneyed 'other' woman. Charles Coburn appeared as music publisher Max Dreyfus, Albert Basserman was Gershwin's benevolent music professor and mentor, Julie Bishop (centre) was Lee Gershwin, Herbert Rudley (2nd left), Ira Gershwin, and Rosemary De Camp and Morris Carnovsky Ma and Pa Gershwin. Oscar Levant (right – who had the best lines in the film), Paul Whiteman, Al Jolson, George White, Hazel Scott and Anne Brown played themselves. Mickey Roth and Darryl Hickman were the young George and Ira. Other roles: Stephen Richards (left, later Mark Stevens), Martin Noble (as Jascha Heifetz), Will Wright (as Rachmaninov), Ernest Golm (as Otto Kahn), Eddie Marr (as Buddy De Sylva) and Oscar Loraine (Ravel). The excellent orchestral arrangements were by Ray Heindorf. LeRoy Prinz choreographed, and the direction was by Irving Rapper. Ray Turner played the piano for Alda, and Louanne Hogan dubbed the vocals for Joan Leslie. It was beautifully photographed in black and white by Sol Polito. Other songs and musical numbers (lyrics by Ira Gershwin unless otherwise indicated): *Somebody Loves Me* Buddy De Sylva, Ballard MacDonald; *Fascinating Rhythm*; *Summertime* Du Bose Heyward; *Delishious*; *The Man I Love*; *Mine*; *Yankee Doodle Blues* De Sylva, Irving Caesar; *Liza* Ira Gershwin, Gus Kahn; *Oh Lady Be Good*; *Clap Yo' Hands*; *Bidin' My Time*; *Love Walked In*; *Do It Again* De Sylva; *I'll Build A Stairway To Paradise* De Sylva, Arthur Francis (pseudonym of Gershwin); *Blue Monday Blues* Buddy De Sylva; *Swanee* by Irving Caesar; *Someone To Watch Over Me*; *Cuban Overture*; *An American In Paris*; *'Swonderful*; *I Got Rhythm*; *Variations on I Got Rhythm*; *My One And Only*; *Embraceable You*.

Instead of Jose Iturbi adorning a trite tale with a few popular classics, producer Joe Pasternak persuaded Wagnerian tenor Lauritz Melchior to handle the long-haired stuff in **Thrill Of A Romance**, a glossy entertainment from MGM with lots of spit and polish, but not much else by way of solid musical entertainment. Mrs Johnson's boy Van (right) topped the cast list as an air force hero on vacation at a Sierra Nevada mountain lodge, with Esther Williams (left) as the girl he woos (between her dips in the resident swimming pool). Except that she's a newlywed whose prosaic businessman husband has had to leave suddenly for Washington. Johnson's romance with water-sprite Williams was the *raison*

d'être of Richard Connell and Gladys Lehman's uneventful screenplay, and pretty predictable it turned out to be. Two hit songs emerged: 'Please Don't Say No, Say Maybe' by Ralph Freed and Sammy Fain, boomingly sung by Mr Melchior, and 'I Should Care' by Sammy Cahn, Axel Stordahl and Paul Weston, sung by Robert Allen. The direction was by Richard Thorpe, who relied on additional musical support from Tommy Dorsey and Xavier Cugat and their orchestras, as well as The King Sisters. Other songs and musical numbers included: *Lonely Night* George Stoll, Richard Connell; *Vive L'Amour* Stoll, Ralph Blane, Kay Thompson; *Schubert's Serenade*; *The Thrill Of A Romance*.

Forties Musicals

Just as Bing Crosby took the mickey out of Frank Sinatra in Paramount's *Here Come The Waves* (1944), so Eddie Bracken did the same to Crosby in **Out Of This World** (Paramount) – and with Crosby's voice too. For every time Bracken opened his mouth to croon, out popped Crosby. A gentle spoof on the type of mellifluous warbling guaranteed to elicit squeals of joy from bobby-soxers everywhere, **Out Of This World** was the story of a crooning telegram boy (Bracken, right) whose life becomes needlessly complicated when he hitches up with a stranded all-girl orchestra led by Diana Lynn, who played Chopin's 'Minute Waltz' as part of a Sam Coslow number called 'The Ghost of Mr Chopin'. Bracken's particular brand of clowning helped plug the cracks in Walter DeLeon and Arthur Phillips's screenplay (based on stories by Elizabeth Mehan and Sam Coslow), and there was energetic support from Cass Daley, who gave a fair imitation of a whirling dervish while delivering a number called 'A Sailor With An Eight Hour Pass' (by Ben Raleigh and Bernie Wayne). Veronica Lake (left) received second billing, but was wasted in the role of a theatrical booking agent secretary who helps turn Bracken from singing messenger into singing sensation. The cast was completed by Parkyakarkus, Donald MacBride, Florence Bates, Don Wilson, Mabel Paige, Olga San Juan and Irving Bacon. Also joining in the fun were the four Crosby sons, Carmen Cavallaro, Ray Noble, Ted Fiorito, Henry King and Joe Reichman. Sammy Lee choreographed it, Sam Coslow produced and the director was Hal Walker. Songs and musical numbers included: *June Comes Around Every Year*; *Out Of This World* Johnny Mercer, Harold Arlen; *I'd Rather Be Me* Eddie Cherkose, Felix Bernard, Sam Coslow; *All I Do Is Beat That Golden Drum*; *It Takes A Little Bit More* Coslow.

The last, and most stylish, of the year's four musical fairy tales was **Yolanda And The Thief** (MGM), set in Latin America and starring Fred Astaire (centre) as a conman-cum-thief, and Lucille Bremer as a wealthy, gullible young heiress he plans to fleece by pretending to be the earthly incarnation of her guardian angel. But love intrudes and his plans go awry. Directed with immense sophistication by Vincente Minnelli, the finished product was a triumph of style over content, with Irving Brecher's mundane screenplay (from a story by Ludwig Bemelmans and Jacques Thery) uncomfortably at variance with the elegant visual flair imposed on the narrative by Minnelli, his cameraman Charles Rosher, art directors Cedric Gibbons and Jack Martin Smith, and costume designer Irene Sharaff. Photographed in superb Technicolor, it looked a dream and, indeed, the best sequence in it was a dream ballet in which Astaire, torn between his love for Bremer and his love of money, agonizes over which to choose. Very surreal and very exotic, it lasted for sixteen ravishing minutes, its only blemish being a regrettable lyric (by Arthur Freed) which interrupted Eugene Loring's choreography and Harry Warren's music with lines like 'Let The Band Begin, Playing Lohengrin . . .' In complete contrast was the film's joyous finale – a conventional 'big finish', set against a roisterous carnival background to the accompaniment of the show's most accessible tune, 'Coffee Time', also by Freed and Warren, who wrote all of the film's five songs. The cast was completed by Frank Morgan, Mildred Natwick, Mary Nash and Leon Ames – all of them hampered by the inanities of Brecher's screenplay. Too whimsical for mass audience appeal, the film lost over $1,600,00 on its initial release and, of all Astaire's MGM musicals, is the least seen and the least known. Other songs: *This Is The Day For Love* (Bremer); *Angel* (Bremer); *Yolanda* (Astaire); *Will You Marry Me* (dream ballet).

Gloria Jean sang four of the songs in **Easy To Look At**, a small-budget programmer from Universal which offered minimal entertainment. She was cast as an ambitious costume designer who comes to New York to make a name for herself in her chosen field, never for a moment thinking that the name she would make would be a bad one. For, as scripted by Henry Blankfort (who also produced), she is unjustly accused of being a design thief. It all came right in the last reel, though, with Kirby Grant having designs of his own on Miss Jean (right), and J. Edward Bromberg (left), a once famous couturier now reduced to foreman of a clothes emporium, being recognized all over again for the genius he is. George Dolenz, Eric Blore, Leon Belasco, Mildred Law, Dick French (centre), and The Delta Rhythm Boys were also featured. The director was Ford Beebe. Songs and musical numbers included: *Come Along My Heart*; *Just For the Devil Of It*; *That Does It*; *Umbrella With A Silver Lining*; *Swing Low Sweet Lariat* Charles Newman, Arthur Altman; *Is You Is Or Is You Ain't My Baby?* Billy Austin, Louis Jordan.

Anchors Aweigh (MGM), produced in Technicolor by Joe Pasternak, was an archetypal Gene Kelly musical, many of whose ideas would be repeated in future Kelly offerings, most notably in *On The Town* (MGM, 1949). The story (by Natalie Marcin, screenplay by Isobel Lennart) concerned a couple of sailors on leave in Hollywood and the romantic adventures they have, particularly between Kelly and would-be singer Kathryn Grayson, whose ambition it is to audition for Jose Iturbi. In order to impress her, Kelly lies to her that his buddy (Frank Sinatra) and Iturbi are good friends and that with a word in the maestro's ear from Frank, the audition is as good as fixed. Grayson believes him and for the rest of the film (which ran 140 minutes) Kelly and Sinatra rush around Hollywood trying to find Iturbi, in the course of which Sinatra meets a girl (Pamela Britton) from Flatbush, his hometown, and pairs off with her, leaving the way clear for his buddy to pursue Miss Grayson and Iturbi (whom he never manages to find, but who finds Grayson instead), thus ensuring a happy ending. So much for the plot – a typical Pasternakian trifle in which audiences were offered equal quantities of popular music and light classics. Though Pasternak's particular brand of middle-European *schmaltz* was thickly spread over the storyline, Kelly's energetic presence gave the narrative a freshness and a vigour it lacked both in synopsis and in director George Sidney's rather pedestrian handling of it, its best sequences being the three major dances Kelly devised for himself. In one of them (a fantasy in which he woos Grayson on a sound-stage at MGM) the set became a romantic Spanish courtyard with Kelly, dressed in a dazzling gold shirt, red and black cape and black trousers, giving full expression to his characteristic athletic prowess in a fandango-style routine (to the accompaniment of *La Cumparsita* by G.H. Matos Rodriguez) that had him scaling battlements, leaping over parapets and making a 45ft vine-swinging jump from a rooftop to the balcony of his señorita in the most romantic Fairbanks style. In the traditional 'Mexican Hat Dance', performed in a studio reconstruction of Olvera Street (the Mexican section of Los Angeles), with its colourful market place, he partnered little Sharon McManus in a routine which, although self-consciously cute, contained some delightful moments. The third and best sequence (illustrated) was a dance that combined live action and cartoon in which sailor Kelly teaches a grumpy mouse (Jerry from the Tom and Jerry cartoons) how to dance 'The Worry Song' by Ralph Freed and Sammy Fain. Apart from Kelly's contribution to the film (he also choreographed it together with Stanley Donen), there were several songs from Grayson and Sinatra and a fair amount of serious music making from Jose Iturbi, including a snatch of Tchaikovsky's Piano Concerto No. 1 in B Flat Minor, and a complete performance of Liszt's Second Hungarian Rhapsody, played by Iturbi and a veritable battalion of young pianists at the Hollywood Bowl. The cast also included Dean Stockwell (as Miss Grayson's small nephew), Rags Ragland, Billy Gilbert, Carlos Ramirez, James Flavin and Edgar Kennedy. Other songs and musical numbers: *Jealousy* (Grayson) Vera Bloom, Jacob Gade; *Donkey Serenade* (Iturbi) Bob Wright, Chet Forrest, Rudolf Friml; *My Heart Sings* (Grayson) Harold Rome, Herpin; *If You Knew Susie* (Kelly, Sinatra) Joseph Meyer, Buddy De Sylva, new lyrics by Sammy Cahn; *What Makes The Sunset?* (Sinatra); *I Begged Her* (Sinatra, Kelly); *We Hate To Leave* (Sinatra, Kelly); *The Charm Of You* (Sinatra); *I Fall In Love Too Easily* (Sinatra) Cahn, Jule Styne; *Cradle Song (Wiegenlied, Opus 49, No 4)* (Sinatra) Brahms; *Waltz (from Serenade in C, Opus 48)* (Grayson) Tchaikovsky; *Largo Al Factotum* (from the opera 'The Barber of Seville') (Ramirez) Rossini; *Anchors Aweigh* (orchestra, conducted by Iturbi) Alfred H. Miles, Royal Lovell, Charles A. Zimmerman.

Forties Musicals

Often similar to *Hello, Frisco, Hello* (20th Century-Fox, 1943), **Nob Hill** was another Technicolored period piece from the Fox lot set in San Francisco during the heyday of the Barbary Coast. It starred George Raft (standing right) as the proprietor of a café, Vivian Blaine (centre) as his singing sweetheart and Joan Bennett as the rich society girl he temporarily deserts her for. Pasted together from bits and pieces of past Fox successes by Wanda Tuchock and Norman Reilly Raine (story by Eleanore Griffin), and directed by Henry Hathaway with no sense of occasion at all, it also featured Peggy Ann Garner, Alan Reed (standing left), B.S. Pully, Emil Coleman, The Three Swifts and Rory Calhoun. Nick Castle choreographed it, and the producer was Andre Daven. Songs and musical numbers included: *I Don't Care Who Knows It; I Walked In; Touring San Francisco; Paris Of The USA* Harold Adamson, Jimmy McHugh; *What Do You Want To Make Those Eyes At Me For?* Howard Johnson, Joseph McCarthy, James V. Monaco; *San Francisco* Gus Kahn, Bronislau Kaper, Walter Jurmann; *On San Francisco Bay* Vincent Bryan, Gertrude Hoffman; *King Chanticleer (Texas Tommy)* Nat D. Ayer; *Chinatown, My Chinatown* William Jerome, Jean Schwartz; *Too-ra-loo-ra-loo-ra* James Royce Shannon.

▽

△

There was nothing much to tell in **Tell It To A Star** (Republic), a 67-minute double feature support which starred Ruth Terry as a cigarette girl who'd rather be a singer, Alan Mowbray as a financier who happens to be stone broke but whose gift of the gab helps Miss Terry realize her ambitions, and Robert Livingston as the bandleader she falls for. Aurora Miranda (illustrated centre) was also featured. It was written by John K. Butler from an original story by Gerald Drayson Adams and John Kraft, and directed by Frank McDonald for producers Armand L. Schafer and Walter Goetz. Songs and musical numbers included: *Tell It To A Star* Shirley Botwin; *Love Me Or Leave Me* Gus Kahn, Walter Donaldson; *You're So Good To Me* Sammy Cahn, Jule Styne; *A Batucada Corazon* Ary Barroso.

Jack Oakie and Peggy Ryan (both illustrated) were teamed as a father and daughter vaudeville partnership in **On Stage Everybody** (Universal), a programmer loosely inspired by the radio show of the same name, and telling a story in which Oakie, having at first rejected radio and everything it stood for, finds himself auditioning a talented group of youngsters for the very medium he once so despised. The slender story and screenplay by Warren Wilson and Oscar Brodney was given a modicum of substance by several specialty acts including The King Sisters, and a fair amount of time was devoted to the winners of the Radio Show Contest, all of whom appeared as themselves. Johnny Coy (a replacement for Donald O'Connor who had enlisted) received second billing to Peggy Ryan, with Julie London (her debut), Otto Kruger, Esther Dale, Wallace Ford, Milburn Stone, Stephen Wayne and Jimmy Clark also in it for producer Warren Wilson and associate producer Lou Goldberg, and director Jean Yarbrough. Songs and musical numbers included: *For Him No Love; It'll All Come Out In The Wash; I'm So At Home With You* Inez James, Sidney Miller; *Stuff Like That There* Ray Evans, Jay Livingston; *Put Put Put Your Arms Around Me* Mann Curtis, Al Hoffman, Jerry Livingston; *Take Me In Your Arms* Mitchell Parish, Fred Markush, Fritz Rotter; *What Do I Have To Do To Be A Star?* Bobby Kroll; *Dance With A Dolly With A Hole In Her Stocking* Terry Shand, Jimmy Eaton, Mickey Leader.

▽

Columbia struck another blow for good neighbourliness between America and Latin America with **The Gay Senorita**, 69 minutes of cheerful propaganda in which Jim Bannon set out to convert the Mexican section of a Californian town into a factory site, but changed his plans after falling madly in love with Jinx Falkenburg, the happy senorita of the title. Also cast: Corinna Mura, Steve Cochran, Thurston Hall, Isabel Withers, Marguerite Sylva, Tommy Cook and Lita Baron (Isabelita – illustrated). It was written by Edward Eliscu from a story by J. Robert Bren, produced by Jay Gorney and directed by Arthur Dreifuss. Songs included: *Buenos Noches* Don George. Serge Walters.

▽

△

Betty Hutton's most important role to date was as Texas Guinan in **Incendiary Blonde** (Paramount), a typical Hollywood biopic that skittered uneasily between fact and fantasy but was never less than entertaining – if one didn't mind Hutton (illustrated) hurling herself head first into the part. Always an energetic worker, she made a frontal attack on the role of Texas with such determined gusto there was hardly time for her to catch her breath between her heavy belting of the numbers, and her heavy emoting in the more dramatic bits. Audiences were left hoarse just watching her! Claude Binyon and Frank Butler's screenplay began in 1909, with Texas winning fifty dollars for riding a bucking bronco. Her days as a Broadway chorine and as a silent screen heroine were also charted, but the film's main concern was with the years between 1923 and her untimely death ten years later after she had become a legend as Broadway's most famous nightclub hostess with her phrase 'Hello Suckers!'. Though no mention was made of her brushes with government prohibition agents, the film dwelt on her association with an assorted collection of bootleggers in several hugely enjoyable, if wildly overplayed scenes. Barry Fitzgerald was cast as Texas's father, a schemer whose numerous ventures always ended in ash, Arturo De Cordova played her gangster lover, with other roles going to Charles Ruggles, Albert Dekker, Mary Philips, Bill Goodwin and Eduardo Ciannelli. Also cast were The Maxellos and Maurice Rocco as themselves. The musical numbers were staged by Danny Dare, Joseph Sistrom produced (in Technicolor), and the numerous switches of mood in the narrative were well handled by director George Marshall. Songs and musical numbers included: *It Had To Be You* (Hutton) Gus Kahn, Isham Jones; *Ragtime Cowboy Joe* (Hutton) Maurice Abrahams, Lewis F. Muir, Grant Clarke; *Oh By Jingo* (Hutton, chorus) Lew Brown, Albert von Tilzer; *Sweet Genevieve* (Fitzgerald, chorus) Henry Tucker, George Cooper; *Row Row Row* (Hutton) William Jerome, James V. Monaco; *Darktown Strutters' Ball* (Rocco) Shelton Brooks; *What Do You Want To Make Those Eyes At Me For?* (Hutton) Howard Johnson, Joseph McCarthy, James V. Monaco; *Ida, Sweet As Apple Cider* (performer unidentified) Eddie Leonard, Eddie Munson.

△

▽

▷

State Fair (20th Century-Fox), a musical remake of Will Rogers's 1933 film of the same name, brought Jeanne Crain (in the role originally played by Janet Gaynor) to prominence as Margy Frake, the brunette heroine of Phil Stong's cosy, homespun novel. Apart from Crain accompanying her parents Charles Winninger (in the Rogers role) and Fay Bainter to Iowa's big state fair, where she meets and falls in love with reporter Dana Andrews (right), not a great deal happened in Oscar Hammerstein II's screenplay (adapted from the novel by Sonya Levien and Paul Green) – unless you considered Winninger's obsession with his prize hog, and his wife's concern over her pickles as happenings. Instead, the pleasures were mainly to be derived from the marvellous score (by Richard Rodgers and Hammerstein II), from the gentle, bucolic atmosphere conveyed in Walter Lang's direction, and from the delightfully fresh and invigorating central performance by Miss Crain (centre). Dick Haymes (left) played her crooning brother Wayne and Vivian Blaine appeared as a dance-band singer, with other roles in William Perlberg's delightful Technicolor production going to Donald Meek, Frank McHugh, Henry Morgan, Percy Kilbride and William Marshall. Jeanne Crain's vocals were dubbed by Louanne Hogan. It was remade again in 1962. Songs and musical numbers: *It's A Grand Night For Singing*; *It Might As Well Be Spring*; *That's For Me*; *Isn't It Kinda Fun?*; *All I Owe I-O-Way*; *Our State Fair*.

The title told it all: **Radio Stars on Parade** (RKO) was little more than a collection of radio celebrities in a 69-minute free-for-all that top-starred Wally Brown and Alan Carney as the managers of a Hollywood talent agency who find themselves caught up in Ralph Edwards's popular show *Truth or Consequences*. Others appearing were Frances Langford (illustrated) as a nightclub singer aspiring to radio work, Rufe Davis, Robert Clarke, Sheldon Leonard, Ralph Peters, Don Wilson, Tony Romano, The Town Criers, The Cappy Barra Boys, and Skinnay Ennis and His Band. Robert E. Kent and Monte Brice wrote it and it was directed by Leslie Goodwins for producer Ben Stoloff. Songs and musical numbers included: *I Couldn't Sleep A Wink Last Night* Jimmy McHugh, Harold Adamson; *That Old Black Magic* Harold Arlen, Johnny Mercer.

One of the songs in Columbia's **I Love A Bandleader** (GB: **Memory For Two**) was called 'Good, Good, Good' (by Allan Roberts and Doris Fisher) – not an accurate appraisal of the film to which it was attached, but a jive-oriented ditty sung by star Phil Harris (foreground left) as a duet with Leslie Brooks (foreground centre). Harris played a nightclub painter who, after literally falling head over heels for Miss Brooks, winds up with amnesia, in which state of mind he becomes a successful bandleader. Taking advantage of Harris's loss of memory, Brooks poses as his fiancée in order to land herself a job as a singer, and when a second blow on the head restores Harris's memory to him, complications proliferate. Paul Yawitz scripted it from a story by John Grey, Del Lord directed, Michael Kraike produced and the cast included Walter Catlett, Frank Sully and the Four V's.

A *pot-pourri* from Paramount, **Duffy's Tavern** (loosely inspired by the radio show of the same name) involved the bar's polygot keeper Archie (Ed Gardner, left) and an inebriated patron of the establishment (Victor Moore, right) in an effort to revive the flagging fortunes of a recording studio. Anyone familiar with plots like this, could tell at a glance that the film was little more than a contrivance to display the variegated talents of the studio's contract artists in a series of musical numbers and sketches of fluctuating quality. Best of the offerings were Betty Hutton's (centre) maniacal rendition of 'Doin' It The Hard Way' (by Johnny Burke and Jimmy Van Heusen), Cass Daley's equally frenetic handling of 'You Can't Blame A Gal For Trying' (by Ben Raleigh and Bernie Wayne), and an amusing parody on Burke and Van Heusen's 'Swinging On A Star' by Bing Crosby, Betty Hutton, Dorothy Lamour, Diana Lynn and Arturo De Cordova. Alan Ladd and Veronica Lake rehearsed a radio murder script, much to the consternation of Victor Moore who thought it was all for real, with other bits and pieces falling to Paulette Goddard, Eddie Bracken, Brian Donlevy, Sonny Tufts, Barry Fitzgerald, Robert Benchley, William Demarest, Walter Abel, Billy De Wolfe, Johnny Coy, Howard Da Silva, and Gary, Phillip, Dennis and Lin Crosby. Melvin Frank and Norman Panama's screenplay also utilized the talents of Marjorie Reynolds and Barry Sullivan (as the love interest), Charles Cantor, Eddie Green and Ann Thomas. Billy Daniels was in charge of the choreography; Joseph Sistrom produced with Danny Dare as his associate, and the director was Hal Walker. Other songs and musical numbers included: *Leave Us Face It* (Frank Loesser, Abe Burrows).

A public relations job for the folks down Mexico way, **Mexicana** (Republic) was a musical travelogue of sorts that featured Tito Guizar (Mexico's answer to Frank Sinatra) as a singing idol who, to discourage his fans from ripping the shirt off his back everytime he appears in public, persuades a visiting soprano (Constance Moore, illustrated lying down) to pose as his wife. And before you could say caramba! – well, you know the rest. Estelita Rodriguez as a long standing admirer of Señor Guizar didn't approve at all, and who could blame her? Frank Gill Jr's screenplay also found parts for Leo Carillo, Jean Stevens (illustrated), Howard Freeman and Steve Geray, as well as The St Luke Choristers and The Peter Meremblum Junior Orchestra. The choreographer was Nick Castle and it was produced and directed by Alfred Santell. Songs and musical numbers: *Mexicana*; *Lupita*; *See Mexico*; *Heartlessness*; *Time out For Dreaming*; *De Corazon A Corazon* Ned Washington, Gabriel Ruiz; *Somewhere There's A Rainbow* Washington, Walter Scharf.

▽

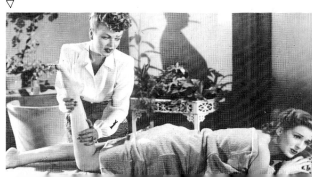

Forties Musicals

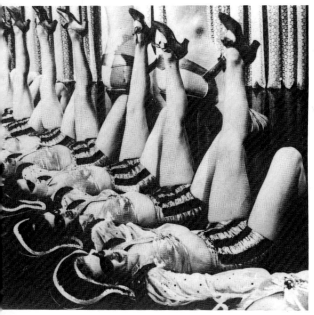

Nothing was scandalous about **George White's Scandals of 1945** (RKO) except, possibly, its woeful lack of originality. A backstage musical, relying for interest on the hazards attendant on putting on a show, its screenplay written in committee by Hugh Wedlock, Howard Snyder, Parke Levy and Howard Green, from a story by Wedlock and Snyder – also involved audiences in a couple of perfunctory romances between stars Joan Davis and Jack Haley and featured players Phillip Terry and Martha Holliday: the former encountering resistance from Haley's spinster aunt (Margaret Hamilton); the latter fraught with misunderstandings. Davis and Haley scored in a number from the 1931 stage edition of the *Scandals* called 'Life Is Just A Bowl Of Cherries' by Lew Brown and Ray Henderson; and from guest star Ethel Smith there was a pyrotechnical display on the organ of 'Liza' by George and Ira Gershwin. And that was about it. George White produced, Ernest Matray choreographed (production number illustrated), and the director was Felix Feist. Other songs and musical numbers included: *I Wake Up In The Morning* (Davis, Haley); *I Want To Be A Drummer* (Gene Krupa and His Band); *Who Killed Vaudeville?* (Davis, Haley) Jack Yellen, Sammy Fain; *Bolero In The Jungle* (Gene Krupa) Tommy Peterson, Krupa; *Wishing* (Smith) Buddy De Sylva.

Susanna Foster (illustrated centre) was so irredeemably stage-struck in **That Night With You** (Universal) that, in order to land herself a part in a Broadway show, she tells producer Franchot Tone she's his daughter – the result of a one-day marriage undertaken in his youth. Miss Foster wasn't the sort of actress to get away with foolishness of this ilk, and had to rely on her pleasant singing voice to see her through the contrivances of producers Michael Fessier and Ernest Pagano's witless screenplay (story by Arnold Belgard). David Bruce, Louise Allbritton, Jacqueline De Wit, Irene Ryan, Barbara Sears, Anthony Caruso and Buster Keaton (seen briefly as a short-order cook) completed the cast. The dances were staged by Lester Horton and Louis Da Pron and the film was directed by William A. Seiter. Songs and musical numbers included: *Once Upon A Dream* Jack Brooks, Hans J. Salter; *Market Place*; *Shadows*; *Largo Al Factotum* from Rossini's 'The Barber of Seville' (a female version performed in a beauty parlour). ▷

Studio head Darryl F. Zanuck purchased John Kenyon Nicholson's story, **The Dolly Sisters**, as a vehicle for Betty Grable (left) and Alice Faye. But, unable to coax Miss Faye out of retirement, Zanuck finally agreed to producer George Jessel's casting of June Haver (right) instead. The result was a typical Fox musical, monotonous in its fidelity to the genre's form, but handled with such pazazz and showmanship that it proved an irresistible (and financially rewarding) splash of Technicolored, turn-of-the-century escapism. Its fictionalized account of the two Hungarian brunettes (not blondes, as the film would have us believe) who achieved stardom after Oscar Hammerstein engaged them to appear at his Music Hall, was the perfect excuse for several old (and several new) numbers, plus a couple of romances to pad out its fragile plot. John Payne as a composer called Harry Fox was Grable's choice, while Haver settled for a far less turbulent relationship with Frank Latimore. The two hit songs to emerge were 'I Can't Begin To Tell You' by Mack Gordon and James V. Monaco, sung by Grable, Payne and Haver; and 'I'm Always Chasing Rainbows' by Joseph McCarthy and Harry Carroll (based on a Chopin melody), sung by Grable. The musical numbers were staged by Seymour Felix with such kitschy vulgarity (especially a gaudy item glorifying a woman's make-up kit called 'Powder, Lipstick and Rouge' by Mack Gordon and Harry Revel) that, viewed today, they ▽

cannot be considered as anything other than monuments to bad taste. At the same time, what cannot be denied is just how compulsively enjoyable they are. The film was stunningly costumed by Orry-Kelly and directed by Irving Cummings with a cheerful disregard for period accuracy. The rest of the capable cast included S.Z. Sakall as the sisters' genial uncle Latsie, Reginald Gardiner, Gene Sheldon, Sig Rumann, Trudy Marshall, Collette Lyons and Frank Middlemass (playing Oscar Hammerstein). Other songs and musical numbers: *Give Me The Moonlight* (Grable, Payne) Lew Brown, Albert von Tilzer; *On The Mississippi* (Male quartet) Ballard MacDonald, Arthur Fields, Harry Carroll; *We Have Been Around* (Grable, Haver) Mack Gordon, Charles Henderson; *Carolina In The Morning* (Grable, Haver) Gus Kahn, Walter Donaldson; *Arrah Go On I'm Gonna Go Back To Oregon* (Payne) Joe Young, Sam Lewis, Bert Grant; *Darktown Strutters' Ball* (Grable, Haver) Shelton Brooks; *The Vamp* (Grable, Haver) Byron Gay; *Hungarian Dance No 5 in F Sharp Minor* (danced by Evon Thomas and Donna Jo Gribble playing the sisters as children, then by Grable and Haver) Brahms; *Smiles* (Soldiers' chorus) J. Will Callahan, Lee S. Roberts; *Oh Frenchie* (Soldiers' chorus) Sam Ehrlich, Con Conrad; *Pack Up Your Troubles* (Soldiers' chorus) Felix Powell, George Asaf; *Mademoiselle From Armentières* (Soldiers' chorus); *The Sidewalks Of New York* (Grable, Haver) James Blake, Charles B. Lawlor.

△

A big grosser for Paramount, **The Stork Club** was an inexpensively produced (by Buddy De Sylva; associate producer Harold Wilson) starring vehicle for Betty Hutton (centre). She played a hat-check girl at the famous nightspot who, on one of her afternoons off, saves an elderly bum (Barry Fitzgerald, right) from drowning. Except that he isn't a bum at all but a millionaire, who rewards her by setting her up in a penthouse complete with limousine, charge account and chauffeur. When her bandleader boyfriend (Don Defore) returns from active service, he isn't at all happy at the set-up, incorrectly suspecting Hutton of paying in kind for the services rendered her. But scriptwriters De Sylva and John McGowan waved their magic pencil over it all, and in the end everyone lived happily ever after – as was usually the way with fairy tales. Musical highlight was Hutton's wildcat performance of 'Doctor, Lawyer, Indian Chief' by Paul Francis Webster and Hoagy Carmichael. She had another solo called 'I'm A Square In The Social Circle' (by Ray Evans and Jay Livingston) and was joined by wishy-washy Andy Russell in an indifferent duet called 'If I Had A Dozen Hearts' by Webster and Harry Revel. Robert Benchley (left) appeared as a counsellor, with Bill Goodwin, Iris Adrian, Mary Young, Charles Coleman, Perce Launders and Mikhail Rasumny completing the cast. The choreography was by Billy Daniels and the direction by Hal Walker. Other songs and musical·numbers included: *Love Me* Sammy Cahn, Jule Styne; *China Boy* Dick Winfree, Phil Boutelje; *Baltimore Oriole* Webster, Carmichael; *In The Shade Of The Old Apple Tree* Harry H. Williams, Egbert Van Alstyne.

The sort of musical one expected to see coming from 20th Century-Fox rather than from Monogram, **Sunbonnet Sue**, set in the colourful Bowery era *circa* 1902, was a nostalgic trip down memory lane to the accompaniment of several popular tunes of the period, and a mere *soupçon* of a plot involving the fortunes of a saloon owner (George Cleveland) who allows his daughter (Gale Storm, centre) to sing and dance to the delight of his customers, but to the disapproval of her socially-minded aunt (Minna Gombell). Miss Storm managed to bring a charm and freshness to the role despite its conventionality, with the rest of the cast (Phil Regan, Edna M. Holland (right), Raymond Hatton, Alan Mowbray (left) and Charles Judels) also responding well to Ralph Murphy's thoroughly professional direction. Murphy also scripted it, together with Richard A. Carroll, from a story by Paul Gerard Smith and Bradford Ropes and the dances were staged by Jack Boyle. Edward J. Kay's musical scoring was particularly good. Songs and musical numbers: *School Days*; *Sunbonnet Sue* Gus Edwards, Will D. Cobb; *The Bowery* Charles H. Hoyt, Percy Gaunt; *Yip-I-Addy-I-Ay* Cobb, John H. Flynn; *Yoo Hoo, Ain't You Comin Out Tonight?* Carson Robison; *By The Light Of The Silvery Moon* Ed Madden, Edwards; *If I Had My Way* Lou Klein, James Kendis; *While Strolling Through The Park One Day* Ed Haley; *Donegal*; *Roll Dem Bones*; *Look For The Rainbow* Ralph Murphy, C. Harold Lewis.

◁

Universal's **Senorita From The West** embellished the oft-told tale of the ambitious youngster who arrives in the big city fresh from the backwoods, with a couple of plot twists that were more contrived than ingenious. The youngster, played by Bonita Granville (centre) is a gold-mine heiress, except that her guardians haven't informed her of the fact lest she should fall prey to some fortune-hunting city slicker. The man she does eventually choose is a bashful singer (Allan Jones) who ghosts for 'crooner' Jess Barker, a con artist who learns of Miss Granville's wealth and immediately sets out to ensnare her. George Cleveland, Fuzzy Knight, Oscar O'Shea, Renny McEvoy, Olin Howlin and Bob Merrill were also in it, with Spade Cooley (centre right foreground) and His Orchestra supplying much of the music. The makeshift direction was by Frank Strayer, the equally makeshift script by Howard Dimsdale, and the producer was Phil Cahn. Songs and musical numbers included: *Lonely Love* Everett Carter, Ray Sinatra; *Lou Lou Louisiana* Everett Carter, Milton Rosen; *What A Change In The Weather* Kim Gannon, Walter Kent; *These Hazy, Lazy Old Hills*; *All The Things I Wanna Say.*

◁

Sing Your Way Home was an unintelligent, wretchedly plotted programmer from RKO which starred Jack Haley (illustrated centre) as a war correspondent *en route* to New York from Europe after V-J Day, and in whose care are a group of hepcat American teenagers hitherto trapped in Europe by the war. The main plot complication – involving a coded message sent by Haley to his editor – defied belief: but then so did everything else about this fabricated yarn (screenplay by William Bowers, story by Edmund Joseph and Bart Lytton), including Haley's shipboard romance with singer Anne Jeffreys. Marcy McGuire (centre left, leg up) showed zest as one of the homeward-bound teenagers, and was the only bright spot in a cast that also included Glenn Vernon, Donna Lee, Patti Brill and James Jordan Jr. Herb Magidson and Allie Wrubel's score was better than producer Bert Granet's film deserved, especially 'I'll Buy That Dream', sung by Anne Jeffreys, which became a standard. Anthony Mann directed. Other songs and musical numbers included: *Heaven Is A Place Called Home*; *Seven O'Clock In The Morning (Waking Up Boogie)*; *Somebody Stole My Poor Little Heart* Magidson, Wrubel; *The Lord's Prayer* arranged by Albert Hay Malotte.

▽

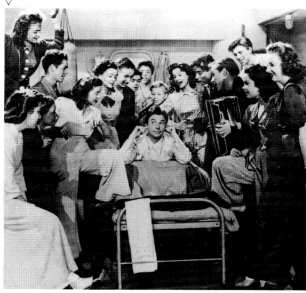

△

1946

Meet Me On Broadway (Columbia) needed a stronger cast than the one assembled for it by producer Burt Kelly. Fred Brady played an arrogant young director whose know-it-all attitude ruins his chances of Broadway success and reduces him to staging a country club show with amateurs; Jinx Falkenburg was the rich gal whose dad owns the country club and Marjorie Reynolds (top billed) was his faithful longstanding sweetheart. Also cast: Loren Tindall, Allen Jenkins, Spring Byington and Gene Lockhart. Several production numbers (staged by Billy Daniels, see illustration) helped pass **Meet Me On Broadway's** 77 minutes painlessly enough but, in the end, the rendezvous was hardly worth keeping. George Bricker, who thought it all up, wrote the screenplay with Jack Henley, and it was directed by Leigh Jason. Songs and musical numbers included: *I Never Had A Chance; Fifth Avenue; Is It Worth It; Only For Me* Saul Chaplin, Edgar De Lange; *She Was A Good Girl* Allan Roberts, Doris Fisher.

Composer Harry Warren (together with lyricist Johnny Mercer) scored his first really big hit at MGM with George Sidney's **The Harvey Girls**, a glorious 'frontier' musical (in Technicolor) whose plot followed a group of ultra-refined waitresses employed by restaurateur Fred Harvey into the wild and woolly West. A veritable army of scenarists (Edmund Beloin, Nathaniel Curtis, Harry Crane, James O'Hanlon, Samson Raphaelson, Kay Van Riper, from a story by Samuel Hopkins Adams, Eleanore Griffin and William Rankin) gave the film its narrative thrust by generally focussing on the conflict between the decorous waitresses and the somewhat less proper women of the town; and in particular on one rather straitlaced lass (Judy Garland, illustrated) and her private war with the proprietor (John Hodiak) of a local bawdy house, with whom she soon falls in love. Garland was enchanting in the role, and there was good work too from Ray Bolger, Virginia O'Brien (marvellous in 'The Wild Wild West') and Angela Lansbury. Cyd Charisse was in it too (vocals dubbed by Betty Russell); so were Marjorie Main, Preston Foster, Kenny Baker, Chill Wills, Selena Royle and Ruth Brady. Warren and Mercer composed eleven songs for the film, eight of which were finally used, the undoubted and most durable hit being the legendary 'On The Atchison, Topeka And The Santa Fe', choreographed by Robert Alton and performed by Garland, Bolger and a train load of Harvey girls. Arthur Freed produced, Conrad Salinger did the memorable orchestrations, Kay Thompson was in charge of the vocal arrangements and Lennie Hayton the musical direction. The associate producer, and one of the most influential and invaluable members of the celebrated 'Freed unit' was Roger Edens. The film grossed over $5,000,000 on its initial release. Other songs and musical numbers: *In The Valley* (Garland); *Wait And See* (Baker, Charisse, Lansbury); *The Train Must Be Fed* (ensemble); *Swing Your Partner Round And Round* (Garland, Bolger, Main, ensemble); *It's A Great Big World* (Garland, Charisse, O'Brien); *Oh You Kid* (Lansbury).

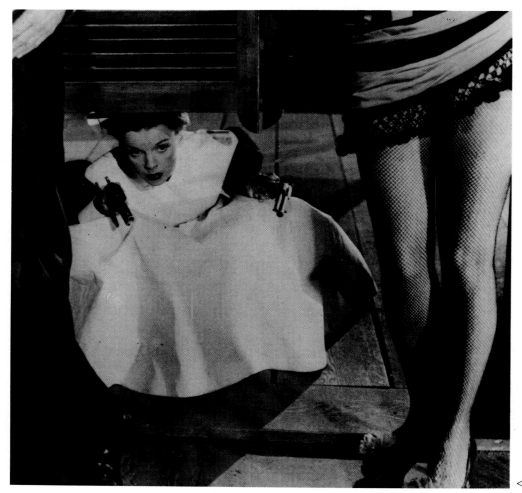

◁

Though most of the youngsters cast by producer Sam Katzman in his youth-orientated **Junior Prom** (Monogram) seemed a trifle too old for their school-kid roles, the film emerged as an exuberant little programmer whose all but invisible plot concerned a campus election campaign and the battle among several contenders for presidency. Freddie Stewart (right) topped the bill, with acrobatic June Preisser (centre) as his co-star, and other roles going to Judy Clark, Noel Neill, Jackie Moran, Frankie Darro, Warren Mills (left) and Murray Davis. Helping to put a beat in it were Abe Lyman and Eddie Heywood with their orchestras, Harry (The Hipster) Gibson, and The Airliners. Erna Lazarus and Hal Collins wrote it and Arthur Dreifuss directed. Songs and Musical numbers included: *Keep The Beat; Teen Canteen* Sid Robin; *Trimball For President* Stanley Cowan; *(All Of A Sudden) My Heart Sings* Herpin, Harold Rome (English lyrics), Jamblan (French lyrics); *Loch Lomond* (traditional); *It's Me Oh Lawd* (negro spiritual).
▽

Music and slapstick were the main ingredients of **People are Funny** (Paramount), a spin-off of the popular radio show of the same name. Written by Maxwell Shane and David Lang (story by Lang), it concerned the attempts of a radio producer (Phillip Reed) to find a replacement show when sponsor Rudy Vallee expresses dissatisfaction with the one currently on the air. What, of course, he comes up with, is 'People Are Funny' – and just how he does so – in the company of Helen Walker (illustrated right), Ozzie Nelson, Bob Graham, Barbara Roche, Art Linkletter, Clara Blandick, and Roy Atwell and The Vagabonds – was what producer-director Sam White's pleasant little film was all about. Frances Langford was prominently billed as guest star, with Jack Haley (left) heading the cast as a small-town radio announcer and the originator of the radio programme in question. Songs included: *I'm In The Mood For Love* Dorothy Fields, Jimmy McHugh; *Angelina* Doris Fisher, Allan Roberts; *The Old Square Dance Is Back Again* Don Reid, Henry Tobias; *Alouette* (traditional French Canadian); *Every Hour On The Hour* Don George, Duke Ellington.
▽

A Coast Guard romance involving Janet Blair and Alfred Drake, **Tars And Spars** (Columbia) relied solely on the comic antics of newcomer Sid Caesar (seen at his best in an hilarious parody of a bad war film) to keep it alive and kicking. Otherwise it was just another routine musical with a wartime background, desperately in need of a few fresh ideas and a couple of good tunes. John Jacoby, Sarett Tobias and Decla Dunning hammered it out from a story by Barry Trivers, the lustreless score was by Jule Styne and Sammy Cahn, Alfred E. Green directed, Jack Cole choreographed, Milton H. Bren produced, and the cast was completed by dancers Anita Alvarez and Marc Platt (illustrated), Jeff Donnell, Ray Walker and James Flavin. Only Caesar came, saw, and conquered. Songs and musical numbers; *I'm Glad I Waited For You; Love Is A Merry-Go-Round; Kiss Me Hello. Baby; I Always Meant To Tell You; He's A Hero; Don't Call On Me; After The War Baby; When I Get To Town; I Love Eggs; I Have A Love In Every Port.*
▽

△

Adequate programmer fare with more music (production number illustrated) than plot, **Swing Parade of 1946** (Monogram) starred Gale Storm as a young lady with a burning desire to become a nightclub entertainer, and Phil Regan as a nightclub owner whose club she finds herself singing in. Russell Hicks played Regan's wealthy father who, after mistakenly believing Miss Storm to be a summons server, employs her to serve a summons on his son's club, with other roles going to Ed Brophy, Mary Treen and Leon Belasco. Also in it were The Three Stooges, Connee Boswell (singing Harold Arlen and Ted Koehler's 'Stormy Weather'), and the bands of Louis Jordan and Will Osborne. It was produced by Lindsley Parsons and Harry A. Romm, written by Tim Ryan from a story by Edmund Kelso, and directed by Phil Karlson. Other songs and musical numbers included: *On The Sunny Side of The Street* Dorothy Fields, Jimmy McHugh; *Oh Brother* Matt Malneck, Allie Wrubel; *Don't Worry About That Mule* William Davis, Duke Groner, Charles Stewart; *A Tender Word Will Mend It All* Doris Fisher, Allan Roberts; *After All This Time* Paul DeFur, Ken Thompson; *Caldonia* Fleecie Moore; *Just A Little Fond Affection* Elton Box, Desmond Cox, Lewis Ilda.

One of the best of all the *Road* pictures, **Road To Utopia** (Paramount), made in 1944 but released two years later, benefitted from a wonderfully zany screenplay (provided by Norman Panama and Melvin Frank) that was as anarchic and as anachronistic as it was funny, and which cast Bing Crosby (left) and Bob Hope (right) as a pair of vaudevillians who, in cahoots with singer Dorothy Lamour (as a soloist in an Alaskan dance hall), set out to locate an old Alaskan goldmine, in the course of which they are hotly pursued by villains Robert Barrat, Nestor Paiva, Douglass Dumbrille and Jack La Rue. Hal Walker's direction was totally in accord with the outrageous antics perpetrated by all concerned, and the songs – by Jimmy Van Heusen and Johnny Burke – most notably 'Personality' sung by Lamour, were first rate. Most of the story was told in flashback and, for once, it was Hope who got the girl, Crosby having been abandoned on an ice-floe and presumed dead. In the film's final scene, however, many years after the events described, he arrives unexpectedly at Hope's residence only to discover that the child Hope and Lamour have had, is the spittin' image of himself. It was an inspired joke on which to end an often inspired piece of screen lunacy. Robert Benchley lent his services as narrator, with other parts going to Hillary Brooke, Will Wright, Jimmy Dundee, Billy Benedict and Arthur Loft. Danny Dare choreographed, and the producer was Paul Jones. Other songs and musical numbers: *Welcome To My Dream* (Crosby); *Put It There Pal* (Crosby, Hope); *It's Anybody's Spring* (Crosby); *Would You* (Lamour); *Good-time Charley* (Crosby, Hope).
▽

William Powell appeared briefly in **Ziegfeld Follies**, again playing the role of Florenz Ziegfeld. He reminisces (in heaven) about his tenure on earth when, as showman *extraordinaire*, he presented a series of revues unparalleled in their opulence. If only, he muses, he could produce just one more show, utilizing all the fabulous talent available at MGM – now that *really* would be something. It would open with Fred Astaire, Lucille Ball and Cyd Charisse in a typical Ziegfeld paean to pulchritude called 'Bring on the Beautiful Girls' (by Earl Brent and Roger Edens). Virginia O'Brien would then reprise the number, this time, however, singing the praises of men ('Bring On Those Wonderful Men'). Next, opera stars James Melton and Marion Bell would be seen and heard in 'The Drinking Song' from Verdi's *La Traviata*. After that Keenan Wynn would appear in a sketch called 'Number Please', to be followed by a cooling water ballet performed by Esther Williams to a musical arrangement by Roger Edens. Another couple of sketches would quickly follow: 'Pay The Two Dollars' with Victor Moore, Edward Arnold, Ray Teal and Joseph Crehan, and 'The Sweepstakes Ticket' with Fanny Brice, Hume Cronyn and William Frawley. Next would come one of the highlights of the entire show – Fred Astaire and Lucille Bremer in a superb Arthur Freed–Harry Warren number called 'This Heart Of Mine'. After that, a scorching performance from Lena Horne, singing 'Love' by Ralph Blane and Hugh Martin. Red Skelton would then appear in

When Television Comes', doing his famous vaudeville routine, 'Guzzler's Gin', as a TV announcer who gets progressively drunker with each mouthful he takes of the product he is advertising. Another highlight, 'Limehouse Blues' (by Philip Braham and Douglas Furber) about a Chinese coolie and his infatuation with a beautiful Oriental woman would again feature Fred Astaire and Lucille Bremer (illustrated), to be followed by Judy Garland doing a wicked impersonation of Greer Garson in 'The Great Lady Gives An Interview' ('Madame Crematon') by Roger Edens and Kay Thompson. Fred Astaire and Gene Kelly would then make the first of only two appearances together in a little-known number by the Gershwin brothers called 'The Babbitt And The Bromide'. Finally, the revue would end with Kathryn Grayson (surrounded by foam) singing 'There's Beauty Everywhere' by Arthur Freed and Harry Warren. Thus thought the Great Ziegfeld, and thus it came to pass. Vincente Minnelli received sole directorial credit, though several other directors, including Charles Walters, Roy Del Ruth and George Sidney, were also involved. Robert Alton was given dance director credit, Roger Edens was in charge of the musical adaptation; Lennie Hayton conducted, and the brilliant orchestrations were by Conrad Salinger and Wally Hegelin, two indispensable members of producer Arthur Freed's celebrated production team. Though inconsistent in quality, **Ziegfeld Follies** was awesomely professional and never dull.

Based on an indifferent play by Louise (Gypsy Rose Lee) Hovick, **Doll Face** (GB: **Come Back To Me**), scripted by Leonard Praskins, was just another 20th Century-Fox backstage musical about a burlesque star with Broadway aspirations. It did, however, give the vivacious Vivian Blaine top billing and the leading role. The men in her life were played by Dennis O'Keefe (right) and Michael Dunne, with other parts in this inexpensively produced (in black and white by Bryan Foy) effort going to Carmen Miranda (illustrated left), Perry Como (whose big moment came in a song called 'Dig You Later' by Harold Adamson and Jimmy McHugh), Martha Stewart, Reed Hadley, Frank Orth and Donald MacBride. The invigorating direction was by Lewis Seiler. Other songs and musical numbers: *Here Comes Heaven Again*; *Chico Chico*; *Somebody's Walking In My Dreams*; *Red Hot And Beautiful* Adamson. McHugh.

△

Robert Alda starred in a small-scale musical called **Cinderella Jones** (Warner Bros.), directed by Busby Berkeley with a score by Sammy Cahn and Jule Styne. Despite its credentials, it was a tepid non-starter. Charles Hoffman's screenplay from a rather mundane story by Philip Wylie told of a young lady who, in order to inherit $10,000,000, has to marry a man of exceptional intelligence by a given date. Made in 1944, it was full of wartime references which might have added to its appeal, but these were edited out when the release of the film was delayed for two years. Reason for the delay was that the studio was hoping to capitalize on Alda's success in the Gershwin biopic *Rhapsody in Blue*. Unfortunately for all concerned, Mr Alda (illustrated 2nd left) never quite made it, and the studio's gamble misfired. Also, director Berkeley was going through an unhappy period in his private life and the film was totally bereft of his characteristic flair. Joan Leslie (left) was cast as the girl at the centre of the plot, and the rest of the cast included Julie Bishop (right foreground), William Prince (centre), S.Z. Sakall (2nd right), Edward Everett Horton, Elisha Cook Jr, Ruth Donnelly (centre left) and Hobart Cavanaugh. The producer was Alex Gottlieb. Songs: *If You're Waitin' I'm Waitin' Too*; *Cinderella Jones*; *You Never Know Where You're Goin' Till You Get There*; *When The One You Love Simply Won't Love Back*.

Moderate programme entertainment, **Talk About A Lady** (Columbia) starred Jinx Falkenburg as an unspoiled country girl who inherits assets worth several million dollars, as well as a nightclub, and finds herself doing battle with socialite Trudy Marshall, who feels the booty should have gone to her. Forrest Tucker and Joe Besser (illustrated) co-starred, and the supporting cast included Richard Lane, Jimmy Little, Frank Sully, Jack Davis, Robert Regent and Mira McKinney. Stan Kenton and His Orchestra also appeared. Richard Weil and Ted Thomas wrote it from a story by Robert D. Andrews and Barry Trivers, it was produced by Michael Kraike and directed by George Sherman. Songs and musical numbers included: *You Gotta Do Watcha Gotta Do*; *Avocado*; *I Never Had A Dream Come True* Allan Roberts, Doris Fisher; *A Mist Is Over The Moon* Oscar Hammerstein II, Ben Oakland.

▽

Freddie Stewart played a dual role in **Freddie Steps Out** (Monogram): a swoon crooner and a young student called Freddie – his physical double. When the crooner disappears, Freddie's chums decide to play a joke on their schoolmate by giving out the news that he is none other than the missing singer. Things get out of hand with the arrival of the real crooner's wife (Julie Gibson) and baby; and much of Hal Collins's screenplay was involved in returning order to the lives of all concerned. Warren Mills, June Preisser (left, as Freddie's girl-friend), Ann Rooney (centre), Noel Neill (right), Jackie Moran and Frankie Darro were also in it for producer Sam Katzman, and director Arthur Dreifuss (who co-scripted). It was a livelier-than-average, low-budget programmer. Songs and musical numbers included: *Patience And Fortitude* Billy Moore Jr, Blackie Warren; *Let's Drop The Subject* Hal Collins, Joe Sanns; *Don't Blame Me* Dorothy Fields, Jimmy McHugh.

▽

Danny Kaye was **The Kid From Brooklyn** (RKO), the best and highest grossing of his three movies to date. In the role first created on screen by Harold Lloyd in Paramount's *The Milky Way* (1936), he played Burleigh, a milkman who inadvertently becomes involved with a prize-fighter and his dim-witted trainer, and finds himself middleweight champion of the world. Don Hartman and Melville Shavelson's screenplay, based on the earlier screenplay by Grover Jones, Frank Butler and Richard Connell which, in turn, was adapted from a Broadway flop by Lynn Root and Harry Clork, gave Kaye every opportunity to demonstrate his versatility, and the result was a knockout. Skilfully negotiating the dramatic change in character Burleigh undergoes when he has his first taste of success in the ring (all his initial fights have been rigged, though he does not realize this), Kaye proved for the first time that he was as good an actor as he was a set-piece performer. Though the bulk of the musical numbers (by Jule Styne and Sammy Cahn) were shared between co-stars Virginia Mayo as Kaye's *vis-à-vis*, and Vera-Ellen (illustrated centre) as his sister, as well as the 18 Goldwyn Girls, Kaye had a specialty of his own – a Martha Graham parody called *Pavlova*, written years earlier for one of his nightclub acts by Sylvia Fine and Max Liebman. Lionel Stander as the trainer repeated the role he originally played in the 1936 version, with other parts going to Walter Abel, Eve Arden, Fay Bainter, and Steve Cochran as prizefighter Speed McFarlane. It was filmed in Technicolor, choreographed by Bernard Pearce and directed by Norman Z. McLeod. Virginia Mayo and Vera-Ellen's vocals were dubbed by Dorothy Ellers and Betty Russell respectively. Songs and musical numbers: *I Love An Old-Fashioned Song*; *You're The Cause Of It All*; *Josie*; *Sunflower Song*; *Hey, What's Your Name?*; *Welcome Burleigh*.

▽

Forties Musicals

Producer Joe Pasternak made the perfect choice ▷
when he signed Henry Koster to direct **Two
Sisters From Boston** (MGM), an enjoyable black
and white musical not dissimilar in mood to
some of the team's Deanna Durbin offerings at
Universal in the mid-thirties. Set at the turn of the
century, it starred Kathryn Grayson (right) and
June Allyson (left) as sisters from Boston, one
of whom (Grayson) arrives in New York where
she is cared for by pianist Jimmy Durante, in
whose saloon she sings. She fancies herself
as an opera singer and tries to push herself
in the direction of the Met, while Miss Allyson
who follows her sister to New York, settles for
the son (Peter Lawford) of an opera sponsor.
Lauritz Melchior was in it, sharing some of the
vocals with Miss Grayson, and performing on his
own (most memorably) 'The Prize Song' from
Wagner's *Die Meistersinger*. Grayson joined Durante for 'The Fire Chief's Daughter', 'There Are
Two Sides To Every Girl' and 'Down By The
Ocean' (by Ralph Freed and Sammy Fain) while,
on his own, Durante made a meal of 'Gwan,
Your Mudder's Callin'' (also by Freed and Fain).
Ben Blue, Isobel Elsom, Harry Hayden, Thurston
Hall and Nella Walker completed the cast. Myles
Connolly wrote the sympathetic screenplay,
with additional dialogue by James O'Hanlon.
Other songs and musical numbers: *Nellie Martin*;
After The Show Freed, Fain, *Hello, Hello, Hello*
Durante; sequences from an opera especially
contrived for the occasion, utilizing melodies by
Mendelssohn and Liszt.

Some doubling up (but not, alas, with laughter)
in **Hit The Hay** (Columbia), with Judy Canova
(illustrated centre) starring as a backwoods
opera *diva* whose agile coloratura belies an
ability to act. She is discovered (by Ross Hunter)
singing operatic arias while milking a cow, and
immediately groomed for a career in grand
opera. When it is realized she cannot act her
way out of a paper bag let alone a convoluted
operatic plot, an actress who looks like her (also
played by Canova) is hired to go on in her place
and mime to the music, while coloratura
Canova stands by singing in the wings. Tiring of
this dishonest ploy, Canova decides to re-vamp
Rossini's *William Tell* as a burlesque calling it
'Tillie Tell', which she does with great success,
thus saving the impecunious opera house which
mounts it and, at the same time, finding herself a
husband (Fortunio Bonanova, left). Two Ca-
novas for the price of one was more than most
audiences could be expected to take, and although her vocalizing was surprisingly good,
her rubber-faced antics were irritatingly unstoppable. The result was that **Hit The Hay** bit the
dust. Doris Merrick, Gloria Holden, Francis
Pierlot, Grady Sutton and Louis Mason were also
in it; Richard Weil and Charles R. Marion wrote
it, Del Lord directed and the producer was Ted
Richmond. The musical items included extracts
from Flotow's *Martha* and a jazz version of
Rossini's *William Tell*.

Frances Langford (illustrated) starred as **The** ▷
Bamboo Blonde (RKO), a nightclub singer who
has a brief romance with a B-29 pilot (Russell
Wade, right) the night before he departs for
active service in the Pacific. The bomber crew
steal the picture of herself Langford has given
him, paint her portrait on their plane, and
christen her the Bamboo Blonde. Back in New
York, the nightclub manager for whom Langford works capitalizes on the fact when the
'Bamboo Blonde' crew (as they become known)
turn out to be the hottest in the force. Romantic
complications occur with Wade's return to New
York (he happens to be engaged to Jane Greer)
but all ends happily, as audiences, after the first
seven minutes running time, predicted it would.
Ralph Edwards, Iris Adrian, Richard Martin,
Glenn Vernon and Paul Harvey were also in it; it
was written by Olive Cooper and Lawrence
Kimble from a story by Wayne Whittaker; had
one of the shortest and silliest 'production'
numbers ever devised (choreography by Charles
O'Curran) and was directed for executive pro-
ducer Sid Rogell by Anthony Mann. Songs: *I'm
Good For Nothing But Love*; *Dreaming Out Loud*;
Moonlight Over The Islands; *Right Along About
Evening* Mort Greene, Lew Pollack.

In order to achieve her ambition and become a
successful Tin Pan Alley song-plugger, Ellen
Drew (right), the heroine of **Sing While You
Dance** (Columbia), embarks on a course of far-
fetched behaviour which includes inducing the
widow (Ethel Griffies) of a deceased millionaire
composer to allow her late husband's music to
undergo certain commercial changes. Too silly
for words (as well as music), it was the brainchild of Robert Stephen Brode, whose screenplay
(from a story by Lorraine Edwards) gave employment to Robert Stanton (left, as an amateur
composer), Andrew Tombes, Edwin Cooper,
Robert Stevens, and Amanda Lane (centre).
Leon Barsha produced and the director was D.
Ross Lederman. Songs included: *Oh What A
Lovely Dream* Milton Drake, Ben Oakland; *It's A
Blue World* Bob Wright, Chet Forrest; *I Don't
Know How You Did It* Doris Fisher, Allan Roberts.

Do You Love Me? (20th Century-Fox), a pleasing Cinderella story shot in Technicolor, starred Maureen O'Hara as a sedate and bespectacled music student whose involvement with a band-leader-cum-trumpeter (Harry James, illustrated centre) and a crooner (Dick Haymes, right) radically alters her outlook on life. Reginald Gardiner (left), who first got to conduct an orchestra (albeit an imaginery one) in *Born To Dance* (MGM, 1936), was given another chance to wield the baton in this one, with other parts in Robert Ellis and Helen Logan's screenplay (story by Bert Granet) in the capable hands of Richard Gaines, Stanley Prager, B.S. Pully, Chick Chandler and Alma Kruger. Also featured was the dance team of Jack Scordi and Diane Ascher. If the story was meagre even by musical comedy standards, there was always Haymes's dreamy crooning. James's wizardry on the trumpet, and O'Hara's stunning red hair to claim one's attention – plus a surprise appearance by Betty Grable at the climax. It was produced (opulently) by George Jessel, and the slick and efficient direction was by Gregory Ratoff. The choreographer was Seymour Felix. Songs and musical numbers included: *As If I Didn't Have Enough On My Mind* Charles Henderson, Lionel Newman, Harry James; *I Didn't Mean A Word I Said* Harold Adamson, Jimmy McHugh; *Moonlight Propaganda* Herb Magidson, Matt Malneck; *Do You Love Me?* Harry Ruby.

In **Cuban Pete** (GB: **Down Cuba Way**), Universal Studios manacled Desi Arnaz (right) to a bottom-rung programmer as a popular Cuban bandleader lured to New York by advertising agent Joan Fulton (centre) in order to star in a commercial radio show whose sponsor (Jacqueline De Wit) has threatened to cancel Fulton's contract unless she can secure Arnaz. The script (by Robert Presnell Sr and M. Coates Webster from a story by Bernard Feins) was as trite as its plot, and relied for support on the musical numbers offered, which included an organ solo from Ethel Smith called 'The Breeze And I' (by Al Stillman and Ernesto Lecuona).

Cole Porter deserved a better tribute to his life and work than **Night And Day** (Warner Bros.), a shoddy Technicolored biopic in the worst Hollywood tradition that even contained the cliché 'Wait a minute, I think I've got it!' uttered by Porter as his muse finally descends to help him complete his most famous song, 'Night And Day'. With the miscasting of Cary Grant (illustrated left) as Porter, the film perpetrated the most serious of its many errors, at the same time setting the tone of fantasy that permeated everything about Arthur Schwartz's misconceived production. Apart from the horse-riding accident in Central Park that crippled Porter for the remainder of his life, his story was hardly one that burst its seams with narrative incident, and it emerged, in its screen incarnation, as little more than a riches-to-riches yarn, devoid of anything remotely resembling the man's true personality or his nature. His homosexuality, for example, was not even hinted at. The result was a story wretchedly thin on incident and offering, instead, a succession of Porter standards. Which would have been fine had they not been so indifferently staged by LeRoy Prinz, or so woefully under-powered in performance. Ginny Simms sang several of the songs first introduced by Ethel Merman ('You're The Top', 'I Get A Kick Out Of You') but with none of Merman's vivacity, leaving the vocal honours to Mary Martin (illustrated centre) whose rendering of 'My Heart Belongs To Daddy', which she introduced to audiences in the 1938 Broadway musical *Leave It To Me*, was by far the best single item in the show. Alexis Smith was cast as Porter's wife Linda, with other roles going to Monty Woolley (playing himself as a bombastic ex-Yale actor-professor), Jane Wyman (illustrated right), Eve Arden, Alan Hale, Victor Francen, Dorothy Malone, Tom D'Andrea, Selena Royle, Donald Woods, Henry Stephenson, Sig Rumann, and Herman Bing. Carlos Ramirez was featured in 'Begin the Beguine'. Milada Mladova and George Zoritch did a dance specialty, and from Estelle Sloan came an energetic tap routine. The film was scripted by Charles Hoffman, Leo Townsend and William Bowers (adaptation by Jack Moffitt) and directed without distinction by Michael Curtiz. Ray Heindorf's orchestrations were, Miss Martin notably excepted, the film's one saving excellence. Other musical numbers: *I've Got You Under My Skin; What Is This Thing Called Love? Miss Otis Regrets; Just One Of Those Things; Do I Love You; An Old-Fashioned Garden; Bullfrog; In The Still Of The Night; Love For Sale; Let's Do It; You Do Something To Me; Easy to Love; You've Got That Thing; Don't Fence Me In; I'm Unlucky At Gambling; I'm In Love Again; Rosalie; Anything Goes* Porter; *I Wonder What's Become Of Sally* Jack Yellen, Milton Ager.

A Technicolor remake of *Libelled Lady* (MGM, 1936), **Easy to Wed** (MGM) was an engaging attraction which featured Keenan Wynn and Lucille Ball (right) in the roles originally taken by Spencer Tracy and Jean Harlow; and starred Van Johnson (centre) and Esther Williams (left) in the parts that were created by William Powell and Myrna Loy. Wynn played a harassed newspaper editor in the midst of a libel suit brought by a millionaire's daughter, with Ball as his helpful fiancée; Williams was the pretty plaintiff, and Johnson an ex-reporter employed by Wynn to persuade Williams to withdraw her charges. Aided and abetted by several musical numbers (staged by Jack Donohue), it emerged as pleasant lightweight entertainment, nicely scripted by Dorothy Kingsley (from the original screenplay by Maurice Watkins, Howard Emmett Rogers and George Oppenheimer) and competently directed by journeyman Edward Buzzell for producer Jack Cummings. Also in the cast were Cecil Kellaway, Carlos Ramirez, Ben Blue, Ethel Smith, June Lockhart, Grant Mitchell, Josephine Whittell and Paul Harvey. Songs and musical numbers included: *Easy To Wed* Ted Duncan, Johnny Green; *Goosey-Lucy; It Shouldn't Happen To A Duck* Robert Franklin, Green; *Continental Polka; Gonna Fall In Love With You* Ralph Blane, Green; *Come Closer To Me* Osvaldo Farres, Al Stewart.

Arnaz had four songs in all, including the title number (by José Norman) which he sang twice; and there was additional vocalizing from the King Sisters. Completing the cast were Don Porter, Pedro de Cordoba, and little Beverly Simmons (left), with Igor de Navrotzki and Yvette von Koris featured as specialty dancers. Will Cowan produced and the director was Jean Yarbrough. Other songs and musical numbers included: *El Cumbanchero* Rafael Hernandez; *Lullaby* (adapted from the traditional Mexican folk song *Cielito Lindo*) Bill Driggs; *After Tonight* Jack Brooks, Milton Schwartzwald; *Rhumba Matumba* Bobby Collaza.

Forties Musicals

◁ Two years after *Meet Me In St Louis* (MGM) came **Centennial Summer**, an unsuccessful attempt on behalf of 20th Century-Fox and producer-director Otto Preminger to recapture some of the family nostalgia and fireside cosiness of the earlier film. Instead of St Louis, 1904, **Centennial**'s setting was Philadelphia, 1876, the time of the big Exposition and, as in the MGM film, the family in question was female-dominated – this time by Jeanne Crain and Linda Darnell (illustrated centre). Dorothy Gish and Walter Brennan were their decent, middle-class parents and Cornel Wilde (left) the handsome Frenchman on a visit to Philadelphia who causes rivalry in romance between the two sisters. The best thing about the film was the music composed for it by Jerome Kern (who died shortly after completing it), but it too often received lacklustre vocal performances, Miss Crain's singing being indifferently dubbed by Louanne Hogan. Nor did Dorothy Fox's tepid choreography do justice to a score bursting with possibilities. Constance Bennett appeared as Gish's Paris-based sister, with other featured roles going to William Eythe (right), Barbara Whiting, Larry Stevens, Kathleen Howard, Buddy Swan and dancer Avon Long. It was written by Michael Kanin from the novel by Albert E. Idell and photographed in Technicolor. Songs and musical numbers: *All Through The Day* (lyrics by Oscar Hammerstein II); *In Love In Vain*; *The Right Romance* (lyrics by Leo Robin); *Cinderella Sue* (lyrics by E.Y. Harburg); *Centennial*; *Up With The Lark*; *Railroad Song* (lyrics for all three by Leo Robin).

A musical remake of *Thanks A Million* (20th Century-Fox, 1937), **If I'm Lucky** (20th Century-Fox) was a colourless piece of arrant nonsense, entirely bereft of convincing performances and without a single good tune. All about a crooner who decides to enter politics and run for State Governor, hoping that his impecunious musical colleagues will, as a result of his switch in careers, find radio employment a bit easier, it starred singer Perry Como (illustrated centre) who, as an actor, displayed limited ability. Vivian Blaine (top-billed), Harry James and His Music Makers, Carmen Miranda, Phil Silvers and Edgar Buchanan were in it too, all floundering hopelessly in the mire of mediocrity provided by scenarists Snag Werris, Robert Ellis, Helen Logan and George Bricker. Kenny Williams choreographed it, Bryan Foy was the producer and it was directed by Lewis Seiler with both eyes closed. Songs and musical numbers: *If I'm Lucky*; *One More Kiss*; *Publicity*; *Bet Your Bottom Dollar*; *Follow The Band*; *That American Look* Josef Myrow, Edgar De Lange.
▽

△

The thrill of Brazil was absent from **The Thrill Of Brazil** (Columbia), a vacuous remake of *His Girl Friday* (Columbia, 1940) whose story concerned itself with producer Keenan Wynn's attempts to prevent the marriage of his ex-wife Evelyn Keyes to Allyn Joslyn, the vice-president of a toothpaste concern. Bolstering this flimsy tale were Latin-American singing star Tito Guizar, Enric Madriguera and His Orchestra, the dancing team of Veloz and Yolanda, and the terpsichorean skills of Ann Miller (illustrated) whose vivacity had never been more welcome! Completing the cast were Felix Bressart, Sid Tomack and Eugene Borden. The choreographic chores were shared between Nick Castle and Jack Cole, and the production chores between Sidney Bidell and Alan Rivkin. S. Sylvan Simon directed, substituting speed for energy. Songs and musical numbers included: *Thrill Of Brazil*; *Copa-Cabana*; *Custom House*; *A Man Is Brother To A Mule*; *That's Good Enough For Me*; *My Sleepy Guitar* Doris Fisher, Allan Roberts.

Fred Brady (left) played twin brothers in **Slightly Scandalous** (Universal), and wasn't much good in either role. One of the brothers has three girl friends and is trying to sell a television show to a fountain pen manufacturer; the other has no girl friend at all, and is a humble insurance man. The quiet one invests money in his twin's TV show and, in the process of protecting his investment, becomes involved with his brother's romances. So much for the plot by Erna Lazarus and David Mathews (who also scripted, with additional dialogue by Joel Malone and Jerry Warner). Partially rescuing it from total tedium were the musical contributions of Isabelita, The Guadalajara Trio, Nico Moro, Frank Yaconelli and specialty dancers Dorese Midgley and Georgann Smith. Paula Drew and Sheila Ryan (right) provided the soporific love interest, with Walter Catlett and Louis Da Pron completing the cast. Stanley Rubin and Marshall Grant produced, and the director was Will Jason. Songs and musical numbers: *I Couldn't Love You Anymore*; *When I Fall In Love*; *Negra Leona*; *Same Old Routine*; *The Mad Hatter*; *Baa Baa To You* Jack Brooks.
▽

Running 127 minutes and out-staying its welcome by a good half-an-hour, **Holiday In Mexico** was Jane Powell's first film for MGM and, although better than her previous efforts for United Artists, was no masterpiece. She played the teenage daughter of a widowed American Ambassador in Mexico (Walter Pidgeon) who, in between running his home for him, finds time to develop a king-sized crush on Jose Iturbi (illustrated right), much to the disapproval of her resident boyfriend Roddy McDowall. Produced by Joe Pasternak in rather garish Technicolor and with a characteristically Pasternakian mixture of popular classics and contemporary music, it appealed to a large cross-section of audiences and registered a healthy box-office gross. The film also featured Hungarian beauty Ilona Massey, as well as Xavier Cugat, Amparo Iturbi (illustrated left), Tonia and Teresa Hero, Hugo Haas, Mikhail Rasumny, Helene Stanley, William 'Bill' Phillips and Linda Christian. Isobel Lennart wrote it from a story by William Kozlenko and it was directed by George Sidney – whose handling of Iturbi's piano solos (with the camera literally placed behind the strings inside the instrument so that one was able to see the hammers pounding away as Iturbi's fingers danced up and down the keyboard) was both bizarre and inventive. The indifferent choreography was by Stanley Donen. Songs and musical numbers: *I Think Of You* (based on 2nd theme of 1st movement of Rachmaninov's Piano Concerto No 2) Jack Elliott, Don Marcotte; *Walter Winchell Rhumba* Carl Sigman, Noro Morales; *Yo Te Amo Mucho (And That's That)* Sammy Stept, Ervin Drake, Cugat, Morales; *You, So It's You* Earl Brent, Nacio Herb Brown; *And Dreams Remain* Ralph Freed, Raoul Soler; *Holiday In Mexico* Freed, Sammy Fain; *Ave Maria* Schubert; *Les Filles De Cadiz* Leo Delibes, Alfred De Musset; *Italian Street Song* Victor Herbert, Rida Johnson Young; *Rachmaninov's Piano Concerto No 2 in C Minor* (abbreviated); *Polonaise in A Flat Major* Chopin; *Goodnight Sweetheart* Ray Noble, James Campbell, Reg Connelly; *Three Blind Mice* (arranged by Andre Previn); *The Music Goes 'Round And Around* Red Hodgson, Ed Farley, Mike Riley; *Liebestod* (from 'Tristan and Isolde') Wagner, arranged for two pianos.

▽

A disastrous flop for all concerned, **No Leave, No Love** (MGM) was indeed a no-no that combined romance with music as a couple of Marine buddies (Van Johnson, left, and Keenan Wynn, right) spent time and money living it up in the big city. Pat Kirkwood, imported from England to play a radio singer and the object of Johnson's affection, made no impact at all in her first (and last) Hollywood film, but with a script as tenuous as the one provided by Charles Martin and Leslie Kardos, the fault was not entirely hers. Also floundering were Edward Arnold, Marie Wilson, Leon Ames and Selena Royle. Musical diversion was provided by Xavier Cugat and Guy Lombardo with their respective orchestras, a specialty dance team called The Garcias, and Marina Koshetz, as well as Sugarchile Robinson and Joey Preston, the former a boy pianist, the latter a child drummer. It was directed by Charles Martin, choreographed by Stanley Donen and produced by Joe Pasternak. Songs and musical numbers: *All The Time* Ralph Freed, Sammy Fain; *Love On A Greyhound Bus* Kay Thompson, Ralph Blane, George Stoll; *Isn't It Wonderful?* Thompson; *It'll Be Great To Be Back Home* Charles Martin; *Old Sad Eyes* Irving Kahal, Fain; *When It's Love* Edgar De Lange, Nicholas Kharito.

▽

△

In **Make Mine Music** (RKO), Walt Disney attempted, with varying degrees of success, to do for popular music what *Fantasia* (RKO, 1940) had done for the classics. 'A Music Fantasy In Ten Parts', it opened with The King's Men singing 'The Martins And The Coys' (by Al Cameron and Ted Weems), using the hillybilly hit to depict a feud between two mountain families. Next came the Ken Darby Chorus singing 'Blue Bayou' (by Bobby Worth and Ray Gilbert), a piece involving the moon and a flamingo. This was followed by 'A Jazz Interlude' featuring Benny Goodman and His Orchestra in a number called 'All The Cats Join In' (by Alec Wilder, Ray Gilbert and Eddie Sauter) about a couple of bobby-soxers in a jitterbug session at the local malt shop. 'Without You' (by Osvaldo Farres and Ray Gilbert) was sung by Andy Russell in an atmospheric item called 'A Ballad In Blue'; while Jerry Colonna appeared next in 'A Musical Recitation', telling the story of 'Casey At The Bat' (by Ray Gilbert, Ken Darby and Eliot Daniel). Ballet dancers Tatiana Riabouchinska and David Lichine of the Ballet Russe performed in 'Ballade Ballet' to a vocal by Charles Wolcott and Ray Gilbert called 'Two Silhouettes' sung by Dinah Shore. Prokofiev's 'Peter and the Wolf' followed, narrated by Sterling Holloway, then The Benny Goodman Quartet (clarinet, drums, bass and piano) offered a wildly surreal version of 'After You've Gone' (by Henry Creamer and Turner Layton). The Andrews Sisters lent their voices to 'Johnny Fedora and Alice Blue Bonnet' (by Allie Wrubel and Ray Gilbert), a story about two hats who fall in love in the window of a department store; and the grand finale was 'Opera Pathetique', the best of the items on offer, featuring the voice of Nelson Eddy in the touching fantasy of Willie, an opera-singing whale (see illustration) whose one ambition in life is to sing at the Met. The music for the entire sequence comprised 'Shortnin' Bread' a traditional song arranged by Jacques Wolfe, and operatic excerpts from Rossini's 'The Barber of Seville', Donizetti's 'Lucia di Lammermoor', Leocavallo's 'I Pagliacci', Wagner's 'Tristan and Isolde', Boito's 'Mefistofele' and Flotow's 'Martha'. All the parts in these excerpts – soprano, tenor, baritone, bass and chorus – were sung by Eddy! **Make Mine Music** was filmed in Technicolor with Joe Grant in charge of the production. The film received a disappointing press on its initial release and was not particularly successful at the box office.

Forties Musicals

If one had to kick the truth around in the service of a commercial biopic, the way to do it was the way producer Sidney Skolsky did it in **The Jolson Story**. A blockbuster from Columbia, it had the distinction of containing practically every known cliché in the musical genre yet, at the same time, was cobbled with such expertise that it emerged as an unashamedly entertaining wallow from its opening scene to its compulsively watchable finale in which Jolson, after a period of self-imposed vocal celibacy, rediscovers the joy of singing and, at the same time, loses his wife who walks out on him. Of course it wasn't like that at all in real life. What audiences were really getting was a retread of *The Jazz Singer* (Warner Bros. 1927) in which a stage-struck Jewish boy defies his Cantor father for a career in show business. In his first major screen assignment, Larry Parks was cast as Jolson (though Jolson's own, somewhat frayed voice was used in the majority of the numbers) and came as close as possible to conveying the dynamism of the man many considered to be the greatest entertainer of them all (see illustration). Jolson himself was seen only once in the film, performing in long shot. Evelyn Keyes was Julie Benson, the show girl he marries (in reality Ruby Keeler, but Miss Keeler refused to allow her name to be used), her best moment being the spirited imitation she gave of Jolson singing 'California Here I Come' (by Buddy De Sylva, Jolson and Joseph Meyer). Jolson's parents were played by Ludwig Donath and Tamara Shayne in performances that, at times, came perilously close to caricature, with William Demarest filling the key role of Steve Martin, the man who discovers young Ase Joelson (Scotty Beckett) in a vaudeville theatre before the lad's voice breaks and thereafter becomes his lifelong friend and mentor. Stephen Longstreet's screenplay (adapted by Harry Chandler and Andrew Solt) attempted to show something of Jolson's arrogance and general unlikeability, but in the main his scenario was a valentine to a man so in love with show business (and himself) that nothing else in life mattered an iota. Jack Cole and Joseph H. Lewis staged the dance numbers, Morris Stoloff and Saul Chaplin were in charge of the musical direction and the director was Alfred E. Green, a veteran who knew exactly how to turn a cliché to enormous profit. It was no surprise to anyone that the film grossed a mammoth $8,000,000 making it the third biggest moneymaker of the year (the other two were Sam Goldwyn's *The Best Years Of Our Lives* at $11,600,000 and David O. Selznick's *Duel In The Sun* at $10,750,000), and the biggest moneymaker in Columbia's history up to that time. Songs and musical numbers: *Swanee* Irving Caesar, George Gershwin; *You Made Me Love You* Joseph McCarthy, James V. Monaco; *By The Light Of The Silvery Moon* Edward Madden, Gus Edwards; *I'm Sitting On Top Of The World* Sam Lewis, Joe Young, Ray Henderson; *There's A Rainbow Round My Shoulder* Jolson, Billy Rose, Dave Dreyer; *My Mammy* Lewis, Young, Walter Donaldson; *Rock-A-Bye Your Baby With A Dixie Melody* Lewis, Young, Jean Schwartz; *Liza* Gus Kahn, George and Ira Gershwin; *Waiting For The Robert E. Lee* L. Wolfe Gilbert, Lewis F. Muir; *April Showers* Buddy De Sylva, Louis Silvers; *About A Quarter To Nine* Al Dubin, Harry Warren; *I Want A Girl Just Like The Girl That Married Dear Old Dad* Will Dillon, Harry von Tilzer; *The Anniversary Song* Jolson, Saul Chaplin, J. Ivanovici; *The Spaniard Who Blighted My Life* Billy Merson; *Let Me Sing And I'm Happy* Irving Berlin; *When You Were Sweet Sixteen* James Thornton; *Toot Toot Tootsie Goodbye* Gus Kahn, Ernie Erdman, Dan Russo; *Eli Eli* (traditional); *On The Banks Of The Wabash* Paul Dresser; *Ma Blushin' Rosie* Edgar Smith, John Stromberg; *Ave Maria* Schubert; *After The Ball* Charles K. Harris; *Blue Bell* Edward Madden, Theodore F. Morse; *Every Little Movement Has A Meaning Of Its Own* Otto Harbach, Karl Hoschna. A short medley comprising: *Lullaby of Broadway*; *42nd Street*; *A Latin From Manhattan*; *We're In The Money* Al Dubin, Harry Warren; *Avalon* Jolson, Vincent Rose.

Songwriters Jule Styne, Sammy Cahn, Byron Stokes, F. Dudleigh Vernon, Slim Gaillard, Lee Ricks, Merle Maddern, Lanier Darwin, Will Jason, Val Burton, Eddie Seiler, Sol Marcus and Al Kaufman gave generously of their talents to ensure that the remake of **Sweetheart Of Sigma Chi** (Monogram) remained buoyant for most of its 76 minutes, the best of the numbers being Styne and Cahn's 'Five Minutes More'. With a campus-full of youngsters – including Anne Gillis (left), Fred Colby, Alan Hale Jr, David Holt, Marjorie Hoerner, William Beaudine Jr, Emmett Vogan Jr and Fred Datig Jr – ready, willing and able to breathe life into a tired old plot about a couple of crooks who set about rigging a rowing race in order to cash in on a large bet, the show had more bounce in it than a bad cheque, proving that when it tried hard, even Monogram could deliver the goods. Ross Hunter as a rowing star lately returned to college after doing war duty was also in it, so were Elyse Knox (right), Phil Regan (centre), Phil Brito, Tom Harmon, Virginia Grey, Paul Guilfoyle and Edward Brophy. Also featured were The Slim Gaillard Trio, and Frankie Carle and His Orchestra. It was written by Frank L. Moss from a story by George Waggner and directed by Jack Bernhard for producer Jeffrey Bernard. Other songs and musical numbers included: *Sweetheart of Sigma Chi* F. Dudleigh Vernon, Byron D. Stokes; *Penthouse Serenade* Will Jason, Val Burton; *It's Not I'm Such A Wolf, It's Just You're Such A Lamb* Merle Maddern, Lanier Darwin; *And Then It's Heaven* Edward Seiler, Sol Marcus, Al Kaufman; *Cement Mixer* Slim Gaillard, Lee Ricks; *Yeproc-Heresi* Gaillard; *Bach Meets Carle* (a Bach pastiche by Frankie Carle).

▽

△

A routine backstage musical from Republic, whose whiff of a plot concerned itself with a romantic misunderstanding between singing star Constance Moore (illustrated left) and her songwriter beau William Marshall, **Earl Carroll Sketchbook** (GB: **Hats Off To Rhythm**) was a sketchy excuse for a musical whose handful of songs by Sammy Cahn and Jule Styne yielded but one worthwhile tune – 'I've Never Forgotten' – unexcitingly sung by Miss Moore, who did better with 'I've Got A Right To Sing The Blues' (by Harold Arlen and Ted Koehler), first heard in one of Carroll's stage revues. For the rest it was formula film-making, with a screenplay by Frank Gill Jr and Parke Levy (original story by Gill) with Bill Goodwin, tap-dancer Johnny Coy, Vera Vague (right) and Edward Everett Horton (centre) also cast for producer Robert North and director Albert S. Rogell. The choreographer was Nick Castle. Other songs and musical numbers included *I Was Silly; Lady With A Mop; Oh Henry; What Makes You Beautiful, Beautiful?*

◁ **Three Little Girls In Blue** (20th Century-Fox), first seen as *Three Blind Mice* (1938), then as *Moon Over Miami* (1941), was a breezy Technicolor romp set in 1902 and starring June Haver, Vivian Blaine and Vera-Ellen (dubbed by Carol Stewart) as the damsels of the title. Pretending to be wealthy, they set out to ensnare millionaire husbands in Atlantic City, only to find that love and a healthy bank balance do not always go arm-in-arm. In the end Haver gets penniless George Montgomery (dubbed by Ben Gage); Vera-Ellen (illustrated left) finishes up with wine waiter Charles Smith (right) – inexplicably uncredited – and Vivian Blaine with wealthy aristocrat Frank Latimore. Josef Myrow and Mack Gordon provided a cheerful score, one of its highlights being a dream ballet danced by Vera-Ellen and Charles Smith (dubbed by Del Porter) called 'You Make Me Feel So Young' (later popularized by Frank Sinatra) and delightfully staged by Babe Pearce. Celeste Holm, fresh from her Broadway triumph as Ado Annie in *Oklahoma*, made her film debut in it and injected a vibrant sense of humour into her number 'Always A Lady'. It was adapted by Brown Holmes, Lynn Starling, Robert Ellis and Helen Logan from a play by Stephen Powys, and scripted by Valentine Davies. Mack Gordon produced and the exuberant direction was by Bruce Humberstone. Other songs and musical numbers (staged by Seymour Felix): *On The Boardwalk In Atlantic City; Somewhere In The Night; I Like Mike; A Farmer's Life Is A Very Merry Life; Oh My Love; Three Little Girls In Blue; Always A Lady* Myrow, Gordon; *If You Can't Get A Girl In The Summertime* Bert Kalmar, Harry Tierney.

△

Monogram's **High School Hero** went back to the thirties for its subject matter, and to somewhere just this side of the Dark Ages for its method of presentation. A typical campus carry-on, it involved two high school football teams – one good, one lousy. The problem posed by scenarists Hal Collins and Arthur Dreifuss (who also directed) was how to bring the inferior team up to scratch. It starred Freddie Stewart and June Preisser with Noel Neill, Anne Rooney, Jackie Moran, Frankie Darro, Warren Mills (foreground centre), Milt Kibbee and Douglas Fowley in support. The orchestras of Freddie Slack and Jan Savitt (with Isabelita) were also featured. Sam Katzman produced, and the dances were staged by Jack Boyle. Songs and musical numbers: *You're For Me; Come To My Arms; Whitney High; Night Time And You* Edward J. Kay; *You're Just What I Crave* Arthur Alexander; *Fairview High* Phil Grayson; *Southpaw Serenade* Freddie Slack.

Forties Musicals

Period specialists 20th Century-Fox went back to the not-too-distant Twenties for **Margie**, an enchanting piece of nostalgic Americana helmed by veteran director Henry King with a great deal of affection. Told in flashback as the grown Margie (Jeanne Crain) recalls her youth to her bobbysoxer daughter (Ann Todd Jr), it evoked the era of racoon coats, flagpole sitting, ragtime and charleston, while telling with warmth and humour of Margie's adolescent adventures – her unspoken rivalry with her flighty friend (Barbara Lawrence), her problems with boys and with the elastic in her bloomers (the latter a running gag that came close to being overworked), her impassioned participation in the debating society and her infatuation (along with the rest of the school females) for the handsome new French teacher (Glenn Langan). All very slight, but utterly charming, and punctuated with over a dozen songs woven throughout the narrative with unobtrusive skill by King and musical director Alfred Newman. The nearest to a production number was a skating sequence in which the camera glided and swirled with the skaters, at one point executing a 360-degree pan as the orchestra played 'Three O'Clock In The Morning' (by Dorothy Terriss and Julian Robledo). Equally captivating was Lawrence's rendition of 'A Cup Of Coffee, A Sandwich And You' (by Billy Rose, Al Dubin and Joseph Meyer) on a twilit porch, the song being

taken up by Crain in her bedroom. Later, while preparing for bed and rehearsing her debating speech, Crain hears the strains of 'I'll See You In My Dreams' (by Gus Kahn and Isham Jones) from a gramophone record outside. She hums a few bars, the song continues and, with supreme confidence in his material and his creation of atmosphere, King allows his camera to linger after Margie is snug beneath her counterpane with the song coming to its close – the mating of music and image a wistful and beguiling paean to youth and innocence, photographed with a soft glow by Charles G. Clarke. Crain (right) was perfection, leading a cast that included Esther Dale (left, as Margie's grandmother), Hobart Cavanaugh (as her father), Lynn Bari, Alan Young, Conrad Janis, Hattie McDaniel and Vanessa Brown. The screenplay was by F. Hugh Herbert from stories by Ruth McKenny and Richard Bransten, and it was produced by Walter Morosco. Other songs: *Margie* Benny Davis, Con Conrad, J. Russel Robinson; *At Sundown* Walter Donaldson; *My Time Is Your Time* Eric Little, Leo Dance; *Avalon* Al Jolson, Vincent Rose; *Collegiate* Mo Jaffe, Nat Bonx; *Charmaine*; *Diane* Erno Rapee, Lew Pollack; *April Showers* Buddy De Sylva, Louis Silvers; *Charleston* Cecil Mack, James P. Johnson; *Wonderful One* Dorothy Terriss, Paul Whiteman, Ferde Grofé, from a theme by Marshall Neilan; *Ain't She Sweet?* Jack Yellen, Milton Ager.

△
Walt Disney's **Song Of The South** (RKO) was partially redeemed by the cartoon sequences illustrating Uncle Remus's stories about Br'er Fox, Br'er Rabbit and Br'er Bear. For the rest it was a syrupy tale about an unhappy youngster (Bobby Driscoll, illustrated), and his friendship with the aforementioned Uncle Remus (James Baskett), as well as with a poor but pretty little moppet (Luana Patten, illustrated) who is equally unhappy because her brothers want to drown her puppy. Scenarists Dalton Raymond, Morton Grant and Maurice Rapf (working from stories by Joel Chandler Harris) reduced them all to caricatures, a fault compounded in Wilfred Jackson's direction (the more successful cartoon sequences were directed by Harve Foster). It was photographed in Technicolor and the associate producer was Perce Pearce. The rest of the cast included Ruth Warrick, Hattie McDaniel, Lucile Watson, Glenn Leedy, George Nokes and Gene Holland. Songs and musical numbers: *How Do You Do* Robert McGimsey; *Song Of The South* Sam Coslow, Arthur Johnston; *Uncle Remus Said* Eliot Daniel, Hy Heath, Johnny Lange; *Sooner Or Later* Charles Wolcott, Ray Gilbert; *Everybody Has A Laughing Place*; *Zip-a-dee-doo-dah* Allie Wrubel, Gilbert; *You'll Always Be The One I Love* Sunny Skylar, Ticker Freeman; *Let The Rain Pour Down*; *Who Wants To Live Like That?* Foster Carling.

Familiarity was the keynote struck by **It's Great To Be Young** (Columbia), with Leslie Brooks (left), Jimmy Lloyd (centre), Jeff Donnell, Robert Stanton, Jack Williams, Jack Fina, Frank Orth, Ann Codee (right) and Milton DeLugg and His Swing Wing featuring in an all too familiar yarn about a group of ex-GIs with greasepaint in their veins who, after landing a Borscht Circuit engagement and suffering the usual heartbreaks endemic to show-biz, stage a show at a summer resort, and finish up on Broadway. Jack Henley wrote it from a story by Karen DeWolfe (as well as an inordinate number of uncredited writers), Ted Richmond produced, and it was directed for the platitude it was by Del Lord. Not one of the performances made any impression. Songs and musical numbers: *It's Great To Be Young*; *A Thousand And One Sweet Dreams*; *Five Of The Best*; *That Went Out With High-Button Shoes*; *Frankie Boogie* Doris Fisher, Allan Roberts; *Bumble Boogie* (based on Rimsky-Korsakov's 'Flight of the Bumble Bee') Jack Fina.
▽

◁ **Susie Steps Out** (United Artists) moved away from the familiar world of radio and into the up-and-coming medium of television, with Cleatus Caldwell (left) second-billed to crooner David Bruce as an employee in an advertising agency. When she loses her job as a result of a mix-up with the boss's wife, her little sister comes to the financial aid of their ailing father (Percival Vivian) by successfully posing as a nightclub singer and, in the final reel, makes the grade as a TV star. A compendium of clichés compiled by Elwood Ullman from an original story by director Reginald Le Borg, and Kurt Neuman, the Buddy Rogers-Ralph Cohn production also featured Howard Freeman, Grady Sutton Ann Hunter (right), Margaret Dumont, John Berkes and Joseph J. Greene. Songs and musical numbers included: *When You're Near*; *For The Right Guy*; *I'm So Lonely*; *When Does Love Begin* Hal Borne; *Bob-Bob That Did It* Borne, Eddie Cherkose.

An inept remake of Carole Lombard's screwball farce *True Confession* (Paramount, 1937), **Cross My Heart** (Paramount) had larger-than-life Betty Hutton (left) confessing to a murder she was totally innocent of in order to give her attorney boyfriend (Sonny Tufts, right) the chance of a lifetime to establish his reputation in the legal profession by defending her. It was hardly surprising that audiences didn't swallow it. Rhys Williams played the prosecuting attorney, Alan Bridge was a detective, Ruth Donnelly was Betty's mother and Michael Chekhov a hammy Russian actor and the murderer in question. He should have done away with scenarists Harry Tugend and Claude Binyon whose screenplay (based on a play by Louis Verneuil and Georges Berr, additional dialogue by Charles Schnee), was equally criminal. Tugend also produced and the director was John Berry. Songs and musical numbers included: *Love Is The Darndest Thing*; *That Little Dream Got Nowhere*; *How Do You Do It?*; *Does Baby Feel Alright?*; *It Hasn't Been Chilly In Chile* Johnny Burke, Jimmy Van Heusen; *Cross My Heart* Robert Emmett Dolan, Larry Neill (all sung by Hutton).
▽

△
Judy Canova (illustrated) did neither herself nor her radio fans any good by appearing in **Singin' in the Corn** (Columbia), a staggeringly poor filler in which she played a carnival mind reader who inherits her uncle's estate on the proviso that, before receiving a cent, she has to return a local ghost town to the Indians. The blame for the screenplay rested with Isabel Dawn and Monte Brice, who wrote it from an equally culpable story by Richard Weil. Allen Jenkins (illustrated) co-starred as Canova's partner, and the cast was completed by Guinn Williams, Alan Bridge, Charles Halton, Robert Dudley and Nick Thompson. Also appearing were The Singing Indian Braves, who had to be just that in order to lend themselves to twaddle of this sort. Ted Richmond produced and the director was Del Lord. Songs and musical numbers included: *I'm A Gal Of Property*; *Pepita Chequita*; *An Old Love Is A True Love* Doris Fisher, Allan Roberts; *Ma, He's Making Eyes At Me* Sidney Clare, Con Conrad.

△
Weighing in at $3,000,000, **Blue Skies** was an efficient entertainment and an almighty smash from Paramount that reunited Bing Crosby and Fred Astaire (first seen together in *Holiday Inn*, Paramount, 1942) in a musical spectacle that echoed, in several instances, their earlier collaboration. Both movies had scores by Irving Berlin, both featured Crosby and Astaire as erstwhile partners in a song-and-dance-team, both had them falling for the same girl and, in both, Crosby got her. As was the case in *Holiday Inn*, the plot of **Blue Skies** (adapted by Allan Scott from an idea by Berlin, and scripted by Arthur Sheekman) was little more than a serviceable framework constructed to support a clutch of Berlin songs, 20 of them featured, and of the 20, four written especially for the film. Recounted in flashback, the story began in 1919 and followed the private and professional lives of the two men for the next 27 years, focussing particularly on Crosby's up and down marriage (which ended in divorce) to Joan Caulfield. Musically, the film was drenched in nostalgia, the choreographic high point being Hermes Pan's staging of 'Puttin On The Ritz', and Astaire's galvanic interpretation of it. With its two male stars (Crosby left, Astaire right) occupying centre stage for most of the remaining time, there weren't many opportunities available for the rest of the cast to register anything other than adequate support, though Billy De Wolfe was allowed to intrude every now and then with some resistible bits of clowning. Also cast: Olga San Juan, Jimmy Conlin, Cliff Nazarro, Frank Faylen, Jack Norton, Will Wright, Victoria Horne, Karolyn Grimes and Roy Gordon. Sol C. Siegel produced (in Technicolor) and the director was Stuart Heisler. Other songs and musical numbers: *A Pretty Girl Is Like A Melody* (Astaire, male chorus); *I've Got My Captain Working For Me Now* (Crosby, De Wolfe); *You'd Be Surprised* (San Juan); *Serenade To An Old-Fashioned Girl* (Caulfield, male quartet); *I'll See You In C-U-B-A* (Crosby, San Juan); *A Couple Of Song And Dance Men* (Astaire, Crosby, Nazarro on piano); *Always* (chorus); *You Keep Coming Back Like A Song* (Crosby, male chorus); *Blue Skies* (Crosby); *The Little Things In Life* (Crosby); *Not For All The Rice In China* (Crosby); *Everybody Step* (Crosby, danced by chorus); *How Deep Is The Ocean?* (Crosby, female chorus); *Getting Nowhere* (Crosby); *Heat Wave* (San Juan, chorus; danced by Astaire and San Juan); *Any Bonds Today?* (Crosby); *This Is The Army Mr Jones* (Crosby); *White Christmas* (Crosby); *Russian Lullaby* (Crosby). Background music: *Nobody Knows*; *Tell Me Little Gypsy*; *Some Sunny Day*; *Mandy*; *When You Walked Out*; *Because I Love You*; *How Many Times*; *The Song Is Ended*; *Lazy*. Interesting sideline: The film was originally scheduled to be produced by Mark Sandrich, who cast Paul Draper in the Astaire role. Nine days into shooting, however, Sandrich suffered a fatal heart attack. The production was taken over by Sol C. Siegel who replaced Draper with Astaire, the latter announcing that it would be his last film. Happily this was not the case, though no musical he made before or after **Blue Skies** was as successful.

Forties Musicals

◁ The usual clichés attendant on the musical ▷ biopic came cascading forth in glorious Technicolor in **Till The Clouds Roll By**, MGM's star-studded salute to the greatest ever melodist of the American musical theatre – Jerome Kern. And with so many of their contract artists on hand to bring his immortal music to life, what did it matter if the accompanying story hardly shook the world? The fact was that Kern's songs spoke louder than actions; the fiction was – well, whatever scenarists Myles Connolly and Jean Holloway (working from a loose adaptation by George Wells of a story by Guy Bolton) cared to dream up. Beginning on 27 December 1927 with the opening night of Kern's masterpiece *Show Boat* (written with Oscar Hammerstein II), the film flashes back in time to the 'early days' with Kern (Robert Walker) a struggling young songwriter, receiving platitudinous counsel from earnest Van Heflin who implores him not to waste his time on 'little tunes' but to 'think big'. Which is exactly what the aspiring composer does, going from one success to another, marrying along the way and, at one point, offering advice of his own to Heflin's stage-struck daughter (Lucille Bremer, vocals dubbed by Trudy Erwin) who throws a tantrum when a number he has written for her is given to Marilyn Miller (Judy Garland) instead. The finale (directed by George Sidney) was a massive production number featuring several Kern ever-greens, and climaxed by Frank Sinatra singing 'Ol' Man River' from *Show Boat*. The film ran 137 minutes, featured nearly two dozen Kern classics and almost the same number of stars. With its vocal arrangements by Kay Thompson, musical direction by Lennie Hayton, superb orchestrations by Conrad Salinger, and the attractive staging of the numbers by Robert Alton (at his best in the title number) and Vincente Minnelli (the latter in charge of Judy Garland's three sequences), the musical side of the show was in the hands of the most capable team of experts in the business. Arthur Freed produced, Richard Whorf directed. Also cast: Dorothy Patrick (as Mrs Kern), Joan Wells, Paul Langton, Mary Nash and Harry Hayden. Songs, musical numbers, performers and lyricists: *Cotton Blossom* (chorus); *Make Believe* (Kathryn Grayson, Tony Martin); *Can't Help Lovin' Dat Man* (Lena Horne); *Ol' Man River* (Caleb Peterson); *Life Upon The Wicked Stage* (Virginia O'Brien); *Who Cares If My Boat Goes Upstream?* (Martin) Oscar Hammerstein II; *Till The Clouds Roll By* (June Allyson, Ray McDonald, illustrated right) P.G. Wodehouse; *How D'You Like To Spoon With Me?* (Angela Lansbury) Edward Laska; *They Didn't Believe Me* (Dinah Shore) Herbert Reynolds; *The Last Time I Saw Paris* (Shore) Hammerstein II; *I Won't Dance* (Van Johnson, Bremer) Otto Harbach, Hammerstein II; *Why Was I Born?* (Horne) Hammerstein II; *Smoke Gets In Your Eyes* (Cyd Charisse, Gower Champion) Harbach; *Who?* (Garland) Harbach, Hammerstein II; *Look For The Silver Lining* (Garland) Buddy De Sylva; *Sunny* (chorus), danced by Garland, illustrated left) Harbach, Hammerstein II; *Cleopatterer* (Allyson); *Leave It To Jane* (Allyson) Wodehouse; *One More Dance* (Bremer) Hammerstein II; *The Land Where The Good Songs Go* (Bremer); *Kalua* (orchestra); *Polka From Mark Twain Suite* (orchestra); *Yesterdays* (chorus) Harbach; *Long Ago And Far Away* (Grayson) Ira Gershwin; *A Fine Romance* (O'Brien) Dorothy Fields; *All The Things You Are* (Martin) Hammerstein II; *She Didn't Say Yes* (Wilde Twins) Harbach.

Warner Bros.' last musical in 1946 was **The Time, The Place And The Girl** (not to be confused with their 1929 pic of the same name). Written by Francis Swann, Agnes Christine Johnston and Lynn Starling (story by Leonard Lee), it involved Jack Carson (left) and Dennis Morgan (right) in an attempt to put on a show against the wishes of a retired opera singer (Florence Bates), but with the assistance of Miss Bates's husband (S.Z. Sakall) and her glamorous grand-daughter (Martha Vickers, centre right). An air of stale familiarity pervaded the movie, but with a solid score by Arthur Schwartz and Leo Robin that included 'A Gal In Calico' and 'A Rainy Night in Rio', some imaginative dance sequences by LeRoy Prinz, and a decent quota of laughs, the movie was a smash. Engaging performances came from Carson, Morgan, Vickers, Janis Paige (centre left), and a supporting cast that included Alan Hale, Donald Woods, and Angela Greene. Carmen Cavallaro and His Orchestra, The Condos Brothers and Chandra Kaly were in it too. It was produced, in Technicolor, by Alex Gottlieb, and directed by David Butler. Other songs: *Oh But I Do; Through A Thousand Dreams; A Solid Citizen Of The Solid South; I Happened To Walk Down First Street.*
▽

1947

Academy Awards

Cinematography (colour)
NOMINATIONS INCLUDED: *Mother Wore Tights* (20th Century-Fox) Harry Jackson

Music
Song
'Zip-A-Dee-Doo-Dah' *Song Of The South* (Disney, RKO) Allie Wrubel *cm*; Ray Gilbert *lyr*.
NOMINATIONS INCLUDED: 'A Gal In Calico' *The Time, The Place And The Girl* (WB) Arthur Schwartz *cm*; Leo Robin *lyr*. 'I Wish I Didn't Love You So' *The Perils Of Pauline* (Paramount) Frank Loesser, 'Pass That Peace Pipe' *Good News* (MGM) Ralph Blane *cm*; Hugh Martin and Roger Edens *lyr*. 'You Do' *Mother Wore Tights* Josef Myrow *cm*; Mack Gordon *lyr*.

Scoring Of A Musical Picture
Mother Wore Tights Alfred Newman
NOMINATIONS INCLUDED: *Fiesta* (MGM) Johnny Green. *My Wild Irish Rose* (WB) Ray Heindorf and Max Steiner. *Road To Rio* (Paramount) Robert Emmett Dolan. *Song Of The South* Daniele Amfitheatrof, Paul J. Smith and Charles Wolcott.

The Annual Top Moneymaking Films
INCLUDED: *Blue Skies* (Paramount). *California* (Paramount). *This Time For Keeps* (MGM). *I Wonder Who's Kissing Her Now* (20th Century-Fox). *The Jolson Story* (Columbia). *Margie* (20th Century-Fox). *Mother Wore Tights*. *No Leave, No Love* (MGM). *The Perils Of Pauline*. *Till The Clouds Roll By* (MGM). *Variety Girl* (Paramount). *Welcome Stranger* (Paramount).

Eddie Bracken should have sued scenarists Edmund Beloin, Jack Rose and Lewis Meltzer (story by William Bowers and Robinson Holbert) for letting him down so badly in **Ladies' Man** (Paramount). Considering the feebleness of the plot (country bumpkin strikes oil, comes to the big city to celebrate, and becomes involved with a radio programme as well as with some gold-digging females), he needed all the assistance he could get, his innocent, village-idiot mien not being a sturdy enough prop on this sorry occasion. Desperately trying to pummel it into life were co-star Cass Daley, tap-dancer Johnny Coy, and Spike Jones and His City Slickers. They were spasmodically successful, but it was uphill for most of the way, with an unusually dull score by the usually reliable Jule Styne and Sammy Cahn, and a few 'oldies', contributing to the pervading mediocrity of it all. Completing the cast were The Virginias, Welles and Field, Lewis Russell, Georges Renavent and Roberta Jonay. Daniel Dare produced, the dances were staged by Billy Daniels, and it was directed by William D. Russell (production number illustrated). Songs and musical numbers: *I Gotta Girl I Love In North And South Dakota*; *What Am I Gonna Do About You?*; *I'm As Ready As I'll Ever Be*; *Away Out West* Styne, Cahn; *Cocktails For Two* Sam Coslow, Arthur Johnston; *Holiday For Strings* David Rose; *Mama Yo Quiero* Al Stillman, Jaraca and Vincente Paiva.
▽

As **The Shocking Miss Pilgrim** (20th Century-Fox) was set in stuffy Boston of 1874, and featured its star, Betty Grable (illustrated) as a woman typist fighting for suffrage in the male-dominated world of big business, there was little chance of her showing off her celebrated legs. Still, despite the lack of flesh, and a really stultifying screenplay by George Seaton (from a story by Ernest and Fredericka Maas), it was a box-office success that proved its star's enormous drawing power regardless of the quality of her scripts. Dick Haymes was her co-star and boss, with other roles going to Anne Revere (as Haymes's progressive aunt), Allyn Joslyn, Gene Lockhart, Elisabeth Risdon, Arthur Shields, Charles Kemper, Roy Roberts, Stanley Prager and 'The Outcasts'. Some hitherto unpublished manuscripts by George Gershwin, collated and adapted by Kay Swift and Ira Gershwin, with new lyrics by the latter, comprised the score, the most durable number being 'For You, For Me, For Evermore' sung as a duet by Grable and Haymes. Scenarist Seaton also directed (flatly) and the dances were staged by Hermes Pan. William Perlberg produced (in Technicolor). Other songs and musical numbers: *Aren't You Kinda Glad We Did?*; *Changing My Tune*; *Back Bay Polka*; *One Two Three*; *But Not In Boston*; *Sweet Packard*; *Stand Up And Fight*; *Waltzing Is Better* ◁ *Sitting Down*; *Waltz Me No Waltzes*; *Demon Rum*.

△

Deanna Durbin sang four songs in **I'll Be Yours** (Universal International), a moderately diverting remake of Ferenc Molnar's *The Good Fairy*, first produced by Universal in 1935 with William Wyler directing from a script by Preston Sturges. In the new version, also with a script by Sturges (adapted from the Hungarian by Jane Hinton), the fantasy inherent in the original was nowhere in evidence, and instead of Margaret Sullavan in the central role of a young woman who helps a struggling young lawyer to find employment with a meat packer by passing him off as her jealous spouse, there was Miss Durbin (illustrated). Adolphe Menjou, in the role originally played by Frank Morgan was somewhat miscast as the meat packer, and there wasn't much sparkle, either, from Tom Drake as the lawyer. Still, director William A. Seiter, aided by a passable performance from his leading lady kept it simmering amiably along its innocuous way. Also cast: Walter Catlett, Franklin Pangborn, William Trenk, Joan Fulton, Patricia Alphin and William Brooks. Felix Jackson produced. Songs: *It's Dreamtime*; *Cobbleskill School Song* Jack Brooks, Walter Schumann; *Granada* Augustin Lara, English lyrics Dorothy Dodd; *Sari Waltz* C.C.S. Cushman, E.P. Heath, Emmerich Kalman; *Lullaby* Brahms.

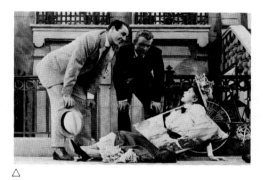
△

Two veterans, producer-director Allan Dwan and silent star Irene Rich, surfaced in **Calendar Girl**, a turn of the century tale from Republic in which Miss Rich was cast as the kindly landlady of a boarding house peopled by the usual motley collection of young hopefuls – including Jane Frazee (top-starred) as a singer, William Marshall as a struggling young composer, and James Ellison (left) as a painter whose calendar portrait of Frazee (illustrated) causes a rift between her and her beau Marshall (centre). Victor McLaglen played an Irish fireman, and Gail Patrick made a token appearance as a wealthy Bostonian. More prominently featured were Kenny Baker and Janet Martin who, together with Frazee and Marshall, handled the bulk of the film's seven songs (by Harold Adamson and Jimmy McHugh). Franklin Pangborn, Gus Schilling and Charles Arnt completed the cast. The script was by Mary Loos, Richard Sale and Lee Loeb from a story by Loeb, and the choreography was by Fanchon. Songs and musical numbers: *Have I Told You Lately?*; *Calendar Girl*; *A Lovely Night To Go Dreaming*; *At The Fireman's Ball*; *New York's A Nice Place To Visit*; *Let's Have Some Pretzels And Beer*; *A Bluebird Is Singing To Me*.

A 67-minute programmer from RKO, **Beat The Band** wrapped several musical numbers around a flimsy box of clichés whose contents contained a second-hand yarn about a gal from the sticks (Frances Langford, right) who comes to the big city to take opera lessons, and falls into the clutches of unscrupulous Phillip Terry (centre right), a bandleader pretending to be a singing teacher. Ralph Edwards (left) was cast as Terry's comic manager, with other parts in Lawrence Kimble's screenplay (adapted by Kimble and Arthur Ross from a play by George Abbott) going to June Clayworth (centre), Mabel Paige, Andrew Tombes and Donald MacBride. Miss Langford did most of the singing, and there was additional musical support from Gene Krupa and His Band. Michael Kraike produced and the director was John H. Auer. Songs and musical numbers included: *Kissin' Well*; *I'm In Love*; *I've Got My Fingers Crossed*; *Beat The Band* Mort Greene, Leigh Harline; *Shadow Rhapsody*.

With the war over, audiences found **Wake Up And Dream** (20th Century-Fox), a Technicolored wadge of whimsy with a wartime background, not at all to their liking. John Payne, though top-starred, only appeared briefly at the beginning of the film – and again at the end – as a soldier believed lost in battle. June Haver (illustrated left) was his waitress girlfriend, and Connie Marshall (sitting left) his kid sister who sets out, in company with Miss Haver and elderly Clem Bevans (right) on the latter's boat, to find him. Based on Robert Nathan's novel *The Enchanted Voyage*, there was nothing enchanted about director Lloyd Bacon's tepid musical voyage of discovery, though one good song 'Give Me The Simple Life' by Harry Ruby and Rube Bloom did emerge. John Ireland (standing right), as a would-be dentist, went along for the ride, with Charlotte Greenwood, George Cleveland, Oliver Blake, Charles Russell, Charles D. Brown and Irving Bacon completing the cast for producer Walter Morosco. The script was by Elick Moll. Other songs and musical numbers included: *I Wish I Could Tell You*; *Into The Sun* Ruby, Bloom; *Who Knows?* Don Raye, Gene De Paul.

Russ Morgan and His Orchestra supplied most of the pleasant music for **Cigarette Girl** (Republic). In between the musical numbers, however, was the decidedly bankrupt business of the plot by Edward Huebach (screenplay by Henry K. Moritz). A story-book romance, it had Leslie Brooks (illustrated) and Jimmy Lloyd wooing each other; he in the guise of an oil company president, she as a famous nightclub singer. In fact, they're nothing of the sort, but, as the story unfurls, he does become a business tycoon and she, in the best Cinderella-like fashion, a Broadway star. Ludwig Donath, Doris Colleen, Howard Freeman, Joan Barton, Mary Forbes, Francis Pierlot, and Eugene Borden were also cast, William Bloom produced and the director was Gunther V. Fritsch. Songs and musical numbers included: *It's All In The Mind*; *The More We Get Together*; *How Can You Tell?*; *They Won't Let Me Sing*; *Honeymoon On A Dime* Doris Fisher, Allan Roberts.

What happened in **It Happened In Brooklyn** (MGM) was that Frank Sinatra, returning home from the war, met and fell in love with pretty music teacher Kathryn Grayson, but lost her to Peter Lawford. And all to the accompaniment of several passable Jule Styne-Sammy Cahn songs, the best being 'Time After Time' which went on to become a Sinatra standard. Jimmy Durante was in it too (as a school janitor), and his duet with Sinatra, 'The Song's Gotta Come From The Heart' (illustrated) was the best novelty item in the show, though Sinatra's charmingly ill-conceived rendering (with Miss Grayson) of 'La Ci Darem La Mano' from Mozart's *Don Giovanni* might equally be con-

When 20th Century-Fox wasn't dispensing dollops of period nostalgia it was acting as a tour agent for Latin America: viz *That Night In Rio* (1941), *A Weekend In Havana* (1941), and *Down Argentine Way* (1940). The studio's latest excursion into the travel business was **Carnival In Costa Rica**, a Technicolored cliché that filled the eye but not the mind. The story of a young couple (Dick Haymes – at the height of his popularity – and second-billed Vera-Ellen, illustrated centre) who, against their bickering parents' wishes, refuse to marry, it starred Cesar Romero as well as Celeste Holm (who was far too talented a lady to waste her time on junk like this), ditto Anne Revere, as well as J. Carrol Naish (who generally wasted his time on junk like this), Pedro de Cordoba, Barbara Whiting, Nestor Paiva and Fritz Feld. It was choreographed by the distinguished Russian choreographer Leonide Massine, scripted by John Larkin, Samuel Hoffenstein and Elizabeth Reinhardt, and directed for producer William A. Bacher by Gregory Ratoff. Songs and musical numbers: *I'll Know It's Love*; *Another Night Like This*; *Mi Vida*; *Costa Rica*; *Rhumba Bomba*; *Maracas* Harry Ruby, Ernesto Lecuona; *Qui Pi Pia* Al Stillman, Sunny Skylar.

sidered the comic highspot – albeit unintentionally. Jack Cummings's modest black and white production also featured Gloria Grahame, Marcy McGuire, Aubrey Mather, Tamara Shayne, Bobby Long, tap-dancer Billy Roy and, heard but not seen, the piano playing of 17-year-old Andre Previn who had recently joined the studio's music department. The dances were staged by Jack Donohue, and the serviceable direction was by Richard Thorpe. Modest it may have been, but it made a box-office killing. Other songs *Brooklyn Bridge*; *It's The Same Old Dream*; *I Believe*; *Whose Baby Are You*; *Otchichornya* (traditional); *The Bell Song* (from 'Lakme') Delibes.

Forties Musicals

An underfed programmer made in Trucolor, **That's My Gal** (Republic) attached several specialty routines to a frail story about a bunch of con-men producers who persuade some gullible show backers to over-invest in a no-chance burlesque show, the idea being to make a quick getaway with the loot when the show folds. Trouble is, the show turns out to be a success. Alas, the same could not be said for the movie, whose hard-working cast – Lynne Roberts, Donald Barry, Pinky Lee, Frank Jenks and Edward Gargan – were entirely unable to animate Joseph Hoffman's tiresome screenplay (from a story by Frances Hyland and Bernard Feins). It was left to Jan Savitt and His Top Hatters, Isabelita, The Guadalajara Trio, The Four Step Brothers, St Clair and Vilova, Dolores and Don Graham (illustrated), and Judy Clark to provide what meagre entertainment there was. Armand Schaefer produced and the director was George Blair. Hal Belfer choreographed. Songs and musical numbers: *That's My Girl*; *The Music In My Heart Is You*; *Take It Away* Jack Elliott; *For You And Me*; *Sentimental*; *Hitchhike To Happiness* Kim Gannon, Walter Kent; *720 In The Books* Jan Savitt.

▽

△

Nine tunes, performed by the orchestras of Russ Morgan and Jack McVea, with contributions from Wingy Manone, Candy Candido, Abe Lyman, Les Paul, Jess Stacy and Joe Venuti, left very little time for **Sarge Goes To College** (Monogram) to develop its plot – which was probably a blessing. All about a rather dumb marine sergeant (Alan Hale Jr) who is sent to college in order to relax before undergoing a serious operation, it was mindless even by Monogram's standards. Romance, and the usual college show, both played a part in Hal Collins's screenplay (story by Henry Edwards); so did Freddie Stewart (right), June Preisser (left), Frankie Darro, Warren Mills, Noel Neill, Arthur Walsh and Monte Collins. Best song: 'Open The Door, Richard' (by Dusty Fletcher, John Mason, Jack McVea and Don Howell), performed by Jack McVea and His Orchestra. It was produced and directed by Will Jason. Other songs and musical numbers included: *I'll Close My Eyes* Buddy Kaye, Billy Reid; *Penthouse Serenade* Will Jason, Val Burton; *Somebody Else Is Taking My Place* Dick Howard, Bob Ellsworth, Russ Morgan; *Two Are The Same As One*; *Blues In B Flat*.

△

Mexican heart throb Ricardo Montalban (right) made his American screen debut in **Fiesta** (MGM), an expensive piece of hokum (filmed on location in Mexico) whose leading characters were a pair of twins (Montalban and Esther Williams). Their father, a retired matador (Fortunio Bonanova), has hopes that his son will follow in his footsteps to the bull-fighting ring, but the boy has other plans. He wants to become a composer. In order to save the family from disgrace, and to clear her brother's name of cowardice, sister Williams dresses up in *torero*'s clothing and steps into the bullring on his behalf. After proving the equal of any man (and striking an early blow for Women's Lib) the masquerade is, eventually, unmasked and Montalban is allowed to continue his music studies. To this unlikely tale (written by George Bruce and Lester Cole) were brought several highly colourful musical sequences, including a version (by musical director Johnny Green) of Aaron Copland's 'El Salon Mexico' retitled 'Fantasia Mexicana', which was excitingly staged by Eugene Loring. Jack Cummings produced, Richard Thorpe directed, and the cast included Akim Tamiroff, John Carroll, Mary Astor, Cyd Charisse (left), Hugo Haas and Alan Napier. Other songs and musical numbers included: *La Bamba* Luis Martinez Serrano; *La Luna Enamorada* Angel Ortiz De Villajos; *Miriano* Bolanos Recio, Leocadio Martinez Durango; *Romeria Vasca* Los Bocheros.

Love And Learn (Warner Bros.) was the feeble tale of two songsmiths, Jack Carson (left) and Robert Hutton (2nd left), who are saved from failure by wealthy Martha Vickers (centre, her vocals dubbed by Trudy Erwin) masquerading as a poverty-stricken girl. One of Warner's worst forties enterprises, it was written by Eugene Conrad, Francis Swann and I.A.L. Diamond

▽

△

An enjoyable entry from Republic, **Hit Parade of 1947** starred Eddie Albert as an ambitious songwriter who, together with a trio of other performers (Constance Moore, Joan Edwards, Gil Lamb), forms a nightclub act. Albert falls in love with Moore (illustrated), the act's a hit, and soon they're signed to a Hollywood contract. When, however, they learn that the reason they were signed was for Miss Moore, and Miss Moore alone, Albert, Edwards and Lamb return to New York leaving Moore to pursue her movie career as a solo artist. What happens to each of them formed the nucleus of Mary Loos's screenplay (original story by Parke Levy) and was a more than adequate foundation for several tuneful songs and one production number ('Chiquita From Santa Anita' by Harold Adamson and Jimmy McHugh, who wrote most of the score). Miss Edwards, a radio favourite making her screen debut, sang pleasingly and so did Eddie Albert; and the comedy routines were in the care of Gil Lamb, an excellent pantomimist. Roy Rogers and Trigger made a guest appearance; also on hand were Woody Herman and His Orchestra, and Bob Nolan and The Sons of the Pioneers. The director was Frank McDonald. Other songs: *Is There Anyone Here From Texas?*; *I Guess I'll Have That Dream Right Now*; *Couldn't Be More In Love*; *The Customer Is Always Wrong*; *The Cats Are Going To The Dogs* Adamson, McHugh; *Brooklyn Buckaroos* Foster Carling; *Out California Way* Tim Spencer.

(from a story by Harry Sauber) with parts as well for Janis Paige (right), Otto Kruger, Barbara Brown, Tom D'Andrea, Florence Bates and Craig Stevens. William Jacobs produced, Frederick De Cordova directed. Songs: *Would You Believe Me?* M.K. Jerome, Charles Tobias, Ray Heindorf; *Happy Me*; *If You Are Coming Back To Me* Jerome, Jack Scholl.

▽

Carnegie Hall (United Artists), produced by Boris Morros and William Le Baron, pegged some superb music on to a really trite tale about a mother (Marsha Hunt) who uses her position as a custodian of Carnegie Hall to further her son's (William Prince) career as a concert pianist. Plot-wise it was a non-starter whose slender narrative could have been dispensed with in half an hour. Far more successful were the musical items on offer by some of the world's greatest exponents of classical music. Artur Rubinstein performed Chopin's Polonaise in A flat and De Falla's 'Ritual Fire Dance'; cellist Gregor Piatigorsky (illustrated) played Saint-Saens' 'The Swan'; Leopold Stokowski conducted the Philharmonic Symphony Orchestra in the second movement of Tchaikovsky's Fifth Symphony, Heifetz gave a movement of the Tchaikovsky Violin Concerto; Rise Stevens sang the 'Seguidilla' from Bizet's *Carmen*, and Lily Pons 'The Bell Song' from Delibes' *Lakme*, Ezio Pinza was heard in the 'Champagne Song' from Mozart's *Don Giovanni*, and Jan Peerce sang 'O Sole Mio' by Capurro and Eduardo Di Capua,

and 'La Danza' by Rossini. The rest was hogwash, whose participants included Frank McHugh, Hans Yaray, Joseph Buloff, Emile Boreo, Eola Galli, *New York Times* music critic Olin Downes (as himself), Walter Damrosch (as himself) and Alfonso D'Artega as Tchaikovsky. Also appearing were The New York Philharmonic Quintet, Bruno Walter, Artur Rodzinski, Fritz Reiner and – less successfully – Vaughan Monroe and His Orchestra and Harry James, the latter being featured in a kitschy piece called 'Fifty-Seventh Street Rhapsody' by Portnoff. The scenario was by Karl Kamb from a story by Seena Owen and the direction by Edgar G. Ulmer. Other musical items included: *Beware My Heart* Sam Coslow; *Sometime We Will Meet Again* Le Baron, Morros, Gregory Stone; *The Brown Danube* Hal Borne; *Quintet in E Flat for Piano and Strings, Opus 44* (John Corigliano Quintette) Schumann; *Prelude To Die Meistersinger* (N.Y. Philharmonic conducted by Bruno Walter) Richard Wagner; *Beethoven Symphony No 5 (section)* (N.Y. Philharmonic conducted by Artur Rodzinski).

A programmer from Columbia, **Little Miss Broadway** starred Jean Porter (right) in a farfetched yarn as an orphan who wrongly believes that her only living relatives are wealthy socialites. What they are, in fact, are a set of colourful Broadway characters who, in order not to shatter Miss Porter's image of them, take possession of an opulent Long Island mansion belonging to a thief doing time, and set out to impress her and her fiancé (John Shelton). Ruth Donnelly (centre left), Edward Gargan (left), Charles Jordan and Vince Barnett were the relatives, with other roles in Arthur Dreifuss, Victor McLeod and Betty Wright's screenplay going to Doris Colleen, Douglas Wood and Milton Kibbee. Also featured were Jerry Wald and His Orchestra. A moderate entertainment, it was directed by co-author Dreifuss and produced by Sam Katzman. Songs: *That's Good Enough For Me*; *A Man Is Brother To A Mule* Allan Roberts, Doris Fisher; *Judy And Dick* Betty Wright, Victor McLeod, Fred Karger; *Cheer For The Team* Walter G. Samuels, Charles Newman, McElbert Moore.

Though Deanna Durbin (right) was top-billed in **Something In The Wind** (Universal International) and sang several Johnny Green-Leo Robin songs pleasantly enough, it was Donald O'Connor (left), exuding bushels of energy in a spoof on radio melodramas (called 'I Love A Mystery'), as well as in a ballet send-up, who was the standout performer in Joseph Sistrom's entertaining production. Durbin, who was far less engaging than her co-star, played a disc jockey mistakenly believed by the grandson (John Dall) of a recently deceased tycoon, to have been the old man's mistress. She's kidnapped by Dall, falls in love with him, and is assisted in her predicament by O'Connor. Harry Kurnitz and William Bowers's screenplay was superior to its plot, and there were entertaining performances from Charles Winninger, Margaret Wycherley and Helena Carter. The Williams Brothers also appeared; so did Jan Peerce, who joined Miss Durbin in the 'Miserere' from Verdi's *Il Trovatore*. The director was Irving Pichel. Songs: *Something In The Wind*; *Turntable Song*; *It's Only Love*; *You Wanna Keep Your Baby Lookin' Right*; *Happy Go Lucky And Free*.

In **Copacabana** (United Artists), a box-office flop, Groucho Marx starred as an artists' agent whose only client is Carmen Miranda (illustrated centre). So when he negotiates a deal requiring a pair of nightclub entertainers, he prevails upon Miranda to accept both assignments: as a veiled chanteuse, and as a Latin-American spitfire. Though most of the movie was inexpensively shot in a couple of nightclub sets, there was a great deal of activity in the Laszlo Vadnay-Allan Boretz-Howard Harris screenplay (story by Vadnay), with roles in it for Steve Cochran and Gloria Jean (the romantic interest), as well as popular crooner Andy Russell, Ralph Sanford and Andrew Tombes. Newspaper columnists Louis Sobol, Earl Wilson and Abel Green also appeared, but contributed nothing to the makeshift goings-on under Alfred E. Green's frantic direction. Larry Ceballos staged the dances and it was produced by Sam Coslow who also wrote the songs. Songs and musical numbers: *Je Vous Aime*; *Stranger Things Have Happened*; *My Heart Was Doing A Bolero*; *Let's Do The Copacabana*; *I Haven't Got A Thing To Sell*; *We've Come To Copa* Coslow; *Tico, Tico* Ervin Drake, Aloysio Oliveira, Zequinha Abreu.

Not one of Walt Disney's more inspired inventions, **Fun And Fancy Free** (RKO) was merely a pleasing animated diversion, introduced by Jiminy Cricket (singing 'I'm A Happy-Go-Lucky-Fellow' by Leigh Harline and Ned Washington), and comprising two sections. The first, narrated by Dinah Shore, recounted the adventures of a badly treated circus bear after he manages to escape his keepers; while the second was a version of the *Jack And The Beanstalk* story featuring Mickey Mouse, Donald Duck and Goofy (see illustration) with live-action cut-ins of Edgar Bergen (who is seen relating the tale to Charlie McCarthy), Mortimer Snerd, and little Luana Patten. The production supervisor was Ben Sharpsteen, William Morgan was in charge of the live-action direction and the cartoon directors were Jack Kinney, Bill Roberts and Hamilton Luske. It was filmed in Technicolor, and also featured the voices of Anita Gordon, Cliff Edwards, Billy Gilbert, Clarence Nash, The Kings Men, The Dinning Sisters and The Starlighters. Songs and musical numbers: *Fun And Fancy Free* Bernie Benjamin, George Weiss; *Lazy Countryside* Bobby Worth; *Too Good To Be True*; *Say It With A Slap* Eliot Daniel, Buddy Kaye; *Fee Fi Fo Fum* Paul J. Smith, Arthur Quenzer; *My Favourite Dream* William Walsh, Ray Noble.

Forties Musicals

According to scenarists Richard English, Art Arthur and Curtis Kenyon – in their screen biography of the Dorsey Brothers called **The Fabulous Dorseys** (United Artists) – Tommy (on trombone) and Jimmy (on saxophone) spent the greater part of their youth bickering with each other: a state of affairs they carried through into manhood. But a happy ending was imposed on their uneasy relationship when a family bereavement reunites them. With most musical biopics, it was the subject's work rather than his life story that people paid to see, and **The Fabulous Dorseys** was no exception. Tommy and Jimmy played themselves (Bobby Ward, left, and Buz Buckley, centre, were the brothers as children), and Sara Allgood and Arthur Shields (right) were their parents. Also cast were Janet Blair, William Lundigan, James Flavin, William Bakewell, Dave Willock and (as himself) Paul Whiteman. There were guest appearances too, from Henry Busse, Bob Eberly, Charlie Barnet, Mike Pingatore, Ziggy Elman, Art Tatum, Helen O'Connell, Ray Bauduc and Stuart Foster. Charles R. Rogers produced and Alfred E. Green directed. Musical numbers included: *At Sundown* (Dorseys, Whiteman) Walter Donaldson; *I'll Never Say Never Again, Again* (Dorseys band) Harry Woods; *To Me* (Tommy Dorsey, Blair, Lundigan) Allie Wrubel, Don George; *Green Eyes* (Jimmy Dorsey, Eberly, O'Connell) Nilo Menendez, Adolfo Utrera, English lyrics E. Rivera, Eddie Woods; *Dorsey Concerto* (Dorseys, Whiteman) Leo Shuken, Ray Bauduc; *Art's Blues* (Dorseys, Tatum, Barnet, Busse, Elman, Bauduc) Tatum; *Everybody's Doin' It* (local band) Irving Berlin; *Marie* (Tommy Dorsey, Blair, Foster, Dorsey Band) Berlin; *The Object Of My Affection* (Dorsey Brothers Band) Pinky Tomlin, Coy Poe, Jimmie Grier; *Runnin' Wild* (Dorsey Brothers Band) Joe Grey, Leo Wood, A. Harrington Gibbs; *When You And I Were Young Maggie* (Dorseys band) James Austin Butterfield, George W. Johnson; *Waitin' At The Gate For Katy* Richard Whiting, Gus Kahn.

Set during the roistering years of the motion picture's infancy, **The Perils of Pauline** (Paramount) gave Betty Hutton (illustrated) her best role to date as serial queen Pearl White. And although the screenplay by P.J. Wolfson and Frank Butler was in many instances sheer fabrication, it made for unbridled, high-spirited entertainment. Several old-timers, including Paul Panzer, Hank Mann, James Finlayson, Creighton Hale, Bert Roach and Chester Conklin were on hand to provide the touch of verisimilitude so conspicuously absent from the scenario; and there were a few amusing scenes depicting the haphazard way movies were shot before they found their voice. John Lund costarred as Hutton's romantic involvement and contributed very little to the boy-meets-girl romance that developed between them, with other roles going to Billy De Wolfe as a Shakespearean ham, William Demarest as a movie director, and Constance Collier as an ageing trouper. Hutton sang several Frank Loesser songs in that inimitable way of hers, the best being 'Poppa Don't Preach To Me', one of her biggest commercial hits. Billy Daniels choreographed, George Marshall directed with little sense of period but with a compensating flair for humour, and the Technicolor production was in the hands of Sol C. Siegel. Other songs and musical numbers: *I Wish I Didn't Love You So*; *Rumble Rumble Rumble*; *The Sewing Machine* Loesser; *Poor Pauline* Raymond Walker, Charles McCarron.

New Orleans from United Artists, wasted a lot of hot jazz on a cold plot (by Elliot Paul and Herbert J. Biberman, screenplay by Paul and Dick Irving Hyland). With such musicians as Louis Armstrong, Billie Holiday, Woody Herman, Kid Ory, Zutty Singleton, Barney Bigard, Bud Scott, Charle Beale, Red Callender and Meade Lux Lewis on hand, it was criminal that its scenarists couldn't have come up with anything stronger than a story about a young girl (Dorothy Patrick) who has to make a choice between the worlds of classical music and jazz. Basically a potted history of jazz, spanning forty years, it was limply directed by Arthur Lubin for producer Jules Levey, the best thing in it being 'Do You Know What It Means To Miss New Orleans' (by Edgar De Lange and Louis Alter) marvellously performed by Armstrong (illustrated centre) and His All Stars, Billie Holiday, Woody Herman and Dorothy Patrick. Arturo de Cordova was the male lead (and the object of Miss Patrick's

affections) and Shelley Winters was seen briefly as his secretary, with other roles going to Irene Rich as Patrick's society-orientated mother, John Alexander, Richard Hageman and Marjorie Lord. Other musical numbers included: *Endie* (Armstrong, Herman); *The Blues Are Brewin'* (Armstrong Holiday, Herman) Alter, De Lange; *Where The Blues Were Born In New Orleans* (Armstrong) Bob Carleton, Cliff Dixon; *New Orleans Stomp* (Patrick) Joe 'King' Oliver; *West End Blues* (Armstrong) 'King' Oliver, Clarence Williams; *Buddy Bolden's Blues* (Armstrong) Jelly Roll Morton; *Dippermouth Blues* (Armstrong) 'King' Oliver; *Shim-Me-Sha-Wabble* (Armstrong) Spencer Williams; *Honky Tonk Train Blues* Meade Lux Lewis; *Basin Street Blues* (Armstrong); Spencer Williams; *Mahogany Hall Stomp* (Armstrong) Spencer Williams; *Farewell To Storyville* (Armstrong, Holiday) Spencer Williams; *Maryland, My Maryland* (Armstrong) James Ryder Randall, Walter de Mapes.

Choreographer Jack Cole made the biggest contribution to **Down To Earth** (Columbia), a lush fantasy in gorgeous Technicolor which reintroduced the character of Mr Jordan (Roland Culver), first seen in the delightful 1941 comedy *Here Comes Mr Jordan* (Columbia) in which he was played by Claude Rains. Jordan, who operates from on high, is capable of manipulating mere mortals to satisfy his own caprices and, on this occasion, sends Terpsichore (Rita Hayworth, illustrated) down to earth as the star of a musical comedy. Enter Jack Cole, whose production numbers gave a basically insubstantial tale what little substance it had. A Greek ballet with music by Mario Castelnuovo-Tedesco, was especially effective, with Hayworth looking breathtakingly beautiful throughout. Larry Parks co-starred as the show's director – a philistine who'd rather have his star perform in swingtime than indulge in classical lyricism, and their very mortal romance padded out much of the plot. Marc Platt was the featured male dancer, with Edward Everett Horton (as Messenger 7013) and James Gleason as fight-manager-turned-agent Max Corkle repeating the roles they had created in the earlier film. Edwin Blum and Don Hartman's screenplay also found parts for Adele Jergens, George Macready, William Frawley, Jean Donahue, Kathleen O'Malley and William Haade. It was produced by Hartman, and the director was Alexander Hall (who had also directed *Here Comes Mr Jordan*). Miss Hayworth's vocals were dubbed by Anita Ellis and Adele Jergens's by Kay Starr. Other songs and musical numbers included: *The Nine Muses*; *They Can't Convince Me*; *This Can't Be Legal*; *People Have More Fun Than Anyone*; *Let's Stay Young Forever* Doris Fisher, Allan Roberts.

△

Another Gay Nineties musical biopic from 20th Century-Fox, **I Wonder Who's Kissing Her Now** gave star billing to June Haver whose blatant lack of star quality did nothing to prevent the film from grossing over $3,000,000. Her co-star Mark Stevens (illustrated) also lacked charisma but had the more substantial role of the two, playing Joe Howard the composer, on whose life the film was ever-so-loosely based. With the Haver-Stevens combination so bereft of personality it was left to Technicolor, some sweetly nostalgic old songs and a few kitschy production numbers (staged by Hermes Pan, the most characteristic being the title number) to inject a few red corpuscles into a basically anaemic entertainment. A running cliché even had composer Stevens (vocals dubbed by Buddy Clark) suddenly finding inspiration for a lyric after Haver walks out on him and, in a mood of regret and remorse, he wonders who's kissing her now. Still, George Jessel's production satisfied all the prerequisites of the period Fox musical, and audiences kindly disposed to moving wallpaper, found it a painless, even pleasant experience. Martha Stewart and Lenore Aubert were the 'other women' involved in Stevens's life, with Reginald Gardiner (whose dialogue mainly consisted of the phrase 'and so forth, and so forth'), William Frawley, dancer Gene Nelson (his debut), Truman Bradley and George Cleveland completing the cast. The screenplay was by Lewis R. Foster, and the director was Lloyd Bacon, who, 14 years earlier, had directed one of the screen's formative musicals, *42nd Street* (Warner Bros.). Songs and musical numbers: *I Wonder Who's Kissing Her Now* Joe Howard, Frank Adams, Will Hough, Harold Orlob; *Honeymoon*; *What's The Use Of Dreaming?* Howard, Hough; *Hello My Baby* Howard, Ida Emerson; *Oh Gee, Be Sweet To me Kid*; *How'd You Like To Be The Umpire?* Howard, Adams, Hough; *Goodbye My Lady Love* Howard; special material by Charles Henderson and George Jessel.

It took three years for Paramount to reunite ▷ Bing Crosby and Barry Fitzgerald after their success in *Going My Way*. The film was **Welcome Stranger** which, in Arthur Sheekman's screenplay (adaptation by Sheekman and N. Richard Nash, story by Frank Butler), found elderly Doctor Fitzgerald (illustrated) baulking at his new assistant's manner of dress and his love of singing. The local townsfolk don't approve of Crosby either, until he saves Fitzgerald's life by performing a successful appendectomy on him. Trying for the same kind of emotional impact as the earlier film, but succeeding only in being fairly genial entertainment, it co-starred Joan Caulfield (right) as a pretty schoolteacher and volunteer worker in Fitzgerald's clinic, and also featured Wanda Hendrix, Frank Faylen, Elizabeth Patterson, Larry Young, Robert Shayne and Percy Kilbride for producer Sol C. Siegel and director Elliott Nugent. Billy Daniels staged the dances. Songs: *As Long As I'm Dreaming*; *Country Style*; *My Heart Is A Hobo*; *Smile Right Back At The Sun* Johnny Burke, Jimmy Van Heusen.

A bewildering mixture of beautiful music and banality, **Song Of Love** (MGM) lent an entirely unconscious sense of the ridiculous to the relationship between Johannes Brahms and Clara Schumann. A comic riot whose intentions were strictly serious, it starred Katharine Hepburn (left) as Clara, Paul Henreid (right) as Robert Schumann, Robert Walker as Brahms and Henry Daniell as Liszt. The real stars of the enterprise, though, were the four anonymous hands who played the eleven pieces of music featured at various intervals throughout the 119-minute running time. Also cast: Leo G. Carroll, Else Janssen, Roman Bohnen, Ludwig Stossel, Tala Birell, Kurt Katch, Henry Stephenson, and Gigi and Janine Perreau. The Metro Goldwyn Mayer Symphony Orchestra was conducted by William Steinberg. It was written by Ivan Tors, Irmgard Von Cube, Allen Vincent and Robert Ardrey from a play by Bernard Schubert and Mario Silva, and produced and directed with a misguided sense of history by Clarence Brown. Musical items included: *Traumerei, Opus 15, No 7*; *Arabeske, Opus 18*; *Dedication, Opus 25, No 1* Schumann; *Mephisto Waltz* Liszt; *Rhapsody No 2 in G Minor*; *Lullaby* Brahms.

▽

▷

Betty Grable, now earning $150,000 a film, played a character called Myrtle McKinley Burt in **Mother Wore Tights**, another of 20th Century-Fox's tunefully sentimental excursions into the not-so-distant past. This time Grable (right) and her co-star Dan Dailey (centre left) were a happily married vaudeville team whose composure is ruffled only when their elder daughter (Mona Freeman), after a bout of finishing school, develops a snobbish resistance to her folks' vaudeville life-style. In the end, of course, pride replaced prejudice – but not before producer-screenwriter Lamar Trotti made

◁ rather heavy weather of the issue. Still, one way and another, **Mother Wore Tights** (in Technicolor) was one of the year's bouncier musicals, with a solid hit song emerging in 'You Do' (by Mack Gordon and Joseph Myrow). Dailey and Grable were both excellent in their undemanding roles, and so were daughters Freeman and young Connie Marshall (the film was narrated by Anne Baxter as the voice of Marshall grown up). All the supporting performances under Walter Lang's assured direction were fine, including those of Vanessa Brown, Robert Arthur, Sara Allgood, William Frawley, Ruth Nelson, Chick Chandler, George Cleveland, Veda Ann Borg, Lee Patrick and Sig Rumann. There was an effective specialty appearance, too, from the talented Señor Wences. Seymour Felix and Kenny Williams provided the film with its appropriate 'meat-and-potatoes' choreography, the attractive period costumes were by Orry-Kelly, and Alfred Newman was in charge of the musical direction. Other songs and musical numbers: *Burlington Bertie From Bow* William Hargreaves; *Kokomo Indiana*; *There's Nothing Like A Song*; *Rolling Down To Bowling Green*; *This Is My Favourite City*; *Fare Thee Well Dear Alma Mater* Gordon, Myrow; *Tra-la-la-la-la* Gordon, Harry Warren; *Swingin' Down The Lane* Gus Kahn, Isham Jones; *Stumbling* Zez Confrey; *Lily Of The Valley* L. Wolfe Gilbert, Anatole Friedland; *Choo'n Gum* Mann Curtis, Vic Mizzy; *Silent Night* Franz Gruber, Joseph Mohr; Title music: *Ta-ra-ra-boom-de-ay* Henry J. Sayers; *M-O-T-H-E-R* Howard Johnson, Theodore F. Morse; *Put Your Arms Around Me Honey* Albert von Tilzer, Junie McCree; *Daddy, You've Been A Mother To Me* Fred Fisher.

◁ Just as banal, but less pretentious and more entertaining than *Song Of Love*, was **Song Of Scheherezade** (Universal International), an exotic hodge-podge in gaudy Technicolor that featured Jean-Pierre Aumont (illustrated right) as Rimsky-Korsakov, and top-starred Yvonne De Carlo (illustrated left) as Cara, a dancer Rimsky meets in a Spanish-Moroccan port while on his way back to Russia after a world cruise. Cara inspires him to write his most famous composition, 'Scheherazade' and, after a series of Hollywood movie plot contrivances, even gets to dance the leading role when the ballet is premiered at the St Petersburg Opera House. One of the 'campest' of all the costume extravaganzas, its mindless screenplay (by Walter Reisch) was matched only by the vulgarity of the direction (also by Reisch) yet, viewed today, it emerges as compulsively entertaining kitsch. Brian Donlevy co-starred as the chain-smoking captain of the ship on which Rimsky is travelling, with Eve Arden as Madame de Talvera, Miss De Carlo's extravagant, pleasure-loving mother! Philip Reed, John Qualen, Charles Kullman, Richard Lane, Terry Kilburn and George Dolenz also appeared for producer Edward Kaufman, the choreography was by Tilly Losch and Miklos Rosza was in charge of the musical adaptation and direction. The lyrics were by Jack Brooks. Musical numbers: *Gypsy Song*; *Navy March*; *Song Of India*; *Arabesque*; *Hymn To The Sun*; *Flight Of The Bumble Bee*; *Capriccio Espagnole, Opus 35 (Fandango)*; *Song Of Scheherazade*; *Dance Of The Tumblers*.

There was a decided sense of *déjà vu* about **Northwest Outpost** (Republic) (GB: **End Of The Rainbow**). An operetta set in 1838 with a score by Rudolf Friml, it starred Nelson Eddy (right) as the brave Captain Jim, Ilona Massey (2nd left) as the beautiful Natalia, and Joseph Schildkraut as Massey's sinister blackmailing husband. Needless to say, Eddy and Massey fall passionately in love and, after the requisite complications to which such plots were prey, find happiness in each other's arms. Hugo Haas and Elsa Lanchester appeared as a governor and his wife, with Lenore Ulric, Peter Whitney (left), Tamara Shayne (centre), Erno Verebes, George Sorel, Rick Vallin and the American GI chorus completing the cast. Elizabeth Meehan and Richard Sale wrote it from a story by Angela Stuart that was clearly inspired by the numerous MacDonald-Eddy operettas that preceded it in the thirties; and the adaptation was by Laird Doyle. Edward Heyman provided the lyrics, and it was produced and directed by Allan Dwan. **Northwest Outpost** was Eddy's last film: what a pity it was so undistinguished an exit for him. Songs and musical numbers: *Weary*; *Tell Me With Your Eyes*; *One More Mile To Go*; *Raindrops On A Drum*; *Love Is The Time*; *Nearer and Dearer* Friml, Heyman; *Russian Easter Hymn* (traditional).
▽

A star-studded tribute to variety clubs and the ▷ excellent work undertaken by them, **Variety Girl** was a variable *pot pourri* that amassed the services of practically every artist under contract to Paramount at the time to give marquee value to a slender story about a pair of hopefuls (Mary Hatcher and Olga San Juan) who head for Hollywood and possible stardom. DeForest Kelley, William Demarest, Frank Faylen, Frank Ferguson and Glenn Tryon were also featured but it was the guest stars who kept interrupting Edmund Hartmann, Frank Tashlin, Robert Welch and Monte Brice's screenplay that the customers came to see. They included: Alan Ladd, Dorothy Lamour, Pearl Bailey, Gary Cooper, Bob Hope (right), Bing Crosby (left), Barry Fitzgerald, Billy De Wolfe, Judy Canova, Diana Lynn, Ray Milland, Spike Jones, Robert Preston, Cass Daley, Paulette Goddard, Barbara Stanwyck, Veronica Lake, Sonny Tufts, Joan Caulfield, William Holden, Lizabeth Scott, Burt Lancaster, Gail Russell, Sterling Hayden, John Lund, William Bendix, Howard Da Silva, MacDonald Carey, and directors Cecil B. De Mille, Mitchell Leisen and Frank Butler. Unaccountably missing: Betty Hutton and Eddie Bracken. Highlights were a golfing sequence with Hope and Crosby, who also sang a song together called 'Harmony' (by Johnny Burke and Jimmy Van Heusen), Pearl Bailey singing 'Tired' (by Doris Fisher and Allan Roberts) and Alan Ladd and Dorothy Lamour doing Frank Loesser's 'Tallahassee', as well as a Puppetoon colour cartoon sequence ('Romeow and Julie-cat'). The dances were staged by Billy Daniels and Bernard Pearce, Daniel Dare produced and the director was George Marshall. Other songs and musical numbers included: *He Can Waltz*; *The French*; *Your Heart Calling Mine*; *Impossible Things*; *I Must Have Been Madly In Love*; *I Want My Money Back* Loesser; *Tiger Rag* Jelly Roll Morton.

Little Margaret O'Brien received star billing in ▷ **The Unfinished Dance** (MGM), a glossy but cloying remake of Jean Benoit-Levy's touching French film *Ballerina* (1938). The story of a poor orphan (O'Brien) and how her hero-worshipping devotion to a famous ballerina (Cyd Charisse) results in a tragic accident when, mistakenly believing newcomer Karin Booth to be a threat to Charisse's supremacy in the company, she inadvertently pulls the wrong switch during a performance (see illustration), causing Miss Booth to fall through a trap door and injure her spine, it pulled all the wrong switches where the emotions were concerned, substituting bathos for pathos. Danny Thomas as O'Brien's guardian added his own particular brand of syrup to Myles Connolly's already oversweet screenplay (based on Paul Morand's story *La Mort Du Cygne*), with Esther Dale, Thurston Hall, Harry Hayden, Mary Eleanor Donahue, Ruth Brady, Ann Codee and Gregory Gaye adequate in supporting roles. David Lichine was in charge of the choreography, it was produced (in Technicolor) by Joe Pasternak and directed by Henry Koster, a measure of whose superficial approach to the film could be judged by the fact that, after Miss Booth's spinal injury, she is never ever seen to be physically afflicted in her manner of walking – thus negating the whole point of the story. Musical numbers: *Holiday For Strings* David Rose; *I Went Merrily On My Way* Sammy Fain, Irving Kahal; excerpts from Smetana's *The Bartered Bride*, Tchaikovsky's *Swan Lake*, Gounod's *Faust*, Kreisler's *Liebesfreud*; Beethoven's *Symphony No. 2*.

Forties Musicals

Like so many musical biopics of the period, **My Wild Irish Rose** (Warner Bros.) chose to inflict on audiences an account of the life of a composer in which it was difficult to tell fact from fantasy. In this case, the subject was Chauncey Olcott, whose claim to fame was a couple of well-known tunes such as 'Mother Machree' (which he wrote with Ernest R. Ball and Rida Johnson Young) and 'When Irish Eyes Are Smiling' (with Ball and George Graff Jr). Dennis Morgan (centre), with a curious Irish brogue, played Olcott, whose existence, if the screenplay (by Peter Milne, story by Rita Olcott) was anything to judge by, must have been extremely dull and depressing. Doing their best to penetrate the clichés were Andrea King as Lillian Russell, George O'Brien as Iron Duke Muldoon and, by way of a cheering bonus, beautiful newcomer Arlene Dahl (right) as the girl Olcott marries. There was an attempt to pep the whole thing up with some interminable specialty dances performed by Igor Dega, Pierre Andre, The Three Dunhills, and Louis Willis Jr, and the rest of the cast included Ben Blue, Sara Allgood, William Frawley and Don McGuire (left). David Butler directed for producer William Jacobs who, in spite of the mediocre quality of the piece, turned in a box-office hit. Other songs and musical numbers: *Wee Rose Of Killarney; Miss Lindy Lou; There's Room In My Heart For Them All; The Natchez And The Robert E. Lee* M.K. Jerome, Ted Koehler; *One Little, Sweet Little Girl* Dan Sullivan; *My Wild Irish Rose* Olcott; *A Little Bit Of Heaven* J. Keirn Brennan, Ball; *My Nellie's Blue Eyes* William J. Scanlan; *Come Down Ma' Evenin' Star* Edgar Smith, John Stromberg.

Undeniably good-looking, but bereft of a single original idea, **This Time For Keeps** (MGM) was a glossy and trivial boy-meets-girl story embroidered with a mixture of pop and classical music in producer Joe Pasternak's corny old way. Esther Williams (as the star of a spectacular 'aquacaper') was the girl, Johnnie Johnston (the wealthy son of an operatic tenor) the boy, and Mackinac Island the setting for their on-off-on romance. Jimmy Durante (illustrated – as Williams's faithful bodyguard-cum-pianist) was in it too, and brightened up the proceedings whenever he was allowed to – most memorably in an attempt to find the lost chord. Lauritz Melchior (as Johnston's tenor-father) received second billing, and redressed the light-hearted musical balance by singing 'M'Appari' from Flotow's *Martha* and 'La Donna E Mobile' from Verdi's *Rigoletto*. He also sang Cole Porter's 'Easy To Love'. Other musical highlights were a water ballet designed to display the aquatic

◁ A programmer from PRC, **Linda Be Good** starred Elyse Knox as an authoress who, while her husband (John Hubbard, centre) is out of town, joins a burlesque show in order to absorb local colour for a new novel she is writing. Complications set in when Miss Knox (centre left), in the company of dumb blonde Marie Wilson (centre right, a strip queen) is dated by her husband's married boss (Gordon Richards). Finale has Knox blackmailing Richards into giving her husband a vice-presidency. It came and went without anyone noticing the difference. Jack Norton, Ralph Sandford, Joyce Compton, Frank Scannell, Sir Lancelot, Lenny Breman and Byron Foulger were also cast, and a guest spot featured Professor Lamberti. The screenplay was by Leslie Vale and George Halasz (original story by Richard Irving Hyland and Howard Harris), Matty Kemp produced, and Frank McDonald directed. Songs and musical numbers included: *Old Woman With The Rolling Pin; Young Girls Of Today* Sir Lancelot; *My Mother Says I Mustn't* Jack Mason, Sy Miller; *Linda Be Good* Mason, Charles Herbert.

talents of Miss Williams, and Durante's singing of his own and Ben Ryan's 'Inka Dinka Doo'. Completing the cast were Dame May Whitty, Sharon McManus, Dick Simmons, Mary Stuart, Ludwig Stossel, Dorothy Porter, Nella Walker, Holmes Herbert and, playing themselves, Tommy Wonder and Xavier Cugat (and his orchestra). The screenplay was by Gladys Lehman from a story by Erwin Gelsey and Lorraine Fielding, it was choreographed by Stanley Donen, and directed with little sense of rhythm or pace by Richard Thorpe. Other musical numbers: *Chiquita Banana* Leonard Mackenzie, Garth Montgomery, William Wirges; *No Wonder They Fall In Love; Ten Per Cent Off* Ralph Freed, Sammy Fain; *The Man Who Found The Lost Chord; A Little Bit Of This And A Little Bit Of That* Durante; *Why Don't They Let Me Sing A Love Song?; Little Big Shot* Benny Davis, Harry Akst; *I Love To Dance* Freed, Burton Lane; *When It's Lilac Time On Mackinac Island* Leslie Kirk.

△

Though purists might argue that **Living In A Big Way** (MGM) was not, strictly speaking, a musical, it did contain three numbers which its star Gene Kelly choreographed (assisted by Stanley Donen) and performed. In the first, Kelly and his co-star Marie McDonald danced in an Astaire-Rogers-like fashion to 'It Had To Be You' (by Gus Kahn and Isham Jones); the second, a number called 'Fido And Me' (by Louis Alter and Edward Heyman), was danced by Kelly and a little dog around a statue in a garden, and was all about rejection (both the dog and Kelly having been rejected by Miss McDonald); while the third took place in, under and over the skeletal frame of an incomplete apartment block and made effective use of metal rings, step-ladders and planks of wood. The number, performed with children, to the accompaniment of 'Ring Around The Rosy', 'In And Out The Windows', 'Loo By Loo' and 'Yankee Doodle', was quint-essential Kelly in its athleticism and in the easy, spontaneous way the youngsters in it were involved. Stylishly directed by Gregory La Cava, the film cast Kelly (illustrated) as a soldier who meets and marries a girl (McDonald) the night before he is drafted, only to discover, once the war is over, that she is a millionairess and always has been. He bitterly regrets the marriage and wants a divorce. A box-office catastrophe and rarely seen today, its theme – that of the proletariat versus the good life – was a favourite of its director who, although working in familiar territory, was able to eschew stereotype characterizations and avoid sentimentality. It deserved a better fate than it received. Also cast: Charles Winninger, Phyllis Thaxter, Spring Byington, Jean Adair, Shelley Winters and Clinton Sundberg. It was written by La Cava and Irving Ravetch; Pandro S. Berman produced.

Two Blondes And A Redhead (Columbia) starred Jean Porter (foreground left) as a society girl who plays hookey from her exclusive girls' school and appears in the chorus of a musical. When the show closes, she invites two of her chorine friends to her hometown, whereupon all sorts of complications filled out the 69-minute running time. June Preisser (foreground right) and Judy Clark (centre) were Miss Porter's chums, with other roles in Sam Katzman's routine production going to Jimmy Lloyd (as a rich lad pretending to be a servant), Rick Vallin, Charles Smith, Douglas Wood and Regina Wallace. Also featured: Tony Pastor (foreground centre) and His Orchestra. It was written by Victor McLeod and Jameson Brewer from a story by Harry Rebuas, and directed by Arthur Dreifuss. Songs: *It's So Easy; All I Know Is Si Si* Doris Fisher, Allan Roberts; *Boogie Woogie From Nowhere* Saul Chaplin; *On The Sunny Side Of The Street* Dorothy Fields, Jimmy McHugh.

▽

Yet another backwoods-to-Broadway yarn, **Glamour Girl** (Columbia) starred Gene Krupa, whose main contribution to the M. Coates Webster-Lee Gold screenplay was an all-out performance on drums of Segar Ellis and George Williams's 'Gene's Boogie'. Otherwise the plot revolved around a zither-plucking singer (Susan Reed, centre) who's discovered in the sticks by a record talent scout (Virginia Grey, right) and brought to New York, where she finds instant anonymity. Undaunted, Grey and partner Michael Duane (left) start a company of their own and, in no time at all (68 minutes), Miss Reed is the talk of the town. Jack Leonard, singer Carolyn Grey, Jimmy Lloyd, Pierre Watkin and Eugene Borden were adequate in support. Sam Katzman produced and Arthur Dreifuss directed. Other songs and musical numbers included: *Anywhere* Jule Styne, Sammy Cahn; *Without Imagination* Allan Roberts, Doris Fisher.

▽

△

June Allyson was not the greatest singer on MGM's roster, and Peter Lawford's song-and-dance efforts would give Astaire no sleepless nights, but that didn't stop **Good News** (MGM), a colourful remake of the campest of all campus comedies, from being knockout entertainment. The plot was pretty similar to the original 1930 version, but this time it was Patricia Marshall who set her sights on the football hero (Lawford) and demure little June who finally got him. With Charles Walters and Robert Alton in charge of the dances, the film rated an 'A' for ebullience, from its rousingly vigorous opening ensemble performance of the title tune to its spirited finale 'The Varsity Drag' (illustrated, with Allyson and Lawford foreground), both numbers by Buddy De Sylva, Lew Brown and Ray Henderson, the latter engagingly performed by Allyson and Lawford as they led the company in a complex, but fluently controlled *mélange* of high-stepping dance patterns. Zesty Joan McCracken, fresh from Broadway's *Bloomer Girl* and *Billion Dollar Baby*, contributed some wry comedy and led the chorus in another choreographic highlight 'Pass That Peace Pipe' (by Roger Edens, Ralph Blane and Hugh Martin) which for *élan* and inventiveness ranks with the Hollywood musical's best. But every number was a gem: Allyson and Lawford's 'The French Lesson', written especially for the film by Roger Edens, with lyrics by Betty Comden and Adolph Green, who also contributed the screenplay (their first), and the other De Sylva, Brown and Henderson numbers from the original score: 'Just Imagine', plaintively warbled by Allyson, 'Lucky In Love' sung by all the principals in turn in another expertly staged ensemble sequence, 'He's A Ladies' Man', buoyantly performed by Lawford, Ray McDonald and Mel Torme and the durable ballad 'The Best Things In Life Are Free', sung first by Allyson, and later reprised by Mel Torme and (in French) by Lawford. Robert Strickland, Donald MacBride, Tom Dugan, Clinton Sundberg, Loren Tindall and Connie Gilchrist were also cast. Arthur Freed produced (in Technicolor) and Charles Walters made an impressive directorial debut. **Good News** originally started life as a Broadway musical by Lawrence Schwab, Frank Mandel, De Sylva, Brown and Henderson in 1927 and ran 557 performances.

1948

Heavy on musical numbers, light on plot (air hostess becomes a bandsinger), **Mary Lou** (Columbia) starred Joan Barton (right), Robert Lowery (as her boyfriend), Glenda Farrell, Abigail Adams, Frank Jenks, Emmett Vogan, Thelma White, Pierre Watkin, Chester Clute, and Frankie Carle and His Orchestra. Passable double-bill support, it was written by M. Coates Webster, choreographed by Jack Doyle, produced by Sam Katzman and directed by Arthur Dreifuss. Songs and musical numbers: *Mary Lou* J.R. Robinson, Abe Lyman, George Waggner; *Don't Mind My Troubles*; *I'm Sorry I Didn't Say I'm Sorry* Allan Roberts, Lester Lee; *That's Good Enough For Me*; *Wasn't It Swell Last Night?* Roberts, Doris Fisher; *Carle's Boogie* Frankie Carle; *Learning To Speak English* Facundo Rivero, Ben Blossner.

A quickie from Republic, **Campus Honeymoon** concerned a marriage of convenience between two young war veterans (Richard Crane, 2nd left, and Hal Hackett, left) and a couple of sisters (the Wilde twins, Lyn and Lee, illustrated). Unmarried, the men are not eligible for a pair of houses in a special veteran's housing project, hence the 'arrangement'. But in no time at all the ex-GIs find they really *are* in love with the girls, and vice versa, the assumption at the end of 61 minutes of lightweight joviality being that they all live happily ever after. It was produced by Fanchon with a cast that also included Adele Mara, Wilson Wood and Stephanie Bachelor, and directed by Richard Sale who also scripted it, with Jerry Gruskin, from a story by Thomas R. St George. Songs included: *How Does It Feel to Fall In Love?*; *Who's Got A Tent For Rent?*; *Are You Happening To Me?* Sale, Gruskin; *Rocked In The Cradle Of The Deep* J.P. Knight, Emma Willard; *It's So Nice To Have A Man About The House* Jack Elliott, Harold Spina; *Opalooka Song* Sale, Nathan Scott.

The fifth, and most conventional of the 'Road' films, **Road To Rio** (Paramount) relied more on its storyline than on the anachronistic 'sight' gags that had hitherto dominated the series and, compared to *Road To Utopia* (Paramount, 1946) was a sober effort indeed. Compared to most other comedies, though, it was a riot. Crosby (left foreground) and Hope (centre) played a pair of musicians who, after accidentally setting fire to a carnival, sail for Rio. On board ship they meet Dorothy Lamour (right) a mysterious beauty whose mercurial changes in temperament baffle them – until they realize that she is being hypnotized by her aunt (Gale Sondergaard) into marrying a man in Brazil she does not love. With its attractive score by Johnny Burke and Jimmy Van Heusen, whose three best numbers were 'You Don't Have To Know The Language' sung by Crosby and The Andrews Sisters (appearing as themselves), 'But Beautiful', which became a Crosby standard, and 'Experience', sung by Lamour, plus a laugh-laden screenplay by Edmund Beloin and Jack Rose, **Road To Rio** was an appealing package of fun that outgrossed every other film in 1948. Frank Faylen and Joseph Vitale were the obligatory heavies, with other roles going to the Wiere Brothers as a trio of whacky Brazilian entertainers, Nestor Paiva, Robert Barrat, Frank Puglia, Jerry Colonna, Charles Middleton and Stanley Andrews. The dances were staged by Bernard Pearce and Billy Daniels, Daniel Dare produced and the director was Norman Z. McLeod. Other songs and musical numbers: *Apalachicola Fla*; *Cavaquinho* Burke, Van Heusen; *Brazil* Ary Barroso, English lyrics Bob Russell.

Though not dissimilar in plot to producer Joe Pasternak's *Three Smart Girls* (Universal, 1937), MGM's **Three Daring Daughters** (GB: **The Birds And The Bees**), also produced by Pasternak, had the advantage of Technicolor and, instead of Miss Durbin dominating the proceedings, top-starred Jeanette MacDonald (in her penultimate film). As a magazine editor, and divorced mother of three self-consciously cute daughters, Miss M. (2nd right) brought a welcome dollop of sophistication to the narrative. Jose Iturbi (playing himself, 2nd left) received second billing and, in his most substantial screen role to date, was required by the Albert Mannheimer-Frederick Kohner-Sonya Levien-John Meehan screenplay, to become Miss MacDonald's husband! Plot pivoted on the objections to the relationship lodged by MacDonald's three young daughters (Jane Powell, centre, Mary Eleanor Donahue, right, Ann E. Todd, left), who are under the much mistaken impression that their divorced father (a newspaperman) is a paragon of virtue. The girls are eventually won over by Iturbi who proves to them that he is just as much at home playing Bobby Troup's 'Route 66', as he is with Liszt's 'Liebestraum'. The film's one durable hit was 'The Dickey Bird Song' by Sammy Fain and Howard Dietz, charmingly sung by MacDonald and her three offspring, and reprised with Iturbi at the piano. The Iturbis – Amparo joined her brother – on twin pianos played Enesco's Rumanian Rhapsody in A, Opus 11, No I, with Larry Adler on the harmonica, and full orchestra. Edward Arnold was cast as the 'thirteenth richest man in the world' and the boss of MacDonald's (unseen) ex-husband, with other parts under the *schmaltzy* eye of director Fred Wilcox going to Harry Davenport, Moyna McGill, Kathryn Card, Richard Simmons, Thurston Hall, and Virginia Brissac. Dorothy Porter also appeared as herself and the Misses Donahue and Todd's singing was dubbed by Beverly Jean Garbo and Pat Hyatt respectively. Interesting sideline: The film was considered 'morally objectionable in part or all' by the Catholic League of Decency as it 'tended to justify as well as accept the respectability of divorce'. Other songs and musical numbers: *Alma Mater* Georgie Stoll, Billy Katz; *Fleurette* Victor Herbert, Ralph Freed; *Passepied* Leo Delibes, Princess Anna Eristoff; *Where There's Love* (based on a waltz from 'Der Rosenkavalier') Richard Strauss, Earl Brent; *Ritual Fire Dance* (El Amor Brujo) Manuel de Falla; *You Made Me Love You* Joseph McCarthy, James V. Monaco; *Happy Birthday* Patty Smith Hill, Mildred J. Hill; *Je Veux Vivre* (Juliet's Waltz from 'Romeo et Juliette') Gounod; *Hungarian Fantasy* Liszt; *Sweethearts* Victor Herbert, Bob Wright, Chet Forrest; *Allegro Appassionato, Opus 10* Saint-Saens; *Springtide* (*An den Fruhling*) *Opus 43, No 6* Edward Grieg, Earl Brent; Coda of the fourth movement of Tchaikovsky's *Fourth Symphony*; *Piano Sonata No 11 in A, K331* Mozart. ▽

That exhausted, if not entirely dead, horse, the backstage musical, was flogged again in **April Showers** (Warner Bros.), a damp excursion into the ups and downs of vaudeville. On this occasion, Jack Carson (left) played Joe Thyme (known as Big Thyme), the head of a family act called 'The Three Happy Thymes'. Joe hits the bottle and causes the disintegration of the act, whose members each go their sad and separate ways. But, as written by Peter Milne from a story by Joe Laurie Jr, an opportunity on Broadway reunites the little band who, unlike the film – become a smash hit. Carson's unfortunate wife and his extrovert son were played by Ann Sothern (right) and Robert Ellis, with the ubiquitous S.Z. Sakall (foreground), Richard Robert and Robert Alda in support, James Kern directed for producer William Jacobs. Songs and musical numbers included: *Little Trouper* Kim Gannon, Walter Kent; *World's Most Beautiful Girl* Gannon, Ted Fetter; *It's Tulip Time In Holland* Dave Radford, Richard A. Whiting; *April Showers* Buddy De Sylva, Louis Silvers; *Carolina In The Morning* Gus Kahn, Walter Donaldson.

Eddie Cantor produced and starred in **If You Knew Susie** (RKO), a nebulous brew of songs and gags mixed in with an idiot plot about a retired vaudevillian (Cantor, 2nd left) who discovers that the US government, as a result of a financial transaction undertaken with his ancestors, owes him a fortune in back interest. Joan Davis (left) co-starred as his wife, with other parts in Warren Wilson and Oscar Brodney's laboured screenplay (additional dialogue by Bud Peterson and Lester A. White) going to Bobby Driscoll (right) and Margaret Kelly (as Cantor's offspring), Allyn Joslyn, Charles Dingle, Sheldon Leonard, Joe Sawyer, Dick Humphreys (centre) and Peggy Lynch (2nd right). Charles O'Curran choreographed, Gordon M. Douglas directed. Songs and musical numbers included: *If You Knew Susie* Buddy De Sylva, Joseph Meyer; *My How The Time Goes By; My Brooklyn Love Song; What Do I Want With Money?; Living The Life I Love* Harold Adamson, Jimmy McHugh.

Tony Martin (left) was cast as Pepe Le Moko in **Casbah** (Universal International), the third version of the story which bears its hero's name (the other two being the French *Pepe Le Moko* with Jean Gabin; and *Algiers* United Artists, 1938, starring Charles Boyer). Though not ideal casting, his handling of the interpolated songs was more than adequate, underlining the impression that he was better at singing than he was at crime. Marta Toren was the woman whose love he dies for, with other featured roles in Ladislaus Bus-Fekete and Arnold Manoff's screenplay (based on the novel by Detective Ashelbe, and a 'musical' adaptation by Erik Charell) going to Hugo Haas as a Casbah guide, Peter Lorre (excellent) as Inspector Slimane and Yvonne De Carlo (centre). Also cast: Thomas Gomez, Douglas Dick (right), Herbert Rudley, Virginia Gregg, and Katherine Dunham and her dancers. It was produced by Nat G. Goldstone, choreographed by Bernard Pearce, and directed by John Berry. Songs and musical numbers: *For Every Man There's A Woman; It Was Written In The Stars; Hooray For Love; What's Good About Goodbye?* Harold Arlen, Leo Robin. ▽

Campus Sleuth (GB: **Smart Politics**) a musical whodunnit, was a time-waster from Monogram that involved Freddie Stewart and June Preisser (both illustrated) in a campus murder. In this instance it was difficult to tell who the victim was: a dead magazine photographer or the paying customers out front. Warren Mills, Noel Neill, Donald MacBride, Monte Collins and Stan Ross were also in it; so were Bobby Sherwood and His Orchestra and Gerri Gallian and his piano. Hal Collins wrote it from a story by himself and Max Wilson, Will Jason produced and directed. It was thankfully all over in 57 minutes. Songs: *Baby You Can Count On Me; What Happened?; Neither Could I; Jungle Rhumba; Sherwood's Forest* Will Jason, Sid Robin. ▽

Donald O'Connor did one excellent number in **Are You With It?** (Universal International) – a really bravura piece of hoofing – and it took place in a restaurant. Most of the film, however, was set in a Carnival, and nothing its young star perpetrated there matched his energetic dancing in the earlier sequence. In fact a boringly, albeit elaborately, staged ballet which climaxed the film was, frankly, an embarrassment (choreography by Louis Da Pron). Top-billed O'Connor (left) played a mathematical genius who joins a carnival when he is fired for misplacing a decimal point, Olga San Juan was his romantic object, and Lew Parker (in the role he originally played in the Broadway show of the same name), a carnival pitch man. Also cast: Martha Stewart, George O'Hanlon (right), Walter Catlett, Pat Dane, Ransom Sherman, Louis Da Pron, Noel Neill and Julie Gibson. O'Connor mugged his way through most of Oscar Brodney's undemanding screenplay (based on the Sam Perrin-George Balzer stageshow), his rubber face working overtime in a routine called 'Down At Baba's Alley' (by Sidney Miller and Inez James, who contributed all of the music). Robert Arthur produced and it was directed by Jack Hively. Other songs and musical numbers were: *It Only Takes A Little Imagination*; *What Do I Have To Do To Make You Love Me?*; *Daddy Surprise Me*; *I'm Looking For A Prince Of A Fellow*; *Are You With It?*.

First seen on Broadway in 1945, with a score by Sigmund Romberg and a book by Herbert and Dorothy Fields, **Up In Central Park** (Universal International) came to the screen shorn of most of its songs – a considerable miscalculation from which the film never recovered, especially as its star, Deanna Durbin (illustrated) was a far better singer than she was an actress. Set in New York when Tammany Hall was in its heyday, it featured Durbin as the immigrant daughter of a park superintendent (Albert Sharpe) who, together with *New York Times* reporter John Matthews (Dick Haymes) manages to uncover the crooked political activities of Boss Tweed (Vincent Price) and his organization. As both Haymes and Price were miscast and Miss Durbin misused, there wasn't much value for money in Karl Tunberg's production (Tunberg also scripted it) and, not surprisingly, it repeated its disappointing Broadway history by failing to find mass audience support. Completing the cast were Tom Powers, Hobart Cavanaugh, Thurston Hall, Howard Freeman, Mary Field, Tom Pedi and Moroni Olsen. The director was William A. Seiter. Songs: *Oh Say, Do You See What I See?*; *When She Walks In The Room*; *Carousel In The Park* Romberg, Fields; *Pace, Pace Mio Dio* (from 'La Forza Del Destino') Verdi.

Scripted by Whitfield Cook and Anne Morrison Chapin (additional dialogue by Aben Kandel) from a story by Miklos Laszlo as adapted by Nanette Kutner, **Big City** (MGM) was the sentimental story of an orphan who finds herself adopted by a Jewish cantor (Danny Thomas), a Protestant minister (Robert Preston) and an Irish-Catholic cop (George Murphy). As the orphan was played by top-starred Margaret O'Brien (illustrated) a dewy-eyed time was had by all. Conflict intruded when cop Murphy marries saloon singer Betty Garrett (her debut) and has the unpopular notion of supplying Miss O'Brien with a *bona fide* mother. But it all worked out satisfactorily, as produced by Joe Pasternak in whose particular make-believe world everything had to be sweetness and light. And musical. Hence little Margaret (dubbed by Marni Nixon) trilled away in company with opera star Lotte Lehmann who (as Thomas's mother) sang 'God Bless America' (by Irving Berlin), Brahms's 'Lullaby', and 'The Kerry Dance' (by James Lyman Molloy). Berlin was also represented by 'What'll I Do?' (sung by Danny Thomas); and from Miss Garrett, fresh from her triumph on Broadway in *Call Me Mister*, came 'Ok'l Baby Dok'l' (by Inez James and Sidney Miller). Also cast: Karin Booth, Edward Arnold, Butch Jenkins, Connie Gilchrist and The Page Cavanaugh Trio. The caring, if over sentimental, direction was by Norman Taurog. Other songs and musical numbers: *Shoo Shoo Baby* Phil Moore; *I'm Gonna See A Lot Of You* Janice Torre, Fred Spielman; *Don't Blame Me* Dorothy Fields, Jimmy McHugh; *Yippee-O-Yippee-Ay Ay* Jerry Seelen, Walter Pepp.

Another *pot-pourri* of animated musical numbers from the Disney studios, **Melody Time** (RKO) was the last of the series and qualitatively on a par with *Make Mine Music* (RKO, 1945). There were seven segments in all, the two best being 'The Story Of Johnny Appleseed' (with Dennis Day's voice as Appleseed), and 'Pecos Bill' which featured Roy Rogers (left), the Sons Of The Pioneers, Bobby Driscoll and Luana Patten (right) in a tale about a youngster raised by coyotes who finds his equal in a wonderhorse called Widowmaker. The film opened with a sequence called 'Once Upon A Wintertime' by Bobby Worth and Ray Gilbert (sung by Frances Langford). This was followed by 'Bumble Boogie', a jazzy version of Rimsky-Korsakov's 'The Flight Of The Bumble Bee' arranged by Jack Fina, and performed by Freddy Martin and His Orchestra, with Fina on piano. 'Johnny Appleseed' came next, and after that The Andrews Sisters sang the story of a young tugboat called 'Little Toot' (by Allie Wrubel). Fred Waring and His Pennsylvanians featured in a rather self-consciously 'arty' sequence called 'Trees' (from the poem by Joyce Kilmer with music by Oscar Rasbach); followed by Ethel Smith and The Dinning Sisters performing 'Blame It On The Samba' (by Ernesto Nazareth and Ray Gilbert) in an item which reunited Donald Duck with Joe Carioca. The finale was the aforementioned 'Pecos Bill'. The production supervisor was Ben Sharpsteen and the cartoon directors Clyde Geronimi, Wilfred Jackson, Hamilton Luske and Jack Kinney. Other songs and musical numbers: *Melody Time* George Weiss, Bennie Benjamin; *The Lord Is Good To Me*; *The Pioneer Song*; *The Apple Song* Kim Gannon, Walter Kent; *Blue Shadows On The Trail*; *Pecos Bill* Eliot Daniel, Johnny Lange.

Three songs, two of which developed into full-scale tap numbers for star Donald O'Connor, helped considerably to enliven **Feudin', Fussin' And A-Fightin'** (Universal International), a slaphappy hunk of hokum in which O'Connor (left) starred as a travelling salesman who, after being kidnapped by the townsfolk of Rimrock, finds himself taking part in their annual footrace against a rival village. O'Connor's taps were tops, and there was some boisterous over-acting from Marjorie Main as Rimrock's stentorian mayor and from Percy Kilbride as a local livery stable owner. Also doing their bit for the backwoods: Joe Besser, Harry Shannon, Fred Kohler Jr, Howland Chamberlin and, for romantic interest, Penny Edwards (right). D.D. Beauchamp scripted it from a story he wrote for *Colliers Magazine*, Leonard Goldstein produced, Louis Da Pron choreographed and the director was George Sherman. Songs and musical numbers included: *S'posin'* Andy Razaf, Paul Denniker; *Me And My Shadow* Al Jolson, Billy Rose, Dave Dreyer; *Feudin' And Fightin'* Al Dubin, Burton Lane.

The Pirate (MGM) produced by Arthur Freed and directed by Vincente Minnelli was, if possible, even more artificial in its 'look' and in the stagey atmosphere it created than the same team's *Yolanda And The Thief* (MGM, 1945). And, like *Yolanda*, it was not a box-office success. The story (with music by Cole Porter) of a strolling player called Serafin who pretends to be the notorious Caribbean pirate, Macoco, in order to win the love of wealthy Manuela, it was pitched at an airless, stifling temperature of 95° in the shade so that the very water in the quay at San Sebastian (the Caribbean Island on which it all takes place) seemed sizzling to the touch. Judy Garland (right) was cast as Manuela and Gene Kelly (left) as Serafin. Giving performances as stylized and as theatrical as Jack Martin Smith's sets, they played all their non-musical scenes in capital letters, and punctuated every gesture with an exclamation mark. The overall results were 'arty' rather than artistic, which explains why the film failed, on its initial release, to find a willing audience for its excesses. The passage of time, however, has allowed for a reassessment of its qualities, and although neither the claustrophobia nor the frenzied quality of the performances has lessened with time, there can be no denying Minnelli's brilliant use of colour throughout. And if the rather tiresome screen-

play (by Albert Hackett and Frances Goodrich, from a play by S.N. Behrman) remains instantly forgettable, what seems to have improved with the years is the dazzling dance direction by Kelly and Robert Alton, 'Nina' being the choreographic highlight of the film. In a routine of sustained inventive brilliance, danced to a catchy bolero rhythm, Kelly, dressed in black trousers, colourful waistcoat and dashing hat, curls himself around decorative poles and clambers over rooftops as he courts every girl in San Sebastian in that overtly masculine manner which is his stylistic trade-mark. It is not only Kelly's *braggadocio* approach to the dance which makes it so appealing, but the editing of the sequence (by Blanche Sewell), the Technicolor photography (by Harry Stradling), the colours chosen by Minnelli to offset it all and, of course, the wizardry of Porter's song. Less inventive, but also visually exciting, is the 'Pirate' ballet, in which Kelly, as Serafin, dances out his fantasy as Macoco, cavorting boisterously up, down and across a screen of billowing mauve clouds and belching smoke. Choreographically it is of much less consequence than 'Nina', and also excrutiatingly noisy. The film's quieter moments arrived in the shape of two Porter ballads, 'You Can Do No Wrong', which followed a wild knock-about scene in which Garland hurled

words as well as objects at Kelly; and 'Love Of My Life', following Kelly and The Nicholas Brothers' energetic 'Be A Clown'. Both ballads were sung, quite marvellously, by Garland, whose other big song was the rousing 'Mack The Black'. Walter Slezak, Gladys Cooper, Reginald Owen and George Zucco all gave supporting performances bordering on caricature. On balance, a memorable failure.

Just as old timer Charles Winninger (right) refused to admit that vaudeville was a thing of the past, and that he and his juggling son and partner, Dan Dailey (left), had missed the boat, so 20th Century-Fox's **Give My Regards To Broadway** refused to admit that backstage sagas of this particular ilk were by now just as *passé*, especially when regurgitated in so makeshift and familiar a fashion as this one was. Fay Bainter played wife and mother to her fretting husband and son, and her two non-show business daughters, Barbara Lawrence (centre) and Jane Nigh. Also cast: Nancy Guild, Charles Russell, Sig Rumann, Howard Freeman, Herbert Anderson and Harry Seymour. Walter Morosco produced, the director was Lloyd Bacon, Seymour Felix staged the routines and it was scripted by Samuel Hoffenstein and Elizabeth Reinhardt from a story by John Klempner. (Technicolor). Songs and musical numbers: *Give My Regards To Broadway* George M. Cohan; *When Frances Dances With Me* Benny Ryan, Sol Violinsky; *Let A Smile Be Your Umbrella* Sammy Fain, Irving Kahal, Francis Wheeler; *Whispering* John Schonberger, Richard Coburn, Vincent Rose; *Where Did You Get That Hat?* J.W. Kelly; *Linger Awhile* Harry Owens, Rose.

Forties Musicals

'There was something about the way she looked at a man that rang bells', claimed the ads for **Lulu Belle**. They were referring to star Dorothy Lamour (illustrated right) as the titular heroine of Charles MacArthur and Edward Sheldon's 1926 Broadway play which came to the screen, via Columbia, in a whitewash job that changed Lulu's profession from prostitute to saloon *chanteuse*, and her face from black to white. Unfortunately, there was nothing about the film that rang bells and nothing about Miss Lamour's underpowered performance to justify the publicity blurb. Set in 1900 and told in flashback, the film catalogued the various romantic dalliances enjoyed by its heroine – from her marriage to attorney George Montgomery, to her liaison with prizefighter Greg McClure, his manager Albert Dekker, and railroad tycoon Otto Kruger who transports her from New Orleans to Broadway where she becomes a star. Not surprisingly, she stops a bullet, at which point the film became something of a whodunnit. Addison Richards, Glenda Farrell (left), Charlotte Wynters, William Haade and Clancy Cooper were also cast by producer Benedict Bogeaus, Everett Freeman scripted it (additional dialogue by Karl Kamb), Nick Castle choreographed, and it was directed by Leslie Fenton. Songs and musical numbers: *Lulu Belle* Edgar De Lange, Henry Russell; *Sweetie Pie* John Lehman, Russell; *I'd Be Lost Without You* Russell; *Ace In The Hole* George Mitchell, James Dempsey; *Sweetheart Of The Blues* Lester Lee, Allan Roberts.
▽

△

Director Billy Wilder's characteristic cynicism was nowhere in evidence in **The Emperor Waltz** (Paramount), a charming fantasy for grown-ups which he both directed and scripted (with producer Charles Brackett). Set against a Technicolored Tyrolean backdrop, in the time of Emperor Franz Joseph, it starred Bing Crosby (right) as a phonograph salesman whose particular assignment is to sell the contraption to a thoroughly uninterested, not to say suspicious, Emperor (Richard Haydn). After being ejected from the royal presence, Crosby attempts to reach the unyielding Emperor through his pretty niece, Johanna Franziska Von Stultzenberg (Joan Fontaine, left). But she, too, will have nothing to do with the travelling salesman, and it is left to their respective pet dogs (his fox terrier, her poodle) to bring them together. Considering the cornball nature of the material, Wilder and Brackett's screenplay was a miracle of invention and resourcefulness that kept it all deliciously palatable. The central performances were completely charming, and there was good work as well from Roland Culver, Lucile Watson, Harold Vermilyea and Sig Rumann. Billy Daniels choreographed. Songs and musical numbers: *Get Yourself A Phonograph* Johnny Burke, Jimmy Van Heusen; *I Kiss Your Hand, Madame* Ralph Erwin, Sam M. Lewis, Joe Young, German lyrics Fritz Rotter; *The Kiss In Your Eyes* Burke (an adaptation, with English lyrics, of 'Im Chambre Separée' from Richard Heuberger's 'Der Opernball'); *Friendly Mountains* (based on traditional Swiss songs) Burke; *The Emperor Waltz* Burke, Johann Strauss (all sung by Crosby).

◁ A former singer with Les Brown's band, Doris Von Kappelhof, better known as Doris Day, achieved international stardom via the Warner Bros. studio in her first film **Romance On The High Seas** (GB: **It's Magic**) much of which, as the title suggested, took place on board a luxury liner. One of those convoluted mistaken identity yarns, the film featured Miss Day (illustrated) as a singer who is hired by a wealthy socialite (Janis Paige) to take her place on an ocean voyage to Rio so that she (Paige) can remain in New York and secretly spy on her husband (Don DeFore) whom she believes is being unfaithful to her. DeFore, meanwhile, suspicious that his wife wants to take a trip without him, hires a detective (Jack Carson, left – top starred) to watch over her! Julius J. and Philip G. Epstein's screenplay (from a story by S. Pondal Rios and Carlos A. Olivari; additional dialogue I.A.L. Diamond) pepped up a basically tired series of situations with several well-written scenes, as did the score by Sammy Cahn and Jule Styne, whose 'It's Magic' and 'Put Em In A Box, Tie 'Em With A Ribbon, And Throw 'Em In The Deep Blue Sea' (both sung by Day) became king-sized hits. Though the star was given fourth billing (the part was originally offered to Judy Garland, then Betty Hutton), she was the undoubted hit of a show whose cast also included Oscar Levant, S.Z. Sakall, Fortunio Bonanova, Eric Blore and Franklin Pangborn, plus specialties Avon Long, Sir Lancelot, The Samba Kings and The Page Cavanaugh Trio. After an absence of nine years Busby Berkeley returned to Warner Bros. to create and stage the dance sequences. Alex Gottlieb produced, and Michael Curtiz directed. Other songs and musical numbers: *It's You Or No One* (Day); *I'm in Love* (Day); *The Tourist Trade* (Sir Lancelot); *Run, Run, Run* (Carson) Cahn, Styne; *Cuban Rhapsody* (Levant) Ray Heindorf, Oscar Levant.

Two Guys From Texas (Warner Bros.) was a lightweight spoof of musical westerns which again teamed Jack Carson (centre) and Dennis Morgan (left) – this time as a couple of not-too-successful song and dance men who end up on a dude ranch where they encounter a series of misadventures and a dose of romance. The screenplay, by I.A.L. Diamond and Allen Boretz (from a play by Louis Pelletier Jr and Robert Sloane), provided a lot of opportunity for comedy which Carson embraced with gusto. Some slick musical numbers, and suitably pacey direction from David Butler, kept the mild diversion going, with adequate support from Dorothy Malone, Penny Edwards (2nd right), Fred Clark, Forrest Tucker, Gerald Mohr and John Alvin. Monte Blue also turned up; so did The Philharmonic Trio. Alex Gottlieb produced. Songs: *Every Day I Love You Just A Little Bit More*; *Hankerin'*; *I Don't Care If It Rains All Night*; *There's Music In The Land*; *I Wanna Be A Cowboy In The Movies* Jule Styne, Sammy Cahn.
▽

It was really Gene Kelly who was responsible for Fred Astaire's return to pictures. A few weeks before shooting on Irving Berlin's **Easter Parade** (MGM) was due to commence, Kelly, who was scheduled to appear in it with Judy Garland, sprained his ankle in a volleyball game and suggested to producer Arthur Freed that Astaire replace him. Freed did not need much persuading; neither, as it turned out, did Astaire. Tired of his period of relative inactivity since his 'retirement' two years earlier, he jumped at the chance of working with Judy Garland and immediately began reworking some of the routines that had been planned for Kelly. The result was the year's best musical. It grossed $4,200,000, making it the second biggest money maker in 1948 (the first was Paramount's *Road To Rio*). Astaire played Don Hewes, a dancer who, at the beginning of the film, is ditched by his partner (Ann Miller) when Ziegfeld beckons her for a part in his new show. Bent on revenge, he determines to prove that he can make a star out of anyone he chooses, selects Garland from a chorus line, and sets about grooming her. At first it isn't easy, the situation being aggravated by the fact that he is still in love with Miller. But time heals everything, makes a thorough pro of Garland and, in the end, she and Astaire find themselves in love with one another – the happy realization coming just in time for them to be seen arm-in-arm in the Fifth Avenue Easter Parade. As backstage romances go, it was no world-beater, but the perfect cue for a casket of Berlin evergreens which its attractive cast (including Peter Lawford as Astaire's best friend) sang and danced with immense *élan*. Of the 17 Berlin standards on offer, the most memorable were Astaire's 'Drum Crazy' solo performed in a toy shop at the start of the film; 'Stepping Out With My Baby', another Astaire routine which innovatively combined slow motion with normal motion at one and the same time; and the joyous 'A Couple Of Swells' sung and danced by Garland and Astaire as tramps (illustrated). Ann Miller's 'The Girl On The Magazine Cover' (sung by Richard Beavers) was the show's big production number, and it was elegantly staged by Robert Alton who was in charge of the dance direction throughout. 'Shaking The Blues Away' was another Miller item (visually stunning in grey and yellow) and, like every other number in this catalogue of delights, was a knockout. Garland's 'Better Luck Next Time' was touchingly delivered to a sympathetic bartender (Clinton Sundberg) and provided a striking contrast to her more energetic numbers, the most exuberant being the catchy title song, and the quartet of oldies ('When the Midnight Choo-Choo Leaves For Alabam', 'Snooky Ookums', 'Ragtime Violin' and 'I Love A Piano') she shared with Astaire. **Easter Parade** was scripted by Sidney Sheldon, Frances Goodrich and Albert Hackett from a story by Hackett and Miss Goodrich, and its cast was completed by Jules Munshin, Jeni Le Gon, Dick Simmons, and specialty dancers Pat Jackson, Dee Turnell and Bobbie Priest. The appropriately bright and breezy direction was by the reliable Charles Walters. Other songs and musical numbers: *Happy Easter* (Astaire); *It Only Happens When I Dance With You* (Astaire, danced by Astaire and Miller, reprised by Garland); *Everybody's Doin' It* (Garland, chorus); *I Want To Go Back To Michigan* (Garland); *Beautiful Faces Need Beautiful Clothes* (Astaire, Garland); *A Fella With An Umbrella* (Lawford, Garland).

A low-budget programmer from Columbia, also low on entertainment, **I Surrender Dear** revolved around a feud between Gloria Jean's (left) orchestra-leader boyfriend (David Street) and her father (Robert Emmett Keane, right) after the former ousts the latter from his radio station job by becoming a disc jockey. All the requisite complications came tumbling out of scenarist M. Coates Webster's screenplay (additional dialogue by Hal Collins) with roles in it for Don McGuire, Alice Tyrrell, Douglas Wood, Byron Foulger, Regina Wallace, and, in brief appearances, disc jockeys Jack Eigen, Dave Garroway and Peter Potter, as well as The Novelties. Sam Katzman produced and it was directed by Arthur Dreifuss. Best song was Allan Roberts and Doris Fisher's 'Amado Mio', first heard in *Gilda* (Columbia 1946). Other songs and musical numbers: *I Surrender Dear* Harry Barris, Gordon Clifford; *How Can You Tell?* Roberts, Fisher; *When You Are In The Room* Oscar Hammerstein II, Ben Oakland; *Nobody Else But Elsie* Allie Wrubel.

MGM's big-hearted (though small-scale) Technicolor musical, **A Date With Judy**, was dominated by adolescents, but it was Carmen Miranda (fourth billed) who, with her delicious performance of 'Cuanto La Gusta' (by Ray Gilbert and Gabriel Ruiz), made the greatest impact in Joe Pasternak's jolly little production. And the scene in which she teaches top-billed Wallace Beery how to rhumba was, unquestionably, the best in the show. For the rest it was a bright, formula entertainment, whose main concern hinged on the rivalry between Jane Powell (illustrated) and Elizabeth Taylor for the attentions of handsome Robert Stack. Young Scotty Beckett (illustrated) played Miss Taylor's brother, and the cast was completed by Selena Royle, Leon Ames, Clinton Sundberg, George Cleveland, Lloyd Corrigan, Jerry Hunter, Jean McLaren and, playing himself, Xavier Cugat. Dorothy Kingsley and Dorothy Cooper concocted a cheerful screenplay from characters originally created by Aleen Leslie, and it was directed with the right spirit by Richard Thorpe. The dances were staged by Stanley Donen, notably a lively duet for Powell and Beckett, 'Strictly On The Corny Side' (by Stella Unger and Alec Templeton). Other songs and musical numbers: *It's A Most Unusual Day* Harold Adamson, Jimmy McHugh; *Judaline* Don Raye, Gene De Paul; *I've Got A Date With Judy*; *I'm Gonna Meet My Mary* Bill Katz, Calvin Jackson; *Temptation* Arthur Freed, Nacio Herb Brown; *Mulligatawny*.

Forties Musicals

◁ The problem with Esther Williams was finding storylines that would allow her to interrupt the scenario every now and then to take to the nearest swimming pool for demonstrations of the combination crawl and backstroke that helped make her one of the most bankable stars on the MGM lot. The problem wasn't particularly licked in **On An Island With You**, a water-logged romance about a film crew in Honolulu and the romance its star, Williams, has with aviator Peter Lawford (both illustrated). Ricardo Montalban was also in it; so was Jimmy Durante who sang the best number in the film – a ditty he wrote called 'I Can Do Without Broadway, But Can Broadway Do Without Me'. Also there: Cyd Charisse, Leon Ames, Kathryn Beaumont, Dick Simmons, and giving it that Latin *quelque chose*, Xavier Cugat and His Orchestra. Jack Donohue staged the numbers, Joe Pasternak produced, and it was breezily directed from a screenplay by Dorothy Kingsley, Dorothy Cooper, Charles Martin and Hans Wilhelm (story by Martin and Wilhelm), for the piece of fluff it was by Richard Thorpe. It made a fortune and became one of the top grossing films of the year. Songs and musical numbers: *On An Island With You*; *If I Were You*; *Taking Miss Mary To The Ball*; *Dog Song*; *Buenas Noches, Buenos Aires* Nacio Herb Brown, Edward Heyman; *Wedding Samba* Abraham Ellstein, Allan Small, Joseph Liebowitz.

Ernst Lubitsch began, but did not live to complete, **That Lady In Ermine** (20th Century-Fox). On his death, Otto Preminger stepped in to finish off the job – and finish it off he certainly did. For what should have been a light, airy, operetta-like romance between a beautiful countess and a dashing hussar, was ruined by Preminger, who pounded the fragile life out of it (it was a remake of *Bride Of The Regiment*, 1st National, 1930). The whimsy inherent in Rudolph Schanzer and Ernest Welisch's story from which Samson Raphaelson wrote his screenplay (the plot jumped backwards and forwards between 1561 and 1861, with the romance initially all taking place in the hussar's dreams), cried out for the celebrated Lubitsch 'touch' – what it got, instead, was the Preminger boot, which was of no help to Betty Grable (right), its star who, in a

▽

dual role, needed all the assistance she could get as far as her acting was concerned. Vocally she was fine, though, and did well by the two best songs: 'OOOh What I'll Do To That Wild Hungarian' and 'This Is The Moment' by Leo Robin and Frederick Hollander. Douglas Fairbanks Jr (left, also in a dual role) played the hussar, with Cesar Romero (centre) mildly amusing as Grable's meek husband of one day's duration. Also cast: Walter Abel, Reginald Gardiner, Harry Davenport, Virginia Campbell, Whit Bissell, Edmund McDonald and David Bond. It was choreographed by Hermes Pan, and Lubitsch received credit for both the production and the direction. (Technicolor). Other songs and musical numbers included: *There's Something About Midnight*; *The Melody Has To Be Right*; *Jester's Song* Robin, Hollander.

Marilyn Monroe's second film was **Ladies Of The Chorus** (Columbia), a 59-minute also-ran in which she played a burlesque chorus girl in love with a wealthy socialite (Rand Brooks). The story had Monroe's mother (Adele Jergens, left), who features in the same burlesque show as her daughter, opposing the match on the grounds that years ago, she herself loved beyond her station, and it didn't work out. In time, however, the conflict was solved to everyone's satisfaction, and the film ended with a double wedding: Monroe (second left) to Brooks, and Jergens to a former burlesque comic (Eddie Carr). Nana Bryant, Steve Geray, Bill Edwards and Marjorie Hoshelle also appeared; Henry Sauber and Joseph Carole wrote it from a story by Sauber; Jack Boyle choreographed, Harry A. Romm produced and Phil Karlson directed. Monroe coped adequately with the inferior material, and did well by Lester Lee and Allan Roberts's 'Everybody Needs A Da-Da-Daddy'. Other songs and musical numbers included: *Ladies Of The Chorus*; *Anyone Can Tell I Love You*; *Crazy For You*; *You're Never Too Old* Lee, Roberts.

▽

Tireless Joe Pasternak was at it again, blending the light with the heavy in **Luxury Liner** (MGM), a musical ocean voyage whose passenger list included Metro's youngest thrush (Jane Powell, just turned twenty), her widowed middle-aged dad (George Brent), tenor Lauritz Melchior (illustrated), soprano Marina Koshetz, bandleader Xavier Cugat, The Pied Pipers, and Frances Gifford as a widow whom interfering Miss Powell is determined shall marry her pa. So much for the plot (by Gladys Lehman and Richard Connell who also scripted). The romantic shipboard setting, with the help of Technicolor and all the handsome production values the studio could accord it, gave the film a glossy veneer that more than compensated for its lack of substance. Contributing to its success, too, was the music, and there was lots of it, from Miss Powell's rendition of the French-Canadian folk song 'Alouette' which she sang with various members of the crew, to Melchior and Powell's dramatic reading of the Act II duet from Verdi's *Aida*. Richard Whorf's direction was competent, and his cast was completed by John Ridgely, Thomas E. Breen and Richard Derr. Other songs and musical numbers: *Spring Came Back To Vienna* (Powell) Janice Torre, Fred Spielman, Fritz Rotter; *The Peanut Vendor* (Powell) L. Wolfe Gilbert, Marion Sunshine, Moisés Simons; *Yes We Have No Bananas* (The Pied Pipers) Frank Silver, Irving Cohn; *Come Back To Sorrento* (Melchior) Ernesto De Curtis, Claude Aveling; *Gavotte* (from Massenet's 'Manon') Massenet (Powell); *Cugat's Nougat* (Cugat) Cugat; *I've Got You Under My Skin* (Koshetz) Cole Porter; *Con Maracas* Cugat, Candido Dimanlig.

The answer to the question in the title of Paramount's **Isn't It Romantic?** was an emphatic no. Nor was it entertaining. A luke-warm period musical set in Indiana and recounting the activities of a trio of sisters (Veronica Lake, right, Mona Freeman, left, and Mary Hatcher), it was charmless, colourless (being photographed in black and white) and, with the notable exception of Pearl Bailey as the household maid, deficient in talent. Bailey sang a number called 'I Shoulda Quit When I Was Ahead' (by Jay Livingston and Ray Evans who wrote most of the score), but failed to heed the advice. Other roles went to Roland Culver as the three sisters' civil war veteran father, Billy De Wolfe (centre) as Miss Lake's beau, and Patric Knowles as a fake oil stock peddler who woos Miss Lake away from De Wolfe without too much difficulty. De Wolfe scored with a send-up of silent screen clichés ('At The Nickleodeon'), and there was a passable tune called 'Miss Julie July'. The rest, however, was tedium. Theodore Strauss, Josef Mischel and Richard L. Breen wrote it from a story by Jeanette Covert Nolan, Josephine Earl staged the dances, Daniel Dare produced and the direction was by Norman Z. McLeod. Other musical numbers: *Wondering When*; *Indiana Dinner* Livingston, Evans; *Isn't It Romantic?* Richard Rodgers, Lorenz Hart.

A frightful bowdlerization of the S.J. Perelman-Ogden Nash-Kurt Weill stage musical on which it was based, **One Touch Of Venus** was a stinker from Universal International which starred Ava Gardner (in the role created by Mary Martin) as a statue of Venus who springs miraculously to life after being kissed by a window dresser in a department store. The man doing the kissing was Robert Walker (illustrated), and it is to be regretted that he did not bring his osculatory skills to bear on Harry Kurnitz and Frank Tashlin's screenplay, on William A. Seiter's dreary direction and on his own and Miss Gardner's lustreless performances. Of the sixteen Weill songs originally featured in the show, only a mere handful were retained, and were indifferently sung. Dick Haymes was also in it, and the cast was completed by Eve Arden, Olga San Juan, Tom Conway, James Flavin and Sara Allgood. The dance routines (such as they were) were staged by Billy Daniels. Lester Cowan produced and Miss Gardner's vocals were dubbed by Eileen Wilson. Songs and musical numbers: *My Week*; *Don't Look Now But My Heart Is Showing*; *That's Him* (lyrics by Ann Ronell); *The Trouble With Women*; *Speak Low* Ogden Nash, Weill.

Danny Kaye's fifth and last film for Samuel Goldwyn was **A Song Is Born** (RKO), a remake in Technicolor by director Howard Hawks of *Ball Of Fire* (RKO, 1941), which Hawks also directed, and which starred Gary Cooper and Barbara Stanwyck. Based on a story by Thomas Monroe and Billy Wilder, and with a screenplay (uncredited) by Harry Tugend, it was the tale of a group of musicologists in general and Kaye in particular who, while in the midst of writing a mammoth history of music in the imposing and monastic confines of The Totten Foundation, have their studies interrupted by a singer called Honey Swanson (Virginia Mayo). Mayo is on the run from the district attorney as well as from her gangster boyfriend and, in seeking sanctuary with the musicologists, unleashed the chain of events which formed the basis of the storyline. The participation of several eminent jazz musicians – including Benny Goodman (as one of the professors), Tommy Dorsey, Louis Armstrong, Lionel Hampton and Charlie Barnet, with their orchestras, as well as Mel Powell, The Golden Gate Quartet, The Page Cavanaugh Trio, Buck and Bubbles, and Russo and The Samba Kings, helped take the edge off the air of desperation that permeated the entire project, but not completely. **A Song Is Born**, despite the talent invested in it, was a walloping bore which denied Kaye (illustrated) the chance to do the sort of things he did best, and in which Mayo was dull and undercast but superbly dubbed by Jerri Sullivan. Appearing as the other professors were Hugh Herbert, J. Edward Bromberg, Felix Bressart, Ludwig Stossel and O.Z. Whitehead, with Steve Cochran, Esther Dale, Mary Field and Howland Chamberlin also cast. Songs and musical numbers: *Stealin' Apples* (Hampton, Goodman, Powell, Harry Babsin, Alton Hendrickson) Andy Razaf, Fats Waller; *Flyin' Home* (Armstrong, Goodman, Dorsey, Barnet, Powell) Hampton, Goodman, Sid Robin; *Bach Boogie* (Buck on piano); *I'm Getting Sentimental Over You* (Dorsey, Orch) George Bassman; *Anitra's Dance* from incidental music to 'Peer Gynt' (Buck on piano, Goodman on clarinet) Grieg; *Blind Barnabas* (Golden Gate Quartet); *Redskin Rhumba* (Barnet, Orch) Barnet; *The Goldwyn Stomp* (Armstrong, with Hampton, Orch); *Mockin' Bird* (Golden Gate Quartet) traditional; *Sweet Genevieve* (Kaye) George Cooper, Henry Tucker; *Gaudeamus Igitur* (Professors) traditional; *Joshua Fit De Battle* (Golden Gate Quartet) traditional spiritual; *A Song Was Born* (Mayo, Armstrong, Goodman, Dorsey, Hampton, Barnet, Powell, Louis Bellson) Don Raye, Gene De Paul; *Daddy-O* (Mayo, Cavanaugh Trio); *Longhair Jam Session* (Mayo, Professors, Bubbles) a medley comprising Act IV Quartet from Verdi's 'Rigoletto'; Rossini's 'William Tell' overture; *Anvil Chorus* from Verdi's 'Il Trovatore' and *Song Of The Volga Boatmen* (traditional).

Falling midway between *Meet Me In St Louis* (MGM, 1944) and a typical Andy Hardy comedy, **Summer Holiday** (MGM) was a palatable slice of Americana which owed more to producer Arthur Freed and his adroit production team than it did to Eugene O'Neill, on whose gentle comedy *Ah Wilderness* it was based. Whereas O'Neill's play was a subtle delineation of a young lad's first faltering steps into manhood, Freed, and his able director Rouben Mamoulian (whose *Love Me Tonight*, Paramount, 1932, was one of the key musicals in the entire genre), while retaining much of the play's basic story-line, opened out the piece to accommodate the prerequisites of musical comedy but, at the same time, blurred the carefully articulated sensibilities of the original, and coarsened most of the characterizations. Yet, for all their tampering (the simplistic screenplay by Frances Goodrich and Albert Hackett, from the adaptation of the play by Irving Brecher and Jean Holloway, was partially written in rhyming couplets), the film succeeded on its own terms thanks, in the main, to Mamoulian's superb visual flair (his use of Technicolor was striking, especially in the bar-room encounter between Mickey Rooney and singer Marilyn Maxwell); and a first-rate score by Harry Warren and Ralph Blane. As the young protagonist at the film's centre, Rooney (illustrated foreground) bulldozed his way through the role with his usual air of super-confidence, and was prettily partnered by Gloria De Haven (foreground right) who was adequate as the girl in his life. Walter Huston (centre) was the *paterfamilias* and Selena Royle (right) his wife, with other parts going to Frank Morgan, Agnes Moorehead (left), Jackie 'Butch' Jenkins, Shirley Johns, Anne Francis and Hal Hackett. The film was gorgeously costumed by Walter Plunkett, and zestfully choreographed by Charles Walters, with Cedric Gibbons and Jack Martin Smith's sets also contributing to its well-evoked period atmosphere. Songs and musical numbers: *Afraid To Fall In Love* (Rooney, De Haven); *It's Our Home Town* (ensemble); *Independence Day* (Moorehead, Royle, Huston, Morgan); *Weary Blues* (Maxwell); *All Hail Danville High* (chorus); *I Think You're The Sweetest Kid I've Ever Known* (Rooney, Maxwell); *The Stanley Steamer* (De Haven, Rooney, Moorehead, Royle, Huston, Jenkins).

Numbingly familiar, **When My Baby Smiles At Me** (20th Century-Fox), adapted by Elizabeth Reinhardt and scripted by Lamar Trotti from George Manker Watters and Arthur Hopkins's Broadway play *Burlesque*, was a remake of two earlier Paramount films: *The Dance Of Life* (1929) with Nancy Carroll, and *Swing High Swing Low* (1937) with Carole Lombard. This time the star was Betty Grable who, though competent and professional in everything she did, was outdistanced by co-star Dan Dailey (illustrated) as a putty-nosed burlesque comedian who winds up in Bellevue Hospital after his successful career hits the skids. A performance of distinction, combining charm, pathos, and vitality, it was the freshest thing in a show turned stale by its reliance on past successes. June Havoc and Jack Oakie purveyed some low comedy; Jean Wallace, Richard Arlen, James Gleason, Vanita Wade, Robert Emmett Keane, Jerry Maren and George Lewis completed the cast. The dance routines were staged by Seymour Felix; Josef Myrow and Mack Gordon provided the film with its two new songs, 'By The Way' and 'What Did I Do?', George Jessel produced (in Technicolor), and the uninspired direction was by Walter Lang. Other musical numbers: *Oui Oui Marie* Alfred Bryan, Joseph McCarthy, Fred Fisher; *Don't Bring Lulu* Billy Rose, Lew Brown, Ray Henderson; *Shoe Shine Blues* (introductory routine to *Birth Of The Blues*); *Birth Of The Blues* Buddy De Sylva, Brown, Henderson; *When My Baby Smiles At Me* Andrew B. Sterling, Ted Lewis, Bill Munro; *The Daughter Of Rosie O'Grady* M.C. Brice, Walter Donaldson; *Say Si-Si* Al Stillman, Ernesto Lecuona.

Frank Sinatra (illustrated) came a cropper in **The Kissing Bandit** (MGM), a musical romance whose vivid colour by Technicolor in no way compensated for the dullness of Isobel Lennart and John Briard Harding's screenplay. Sinatra, at his scrawniest, seemed ill at ease throughout as a meek young fellow who finds himself having to step into his father's *braggadocio* role as a womanizing desperado. Kathryn Grayson, his co-star and romantic *vis-a-vis* fared somewhat better and got to sing the best song in the film, 'Love Is Where You Find It' (by Nacio Herb Brown and Earl Brent who, with Edward Heyman, provided the rest of the score as well); and from Ann Miller, Ricardo Montalban and Cyd Charisse there was a frenetic show-stopper called 'Dance Of Fury', excitingly staged by Stanley Donen (added after the film's completion). J. Carrol Naish, Mildred Natwick, Mikhail Rasumny, Billy Gilbert, Clinton Sundberg, Carleton E. Young and dancer Sono Osato were also in it for producer Joe Pasternak, and director Laszlo Benedek. Other songs and musical numbers: *If I Steal A Kiss*; *Señorita*; *Siesta*; *What's Wrong With Me?*; *Tomorrow Means Romance*; *I Like You* (Whip Dance).

Set in the twenties, **You Were Meant For Me** (20th Century-Fox) – a loose remake of the same studio's *Orchestra Wives* (1941) – strung a series of familiar old songs on to a thread of a plot involving a bandleader and his girl. Dan Dailey (right) was the bandleader; Jeanne Crain (left) the girl. They marry, and all goes well until Crain tires of following her husband and his band from one small town to another. Matters reach a head with the advent of the Depression, at which point true love happily reasserts itself, saving them from bankruptcy and a trip to the divorce courts. Elick Moll and Valentine Davies's screenplay gave it all a lot more credibility than the plot summary might suggest was possible, and there was solid support from Oscar Levant (who played Dailey's business manager, as well as George Gershwin's 'Concerto in F'), Barbara Lawrence, Selena Royle, Bob McCord, Harry Barris, Percy Kilbride and Herbert Anderson. Lee Clark and Kenny Williams staged the dance routines, Fred Kohlmar produced and the director was Lloyd Bacon. Songs and musical numbers: *Crazy Rhythm* Irving Caesar, Roger Wolfe Kahn, Joseph Meyer; *You Were Meant For Me* Arthur Freed, Nacio Herb Brown; *Goodnight Sweetheart* James Campbell, Reginald Connolly, Ray Noble; *If I Had You* Campbell, Connolly, Ted Shapiro; *Ain't She Sweet* Jack Yellen, Milton Ager; *Ain't Misbehavin'* Andy Razaf, Fats Waller; *I'll Get By* Roy Turk, Fred Ahlert.

A featherweight *mélange* of comedy and songs from Columbia, **Manhattan Angel** took 61 minutes to show how Gloria Jean (centre), the linchpin of a Youth Centre, manages to raise $25,000 to save the premises from demolition. A passable programmer which Arthur Dreifuss directed from a screenplay by Albert Deer (story by Deer and George H. Plympton), it was produced by Sam Katzman with a cast that included singer Toni Harper, Ross Ford, Patricia White, Thurston Hall, Alice Tyrrell, Benny Baker, Russell Hicks and Fay Baker. Songs included: *I'll Take Romance* Oscar Hammerstein II, Ben Oakland; *Candy Store Blues* Nick Castle, Herb Jeffries, Eddie Beal; *Naughty Aloysius* Robert Wilder; *It's A Wonderful, Wonderful Feeling* Jack Segal, Dewey Bergman.

A Walt Disney live-action feature with three short animated sequences, **So Dear To My Heart** (RKO) was specifically aimed at the kids with its simple story of a young, rural lad (Bobby Driscoll, illustrated right) and his endeavours to enter his pet ram at the county fair. His efforts are successful, and he wins first prize. Set in Indiana in 1903, its charming rustic atmosphere permeated every frame, with Beulah Bondi as Master Driscoll's kindly old granny and Burl Ives as Uncle Hiram, the local handyman-cum-blacksmith, thickly laying on the nostalgia in convincing 'backwoods' performances that were a credit to John Tucker Battle's screenplay (adapted by Maurice Rapf and Ted Sears from the story by Sterling North). Particularly enjoyable was Ives's singing of such folk songs as 'Sourwood Mountain' and 'Billy Boy'. Completing the cast were Harry Carey, Luana Patten (illustrated left), Raymond Bond, Walter Soderling, Mat Willis and Spelman B. Collins, plus the voices of John Beal, Ken Carson, Bob Stanton and The Rhythmaires. It was photographed in Technicolor, and the director was Harold Schuster. Other songs: *So Dear To My Heart* Ticker Freeman, Irving Taylor; *Ol' Dan Patch*; *Lavender Blue (Dilly Dilly)*; *Stick-to-it-ivity* Elliot Daniel, Larry Morey; *It's Whatcha Do With Whatcha Got* Don Raye, Gene De Paul; *County Fair* Robert Wells, Mel Torme.

Producer Arthur Freed should never have bothered to attach a largely fictitious story to **Words And Music** (MGM), his Technicolor biopic of the lives and careers of Richard Rodgers and Lorenz Hart. Far greater justice to the incomparable songwriting team would have been done had the studio simply paid tribute to their talents by stringing together, in a revue-type format, a collection of their songs. As Rodgers's life wasn't particularly exciting (he simply went from one success to another) and Hart, the more complex and interesting of the two, was homosexual (a taboo cinematic subject in 1948), it would surely have been kinder to let their words and music speak for themselves, rather than to allow the pack of half-truths and downright lies perpetrated in Fred Finklehoffe's anachronistic screenplay (from a story by Guy Bolton and Jean Holloway) to be passed off as fact. Mickey Rooney starred as Lorenz Hart and, although he made some sort of attempt to capture the mercurial nature of the man, it was basically a hammy and superficial performance as broad as Rooney was short. As for Tom Drake as Rodgers, the less said the better. Which left the musical numbers, most of which were staged by Robert Alton with his characteristic panache. Best sequences were Lena Horne's renditions of 'The Lady Is A Tramp' and 'Where or When'; Judy Garland's powerhouse performance of 'Johnny One Note'; June Allyson and The Blackburn Twins in 'Thou Swell' and, best of all, Gene Kelly and Vera-Ellen's 'Slaughter On Tenth Avenue' (illustrated) from *On Your Toes* (choreographed by Kelly). Also on hand: Cyd Charisse, Ann Sothern, Mel Torme, Dee Turnell, Allyn McLerie, Perry Como, Betty Garrett, Marshall Thompson, Janet Leigh, Jeanette Nolan, Harry Antrim, Richard Quine, Clinton Sundberg, Ilka Gruning, Emory Parnell, Helen Spring and Edward Earle. The musical direction was by Lennie Hayton and the superb orchestrations by Conrad Salinger. Norman Taurog directed. Other songs and musical numbers: *Lover* (orchestra over titles); *I Wish I Were In Love Again* (Garland, Rooney); *The Girl Friend* (instrumental); *This Can't Be Love* (Charisse, Turnell); *Blue Room* (Como, Charisse); *With A Song In My Heart* (Como); *Manhattan* (Rooney); *There's A Small Hotel* (Garrett); *Where's That Rainbow* (Sothern); *On Your Toes* (instrumental); *Way Out West* (Garrett); *Blue Moon* (Torme); *Mountain Greenery* (Como, McLerie); *Spring Is Here* (Rooney).

One Sunday Afternoon (Warner Bros.), a Technicolor musical starring Dennis Morgan (2nd left), Don De Fore (centre), Janis Paige (right) and Dorothy Malone, was the third screen version of James Hagan's play, first made by Paramount in 1933 as *One Sunday Afternoon*, and remade by Warner's in 1941 as *The Strawberry Blonde*. The bitter-sweet tale of a dentist (Morgan) who loses his strawberry blonde love (Paige) to his smoothie, man-about-town, not to mention crooked, friend (De Fore), and marries a more reliable girl (Malone) on the rebound, it suffered from a lack of pace which left audiences uninvolved. The culprit was director Raoul Walsh who, having directed the 1941 version with James Cagney, Olivia De Havilland, Jack Carson and Rita Hayworth, seemed unable to raise any enthusiasm the second time around. In fact, sad to relate, it was all a bore. Ralph Blane composed a set of songs which, while not unpleasant, failed to capture the period lilt of the piece (the sets and costumes, however, were admirable in this respect). Robert L. Richards pounded out the screenplay, LeRoy Prinz staged the dances, Jerry Wald produced, and the supporting cast included Ben Blue (left), Dorothy Ford, Oscar O'Shea, Alan Hale Jr (centre right) and George Neise. Songs: *Girls Were Made To Take Care Of Boys*; *Some Day*; *Johnny And Lucille*; *Sweet Corner Girl*; *One Sunday Afternoon* Blane; *Amy, You're A Little Bit Old-Fashioned* Marion Sunshine, Henry I. Marshall; *In My Merry Oldsmobile* Vincent Bryan, Gus Edwards; *Daisy Bell* Harry Dacre; *Deck The Halls With Boughs Of Holly* (traditional carol); *Auld Lang Syne* (traditional melody, words by Robert Burns).

After an absence of almost four years, Sonja Henie (illustrated) returned to the screen in **The Countess Of Monte Cristo** (Universal International). It was to be her last American film and, in terms of quality and box-office appeal, her least successful. Olga San Juan co-starred, and together they played a pair of Norwegian barmaids who, after landing jobs at a film studio in Oslo, utilize certain props in the prop department to help them masquerade as a countess (Henie) and her servant in an elegant resort hotel. Six ice-skating sequences and three songs comprised the musical programme – but the magic was missing and the film bombed. Also in it were Dorothy Hart, Michael Kirby, Arthur Treacher, Hugh French, Freddie Trenkler and Arthur O'Connell. Frederick De Cordova directed from a tired screenplay by William Bowers (story by Walter Reisch), and the producer was John Beck. Songs: *Friendly Polka*; *Count Your Blessings*; *Who Believes In Santa Claus?* (all sung by San Juan) Jack Brooks, Saul Chaplin.

Writing (New Classification)
(Story and Screenplay)
NOMINATIONS INCLUDED: *Jolson Sings Again*
(Columbia) Sidney Buchman

Cinematography (colour)
NOMINATIONS INCLUDED: *The Barkleys Of
Broadway* (MGM) Harry Stradling. *Jolson
Sings Again* William Snyder.

Music
Song
'Baby It's Cold Outside' *Neptune's Daughter*
(MGM) Frank Loesser
NOMINATIONS INCLUDED: 'It's A Great Feeling'
It's A Great Feeling (WB) Jule Styne *cm*;
Sammy Cahn *lyr*. 'Lavender Blue' *So Dear To
My Heart* (Disney, RKO) Eliot Daniel *cm*;
Larry Morey *lyr*. 'My Foolish Heart' *My
Foolish Heart* (Goldwyn, RKO) Victor Young
cm; Ned Washington *lyr*.

Scoring Of A Musical Picture
On The Town (MGM) Roger Edens and
Lennie Hayton
NOMINATIONS INCLUDED: *Jolson Sings Again*
Morris Stoloff and George Duning. *Look For
The Silver Lining* (WB) Ray Heindorf.

Special Awards
To Fred Astaire, for his unique artistry and
his contributions to the technique of musical
pictures. (statuette)

The Annual Top Moneymaking Films
INCLUDED: *Jolson Sings Again*. *Words and
Music* (MGM). *Neptune's Daughter*. *In The
Good Old Summertime* (MGM). *Take Me Out
To The Ball Game* (MGM). *The Barkleys Of
Broadway*. *A Connecticut Yankee In King
Arthur's Court* (Paramount).

Warner Bros.' **My Dream Is Yours** (a remake in
Technicolor of their *20 Million Sweethearts*,
1934) was an agreeable if utterly undistinguished movie about the struggles of a young
hopeful to become a radio star. It starred Doris
Day (centre) as a girl-next-door who just happens to have talent, co-starred Jack Carson
(right) as a radio talent scout, and boasted, in its
supporting cast, such stalwarts as Eve Arden
(left), S.Z. Sakall, Adolphe Menjou, Lee Bowman
(as a conceited crooner), and in one of its best
sequences, the very welcome Bugs Bunny. Also:
Selena Royle, Edgar Kennedy, Sheldon Leonard,
Franklin Pangborn and Frankie Carle and His
Orchestra. The dull script was by Harry Kurnitz
and Dane Lussier (adapted by Allen Rivkin and
Laura Kerr), and Michael Curtiz produced and
directed. Songs and musical numbers: *My
Dream Is Yours*; *Someone Like You*; *Tic Tic Tic*; *Love
Finds A Way* Harry Warren, Ralph Blane; *I'll
String Along With You* Warren, Al Dubin; *Cana-
dian Capers* Gus Chandler, Bert White, Henry
Cohen; *You Must Have Been A Beautiful Baby*
Johnny Mercer, Harry Warren; *Nagasaki* Mort
Dixon, Warren; *Jeepers Creepers* Mercer, Warren;
With Plenty Of Money And You Dubin, Warren.

◁ Betty Grable was **The Beautiful Blonde From
Bashful Bend** (20th Century-Fox), and her performance in this knockabout musical satire on
the wild West (written, produced and directed by
Preston Sturges from a story by Erle Felton) was
tentative, to say the least. Miss Grable (right)
played a pistol-packin' saloon gal mistaken by a
pince-nez'd Rudy Vallee (left, as a Sunday school
organist) for a mild-mannered school marm.
The whole production (photographed in Technicolor) suffered from the makeshift, anything-
goes air of improvisation that underlined it, and
the finished result was emphatically unfunny,
unappetising and unsuccessful. Also caught up
in the circumlocutions of the plot were Cesar
Romero, Olga San Juan (as an Indian half-
breed), Sterling Holloway and Danny Jackson
(as a pair of village idiots), Hugh Herbert, El
Brendel, Porter Hall, Pati Behrs, Margaret Hamilton and Emory Parnell. Songs and musical
numbers included: *Beautiful Blonde From Bashful
Bend* Don George, Lionel Newman; *Everytime I
Meet You* Mack Gordon, Josef Myrow; *In The
Gloaming* Meta Orred, Annie F. Harrison.

△
MGM's **Take Me Out To The Ball Game** (GB:
Everybody's Cheering), set at the turn of the
century, centred around the amorous exploits of
Gene Kelly (left foreground) and Frank Sinatra
(foreground centre right) as baseball players-
cum-vaudevillians. As in *Anchors Aweigh* (MGM
1945), Sinatra (top cast) was the more shy and
retiring of the two men with, this time, Esther
Williams (left), who also happens to be the
manager of his baseball team, as the object of his
affections. Williams, however, only has eyes for
Kelly, which leaves Sinatra open to the advances
of a determined Betty Garrett. Plot complications insinuated themselves in the form of a
gang of crooks who want Kelly and his team to
lose a vitally important game, but the narrative
shenanigans were speedily disposed of and the
film ended with a patriotic flag-waving finale
called 'Strictly USA' written by Roger Edens,
Betty Comden and Adolph Green who, apart
from the title number (by Albert von Tilzer and
Jack Norworth) and one other, wrote all the
songs. Though **Ball Game** set out to glorify the
all-American male, and was basically a Kelly-
Sinatra vehicle, MGM gave Esther Williams
second billing, and it was the unenviable task of
scenarists Harry Tugend and George Wells
(working from a story by Kelly and Stanley
Donen who were paid $25,000 for the outline
they handed to producer Arthur Freed) to devise
situations in which she could take to the water.
They only came up with one. Jules Munshin (left
of Sinatra) was cast as a baseball-playing buddy
of Kelly and Sinatra's, and the chemistry of the
trio pleased the studio sufficiently to bring
them together again in *On The Town* (1950).
Also cast: Edward Arnold, Richard Lane (2nd
right), Tom Dugan (far right), Murray Alper,
William Graff. Though the film, directed in
Technicolor by Busby Berkeley (his last as
overall director), was by no means epoch-
making, it had the sort of vitality that would
characterize the three great Kelly musicals (*On
The Town*, 1949, *An American In Paris*, 1951 and
Singin' In The Rain, 1952) that would follow it.
On the evidence of **Ball Game**'s story, Kelly and
Donen were grossly overpaid for their efforts.
The musical numbers, however, were delightful,
and although Kelly clearly danced down to
Sinatra in the simple but effective soft-shoe
treatment of the title number, and mugged
somewhat over enthusiastically with him and
Munshin in 'O'Brien To Ryan To Goldberg', he
came into his own in an exciting solo called 'The
Hat My Father Wore On St Patrick's Day' (by
William Jerome and Jean Schwartz) in which he
executed a series of 'barrel rolls', akin to the
backbend pirouette of ballet, which were breathtaking. Other musical numbers: *The Right Girl
For Me* (Sinatra); *It's Fate, Baby It's Fate* (Garrett,
Sinatra); *Yes Indeedy* (Kelly, Sinatra).

Bing Crosby (right) starred as New England blacksmith Hank Martin in the third and most elaborate screen version of Mark Twain's **A Connecticut Yankee In King Arthur's Court** (Harry C. Meyers was top-cast in the first version which William Fox made in 1921; and Will Rogers in Fox's remake of it in 1931). This version, from Paramount, was lavishly mounted by producer Robert Fellows and dazzlingly photographed in Technicolor by Ray Rennahan, with sets by Hans Dreier that were sumptuous and spectacular. The film was not only lovely to look at, but pretty good to listen to, with its catchy score by Johnny Burke and Jimmy Van Heusen. All about a blacksmith who, after being knocked unconscious in an accident during a rainstorm, wakes up and finds himself in Camelot at the time of King Arthur, Twain's story benefited from the addition of music and colour, and if Crosby's performance didn't quite carry the same conviction as Will Rogers's, it wasn't short on charm. Technicolor did wonders for his co-star Rhonda Fleming (as Lady Alesande) whose attractive red hair was far more striking than her performance; and as Sir Sagrimore, one of King Arthur's Knights, William Bendix (left) was, well, William Bendix. King Arthur himself was played by Sir Cedric Hardwicke, and the cast was completed by Henry Wilcoxon, Murvyn Vye, Joseph Vitale, Richard Webb, Alan Napier, Virginia Field and Julia Faye. It was written by Edmund Beloin, and directed with a pleasing sense of fantasy by Tay Garnett. Songs and musical numbers: *Once And For Always* (Crosby, Fleming); *Busy Doing Nothing* (Crosby, Hardwicke, Bendix); *If You Stub Your Toe On The Moon* (Crosby); *When Is Sometime?* (Fleming).

▽

△

As with most showbiz biopics, William Jacobs's Technicolor production **Look For The Silver Lining** (Warner Bros.) reduced the life of Marilyn Miller, whose story it was purportedly telling (in flashback), to the usual vaudeville-to-Broadway format, with all its ups and downs. Although nominally the star of the proceedings, the anaemic June Haver (illustrated centre) was consistently upscreened by Ray Bolger, who played Miss Miller's mentor Jack Donahue, and gave this cloud of a musical its only silver lining with his tap rendition of Jerome Kern's immortal 'Who' (lyrics by Otto Harbach and Oscar Hammerstein II). Otherwise, it was boringly routine, with a routine cast that included Gordon MacRae as the star's first husband, Charles Ruggles (right), Rosemary De Camp (left), S.Z. Sakall and Walter Catlett. The sluggish dance numbers were by LeRoy Prinz and the dull direction by David Butler. The Ephrons, Phoebe and Henry, wrote it with Marian Spitzer from a story by Bert Kalmar and Harry Ruby. Songs and musical numbers: *Sunny* Kern, Harbach, Hammerstein II; *Look For The Silver Lining*; *Whip-Poor-Will* Buddy De Sylva, Jerome Kern; *A Kiss In The Dark* De Sylva, Victor Herbert; *Pirouette* Herman Finck; *Just A Memory* De Sylva, Lew Brown, Ray Henderson; *Time On My Hands* Mack Gordon, Harold Adamson, Vincent Youmans; *Wild Rose* Clifford Grey, Kern; *Shine On Harvest Moon* Nora Bayes, Jack Norworth; *Back, Back, Back To Baltimore* Harry Williams, Egbert Van Alstyne; *Jingle Bells* J.S. Pierpont; *Can't You Hear Me Callin', Caroline?* William H. Gardner, Caro Roma; *Carolina In The Morning* Gus Kahn, Walter Donaldson; *Yama Yama Man* George Collin Davis, Karl Hoschna; *Dengozo* Ernesto Nazareth; *Oh Gee! Oh Joy!* P.G. Wodehouse, the Gershwins.

Dorothy Lamour (illustrated) was the star of **Slightly French** (Columbia), a remake of *Let's Fall In Love* (Columbia, 1934) which starred Ann Sothern. A nothing-to-get-excited-about programmer, it featured Lamour as an Irish cooch dancer who, through the Professor Higgins-like determination of a fallen film producer (Don Ameche), is transformed from Irish Mary O'Leary into famous French actress Rochelle Olivia, in which guise she successfully attempts the Can-Can in a number (by Lester Lee and Allan Roberts) called 'Fifi From The Folies Bergère'. Her accent wasn't bad either. Others flitting in and out of Karen De Wolfe's screenplay (from a story by Herbert Fields) were Janis Carter, Willard Parker, Adele Jergens, Jeanne Manet and Frank Ferguson. Irving Starr produced and the solid direction was by Douglas Sirk. Other songs: *I Want To Learn About Love*; *Night*; *I Keep Telling Myself* Lee, Roberts; *Let's Fall In Love* Harold Arlen, Ted Koehler.

◁

△

Make Believe Ballroom (Columbia) starred Jerome Courtland (left) and Virginia Welles (right) as a couple of collegiate carhops who enter a musical quiz show, fall in love, and win the top prize. The prize in producer Ted Richmond's low-budgeter wasn't its eye-glass full of plot nor its featured players (who included Ruth Warrick, Ron Randell, Al Jarvis, Adele Jergens, Paul Harvey and Louis Jean Heydt) but its roster of guest artists: Frankie Laine, The King Cole Trio, Toni Harper, Jack Smith, Kay Starr, The Sportsmen, Charlie Barnet, Jimmy Dorsey, Jan Garber, Gene Krupa and Ray McKinley. With so much musical talent on offer, there was nothing for Albert Duffy and Karen De Wolfe's screenplay (based on the radio programmes of Al Jarvis and Martin Block) to do but take a back seat, which it frequently did. The director was Joseph Santley. Songs and musical numbers: *Miss In Between Blues* Allan Roberts, Lester Lee; *The Way The Twig Is Bent* Roberts, Doris Fisher; *Make Believe Ballroom* Leon Rene, Johnny Mercer, Al Jarvis; *I'm The Lonesomest Gal In Town* Lew Brown, Albert von Tilzer; *On The Sunny Side Of The Street* Dorothy Fields, Jimmy McHugh; *It's A Blue World* Bob Wright, Chet Forrest; *The Trouble With You Is Me* Jack Segal, George Handy; *Hello Goodbye* Alex Sullivan, Lew Pollack; *Disc Jockey Jump* Gene Krupa, Gerry Mulligan; *Coming Out* M. Christiance, Harry J. Cole.

◁ After the enormous success of *Easter Parade* (MGM, 1948), producer Arthur Freed planned a follow-up for its two stars, Fred Astaire and Judy Garland, called **The Barkleys Of Broadway**. Garland, however, cried off the assignment (or rather, she simply didn't show up for work) and was replaced by Ginger Rogers, whose last film with Astaire had been *The Story Of Vernon And Irene Castle* (RKO) ten years earlier. Thus, at a stroke, the world was deprived of a Garland musical, but enriched by one more Astaire-Rogers (both illustrated) offering. In it, the famous team seemed, almost, to parody themselves by playing a husband-and-wife dance team who temporarily go their separate ways when the wife decides she'd rather be a straight actress than a musical comedy star. They're finally reunited to the haunting strains of 'They Can't Take That Away From Me' by George and Ira Gershwin (reprised from Astaire and Rogers's 1937 success, *Shall We Dance*, RKO). The rest of the new songs were by Harry Warren with lyrics by Ira Gershwin, the highlight being Astaire's memorable and imaginative 'Shoes With Wings On' choreographed by himself and Hermes Pan, in which the star, as a repair man in a shoe shop, puts on a pair of white shoes after they miraculously begin to dance on their own. The other shoes in the shop suddenly spring to life as well, and only stop when Astaire shoots at them with a couple of pistols. Best of the rest was 'My One And Only Highland Fling' sung by Fred and Ginger in a thick Scots brogue, and Harry Warren's 'Bouncin' The Blues', a rapid rehearsal tap routine. Plot-wise, scenarists Betty Comden and Adolph Green made the most of the least, their screenplay skilfully negotiating the inherent clichés, and providing parts for Oscar Levant (as the team's jaundiced composer-cum-wet nurse), Billie Burke, Gale Robbins, Jacques Francois (as a French Playwright convinced that Miss Rogers is capable of playing Sarah Bernhardt), George Zucco and Clinton Sundberg. Robert Alton directed the dance sequences and Charles Walters the film. Other songs and musical numbers: *You'd Be Hard To Replace* (Astaire); *Manhattan Downbeat* (Astaire, Rogers); *A Weekend In The Country* (Astaire, Rogers, Levant) Warren, Gershwin; *Swing Trot* (credit sequence, danced by Astaire and Rogers) Warren, Gershwin; *Piano Concerto No 1* (Levant) Tchaikovsky; *Sabre Dance* (Levant) Khatchaturian; *This Heart Of Mine* (orchestral) Warren, Arthur Freed.

Set in the last years of the 'silent film' era, and continuing into the thirties, **You're My Everything** (20th Century-Fox) was a pleasant, well-written backstage story which starred Dan Dailey (illustrated centre in blackface) as a vaudeville hoofer and Anne Baxter as his wife, a one-time silent screen actress (known as the Hotcha Girl) who becomes a major film star with the arrival of talkies. Shari Robinson (illustrated) played their daughter and, encouraged by Dailey, lands a part in a movie. Her mother is furious, insisting that Shari lead a 'normal' non-showbiz life on the farm Dailey has bought for them. Dailey mollifies her by promising not to allow the child to make more than one film. But Shari turns out to be a sensation and is immediately put under contract by the studio. Baxter ups and leaves in a huff, taking Shari with her. A reconciliation is contrived by Baxter's wise Aunt Jane (Anne Revere) and all ends happily. A serviceable enough plot on which to mount several well-staged numbers (by Nick Castle), it also brought out the best in Dailey and Miss Baxter, but over-extended little Miss Robinson, whose success in the movies was clearly intended to mirror Shirley Temple's (she even sang

'On The Good Ship Lollipop', by Sidney Clare and Richard Whiting, from 20th Century-Fox's 1934 production *Bright Eyes*). Alas, the only thing Shari appeared to have in common with Shirley was the first two letters of her name – and watching the former work, it was hard to see what all the fuss was about. Still, that detail apart, **You're My Everything**, photographed in Technicolor, with a cast that also included Stanley Ridges, Henry O'Neill, Selena Royle, Alan Mowbray (as a director of silent movies), Robert Arthur, and, in two small scenes, Buster Keaton and lyricist Mack Gordon, was good, solid entertainment. Lamar Trotti (who also wrote it, with Will H. Hayes Jr, from a story by George Jessel) produced. Alfred Newman was in charge of the music, and it was most efficiently directed by Walter Lang. Songs and musical numbers included: *You're My Everything* Harry Warren, Mort Dixon, Joe Young; *Varsity Drag* De Sylva, Brown, Henderson; *I May Be Wrong* Harry Ruskin, Henry Sullivan; *Chattanooga-Choo-Choo*; *Serenade In Blue* Warren, Mack Gordon; *I Can't Begin To Tell You* James V. Monaco, Gordon; *Would You Like To Take A Walk?* Warren, Mort Dixon, Billy Rose.

▷

Neptune's Daughter (MGM) starred Esther Williams, Ricardo Montalban, Betty Garrett and Red Skelton, all of whom sang the disarmingly catchy 'Baby, It's Cold Outside'. Garrett belted out 'I Love Those Men', and Montalban crooned 'My Heart Beats Faster' (all by Frank Loesser). Plot-wise it had Williams, as a chic manufacturer of chic swimwear, spending a great deal of time rejecting the persistent advances of Latin-American polo star Montalban. Far more entertaining, though, was its sub-plot which involved Garrett (right) in a mistaken identity romance with Skelton (left), a polo club masseur whom she believes to be millionaire Montalban. Dorothy Kingsley's racy screenplay was full of fun and skilfully accommodated the musical interpolations, including an elaborate voodoo dance number, and an eye-filling water ballet (staged by Jack Donohue). There were parts in it too for Keenan Wynn, Ted De Corsia, Mike Mazurki and Mel Blanc. Also: Xavier Cugat and His Orchestra. The Technicolor production was under the supervision of Jack Cummings, and the director was Edward Buzzell.

Red Hot And Blue (Paramount), a musical comedy thriller and a starring vehicle for Betty Hutton, had nothing in common with Cole Porter's 1936 Broadway show. Miss Hutton played a would-be actress whose romance with stage director Victor Mature is temporarily fouled up when a gangster-turned-backer is murdered while she is in his apartment. From this point on Hagar Wilde and John Farrow's screenplay (from a story by Charles Lederer) becomes a backstage whodunnit, with both the police and the dead man's cronies anxious to nail the killer, and with suspicion of course, falling on none other than Miss Hutton (illustrated centre). An ineffectually staged chase towards the end robbed the film of much of its potential, leaving Hutton with four Frank Loesser songs to justify the price of admission, the most effective being a parody on Shakespearean acting technique called 'Hamlet'. Loesser himself appeared, as a piano-playing hood. As an actor he was a pretty good tunesmith! Also cast: William Demarest (2nd left), June Havoc (left), Jane Nigh (right), William Talman, Raymond Walburn, Onslow Stevens and Joseph Vitale. Produced by Robert Fellows and directed unevenly by John Farrow. Other songs: *That's Loyalty; I Wake Up In The Morning Feeling Fine; (Where Are You) Now That I Need You*.

Make Mine Laughs (RKO) was an enjoyable and varied compilation of celluloid clips from the RKO vaults; some of the material was new, most of it familiar. The show ran 63 minutes and featured Gil Lamb as master of ceremonies, Ray Bolger, Dennis Day (right), Frances Langford, Anne Shirley (left), Joan Davis, Jack Haley, Leon Errol, Robert Lamouret and his dummy duck in a ventriloquist routine, Manuel and Marita Viera with their monkey orchestra, Freddie Fisher and His Schnickelfritzers, Spanish dancers Rosario and Antonio, a muscle act called The Titans, Frankie Carle at the piano, a 1920 Pathe newsreel showing bathing beauties, and a tear-jerker of silent vintage. George Bilson produced, the Leon Errol sequence was scripted and directed by Hal Yates, while Richard Fleischer was in charge of the overall direction. Songs and musical numbers included: *You Go Your Way And I'll Go Crazy* (Bolger) Mack Gordon, Harry Revel; *Poor Little Fly On The Wall* (Fisher) Fisher; *If You Happen To Find My Heart* (Day, Shirley) Herb Magidson, Lew Pollack; *Carle Meets Mozart (Turkish Rondo from Mozart's Piano Sonata in A, K311)* (Carle) Carle, Frank De Vol; *Who Killed Vaudeville?* (Davis, Haley) Jack Yellen, Sammy Fain; *Moonlight Over The Islands* (Langford) Mort Greene, Pollack; *Send Back My Love To Me* (Langford).

An amiable and mildly amusing spoof on Hollywood, **It's A Great Feeling** (Warner Bros.) starred Jack Carson (right) as an egotistical ham attempting, with the help of his buddy Dennis Morgan (left), to direct himself in a movie. The screenplay, by Jack Rose and Melville Shavelson from an original story by I.A.L. Diamond, took place for much of the time on the Warner lot, with such studio luminaries as Gary Cooper, Joan Crawford, Errol Flynn, Sydney Greenstreet, Danny Kaye, Patricia Neal, Eleanor Parker, Ronald Reagan, Edward G. Robinson and Jane Wyman on hand for token guest-star appearances. Also featured were directors Michael Curtiz, Raoul Walsh, King Vidor, and David Butler (who actually directed the film). Doris Day was second-billed as a waitress waiting for her big break, and one number in the pleasant Jule Styne-Sammy Cahn score, 'At The Cafe Rendezvous', had her singing in a strong French accent. It was produced, in Technicolor, by Alex Gottlieb, and choreographed by LeRoy Prinz whose big dream sequence was as uninspired as it was unnecessary. Also cast: Irving Bacon, Claire Carleton, Harlan Warde, Jacqueline De Wit. Other songs and musical numbers: *It's A Great Feeling; There's Nothing Rougher Than Love; That Was A Big Fat Lie; Give Me A Song With A Beautiful Melody; Blame My Absent-Minded Heart; Fiddle-dee-dee*.

The blarney concocted by Edmund Beloin and Richard Breen to reunite Bing Crosby (left) and Barry Fitzgerald (centre left) for the third (and final) time, was called **Top O' The Morning** (Paramount), a bottom of the barrel entertainment, drenched in sentimentality, and overrun by a regiment of clichés to which Irish stories such as this one are prone. All about an American insurance investigator (Crosby) who arrives in the land of the shamrock to investigate the looting of the famous Blarney Stone, it featured Fitzgerald as a cantankerous, but lovable, old member of the Civil Guard and Ann Blyth as his pretty daughter who, in no time at all, captures Crosby's affections. Miss Blyth's fresh and engaging personality helped neutralize some of the film's more treacly passages; ditto a handful of new songs by Johnny Burke and Jimmy Van Heusen. Nor was there much wrong with the performances. It was the below-par quality of the story and screenplay that sabotaged the stars' efforts and made for 100 minutes of indigestible whimsy. Also cast: Hume Cronyn (centre right), Eileen Crowe, John McIntire, John Eldredge and John Costello. David Miller directed, Robert L. Welch produced. Songs: *Top O' The Morning; Oh 'Tis Sweet To Think; The Donovans; You Are In Love With Someone?* Burke, Van Heusen; *When Irish Eyes Are Smiling* Chauncey Olcott, George Graff Jr, Ernest R. Ball.

Forties Musicals

Judy Garland (illustrated right) was given ample opportunity to exploit her infectious sense of comedy in **In The Good Old Summertime** (MGM), a small-scale treat from producer Joe Pasternak that concerned the tender and touching romance between two pen pals, both of whom are unaware that they work in the same music shop. Not only do they see each other practically every day of their lives, but to spice the situation, a certain animosity exists between them. Based on Miklos Laszlo's play *The Shop Around The Corner* (filmed by MGM in 1940 with James Stewart and Margaret Sullavan) and scripted by Albert Hackett, Frances Goodrich and Ivan Tors from an extant screenplay by Samson Raphaelson, it also gave co-star Van Johnson (left) a marvellous chance to flex his comedic muscles and reveal himself as a lightweight performer of immense charm and a
▽

certain amount of style. S.Z. Sakall (as Otto Oberkugen, the owner of the emporium in which Garland and Johnson are employed) actually gave a performance rather than a caricature of himself, with Spring Byington (the secretary he has secretly loved for twenty years), Clinton Sundberg, Marcia Van Dyke and Lillian Bronson fine in support. Completing the cast was Buster Keaton who, as another employee of Sakall's, had one side-splitting moment when he steps on to a dance floor, slips, and crushes under his weight what he believes to be a priceless Stradivarius. The musical numbers were simply but effectively staged by Robert Alton, whose creative gifts could always be relied upon, the two best being 'I Don't Care' (by Jean Lenox and Harry Sutton) and 'Play That Barber Shop Chord' (by Ballard MacDonald, William Tracey and Lewis Muir), both sung by

Garland, with the latter backed by a splendid barber-shop quartet. One of the sweetest, most unpretentious entertainments of the year, it was subtly photographed in Technicolor, looked a dream in Cedric Gibbons and Randall Duell's period settings, and was directed with just the right lightness of touch by Robert Z. Leonard. Other songs and musical numbers: *In The Good Old Summertime* George Evans, Ren Shields; *Put Your Arms Around Me Honey* Junie McCree, Harry von Tilzer; *Meet Me Tonight In Dreamland* Beth Slater Whitson, Lee Friedman; *Merry Christmas* Janice Torre, Fred Spielman; *Chicago* (title music) Fred Fisher; *Wait Till The Sun Shines Nellie* Harry von Tilzer, Andrew B. Sterling. Interesting sideline: Liza Minnelli – aged 18 months – made her screen debut in the very last scene, as the child of Garland and Johnson who, in the plot, marry.

△

The first Walt Disney feature in seven years that didn't combine cartoon characters with live action was **The Adventures Of Ichabod And Mr Toad** (RKO). Taken from Kenneth Grahame's *The Wind In The Willows* and Washington Irving's *The Legend Of Sleepy Hollow*, the film told two separate stories. The first was about Mr Toad (illustrated) whose love of anything on wheels causes his downfall; the second was about Ichabod Crane, a superstitious school master, and his encounter with the Headless Horseman. Beautifully drawn and bristling with imaginative touches, it marked a return to form for Disney and his band of animators and was appreciatively welcomed by the press, though commercially it hardly matched the success of *Snow White And The Seven Dwarfs* (1937) or even *Bambi* (1942). Ichabod was narrated by Bing Crosby and Mr Toad by Basil Rathbone, with the voices of Eric Blore as Mr Toad, Pat O'Malley as Cyril, Claude Allister as Water Rat, John Ployardt as the prosecutor, Colin Campbell as Mole, Campbell Grant as Angus MacBadger and Ollie Wallace as Winky. The production supervisor was Ben Sharpsteen and the directors Jack Kinney, Clyde Geronimi and James Algar (Technicolor). Songs: *Ichabod*; *Katrina*; *The Headless Horseman* Don Raye, Gene De Paul; *Merrily On Our Way* Frank Churchill, Charles Wolcott, Larry Morey, Ray Gilbert.

△

S.Z. Sakall, having acquitted himself so favourably in *In The Good Old Summertime*, received third billing in **Oh You Beautiful Doll** (20th Century-Fox), a George Jessel-produced saunter down Nostalgia Lane in which he was given the most substantial role of his career. He gave a most effective performance as real-life composer Fred Fisher, a serious musician who found success, not in the concert hall or the opera houses of the world, but in Tin Pan Alley. According to Albert and Arthur Lewis's well-turned screenplay, Fisher (real name Alfred Breitenbach) was a struggling composer until a song plugger, spotting the commercial potential in some of his operatic arias, up-tempo'd some of the tunes and added popular lyrics. So ashamed was Breitenbach of his new found success, that he changed his name to Fisher, in which deception he continued to flourish as a songsmith-cum-publisher for forty years. As audiences were hardly aware of Fisher's existence, it hardly mattered that certain liberties were taken with his life. It was his tunes that counted, and as staged by Seymour Felix and performed by June Haver (illustrated), top-starred as Fisher's daughter, and leading man Mark Stevens (vocals dubbed by Bill Shirley), they sprang pleasingly to life. Charlotte Greenwood did some high kicking as Fisher's wife Anna, with other roles under John M. Stahl's direction going to Gale Robbins, Jay C. Flippen, Andrew Tombes, Eduard Franz, Eula Morgan and Nestor Paiva. (Technicolor). Songs (and lyricists) included: *Oh You Beautiful Doll* (Nat D. Ayer, A. Seymour Brown only); *There's A Broken Heart For Every Light On Broadway* (Howard Johnson); *Peg O' My Heart* (Alfred Bryan); *Chicago*; *I Want You To Want Me To Want You* (Bob Schafer, Bryan); *Come Josephine In My Flying Machine* (Bryan); *Who Paid The Rent For Mrs Rip Van Winkle?* (Bryan); *Daddy, You've Been More Than A Mother To Me*; *When I Get You Alone Tonight* (Joseph McCarthy, Joe Goodwin); *Dardanella* (Felix Bernard, Johnny S. Black, lyrics Fisher); *Ireland Must Be Heaven For My Mother Came From There* (McCarthy, Johnson).

▽

Jolson Sings Again (Columbia) literally began where *The Jolson Story* (1946) left off (i.e. in a nightclub with Jolie giving an impromptu performance to the disapproval of his first wife, who walks out on him) and continued the story through the War when, after a period of despondency and dissipation, he regains his spirit by undertaking a series of USO camp shows. The strain of these shows proves detrimental to his health, resulting in the removal of a lung. It is while convalescing in hospital (according to Sidney Buchman's screenplay) that he meets and falls in love with Nurse Ellen Clark (Barbara Hale) from Arkansas, and marries her. From then on the film concerned itself with Jolson's recuperation and the making of *The Jolson Story*, offering some interesting insights into the way Jolson's voice was dubbed on to the soundtrack. Jolson himself never appeared, and in one curious scene audiences saw a double-exposure Larry Parks (illustrated) playing himself as well as Jolson. Barbara Hale did the best she could in a role that was never substantially scripted, and, of the principals, was the only newcomer to the cast. The rest were hold-overs from the earlier film, and included William Demarest as Steve Martin, Jolson's faithful friend and companion, Ludwig Donath and Tamara Shayne as Mama and Papa Joelson (Mama dying early on in the story) and Bill Goodwin as playwright Tom Baron. As was the case in *The Jolson Story*, it was Jolson's singing that proved the main attraction, and there were almost as many songs in the sequel as in the original, many of them repeats. Though **Jolson Sings Again** (produced in Technicolor by Buchman, and directed by Henry

Levin) wasn't nearly as good as its predecessor, it was the biggest grossing film of 1949 with a box-office take of over $5,500,000. Songs: *After You've Gone* Harry Creamer, Turner Layton; *Chinatown, My Chinatown* Joe Young, Sam Lewis, Jean Schwartz; *Give My Regards To Broadway* George M. Cohan; *I Only Have Eyes For You* Al Dubin, Harry Warren; *I'm Just Wild About Harry* Noble Sissle, Eubie Blake; *You Made Me Love You* Joseph McCarthy, James V. Monaco; *I'm Looking Over A Four Leaf Clover* Mort Dixon, Harry M. Woods; *Is It True What They Say About Dixie?* Sammy Lerner, Irving Caesar, Gerald Marks; *Ma Blushin' Rosie* Edgar Smith, John Stromberg; *Let Me Sing And I'm Happy* Irving Berlin; *Baby Face* Benny Davis, Harry Akst; *Sonny Boy* Buddy De Sylva, Lew Brown, Ray Henderson; *About A Quarter To Nine* Al Dubin, Harry Warren; *Anniversary Song* Saul Chaplin, Al Jolson, J. Ivanovici; *For Me And My Gal* Edgar Leslie, E. Ray Goetz; *California Here I Come* De Sylva, Jolson, Joseph Meyer; *Rockabye Your Baby* Sam Lewis, Joe Young, Jean Schwartz; *Carolina In The Morning* Gus Kahn, Walter Donaldson; *Toot Toot Tootsie Goodbye* Gus Kahn, Ernie Erdman, Dan Russo; *April Showers* De Sylva, Louis Silvers; *Swanee* George Gershwin, Irving Caesar; *My Mammy* Sam Lewis, Joe Young, Walter Donaldson (all sung by Jolson); *I'll Take Romance* (orchestral) Oscar Hammerstein II, Ben Oakland; *It's A Blue World* (orchestral) Bob Wright, Chet Forrest; *Learn To Croon* (Bing Crosby) Sam Coslow, Arthur Johnston; *Back In Your Own Backyard* Jolson, Billy Rose, Dave Dreyer; *When The Red Red Robin Comes Bob, Bob, Bobbin' Along* Harry Woods.

Forties Musicals

△

Mario Lanza, hailed by MGM as the new Caruso, made an auspicious debut in **That Midnight Kiss**, produced (in glowing Technicolor) by producer Joe Pasternak with all the quintessential Pasternakian ingredients in ample evidence to ensure many happy box-office returns for the studio. With its full-to-overflowing mixture of classical music and popular standards, an easy-going, undemanding screenplay (by Bruce Manning and Tamara Hovey), plus a cast that top-starred Kathryn Grayson and included Jose Iturbi (as Jose Iturbi), Ethel Barrymore, Keenan Wynn, J. Carrol Naish, Jules Munshin, Thomas Gomez, Marjorie Reynolds and Arthur Treacher, it had the sweet smell of success stamped on

to every frame. Grayson played a Philadelphia heiress determined to become an opera star, and Lanza (illustrated right) a singing truck driver whose virile good looks and powerful high C's sweep her off her feet. Several misunderstandings helped thicken a very thin plot. In the end, however, music rather than words proved to be the food of love, with the warring couple singing their way into each other's hearts (and ours). It was high-grade *schmaltz*, quite irresistible in its shameless disregard for the mundane realities of life. Norman Taurog's sure-footed direction didn't miss a trick. Musical programme: *I Know, I Know, I Know* (Grayson) Bronislau Kaper, Bob Russell; *Three O'Clock In The Morning* (Naish)

Dorothy Terriss, Julian Robledo; *They Didn't Believe Me* (Grayson, Lanza) Jerome Kern, Herbert Reynolds; *Santa Lucia* (Naish) Teodoro Cottrau; *Down Among The Sheltering Palms* (Wynn, and quartet) James Brockman, Abe Olman; *Revolutionary Etude* (Jose and Amparo Iturbi) Chopin; *Caro Nome* (Grayson, Iturbi) from Verdi's 'Rigoletto'; *Celeste Aida* (Lanza) from Verdi's 'Aida'; *Una Furtiva Lacrima* (Lanza, Iturbi) from Donizetti's 'L'Elisir d'Amore'; *Piano Concerto In E Flat* Liszt; *Piano Concerto No 1* Tchaikovsky (segments only, Iturbi); *Mama Mia Che Vo Sape* (Lanza) from Mascagni's 'Cavalleria Rusticana'; *Finale: themes from Tchaikovsky's 5th Symphony* (Lanza, Grayson); *Russian Nightmare* (Grayson).

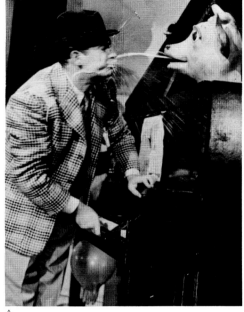

Coming four years before MGM's celebrated hit, *The Bandwagon*, **Dancing In The Dark** was a minor entry in Technicolor (from 20th Century-Fox) whose silly storyline concerned the efforts of the studio's production head, a man named Crossman (Darryl F. Zanuck, Fox's boss, wrote screenplays under the pseudonym Melville Crossman), to mount a film version of the Arthur Schwartz-Howard Dietz Broadway revue *Bandwagon*. The first thing Crossman (played by Adolphe Menjou) does, is to send a conceited has-been actor to New York in order to sign up a star to play the lead role in the impending film. William Powell (left) was top-starred as the disdainful erstwhile thespian, and the girl he chose was Betsy Drake (right), an unknown young actress – rather than the star Crossman wants – who throws all sorts of tantrums when she discovers that Powell is none other than the father who deserted her mother before she was born. Miss Drake's performance was on a par with Mary C. McCall Jr's fair-to-middling screenplay (adaptation by Marion Turk), but was no match for the Schwartz-Dietz evergreens she was expected to sing. Mark Stevens (centre) was second-billed as a press agent, with other roles going to Randy Stuart, Lloyd Corrigan, Hope Emerson, Walter Catlett, Don Beddoe, Jean Hersholt, Sid Grauman and Byron Foulger. George Jessel produced and the director was Irving Reis. Songs and musical numbers included: *Dancing In The Dark*; *I Love Louisa*; *New Sun In The Sky*; *Something To Remember You By*.

Warner Bros.' **The Inspector General** might have been termed 'suggested by' rather than 'based on' Gogol's classic, for, as played by Danny Kaye, Gogol's illiterate buffoon (who is mistaken for an important visiting dignitary in a small town) owed more to the spirit of burlesque than to European comic theatre. Kaye (illustrated centre) played the part of Georgi, a medicine show helper, to the hilt, unrestrainedly relishing the farcical confusion provided by Phillip Rapp and Harry Kurnitz's script and the witty patter songs written for him by his wife, Sylvia Fine, and Johnny Mercer. Although the supporting cast was long and, by the studio's standards, relatively distinguished, with Gene Lockhart (as a crooked mayor), Elsa Lanchester (as the mayor's flighty wife), Walter Slezak, Alan Hale, Walter Catlett, Rhys Williams and Benny Baker, director Henry Koster understood exactly where the film's appeal lay and resigned himself to recording, in Technicolor, a very funny one-man-show. The producer was Jerry Wald. Songs and musical numbers: *Onward Onward*; *The Medicine Show*; *The Inspector General*; *Lonely Heart*; *Gypsy Drinking Song*; *Soliloquy For Three Heads*; *Happy Times*; *Brodny*.

One of the rare feature films to star Milton Berle (illustrated), **Always Leave Them Laughing** (Warner Bros.), about the progression of a comedian from acting as master of ceremonies at a mosquito-plagued resort to becoming top banana on television, admirably geared its cliché-ridden plot to Berle's particular talents, allowing him to perform as many sketches as possible. There was a score of sorts, mixing some dispensable new songs with a couple of golden oldies, but it was the jokes that audiences came out humming. Adding to the general good humour was Bert Lahr proving all over again just how stunning and original a comedian he was; Virginia Mayo played his scheming wife, and Ruth Roman was Berle's romantic interest. Jack Rose and Melville Shavelson wrote the screenplay (from a story by Max Shulman and Richard Mealand), Roy Del Ruth directed and Jerry Wald produced. Songs and musical numbers included: *You're Too Intense*; *Always Leave Them Laughing* Milton Berle, Sammy Cahn; *Say Farewell* Cahn, Ray Heindorf; *Clink Your Glasses* Cahn, Johnny Mercer; *Embraceable You* George and Ira Gershwin; *By The Light Of The Silvery Moon* Edward Madden, Gus Edwards.

A love affair between Desi Arnaz (illustrated centre) and his co-star Mary Hatcher (as a couple of wooing Cubans) formed the meagre content of **Holiday In Havana** (Columbia), a low-budget filler whose screenplay by Robert Lees, Frederick I. Rinaldo and Karen De Wolfe (from a story by Morton Grant) was as undistinguished as its score. Ann Doran, Steve Geray, Minerva Urecal and Sig Arno were also in it; Ted Richmond produced, and the director was Jean Yarbrough. Songs and musical numbers included: *Straw Hat Song* Fred Karger, Allan Roberts; *Rhumba Rumbero* Albert Gamse, Miguelito Valdez; *Copacabana* Doris Fisher, Allan Roberts; *Made For Each Other* Ervin Drake, Jimmy Shirl, Rene Touzet; *Holiday In Havana* Desi Arnaz; *I'll Take Romance* Oscar Hammerstein II, Ben Oakland.

◁ More campus shenanigans in **Yes Sir That's My Baby** (Universal), a low-voltage offering whose one bid for originality lay in the fact that the college kids on parade weren't kids at all but war veterans completing their education. Problems arise when biology professor Charles Coburn tries to form a football team against the wishes of the students' wives (who'd rather their spouses stayed at home and helped bring up baby). But the women relent in the last reel when they learn that Coburn will lose his job if the local team fails to come through in an important match. Donald O'Connor (illustrated) and Gloria De Haven were the main husband-and-wife embroiled in the so-called conflict, with other parts in Oscar Brodney's laugh-sparse screenplay going to Barbara Brown (as a psychology professor), Joshua Shelley, Jack Lambert, Jack Overman, George Spaulding, Michael Dugan and June Fulton. George Sherman directed and the producer was Leonard Goldstein, (Technicolor). Songs and musical numbers: *Men Are Little Children*; *They've Never Figured Out A Woman*; *Look At Me* Jack Brooks, Walter Scharf; *Yes Sir, That's My Baby* Gus Kahn, Walter Donaldson.

On The Town (MGM) started life as a Jerome Robbins ballet called *Fancy Free*. The material was reworked by composer Leonard Bernstein with a book and lyrics by Betty Comden and Adolph Green, and surfaced as a hit Broadway musical in 1944. Producer Arthur Freed prevailed on Louis B. Mayer to purchase the property – which he reluctantly did while, at the same time, condemning the show as 'smutty' and 'Communistic' because of a scene in it in which a black girl danced with a white man. Five years later, Freed, now securely entrenched as the studio's top producer of musicals, was finally given the green light by Mayer to proceed with the project. The result was the freshest, most invigorating and innovative screen musical of the decade, and the perfect vehicle for Gene Kelly who not only starred in it, but directed and choreographed it together with Stanley Donen. The story of **On The Town** was not nearly as innovative as its production. Three sailors disembark from their battleship in the Brooklyn Navy Yard at six o'clock one morning and spend the next 24 hours in search of women and fun. Kelly falls in love with a poster of the subway's Miss Turnstiles (Vera-Ellen, illustrated with Kelly in main picture) and spends half the film searching for its model whom he finally tracks down at Symphonic Hall where she is receiving ballet instruction from an inebriated Maria Ouspenskaya-type ballet mistress (Florence Bates). Sinatra, again cast as the timid butter-wouldn't-melt-in-the-mouth innocent, is chased with relentless zeal by a lady cab driver called Brunnhilde Esterhazy (Betty Garrett), while the third (Jules Munshin) makes quite a hit with an anthropologist (Ann Miller) he happens to meet at the Anthropological Museum. Which more or less took care of the story, except that Kelly and Donen invested it with so much that was new and exciting – from the expressive 'Miss Turnstiles' Ballet (Bernstein) to the scintillating sequence atop the Empire State building where the three couples rendezvous – that they changed the entire concept of the film musical, opening it out (some of it was actually filmed on location in New York and its environs) and relying on the dance for its chief mode of musical expression. The underlying feeling of the film was essentially balletic, and even when its cast were standing still (which wasn't very often) you felt they were about to take off any second. In fact, so concerned was Kelly that **On The Town** should retain its balletic flavour, that in the 'Day In New York' ballet (Bernstein) he substituted four trained ballet dancers (Alex Romero, Gene Scott, Carol Haney and Marie Grosscup) for Sinatra, Munshin, Betty Garrett and Ann Miller. Agnes de Mille had done this six years earlier on stage in the Dream Ballet for *Oklahoma!*, but it had never been attempted on the screen before. The less overtly balletic numbers were equally successful, such as Roger Edens, Betty Comden and Adolph Green's 'Prehistoric Man', danced by Miller in the anthropology museum with support from the rest of the principals; and the rousing 'New York, New York' (by Leonard Bernstein, Comden and Green) exuberantly performed by Kelly, Sinatra and Munshin. It wasn't until the last 20 minutes or so that the high standard the film set for itself flagged and became bogged down in plot. And if, while watching the movie today, a slight feeling of *déjà vu* insinuates itself, it is because films such as *Hit The Deck* (MGM, 1955), *Skirts Ahoy* (MGM,

1952), *It's Always Fair Weather* (MGM, 1955), *All Ashore* (Columbia, 1953), *So This Is Paris* (Universal International, 1955), and *Three Sailors And A Girl* (Warner Bros, 1953), all of which contained similar ingredients to **On The Town**, have, over the years, blunted one's appetite for this kind of simple-minded yarn. Also, it is to be regretted that most of Leonard Bernstein's original Broadway score was jettisoned in favour of a more 'commercial' one by Roger Edens, a particularly unfortunate loss being 'Lonely Town', one of Bernstein's most poignant songs. All the same, **On The Town**, which cost $2,111,250 to make (and grossed over $4,500,000 on its initial release) pushed the Hollywood musical out of its claustrophobic confines in search of new ideas, and was a landmark of its time. Edens, Conrad Salinger and Lennie Hayton scored it, it was photographed by Harold Rosson, costumed by Helen Rose and designed by Cedric Gibbons and Jack Martin Smith. Completing the cast were Alice Pearce as ugly-duckling Lucy Schmeeler, George Meader, Bea Benedaret, Hans Conried and, making a brief appearance, singer Bern Hoffman. It was filmed in Technicolor. The inset picture shows (from left) Sinatra, Garrett, Munshin, Miller, Kelly and Vera-Ellen. Other songs and musical numbers: *I Feel Like I'm Not Out Of Bed Yet* (Hoffman); *Come Up To My Place* (Sinatra, Garrett) Bernstein, Comden, Green; *Miss Turnstiles Ballet* (Vera-Ellen) Bernstein; *Main Street* (Kelly, Vera-Ellen); *You're Awful* (Sinatra, Garrett); *On The Town* (Kelly, Sinatra, Munshin, Miller, Garrett, Vera-Ellen); *You Can Count On Me* (Kelly, Sinatra, Munshin, Miller, Garrett, Pearce); *Pearl Of The Persian Sea*; *That's All There Is, Folks* Edens, Comden, Green.

1950

Producer William Jacobs invaded 20th Century-Fox territory with David Butler's Technicolor musical **The Daughter Of Rosie O'Grady** (Warner Bros.) in which the eponymous heroine (inoffensively played by June Haver, centre right) falls in love with the great Tony Pastor himself (Gordon MacRae, centre), to the disapproval of her tediously alcoholic father (James Barton, centre left). The script by Jack Rose, Melville Shavelson and Peter Milne was pure formula fare trading in turn-of-the-century nostalgia – though not nearly as effectively or with the panache of the Fox counterpart. Also in it: S.Z. Sakall, Gene Nelson (on Haver's right), Jane Darwell and a very young Debbie Reynolds. The sluggish dance direction was by LeRoy Prinz. Songs and musical numbers: *My Own True Love And I* M.K. Jerome, Jack Scholl; *As We Are Today* Ernesto Lecuona, Charles Tobias; *Ma Blushin' Rosie* Edgar Smith, Jan Stromberg; *The Rose Of Tralee* Charles Glover, C. Mordaunt Spencer; *A Farm Off Old Broadway*; *A Picture Turned To The Wall*; *Winter, Winter* A. Bryan-Gumble; *Winter Serenade*; *The Daughter Of Rosie O'Grady* Monty C. Brice, Walter Donaldson.

Michael Curtiz's **Young Man With A Horn** (GB: **Young Man Of Music**) involved a jazz trumpeter (Kirk Douglas, left) who, through a fanatical devotion to his art, wrecks his private life and almost forfeits the love of a long-suffering young singer (Doris Day). One of the less embarrassing biopics (the screenplay by Carl Foreman and Edmund H. North was inspired by a Dorothy Baker novel based on the legendary Bix Beiderbecke), it benefited from the customary intensity of Douglas's playing (both of the role itself and, via Harry James dubbed on the soundtrack, the trumpet) and the potent evocation, chiefly through music, of the '20s and '30s. Lauren Bacall (right) featured as a rich bitch who helps drive the musician to drink, with other roles going to Juano Hernandez, Jerome Cowan, Nestor Paiva and Mary Beth Hughes. It was narrated by Hoagy Carmichael, who also played a prominent supporting role, and produced for Warner Bros. by Jerry Wald. Songs: *The Very Thought Of You* Ray Noble; *I May Be Wrong* Henry Sullivan, Harry Ruskin; *The Man I Love* George and Ira Gershwin; *Too Marvellous For Words* Johnny Mercer, Richard A. Whiting; *Get Happy* Harold Arlen, Ted Koehler; *I Only Have Eyes For You* Al Dubin, Harry Warren; *Lullaby Of Broadway* Dubin, Warren; *With A Song In My Heart* Richard Rodgers, Lorenz Hart; *Can't We Be Friends* Paul James, Kay Swift; *Blue Room* Rodgers, Hart; *Chinatown* William Jerome, Jean Schwartz; *Manhattan Rhapsody* Ray Heindorf.

Romance, Music and Laughter were, according to the blurb circulated by Allied Artists, the chief ingredients of **There's A Girl In My Heart**. What the publicity boys failed to mention was its plot, whose chief ingredient was cobwebs. The story of a property developer who attempts (unsuccessfully) to acquire a valuable piece of property from an attractive widow and falls in love with her instead, it starred Lee Bowman as the developer and Elyse Knox as the widow, with Iris Adrian (illustrated centre), Gloria Jean, Peggy Ryan and Ray McDonald roped in for musical support. Lon Chaney (as Bowman's pal), Ludwig Donath, Joel Marston and Irene Ryan were also featured in Arthur Hoerl and the aptly named John Eugene Hasty's screenplay, and it was produced and directed by Arthur Dreifuss. Songs and musical numbers: *There's A Girl In My Heart* Arthur Dreifuss, Robert Bilder; *The Roller Skating Song*; *Be Careful Of The Tidal Wave*; *We Are The Main Attraction*; *Any Old Street* Robert Bilder; *A Bicycle Built For Two (Daisy Bell)* Harry Dacre; *After The Ball* Charles K. Harris.

Monogram's Bowery Boys made their only musical in **Blues Busters**, a pleasant programmer in which Huntz Hall (right), playing a character called Satch Debussy Jones suddenly finds himself the proud possessor of a marvellous crooning voice after undergoing a tonsillectomy. Bowery mastermind Leo Gorcey capitalizes on the discovery by remodelling a sweet shop owned by Louis Dumbrowsky (Bernard Gorcey) and turning it into a nightclub with Hall the stellar attraction. Adele Jergens appeared as rival club owner Craig Stevens's resident thrush, with other roles in Jan Grippo's production going to Gabriel Dell (left), Phyllis Coates, William Benedict, David Gorcey and Marty King. Charles R. Marion wrote it (additional dialogue by Bert Lawrence) and the director was William Beaudine. Songs included: *Wasn't It You; You Walk By* Ben Raleigh, Bernie Wayne; *Bluebirds Keep Singin' In The Rain* Johnny Lange, Eliot Daniel.

Walt Disney's version of **Cinderella** (RKO) was warmly welcomed by the press, but in no way showered with the kind of superlatives that greeted the same studio's *Snow White And The Seven Dwarfs* (1938) or *Pinocchio* (1940). Viewed today, it is every bit the equal of the two earlier films, matching them both in the skill of its animation (see illustration) and the scope of its invention. Based on the famous Charles Perrault fairy tale, the story was boldly reshaped by scenarists William Peed, Ted Sears, Erdman Penner, Winston Hibler and Harry Reeves to accommodate a host of Disneyesque characters, the most lovable being two household mice called Jacques and Gus-Gus who, in one of the film's most memorable sequences, join forces with several bluebirds to create a dress for Cinderella so that she might go to the ball after all. The more familiar *Cinderella* characters were traditionally realized in terms of good or evil, the ugly stepmother being almost too frightening for the comfort of the very young. Anastasia and Drusilla, the stepsisters, were, however, just right. Apart from the brilliance of its animation, **Cinderella** benefited, too, from a marvellous set of songs and, of course, from its vivid Technicolor. The production supervisor was again Ben Sharpsteen, and the voices on the soundtrack belonged to Ilene Woods (Cinderella), William Phipps (Prince Charming), Eleanor Audley (stepmother), Rhoda Williams and Lucille Bliss (Anastasia and Drusilla), Verna Felton (fairy godmother), Luis Van Rooten (King and Grand Duke) and James McDonald (Gus-Gus and Jacques). Songs: *Bibbidi-Bobbidi-Boo*; *So This Is Love*; *A Dream Is A Wish Your Heart Makes*; *Cinderella*; *The Work Song*; *Sing Sweet Nightingale* Mack David, Jerry Livingston, Al Hoffman.
▽

A minor entry from Columbia, **The Petty Girl** (GB: **Girl Of The Year**), photographed in Technicolor, starred Robert Cummings as a painter called George Petty and Joan Caulfield (illustrated foreground) as the prudish burlesque stripper who poses for him, then becomes his bride. Third-billed Elsa Lanchester committed grand larceny in every scene she was in, with other roles in producer Nat Perrin's screenplay (from a story by Mary McCarthy) going to Melville Cooper, Audrey Long, Mary Wickes, Frank Orth, John Ridgely, Raymond Largay, Ian Wolfe, Frank Jenks and Tim Ryan. Musical highlight: a production number featuring a dozen other 'Petty' girls in various stages of *deshabille* as each represents a different month of the year. The director of this lively little show was Henry Levin. Songs and musical numbers included: *Petty Girl*; *Fancy Free*; *Calypso Song*; *Ah Loves You* Harold Arlen, Johnny Mercer. ▷

Two lavish production numbers (staged by Jack Donohue), guest-star Lena Horne's singing of 'Baby Come Out Of The Clouds' (by Lee Pearl and Henry Nemo), and a lively routine by Mrs Glenn Ford (better known as Eleanor Powell, who tapped her way out of retirement for the occasion), were among the musical highlights in **The Duchess Of Idaho** (MGM), a Joe Pasternak-produced trifle, dazzlingly photographed in Technicolor, and starring Esther Williams and Van Johnson (both illustrated foreground). When not demonstrating the crawl and the backstroke, Miss Williams (playing a well-known swimming star) was helping her rather forlorn room-mate (Paula Raymond) to lead her wealthy playboy boss (John Lund) to the altar, in the process of which she and bandleader Van Johnson realize that they're mutually attracted. Scenarists Dorothy Cooper and Jerry Davis ensured a happy ending to their predictable story (the only surprise was an unbilled guest appearance by Red Skelton), and the director was Robert Z. Leonard. Also in it: Mel Torme, Clinton Sundberg, Connie Haines, Amanda Blake, Tommy Farrell, Sig Arno and Dick Simmons. Other songs and musical numbers: *You Can't Do Wrong Doin' Right*; *Let's Choo Choo Choo To Idaho*; *Of All Things*; *Or Was It Spring*; *Warm Hands, Cold Heart* Al Rinker, Floyd Huddleston; *Singlefoot Serenade* G.M. Beilenson, M. Beelby; *You Won't Forget Me* Kermit Goell, Fred Spielman.
▽

A remake of Frank Capra's *Broadway Bill* (Columbia, 1934), **Riding High** (Paramount) starred Bing Crosby (in the role originally played by Warner Baxter) as a horse-trainer whose devotion to a faithful horse, at the expense of a romance with a millionairess, pays off with a handsome win. Unfortunately though, the horse dies in the process. Written by Robert Riskin, with additional dialogue by Melville Shavelson and Jack Rose, and again directed by Capra with a sureness of touch and a real feeling for its racing milieu, it was a perfect vehicle for Crosby (centre) who was marvellous in it. Four songs by Johnny Burke and Jimmy Van Heusen were neatly interspersed into the narrative and were a pleasing bonus to a screenplay that didn't really need musical embellishment. Coleen Gray (right) was the leading lady, with other roles going to Charles Bickford, William Demarest, and, repeating the roles they originally played, Clarence Muse (left, as Crosby's stableboy), Raymond Walburn, Douglass Dumbrille, Ward Bond, Paul Harvey. Also: Frankie Darro, Gene Lockhart, Charles Lane, Percy Kilbride, Frances Gifford and Margaret Hamilton. Capra produced. Songs: *The Horse Told Me*; *Sunshine Cake*; *We've Got A Sure Thing*; *Someplace On Anywhere Road* Burke, Van Heusen; *De Camptown Races* Stephen Foster; *Whiffenpoof Song* Meade Minnigerode, George S. Pomeroy, Tod B. Galloway.

◁ Producer Joe Pasternak dusted off one of Deanna Durbin's old scripts (*It's A Date*, Universal, 1940) and hired Sidney Sheldon to refurbish it (from the story by Jane Hall, Frederick Kohner and Ralph Block) as a starring vehicle for petite and pretty Jane Powell (centre left) and, in the role played a decade earlier by Kay Francis, Ann Sothern. The story of a mother and daughter who, while on an ocean voyage to Rio, both covet the same parts in a play, as well as the same man (Barry Sullivan), the slender narrative of **Nancy Goes To Rio** was padded out by a misunderstanding that arises when Miss Powell is thought to be pregnant. The musical programme accompanying the plot was a typical Pasternakian lucky-dip of the old and the new and the classical, the best of the middle category being 'Time And Time Again' by Earl Brent and Fred Spielman, pleasantly sung by Miss Powell. Pleasing too was Nick Castle's staging of 'Shine On Harvest Moon' (by Jack Norworth and Nora Bayes), delightfully rendered in song and dance by Powell, Sothern and Louis Calhern. Carmen Miranda was also in it (doing a number called 'Cha Bomm Pa Pa' by Ray Gilbert) with other parts going to Scotty Beckett (centre right with Powell), Fortunio Bonanova, Glenn Anders, Nella Walker, Hans Conried and Frank Fontaine. The glossy direction (in Technicolor) was by Robert Z. Leonard. Other songs and musical numbers: *Magic Is The Moonlight* Charles Pasquale, Maria Grever; *Love Is Like This* Ray Gilbert, Vianna; *Nancy Goes To Rio* George Stoll, Earl Brent; *Yipsee-I-O* Gilbert; *Musetta's Waltz* (from 'La Boheme') Puccini.

Despite the generous selection of operatic extracts in producer Joe Pasternak's **The Toast of New Orleans** (MGM), the song that made the biggest impression on audiences was 'Be My Love', composed by Nicholas Brodszky and Sammy Cahn, and sung by Kathryn Grayson and Mario Lanza, at the tops of their ample voices. Lanza (right), in a role not dissimilar to the one he played in *That Midnight Kiss* (MGM), was cast as a singing fisherman in a Louisiana bayou. Kathryn Grayson (left) was a famous soprano, David Niven was third-billed as Grayson's urbane manager who decides to groom Lanza for an operatic career. Cy Gomberg and George Wells's exiguous plot focused largely on Lanza's rough-and-ready behaviour as Niven's protégè, and his stormy romance with Grayson which only narrowly averts blows during the tender love duet from Act I of Puccini's *Madam Butterfly*. Though the narrative traded mainly in clichés, director Norman Taurog, aided by Technicolor, some glorious music and the volatile personality of his two stars, managed to impart to it a veneer of sophistication that went some way to disguise its basic lack of originality. Brodszky and Cahn contributed several other numbers to the jolly proceedings, most notably 'The Tina Lina' and 'Boom Biddy Boom Boom', and the supporting cast was completed by J. Carrol Naish as Lanza's doting, fisherman uncle, dancer James Mitchell (underused), Richard Hageman (centre), Clinton Sundberg, Sig Arno, Rita Moreno and Romo Vincent. The choreography was by Eugene Loring, and the musical direction by George Stoll and Johnny Green. Other songs, musical numbers, and operatic extracts: *Brindisi* (from 'La Traviata') Verdi; *O Paradiso* (from 'La Gioconda') Ponchielli; *The Toast Of New Orleans*; *I'll Never Love You*; *Song Of The Bayou* Brodszky, Cahn; *Flower Song* (from 'Carmen') Bizet; *Je Suis Titania* (from 'Mignon') Thomas; *M'Appari* (from 'Martha') Flotow.

Ethel Merman belted it out on stage for 1,159 performances; Judy Garland was signed for the screen version, and Betty Hutton finally got to play it. The role was Annie Oakley, the show was Irving Berlin's **Annie Get Your Gun**, which George Sidney directed (replacing Busby Berkeley and Charles Walters) to give MGM its top money-making musical of 1950. Sidney Sheldon's adaptation and screenplay from Herbert and Dorothy Fields's original book stuck as closely to the Broadway version of the show as was considered decent by Hollywood's meddlesome standards – and although the score lost a few numbers between Times Square and Culver City (most notably 'Moonshine Lullaby' and 'Who Do You Love, I Hope') the spirit of the piece was left intact. The simple story of an unorthodox love affair between two prize sharpshooters who are attached to different Wild West shows, the film co-starred Howard Keel in the role played on stage by Ray Middleton, with Louis Calhern (who replaced Frank Morgan after the latter's death) as Buffalo Bill, J. Carrol Naish as Sitting Bull, and Edward Arnold as Pawnee Bill. Keenan Wynn, Benay Venuta and Clinton Sundberg completed the cast. It was photographed in Technicolor, and was another triumph for producer Arthur Freed, and for Robert Alton, whose staging of the musical numbers (Hutton in 'I'm An Indian Too' illustrated) did Berlin's magnificent score proud. All the performances were spot-on, especially Hutton's, which, after a slightly frenetic start, settled down to become the highwater mark of her career. The musical director was Adolph Deutsch. Songs and musical numbers: *Colonel Buffalo Bill* (chorus); *I've Got The Sun In The Morning* (Hutton); *You Can't Get A Man With A Gun* (Hutton); *They Say That Falling In Love Is Wonderful* (Hutton, Keel); *My Defences Are Down* (Keel); *There's No Business Like Show Business* (Hutton, Keel, Wynn, Calhern); *Doin' What Comes Naturally* (Hutton, and children); *The Girl That I Marry* (Keel); *Anything You Can Do* (Hutton, Keel).

Tea For Two, competently directed by David Butler, proved to be among the most delightful and successful of Warner Bros.' cycle of Doris Day musicals. Very loosely based on the Otto Harbach-Frank Mandel Broadway hit of 1924 *No, No, Nanette* (and its subsequent revivals), Harry Clork's screenplay concerned Doris's attempts to say 'no' to every offer or proposition not, as in her later Universal-International comedies, to preserve her virginity, but to win a bet whose stake would allow her to finance (and, naturally, star in) a Broadway show. The movie, told in flashback, was absolutely without pretensions, benefited from a collection of watertight standards and, ably supported by Gordon MacRae, Gene Nelson (illustrated), Patrice Wymore, Eve Arden, Billy De Wolfe, dancer Virginia Gibson, and the inevitable S.Z. Sakall, Miss Day's bright, scrubbed, American-as-apple-pie energy, especially in LeRoy Prinz's better than usual dance numbers, charmed even the most curmudgeonly spectator. It was produced, in Technicolor by William Jacobs. Songs and musical numbers: *I Want To Be Happy*; *Tea For Two* Vincent Youmans, Irving Caesar; *No, No Nanette* Youmans, Otto Harbach; *Oh Me, Oh My!* Youmans, Ira Gershwin; *I Know That You Know* Youmans, Anne Caldwell; *Do Do Do* George and Ira Gershwin; *Crazy Rhythm* Irving Caesar, Joseph Meyer, Roger Wolfe Kahn; *Charleston* Cecil Mack, Jimmie Johnson; *I Only Have Eyes For You* Al Dubin, Harry Warren; *The Call Of The Sea* Youmans, Caesar, Harbach.

After the beautiful music they made together in Fox's *When My Baby Smiles At Me* (1948), Betty Grable (left) and Dan Dailey (right) were again teamed for **My Blue Heaven** (20th Century-Fox) – but this one was a black mark for both their careers. The banal story of a husband-and-wife TV team who, after adopting a child, discover they're about to have one of their own, it was notable only in that it introduced movie audiences to Mitzi Gaynor. Apart from the title song, sung by Grable and Dailey and written by George Whiting and Walter Donaldson, the rest of the score was by Ralph Blane and Harold Arlen, the best of the batch being Gaynor's 'Live Hard, Work Hard, Love Hard'. David Wayne co-starred, and the cast was completed by Una Merkel, Louise Beavers and Laura Pierpont. Sol C. Siegel produced (in Technicolor), the schmaltzy direction was by Henry Koster, and it was written by Lamar Trotti and Claude Binyon from a story by S.K. Lauren. Other songs and musical numbers: *Don't Rock The Boat Dear*; *Friendly Islands*; *Halloween*; *I Love A New Yorker*; *It's Deductible*; *What A Man*.

Popular music stars Frankie Laine, Billy Daniels, The Mills Brothers, Bob Crosby, Kay Starr, and The Modernaires were the chief attractions of **When You're Smiling**, a low-budget entertainment from Columbia with a plot of sorts involving the unscrupulous activities of a recording-company boss (Jerome Cowan) who happens to be heavily in debt to a bookmaker. In order to alleviate his financial situation, he attempts to marry off his daughter (Margo Woode) to a supposedly wealthy Texas·cowhand (Jerome Courtland, left). The cowhand, however, has a mind of his own, preferring Cowan's pretty secretary (Lola Albright, right). Miss Albright reciprocates his affections, and helps turn him into a star. Karen De Wolf and John R. Roberts were responsible for writing the clap-trap, Jonie Taps produced, and the director was Joseph Santley. Songs and musical numbers included: *When You're Smiling* Mark Fisher, Joe Goodwin, Larry Shay; *That Old Black Magic* Harold Arlen, Johnny Mercer; *When The Wind Was Green* Don Hunt.

After Betty Hutton's enormous personal success in MGM's *Annie Get Your Gun*, Paramount wasted no time in putting their top female star to work. Unfortunately, **Let's Dance** was an inferior little item in spite of the presence of Fred Astaire (second billed). It cast them as wartime entertainers whose act splits up when Betty's flyer husband is killed in action. She returns to Boston, her home town, and spends the next five years raising her child; meanwhile, Astaire becomes a business man. Tired of domesticity, Hutton (right) decides to make a show-biz comeback, persuades Astaire (left) to rejoin the act and, before you can say 'I told you so', the couple fall in love. Apart from its indifferent screenplay by Allan Scott and Dane Lussier (from a story by Maurice Zolotow), the thing that was really wrong with **Let's Dance** was the uneasy melding of the personalities of its two stars who never really seemed right together. A couple of lively dance routines – notably 'Can't Stop Talking' and 'Oh Them Dudes' (by Frank Loesser, who supplied all the lyrics and music) – were passingly enjoyable, but the sparkle wasn't there. Lucille Watson played a hissable mother-in-law out to gain custody of Miss Hutton's child, and Roland Young and Melville Cooper provided comic relief as her two attorneys, with other roles under Norman Z. McLeod's direction going to Ruth Warrick, Gregory Moffett, Barton MacLane, Shepherd Strudwick, Harold Huber and George Zucco. It was choreographed by Hermes Pan and the producer was Robert Fellows. Other songs and musical numbers: *Piano Dance* (interpolating *Tiger Rag*); *Jack And The Beanstalk*; *Why Fight The Feeling?*; *The Hyacinth*; *Tunnel Of Love*.

Three Little Words (MGM), a biopic of composers Bert Kalmar and Harry Ruby, was one of the better musicals of 1950. Relying more on plot than on a series of elaborately staged production numbers (though there were a few of those as well) it was an entertaining account of two showbiz careers, with Fred Astaire top-billed as lyricist Kalmar and a subdued Red Skelton as composer Ruby. George Wells's scenario took in the main points of the two men's lives, showing Kalmar to have been a vaudeville song-and-dance man (with a hankering to be a magician) who turns to lyric writing when a knee injury ends his career as a dancer; and Ruby to have been a honky-tonk pianist with a yearning to play baseball. The two men get together to form a songwriting team, take Broadway and Hollywood by storm, then split up over a misunderstanding. It is their wives (according to Wells's fanciful screenplay) who bring them together again. Vera-Ellen (whose vocals were dubbed by Anita Ellis) played Mrs Kalmar, Arlene Dahl was Mrs Ruby, with other parts going to Keenan Wynn, Gale Robbins, Phil Regan (as himself), Harry Shannon, Paul Harvey, Carleton Carpenter, George Metkovich and The Great Mendoza (as himself). In her third film, Debbie Reynolds

was seen as 'Boop-Boop-a-Doop' girl Helen Kane, with Miss Kane herself dubbing the vocals in Kalmar, Ruby and Herbert Stothart's 'I Wanna Be Loved By You'; while Gloria De Haven played her mother, Mrs Carter De Haven, and sang 'Who's Sorry Now' (Kalmar, Ruby and Ted Snyder). Other highlights were 'Mr And Mrs Hoofer At Home' danced by Astaire and Vera-Ellen (both illustrated) and the same team's 'Thinking Of You'. The choreography was by Hermes Pan, Andre Previn was the musical director, it was produced (in Technicolor) by Jack Cummings, and directed by Richard Thorpe. Other songs and musical numbers: *Three Little Words* (Astaire, Skelton, Vera-Ellen); *I Love You So Much* (Dahl, male chorus); *She's Mine, All Mine* (Barber Shop Quartet); *So Long Oo-Long* (Astaire, Skelton); *Hooray For Captain Spaulding* (incomplete) (Skelton, Astaire); *Up In The Clouds* (chorus); *All Alone Monday* (Robbins) Kalmar, Ruby; *Nevertheless* (Astaire, Vera-Ellen); *Where Did You Get That Girl?* (Astaire, Vera-Ellen) Kalmar, Ruby, Harry Puck; *My Sunny Tennessee* (Astaire, Skelton) Kalmar, Ruby, Herman Ruby; *Come On Papa* (Vera-Ellen, chorus) Harry Ruby, Edgar Leslie; *You Are My Lucky Star* (Regan) Arthur Freed, Nacio Herb Brown.

Fifties Musicals

John Carroll played a dual role in **Hit Parade of 1951** (Republic): a reckless Las Vegas gambler and a rather effeminate crooner. That old standby, mistaken identity, loomed large in Elizabeth Reinhardt, Aubrey Wisberg and Lawrence Kimble's screenplay (story by Wisberg), causing chaos and confusion when the gambler loses $200,000 and the crooner loses his dissatisfied girlfriend (Marie McDonald, illustrated). Euphemistically speaking, it was a routine affair, with several songs and production numbers included as garnishing. Estelita Rodriguez, Frank (John L.C. Sevony) Fontaine, Grant Withers, Mikhail Rasumny and Steve Flagg also appeared for producer-director John H. Auer, and the dances were staged by Val Raset. Songs and musical numbers included: *Square Dance Samba*; *You're So Nice*; *How Would I Know?*; *Wishes Come True*; *You Don't Know The Other Side Of Me* Al Rinker, Floyd Huddleston.

▽

△

Bing Crosby hardly extended his range in **Mr Music** (Paramount), a genial, albeit insubstantial effort that benefited from an agreeable score by Johnny Burke and Jimmy Van Heusen, the best number being the oft-reprised 'Life Is So Peculiar' – sung by Crosby and guest stars Peggy Lee and The Merry Macs. Marge (illustrated) and Gower Champion (as themselves) did it as a dance; and Groucho Marx (another guest star) joined Crosby to do it in a sketch. Also guesting was Dorothy Kirsten, who sang a duet with Crosby called 'Accidents Will Happen'. As for the plot, it was all about a songwriter who'd rather play golf than write songs . . . Nancy Olson as Bing's faithful secretary and Charles Coburn as a Broadway producer co-starred, with other parts in Arthur Sheekman's screenplay ('suggested' by Samson Raphaelson's play *Accent On Youth*) going to Ruth Hussey, Robert Stack, Tom Ewell, Ida Moore, Charles Kemper, Donald Woods and Richard Haydn. Haydn also directed, and the producer was Robert L. Welch. Other songs: *Mr Music*; *And You'll Be Home*; *High On The List*; *Wouldn't It Be Funny*; *Wasn't I There?*

316

Judy Garland's last film for MGM was **Summer Stock** (GB: **If You Feel Like Singing**) an old-fashioned 'let's put on a show in a barn' yarn, but with adults rather than adolescents in the star parts. Gene Kelly was cast opposite Garland, with other roles in George Wells and Cy Gomberg's screenplay going to Phil Silvers, Gloria De Haven, Eddie Bracken, Marjorie Main, Ray Collins, Nita Bieber, Carleton Carpenter and Hans Conried. Its simple story ran thus: Jane, New England farm girl (Garland), has her peaceful, bucolic existence interrupted when her sister Abigail (De Haven) invites a troupe of show folk to use their barn as a summer theatre. Garland is furious at this invasion of her privacy, and insists that the actors help out on the farm to pay for the use of the barn and the food they eat. In time, however, she falls in love with Ross (Kelly), the show's author, and, on opening night becomes a star when she has to step into De Haven's shoes. This juvenile scenario, unworthy of the talents of its two leading players, was redeemed by a series of splendidly staged musical numbers, the two most outstanding being Kelly's solo dance with a piece of newspaper and a squeaking floorboard (which he choreographed and devised himself to 'You Wonderful You' by Harry Warren, Jack Brooks and Saul Chaplin) and Garland's 'Get Happy' (by Harold Arlen and Ted Koehler), filmed three months after the movie's completion by Charles Walters. The sequence featured a slimline Garland – she was decidedly over-weight in the rest of the footage – sexily dressed in a man's tuxedo jacket and wearing a natty hat whose brim covered her right eye (see illustration). It was the classiest thing in the show and one of the best numbers Garland ever committed to film. **Summer Stock** was produced in Technicolor by Joe Pasternak and directed by Charles Walters. Other songs and musical numbers: *If You Feel Like Singing*; *Happy Harvest*; *Friendly Star*; *Blue Jean Polka*; *Mem'ry Island*; *Dig-Dig-Dig For Your Dinner* Harry Warren, Mack Gordon; *Heavenly Music* Saul Chaplin.

▷

△

Eight years after his triumph in Warner Bros.' *Yankee Doodle Dandy*, James Cagney returned to musicals in the same studio's **The West Point Story** (GB: **Fine And Dandy**). The Louis F. Edelman production told the lack-lustre story of a failed Broadway producer (Cagney, right) making his comeback with a spectacular show at the famous military academy and becoming, in the process, a cadet himself. In spite of Cagney's zestful and cocky central performance, and the efforts of a cast that included Doris Day, Gordon MacRae, Virginia Mayo (left), Gene Nelson, Alan Hale Jr, Jerome Cowan and Roland

Winters, the film's rather mindless endorsement of military life hardly met the requirements of musical comedy, and the score by Jule Styne and Sammy Cahn was one of the team's weakest. The credits (or debits) included John Monks Jr, Charles Hoffman and Irving Wallace for the longueur-filled script, Roy Del Ruth for the flabby direction, and LeRoy Prinz for the indifferent choreography. Songs and musical numbers: *Ten Thousand Four Hundred And Thirty Two Sheep*; *By The Kissing Rock*; *You Love Me*; *Military Polka*; *Long Before I Knew You*; *It Could Only Happen In Brooklyn*; *The Corps*; *Brooklyn*.

△

Though Jane Powell (left), Ricardo Montalban (right), Louis Calhern and Ann Harding were all billed above her, it was cute little Debbie Reynolds who hogged most of the notices for **Two Weeks With Love** (MGM), a nostalgic, turn of the century musical, set in the Catskills and all about the romantic adventures of Patti and Melba Robinson (Powell and Reynolds) who are spending a two-week vacation in the famous mountain resort with their parents (Calhern and Harding), and younger brothers (Gary Gray and Tommy Rettig). Powell, the elder of the two sisters (but still too young to wear corsets), falls for handsome Montalban (and has to compete for his affections with a more experienced Phyllis Kirk); while Reynolds makes a successful bee-line for gangly Carleton Carpenter. Together Reynolds and Carpenter performed 'Aba Daba Honeymoon' (by Arthur Fields and Walter Donovan) which was the highlight of producer Jack Cummings's entrancing little film. Less successful was a somewhat Freudian dream sequence, which combined Powell's fervent wish to be clothed in a corset with her equally fervent desire to be swept off her feet by Montalban. The number was staged by Busby Berkeley, who was in charge of the dance direction throughout and who, in 'The Oceana Roll' (by Roger Lewis and Lucien Denni), performed by Powell and a group of kids in the lounge of a hotel, again proved how effective a number could be without recourse to elaborate overhead shots or armies of extras. The director was Roy Rowland, and the cast was completed by Clinton Sundberg and Charles Smith. (Technicolor). Other songs and musical numbers: *A Heart That's Free* Thomas T. Railey, Alfred G. Robyn; *By The Light Of The Silvery Moon* Gus Edwards, Edward Madden; *My Hero* Stanislaus Stange, Oscar Straus; *Row Row Row* William Jerome, James V. Monaco; *That's How I Need You* Joe McCarthy, Joe Goodwin; *Beautiful Lady* Ivan Caryll, C.H.S. McClellan.

◁ A remake of *Tin Pan Alley* (20th Century-Fox, 1940), **I'll Get By**, also from the Fox factory, starred June Haver (2nd right) as a vocalist, William Lundigan (right) as a struggling music publisher whose career she helps to promote, and Dennis Day (centre) as a composer who becomes Lundigan's partner in a publishing business. Though no fewer than five (count 'em) writers were credited with the story (Robert Ellis, Helen Logan, Pamela Harris) and screenplay (Mary Loos, Richard Sale), the narrative was washed away in a tidal wave of music, leaving Haver and Lundigan very little to do in the way of acting. The same applied to co-stars Gloria De Haven (2nd left, as Haver's sister), Harry James (as himself, left) and Thelma Ritter. The story was updated from World War I to World War II, and the musical highlights included Haver and De Haven singing 'Taking A Chance On Love' (by John Latouche, Ted Fetter and Vernon Duke), as well as Haver's pleasant account of the title number (by Roy Turk and Fred Ahlert). Jeanne Crain, Victor Mature, Reginald Gardiner and Dan Dailey (who did a brief dance with Haver and De Haven) made guest appearances, it was directed by Richard Sale, choreographed by Larry Ceballos, and produced (in Technicolor) by William Perlberg. Other songs and musical numbers included: *Deep In The Heart Of Texas* June Hershey, Don Swander; *You Make Me Feel So Young* Mack Gordon, Josef Myrow; *I've Got The World On A String* Ted Koehler, Harold Arlen; *Once In A While* Bud Green, Michael Edwards; *Yankee Doodle Blues* Buddy De Sylva, Irving Caesar, George Gershwin; *Fifth Avenue*; *There Will Never Be Another You* Mack Gordon, Harry Warren; *McNamara's Band* Shamus O'Connor, J.J. Stamford; *It's Been A Long, Long Time* Sammy Cahn, Jule Styne; *No Love, No Nothin'* Leo Robin, Harry Warren; *Auld Lang Syne* music traditional, lyrics Robert Burns.

Despite its colourful Tahitian settings, the at-   ▷ tractive presences of Esther Williams and Howard Keel, and a passable score, largely provided by Harry Warren and producer Arthur Freed, **Pagan Love Song** (MGM) was, artistically, the least successful of Freed's films, even though it grossed over $3,200,000 on the marquee value of Williams's name. The fault lay in Robert Nathan and Jerry Davis's amorphous screenplay (from the book *Tahiti Landfall* by William S. Stone), a mere bagatelle which had Keel as a schoolteacher arriving in Tahiti to take over his late uncle's coconut plantation and mistaking American-born Williams (illustrated foreground centre) for a *bona fide* island native. How he successfully woos her, and learns that when in Tahiti one does as the Tahitians do, provided the film with its dreary content. Freed and Nacio Herb Brown's famous 'Pagan Love Song' (first sung by Ramon Novarro in MGM's *The Pagan*, 1929) was given due prominence in the musical programme, and from Roger Edens came a number called 'Mata'. One lavish water ballet helped brighten the proceedings, and Williams sang 'The Sea Of The Moon' (by Warren and Freed) most pleasingly. Rita Moreno was in it too, so were Minna Gombell, Charles Mau, Philip Costa, Dione Leilani and Charles Freund. It was photographed in Technicolor, and directed and choreographed by Robert Alton, who replaced Freed's original choice, Stanley Donen, after Williams refused to work with him. Other songs and musical numbers: *The House Of Singing Bamboo; Singing In The Sun; Tahiti; Why Is Love So Crazy?; Etiquette* Warren, Freed.

△

Wabash Avenue (20th Century-Fox), a colourful remake of the same studio's *Coney Island* (1943), was set at the time of the 1892 Chicago World Fair, and starred 34-year-old Betty Grable (centre left), and Victor Mature (right foreground) and Phil Harris (seated 2nd left) as a couple of con-men artists who are both in love with her. Grable played a shimmy dancer in a gas-lit saloon and apart from bringing the house down with 'I Wish I Could Shimmy Like My Sister Kate' (by Armand J. Piron and Peter Bocage) was given ample opportunity to reveal that she still had the greatest pair of legs in the business. Mack Gordon and Josef Myrow provided her with several excellent new songs, the two best being a little item called 'Walking Along With Billy' and 'Baby Won't You Say You Love Me'. Though the storyline couldn't have been more hackneyed, scenarists Harry Tugend and Charles Lederer somehow managed to doll it up, imparting to it the kind of zest that had characterized the best of Fox's period musicals in the forties. The supporting cast included Reginald Gardiner (back left), James Barton, Barry Kelley (seated centre), Margaret Hamilton, Jacqueline Dalya, Robin Raymond, Hal K. Dawson and Irving Bacon. Henry Koster directed and it was produced by William Perlberg. Other songs and musical numbers: *Wilhelmina; May I Tempt You With A Big Red Rosy Apple?; Clean Up Chicago; Down On Wabash Avenue* Gordon, Myrow; *I've Been Floating Down The Old Green River* Bert Kalmar, Joe Cooper.

1951

Academic Awards

Best Picture
An American In Paris (MGM) produced by
Arthur Freed

Direction
NOMINATIONS INCLUDED: Vincente Minnelli *An
American In Paris*

Writing (Story and Screenplay)
An American In Paris Alan Jay Lerner

Cinematography (colour)
An American In Paris Alfred Gilks and John
Alton
NOMINATIONS INCLUDED: *Show Boat* (MGM)
Charles Rosher

**Art Direction (Set Decoration)
(colour)**
An American In Paris Cedric Gibbons and
Preston Ames; Edwin B. Willis and Keogh
Gleason.

Music
Song
'In The Cool, Cool, Cool Of The Evening'
Here Comes The Groom (Paramount) Hoagy
Carmichael *cm*; Johnny Mercer *lyr*.
NOMINATIONS INCLUDED: 'A Kiss To Build A
Dream On' *The Strip* (MGM) music and lyrics
by Bert Kalmar, Harry Ruby and Oscar
Hammerstein II. 'Never' *Golden Girl* (20th
Century-Fox) Lionel Newman *cm*; Eliot
Daniel *lyr*. 'Too Late Now' *Royal Wedding*
(MGM) Burton Lane *cm*; Alan Jay Lerner *lyr*.
'Wonder Why' *Rich, Young And Pretty*
(MGM) Nicholas Brodszky *cm*; Sammy Cahn
lyr.

Scoring Of A Musical Picture
An American In Paris Johnny Green and Saul
Chaplin
NOMINATIONS INCLUDED: *Alice In Wonderland*
(Disney, RKO) Oliver Wallace. *The Great
Caruso* (MGM) Peter Herman Adler and
Johnny Green. *On The Riviera* (20th Century-
Fox) Alfred Newman. *Show Boat* Adolph
Deutsch and Conrad Salinger.

Costume Design (colour)
An American In Paris Orry-Kelly. Walter
Plunkett and Irene Sharaff
NOMINATIONS INCLUDED: *The Great Caruso*
Helen Rose and Gile Steele

Sound Recording
The Great Caruso Douglas Shearer, sound
director.
NOMINATIONS INCLUDED: *Two Tickets To
Broadway* (RKO) John Aalberg, sound
director.

Honorary Award
To Gene Kelly, in appreciation of his
versatility as an actor, singer, director and
dancer and specifically for his brilliant
achievements in the art of choreography of
film. (statuette)

The New York Times Annual 'Ten Best'
7th *An American In Paris*

The Annual Top Moneymaking Films
INCLUDED: *Show Boat. An American in Paris.
The Great Caruso* (Paramount).
At War With The Army (Paramount).
*Royal Wedding. Here Comes The Groom.
On Moonlight Bay* (WB). *On The
Riviera.*

Of Men And Music (20th Century-Fox) was a showcase for the extraordinary talents of pianist Arthur Rubinstein, tenor Jan Peerce, soprano Nadine Connor, violinist Jascha Heifetz and conductor Dimitri Mitropoulos. In four unrelated sequences, and via four embarrassingly contrived little scenarios, they were put to work, with musical results that were more satisfactory than the flimsy narrative content. Rubinstein opened the programme with performances of Mendelssohn's 'Spinning Song', Liszt's 'Liebestraum', and Chopin's Waltz in C Sharp Minor and Polonaise in A Major. The sequence ended with the maestro playing 'Pop Goes The Weasel' for his children. Next Jan Peerce and Nadine Connor (see illustration) entered a bare stage and launched into a series of songs and arias. Peerce began with 'O Paradiso' from Meyerbeer's 'L'Africaine', and 'Matinata' by Leoncavallo, followed by Miss Connor who sang an aria from Donizetti's 'Don Pasquale'. They then joined forces for a duet from Donizetti's 'Lucia Di Lammermoor'. Next, Jascha Heifetz was introduced in his comfortable home in California and, accompanied by Emanuel Ray, played Bach's Partita Prelude, Debussy's 'The Girl With The Flaxen Hair', Wienieawski's 'Scherzo Tarantelle' and Paganini's Caprice No 24. The fourth,

and most satisfactory, sequence was a rehearsal session in which Dimitri Mitropoulos conducted the Philharmonic Symphony Orchestra in a performance of the third movement of Liszt's 'Faust' Symphony. **Of Men And Music** was directed by Irving Reis and Alex Hammid, written by Liam O'Brien, Harry Kurnitz, John Paxton and David Epstein, featured Deems Taylor in an introductory segment, and was produced by Rudolph Polk and Bernard Luber.
▽

Rhythm Inn, a programmer from Monogram, involved some pawned musical instruments belonging to a Dixieland band having to be smuggled out of the pawnshop every night so that the group can fulfil a contractual obligation. It also involved a music store clerk with a yen to be a songsmith, as well as his girlfriend whose dream it is to become a successful vocalist. What it failed to involve was audiences. Charles Smith was the would-be writer, Lois Collier the would-be singer, and Kirby Grant the bandleader. Jane Frazee (illustrated) also appeared as a band singer, so did Fritz Feld, Ralph Sanford, and specialties Armida, Anson Weeks and His Orchestra, skater Jean Ritchie, Ames and Arno, and Ramon Ros. Bill Raynor wrote it, Paul Landres directed and the producer was Lindsley Parsons. Songs and musical numbers included: *It's A Big Wide Wonderful World* John Rox; *Chi Chi* Armida; *Love* Bill Raynor, Edward J. Kay; *B Flat Blues*; *Return Trip*; *What Does It Matter?* Kay; *With A Twist Of The Wrist* Irvin Graham.
▽

△
On The Riviera (20th Century-Fox), first seen as a Broadway play (by Rudolph Lothar and Hans Adler) in 1934, then, a year later, as a showcase for Maurice Chevalier (*Folies Bergère*) and, in 1941 as a starring vehicle for Don Ameche (*That Night In Rio*) was the story of a nightclub entertainer whose striking physical resemblance to a well-known financier deceives even the financier's wife. This version starred Danny Kaye in the double lead, with Gene Tierney as the deceived wife and Corinne Calvet as the entertainer's girlfriend. Also: Marcel Dalio, Henri Letondal, Clinton Sundberg, Sig Rumann, Joyce MacKenzie, Marina Koshetz, Ann Codee and dancer Gwen Verdon. The familiar story was given a slight overhaul by Valentine Davies and Phoebe and Henry Ephron, its glamorous Riviera setting this time taking the place of Paris and Rio. Sylvia Fine provided a quartet of songs, best of which was 'Popo The Puppet' (illustrated, with Kaye) staged, as were the rest of the numbers, by Jack Cole. It was produced (in Technicolor) by Sol C. Siegel, and the pedestrian direction was by Walter Lang. Other songs and musical numbers: *On The Riviera; Rhythm Of A New Romance; Happy Ending* Fine; *Ballin' The Jack* Jim Burris, Chris Smith.

Call Me Mister (20th Century-Fox) reunited its dance director Busby Berkeley with its director Lloyd Bacon for the first time since *42nd Street* (Warner Bros. 1933), and once again teamed Betty Grable with Dan Dailey. Not a great deal (three songs, to be precise) of Harold Rome's 1946 Broadway revue remained in the updated screen version of it and Albert E. Lewin and Burt Styler's screenplay, based on Rome and Arnold M. Auerbach's original book, was, heaven knows, no masterpiece. Yet Grable, as an entertainer with the Civilian Actress Technician Service in Japan, and Dailey as her GI husband from whom she had been separated, were in fine form throughout. Storyline had Dailey (right) forging an assignment paper in order to stage an army camp show in the hope of winning Grable (centre) back. They both displayed their respective musical wares on several enjoyable occasions, Grable dominating the scene in an excellent Mack Gordon-Sammy Fain number called 'Japanese Girl Like American Boy'. Other highlights were her and Dailey's dancing of the title number (by Harold Rome), co-star Danny Thomas's delightful 'Lament To The Pots And Pans', written especially for him by Jerry Seelen and Earl K. Brent, and an energetic dance routine by a trio of male dancers called The Dunhills. Apart from 'Love Is Back In Business' (by Gordon and Fain), an over-elaborate finale, all the routines were modestly and effectively staged. Dale Robertson (left), Benay Venuta, Richard Boone, Jeffrey Hunter and Frank Fontaine were also cast, and it was produced (in Technicolor) by Fred Kohlmar. Other songs and musical numbers included: *Going Home Train*; *Military Life* Rome; *I Just Can't Do Enough For You Baby* Gordon, Fain; *I'm Gonna Love That Guy* Frances Ash, Bobby Short also made an unbilled appearance.

The title of Warner Bros.' **Lullaby Of Broadway** came, of course, from the Al Dubin-Harry Warren song indelibly associated with Busby Berkeley's masterful production number in the same studio's *Gold Diggers Of 1935*, a sequence whose memory nothing in the new film could eclipse. The Earl Baldwin story and screenplay involved a musical comedy star (Doris Day) who arrives in New York from London believing that her mother (Gladys George), now a drunken singer in a sleazy Greenwich Village nightclub, is still the Broadway hit she once was. The truth is kept from Doris by Billy De Wolfe and Anne Triola, as a song-and-dance team working temporarily as servants for a lovable millionaire (played by S.Z. Sakall — who else?), until complications arise with the millionaire's wife (Florence Bates). The songs, with a couple of exceptions, were no less familiar than the plot, but infinitely more welcome. Unfortunately, LeRoy Prinz, who staged the dance numbers, could not match Berkeley's delirious invention. Gene Nelson (illustrated) played the romantic lead, and the film, produced in gorgeous Technicolor by William Jacobs, was competently directed by Roy Del Ruth. Songs and musical numbers included: *Lullaby Of Broadway*; *You're Getting To Be A Habit With Me* Al Dubin, Harry Warren; *Just One Of Those Things* Cole Porter; *Somebody Loves Me* George Gershwin, Buddy De Sylva, Ballard MacDonald; *I Love The Way You Say Goodnight* Eddie Pola, George Wyle; *Please Don't Talk About Me When I'm Gone* Sam Stept, Sidney Clare; *In A Shanty In Old Shanty Town* Little Jack Little, John Siras, Joe Young; *Zing Went The Strings Of My Heart* James Hanley. ▷

Though Betty Grable topped the bill in **Meet Me After The Show** (20th Century-Fox), the real star was its choreographer, Jack Cole, whose lively production numbers went some considerable distance to lend enchantment to an otherwise arid story about a musical comedy star (Grable, illustrated centre) and the bickering relationship she shares with her producer husband (Mac-Donald Carey). After seven years of marriage the couple have a serious fall-out, at which point in the plot (by Erna Lazarus and W. Scott Darling, screenplay by Mary Loos and director Richard Sale), Eddie Albert (as a singer) and Rory Calhoun (as a beachcomber), admirers of Miss Grable, decide to try their chances with her. The production numbers included 'It's A Hot Night In Alaska', 'No Talent Joe' and 'I Feel Like Dancing' (in which co-choreographer Gwen Verdon also appeared); while the best of an indifferent batch of Jule Styne-Leo Robin songs was Grable's 'Bettin' On A Man'. It was produced (in Technicolor) by George Jessel, whose cast also included Fred Clark, Irene Ryan and Lois Andrews. Other songs and musical numbers: *Meet Me After The Show*; *Let Go Of My Heart*. ▽

It seemed, at one point, that producer Arthur Freed would never get MGM's **Royal Wedding** (GB: **Wedding Bells**) off the ground. Ten days into shooting, leading lady June Allyson discovered she was pregnant and in the time it took to find a replacement (Judy Garland), director Charles Walters moved on to another project. Garland, however, soon began to behave in her characteristically unprofessional manner and was fired. Freed then learned of the availability of Jane Powell (hitherto the property of producers Joe Pasternak and Jack Cummings) and decided to give her a chance in what turned out to be her most prestigious musical to date, and the one in which she finally came of age. Never before had she worked so hard or so well, and her performance as part of a brother and sister act who travel to London to take part in the festivities leading up to Princess Elizabeth's wedding to Philip Mountbatten, was a revelation. Her brother was none other than Fred Astaire and, while in London, they both fall in love: he with a music hall dancer (Sarah Churchill – the role was originally offered to Moira Shearer who was unavailable); she with a handsome English lord (Peter Lawford). The ending had both couples marrying on the same day as the Princess. Keenan Wynn was featured in a dual role as twin brothers, with other parts going to Albert Sharpe, Viola Roache, Henri Letondal, James Finlayson and Mae Clarke. Stanley Donen made his solo directorial debut with this one, and it was a first, too, for Alan Jay Lerner who contributed the serviceable screenplay. The patter, however, was of tertiary importance to the singing and the dancing, and with an engaging score by Lerner and Burton Lane, choreography by Nick Castle and orchestrations by Conrad Salinger and Skip Martin, the musical side of Freed's production never faltered. Highlights were Astaire's 'Sunday Jumps' number performed with a hat-stand; the celebrated 'You're All The World To Me' whose melody was first heard as 'I Want To Be A Minstrel Man' in Goldwyn's *Kid Millions* (1934) and in which he dances on the walls and ceiling of a hotel room (illustrated); as well as the rough-and-ready duet he did with Powell called 'How Could You Believe Me When I Said I Love You When You Know I've Been A Liar All My Life?', and Powell's touching rendition of 'Too Late Now', which became a huge hit. An exhilarating Technicolor entertainment. Other songs and musical numbers: *Ev'ry Night At Seven*; *Open Your Eyes*; *The Happiest Day Of My Life*; *I Left My Hat In Haiti*; *What A Lovely Day For A Wedding*. ▽

Ten specialty acts and a handful of songs were ▷
the main features of **Casa Mañana**, a programmer from Monogram whose skeletal story involved a triangle situation between a would-be singer (Virginia Welles, illustrated), a nightclub owner (Robert Clarke) who wants to make her the star of his new club, and Robert Karns, Clarke's rival in love. Tony Roux, Carol Brewster, Paul Mazey and Jean Richey also had parts in Bill Raynor's nondescript screenplay, with the Rio Bros, Eddie Le Baron and His Orchestra (illustrated), Spade Cooley, Yadira Jiminez, Zaree and Dolores, The Mercer Brothers, Armande and Lita, Betty and Beverley, Olga Perez, and Davis and Johnson roped in for support. Jean Yarbrough directed and it was produced by Lindsley Parsons. Songs and musical numbers included: *Bounce* Olsen and Johnson, Ray Evans, Jay Livingston; *People Like You* Otis Bigelow, Harold Cooke; *I Hear A Rhapsody* Jack Baker, George Fragos, Dick Gasparre; *Fifty Games Of Solitaire On Saturday Night* Ruth and Louis Herscher.

△

Mario Lanza (illustrated) received top billing in the third and most successful film of his erratic career, **The Great Caruso** (MGM). A heavyweight entry in every respect – from Lanza's own (220 lbs) to the box-office gross ($4,500,000), it was the high-water mark of producer Joe Pasternak's career, and the most successful 'long-haired' entertainment ever to emerge from Hollywood. As an authentic biopic of the life of the celebrated Italian tenor Enrico Caruso, it owed more to the imaginations of scenarists Sonya Levien and William Ludwig than it did to truth, and fluctuated between total fiction and gross distortion, even giving Caruso one wife instead of two. Little more than a series of clichés, the film sketched in some obligatory early struggles in which Caruso is seen to be a Neapolitan café singer (cue for 'Mattinata'), then quickly went on to record his triumphs in the opera houses of the world (especially New York's Metropolitan), his marriage, his illness, and his death (during a performance of Flotow's *Martha*). It was all over in 109 minutes that were mainly devoted to the music most closely associated with Caruso's career. In addition to the numerous operatic extracts (staged by the Metropolitan's Peter Herman Adler), a popular hit emerged in 'The Loveliest Night Of The Year', adapted by Irving Aaronson from 'Over The Waves' by Juventino Rosas, and with a new lyric by Paul Francis Webster. Ann Blyth received second billing as Dorothy Benjamin, Caruso's wealthy socialite wife, with other roles going to sopranos Dorothy Kirsten and Jarmila Novotna, Richard Hageman, Carl Benton Reid, Eduard Franz, Ludwig Donath and Alan Napier. There was additional operatic participation by Blanche Thebom, Teresa Celli, Nicola Moscona, Giuseppe Valdengo, Lucine Amara and Marina Koshetz. Directed by Richard Thorpe, it was 40 carat corn, and quite irresistible. The musical supervision and the background score were by Johnny Green. Other operatic extracts and songs: *Vesti La Giubba* (from 'Pagliacci') Leoncavallo; *The Last Rose Of Summer* Thomas Moore, Richard Alfred Milliken; *M'Appari* (from 'Martha') Flotow; *Celeste Aida; Numi Pieta; O Terra Addio* (from 'Aida') Verdi; *The Sextet* (from 'Lucia Di Lammermoor') Donizetti; *La Donna E Mobile* (from 'Rigoletto') Verdi; *Che Gelida Manina* (from 'La Bohème) Puccini; *E Lucevan Le Stelle* (from 'Tosca') Puccini; *Ave Maria* Bach-Gounod; *Because* Teschemacher, Guy d'Hardelot; *Sweethearts* Victor Herbert, Robert B. Smith.

△

Technicolor added an important dimension to the third screen version of Jerome Kern and Oscar Hammerstein II's **Show Boat** (MGM), previous versions being the bowdlerized Universal offering in 1929, and the same studio's glowing remake of it in 1936. Arthur Freed's production at MGM (see illustration) was less faithful to the original stage show than the middle version, and scenarist John Lee Mahin tidied up the ending by keeping the storyline in the 19th century, and eliminating all references to Magnolia's success as an actress. In Mahin's treatment of the story, Kim, the daughter of Magnolia and Ravenal, remains a child, whereas in Hammerstein's original libretto and in the 1936 screen version, she follows in her mother's footsteps and becomes a Broadway star. As the ending of **Show Boat** (from the novel by Edna Ferber) has never really been satisfactorily resolved, Freed and Mahin can be forgiven for their interference. What their version lacked in narrative weight, it more than compensated for in the neatness of its structure. From its jaunty opening scenes aboard The Cotton Blossom, to its tearful finale, MGM's multi-million dollar production unfurled with all the gloss and expertise audiences had come to expect from the studio. Kathryn Grayson, top billed as Magnolia sang better than she acted; Ava Gardner (vocals dubbed by Eileen Wilson) was second-billed as the mulatto Julie and, although beautiful to look at and certainly very moving in the role, could not match the performance in the same part given by Helen Morgan in the 1936 film. Howard Keel played Ravenal, Joe E. Brown Cap'n Andy, Robert Sterling was Steve, William Warfield Joe, Agnes Moorehead Parthenia Hawks and, lending unbridled zest to it all, Marge and Gower Champion as Ellie and Frank. Their two big dances, 'I Might Fall Back On You' and 'Life Upon The Wicked Stage', choreographed by Robert Alton, were both winners. The solid, workmanlike direction was by George Sidney, with Adolph Deutsch in charge of the musical direction. Other songs and musical numbers: *Cotton Blossom* (chorus); *Buck and Wing Dance* (Champions); *Where's The Mate For Me?* (Keel); *Make Believe* (Keel, Grayson); *Can't Help Lovin' Dat Man* (Gardner, reprised Grayson, Gardner); *Mis'ry's Comin' Around* (chorus); *Ol' Man River* (Warfield, chorus); *You Are Love* (Grayson, Keel); *Why Do I Love You?* (Grayson, Keel); *Bill* (Gardner) lyrics P.G. Wodehouse; *After The Ball* (Grayson) by Charles K. Harris.

Jane Powell (2nd right) starred in **Rich Young And Pretty** (MGM), a handsomely packaged (in Technicolor) feather-light *bon-bon* which introduced Vic Damone (2nd left) and Fernando Lamas (left) to moviegoers, and also saw the return to Hollywood of Danielle Darrieux (right). It was all about a lass from Texas (Powell), who, while visiting Paris with her rancher father (Wendell Corey), meets the man of her dreams (Damone) as well as her mother (Darrieux), a lady of independent spirit who deserted her husband many years before for a sophisticated life in Europe. Several attractive songs by Nicholas Brodszky and Sammy Cahn were appliquéd on to Dorothy Cooper and Sidney Sheldon's screenplay (story by Miss Cooper), the catchiest being 'We Never Talk Much' delightfully sung by Miss Darrieux and Mr Lamas (her beau), and later reprised by Powell and Damone who, together with The Four Freshmen, acquitted themselves well in 'How Do You Like Your Eggs In The Morning?'; while from Miss Darrieux there was a sexy rendition of 'There's Danger In Your Eyes, Chérie' (by Jack Meskill and Pete Wendling). The dances were staged by Nick Castle, it was produced by Joe Pasternak with a cast that included Marcel Dalio, Una Merkel, Richard Anderson, Jean Murat and Hans Conried, and directed by Norman Taurog. Other musical numbers: *Wonder Why*; *Dark Is The Night*; *Paris*; *L'Amour Toujour, Tonight For Sure*; *I Can See You* Brodszky, Cahn; *The Old Piano Roll Blues* Cy Coben; *Deep In The Heart Of Texas* June Hershey, Don Swander.
▽

If Bud Abbott (right) and Lou Costello (centre) were an acquired taste, only the most undemanding of tots was likely to acquire it from **Jack And The Beanstalk**, Warner Bros'. musical fantasy which began in black and white and reverted to Super Cinecolor *á la The Wizard Of Oz* (MGM, 1939), when Costello dreams himself into a fairy-tale world where he is pitted against the giant, played by ex-prizefighter Buddy Baer. Jean Yarbrough directed the Nat Curtis screenplay (from a treatment by Pat Costello) with an impossibly heavy hand, and Alex Gottlieb produced. Also featured were Dorothy Ford (left), Barbara Brown, David Stollery, Patrick the Harp, and James Alexander and Shaye Cogan as the romantic leads. Songs and musical numbers: *He Never Looked Better In His Life*; *I Fear Nothing*; *Darlene*; *Dreamer's Cloth* Lester Lee, Bob Russell.
▽

Twenty-eight disc jockeys, as well as Ginny Simms (centre right), Michael O'Shea, Tom Drake (left), Jane Nigh (right), Russ Morgan (centre left), Lenny Kent, Tommy Dorsey, George Shearing, Nick Lucas, Herb Jeffries, Sarah Vaughan, The Weavers, Jerome Cowan, Foy Willing and The Riders Of The Purple Sage, Red Nichols, Red Norvo, Ben Pollack, Joe Venuti and Jack Fina appeared in **Disc Jockey** (Allied Artists). As each made his presence felt, there was very little room left for plot – and what there was of it concerned the efforts of disc jockey radio promoter O'Shea to make a star out of an unknown singer (Ginny Simms) through recordings and the help of disc jockeys. Clark E. Reynolds thought it all up, Maurice Duke produced, and the direction was by Will Jason. Songs and musical numbers included: *Let's Meander Through The Meadow*; *Show Me You Love Me* S. Steuben, Roz Gordon; *Nobody Wants Me*; *After Hours* Gordon; *Disc Jockey*; *In My Heart* Herb Jeffries, Dick Hazard; *Peaceful Country*; *Riders Of The Purple Sage* Foy Willing; *Brain Wave* George Shearing; *Oh Look At Me Now* John De Vries, Joe Bushkin; *The Roving Kind* Jessie Cavanaugh, Arnold Stanton.
▽

△

On Moonlight Bay (Warner Bros.), written by Jack Rose and Melville Shavelson from some of Booth Tarkington's evergreen Penrod stories, starred Doris Day as the-girl-next-door who woos and eventually marries boy-next-door Gordon MacRae (illustrated centre with Day); with Leon Ames, Rosemary De Camp and Mary Wickes in support. Apart from 'Love Ya' by Charles Tobias and Peter De Rose sung by Doris, and third-billed Jack Smith, (illustrated right), the songs were all standards culled from the period in which the film was set. Roy Del Ruth directed the William Jacobs Technicolor production and LeRoy Prinz choreographed. Songs and musical numbers: *Moonlight Bay* Percy Wenrich, Edward Madden; *Till We Meet Again* Ray Egan, Richard Whiting; *Pack Up Your Troubles* Felix Powell, George Asaf; *Cuddle Up A Little Closer*; *Every Little Movement Has A Meaning All Its Own* Otto Harbach, Karl Hoschna; *I'm Forever Blowing Bubbles* Jaan Kenbrovin, John W. Kellette; *Christmas Story* Pauline Walsh; *Tell Me* J. Will Callahan, Max Kortlander.

The highlight of **Excuse My Dust** (MGM), a Technicolorful, Gay Nineties romp in which Red Skelton (left) starred as an automobile inventor, was a cross-country auto race in the best Keystone tradition. But it took a long time coming, and most of the film's running time was devoted to Skelton's unpopular tinkering with his assorted gadgets to the annoyance of the neighbours in general and the father of his sweetheart (a livery stable man) in particular. Sally Forrest was Skelton's pretty inamorata and together they sang 'Spring Is Sprung', one of the better bits of musical embroidery (by Arthur Schwartz and Dorothy Fields, who composed the rest of the score as well). William Demarest played Forrest's ill-tempered father, with Monica Lewis, MacDonald Carey, Raymond Walburn (right), Jane Darwell (centre), Lillian Bronson, Guy Anderson and Paul Harvey completing the cast for producer Jack Cummings. The broad direction was by Roy Rowland and the dances were staged by Hermes Pan. Sally Forrest's vocals were dubbed by Gloria Grey. Other songs and musical numbers: *Lorelei Brown*; *Get A Horse*; *That's For Children*; *I'd Like To Take You Out Dreaming*; *Going Steady*.
▽

In **Comin' Round The Mountain** (Universal International), Bud Abbott (standing centre left) and Lou Costello (standing right) found themselves searching for hidden treasure, while their scriptwriters Robert Lees and Frederick I. Rinaldo searched for a few fresh ideas and the audiences for their promised share of laughs. Messrs A. and C. found Fort Knox; but there was only dross for the paying customers. A running gag about a love potion soon ran itself into them thar Kentucky hills, and a lot of unentertaining feudin', fussin' and fightin' between the McCoys and the Winfields seemed to dominate the action. Dorothy Shay (2nd right) as a singing Park Avenue hillbilly provided muscial accompaniment throughout, with Kirby Grant, Joe Sawyer (standing left), Glenn Strange, Ida Moore (centre) and Shaye Cogan completing the cast. Howard Christie produced and the director was Charles Lamont. Songs included: *You Broke Your Promise* George Wyle, Irving Taylor, Eddie Pola; *Agnes Clung* Hessie Smith, Dorothy Shay; *Why Don't Someone Marry Mary Ann?* Wilbur Beatty, Britt Wood; *Sagebrush Sadie* Britt Wood.
▽

A melodrama with a musical accompaniment, **The Strip**, produced in black and white by Joe Pasternak, was a low-budget entry from MGM that starred Mickey Rooney as a drummer discharged from the army who arrives in Hollywood where he falls in with bookie James Craig. He meets a dancer-cum-cigarette girl (Sally Forrest), and introduces her to Craig who shows a decided interest in her. Rooney is beaten up, the bookie killed and Forrest fatally wounded. Written by Allen Rivkin, and told largely in flashback, the film relied heavily on its musical interludes to lighten the gloom, and these were supplied by Louis Armstrong, Jack Teagarden, Earl 'Fatha' Hines, Barney Bigard, and guest stars Vic Damone, who sang 'Don't Blame Me' (by Dorothy Fields and Jimmy McHugh) and Monica Lewis, who sang 'La Bota' (by Haven Gillespie II and Charles Wolcott). Rooney banged the drums on several occasions (see illustration), Miss Forrest danced, and the hit song, reprised a number of times, was 'Give Me A Kiss To Build A Dream On' by Bert Kalmar, Harry Ruby and Oscar Hammerstein II (composed in 1935). The dances were staged by Nick Castle, it was directed by Leslie Kardos, and the cast was completed by William Demarest as a nightclub owner, Kay Brown, Tommy Rettig, Tom Powers, Jonathan Cott and Tommy Farrell. Other musical numbers: *Basin Street Blues* (Armstrong, Teagarden) Spencer Williams; *Shadrack* (Armstrong) Robert MacGimsey; *Rose Room* (Armstrong) Harry Williams, Art Hickman; *Ain't Misbehavin'* (Rooney, Armstrong) Andy Razaf, Fats Waller.

Considering television's threat to the industry in the early 50s, it received a surprising 'plug' in **Sunny Side Of The Street** (Columbia), a mediocre vehicle (in Super Cinecolor) for Frankie Laine and Billy Daniels (illustrated), whose plot (by Harold Conrad, screenplay by Lee Loeb) was basically concerned with would-be singer Jerome Courtland's attempt to break into TV via a former sweetheart (Audrey Long) – to the chagrin of his present lady (Terry Moore). About as substantial as a commercial, it was directed by Richard Quine, produced by Jonie Taps, and featured, in support, Toni Arden, Dick Wesson, William Tracy and, in a small part, Lynn Bari. Songs and musical numbers included: *On The Sunny Side Of The Street* Dorothy Fields, Jimmy McHugh; *I'm Gonna Live Till I Die* Al Hoffman, Mann Curtis, Walter Kent; *I May Be Wrong But I Think You're Wonderful* Harry Ruskin, Henry Sullivan; *Let's Fall In Love* Ted Koehler, Harold Arlen; *I Get A Kick Out Of You* Cole Porter.

▽

A light-hearted, thoroughly engaging entertainment from the pens of Virginia Van Upp, Liam O'Brien and Myles Connolly (story by O'Brien and Robert Riskin), **Here Comes The Groom** (Paramount) was also the perfect vehicle for both its star (Bing Crosby) and its producer-director (Frank Capra). The tale of an easy-going roving reporter (Crosby, centre in suit) who adopts a couple of French orphans and is given five days either to find a wife for himself or give up the two children, it co-starred Jane Wyman as the woman he decides on, and Franchot Tone as the Boston millionaire she is just about to marry. Tone may be wealthy, but Crosby is rich in charm – and it's no surprise when, in the end, he gets the girl of his choice. Alexis Smith, James Barton, Connie Gilchrist, Robert Keith, Jacques Gencel, Walter Catlett and Beverly Washburn were also in it; so were Anna Maria Alberghetti, who sang 'Caro Nome' from Verdi's *Rigoletto*, and Dorothy Lamour, Phil Harris, Louis Armstrong and Cass Daley (centre right) who joined Crosby in a number called 'Misto Cristofo Columbo' (by Jay Livingston and Ray Evans). But the hit number was 'In The Cool Cool Cool Of The Evening', by Johnny Mercer and Hoagy Carmichael. The dances were staged by Charles O'Curran. Other songs: *Bonne Nuit; Your Own Little House* Livingston, Evans.

△

Walt Disney's full-length animated cartoon version of RKO's **Alice In Wonderland** (illustrated) was more Disney than Lewis Carroll, its original creator. Though full of clever little touches, and not without entire sequences that worked extremely well (such as 'The Mad Hatter's Tea Party' and 'The Caucus Race') the film, which also borrowed heavily from *Alice Through The Looking Glass*, lacked the surreal and satiric qualities of the book and, visually, as was to be expected, bore no relation to the famous Tenniel illustrations that accompanied the first edition of the text. Still, there was much to enjoy, not least of which were the songs and the delicious characterizations of The Mad Hatter, The March Hare and The Cheshire Cat as interpreted (vocally) by Ed Wynn, Jerry Colonna, and Sterling Holloway. Other voices: Kathryn Beaumont as a very English Alice, Pat O'Malley as The Walrus, The Carpenter and Tweedledum and Tweedledee, Bill Thompson as The White Rabbit and Dodo, Richard Haydn as The Caterpillar, and Verna Felton as The Queen of Hearts. The production supervisor was Ben Sharpsteen and the directors Clyde Geronimi, Hamilton Luske and Wilfred Jackson. It was photographed in Technicolor. Songs included: *Very Good Advice; In A World Of My Own; All In A Golden Afternoon; Alice In Wonderland; The Walrus And The Carpenter; The Caucus Race; I'm Late; Painting The Roses Red; March Of The Cards* Bob Hilliard, Sammy Fain.

Written by Sid Silvers and Hal Kanter from a story by Sammy Cahn, **Two Tickets To Broadway** (RKO) was the one about a group of hopefuls and their bid for the big-time – except that, contrary to the title, what they have their eyes on is TV. So much for the scenarists' nod in the direction of topicality. Yet, despite an almost absurdly familiar narrative line, it was agreeably cast with Tony Martin as an unemployed tenor, Janet Leigh as his girlfriend, Eddie Bracken (on floor) as a thoroughly incompetent wheeler-dealing agent, Gloria De Haven (centre) as Bracken's singing sweetheart, and Ann Miller (right) as the dancer of the group. Other plus factors were the appearances of Joe Smith and Charles Dale as a couple of delicatessen proprietors, an acrobatic troupe called The Charlivels, seven enjoyable Jule Styne-Leo Robin tunes, and the dance direction of Busby Berkeley. Also appearing was Bob Crosby, on whose TV show agent Bracken hopes to place his enthusiastic hopefuls. Of course, he eventually succeeds. Ann Miller was terrific in a routine called 'Let The Worry Bird Worry For You' (by Styne and Robin), and from Martin there was some heavy vocalizing in the Prologue from Leoncavallo's 'Pagliacci'. He also sang two of his standards, 'There's No Tomorrow' (by Al Hoffman, Leo Corday and Leon Carr) and 'Manhattan' (by Richard Rodgers and Lorenz Hart). James V. Kern directed, and Howard Hughes received the producer's credit, though it was Jerry Wald who was in charge of the Technicolor production. Also cast: Barbara Lawrence (left), Taylor Holmes, Buddy Baer. Other songs and musical numbers: *The Closer You Are; Baby, You'll Never Be Sorry; Big Chief Hole In The Ground; Pelican Falls High; It Began In Yucatan* Styne, Robin; *Let's Make Comparisons* Crosby, Sammy Cahn.
▽

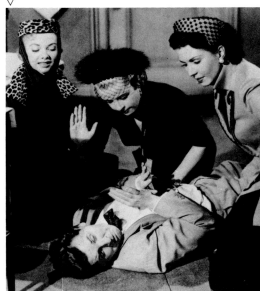

Though Esther Williams (illustrated), playing a ▷ carnival performer who is dunked every time a customer succeeds in hitting a target with a ball, was billed above Red Skelton in **Texas Carnival** (MGM), she had very little to do in producer Jack Cummings's damp squib of a show. She swam once (in a dream sequence) and that was more or less it. The same applied to co-stars Howard Keel and tap-happy Ann Miller, the latter brightening up the decidedly dreary proceedings with one characteristically exuberant solo called 'It's Dynamite' (by Harry Warren and Dorothy Fields). For the rest it was left to Skelton to make what he could of a mistaken identity story (by Dorothy Kingsley and George Wells, screenplay by Kingsley) in which he is assumed to be a millionaire oil and cattle tycoon when, in fact, he's nothing but a carnival bum, pitching for Miss Williams. Lasting only 77 minutes, the film appeared to have been the victim of some drastic editing which might well explain why the rest of the cast - including Keenan Wynn (as the millionaire Skelton's mistaken for), Paula Raymond, Tom Tully and Glenn Strange, seemed so under-employed. Also appearing: The Red Norvo Trio, and Foy Willing and His Band. The score was, to be euphemistic, indifferent; so was Hermes Pan's dance direction. It was sluggishly directed by the usually able Charles Walters. (Technicolor). Other musical numbers included: *Whoa! Emma*; *Young Folks Should Get Married*; *Carnie's Pitch* Dorothy Fields, Harry Warren; *Clap Your Hands* David Rose, Earl Brent; *Deep In The Heart Of Texas* June Hershey, Don Swander.

△
Judy Canova (right), appearing for the first time in 'glorious New Trucolor', was the star of **Honeychile** (Republic), another hillbilly adventure, set in Cactus Junction, Wyoming, and all about the efforts of a couple of music publishers (Eddie Foy Jr, left, and Walter Catlett) to secure the rights of a song called 'Honeychile' written by Miss C. The lady doggedly refuses to sell — until she needs some ready cash to free her fiancé (Alan Hale Jr) from the clutches of a pair of crooked bookies who have rigged a chuckwagon race. Claire Carleton, Karolyn Grimes, Brad Morrow, Roy Barcroft, Leonid Kinskey and Gus Schilling supported, the serviceable screenplay was by Jack Townley and Charles E. Roberts, Herbert J. Yates produced and the director was R.G. Springsteen. Songs and musical numbers: *Honeychile* Jack Elliott, Harold Spina; *Tutti Frutti* Elliott, Ann Canova; *More Than I Care To Remember* Ted Johnson, Matt Terry; *Rag Mop* Johnny Lee Wills, Deacon Anderson.

Loosely based on the life and times of Lotte Crabtree, that popular little entertainer from Rabbit Creek, California, **Golden Girl** (20th Century-Fox), produced by George Jessel in Technicolor, was first class entertainment that starred Mitzi Gaynor (centre) as the lady in question, Dale Robertson as handsome Tom Richmond of Alabama (the man to whom she loses her heart but who turns out to be a Confederate spy); Una Merkel as her disapproving ma, James Barton as her reprobate father, and Dennis Day as a timid admirer. The period atmosphere (1861) was aptly caught in Lloyd Bacon's stalwart direction and in Seymour Felix's choreography; and the screenplay, by Walter Bullock, Charles O'Neal and Gladys Lehman (from a story by Albert and Arthur Lewis and Edward Thompson) gave sufficient idea of what theatrical life 'on the road' must have been like during the Civil War. Lotte Crabtree reached the peak of her career when she played Niblo's Gardens in New York, and one of the best scenes in the film had her singing 'Dixie' (by Daniel Decatur Emmett) to the vehement disapproval of her booing audience when news of the North's victory comes through. Also cast: Raymond Walburn, Gene Sheldon, Carmen D'Antonio, Michael Ross and Harry Carter. Songs and musical numbers: *Carry Me Back To Old Virginny*; *Oh, Dem Golden Slippers* James A. Bland; *California Moon* George Jessel, Sam Lerner, Joe Cooper; *Sunday Mornin'* Eliot Daniel, Ken Darby; *Kiss Me Quick And Go My Honey* Daniel; *Never* Daniel, Lionel Newman; *When Johnny Comes Marching Home* Patrick S. Gilmore; *Believe Me If All Those Endearing Young Charms* Thomas Moore, Matthew Locke; *La Donna E Mobile* (from 'Rigoletto') Verdi. ▷

Filmed in a sepia tone, **Purple Heart Diary** (GB: **No Time For Tears**), produced for Columbia by Sam Katzman, directed by Richard Quine and starring Frances Langford (centre), was a series of simply presented songs (performed by Langford, Ben Lessy and Tony Romano, all playing themselves) attached to a perfunctory story about a trio of performers in the war-torn Pacific and the pleasure they bring to the troops – especially an amputee (Brett King) whose feelings of frustration threaten to ruin a romance he is having with a nurse (Aline Towne). Basically a PR job for the United Service Organisation (the entertainment industry's establishment for troop entertainment), it was written by William Sackheim and also featured Warren Mills, Larry Stewart, Joel Marston, Richard Grant and Lyle Talbot. Songs included: *Hold Me In Your Arms*; *Hi, Fellow Tourists*; *Where Are You From?* Johnny Bradford, Barbara Hayden, Tony Romano; *Bread And Butter Woman* Allan Roberts, Lester Lee; *Tattle-Tale Eyes* John Bradford, Romano. ▷

Ezio Pinza, operatic bass turned Broadway star (in Rodgers and Hammerstein's *South Pacific*), made an undistinguished movie debut in **Mr Imperium** (GB: **You Belong To My Heart**), a stinker of such proportions that MGM decided to release it after Pinza's second film, *Strictly Dishonorable*. But it bombed just the same. Lana Turner (illustrated left) received top billing in Edwin H. Knopf's production, playing a singer (Fran Warren dubbed for her) with a cowboy quartet who falls in love with a European prince (Pinza) on the Italian Riviera. The affair is doomed as Pinza soon becomes king and is not in a position to marry a commoner. Pinza sang pleasantly enough, the settings were suitably sumptuous, and Miss Turner was gorgeously costumed by Walter Plunkett. The script (by Knopf and Don Hartman from a play by Knopf) and direction (by Hartman) did not bear thinking about. Also cast: Marjorie Main, Barry Sullivan, Sir Cedric Hardwicke, Debbie Reynolds, Keenan Wynn. Songs: *My Love And My Mule*; *Andiamo*; *Let Me Look At You* Harold Arlen, Dorothy Fields; *You Belong To My Heart* Ray Gilbert, Augustin Lara.
▽

Fifties Musicals

Like the Impressionist and post-Impressionist canvases from which it drew its inspiration, the superb ballet that climaxed **An American In Paris** (MGM) was full of light and movement. Nothing of its kind from Hollywood had quite possessed its class, sense of style, and chic. It began at the Beaux Arts Ball where a painter (Gene Kelly), after finding himself separated from the girl he loves (Leslie Caron), wanders, heavy-hearted, out onto a terrace, and begins a sketch with a black crayon. He tears it up, But suddenly there is a breeze and the two halves of the torn sketch come together to form a backdrop against which the artist appears. At his feet he sees a red rose. He picks it up, the black and white background bleeds into colour and the scene changes to the Place de la Concorde, with sets and costumes after Dufy. Then, as the painter sees and pursues the girl he loves, the setting becomes a flower market near La Madeleine, the mood sad but tranquil, the style and decor now paying homage to Renoir. The pastel colours of Utrillo inspire a street scene followed by a spirited George M. Cohanesque dance, this time in a Rousseau setting, performed by four Americans in Paris celebrating the Fourth of July. The mood changes from exuberance to passion as the painter, filled with longing and regret, dances in and around a fountain in the Place de la Concorde. The scene now changes to the Paris Opera, *à la* Van Gogh, and after that to Lautrec's Montmartre, where the painter becomes the character of Chocolat. The final sequence sees a return to the fountain, accompanied by a frenzied eruption of music. Everyone disappears and the painter is left alone. Designed by Preston Ames, costumed by Irene Sharaff, and choreographed by Kelly, it was 18 minutes of screen magic, unsurpassed in the boldness of its design and the dazzle of its execution. It took six months to rehearse, a month to shoot, and

cost $450,000. The rest of the film was, in every way, more conventional – telling a rather trite story of an American GI-painter's love for a perfume shop assistant (Caron) and the complications that arise when a wealthy patron of the arts (Nina Foch) tries to ensnare him. The screenplay was by Alan Jay Lerner and what it lacked in originality, it compensated for in the opportunities it provided for Kelly (left), Caron (right), and co-stars Oscar Levant and Georges Guetary to interrupt the narrative with song and dance. The music was by George and Ira Gershwin, whose complete catalogue of songs producer Arthur Freed purchased from the Gershwin estate for $300,000. The best of these were 'I Got Rhythm' sung and danced by Kelly to a group of French children, and 'Tra-La-La', played on the piano (by Levant) and danced by Kelly in a Paris attic. Less successful was the rather self-consciously endearing 'By Strauss' (performed by Kelly, Guetary and Levant), and Levant's dream sequence in which he imagines himself as conductor, soloist and every member of the orchestra in the third movement of Gershwin's Concerto in F. It was a pleasing Walter Mitty-ish idea which somehow did not quite come off. Leslie Caron (making her screen debut) was enchanting, especially in her introductory dance solos to various arrangements of 'Embraceable You'. Contributing incalculably to the overall success of **An American In Paris** was director Vincente Minnelli, whose unerringly sophisticated visual sense made sure that it was always good to look at. The musical direction was by Johnny Green and Saul Chaplin. Other songs and musical numbers: *S'Wonderful* (Kelly, Guetary); *Love Is Here To Stay* (Kelly, Caron); *I'll Build A Stairway To Paradise* (Guetary) lyrics by E. Ray Goetz and Buddy De Sylva; *Nice Work If You Can Get It* (Guetary, Levant); *I Don't Think I'll Fall In Love Today* (Levant); *Liza* (Levant).

△

With a minimal plot – the romance between a Hollywood actress and an Air Force corporal – and a plethora of guest appearances, **Starlift** (Warner Bros.) was a Korean War updating of the stars-and-stripes *Hollywood Canteen* format. The title was derived from Operation Starlift, by which movie performers were flown up to Travis Air Base near San Francisco to entertain outgoing or incoming troops and, as usual, more pleasure was to be gained from spotting familiar faces – Doris Day, Gordon MacRae, Virginia Mayo (illustrated), Gene Nelson, Ruth Roman, James Cagney, Gary Cooper, Virginia Gibson, Phil Harris, Frank Lovejoy, Lucille Norman, Louella Parsons, Randolph Scott, Jane Wyman and Patrice Wymore – than from following the romantic peregrinations of the nominal leads (Janis Paige and Ron Haggerthy). It was written by John Klorer and Karl Kamb, directed by Roy Del Ruth, choreographed by LeRoy Prinz, and produced by Robert Arthur. Songs and musical numbers included: *Liza*; *S'Wonderful* George and Ira Gershwin; *You Do Something To Me*; *What Is This Thing Called Love?* Cole Porter; *It's Magic* Sammy Cahn, Jule Styne; *I May Be Wrong But I Think You're Wonderful* Harry Ruskin, Henry Sullivan; *Good Green Acres Of Home* Irving Kahal, Sammy Fain; *You Oughta Be In Pictures* Edward Heyman, Dana Suesse; *You're Gonna Lose Your Gal* Joe Young, James V. Monaco.

Painting The Clouds With Sunshine (Warner Bros.) was yet another adaptation of the Avery Hopwood *Gold Diggers* story which had inspired some of the studio's most memorable musicals in the '30s. Virginia Mayo, Lucille Norman and Virginia Gibson were three showgirls on the make in Las Vegas; Gene Nelson (illustrated), Tom Conway and Dennis Morgan the three guys who convince them that true love is worth more than tiaras; S.Z. Sakall and Wallace Ford provided the inevitable comic relief. The weak screenplay was the work of Harry Clork, Roland Kibbee and Peter Milne, LeRoy Prinz choreographed, the film was produced, in Technicolor, by William Jacobs, and directed by David Butler. Songs and musical numbers: *Painting The Clouds With Sunshine*; *Tip-Toe Through The Tulips* Al Dubin, Joe Burke; *Vienna Dreams* Irving Caesar, Rudolf Sieczynski; *With A Song In My Heart* Richard Rodgers, Lorenz Hart; *Birth Of The Blues* Buddy De Sylva, Lew Brown, Ray Henderson; *You're My Everything* Harry Warren, Mort Dixon; *Jealousy* Vera Bloom, Jacob Gade; *Man Is A Necessary Evil*; *Mambo Man* Jack Elliott, Sonny Burke.

▽

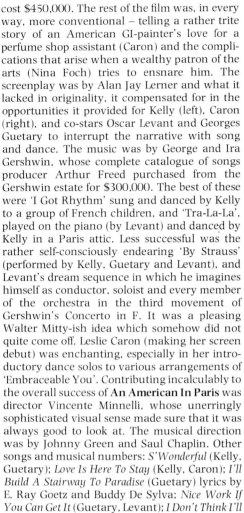

1952

She's Working Her Way Through College (Warner Bros.) was an adaptation of the James Thurber-Elliott Nugent stage comedy *The Male Animal* (already filmed by the studio in 1942 with Henry Fonda and Olivia de Havilland) with songs added and most of the original plot subtracted. In its new incarnation, the Peter Milne screenplay involved a burlesque star (Virginia Mayo, foreground centre) with ambitions to be a serious actress, who enrols in the drama course at a small mid-west college, and the complications that all too predictably ensue. Ronald Reagan (2nd right) played the professor who injudiciously befriends her, and Phyllis Thaxter (right) his suspicious wife. Also on the campus were Don DeFore (who played in the 1942 version), Gene Nelson (left), Patrice Wymore, Roland Winters, Raymond Greenleaf, The Blackburn Twins and Ginger Crowley. The lacklustre musical numbers were staged by LeRoy Prinz, and the film was produced (in Technicolor) by William Jacobs. Songs and musical numbers: *I'll Be Loving You*; *The Stuff That Dreams Are Made Of*; *Give 'Em What They Want*; *Am I In Love?*; *Love Is Still For Free*; *She's Working Her Way Through College* Sammy Cahn, Vernon Duke; *With Plenty Of Money And You* Al Dubin, Harry Warren.

Frank Sinatra starred in **Meet Danny Wilson** (Universal-International), a tuneful platitude about a saloon-room singer's rise to stardom. Alex Nicol played his pianist buddy, and Shelley Winters the gal they both fancy, with Raymond Burr as a racketeer villain who gets what's coming to him in a climactic scene in an empty, floodlit ball park. Sinatra (illustrated) showed positive signs of developing into the fine actor he later became, and his singing was, as usual, terrific. There were nine songs in all including 'A Good Man Is Hard To Find' (by Eddie Green) sung by Sinatra and Miss Winters, and such old favourites as 'I've Got A Crush On You' (by the Gershwins) and 'That Old Black Magic' (by Harold Arlen and Johnny Mercer). Don McGuire wrote it, Leonard Goldstein produced, and it was directed by Joseph Pevney. Other songs: *When You're Smiling* Mark Fisher, Joe Goodwin, Larry Shay; *All Of Me* Seymour Simons, Gerald Marks; *How Deep Is The Ocean?* Irving Berlin; *She's Funny That Way* Neil Moret, Richard Whiting; *You're A Sweetheart* Harold Adamson, Jimmy McHugh; *Lonesome Man Blues* Sy Oliver.

There were so many special effects in **The Belle Of New York** (MGM) that it took producer Arthur Freed 24 weeks to complete. Based on the 1897 stage show of the same name (it was a mild flop in New York, but a huge hit in London where, as the first American musical to play the West End, it ran for 674 performances), Freed's version retained the show's turn of the century setting and its basic plot, but Hugh Morton's original book and lyrics were entirely ditched, as was Gustav Kerker's score. Instead Freed commissioned Johnny Mercer and Harry Warren to provide the words and music, and Robert O'Brien and Irving Ellinson to script it (from an adaptation by Chester Erskine). For the lead role of the playboy who, to date, has left five brides stranded at the altar, Freed cast Fred Astaire (illustrated) who, six years earlier, had declined the part, with Vera-Ellen co-starring as the straitlaced Salvation Army lass he finally settles for. Marjorie Main was Astaire's equally strait-laced Aunt on whom he depends for his income. The rest of the cast was completed by Keenan Wynn, Alice Pearce, Clinton Sundberg, Gale Robbins, and Lisa Ferraday. The meagre plot was augmented by nine songs, one of which literally had Astaire dancing solo in the clouds to the tune of 'Seeing's Believing'. Best song, though, was 'Baby Doll' sung and danced by Vera-Ellen and Astaire, and the only number in the score to make it into the pop charts. Pleasing, too, was 'Thank You Mr Currier, Thank You Mr Ives' ('The Bride's Wedding Song') in which Vera-Ellen, against backdrops inspired by Currier and Ives prints, imagines herself dancing through the four seasons with Astaire. The first-class choreography was by Robert Alton, the gorgeous settings by Cedric Gibbons and Jack Martin Smith, and the costumes by Helen Rose. Charles Walters's direction had the lush MGM 'feel' to it, and it was photographed in Technicolor. Other songs and musical numbers: *When I'm Out With The Belle Of New York*; *Bachelor's Dinner Song*; *Oops*; *Naughty But Nice*; *I Wanna Be A Dancin' Man* Mercer, Warren; *Let A Little Love Come In* Roger Edens.

Fifties Musicals

Singin' In The Rain (MGM) was the story of a matinée idol called Don Lockwood (Gene Kelly) and his romance with chorus girl Kathy Selden (Debbie Reynolds). One of the best, and best written story-lines (by Betty Comden and Adolph Green) to grace a Hollywood musical, it was the perfect subject on which to hang the Arthur Freed-Nacio Herb Brown songs that accompanied it, and a marvellous opportunity to take a light-hearted and often satirical look at the early days of talking pictures. With the exception of three numbers – 'Fit As A Fiddle' (by Freed, Al Hoffman and Al Goodhart), 'Moses Supposes', and 'Make 'Em Laugh' (both written specially by Roger Edens, Comden and Green) – all the Freed-Brown numbers featured in **Singin' In The Rain** were from earlier MGM movies: 'All I Do Is Dream Of You' sung by Debbie Reynolds (after popping out of an enormous cake at a typical Hollywood party) was first heard in *Sadie McKee* (1934); 'Should I?' was featured in *Lord Byron Of Broadway* (1929); 'Singin' In The Rain' came from *Hollywood Revue Of 1929*; 'I've Got A Feelin' You're Foolin', 'You Are My Lucky Star' and 'Broadway Rhythm', all from *Broadway Melody Of 1936* (1935); 'The Wedding Of The Painted Doll' from *Broadway Melody* (1929); 'You Were Meant For Me' from *Broadway Melody* (1929); 'Would You' from *San Francisco* (1936); 'Good Morning' from *Babes In Arms* (1939), 'Beautiful Girl' (sung here with flair by Jimmy Thompson) from *Going Hollywood* (1933), and 'Broadway Melody' from *Broadway Melody* (1929). Just as most of its music had featured prominently in past films, so everything else in **Singin' In The Rain** drew its inspiration from the movies. In fact most of the film was a compendium of borrowings drawn from a variety of real-life sources and personalities. The scene on the sound stage, for example, with dumb blonde Jean Hagen, in a *tour-de-force* performance, desperately trying to 'speak into the bush' where the microphone has been hidden, had its origins in reality. Douglas Shearer, head of MGM's sound department, was consulted regularly about the hazards of early sound recording, and most of the tribulations suffered by the artists and technicians in **Singin' In The Rain's** reconstruction of those times, actually happened. Roscoe Dexter (Douglas Fowley) the director in that particular scene, was modelled on Busby Berkeley, while R.F. Simpson, the studio boss (Millard Mitchell), was inspired by producer Arthur Freed, Dora Bailey the columnist (played by Madge Blake) was modelled on Louella Parsons, Kelly himself on a composite of several matinée idols (particularly Fairbanks, in the 'Duelling Cavalier' sequences) and Cyd Charisse, in the 'Broadway Ballet', on Louise Brooks. Musically, the ballet, choreographed by Kelly, was the film's most ambitious sequence, also drawing its inspiration from the movies. Entirely new, however, was what Kelly calls the 'Crazy Veil' sequence in which Cyd Charisse danced with a soft piece of voile, and which required the use of three aeroplane motors to control the veil's movement. Choreographically, it was Kelly at his most lyrical, and a highspot in a film crowded with them. In fact, **Singin' In The Rain**, directed and choreographed by Kelly and Stanley Donen, remains an undoubted masterpiece and the finest, most durable musical ever to have come out of Hollywood. If the test of a great musical is that you can see it over and over again without longing for the dialogue to end and the musical numbers to begin, then **Singin' In The Rain**

passes *cum laude*. And it is more popular in today's nostalgia-addicted world than it was on its initial release. But even to those not seduced by nostalgia, it remains an invigorating musical, perfect in its reconstruction of a world gone forever, and unforgettable if only for Kelly's joyous dancing in the title number as he abandons himself to a Californian cloudburst, kicks and stamps in a gutterful of water, and climbs halfway up a lamp-post, arms outstretched, and water pouring onto his face, defying adversity. The number, an 'irrepressible ode to optimism' as it has been described by Comden and Green, was the apotheosis of his art, and the climax of an adventurous career. Though the rest of the film never quite equalled the magic of those five glorious minutes, every other number was still head and shoulders above most of the musicals of the fifties. Donald O'Connor has never been as good again, most notably in his justly celebrated 'Make 'Em Laugh' routine, in which he danced, sang, and clowned as if his artistic life depended on the success of it. Every trick in his repertoire was aired afresh and the cumulative effect was

devastating in its virtuosity. As for Debbie Reynolds, her dancing in the buoyant 'Good Morning' never for an instant betrayed her lack of experience, and she was a most sympathetic partner for Kelly in the lyrical 'You Were Meant For Me' into which Kelly attempted to inject the perfect romantic atmosphere on a sound stage through the auspices of five hundred kilowatts of stardust and a soft, summer breeze. It was the third time he had used this 'make-believe' device – first with Kathryn Grayson in *Anchors Aweigh* (MGM, 1945), and next in *Summer Stock* (MGM, 1950) where he wooed Judy Garland. The producer was Arthur Freed, Harold Rosson photographed it (in Technicolor), Cedric Gibbons and Randall Duell were the art directors, Walter Plunkett created the costumes, Lennie Hayton was the musical director; Conrad Salinger, Wally Heglin and Skip Martin orchestrated the numbers, and the cast was completed by Rita Moreno, Kay Donovan, Kathleen Freeman and Mae Clark. Illustrations: Kelly dances the title number; Inset: Kelly dancing with Cyd Charisse.

△

The life and lyrics of Gus Kahn were the inspiration for Warner Bros.' **I'll See You In My Dreams** which, though it followed the well-trodden path of a hundred other such movie biographies wherein hard-won success in Tin Pan Alley and marital difficulties at home were the underlying factors in the plot, was sensitively directed by Michael Curtiz from a skilful screenplay by Melville Shavelson and Jack Rose, and proved to be a well-deserved box-office hit. Danny Thomas (illustrated), making a bid for the movie stardom that had always eluded him, played Gus, Doris Day (illustrated) was his wife Grace, while Frank Lovejoy, Patrice Wymore, James Gleason, Mary Wickes, Jim Backus and Minna Gombell excelled in support. Louis F. Edelman produced, and the dance director was LeRoy Prinz. Songs and musical numbers – all by Kahn, co-composers listed – included: *Ain't We Got Fun*; *Ukelele Lady* Richard Whiting, Ray Egan; *The One I Love Belongs To Somebody Else*; *I'll See You In My Dreams*; *It Had To Be You*; *Swingin' Down The Lane* Isham Jones; *Makin' Whoopee*; *Yes, Sir, That's My Baby*; *Carolina In The Morning*; *Love Me Or Leave Me* Walter Donaldson; *Pretty Baby* Egbert Van Alstyne, Tony Jackson; *Memories* Van Alstyne; *Nobody's Sweetheart* Ernie Erdman, Billy Meyers, Elmer Schoebel; *My Buddy* Donaldson; *Toot Toot Tootsie* Erdman, Dan Russo; *No, No, Nora* Erdman, Ted Fiorito; *Your Eyes Have Told Me So* Van Alstyne, Walter Blaufuss; *I Wish I Had A Girl* Grace LeBoy Kahn; *San Francisco* Bronislau Kaper; *I Never Knew* Fiorito; *The Carioca* Edward Eliscu, Vincent Youmans; *I'm Through With Love* Fud Livingston, Matt Malneck; *Liza* George and Ira Gershwin; *Shine On Harvest Moon* Jack Norworth, Nora Bayes (not a Kahn composition).

Based on a hoary old 1919 play by Walter B. Hare, and brought to the screen in Technicolor, with a scenario by Claude Binyon, Paramount's **Aaron Slick From Punkin Crick** (GB: **Marshmallow Moon**) was a stultifying bore that made little attempt to lampoon the time-worn saga of the innocent country lass who almost loses her farm to a city slicker but is saved in the nick of time by a shy but determined local yokel. Dinah Shore (left) was the hapless heroine, Alan Young (right) the diffident hero, and Robert Merrill the villain. Hisses and boos all round, especially to Mr Binyon whose direction was as leaden as his screenplay. William Perlberg and George Seaton produced, Jay Livingston and Ray Evans contributed several unmemorable songs, and the supporting cast included Adele Jergens, Minerva Urecal, Martha Stewart, Fritz Feld, Veda Ann Borg and Chick Chandler. Songs: *Life Is A Beautiful Thing*; *I'd Like To Baby You*; *My Beloved*; *Marshmallow Moon*; *Why Should I Believe In Love?*; *Purt Nigh But Not Plumb* (sic); *Still Water*; *Saturday Night In Punkin Creek*; *Step Right Up*.

After the enormous success of *The Great Caruso* (MGM) the previous year, Mario Lanza took a backward step, and **Because You're Mine** (MGM), though not exactly a box-office dud, was the least successful of the oversized tenor's four films to date. The plot contrived by Ruth Brooks Flippen and Cy Gomberg, and scripted by Karl Tunberg and Leonard Spigelgass, had Lanza (illustrated) playing an opera star who is drafted into the army. Fortunately his sergeant (James Whitmore) loves classical music and, furthermore, has a sister (Doretta Morrow) who is herself an aspiring young singer. Paula Corday played a temperamental soprano jealous of Lanza's new-found *amour*, with other roles in producer Joe Pasternak's Technicolor production going to Dean Miller, Celia Lovsky, Jeff Donnell, Spring Byington and Curtis Cooksey. There were several operatic extracts in the musical programme and some new songs by an assortment of composers, plus a reprise of Nicholas Brodszky and Sammy Cahn's 'Be My Love' – sung by Miss Morrow over the telephone as part of an audition. The film was directed by Alexander Hall. Songs and operatic excerpts: *Lee-Ah-Loo* John Leeman, Ray Sinatra; *The Song Angels Sing* Paul Francis Webster, Irving Aaronson (melody adapted from 3rd movement of Brahms's Symphony No 3); *You Do Something To Me* Cole Porter; *All The Things You Are* Jerome Kern, Oscar Hammerstein II; *The Lord's Prayer* Albert Hay Malotte; *Granada* Augustin Lara; *Addio Alla Madre* (from 'Cavalleria Rusticana') Mascagni; *Addio* (from 'Rigoletto'); *Il Balen Del Suo Sorriso* and *Miserere* (from 'Il Trovatore') Verdi; *Casta Diva* (from 'Norma') Bellini; *O Paradiso* (from 'L'Africaine') Meyerbeer; *The Sextet* (from 'Lucia Di Lammermoor') Donizetti.

◁

With A Song In My Heart (20th Century-Fox), written and produced by Lamar Trotti and directed by Walter Lang, was a colourful, tearjerking biopic of Jane Froman whose career as a popular songstress was interrupted when she was badly injured in an aeroplane crash in Lisbon in 1943. Susan Hayward (illustrated right) starred as Miss Froman (with Froman herself doing the singing) and gave one of the best performances in a musical since James Cagney unleashed his George M. Cohan onto the world in *Yankee Doodle Dandy* (Warner Bros. 1942). Starting as a modest radio singer in Cincinnati, Froman worked her way to Broadway stardom in the familiar biopic format, taking time off from vocalizing to undergo a series of operations as a result of the accident. Much of the screenplay was involved with Froman's courageous battle to survive her painful ordeal, in the process of which two men dominate her life: Don Ross (David Wayne, illustrated left), the man who helped shape her career; and John Burn (Rory Calhoun), the pilot who rescued her from the Tagus River when their plane went down. In real life Froman divorced Ross and married the pilot, but in the film she remains married to Wayne. Thelma Ritter was fourth-billed as Clancy, a hospital nurse who becomes a life-long friend of Hayward's, with Helen Westcott, Una Merkel, Richard Allan, Max Showalter, Lyle Talbot and Leif Erickson in support. Also in it, as a handsome young paratrooper with shell-shock, was Robert Wagner. For every tear shed throughout, there was an accompanying song, an American medley of old favourites sung by Hayward at an army camp being the musical highlight. Splendid, too, was Miss Froman's stirring singing of the title number (by Richard Rodgers and Horenz Hart) staged at the Roxy Theatre. The superb musical direction was by Alfred Newman, and the choreography by Billy Daniels. The many other songs and musical numbers included: *Blue Moon* Rodgers, Hart; *Tea For Two* Irving Caesar, Vincent Youmans; *That Old Feeling* Lew Brown, Sammy Fain; *I've Got A Feelin' You're Foolin'* Arthur Freed, Nacio Herb Brown; *They're Either Too Young Or Too Old* Frank Loesser, Arthur Schwartz; *It's A Good Day* Peggy Lee, Dave Barbour; *I'll Walk Alone* Sammy Cahn, Jule Styne; *I'm Thru With Love* Gus Kahn, Fud Livingston, Matt Malneck; *Embraceable You* George and Ira Gershwin; *On The Gay White Way* Ralph Rainger, Leo Robin; *Get Happy* Ted Koehler, Harold Arlen; *Jim's Toasted Peanuts*; *Wonderful Home Sweet Home* Ken Darby; American medley: *Deep In The Heart Of Texas* June Hershey, Don Swander; *Carry Me Back To Old Virginny* James Bland; *Give My Regards To Broadway* George M. Cohan; *Alabamy Bound* Bud Green, Buddy De Sylva, Al Jolson, Joseph Meyer; *Chicago* Fred Fisher; *America The Beautiful* Katherine Lee Bates, Samuel A. Ward; *Dixie* Daniel Decatur Emmett; *California Here I Come* Buddy De Sylva, Jolson, Meyer.

▽

Skirts Ahoy! (MGM) starred Esther Williams (centre), Joan Evans (left) and Vivian Blaine (right) as three pretty girls who decide to join the Waves. Scenarist Isobel Lennart's plot, which was red-eyed with tiredness, blearily focused on their respective amorous exploits with Barry Sullivan, Keefe Brasselle and Dean Miller. There were eight new songs by composer Harry Warren (his last score at MGM) and lyricist Ralph Blane; and one ('Oh By Jingo') by Lew Brown and Albert von Tilzer which producer Joe Pasternak dragged in at the last minute for guest stars Debbie Reynolds and Bobby Van who appeared as themselves at a naval show. None of the songs was particularly memorable, though Williams's 'What Makes A Wave?' performed together with the five De Marco Sisters; and 'What Good Is A Gal Without A Guy?' (sung by Williams, Evans and Blaine) were serviceable enough. Two swimming sequences, plus a guest appearance by Billy Eckstine (singing 'Hold Me Close To You') were other minor embellishments in an entertainment that newly defined the word routine. The dances were staged by Nick Castle and the direction was by Sidney Lanfield. Also cast: Mary Foran (seated centre), Jeff Donnell, Margalo Gillmore, Thurston Hall, Russell and Kathy Targay and Roy Roberts. (Technicolor). Other songs and musical numbers: *I Get A Funny Feeling*; *We Will Fight*; *Hilda Matilda*; *Glad To Have You Aboard*; *The Navy Waltz*.

Joe Pasternak's expensive Technicolor production of Franz Lehar's **The Merry Widow** (MGM) couldn't compare in either style or sophistication with Ernst Lubitsch's celebrated 1934 screen version for the same studio. Rewritten by Sonya Levien and William Ludwig so as not to over-tax the limited acting abilities of its star, Lana Turner (vocals by Trudy Erwin), and with Fernando Lamas in support, it emerged as little more than a far-fetched romance between a widowed American millionairess who, on returning to Marshovia, the country of her late husband's birth, meets and falls in love with the dashing Count Danilo. Gone was the sense of fun that permeated the Lubitsch film, and gone was the subtle sexual interplay between the two flirting protagonists. Instead, audiences were left with a rather coarse performance from Turner, an operetta stereotype from Lamas (who, despite the fact that it was written for the widow, sang 'Vilia'), and direction from Curtis Bernhardt that was as heavy as Lubitsch's was light. Jack Cole staged the dances ('The Can-Can' illustrated) and not once approached, in splendour or invention, the climactic 'Merry Widow' waltz from the earlier film. Una Merkel was third-billed as Turner's lady in waiting, with other roles going to Richard Haydn as Baron Popoff, Thomas Gomez as the King of Marshovia, John Abbott as the Marshovian Ambassador, Marcel Dalio as a police sergeant, King Donovan as Nitki and Robert Coote as the Marquis de Crillo. Gwen Verdon (right) was prominent among the dancers. Other musical numbers: *Girls, Girls, Girls*; *I'm Going To Maxim's*; *Can-Can*; *Night* all lyrics by Paul Francis Webster.

A remake of the Jerome Kern-Dorothy Fields musical *Roberta* (RKO, 1935), **Lovely To Look At** (MGM), produced in Technicolor by Jack Cummings, starred Kathryn Grayson, Red Skelton, Howard Keel, Marge and Gower Champion and Ann Miller. In George Wells and Harry Ruby's new adaptation of Alice Duer Miller's story (additional dialogue by Andrew Solt) Skelton played an American comedian who inherits a half interest in a Parisian dress salon. He and pals Keel and Champion travel to Paris where they discover that the salon – run by two sisters (Grayson and Marge Champion) – is almost bankrupt. So Skelton, instead of selling his share of the inheritance in order to raise finances for a Broadway show, decides to take over the running of the salon himself. Helping to flesh out the fragile story were the romances that blossomed between the leading players, Grayson pairing off with Keel, Miller with Skelton and Champion with Champion. Also cast: Zsa Zsa Gabor, Kurt Kasznar, Marcel Dalio and Diane Cassidy. If, musically, the film never quite reached the sublime heights attained in the earlier Astaire-Rogers version, it was not without its good things – notably Miss Miller's torrid 'I'll Be Hard To Handle' (see illustration), Grayson's glorious singing of the miraculous 'Smoke Gets In Your Eyes', and the Champions dancing 'I Won't Dance' (performed in a roomful of fashion dummies). The dances were staged by Hermes Pan, and it was directed by Mervyn LeRoy. Kern composed all the numbers, but with a variety of collaborators. Songs and musical numbers (lyricists listed): *Yesterdays* (Grayson; ballet danced by Champions); *The Touch Of Your Hand* (Keel, Grayson); *Smoke Gets In Your Eyes* (Grayson; danced by Champions) Otto Harbach; *LaFayette* (Keel, Gower Champion, Skelton) Dorothy Fields; *Lovely To Look At* (Keel, chorus) Fields, Jimmy McHugh; *The Most Exciting Night* (Keel); *You're Devastating* (Keel, Grayson) Harbach, Fields; *I Won't Dance* (Champions) Fields, McHugh, Harbach, Hammerstein II; *I'll Be Hard To Handle* (Miller) Fields, Bernard Dougall; *Opening Night* (chorus) Fields, McHugh (not Kern).

Although the title might have suggested a sequel to the previous year's *She's Working Her Way Through College* – with Virginia Mayo's stripper, her newly won Ph.D demurely concealing her charms, on the way to success in the legitimate theatre – **She's Back On Broadway** (Warner Bros.) bore no relation to the earlier film, being the routine account of a Hollywood star (Mayo, left) who hopes to shore up a flagging career with a big stage hit, *Breakfast In Bed*. Not even a strong supporting cast – Steve Cochran as the show's director, Patrice Wymore as a bitchy singer, Frank Lovejoy as a long-suffering producer, and Gene Nelson (right) – could help fill the holes created by Orin Jannings's uneven screenplay or the totally unmemorable score by Bob Hilliard and Carl Sigman. Larry Keating, Paul Picerni, Condos and Brandow, Douglas Spencer and Jacqueline de Wit were also on view. LeRoy Prinz staged the dance numbers (in the studio's new colour process, thoughtfully named WarnerColor), Gordon Douglas directed and Henry Blanke produced. Songs and musical numbers included: *I'll Take You As You Are*; *One Step Ahead Of Everybody*; *The Ties That Bind*; *Breakfast In Bed*; *Behind The Mask* Bob Hilliard, Carl Sigman; *I Think You're Wonderful*.

The original premise of **April In Paris** (Warner Bros.) – a chorus girl, Ethel Jackson (Doris Day), is sent on a cultural junket to Paris instead of Ethel Barrymore for whom the invitation was intended – was so puerile that the film was quite unable to survive it. A shipboard romance that developed between Day, and Ray Bolger (illustrated centre), playing a State Department official, was rendered implausible by Bolger's strenuous hamming, and apart from the title song by Vernon Duke and E.Y. Harburg, the score was undistinguished. The brightest spot in this otherwise awful David Butler-directed film was the lively staging in the ship's galley of 'I'm Gonna Ring The Bell Tonight'. The production numbers by LeRoy Prinz were numbingly forgettable, and the screenplay by Jack Rose and Melville Shavelson, with parts in it for Eve Miller, George Givot, Paul Harvey and Herbert Farjeon, thoroughly inept. Produced (in Technicolor) by William Jacobs. Songs and musical numbers: *It Must Be Good*; *That's What Makes Paris Paree*; *Give Me Your Lips*; *I Know A Place*; *I Ask You* Sammy Cahn, Vernon Duke.

The third and least successful biopic to deal with the life of Stephen Foster (the other two being *Harmony Lane*, Mascot, 1935, and *Swanee River*, 20th Century-Fox, 1939) was Republic's Trucolor production, **I Dream Of Jeanie**. Allan LeMay's screenplay was no more accurate a reflection of how it really was than were the earlier versions, and depicted Foster (Bill Shirley – illustrated) as a thick-skulled, bookkeeping dilettante who dabbled in composition when he wasn't throwing himself at a selfish and unworthy Southern belle (Muriel Lawrence). The girl who eventually nabs him is Lawrence's more appealing sister Jeanie (Eileen Christy). There was, alas, nothing very appealing about the film in general or the performances in particular – with one notable exception: Ray Middleton as Minstrel Man E.P. Christy. Veteran Allan Dwan directed for producer Herbert J. Yates, and the dances were staged by Nick Castle. Also cast: Lynn Bari, Richard Simmons and Rex Allen. Songs included: *My Old Kentucky Home*; *Swanee River*; *Oh Susanna*; *Old Dog Tray*; *Old Folks At Home*; *Ring De Banjo*; *De Camptown Races*; *I Dream Of Jeanie With The Light Brown Hair*; *Come Where My Love Lies Dreaming* Foster.
▽

△

The Dean Martin-Jerry Lewis formula (Lewis illustrated) was successfully put to the test once again in **Jumping Jacks** (Paramount). They played a pair of cabaret entertainers who become paratroopers with amusing, if wholly predictable, results. Slight romantic interest was supplied by Mona Freeman, and Robert Strauss (who appeared with the boys in *Sailor Beware*, Paramount, 1951) was again cast as their superior, with other roles in Hal Wallis's production going to Don DeFore, Dick Erdman, Ray Teal, Marcy McGuire and Danny Arnold. Mack David and Jerry Livingston provided the score, and it was directed without restraint by Norman Taurog. Funniest moment: Lewis attempting to pack a parachute in mime. Songs and musical numbers: *Keep A Little Dream Handy*; *Do The Parachute Jump*; *I Can't Resist A Boy In Uniform*; *What Have You Done For Me Lately?*; *I Know A Dream When I See One*; *Big Blue Sky*.

Shortly after having had a growth on her vocal chords removed, Betty Hutton starred in her penultimate film, and her last for Paramount, **Somebody Loves Me**. It was a Technicolor biopic based on the lives of vaudeville headliners Blossom Seeley and her husband Benny Fields. Hutton (right)was of course, Seeley, and Ralph Meeker (left) played Fields. Starting in 1906 on San Francisco's Barbary Coast, the film sketched out Seeley's career through World War 1 (and the volunteer war work she did) to her success on Broadway. It was the usual rags-to-riches story, with the usual dosage of heartache thrown in for the furtherance of the largely fictional storyline – despite which trials and tribulations Seeley, in the person of Hutton continued to face life with a song, and sang a good many of them, including such old favourites as 'Rose Room' (by Harry Williams and Art Hickman), 'Way Down Yonder In New Orleans' (by Henry Creamer and J. Turner Layton), 'Teasing Rag' (by Joe Jordan), 'Dixie Dreams' (by Arthur Johnston, George W. Meyer, Grant Clarke and Roy Turk) and 'On San Francisco Bay' (by Vincent Bryan and Gertrude Hoffman). There were three new songs: 'Love Him', 'Thanks To You', and 'Honey Oh My Honey' by Ray Evans and Jay Livingston, the latter sung by co-star Adele Jergens (as an arrogant vaudeville star). Also cast: Robert Keith as Hutton's agent, Billie Bird as her wise-cracking confidante, and Henry Slate and Sid Tomack as her first partners, a group called The Chez Paree Adorables; also, in an unbilled appearance, Jack Benny doing one of his well-known routines. The film was choreographed by Charles O'Curran, produced by William Perlberg and directed by Irving Brecher who also wrote the screenplay. Other songs included: *Somebody Loves Me* Buddy De Sylva, George Gershwin; *Jealous* Jack Little, Tommy Malie, Dick Finch; *June Night* Cliff Friend, Abel Baer; *I Cried For You* Gus Arnheim, Arthur Freed, Abe Lyman; *I'm Sorry I Made You Cry* N.J. Clesi, Theodore Morse; *Toddling The Todalo* E. Ray Goetz, A. Baldwin Sloane; *Smiles* J. Will Callahan, Lee S. Roberts; *Wang Wang Blues* Gus Mueller, Buster Johnson, Henry Busse; *I Can't Tell You Why I Love You* Will J. Cobb, Gus Edwards.
▽

△

Although much of the material had worn badly, **Where's Charley?** (Warner Bros.), based on the George Abbott-Frank Loesser musical adaptation of Brandon Thomas's venerable farce *Charley's Aunt*, was pleasantly viewable for two reasons: the lively score, and Ray Bolger (centre)who, repeating his Broadway success as the Oxford student obliged to impersonate his own aunt from Brazil ('where the nuts come from') in order that two young lovers might be respectably chaperoned, was determined to prove there was life in the old warhorse yet, and almost single-handedly saved the proceedings from tedium. Also featured were Allyn McLerie, who had played Amy in the stage version, Robert Shackleton, Mary Germaine, Horace Cooper (left), Howard Marion Crawford (right) and, as the real aunt, Margaretta Scott. John Monks Jr wrote the screenplay, David Butler directed, and Michael Kidd – using mainly English chorus girls and boys – choreographed. The Technicolor production was shot in England, partly on location in Oxford. Songs and musical numbers: *Make A Miracle*; *The New Ashmolean Marching Society And Students' Conservatory Band*; *My Darling, My Darling*; *Once In Love With Amy*; *At The Red Rose Cotillon*; *Better Get Out Of Here* Frank Loesser.

△

A public relations job for Columbia Pictures (in and around whose studios much of it was set), **Rainbow Round My Shoulder**, by the same team that brought you *Sunny Side Of The Street* (Columbia, 1951), top-starred Frankie Laine and Billy Daniels, but the plot, such as it was, concerned the efforts of young Charlotte Austin to become a film star against vehement opposition from her socialite grandmother and guardian (Ida Moore). Blake Edwards and Richard Quine wrote it (the latter also directing). Lee Scott was the choreographer (production number illustrated), the supporting cast included Arthur Franz, Eleanore Davis, Lloyd Corrigan, Barbara Whiting and Ross Ford, and the production (in Technicolor) was under the supervision of Jonie Taps. Solid, programmer entertainment. Songs and musical numbers: *There's A Rainbow Round My Shoulder* Dave Dreyer, Billy Rose, Al Jolson; *Bye Bye Blackbird* Mort Dixon, Ray Henderson; *She's Funny That Way* Neil Moret, Richard Whiting; *Wrap Your Troubles In Dreams* Harry Barris, Ted Koehler, Billy Moll; *The Last Rose of Summer* Thomas Moore, R.A. Milliken; *Wonderful, Wasn't It?* Hal David, Don Rodney; *Girl In The Wood* Terry, Neal & Stuart Gilkyson; *Pink Champagne* Bob Wright, George Forrest.

Fifties Musicals

Although the navy had been the inspiration for innumerable hits, most notably MGM's *On The Town* (1949), for some reason musicals with an army setting rarely proved satisfactory, and **About Face** (Warner Bros.) was no exception. Although the principals – Gordon MacRae (centre), Dick Wesson (right) and Eddie Bracken, matched with Virginia Gibson (2nd left), Aileen Stanley Jr (left) and Phyllis Kirk – were likeable enough, the Peter Milne screenplay, recounting the adventures (both military and romantic) of three cadets was derivative and inane. Also featured were Larry Keating, Cliff Ferre, John Baer and, years before his name went up in lights on Broadway, Joel Grey. Roy Del Ruth directed this William Jacobs Technicolor production, which was based on a successful 1936 play, *Brother Rat*, by John Monks Jr and Fred Finklehoffe (already filmed by Warner Bros. in 1938 with Ronald Reagan, Wayne Morris and Eddie Albert). Songs and musical numbers: *If Someone Had Told Me*; *Piano, Bass And Drums*; *No Other Girl For Me*; *I'm Nobody*; *Spring Has Sprung*; *Wooden Indian*; *Reveille*; *Tar Heels*; *They Haven't Lost A Father Yet* Charles Tobias, Peter De Rose.

Husband and wife team Marge and Gower Champion (illustrated centre) played a husband and wife team in **Everything I Have Is Yours** (MGM), the first film in which they enjoyed star billing. Acting, however, was not their particular *forte* and it needed performances stronger than they were able to deliver to rescue producer George Wells's story and screenplay from being just another piece of musical flim-flam. Focusing mainly on the couple's domestic set-up, the plot concerned Gower's gallivanting with Monica Lewis while Marge sits home minding the baby and having day dreams about dancing with her husband. This ploy at least gave choreographers Nick Castle and Mr Champion an excuse for yet one more dance sequence in a film that only came alive when its protagonists were on their toes. On various occasions Champion danced with his wife, with Miss Lewis and even with some toys, while Mrs Champion came into her own in a solo called 'Derry Down Dilly' by Johnny Green and Johnny Mercer. Dennis O'Keefe, Dean Miller, Eduard Franz, John Gallaudet, Diane Cassidy and Elaine Stewart completed the cast, and it was directed by Robert Z. Leonard. (Technicolor). Other songs and musical numbers: *Like Monday Follows Sunday* Green, Clifford Grey, Rex Newman, Douglas Furber; *17,000 Telegraph Poles* Saul Chaplin; *Serenade For A New Baby* Green; *My Heart Skips A Beat* Bob Wright, Chet Forrest, Walter Donaldson; *Everything I Have Is Yours* Harold Adamson, Burton Lane.

The one undeniably rousing element in 20th Century-Fox's **Stars And Stripes Forever** (GB: **Marching Along**) was its music. For the rest, it was a tedious reconstruction of incidents in the life of march king John Philip Sousa that plodded listlessly along in producer Lamar Trotti's enervating screenplay. A bewhiskered Clifton Webb (illustrated foreground) was called on to impersonate Sousa, which he did with his usual haughty veneer, and was co-starred with Debra Paget and Robert Wagner who, as a pair of young lovers, shouldered a substantial portion of the 'plot' – he as a horn player in Sousa's band, she as a singer. Ruth Hussey was cast as Sousa's sensible wife with other roles in the Technicolor production going to Finlay Currie (2nd right), Roy Roberts, Tom Browne Henry, Lester Matthews (right) and Maude Prickett. The film was directed by Henry Koster, and contained a ballet sequence staged by Nick Castle and Al White Jr built around Percy Gaunt and Charles Hoyt's popular song, 'The Bowery'. Best moments were a negro choir's singing of 'The Battle Hymn Of The Republic' (by Julia Ward Howe and William Steffe) and a performance of 'Dixie' (by Daniel Decatur Emmett) played by Sousa and his musicians as they enter the Cotton States Exposition in Atlanta. Other musical numbers: *Stars And Stripes Forever*; *El Capitan*; *Washington Post*; *King Cotton* Sousa; *Light Cavalry* Von Suppe; *Turkey In The Straw* (traditional); *Hail To The Chief* John Sanderson.

After the successful box-office returns from *Paleface* (Paramount, 1948), it was inevitable that a sequel would follow, and only surprising that it took so long. But it finally happened, and was called **Son Of Paleface** (Paramount). Bob Hope (illustrated foreground centre) played the son of the late pioneer dentist, Painless Potter, and Jane Russell was a lady bandit whose front (you should pardon the expression) was saloon singing. They were joined by Roy Rogers and Trigger who, playing themselves, offered Hope valiant assistance in tracking down his inheritance. Director Frank Tashlin, together with Robert L. Welch and Joseph Quillan, provided the trio with a gloriously anachronistic screenplay (redolent of some of the more inspired 'Road' films), and there were several new and appealing songs as well as a reprise of Jay Livingston and Ray Evans's world-wide smash, 'Buttons And Bows'. The dances were staged by Josephine Earl, and it was produced, in Technicolor, by Robert L. Welch with a cast that also included Bill Williams, Lloyd Corrigan, Paul E. Burns, Douglass Dumbrille, Harry Von Zell, Iron Eyes Cody, Wee Willie Davis, and Charles Cooley. Other songs and musical numbers included: *There's A Cloud In My Valley Of Sunshine* (Rogers) Jack Hope, Lyle Morraine; *California Rose* (Rogers); *Wing-Ding Tonight* (Hope, Russell); *What A Dirty Shame* (chorus) Jay Livingston, Ray Evans; *Am I In Love?* (Hope, Russell); *Four Legged Friend* (Rogers) Jack Brooks.

George Jessel's Technicolor production for 20th Century-Fox of Damon Runyon's **Bloodhounds of Broadway** owed very little in spirit to the original. But with Mitzi Gaynor (centre) at her exuberant best, heading an agreeable cast that also included Scott Brady, Mitzi Green, Marguerite Chapman, Michael O'Shea, Wally Vernon, Henry Slate, George E. Stone and Charles Buchinsky (later Bronson) this amiable story of how a crooked New York bookie (Brady), who, while lying low in Georgia, meets and is ultimately reformed by a hillbilly (Gaynor) with show-biz aspirations, was a merry enough entertainment in its own right. Gaynor's dancing helped it along most pleasurably and her singing of Eliot Daniel's 'Bye Low' was enchanting. Harmon Jones directed from a screenplay by Sy Gomberg and Robert Sidney choreographed. Other songs: *Jack O'Diamonds* Ben Oakland, Paul Webster; *Broadway Rhythm*; *I've Got A Feelin' You're Foolin'* Arthur Freed, Nacio Herb Brown; *I Wish I Knew* Mack Gordon, Harry Warren.

'A *bona fide* Goldwyn dazzler' was how one critic at the time described Sam Goldwyn's 78th production, **Hans Christian Andersen** (RKO). Weighing in at over four million dollars, $400,000 of it going on a 17-minute ballet sequence, $175,000 on the salary of its star, Danny Kaye, $14,000 on shoes alone and umpteen thousands on the 16 screenplays Goldwyn commissioned over a 15-year period of germination and gestation – it justified the expenditure, and was a visual and aural delight with a tuneful and imaginative score by Frank Loesser. Though critical opinion was divided on the merits of Danny Kaye's performance in the central role, the film grossed over $6,000,000 to become the third biggest money-maker in Goldwyn's history, outdistanced only by *The Best Years Of Our Lives* (1946), and the yet to come *Guys And Dolls* (1955). Kaye's performance was, in fact, just what Moss Hart's gentle screenplay (from a story by Myles Connolly) called for. Toning down the facial tics usually associated with him, the comedian was particularly effective in the musical numbers, especially the enchanting 'Thumbelina' and 'The Ugly Duckling'. Apart from the lengthy ballet sequence (choreographed, as were all the dance sequences, by Roland Petit, whose wife Zizi Jeanmaire, was cast opposite Kaye) Kaye was hardly off the screen. As a disclaimer at the beginning of the film made clear, **Hans Christian Andersen** was not a biography of the great Danish writer, but a fairy tale about a cobbler's unrequited love for a ballerina (Jeanmaire, illustrated centre with Kaye) and how, instead of finding romance, he finds fame as a writer of children's stories. Joey Walsh played Andersen's faithful companion Peter, with other roles under Charles Vidor's direction going to Farley Granger as Jeanmaire's husband Niels, Philip Tonge, John Brown, John Qualen and ballet dancer Erik Bruhn as 'The Hussar' in the Ice-Skating Ballet. Roland Petit also appeared, as The Prince in 'The Little Mermaid' sequence. It was photographed by Harry Stradling (in Technicolor) with Richard Day and Antoni Clave on art direction. Other musical numbers: *The King's New Clothes*; *Inchworm*; *I'm Hans Christian Andersen*; *Wonderful Copenhagen*; *Dream Fantasy*; *Anywhere I Wander*; *Wedding Fantasy*; *No Two People*.
▽

The spectacular water ballets created by Busby ▷ Berkeley for MGM's **Million Dollar Mermaid** (GB: **One Piece Bathing Suit**) saved an otherwise pedestrian biopic that purported to tell the story of Annette Kellerman, the Australian swimming champion who, in the 1920s, found fame and fortune as the aquatic star attraction in the New York Hippodrome, and notoriety as the girl who first introduced the world to the 'daring' one-piece bathing suit and got herself arrested in Boston for doing so. Esther Williams (illustrated foreground centre) in a role tailor-made for her, was top-cast as Miss Kellerman, Victor Mature co-starred as the American promoter she first meets in England, and who, after inducing her to swim 26 miles down the Thames as a publicity stunt, launches her in America. Also cast: David Brian as the manager of the Hippodrome and Mature's rival for Miss Williams's affections, and Walter Pidgeon as Williams's father. But, as was so often the case when Busby Berkeley had a hand in things, he was the real star of the film, with his two elaborately staged sequences again proving that, when it came to pulling out the stops in a musical routine – be it on water or on *terra firma* – he was still the best in the business. Everything else in the film, including Mervyn LeRoy's direction, was anaemic by comparison. It was produced (in Technicolor) by Arthur Hornblow Jr with a cast that included Donna Corcoran, Jesse White, Maria Tallchief, Howard Freeman, Charles Watts and Wilton Graff. The screenplay was by Everett Freeman.

△

Bing Crosby (left) playing a widowed Broadway producer, and Jane Wyman (as his fiancée) appeared together for a second time in **Just For You** (Paramount), a sentimental little piece in Technicolor which found Crosby – between songs – trying to improve his image as a parent. To this end he decides to cut down his production schedule and take his hitherto neglected 18-year-old son (Robert Arthur) and younger daughter (Natalie Wood, centre) on an extended holiday to a country resort. Finding it difficult to communicate with them, he sends for fiancée Wyman, whose presence, far from alleviating the situation, aggravates it when young Robert falls in love with her. After several plot complications via scenarist Robert Carson, whose inconsequential screenplay was adapted from a novel by Stephen Vincent Benet, Robert enlists in the air force and pulls himself together, while Miss Wood is sent to a swanky finishing school run by Ethel Barrymore. The Harry Warren-Leo Robin score was far better than the material deserved. Best numbers: 'Zing A Little Zong', 'I'll Si-Si Ya In Bahia' and 'On The 10.10 From Ten-Ten-Tennessee'. Pat Duggan produced, Elliott Nugent directed, and the supporting cast included Cora Witherspoon (right), Regis Toomey, Ben Lessy and Art Smith. Other songs and musical numbers: *Just For You*; *He's Just Crazy For Me*; *Checkin' My Heart*; *The Maiden Of Guadalupe*; *The Live Oak Tree*; *Call Me Tonight*.

An enjoyable period piece (set in 1904), **Meet Me At The Fair** (Universal International) starred Dan Dailey (left) as a fantasy-prone, easy-going travelling medicine show operator who sets the wheels of Irving Wallace's screenplay (adapted by Martin Beckley from a novel by Gene Markey) in motion when he befriends a runaway orphan (Chet Allen, right) and is soon after accused of kidnapping him. Romance intruded in the shape of Diana Lynn (2nd left), a social worker strongly opposed to Dailey's friendship with the boy. In the end, however, she becomes his ally and wins a successful battle against a crooked district attorney (High O'Brian, 2nd right) who also happens to be her fiancé. Carole Mathews was also in it, as a fairground singer in love with Dailey, and the rest of the cast comprised 'Scat Man' Crothers as Dailey's assistant, Rhys Williams, Russell Simpson, Thomas E. Jackson and George Chandler. The smooth and efficient direction was by Douglas Sirk, the dances were staged by Kenny Williams, and the producer was Albert J. Cohen. Songs and musical numbers: *Meet Me At The Fair* Milton Rosen, Frederick Herbert; *I Was There* F.E. Miller, 'Scat Man' Crothers; *Remember The Time* Kenneth Williams, Marvin Wright; *I Got The Shiniest Mouth In Town* Stan Freeberg; *Bill Bailey Won't You Please Come Home?* Hughie Cannon; *Oh Susanna* Stephen Foster; *Sweet Genevieve* George Cooper, Henry Tucker; *Ave Maria* Schubert; *Ezekiel Saw De Wheel*; *All God's Chillun Got Wings* (traditional).
▽

1953

Road To Bali (Paramount) was the first *'Road'* film made by the team of Crosby, Hope and Lamour for five years, and although not as spontaneously zany as their last adventure, was nothing to be ashamed of. Messrs Crosby and Hope (illustrated) were, as usual, a couple of vaudevillians on the run, this time finishing up in the South Seas where, together with a sarong-clad Miss L., they become embroiled in a plot involving hidden treasure. Making unbilled guest appearances were Humphrey Bogart (in his 'African Queen' get-up), Bob Crosby (who fires a rifle, explaining that brother Bing promised him 'one shot' in it), Dean Martin, Jerry Lewis, and Jane Russell. Frank Butler, Hal Kanter and William Morrow's screenplay lacked the freshness of some of the earlier *'Road'* films, and if Crosby, Lamour and Hope were definitely getting older, so were the gags. Johnny Burke and Jimmy Van Heusen provided the undistinguished score and Charles O'Curran staged the dances. Produced (in Technicolor) by Harry Tugend, directed by Hal Walker and, in support featured Murvyn Vye, Peter Coe, Ralph Moody, Leon Askin, Donald Lawton and Michael Ansara. Songs: *The Merry-Go-Runaround*; *Chicago Style*; *Hoots Mon*; *To See You*; *Moonflowers* Burke, Van Heusen; *Chorale For Brass, Piano And Bongo* Stan Kenton, Pete Rugolo.

Although screenwriters Frank Davis, Leonard Stern and Lewis Meltzer dutifully updated narrative elements for the remake of **The Jazz Singer** (Warner Bros.), they were incapable of disguising the sentimentality ingrained in Samson Raphaelson's play which, at this late date, was an irrefutable argument for a return to the silent cinema. Danny Thomas (left) played the cantor's son who, in this version, is a Korean War veteran returning home and discovering, to the distress of his father (Eduard Franz), that he is more attracted by the rewards of Broadway than those of heaven. The basic material proved intractably *schmaltzy*, rendering the movie as much an anachronism as it had originally been epoch-making. Peggy Lee (right), played the girl Thomas loves, Mildred Dunnock, Tom Tully Alex Gerry, Allyn Joslyn and Harold Gordon supported, Michael Curtiz directed, LeRoy Prinz staged the dance numbers, Louis F. Edelman produced (in Technicolor) and it was edited by Alan Crosland Jr, the son of the man who had directed the original version in 1927. Songs and musical numbers included: *Lover* Richard Rodgers, Lorenz Hart; *Just One Of Those Things* Cole Porter; *This Is A Very Special Day* Peggy Lee; *Clover* Mort Dixon, Harry Woods; *Birth Of The Blues* De Sylva, Brown, Henderson; *Living The Life I Love*; *I Hear The Music Now*; *What Are New Yorkers Made Of*; *Hush-A-Bye*; *Oh Moon* Sammy Fain, Jerry Seelen; *I'll String Along With You* Al Dubin, Harry Warren; *Breezin' Along With The Breeze* Richard A. Whiting, Seymour Simons, Haven Gillespie; *If I Could Be With You* Henry Creamer, Jimmy Johnson; *Kol Nidrei* (Hebrew traditional).

Paramount sat on **The Stooge** for two years before releasing it in 1953. Though it starred the popular team of Dean Martin and Jerry Lewis (illustrated), the screenplay fashioned for it by Fred Finkelhoffe and Martin Rackin (story by Finkelhoffe and Sid Silvers) veered from the usual formula fare M. and L.'s fans had come to expect in that it introduced an element of mawkishness and sentimentality totally at variance with the team's basic zaniness. The result was an unsatisfying effort in which Martin appeared as a thoroughly conceited and objectionable vaudeville star and Lewis as his good-natured, frequently put-upon stooge. There was an excellent performance from Eddie Mayehoff as Martin's agent, the direction was by Norman Taurog, and it was produced by Hal Wallis with a cast including Marion Marshall, Polly Bergen, Richard Erdman and Frances Bavier. Songs: *A Girl Named Mary And A Boy Named Bill* Mack David, Jerry Livingston; *Who's Your Little Whozis?* Al Goering, Ben Bernie, Walter Hirsch; *Just One More Chance* Arthur Johnston, Sam Coslow; *With My Eyes Wide Open I'm Dreaming* Mack Gordon, Harry Revel; *Louise* Leo Robin, Richard A. Whiting; *I'm Yours* E.Y. Harburg, Johnny Green.

A bargain-basement *On The Town* (MGM, 1949), **All Ashore** (Columbia) starred Mickey Rooney (left), Dick Haymes (right) and Ray McDonald as three sailors on shore leave at Catalina Island. Their adventures (with Rooney playing the fall guy of the trio) formed the basis of Blake Edwards and Richard Quine's screenplay (story by Edwards and Robert Wells) and also involved Peggy Ryan, Jody Lawrance (centre) and Barbara Bates as the available gals, with Fay Roope, Jean Willes, Rica Owen, Patricia Walker and Edwin Parker also cast for producer Jonie Taps. It was photographed in Technicolor, and relied solely on the multi-talented Rooney – seen at his best in a dream sequence in which he imagines he is a brave, mediaeval knight – for its laughs and general entertainment value. The director was co-author Quine. Songs included: *You're A Buddy*; *Boy Meets Girl*; *Heave Ho, My Hearties*; *I Love No One But You* Robert Wells, Fred Karger.

A really lousy script by Walter Bullock was the cardinal fault of **The I-Don't-Care Girl**, a Technicolor biopic from 20th Century-Fox that attempted crudely, and wholly unsatisfactorily, to find out (via flashbacks) what made tempestuous vaudeville star Eva Tanguay tick. Mitzi Gaynor (illustrated) starred (in a role tailor-made for Betty Hutton), but was unable to breathe life into the character, or to make Bullock's hodge-podge of a screenplay seem plausible. Even the number 'I Don't Care' (by Jean Lenox and Harry O. Sutton) which made Tanguay famous, was more convincingly sung by Judy Garland in *In The Good Old Summertime* (MGM 1949). What the film did have going for it (apart from its splendid Technicolor) were three production numbers staged by Jack Cole (though none of them true to the period in which the film was set) and a trio of tap routines (choreographed by Seymour Felix) for Gaynor and co-star David Wayne (as Tanguay's first dancing partner). Cole's work could be seen in 'The Beale Street Blues' (by W.C. Handy), 'I Don't Care' and 'The Johnson Rag' (by Jack Lawrence, Guy H. Hall and Henry Kleinkauf); and Felix's in 'This Is My Favourite City' (by Mack Gordon and Josef Myrow), 'I Don't Care' (a second version) and 'Pretty Baby' (by Gus Kahn, Tony Jackson and Egbert Van Alstyne). Gaynor's other co-stars were Oscar Levant, and Bob Graham, a singer, and the object of Gaynor's affections. Also cast: Craig Hill, Warren Stevens, Hazel Brooks, Marietta Canty and Sam Hearn. Producer George Jessel appeared as himself, the idea behind Bullock's screenplay being to feature Jessel as a producer about to begin a motion picture of Eva Tanguay's life, and seeking out some pertinent facts about the star from those who knew her best. Lloyd Bacon directed. Other songs and musical numbers: *As Long As You Care (I Don't Care)* George Jessel, Joe Cooper; *Oh, You Beautiful Doll* Nat D. Ayer, A. Seymour Brown; *Liebestraum* Liszt; *Piano Concerto No 1* (excerpt) Liszt; *Hello, 'Frisco, Hello* Louis A. Hirsch, Gene Buck; *On The Mississippi* Ballard MacDonald, Harry Carroll, Arthur Fields; *Here Comes Love Again* Jessel, Eliot Daniel; *Little G Minor Fugue* Bach (used to frame *The Johnson Rag* sequence); *Largo Al Factotum* (from 'The Barber Of Seville', also used in *Johnson Rag* sequence) Rossini.

As technically stunning as anything Walt Disney had achieved in the past (or would achieve in the future), **Peter Pan** (RKO) owed more to the imagination of Disney's team of animators than it did to its original creator, J.M. Barrie. Though the storyline was basically unchanged, the characters and their visual realization were all Disney stereotypes – the least successful being Tinker Bell, a sexy nymphet who wouldn't have been tolerated in fairyland for a second. And if the plotting was bold and vigorous something of the magic of Barrie's story was missing. Yet, it was fun while it lasted – the highlight being Captain Hook's encounter with the dreaded crocodile. The music and songs were skilfully integrated into the narrative, and although the score wasn't as memorable as *Cinderella*'s (RKO, 1950), it was perfectly serviceable. Bobby Driscoll's voice was heard as Peter, Kathryn Beaumont's as Wendy, with other vocal characterizations by Hans Conried (Captain Hook), Bill Thompson (Smee), Heather Angel (Mrs Darling), Paul Collins (Mr Darling) Tommy Luske (John), Candy Candido (Indian Chief) and Tom Conway (narrator). It was directed by Hamilton Luske, Clyde Geronimi and Wilfred Jackson and produced, in Technicolor, at a cost of $4,000,000, by Walt Disney. (Peter Pan and Wendy illustrated). Songs: *The Elegant Captain Hook; You Can Fly; Your Mother And Mine; What Makes The Red Man Red?* Sammy Cahn, Sammy Fain; *A Pirate's Life* Oliver Wallace, Erdman Penner; *Tee Dum-Tee Dee* Wallace, Ted Sears, Winston Hibler; *Never Smile At A Crocodile* Frank Churchill, Jack Lawrence.

It is not often that the word 'enchanting' can accurately be applied to a musical, but it was the best way to describe **Lili** (MGM), as well as Leslie Caron's genuinely touching performance in it. Adapted by Helen Deutsch from a story by Paul Gallico, it told the tender tale of a 16-year-old orphan who becomes a waitress with a travelling carnival show. She's fired for spending too much time watching the show's magic act, and is comforted in her grief by a group of puppets, (illustrated, with Caron) operated unbeknownst to the naive Miss Caron, by Mel Ferrer, a cripple whom she loathes, believing him to be cruel and heartless. It is only after Ferrer, who is in love with the waif, slaps her in a jealous rage (for Miss Caron prefers Jean-Pierre Aumont, the show's handsome magician, to him), that she begins to understand that the love exuding from the puppets comes from the love Ferrer feels for her. Bronislau Kaper provided the music for this absorbing, bitter-sweet film and the hit song 'Hi-Lili, Hi-Lo' (performed by the puppets) had a lyric by scenarist Deutsch. The film also contained a delightful dream ballet, choreographed by Charles Walters and Dorothy Jarnac. Walters directed, and it was produced (in Technicolor) by Edwin H. Knopf with a cast that was completed by Zsa Zsa Gabor, Kurt Kasznar, Amanda Blake, Alex Gerry, Ralph Dumke, Wilton Graff and George Baxter. In 1961, a Broadway musical based on the film, and called *Carnival*, reversed the usual procedure of Hollywood always sponging off Broadway. It starred Anna Maria Alberghetti and was a Broadway success, running for 719 performances.

A jolly, brightly-packaged Technicolor offering from MGM that could have done with a slightly more substantial screenplay, **I Love Melvin** starred Donald O'Connor and Debbie Reynolds (centre) in a simple story about a photographer's assistant who rashly promises a would-be film star (Reynolds) that he will put her picture on the cover of *Look* magazine. Such was the lightweight situation concocted by Laslo Vadnay, and which producer George Wells scripted (additional dialogue by Ruth Brooks Flippen), with parts in it for Una Merkel and Allyn Joslyn (as Reynolds's parents), Richard Anderson, Les Tremayne, Noreen Corcoran, Jim Backus, Barbara Ruick, and guest star Robert Taylor. O'Connor and Reynolds's musical comedy talents were exploited in several full-scale production numbers, the three best being 'A Lady Loves', in which Reynolds imagines herself as a famous film star; 'Saturday Afternoon Before the Game', a football routine featuring Reynolds as the football; and 'I Wanna Wander', a knockabout item for the versatile and energetic O'Connor. All the songs were by Mack Gordon and Josef Myrow, and they were excellently staged by Robert Alton. Don Weis's direction drew engaging performances from the two stars. Other songs and musical numbers: *We Have Never Met As Yet; Life Has Its Funny Little Ups And Downs; Where Did You Learn To Dance?; And There You Are.*

△

Irving Berlin's mammoth Broadway hit, **Call Me Madam**, gave Ethel Merman (illustrated) the best screen role of her career and she devoured it greedily. As Mrs Sally Adams, 'the hostess with the mostest' and Ambassadress to Lichtenberg, she recreated the part she played 644 times on Broadway in a no-holds-barred performance that left critics and audiences alike breathless. However, for those unfortunate enough to remain unresponsive to the lady's particular brand of scenery-chewing, sock-it-to-'em tactics, the experience must, indeed, have been a painful one. For the film was Merman, and Merman was the film. And anyone else – such as Donald O'Connor (as her press attaché), Vera-Ellen (as the princess O'Connor falls for) and George Sanders (as the Lichtenberg general who proves the hostess has a heart by stealing it), were little more than agreeable appendages to the main business at hand – which is not to discredit O'Connor and Ellen's superb dancing to Robert Alton's notable choreography. Also trying to get a look in were Billy De Wolfe, Helmut Dantine, Walter Slezak, Steve Geray, and Ludwig Stossel. Musically, too, Merman had it all her own way, completely dominating O'Connor in their duet 'You're Just In Love' and overpowering the rest of the cast with her high voltage belting of 'The Hostess With The Mostest', 'International Rag' and 'Can You Use Any Money Today?'. Sanders coped well enough with his solo, 'Marrying For Love', and from Vera-Ellen (her vocals dubbed by Carole Richards) and Donald O'Connor there was a spirited rendition of 'It's A Lovely Day Today'. But it was the redoubtable Merman who carried the movie to success, making one regret that her screen appearances were so few and far between. It was adapted from Howard Lindsay and Russel Crouse's book by Arthur Sheekman, produced (in Technicolor) for 20th Century-Fox by Sol C. Siegel, and directed by Walter Lang. Other songs and musical numbers: *Welcome To Lichtenberg* (chorus); *Mrs Sally Adams* (girls); *The Ocarina* (Vera-Ellen, chorus); *What Chance Have I With Love?* (O'Connor); *Something To Dance About* (O'Connor, Vera-Ellen); *The Best Thing For You* (Merman, Sanders).

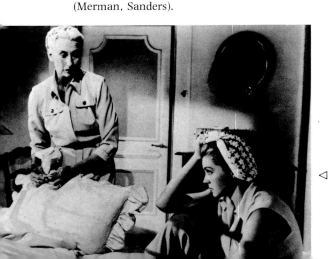

Warner Bros. unwisely opted to give Sigmund Romberg's operetta **The Desert Song** another airing (its third on film), but neither the principals, Gordon MacRae and Kathryn Grayson, nor director Bruce Humberstone could do much to conceal the ancient origins of the material. MacRae (foreground centre) played the Riff chieftain (no longer referred to as 'The Red Shadow', doubtless because, in a period jumpy with McCarthyism, the adjective had too many communistic associations) who saves the French garrison from the wicked Sheik Youssef (Raymond Massey) and wins the hand of the general's daughter (Grayson). It may have worked back in 1926 (the show's original libretto was by Lawrence Schwab, Otto Harbach, Frank Mandel, Sigmund Romberg and Oscar Hammerstein II) but, 27 years later, in Roland Kibbee's idiotic screenplay, it was a case of too little, too late. Also featured were Steve Cochran (as a legionnaire), Ray Collins, Dick Wesson (foreground left) and Allyn McLerie. The musical numbers, including a weird houri dance for McLerie, were staged by LeRoy Prinz, and the film was produced, in Technicolor, by Rudi Fehr. Songs and musical numbers: *The Desert Song*; *Long Live The Night*; *The Riff Song*; *Romance*; *One Alone*; *One Flower* Romberg, Hammerstein; *Gay Parisienne* Jack Scholl, Serge Walter.

▽

Dangerous When Wet (MGM) didn't offer very much by way of plot (its star, Esther Williams, right, spends most of her time preparing to swim across the English Channel), but it was brimful of attractive people and attractive performances. Handsome Fernando Lamas played an amorous and wealthy peddler of French champagne, Jack Carson was a producer-cum-travelling salesman. Charlotte Greenwood (left) Williams's high-kicking Ma, William Demarest her Pa, and Barbara Whiting and Donna Corcoran her sisters. The score was by Arthur Schwartz and Johnny Mercer, and contained a pip of a number in 'I Got Out Of Bed On The Right Side' as well as the pleasant 'Ain't Nature Grand' sung, at various stages, by practically every member of the cast. In addition, there was a lengthy animated dream sequence directed by Fred Quimby, William Hanna and Joseph Barbera, featuring Tom and Jerry, as well as a live-action Miss Williams – the highlight of the film. Dorothy Kingsley's screenplay was slightly better than serviceable, the 'dramatic' climax being the Channel swim itself. It was directed by Charles Walters for producer George Wells, and the cast was completed by Denise Darcel, Bunny Waters, Henri Letondal, Paul Bryer, Jack Raine, Richard Alexander, Tudor Owen and Ann Codee. (Technicolor). Other songs: ◁ *I Like Men*; *Liquapep*; *Fifi*; *In My Wildest Dreams*.

△

William Lundigan, Jane Greer (illustrated), Mitzi Gaynor, Gloria De Haven and David Wayne starred in **Down Among The Sheltering Palms** (20th Century-Fox), a minor musical whose lush and exotic Pacific island background provided the scene for a really weather-beaten story (by Edward Hope, screenplay by Claude Binyon, Albert Lewin and Burt Styler) in which a decorous officer (Lundigan), while attempting to see that his GIs keep their distance from the island's bevy of local lovelies, finds himself ensnared by an American newspaper columnist (Greer), an amorous civilian (De Haven) and one of the native islanders (Gaynor). Wayne played Lundigan's sidekick, and together they sang the best tune in the show, 'I'm A Ruler Of A South Sea Island' (by Harold Arlen and Ralph Blane, who wrote all the new songs). From Miss Greer came 'Who Will It Be When The Time Comes?', Gaynor's high point was 'What Makes De Difference?' while Gloria De Haven gave out with 'All Of Me' (by Seymour Simons and Gerald Marks). The dances were staged by Seymour Felix, it was produced in Technicolor by Fred Kohlmar, and directed by Edmund Goulding. Other musical numbers included: *Down Among The Sheltering Palms* Abe Olman, James Brockman; *When You're In Love* Arlen, Blane.

Betty Grable (left) didn't so much as show an ankle in **The Farmer Takes A Wife** (20th Century-Fox), a Technicolor remake of the 1935 version which had starred Janet Gaynor in the Grable role and Henry Fonda in the role played in the musical version by Dale Robertson (right). Based on a novel by Walter D. Edmonds, and a stage play by Frank B. Elser and Marc Connelly, its folksy story, set on the Erie Canal in 1850, concerned Molly Larkin (Grable), a cook on a canal boat owned by Jotham Klore (John Carroll), and her romance with driver Daniel Harrow (Robertson), much to rival Carroll's aggressive disapproval. To give it the zest it so pitifully lacked, it needed a screenplay far racier than the one Walter Bullock, Sally Benson and Joseph Fields provided, and performances of more conviction than its leads were capable of. Its redeeming feature was its score by Harold Arlen and Dorothy Fields, especially a number called 'We're In Business' sung by Grable and Robertson, as well as by practically every one else in a cast that also included Thelma Ritter, Eddie Foy Jr, Gwen Verdon, Charlotte Austin, Kathleen Crowley and Merry Anders. Jack Cole was in charge of the dance direction, Frank P. Rosenberg produced, and Henry Levin called the shots. Other songs and musical numbers: *On The Erie Canal*; *We're Doing It For The Natives In Jamaica*; *When I Close My Door*; *Today I Love Everybody*; *Somethin' Real Special*; *With The Sun Warm Upon Me*; *Can You Spell Schenectady*.
▽

Sol Hurok always loved music, but as he had no performer's talents the only way he could participate in the art he so passionately adored was to become an impresario, a fact which was duly celebrated in a gaudy biopic from 20th Century-Fox called **Tonight We Sing**. Barring some domestic upheavals when his wife (Anne Bancroft) temporarily walks out on him, the film concentrated mainly on Hurok's entrepreneurial activities with such stars as Chaliapin (Ezio Pinza, here illustrated as Mussorgsky's *Boris Godounov*), Anna Pavlova (Tamara Toumanova), and the great violinist Eugene Ysaye (Isaac Stern), thus providing the cue for an outpouring of glorious music. As Hurok himself, David Wayne gave one of the least convincing performances of his indifferent career, but then, apart from the music, nothing about George Jessel's synthetic, Technicolor production was overburdened with anything as weighty as conviction. Harry Kurnitz and George Oppenheimer pasted the script together from incidents related in a book written by Hurok and Ruth Goode, and it was unimaginatively directed by Mitchell Leisen. Also cast: Byron Palmer (with vocals dubbed by Jan Peerce), Roberta Peters, Oscar Karlweis (as Hurok's partner), Mikhail Rasumny (as Hurok's valet), Steve Geray, Walter Woolf King and John Meek (as Hurok aged 10). The musical direction was by Alfred Newman, choral direction by Ken Darby, and ballet choreography by David Lichine. Musical extracts: *Le Cygne* (Toumanova) Saint-Saëns; *Sempre Libera* (Peters) from Verdi's 'La Traviata'; *Jewel Song* (Peters) from Gounod's 'Faust'; *Qu'Attendez-Vous Encore* (Pinza, Palmer) from 'Faust'; *Vous Qui Faites L'Endormie* (Pinza, Palmer) from 'Faust'; *Love Duet* (Palmer, Peters) from Act 1 of Puccini's 'Madam Butterfly'; *Andante Le Triste Vero* (Palmer) from 'Madam Butterfly'; *Addio Fiorito Asil* (Palmer) from 'Madam Butterfly'; *Mattinata* (Palmer) Leoncavallo; *Valse Caprice in E Flat* (Stern) Anton Rubinstein; *Processional* (from 'Boris Godounov') Mussorgsky.

As he had done on so many occasions in the past, the legendary Busby Berkeley came to the rescue of a musical desperately in need of a few good ideas. This time it was on **Small Town Girl** (MGM) that he worked his special brand of alchemy, turning a routine song-and-dance show into a good one. The simple story was of a millionaire playboy (Farley Granger) who, after being given a 30-day sentence for speeding through the quiet streets of small-town Duck Creek, falls out of love with his fiancée (Ann Miller) and into love with the daughter (Jane Powell) of the local Judge. Apart from Berkeley's inventive dance direction, the film was also blessed with Bobby Van, as a small-town clerk aching for a career in the theatre. Van stopped the show with a dance routine called 'Take Me To Broadway' performed entirely in energetic hops, and was the freshest talent on display. There was reliable work too, from Ann Miller, whose 'I've Got To Hear That Beat' was effectively staged by Berkeley in a set whose floor comprised dozens of holes through which appeared the disembodied hands of over fifty musicians, each of them holding a musical instrument. (illustrated). Other musical highlights included Jane Powell singing 'Small Towns Are Smile Towns', and guest star Nat King Cole's 'My Flaming Heart'. All the songs were by Nicholas Brodszky and Leo Robin, with Andre Previn as the musical director. Joe Pasternak produced, it was photographed in Technicolor, and the director was Leslie Kardos. Also cast: S.Z. Sakall, Billie Burke, Fay Wray, Dean Miller, William Campbell, Philip Tonge. Other songs and musical numbers: *Fine Fine Fine*; *The Fellow I'd Follow*; *Lullaby Of The Lord*; *My Gaucho*.

Chart-topper Rosemary Clooney (right) made a pleasing screen debut in **The Stars Are Singing**, slamming home such Jay Livingston-Ray Evans hits as 'I Do I Do I Do', 'Haven't Got A Worry To My Name' and 'Lovely Weather For Ducks'; and Ross Bagdasarian and William Saroyan's 'Come On-A-My-House' (a big hit which had established Clooney as a major singing star in 1951). Musically, she was well assisted by Anna Maria Alberghetti (left) and Lauritz Melchior, though as far as the story (by Paul Hervey Fox) was concerned, she received no assistance at all from scenarist Liam O'Brien. A trifle about a group of undiscovered talents (Clooney in company with dancer Tom Morton and comedian Bob Williams) who do their best to promote the career of a young Polish soprano (Alberghetti), it relied for dramatic emphasis solely on the fact that Miss Alberghetti had entered the States illegally. Still, all the performances were agreeable enough, the songs were first class, and Bob Williams's celebrated act with a recalcitrant dog called Red Dust, was hilarious. The Technicolor production was by Irving Asher, whose cast also included Fred Clark, John Archer, Mikhail Rasumny, Lloyd Corrigan and Don Wilson, and the seasoned direction was by Norman Taurog. Other songs, musical numbers and operatic extracts: *My Heart Is Home* (Alberghetti, Melchior); *My Kind Of Day* (Alberghetti); *Feed Fido Some Rruff* (Clooney, Alberghetti, Morton, Williams); *New Father* (Morton) Livingston, Evans; *Voices Of Spring* (Alberghetti) Johann Strauss; *Una Voce Poco Fa* (Alberghetti) from Rossini's 'Barber of Seville'; *Because* (Melchior) Edward Teschemacher, Guy d'Hardelot; *Ah! Fors'è Lui Che L'Anima* (Alberghetti) from Verdi's 'La Traviata'; *Vesti La Giubba* (Melchior) from Leoncavallo's 'Pagliacci'.

An imaginative musical fantasy, **The 5,000 Fingers Of Dr T** (Columbia) was a Stanley Kramer production that was always interesting to look at but, in the end, not particularly successful dramatically. All about a youngster (Tommy Rettig, centre) who'd rather be out with the rest of his chums playing baseball than practising the piano for his teacher Dr Terwilliker, it took the form of an elaborate and extended dream sequence set in a nightmarish land dominated by the evil Dr T. who runs a piano school for 500 boy prisoners and whose dungeon, below his uninviting fortress dwelling, houses a group of unfortunate creatures imprisoned for having the audacity to play musical instruments other than pianos. In the best sequence in the film the hapless prisoners, grown green and mouldy with age, perform a bizarre ballet (choreographed by Eugene Loring) that made for genuinely original cinema. The Dr T. of the title (as well as Dr Terwilliker) was played – with a delicious sense of the sinister – by Hans Conried, (left foreground), with Peter Lind Hayes (right foreground) top cast as a plumber who, together with young Rettig, comes to the aid of Rettig's mother (Mary Healy), another of the dreaded Doctor's victims. It was thought up by humorist Ted Geisel (better known as Dr Seuss, under which name he was credited as co-author of the screenplay with Allan Scott) and directed by Roy Rowland, whose grip on the unorthodox material was variable. Dr Seuss also wrote the lyrics for the show's songs, and the music was by Frederick Hollander. The imaginative art direction was by Rudolph Sternad. (Technicolor). Songs: *The Kid's Song*; *Ten Happy Fingers*; *Get Together Weather*; *Dream Stuff*; *The Dressing Song (My Do-Me-Do-Duds)*; *Dungeon Elevator*; *Hypnotic Duel*; *Victorious*.

Fifties Musicals

The Band Wagon (MGM) was the apotheosis ▷ of the backstage musical. Betty Comden and Adolph Green's witty screen play (written around songs by Howard Dietz and Arthur Schwartz) was able to include the line 'Gosh, with all this raw talent around, why can't us kids get together and put ourselves on a show', which was both tongue in cheek and lump in the throat. It was not only a sophisticated tribute to all those innocent backstage movies that had preceded it, but was also a brilliantly double-edged tribute to its star, Fred Astaire. Exactly twenty years since Astaire (left) made his film debut in *Dancing Lady* (MGM), producer Arthur Freed gave him what could be considered his finest role in the best film he ever made. Behind the titles, Fred's talismanic top hat and cane are seen, but as the film opens we hear that 'perhaps the most famous top hat and stick of our generation' are being auctioned off. They belong, in the movie's context, to fading Hollywood musical star, Tony Hunter (Astaire), persuaded by his friends Nanette Fabray and Oscar Levant (playing two Broadway librettists modelled on Comden and Green), to make a come-back on the Great White Way. They have asked ballet dancer Gabrielle Gerard (Cyd Charisse, centre, in her first starring role) to co-star, and theatrical *wunder-kind* Jeffrey Cordova (Jack Buchanan) to direct. Buchanan, in a role originally meant for Clifton Webb, played it to perfection, and his top hat and white tie duo, 'I Guess I'll Have To Change My Plan', with Fred, was a delightful moment of Anglo-American harmony, a harmony achieved in the plot only after various trials and tribulations. Buchanan, who is first seen as Oedipus Rex, tries to turn the show into a modern Faust which results in a huge flop, giving rise to one of director Vincente Minnelli's best visual jokes – a close-up of an enormous egg. Other outstanding visual moments: the machine in the penny arcade opening up after Astaire kicks it at the end of his energetic 'A Shine On Your Shoes' number, and Fred, Buchanan and Fabray as tiny babies in the hilarious 'Triplets'. Oliver Smith (from Broadway) designed the sets, including those for the brilliant Mickey Spillane-inspired 'Girl Hunt' ballet which was a high-water mark in a genre that the Freed unit had virtually invented. Alan Jay Lerner (uncredited) wrote Astaire's spoof narration, Roger Edens adapted themes from Dietz–Schwartz songs, and Michael Kidd choreographed (dazzlingly). In the ballet, Astaire was a private eye caught up with 'bad, dangerous' blonde/brunette Cyd Charisse who (her vocals dubbed by India Adams) proved an exciting partner for Astaire. She seemed to bring out an erotic quality in his dancing, especially in the exquisite 'Dancing in the Dark', with its Central Park setting which recalled some of the more lyrical of the Astaire-Rogers dances in the thirties. There was only one new song in the film, 'That's Entertainment', written in 30 minutes by Schwartz and Dietz in answer to Freed's request for a 'There's No Business Like Show Business' type number, and it summed up perfectly what the film was all about. Completing the cast were James Mitchell (foreground right) Robert Gist, Thurston Hall, and LeRoy Daniels. Ava Gardner made a guest appearance. Other songs and musical numbers: *By Myself* (Astaire); *I Love Louisa* (Astaire, Levant, Charisse, Fabray, chorus); *New Sun In The Sky* (Charisse); *Louisiana Hayride* (Fabray, chorus); *You And The Night And The Music* (chorus); *High And Low* (orchestra); *Something To Remember You By* (chorus); *Beggar's Waltz* (Charisse, corps de ballet).

The screenplay fashioned by Charles Lederer for ▷ 20th Century-Fox's version of Joseph Fields and Anita Loos's smash musical comedy **Gentlemen Prefer Blondes** (from Loos's celebrated novel) was spot-on for three-quarters of its playing time, but deteriorated sadly towards the end. A pity, for until its decline and fall, this lavishly produced (by Sol C. Siegel) yarn about a couple of big girls from Little Rock was smashing entertainment. Fortunately, its two stars, Marilyn Monroe (right, as Lorelei Lee, in the role created on Broadway by Carol Channing) and Jane Russell (left) as Dorothy, both giving their best performances to date, never for an instant faltered. And in the witty dance sequences created for them by choreographer Jack Cole, they were sensational – particularly Monroe, who benefited greatly from Cole's really classy staging of the film's best song, 'Diamonds Are A Girl's Best Friend' (by Jule Styne and Leo Robin, who wrote the original Broadway score). Russell was at her best in Hoagy Carmichael-Harold Adamson's 'Ain't There Anyone Here For Love', staged by Cole in a ship's gymnasium, and featuring a couple of dozen of the world's most beautifully built men. Together the girls did 'Bye Bye Baby', and the stunning opening number, 'A (Two) Little Girl(s) From Little Rock' (the two remaining Styne-Robin songs held over from the stage production), as well as another Carmichael-Adamson contribution called 'When Love Goes Wrong'. On each occasion they ignited the screen with their particular brands of sex appeal, their combustible presences enriching the studio coffers by over $5,000,000. Charles Coburn was delightful as a diamond millionaire Monroe temporarily sets her sights on, Tommy Noonan (as Monroe's fiancé) gave his usual interpretation of a 'nebbish', Elliot Reid played a private detective hired by Noonan's millionaire father (Taylor Holmes) to see that his son and Monroe remain apart, and young George Winslow as a precocious six-year-old called Henry Spofford III, gave the best supporting performance of all. The direction, unhampered by subtlety, was by Howard Hawks.

There was an air of desperation about Paramount's **Scared Stiff**, an inferior remake of Bob Hope's 1940 comedy *The Ghost Breakers* (Paramount). It starred Dean Martin and Jerry Lewis (illustrated) as the hapless victims of a haunted house, and Lizabeth Scott as the gal that got them there. As part of the desperation tactics employed by producer Hal Wallis, Carmen Miranda was drawn into the sorry business too, and, in unbilled guest appearances, so were Bing Crosby and Bob Hope. But nothing and no one could save the show from disaster. Herbert Baker and Walter DeLeon wrote it (from the play by Paul Dickey and Charles W. Goddard), the musical numbers were staged by Billy Daniels and included 'San Domingo' and 'Song of The Enchilada Man' (by Jerry Livingston and Mack David) performed by Martin, Lewis and Miranda as well as 'Mama Yo Quiero' (by Al Stillman, and Jaraca and Vincente Paiva) in which Lewis mimed (indifferently) to a recording made by Miranda, and the supporting cast included George Dolenz, Dorothy Malone, William Ching, Paul Marion, Jack Lembert and Tom Powers. It was directed by George Marshall, who was more successful when he directed it the first time round. Other songs and musical numbers: *You Hit The Spot* Mack Gordon, Harry Revel; *I Don't Care If The Sun Don't Shine* David; *I'm Your Pal* David, Livingston; *When Somebody Thinks You're* ◁ *Wonderful* Harry Woods.

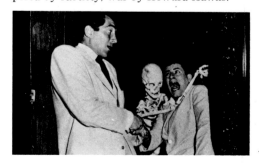

△

A small-scale, but pleasant little Technicolor offering, **Cruisin' Down The River** (Columbia) used flashbacks to recall a long-standing feud between riverboat owner Cecil Kellaway and a gambler called Beauregard Clemment (Dick Haymes) who wins Kellaway's boat from him. Years later, Beau III (also played by Haymes) offers to return the riverboat but Kellaway proudly refuses. A compromise is reached and, with the help of Kellaway's granddaughter (Audrey Totter) and servant (Billy Daniels), the boat – called the 'Chattahoochee Queen' – is turned into a floating nightclub. It was written by Blake Edwards and Richard Quine, choreographed by Lee Scott, directed by Jack Corrick and produced by Jonie Taps, with a cast that also included Connie Russell, Douglas Fowley, Larry Blake, Johnny Downs, Benny Payne, The Bell Sisters, specialty dancer Erze Ivan, and The Lee Scott Dancers (illustrated). Songs and musical numbers included: *Cruisin' Down The River* Eily Beadell, Nell Tollerton; *There Goes That Song Again* Sammy Cahn, Jule Styne; *Pennies From Heaven* Johnny Burke, Arthur Johnston; *Sing You Sinners* Sam Coslow, W. Frank Harling; *Swing Low Sweet Chariot* (traditional); *Father Dear Father* Emmet G. Coleman

June Haver's last movie before entering a convent was **The Girl Next Door** (20th Century-Fox), a piece of inconsequentiality in which she starred opposite Dan Dailey. Plot by L. Bus-Fekete and Mary Helen Fry (screenplay by Isobel Lennart) was an elongated cliché in which Haver (left), a musical comedy star eager for the quiet life, becomes romantically involved with a widower (Dailey, right) who also happens to be a newspaper strip cartoonist by profession. In this instance music spoke louder than words, with Haver seen and heard at her best in Mack Gordon and Josef Myrow's 'Nowhere Guy' – Messrs Gordon and Myrow supplying all of the songs. Dennis Day was cast as Haver's business manager, with other roles in Robert Bassler's Technicolor production going to Billy Gray, Cara Williams, Natalie Schaefer and Clinton Sundberg. It was directed by Richard Sale and choreographed by Richard Barstow. UPA supplied a cartoon sequence which made no impact at all. Other songs and musical numbers: *If I Love You A Mountain*; *I'd Rather Have A Pal Than A Gal – Anytime*; *We Girls Of The Chorus*; *The Great White Way*; *A Quiet Little Place In The Country*; *You're Doing Allright*; *The Girl Next Door*; *You Walk By*.
▽

The only major hit song to emerge from a Dean Martin-Jerry Lewis film was 'That's Amore' by Harry Warren and Jack Brooks, and it was featured in **The Caddy** (Paramount), a middling effort about a couple of show business celebrities who originally started out as professional golfers. As scripted by Edmund Hartmann and Danny Arnold, there weren't that many laughs *per se*, but Lewis (right, with Martin), pretending on one occasion to be an elegant Continental swell and, on another, an English man of letters, proved himself a mimic of superb ability. Donna Reed and Barbara Bates were the girls in their lives, and the cast was completed by Joseph Calleia, Fred Clark, Clinton Sundberg, Howard Smith, Marshall Thompson, Marjorie Gateson, Frank Puglia and Lewis Martin. Norman Taurog directed, and it was produced by Paul Jones. Other songs: *What Would You Do Without Me?*; *It's A Whistling Kinda Morning*; *The Gay Continental*; *It Takes A Lot Of Little Likes To Make One Big Love*; *You're The Right One* Warren, Brooks.
▽

△

Like *On Moonlight Bay* (1951), **By The Light Of The Silvery Moon** (Warner Bros.) offered more turn-of-the-century nostalgia in which plot – the travails of a small-town girl (Doris Day, illustrated), to keep her father (Leon Ames) from the clutches of a group of actresses who wish to lease the local theatre, and the problems this causes her steady beau (Gordon MacRae) – was decidedly subservient to the chance of hearing the principals sing an impressive roster of long-established standards. The supporting cast – Rosemary De Camp, Mary Wickes and Billy Gray – were recruited from the earlier film, imparting a cosy family aspect to the wholesome proceedings which David Butler directed for producer William Jacobs and which was choreographed by LeRoy Prinz. (Technicolor). Songs and musical numbers: *By The Light Of The Silvery Moon* Gus Edwards, Edward Madden; *I'll Forget You* Ernest R. Ball, Annalu Burns; *Your Eyes Have Told Me So* Gus Kahn, Egbert Van Alstyne, Walter Blaufuss; *Be My Little Baby Bumble Bee* Stanley Murphy, Henry I. Marshall; *If You Were The Only Girl In The World* Clifford Grey, Nat D. Ayer; *Ain't We Got Fun* Kahn, Ray Egan, Richard A. Whiting; *King Chanticleer* Ayer.

△

Rhonda Fleming (centre) starred in **Those Red-heads From Seattle** (Paramount), a 3-D musical with 2-D characters and a 1-D plot, concerning a mother (Agnes Moorehead) who takes her four daughters (Fleming, Teresa Brewer, right, Cynthia Bell, left, and Kay Bell) to the Yukon to join their father (Frank Wilcox) in the gold rush. Wilcox, however, is killed before his family arrives, forcing the girls to turn to assorted work until the romantic problems they encounter along the way are all satisfactorily resolved. Gene Barry co-starred opposite Fleming as a saloon keeper, with other roles in director Lewis R. Foster, Geoffrey Homes and George Worthington Yates's screenplay going to singer Guy Mitchell, Jean Parker, Roscoe Ates, John Kellogg, and Walter Reed. It was produced, in Technicolor, by William H. Pine and William C. Thomas. Songs and musical numbers: *Baby Baby Baby* Mack David, Jerry Livingston; *Mr Banjo Man* Jay Livingston, Ray Evans; *I Guess It Was You All The Time* Johnny Mercer, Hoagy Carmichael; *Chick-A-Boom* Bob Merrill; *Take Back Your Gold* M.H. Rosenfeld, Louis W. Pritzkow.

So This Is Love (GB: **The Grace Moore Story**), a satisfactory biography of soprano Grace Moore related, in flashback, her rise from a rural childhood in Tennessee to a wildly successful debut at New York's Metropolitan Opera House, where her Mimi in *La Boheme* commanded no fewer than 28 curtain calls. Although the John Monks Jr screenplay trod the familiar path of the Hollywood biopic (and omitted Miss Moore's tragic death in a plane crash), it made for an entertaining and convincing narrative, benefiting enormously from Kathryn Grayson's ability (as Miss Moore) to move easily from popular to operatic standards. The singer's first love was played by newcomer Merv Griffin, later to become famous as the host of a TV talk show; while the suitor whom she finally rejects for the greater glory of her career was Douglas Dick. Walter Abel played her father, with Rosemary De Camp, Jeff Donnell, Fortunio Bonanova (illustrated, with Grayson) Ann Doran, Joan Weldon and Mabel Atherton (as *diva* Mary Garden) also cast, Gordon Douglas directed, LeRoy Prinz staged the musical sequences and Henry Blanke produced (in Technicolor) for Warner Bros. Songs: *Time On My Hands* Harold Adamson, Mack Gordon, Vincent Youmans; *Remember* Irving Berlin; *I Wish I Could Shimmy Like My Sister Kate* Armand J. Piron, Peter Bocage; *Ciribiribin* Harry James, Jack Lawrence, A. Pestalozza; *The Kiss Waltz*; extracts from Mozart's *The Marriage Of Figaro*, Gounod's *Faust*; Puccini's *La Boheme*.
▽

△

Joan Crawford's first MGM film in ten years, and her first ever in Technicolor, was **Torch Song**. Looking gorgeous in costumes designed by Helen Rose, she played a school-of-hard-knocks Broadway star who, having reached the top, is determined to stay there, regardless of whom she hurts – herself included. Her obsessional quest for perfection frightens off possible suitors, except for co-star Michael Wilding (illustrated, with Crawford) as her new piano-playing accompanist. Blinded in the war, Wilding has certain insights into Miss Crawford's personality and soon tames her. **Torch Song** was filmed in 18 days, contains one of the worst production numbers ever put on film – 'Two Faced Woman' by Arthur Schwartz and Howard Dietz, staged, to a playback originally intended for Cyd Charisse in *The Band Wagon* (MGM, 1953), by Charles Walters, who also directed – and was the kind of story women used to read under dryers at the hairdresser. Still, Crawford's performance was compulsively watchable, and the screenplay, by John Michael Hayes and Jan Lustig, while largely trading in platitudes, was not without its moments of wit. It was produced by Henry Herman and Sidney Franklin Jr with a cast that included Gig Young, Nancy Gates, Marjorie Rambeau, Henry Morgan and Dorothy Patrick. Also: Eugene Loring, James Todd, Paul Guilfoyle and Benny Rubin. Crawford's vocals were dubbed by India Adams, and Wilding's piano playing by Walter Cross. Other songs and musical numbers: *Follow Me* Adolph Deutsch; *Tenderly* Jack Lawrence, Walter Gross; *You Won't Forget Me* Kermit Goell, Fred Spielman; *Blue Moon* Richard Rodgers, Lorenz Hart.

Three years after MGM's success with Betty ▷ Hutton in *Annie Get Your Gun* (MGM), Warner Bros. starred Doris Day (illustrated) as **Calamity Jane**. Although Doris misguidedly tried to prove that anything Betty could do she could do better – or, at least, louder and more frenetically – and on occasion even succeeded, the movie was blessed with a tuneful score by Sammy Fain and Paul Francis Webster (giving Doris one of her biggest hits ever with 'Secret Love') and some gorgeous Technicolor photography by Wilfrid M. Cline. A wooden Howard Keel (illustrated) was co-starred as Wild Bill Hickock, with other roles going to Allyn McLerie, Philip Carey, Dick Wesson, Paul Harvey, Chubby Johnson and Gale Robbins. David Butler directed from James O'Hanlon's screenplay and Jack Donohue staged the lively and energetic musical numbers. It was producer William Jacobs's very last production. Other musical numbers: *The Deadwood Stage*; *Higher Than A Hawk*; *'Tis Harry I'm Plannin' To Marry*; *The Black Hills Of Dakota*; *Just Blew In From The Windy City*; *A Woman's Touch*; *I've Got A Heart Full of Honey*; *I Can Do Without You*; *Keep It Under Your Hat*.

Although **Three Sailors And A Girl** (Warner Bros.) was based on George S. Kaufman's play *The Butter And Egg Man* which had already undergone numerous transformations on screen (in 1928 also as *The Butter And Egg Man*, in 1932 as *The Tenderfoot*, in 1937 as *Dance, Charlie, Dance* and only three years later as *An Angel From Texas*), its plot – the three sailors of the title attempt to turn an out-of-town flop into a Broadway smash with the aid of an impoverished producer and a sweet young singer – was pure formula. The sailors were Gordon MacRae (seated), Jack E. Leonard (left) and Gene Nelson (right – one of whose dances took place inside a submarine), the girl was Jane Powell (centre), and the producer Sam Levene. George Givot, Veda Ann Borg, Archer McDonald and Raymond Greenleaf were also cast. Roy Del Ruth directed from an insubstantial screenplay by Roland Kibbee and Devery Freeman; Sammy Cahn doubled as producer and, with Sammy Fain, songwriter. LeRoy Prinz and Gene Nelson choreographed, the standout number being 'The Lately Song', sung and danced by the four leads. It was filmed in Technicolor. Other songs and musical numbers included: *Show Me A Happy Woman And I'll Show You A Miserable Man*; *Kiss Me Or I'll Scream*; *Face To Face*; *You're But Oh So Right*; *Home Is Where The Heart Is*; *There Must Be A Reason*; *My Heart Is A Singing Heart* Fain, Cahn.

▽

△

A classic musical from MGM and producer Jack Cummings, **Kiss Me Kate** was a literate, witty, and thoroughly beguiling screen adaptation of Cole Porter and Sam and Bella Spewack's 1948 Broadway smash. Kathryn Grayson (left), in the meatiest role of her career, played fiery actress Lilli Vanessi (and Katharine in the show-within-a-show performance of 'Kiss Me Kate'); Howard Keel (right) was Fred Graham, Grayson's erstwhile spouse (Petruchio in the show), and Ann Miller dancer Lois Lane (Bianca). They were brilliantly supported by Keenan Wynn, Bobby Van, Tommy Rall, James Whitmore, Kurt Kasznar and Bob Fosse. Basically a series of backstage intrigues played out in tandem with a performance of a musical version of Shakespeare's *The Taming Of The Shrew*, the behind-the-scenes shenanigans (especially the spitfire relationship between Grayson and Keel) neatly paralleled many of the incidents in *The Shrew* itself, thus giving to the Spewacks' screenplay a density and consistency of structure unusual in musicals. In fact, **Kiss Me Kate** had the distinction of being one of the best and most neatly plotted musicals of the decade. It also had a score whose every number was a show stopper, most notably Ann Miller's torrid 'Too Darn Hot' and the infectious 'From This Moment On' (which Porter originally wrote for his 1950 show *Out Of This World* and which was sung and danced by Miller, Rall, Van, Fosse, Jeannie Coyne and Carol Haney. The choreography was by Fosse and Hermes Pan and, in such numbers as 'Tom, Dick and Harry' (Miller, Rall, Fosse, Van) hit the heights. The musical direction was by Andre Previn and Saul Chaplin, Walter Plunkett designed the clothes, the sets and art direction were in the hands of Cedric Gibbons and Urie McCleary, it was photographed in Ansco Color and 3-D (the latter process being dropped after its initial release) and directed by George Sidney. Other songs and musical numbers: *So In Love* (Grayson, Keel); *I Hate Men* (Grayson); *Wunderbar* (Grayson, Keel); *Were Thine That Special Face* (Keel); *I've Come To Wive It Wealthily In Padua* (Keel); *Where Is The Life That Late I Led?* (Keel); *We Open In Venice* (Grayson, Keel, Miller, Rall); *Always True To You Darling In My Fashion* (Miller, Rall); *Brush Up Your Shakespeare* (Wynn, Whitmore); *Kiss Me Kate* (Grayson, Keel, chorus); *Why Can't You Behave?* (Miller, Rall).

△ △ △

Director Alfred E. Green, who had been responsible for one of Columbia's biggest ever hits with *The Jolson Story* (1946), was signed by Warner Bros. to repeat his success with another biopic, **The Eddie Cantor Story**. Unfortunately, he couldn't. Casting was at the heart of the problem with Keefe Brasselle (left) as Cantor lacking the manic energy of the original and encouraged, at times, to portray Cantor as a certifiable eye-popping, hand-waving clown. The screenplay (by Jerome Weidman, Ted Sherdeman and Sidney Skolsky, from a story by Skolsky, who also produced) was full of incident, the songs were Cantor classics, and the reconstruction of vaudeville's Golden Age nicely done; but the film never recovered from its central casting error. Marilyn Erskine (right) co-starred as Cantor's wife Ida and Aline MacMahon was his devoted Grandma. Florenz Ziegfeld was played by William Forrest, Lillian and Gus Edwards by Ann Doran and Hal March, and Will Rogers by Will Jr, who had played his father once before in *The Story Of Will Rogers* (Warner Bros. 1952). Also in it were Arthur Franz, Gerald Mohr, Tristram Coffin and Marie Windsor. The cornucopia of songs and musical numbers included: *If You Knew Susie* Joseph Meyer, Buddy De Sylva; *Yes Sir, That's My Baby*; *Making Whoopee* Gus Kahn, Walter Donaldson; *How Ya Gonna Keep 'Em Down On The Farm* Donaldson, Sam M. Lewis, Joe Young; *Now's The Time To Fall In Love* Al Lewis, Al Sherman; *Will You Love Me In December As You Do In May* James J. Walker, Ernest R. Ball; *Be My Little Baby Bumble Bee* Stanley Murphy, Henry I. Marshall; *Oh, You Beautiful Doll* A. Seymour Brown, Nat D. Ayer; *Bye, Bye, Blackbird* Mort Dixon, Ray Henderson; *If I Were A Millionaire* Will Cobb, Gus Edwards; *Yes, We Have No Bananas* Frank Silver, Irving Cohn; *Ma (He's Making Eyes At Me)* Sidney Clare, Con Conrad; *Margie* Benny Davis, Conrad, J. Russell Robinson; *Ida, Sweet As Apple Cider* Eddie Leonard, Eddie Munson; *You Must Have Been A Beautiful Baby* Johnny Mercer, Harry Warren.

Debbie Reynolds (centre right) and Bobby Van (right) were joined by Bob Fosse (centre left) for **The Affairs Of Dobie Gillis** (MGM), an energetic musical farce with a campus setting and an effulgent screenplay by Max Shulman in which students Reynolds and Van literally have an explosive romance at Grainbelt University – their youthful exuberance causing the chemistry block to be blown to smithereens. As a result of the incident, they're separated – but not for very long. Arthur M. Loew Jr produced, Don Weis directed, Alex Romero staged the dances, and the cast included Barbara Ruick (left) in her first substantial role, as well as Hanley Stafford, Lurene Tuttle (Ruick's real-life mother), and Hans Conried. Songs included: *All I Do Is Dream Of You* Arthur Freed, Nacio Herb Brown; *You Can't Do Wrong Doin' Right* Al Rinker, Floyd Huddlestone; *Believe Me If All Those Endearing Young Charms* Thomas Moore, Matthew Locke.
▽

Donald O'Connor (right) did all that was humanly possible to sing, dance, clown and act some life into **Walking My Baby Back Home** (Universal International), but the combination of a dreary screenplay by Don McGuire and Oscar Brodney (story by McGuire), the slow-paced direction of Lloyd Bacon and the unimaginatively staged routines made the task impossible. The story of a socialite (O'Connor) who, after being discharged from the army, involves himself in several abortive music ventures until finally hitting on the successful idea of giving Dixieland music symphonic treatment, it co-starred Janet Leigh (left), with Buddy Hackett, Scat Man Crothers, Lori Nelson, Kathleen Lockhart, George Cleveland, John Hubbard and Paula Kelly (who dubbed for Janet Leigh) and The Modernaires in support. The producer was Ted Richmond, and it was photographed in Technicolor. Songs and musical numbers included: *Walkin' My Baby Back Home* Roy Turk, Fred Ahlert; *Glow Worm* Paul Lincke, Johnny Mercer; *Honeysuckle Rose* Fats Waller, Andy Razaf; *South Rampart Street Parade* Ray Bauduc, Bob Haggart, Steve Allen; *De Camptown Races* Stephen Foster; *Muskrat Ramble* Kid Ory, Ray Gilbert.

Bob Hope (left) needed a much better script than the one he got from Edmund Hartmann and Hal Kanter (story by Hartmann) in **Here Come The Girls** (Paramount), a laboured caper in which he overacted grossly as a clumsy, overgrown chorus boy who, after being fired from a show for incompetence by irate producer Fred Clark (right), suddenly finds himself catapulted to stardom when the same Mr Clark offers him the lead in a new musical because the real star of the show (Tony Martin) is being hunted down by Jack The Slasher (Robert Strauss). Martin's murderous rival for the affections of leading lady Arlene Dahl. Rosemary Clooney appeared as Hope's neglected girlfriend, with Millard Mitchell, William Demarest, Zamah Cunningham, Frank Orth and The Four Step Brothers completing the cast for producer Paul Jones. There were several fair-to-middling songs by Jay Livingston and Ray Evans, and several production numbers, each one of which was interrupted and ruined by Hope who, in the course of the plot, found himself being pursued on stage by the aforementioned killer. Claude Binyon directed. (Technicolor). Songs and musical numbers: *Girls Are Here To Stay*; *Never So Beautiful*; *You Got Class*; *Desire*; *When You Love Someone*; *Ali Baba Be My Baby*; *Heavenly Days*; *See The Circus*; *Peace*.
▽

Give A Girl A Break was a second division MGM musical with some lively production numbers in its favour (choreographed by Gower Champion), a passable score by Ira Gershwin and Burton Lane, and a pleasing cast in Marge (centre) and Gower Champion, Debbie Reynolds (right), Helen Wood (left), Bob Fosse and Kurt Kasznar. The story (by Vera Caspary, screenplay by Albert Hackett and Frances Goodrich) had the three above-mentioned girls vying for the same lead in a Broadway musical, with each of them in the fortunate position of having one member of the production staff rooting for her. In the end it's Reynolds who gets it – but not before several plot complications made the going anything but smooth for her. It was directed by Stanley Donen for producer Jack Cummings, photographed in Technicolor and, in supporting roles, featured Richard Anderson, William Ching, Lurene Tuttle, Larry Keating and Donna Martell. Songs and musical numbers: *Give A Girl A Break*; *In Our United State*; *It Happens Every Time*; *Nothing Is Impossible*; *Applause, Applause* (not to be confused with the title number of the 1970 Broadway musical *Applause* by Charles Strouse and Lee Adams) Gershwin, Lane; *Challenge Dance* Andre Previn, Saul Chaplin.

Another aquatic spectacular for Esther Williams, **Easy To Love** (MGM), filmed on location at Cypress Gardens, Florida, in CinemaScope and Technicolor, was nothing to shout about as far as its plot was concerned: Williams is in love with her boss, Van Johnson, for whom she doubles as secretary and star of his aqua-show, but her love is unrequited until she allows herself to be courted by swimming instructor John Bromfield and singer Tony Martin. Johnson becomes jealous and realizes he has been in love with her all along. End of plot. It was written by Laslo Vadnay and William Roberts, with other roles going to Edna Skinner, King Donovan, Paul Bryar, Carroll Baker and Eddie Oliver. Cyd Charisse was also in it, making a token 'walk on' appearance. Williams got her bathing suit wet on three occasions: in a pool swimming with a chimpanzee, with Bromfield in a romantic, moonlit gardenia-strewn cove and, finally, in the spectacular finale (illustrated) created by Busby Berkeley which turned out to be one of his most exhilarating sequences ever, and also the last great spectacle he was to create for the screen, nothing in his last two films, *Rose-Marie* (MGM, 1954) and *Billy Rose's Jumbo* (MGM, 1962) equalling it in daring invention. The rest of **Easy To Love**'s musical numbers were handled by Tony Martin who, as well as singing the Cole Porter title song, sang Carmen Lombardo, Johnny Green and Gus Kahn's hit 'Coquette'. The water-ski ballet, 'Beautiful Spring', was by Paul Lincke, Joe Pasternak produced, and it was directed by Charles Walters. Other songs: *That's What A Rainy Day Is For*; *Look Out! I'm Romantic*; *Didja Ever* Vic Mizzy, Mann Curtis.
▽

1954

Academy Awards

Best Picture
NOMINATIONS INCLUDED: *Seven Brides For Seven Brothers* (MGM) produced by Jack Cummings.

Best Actor
NOMINATIONS INCLUDED: James Mason *A Star Is Born* (Transcona, WB).

Best Actress
NOMINATIONS INCLUDED: Dorothy Dandridge *Carmen Jones* (Preminger, 20th Century-Fox) Judy Garland *A Star Is Born.*

Writing (Motion Picture Story)
NOMINATIONS INCLUDED: *There's No Business Like Show Business* (20th Century-Fox) Lamar Trotti
(Screenplay)
NOMINATIONS INCLUDED: *Seven Brides For Seven Brothers* Albert Hackett, Frances Goodrich and Dorothy Kingsley.
(Story and Screenplay)
NOMINATIONS INCLUDED: *The Glenn Miller Story* (U-I) Valentine Davies and Oscar Brodney.

Cinematography (colour)
NOMINATIONS INCLUDED: *Seven Brides For Seven Brothers* George Folsey

Art Direction (Set Decoration) (colour)
NOMINATIONS INCLUDED: *Brigadoon* (MGM) Cedric Gibbons and Preston Ames; Edwin B. Willis and Keogh Gleason. *Red Garters* (Paramount) Hal Pereira and Roland Anderson; Sam Comer and Ray Moyer. *A Star Is Born* Malcolm Bert, Gene Allen and Irene Sharaff; George James Hopkins.

Costume Design (colour)
NOMINATIONS INCLUDED: *Brigadoon* Irene Sharaff. *A Star Is Born* Jean Louis, Mary Ann Nyberg and Irene Sharaff. *There's No Business Like Show Business* Charles LeMaire, Travilla and Miles White.

Sound Recording
The Glenn Miller Story Leslie I. Carey, sound director.
NOMINATIONS INCLUDED: *Brigadoon* Wesley C. Miller, sound director.

Film Editing
NOMINATIONS INCLUDED: *Seven Brides For Seven Brothers* Ralph E. Winters

Music
Song
NOMINATIONS INCLUDED: 'Count Your Blessings Instead Of Sheep' *White Christmas* (Paramount) Irving Berlin. 'The Man That Got Away' *A Star Is Born* Harold Arlen *cm*; Ira Gershwin *lyr.*

Scoring Of A Musical Picture
Seven Brides For Seven Brothers Adolph Deutsch and Saul Chaplin
NOMINATIONS INCLUDED: *Carmen Jones* Herschel Burke Gilbert. *The Glenn Miller Story* Joseph Gershenson and Henry Mancini. *A Star Is Born* Ray Heindorf. *There's No Business Like Show Business* Alfred Newman and Lionel Newman.

Honorary Award
To Danny Kaye, for his unique talents, his service to the Academy, the motion picture industry and the American people.
(statuette)

The New York Times Annual 'Ten Best'
1st *The Glenn Miller Story.* 5th *Seven Brides For Seven Brothers.*

The Annual Top Moneymaking Films
INCLUDED: *White Christmas. The Glenn Miller Story. Seven Brides For Seven Brothers. Living It Up* (Paramount).

One of the best, most endearing, and enduring biopics to emerge from Hollywood, **The Glenn Miller Story** (Universal International) was, in every respect, a fitting tribute to one of the greatest of the Big Band bandleaders. And, in James Stewart (right), producer Aaron Rosenberg found just the right man to portray him. A lovingly scripted (by Valentine Davies and Oscar Brodney) rags-to-riches account of Miller's rise to eminence (ending with his untimely death in 1944, when the military plane on which he was travelling from England to France, went missing), it was not merely a simple-minded excuse for a series of musical interpolations, but a well-told account of an interesting life, and particularly successful in the way it showed Miller struggling for, and ultimately achieving, the special 'sound' which characterized his most celebrated arrangements. June Allyson (left) had the best role of her career as Mrs Miller, and there was good work too from Irving Bacon and Kathleen Lockhart as Miller's parents, as well as from Henry Morgan, Charles Drake, George Tobias, Marion Ross, Barton MacLane, Sig Rumann, James Bell and Katherine Warren. Also appearing – as themselves – were Louis Armstrong and Gene Krupa (marvellous together in 'Basin Street Blues' by Spencer Williams), Frances Langford, Ben Pollack, The Archie Savage Dancers and The Modernaires. The musical numbers were staged by Kenny Williams; Joseph Gershenson and Henry Mancini were in charge of the musical direction, and it was sensitively directed by Anthony Mann (Technicolor). Stewart's trombone playing was dubbed by Murray MacEachern. Musical numbers included: *Moonlight Serenade* Mitchell Parish, Miller; *In The Mood* Andy Razaf, Joe Garland; *Tuxedo Junction* Buddy Feyne, Erskine Hawkins, William Johnson, William Dash; *Little Brown Jug* J.E. Winner; *Adios* Eddie Woods, Enric Madriguera; *String of Pearls* Eddie DeLange, Jerry Grey; *Pennsylvania 6-5000* Gray, Carl Sigman; *Stairway To The Stars* Mitchell Parish, Matt Malneck, Frank Signorelli; *American Patrol* E.H. Meacham; *I Know Why*; *Chattanooga Choo Choo* Mack Gordon, Harry Warren; *Bidin' My Time* George and Ira Gershwin; *I Dreamed I Dwelt In Marble Halls* Alfred Bunn, Michael Balfe; *St Louis Blues March* arrangement of W.C. Handy's *St Louis Blues* by Ray McKinley, Perry Burgett, Jerry Gray, Glenn Miller.
▽

◁ **Top Banana** (United Artists) was a filmed transcript of the 1951 stage show of the same name. Shot at the Winter Garden Theatre, New York, by producers Al Zugsmith and Ben Peskay and directed by Alfred E. Green, its chief attraction was its star Phil Silvers (illustrated). Playing a character reputedly modelled on comedian Milton Berle, Silvers, as a TV clown with his own show, is ordered by his sponsors to introduce some love interest into the programme. He does so by hiring a pair of young lovers (Judy Lynn, Danny Scholl). Then, much to his dismay, watches as a real love affair develops between them, for he, too, has fallen in love with his ingenue. Hy Kraft wrote the burlesque-inspired book, Johnny Mercer the songs, and it was presented by Harry M. Popkin. Others in the cast were Rose Marie, Jack Albertson, Johnny Coy, Joey and Herbie Faye, Walter Dare Wahl, Bradford Hatton and Dick Dana. Songs and musical numbers included: *A Word A Day*; *If You Want To Be A Top Banana*; *I Fought Every Step Of The Way*; *Sans Souci*; *Only If You're In Love*; *The Man Of The Year This Week*; *My Home Is In My Shoes.*

Performing talent rather than cinematic technique – it was one of the early ventures into CinemaScope – was on display in **New Faces** (20th Century-Fox), a flatly filmed version (with a silly plot appended) of Leonard Sillman's successful Broadway revue which, directed by John Murray Anderson, opened in 1952 and ran for 365 performances. In a cast ranging in quality from brilliant to superb, the stand-out (and most durable) performer was Eartha Kitt (illustrated) who sang 'Bal, Petit Bal' (by F. Lemarque) and gave new meaning to the word 'Monotonous' in a song of the same name by Arthur Siegel and June Carroll. In the filmed version of the show, Kitt's popularity resulted in her being given three additional numbers: 'Uskadara' (adapted from a Turkish folk song), 'C'Est Si Bon' (by Jerry Seelen and Henri Betti) and 'Santa Baby' (by Joan Javits, Phil Springer and Tony Springer). She devoured them all. June Carroll made quite an impression too in a marvellous ballad of infidelity by Murray Grand and Elisse Boyd called 'Guess Who I Saw Today', and, from pint-sized Robert Clary, came the poignant 'I'm In Love With Miss Logan', and 'Lucky Pierre' (both by Ronny Graham). Alice Ghostley's 'Boston Beguine' (by Sheldon Harnick) was another stand-out number; so was 'Penny Candy' (by Siegel and Carroll) sung by June Carroll and danced by Carol Lawrence. There were some excellent sketches too, notably a take-off of Arthur Miller's *Death Of A Salesman*; a wicked send-up of Truman Capote as an effete Southern writer in an item written and performed by Ronny Graham; and Michael Brown's 'Lizzie Borden', performed by about half the company led by Paul Lynde, who featured prominently in the show. The film was directed by Harry Horner, produced by Edward L. Alperson, Berman Swartz and Leonard Sillman, and scripted by various writers including Mel Brooks. The choreography was by Richard Barstow. Also in it were: Virginia de Luce, Bill Mullikin, Rosemary O'Reilly, Allen Conroy, Jimmy Russell, George Smiley, Polly Ward, Johnny Laverty, Elizabeth Logue, Faith Burwell and Clark Ranger. Other items: *Take Off The Mask* Alice Ghostley, Ronny Graham; *Waltzing In Venice*; *Raining Memories*; *He Takes Me Off His Income Tax* Graham; *We've Never Seen You Before* Graham, P. DeVries.

A stagy western spoof in vibrant colour and with a parcel of songs by Jay Livingston and Ray Evans, **Red Garters** (Paramount) always promised a great deal more than it delivered. By inverting every horse-opera cliché, such as the cavalry failing to arrive at the last moment, and the hero failing to score in the climactic shoot-out etc. etc. Michael Fessier's screenplay drew a certain amount of laughs from its subject. But it wasn't strong enough to underline producer Pat Duggan's satirical point of view; nor were the songs or Nick Castle's staging of them, particularly memorable. Which left a talented and energetic cast, headed by Rosemary Clooney (featured centre) as a saloon songstress and Jack Carson as the sheriff, and the man she intends to land, working overtime to create something out of very little. They partially succeeded, with help from co-stars Guy Mitchell (as a cowboy who feuds with Gene Barry), Pat Crowley, Joanne Gilbert (Whose 'Love Is Greater Than I Thought' was one of the show's better tunes), Frank Faylen, Reginald Owen, Cass Daley, Richard Hale and, in a fairly minor role, Buddy Ebsen. Clooney succeeded, in one of the film's best sequences, in creating a hit with 'Brave Man'. The leaden direction was by George Marshall. Other songs and musical numbers: *Bad News*; *Red Garters*; *Meet A Happy Guy*; *A Dime And A Dollar*; *Man And Woman*; *Good Intentions*; *Vaquero*; *Lady Killer*; *Specialty Dance*; *Big Doin's*.

Rhapsody, from a novel by Henry Handel Richardson, came to the screen in CinemaScope and colour, in an adaptation by Ruth and Augustus Goetz and a screenplay by Fay and Michael Kanin, with a cast headed by Elizabeth Taylor (centre, double image), Vittorio Gassman (left) and John Ericson (right). Lavishly presented by MGM and set in such picturesque spots as Zurich and Paris, it told the novelettish story of an extremely wealthy young woman (Taylor) and the romantic problems she encounters with a handsome violinist called Paul Bronte (Gassman). The fact that Miss Taylor insists on nibbling his ears while he practises may have had something to do with Gassman's decision to leave her and devote himself to his career, whereupon Taylor – on the rebound – marries pianist John Ericson and makes his life a misery. But it all came right in the end, with Taylor seeing the error of her spoilt and selfish ways. A soap opera adorned with generous chunks of musical war horses, most notably the Tchaikovsky *Violin Concerto* and the Rachmaninov *Piano Concerto No 2*, it was directed by Charles Vidor for producer Lawrence Weingarten with a cast that also included Louis Calhern, Michael Chekhov, Barbara Bates, Richard Hageman, Richard Lupino, Celia Lovsky, Stuart Whitman and Madge Blake. Michael Rubin dubbed Gassman's violin sequences, and Claudio Arrau played the piano for Ericson.

With *Gentlemen Prefer Blondes* (20th Century-Fox, 1953) very much in mind, producer Edmund Grainger flung together **The French Line** (RKO), a tawdry spin-off of the Marilyn Monroe-Jane Russell hit with Russell (foreground centre left) heading a cast that included Gilbert Roland, Arthur Hunnicutt, Mary McCarty (foreground centre right) and Joyce MacKenzie. A mistaken identity plot involved an inordinately wealthy Texan oil heiress (Russell), seen in various stages of *déshabille*, who takes an ocean trip to Gay Paree after being jilted shortly before her wedding. Roland, as a musical comedy star, turns out to be the man of Russell's dreams, though Hunnicutt, as her drawling Texan guardian, was clearly the better actor. Also cast: Paula Corday, Scott Elliott, Craig Stevens, Laura Elliot, Jayne Mansfield (debut) and Michael St Angel. It was written by Mary Loos and Richard Sale from a story by Matty Kemp and Isabel Dawn, Lloyd Bacon directed, and Billy Daniels staged the dances. The film was photographed in Technicolor and initially released in 3-D. Songs and musical numbers: *Comment Allez-Vous?*; *What Is This That I Feel?*; *Well I'll Be Switched*; *Any Gal From Texas*; *With A Kiss*; *Wait Till You See Paris*; *The French Line*; *By Madame Fuelle*; *Lookin' For Trouble*; *Poor Andre* Josef Myrow, Ralph Blane, Robert Wells.

A story of a group of theatrical entertainers stranded in Miami, **Lucky Me** – Warner Bros.' first musical in CinemaScope – was a singularly undistinguished effort whose trite screenplay (by James O'Hanlon, Robert O'Brien, and Irving Ellison, story by O'Hanlon), sabotaged the combined efforts of Doris Day (left), Robert Cummings, Phil Silvers (right), Eddie Foy Jr, Nancy Walker and Martha Hyer, all of whom looked, in the CinemaScope close-ups, as if they were peering into a giant letter box. Jack Donohue directed it, LeRoy Prinz staged the numbers, and it was produced by Henry Blanke in Warnercolor. Songs and musical numbers: *Lucky Me*; *Superstition Song*; *I Speak To The Stars*; *Take A Memo To The Moon*; *Bluebells Of Broadway*; *High Hopes*; *Men*; *Love You Dearly*; *I Wanna Sing Like An Angel* Sammy Fain, Paul Francis Webster.

△

Not since *On The Town* (MGM, 1949) was there a musical as dance-orientated as director Stanley Donen's exuberant **Seven Brides For Seven Brothers** (MGM). Based on a story by Stephen Vincent Benet called *The Sobbin' Women*, it was blessed with a witty screenplay by Albert Hackett, Frances Goodrich and Dorothy Kingsley, and had an original score by Gene De Paul and Johnny Mercer that was a pip. The unusually strong story concerned the seven Pontipee brothers, all of whom lead a rough lonely existence on their farm in Oregon, and their successful – if somewhat unorthodox – attempts to find themselves wives. As Adam Pontipee, the eldest of the brothers, Howard Keel (left) was at his commanding best, while, as Milly, Jane Powell (right) proved that her performance in *Royal Wedding* (MGM, 1951) was no fluke and that, given the right material, she was as splendid a trouper as anyone who ever graced an MGM musical. Making, perhaps, the biggest impact, though, were the six brothers, whose collective presence was simply dynamic. Chosen for their ability to dance, they imbued the film with a balletic quality (particularly in 'The Lonesome Polecat Lament') without ever losing the essentially masculine 'feel' of the piece. Indeed, **Seven Brides For Seven Brothers** remains one of the most virile of all musicals, its memorable house-raising sequence being the most vigorously acrobatic dance routine ever filmed. The choreographer, Michael Kidd, was fast becoming one of the greatest dance directors both in Hollywood and on Broadway. Other musical highlights: Powell teaching the brothers to court in the lilting 'Goin' Courtin' and the lyrical 'June Bride', sung and danced by Powell and the six 'brides'; Keel's solo 'Bless Yore Beautiful Hide' sung on his first visit into town as he appraises the qualities of womanhood in general was a splendid example of the 'integrated' nature of the De Paul-Mercer score; and for engendering high-spirited exhilaration, there was nothing to touch Powell's 'Wonderful, Wonderful Day'. Adolph Deutsch and Saul Chaplin were in charge of the musical direction, and the film was produced by Jack Cummings. Jeff Richards, Russ Tamblyn, Tommy Rall, Marc Platt, Matt Mattox and Jacques D'Amboise played the six Pontipee brothers; Julie Newmeyer, Nancy Kilgas, Betty Carr, Virginia Gibson, Ruta Kilmonis and Norma Doggett the six brides. Completing the cast were Ian Wolfe, Harold Petrie, Dante Di Paolo, Kelly Brown, Matt Moore, Dick Rich, Marjorie Wood, Russell Simpson and Anna Q. Nilsson. It was photographed in CinemaScope and Ansco Color. Other songs and musical numbers: *When You're In Love* (Powell, Keel); *Spring, Spring, Spring* (brothers, brides); *Sobbin' Women* (Keel, brothers).

342

MGM's third version of Rudolf Friml's operetta **Rose-Marie** was the first musical to be photographed in CinemaScope (but not the first to be released), and although it was neither artistically nor commercially as successful as the 1936 production, it looked impressive on the big screen, especially as much of it was filmed in colour on location in the Canadian Rockies. While based on the book by Otto Harbach and Oscar Hammerstein II, the new version, scripted by Ronald Miller and George Froeschel, differed extensively from previous versions in that it introduced a major sub-plot involving Wanda, the beautiful daughter of a tribal chief, and her unrequited infatuation for Mike Malone, the mountie who loves Rose-Marie. Howard Keel was the mountie, Ann Blyth (top-billed, illustrated left) played Rose-Marie, Joan Taylor was Wanda, Fernando Lamas (right) appeared as Duval the trapper (who in this instance got the woman), with other roles going to Bert Lahr as a comic mountie, Marjorie Main as the proprietress of a saloon-cum-hotel, Ray Collins, and Chief Yowlachie. In addition to four songs from the original 1924 stage production ('Rose Marie', 'The Indian Love Call', 'The Mounties' and 'Totem Tom Tom'), producer-director Mervyn LeRoy asked 72-year-old Rudolf Friml and lyricist Paul Francis Webster to provide three more, which they did: 'The Right Place For A Girl', 'Free To Be Free', and 'I Have The Love'. One additional song was needed as a specialty number for Bert Lahr, and this was written by George Stoll and Herbert Baker. Called 'The Mountie Who Never Got His Man', it was the second brightest spot in the show, pride of place definitely going to Busby Berkeley's elaborate staging of 'Totem Tom Tom', a ceremonial Indian war-dance featuring Joan Taylor and 100 brightly painted braves.

◁ The two-dimensional stereotypes created by Oscar Hammerstein II for **Carmen Jones**, an all-black updating of Georges Bizet and Prosper Mérimée's operatic masterpiece *Carmen*, were always at odds with the glorious music the characters kept singing. The result was that, while admiring the carpentry of the exercise, it was difficult to become involved with it or with any of the protagonists in this torrid musical melodrama. In Hammerstein's version, cigarette-maker Carmen (Dorothy Dandridge, left) became a worker in a parachute factory, dragoon Don José, renamed Joe (Harry Belafonte, right), was a GI about to go to flying school, Micaela (Olga James) became Cindy Lou, and toreador Escamillo a prizefighter called Husky Miller (Joe Adams). Also cast: Pearl Bailey, Diahann Carroll, Brock Peters, Roy Glenn and Nick Stewart. Dandridge's singing was dubbed by mezzo-soprano Marilyn Horne, Belafonte's by Laverne Hutchinson, Carroll's by Bernice Peterson and Adams's by Marvin Hayes. The musical numbers were well staged by Herbert Ross and Herschel Burke Gilbert, Dimitri Tiomkin conducted it, Harry Kleiner wrote the screenplay (based on Hammerstein's book for the 1943 Broadway production) and the heavy-handed direction was by Otto Preminger, who also produced it (in CinemaScope and Colour De Luxe) for 20th Century-Fox. Songs: (all lyrics by Oscar Hammerstein II): *Dat's Love (Habanera)*; *You Talk Just Like My Maw*; *Dere's A Café On De Corner*; *Dis Flower (Flower Song)*; *Beat Out Dat Rhythm On A Drum*; *Stand Up And Fight (Toreador Song)*; *Card Song*; *My Joe*; *Whizzin' Away Along De Tracks*; *Duet And Finale*.

The best of the Dean Martin-Jerry Lewis films to date, **Living It Up** was a remake of David O. Selznick's 1937 comedy *Nothing Sacred*, with songs by Jule Styne and Bob Hilliard (who had made it into a musical for the 1953 Broadway season, calling it *Hazel Flagg*). Lewis (right) played the stationmaster of a small mid-western town who believes he is dying of radiation poisoning – in reality, there's nothing wrong with him, except for a slight sinus condition. Persuaded by his doctor (Martin, left) not to reveal this fact, Lewis accepts an all expenses paid invitation from newspaper reporter Janet Leigh to come to New York for one last fling – Leigh, of course, still believing that he is soon to die. Musically, the film's highlight came and went with 'Every Street's A Boulevard In Old New York', engagingly performed by the comedy team; while from Martin on his own came the appealing 'How Do You Speak To An Angel'. Otherwise, the comedy spoke louder than the music, with Fred Clark (as Miss Leigh's editor) in particularly good form. Also contributing to the general merriment purveyed in Jack Rose and Melville Shavelson's screenplay and Norman Taurog's direction, were Edward Arnold, Sammy White, Sig Rumann and Sheree North. Nick Castle staged the numbers and the producer was Paul Jones. Other songs: *Money Burns A Hole In My Pocket*; *That's What I Like*; *You're Gonna Dance With Me, Baby*; *Champagne And Wedding Cake*.

▽

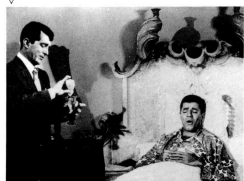

Judy Garland (illustrated) gave the greatest ▷
performance of her career in **A Star Is Born**
(Warner Bros.), a remake of the 1937 United
Artists release that starred Janet Gaynor and
Fredric March, directed by William Wellman,
and which was itself a re-working of *What Price
Hollywood* (RKO, 1932) which starred Constance
Bennett and Lowell Sherman, with direction by
George Cukor. Cukor, who also directed the
Garland version, was seen at his best too, the
opening, in which a drunken James Mason (as
film star Norman Maine) all but ruins a Hollywood benefit, being the most authentic backstage sequence ever filmed. Garland's tremendous energy, coupled with the quivering vulnerability that made her so special a performer,
was given full rein in Moss Hart's tautly written
screenplay (based on the 1937 screenplay by
Dorothy Parker, Alan Campbell and Robert
Carson from a story by William Wellman), and
not once in the film's 154-minute running time
was she less than superb. Whether acting her
heart out – as in the scene in her studio dressing-
room, where, incongruously made up as a
freckled urchin in readiness for a production
number, she agonizes to studio boss Charles
Bickford over husband Mason's deteriorating
condition; or in the light-hearted sequence in
which she puts on a rehearsal record and, for the
benefit of her out-of-work spouse, runs through
'a production number to end all production
numbers', her timing never faltered. Marvellous
too, were her purely comic scenes – such as her
transformation from Esther Blodgett to Vicki
Lester; while vocally she was at the peak of her
powers in 'The Man That Got Away' (by Harold
Arlen and Ira Gershwin, who also provided
five more new songs, two of which, 'Lose That
Long Face' and 'Here's What I'm Here For', were
cut) and the lengthy but entertaining 'Born In A
Trunk' routine (by Leonard Gershe). Mason's
performance was equally fine, his sorry deterior-
ation from super-star to washed-up alcoholic
painfully and accurately charted. In fact, as a
study of the corrosive effects of failure, **A Star Is
Born** has never been surpassed. Its impact today
remains as great as it was on its initial release,
one's only regret being that studio head Jack
Warner saw fit to remove almost a half an hour
from the final release print. But it must rate as
one of the great musicals of all time. It was
produced by Sid Luft, choreographed by Richard
Barstow, and photographed in CinemaScope
and Technicolor by Sam Leavitt with Ray
Heindorf in charge of the musical direction.
Completing the cast were Tom Noonan, Lucy
Marlowe, Amanda Blake, Irving Bacon, Hazel
Shermet and James Brown. Other songs and
musical numbers: *Gotta Have Me Go With You;
It's A New World; Someone At Last (Somewhere
There's A Someone)* Gershwin, Arlen; *Born In A
Trunk:* including *I'll Get By* Roy Turk, Fred
Ahlert; *You Took Advantage Of Me* Richard
Rodgers, Lorenz Hart; *Black Bottom* De Sylva,
Brown, Henderson; *Peanut Vendor* L. Wolfe
Gilbert, Marion Sunshine, Moisés Simon; *My
Melancholy Baby* George A. Norton, Ernie Bur-
nett; *Swanee* Irving Caesar, George Gershwin.

Athena (MGM), dedicated to the proposition
that a healthy body and a healthy mind are the
prerequisites for romance and everlasting happiness, wrapped a slight, and slightly off-beat,
story in a routine screenplay (by William Ludwig and Leonard Spigelgass) and an equally
routine set of songs (by Hugh Martin and Ralph
Blane). Jane Powell and Debbie Reynolds played
two nubile and remarkably healthy sisters (with
five more equally healthy sisters in the background), with Edmund Purdom (left) as a Back
Bay attorney, and Vic Damone (a crooner) the
men in their lives. Certain romantic complications arose in the shape of Louis Calhern
and Evelyn Varden, the eccentric vegetarian
grandparents of the seven sisters – but without
them, there'd have been even less to the plot
than there was. Steve Reeves (Mr Universe) was
on hand to help demonstrate the beauty of
physical perfection in the male of the species,
with other parts in Joe Pasternak's Technicolor
production going to Linda Christian (right) – no
slouch in the body department either, Henry
Nakamura, Ray Collins, Carl Benton Reid, Howard Wendell and, as the five remaining sisters,
Virginia Gibson, Nancy Kilgas, Dolores Starr,
Jane Fischer and Cecile Rogers. Valerie Bettis
staged the dances, and Richard Thorpe directed.
Musical highlights: 'The Girl Next Door' sung by
Vic Damone (first heard in *Meet Me In St Louis*,
MGM, 1944, when Judy Garland sang it as 'The
Boy Next Door') and 'I Never Felt Better' sung by
both Powell and Reynolds. Other songs and
musical numbers: *Love Can Change The Stars;
Venezia; Imagine; Vocalize; Chacun le Sait* from
Gaetano Donizetti's 'Daughter Of The Regiment'
(Powell). ◁

◁ Studio boss Dore Schary's decision to confine the
screen version of MGM's **Brigadoon** to a sound
stage rather than have it shot on location, was a
bad one, and the film, unfortunately, never
recovered from it. A whimsical fantasy (screenplay and lyrics: Alan Jay Lerner, Music: Frederick Loewe) in which two Americans from
Manhattan stumble across the fairytale village
of Brigadoon while out grouse-shooting and
learn that it only materializes out of the highland mists once every 100 years, needed either
the stylized limitations imposed on it by the
theatre or the spaciousness of the real outdoors,
but not the compromise offered by MGM. The
awkward dimension of the CinemaScope screen
only accentuated the staginess of Cedric Gibbons
and Preston Ames's sets and, as in *The Pirate*
(MGM, 1948), the direction, by Vincente Minnelli, was singularly airless and confining. Gene
Kelly (illustrated foreground centre) and Van
Johnson (foreground right) were cast as the two
Americans, with Cyd Charisse as Fiona, the
beautiful Scottish lass with whom Kelly falls in
love and who forces him to choose between her
and his fiancée back home in Manhattan. Apart
from Charisse's duet with Kelly in 'The Heather
On The Hill', Kelly's solo dance to 'Almost Like
Being In Love', and an ensemble tap dance
energetically rattled out to 'I'll Go Home With
Bonnie Jean', **Brigadoon** offered very few
pleasures. Johnson's dancing, even in the soft-
shoe routine he did with Kelly, looked ponderous; Charisse moved exquisitely, but her acting
was colourless, while Kelly himself, instead of
playing against the whimsy of the piece, tended
to squeeze every groan out of this bagpipe of a
musical. Minnelli's direction was undistinguished and even his usually exceptional use of colour
disappointing. It was produced by Arthur Freed
with a cast that also included Elaine Stewart,
Barry Jones, Hugh Laing, Albert Sharpe, Virginia Bosler, Jimmy Thompson, Tudor Owen
and Eddie Quillan, and the choreography was by
Gene Kelly. Cyd Charisse's vocals were dubbed
by Carole Richards. Other songs and musical
numbers: *Prologue; Entrance Of The Clans; Brigadoon; Waitin' For My Dearie; Once In The
Highlands; Down On MacConnachy Square; Wedding Dance; The Chase.*

Fifties Musicals

Deep In My Heart (MGM), an all-star biopic of Hungarian-born composer Sigmund Romberg, was produced in Technicolor by Roger Edens, directed by Stanley Donen and, as Sigmund Romberg, starred the versatile Jose Ferrer. Less felicitously cast was the insipid Doe Avedon as Mrs Romberg. Taking the usual liberties with the facts, scenarist Leonard Spigelgass, working from a biography of the composer by Elliott Arnold, came up with the usual ladder-of-fame narrative, showing the composer's step-by-step rise to Broadway eminence after humble beginnings as a musician in a modest Second Avenue café owned by Anna Mueller (a winning performance from opera star Helen Traubel). A song plugger (flashily played by David Burns) persuades Romberg to up-tempo his approach to music, and the result is 'The Leg Of Mutton Rag', Romberg's first commercial success (gloriously performed by Ferrer and Traubel). A string of minor songs in minor shows for the Shubert brothers followed, until *Maytime* – whose success resulted in two Broadway productions of it appearing at the same time. Slightly padding out the non-existent plot was Romberg's romance with Miss Avedon which did, at least, give rise to the best scene in the film: a run-through at a Catskill resort of a new (fictitious) Romberg show called *Jazz A Doo* with all the parts in it being played by Ferrer. Other musical highlights included Ann Miller's dancing of 'It' (not from *Artists And Models* as the film claimed, but from *The Desert Song*, lyrics by Otto Harbach and Oscar Hammerstein II) and Cyd Charisse and James Mitchell's erotic *pas de deux* to 'One Alone' from *The Desert Song* (lyrics Harbach, Hammerstein II). Gene Kelly and his brother Fred (as the O'Ryan

brothers, illustrated centre – Fred left) danced together for the first and last time in a film in 'I Love To Go Swimmin' With Wimmen' (from *Dancing Around* though no such dancers and no such song existed in that particular 1914 production; the number – lyrics by Ballard MacDonald – was in fact written for *Love Birds*, 1921, but dropped). Ferrer (excellent throughout as Romberg) joined his real-life wife Rosemary Clooney in 'Mr and Mrs' (lyrics by Cyrus Wood). Merle Oberon was cast as lyricist Dorothy Donnelly, Walter Pidgeon was J.J. Shubert, Paul Henreid Florenz Ziegfeld, and Tamara Toumanova Gaby Deslys, Paul Stewart and Jim Backus completed the cast, and the remaining guest stars were Jane Powell and Vic Damone (who sang 'The Road To Paradise' solo and 'Will You Remember' from *Maytime*, lyrics by Rida Johnson Young, with Powell), William Olvis (singing 'Serenade' from *The Student Prince*, lyric by Dorothy Donnelly), Howard Keel (in 'Your Land And My Land', lyrics by Donnelly, from *My Maryland*) and Tony Martin and Joan Weldon (in 'Lover Come Back To Me' from *The New Moon*, lyric by Oscar Hammerstein II). The choreography was by Eugene Loring. Other songs, musical numbers with their lyricists: *You Will Remember Vienna* (Traubel) Hammerstein II; *Auf Wiedersehn* (Traubel) Herbert Reynolds; *Softly As In A Morning Sunrise* (Toumanova, Traubel) Hammerstein II; *When I Grow Too Old To Dream* (Ferrer, chorus) Hammerstein II; *Stout-Hearted Men* (Traubel) Hammerstein II; *Riff Song* (orchestral); *The Desert Song* (orchestral); *One Kiss* (orchestral); *Deep In My Heart* (chorus) Donnelly; *I Love To Say Hello* (Toumanova) Alex Gerber.

The problems Mario Lanza continued to have with his weight led, ultimately, to his relinquishing the role of Prince Karl in Joseph Pasternak's CinemaScope production of Sigmund Romberg's **The Student Prince** (MGM) to Edmund Purdom (illustrated centre left). Lanza's voice, however, was used in the vocals, with slightly disconcerting results in view of Purdom's tall, slim, rather 'pretty' good looks. Still, after the first half hour or so, audiences began to accept the fact that the Prince's face and the voice emanating from it weren't a perfect match, and settled back to enjoy the glorious outpouring of melody which was the film's *raison d'être*, no one in 1954 being able to take seriously the operetta romance between a handsome aristocrat and a workaday barmaid in 1894 Heidelberg. Ann Blyth (left) was pleasant on both eye and ear as the barmaid Kathie, and there were several stereotyped performances from Louis Calhern as The King of Karlsburg, Edmund Gwenn as the prince's tutor and S.Z. Sakall as a hotelier. Also cast: Betta St John (centre right) as the princess Purdom finally marries, John Williams, John Ericson (right), John Hoyt, Evelyn Varden and Richard Anderson. In addition to such Romberg classics as 'Deep In My Heart', 'Golden Days', 'The Drinking Song' and 'Serenade', were three new ones by Nicholas Brodszky and Paul Francis Webster: 'Beloved', 'Summertime In Heidelberg' and 'I'll Walk With God', as well as the traditional 'Gaudeamus Igitur'. Most unfortunate scene in the film to a present-day viewer: a group of brightly caparisoned students interlocking arms and warbling: 'Come boys, let's all be gay boys'! It was written by William Ludwig and Sonya Levien (based on the operetta by Dorothy Donnelly and a play by William Meyer-Foerster) and directed by Richard Thorpe (Anscocolour).

White Christmas (Paramount) grossed $12,000,000 and was the top money-making film of 1954. With a score by Irving Berlin, and with Bing Crosby and Danny Kaye – the latter fresh from his triumph in Paramount's *Knock On Wood* – heading the cast, it was bespoke entertainment for all the family. Kaye, in fact, was a replacement for Donald O'Connor who had injured his leg, which led to the additional casting of John Brascia to partner Vera-Ellen (which he did very well) in several of the dance numbers. A throwback to the days of *Holiday Inn* (Paramount, 1942) and *Blue Skies* (Paramount, 1946), its screenplay, by Norman Panama, Melvin Frank and Norman Krasna, featured Crosby (standing centre right) and Kaye (standing centre left) as – would you believe – a song-and-dance team who, after first meeting while on active service, become pals as well as two of the big names in show business. Deciding to take time off in the company of showgirls Rosemary Clooney (left of Kaye) and Vera-Ellen (right of Crosby), they travel to a New England ski resort only to discover that its owner (Dean Jagger) who had been their general in the army is on the verge of bankruptcy because there hasn't been any snow that year. So they stage a mammoth Christmas benefit for him. It's a roaring success, snow suddenly begins to fall, and the film ends with the resort being saved from closure, and with Crosby and Kaye happy in the arms of Clooney and Vera-Ellen respectively. Fortunately the Berlin songs – most notably 'Sisters', first sung by Clooney and Vera-Ellen, and then by Crosby and Kaye miming to the girls' voices – were a lot better than the plot and, as there were quite a few of them, they helped pass the time agreeably enough. Robert Alton choreographed the two big production numbers, 'I'd Rather See A Minstrel Show' and 'Choreography', though far more effective were the modestly staged 'The Best Things Happen When You're Dancing', performed by Kaye and Vera-Ellen, and Clooney's 'Love, You Didn't Do Right By Me', whose male line-up featured a young George Chakiris. Michael Curtiz directed and it was produced in Vistavision (the first film to use it) and Technicolor by Robert Emmett Dolan with a cast that included Mary Wickes, Anne Whitfield, Grady Sutton and Sig Rumann. Other songs and musical numbers: *White Christmas* (Crosby, Kaye, Clooney, Vera-Ellen); *The Old Man* (Crosby, Kaye); *Gee, I Wish I Was Back In The Army* (Crosby, Kaye, Clooney, Vera-Ellen); *Snow* (Crosby, Kaye, Clooney, Vera-Ellen); *Count Your Blessings Instead Of Sheep* (Crosby, Clooney); *What Can You Do With A General* (Crosby); *Abraham* (Vera-Ellen, Brascia); *Mandy* (Vera-Ellen, Brascia, ensemble); *Heat Wave*; *Let Me Sing*; *Blue Skies* (Crosby, Kaye).

Another bumper musical extravaganza featuring a further batch of Irving Berlin standards, **There's No Business Like Show Business** (20th Century-Fox) was, perhaps, the splashiest of the year's musicals, and – with a cast that included Ethel Merman (top starred), Donald O'Connor, Marilyn Monroe, Dan Dailey, Johnnie Ray (his debut) and Mitzi Gaynor – one of the most entertaining in a seen-it-all-before kind of way. It dealt with the joys and heartaches experienced by a vaudeville family called the Donahues, with Merman and Dailey as Ma and Pa, and Ray, Gaynor and O'Connor as their talented offspring. Though the film ran 117 minutes, not a great deal actually happened in Phoebe and Henry Ephron's screenplay (from a story by Lamar Trotti) other than an alcohol-prone O'Connor having a turbulent on-off love affair with nightclub singer Monroe and (in the film's most nauseating scenes) Johnnie Ray deciding to become a priest. Berlin's 'Alexander's Ragtime Band' was made the subject of the film's big production number, being interpreted by various members of the Donahue family in a number of different ways. Thus Dailey and Merman performed it as heavily accented Swiss might; O'Connor did it Scottish, Gaynor gave it a bit of the 'oo-la-la', while Ray made of it something quite unbelievably lugubrious. Marilyn Monroe did a sexy version of 'Heat Wave', and from O'Connor came some nifty dancing with 'A Man Chases A Girl Until She Catches Him'. Monroe's routines were staged by Jack Cole and all the others by Robert Alton, it was produced in CinemaScope and Colour by Sol C. Siegel, directed by Walter Lang and, in secondary roles, featured Richard Eastham, Hugh O'Brian, Rhys Williams, Lee Patrick, Eve Miller, Robin Raymond and Lyle Talbot. Illustration shows left to right: Merman, Dailey, Gaynor, O'Connor, Monroe. Other songs and musical numbers: *There's No Business Like Show Business* (Merman, Dailey, O'Connor, Ray, Gaynor, Monroe); *When The Midnight Choo Choo Leaves For Alabam* (Merman, Dailey, Gaynor, O'Connor); *Let's Have Another Cup Of Coffee* (Merman); *Play A Simple Melody* (Merman, Dailey); *After You Get What You Want You Don't Want It* (Monroe); *You'd Be Surprised* (Dailey); *A Sailor's Not A Sailor* (Merman, Gaynor); *A Pretty Girl Is Like A Melody* (Merman, Dailey); *Remember* (chorus); *Lazy* (Gaynor, O'Connor, Monroe); *If You Believe* (Ray); *Marie* (trio).

▽

With a more assured director than Gordon Douglas and a sharper script than that provided by Julius J. Epstein and Lenore Coffee, **Young At Heart** (Warner Bros.), a musical remake of the Claude Rains-John Garfield melodrama, *Four Daughters* (1938), might just have worked. Certainly, the unusual teaming of Doris Day (right) as a respectable New England Miss with Frank Sinatra (left) as the embittered songwriter she marries on the rebound, promised more than it delivered, though perhaps their respective styles could never have fruitfully co-existed. Doris's two sisters (the fourth sister was dropped for this version) were charmingly played by Dorothy Malone and Elizabeth Fraser; Gig Young was the composer on whom she originally set her sights, and Ethel Barrymore and Robert Keith her aunt and father. It was produced, in Warnercolor (print by Technicolor), by Henry Blanke. Songs and musical numbers: *Young At Heart* Johnny Richards, Carolyn Leigh; *Hold Me In Your Arms* Ray Heindorf, Charles Henderson, Don Pippin; *Ready, Willing And Able* Floyd Huddleston, Al Rinker, Dick Gleason; *Till My Love Comes To Me* lyrics Paul Francis Webster, music adapted by Ray Heindorf from Mendelssohn's 'On Wings of Song'; *There's A Rising Moon (For Every Falling Star)* Sammy Fain, Webster; *Someone To Watch Over Me* George and Ira Gershwin; *Just One Of Those Things* Cole Porter; *One For My Baby* Harold Arlen, Johnny Mercer; *You, My Love* Mack Gordon, Jimmy Van Heusen.
▽

△

Jupiter's Darling (MGM) was the one with all those painted elephants. It was also the one in which Esther Williams (illustrated) played Amytis to Howard Keel's Hannibal, and the one which laid an egg bigger than all the elephants in it put together. Based on the play *Road To Rome* by Robert E. Sherwood, the screenplay by Dorothy Kingsley concerned itself with a romantic liaison between Williams and Keel, and the promise given by Keel to Williams that he will desist from sacking Rome. In 96 minutes Williams took to the water on three separate occasions, but only once – to a tune called 'I Have A Dream' by Burton Lane and Harold Adamson (who provided the entire serviceable score) – did she actually 'perform'. George Sanders was cast as Williams's fiancé Fabius Maximus, while Marge and Gower Champion, as an unlikely pair of Romans called Meta and Varius, interrupted the highly interruptible narrative with 'If This Be Slav'ry' and 'The Life Of An Elephant'. Completing the cast for producer George Wells were Richard Haydn, William Demarest, Norma Varden and Douglass Dumbrille. The director was George Sidney. (CinemaScope and Eastmancolor). Other songs and musical numbers: *Hannibal's Victory March*; *I Never Trust A Woman*; *Don't Let This Night Get Away*.

Betty Grable's first film for two years, and her first away from 20th Century-Fox since 1939, was **Three For The Show** (Columbia), a remake, in CinemaScope and Technicolor, of *Too Many Husbands* (Columbia, 1940) from the play by Somerset Maugham. She starred as a showgirl who discovers to her dismay that she is the possessor of two husbands: dancer Gower Champion, her present spouse, and Jack Lemmon (centre right) a World War II pilot and composer who suddenly turns up again, having hitherto been reported dead. Marge Champion (right) was also in it as a none-too-fussy dancer prepared to settle for whichever man Grable (centre left), who loves both Champion and Lemmon, finally decides to relinquish. Several well-staged dances by choreographer Jack Cole gave the commonplace proceedings a much-needed fillip – the two best being Grable's dream sequence in a male harem, and Marge and Gower Champion's stylish dancing to the strains of the Gershwins' 'Someone To Watch Over Me'. It was written by Edward Hope and Leonard Stern, directed by H.C. Potter and produced by Jonie Taps whose cast included Myron McCormick (left), Paul Harvey, Robert Bice and Hal K. Dawson. Other songs and musical numbers: *How Come You Do Me Like You Do* Gene Austin, Roy Bergere; *I've Got A Crush On You* George and Ira Gershwin; *Down Boy* Hoagy Carmichael, Harold Adamson; *Which One* Lester Lee, Ned Washington; *Swan Lake* (ballet excerpt) Tchaikovsky; *I've Been Kissed Before* Bob Russell, Lester Lee.

△

So This Is Paris was straight off the Universal-International assembly line. The story of three American sailors in Paris, and the three Parisian girls they meet, it was (like Columbia's 1953 *All Ashore*) another cut-price *On The Town* (MGM, 1949) and tediously familiar, with neither its cast – Tony Curtis (illustrated) Gloria De Haven, Gene Nelson, Corinne Calvet, Paul Gilbert and Mara Corday, nor its scenarist (Charles Hoffman, from a story by Ray Buffum) able to impart even the merest soupçon of freshness or originality to it. Gene Nelson and Lee Scott, who were in charge of the dance numbers, were impeded in their efforts to give them snap and crackle by a score (from Pony Sherrell and Phil Moody) that was thoroughly bottom drawer, the only number of any merit being the Dorothy Fields-Jimmy McHugh oldie 'I Can't Give You Anything But Love, Baby' sung by Miss De Haven in French. Richard Quine directed and it was produced, in Technicolor, by Albert J. Cohen, with Allison Hayes, Christiane Martel and Myrna Hansen among the supporting players. Other songs and musical numbers: *So This Is Paris*; *Two Of Us*; *A Dame's A Dame*; *If You Were There*; *Looking For Someone To Love*; *Wait Till Paris Sees Us*; *Three Bon Vivants*; *If You Want To Be Famous*.

▷

◁ Walt Disney's first full-length animated cartoon in CinemaScope was **Lady And The Tramp** (Buena Vista) and, although it had its moments, most notably a delicious sequence involving a pair of scheming Siamese cats, it lacked the flair and the imagination – both in its narrative line and in execution – of some of the studio's earlier works. The story of a romance between a cocker spaniel called Lady and a mutt named Tramp (see illustration) whom she meets while braving the harsh realities of the outside world, the cleverest scenes were those in which Disney's band of animators brought a decidedly human likeness to their canine subjects – but its overall tendency to cuteness was more appealing to children than to their parents. Lending their voices for the occasion were Peggy Lee, Barbara Luddy, Larry Roberts, Bill Thompson, Bill Baucon, Stan Freberg, Verna Felton, George Givot and The Mello Men. It was adapted by Erdman Penner, Joe Rinaldi, Ralph Wright and Donald Da Gradi from a story by Ward Greene, and directed by Hamilton Luske, Clyde Geronimi and Wilfred Jackson. (Technicolor) Songs: *He's A Tramp*; *La La Lu*; *Siamese Cat Song*; *Peace On Earth*; *Bella Notte* Sonny Burke, Peggy Lee.

△

Pete Kelly's Blues (a Mark VII Ltd Production for Warner Bros.), starring Jack Webb (illustrated), who also produced and directed, was the story of a nightclub trumpeter (Webb) who decides to make a stand against protection racketeers in Kansas *circa* 1927. But it never quite made up its mind whether to be a musical or a melodrama, and is best remembered as an unusually violent (for 1955) gangster movie with a strong musical background, mostly composed of songs from the period but with a title number by Sammy Cahn and Ray Heindorf that continued to haunt the memory long afterwards. Peggy Lee (illustrated) as a fading singer who takes to drink was also in it; so were Janet Leigh, Edmond O'Brien, Andy Devine, Lee Marvin, Jayne Mansfield, Martin Milner and Ella Fitzgerald. Webb's trumpet playing was dubbed by Dick Cathcart. (CinemaScope and Warnercolor) Songs and musical numbers included: *Pete Kelly's Blues* Cahn, Heindorf; *Sing A Rainbow*; *He Needs Me* Arthur Hamilton; *Somebody Loves Me* Buddy De Sylva, Ballard MacDonald, George Gershwin; *Sugar* Maceo Pinkard, Sidney Mitchell, Edna Alexander; *I Never Knew* Gus Kahn, Ted Fiorito; *Hard-Hearted Hannah* Jack Yellen, Milton Ager, Bob Bigelow, Charles Bates; *Bye, Bye Blackbird* Mort Dixon, Ray Henderson; *What Can I Say After I Say I'm Sorry* Walter Donaldson, Abe Lyman; *Oh, Didn't He Ramble* Bob Cole, J. Rosamond Johnson (published under composite pseudonym Will Handy).

A handful of excellent songs sung by some
excellent voices – most notably those belonging
to Kay Armen, Jane Powell, Vic Damone and
Tony Martin – considerably brightened the entertainment value of MGM's remake of Radio
Pictures' **Hit The Deck**. For without them,
Joe Pasternak's CinemaScope production would
have had very little to offer other than a familiar
story of a trio of sailors on shore leave and the
romantic complications they're heir to. Debbie
Reynolds was also in it, so were Walter Pidgeon
(as Powell's admiral father), Gene Raymond,
Russ Tamblyn, J. Carrol Naish, Richard Anderson, Jane Darwell and, as a nightclub dancer,
Ann Miller. The romantic programme went
something like this: Miller loves Martin; Damone
loves Powell; Reynolds loves Tamblyn, and
Armen loves J. Carrol Naish. The musical programme was far more interesting. Miller had a
show stopper with 'The Lady From The Bayou'
(by Leo Robin and Vincent Youmans), Messrs
Martin, Damone and Tamblyn did some close
harmonizing to 'Hallelujah' (by Vincent Youmans, Clifford Grey and Leo Robin), and from
Miss Powell and Damone came 'Sometimes I'm
Happy' (another standard by Youmans, Grey
and Irving Caesar) and 'I Know That You Know'
(by Youmans and Anne Caldwell). Kay Armen
sang 'Ciribiribee' (by A. Pestalozza). Reynolds
and Tamblyn did a hum-dinger of a dance in an
amusement park fun-house, and from Tony
Martin came the haunting 'More Than You
Know' (by Youmans, Billy Rose and Edward
Eliscu). It was written by Sonya Levien and
William Ludwig from the stage show by Herbert
Field and the play *Shore Leave* by Hubert
Osborne, robustly choreographed by Hermes Pan, and
directed by Roy Rowland (Eastmancolor). Illus-
tration left to right: Powell and Damone, Miller
and Martin, Reynolds and Tamblyn. Other songs
and musical numbers: *Keepin' Myself For You*
Youmans, Sidney Clare; *A Kiss Or Two* Robin,
Youmans; *Lucky Bird*; *Loo-Loo*; *Join The Navy*;
Why Oh Why Robin, Grey, Youmans.

Though Bob Hope portrayed vaudevillian and
father of seven, Eddie Foy, in **The Seven Little
Foys** (Paramount), the personality he projected
throughout Jack Rose and Melville Shavelson's
screenplay was very much his own. All about
the attempts of the un-paternal Foy to rear his
kids and turn them into a vaudeville act (see
illustration – Hope left) after the death of his
ballet dancer wife (Milly Vitale), there was
something unendearing about it all – and it was
left to James Cagney, appearing for the second
time as George M. Cohan, to give it a much
needed boost in a scene he shared with Hope at
New York's Friar's Club. Together they hoofed to
'Mary's A Grand Old Name' and 'Yankee Doodle
Boy' (both by Cohan), and exuded a warmth
that was never in evidence elsewhere. George
Tobias featured as a theatrical agent, with other
roles going to Angela Clarke, Herbert Heyes,
Richard Shannon and, as the seven little Foys,
Billy Gray, Lee Erickson, Paul De Rolf, Lydia
Reed, Linda Bennett, Jimmy Baird, and Tommy
Duran. Shavelson directed, Rose produced (in
Vistavision and Technicolor), and the choreo-
grapher was Nick Castle. Miss Vitale's vocals
were dubbed by Viola Vonn. Other songs and
musical numbers: *I'm The Greatest Father Of
Them All* William Jerome, Foy, Joseph J. Lilley;
Row Row Row Jerome, James V. Monaco; *China-
town My Chinatown*; *I'm Tired* Jerome, Jean
Schwartz; *Comedy Ballet* Lilley; *Nobody* Bert
Williams, Alex Rogers.

Fred Astaire's only film for 20th Century-Fox
was **Daddy Long Legs**. Written as a novel in
1912 by Jean Webster (who also turned it into a
play), then filmed twice – in 1919 by First
National with Mary Pickford and Mahlon Hamilton, and in 1931 by Fox with Janet Gaynor and
Warner Baxter – its third version underwent
certain plot alterations, mainly to accommodate
the talents of Leslie Caron (illustrated) who was
unmistakeably French. Phoebe and Henry
Ephron's screenplay therefore involved Astaire
(illustrated) in some State Department business,
a ploy which conveniently takes him to France
where, at an orphanage near Paris, he first
becomes aware of (and enchanted by) the waif-
like Miss Caron. From then on the story was
pretty much the same as its author originally
intended, with Astaire offering to sponsor
Caron's education in America without revealing
his true identity; and Caron, having met Astaire,
falling in love with him without realizing who
he is. At Astaire's request, Johnny Mercer was
commissioned to write the score and, on this
occasion, he supplied the music as well as the
words. Best song was the lilting 'Something's
Gotta Give', sung by Astaire on a hotel balcony,
then danced by him and Caron. For the rest, the
music was serviceable rather than inspired –
'The Slew-Foot' danced by Astaire, Caron and a
ballroom full of students, nowhere approaching
in quality Astaire's more celebrated routines
with Ginger Rogers. There were two lengthy
dream ballets called 'The Daydream Sequence'
and 'Dancing Through Life'. They were choreographed by Roland Petit, and were garish and
uninspired. The film was produced in Cinema-
Scope and Color by De Luxe, by Samuel G. Engel,
directed by Jean Negulesco and, in secondary
roles, featured Fred Clark as Astaire's business
manager, Thelma Ritter as his secretary and
Terry Moore as his pretty niece. Also: Larry
Keating, Charlotte Austin, Kathryn Givney,
Kelly Brown, Ann Codee, and Ray Anthony and
His Orchestra. Sharing the choreographic duties
with Petit was David Robel. Other songs and
musical numbers: *History Of The Beat*; *C-A-T
Spells Cat*; *Daddy Long Legs*; *Welcome Egghead*;
Dream.

It was the icing – in the shape of CinemaScope,
Technicolor and the glamorous Paris and
Riviera settings, as well as the costumes by
Travilla and Christian Dior – that gave **Gentlemen Marry Brunettes**, set in the 1920s, what
little taste and entertainment value it had.
Otherwise, the film didn't offer much in the
telling of a tired old story of a couple of sisters
who, irritated by the attentions of seemingly
every stage-door Johnny in New York, and the
inability of one of them ever to say no, answer
the call of a theatrical agent (Scott Brady, vocals
dubbed by Paul Carpenter) in Paris, and journey
to the City of Light where, among other things,
they become involved with Rudy Vallee (left, as
himself), Guy Middleton (as a wealthy earl) and
Alan Young as a stage-struck young man who
also happens to be a millionaire. Jeanne Crain
(centre, vocals dubbed by Anita Ellis) and Jane
Russell (right) were the brunettes in question,
with other parts in Mary Loos and Richard Sale's
vacuous screenplay going to Eric Pohlmann,
Ferdy Mayne, Leonard Sachs and Guido Lorraine. Co-author Sale was also the director of this
disappointingly stale trifle. It was produced by
Sale and Robert Waterfield, with Robert Bassler
as executive producer, and choreographed by
Jack Cole. A Voyager Production, it was pre-
sented by Russ-Field Corporation, and released
by United Artists. Songs and musical numbers
included: *Gentlemen Marry Brunettes* Herbert
Spencer, Earle Hagen; *You're Driving Me Crazy*
Walter Donaldson; *Miss Annabelle Lee* Sidney
Clare, Lew Pollack; *Have You Met Miss Jones?*; *My
Funny Valentine* Richard Rodgers, Lorenz Hart; *I
Wanna Be Loved By You* Bert Kalmar, Harry Ruby;
Ain't Misbehavin' Andy Razaf, Fats Waller.

Interrupted Melody (MGM) charted the heroism of opera singer Marjorie Lawrence, whose international career was blighted at its zenith when she contracted poliomyelitis. It was a moving and inspirational story, told with love and tenderness by scenarists William Ludwig and Sonya Levien, solidly directed by Curtis Bernhardt, and performed by Eleanor Parker (as Lawrence) with superb conviction. Glenn Ford was top-billed as the doctor who becomes her husband; and together they shared the film's most affecting scene in which Ford, against his wife's wishes, puts on a record of her singing 'My Heart At Thy Sweet Voice' from Saint-Saens's *Samson and Delilah*, hoping that it will force her to drag her immobile body across the room in an attempt to stop the music by sending the record player crashing to the floor. The ploy works, proving to Parker that, with effort, she *can* move and that, with persistence, there is hope for at least a partial recovery of her limbs. Her return to the world of grand opera took place in the film's climactic scene at the Metropolitan where, in a performance of Wagner's *Tristan Und Isolde*, Lawrence reasserts herself as one of the world's great dramatic sopranos. It was the most moving moment in a well-crafted piece of screen biography, credit having to go not only to Parker for her magnificent central performance, but to Eileen Farrell, who dubbed all her vocals. There was also a dramatically staged excerpt from Brunnhilde's Immolation in Wagner's *Götterdämmerung* (illustrated). The rest of the cast was completed by Roger Moore as Marjorie's brother Cyril and Cecil Kellaway as her father, as well as by Peter Leeds, Evelyn Ellis, Walter Baldwin, Ann Codee, Stephen Bekassy and, as himself, Leopold Sachs. It was produced in CinemaScope and Eastmancolor by Jack Cummings, with Walter Du Clouy in charge of the musical direction. Other songs and operatic excerpts: *Musetta's Waltz* (from 'La Boheme') Puccini; *Habanera* (from 'Carmen') Bizet; *Seguidilla* (from 'Carmen'); *Finale to Act I* of 'Il Trovatore' Verdi; *One Fine Day* (from 'Madame Butterfly') Puccini; *Waltzing Matilda* A.B. Paterson, Marie Cowan; *Over The Rainbow* Harold Arlen, E.Y. Harburg.

The best of Gene Kelly's CinemaScope musicals and a return to form for him after the undiluted whimsy purveyed in *Brigadoon* (MGM) the previous year, **It's Always Fair Weather** was the last film he and Stanley Donen would co-direct, and one of the last of the better MGM musicals under the producership of Arthur Freed. It originated from an idea by Betty Comden and Adolph Green who saw it, initially, as a Broadway sequel to *On The Town*, but Kelly persuaded them to turn it into a film, believing it to be the perfect vehicle for himself, Frank Sinatra and Jules Munshin. Sinatra, however, having won an Oscar for his performance in Columbia's *From Here To Eternity* two years earlier, did not wish to return to musicals: a decision which forced Kelly to change his approach to the subject. So, instead of having sailors, Comden and Green wrote a scenario involving a trio of soldiers; and instead of Sinatra and Munshin, Kelly (centre) cast Dan Dailey (right) and choreographer Michael Kidd (left), with the two main female roles going to Cyd Charisse and Dolores Gray. The story was simple enough – three wartime buddies pre-arrange a reunion meeting to take place ten years after demobilization to see how each is coping with civilian life. When, reluctantly, the three show up as planned, they realize they no longer have anything in common. Though **It's Always Fair Weather** did not have the expensive MGM look of *An American In Paris* (1950) or *Singin' In The Rain* (1952), there was no cut-back on the talent invested in it, and the result was extremely enjoyable. Its theme dealing, albeit lightheartedly, with the incompatibility of three men who, a decade earlier would have died for one another, was treated by scenarists Comden and Green in a manner more cynical and hard-hitting than audiences had come to expect from them, and the satirical swipes the film took at television left a smarting sting. The musical numbers were effective too (though several of them had absolutely nothing to do with the plot), notably Kelly's 'I Like Myself' (music by Andre Previn, lyrics by Comden and Green who wrote all the songs), sung and danced on rollerskates. Charisse, as a lady fanatically interested in everything, did an energetic number called 'Baby, You Knock Me Out' with a bunch of pugilists in a gym; Kelly, Kidd and Dailey had some interesting moments dancing with garbage lids attached to their feet, and from Dolores Gray came one of the best songs in the film, a ditty called 'Thanks A Lot But No Thanks'. The cast was completed by Lou Lubin, David Burns and Jay C. Flippen. Kelly and Donen were responsible for the choreography, and Previn for the musical direction. Other songs and musical numbers: *March, March; Once Upon A Time; The Time For Parting; Why Are We Here (Blue Danube); Music Is Better Than Words; Situation-Wise; Stillman's Gym.*

Liberace's fulsome personality proved rather too flamboyant to generate the slightest credibility in a feature film, as Warner Bros. discovered with **Sincerely Yours**, a truly horrendous musical reworking of the 1932 George Arliss vehicle *The Man Who Played God* (from the Jules Eckert Goodman melodrama). The smirking Maestro (right) played, not exactly God, but a self-centred concert pianist who, when he falls victim to an attack of deafness, learns to read lips and becomes involved in other people's problems, thereby solving his own. Sincerely, a load of old garbage, for which neither director Gordon Douglas nor the unfortunate supporting company – co-star Joanne Dru as the pianist's adoring secretary, Dorothy Malone (left), Alex Nicol, William Demarest and Lori Nelson – should be held responsible. Irving Wallace perpetrated the script and Henry Blanke produced (for International Artists Ltd). Music included: *Minuet in G* Paderewski; *Sonata No 9* Mozart; *Traumerei* Schumann; *Liebestraum* Liszt; *Rhapsody In Blue* George Gershwin; *Gershwin Medley: Embraceable You, The Man I Love, I Got Rhythm, Liza; Cornish Rhapsody* Hubert Bath; *Tea For Two* Vincent Youmans, Irving Caesar; *Sincerely Yours* Paul Francis Webster, Liberace.

A backstage programmer prominently featuring Frank Sennes's Moulin Rouge theatre-restaurant in Hollywood, **Paris Follies of 1956** (Allied Artists) – made in five days (and it showed) – was a hoary old chestnut about a producer (Forrest Tucker) who discovers that the millionaire (Lloyd Corrigan) who has promised to finance his latest show isn't a millionaire at all, but a common-or-garden nutter. Margaret Whiting (illustrated) co-starred as a flighty singer, with other roles being Bernard Tabakin's production (for Mercury-International) going to Dick Wesson, Martha Hyer and Wally Cassell. The Sportsmen and Frank Parker also put in an appearance as themselves (it didn't help). It was written by Milton Lazarus, directed by Leslie Goodwins and choreographed by Donn Arden. Songs and musical numbers included : *Can This Be Love?; I Love A Circus; Have You Ever Been In Paris?; I'm All Aglow Again; I'm In A Mood Tonight* Pony Sherrell, Phil Moody; *The Hum Song* Sid Kuller.

Ruth and Eileen Sherwood, two sisters from Ohio who arrive in New York looking for life and love and take up residence in a Greenwich Village basement apartment, first appeared as characters in several *New Yorker* short stories by Ruth McKenney. In 1940, they became the protagonists of a comedy called *My Sister Eileen* by Joseph Fields and Jerome Chodorov. A movie version followed a couple of years later with Rosalind Russell top-starred and, in 1953, parading under the title *Wonderful Town*, the girls were at it again for 559 performances in a Broadway musical (again starring Miss Russell) with music by Leonard Bernstein and book and lyrics by Betty Comden and Adolph Green. A second musical version called **My Sister Eileen** emerged from Columbia in 1955 with Betty Garrett as the literary Ruth and Janet Leigh as her sister Eileen. Blake Edwards and Richard Quine wrote it, with songs by Jule Styne and Leo Robin. Though not as clever as the Bernstein-Comden-Green version, it was nothing to be ashamed of and, if only for Betty Garrett's dynamic performance in a role that for once revealed her versatility and scope as a musical comedy star, was worth spending time and money on. Jack Lemmon co-starred as a magazine publisher and consolidated his reputation as one of the screen's brightest new male talents, with other roles going to Kurt Kasznar, Bob Fosse (who also choreographed), Tommy Rall, Dick York, Barbara Brown, Horace McMahon and Henry Slate. The Styne-Robin score was not in the same league as Bernstein's, but in 'Give Me A Band And My Baby' (illustrated) sung by Garrett (centre left), Leigh (centre right), Fosse (left) and Rall (right) and 'It's Bigger Than You And Me', sung by Lemmon to Garrett, they came up with a couple of knockouts. Richard Quine directed and it was produced by Fred Kohlmar, in Technicolor. Other songs and musical numbers: *We're Great But No One Knows It*; *There's Nothing Like Love*; *Competition Dance*; *As Soon As They See Eileen*; *This Is Greenwich Village*; *Conga*.
▽

A totally fictitious biopic relating to the life and times of Peter Ilyitch Tchaikovsky, **Song Of My Heart** (Allied Artists) was a travesty that had the composer falling in love with a princess, but being prevented from marrying her by the princess's disapproving father. This wholly distorted view of Tchaikovsky's love life (he was, in fact, a homosexual whose misguided marriage ended in disaster within days of the ceremony taking place) was told in flashback by a Russian lieutenant whose father had been the composer's valet. Frank Sundstrom was Tchaikovsky, Audrey Long (right) his princess sweetheart and Sir Cedric Hardwicke (left) her father, with other parts in writer-director Benjamin Glazer's bungle going to Mikhail Rasumny, Gale Sherwood, Serge Krizman, Charles Trowbridge and Kate Lawson. The producers were Nathaniel Finston and J. Theodore Reed, and the music featured included extracts from the fourth, fifth and sixth symphonies, the *B Flat Piano Concerto*, *The Nutcracker Suite*, *Swan Lake*, *The Romeo And Juliet Fantasy*, *The 1812 Overture*, *Marche Slave*, and *Caprice Italien*.
▽

Artists And Models (Paramount) was the sixteenth Dean Martin-Jerry Lewis film and one of their liveliest. In it, Martin played a struggling artist and Lewis a struggling writer of children's stories who live in a garret in Greenwich village and have no idea where their next meal is coming from. The windfall that changes their lives is Lewis's penchant for talking in his sleep and recounting the most lurid of tales, all of which Martin writes down then sells to a comic-book publisher. With success comes girls – in this instance Eva Gabor, Anita Ekberg and, in a less flashy sort of way, neighbours Dorothy Malone and Shirley MacLaine. Frank Tashlin, Hal Kanter and Herbert Baker wrote it from an adaptation by Don McGuire of a play by Michael Davidson and Norman Lessing. Eddie Mayehoff appeared as a comic-book publisher, with other roles in producer Hal Wallis's Vistavision and Technicolor production going to George Winslow, Jack Elam, Herbert Rudley, Richard Shannon and Richard Webb. The score was by Harry Warren and Jack Brooks whose 'Inamorata', sung by Martin, and also sung and danced by MacLaine, came closest to being a hit. Charles O'Curran created and staged the musical numbers, and it was directed by Frank Tashlin (illustration: featured quartet in the centre are, left to right, Maclaine, Lewis, Malone, Martin). Other songs and musical numbers: *When You Pretend*; *Lucky Song*; *You Look So Familiar*; *Artists And Models*.
◁

Samuel Goldwyn's penultimate film was an expensive recreation of the Jo Swerling-Abe Burrows-Frank Loesser masterpiece **Guys And Dolls**. Having paid $1,000,000 for the rights from Broadway producers Feuer and Martin, Goldwyn spent a further $4,500,000 on his production, a hefty chunk of which went on the casting of Marlon Brando (left) as Sky Masterson (the role was originally offered to Gene Kelly but MGM, to whom Kelly was still under contract, refused to release him) and Frank Sinatra (centre right) as Nathan Detroit. Jean Simmons (centre left) was cast as missionary Sarah Brown, Vivian Blaine (right, repeating the role she created on stage) was Miss Adelaide, with Stubby Kaye, B.S. Pully and Johnny Silver (also recruits from the original stage production) as Nicely Nicely Johnson, Big Jule and Benny Southstreet. Joseph L. Mankiewicz, who had never directed a musical before, was handed the choice directorial assignment, and also provided a screenplay based on Swerling and Burrows's book which, in turn, was culled from Damon Runyon's short story *The Idylls Of Sarah Brown*. The result was a show which, while totally failing to capture the convivial intimacy of the stage presentation was, nonetheless, full of good things – the best being Michael Kidd's spirited, high-octane choreography, seen at its best in the opening sequence and in 'The Crap Game Dance' performed in a sewer. Sinatra sauntered through the role of Nathan with the air of a lovable heel, and although he only had one solo – 'Adelaide', specially written for the film by Loesser – was vocally at the peak of his powers. Vivian Blaine was delightful as his showgirl fiancée of 14 years standing, though the most authentically Runyonesque performance of all came from Stubby Kaye. Brando as gambler Masterson, and Simmons as the missionary lady he falls for after a romantic stint in Havana (undertaken, initially, as a bet with Sinatra), were both better than expected; Brando, using his own singing voice, was particularly effective in 'Luck Be A Lady'. Two of the stage show's songs – 'A Bushel And A Peck', and the melodious 'I've Never Been In Love Before' were replaced by 'Pet Me Poppa' and 'A Woman In Love' – good songs both of them, but no improvements on the originals. **Guys And Dolls** ran 158 minutes, was filmed in CinemaScope and Eastmancolor, and was released by MGM. Apart from the 1955 Goldwyn Girls, the cast also included Sheldon Leonard, Dan Dayton, Johnny Silver, George E. Stone, Kay Kuter, Regis Toomey, Kathryn Givney, Veda Ann Borg, Alan Hokanson and Joe McTurk. Other songs and musical numbers: *Fugue For Tin Horns* (Sinatra, Silver, Dayton); *Follow The Fold* (Simmons, Kuter, group); *The Oldest Established* (Sinatra, Silver, Kaye, ensemble); *I'll Know* (Brando, Simmons); *Adelaide's Lament* (Blaine); *A Woman In Love* (Brando, Simmons, Ruben De Fuentes, trio, Renee Renor); *If I Were A Bell* (Simmons, Brando); *Take Back Your Mink* (Blaine, girls); *Sue Me* (Sinatra, Blaine); *Sit Down You're Rockin' The Boat* (Kaye, Givney, Hokanson, Simmons); *Guys And Dolls* (Sinatra, Silver, Kaye); *Pet Me Poppa* (Blaine, girls).

Fifties Musicals

In scenarist Helen Deutsch's version of the Cinderella story, here called **The Glass Slipper** (MGM), Cindy, played by Leslie Caron, was a petulant, defiant, altogether unappealing young woman; while her two stepsisters (Amanda Blake and Lisa Daniels) were, contrary to the original Charles Perrault story, beautiful and accomplished. Cindy's stepmother, as played by Elsa Lanchester, wasn't particularly mean or unkind; and there was very little magic about Estelle Winwood's fairy godmother: an eccentric old biddy who lives in the woods and has a collection of favourite words ('apple dumpling' being two of them). Michael Wilding – looking very self-conscious in white leotards – was the handsome Prince (illustrated with Caron), with other parts in producer Edwin H. Knopf's Eastman-color, all-expense-spared production going to Keenan Wynn, Barry Jones, Lurene Tuttle and Liliane Montevecchi. Bronislau Kaper provided a score which was little more than musical wallpaper, its 'highlight' being two Roland Petit-choreographed ballets in which Wilding – misguidedly – took an active part. The better of these two excursions into dance was an item called 'Son Of The Cook' in which Caron, believing that the Prince is 'the son of the cook of the dook' imagines what it would be like dancing with him. The ballet librettos were provided by Miss Deutsch, who also supplied the lyrics for a moony love song (sung by Wilding) called 'Take My Love'. The narration, with its 'psychological' overtones, was solemnly spoken by Walter Pidgeon. Charles Walters directed.

After her Broadway success in *Wonderful Town*, Rosalind Russell returned to the screen in an inferior effort (produced by her husband Frederick Brisson) called **The Girl Rush** (Paramount). Set for most of its running time in Las Vegas, the story had Russell believing that she owns a half share in the fabulous Flamingo Hotel when, in fact, all she owns is a half interest in a derelict old shack whom nobody patronizes. Real owner of the Flamingo turns out to be Fernando Lamas who, after playing along with Russell's mistaken belief in her ownership, predictably finds himself romantically involved with her. James Gleason was cast as Russell's business partner, with other roles in the Vistavision and Technicolor production going to Eddie Albert and Gloria De Haven (illustrated) – who also paired up in time for the final clinch – Marion Lorne and Robert Fortier (standing, right). Robert Pirosh directed it and, together with Jerome Davis, wrote the screenplay from a story by Phoebe and Henry Ephron; the score was by Hugh Martin and Ralph Blane, and the choreography by Robert Alton. Best tune was a production number called 'An Occasional Man' sung by De Haven, with the overlong 'Homesick Hillbilly' (sung by Russell) coming a close second. The rest of the songs and musical numbers were nothing special and included *Champagne*; *Birmin'ham*; *Choose Your Partner*; *Out Of Doors*; *Take A Chance*; *At Last We're Alone*; *The Girl Rush*.

Having successfully adapted the music of Edvard Grieg into a Broadway hit *(Song Of Norway)*, the team of Bob Wright and Chet Forrest dipped into the musical output of Alexander Borodin and surfaced with **Kismet**, a smash hit which ran for 583 performances on Broadway, and 648 in London's West End, not counting its numerous revivals – the latest being an all-black version called *Timbuktu* with a cast headed by Eartha Kitt. With its sumptuous and exotic settings, the Arabian Nights flavour of its story, and its generous outpouring of melody it was, in theory at any rate, the ideal subject for a film musical. Kismet, however, was against **Kismet** (MGM) and, as directed by Vincente Minnelli for producer Arthur Freed, the film was an eye-filling bore that completely failed to capture the magic of the stage presentation. Howard Keel (left), in the role created by Alfred Drake, played the poet-beggar Hajj, Ann Blyth (right) was his daughter and Vic Damone the young Caliph she loves, with Sebastian Cabot the Wazir who forces Hajj to use his so-called magic powers as a means of marrying off Damone (his son) to a princess; Dolores Gray was cast as the luscious Lalume, wife of the Wazir. Hollywood kitsch at its most expensive, it was choreographed without much excitement by Jack Cole, written by Charles Lederer and Luther Davis from the play by Edward Knoblock and, in other roles, featured Monty Woolley, Jay C. Flippen, Mike Mazurki, Jack Elam, Ted De Corsia and Julie Robinson. Kismet was first seen on Broadway in 1911 as a vehicle for Otis Skinner who, in 1930, recreated his role for Warner Bros. It was remade in 1944 by MGM in a Technicolor version with a cast that was headed by Ronald Colman, and which included Marlene Dietrich and Edward Arnold, but was as unsuccessful as this latest attempt. Songs and musical numbers: *Fate*; *Gesticulate*; *The Olive Tree*; *The Sands Of Time*; *Not Since Nineveh*; *Bored*; *Baubles, Bangles And Beads*; *Stranger In Paradise*; *Night Of My Nights*; *And This Is My Beloved*; *Rahadlakum*; *Dance Of The 3 Princesses Of Ababu*.

Ruth Etting, the nightclub singer and Follies star who flourished during the twenties and thirties, was unhappily married to Martin 'The Gimp' Snyder, a limping laundryman who discovered her when she was a dance hostess in a Chicago niterie. Bettering his position in the world in direct ratio to Etting's rise to stardom 'The Gimp', while unable to manacle his wife's emotions, was perfectly capable of plugging a couple of bullets into the man she really loved – which is exactly what he did. Fortunately, the man, whom Etting later married, lived – thus providing producer Joe Pasternak with a conveniently happy ending for **Love Me Or Leave Me** (MGM), his screen version of Miss Etting's often turbulent life story. And to play Etting, Pasternak chose Doris Day (left) who, in her first movie away from Warner Bros., proved there was more to her than just her girl-next-door image. In her most dramatic role to date, she shared the acting honours with co-star James Cagney (right) as 'The Gimp' and, although his performance was the more mesmeric of the two, she coped well enough with the demands of Daniel Fuchs and Isobel Lennart's often abrasive screenplay (story by Fuchs). Two new songs, 'I'll Never Stop Loving You' by Nicholas Brodszky and Sammy Cahn and 'Never Look Back' by Chilton Price, were specially composed for the film – the rest were oldies that included Irving Berlin's 'Shaking The Blues Away', staged by Alex Romero, and the only production number as such. Cameron Mitchell played Johnny Alderman, a pianist and the man Etting really loved, with other roles under Charles Vidor's assured direction going to Robert Keith as an agent, Harry Bellaver as Cagney's all-purpose dogsbody, Tom Tully, Richard Gaines, Peter Leeds, Claude Stroud and Audrey Young. Georgie Stoll was the overall musical director, with Percy Faith in charge of Miss Day's music (Cinema-Scope and Eastmancolor). Other songs included: *Mean To Me* Roy Turk, Fred Ahlert; *Love Me Or Leave Me* Walter Donaldson, Gus Kahn; *Sam The Old Accordion Man*; *At Sundown* Donaldson; *Everybody Loves My Baby* Jack Palmer, Spencer Williams; *Stay On The Right Side Sister* Ted Koehler, Rube Bloom; *It All Depends On You* De Sylva, Brown, Henderson; *Ten Cents A Dance* Richard Rodgers, Lorenz Hart; *My Blue Heaven* Donaldson, George Whiting; *You Made Me Love You* Joseph McCarthy, James V. Monaco (all sung by Day); *I'm Sitting On Top Of The World*; *Five Foot Two* Sam M. Lewis, Joe Young, Ray Henderson.

Clearly inspired by MGM's *Seven Brides For Seven Brothers* (1954), Universal assembled a cast which included Jeanne Crain, George Nader (both top-starred, illustrated), Kitty Kallen, Bert Lahr, Paul Gilbert, Keith Andes, Mamie Van Doren, Tommy Rall and The Midwesterners to re-tell the Lysistrata story in **The Second Greatest Sex**. On this moderately bouncy occasion, it is the women of Osawkie, Kansas who, in 1880, hold back their favours when the men spend too much time in pursuit of a safe containing the official records of Kanaba County – the possessor of which gains control of the county seat. It was produced (in Technicolor) by Albert J. Cohen, choreographed by Lee Scott and directed by George Marshall. Songs and musical numbers: *Lysistrata*; *Send Us A Miracle*; *Travellin' Man*; *My Love Is Yours*; *What Good Is A Woman Without A Man?*; *There's Gonna Be A Wedding* Pony Sherrell, Phil Moody; *The Second Greatest Sex* Jay Livingston, Ray Evans; *How Lonely Can I Get* Joan Whitney, Alex Kramer.

Too familiar by half, **Ain't Misbehavin'** (Universal) was the one about the wealthy young man who falls for a chorus girl – with Rory Calhoun and Piper Laurie (centre) as the lovers. Jack Carson was third-billed in Edward Buzzell, Phillip Rapp and Devery Freeman's routine screenplay (story by Robert Carson) – as the cynical protector of Calhoun's fortune, with Mamie Van Doren, Reginald Gardiner, Barbara Britton, Lisa Gaye (left) and Dani Crayne completing the cast for producer Samuel Marx. Edward Buzzell directed (in Technicolor), and the choreographers were Kenny Williams and Lee Scott. Songs and musical numbers: *A Little Love Can Go A Long Way* Paul Francis Webster, Sammy Fain; *The Dixie Mambo* Charles Henderson, Sonny Burke; *I Love That Rickey Tickey Tickey* Sammy Cahn, Johnny Scott; *Ain't Misbehavin'* Fats Waller, Andy Razaf.

Twelve years after it first took Broadway by storm, Rodgers and Hammerstein's **Oklahoma!** reached the screen in a new process known as Todd-AO. The show itself was far better than the process it launched in which the colour varied from scene to scene and some of the images appeared decidedly distorted. Despite the shedding of one of the stage version's songs, this watershed musical transferred triumphantly to celluloid and was almost as entertaining, if not quite as magical, as it was when it first opened. Gordon MacRae (right) was cast as Curly, Shirley Jones (left) was Laurey, the girl he loves, Charlotte Greenwood was Aunt Eller and, as Will Parker and his girl Ado Annie, Gene Nelson and Gloria Grahame couldn't have been improved upon. Rod Steiger was a suitably unlikeable Jud Fry, and the cast was completed by Eddie Albert (as Ali Hakim), James Whitmore, Barbara Lawrence, Jay C. Flippen, Roy Barcroft and, substituting for MacRae and Jones in the 'Out Of My Dreams' ballet – dancers James Mitchell and Bambi Lynn. Greatly contributing to the richness of sound that was a feature of the new Todd-AO process, was Robert Russell Bennett's orchestration and the marvellous orchestral playing under the direction of Jay Blackton and Adolph Deutsch. Agnes De Mille (who helped create the show on Broadway) was again responsible for the choreography and, in numbers such as 'The Farmer And The Cowman' and 'Everything's Up To Date In Kansas City' (dynamically danced by Nelson) revealed just why she was such a major force among contemporary American choreographers. The screenplay, based on Oscar Hammerstein II's original book, was by Sonya Levien and William Ludwig, and if today it seems unavoidably dated – the corn indeed being 'as high as an elephant's eye' – 25 years ago it sounded just fine. Other songs and musical numbers: *Oh What A Beautiful Morning* (MacRae); *Surrey With The Fringe On Top* (MacRae, Jones, Greenwood); *I Cain't Say No* (Grahame); *Many A New Day* (Jones and chorus); *People Will Say We're In Love* (MacRae, Jones); *Poor Jud Is Dead* (Steiger, MacRae); *All Or Nothin'* (Nelson, Grahame); *Oklahoma!* (MacRae, Jones, Nelson, Greenwood and company).

The most original thing about **Bring Your Smile Along** (Columbia) was that the small-town boy whom Constance Towers (her debut) ditches in favour of Keefe Brasselle was personable William Leslie and not the traditional unsophisticated 'schnook' one had come to expect from stories of this kind. Written by Blake Edwards (who also directed) from a story by Edwards and Richard Quine, it was all about a New England school teacher (Towers, centre right), who leaves her biology-teacher fiancé (Leslie) to 'find herself' in New York as a lyric writer. In the big city she meets tunesmith Brasselle (right), forms a songwriting partnership with him and, in no time at all, is producing hit after hit – all of them recorded by Frankie Laine (centre left), who received top-billing in the venture. Also cast were Ida Smeraldo (left) and Mario Siletti (seated). It was choreographed by Miriam Nelson and produced in Technicolor by Jonie Taps. Songs and musical numbers: *Bring Your Smile Along* Benny Davis, Carl Fischer; *If Spring Never Comes* Bill Carey, Fischer; *Gandy Dancers Ball* Paul Mason Howard, Paul Weston; *Don't Blame Me* Dorothy Fields, Jimmy McHugh; *Side By Side* Harry Woods; *When A Girl Is Beautiful*; *Every Baby Needs A Da Da Daddy* Allan Roberts, Lester Lee; *Italian Mother Song* Ned Washington, Lee.

Filmed by 20th Century-Fox in their large-screen CinemaScope 55 process (altogether more successful than Todd-AO), Rodgers and Hammerstein's most tuneful musical, **Carousel**, offered audiences an ear and eyeful of well packaged sentimentality as Gordon MacRae and Shirley Jones re-enacted what was originally Ferenc Molnar's bitter-sweet fantasy *Liliom*. All about a carnival barker called Billy Bigelow (MacRae) who marries a cotton mill girl (Jones), is killed in an attempted robbery, then, years later, is briefly allowed to return to earth to redeem himself and to see his now grown-up daughter, it stuck faithfully to Molnar's original story while, at the same time, undergoing a change of locale from Budapest to New England. Containing some of Rodgers's finest music, it remains one of the most poignant of all Broadway musicals but, at the same time, because of the tightrope it treads between whimsy and *schmaltz*, one of the most difficult to pull off successfully. For most of the time the screen version, with a scenario by Phoebe and Henry Ephron (adapted from the stage show by Oscar Hammerstein II, from an adaptation of Molnar's play by Benjamin F. Glazer), skilfully negotiated the stickier moments in the narrative, thanks mainly to the vigorous, whole-hearted performances of a company that included Cameron Mitchell, Barbara Ruick, Claramae Turner, Robert Rounseville, Susan Luckey, Jacques D'Amboise and Gene Lockhart, as well as the sheer energy generated by Rod Alexander's choreography, especially in the exuberant 'June Is Bustin' Out All Over' (production number illustrated). Charles E. Clarke's Eastmancolor photography was superb; so was the full-bodied playing of the 20th Century-Fox studio orchestra under the direction of Alfred Newman and Ken Darby. Other songs and musical numbers: *Carousel Waltz* (orchestra); *When I Marry Mister Snow* (Ruick); *If I Loved You* (MacRae, Jones); *When The Children Are Asleep* (Rounseville, Ruick); *Soliloquy* (MacRae); *Stonecutters Cut It On Stone* (Mitchell, chorus); *What's The Use Of Wondrin'* (Jones); *A Real Nice Clambake* (Rounseville, Ruick, Mitchell, Turner); *You'll Never Walk Alone* (Jones, Turner); *Carousel Ballet* (Luckey, D'Amboise).

▽

◁ Ye olde mediaeval plotte involving, among other things, wicked olde usurpers to the throne, formed the riotous content of **The Court Jester** (Paramount). The second best thing about it was its total lack of inhibition in matters farcical; the first was the happy casting of Danny Kaye (illustrated) as the titular hero of the piece. Beginning as a potboy to a forest leader, Kaye champions an heir to the throne of England and, in the guise of court jester, gains access to the court of evil Basil Rathbone, whom he schemes to overthrow. Angela Lansbury was cast as Princess Gwendolyn, Glynis Johns was Maid Jean, with other parts in producer-directors Norman Panama and Melvin Frank's knock-about screenplay going to Cecil Parker, Mildred Natwick (as necromancer Griselda), Robert Middleton, Michael Pate, Herbert Rudley, Noel Drayton, John Carradine, Alan Napier and Hermine's Midgets. The songs were by Mrs Danny Kaye (Sylvia Fine) and Sammy Cahn, and the choreography by James Starbuck. (Vistavision and Technicolor). Songs and musical numbers: *Life Could Not Better Be*; *Outfox The Fox*; *I'll Take You Dreaming*; *My Heart Knows A Love Song* Fine, Cahn; *Maladjusted Jester* Fine.

△

Long-legged, loose-limbed Cyd Charisse (illustrated), billed second to Dan Dailey, was the best thing in and about MGM's **Meet Me In Las Vegas** (GB: **Viva Las Vegas**). A simple-minded little yarn, gaudily accoutred in CinemaScope and Eastmancolor, it was set in and about The Sands Hotel, Nevada, and told what happens when a gambling rancher (Dailey) discovers that all he has to do to win at roulette is take hold of ballerina Charisse's hand. Joe Pasternak's high-gloss production gave potential visitors to Vegas a pretty good idea of what the place looks like; Isobel Lennart's screenplay was not without its quota of gags and wisecracks, and the dance routines, by Hermes Pan and Eugene Loring (the latter responsible for the 'Frankie and Johnny Ballet', lyrics by Sammy Cahn), danced by Charisse, John Brascia and Liliane Montevecchi, and sung offstage by Sammy Davis Jr, were entertaining enough. Agnes Moorehead appeared as Dailey's mother, with other parts under Roy Rowland's commonplace direction going to Lili Darvas, Jim Backus, Paul Henreid and Oskar Karlweis. Making guest appearances were Lena Horne, Frankie Laine, Jerry Colonna, Mitsuko Sawamura, Frank Sinatra, Tony Martin and Debbie Reynolds. Other songs and musical numbers: *The Gal With The Yaller Shoes* (Dailey); *If You Can't Dream* (Horne); *My Lucky Charm* (Dailey and Japanese child); *Hell Hath No Fury* (Laine) Sammy Cahn, Nicholas Brodszky; *Rondo Brilliante* (Charisse) Mendelssohn; *Sleeping Beauty* (excerpt, Charisse) Tchaikovsky.

With **The Benny Goodman Story**, Universal-International attempted to do for the clarinettist what *The Glenn Miller Story* (1954) had done for the trombonist but, unfortunately, although the production team was to some extent the same, the results were not nearly as successful. Labouring under a plodding and unimaginative screenplay by Valentine Davies, who also directed, was a cast headed by Steve Allen (right) – making his motion picture debut as Goodman – Donna Reed (left) as his wife, and Berta Gersten as his mother. Also: Herbert Anderson, Robert F. Simon, Sammy Davis Jr, Dick Winslow, Barry Truex, David Kasday, Hy Averback and Wilton Graff. The familiar story of the slum kid who makes good, forms his own swing band, struggles a bit, becomes a successful impresario, then marries into society, its best moments had nothing whatsoever to do with the narrative, but were the result of the copious amount of music appended to it. And, with the participation of Harry James, Gene Krupa, Martha Tilton, Lionel Hampton, Ziggy Elman and Kid Ory – the music was in good hands. It was produced, in Technicolor, by Aaron Rosenberg. Steve Allen's clarinet playing was dubbed by Goodman himself. Musical numbers included: *Let's Dance* Fanny Baldridge, Gregory Stone, Joseph Bonine; *Down South Camp Meeting* Irving Mills, Fletcher Henderson; *It's Been So Long* Walter Donaldson, Harold Adamson; *Bugle-Call Rag* Elmer Schoebel, Billy Meyers, Jack Pettis; *Goody, Goody* Johnny Mercer, Matt Malneck; *Don't Be That Way* Goodman, Mitchell Parish, Edgar Sampson; *Shine* (Harry James) Cecil Mack, Lew Brown, Ford Dabney; *Sing, Sing, Sing* (James, Krupa) Louis Prima; *Stompin' At The Savoy* Goodman, Sampson, Chick Webb, Andy Razaf; *One O'Clock Jump* Count Basie; *Memories Of You* (trio) Eubie Blake, Andy Razaf; *And The Angels Sing* (Tilton) Johnny Mercer, Ziggy Elman; *China Boy* Dick Winfree, Phil Boutelje; *Moonglow* Will Hudson, Eddie DeLange, Irving Mills; *Avalon* Al Jolson, Vincent Rose; *Sensation Rag* E.B. Edwards; *Original Dixieland One Step* (Allen, Ory) Nick La Rocca; *On The Sunny Side Of The Street* (Teddy Wilson) Jimmy McHugh, Dorothy Fields; *King Porter Stomp* Jelly Roll Morton; *Roll 'Em* Mary Lou Williams; *Clarinet Concerto* Mozart.

△

A vintage MGM musical, **High Society**, with a melodious score by Cole Porter, was a Technicolor remake of Philip Barry's *The Philadelphia Story*, first seen as a Broadway play in 1939, then as an MGM film the following year starring Katharine Hepburn, Cary Grant and James Stewart. The musical remake boasted an equally glittering cast with Bing Crosby (left) top-starred as C.K. Dexter Haven, and Grace Kelly (centre) as his ex-wife, a Philadelphia heiress on the verge of marrying husband number two (John Lund). Frank Sinatra (right) was third-billed as a newspaper reporter assigned to cover Miss Kelly's impending marriage, with Celeste Holm also in it as his chic assistant. The rest of the cast was completed by Louis Calhern, Sidney Blackmer, Margalo Gillmore, Lydia Reed, Richard Keene, Hugh Boswell and, prominently featured as himself, Louis Armstrong. John Patrick's screenplay stuck closely to the guide-lines laid down in Barry's play, with Crosby successfully wooing Kelly away from Lund to ensure a happy ending. All the performances under Charles Walters's direction sparkled, the undoubted musical highlight being Crosby and Armstrong's memorable foray into 'Now You Has Jazz', with Sinatra and Holm's 'Who Wants To Be A Millionaire?' running a close second. Sol C. Siegel produced. Other songs: *High Society Calypso* (Armstrong); *Little One* (Crosby); *True Love* (Crosby, Kelly); *You're Sensational* (Sinatra); *I Love You Samantha* (Crosby, Armstrong); *Well, Did You Evah* (Crosby, Sinatra); *Mind If I Make Love To You?* (Sinatra).

Dean Martin and Jerry Lewis's final film as a team was **Hollywood Or Bust** (Paramount), the bust of the title belonging to Anita Ekberg who, although appearing only towards the end of the film, was referred to throughout as the star film-fan Jerry Lewis most wants to meet. How, in the company of bookie Dean Martin, and Pat Crowley (both illustrated) a girl they encounter while motoring from New York to Hollywood, he finally succeeds in doing so, formed the undernourished content of Erna Lazarus's screenplay. Fortunately director Frank Tashlin managed to endow it with a sense of humour not apparent in the dialogue, his staging of the title number being almost surreal as hordes of pretty, waving girls decorate the roadside from coast to coast. A few comic routines – such as Lewis attempting to fix Miss Crowley's broken-down car, and his skirmish with an aggressive bull – hardly extended the comedian's gifts, nor did the songs written by Sammy Fain and Paul Francis Webster for Martin stretch him as a crooner. In short, predictable entertainment (Vistavision and Technicolor). Maxie Rosenbloom and Jack McElroy completed the cast for producer Hal Wallis. Other songs: *A Day In The Country*; *Let's Be Friendly*; *It Looks Like Love*; *The Wild And Woolly West*. ▷

△

Gene Kelly began work on **Invitation To The Dance** (MGM) as early as 1952. It was to be a specialized, yet popular, film in four separate parts, utilizing the talents of some of Europe and America's best dancers. Four years later it was finally released having, in the interim, shed sequence number three, in which Kelly and several other dancers interpreted, through the medium of dance, a dozen popular songs. The first of the three remaining ballets was 'Circus'. Composed by Jacques Ibert, it was the tale of a love-sick Pierrot (Kelly) who falls to his death from a high-wire trapeze while trying to impress the girl he loves (Claire Sombert), who loves another (Igor Youskevitch). The second segment, 'Ring Around The Rosy', had music by Andre Previn and was a *La Ronde* type of story which traced the history of a bracelet given by a doting husband to his wife who, in turn, gives it to an artist, who gives it to a model whence it passes to a crook, a nightclub siren, a crooner, a hat-check girl, a sailor, a whore and, finally, back to the husband. It was danced by Kelly (right), Tamara Toumanova (left), Tommy Rall, Claude Bessy, Diane Adams, Igor Youskevitch, Paddy Stone and Irving Davies. The third and final item was 'Sinbad The Sailor', with music from Rimsky-Korsakov's *Scheherazade*. It combined live-action with animated cartoon figures, featured Kelly as a sailor, young David Kasday as a genie, and Carol Haney as Scheherazade. Of the three sections, the middle, being closest in spirit to a typical large scale MGM production number, was the most successful, with some marvellous dancing in it from Tommy Rall. The finale was effective, too, while the first, despite an excellent *pas de deux* by Kelly and Claire Sombert, was relentlessly mannered and pretentious. In it Kelly strove to be the kind of classical dancer he patently was not and the strain showed. The cartoon sequences were directed by Fred Quimby, William Hanna and Joseph Barbera; Kelly served throughout as both choreographer and director, with Arthur Freed in charge of the production. It was photographed in Technicolor by Joseph Ruttenberg and F.A. Young.

Fifties Musicals

Yul Brynner's justly celebrated performance as the King of Siam in Rodgers and Hammerstein's long-running Broadway smash was dynamically captured in the screen version of **The King And I** (20th Century-Fox), lavishly produced by Charles Brackett. Though Gertrude Lawrence was not on hand to repeat her performance as Anna, the school teacher who, with a son of her own, journeys from England to Siam to undertake the education of the King's children, Deborah Kerr was, and, happily – with her vocals dubbed by Marni Nixon – proved to be more than a match for the dominating Brynner (illustrated centre). It was a performance full of warmth and tenderness and, although her role in *From Here To Eternity* (Columbia, 1953) was showier, it was one of the best things she has ever done. Under the direction of Alfred Newman and Ken Darby, Rodgers's marvellous score had never sounded so good, nor had choreographer Jerome Robbins's set-piece, 'The Little House Of Uncle Thomas', ever looked as good. And although four numbers – 'My Lord and Master', 'Shall I Tell You What I Think Of You', 'Western People Funny' and 'I Have Dreamed' – were excised for the film, it did not prevent the celluloid version of the show from achieving the rare distinction of being even more satisfying than the original stage presentation. Rita Moreno was cast as the King's slave Tuptim, and Carlos Rivas as her lover Lun Tha, with other roles under Walter Lang's stylish direction going to Martin Benson, Terry Saunders, Rex Thompson (as Kerr's young son), Alan Mowbray, Patrick Adiarte, and, in the 'Uncle Thomas' ballet, Yuriko, Marion Jim, Robert Banas and Dusty Worrall. It was photographed in CinemaScope 55 and Eastmancolor by Leon Shamroy; the superb costumes were by Irene Sharaff, the sets by Walter M. Scott and Paul S. Fox, and the art direction by Lyle Wheeler and John De Cuir. The screenplay, based on Oscar Hammerstein II's book which, in turn, was based on Anna Leonowens's book *Anna And The King Of Siam*, was by Ernest Lehman. Other songs and musical numbers: *I Whistle A Happy Tune* (Kerr, Thompson); *Hello Young Lovers* (Kerr); *March Of The Siamese Children*; *A Puzzlement* (Brynner); *Getting To Know You* (Kerr, children); *We Kiss In A Shadow* (Moreno, Rivas); *Something Wonderful* (Saunders); *Song Of The King* (Brynner); *Shall We Dance* (Brynner, Kerr).

Director Anthony Mann, who was responsible for some of the best Westerns of the 50s, contended successfully with the wide open spaces of Mario Lanza's girth in **Serenade**, a melodrama from Warner Bros. which told the story of a Californian vineyard worker's rise to operatic eminence, and the rivalry of two women – one American and rich, the other Mexican and poor – who are attracted to him. In their adaptation of James M. Cain's novel, screenwriters Ivan Goff, Ben Roberts and John Twist eliminated the homosexual elements, making it considerably less gritty and *noir*; but, as a vehicle for Lanza, it proved more effective than most, and offered him ample opportunity to tackle numerous operatic excerpts, folk numbers, and two romantic songs, 'Serenade' and 'My Destiny', written for the film by Nicholas Brodszky and Sammy Cahn. Joan Fontaine played the society patroness who collects talent, and Sarita Montiel (illustrated with Lanza) the fiery Latin ready to kill for love. Also featured were Vincent Price as a smooth impresario, Harry Bellaver as Lanza's manager, and Joseph Calleia as his voice coach. It was photographed in WarnerColor (there was some splendid location shooting at San Miguel de Allende) by J. Peverell Marley, and produced by Henry Blanke. Other songs and operatic excerpts: *Torna A Sorrento* Ernesto de Curtis, Claude Aveling; *La Danza* Rossini; *Ave Maria* Schubert; *Lamento di Federico* (from 'L'Arlesiana') Cilea; *O Soave Fanciulla* (from 'La Boheme', sung with Jean Fenn) Puccini; *Italian Tenor Aria* (from 'Der Rosenkavalier', Act 1) Richard Strauss; *Amor Ti Vieta* (from 'Fedora') Giordano; *Di Quella Pira* (from 'Il Trovatore') Verdi; *Dio Ti Giocondi* (from 'Otello' sung with Licia Albanese) Verdi; *Il Mio Tesoro* (from 'Don Giovanni') Mozart; *O Paradis, Sorti De L'Onde* (from 'L'Africaine') Meyerbeer; *Nessun Dorma* (from 'Turandot') Puccini.

A programmer with a Latin-American beat to it, **Cha-Cha-Cha-Boom** (Columbia) featured Perez Prado, The Mary Kaye Trio (illustrated), Helen Grayce, and bandleaders Luis Arcaraz and Manny Lopez (as themselves) in a serviceable story (by James B. Gordon) involving the efforts of a talent scout (Steve Dunne) – who also happens to own a recording company – to find some exciting new talent. Alix Talton, José Gonzales Gonzales, Sylvia Lewis, Dante De Paulo, Charles Evans and Howard Wright completed the cast for producer Sam Katzman; the dances were staged by Earl Barton, and it was directed by Fred F. Sears. Songs and musical numbers included: *Get Happy* Ted Koehler, Harold Arlen; *Lonesome Road* Gene Austin, Nathaniel Shilkret; *Save Your Sorrow* Buddy De Sylva, Al Sherman; *Lily's Lament*; *Year Round Love*; *Cuban Rock And Roll*; *Voodoo Suite*; *Crazy Crazy*; *Mambo No. 8*.

Filmed three times before – by Fox in 1920 (with William Farnum), and by Paramount in 1930 and 1938 (with Dennis King and Ronald Colman respectively) – **The Vagabond King** reached the screen yet again, but this time in Vistavision and Technicolor and with a strapping young Maltese tenor called Oreste (full name Oreste Kirkop, illustrated centre) making his screen debut as the dashing poet François Villon. The heroine of the Rudolf Friml-William H. Post-Brian Hooker warhorse (it was first seen on stage in 1902) was Kathryn Grayson, with other roles in Ken Englund and Noel Langley's new version of it assigned to Rita Moreno (centre left) as the doomed tavern maid Huguette, Walter Hampden (excellent) as wily King Louis XI, a monarch who'd gamble the fate of France to ensure Villon's powerful support, Sir Cedric Hardwicke as Louis's counsellor Tristan, and Leslie Nielsen and William Prince as the traditional villains of the piece. All the music was by Friml, some of it – such as 'Only A Rose', 'Song of the Vagabonds', 'Some Day', 'Vive Le You' and the attractive 'Valse Huguette' – from the original score with lyrics by Brian Hooker; the rest specially composed with lyrics by Johnny Burke. These included a spirited dance called 'Watch Out For The Devil', 'Bon Jour' and 'This Same Heart'. The choreography was by Hanya Holm, Michael Curtiz directed with as much vigour as the tired old subject would allow, and it was produced for Paramount by Pat Duggan. The cast was completed by Jack Lord, Billy Vine, Henry MacNaughton, Lucie Lancaster, Gregory Morton and Gavin Gordon.

△

Bing Crosby's twenty-two-year stint at Paramount came to an end with **Anything Goes** – a remake, in Vistavision and Technicolor, of Cole Porter's celebrated Broadway success, first unspooled in 1936 with Crosby and Ethel Merman in the leads. Flinging out the original P.G. Wodehouse-Guy Bolton story (which wasn't much good anyway), scenarist Sidney Sheldon came up with one that wasn't much better. It teamed Donald O'Connor with Crosby for the first time since *Sing You Sinners* (Paramount, 1938) – and together they were cast as a couple of big-name stars who embark on a round-the-world cruise in search of a suitable female lead for their forthcoming show. Love enters their lives in the pleasing shapes of Jeanmaire and Mitzi Gaynor (illustrated with Crosby), and that was about the gist of it. Fortunately Porter's score was more substantial than the narrative it embellished and, with the addition of three new passable Jimmy Van Heusen-Sammy Cahn numbers, it was musically satisfying. Crosby sang such standards as 'You're The Top' (together with the other leads) and the immortal 'All Through The Night'; Gaynor gave out with a lively performance of the title number; O'Connor was at his best in 'You Can Bounce Right Back' (by Van Heusen and Cahn); and Jeanmaire – in a dream ballet choreographed by her husband Roland Petit – brought a *soupçon* of 'culture' to the decidedly uncultural proceedings. Sharing the choreography credit were Nick Castle and Ernie Flatt; it was directed without much flair by Robert Lewis and produced by Robert Emmett Dolan with a cast that also included Phil Harris as Gaynor's tax-dodging father, Kurt Kasznar, Richard Erdman, Walter Sande and Argentina Brunetti. Other songs and musical numbers: *I Get A Kick Out Of You* (Jeanmaire); *It's DeLovely* (O'Connor, Gaynor); *Blow, Gabriel, Blow* (Crosby, O'Connor, Gaynor, Jeanmaire) Porter; *You Gotta Give The People Hoke* (Crosby, O'Connor); *A Second-Hand Turban And A Crystal Ball* (Crosby, O'Connor) Van Heusen, Cahn.

A dispiriting remake of *Bachelor Mother* (RKO, 1939), **Bundle Of Joy** (RKO), with Debbie Reynolds (right) in the role originally played by Ginger Rogers, was the story of a saleslady in a department store who is fired just before Christmas, finds a baby on a doorstep, is reinstated in her job, becomes something of a celebrity, attracts the attention of Eddie Fisher (left – his movie debut), the son of the store's owner (Adolphe Menjou), and marries him after the parentage of the foundling has satisfactorily been settled. With little assistance from scenarists Norman Krasna, Robert Carson and Arthur Sheekman (story by Felix Jackson), or from Josef Myrow and Mack Gordon whose score was as unexciting as the plot it accompanied, the strain of injecting credulity into it all was more than its principal players could endure and the whole thing collapsed with a dull thud. The perfunctory dance routines were staged by Nick Castle, Edmund Grainger produced it (in Technicolor), Norman Taurog directed, and the cast included Nita Talbot, Tommy Noonan, Una Merkel, Melville Cooper, and Bill Goodwin. Songs and musical numbers: *I Never Felt This Way Before*; *Lullaby In Blue*; *Worry About Tomorrow Tomorrow*; *All About Love*; *Someday Soon*; *Bundle Of Joy*; *What's So Good About Morning*.

▽

Top recording star Elvis Presley made his motion picture debut in **Love Me Tender** (20th Century-Fox), a western whose narrative line (by Maurice Geraghty, screenplay by Robert Buckner) was interrupted on four occasions by Presley's unique way with a song. For the rest it was a routine backwoods drama in which Presley (right) was cast as a Texas farm boy who, during the civil war, marries his cavalryman brother's sweetheart when news of his brother's death filters through. But the brother – played by Richard Egan (left) – isn't dead at all and, after returning home, incurs Presley's jealousy by resuming his friendship with his former sweetheart (Debra Paget, centre). The situation went from bad to worse; so, alas, did the film. David Weisbart produced, Robert D. Webb directed, and the cast included Robert Middleton, William Campbell, Neville Brand, Mildred Dunnock, Bruce Bennett, Russ Conway, James Drury and Ken Clark. It was photographed in CinemaScope and black and white. Songs: *Love Me Tender* (adapted from 'Aura Lea') W.W. Fosdick, George R. Poulton; *Poor Boy*; *We're Gonna Move*; *Let Me* Elvis Presley, Vera ◁ Matson.

In 1939 Clare Booth Luce's long-running Broadway hit *The Women* was turned into a classic MGM comedy. Seventeen years later, with the addition of CinemaScope, Metrocolor, six songs, several gentlemen, and a new title **The Opposite Sex**, it lost its classic status in the remake under producer Joe Pasternak's supervision but, as an extended cat fight, was pretty good entertainment just the same. Demure little June Allyson headed the cast in the role created by Norma Shearer, and what little plot there was between the gossiping and the ruining of reputations, concerned Allyson's 10-year-old marriage to producer Leslie Nielsen and whether or not it would last much longer. Though Fay and Michael Kanin's updating of Miss Booth's acerbic observations about the female sex lacked the barbed sting of the original, it was not without its more satiric moments, though none of the performances – with the possible exception of Miss Allyson (illustrated in production number) – came anywhere near those given by the stellar cast assembled by producer Hunt Stromberg in 1939. Nor was the direction, by David Miller, anything like as effective as George Cukor's. However, the performances of Joan Collins (as Crystal), Dolores Gray (Sylvia), Ann Sheridan (Amanda), Ann Miller (Gloria), Agnes Moorehead (the Countess) and Joan Blondell (Edith) were as good as the screenplay allowed them to be. Completing the cast were Charlotte Greenwood, Sam Levene, Jeff Richards, Bill Goodwin, Alice Pearce, Barbara Jo Allen, Jerry Antes and Carolyn Jones, with appearances by Harry James, Dick Shawn, Jim Backus and Art Mooney. Songs: *Now Baby Now*; *A Perfect Love*; *Rock And Roll Tumbleweed*; *Yellow Gold*; *The Opposite Sex* Nicholas Brodszky, Sammy Cahn, and *Young Man With A Horn* Ralph Freed, George Stoll, first heard in MGM's *Two Girls and a Sailor* (1944).

▽

There was something decidedly maudlin about **The Eddie Duchin Story** (Columbia) which the accompanying music only served to underline. A four-handkerchief weepie almost from start to finish, it chronicled, with a constant lump in its throat, the sad life that dogged pianist-cum-bandleader Duchin during the thirties and forties. Starting with his arrival in New York and his failure to land the job he was after, and ending with his death, the narrative fashioned by scenarist Samuel Taylor, from a story by Leo Katcher, was little more than a catalogue of woes, the most poignant being the death of Duchin's wife, Marjorie Oelrichs, shortly after the birth of their son. Tyrone Power (left) was top-cast as Duchin, Kim Novak was adequate (but only just) as his wife, Victoria Shaw played Chiquita, an English girl and the second love of his life, and Rex Thompson (right) was his 12-year-old son, with other roles in Jerry Wald's lugubrious production going to James Whitmore, Mickey Maga, Shepperd Strudwick, Frieda Inescort, Gloria Holden, Larry Keating and John Mylong. The director was George Sidney. Power's piano playing was dubbed by Carmen Cavallaro. Among nearly thirty numbers played were: *La Vie En Rose* Edith Piaf, R.S. Louiguy; *Manhattan* Richard Rodgers, Lorenz Hart; *Shine On Harvest Moon* Jack Norworth, Nora Bayes; *It Must Be True* Gus Arnheim, Gordon Clifford, Harry Barris; *Let's Fall In Love* Harold Arlen, Ted Koehler; *Exactly Like You* Dorothy Fields, Jimmy McHugh; *Dizzy Fingers* Zez Confrey; *I'll Take Romance* Oscar Hammerstein II, Ben Oakland; *Smiles* J. Will Callahan, Lee S. Roberts; *Shine* Cecil Mack, Lew Brown, Ford Dabney; *You're My Everything* Harry Warren, Mort Dixon, Joe Young; *Brazil* Ary Barrosa, Bob Russell; *Sweet Sue* Will J. Harris, Victor Young; *Ain't She Sweet* Jack Yellen, Milton Ager; *April Showers* Buddy De Sylva, Louis Silvers; *Three O'Clock In The Morning* Dorothy Terriss, Julian Robledo; *Till We Meet Again* Ray Egan, Richard A. Whiting; *The Man I Love* George and Ira Gershwin; *Blue Room* Rodgers, Hart; *What Is This Thing Called Love?* Cole Porter.

By 1956 Hollywood was fast running out of songsmiths whose lives could be glorified and/or mangled in some distorted biopic. Mining the last vein in this particular area of the musical, 20th Century-Fox surfaced with **The Best Things In Life Are Free** – a tribute, in CinemaScope and Color De Luxe, to the work of Buddy De Sylva, Ray Henderson and Lew Brown who were as active in Hollywood in the thirties as they were on Broadway in the twenties. As written by William Bowers and Phoebe Ephron from a story by John O'Hara, the film was little more than a compendium of incidents culled from the three men's lives (starting with their meeting in Atlantic City, and taking in such monumental show-biz events as the composing of 'Sonny Boy' for Al Jolson) without much emphasis on characterization. Gordon MacRae (centre), Ernest Borgnine (left) and Dan Dailey (right) were De Sylva, Brown and Henderson respectively; but for all the acting they were called on to do, they might just as well have been playing themselves. As Kitty Kane, the female lead (and the girl De Sylva/MacRae falls for), Sheree North (front right) was prettier than all three of them put together and, with dancer Jacques D'Amboise and chorus, gave the movie two of its few cherishable moments in the 'Black Bottom' and 'The Birth Of The Blues', the latter danced by North and sung by MacRae. Rod Alexander choreographed, Henry Ephron produced, Michael Curtiz directed with pace and Tommy Noonan, Murvyn Vye, Phyllis Avery, Larry Keating, Byron Palmer, Roxanne Arlen, Tony Galento and Norman Brooks (as Jolson) completed the cast. Sheree North's vocals were dubbed by Eileen Wilson. Other songs and musical numbers: *The Best Things In Life Are Free; Sonny Boy; You Try Somebody Else; Without Love; This Is The Missus; Button Up Your Overcoat; This Is My Lucky Day; Sunny Side Up; Together; One More Time; It All Depends On You; Broken Hearted; If I Had A Talking Picture Of You; Don't Hold Everything; Just A Memory; Good News; Lucky In Love.*

A slick musical remake, in CinemaScope and Technicolor, of Columbia's Academy Award winning 1934 comedy *It Happened One Night*, **You Can't Run Away From It** (Columbia), starred June Allyson (left) as the runaway heiress originally played by Claudette Colbert, and Jack Lemmon (right), in the role originated by Clark Gable, as the out of work reporter she meets and with whom she travels across country, unaware of his profession and of his intentions of returning her to her distraught father (Charles Bickford) for the reward money. The update was by Claude Binyon and Robert Riskin (who wrote the original screenplay) from a short story by Samuel Hopkins Adams, and the cast for producer-director Dick Powell (husband of June Allyson) included Paul Gilbert, Jim Backus, Stubby Kaye, Henny Youngman, Allyn Joslyn, Jacques Scott, Walter Baldwin, Byron Foulger, Louise Beavers and, heard but not seen, The Four Aces. The songs were by Johnny Mercer and Gene De Paul and included: *You Can't Run Away From It; Howdy Friends And Neighbours; Temporarily; Thumbing A Ride; Scarecrow Ballet.*

Academy Awards

Writing (New Classifications)
Two awards for writing instead of three as given since 1940

(Story and Screenplay)
written directly for the screen
NOMINATIONS INCLUDED: *Funny Face* (Paramount) Leonard Gershe

Cinematography (New Classification)
One award instead of separate awards for black-and-white and colour films, for the first year since 1938
NOMINATIONS INCLUDED: *Funny Face* Ray June

Jayne Mansfield (left) of limited talent and squeaky voice fame, made her first starring appearance in **The Girl Can't Help It** (20th Century-Fox), a spoof, with intermittent moments of fun, on the rock craze. Borrowing quite heavily from Garson Kanin's plot of *Born Yesterday* (first seen as a Broadway play, then as a Columbia film in 1950), Frank Tashlin and Herbert Baker's screenplay was all about an agent's attempts to groom a gangster's moll (Mansfield) for stardom, with the accent throughout being on Miss M.'s vital – in this instance very vital – statistics. Tom Ewell (right) was top-billed as the agent and Edmond O'Brien was cast as the gangster; with other parts going to Henry Jones, John Emery and Juanita Moore. Musically, there was a full programme and, on numerous occasions, performers such as Julie London, Ray Anthony, Fats Domino, The Platters, The Treniers, Little Richard, Gene Vincent, The Chuckles, Eddie Fontaine, Abbey Lincoln, Johnny Olen, Nino Tempo and Eddie Cochran, came to the rescue of the leading players when the script simply ground to a halt. It was produced and directed by Tashlin, and photographed in CinemaScope and Eastmancolor. Songs included: *Rock Around The Rockpile; The Girl Can't Help It; She's Got It; Ready Teddy* John Marascalco, Robert A. Blackwell; *Be-Bop-A-Lu-La* Vincent, Sheriff Tom Davis; *Cool It Baby; Everytime; Big Band Boogie; 20 Flight Rock; Spread The Word; Blue Monday* Domino, Dave Bartholomew; *The Great Pretender* Buck Ram; *Cry Me A River* Arthur Hamilton.

Art Direction (Set Decoration)
(New Classification)

One award instead of separate awards for black-and-white and colour films, for the first year since 1939.

NOMINATIONS INCLUDED: *Funny Face* Hal Pereira and George W. Davis; Sam Comer and Ray Moyer. *Les Girls* (MGM) William A. Horning and Gene Allen; Edwin B. Willis and Richard Pefferle. *Pal Joey* (Columbia) Walter Holscher; William Kiernan and Louis Diage.

Costume Design (New Classification)

One award instead of separate awards for black-and-white and colour films, for the first time in this category)

Les Girls Orry-Kelly

NOMINATIONS INCLUDED: *Funny Face* Edith Head and Hubert de Givenchy. *Pal Joey* Jean Louis.

Sound Recording

NOMINATIONS INCLUDED: *Les Girls* M-G-M Studio Sound Dept.; Dr Wesley C. Miller,

sound director. *Pal Joey* Columbia Studio Sound Dept.; John Livadary, sound director.

Film Editing

NOMINATIONS INCLUDED: *Pal Joey* Viola Lawrence and Jerome Thoms

Music
Song

'All The Way' *The Joker Is Wild* (Paramount) Jimmy Van Heusen *cm*; Sammy Cahn *lyr*.

NOMINATIONS INCLUDED: 'April Love' *April Love* (20th Century-Fox) Sammy Fain *cm*; Paul Francis Webster *lyr*.

The New York Times Annual 'Ten Best'

2nd *Funny Face*. 6th *Silk Stockings* (MGM). 8th *Les Girls*.

The Annual Top Moneymaking Films

INCLUDED: *Pal Joey*. *Love Me Tender* (20th Century-Fox). *April Love*. *Jailhouse Rock* (MGM). *Loving You* (Paramount)

△
Stylish, elegant, ultra-sophisticated, and fun to experience, **Funny Face** was a Paramount production which had all the panache of a vintage MGM musical. No accident this, since its producer, Roger Edens, and its director, Stanley Donen, were members of Arthur Freed's unit at Culver City. Also in its favour were a handful of George and Ira Gershwin standards (four of them from the original *Funny Face* stage show of 1927), plus a superb cast headed by Audrey Hepburn (right), Fred Astaire (left), and the delicious Kay Thompson. The simple story of a waif-like Greenwich Village bookseller (Hepburn), who is discovered by fashion photographer Astaire and whisked off to Paris where, with a bit of help from fashion magazine editor Thompson, she is transformed into a top model, it had its tongue well in its cheek in its attitudes to the synthetic *milieu* of high fashion, and also took a few satiric jibes at the then popular Existentialist movement – Hepburn becoming an *habitué* of a dimly-lit Existential hang-out. Though Astaire was getting too old to play the kind of romantic lead Leonard Gershe's screenplay (based on an unproduced stage musical called *Wedding Day*) called for, he substituted charm for youth and, in such numbers as 'Let's

Kiss And make Up' and 'He Loves And She Loves' (both by the Gershwins), he still had magic. As the character he played was based on photographer Richard Avedon, it was fitting that Avedon was engaged as visual consultant on the film – a move which resulted in **Funny Face** being the most ravishingly photographed musical since *An American In Paris* (MGM, 1950). From the opening 'Think Pink' production number (by Leonard Gershe and Roger Edens) – in which Thompson exhorts the women of the world to do just that – to Hepburn's 'Basal Metabolism' dance in a smoky Paris bistro, colour was one of the film's chief ingredients and a contributing factor to its success. Stanley Donen staged the songs, and Eugene Loring was in charge of the dance direction with Astaire; it was photographed (in Vistavision and Technicolor) by Ray June and John P. Fulton, costumed by Edith Head and Hubert de Givenchy and, in secondary roles, featured Michel Auclaire as 'Empathicalist' Emile Flostre, Robert Flemyng, Dovima, Virginia Gibson, Ruta Lee, Alex Gerry and the glamorous Suzy Parker. Other songs and musical numbers: *Funny Face* (Astaire, Hepburn); *How Long Has This Been Going On?* (Hepburn); *Clap Yo' Hands* (Astaire, Thompson); *S'Wonderful* (Astaire, Hepburn) the Gershwins; *Bonjour Paris* (Astaire, Thompson, Hepburn); *On How To Be Lovely* (Thompson, Hepburn) Gershe, Edens; *Marche Funebre* Edens.

Dean Martin's first film *sans* Jerry Lewis was **Ten Thousand Bedrooms** (MGM), and it wasn't only his erstwhile partner that was missing, but a workable screenplay. In one of his feeblest productions to date, Joe Pasternak was content to rely on the star's easygoing manner and relaxed way with a tune to see him through this tale of a wealthy owner (Martin, right) of a chain of luxury hotels who, while on a business trip to the Eternal City, becomes involved with a couple of sisters, one of whom was played by Eva Bartok, the other by Anna Maria Alberghetti (left). Miss B. knows how to behave herself in the company of a man (even a millionaire); Miss A. does not – yet almost succeeds in hooking him. Trite beyond endurance, it was far better to look at (in CinemaScope and Metrocolor) than it was to listen to, with the location footage of Rome enough of an attraction to make one wish one was there rather than in the cinema. Richard Thorpe's direction was as enervating as the script, a condition which also affected supporting players Paul Henreid, Marcel Dalio (centre), Jules Munshin, Dewey Martin, Walter Slezak and Dean Jones. Nicholas Brodszky and Sammy Cahn wrote the mediocre score. Songs: *Ten Thousand Bedrooms*; *Money Is A Problem*; *You I Love*; *Only Trust Your Heart* Brodszky, Cahn; *Guaglione (The Man Who Plays The Mandolin)* George Fancuilli; *Nisa* Marilyn Keith, Alan Bergman.
▽

Another Joe Pasternak production, **This Could Be The Night** (MGM)· was, in a less colourful way, just as trite and silly as *Ten Thousand Bedrooms*. Set in a nightclub run by two Runyonesque gangster types – Paul Douglas (left) and Anthony Franciosa – it was the story of a love affair that blossoms between Franciosa and Jean Simmons (right), who is a schoolteacher by day and a secretary by night. Based on short stories by Cordelia Baird Gross, Isobel Lennart's screenplay set out to show that, with the right sort of personnel, a nightclub can be just as cosy as a home! The personnel in this instance were chef J. Carrol Naish – a real father to his staff – nightclub cuties Julie Wilson and Neile Adams, and an assortment of characters played by Joan Blondell, Rafael Compos, ZaSu Pitts, Tom Helmore, Murvyn Vye and Frank Ferguson. Supplying the music – and there was a great deal of it – were Ray Anthony and His Orchestra and the Misses Wilson and Adams. Aiming for atmosphere (it was photographed in CinemaScope and black and white) but failing to achieve it was director Robert Wise. Songs included: *This Could Be The Night*; *Hustlin' News Gal*; *I Got It Bad* Duke Ellington, Paul Francis Webster; *I'm Gonna Live Till I Die* Al Hoffman, Walter Kent, Mann Curtis; *Taking A Chance On Love* John Latouche, Ted Fetter, Vernon Duke; *Blue Moon* Richard Rodgers, Lorenz Hart; *Dream Dancing* Cole Porter; *The Tender Trap* Sammy Cahn, Jimmy Van Heusen; *Trumpet Boogie*; *Mamba Combo*.

△

Silk Stockings (MGM) played 478 performances on Broadway, its source being the 1939 MGM comedy *Ninotchka* which starred Greta Garbo, and which came from a story by Melchior Lengyal, with a screenplay by Charles Brackett, Billy Wilder, Ernst Lubitsch and Walter Reisch. With Fred Astaire in the lead, the screen version of **Silk Stockings**, produced by Arthur Freed, stuck more closely in plot outline to the Broadway musical (by George Kaufman, Leueen McGrath and Abe Burrows) than it did to the earlier film, with scenarists Leonard Gershe and Leonard Spigelgass structuring their screenplay to allow dance to predominate whenever possible. Which was fortunate, for **Silk Stockings** turned out to be Astaire's last appearance in a musical worthy of him, and the last film in which his dancing was seen at its best. Nina 'Ninotchka' Yoshenka, the Communist sent from Moscow to check on three Russian emissaries who, in turn, have orders to bring back with them a Communist composer about to lend his talents to Hollywood, was played by Cyd Charisse (Garbo played it in the non-musical film; Hildegarde Neff on the stage.) It was the best role of Charisse's career and, despite her distinctly limited range as an actress, she worked well under Rouben Mamoulian's direction, and carried it off splendidly, her vocals being dubbed by Carole Richards, Peter Lorre, Jules Munshin and Joseph Buloff were the trio of emissaries who fall into wicked capitalist ways, and Janis Paige (third-billed) an Esther Williams-type swimming star for whom producer Astaire is preparing a musical about Napoleon and Josephine. George Tobias, who appeared both in the original 1939 film and the stage show, played the Soviet Arts Commissar, with other parts going to Wim Sonneveld as the composer Boroff whom all the fuss is about, Betty Uitti, Barrie Chase, Tybee Afra and Belita. Apart from the incomparable dancing of Astaire and Charisse (illustrated), seen at its most glorious in 'All Of You' and 'Fated To Be Mated' (especially composed for the film), the best thing about **Silk Stockings** was its Cole Porter score, orchestrated by Conrad Salinger, Skip Martin and Al Woodbury, and conducted by Andre Previn and Johnny Green. Whether satirically jocular, as in Lorre, Munshin and Buloff's 'Siberia', or lyrical as in 'Paris Loves Lovers' (Astaire and Charisse), it so perfectly captured the mood and spirit of the moment that, when reviewing the original 1939 version, one often wishes that it, too, would burst into song at the appropriate moments. The choreography was by Hermes Pan and Eugene Loring, one of the high-

lights being a novelty number called 'The Ritz Roll and Rock' (specially written for Astaire) which resourcefully combined the current rock fad with Astaire's traditional top hat, white tie and tails. Other songs and musical numbers: *Too Bad (We Can't Go Back To Moscow)* (Lorre, Munshin, Buloff, Astaire, Uitti, Chase, Afra); *Stereophonic Sound* (Paige, Astaire); *It's A Chemical Reaction That's All* (Astaire, Charisse); *Satin And Silk* (Paige); *Silk Stockings* (Charisse); *Without Love* (Charisse); *Josephine* (Paige); *The Red Blues* (Sonneveld, Charisse, dancers).

△

The rags to riches or – in this instance – faded jeans to fast cars and fancy gear – story of a simple Southern lad promoted to pop stardom by a resourceful press agent, **Loving You** (Paramount) was Elvis Presley's second film. In Vistavision and Technicolor, it found him in a quandary for, being a modest country lad at heart, he'd willingly swop his new, faintly ridiculous looking attire for his faded old jeans, and his status-symbol car for his battered old hot rod anytime. Lizabeth Scott (right, with Presley) co-starred as an agent, and Wendell Corey was her bandleader husband whose band she promotes by having Presley sing with it, with other roles in Hal Wallis's routine production going to Dolores Hart (as the romantic interest), James Gleason, Paul Smith, and The Jordanaires. It was written by Hal Kanter, who also directed, and Herbert Baker. Songs: *Lonesome Cowboy* Sid Tepper, Roy C. Bennett; *Teddy Bear* Kal Mann, Bernie Lowe; *Got A Lot Of Livin' To Do* A. Schroeder, Ben Weisman; *Party* Jessie Mae Robinson; *Mean Woman Blues* Claude DeMetrius; *Hot Dog*; *Loving You* Jerry Lieber, Mike Stoller.

Seventeen years after it appeared on Broadway, the Richard Rodgers-Lorenz Hart-John O'Hara musical **Pal Joey** reached the screen via Columbia Pictures, with Frank Sinatra (left) as the hero-cum-heel of the title. And although there was evidence throughout of Hollywood's obsessively interfering fingers having picked and prodded at various aspects of the original show (the setting was changed from Chicago to San Francisco; the score became a hybrid of several Rodgers and Hart shows; the language was sanitized etc. etc.), the strength of its storyline, the irresistible charm of the central performance, the durability of the music, and the glamour invested in the distaff side by co-star Rita Hayworth (right, as the ex-stripper turned society dame who offers to buy Joey the night-club of his dreams) and Kim Novak (as the 'mouse' in the chorus line Joey falls for), added up to more positives than negatives. It was to be regretted that Dorothy Kingsley's screenplay was far less courageous than O'Hara's original. More of the heel and less of the hero was what was needed to give Sinatra's performance additional edge; and, to help keep his relationship with Hayworth well-spiced, she should have remained a married woman (as she was in the original), and not have conveniently become a widow. The songs from the 1940 Broadway production that were retained included 'Zip' (performed by Hayworth, her vocals dubbed by Jo Ann Greer), 'Bewitched, Bothered And Bewildered' (Sinatra and Hayworth), 'I Could Write A Book' (Sinatra and Novak, the latter dubbed by Trudy Erwen), and 'That Terrific Rainbow' (Novak); while from other Rodgers and Hart shows came 'My Funny Valentine' (*Babes In Arms*) sung by Novak, 'There's A Small Hotel' (*On Your Toes*) sung by Sinatra, and 'I Didn't Know What Time It Was' (*Too Many Girls*), also sung by Sinatra. The film's undisputed hit however, was Sinatra's 'The Lady Is A Tramp'. also from *Babes In Arms*. The spectacularly stunning costumes were by Jean Louis, Morris Stoloff and Nelson Riddle were in charge of the musical direction, Hermes Pan choreographed, it was produced (in Technicolor) by Fred Kohlmar and, until he allowed it to turn sentimental towards the end, well directed by George Sidney. The rest of the cast included Barbara Nichols, Bobby Sherwood, Hank Henry and Elizabeth Patterson. Interesting sideline: In 1944, Columbia's studio head Harry Cohn purchased the rights of **Pal Joey** as a vehicle for Gene Kelly who, in 1940, created the role on Broadway. But MGM's Louis B. Mayer, to whom Kelly was under contract, asked Cohn for too much money in return for Kelly's services, and the project was shelved. Other songs and musical numbers: *What Do I Care For A Dame*; *Great Big Town*.

▽

The Joker Is Wild (Paramount) also starred Frank Sinatra, this time as Joe E. Lewis, the prohibition nightclub singer whose career changed direction when, after a *fracas* with some gangsters in which his vocal chords were slashed, he was forced to become a comedian. Abrasively scripted by Oscar Saul (from a book by Art Cohn) with a wry, unsentimental, even jaundiced, central performance from its impressive star, it was twenty minutes too long (at 126 minutes), with the final half hour – as the comedian grows progressively more inebriated – becoming maudlin and indulgent. As Lewis's faithful accompanist, Eddie Albert was excellent, with Mitzi Gaynor (illustrated with Sinatra) as his chorus girl wife, Martha Stewart, and Jeanne Crain as the woman he really loves, holding up the feminine side adequately enough. But it was Sinatra's film all the way, and as the subject was so close to his heart in more senses than one (not only did he understand the nightclub milieu in which most of the film was set, but he was also a personal friend to Lewis), his performance had the imprimatur of authenticity. Josephine Earl staged the musical numbers, the no-punches-pulled direction was by Charles Vidor, and it was produced by Samuel J. Briskin, whose cast was completed by Beverly Garland, Jackie Coogan, Ted de Corsia, Barry Kelley and Sophie Tucker. Songs included: *All The Way* Sammy Cahn, Jimmy Van Heusen; *Out Of Nowhere* John Green, new lyrics by Harry Harris; *At Sundown* Walter Donaldson; *I Cried For You* Arthur Freed, Gus Arnheim, Abe Lyman; *If I Could Be With You* Jimmie Johnson, Henry Creamer; *Mimi* Richard Rodgers, Lorenz Hart; *Swinging On A Star* Van Heusen, new lyrics by Harris; *Naturally* lyrics by Harris, music from Flotow's 'Martha'; *June In January* Leo Robin, Ralph Rainger; *Chicago* Fred Fisher; *I Love My Baby* Bud Green, Harry Warren.

◁ Scriptwriters Jack Rose and Melville Shavelson (working from a book by Gene Fowler) toned down the wisecracks in **Beau James** (Paramount), a semi-serious, commercially unsuccessful vehicle for Bob Hope (right) in which he played New York's colourful mayor, Jimmy Walker. An adulterer whose political career ended under a cloud of financial corruption, Walker was nonetheless a personality to whom it was difficult not to respond with affection, and it was this quality, admirably reproduced by Hope, that gave the film its appeal. Vera Miles (left) co-starred as Betty Compton, the Broadway actress who captivates the mayor despite the fact that he is a Catholic and already married (to Alexis Smith), with other roles in Rose's Vistavision (and Technicolor) production going to Paul Douglas, Darren McGavin, Joe Mantell, Walter Catlett and, playing themselves, Jimmy Durante, George Jessel, Sammy Cahn. Vera Miles's vocals were dubbed by Imogene Lynn. As Walker always had show business aspirations, the songs featured throughout the film fitted into the narrative without too much strain. Jack Baker choreographed, Walter Winchell narrated, and the director was Melville Shavelson. Songs: *Manhattan* Richard Rodgers, Lorenz Hart; *Will You Love Me In December (As You Do In May?)* James J. Walker, Ernest R. Ball; *Someone To Watch Over Me* George and Ira Gershwin; *His Honour The Mayor Of New York* Sammy Cahn, Joseph J. Lilley; *The Sidewalks Of New York* James Blake, Charles Lawlor (special Yiddish lyrics for the film by Sammy Cahn); *When We're Alone* (Penthouse Serenade) Will Jason, Val Burton.

△
20th Century-Fox's **April Love**, an antiseptic musical reworking of Fox's 1944 *Home In Indiana*, asked audiences to believe in wholesome Pat Boone (his second film, Fox's *Bernadine* being the first) as a juvenile delinquent who is sent to his uncle's stud farm in Kentucky after stealing a car. Scripted by Winston Miller from a novel by George Agnew Chamberlain, it hardly gave audiences value for money, its so-called plot centring on Boone's inconsequential romance with his pretty neighbour Shirley Jones and his winning of a climactic trotting race. The marshmallow direction was by Henry Levin, Sammy Fain and Paul Francis Webster provided the songs (the best was the title number), it was produced by David Weisbart in CinemaScope and Eastmancolor and, in secondary roles, featured Arthur O'Connell as Boone's acerbic uncle, Dolores Michaels, Jeanette Nolan (illustrated, with Boone) and Brad Jackson. Songs: *April Love*; *Clover In The Meadow*; *Give Me A Gentle Girl*; *Do It Yourself*; *Bentonville Fair*.

Gene Kelly's last film for MGM, and the last major musical in which he was to star, was **Les Girls**, produced in CinemaScope and Metrocolor by Sol C. Siegel and directed by George Cukor. Jack Cole, with whom Kelly had never worked before, was the choreographer. Not a Kelly musical in the strictest sense, its accent, as the title proclaimed, was on the female of the species, hence the studio's choice of Cukor, whose reputation for drawing good performances from women – represented on this unremarkable occasion by Mitzi Gaynor, Taina Elg, and the luminous Kay Kendall – was well known. The words and music were by Cole Porter who was extremely ill at the time, and needed the invaluable assistance of Saul Chaplin to enable him to complete the score. John Patrick wrote the screenplay from a story by Vera Caspary which began in a London courtroom where Lady Wren (Kendall, illustrated with Kelly), a former show girl who was once part of an act called 'Les Girls', is facing a libel action as a result of her recently published memoirs in which she has recounted certain incidents involving her boss (Kelly) and the two other show girls (Gaynor and Elg) who were part of his act. Kendall's confessions, however, seem to be at variance with the stories her colleagues have to relate and, as each woman takes the stand, out pour several *Rashomon*-style versions of the truth. A perfectly workable idea for a musical comedy, it unfortunately became confused in the telling and emerged as something of a shambles. The three parts of Patrick's screenplay failed to balance, and Porter's score turned out not only to be his last but, in terms of quality, his least. Apart from a really delightful performance from Kay Kendall, the only other good thing about **Les Girls** was a number called 'Why Am I So Gone About That Gal?', a musical parody of Marlon Brando's 1953 Columbia film *The Wild Ones*, performed by Kelly and Gaynor. Completing the cast were Jacques Bergerac, Leslie Phillips, Henry Daniell, Patrick MacNee, Stephen Vercoe and Philip Tonge. Other songs and musical numbers: *Les Girls*; *You're Just Too, Too*; *Ca C'est L'Amour*; *Ladies In Waiting*.
▽

△

△

Not only was **The Pajama Game** (Warner Bros.) – set in a pajama factory and all about a 7½ cents wage dispute – one of the best and most profitable musicals of the decade, it also furnished proof that it was possible to transfer a Broadway hit to the screen almost intact without its becoming stage-bound in the process. Directors George Abbott and Stanley Donen so skilfully opened out the material that one soon forgot its theatrical origins. The 'Once-A-Year Day' picnic scene, for example, was a real movie-stopper, with the camera, no less mobile than Bob Fosse's marvellous dancers, swooping, panning, tracking and practically performing cartwheels. But just as memorable were numbers with an apparently much smaller potential for movie pyrotechnics, such as 'I'll Never Be Jealous Again', sung by Eddie Foy Jr and Reta Shaw as the camera itself seems to do a soft-shoe shuffle over the factory floor; or the hilarious tango 'Hernando's Hideaway' (with Carol Haney). Numbers like these demonstrated that, in a truly cinematic musical, the camera is not a spectator but a performer. Doris Day (left) gave her most enchanting performance ever as the head of the factory's grievance committee, conspiring to look both sexy and wholesome in pajamas, and John Raitt (right) repeated his role as the workshop superintendent, and dancers Buzz Miller and Kenneth LeRoy accompanied Haney in 'Steam Heat'. The screenplay was by George Abbott and Richard Bissell (from the latter's novel *Seven And A Half Cents*) and the superlative score, which included the hit ballad 'Hey, There', by Richard Adler and Jerry Ross. This rejuvenating movie was produced by Abbott and Donen, with Fred Brisson, Robert E. Griffiths and Harold Prince as associate producers. Other musical numbers included: *The Pajama Game*; *I'm Not At All In Love*; *Small Talk*; *There Once Was A Man*; *Seven And A Half Cents*; *Racing With The Clock*.

△

The efforts of a former fan dancer (Virginia Field) to live down her past and, together with her two teenage children (Cary Vinson, right, and Judy Busch), to find acceptance in the small town of Springville, was what **Rockabilly Baby** (20th Century-Fox) was all about. Average programmer material with a cast that also included Douglas Kennedy, Irene Ryan, Ellen Corby, Marlene Willis (left), singer Luis Amando and, as himself, Les Brown, it whiled away 82 minutes painlessly enough, featured six songs, and sufficient plot complications (screenplay by Will George and William Driskill) to engage one's attention without undue strain. It was produced and directed by William F. Claxton. Songs: *We're On Our Way*; *Why Can't I?*; *Is It Love?*; *I'd Rather Be*; *My Calypso Baby* Paul Dunlap; *Teenage Cutie* Dick Kallman.

360

Elvis Presley (illustrated) signed up with MGM for **Jailhouse Rock**, the best of his three films to date, in which he played an ex-jail-bird (imprisoned on a manslaughter charge) who becomes a rather unlovable pop star on his release. Very much a Presley vehicle from first to last, the film wasted the talents of co-star Judy Tyler (a Broadway singer who, tragically, died shortly after the film's completion), with whom Presley forms a record company and falls in love; and Mickey Shaughnessy as Presley's prison cellmate and a former folk singer. Completing the cast were Vaughn Taylor, Jennifer Holden and Anne Neyland. Presley's songs were by Jerry Lieber and Mike Stoller, the two best being the title number, sung in prison, and 'Treat Me Nice'. It was produced in CinemaScope and black and white by Pandro S. Berman and the director was Richard Thorpe. Other songs: *Young And Beautiful*; *I Wanna Be Free*; *Don't Leave Me Now*; *Baby I Don't Care* (all sung by Presley).

Yet another case of a minor talent helplessly trying to impersonate a major one, Warner Bros.' **The Helen Morgan Story** (GB: **Both Ends Of The Candle**) was doomed to failure by the casting of Ann Blyth (illustrated) as the great torch singer of the twenties. Although director Michael Curtiz vividly recaptured both the squalor of the carnival sideshows in which Helen Morgan began her career, and the glittering speakeasies which saw her rise to stardom, he could not disguise the void at the centre of the film. Nor was he aided by a routine biopic screenplay by Oscar Saul, Dean Reisner, Stephen Longstreet and Nelson Gidding. Paul Newman played the unscrupulous hustler who helps launch Morgan's career, and Richard Carlson the married man to whom she becomes disastrously attached. Gene Evans, Alan King, Cara Williams and Virginia Vincent led the solid supporting cast. Although Miss Blyth was the possessor of a soprano voice, she was dubbed by Gogi Grant. The producer was Martin Rackin, and the songs and musical numbers were staged by LeRoy Prinz. They included: *Bill* Jerome Kern, P.G. Wodehouse; *Can't Help Lovin' Dat Man*; *Don't Ever Leave Me*; *Why Was I Born?* Kern, Oscar Hammerstein II; *If You Were The Only Girl In The World* Clifford Grey, Nat D. Ayer; *I Can't Give You Anything But Love* Dorothy Fields, Jimmy McHugh; *Avalon* Vincent Rose, Al Jolson; *Breezin' Along With The Breeze* Haven Gillespie, Seymour Simons, Richard Whiting; *Someone To Watch Over Me*; *I've Got A Crush On You*; *Do Do Do* George and Ira Gershwin; *Body And Soul* Edward Heyman, Robert Sour, Frank Eyton, John Green; *I'll Get By* Roy Turk, Fred Ahlert; *The Love Nest* Otto Harbach, Louis A. Hirsch.
▽

1958

Academy Awards
Best Picture
Gigi (MGM) produced by Arthur Freed

Direction
Vincente Minnelli *Gigi*

Writing (Screenplay)
based on material from another medium
Gigi Alan Jay Lerner

Cinematography
After a one-year change in 1957, two awards again given for cinematography achievement
Gigi Joseph Ruttenberg
NOMINATIONS INCLUDED: *South Pacific* (Magna Corp., 20th Century-Fox) Leon Shamroy

Art Direction (Set Decoration)
(black and white or colour)
Gigi William A. Horning and Preston Ames; Henry Grace and Keogh Gleason

Costume Design
(black and white or colour)
Gigi Cecil Beaton

△

Some splendid aerial shots of Rome – gorgeous in Technirama and colour – the unexpected sight of Mario Lanza (illustrated) doing impersonations of Dean Martin, Frankie Laine, Louis Armstrong and Perry Como, plus the haunting strains of 'Arrivederci Roma' (by Renato Rascel and Carl Sigman) powerfully sung by Lanza, were the best things about **The Seven Hills Of Rome** (MGM). The worst were its glossy selection of clichés in which Lanza was featured as an American TV star who journeys to Rome in pursuit of his heiress girlfriend (Peggie Castle) after a lovers' quarrel, meets pretty Maria Alassio, and only towards the end of the film realizes he loves *her* rather than Miss Castle. Composer Rascel was second-billed as Lanza's Roman cousin, with other roles in producer Lester Welch's predominantly Italian cast going to Celia Matania, Rossella Como, Amos Davoli, Guido Celano and Carlo Rizzo. The director was Roy Rowland, and it was written by Art Cohn and Giorgio Prosperi. Other songs: *Seven Hills Of Rome*; *Never Till Now* John Green, Paul Francis Webster; *Earthbound* Jack Taylor, Clive Richardson, Bob Muset; *Come Dance With Me*; *Lolita*; *There's Gonna Be A Party Tonight*; *Italian Calypso*; *Questa o Quella* (from 'Rigoletto') Verdi; *Imitation Routine*; *Temptation* Arthur Freed, Nacio Herb Brown; *Jezebel* Wayne Shanklin; *When The Saints Go Marching In* (trad.); *Memories Are Made Of This* Terry Gilkyson, Richard Dehr, Frank Miller.

Sound
No longer categorized as Sound Recording
South Pacific Todd-AO Sound Dept., Fred
Hynes, sound director

Film Editing
Gigi Adrienne Fazan

Special Effects
Tom Thumb (MGM) Tom Howard

Music
Song
'Gigi' *Gigi* Frederick Loewe *cm*; Alan Jay
Lerner *lyr*.

Scoring Of A Musical Picture
Gigi Andre Previn
NOMINATIONS INCLUDED: *Damn Yankees* (WB)
Ray Heindorf, *Mardi Gras* (20th
Century-Fox) Lionel Newman. *South Pacific*
Alfred Newman and Ken Darby

Honorary Award
To Maurice Chevalier for his contributions
to the world of entertainment for more than
half a century. (statuette)

The New York Times Annual 'Ten Best'
2nd *Gigi*. 7th *Damn Yankees*

The Annual Top Moneymaking Films
INCLUDED: *South Pacific*

Pop idol Tommy Sands (illustrated) made his
screen debut in **Sing Boy Sing** (20th Century-
Fox) whose screenplay by Claude Binyon, from a
story by Paul Monash, was a cross between
Loving You (Paramount, 1957) and *The Jazz
Singer* (Warner Bros. 1927). As was the case in
the Presley film, Sands was a simple lad from
Dixie who is promoted to stardom by a ruthless
manager (Edmond O'Brien). Its *Jazz Singer* overtones intruded when, with his preacher grandfather (John McIntire) on the verge of dying,
Sands returns home, determined to forsake the
$300,000 a year he could be earning in the glare
of the spotlights, and becomes a preacher himself. But his heart isn't in it, and it is his wise old
Aunt Caroline (Josephine Hutchinson) who, in
an impassioned speech, implores him to lead his
own life. Giving a performance that was both
credible and likeable, Sands made the best of
Binyon's familiar but serviceable screenplay,
sang a dozen songs (including 'Rock Of Ages')
pleasantly, and generally proved himself to be
more than just another pretty face. His supporting cast included Nick Adams, Lili Gentle, Diane
Jergens and Jerry Paris. It was produced and
directed by Henry Ephron. Songs: *Sing Boy Sing*;
Gonna Talk With My Lord; *Who Baby?*; *Crazy
'Cause I Love You*; *Bundle Of Dreams*; *Your Daddy
Wants To Do Right*; *Just A Little Bit More*; *That's
All I Want From You*; *People In Love*; *Soda-Pop
Song*; *Would I Love You.*
▽

Merry Andrew (MGM) was basically a one-idea ▷
show – the idea being to present an English
schoolmaster's hilariously inept adventures as a
performer in a circus. Danny Kaye (left) was the
teacher turned ringmaster-cum-tumbler-cum-
trapeze artist, and it all began when he set out
from school one day on an archaeological dig in
search of an ancient statue of Pan. What he
unearths instead, is Pier Angeli (right), a
member of Gallini's Circus, who attracts him
even more than the study of antiquities. It was
amiable albeit uninspired fare, enlivened by
several Saul Chaplin-Johnny Mercer songs, the
best being a number called 'Salud' featuring
Kaye, Angeli and Salvatore Baccaloni (as the
circus owner), plus several excellent dancers all
energetically responding to director Michael
Kidd's assertive choreography. Based on a Paul
Gallico story with a screenplay by Isobel Lennart
and I.A.L. Diamond, it also featured Robert
Coote, Noel Purcell, Patricia Cutts, Rex Evans,
Tommy Rall, Walter Kingsford and Rhys Wil-
liams, and was produced by Sol C. Siegel in
CinemaScope and Metrocolor. Other songs and
musical numbers: *Pipes Of Pan*; *Chin Up Stout
Fellows*; *Everything Is Tickety Boo*; *You Can't
Always Have What You Want*; *Square Of The
Hypotenuse*; *Here's Cheers*.

△

Another fair lady from the team of Alan Jay
Lerner and Frederick Loewe, **Gigi** was the last of
the great MGM musicals and it justly deserved its
eight Academy Awards. The delightful story of
a young girl reared by her grandmother and
her great-aunt to follow the family tradition by
becoming a courtesan, it starred Leslie Caron
(right, giving the performance of her career)
as Gigi, Louis Jourdan (left) as the handsome,
outrageously eligible Gaston Lachaille who scan-
dalizes Gigi's family by actually proposing marriage to her, Maurice Chevalier as his wordly
grandfather Honoré, and Hermione Gingold and
Isabel Jeans as Gigi's grandmother and great-
aunt respectively. Set in *fin de siécle* Paris, it was
brilliantly costumed by Cecil Beaton, directed by
Vincente Minnelli and scripted by Alan Jay
Lerner from the novel by Colette with grace and
elegance. In fact, **Gigi** was a stylish triumph from
start to finish which sadly – but gloriously –
marked the end of an era. (Its producer Arthur
Freed would make only one more musical, *Bells
Are Ringing*, MGM 1960.) If **Gigi** was one of Freed's
finest achievements, it also showed Minnelli on
top of his form. For sheer sustained visual
opulence and the brilliant use it made of colour,

the film ranks with his work on *Meet Me In St
Louis* (MGM, 1944) and *An American In Paris*
(MGM, 1951). Musically, too, it was perfection;
the highlight of its ravishing and extraordinarily
durable score being whatever number you may
care to choose: be it the rousing 'The Night They
Invented Champagne' (Caron, Jourdan, Gingold), the incomparable 'Gigi' (Jourdan), the
tender 'Say A Prayer For Me Tonight' (Caron),
Chevalier's jaunty ode to old age 'I'm Glad I'm
Not Young Anymore' or, perhaps best of all, the
touching 'I Remember It Well', magnificently
performed by Chevalier and Gingold on the
terrace of a Deauville Hotel against a calculatedly
romantic sunset. The richly textured orchestra-
tions throughout were by Conrad Salinger, with
Andre Previn in charge of the musical direction.
Leslie Caron's vocals were dubbed by Betty
Wand, and the cast was completed by Eva Gabor,
Jacques Bergerac and John Abbott. It was mag-
nificently photographed in Metrocolor and Cine-
maScope by Joseph Ruttenberg. Other songs:
Thank Heaven For Little Girls (Chevalier); *It's A
Bore* (Jourdan, Chevalier); *The Parisians* (Caron);
Waltz At Maxim's (She's Not Thinking Of Me)
(Jourdan); *Gossip* (chorus).

Composer Harry Warren and lyricist Sammy Cahn were signed by producer Jerry Lewis for **Rock-A-Bye Baby** (Paramount), a *schmaltzy* but moderately likeable item in which Lewis top-starred himself as a TV repair man in a small town, the love of whose life is co-star Marilyn Maxwell. Unfortunately Maxwell, who has become a movie star, does not love him, the man of her choice being a Mexican bullfighter. Trouble sets in when the Mexican dies in the ring a day after their marriage and Maxwell (left) discovers, just as she is about to appear in an epic production called 'The White Virgin Of The Nile', that she is pregnant. Lewis comes to the rescue by agreeing to look after Maxwell's baby – which turns out to be triplets. Story ends with Lewis (centre) finally marrying Maxwell's sister (Connie Stevens, right) and finding himself the father of quintuplets. It was written and produced by Frank Tashlin with a cast that also included Salvatore Baccaloni as Maxwell and Stevens' fiery father, Reginald Gardiner, Hans Conried, Isobel Elsom, Ida Moore and Lewis's son Gary. It was photographed in Vistavision and Technicolor, and choreographed by Nick Castle who staged Maxwell's 'White Virgin' number, a duet song and dance for Lewis and his son called 'In The Land Of La La La' and a duet for Lewis and Baccaloni (sung as a lullaby to the triplets) called 'Dormi, Dormi, Dormi'. Other songs and musical numbers included: *Love Is A Lonely Thing; Why Can't He Care For Me.*
▽

◁ Richard Rodgers, Oscar Hammerstein II and Joshua Logan's **South Pacific** (based on James A. Michener's *Tales Of The South Pacific*) reached the screen via 20th Century-Fox in Todd-AO and Technicolor, and with a cast headed by Rossano Brazzi and Mitzi Gaynor (both illustrated) in the roles played on Broadway by Ezio Pinza and Mary Martin. Only Juanita Hall, as Bloody Mary, was retained from the stage show – her enchanting 'Happy Talk' being the highlight of a production (by Buddy Adler) that unsuccessfully strove to capture the exoticism and the magic of the original. Largely to blame was Joshua Logan's sledge-hammer direction, and the intrusive use of colour filters in the musical numbers. As Emile de Becque the French planter, and Nellie Forbush the Navy nurse with whom he falls in love, Brazzi (whose vocals were dubbed by Giorgio Tozzi) and Gaynor were fine; so were John Kerr (vocals dubbed by Bill Lee) as the sub-plot's Lieutenant Cable and France Nuyen as his native girl Liat. Ray Walston made a meal of Luther Billis, with other roles going to Russ Brown, Jack Mullaney, Ken Clark, Floyd Simmons, Candace Lee and Tom Laughlin. The screenplay was by Paul Osborn, it was photographed by Leon Shamroy and L.B. Abbott, with Alfred Newman in charge of the musical direction and LeRoy Prinz handling the choreography. Interesting sideline: Though Juanita Hall sang the role of Bloody Mary on Broadway, Richard Rodgers was unhappy with her vocal quality when the film's soundtrack came to be recorded, so her vocals were dubbed in by Muriel Smith. Other songs and musical numbers: *Dites-Moi* (Gaynor, Brazzi, children); *A Cockeyed Optimist* (Gaynor); *Twin Soliloquies* (Gaynor, Brazzi); *Some Enchanted Evening* (Brazzi, Gaynor); *Bloody Mary* (Sailors); *There Is Nothing Like A Dame* (Sailors); *I'm Gonna Wash That Man Right Outa My Hair* (Gaynor); *I'm In Love With A Wonderful Guy* (Gaynor); *Younger Than Springtime* (Kerr); *Honey Bun* (Gaynor, Walston); *Carefully Taught* (Kerr); *This Nearly Was Mine* (Brazzi); *Bali Ha'i* (Hall) and *My Girl Back Home* (Gaynor, Kerr) – which was not featured in the stage show.

The Jordanaires, Drifting Johnny Miller, Lonzo and Oscar, The La Dell Sisters and Bernie Nee joined Ferlin Husky, Zsa Zsa Gabor (right), Rocky Graziano, Faron Young, Al Fisher and Lou Marks in **Country Music Holiday**, a cornball country-and-western entry from Paramount about a bumpkin (Husky) who finds that half of himself (contract-wise) belongs to agent Jesse White (left); while the other half, much to the consternation of Husky's girlfriend (June Carter), as well as his father (Rod Brasfield), belongs to Miss Gabor. Cliff Norton, Patty Duke, Hope Sansberry, Lou Marks and Lew Parker completed the cast for producers Ralph Serpe and Howard B. Kreitsek; it was written by H.B. Cross and directed by Alvin Ganzer. Songs and musical numbers: *Somewhere There's Sunshine; Terrific Together; Don't Walk Away From Me; Wide Wide World; My Home Town; Just One More Chance; The Face Of Love; When It Rains it Pours.*
▽

Though New Orleans was also the setting for **Mardi Gras** (20th Century-Fox), there was nothing sleazy about the events perpetrated in Winston Miller and Hal Kanter's jolly but harmless little screenplay adapted from a story by Curtis Harrington. It starred Pat Boone (centre), Tommy Sands (right) and Gary Crosby (his debut, left), as members of the Virginia Military Institute, and what little plot there was was inspired by MGM's 1943 *Best Foot Forward*, and concerned Boone's winning a date with a Hollywood starlet (Christine Carere) in a raffle and, in due course, falling in love with her. Joining the Cadets of the V.M.I. were Sheree North as Miss Carere's secretary-cum-confidante and Barrie Chase as a stripper, as well as Fred Clark and Richard Sargeant. Sammy Fain and Paul Francis Webster provided the utilitarian score, Jerry Wald produced (in CinemaScope and Color by De Luxe) and the director was Edmund Goulding. Songs: *Bigger Than Texas; I'll Remember Tonight; Mardi Gras March; Bourbon Street Blues; Loyalty; A Fiddle, A Rifle.*
▽

△
An unworthy and enervating biopic of jazz composer W.C. Handy, written by Robert Smith and Ted Sherdeman, **St Louis Blues** (Paramount) starred Nat King Cole (left) as Handy and Eartha Kitt as the woman he loved. Despite the several classic Handy compositions on offer, the film made little impact due to the lack of conviction in the screenplay, the central performances, the unimaginative staging of the songs, and the overall listlessness of Allen Reisner's direction. Ruby Dee was cast as the other woman in Handy's life and, as played by Miss Dee, what a little ninny she was. Other roles in Robert Smith's production were given to Juano Hernandez (as Handy's pious and disapproving father), Pearl Bailey (right), Cab Calloway, Mahalia Jackson, Billy Preston (as young Handy) and, playing herself, Ella Fitzgerald. Songs (all music and lyrics by Handy unless otherwise stated) included: *Hesitating Blues; Chantez Les Bas; Beale Street Blues; Careless Love* adapted from folk music by Handy; lyrics by Spencer Williams and Martha Koenig; *Morning Star; Way Down South Where The Blues Began; Mr Bayle; Aunt Hagar's Blues* (lyrics Tim Brymn); *They That Sow* (hymn); *Going To See My Sarah* (spiritual).

◁ Elvis Presley (illustrated), as 'a hustler out to make a fast buck', actually gave something resembling a performance in **King Creole** (Paramount), a melodrama set in New Orleans and based on Harold Robbins's novel *A Stone For Danny Fisher*. Scripted by Herbert Baker and Michael V. Gazzo as a Presley show piece, it allowed room for several numbers (including the popular title song by Jerry Lieber and Mike Stoller) as well as 'Hard Headed Woman' (by Claude DeMetrius), at appropriate points in a story which saw Presley's rise from earnest bus boy-cum-musician to Bourbon Street nightclub singer in the company of several decidedly unsavoury heavies – including Walter Matthau and Vic Morrow. Also cast: Carolyn Jones giving the best performance in the film as Matthau's ex-girlfriend for whom Presley falls, Dean Jagger as Presley's ineffectual father and Jan Shephard as his sister, as well as Paul Stewart and Dolores Hart. Michael Curtiz's direction successfully captured the essentially seedy atmosphere of the film's milieu and managed to extend Presley's hitherto limited range as an actor. Hal Wallis produced. Other songs: *Dixieland Rock* Schroeder, Frank; *As Long As I Have You*; *Crawfish* Fred Wise, Ben Weisman; *Don't Ask Me Why*; *New Orleans* Sid Tepper, Roy C. Bennett; *Lover Doll* Sid Wayne, Abner Silver; *Trouble*; *Steadfast, Loyal And True* Jerry Lieber, Mike Stoller; *Young Dreams* Schroeder, Kalmanoff.

Completed in 1956 but released two years later, **The Girl Most Likely**, a musical remake of *Tom, Dick And Harry* (RKO, 1940) was the very last film made by RKO, and the last to be directed by Mitchell Leisen, from a screenplay by Devery Freeman (based on Paul Jarrico's original screenplay). The story of a rather hare-brained young lady who finds herself engaged to three men without knowing which one, finally, to choose, it top-starred Jane Powell with Cliff Robertson, Keith Andes and Tommy Noonan as her trio of beaus. Also: singer Kaye Ballard and dancer Kelly Brown, as well as Judy Nugent, Una Merkel, Frank Cady and – on soundtrack only – The Hi-Lo's. Hugh Martin and Ralph Blane provided a fairly jolly score, the best number being a ballad called 'I Don't Know What I Want', beautifully sung by Miss Powell. Gower Champion master-minded a couple of brawny dance routines, one of which (called 'Balboa', illustrated) took place on a quayside at Balboa, the other (called 'All The Colors Of The Rainbow') in a bazaar at Tia Juana. Stanley Rubin produced (in Technicolor). Other songs and musical numbers: *Keeping Up With The Joneses*; *The Girl Most Likely*; *Travelogue*; *Crazy Horse*.
▽

After their triumph with *The Pajama Game* the previous year, producer-directors George Abbott and Stanley Donen tackled another Richard Adler-Jerry Ross Broadway smash, **Damn Yankees** (GB: **What Lola Wants**), for Warner Bros. It told the Faustian tale of a middle-aged baseball fan (Robert Shafer) who makes the traditional pact with the Devil (Ray Walston), not for the purpose of acquiring universal knowledge but, more practically, to play long-ball hitter with the Washington Senators – and who becomes Tab Hunter in the process. Apart from Hunter, the whole cast, plus the creators – from writer Douglass Wallop (on whose novel *The Year The Yankees Lost The Pennant* the musical was based) to choreographers Bob Fosse (who himself partnered the star, Gwen Verdon, in the fast-moving 'Who's Got The Pain') and Pat Ferrier – were recruited from the original show so that, with Donen once again breathing cinematic life into the material, even indulging in his favourite split-screen effects, the result was the happiest possible marriage between Broadway and Hollywood. And the matchmaker of this marriage was unquestionably Verdon (illustrated centre, with Hunter), repeating her stage success as the 172-year-old witch Lola, conjured up by the Devil to lure the baseball player away from his devoted but middle-aged wife. Perhaps because her appeal was too sophisticated, larger than life, and Broadway-based, Verdon was never to gain stardom in films, but her marvellous gift for zany comedy, combined with the exuberant eroticism she projected in the dance numbers, have assured her with **Damn Yankees** alone, a slight but secure niche in the history of the Hollywood musical. Also prominently featured in the musical numbers were Russ Brown, Shannon Bolin, Rae Allen and Jean Stapleton. Other songs and musical numbers included: *Heart*; *Whatever Lola Wants*; *Shoeless Joe From Hannibal Mo*; *There's Something About An Empty Chair*; *Two Lost Souls*; *A Little Brains, A Little Talent*; *Those Were The Good Old Days*; *Goodbye, Old Girl*; *Six Months Out Of Every Year*; *The Game*.
◁

If Tom Thumb, the character, was no bigger than a grown man's thumb, neither, as it turned out, was the entertainment value of MGM's **Tom Thumb** – an Eastmancolor account of the famous Grimm fairy tale – except, possibly, to the very, very young. It was directed by George Pal with far too much reliance on trick photography at the expense of genuine humour and fantasy, and with no restraint in the two wildly caricatured performances of Terry-Thomas and Peter Sellers as the villains of the piece. Top-cast Russ Tamblyn (right) was characteristically energetic as Tom, and some of his dance routines, staged by Alex Romero, were splendid. But Ladislas Fodor's screenplay, like Pal's direction, was devoid of enchantment and, for most of the time, was as wooden as Pal's puppet creations, making it difficult for any of the flesh and blood characters – including lovers Alan Young and June Thorburn (left, as the wish-granting Forest Queen) as well as Bernard Miles and Jessie Matthews as Tom's parents, to emerge as anything other than two-dimensional fairy tale stereotypes. The songs by Peggy Lee, Kermit Goell, Janice Torre and Fred Spielman lacked inspiration – the best of the bunch being 'The Yawning Song', sung by one of the puppets with a vocal by Stan Freberg. Pal also produced, and his cast was completed by Ian Wallace, Peter Bull, Barbara Ferris and Dal McKennon. Jessie Matthews's vocals were dubbed by Norma Zimmer. Other songs and musical numbers: *Tom Thumb's Tune*; *Talented Shoes*; *After All These Years*; *Are You A Dream?*.
▽

A well-turned programmer from producer Sam
Katzman and Columbia, **Juke Box Rhythm**
starred Jo Morrow as a European princess who,
together with her aunt (Frieda Inescort), arrives
in New York to purchase her coronation wardrobe. Mary C. McCall Jr and Earl Baldwin's
screenplay had co-star Jack Jones (on the verge
of making an international career for himself)
attempting to have the princess and her chape-
rone give the wardrobe concession to Hans
Conried, an unknown designer and former junk
man. Nonsensical but amiable, it was adroitly
directed by Arthur Dreifuss, choreographed by
Hal Belfer (see illustration), and also featured
Brian Donlevy as a Broadway producer (and
Jones's father), Karin Booth, Marjorie Reynolds,
Edgar Barrier, Fritz Feld and Hortense Betra.
George Jessel appeared in a special guest role;
and also playing themselves were The Nitwits,
Johnny Otis, The Treniers, and The Earl Grant
Trio. Songs and musical numbers: *Let's Fall In
Love*; *Juke Box Rhythm*; *The Freeze*; *Make Room
For The Joy*; *I Feel It Right Here*; *Last Night*; *Get
Out Of The Car*; *Willie And The Hand Jive*; *Spring Is
The Time For Remembering*.

Nearer in mood, atmosphere and in the style of
its animation to *Snow White And The Seven
Dwarfs* (RKO, 1937) than, say, *The Lady And The
Tramp* (Buena Vista, 1955), but not as melodious
or as inventive as either film, **Sleeping Beauty**,
(Buena Vista, illustrated) photographed in Technirama and Technicolor, was an elaborate re-
telling of the famous Charles Perrault fairy tale
which introduced the world to three new Disney
creations – the good fairies Flora, Fauna and
Merriweather who, to save Princess Aurora
from a jealous witch parading under the name of
Maleficent, spirit her off to their cottage in the
forest for protection. Though gorgeous to look
at, and containing some remarkable feats of
animation (such as the exciting dragon fight and
the frightening chase of the prince by the witch's
evil gargoyles) **Sleeping Beauty**, which cost a
mammoth $6,000,000, explored all the old
familiar Disney territory and, at its best, was an
above average children's entertainment. Mary
Costa's voice was heard as Aurora, Bill Shirley
was the Prince, Eleanor Audley Maleficent,
Verna Felton, Barbara Jo Allen and Barbara
Luddy Flora, Fauna, and Merriweather, Taylor
Holmes King Stefan, Bill Thompson King Hubert
and Candy Candido the Goons. The production
supervisor was Ken Peterson and the supervis-
ing director Clyde Geronimi. Songs: *Once Upon A
Dream* Sammy Fain, Jack Lawrence; *Hail The
Princess Aurora* Tom Adair, George Bruns; *I
Wonder* Winston Hibler, Ted Sears, Bruns; *The
Skump Song* Adair, Erdman Penner, Bruns; *The
Sleeping Beauty Song* Adair, Bruns; and themes
from Tchaikovsky's ballet *Sleeping Beauty*.

Bing Crosby's first film for 20th Century-Fox was
Say One For Me, a good looking (in Cinema-
Scope and Color De Luxe) cousin to *Going My
Way* (Paramount, 1944) in which, for the third
time in his career, Der Bingle played a priest. This
time he was Father Conroy, a mild-mannered,
easygoing clergyman whose off-Broadway
church is a haven largely for show folk. Robert
O'Brien's screenplay, while mainly concerned
with Crosby and his parish activities, also incorporated a sub-plot in which Debbie Reynolds
(illustrated), as a showgirl who's only in the business to earn enough money to look after her
ailing father, finds herself involved with a
sinful nightclub impresario (Robert Wagner) whose
soul she successfully determines to save. Ray
Walston played a down-and-out piano player
whom Bing rescues from the bottle, with other
parts in producer-director Frank Tashlin's film
going to Connie Gilchrist (as Crosby's house-
keeper), Les Tremayne, Frank McHugh, Joe
Besser, Sebastian Cabot, and Judy Harriet whose
vocals were dubbed by Rosemary June. The
score was by Jimmy Van Heusen and Sammy
Cahn. Songs: *I Couldn't Care Less*; *The Secret Of
Christmas*; *You Can't Love 'Em All*; *The Girl Most
Likely To Succeed*; *Chico's Choc-Choc*; *Hanoveh*; *The
Night That Rock And Roll Died*.

364

At the age of 75, Samuel Goldwyn made his last ▷ film – the George and Ira Gershwin-Du Bose Heyward folk opera **Porgy And Bess** (Columbia). It was a bold and expensive cinematic venture, filmed in Technicolor and Todd-AO at a cost of over $6,500,000, but it never reached the heights – either musically or dramatically – that Goldwyn had aimed for. From a musical standpoint, the singing was good, but not as good as the score demanded; while dramatically, the entire production laboured under the heavy hand of its director, Otto Preminger. (Rouben Mamoulian who directed the original stage version, had initially been engaged by Goldwyn to repeat the assignment, but after eight months of pre-production work, differences of opinion with Goldwyn led to him being replaced by Preminger.) Sidney Poitier was cast as the crippled beggar Porgy (the role was originally offered to Harry Belafonte who turned it down), and Dorothy Dandridge (illustrated, with Poitier) as Bess, the slumgirl he loves. Their glossy, Hollywood good looks somehow seemed out of place in Catfish Row, the opera's ghetto-like setting, which left the acting honours to Brock Peters as the murderous Crown, and to Sammy Davis Jr, marvellous as Sporting Life. Diahann Carroll played Clara, Pearl Bailey was a spirited Maria and Ruth Attaway was Serena, with other parts going to Clarence Muse, Leslie Scott, Everdinne Wilson, Joel Fluellen and Earl Jackson. Poitier's vocals were dubbed by Robert McFerrin, Dandridge's by Adele Addison, Carroll's by Loulie Jean Norman and Attaway's by Inez Matthews. N. Richard Nash wrote the screenplay, based on the opera by the Gershwins and Heyward, the novel (by Heyward), and the play by Heyward and his wife Dorothy. Andre Previn and Ken Darby were in charge of the musical direction, Hermes Pan the choreography and Leon Shamroy the photography. Songs: *Summertime* (Carroll, chorus); *Crap Game* (Fluellen, Carroll, chorus); *A Woman Is A Sometime Thing* (Scott, Jackson, Davis, Carroll, chorus); *Honey Man's Call* (Muse); *They Pass By Singing* (Poitier); *Yo' Mammy's Gone* (Jackson); *Gone, Gone, Gone* (Scott, chorus); *Porgy's Prayer* (Poitier); *My Man's Gone Now* (Attaway, chorus); *The Train Is At The Station* (Dandridge, chorus); *I Got Plenty O' Nuttin'* (Poitier, chorus); *Bess, You Is My Woman* (Poitier, Dandridge); *Oh, I Can't Sit Down* (Bailey, Davis, chorus); *I Ain't Got No Shame* (chorus); *It Ain't Necessarily So* (Davis, chorus); *What You Wan' Wid Bess* (Dandridge, Peters); *It Take A Long Pull To Get There* (Scott, male chorus); *De Police Put Me In* (Muse); *Time And Time Again* (Attaway); *Strawberry Woman's Call* (Helen Thigpen); *Crab Man's Call* (Vince Townsend Jr); *A Red-Headed Woman* (Peters); *Dere's A Boat Dat's Leavin' Soon For New York* (Davis); *Good Mornin' Sistuh* (chorus); *Bess, Oh Where's My Bess* (Poitier); *I'm On My Way* (Poitier, chorus).

Produced by Alexander Gruter for Corona Films in Germany and Astor Film, Italy, and released by MGM, **For The First Time**, in Technirama, was an unashamed tear-jerker that starred a comparatively slim Mario Lanza (left) as an opera star who, while on an incognito visit to Capri, falls in love with a deaf girl (Johanna Von Koszian), then spends a large part of the film's running time giving concerts in various European capitals to raise funds for Miss Koszian's medical treatment. Rudolph Maté's direction and Andrew Solt's screenplay rigorously manipulated the emotions throughout, but nowhere more blatantly than the scene in which Lanza, to test his hospitalized sweetheart's hearing, sings Schubert's 'Ave Maria' to her, with the resultant sobbing and sniffing in the audience all but drowning out the soundtrack. Kurt Kasznar (right) appeared as Lanza's manager, with other parts in it for Zsa Zsa Gabor (as a countess), Hans Sohnker, Peter Capell and Renzo Cesana. It was photographed on location in Rome, Naples, Salzburg, Vienna and Capri and, with Lanza in particularly good voice, was as good to listen to as to look at. Pity about the script, though. Songs and operatic excerpts: *Oh Mon Amour*; *Bavarian Drinking Song*; *Vesti La Giubba* (from 'Pagliacci') Leoncavallo; *La Donna è Mobile* (from 'Rigoletto') Verdi; *O Sole Mio* Eduardo di Capua; *I Love Thee* Grieg; *Niun Mi Tema* (from 'Otello') Verdi; *Come Prima* M. Panzeri, S. Paola-Tacani, Mary Bond (all sung by Lanza); Orchestral: ◁ *Grand March* from Verdi's 'Aida'.

Sixteen-year-old Fabian made his screen debut in **Hound Dog Man** (20th Century-Fox), a cosy, homespun affair – in CinemaScope and Color DeLuxe – set in rural America in 1912. Basically about the growing pains of a teenager (Fabian, right) and his younger brother (Dennis Holmes, centre left), Fred Gipson and Winston Miller's screenplay (from Gipson's novel) also starred Arthur O'Connell (left) and Stuart Whitman (centre right), with romantic interest in the shape of Carol Lynley (a hillbilly) and Margo Moore (a married lady) both of whom Fabian, in the course of the tale, falls for. It was directed by Don Siegel, and the songs, by Ken Darby, Frankie Avalon, Saul Ponti, Robert Marcucci, Pete De Angelis, Doc Pomus and Morty Shuman included: *What Big Boy?*; *This Friendly World*; *Pretty Little Girl*; *Single*; *I'm Giving Up*; *Hill-Top Song*; *Hay Foot, Straw Foot*. ▽

Fifties Musicals

Associate producer Sylvia Fine contributed three new songs to **The Five Pennies** (Paramount), but as the film was a biopic of the renowned twenties cornet player Red Nichols, most of the music featured – such as 'After You've Gone' (by Henry Creamer and Turner Layton), 'Runnin' Wild' (Joe Grey, Leo Wood and A. Harrington·Gibbs), 'Out Of Nowhere' (Edward Heyman and John Green) and 'Indiana' (Ballard MacDonald and James Hanley) – was of the appropriate period. Danny Kaye (centre right) starred as Nichols (with Nichols himself on cornet), and the script fashioned by Melville Shavelson and Jack Rose was a *schmaltzy* amalgam of fact and fantasy recalling Nichols's early years as an idealist rebelling against the inferior popular music of the day, his success, his emotional set-back (as penance for his daughter's poliomyelitis he temporarily abandons his cornet), and his triumphant return to the world of jazz. Though much of it was soggy and lugubrious to the point of indigestibility, musically it was full of good things, the undoubted highlight being Kaye and Louis Armstrong's (left) rousing rendition of 'When The Saints Go Marching In'. Barbara Bel Geddes (vocals dubbed by Eileen Wilson) gave a likeable performance as Nichols's wife; Susan Gordon was their daughter aged six who, at 14, turns into Tuesday Weld, with other parts in Rose's production (for Dena Pictures) going to Harry Guardino, Bob Crosby (as Will Paradise), Ray Anthony (as Jimmy Dorsey), Shelly Manne, Bobby Troup, Ray Daley and Valerie Allen. Melville Shavelson directed. (Vistavision and

Technicolor). Other songs: *Lullaby In Ragtime* (Kaye, Bel Geddes); *Good Night Sleep Tight* (Kaye, Armstrong, Bel Geddes); *The Five Pennies* (Kaye, Armstrong) Fine; *Battle Hymn Of The Republic* (Kaye, Armstrong) William Steffe, Julia Ward Howe; *The Music Goes 'Round And Around* (Kaye, Gordon) Red Hodgson, Edward Farley, Michael Riley; *Carnival Of Venice* (Kaye) J. Bellak; *Jingle Bells* (Kaye) J.S. Pierpont; *Paradise* (Crosby) Gordon Clifford, Nacio Herb Brown.

Though far too young for the role, Sal Mineo (right) played drummer Gene Krupa in **The Gene Krupa Story** (Columbia) and, while fine in the early stages of the biopic, was never really convincing as Krupa the heavy drinker and habitual marijuana smoker. Following the familiar pattern of the idealistic young musician who, after deserting his wholesome upbringing (and the priesthood) for the more exciting world of jazz, goes through a rough patch, but bounces back etc. etc,, it was a solid but uninspired effort which relied more on its musical sequences than its screenplay (by Orin Jannings) for its entertainment value. Susan Kohner (left) played Mineo's hometown sweetheart and James Darren his best pal, with other parts in Philip A. Waxman's production going to Susan Oliver, Celia Lovsky and Yvonne Craig. Though Mineo was seen banging at the drums, it was Krupa audiences heard. Also lending their talents: Red Nichols, Ruby Lane, Shelly Manne, Anita O'Day, Buddy Lester and Bobby Troup as well as the Gene Krupa Orchestra. Musical numbers: *I Love My Baby* (Lane) Bud Green, Harry Warren; *Memories Of You* (O'Day) Eubie Blake, Andy Razaf; *Royal Garden Blues* (Krupa Orchestra) Spencer Williams, Clarence Williams; *Cherokee* (Krupa Orchestra) Ray Noble; *Indiana* (Krupa Orchestra, Nichols) Ballard MacDonald, James Hanley; *Way Down Yonder In New Orleans* (Krupa Orchestra) Henry Creamer, J. Turner Layton; *Let There Be Love* (Darren) Ian Grant, Lionel Rand; *Song Of India* (Studio Orchestra) Rimsky-Korsakov; *Drum Crazy* (Studio Orchestra); *Spiritual Jazz* (Studio Orchestra).

An inconsequential musical from Warner Bros. set in the world of rodeo, **Born Reckless** starred Jeff Richards as a cowboy down on his luck, Arthur Hunnicutt as his grizzled partner and Mamie van Doren (illustrated) as the trick rider who hitches up with the two men along the way. A totally forgettable programmer, it was scripted by Richard Landau (from a story by Landau and the film's producer, Aubrey Schenk) and directed by Howard W. Koch. Supporting the principals (who needed all the support they could get) were Carol Ohmart, Tom Duggan, Tex Williams, Nacho Galindo, Orlando Rodriguez and Johnny Glenn and His Group. Songs and musical numbers included: *Song Of The Rodeo* Buddy Bregman, Stanley Styne; *Home Type Girl*; *Seperate The Men From The Boys*; *A Little Longer*; *Born Reckless* Bregman; *Something To Dream About* Charles Singleton, Larry Coleman.
▽

△

An ageing James Cagney became a song and dance man one more time in Universal's **Never Steal Anything Small**. A decidedly amoral entertainment – based on Maxwell Anderson and Rouben Mamoulian's unproduced musical 'Devil's Hornpipe' – it featured Cagney (centre) as a sentimental, even lovable, waterfront hood who'll stop at nothing, including perjury, bribery and grand larceny to get what he wants; and what he wants is to become president of United Stevedores. Shirley Jones (left) co-starred as Linda, the girl he loves (and whose marriage to a young lawyer he attempts to destroy by laying a trumped-up charge of corruption on the lawyer) with other roles under Charles Lederer's uncertain direction going to Roger Smith (right, as the lawyer), Cara Williams, Nehemiah Persoff, Anthony Caruso, Royal Dano and Jack Albertson. Lederer also wrote it, Aaron Rosenberg produced (in CinemaScope and Eastmancolor) and Hermes Pan choreographed. Allie Wrubel composed the music, and Maxwell Anderson the lyrics, the best of which, an item called, 'I'm Sorry, I Want A Ferrari' featured Cagney and Cara Williams in a duet. Other songs and musical numbers included: *Never Steal Anything Small*; *I Haven't Got A Thing To Wear*; *It Takes Love To Make A Home*; *Helping Out Friends*.

Apart from the casting of Leslie Parrish (right, as Daisy Mae), Stella Stevens (as Appassionata von Climax), and a few other minor actors who had not appeared in the stage show, the screen version of Norman Panama and Melville Frank's Broadway hit **Li'l Abner** (based on the cartoon characters created by Al Capp) came to the screen in a production (by Panama) as close to the original as was possible, without it simply being a filmed version of the stage show. Peter Palmer repeated his super central performance as the beefcake hero of the piece, Pappy and Mammy Yokum were played by Joe E. Marks and hoydenish Billie Hayes, the marvellous Stubby Kaye (left) was Marryin' Sam the marriage vendor, with other deliciously Capp-like performances coming from Bern Hoffman (centre) as Earthquake McGoon, the dirtiest wrestler in the world, Al Nesor as Evil Eye Fleagle, Howard St John as General Bullmoose and Julie Newmar as Stupefyin' Jones. All about the fight put up by the citizens of Dogpatch (whose community is deemed the most useless in the whole of America) to prevent the government from using the place as a test site for the A-bomb, its mildly satirical content took second place to the energy engendered by the frenetic performances, and by Michael Kidd and Dee Dee Wood's infectious, foot-stomping choreography, seen at its bracing best in 'Don't Take The That Rag Off'n The Bush' and Stubby Kaye's showstopper 'Jubilation T. Cornpone'. The excellent score was by Gene De Paul and Johnny Mercer, and it was written and directed (in Technicolor and Vistavision) by Frank and Panama, with a cast that was completed by Ted Thurston, William Lanteau, Carmen Alvarez, Alan Carney, Joe Ploski and Diki Lerner. Other songs and musical numbers: *A Typical Day*; *If I Had My Druthers*; *Room Enuff For Us*; *Namely You*; *The Country's In The Very Best Of Hands*; *Unnecessary Town*; *I'm Past My Prime*; *I Wish It Could Be Otherwise*; *Put 'Em Back The Way They Wuz*; *Matrimonial Stomp*.
▽

A competent low-budgeter from the Columbia stable, **Hey Boy, Hey Girl** starred Louis Prima (as himself) and Keely Smith (both illustrated) as a parishioner who helps her parish priest by securing the services of Prima to boost attendances for the local church bazaar. Eighty-one minutes and several songs later, they're madly in love. Such was the storyline devised and written by Raphael Hayes and James West, which also found room to accommodate the talents of Sam Butera and The Witnesses, as well as James Gregory, Henry Slatem, Kim Charney and Barbara Heller. The producer was Harry Romm and the director David Lowell Rich. Songs and musical numbers: *Oh Marie*; *Autumn Leaves* Joseph Kosma, Jacques Prevert, Johnny Mercer; *Hey Boy, Hey Girl*; *Lazy River* Hoagy Carmichael, Sidney Arodin; *When The Saints Go Marching In* (traditional); *Fever* J.R. Davenport, Eddie Cooley; *Nitey Nite*; *A Banana Split For My Baby*; *You Are My Love*.
▽

AL presents SHIRLEY MacLAINE in "SWEET CHARITY" A PANAVISION
OHN McMARTIN · CHITA RIVERA · PAULA KELLY
STUBBY KAYE
MONTALBAN as The Actor
AVIS JR. as Big Daddy

LEE MARVIN · CLINT EASTWOOD · JEAN SEBERG
PAINT YOUR WAGON

1960

Academy Awards

Cinematography (colour)
NOMINATIONS INCLUDED: *Pepe* (Columbia)
Joe MacDonald

Art Direction (Set Decoration) (colour)
NOMINATIONS INCLUDED: *Pepe* Ted Haworth;
William Kiernan

Costume Design (colour)
NOMINATIONS INCLUDED: *Can-Can* (20th
Century-Fox) Irene Sharaff. *Pepe* Edith Head.

Sound
NOMINATIONS INCLUDED: *Pepe* Columbia Studio
Sound Dept.; Charles Rice, sound director

Film Editing
NOMINATIONS INCLUDED: *Pepe* Viola Lawrence
and Al Clark

Music
Song
NOMINATIONS INCLUDED: 'Faraway Part Of
Town' *Pepe* Andre Previn *cm*; Dory Langdon
lyr. 'The Second Time Around' *High Time*
(20th Century-Fox) Jimmy Van Heusen *cm*;
Sammy Cahn *lyr*.

Scoring Of A Musical Picture
Song Without End (Columbia) Morris Stoloff
and Harry Sukman.
NOMINATIONS INCLUDED: *Bells Are Ringing*
(MGM) Andre Previn, *Can-Can* Nelson Riddle.
Let's Make Love (20th Century-Fox)
Lionel Newman and Earle H. Hagen.
Pepe Johnny Green

The Annual Top Moneymaking Films
INCLUDED: *Li'l Abner* (Paramount). *Can-Can*.

Bing Crosby (right) was ill served by Tom and Frank Waldman's script (story by Garson Kanin) for **High Time** (20th Century-Fox), a minor effort in which he played a middle-aged widower and successful owner of a chain of restaurants, who surprises his grown-up children by enrolling in a university, determined to further his education by taking a degree. Though patently too old for this sort of college caper, he did have one good scene in which, as part of his initiation ceremony, he attends a swanky ball in drag (illustrated). He also had one good song: 'The Second Time Around' by Jimmy Van Heusen and Sammy Cahn. Nicole Maurey played a French professor Crosby finds himself attracted to, with the younger members of the cast represented by Tuesday Weld, Fabian, and Richard Beymer (left). Also in it: Yvonne Craig, Patrick Adiarte, Jimmy Boyd and Kenneth MacKenna. A Bing Crosby production, it was directed by Blake Edwards. Other songs: *Nobody's Perfect; I Had A Dream Dear; Lovely Lady* Van Heusen, Cahn; *The Foggy Foggy Dew* (trad.; *It Came Upon A Midnight Clear* (trad).

◁ Director Vincente Minnelli brought nothing to the screen version of the Broadway smash **Bells Are Ringing** (MGM) that wasn't already apparent in Jerome Robbins's original production. Two new numbers ('Better Than A Dream' and 'Do It Yourself') were added, five others dropped and the lively 'Mu-cha-cha' dance unnecessarily shortened. Otherwise it was a fairly faithful transposition, all of whose best assets were rolled up into one big clump of talent called Judy Holliday. As she had done for 924 performances on Broadway, Holliday played Ella Peterson, an answering girl at 'Susanswerphone', who'll stop at nothing to keep her numerous clients (including a playwright, and a dentist with songwriting aspirations), happy. It's after the playwright – suavely played by Dean Martin (illustrated, with Holliday) – oversleeps and fails to respond to his 'wake up' call, causing Holliday to rush over to his apartment to see that he keeps an important appointment, that love begins to bloom. A subplot involving a bookmaker (Eddie Foy Jr) gave the show one of its best numbers – 'It's A Simple Little System' – sung by Foy Jr as an explanation of his betting techniques. But it was Holliday's show – and she was a joy throughout, especially in a typical show-biz party sequence in which, unlike all the other guests present, she was unable to 'Drop That Name' (she also sang 'Better Than A Dream' with Martin – he sang 'Do It Yourself'). Her big solo moment, though, came at the end of the film, in a number called 'I'm Goin' Back (to the Bonjour Tristesse Brassiere Company)'. **Bells Are Ringing**'s lyrics and screenplay were by Betty Comden and Adolph Green, the score was by Jule Styne, Andre Previn was the musical director, and Charles O'Curran the choreographer. Arthur Freed produced (in CinemaScope and Metrocolor) and his cast was completed by Hal Linden, Fred Clark, Jean Stapleton, Frank Gorshin (doing a good impression of Marlon Brando), Ruth Storey, Dort Clark, Bernie West, Valerie Allen, Steven Peck and Gerry Mulligan. Other songs and musical numbers: *Bells Are Ringing* (chorus); *It's A Perfect Relationship* (Holliday); *The Party's Over* (Holliday); *I Met A Girl* (Martin); *The Midas Touch* (Linden); *Just In Time* (Holliday, Martin).

Can-Can (20th Century-Fox) had everything ▷ going for it: a pre-sold title, a buoyant Cole Porter score which included such numbers as 'C'Est Magnifique' and 'It's All Right With Me', and a cast headed by Frank Sinatra (who sang both the above mentioned songs), Shirley MacLaine (right), Maurice Chevalier and Louis Jourdan. That it all turned out to be such an unmitigated bore was as mysterious as it was disappointing. The story of a café owner (MacLaine) who faces prosecution for allowing the Can-Can to be performed at her establishment, and her romantic entanglements with the two men in her life (Sinatra and Jourdan), it simply lacked sparkle – both in the performances and in Walter Lang's direction – and was far too long at 134 minutes. In fact, the only good thing was Juliet Prowse (centre left) as Claudine, the snake. Her dancing (choreographed by Hermes Pan), at least, had class. Producer Jack Cummings tampered with Porter's score, replacing several of the shows's numbers with 'safer' Porter standards, such as 'Let's Do It' (Sinatra, MacLaine), 'Just One Of Those Things' (Chevalier), and 'You Do Something To Me' (Jourdan). Nelson Riddle arranged and conducted the music. The tiresome screenplay, based on the book by Abe Burrows, was by Dorothy Kingsley and Charles Lederer, with

parts in it for Marcel Dalio, Leon Belasco, Nestor Paiva and Marc Wilder. It was photographed in Todd-AO and Technicolor by William H. Daniels. Other songs and musical numbers: *Maidens Typical Of France* (chorus); *Come Along*

With Me (MacLaine); *Live And Let Live* (Jourdan, Chevalier); *Adam And Eve Ballet* (MacLaine, Prowse, chorus); *Montmartre* (Sinatra, Chevalier); *Snake Dance* (Prowse); *Apache Dance* (MacLaine).

Song Without End (Columbia) was a colourfully produced (by William Goetz) biopic that pleased the eye and the ear, but left the intellect thoroughly undernourished. Between its effusive outpourings of music, Oscar Millard's screenplay attempted to show the conflict faced by Liszt as to whether he was marked out by God to be a pianist or a composer. Dirk Bogarde (illustrated) bravely tried to portray the musician, whose love life was represented by newcomer Capucine as the unattainable Princess Carolyne whom he worships; as well as by his mistress Genevieve Page (giving a much more spirited performance than the glacial Capucine) who worships him. Patricia Morison played George Sand, with other roles taken by Ivan Desny, Martita Hunt, Lou Jacobi, Albert Rueprecht, Marcel Dalio, Lyndon Brook (as Wagner) and Alex Davion (as Chopin). The film was co-directed by Charles Vidor, who died before its completion, and George Cukor, who took over from him. It was photographed in CinemaScope and Eastmancolor. Dirk Bogarde's piano playing was dubbed by Jorg Bolet. Musical extracts: *Mephisto Waltz*; *Un Sospiro*; *Consolation in D Flat*; *Fantasy On Themes From Rigoletto*; *Les Preludes*; *Liebestraum*; *Piano Concerto No 1*; *Hungarian Fantasy*; *Venezia é Napoli*; *Valse Oubliée*; *Sonata In B Minor*; *Spozalizio* Liszt; *Pilgrim's Chorus* from Wagner's 'Tannhauser'; *Rakoczy March* arr. Liszt; *La Campanella* Paganini; Handel's *Largo*; *Rondo Capriccioso* Mendelssohn.

Elvis Presley's first film after returning from military training in Germany was **GI Blues** (Paramount), and it gave the world its first glimpse of a 'new-look', clean-cut, all-American Elvis (illustrated). Based on an idea perpetrated several years earlier in a play called *Sailor Beware*, it was a favourite Paramount plot theme which the studio also used in *The Fleet's In* (1928), *Lady Be Careful* (1936), *The Fleet's In* (1942) and *Sailor Beware* (1951). It had Presley, as an American GI in West Germany, accepting a $300 wager that he'll spend the night with an unforthcoming, rather glacial cabaret 'singer' called Lili (Juliet Prowse). How he eventually wins the wager, as well as Miss Prowse's love, was what Edmund Beloin and Henry Garson's screenplay was all about and it provided our hero with several opportunities to knock his

knees and thump his guitar in the manner so beloved by his millions of fans. In one scene he even worked with puppets, singing the hit number 'Wooden Heart' by Fred Wise, Ben Weisman, Kay Twomey and Bert Kaempfert. James Douglas, Robert Ivers, Leticia Roman, Sigrid Maier, Arch Johnson and The Jordanaires completed the cast, it was produced (in Technicolor) by Hal Wallis, and zestfully directed by Norman Taurog. The choreography was by Charles O'Curran. Other songs and musical numbers: *GI Blues* Sid Tepper, Roy C. Bennett; *Shoppin' Around* Tepper, Bennett, Schroeder; *Tonight Is So Right For Love*; *What's She Really Like* Sid Wayne, Silver; *Frankfurt Special*; *Didya Ever*; *Big Boots* Wayne, Edwards; *Pocketful Of Rainbows* Wise, Weisman; *Doin' The Best I Can* Thomas, Schumann; *Blue Suede Shoes* Perkins.

In **Let's Make Love** (20th Century-Fox), inspired by the same studio's *On The Avenue* (1937), Yves Montand played a Franco-American billionaire who thinks nothing of hiring Milton Berle, Bing Crosby and Gene Kelly to teach him how to be funny, how to sing, and how to dance. Either M. Montand was a very bad pupil, or his trio of teachers useless, because he was just as dull after their collective onslaught on his rather dry personality as he was before it. All the same, he got the girl in the end – the girl being Marilyn Monroe, a singer and dancer in an off-Broadway revue whom Montand meets after learning that he is about to be lampooned in one of the show's sketches. Pretending to be a look-alike of himself, Montand joins the show as an actor – and in no time at all falls head over heels in love with Monroe who, initially, only has eyes for singer Frankie Vaughan. Apart from Mr Berle's brief appearance and Jack Cole's brilliant staging of Cole Porter's 'My Heart Belongs To Daddy' (marvellously performed by Monroe, illustrated) there was little else, apart from the sheer opulence of Jerry Wald's CinemaScope and Color by De Luxe production, to admire. Tony Randall was third-billed as Montand's harassed public relations man, with other parts under George Cukor's bland direction going to Wilfrid Hyde-White, David Burns, Michael David, Mara Lynn, Dennis King Jr, Joe Besser and Madge Kennedy. The screenplay was by Norman Krasna. Other songs and musical numbers: *Specialization*; *Let's Make Love*; *Incurably Romantic*; *You With The Crazy Eyes*; *Sing Me A Song That Sells* Jimmy Van Heusen, Sammy Cahn; *Give Me The Simple Life* Rube Bloom, Harry Ruby.

Pepe (Columbia) was an unconscionably long (195 minutes) disaster that dissipated the gentle talents of its Mexican star, Cantinflas, in a silly protracted story (by Leonard Spigelgass and Sonya Levien, screenplay by Dorothy Kingsley and Claude Binyon) about a Mexican peasant who is brought north of the border by a boozy Hollywood film director (Dan Dailey) to serve as a groom for a horse purchased by Dailey in Mexico. Shirley Jones (left), Carlos Montalban, Edward G. Robinson (as a producer), Vicki Trickett, William Demarest, Hank Henry, Ernie Kovacs and dancer Matt Mattox completed the cast of featured characters, with heavyweight guest star appearances by – among others – Maurice Chevalier (singing Kurt Weill and Maxwell Anderson's 'September Song' and Rodgers and Hart's 'Mimi'), Bing Crosby (singing Johnny Burke and Arthur Johnston's 'Pennies from Heaven', Jimmy Kennedy and Michael Carr's 'South Of The Border' and Harold Arlen and Ted Koehler's 'Let's Fall In Love'), Michael Callan (right). Sammy Davis (singing Mercer and Whiting's 'Hooray for Hollywood'); Jimmy Durante, Zsa Zsa Gabor, Jack Lemmon (in his 'Some Like It Hot' attire), Andre Previn (playing his own composition 'The Rumble'); Debbie Reynolds, Frank Sinatra, Bobby Darin and Billie Burke. New songs were by Andre Previn and Dory Langdon, Eugene Loring choreographed, and it was produced and directed in CinemaScope and Eastmancolor by George Sidney. Other songs and musical numbers: *Pepe* (Jones); *That's How It Went Allright* (Darin, Jones, Mattox, Callan); *Faraway Part Of Town* (Judy Garland, vocal only); *Lovely Day* (Jones); *Suzy's Theme* (orchestral).

1961

Although the sight of the aggressively masculine Jets and their equally macho enemies, the Sharks, donning balletic poses as they sauntered down a grimly realistic West Side back street in New York was initially a jolt to the system, there was no denying the power and impact of producer Robert Wise's Panavision adaptation of the Arthur Laurents-Leonard Bernstein-Stephen Sondheim Broadway hit **West Side Story** (United Artists/Mirisch). A contemporary reworking of the Romeo and Juliet tragedy concerning the doomed love of a white boy for a pretty Puerto Rican girl, it was originally conceived by Jerome Robbins with the emphasis on dance – an emphasis which prevailed in the screen version since Robbins, who received a co-director credit with Robert Wise, was also its choreographer. The most galvanic, award-laden movie musical to emerge in the sixties, **West Side Story** was a brilliant fusion of talents, the only element in it which has since dated being Laurents's book (adapted for the screen by Ernest Lehman) with its rather quaint-sounding street-gang lingo. For the rest, the film, like the stage show, was magnificent entertainment. Natalie Wood received top billing as Maria and was enchanting, though her co-star Richard Beymer (left) as Tony was critically lambasted (unfairly) for
▽

giving what was considered an underpowered performance in a dynamic cast that included Rita Moreno as Anita, George Chakiris as Moreno's Puerto Rican lover Bernardo and Russ Tamblyn (right) as Riff. Also: Tucker Smith (Ice), Tony Mordente (Action), David Winters (A-rab), Eliot Feld (Baby John), Burt Michaels (Snowboy), Sue Oakes (Anybody's) and Carole D'Andrea, Jose de Vega and Simon Oakland. The musical directors were Johnny Green and Saul Chaplin, with Sid Ramin and Irwin Kostal in charge of the orchestrations. Boris Leven was the art director and it was stunningly photographed, in Technicolor and Panavision 70 by Daniel Fapp. Marni Nixon dubbed the vocals for Wood, Jim Bryant for Beymer and Betty Wand for Moreno. Songs and musical numbers: *Prologue* (orchestra); *Jet Song* (Tamblyn, Jets); *Something's Coming* (Beymer); *Dance At The Gym* (orchestra and ensemble); *Maria* (Beymer); *America* (Chakiris, Moreno, chorus); *Tonight* (Beymer, Wood); *Gee Officer Krupke* (Tamblyn, Jets); *I Feel Pretty* (Wood); *One Hand, One Heart* (Wood, Beymer); *Quintet* (Wood, Beymer, Chakiris and Sharks, Moreno, Tamblyn and Jets); *Rumble* (orchestral); *Cool* (Smith, Jets); *A Boy Like That* (Moreno, Wood); *I Have A Love* (Wood, Moreno); *Somewhere* (Wood, Beymer); *Roof Dance* (Wood).

Not nearly as risible as it might have been, 20th Century-Fox's **Snow White And The Three Stooges** (GB: **Snow White And The Three Clowns**) was a showcase for Carol Heiss, the 1960 Olympic figure-skating champion who, in Noel Langley and Elwood Ullman's perfectly acceptable screenplay (special material by Ivan Lane from a story by Charles Wick), based in turn on the famous story by the Brothers Grimm, finds herself protected – not by seven dwarfs – but by 'Ye Stooges Three' (illustrated, with Heiss). Edson Stroll was her personable Prince Charming, and Patricia Medina the wicked witch (as well as the Queen). Completing the cast were Guy Rolfe, Buddy Baer, Michael David and Edgar Barrier. It was beautifully designed by Jack Martin Smith and Maurice Ransford, produced in CinemaScope and Color De Luxe by Charles Wick, and directed by Walter Lang with unexpected lightness of touch considering that most of the film's comedy was supplied by Larry Fine, Moe Howard and Joe de Rita. There were five songs (by Harry Harris and

Earl Brent) and two lavishly mounted ice-ballets by Ron Fletcher. Songs and musical numbers: *Day Like This (Once In A Million Years)*; *Place Called Happiness*; *Because I'm In Love*; *I Said It Then*; *We're Looking For People*.
▽

After his success with the independently produced *Shadows*, John Cassavetes made **Too Late
Blues**, his first Hollywood film, which Paramount released. A 'psychological' musical
drama with a jazz background, it starred Bobby
Darin (left) as an idealistic small-time jazz composer and pianist who 'loses his way' when, after
an act of physical cowardice in a pool room
brawl, his girl friend (Stella Stevens, right) walks
out on him. From then on it's downhill all the
way. Darin becomes a gigolo, and Miss Stevens a
tramp. It ends optimistically, though, when
Darin, battered in spirit and unable to tolerate
further degradation, determines to find his way
back to self-respect and musical creativity. More
interesting for the atmosphere rather than the
characters it created, and with performances by
Darin (who did not sing a single note throughout) and Stella Stevens that carried more conviction than Cassavetes and Richard Carr's
rather pretentious screenplay, **Too Late Blues**
was too off-beat to find widespread favour and
was a box-office flop. David Raksin's marvellous
jazz score, with such titles as 'Sax Raises Its Ugly
Head', 'Look Inward Angel', 'The Rim Shot
Heard Around The World', 'Benny Splits While
Jimmy Rowles', 'Bass Canard', and 'Drum Talk',
was well interpreted by Shelly Manne, Red
Mitchell, Benny Carter, Uan Rasey, Jimmy
Rowles and, in a party sequence, Slim Gaillard
doing 'Something Like That'. Also cast: Cliff
Carnell, Everett Chambers, Seymour Cassell, Bill
Stafford, Marilyn Clark, and James Joyce. Cas-
savetes produced. Other musical numbers: *Move
Over*; *A Song After Sundown*; *When Your Time
Comes*; *Samba Do Cabeza Vermelha*; *Danzon Del
Galante*; *Ciudad De Mexico*.

A really aimless offering from United Artists,
Paris Blues, produced in Technicolor by Sam
Shaw, George Glass and Walter Seltzer, starred
Paul Newman and Sidney Poitier (right) as a
couple of jazz musicians in Paris, and Joanne
Woodward and Diahann Carroll (left) as a pair of
tourists who try to sweet-talk them into returning to the States. Louis Armstrong was also
involved – for no purpose other than to take part
in an entertaining jam session featuring a
number called 'Battle Royal'. Fortunately for the
paying customer, there was more music (most of
it written by Duke Ellington, whose orchestra
was heard but never seen) than plot. Jack Sher
and Walter Bernstein were credited with the
screenplay despite the air of improvization that
permeated it all, and the director was Martin
Ritt. Also cast: Serge Reggiani, Barbara Laage,
Andre Luguet and Marie Versini. Paul Newman's trombone playing was dubbed by Murray
MacEachern, Poitier's saxophone by Paul Gon-
salves, and Reggiani's guitar by Les Span.
Musical numbers: *Mood Indigo* Ellington, Irving
Mills, Albany Bigard; *Take The 'A' Train* Billy
Strayhorn; *Sophisticated Lady* Ellington, Mills,
Mitchell Parish; *Paris Stairs*; *Paris Blues*; *Nite*;
Unclothed Woman; *Wild Man Moore*; *Autumnal
Suite* Ellington; *Guitar D'Amour*; *Birdie Jingle*.

Walt Disney's first live-action musical was **Babes
In Toyland** (Buena Vista), a really dismal experience for anyone over the age of five. An
elaborate, but ultimately cloying and inert reworking of Victor Herbert and Glenn Mac-
Donough's famous operetta, it suffered badly
from the casting of Ray Bolger as the villain of
the piece, and Tommy Sands (right) and Annette
Funicello (left) as the youthful hero and heroine.
Bolger simply wasn't frightening or menacing
enough – and Sands and Funicello were just
plain antiseptic. Ed Wynn went over the top as
the Toymaker, which left Henry Calvin and
Gene Sheldon as Bolger's Laurel and Hardy-type
henchmen. Happily, they were fine. The film's
best moments were supplied by choreographer
Tommy Mahoney, whose staging of Bolger's
'Castle In Spain', involving a fountain of dancing
water, and Funicello's 'I Can't Do The Sum' (both
by Victor Herbert and Glenn MacDonough) was,
at least, inventive. Mary McCarty played Mother
Goose and Tommy Kirk was Grumio, with other
parts going to Brian Corcoran, Ann Jillian,
Marilee and Melanie Arnold, John Glenn and
John Perri. Most of the music was by Victor
Herbert, with additional songs by George Bruns
and Mel Leven. It was written by Joe Rinaldi,
Ward Kimball and Lowell S. Hawley, and
directed without any flair at all by Jack
Donohue. (Technicolor). Other songs and musi-
cal numbers included: *Just A Toy*; *Floretta*; *We
Won't Be Happy Till We Get It*; *Lemonade*; *Just A
Whisper Away*; *March Of The Toys*; *Toyland*
Herbert, MacDonough; *Slowly He Sank Into The
Sea*; *The Workshop Song*; *The Forest Of No Return*
Bruns, Leven.

Producer Ross Hunter and director Henry
Koster brought a high surface gloss to their
screen adaptation of the Rodgers and Hammer-
stein-Joseph Fields long-running Broadway
musical **Flower Drum Song** (Universal International) – as well as an almost unbearable
cuteness that was nothing if not patronizing to
San Francisco's Chinese community among
whom the film was set. The story of a Hong Kong
bride (Myoshi Umeki) who arrives in San Francisco for an arranged marriage to a nightclub
owner (Jack Soo) she has never seen but, happily
for everybody, especially Nancy Kwan, Soo's
nightclub singer sweetheart, finishes up with a
far more desirable college boy called Wang Ta
(James Shigeta), it wasn't one of Rodgers and
Hammerstein's better efforts, though it did have
a few agreeable tunes, the two most durable
being 'I Enjoy Being A Girl' (Kwan, dubbed by B.J.
Baker) and 'A Hundred Million Miracles' (Umeki
and Kam Tong, Tong being dubbed by John
Dodson). Juanita Hall (like Soo and Miss
Umeki) was recruited from the Broadway production and brought her own special brand of
magic to 'Chop Suey'. Final item on the credit
side was Reiko Sato's 'Love Look Away' dream
ballet (dubbed by Marilyn Horne) which briefly
married a passable tune to some exquisite
dancing (choreography by Hermes Pan, see
illustration, with music supervised and conducted by Alfred Newman). It was scripted by
Joseph Fields, and photographed in Panavision
and Technicolor by Russell Metty. Other songs
and musical numbers: *Fan Tan Fanny*; *Grant
Avenue*; *You Are Beautiful*; *I Am Going To Like It
Here*; *The Other Generation*; *Gliding Through My
Memoree*; *Sunday*; *Don't Marry Me*.

Best Picture

NOMINATIONS INCLUDED: *The Music Man* (WB) produced by Morton Da Costa.

Cinematography (colour)

NOMINATIONS INCLUDED: *Gypsy* (WB) Harry Stradling, Sr *The Wonderful World Of The Brothers Grimm* (MGM and Cinerama) Paul C. Vogel.

Art Direction (Set Decoration) (colour)

NOMINATIONS INCLUDED: *The Music Man* Paul Groesse; George James Hopkins. *The Wonderful World Of The Brothers Grimm* George W. Davis and Edward Carfagno; Henry Grace and Dick Pefferle.

Costume Design (colour)

The Wonderful World Of The Brothers Grimm Mary Wills

NOMINATIONS INCLUDED: *Gypsy* Orry-Kelly. *The Music Man* Dorothy Jeakins.

Sound

NOMINATIONS INCLUDED: *The Music Man* Warner Bros. Studio Sound Dept.; George R. Groves, sound director.

Film Editing

NOMINATIONS INCLUDED: *The Music Man* William Ziegler

**Music (New Classification)
Scoring Of Music (Adaptation or Treatment)**

The Music Man Ray Heindorf

NOMINATIONS INCLUDED: *Billy Rose's Jumbo* (MGM) George Stoll. *Gypsy* Frank Perkins. *The Wonderful World Of The Brothers Grimm* Leigh Harline

The Annual Top Moneymaking Films

INCLUDED: *West Side Story* (Mirisch-Seven Arts, United Artists). *The Music Man. Flower Drum Song* (Universal-International). *Blue Hawaii* (Paramount). *Babes In Toyland* (Disney, Buena Vista).

State Fair (20th Century-Fox) was Alice Faye's first film for seventeen years. A third version of Philip Stong's cosy homespun novel (the first two appeared in 1932 and 1945, the latter with a melodious score by Richard Rodgers and Oscar Hammerstein II), Richard Breen's screenplay switched locales from Iowa to Texas and de-countrified it in the process. The small-town atmosphere so necessary to buttress its slender narrative was fatally absent, making the domestic obsessions of the Frake family appear more trivial than ever. Pat Boone (left) played the handsome young hero and, in comparison to his co-stars Bobby Darin and Pamela Tiffin positively sparkled. Putting them all in the shade, however, was Ann-Margret (right), as an entertainer to whom Boone loses his manly heart. She exuded more personality and energy and revealed more talent and ability in her one big production number, 'Isn't It Kinda Fun', than the rest of the cast, including Tom Ewell as Mr Frake, Wally Cox, David Brandon, Clem Harvey and Robert Foulk, combined. The score also contained four other songs originally featured in the 1945 version, and five new ones specially composed by Richard Rodgers (who, on this occasion, supplied both the words and the music) including 'Never Say No' pleasingly sung by Alice Faye who, as Ewell's wife, handled the undemanding role with her characteristic warmth. None of Rodgers's new material, however, was memorable. It was produced (in CinemaScope and Color De Luxe) by Charles Brackett, charmlessly directed by José Ferrer, and choreographed by Nick Castle. Miss Tiffin's vocals were dubbed by Marie Green. Other songs and musical numbers: *Our State Fair*; *It Might As Well Be Spring*; *It's A Grand Night For Singing*; *That's For Me* Rodgers, Hammerstein II; *More Than Just A Friend*; *It's The Little Things In Texas*; *Willing And Eager*; *This Isn't Heaven* Rodgers.

Elvis Presley (illustrated) again played a returning GI in **Blue Hawaii** (Paramount), a colourful, animated travel brochure with 15 songs and a pin-prick of a plot, which found its star taking a job as a courier to a tourist agency rather than settling down in the family pineapple business. His first assignment is to accompany a quartet of schoolgirls (chaperoned by Nancy Walters) around Honolulu. One of them (Jenny Maxwell) falls in love with him but, as Presley already has a steady girl (Joan Blackman), this situation provided Hal Kanter's simple screenplay (story by Allan Weiss) with what little conflict it possessed. It looked splendid in Panavision and Technicolor and, in supporting roles, featured Angela Lansbury, Roland Winters, John Archer, Howard McNear, Flora Hayes, Gregory Gaye, Steve Brodie and Iris Adrian. Vocal accompaniment came from The Jordanaires, Charles O'Curran choreographed, Norman Taurog directed and Hal B. Wallis produced. Songs and musical numbers: *Blue Hawaii* Ralph Rainger, Leo Robin (first sung by Bing Crosby in Paramount's 1937 production *Waikiki Wedding*); *Almost Always True* Fred Wise, Ben Weisman; *Aloha Oe* Lydia Kamekeha Liliukalani, arranged and adapted Elvis Presley; *No More* Don Robertson, Hal Blair; *I Can't Help Falling In Love*; *Ku-U-I-Po* Hugo Peretti, Luigi Creatore, George David Weiss; *Rock-a-Hula Baby* Wise, Weisman, Dolores Fuller; *Moonlight Swim* Sylvia Dee, Weisman; *Ito Eats*; *Slicin' Sand*; *Hawaiian Sunset*; *Beach Boy Blues*; *Island of Love* Sid Tepper, Roy C. Bennett; *Hawaiian Wedding Song* Charles E. King, Al Hoffman, Dick Manning.

Bing Crosby (right) and Bob Hope (left) took to the 'Road' for the last time in **The Road To Hong Kong** (United Artists), but with Joan Collins (centre), not Dorothy Lamour, as the girl in the middle. Lamour, however, wasn't entirely neglected in Norman Panama and Melvin Frank's screenplay: she appeared as a nightclub performer whose new act her erstwhile partners briefly augment. The story (as per usual) featured Crosby and Hope as a couple of conmen, this time selling do-it-yourself spaceships to native Tibetans. A bout of amnesia suffered by Hope brings the pair into contact with a high lama (Felix Aylmer) who restores both Hope's memory and his knowledge of a secret rocket fuel formula sought after by a group of spies. After fleeing to Hong Kong (where they meet Lamour and become involved with shapely spy Collins), they are finally rocketed into space where they encounter Frank Sinatra and Dean Martin, guest-starring as a couple of spacemen. Peter Sellers, Jerry Colonna and David Niven also appeared as themselves, with other parts going to Robert Morley, Roger Delgardo, Walter Gotell and Peter Madden. The production, which in no way captured the effortless zaniness of the earlier 'Road' shows, was mounted in England for Melnor Films Ltd, with Panama and Frank producing as well as directing. The score was by Sammy Cahn and Jimmy Van Heusen (whose best song was 'Teamwork', sung by Crosby, Collins and Hope), and the choreography was by Jack Baker and Sheila Myers. Other songs and musical numbers: *The Road To Hong Kong*; *Warmer Than A Whisper*; *Let's Not Be Sensible*; *Warmer Than A Whisper* (Secret Formula Version).

The Wonderful World Of The Brothers Grimm (MGM) in Cinerama was (quite literally) blown up out of all proportion to its modest and familiar content, the imperfections still in evidence in the process in no way improving matters. Laurence Harvey and Karl Boehm played the story-telling brothers and Oscar Homolka the Duke who gives them a hard time because he disapproves of fairy tales, with David Hampton, Charles Beaumont and William Roberts's screenplay also creating parts for Claire Bloom (as Dorothea Grimm), Barbara Eden, Walter Slezak, Ian Wolfe, Elisabeth Neumann, Arnold Stang and Martita Hunt. The three fairy tales featured were 'The Dancing Princess' with Yvette Mimieux, Russ Tamblyn (both illustrated), and Jim Backus, 'The Cobbler and the Elves' with Laurence Harvey, and George Pal's Puppetoons and, best of all, 'The Singing Bone', with Terry-Thomas, Buddy Hackett, Robert Crawford Jr and Otto Kruger. The background score was by Leigh Harline, the songs by Bob Merrill, the dances by Alex Romero, and the sugar-coated direction – devoid of both magic and menace – by Henry Levin and George Pal, the latter also serving as producer. Songs and musical numbers: *Brothers Grimm Theme*; *Ah-oom*; *The Dancing Princess*; *The Singing Bone*; *Christmas Land*; *D-R-A-G-O-N*; *Gypsy Fire*; *Above The Stars*.

Guest stars Ray Charles, Roger Williams and Bobby Vee were brought in by producer Jack Leewood to bolster the entertainment value in a bantamweight offering called **Swingin' Along** (20th Century-Fox), whose story homed in on the misadventures of a San Francisco-based songwriting nebbish (Tommy Noonan, left) and his successful teaming with con-man Pete Marshall (right). Together they enter a songwriting competition and win first prize. No prizes, however, for Jameson Brewer's nebbish of a screenplay, Charles Barton's direction, or the bulk of the performances from a cast that included Connie Gilchrist, Barbara Eden, Carol Christensen, Alan Carney, Mike Mazurki, Tommy Farrell and Lennie Breman. Best songs were 'Song Of The City' by Walter Kent and Walton Farrar, and Ray Charles's 'What'd I Say' performed by Charles in the film's only memorable sequence. (CinemaScope and Color by De Luxe).

Elvis Presley's torso was publicly on view in **Kid Galahad** (United Artists), a remake of the 1937 Edward G. Robinson drama of the same name (Warner Bros.) but not nearly as effective. Presley (right) played a sparring partner in co-star Gig Young's training camp, and the plot (by Francis Wallace, screenplay by William Fay) had him being sadistically paired with a far superior opponent in a bout arranged by gangster David Lewis, to whom Young owes money. Joan Blackman was Young's sister (and Presley's romance), Lola Albright (left) Young's girlfriend; Charles Bronson, Ned Glass, Robert Emhardt, Michael Dante, Judson Pratt, George Mitchell and Richard Devon completed the cast for producer David Weisbart. It was directed by Phil Karlson (in Color De Luxe) for the Mirisch Company. Songs: *King Of The Whole Wide World* Ruth Batchelor, Bob Roberts; *This Is Living*; *Riding The Rainbow* Fred Wise, Ben Weisman; *Home Is Where The Heart Is*; *A Whistling Tune* Sherman Edwards, Hal David; *I Got Lucky* Dee Fuller, Wise, Weisman (all sung by Presley).

Warner Bros. might easily have secured more famous names than producer-director Morton DaCosta and star Robert Preston (right) for their handsomely staged film version of Meredith Willson's hit Broadway musical **The Music Man**, but Jack Warner astutely decided that those responsible for the theatrical success were most capable of retaining that success on the screen. The gamble paid off: DaCosta's direction proved to be entirely cinematic, especially in the showstoppin' '76 Trombones'; and Robert Preston, as the bogus music master whose presence in River City, Iowa, changes the lives of everyone, young and old, who comes in contact with him, charged across the screen like a midwestern hurricane, leaving only warmth and good humour in his wake. To the song 'Trouble' he brought all the authority of 883 stage performances without ever losing his spontaneity. Shirley Jones was perfectly cast as Marian the librarian who succumbs to Preston's spellbinding charms, and Buddy Hackett (left), Hermione

Elvis Presley (illustrated) turned up in Florida for **Follow That Dream** (United Artists), playing the singing member of an itinerant family, comprising pa Arthur O'Connell and three unofficially adopted children, who claim squatter's rights on some abandoned government property and find themselves up against a couple of gangsters (Simon Oakland and Jack Kruschen). Charles Lederer's unexciting screenplay (from a play by Richard Powell) allowed Presley an opportunity to prove his prowess as a judo expert, as well as to sing five indifferent songs. Ann Helm played the girl who loves him, Joanna Moore (illustrated) a State Welfare superintendent, with other roles in David Weisbart's production going to Gavin and Robert Koon, Pam Ogles and Roland Winters. Gordon Douglas directed in Panavision and Color De Luxe. Songs: *Follow That Dream* Fred Wise, Ben Weisman; *What A Wonderful Life* Sid Wayne, Jerry Livingston; *I'm Not The Marrying Kind* Mack David, Sherman Edwards; *Sound Advice* Bill Giant, Bernie Baum, Florence Kaye; *Angel* Sid Tepper.

Gingold, Paul Ford, Timmy Everett, Pert Kelton, The Buffalo Bills and a very appealing Ronnie Howard played assorted inhabitants of the small town. Both Onna White's galvanic choreography and the orchestrations of Ray Heindorf, Frank Comstock and Gus Levene showed off Willson's cheerful score to its best advantage; and Marion Hargrove's screenplay remained faithful to the original book by Willson and Franklin Lacey. Other songs and musical numbers: *Rock Island*; *Iowa Stubborn* (chorus); *If You Don't Mind* (Jones, Kelton); *Goodnight My Someone* (Preston, Jones); *Sincere* (Buffalo Bills); *The Sadder But Wiser Girl* (Preston, Hackett); *Pick A Little* (Gingold, women); *Marian The Librarian* (Preston); *Being In Love* (Jones); *Gary, Indiana* (Preston, Howard); *The Wells Fargo Wagon* (Howard); *Lida Rose/Will I Ever Tell You* (Jones, Buffalo Bills); *Shipoopi* (Hackett, chorus); *Till There Was You* (Preston, Jones) Willson; *Goodnight Ladies* (Buffalo Bills) Harry H. Williams, Egbert Van Alstyne.

△

Brought to the screen with enough fidelity to maintain the original's quality and flavour, but given sufficient cinematic flair to work purely as film, **Gypsy** was the finest stage-to-film transcription of all the Broadway hits slavishly adapted for the big screen during the sixties and early seventies. The original stage show, with its Arthur Laurents book (adapted from Gypsy Rose Lee's memoirs) and brilliant Jule Styne-Stephen Sondheim score, was the apotheosis of the Broadway musical in its integration of story, character, music and dance, and has become a milestone in the history of the American musical theatre. Leonard Spigelgass's screenplay subtly added depth and texture to the characterizations, plus an immeasurable amount of substance and wit. Other plus factors in the film were producer-director Mervyn LeRoy's loving recreation of a bygone theatrical era, and his use of a perfect cast. The central role of Mama Rose, the stage mother to end them all, had been played on Broadway by Ethel Merman, and where Merman had been volcanic, Rosalind Russell, the screen Rose, was merely dynamic, with Miss Russell accurately conveying Rose's unflagging energy and zeal, her almost frightening ambition and, at the same time, the enthusiasm, warmth and humour that made it feasible that her children loved her while being frustrated by her. As the candy-man Herbie, who becomes Rose's manager, lover, companion and trouble shooter, Karl Malden maintained his masculinity and an attractive simplicity while playing second fiddle to Rose, whose inability to commit herself to marriage finally forces him to desert her. Natalie Wood as the child-woman Louise, later Gypsy (see illustration), was at her loveliest, perfectly capturing the note of gaucheness and vulnerability of the youngster; while her transformation into a sophisticated, determinedly independent (and beautiful) woman, was breathtaking. LeRoy's production, progressing from the heyday of vaudeville, through its dying gasps, to the gaudy world of burlesque, was theatrically stylized, sometimes to bewitching effect – notably in a steamy back alley where one of the chorus boys (Paul Wallace) demonstrates his dreamed-of nightclub act to an adoring Louise. Only after Rose has decided that she will make Louise into a star, does the film momen-

tarily flag, and partial blame must rest with the distributors who cut the lively trio 'Together, Wherever We Go'. The lapse is brief, however, and with the act's erroneous booking into a seedy burlesque house, the stage is set for Louise's debut as a stripper – on which subject she is the recipient of some hilarious tuition from three hardened professionals (Faith Dane, Betty Bruce and Roxanne Arlen) in one of the show's standout numbers, 'You Gotta Have A Gimmick'. Apart from the mentioned excision, the original score was left intact, from the excitingly orchestrated overture (conducted on screen by composer Styne) to Russell's devastating 'Rose's Turn' in which her hopes, regrets, frustrations, her bitterness, and her pent-up desires to be a performer, come blazing out in a musical *tour-de-force*. Russell was partially dubbed by Lisa Kirk in a skilful 'ghosting' blend, and this mesmeric finale, along with other show stoppers like the forceful 'Some People' and the defiantly optimistic 'Everything's Coming Up Roses', were given their full measure of authority. Louise's sister, June (Ann Jilliann) bursting onto the Ziegfeld stage with 'Broadway, Broadway', June and Louise's plaintive waltz duet 'If Mama Was Married', and Louise's increasingly confident renditions of 'Let Me Entertain You' – the *leitmotif* which transforms itself from 'cute' kiddies' number into Gypsy's artful, sexually suggestive accompaniment to her striptease act were other notable numbers. Frank P. Perkins was the musical supervisor, Harry Stradling was responsible for the evocative photography (Technirama and Technicolor) and Robert Tucker choreographed. One must, however, acknowledge the debt that the whole creative team owed to Jerome Robbins who directed and choreographed the stage original. The cast was completed by Diane Pace and Suzanne Cupito (June and Louise as children), Harry Shannon, Parley Baer, Jean Willes, Louis Quinn, George Petrie, Ben Lessy and Guy Raymond. Other numbers: *Small World* (Russell); *Baby June And Her Newsboys* (Cupito, Pace, boys); *Mr Goldstone, I Love You* (Russell, ensemble); *Little Lamb* (Wood); *All I Need Is The Girl* (Wallace, with Wood); *Dainty June And Her Farmboys* (Jilliann, Wood, boys); *Cow Song* (Jillian); *You'll Never Get Away From Me* (Russell, Malden).

Made entirely on location in Europe by Walt Disney Productions, **Almost Angels** (GB: **Born To Sing**) set out to show that there was nothing 'softie' about the numerous youngsters who comprise the famed Vienna Boys' Choir, and that basically they are as regular a bunch of kids as you'd expect to find back home in the States even though one scene showed them dressed up as little girls! Still, the singing was glorious – and there was even something of a plot (by R.A. Stemmle, screenplay by Vernon Harris) concerning a choir boy (Peter Weck) whose voice breaks on the eve of a major tour. Hans Holt, Fritz Eckhardt, Bruni Lobel, Gunther Phillipp, Vincent Winter (illustrated), Sean Scully and Denis Gilmore were also in it, the choreographer was Norman Thomson, the musical director Heinz Schreiter (with Helmuth Froschauer conducting the Vienna Philharmonic Orchestra), and Peter V. Herald was the production supervisor. Steve Perrin directed. The Technicolor production was released by Buena Vista. Songs: *Blue Danube*; *Emperor Waltz*; *Vienna Bonbons*; *Vienna Blood*; *Stadt Und Land*; *Lustiger Rat*; *Tritsch-Tratsch Polka*; *Roses From The South* Johann Strauss II; *Radetsky March* Johann Strauss Sr; *Chicken And The Trout* Froschauer; *Rose On The Meadow*; *The Linden Tree* Franz Schubert; *Cradle Song* Johannes Brahms; *Der Postillon*; *Well Then, The Time Has Come*; *Gay Is The Gypsy Life*; *Winter Is Almost Over*; *Greensleeves* (traditional).

▽

Busby Berkeley was the Second Unit director on ▷
Billy Rose's **Jumbo** (MGM), the last film on which
he worked. An old-fashioned circus extravaganza based on Rose's mammoth 1935 stage
production at New York's Hippodrome, it came
nowhere near Cecil B. De Mille's *The Greatest
Show On Earth* (Paramount, 1952) in quality,
spectacle or excitement, and was little more
than an excuse for a series of pleasant but
undistinguished circus routines and musical
numbers. These were tacked on to a familiar plot
which featured Doris Day (left) as the daughter
of an all-but-bankrupt circus owner (Jimmy
Durante, centre right) whose only bankable
asset is his elephant Jumbo; and Stephen Boyd
(right) as the son of a rival circus owner (Dean
Jagger) who infiltrates Durante's circus with
sabotage on his mind, but finishes up on
Durante's side, and in love with his daughter.
The score, by Richard Rodgers and Lorenz Hart,
retained the bulk of the numbers originally
featured in the 1935 stage presentation, the
most imaginatively staged being 'Over And Over
Again' performed by Doris Day and several
trapeze artists under the Big Top. 'Why Can't I',
sung by Day and co-star Martha Raye (as the
circus's resident comedienne, centre left) was
lifted from Rodgers and Hart's *Spring Is Here*
(1929) and, from *The Boys From Syracuse* (1938),
came 'This Can't Be Love' (Day). The finale was
supplied by Roger Edens and was called 'Saw-
dust, Spangles And Dreams'. Using material
originally written by Rodgers and Hart, it was
effectively belted out by the film's four principals,
as was the opening, 'The Circus Is On Parade'.
Despite the energy and the enthusiasm that
went into the project, **Jumbo**, directed by Charles
Walters, was somewhat less than jumbo entertainment. The screenplay was by Sidney Sheldon, based on a musical play by Ben Hecht and
Charles MacArthur. Joseph Waring, Lynn
Wood, Charles Watts, James Chandler, Robert
Burton, Wilson Wood, Norman Leavitt and
Grady Sutton completed the cast for producers
Joe Pasternak and Martin Melcher (Mr Doris
Day). The score was orchestrated by Conrad
Salinger who, after completing the arrange-
ments for the song 'Little Girl Blue' committed
suicide. Other songs and musical numbers: *My
Romance*; *The Most Beautiful Girl In The World*.

Except for an ingenious use of backgrounds by ▷
Matisse, Modigliani, Toulouse-Lautrec, Cézanne
and Van Gogh, the UPA cartoon **Gay Purr-ee**
(illustrated), released by Warner Bros., was derivative of Disney but inferior to the best of his
studio's output. The screenplay by Chuck and
Dorothy Jones (about a country cat Mewsette,
town cat Jaune-Tom, and their misadventures
with some city slickers led by smooth, sleek
Meowrice) was pleasant if unoriginal, but the
Harold Arlen-E.Y. Harburg score didn't quite hit
the right note for children and the dubbing by
several famous voices – Judy Garland, Robert
Goulet, Red Buttons, Hermione Gingold and Mel
Blanc – was perhaps not sufficient an attraction
for their parents. Paul Frees and Morey Amster-
dam were also heard. It was directed (in Techni-
color) by Abe Levitow for executive producers
Henry J. Saperstein and Lee Orgel. Songs: *Paris
Is A Lonely Town*; *The Money Cat*; *Take My Hand,
Paree*; *Mewsette*; *Little Drops Of Rain*; *Roses Red,
Violets Blue*; *Bubbles*; *The Horse Won't Talk*.

Elvis Presley's fourth film in 1962 was **Girls!
Girls! Girls!** (Paramount) and in it he took to the
open seas as an impecunious charter boat pilot
(illustrated). Laurel Goodwin supplied the romantic interest as a wealthy girl pretending to be a
working girl with other parts in Edward Anhalt
and Allan Weiss's thoroughly undistinguished
screenplay going to Stella Stevens (wasted as a
torch singer – although she did have three songs
of her own to sing, including 'The Nearness Of
You' by Ned Washington and Hoagy Carmichael, and 'Never Let Me Go' by Jay Livingston and Ray Evans), Jeremy Slate, Guy Lee,
Benson Fong, Beulah Quo, Robert Strauss,
Frank Puglia, Lili Valenti and Barbara and Betty
Beall. The film was more convincing musically
than dramatically, its numerous songs (staged
by Charles O'Curran) being its *raison d'être*. Hal
Wallis produced (in Panavision and Techni-
color) and Norman Taurog directed. Songs and
musical numbers: *Girls, Girls, Girls* Jerry Leiber,
Mike Stoller; *Return to Sender*; *We're Coming In
Loaded* Otis Blackwell, Winfield Scott; *A Boy Like
Me, A Girl Like You*; *Song Of The Shrimp*; *Earth
Boy*; *The Walls Have Ears* Sid Tepper, Roy C.
Bennett; *Thanks To The Rolling Sea*; *Because Of
Love*; *Where Do You Come From?* Ruth Batchelor,
Bob Roberts; *We'll Be Together, Mama* Charles
O'Curran, Dudley Brooks; *I Don't Wanna Be Tied*
Bill Giant, Bernie Baum, Florence Kaye; *I Don't
Want To* Janice Torre, Fred Spielman. ◁

1963

Academy Awards

Sound
NOMINATIONS INCLUDED: *Bye Bye Birdie*
(Columbia) Columbia Studio Music Dept.;
Charles Rice, sound director

Music
Scoring Of Music (Adaptation or Treatment)
NOMINATIONS INCLUDED: *Bye Bye Birdie* John
Green. *The Sword In The Stone* (Disney,
Buena Vista) George Bruns.

The Annual Top Moneymaking Films
INCLUDED: *Bye Bye Birdie. Gypsy* (WB). *The
Wonderful World Of The Brothers Grimm*
(MGM and Cinerama).

An exuberant and cinematically inventive adaptation of Charles Strouse, Lee Adams and Michael Stewart's Broadway hit, **Bye Bye Birdie** (Columbia) drew its inspiration from the Presley hysteria that was sweeping the country, telling the story of singing idol Conrad Birdie who, to the dismay of his millions of fans, is about to be drafted into the army. The news is equally upsetting to a songwriter called Albert Peterson who has written the title tune for Birdie's latest movie. For if Birdie is drafted, the film won't be made, and Albert won't receive the royalties that will enable him to break away from his possessive mother and marry his secretary, Rosie. Disaster is averted when Rosie persuades Albert to write another tune for Birdie – called 'One Last Kiss' – and talks Ed Sullivan into letting Birdie introduce it on his famous Sunday evening TV show where it is sung by small-towner Kim McAfee. The plot was solid enough to support the series of Strouse-Adams songs that went with it, and gave showy parts to Janet Leigh (top billed) as Rosie, Dick Van Dyke as songwriter Albert, Ann-Margret (in a stand-out performance) as Kim McAfee, Maureen Stapleton as Van Dyke's clinging mother, Jesse Pearson as the hip-notising Conrad Birdie, and Bobby Rydell. The musical numbers were zippily staged by Onna White (see illustration), most outstandingly in 'The Telephone Hour' (Rydell and ensemble), and the hilarious 'Sultan's Ballet', performed on the Ed Sullivan show at breakneck speed. Also cast: Paul Lynde, Mary LaRoche, Michael Evans, Robert Paige, Bobby Russell, Gregory Morton and (as themselves) John Daly and Ed Sullivan. It was scripted by Irving Brecher, produced by Fred Kohlmar for Kohlmar-Sidney Productions, and directed with a sharp satirical eye by George Sidney. The music was supervised, arranged and conducted by Johnny Green. (Panavision and Technicolor). Other songs and musical numbers: *How Lovely To Be A Woman* (Ann-Margret); *Put On A Happy Face* (Leigh, Van Dyke); *Bye Bye Birdie* (Ann-Margret, Lynde, Roche, Russell); *Honestly Sincere* (Pearson); *One Boy (Girl)* (Rydell, Ann-Margret, Leigh); *Kids* (Van Dyke, Lynde, Stapleton, Russell); *Rosie* (Leigh, Van Dyke); *A Lot Of Livin' To Do* (Ann-Margret, Pearson, Rydell); *One Last Kiss* (Ann-Margret, Rydell, Pearson); *We Love You Conrad* (Ann-Margret, Ensemble); *Hymn For A Sunday Evening* (Ensemble). ▷

Connie Francis (centre left), Paula Prentiss ▷ (right), Dany Robin (centre right), Janis Paige (left), Russ Tamblyn, Richard Long, Ron Randell and Roger Perry were seen to no particular advantage in **Follow The Boys** (MGM), a sequel of sorts to the same studio's *Where The Boys Are*. Written by David T. Chantler and David Osborne – whose story involved a quartet of girls dubbed 'seagulls', and the four sailors they follow from port to port – it gave Miss Francis (top-billed) a chance to sing four songs, which she did most professionally. For the rest, however, it was an unfunny farrago of romantic complications that totally failed to jell under Richard Thorpe's pedestrian and heavy-handed direction. It was produced in Panavision and Metrocolor by Lawrence P. Bachmann, who also provided the original storyline. Songs: *Follow The Boys; Tonight's My Night; Intrigue; Waiting For Billy; Sleepyland* Benny Davis, Ted Murry, Dramato Palumbo; *Italian Lullabye* Connie Francis.

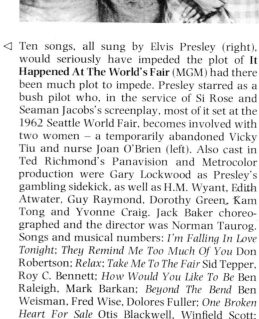

◁ Ten songs, all sung by Elvis Presley (right), would seriously have impeded the plot of **It Happened At The World's Fair** (MGM) had there been much plot to impede. Presley starred as a bush pilot who, in the service of Si Rose and Seaman Jacobs's screenplay, most of it set at the 1962 Seattle World Fair, becomes involved with two women – a temporarily abandoned Vicky Tiu and nurse Joan O'Brien (left). Also cast in Ted Richmond's Panavision and Metrocolor production were Gary Lockwood as Presley's gambling sidekick, as well as H.M. Wyant, Edith Atwater, Guy Raymond, Dorothy Green, Kam Tong and Yvonne Craig. Jack Baker choreographed and the director was Norman Taurog. Songs and musical numbers: *I'm Falling In Love Tonight; They Remind Me Too Much Of You* Don Robertson; *Relax; Take Me To The Fair* Sid Tepper, Roy C. Bennett; *How Would You Like To Be* Ben Raleigh, Mark Barkan; *Beyond The Bend* Ben Weisman, Fred Wise, Dolores Fuller; *One Broken Heart For Sale* Otis Blackwell, Winfield Scott; *Cotton Candy Land* Ruth Batchelor, Bob Roberts; *A World Of Our Own* Bill Giant, Bernie Baum, Florence Kaye; *Happy Ending* Sid Wayne, Weisman.

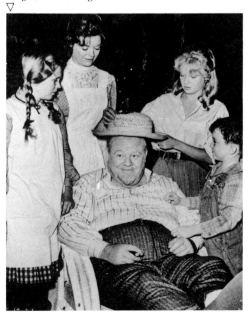

A cloying remake of *Mother Carey's Chickens* (RKO, 1938), **Summer Magic** (Buena Vista), produced by Walt Disney, was the story (by Kate Douglas Wiggins) of the Carey family who move to Maine after the death of their father and, with a little help from Burl Ives, the kindly local postmaster (centre foreground), turn a run-down house belonging to a certain Mr Hamilton (conveniently away in Europe for an extended time) into what estate agents generally describe as a desirable family residence. Dorothy McGuire (centre) was Mother Carey, and her brood were top-starred Hayley Mills (2nd right), Eddie Hodges and Jimmy Mathers (right). Tom Brown played Hamilton who, to the inconvenience of the family, returns unexpectedly from abroad, but who keeps his identity a secret after he meets and falls for Miss Mills. Also cast: Deborah Walley (left), Michael Pollard, Wendy Turner, Una Merkel and Eddie Quillan. Apart from 'The Ugly Bug Ball' written by Richard M. and Robert B. Sherman (who wrote the rest of the score as well) and sung by Ives in a sequence similar to any one might expect to find in a Disney True-Life Adventure short, the songs were unmemorable. So was Sally Benson's screenplay, and James Neilson's cutesy-cutesy direction. Miss McGuire's vocals were dubbed by Marilyn Hooven. Other songs: *Railroad Rag*; *Flitterin'*; *Beautiful Beulah*; *The Pink Of Perfection*; *Summer Magic*; *Femininity*; *On The Front Porch*.

Based on T.H. White's celebrated novel about the boyhood of King Arthur (see illustration), **The Sword In The Stone** (Buena Vista) was Walt Disney's first full-length feature cartoon since *101 Dalmations* in 1961. Belonging more to the 20th century than the 5th century in atmosphere (there was even a sequence at the end of the film that spoofed a popular TV commercial), and relying too often on words rather than actions, the film was in no way vintage Disney, but there was enough humour and wit in it – especially in the characters of Merlin and his pet owl Archimedes (the most successful creation in the film) – to keep the kids and their parents sufficiently amused. Richard M. and Robert B. Sherman wrote half a dozen serviceable songs for it, Wolfgang Reitherman directed, the production supervisor was Ken Peterson, and the voices heard on the soundtrack belonged to Ricky Sorenson (Wart), Sebastian Cabot (Sir Hector), Karl Swenson (Merlin), Junius Matthews (Archimedes), Alan Napier (Sir Pelinore), Norman Alden (Kay), Martha Wentworth (Madam Mim, the second best character in the film), and Robert Reitherman and The Mello Men. Art direction was by Ken Anderson, and the directing animators were Franklin Thomas. Milt Kahal, Oliver Johnston Jr and John Lounsbery. Songs: *A Most Befuddling Thing*; *Blue Oak Tree*; *Mad Madam Mim*; *That's What Makes The World Go Round*; *Higitus Figitus*; *The Legend Of The Sword In The Stone*.

After fifteen years with Columbia, producer Sam Katzman moved to MGM, his first film for that studio being **Hootenanny Hoot** – an underwhelming little entertainment that married a pussy-willow of a plot to a series of musical acts, predominantly 'folk' in their appeal. The best thing that could be said for it was that it made a change from rock'n'roll and twist. All about a TV director (with problems both in his personal and professional life) who, while travelling across country, stumbles on a new 'folk' musical craze in a small mid-western town, promotes it into big business and, in the process, solves his romantic problems, it starred Peter Breck as the director and Ruth Lee as his personal problem, with Joby Baker, Pam Austin, Bobo Lewis, Loren Gilbert and Nick Novarro in support. The script was supplied by James B. Gordon, the music by The Four Brothers, Johnny Cash, The Gateway Trio, Judy Henske, George Hamilton IV, Joe and Eddie, Cathie Taylor and Chris Crosbie – all guest-starred. Hal Belfer choreographed (see illustration), Gene Nelson directed. ▷

◁ The sight of a plumpish Judy Garland (centre) acting out certain scenes in **I Could Go On Singing** (United Artists) which might have been torn from her own life story (and probably were), brought a poignancy to director Ronald Neame's unashamedly sentimental tear-jerker that its hackneyed storyline and general presentation, quite frankly, did not deserve. Garland (in her 35th and final film) played a famous American singer who, while on a concert tour of Britain, looks up an erstwhile flame of hers – a doctor (Dirk Bogarde) by whom she had a son (Gregory Phillips, left). Though the agreement at the time of the child's birth was that Bogarde would raise the boy (now 12) if Garland would slip quietly out of their lives, she now wishes to see the lad and persuades Bogarde to let her do so. The subsequent encounters between mother and son, and the boy's reaction to the truth about his parenthood, formed the basis of Mayo Simon's banal screenplay (story by Robert Dozier). Apart from the four big numbers – including the all-out title number by Harold Arlen and E.Y. Harburg – sung by Garland, and a dramatic scene between Garland and Bogarde in which he upbraids her for keeping an audience waiting (as she had done so many times in real life), the movie had little to offer but a collection of maudlin clichés. Bogarde was miscast and ill at ease as the erstwhile lover, while Jack Klugman, veteran Aline MacMahon (right), Pauline Jameson, Jeremy Burnham and Russell Waters didn't fare much better in support. It was produced in Panavision and Eastmancolor by Lawrence Turman and Stuart Miller for Barbican Productions. Other songs: *By Myself* Howard Dietz, Arthur Schwartz; *Hello Bluebird* Cliff Friend; *It Never Was You* Maxwell Anderson, Kurt Weill; *I Am The Monarch Of The Sea* W.S. Gilbert, Sir Arthur Sullivan.

1964

Academy Awards

Best Picture
My Fair Lady (WB) produced by Jack L. Warner
NOMINATIONS INCLUDED: *Mary Poppins* (Disney, Buena Vista) produced by Walt Disney and Bill Walsh

Best Actor
Rex Harrison *My Fair Lady*

Best Actress
Julie Andrews *Mary Poppins*
NOMINATIONS INCLUDED: Debbie Reynolds *The Unsinkable Molly Brown* (MGM)

Supporting Actor
NOMINATIONS INCLUDED: Stanley Holloway *My Fair Lady*

Supporting Actress
Gladys Cooper *My Fair Lady*

Direction
George Cukor *My Fair Lady*
NOMINATIONS INCLUDED: Robert Stevenson *Mary Poppins*

Writing (Screenplay)
based on material from another medium
NOMINATIONS INCLUDED: *Mary Poppins* Bill Walsh and Don DaGradi. *My Fair Lady* Alan Jay Lerner

Cinematography (colour)
My Fair Lady Harry Stradling
NOMINATIONS INCLUDED: *Mary Poppins* Edward Colman. *The Unsinkable Molly Brown* Daniel L. Fapp

Art Direction (Set Decoration) (colour)
My Fair Lady Gene Allen and Cecil Beaton; George James Hopkins
NOMINATIONS INCLUDED: *Mary Poppins* Carroll Clark and William H. Tuntke; Emile Kuri and Hal Gausman. *The Unsinkable Molly Brown* George W. Davis and Preston Ames; Henry Grace and Hugh Hunt.

Costume Design (colour)
My Fair Lady Cecil Beaton
NOMINATIONS INCLUDED: *Mary Poppins* Tony Walton. *The Unsinkable Molly Brown* Morton Haack.

Sound
My Fair Lady Warner Bros. Studio Sound Dept.; George R. Groves, sound director
NOMINATIONS INCLUDED: *Mary Poppins* Walt Disney Studio Sound Dept.; Robert O. Cook, sound director. *The Unsinkable Molly Brown* MGM Studio Sound Dept.; Franklin E. Milton, sound director

Film Editing
Mary Poppins Cotton Warburton
NOMINATIONS INCLUDED: *My Fair Lady* William Ziegler

Special Visual Effects
Mary Poppins Peter Ellenshaw, Hamilton Luske and Eustace Lycett

Music
Song
'Chim Chim Cher-ee' *Mary Poppins* music and lyrics by Richard M. Sherman and Robert B. Sherman
NOMINATIONS INCLUDED: 'My Kind Of Town' *Robin And The 7 Hoods* (WB) Jimmy Van Heusen *cm*; Sammy Cahn *lyr*.

Score (Substantially Original)
Mary Poppins Richard M. Sherman and Robert B. Sherman

Scoring Of Music (Adaptation or Treatment)
My Fair Lady Andre Previn
NOMINATIONS INCLUDED: *Mary Poppins* Irwin Kostal. *Robin And The 7 Hoods* Nelson Riddle. *The Unsinkable Molly Brown* Robert Armbruster, Leo Arnaud, Jack Elliot, Jack Hayes, Calvin Jackson and Leo Shuken.

The New York Film Critics Awards
Best Motion Picture
My Fair Lady

Best Actor
Rex Harrison *My Fair Lady*

The New York Times Annual 'Ten Best'
7th *Mary Poppins*. 8th *My Fair Lady*

The Annual Top Moneymaking Films
INCLUDED: *The Unsinkable Molly Brown*. *My Fair Lady*. *Viva Las Vegas* (MGM). *Sword In The Stone* (Disney, Buena Vista).

A colourful tourist brochure for Mexico's famous holiday resort, **Fun In Acapulco** (Paramount) tied its exotic locale to a story and screenplay (by Allan Weiss) that featured Elvis Presley (illustrated) as a trapeze artist who, after a tragic incident in which he is responsible for a colleague being seriously maimed, arrives in Acapulco to start life afresh. A shoe-shine lad (Larry Domasin) hears Presley singing, volunteers to become his manager, and finds him a job as a singer-cum-lifeguard at a plush Acapulco hotel. Between songs, Presley became romantically attached to Ursula Andress and a lady bullfighter (Elsa Cardenas), settling in the end for the former, and even managing to overcome his understandable fear of heights by diving off the famous 136 ft cliff at La Quebrada. A light-hearted, lightweight entertainment that left Presley fans light-headed at the physical, romantic and vocal accomplishments of their hero, it also featured Paul Lukas, Alejandro Rey, Robert Carricart and Terry Hope, was directed by Richard Thorpe and glossily produced by Hal Wallis. (Technicolor). Songs: *Bossa Nova Baby* Jerry Leiber, Mike Stoller; *Fun In Acapulco* Ben Weisman, Sid Wayne; *Vino Dinero Y Amor*; *Mexico*; *The Bullfighter Was A Lady* Sid Tepper, Roy C. Bennett; *(There's) No Room To Rhumba In A Sports Car* Fred Wise, Dick Manning; *El Toro* Bill Giant, Bernie Baum, Florence Kaye; *Marguerita* Don Robertson; *I Think I'm Gonna Like It Here* Don Robertson, Hal Blair; *You Can't Say No In Acapulco* Sid Feller, Dolores Fuller, Lee Morris; *Guadalajara* Tito Guizar.

After his fun in Acapulco, Elvis Presley (centre) found himself in hillbilly territory in **Kissin' Cousins** (MGM), a poor man's *Li'l Abner* (Paramount, 1959) in which he played a dual role: an Air Force officer sent to Tennessee to persuade a stubborn hillbilly family to lease their property to the government as a missile launching site; and the blonde backwoods cousin who hates his guts. GI Elvis spends much of his time romancing Yvonne Craig (right); while his cousin sets his sights on shapely Cynthia Pepper. Several songs and dances later, Gerald Drayson Adams and director Gene Nelson's screenplay reached a happy ending for everyone. Two Elvis's for the price of one should have been the bargain offer of the year, but Sam Katzman's Panavision and Metrocolor Production, indifferently directed by Nelson with choreography to match by Hal Belfer, arrived with a dull thud. Also ·cast: Arthur O'Connell, Glenda Farrell, Jack Albertson, Pamela Austin, Donald Woods. Songs: *Kissin' Cousins* Fred Wise, Randy Starr; *Kissin' Cousins* (No 2); *There's Gold In The Mountains*; *One Boy, Two Little Girls*; *Catchin' On Fast*; *Tender Feeling* Bill Giant, Bernie Baum, Florence Kaye; *Smokey Mountain Boy* Lenore Rosenblatt, Victor Millrose; *Anyone (Could Fall In Love With You)* Bennie Benjamin, Sol Marcus, Louis A. De Jesus; *Barefoot Ballad* Dolores Fuller, Lee Morris; *One Is Enough* Sid Tepper, Roy C. Bennett; *Echoes Of Love* Bob Roberts, Paddy McMains; *(It's A) Long Lonely Highway* Doc Pomus, Mort Shuman (all sung by Elvis).

Julie Andrews made a spectacular movie debut ▷ in **Mary Poppins** (Buena Vista), an appropriately spectacular screen entertainment which, if it did nothing else, served to point an admonishing finger at Jack Warner's temerity (and timidity) in overlooking its star for the plum role of Eliza Doolittle in his production of *My Fair Lady*. **Mary Poppins** set Miss Andrews firmly on the road to international stardom, and heaped adulation on Disney and his creative team of movie magicians. Probably the best, most inventive, original screen musical of the decade, it was as near perfect a realization of the Mary Poppins stories created by P.L. Travers as was possible, with Andrews (right) as the embodiment of the much beloved nanny who takes over the running of the father-dominated Banks household to the delight and wonderment of both the adults and the children. Contributing hugely to the magic purveyed throughout its 140-minute running time were, of course, its special effects, which made **Mary Poppins** the best live-action film in Disney studio's history. Animation played a part in it too, most notably in the scenes in which Mary Poppins, accompanied by young Karen Dotrice and Matthew Garber as Jane and Michael Banks, and co-star Dick Van Dyke (left) as chimney sweep Bert, walks into a typically Disneyesque cartoon land full of frolicking barnyard animals. Another highlight was a cartoon fox hunt to the accompaniment of 'Jolly Holiday', one of the several memorable Richard M. and Robert B. Sherman songs composed especially for the film. Best of all, though, were Van Dyke's two marvellous dances, first with animated penguins, then with several chimney sweeps (and Miss Andrews) across the rooftops of London. Technically they were as fine an achievement as anything Disney had ever done, and choreographically a delight (the dance directors were Marc Breaux and Dee Dee Wood). Other musical highlights included the tonguetwisting 'Supercalifragilisticexpialidocious' sung by Andrews and Van Dyke, 'Chim Chim Cheree' (Van Dyke) and 'A Spoonful Of Sugar' (Andrews). David Tomlinson and Glynis Johns were splendid as Mr and Mrs Banks, with other parts in co-producer Bill Walsh and Donald Da Gradi's screenplay going to Ed Wynn (as Uncle Albert), Hermione Baddeley, Elsa Lanchester, Arthur Treacher, Reginald Owen, Reta Shaw and Jane Darwell. It was photographed in Technicolor by Edward Colman, the special effects were by Peter Ellenshaw, the musical director was Irwin Kostal, and the overall director Robert Stevenson. Other songs and musical numbers: *The Perfect Nanny* (Dotrice, Garber); *Sister Suffragette* (Johns); *The Life I Lead* (Tomlinson); *Stay Awake* (Andrews, Van Dyke, Wynn); *Feed The Birds* (Andrews); *Fidelity Fiduciary Bank* (Van Dyke, Tomlinson); *Let's Go Fly A Kite* (Johns, Tomlinson).

Having already journeyed to Acapulco and Tennessee in 1964, Elvis Presley's third movie ▷ stopover of the year was Las Vegas in MGM's **Viva Las Vegas** (GB: **Love In Las Vegas**), the best and most successful of all Presley's musicals so far. Apart from the man of the moment himself (playing a singing racing car driver who arrives in Vegas to take part in the Grand Prix only to discover that he has engine trouble), the film co-starred Ann-Margret (right) as the swimming instructress he falls for, and with whom he shares a quartet of better-than-average numbers: the title song (by Doc Pomus); 'The Lady Loves Me' (by Sid Tepper and Roy C. Bennett), 'What'd I Say?' (by Ray Charles) and 'The Climb'. The two stars were dynamite together and helped inject into Sally Benson's flimsy screenplay more personality and zest than its meagre ration of plot deserved. David Winters's choreography brought out the best in both Elvis and his leading lady; so did George Sidney's assured direction. It was photographed in Panavision and Metrocolor for producers Sidney and Jack Cummings and, in other roles, featured Cesare Danova as Presley's racing rival, as well as William Demarest, Jack Carter and Nicky Blair. Other songs and musical numbers: *I Need Somebody To Lean On* Doc Pomus; *Come On, Everybody* Stanley Chianese; *Today, Tomorrow and Forever* Bill Giant, Bernie Baum, Florence Kaye; *If You Think I Don't Need You* Bob 'Red' West; *Appreciation*; *My Rival* Marvin More, Bernie Wayne.

Elvis Presley fetched up as handyman to carnival owner Barbara Stanwyck in **Roustabout** (Paramount), his main purpose in scenarist Anthony Lawrence and Allan Weiss's very thin story being to boost business by drawing the crowds with his singing. Which he does most satisfactorily, until a *fracas* with one of the customers results in his accepting a job at a rival carnival. Presley's departure spells gloom and doom for Stanwyck, but all ends happily when his girlfriend, Joan Freeman (illustrated left, with Presley), finally persuades him to return. Leif Erickson, Sue Ane Langdon, Pat Buttram, Joan Staley, Dabs Greer and Steve Brodie were also in it, Joseph Lilley was musical director, the numbers were staged by Earl Barton, and it was photographed in Techniscope and Technicolor by Lucien Ballard. The good-looking production was by Hal Wallis whose director, John Rich, succeeded in making the most of the least. Songs and musical numbers: *Roustabout*; *Poison Ivy League*; *One Track Heart* Bill Giant, Bernie Baum, Florence Kaye; *Little Egypt* Jerry Leiber, Mike Stoller; *Wheels On My Heels*; *It's A Wonderful World* Sid Tepper, Roy C. Bennett; *It's Carnival Time* Ben Weisman, Sid Wayne; *Carny Town* Fred Wise, Randy Starr; *Hard Knocks*; *There's A Brand New Day On The Horizon* Joy Byers; *Big Love, Big Heartache* Fuller, Morris, Hendrix (all sung by ◁ Presley).

Made specifically with youth appeal in mind, producer Joe Pasternak's **Looking For Love** (MGM) combined music and romance in a light-as-air plot that had Connie Francis (illustrated) as a switchboard operator with show business aspirations determinedly pursuing lanky Jim Hutton, but realizing after their first kiss that he isn't for her. The final romantic accounting in Ruth Brooks Flippen's flippant screenplay had Francis finally pairing with a grocery assistant called Cuz Rickober (Joby Baker) leaving Hutton free to fall into the arms of her room-mate (Susan Oliver). There were seven songs in the film, including a reprise (yet again) of Nicholas Brodszky and Sammy Cahn's 'Be My Love' – and they were all sung by Miss Francis. Johnny Carson, Yvette Mimieux, George Hamilton, Paula Prentiss and Danny Thomas made guest appearances, with Barbara Nichols, Jay C. Flippen, Jesse White, Charles Lane and Joan Marshall completing the cast. The director was Don Weiss and it was choreographed by Robert Sidney. A Euterpe Inc.-Franmet Production in Panavision and Metrocolor. Other songs: *Looking For Love*; *Let's Have A Party*; *When The Clock Strikes Midnight* Hank Hunter, Stan Vincent; *Whoever You Are I Love You* Peter Udell, Gary Gold; *This Is My Happiest Moment* Ted Murray, Benny Davis; *I Can't Believe That You're In Love With Me* Jimmy McHugh, Clarence Gaskill.

Jack Warner, who personally supervised the filming of **My Fair Lady** (Warner Bros.), faced almost as many problems in transferring Alan Jay Lerner and Frederick Loewe's blockbuster musical (based, of course, on Shaw's *Pygmalion*) to the screen as did Professor Higgins in turning Eliza Doolittle from a cockney flowerseller into a lady. The initial difficulty lay in the casting: Warner, judging Julie Andrews insufficiently familiar to movie audiences, opted for Audrey Hepburn (a mistake he was later to rue, with the phenomenal success of Miss Andrews in *Mary Poppins* and in *The Sound Of Music*). For Higgins, he had decided on Cary Grant, who wisely declined, remarking that not only would he not play the part, he would not even bother to see the film if someone other than Rex Harrison (right) were chosen. Thus it was that the film became, apart from its other qualities, quite simply a document recording one of the greatest of all musical comedy performances, with familiarity breeding, for Harrison, an even more subtly attuned reading of the role and, for the spectator, an ever increasing admiration. Miss Hepburn (left), on the other hand, made a game attempt but was visibly a lady all the time, which removed much of the story's credibility. Still, with Cecil Beaton's sets and costumes and Hermes Pan's choreography, **My Fair Lady** proved indestructible. George Cukor directed tastefully, making a real show-stopper out of 'Get Me To The Church On Time' with the sublime Stanley Holloway as Doolittle (another second choice: Warner preferred James Cagney!), while other highlights included the 'Ascot Gavotte', whose elegant Edwardian ladies and gentlemen were decked out by Beaton in glorious black and white; 'The Rain In Spain' (Hepburn, Harrison and Wilfrid Hyde-White as Colonel Pickering) and, perhaps most memorable of all, Harrison's unexpectedly touching rendition of 'I've Grown Accustomed To Her Face'. Gladys Cooper was cast as Mrs Higgins, Isobel Elsom as Mrs Eynsford Hill and Jeremy Brett as her lovesick son Freddy. The film, with a screenplay by Alan Jay Lerner, was beautifully photographed in Super Panavision and Technicolor by Harry Stradling. Audrey Hepburn's vocals were dubbed by Marni Nixon. Other songs and musical numbers: *With A Little Bit Of Luck* (Holloway, chorus); *Why Can't The English Teach Their Children How To Speak?* (Harrison); *Show Me* (Hepburn, Brett); *I Could Have Danced All Night* (Hepburn); *Just You Wait*, *'Enry 'Iggins* (Hepburn); *Wouldn't It Be Luverly* (Hepburn, chorus); *I'm An Ordinary Man* (Harrison); *Embassy Waltz* (orch.); *On The Street Where You Live* (Brett); *You Did It* (Harrison, Hyde-White); *Without You* (Hepburn); *Servants' Chorus* (chorus); *A Hymn To Him* (Harrison).

Meredith Willson's 1960 Broadway hit, **The Unsinkable Molly Brown**, reached the screen via MGM with Debbie Reynolds in the role created on stage by Tammy Grimes. Harve Presnell, making his movie debut, co-starred as Johnny Brown, the role he played on Broadway, and if the pairing wasn't exactly explosive, neither was the film. Rather, it was a solid workmanlike transfer from stage to screen of a solid workmanlike piece of Broadway carpentry that didn't have an original idea in its head. The story of a hoydenish foundling from Colorado who strikes it rich after marrying handsome Harve – its main plot emphasis centred on *nouveau riche* Molly's fight to become accepted into snobby Denver society. She embarks on a self-improvement tour of Europe, and her new-found sophistication, plus her heroism while returning to the States on the *Titanic*, changes her backwoods status overnight and, after nearly losing her man, she not only wins back his love, but also the undivided approval of the Denverites. Reynolds gave her all, but was unable to hide the fact that she was acting her head off. Presnell, on the other hand, underplayed to the point of vapidity. Just the right note of exuberance, however, was struck by Peter Gennaro's choreography – seen at its buoyant best in a number (not in the stage show) called 'He's My Friend', as well as in the infectious 'Belly Up To The Bar Boys' (illustrated, with Reynolds). Helen Deutsch's screenplay stuck fairly closely to Richard Morris's original book, and had featured parts in it for Ed Begley as Reynolds's foster father, Hermione Baddeley and Jack Kruschen as two of Begley's colourful cronies, Martita Hunt and Vassili Lambrinos. Also: George Mitchell, Harvey Lembeck, Fred Essler, Gus Trikonis, Grover Dale and Hayden Rorke. Laurence Weingarten produced (in CinemaScope and Metrocolor) and it was directed, with verve substituting for inspiration, by Charles Walters. Other songs and musical numbers: *I'll Never Say No*; *I Ain't Down Yet*; *Colorado My Home*; *Soliloquy*; *Dolce Far Niente* (background); *Up Where The People Are* (shorter version of Broadway original).

If Warner Bros.' **Robin And The 7 Hoods** had been as amusing an experience for audiences as it patently was for the cast, it would have broken box-office records. A Robin Hood parody whose basic joke was that the skulduggery took place in gangland Chicago *circa* 1928, it was marred by the self-indulgent fooling of such talents as Frank Sinatra (left), Dean Martin (right), Sammy Davis Jr, Peter Falk and (as Allen A. Dale) Bing Crosby (centre), and by a rambling screenplay by David R. Schwartz. Edward G. Robinson made an extremely brief guest appearance (he was killed off before you could say 'Edward G. Robinson'), with Barbara Rush, Victor Buono, Hank Henry, Allen Jenkins and Jack La Rue also in it. Unfortunately, director Gordon Douglas made little effort to keep The Clan in check, and the film's most deserved credit was William H. Daniels's for his brilliant colour photography. A P.E. Production, it was filmed in Technicolor and Panavision and produced by Sinatra, with Howard W. Koch as executive producer. The songs were by Jimmy Van Heusen and Sammy Cahn – the two best being Sinatra's 'My Kind Of Town', and 'Style' – stylishly sung and danced by Sinatra, Crosby and Martin. Other songs and musical numbers: *All For One* (Falk); *Don't Be A Do-Badder* (Crosby); *Any Man Who Loves His Mother* (Martin); *Mr Booze* (Sinatra, Crosby, Martin, Davis); *Bang Bang* (Davis); *Charlotte Couldn't Charleston* (Chorus); *Give Praise* (Chorus).

Producer Sam Katzman, who was nothing if not a trend follower, caught on to the currently popular (and profitable) craze for the Watusi with MGM's **Get Yourself A College Girl** (GB: **The Swingin' Set**), billing music-makers The Dave Clark Five, The Animals, The Jimmy Smith Trio, Stan Getz, Astrud Gilberto, The Standells and Roberta Linn and Freddie Bell and The Bell Boys, above both the title and his dramatic cast – which showed precisely in which direction his priorities lay. And – considering the unutterable banality of Robert E. Kent's story and screenplay (about a goodlooking student in an exclusive girls' school who endangers her tenure there when it is discovered that she is the composer of several hit tunes, but who is saved from dismissal by a descendant of the school's founder, now a would-be senator badly in need of some young folks' votes) – who could blame him? Mary Ann Mobley (a former Miss World, right) played the undergraduate tunesmith and Willard Waterman was the would-be senator, with other roles under Sidney Miller's perfunctory direction going to Chad Everett, Joan O'Brien, Nancy Sinatra (left), Chris Noel and Fabrizio Mioni. Hal Belfer staged the numbers. (Metrocolor). Songs included: *Get Yourself A College Girl* Sidney Miller, Fred Karger; *The Swingin' Set* Donnie Brooks, Miller, Karger.

1965

Fort Lauderdale during Easter was the setting of Elvis Presley's latest romp, **Girl Happy** (MGM), and although art directors George W. Davis and Addison Hehr saw fit to provide the Florida landscape with mountains, at least the music was authentic Presley, and his fans gave it the thumbs up. Storyline had Presley (illustrated) being hired by a Chicago nightclub owner (Harold J. Stone) to look after his over-exuberant daughter (Shelley Fabares, illustrated) for the duration of her Fort Lauderdale vacation, which was easier said than done. Harvey Bullock and R.S. Allen's screenplay won no awards for originality or invention, but it provided a solid enough foundation on which to balance the show's twelve musical numbers – the best being 'She's Evil' sung by Presley and Fabares, and Presley's 'Wolf Call' (by Bill Giant, Bernie Baum and Florence Kaye). Nita Talbot, as a stripper, also did well by a number called 'Good News' (by Sam Cooke) in which she was covered in newspaper. It was produced by Joe Pasternak in Panavision and Metrocolor, with a cast that included Gary Crosby (left), Joby Baker (2nd left),

A modest but entertaining biopic of country and western singer Hank Williams, **Your Cheatin' Heart** (MGM) starred George Hamilton (left) as the composer-singer (his vocals were dubbed by the subject's son, Hank Williams Jr) and Susan Oliver (right) as Audrey, the girl he meets while performing in a travelling medicine show, and marries. A familiar rags to riches story, its screenplay, by Stanford Whitmore, alternated the joy and the tragedy that featured so prominently in Williams's life, providing an excellent part for Red Buttons as Shorty Younger, the trouper who became Williams's life-long friend and who tried desperately to rehabilitate him when success robbed him of his touch with the common folk and drove him to drink. Arthur O'Connell played Fred Rose, the music publisher who gave Williams his first important break, with other roles under Gene Nelson's caring direction going to Shary Marshall, Chris Crosby, Rex Holman, Hortense Petra and Roy Engel. The producer, for Four Lead Productions, was Sam Katzman. Songs: *Your Cheatin' Heart*; *Hey, Good Lookin'*; *I Saw The Light*; *Jambalaya*; *Ramblin' Man*; *I'm So Lonesome I Could Cry*; *Cold Cold Heart*; *Kaw-Liga*; *I Can't Help It*; *Long Gone Lonesome Blues*; *You Win Again* all by Williams.

Mary Ann Mobley, Jimmy Hawkins (right) and Jackie Coogan; the choreographer was David Winters and it was directed by Boris Sagal. Other songs and musical numbers: *Girl Happy* Doc Pomus, Norman Meade; *Cross My Heart And Hope To Die* Ben Weisman, Sid Wayne; *Do Not Disturb*; *Spring Fever* Giant, Baum, Kaye; *Fort Lauderdale Chamber Of Commerce*; *Puppet On A String* Sid Tepper, Roy C. Bennett; *I've Got To Find My Baby*; *The Meanest Girl In Town* Joy Byers; *Startin' Tonight* Lenore Rosenblatt, Victor Millrose; *Do The Clam* Weisman, Wayne, Dolores Fuller.

Louis M. Heyward's screenplay for American International's **Sergeant Deadhead** centred on the switch made by bumbling airman Frankie Avalon when, after changing personality during a space trip following a guardhouse breakout, he becomes a snooty extrovert. At the end of the film's 89-minute running time, he is rehabilitated back into his old, likeable self, in which guise he and co-star Deborah Walley are paired to provide the final clinch. Far more interesting than the youngsters were some of the older members of the cast, especially Fred Clark and Eve Arden (both illustrated) as a WAF commander and his sweetheart, the latter doing well by Guy Hemric and Jerry Styner's 'You Should've Seen The One That Got Away'. Cesar Romero, Gale Gordon and Reginald Gardiner were also in it (as a trio of inspectors who come to witness a missile launch); so were Harvey Lembeck, John Ashley and Buster Keaton. James H. Nicholson and Samuel Arkoff produced (in Pathecolor and Panavision), it was choreographed by Jack Baker, and the director was Norman Taurog. Other songs and musical numbers: *Sergeant Deadhead*; *The Difference In Me Is You*; *Let's Play Love*; *Two-Timin' Angel*; *How Can You Tell?*; *Hurry Up And Wait* Hemric, Styner.

Though Rodgers and Hammerstein's monumentally successful **The Sound Of Music** (20th Century-Fox) – which has grossed over $80,000,000 to date – was a decided improvement on the long-running Broadway hit from whence it came, the mawkish sentimentality it oozed from every frame of its 174-minute running time made it difficult to enjoy without the uneasy feeling that one's emotions were being mercilessly manipulated. Yet, as a piece of old-fashioned popular entertainment with both eyes firmly on the box-office cash registers of the world, it was a shrewdly professional piece of work, stunningly presented, and crafted with awesome expertise. It also starred Julie Andrews (centre left) who, alone in a cast that included an unsympathetic and wooden Christopher Plummer (centre), as well as Eleanor Parker (as the Baroness), Richard Haydn (as Max Detweiler), Peggy Wood (as Mother Abbess) and Charmian Carr (as Liesl), managed to wade through the molasses of Ernest Lehman's screenplay (from the book by Howard Lindsay and Russel Crouse) while keeping her head above it all. She played Maria, the postulant nun who forsakes the abbey for a position as governess to the seven children (illustrated) of martinet widower Captain Von Trapp (Plummer), and remains on in his household (after the obligatory set-backs) to become his wife. It was Andrews's extraordinarily assured and appealing central performance – coupled with some magnificent Todd-AO and Color by De Luxe aerial views of Salzburg (the story's setting), photographed by Ted McCord, that was largely responsible for the film's enormous success. Marc Breaux and Dee Dee Wood choreographed the simple but effective dance routines, Boris Leven, the art director, made excellent use of Salzburg's architectural landmarks, and the production and direction were by Robert Wise. Completing the cast: Heather Menzies, Nicolas Hammond, Duane Chase, Angela Cartwright, Debbie Turner, Kym Karath, Anna Lee, Portia Nelson, Ben Wright, Daniel Truhitte, Norma Varden, Gil Stuart, Marni Nixon, and Evadne Baker. Christopher Plummer's vocals were dubbed by Bill Lee. Songs and musical numbers: *The Sound Of Music* (Andrews); *Praeludium* (nun's chorus); *Morning Hymn And Alleluia* (nun's chorus); *Maria* (Lee, Nixon, Nelson, Baker); *I Have Confidence In Me* (Andrews); *Sixteen Going On Seventeen* (Carr, Truhitte); *Climb Every Mountain* (Wood); *Lonely Goatherd* (Andrews, Baird Marionettes); *Do-Re-Mi* (Andrews, children); *Something Good* (Andrews, Plummer); *Edelweiss* (Plummer, Andrews, children); *So Long, Farewell* (children); *Processional* (orchestra); *My Favourite Things* (Andrews).

I'll Take Sweden (United Artists), was a self-conscious effort on behalf of its writers – Nat Perrin, Bob Fisher and Arthur Marx – to be 'with it'. Bob Hope played a widowed oil company executive who, to free his perfectly contented daughter (Tuesday Weld) from the clutches of her impoverished boyfriend (Frankie Avalon), gets himself transferred to Sweden. In Sweden the situation, as far as the harassed Hope is concerned, is even worse, for, in that country's climate of free love, Weld is soon taken up by a suave lecher (Jeremy Slate) of whom papa disapproves even more than he did of Avalon. As for Hope himself, he too finds himself romantically involved – with an interior decorator (Dina Merrill). Avalon (centre) sang the title number (by Diane Lampert and Ken Lauber) as part of a lakeside production number, Hope sang 'Nothing Can Compare With You' (by 'By' Dunham), a group called The Vulcans were featured in 'Watusi Joe' (by Jimmie Haskell and Jim Economides) and Miss Weld was heard but once in 'Give It To Me' (by Haskell and Dunham). Edward Small and Alex Gottlieb were the producer and associate producer of this tedious Technicolor frolic, with Frederick De Cordova directing. Also cast: Rosemarie Frankland, Walter Sande, John Qualen, Peter Bourne, Fay De Witt, Alice Frost and Roy Roberts. Other songs: *Killin' Polka*; *Mad Latina*; *Take It Off*; *Tell Me, Tell Me* Jimmie Haskell, 'By' Dunham; *The Bells Keep Ringin'*; *Peep Show*; *There'll Be Rainbows Again* Dunham, Bobby Beverly; *Would Ya Like My Last Name* Kenneth Lampert, Diane Lampert.

Elvis Presley's **Tickle Me** (Allied Artists) certainly didn't tickle the fancy of the critics who justifiably consigned it to the trash can where it belonged. The story of a rodeo rider who signs on as a horse wrangler at an expensive Arizona dude ranch-cum-beauty spa, it thrust its star among a bevy of lovelies (see illustration), while at the same time involving him in a plot to rescue a cache of gold from a bunch of crooks. Jocelyn Lane was the rightful owner of the hidden fortune, Julie Adams the owner of the dude ranch, with other parts in Elwood Ullman and Edward Bernds's silly screenplay falling to Jack Mullaney, Merry Anders, Connie Gilchrist, Edward Faulkner, Bill Williams and Louis Elias. There were nine songs, all of which came from previous Presley albums and all of which were staged by David Winters. It was produced by Ben Schwalb in Panavision and Color by De Luxe, and directed by Norman Taurog with the accent on slapstick. Songs: *(It's A) Long, Lonely Highway*; *Night Rider* Doc Pomus, Mort Shuman; *It Feels So Right* Ben Weisman, Fred Wise; *Dirty Dirty Feeling* (English version of *Si Seulement!*) Jerry Leiber, Mike Stoller; *(Such An) Easy Question* Otis Blackwell, Winfield Scott; *Put The Blame On Me* Norman Blagman, Kathleen G. Twomey, Wise; *I'm Yours* Don Robertson, Hal Blair; *I Feel That I've Known You Forever* Pomus, Alan Jeffreys; *Slowly But Surely* Sid Wayne, Weisman.

Box-office wise, it appeared that Elvis Presley (illustrated) could do no wrong. His films from 1957 to 1965 grossed in excess of $175,000,000 – even with such dyed-in-the-wool stinkers as **Harum Scarum** (GB: **Harum Holiday**). A frightful *mélange* of this and that from MGM, it featured Presley as a movie star who is kidnapped by a group of assassins while on a personal appearance tour of the Middle East. In no time at all he finds himself decked out like Rudolph Valentino in *The Sheikh*, and involved in a plot to kill the king. Gerald Drayson Adams's screenplay, trading in one absurdity after another, must have given even the lad from Memphis's most ardent admirers a bit of a headache; ditto Gene Nelson's plodding direction. Mary Ann Mobley co-starred as a princess, with other roles in this Technicolored, Four Leaf Production going to Fran Jeffries, Michael Ansara, Jay Novello, Philip Reed, Theo Marcuse, Dick Harvey, and Busby Berkeley's favourite midget, Billy Barty. The dances were staged by Earl Barton. Songs and musical numbers: *Harum Scarum* Peter Andreoli, Vince Poncia Jr, Jimmie Crane; *Golden Coins*; *Go East, Young Man*; *Shake That Tambourine*; *Animal Instinct*; *Wisdom Of The Ages*; *Mirage* Bill Giant, Bernie Baum, Florence Kaye; *Hey Little Girl*; *So Close, Yet So Far (From Paradise)* Joy Byers; *My Desert Serenade* Stanley Jay Gelber; *Kismet* Sid Tepper, Roy C. Bennett.

1966

Academy Awards

Music
Scoring Of Music (Adaptation or Treatment)
A Funny Thing Happened On The Way To The Forum (United Artists) Ken Thorne
NOMINATIONS INCLUDED: *The Singing Nun* (MGM) Harry Sukman

Despite the five golden Gershwin oldies featured in MGM's **When The Boys Meet The Girls**, the film was a depressing retread of *Girl Crazy* – first seen as an RKO film in 1932, then as a vehicle for Mickey Rooney and Judy Garland from MGM in 1943. Connie Francis (left) and Harve Presnell (right) were top-starred as a couple who run a dude ranch for divorcées, with Sue Ane Langdon as the 'other' woman. Fred Clark, Frank Faylen and Joby Baker were in it too; so were Sam The Sham and The Pharaohs, Herman's Hermits, Louis Armstrong and, playing a number called 'Aruba', which he wrote himself, Liberace. It was produced in Panavision and Metrocolor for Four Leaf Productions by Sam Katzman, choreographed by Earl Barton, and directed by Alvin Ganzer. Robert E. Kent wrote it from the stage musical *Girl Crazy* by Guy Bolton and John McGowan. Songs and musical numbers: *But Not For Me* (Francis, Presnell); *I Got Rhythm* (Francis, Presnell, Armstrong); *Bidin' My Time* (Herman's Hermits); *Embraceable You* (Presnell); *Treat Me Rough* (Langdon) George and Ira Gershwin; *When The Boys Meet The Girls* (Francis) Jack Keller, Howard Greenfield; *Mail Call* (Francis) Fred Karger, Ben Weisman, Sid Wayne; *Monkey See, Monkey Do* (Sam and Pharaohs) Johnny Farrow; *Listen People* (Herman's Hermits) Graham Gouldman; *Throw It Out Of Your Mind* (Armstrong) Armstrong, Bill Kayle.
▽

The problem in bringing the Bert Shevelove-Larry Gelbart-Stephen Sondheim Broadway hit, **A Funny Thing Happened On The Way To The Forum** (United Artists) to the screen, was finding a cinematic counterpart for the stage show's near perfect construction. It was a problem only partially solved by director Dick Lester, whose approach to the material was to drop several of the original songs and to impose a completely new rhythm and pace onto the convoluted story of Pseudolus, a house slave in ancient Rome, who hopes to win his freedom by organizing things so that his young master and an innocent courtesan in a neighbouring bawdy house can elope. Lester also indulged in a series of sight gags, jump cuts and (as in the Beatles films), flashy editing, often to the detriment of Melvin Frank and Michael Pertwee's deliciously anachronistic screenplay. Very much a hit and miss affair in which the hits, fortunately, outnumbered the misses, it scored a bull's eye everytime where its performances were concerned, with the larger-than-life Zero Mostel (right) heading a glorious cast that included Phil Silvers (left), Michael Crawford and Annette Andre (as the suitably simple-minded young lovers), Michael Hordern, Leon Greene and, best of all, Jack Gilford (centre right) as the aptly named slave Hysterium. Buster Keaton (centre left), in his last film appearance, was in it too. The one cherishable musical moment was the brilliant 'Everybody Ought To Have A Maid' ('sweeping out, sleeping in') sung by Mostel, Silvers, Gilford and Hordern. Ethel and George Martin staged the numbers, the production and costumes were designed by Tony Walton, and it was produced in Color by De Luxe by Melvin Frank. Other songs and musical numbers: *Comedy Tonight* (Mostel); *Lovely* (Mostel, Crawford, Andre, Gilford); *Bring Me My Bride* (Greene); *The Dirge* (Greene).

British pop group Herman's Hermits (illustrated, leader Peter Noone, foreground) received star billing in **Hold On!** (MGM), a witless encumbrance which found the five Hermits being shadowed, while on a tour of the USA, by a space agency scientist (Herbert Anderson) out to check their credentials and to see whether they are worthy enough to have a nose-cone named after them. Female interest was supplied by Sue Ane Langdon as a pushy starlet out to make the headlines, and by Shelley Fabares as Noone's other half. Also cast: Bernard Fox, Harry Hickock, Hortense Petra and Mickey Deems. Sam Katzman produced in Panavision and Metrocolor and Arthur Lubin directed from a screenplay by James B. Gordon. Wilda Taylor choreographed. Songs and musical numbers: *Hold On!*; *A Must To Avoid*; *All The Things I Do For You Baby*; *Where Were You When I Needed You?* P.F. Sloan, Steve Barri; *Make Me Happy*; *The George And Dragon*; *Got A Feeling*; *We Want You, Herman*; *Wild Love*; *Gotta Get Away* Fred Karger, Sid Wayne, Ben Weisman; *Leaning On A Lamp Post* Noel Gay.
▽

Elvis Presley's 22nd film in ten years was **Spinout** (GB: **California Holiday**), and in it he played the leader of a touring musical combo who prefers his Dusenberg to the quartet of girls who inundate his life – namely millionaire's daughter Shelley Fabares, best-selling authoress Diane McBain, Deborah Walley and, briefly, Dodie Marshall (left, with Presley). In the end he marries all four of them. Theodore J. Flicker and George Kirgo were actually paid for writing it, the eight musical numbers were staged by Jack Baker, and it was directed by Norman Taurog with a cast that also included Jack Mullaney, Will Hutchins, Warren Berlinger, Jimmy Hawkins, Cecil Kellaway and Una Merkel. A Euterpe Picture distributed by MGM, it was produced in Panavision and Metrocolor by Joe Pasternak. Songs and musical numbers: *Stop, Look, Listen* Joy Byers; *Adam And Evil* Fred Wise, Randy Starr; *All That I Am*; *Am I Ready*; *Smorgasbord* Sid Tepper, Roy C. Bennett; *Never Say Yes* Doc Pomus, Mort Shuman; *Beach Shack* Bill Giant, Florence Kaye, Bernie Baum; *I'll Be Back* Sid Wayne, Ben Weisman.
◁

A slightly overweight Elvis Presley (right) returned to Hawaii in **Paradise Hawaiian Style** (Paramount), a decidedly underweight entertainment in which he played a helicopter charter service pilot who finds himself grounded after his machine loses control and forces a member of the Federal Aviation Agency to drive his car into a ditch. James Shigeta played his sidekick, Suzanne Leigh his secretary-cum-sweetheart. Prominently featured too (in bikinis), were Linda Wong, Marianna Hill and Julie Parrish, with John Doucette, Gigi Verone (left), Irene Tsu, Jan Shephard, Philip Ahn, Grady Sutton and old-timer Mary Treen also in it for producer Hal Wallis and director Michael Moore. Allan Weiss and Anthony Lawrence (story by Weiss) wrote it and the choreographer was Jack Regas. (Technicolor). Songs and musical numbers: *Paradise, Hawaiian Style*; *Scratch My Back (Then I'll Scratch Yours)*; *Stop Where You Are*; *This Is My Heaven* Bill Giant, Bernie Baum, Florence Kaye; *House Of Sand*; *Queenie Wahine's Papaya* Giant, Baum, Kaye, Donna Butterworth; *Drums Of The Islands* Sid Tepper, Roy C. Bennett; *A Dog's Life* Sid Wayne, Ben Weisman; *Sand Castles* Herb Goldberg, David Hess, Butterworth; *Bill Bailey, Won't You Please Come Home?* Hughie Cannon.
▽

Following in the footsteps of Ingrid Bergman, Loretta Young, and Julie Andrews, Debbie Reynolds (illustrated) played a somewhat unruly nun in **The Singing Nun**, a nauseatingly sentimental offering from MGM, in which Sister Reynolds, as a Dominican nun in a Belgian hospice, apart from finding herself (in company with two other nuns) the star of a million-seller record, befriends an underprivileged motherless youngster (Ricky Cordell) whose father is a drunkard and whose sister is a tramp. It was written in treacle by Sally Benson and John Furia Jr, the latter providing the storyline (which, in turn, was inspired by Belgian nun Soeur Sourire's hit song 'Dominique', lyrics by Randy Sparks), and co-starred Ricardo Montalban as Father Clementi, and an asphyxiatingly benign Greer Garson (given guest-star billing) as Mother Prioress. Also: Agnes Moorehead, Chad Everett, Katharine Ross, Juanita Moore and Ed Sullivan, on whose TV show the song is aired (just as the original 'Dominique' had been several years before). It was produced by John Beck in Panavision and Metrocolor and sluggishly directed by Henry Koster. Other songs: *Sister Adele*; *It's A Miracle*; *Beyond The Stars*; *A Pied Piper's Dream* Soeur Sourire, Randy Sparks; *Brother John*; *Loverly* Sparks; *Raindrops* Sparks, inspired by *Chante Riviere* by Soeur Sourire; *Je Voudrais*; *Mets Ton Joli Jupon*; *Avec Toi*; *Alleluia* Soeur Sourire.

Frankie And Johnny (United Artists) was an Elvis Presley no-no which found him adrift on a Mississippi showboat as a singing gambler in love with Donna Douglas (of TV's *Beverly Hillbillies* fame). He changes his romantic allegiance, however, to redhead Nancy Kovacks (right) after a fortune teller assures him that this will result in a better run of luck at roulette. Alex Gottlieb wrote it from a story by Nat Perrin, leaving enough gaps in his boring screenplay for a dozen songs, including the title number, 'When The Saints Go Marching In', and a new one by Fred Wise and Randy Starr called 'Look Out Broadway' which, together with a bouncy little item called 'Shout It Out' (by Bill Giant, Bernie Baum and Florence Kaye) were the best things in the show. It was produced in Technicolor by Edward Small, featured Harry Morgan (left), Sue Ane Langdon, Audrey Christie, Robert Strauss, Anthony Eisley and Jerome Cowan, was choreographed by Earl Barton, and directed by Frederick De Cordova. Other songs and musical numbers: *Frankie And Johnny* new words and arrangement Fred Karger, Alex Gottlieb, Ben Weisman; *Chesay* Weisman, Sid Wayne, Karger; *Come Along* David Hess; *Petunia, The Gardener's Daughter*; *Beginner's Luck* Sid Tepper, Roy C. Bennett; *What Every Woman Lives For* Doc Pomus, Mort Shuman; *Everybody Come Aboard* Giant, Baum, Kaye; *Hard Luck* Weisman, Sid Wayne; *Please Don't Stop Loving Me* Joy Byers. ▷

1967

Academy Awards

Best Picture
NOMINATIONS INCLUDED: *Doctor Dolittle* (20th Century-Fox) produced by Arthur P. Jacobs

Supporting Actress
NOMINATIONS INCLUDED: Carol Channing *Thoroughly Modern Milly* (Universal)

Cinematography (New Classification)
One award instead of separate awards for black-and-white and colour.
NOMINATIONS INCLUDED: *Camelot* (WB, Seven Arts) Richard H. Kline. *Doctor Dolittle* Robert Surtees.

Art Direction (Set Decoration) (New Classification)
One award instead of separate awards for black-and-white and colour. *Camelot* John Truscott and Edward Carrere; John W. Brown
NOMINATIONS INCLUDED: *Doctor Dolittle* Mario Chiari, Jack Martin Smith and Ed Graves; Walter M. Scott and Stuart A. Reiss. *Thoroughly Modern Millie* Alexander Golitzen and George C. Webb; Howard Bristol.

Costume Design (New Classification)
One Award instead of separate awards for black-and-white and colour. *Camelot* John Truscott
NOMINATIONS INCLUDED: *The Happiest Millionaire* (Disney, Buena Vista) Bill Thomas. *Thoroughly Modern Millie* Jean Louis.

Sound
NOMINATIONS INCLUDED: *Camelot* Warner Bros. – Seven Arts Studio Sound Dept. *Doctor Dolittle* 20th Century-Fox Studio Sound Dept. *Thoroughly Modern Millie* Universal City Sound Dept.

Film Editing
NOMINATIONS INCLUDED: *Doctor Dolittle* Samuel E. Beetley and Marjorie Fowler

Special Visual Effects
Doctor Dolittle L.B. Abbott

Music
Song
'Talk To The Animals' *Doctor Dolittle* music and lyrics by Leslie Bricusse
NOMINATIONS INCLUDED: 'The Bare Necessities' *The Jungle Book* (Disney, Buena Vista) music and lyrics by Terry Gilkyson. 'Thoroughly Modern Millie' *Thoroughly Modern Millie* music and lyrics by Jimmy Van Heusen and Sammy Cahn

Original Music Score
Thoroughly Modern Millie Elmer Bernstein
NOMINATIONS INCLUDED: *Doctor Dolittle* Leslie Bricusse

Scoring Of Music (Adaptation or Treatment)
Camelot Alfred Newman and Ken Darby
NOMINATIONS INCLUDED: *Doctor Dolittle* Lionel Newman and Alexander Courage. *Thoroughly Modern Millie* Andre Previn and Joseph Gershenson

Honorary Award
To Arthur Freed for distinguished service to the Academy and the production of six top-rated Awards telecasts. (statuette)

The Annual Top Moneymaking Films
INCLUDED: *Thoroughly Modern Millie*.

The best musical of 1967 was **Thoroughly Modern Millie** (Universal). An original, written by Richard Morris with two new Sammy Cahn-Jimmy Van Heusen tunes and a handful of old favourites, it was an irresistible mixture of brashness, charm and nostalgia put together with expertise. It cast an affectionate backward glance at the shimmering twenties, evoking its fads, and its eccentricities, as well as the Golden Days of silent screen entertainment. Ross Hunter's lavishly mounted Technicolor production plunged the delectable Julie Andrews (right) into this era as a secretary newly arrived in New York, and looking for a wealthy husband. Mary Tyler Moore (left) was co-starred, and Beatrice Lillie was in it, too, as Mrs Meers, a white-slave trafficker who runs the hotel the Misses Andrews and Moore are living in. Other featured parts under George Roy Hill's racy direction went to Charol Channing (in one of her rare screen appearances) as thoroughly modern Muzzy, the wealthiest widow in the world, James Fox as a paper clip salesman-cum-millionaire who is madly in love with Miss Andrews, and John Gavin who is madly in love with Miss Moore. Also Jack Soo, Pat Morita, Cavada Humphrey, Ann Dee, Anthony Dexter, Lou Nova and Michael St Clair. Though Hill's direction lost its grip on the melodramatic proceedings that helped bring the film to its climax, it was, for most of the time spot-on, deliciously lampooning a much-lampooned era with a freshness and sparkle that was mirrored in Julie Andrews's thoroughly captivating star performance in the title role, and in Joe Layton's choreography. Songs and musical numbers: *Thoroughly Modern Millie* (Andrews); *The Tapioca* (Andrews, Fox) Van Heusen, Cahn; *Jimmy* (Andrews) Jay Thompson; *Baby Face* (Andrews) Benny Davis, Harry Akst; *Do It Again* (Channing) Buddy De Sylva. George Gershwin; *Jewish Wedding Song* (Andrews, Moore) Sylvia Neufeld; *Poor Butterfly* (Andrews) John Golden, Raymond Hubbell; *Rose Of Washington Square* (Dee) James Hanley, Ballard MacDonald; *I Can't Believe That You're In Love With Me* (orchestral) Jimmy McHugh, Clarence Gaskill; *I'm Sitting On Top Of The World* (girl singer) Sam M. Lewis, Joe Young, Ray Henderson; *Stumbling* (Andrews, Moore) Zez Confrey; *Japanese Sandman* (Soo, Morita) Ray Egan, Richard A. Whiting; *Charmaine* (orchestral) Erno Rapee, Lew Pollack; *Jazz Baby* (Channing).

Having explored the fun spots in America and Mexico, Elvis Presley (left) moved to Europe for **Double Trouble** (MGM) and, in his feeblest film since *Harum Scarum* (MGM, 1965), played an American singer who, while on a tour of the European club circuit is pursued not only by a couple of eager women – a 17-year-old English heiress played by Annette Day, and sultry, aggressive Yvonne Romain, but by a pair of jewel thieves (Chips Rafferty, right, and Norman Rossington) who have planted a fortune in diamonds in his luggage. Throughout the resultant confusion Presley sang a number of indifferent songs and generally did his best to salvage what he could of Jo Heim's insubstantial screenplay (story by Marc Brandel). The Wiere Brothers (as a trio of zany detectives), Monty

Landis, Michael Murphy, Leon Askin, John Alderson and Stanley Adams completed the cast of the B.C.W. (Judd Bernard-Irwin Winkler) production, whose director was Norman Taurog. Songs and musical numbers: *Double Trouble* Doc Pomus, Mort Shuman; *Baby, If You'll Give Me All Of Your Love* Joy Byers; *Could I Fall In Love?* Randy Starr; *Long Legged Girl* J. Leslie McFarland, Winfield Scott; *City By Night* Bill Giant, Florence Kaye, Bernie Baum; *Old MacDonald Had A Farm* arranged by Randy Starr; *I Love Only One Girl* Sid Tepper, Roy C. Bennett; *There's So Much Of The World To See*; *It Won't Be Long* Sid Wayne, Ben Weisman; *Blue River* Paul Evans, Fred Tobias; *What Now, What Next, Where To?* Don Robertson, Hal Blair; *Never Ending* Buddy Kaye, Philip Springer.

SIXTIES MUSICALS

One of the great Broadway musicals of the sixties, **How To Succeed In Business Without Really Trying** (Mirisch-United Artists), in the loving and capable hands of producer-director David Swift, transferred felicitously from stage to screen with Robert Morse (illustrated in white) and Rudy Vallee happily recreating their original roles in Abe Burrows's memorable stage production. The beguilingly simple story of a window cleaner's rise to executive glory in a large Madison Avenue company hazily named World Wide Wickets, its trenchantly satirical approach to the world of big business was just as humorous in Panavision as in the proscenium arch, thanks in the main to Swift's faithful adaptation of the Burrows-Jack Weinstock-Willie Gilbert book (music and lyrics by Frank Loesser) which, in turn, was based on a work by Shepherd Mead. And although certain numbers were dropped from the original – 'Cinderella Darling', 'Love From A Heart Of Gold', 'Happy To Keep His Dinner Warm', and, most regrettably, the 'Pirate Ballet' – or heard only in the background ('Paris Original'), there were enough holdovers from the Broadway show to keep the customers happy. The best of these included Vallee's college song lampoon, 'Grand Old Ivy', in which he was joined by Morse, and the rousing 'Brotherhood of Man' (Morse, Vallee and Ruth Kobart). Anthony Teague was excellent as Vallee's fink of a nephew Bud Frump, and there was good work too from Maureen Arthur (as sexpot Hedy LaRue), Michelle Lee (as Morse's girlfriend), Kay Reynolds, Sammy Smith and John Myhers. Nelson Riddle was the musical director and it was choreographed by Dale Moreda, based on routines originally created for the stage by Bob Fosse. Other songs and musical numbers: *How To Succeed* (Morse); *Coffee Break* (Teague, Reynolds); *The Company Way* (Morse, Teague, Smith); *A Secretary Is Not A Toy* (Myhers); *Been A Long Day* (Morse, Reynolds, Lee); *Finch's Frolic* (Morse, orchestra); *Rosemary* (Morse); *I Believe In You* (Morse, Lee).

◁ The two best things about **C'Mon Let's Live A Little**, an Allstar Pictures-Hertelandy Associates Production released by Paramount, were the appearances in it of Patsy Kelly and Ethel Smith (albeit without her electric organ). For the rest, there was nothing to shout hurrah about in June Starr's moderately pleasant little screenplay – a campus yarn in which recording artist Bobby Vee (right) starred as a young Arkansas folk singer who, after passing his entrance exam to Waymount College, becomes the innocent instrument of some campus politicking by the college radical, an egotistical senior (John Ireland Jr), who has started a 'free speech' movement directed against the college dean (Mark Evans, left). Jackie De Shannon (centre) co-starred as the Dean's pretty daughter (in love with Vee, naturally), with other roles going to Eddie Hodges, Suzie Kaye, Bo Belinsky, Russ Conway and The Pair Extraordinaire. The songs were by Don Crawford, whose 'Over and Over', sung by Miss Shannon, and 'Baker Man', sung by Miss Kaye, were the two stand-out items. June Starr and John Hertelandy produced, and David Butler directed. (Techniscope) Other songs and musical numbers: *C'Mon Let's Live A Little*; *Instant Girl*; *What Fool This Mortal Be*; *Tonight's The Night*; *For Granted*; *Back Talk*; *Let's Go Go*; *Way Back Home*.

Easy Come, Easy Go (Paramount) was the title of Elvis Presley's latest – a title that was an accurate reflection of its producer Hal Wallis's attitude to his star's subject matter. A couldn't-care-less story (by Allan Weiss and Anthony Lawrence, who also scripted), it featured Presley (illustrated) as a navy frogman who, with the help of co-star Dodie Marshall (as a student of yoga and a go-go dancer), and veteran Frank McHugh (a nautical expert) sets out to reclaim a valuable cargo of Spanish pieces-of-eight. What he eventually finds is a chest filled with copper coins whose value is under $4,000. Magnanimously, Elvis contributes the money to an arts centre, a gesture which helps win him Miss Marshall's undying love. There was little in the film to generate the same sentiment among audiences. Also cast: Pat Priest, Pat Harrington, Skip Ward, and Elsa Lanchester (illustrated standing). David Winters staged the six songs, the associate producer was Paul Nathan, and it was directed by John Rich. (Technicolor). Songs and musical numbers: *Easy Come, Easy Go* Sid Wayne, Ben Weisman; *The Love Machine* Gerald Nelson, Chuck Taylor, Fred Burch; *Yoga Is As Yoga Goes*; *Sing, You Children* Gerald Nelson, Burch; *You Gotta Stop* Bill Giant, Florence Kaye, Bernie Baum; *I'll Take Love* Dee Fuller, Mark Barkan.

Good Times, a Steve Broidy Production, produced by Lindsley Parsons and released by Columbia, featured recording artists Sonny and Cher (illustrated) in a breezy, well-written (by Tony Barrett, story by Nicholas Hymans) screenplay which had them accepting an offer from producer George Sanders to launch them in pictures. The bulk of the film (in Color by De Luxe) comprised Sonny's fantasies about a career in Hollywood, showing him and Cher in a series of stereotyped characterizations, such as gun-slinging sheriff and dance-hall hostess, Tarzan and Jane and, finally, a private investigator and his moll. Inconsequential, but imaginatively handled by director William Friedkin, with choreography by Andre Tayir, songs by Sonny (Bono), and a supporting cast who included Norman Alden, Larry Duran, Kelly Thordsen, Lennie Weinrib and Peter Robbins. Songs and musical numbers: *I Got You, Babe*; *It's The Little Things*; *Good Times*; *Trust Me*; *Don't Talk To Strangers*; *I'm Gonna Love You*; *Just A Name*.

Country and western singer Roy Orbison (illustrated, with guitar) made an unexciting screen debut for producer Sam Katzman in MGM's **The Fastest Guitar Alive**, a Civil War oater with comedy and songs and the merest smidgin of a plot (story and screenplay by Robert E. Kent), in which Orbison and co-star Sammy Jackson were seen as a pair of Confederate soldiers who, pretending to be medicine men, set out in a covered wagon for San Francisco where they hope to rob the mint in order to help the destitute South. Going along for the ride were The Chestnut Sisters (Maggie Pierce and Joan Freeman) and their bevy of dancing barmaids. So much for the female interest. Orbison sang eight songs, seven of which he wrote with Bill Dees. The eighth, a number called 'Snuggle Huggle', was the work of scenarist Kent and Fred Karger. Wilda Taylor choreographed, and the movie was directed by Michael Moore. It was a Four Leaf Production, photographed in Metrocolor. Other songs: *The Fastest Guitar Alive*; *Pistolero*; *Good Time Party*; *River*; *Whirlwind*; *Medicine Man*; *Rollin' On*.

How sad that **The Happiest Millionaire** (Buena Vista), the last film by Walt Disney before his death, should also have been his worst. It took 141 minutes to tell the story of an eccentric Philadelphia millionaire (who shares his mansion with pet alligators) and the problems he and his wife have when their teenage daughter falls in love. In the non-musical 1956 play (by Kyle Crichton, from his and Cordelia Drexel Biddle's book, on which the film was based), the central role was played by Walter Pidgeon. The Disney version gave it to Fred MacMurray who, instead of being lovable and endearing, as was clearly the authors' intention, was a boor and a bore, an error of judgment from which the film never recovered. Not even an interpolated score by the Sherman brothers, or the beaming, good-natured performance of Tommy Steele (illustrated) as the household butler, could enliven this miserable and thoroughly depressing occasion. A.J. Corothers's screenplay totally defeated such stalwart players as Greer Garson (as MacMurray's wife), Geraldine Page, Gladys Cooper and Hermione Baddeley. Lesley Ann Warren played the teenage daughter over whom all the fuss was, with John Davidson (as her beau), Paul Petersen, Eddie Hodges, Joyce Bulifant and Sean McClory completing the cast. Marc Breaux and Dee Dee Wood staged the musical numbers, with Norman Tokar in charge of the leaden direction. The co-producer was Bill Anderson and it was photographed in Technicolor. Songs and musical numbers: *Fortuosity*; *What's Wrong With That*; *Watch Your Footwork*; *Valentine Candy*; *Strengthen The Dwelling*; *I'll Always Be Irish*; *Bye Yum Pum Pum*; *I Believe In This Country*; *Detroit*; *There Are Those*; *When A Man Has A Daughter*; *Let's Have A Drink On It*; *Are We Dancing*; *La Belle Fille d'Amour* Richard B. and Robert M. Sherman.

A real dud from Elvis Presley (illustrated) and United Artists, **Clambake** was assembly line entertainment, set in a studio-manufactured Miami, with millionaire Presley changing identities with an impecunious water-ski instructor (Will Hutchins) in an attempt to see if he can make the grade female-wise without being burdened by wealth. A climactic boat race in which our hero risks life and limb to prove his worth brought Jules Levey, Arthur Gardner and Arnold Laven's Techniscope and Technicolor production to its predictable conclusion, with Shelley Fabares as Presley's prize. Also cast: Bill Bixby, James Gregory, Gary Merrill, Amanda Harley, Suzie Kaye and Angelique Pettyjohn. Arthur Brown Jr wrote it (during his lunch break, probably), and it was directed by Arthur Nadel. Songs and musical numbers: *Clambake* Sid Wayne, Ben Weisman; *A House That Has Everything*; *Confidence* Sid Tepper, Roy C. Bennett; *Hey Hey Hey* Joy Byers; *Who Needs Money?*; *The Girl I Never Loved* Randy Starr.

Based on David Heneker and Beverley Cross's stage musical (adapted in turn from the H.G. Wells novel *Kipps*), Paramount's **Half A Sixpence** was bright, shiny and welcome. Tommy Steele, who created the role in the West End and on Broadway, played Kipps, a draper's son who inherits a fortune and acquires a taste for high society until, his money gone, he realizes where true happiness lies. Julia Foster (illustrated with Steele) as the devoted parlourmaid who loves him for himself and not for his wealth, and veteran Cyril Ritchard as an eccentric actor-manager, contributed pleasant vignettes; and the evocation of lazy Edwardian luxury – whether boating at Henley or bathing at Eastbourne – made the film one long feast for the eye. But it was Tommy's show. With tireless cockney verve and ebullience, he romped through Heneker's tuneful score and Gillian Lynne's lively choreography, perfectly gearing himself to the appeal of such numbers as the haunting title song and the explosive 'Flash, Bang, Wallop!'. Penelope Horner was 'the other woman', Pamela Brown and James Villiers her snobbish family, with Grover Dale, Elaine Taylor, Hilton Edwards and Julia Sutton in support. Beverley Cross's screenplay (adapted by Dorothy Kingsley) was a skilful reworking of his own stage book, and George Sidney's direction almost matched his leading performer in zest. It was a George Sidney-Charles Schneer production in Technicolor. Other songs and musical numbers: *All In The Cause Of Economy*; *I'm Not Talking to You*; *Money To Burn*; *The Race Is On*; *I Don't Believe A Word Of It*; *A Proper Gentleman*; *She's Too Far Above Me*; *This Is My World*; *If The Rain's Got To Fall*; *I Know What I Am*.

Camelot cost a great deal of money – fifteen million dollars – to make, and Jack Warner, whose last major film project (for his studio) it was, wisely decided that as much of his investment as possible should be visible up there on the Technicolor and Panavision screen, in a stunning recreation of the sites of Arthurian legend. Since the original stage musical by Alan Jay Lerner and Frederick Loewe (who also wrote the screenplay), based on T.H. White's novel *The Once And Future King*, had failed to repeat the success of their *My Fair Lady*, Warner Bros. were obviously taking no chances, but neither the expensive gloss, nor such performers as the enchanting and extraordinarily gifted Vanessa Redgrave as Guenevere, Richard Harris as King Arthur (both illustrated) and Franco Nero (dubbed by Gene Merlino) as Lancelot – the classic Round Table triangle – and the first rate score, could prevent the film from being a costly flop (it recouped less than half of its initial outlay). Joshua Logan's vulgar direction, with his customary abuse of colour filters, also weighed heavily on the proceedings. David Hemmings played Mordred, Lionel Jeffries was King Pellinore and Lawrence Naismith was cast as Merlin. Also in it were Pierre Olaf, Estelle Winwood, Gary Marshall, Anthony Rogers and Peter Bromilow. The production was designed by John Truscott and Edward Carrere. Songs and musical numbers: *Camelot*; *If Ever I Would Leave You*; *Then You May Take Me To The Fair*; *C'Est Moi*; *How To Handle A Woman*; *The Lusty Month Of May*; *Guenevere*; *What Do The Simple Folk Do?*; *I Wonder What The King Is Doing Tonight*; *Follow Me*; *I Loved You Once In Silence*; *Wedding Ceremony*; *The Simple Joys Of Maidenhood*.

1968

Academic Awards

Best Picture
NOMINATIONS INCLUDED: *Funny Girl* (Rastar, Columbia) produced by Ray Stark

Best Actress
Barbra Streisand *Funny Girl* and Katherine Hepburn *The Lion In Winter* (Haworth, Avco Embassy) non-musical

Supporting Actor
NOMINATIONS INCLUDED: Daniel Massey *Star!* (20th Century-Fox)

After the fiasco of *The Happiest Millionaire*, the Walt Disney Studio redeemed itself – completely – with **The Jungle Book** (Buena Vista, illustrated). A joyously inventive re-telling of Rudyard Kipling's *Mowgli* stories, it was about an Indian boy who is abandoned at birth and raised as a wolf cub by Bagheera, the panther. When the boy, whose name is Mowgli, is 10 years old, Bagheera – on learning of the return of the tiger Shere Khan – decides the time has come to return the boy to his people, and it is their trip through the jungle that formed the basis of Larry Clemmons, Ralph Wright, Ken Anderson and Vance Gerry's delightful screenplay. The Sherman brothers and Terry Gilkyson provided a handful of super songs to help speed the intrepid travellers on their way – the catchiest being a number called 'I Wanna Be Like You' performed by Louis Prima, who lent his voice to the Technicolor production as King Of The Apes. Other vocal contributions came from Phil Harris as Baloo the Bear, Sebastian Cabot as Bagheera, George Sanders as Shere Khan, Sterling Holloway as Kaa the Snake, J. Pat O'Malley as Colonel Hathi the Elephant, and Bruce Reitherman as Man-cub Mowgli. The director was Wolfgang Reitherman. Other songs: *Trust In Me*; *Colonel Hathi's March*; *That's What Friends Are For*; *My Own Home* Richard B. and Robert M. Sherman; *The Bare Necessities* Terry Gilkyson.

Rex Harrison (illustrated) gave one of his most endearing performances in the expensive and, at 152 minutes, over-long **Doctor Dolittle** (20th Century-Fox), a family entertainment based on the stories of Hugh Lofting. Though Harrison's co-stars in Arthur P. Jacobs's Todd-AO and Color by De Luxe production were Samantha Eggar, Anthony Newley and Richard Attenborough, they were all eclipsed by the menagerie of fantasy creatures that passed through Leslie Bricusse's screenplay – such as Polynesia, the parakeet who taught Dolittle his 498 animal languages, Chee-Chee the chimp, Pushmi-Pullyu, the double-ended llama, Sophie the homesick seal, the Great Pink Sea Snail (illustrated right), and The Giant Lunar Moth. Richard Fleischer's direction was, on occasion, too heavy-handed for Lofting's lightweight creations, and Leslie Bricusse's songs, though pleasant and serviceable in context, have not passed the test of time, an observation which applies equally to the film itself. In the final analysis, it had everything going for it – except magic. Completing the cast were William Dix, Geoffrey Holder, Peter Bull, Muriel Landers, Portia Nelson and Norma Varden. The choreography was by Herbert Ross. (An Apjac Production). Songs and musical numbers: *Doctor Dolittle*; *I've Never Seen Anything Like It*; *After Today*; *My Friend The Doctor*; *When I Look In Your Eyes*; *Talk To The Animals*; *Beautiful Things*; *Fabulous Places*; *I Think I Like You*; *At The Crossroads*; *The Vegetarian*; *Like Animals*; *Something In Your Smile*; *Where Are The Words*. (The last two deleted in G.B.)

As a young girl Fanny Brice, who grew up to become one of the great personalities of the Ziegfeld Follies, lacked all the obvious ingredients of which stars were made. Ugly, skinny, flat-chested, and awkward, her obsessive ambition to make the big time met with derision from her friends and neighbours. Yet nothing could dis-

suade Fanny from pursuing anything other than a life in the theatre, and it was her stubborn determination to make it against all the odds that was so powerfully conveyed in **Funny Girl** (Columbia) which came to the screen via a lengthy (1348 performances) run on Broadway, with its volatile star – Barbra Streisand (illus-

trated) – repeating her award-winning role as Fanny Brice. Streisand's performance was mesmeric, and, following the maxim that it takes a star to play a star, she riveted audiences' attention for the film's 151-minute running time. Remove her and you'd be left with a random collection of backstage clichés and, plot-wise, a re-run of *Rose Of Washington Square* (20th Century-Fox, 1939). And although Isobel Lennart's screenplay, based on her book for the Broadway production, was an improvement on the original, it was still the weakest element in the production; this was especially apparent in the second half when, for much of the time, plot took over from Jule Styne and Bob Merrill's marvellous score with tedious results. Nor was the narrative helped by the off-beat casting of heart-throb Omar Sharif as gambler Nicky Arnstein, the man responsible for most of Miss Brice's unhappiness. What little pathos their scenes together generated was due entirely to Streisand, whose ability to draw blood from a stony co-star must be notched up as one of her several notable achievements. Even during the show's most sentimental moments, Streisand's magnetism, in a remarkable screen debut, rode rough-shod over the *schmaltz*. Impressive, too, was Herb Ross's choreography, at its most effective in the simple 'I'm The Greatest Star', and at its wittiest in the more elaborate 'His Love Makes Me Beautiful' in which Fanny, against the wishes of the great Ziegfeld (Walter Pidgeon), turns a lavish production number extolling the virtues of the beautiful bride into a wildly funny parody. Other musical highlights included the star's equally devastating parody of 'Swan Lake' (with Tommy Rall), her passionate 'Don't Rain On My Parade', her tender 'People' and, for the finale, a moving version of Brice's famous hit 'My Man' (by Maurice Yvain and Channing Pollock). The old-fashioned but solid direction was by William Wyler, whose cast was completed by Kay Medford (as Mrs Brice), Anne Francis, Lee Allen, Mae Questel, Gerald Mohr, Frank Faylen, and Mittie Lawrence. It was photographed in Panavision 70 and Technicolor by Harry Stradling and produced by Ray Stark. Other songs and musical numbers: *Temporary Arrangement* (Sharif); *If A Girl Isn't Pretty* (Streisand, Medford, Questel); *Roller Skate Rag* (Streisand and chorus); *You Are Woman, I Am Man* (Streisand, Sharif); *Sadie Sadie* (Streisand); *Funny Girl* (Streisand) Styne, Merrill; *I'd Rather Be Blue* (Streisand) Billy Rose, Fred Fisher; *Second Hand Rose* (Streisand) Grant Clarke, James Hanley.

The underwhelming story of a talented country and western musician (Hank Williams Jr, right) and the friction that exists between him and his uncle Kermit (Ed Begley), a crusty old tobacco farmer who believes music-making is no way to earn a living, **A Time To Sing**, produced by Sam Katzman for Four Leaf Productions and released by MGM, was also a time to sleep. Romantic interest was supplied by Shelley Fabares (left), with Charles Robinson, D'Urville Martin, Donald Woods, Clara Ward and The X-L's (as themselves) completing the cast for director Arthur Dreifuss. The script was by Robert E. Kent and Orville H. Hampton. Songs and musical numbers: *The Humming Bird*; *It's All Over But The Crying*; *Rock In My Shoe* Hank Williams Jr; *A Man Is On His Own* John Scoggins, Williams; *Money Can't Buy Happiness*; *Old Before My Time* Steve Karliski; *Next Time I Say Goodbye, I'm Leaving* Larry Kusik, Eddie Snyder; *A Time To Sing* Scoggins.
▽

Elvis Presley's 27th film in eleven years was **Speedway** (MGM) and it found him embroiled in a very silly screenplay by Phillip Shuken in which he was cast as a generous, easygoing racing champion whose lackadaisical approach to money matters results in his manager (Bill Bixby) gambling away a fortune of Presley's winnings on the race track. Nancy Sinatra co-starred as an internal revenue agent out to claim a mere $145,000 in income tax owed by Presley (illustrated) – thanks to further mismanagement on Bixby's part. She got her dough (and Elvis), and even got to sing a couple of numbers. Gale Gordon, Carl Ballantine, William Schallert, Ross Hagen, Victoria Myerink and Poncie Ponce were also featured. Douglas Laurence produced (in Metrocolor and Panavision) and the director was Norman Taurog. Songs and musical numbers: *Your Groovy Self* Lee Hazlewood; *Speedway*; *He's Your Uncle, Not Your Dad*; *Who Are You (Who Am I?)*; *Let Yourself Go*; *Your Time Hasn't Come Yet, Baby*; *There Ain't Nothing Like A Song*; *Five Sleepy Heads*; *Western Union*; *Mine*; *Goin' Home*; *Suppose* Mel Glazer, Stephen Schlaks.
▽

Sixteen years after the death of Gertrude Lawrence, 20th Century-Fox accorded her a colourful accolade of sorts in **Star!**, a glittering $12,000,000 worth of celluloid biography in which they cast Julie Andrews as the legendary Gertie – not because she was ideal for the part, but because she happened to be the hottest star around at the time. And it says much for Miss Andrews that, despite the polarities in temperament of the two ladies, she did a most credible and creditable job. Like many show-biz stories, this one began in poverty – in Clapham, London, where Gertrude Lawrence was born. Scenarist William Fairchild's handling of his subject's early struggles during her music hall and chorus girl days was the best thing in a long (165 minutes), familiar, rags-to-riches chronicle that tended to run out of dramatic steam in direct ratio to its star's rise to fame. Which is not to say that the film was short on narrative incident. On the contrary, it was just that the sight of a successful but destructively selfish Gertie becoming the toast of two continents was less compelling than the zestful struggles she faced before her career took off. Fortunately, though, the film was also a veritable sardine-tin of musical numbers on to which one could anchor one's restless spirits. And with such composers as Noel Coward (played by Daniel Massey), Cole Porter and the Gershwins providing many of the tunes, the numbers (choreographed by Michael Kidd) were decidedly welcome in their own right. Julie Andrews (illustrated, as Coward's 'Parisian Pierrot') sang virtually all the songs, generally solo, sometimes with one of her male co-stars or accompanied by dancers. There were many musical standouts, three of which were Miss Andrews's renditions of Kurt Weill and Ira Gershwin's 'Jenny' and Cole Porter's 'The Physician' – both a far cry from the *Mary Poppins – Sound Of Music* image generally associated with her – and Daniel Massey's urbane presentation of Noel Coward's 'Forbidden Fruit'. Richard Crenna was second-billed as Richard Aldrich, Gertie's forceful, sympathetic and supportive second husband, with other parts going to Jenny Agutter (Gertie's daughter), Bruce Forsyth as her music hall performer father, Beryl Reid as her mother, as well as Michael Craig, Robert Reed, John Collin, Alan Oppenheimer, Richard Karlin and Lynley Laurence. The production was designed by Boris Leven, photographed in Todd-AO and Color by De Luxe by Ernest Laszlo, produced

by Saul Chaplin, and directed by Robert Wise. Songs and musical numbers: *Star!* Jimmy Van Heusen, Sammy Cahn; *Piccadilly* Walter Williams, Bruce Seiver, Paul Morande; *Oh It's A Lovely War* J.P. Long, Maurice Scott; *My Garden Of Joy* Saul Chaplin; *'n Everything* Buddy De Sylva, Gus Kahn, Al Jolson; *Burlington Bertie From Bow* William Hargreaves; *Limehouse Blues* Philip Brahm, Douglas Furber; *Someone To Watch Over Me*; *Dear Little Boy*; *Do Do Do* George and Ira Gershwin; *Someday I'll Find You*; *Has Anybody Seen Our Ship?* Coward; *My Ship* Kurt Weill, Ira Gershwin. The film also contained an extract from Noel Coward's play *Private Lives*. Interesting sideline: After the film's release, and its failure to garner the hoped-for box-office returns, it was shortened and re-released under a new title, *Those Were The Happy Days*. It remained, however, a financial failure in both versions.

Though the fictitious storyline attached to United Artists' **The Night They Raided Minsky's** (GB: **The Night They Invented Striptease**) told of an innocent lass (Britt Ekland) from the Amish country – an area inhabited by a puritan religious sect – who arrives in New York's East Side hoping to find fame as a dancer, but finds it, instead, as the inventor of the strip tease (the top of her dress accidentally falls off while she is in the middle of a 'bible dance' at Minsky's famous burlesque theatre), the film's strength derived not from its plot but from its sleazy atmosphere, and the period nostalgia it evoked. It also benefited from the performances of Jason Robards (right) as Minsky's fast-talking 'straight man', his comedian rival Norman Wisdom (left), and Bert Lahr as a retired comedian responsible for introducing Miss Ekland (centre) into the seltzer bottle, bawdy skit, beefy chorus line world of burlesque. Completing the excellent cast were Forrest Tucker, Harry Andrews (as Ekland's father), Joseph Wiseman, Denholm Elliott, Elliott Gould and Jack Burns. The lively, affectionate screenplay (unburdened by such strictures as good taste) was by Arnold Schulman, Sidney Michaels and Norman Lear (the latter producing for Bud Yorkin-Norman Lear Productions), and William Friedkin directed. The narration was spoken and the title song (by Lee Adams and Charles Strouse) performed by Rudy Vallee, and the choreography was by Danny Daniels. Songs and musical numbers: *The Night They Raided Minsky's*; *A Perfect Gentleman*; *Take Ten Terrific Girls*; *You Rat, You*; *Penny Arcade*; *How I Loved Her*; *Wait For Me (love theme)* Adams, Strouse.

Although the E.Y. Harburg-Burton Lane musical fantasy **Finian's Rainbow** (Warner Bros.) clocked up more than seven hundred performances on stage, its unique blend of blarney, social comment and sheer Broadway know-how was a decidedly tricky substance to recapture on film and it eluded Francis Ford Coppola, still a relative newcomer to Hollywood, who directed it. Harburg's plotline (which he and co-librettist Fred Saidy adapted and slightly updated for the screen) concerned a whimsically naive Irish immigrant living in Rainbow Valley, Missitucky, somewhere near Fort Knox, who argues that America's riches have blossomed as a result of the country's buried gold underground at Fort Knox, and decides to reap the same reward by 'planting' a crock of gold he had once stolen from a leprechaun. A sub-plot involving a racist southern senator who, abusing one of the three wishes granted by the gold, is turned into a black, further emphasized the moral of the tale: that gold *is* a base metal and people constitute the world's true wealth. Fred Astaire (left), as Finian McLonergan, looked like an oversized leprechaun and would have been ideal for the role ten years earlier; Petula Clark (right) played his daughter and Don Francks the object of her affections. Tommy Steele, Barbara Hancock, Keenan Wynn, Al Freeman Jr, Jester Hairston, Avon Long, Roy Glenn and Ronald Colby were also to be seen, it was choreographed by Hermes Pan, and produced in Technicolor and Panavision by Joseph Landon. Songs and musical numbers: *How Are Things In Glocca Morra?*; *If this Isn't Love*; *Look To The Rainbow*; *Old Devil Moon*; *Something Sort Of Grandish*; *The Begat*; *This Time Of The Year*; *That Great Come-And-Get-It Day*; *When The Idle Poor Become The Idle Rich*; *When I'm Not Near The Girl I Love*; *Rain Dance Ballet*.

A sort of *Hellzapoppin'* 1968 style, **Head** (Columbia) took the synthetically manufactured and patently untalented pop group, the Monkees (illustrated), through a series of psychedelic-type situations best experienced under the influence of marijuana. A few amusing moments – such as an assault on a Coca Cola machine, and a sequence in which the pop group appear as dandruff in guest-star Victor Mature's hair – revealed a certain visual imagination in producer-director Bob Rafaelson's approach to the plotless material (he also 'wrote' it together with co-producer Jack Nicholson). But for the most part it was a free-wheeling, hit-or-miss affair. Also cast: Annette Funicello, Timothy Carye, Logan Ramsay, Abraham Sofaer, Vito Scotti, and female impersonator T.C. Jones. Nicholson and Rafaelson also appeared – as themselves – and Toni Basil choreographed. (Technicolor). Songs and musical numbers: *Porpoise Song* Gerry Goffin, Carole King; *Circle Sky* Michael Nesmith; *As We Go Along* King, Toni Stern; *Daddy's Song* Nilsson; *Long Title: Do I Have To Do This All Over Again?*; *Can You Dig It?* Peter Tork.

Owing more to *The Happiest Millionaire* (Buena Vista, 1967) than *Mary Poppins* (Buena Vista, 1964), Buena Vista's **The One And Only Genuine Original Family Band** (see illustration) was another clanger from the Disney stable whose uninviting subject was the political race between Grover Cleveland and Benjamin Harrison. Based on the autobiography of Laura Bower Van Nuys, of Rapid City, South Dakota (who was one of the children featured in the story), its screenplay, by Lowell S. Hawley, attempted to draw mileage from the fact that grandpa Walter Brennan was an ardent Democrat while the rest of his brood were staunch Republicans. Hawley's attempts were unsuccessful, and his failure reflected badly in Brennan's tiresome performance, as well as on the perfomances of Buddy Ebsen and Janet Blair in the thankless roles of Ma and Pa Bower. Lesley Ann Warren and John Davidson (stale from their failure in *The Happiest Millionaire*) were the young lovers, with other parts in Bill Anderson's flaccid, Technicolor production going to Kurt Russell, Steve Harmon, Richard Deacon, Wally Cox, Debbie Smith, Goldie Hawn, Bobby Riha and Smitty Wordes. Trying unsuccessfully to hang it all together was director Michael O'Herlihy, the Sherman brothers provided the lack-lustre score, and the dull choreography was by Hugh Lambert. Songs and musical numbers: *The One And Only Genuine Original Family Band*; *Dakota*; *Drummin' Drummin' Drummin'*; *Let's Put It Over With Grover*; *Ten Feet Off The Ground*; *'Bout Time*; *The Happiest Girl Alive*; *Oh Benjamin Harrison*; *West Of Wide Missouri*.
▽

△
With MGM's musical remake of their wonderful 1939 weepie, **Goodbye, Mr Chips**, audiences were ready to cry 'Good riddance!', and who could blame them? James Hilton's best seller about the shy, retiring and soon to be retired schoolmaster looking back over his life was totally unsuited to big-budget musical treatment, nor was the enterprise helped one bit by Peter O'Toole's unconvincing and unappealing performance in the title role (it could not be mentioned in the same breath as Robert Donat's in the earlier version), or by Leslie Bricusse's thoroughly undistinguished score. Petula Clark (illustrated, with O'Toole) played the musical comedy star whom Chips marries to the dismay of headmaster Michael Redgrave; with George Baker, Jack Hedley and Sian Phillips offering stalwart, but futile support. Terence Rattigan wrote the screenplay, Herbert Ross directed, and Arthur P. Jacobs produced (in Panavision and Metrocolor). Songs and musical numbers: *Fill The World With Love*; *Where Did My Childhood Go?*; *London Is London*; *And The Sky Smiled*; *Apollo*; *When I Am Older*; *Walk Through The World*; *What Shall I Do With Today?*; *What A Lot Of Flowers*; *Schooldays*; *When I Was Younger*; *You And I*.

Based on the hit recording, 'The Alice's Restaurant Massacree', in which Arlo Guthrie (right), son of Woody, recounted incidents from his past, including an arrest for littering and his fleeting induction into the US Army – **Alice's Restaurant** (United Artists), written by Venable Herndon and its director, Arthur Penn, was a strikingly original, often hauntingly beautiful account of life in the sixties as experienced by a young man at odds with society. Guthrie's early years – his short-lived college career, his home life and his friendships, especially with a young couple called Alice and Ray Brook who live in a deconsecrated church in Stockbridge and own a restaurant that becomes a haven for hippies – was handled with charm and insight. The Brooks were superbly played by Pat Quinn and James Broderick, with other parts in Hillard Elkins and Joe Manduke's commendable production going to Geoff Outlaw, Tina Chen (left), Kathleen Dabney, Shelley Plimpton, and, as themselves, Pete Seeger and Police Chief William Obanhein. Although basically Guthrie could not be called an actor, he knew how to make his likeable presence felt, and supplied most of the songs. It was stunningly photographed by Michael Nebbia in Color De Luxe. Songs: *Alice's Restaurant Massacree*; *Chilling Of The Evening*; *Ring Around A Rosy Rag*; *Now And Then*; *I'm Going Home*; *Motorcycle Song*; *Highway In The Wind* (Guthrie) Arlo Guthrie; *Amazing Grace* (choir); *Songs For Ageing Children* (Joni Mitchell) Mitchell; *The Pastures Of Plenty* (Pete Seeger) Woody Guthrie.
▽

SIXTIES MUSICALS

Determined, at considerable cost, to duplicate the success he had had on stage with **Sweet Charity**, director-choreographer Bob Fosse transferred his massive hit to the big Panavision 70 screen with all the pazazz he could muster. The result was a gaudy, inflated, would-be blockbuster that not only violated the memory of the original Fellini film on which it was based (*Nights Of Cabiria*), but also the memory of the Broadway musical from whence, more directly, it came. Shirley MacLaine's (centre) over-zealous, over-stressed central performance, un-like Gwen Verdon's on Broadway, strained too hard for audience acceptance. The tale of a taxi-dancer at a seedy Manhattan nightspot who keeps being jilted in love, its modest storyline (screenplay by Peter Stone, based on the book by Neil Simon and a screenplay by Fellini, Tullio Pinelli and Ennio Flaiano) got lost amidst Fosse's indulgent, self-consciously clever direction, leaving little to admire other than his choreography which, happily, was galvanic; and to which his febrile visual approach was eminently suited. There was nothing to touch the imaginative and atmospheric 'Hey Big Spender' number which featured, among others, the dynamic Chita Rivera (right) and the sexy Paula Kelly (left); or a sequence of dances, including 'The Rich-man's Frug' and 'The Hustle', performed by a knockout chorus line in a ritzy disco frequented by matinée idol Vittorio Vitale (Ricardo Montalban). Effective, too, was evangelist Sammy Davis Jr's 'Rhythm Of Life' as well as a rousing rooftop routine by MacLaine, Kelly and Rivera called 'There's Got To Be Something Better Than This' (illustrated); and both Fosse and MacLaine, and the style of the movie, showed to advantage in 'I'm A Brass Band'. Stubby Kaye made a welcome appearance as Herman, who works at MacLaine's club, with other roles going to John McMartin, Barbara Bouchet, Alan Hewitt, Dante De Paulo, John Wheeler and John Craig. The excellent score was by Cy Coleman and Dorothy Fields, Ralph Burns was the musical director and the Technicolor photography was by Robert Surtees. A Universal picture, it was produced by Robert Arthur. Other songs and musical numbers: *Sweet Charity*; *Where Am I Going*; *My Personal Property*; *If They Could See Me Now*; *It's a Nice Face*; *I Love To Cry At Weddings*.

△

▽

Seventeen million dollars, but not a great deal else, went into the screen version of Alan Jay Lerner and Frederick Loewe's 1951 Broadway success **Paint Your Wagon** (Paramount) which, like the stage show, suffered chronically from an inferior book by Lerner, whose screenplay – adapted by Paddy Chayefsky (concerning a small gold-mining town called No Name City, in the California of the late 1840's) was as dull and as muddled as it was on Broadway. The main narrative thrust had drunken, disreputable Lee Marvin (right) and his 'pardner' (Clint Eastwood, left) living in a *ménage à trois* with beautiful Jean Seberg (dubbed by Anita Gordon) who, as the wife Marvin bought from a Mormon, declares her love for them both. Marvin scored quite a hit with his distinctly unmusical interpretation of 'Wandrin' Star' and, from Harve Presnell as Rotten Luck Willie, came the lovely 'They Call The Wind Maria', as well as the rousing 'There's A Coach Comin' In' – both aided by a lusty male chorus. The best song of all, though, 'I Talk To The Trees', went to Eastwood. Lerner and Andre Previn collaborated on five additional songs of which not one turned out to be of any consequence. Much of the film was photographed (in Panavision and Technicolor) on location in Baker, Oregon, and was, at least, always good to look at. The static,

heavy-handed direction was by Joshua Logan whose cast included Alan Dexter, Ray Walston, Tom Ligon, William O'Connell, Ben Baker, Paula Trueman and The Nitty Gritty Dirt Band. The undistinguished choreography was by Jack Baker. Other songs and musical numbers: *I'm On My Way*; *I Still See Elisa*; *Hand Me Down That Can O'Beans*; *Whoo-Ti-Ay*; Lerner, Loewe; *Gold Fever*; *The First Thing You Know*; *A Million Miles Away Behind The Door*; *Gospel Of No Name City*; *Best Things*; Previn, Lerner.

△

Written by Charles M. Schulz, **A Boy Named Charlie Brown** (National General), based on the United Features Syndicate cartoon strip, was an animated feature (see illustration) in Technicolor whose main plot point had Charlie entering a spelling bee, and being eliminated in the final round for not knowing how to spell 'beagle'. Also featured in Lee Mendelson and Bill Melendez's delightful little production were such Schulz favourites as Lucy (the neighbourhood psychiatrist), Snoopy, Lucy's brother Linus, and Schroeder. The vocal characterizations were supplied by Peter Robbins, Pamelyn Ferdin, Glenn Gilger, Andy Pforsich, Sally Dyer and Ann Altieri. Bill Melendez directed and the songs were by Rod McKuen and Vince Guaraldi. Also heard was an extract from Beethoven's *Piano Sonata Opus 13 (The 'Pathetique')* played by Ingolf Dahl. The choreographer for Snoopy's skating sequence was Skippy Baxter. Songs and musical numbers: *Cloud Dreams*; *Charlie Brown And His All-Stars*; *We Lost Again*; *Blue Charlie Brown*; *Time To Go To School*; *I Only Dread One Day At A Time*; *Failure Face*; *By Golly I'll Show 'Em*; *Class Champion*; *I Before E*; *School Spelling Bee*; *Champion Charlie Brown*; *Start Boning Up On Your Spelling, Charlie Brown*; *You'll Either Be A Hero . . . Or A Goat*; *Bus Station*; *Do Piano Players Make A Lot Of Money*; *I've Got To Get My Blanket Back*; *Big City*; *Found Blanket*; *National Spelling Bee*; *B-E-A-G-E-L*; *Homecoming*; *I'm Never Going To School Again*; *Welcome Home, Charlie Brown*.

Though 1969 was far from being a vintage year for screen musicals, it did produce a humdinger of a show in Jerry Herman's **Hello Dolly!** which, although presented by 20th Century-Fox, was in essence an MGM musical. Its director was Gene Kelly; Harry Stradling, its photographer, had worked with Kelly on *The Pirate* (MGM, 1948) and with Fred Astaire on *The Barkleys Of Broadway* (MGM, 1949); Roger Edens, the associate producer, was a founder member of Arthur Freed's famed unit at Culver City as, indeed, were both Kelly and the show's co-musical director (with Lionel Newman) Lennie Hayton. Choreographer Michael Kidd received his early training under Freed's guidance as well; Irene Sharaff, the costume designer, was an important fixture at MGM for years, as was Jack Martin Smith who, with Herman Blumenthal and John De Cuir, designed **Dolly**'s sets. Their combined talents resulted in a show that, like so many vintage MGM musicals, required nothing more of audiences than to sit back and enjoy it. The

fact that its leading lady, Barbra Streisand (right) was far too young (Carol Channing created the role on stage) mattered not a jot to the Fox hierarchy. With a budget of $24,000,000 at stake, they needed a major star in the title role – and a major talent. They got both. Walter Matthau co-starred as Horace Vandergelder, 'the well-known half a millionaire' hay and feed merchant from Yonkers, New York, on whom the widowed Dolly Levi has set her matrimonial sights, with other parts going to Britain's Michael Crawford as Cornelius Hackl, Vandergelder's chief clerk, Danny Lockin as Barnaby the assistant clerk, Marianne McAndrew as milliner Irene Molloy, and E.J. Peaker as Minnie Fay. Also: Joyce Ames, Tommy Tune, Judy Knaiz and, making a special guest appearance in the brilliantly staged title number at the Harmonia Gardens, Louis Armstrong (left). Jerry Herman supplied two new songs for Streisand: the introductory 'Just Leave Everything To Me' (replacing the original 'I Put My Hand In'), and the

quiet 'Love Is Only Love' (a reject from his score of *Mame*) which was sandwiched between the spectacular 'Before The Parade Passes By' (Streisand) and the title number. One other stage number 'Motherhood', was omitted. Producer Ernest Lehman's screenplay was a decided improvement on the stage musical book (which had been based originally on Thornton Wilder's play, *The Matchmaker*), and at least ironed out and tied up the many loose ends which blemished the Broadway version. The film was photographed in Todd-AO and Color De Luxe and the stunning choreography was by Michael Kidd. Other songs and musical numbers: *Put On Your Sunday Clothes* (Streisand, Crawford, Lockin, chorus); *So Long Dearie* (Streisand); *It Takes A Woman* (Matthau, Crawford, Lockin, chorus, reprised Streisand); *Ribbons Down My Back* (McAndrew); *Elegance* (Crawford, Lockin, McAndrew, Peaker); *It Only Takes A Moment* (Crawford, McAndrew, chorus); *Dancing* (principals, chorus); *Waiter's Gavotte* (chorus).

1970

Academy Awards

Costume Design
NOMINATIONS INCLUDED: *Darling Lili* (Paramount) Donald Brooks and Jack Bear.

Music
Song
NOMINATIONS INCLUDED: 'Whistling Away The Dark' *Darling Lili* Henry Mancini *cm*; Johnny Mercer *lyr*.

Original Song Score
NOMINATIONS INCLUDED: *Darling Lili* Henry Mancini and Johnny Mercer. *A Boy Named Charlie Brown* (Mendelson-Melendez. Cinema Center Films, National General) Rod McKuen, John Scott Trotter, Bill Melendez, Al Shean and Vince Guaraldi

Jean Hersholt Humanitarian Award
Frank Sinatra

The Annual Top Moneymaking Films
INCLUDED: *Hello, Dolly!* (Chenault, 20th Century-Fox).

The Aristocats (Buena Vista) cost the Walt ▷ Disney organization $4,000,000 to draw, and it was worth every cent. The delightful story of a 'catnapping' (the victims being a mama cat and her three offspring, Toulouse, Berlioz and Marie) perpetrated by a greedy, evil old butler who'd rather his mistress left her fortune to him than to her cats (illustrated), its strength, and most of its fun, lay in the instantly recognizable 'human' elements embodied in the animals on display. Apart from the feline family around which Tom Rowe and Tom McGowan's amusing little story revolved, other characters who featured prominently included a group of Bohemian hip-cat musicians headed by Scat Cat, the romantic alley cat O'Malley, a mouse called Roquefort, a pair of hounds named Napoleon and Lafayette and, most endearing of all, a couple of spinster geese called Agatha and Abigail. Lending their voices to these creations were Phil Harris, Eva Gabor, Sterling Holloway, Scatman Crothers, Paul Winchell, Lord Tim Hudson, Carole Shelley, Hermione Baddeley, Nancy Kulp, Dean Clark, Liz English, Gary Dubin and Pat Buttram. It was produced in Technicolor by Wolfgang Reitherman and Winston Hibler, with Reitherman directing from a screenplay by Larry Clemmons. Songs and musical numbers: *The Aristocats* (title song sung by Maurice Chevalier); *She Never Felt Alone* (Gabor); *Scales And Arpeggios* (Gabor and 'kittens') Richard M. and Robert B. Sherman; *Thomas O'Malley Cat* (Harris) Terry Gilkyson; *Everybody Wants To Be A Cat* (Harris, Crothers) Floyd Huddlestone, Al Rinker.

The sight of Julie Andrews doing a strip-tease gave **Darling Lili** (Paramount) what little novelty value it had. For most of its 136-minute running time, producer-director Blake Edwards's multi-million dollar extravaganza was an utter bore that mixed music, melodrama, adventure, and romance to indigestible effect. The Mata Hari story of a World War I stage star who also happens to be a German spy called Lili Smith, it top-cast Julie Andrews (illustrated) as the darling of the title, co-starred Rock Hudson (as an American air squadron commander who knows all about her treacherous activities but loves her just the same) with Jeremy Kemp, Lance Percival, Michael Witney, Jacques Marin, Andre Marianne and Gloria Paul in support. It was written by Edwards and William Peter Blatty who failed to bring a point of view to their material resulting in their star's performance carrying even less conviction than the screenplay and the indifferent numbers written for the star by Henry Mancini and Johnny Mercer. Musically speaking, the film temporarily flickered into life only when Andrews was belting out some well-worn World War I favourites such as 'Pack Up Your Troubles In Your Old Kit Bag' by Felix Powell and George Asaf, 'It's A Long Way To Tipperary' by Jack Judge and Harry Williams, and 'Keep The Home Fires Burning' by Ivor Novello and Lena Guilbert-Ford. Physically, the production looked far better than it sounded, its French and Belgian exteriors appearing especially inviting in Russell Harlan's splendid Technicolor photography. Hermes Pan choreographed. Songs and musical numbers: *Darling Lili*; *Smile Away Each Rainy Day*; *Whistling Away The Dark*; *Little Birds*; *A Girl In No-Man's Land*; *I'll Give You Three Guesses*; *Skol*; *Your Goodwill Ambassador*.
▽

△

Not even Barbra Streisand could save **On A Clear Day You Can See Forever** (Paramount) from being the confused mish-mash it was under Vincente Minnelli's unusually faltering direction. Based on the stage show (book and lyrics by Alan Jay Lerner and music by Burton Lane), its theme was reincarnation as demonstrated by heroine Streisand who, when not under co-star Yves Montand's hypnotic spell, is just plain Daisy Gamble from Flatbush, Brooklyn. Under hypnosis, however, she regresses to the 18th century, taking on the persona of a breath-taking aristocratic beauty called Melinda Wainwhistle whose childhood was spent in an orphanage (see illustration, Streisand centre). Though Lerner's screenplay differed a great deal from his book for the stage version – and, indeed, was a distinct improvement on it – it was, nonetheless, the victim of some brutal editing which rendered much of the narrative unintelligible. Another victim of the editor's scissors was Jack Nicholson

as Streisand's guitar-strumming hippy-type ex-step-brother, whose one song (as well as an elaborate production number) was completely elminated from the final release print. Larry Blyden played Streisand's boring fiancé, with other parts in the Howard W. Koch-Alan Jay Lerner production going to Bob Newhart, Simon Oakland, John Richardson, Pamela Brown and Irene Handl. The numbers were staged by Howard Jeffrey without much flair, the best being Montand's visually quite interesting 'Come Back To Me'. Streisand's singing of the half a dozen numbers retained for her from the original Broadway production (which had starred the volatile Barbara Harris) was dynamic, and provided the only bright spots in a dull and top-heavy show. (Panavision and Technicolor) Other songs: *He Isn't You*; *Go To Sleep*; *Hurry, Its Lovely Up Here*; *Love With All The Trimmings*; *Melinda*; *On A Clear Day You Can See Forever*; *What Did I Have That I Don't Have?*

△

In a misguided attempt to recreate the phenomenal success of *The Sound Of Music* (20th Century-Fox, 1965), producers Virginia and Andrew Stone poured into their vast Super Panavision 70 and Color De Luxe screen version of the 1944 Broadway success **Song Of Norway** (ABC) about as much treacle as it could comfortably contain, and then some. A monument to kitsch (including cartoon and puppet sequences), the only element to emerge unscathed was its sublime Norwegian scenery – a setting appropriate to the story it told of the life and times of composer Edvard Grieg. Heading a cast whose multi-national flavour resembled something out of the United Nations, was Toralv Maurstadt as the maestro himself and Florence Henderson (illustrated) as his wife Nina, with other roles in Stone's cliché-cramped screenplay (based on the musical by Milton Lazarus from a play by Homer Curran) being caricatured to the hilt by Frank Poretta, Harry Secombe, Robert Morley, Edward G. Robinson, Oscar Homolka, Christina Schollin and Elizabeth Larner. The music was by Grieg and the lyrics by Bob Wright and Chet Forrest – the same team who put words to Borodin's music in *Kismet*. Lee Theodore was responsible for the energetic but numbingly familiar dance routines, Davis Boulton for the picture-postcard views of the fjords and mountains, and John Ogden for the piano playing. Andrew Stone directed. Songs and musical numbers: *Solveig's Song*; *Piano Concerto In A Minor*; *Life Of A Wife Of A Sailor*; *Freddy And His Fiddle*; *A Rhyme And A Reason*; *Strange Music*; *Song Of Norway*; *Ribbons And Wrappings*; *The Little House*; *When We Wed*; *At Christmastime*; *In The Hall Of The Mountain King*; *Wrong To Dream*; *Hill Of Dreams*; *Hymn Of Betrothal*; *Be A Boy Again*; *Hand In Hand*; *Three There Were*; *The Solitary Wanderer*; *I Love You*.

△

Based on the NBC television series for children, **Pufnstuf** (Universal) was a totally forgettable, and soon forgotten, musical fantasy about a little boy (Jack Wild, illustrated) and his adventures with a dragon, a gopher and various witches (most notably Martha Raye and Mama Cass). Also featured were Billy Hayes, Roberto Gamonet, Sharon Baird and Johnny Silver; it was produced by Si Rose, who also wrote the screenplay with John Fenton Murray, and directed by Hollingsworth Morse. Songs and musical numbers: *Pufnstuf*; *Angel Raid*; *Charge*; *Fire In The Castle*; *Happy Hour*; *Leaving Living Island*; *Rescue Racer To The Rescue*; *Witchiepoo's Lament*; *Different* Charles Fox, Norman Gimbel.

1971

Academy Awards

Best Picture
NOMINATIONS INCLUDED: *Fiddler On The Roof* (Mirsch, United Artists) produced by Norman Jewison

Best Actor
NOMINATIONS INCLUDED: Topol *Fiddler On The Roof*

Supporting Actor
NOMINATIONS INCLUDED: Leonard Frey *Fiddler On The Roof*

Direction
NOMINATIONS INCLUDED: Norman Jewison *Fiddler On The Roof*

Art Direction (Set Decoration)
NOMINATIONS INCLUDED: *Bedknobs And Broomsticks* (Disney, Buena Vista) John B. Mansbridge and Peter Ellenshaw; Emile Kuri and Hal Gausman. *Fiddler On The Roof* Robert Boyle and Michael Stringer, Peter Lamont.

Costume Design
NOMINATIONS INCLUDED: *Bedknobs And Broomsticks* Bill Thomas

Sound
Fiddler On The Roof Gordon K. McCallum and David Hildyard

Cinematography
Fiddler On The Roof Oswald Morris

Special Visual Effects
Bedknobs And Broomsticks Alan Maley, Eustace Lycett and Danny Lee

Music
Song
NOMINATIONS INCLUDED: 'The Age Of Not Believing' *Bedknobs And Broomsticks* music and lyrics by Richard M. Sherman and Robert B. Sherman

Scoring (Adaptation and Original Song Score)
Fiddler On The Roof John Williams
NOMINATIONS INCLUDED: *Bedknobs And Broomsticks* Richard M. Sherman, Robert M. Sherman and Irwin Kostal. *The Boy Friend* (MGM) Peter Maxwell Davies and Peter Greenwell. *Willy Wonka And The Chocolate Factory* (Paramount) Leslie Bricusse, Anthony Newley and Walter Scharf.

The Annual Top Moneymaking Films
INCLUDED: *The Aristocats* (Disney, Buena Vista).

△

Another entertaining full-length animated cartoon, but not really for children, **Shinbone Alley**, with a screenplay by Mel Brooks and Joe Darion (based on characters created by Don Marquis, and on Darion's book of the 1957 Broadway musical), told of the misadventures of a cockroach called archy (a reincarnation of a poet who does his free verse writing on an old typewriter belonging to a newspaper columnist, but cannot manage the key that provides the capital letters) and his unrequited romance with Mehitabel (illustrated) a friendly neighbourhood cat who claims her soul once belonged to Cleopatra. Eddie Bracken (who played archy on Broadway) lent only his voice on this occasion, while Carol Channing was heard as Mehitabel (Eartha Kitt played the role on stage). The other voices on the sound track belonged to Alan Reed, Ken Sanson, Hal Smith, Joan Gerber, Sal Delano and The Jackie Ward Singers. The music and lyrics were by George Kleinsinger and Joe Darion, the best number being an item called 'Flotsam and Jetsam'. An Allied Artists release of a Fine Arts Films Production, it was produced (in Technicolor) by Preston M. Fleet and directed by John David Wilson. Other songs: *Toujours Gai*; *A Woman Wouldn't Be A Woman*; *Cheerio My Deario*.

Roald Dahl's **Willie Wonka And The Chocolate Factory** (based on his story *Charlie And The Chocolate Factory*) was the tale of a young lad called Charlie who, together with four obnoxious children, is given a chance to tour a magic chocolate factory while, at the same time, having his character tested by Willy Wonka, the factory's rather eccentric owner. In theory, and with all its obvious ingredients for success, it should have been ideal family entertainment. And had it been made by the Walt Disney studios it probably would have been. The Stan Margulies-David Wolper production, however, filmed in Bavaria and released by Paramount, was as hard to swallow as a toffee. Lacking visual flair, creative imagination and a hummable song or two (the thoroughly mundane score was by Anthony Newley and Leslie Bricusse), it simply failed to come to life, resulting in a lot of very bored six-year-olds wondering what on earth it was all about. Gene Wilder (illustrated centre) worked hard as Wonka, but to no avail; young Peter Ostrum was Charlie and Jack Albertson was his grandpa Joe, with other parts under Mel Stuart's galumphing direction going to Roy Kinnear, Julie Dawn Cole, Leonard Stone, Denise Nickerson, Dodo Denney, Paris Themmen, Michael Bollner and Ursula Reit. Howard Jeffrey choreographed, and it was photographed in Technicolor by Arthur Ibbetson. Songs and musical numbers: *Candy Man*; *Cheer Up Charlie*; *I've Got A Golden Ticket*; *Pure Imagination*; *Oompa-loompa-doompa-dee-doo*; *I Want It Now*.

▽

The latest in a spate of stage-to-screen transfers ▷
was **Fiddler On The Roof** (Mirisch-United
Artists) which, at 3,242 performances, was one
of the longest running Broadway musicals of all
time. Producer-director Norman Jewison clearly
had no choice but to replace the stage show's
stylized, Chagall-inspired settings with the real
thing, but the consequence was that the whole
conception of the show as originally directed
and choreographed by Jerome Robbins, underwent a change which was not, unfortunately,
for the better. On stage, **Fiddler On The Roof** was
a work of art that was a tribute to the American
musical comedy theatre. On screen, in Panavision 70 and Technicolor (and at 180 minutes), it
was merely another big-budget Broadway
transfer whose 'opening up' served only to
minimize its impact. Also missing from the
screen version was the sheer exuberance and
exhilaration engendered by Robbins's choreography. Director Jewison seemed to cut away
from the dances at all the wrong moments with
the result that at no time were audiences swept
up by the infectious rhythms of Jerry Bock and
Sheldon Harnick's memorable score as they had
been in the theatre. Israeli actor Chaim Topol
(illustrated) who played the role of the milkman
Tevye with great charisma and success on the
London stage (it was created on Broadway, most
memorably, by Zero Mostel) brought immense
charm to his screen performance, but not much
conviction or authority. Norma Crane as his
wife Golde was even less convincing, which left
the acting honours to Molly Picon as Yente the
Matchmaker and Leonard Frey as Motel the
tailor. The rest of the cast included Paul Mann as
Lazar Wolf the Butcher, Rosalind Harris, Michele Marsh, and Neva Small as Tevye's eldest
daughters Tzeitel, Hodel and Chava, Michael
Glaser as Perchick, Patience Collier as Grandma
Tzeitel and Tutte Lemkow as the Fiddler (violin
dubbed by Isaac Stern). The village of Anatevka
in which this simple Sholem Aleichem tale
about a milkman, his wife, and five dowryless
daughters, takes place (in 1905), was designed
by Robert Boyle and photographed by Oswald
Morris at Pinewood Studios, England, and on
location in Yugoslavia. It was written by Joseph
Stein with admirable fidelity to his stage play,
and choreographed by Robbins, Tom Abbott
and Sammy Bayes. The musical director was
John Williams. Songs and musical numbers:
Prologue – Fiddler On The Roof (Stern); *Tradition*
(Topol, chorus); *Matchmaker, Matchmaker* (Har-
ris, Marsh, Small, Edwards, Candy Bonstein); *If I
Were A Rich Man* (Topol); *Sabbath Prayer* (Topol,
Crane, chorus); *To Life* (Topol, Mann, chorus);
Miracle Of Miracles (Frey, Harris); *Tevye's Dream*
(Topol, Collier, chorus); *Sunrise, Sunset* (Topol,
Crane, chorus); *Wedding Celebration And Bottle
Dance* (chorus); *Do You Love Me?* (Topol, Crane);
Far From The Home I Love (Marsh); *Chava Ballet*
(Harris, Marsh, Small); *Anatevka* (Topol, Crane,
Picon, Mann, chorus).

More successful on every level than *Willie
Wonka* was the latest entry from the Disney
stable, **Bedknobs And Broomsticks** (Buena
Vista). Written by producer Bill Walsh and Don
DaGradi (from the book by Mary Norton) it
employed animation and special effects to
superb advantage in telling its story of three
Cockney children who, during World War II, are
evacuated to the seaside home of Eglantine Price
– a lady who, it transpires, is an apprentice witch
studying witchcraft by correspondence in the
hope of using her newly acquired craft against
the Germans. Suddenly life for the three Cockney kids couldn't be rosier, and after learning
the art of magic themselves, they perform all
sorts of wonderful tricks – such as flying to
London on a bedstead. It was sheer enchantment in the best, most inventive Disney tradition, with Angela Lansbury (illustrated) in fine
form as the would-be witch. Her co-star was
David Tomlinson as Emelius Browne – phoney
founder of the Emelius Browne College of Witchcraft, with Roddy McDowall, Sam Jaffe, John
Ericson, Bruce Forsyth, Tessie O'Shea, Reginald
Owen, Arthur E. Gould-Porter and Ben Wrigley
in support. The three children were played by
Cindy O'Callaghan, Roy Snart and Ian Weighill.
Alan Maley, Eustace Lycett and Danny Lee were
in charge of the special effects and Ward Kimball
of the animation; the songs were by the prolific
Sherman brothers, Donald McKayle choreographed, it was photographed in Technicolor by
Frank Phillips, and directed with a gleeful sense
of fun by Robert Stevenson. Songs and musical
numbers: *The Old Home Guard*; *Eglantine*; *Portobello Road*; *Portobello Street Dance*; *The Beautiful
◁ Briny*; *Substitutiary Locomotion*.

Though Sandy Wilson's **The Boy Friend** (MGM-
EMI) began life as a delectable stage show which
satirized the musicals of the twenties, it finally
reached the screen as a homage to the Hollywood musicals of the early thirties – and involved two 'Boy Friends'; one being performed by
a tacky provincial repertory company, the other
imagined – by a Hollywood producer sitting in
the stalls – as a big Busby Berkeley-style musical.
The idea (devised by producer-director Ken
Russell) was ingenious and might, indeed, have
worked, except that visually there was little
difference between the two versions. Former
model Twiggy (left) made an enchanting debut
as the young unknown forced on opening night
to replace the star (an uncredited Glenda Jackson hugely enjoying it all), and she was pleasantly partnered by former Royal Ballet dancer
Christopher Gable (right, who also choreographed). Max Adrian played the company's
flyblown impresario and Vladek Sheybal the
Hollywood producer, with Bryan Pringle,
Barbara Windsor, Antonia Ellis, Georgina Hale,
Moyra Fraser and long-legged Tommy Tune in
support. The confused and confusing adaptation
and screenplay were by director Russell, and the
evocative sets by Tony Walton. Songs and
musical numbers: *I Could Be Happy*; *Perfect
Young Ladies*; *The Boy Friend*; *Won't You Charles-
ton With Me?*; *Fancy Forgetting*; *Sur La Plage*; *A
Room In Bloomsbury*; *Safety In Numbers*; *It's
Never Too Late To Fall In Love*; *Poor Little Pierrette*;
Riviera; *The You Don't Want To Play With Me
Blues* Sandy Wilson; *All I Do Is Dream Of You*;
You Are My Lucky Star Nacio Herb Brown,
Arthur Freed; *Any Old Iron* Charles Collins, E.A.
Shepherd, Fred Terry.

1972

Academy Awards

Best Picture
NOMINATIONS INCLUDED: *Cabaret* (ABC Pictures, Allied Artists) produced by Cy Feuer

Best Actress
Liza Minnelli *Cabaret*
NOMINATIONS INCLUDED: Diana Ross *Lady Sings The Blues* (Paramount)

Supporting Actor
Joel Grey *Cabaret*

Direction
Bob Fosse *Cabaret*

Writing (Screenplay)
based on material from another medium
Cabaret Jay Allen

(Story and Screenplay)
based on factual material or material not previously published or produced
NOMINATIONS INCLUDED: *Lady Sings The Blues* Terence McCloy, Chris Clark and Suzanne de Passe

Cinematography
Cabaret Geoffrey Unsworth
NOMINATIONS INCLUDED: *"1776"* (Columbia) Harry Stradling, Jr

Art Direction (Set Decoration)
Cabaret Rolf Zehetbauer and Jurgen Kiebach, Herbert Strabel
NOMINATIONS INCLUDED: *Lady Sings The Blues* Carl Anderson; Reg Allen

Costume Design
NOMINATIONS INCLUDED: *Lady Sings The Blues* Bob Mackie, Ray Aghayan and Norma Koch

Sound
Cabaret Robert Knudson and David Hildyard

Film Editing
Cabaret David Bretherton

Music
Scoring
Adapatation and Original Song Score
Cabaret Ralph Burns
NOMINATIONS INCLUDED: *Lady Sings The Blues* Gil Askey. *Man Of La Mancha* (United Artists) Laurence Rosenthal.

The Annual Top Moneymaking Films
INCLUDED: *Fiddler On The Roof* (Mirisch, United Artists). *Cabaret*. *Bedknobs And Broomsticks* (Disney, Buena Vista) *Song Of The South* (Disney, Buena Vista, re-issue).

△
Enjoyment of **Lady Sings The Blues** (Paramount) was largely dependent on how much (or how little) one knew about its subject – the great blues singer Billie Holiday – and on whether or not one responded to Diana Ross (illustrated) in her debut screen performance as the lady in question. For audiences *au fait* with the depressing facts of Holiday's sad and often turbulent existence (which ended in 1959 when she was 44 years old), her unhappy romances, her losing battle with drugs etc. etc., there was more to offend than to admire in this travesty of the truth. On the other hand, Diana Ross fans, and those with no knowledge of the facts, were amply catered for in Jay Weston and James S. White's basically old fashioned, forties-type biopic, crisply scripted (but loosely adapted) by Terence McCloy, Chris Clark and Suzanne de Passe from the book by Miss Holiday and William Duffy, with only the merest nod in the direction of verisimilitude. Musically the many standards sung by Miss Ross lacked the authenticity of the Holiday era, sounding more like Motown than Harlem. Billy Dee Williams co-starred as Louis McKay (in reality Holiday's third husband but the only man in her life in the film), with other parts under Sidney J. Furie's competent direction going to Richard Pryor, James Callahan, Paul Hampton, Sid Melton, Virginia Capers, Yvonne Fair, Scatman Crothers, Harry Caesar and Robert L. Gordy. (Panavision and colour). Songs: *Lady Sings The Blues* Holiday, H. Nichols; *T'Ain't Nobody's Bizness If I Do* Porter, Grainger, Graham Prince, Clarence Williams; *All Of Me* Seymour Simons, Gerald Marks; *The Man I Love*; *Our Love Is Here To Stay* George and Ira Gershwin; *Them There Eyes* Maceo Pinkard, William Tracy, Doris Tauber; *I Cried For You* Abe Lyman, Gus Arnheim, Arthur Freed; *Mean To Me* Roy Turk, Fred Ahlert; *What A Little Moonlight Can Do* Harry Woods; *Lover Man (Oh Where Can You Be?)* Jimmy Davis, Jimmy Sherman, Roger 'Ram' Ramirez; *You've Changed* Bill Carey, Carl Fischer; *Gimme A Pigfoot And A Bottle Of Beer* 'Kid' Wesley, 'Sox' Wilson; *Good Morning Heartache* Irene Higginbotham, Ervin Drake, Dan Fisher; *My Man* Channing Pollock, Maurice Yvain; *Strange Fruit* Lewis Allan; *God Bless The Child*; *Don't Explain* Holiday, Arthur Herzog Jr.

△
Broadway's musical version of the events leading up to the signing of the Declaration of Independence, **1776**, was reverentially brought to the screen by its original director Peter L. Hunt together with most of the original creative team, assembled in Hollywood by producer Jack L. Warner for Columbia. The stage version had conquered Broadway for 1,217 performances, but the Panavision screen emphasized the piece's pretensions: its coy, self-congratulatory pomposity, its flaccid score and arch lyrics. Peter Stone's script, from his original libretto, still had some gripping moments of drama as the congressional members wrangled and manoeuvred to assert their points of view, but couldn't disguise the fact that the chief protagonist John Adams (William Daniels, left) was something of a bore, or that the mood shifted uneasily as great figures of history like Benjamin Franklin (Howard Da Silva, right) and Thomas Jefferson (Ken Howard) were diminished and trivialized in the name of humour; while numbers like 'Mama, Look Sharp' (about war's young casualties) and 'Molasses to Rum' (about the North's double standards regarding slavery) proclaimed their messages with high-toned solemnity. When not being overtly serious, Sherman Edwards's lyrics were twee, with titles like 'Piddle, Twiddle and Resolve' and lines like 'He plays the violin, he tucks it right under his chin'. Not surprisingly, the film failed to repeat its Broadway success. Harry Stradling Jr photographed it, Onna White was in charge of the minimal choreography and Ray Heindorf supervised the music. The cast included Donald Madden, John Cullum, Blythe Danner (centre), Roy Poole, David Ford, Virginia Vestoff and Ron Holgate. Other songs: *But, Mr Adams*; *The Lees of Old Virginia*; *Sit Down, John*; *Till Then*; *Yours, Yours, Yours*; *The Egg*; *Is Anybody There?* Edwards.

Seventies Musicals

△

The main trouble with the screen version of the Dale Wasserman-Mitch Leigh-Joe Darion long-running (2,338 performances) hit musical **Man Of La Mancha** (a Produzioni Europee Associate Production, released by United Artists in Color by De Luxe), was that the three leads – Peter O'Toole (left) who was cast to play the triple roles of Don Quixote, Miguel de Cervantes and Alonso Quijana, Sophia Loren (Dulcinea and Aldonza), and James Coco (Sancho Panza, right) – couldn't sing. They were first class in bringing to life scenarist Wasserman's words, but sabotaged Leigh's music and Darion's lyrics in no uncertain terms. A terrible shame this, since the songs were the show's only redeeming feature in the face of the plodding and pretentious book, matched by Arthur Hiller's heavy-handed direction (he also produced). Rounding out the cast were Harry Andrews, John Castle, Brian Blessed, Ian Richardson, Julie Gregg, Rosalie Crutchley and Gino Conforti. Gillian Lynne's choreography was deficient in flair and the musical direction, by Laurence Rosenthal, lacked sparkle. Songs and musical numbers: *It's All The Same; The Impossible Dream; Barber's Song; Man Of La Mancha; Dulcinea; I'm Only Thinking Of Him; I Really Like Him; Little Bird, Little Bird; The Dubbing; Life As It Really Is; Aldonza; A Little Gossip; The Psalm; Golden Helmet of Mambrino.*
▽

Compared with his ridiculous big-screen account of the champagne life of waltz king Johann Strauss II called, with mind-blowing originality, **The Great Waltz** (MGM), Andrew L. Stone's *Song Of Norway* (ABC 1970) was positively sublime! For his latest venture into biopic territory, which he also wrote and directed (sample dialogue: Strauss to Offenbach, 'I admire your versatility . . . operettas, waltzes, fast gallops, quadrilles . . . how *do* you do it?'!) he cast Horst Bucholz (illustrated) as the composer of 'The Blue Danube', Mary Costa as his wife, Yvonne Mitchell as his mother, Nigel Patrick as Strauss senior, Rossano Brazzi as Baron Tedesco and James Faulkner as Josef Strauss, plus the voice of Kenneth McKellar. Bob Wright and Chet Forrest provided the lyrics to Strauss's immortal melodies, and the three-quarter time choreography was by Onna White. Musical programme: *The Blue Danube Waltz; Tritsch-Tratsch Polka; Louder and Faster (Leichtes Blut); Pitter Patter Polka (Thunder And Lightning); Love Is Music (Wine, Women And Song); Say Yes* (from 'The Gypsy Baron'); *Crystal and Gold; Six Drinks; Nightfall; Warm; Who Are You* Johann Strauss II; *The Radetzky March* Johann Strauss Sr; *With You Gone (Brennende Liebe)* Josef Strauss.
◁

Resisting the tendency to 'open out' the musical numbers as he had done in *Sweet Charity* (Universal, 1969) Bob Fosse, in his *tour de force* **Cabaret** (Allied Artists), went to the other extreme in the film version, and confined almost all of them to the small stage of a smoky, crowded cabaret in Berlin just before the outbreak of hostilities in the late thirties. It was part of a radical re-assessment of the Joe Masteroff-John Kander-Fred Ebb stage show on which it was based and, like everything else in the movie, was a distinct improvement on its Broadway counterpart. All the songs (several were specially written for the film by its composers Kander and Ebb) commented on the action as opposed to being integrated into it; the screenplay, by Jay Presson Allen and Hugh Wheeler (the latter billed as 'research consultant') based on John van Druten's play *I Am A Camera* and Christopher Isherwood's *Goodbye To Berlin*, was much sounder in both content and construction than Masteroff's book for the stage show; and, with Liza Minnelli (illustrated) cast as Sally Bowles (a fifth rate American singer ekeing out a living in a decadent, sexually ambiguous *milieu*) the central character sprang vividly and memorably to life. The fact that the hugely talented Miss Minnelli was called upon to play a performer of no conspicuous ability whatsoever – and got away with it without throwing the entire plotline off balance, was a remarkable testament to her unique qualities as an actress and as a star 'presence'. She shared the majority of the songs with Joel Grey, who repeated his mesmeric stage performance as the cabaret's cynical MC – the most effectively staged (by Fosse) of these being 'Money, Money' and 'Mein Herr', both written

specially for the film. Other musical highlights were an explosive performance of the title number by Minnelli and, from Grey, 'Wilkommen', the lascivious 'Two Ladies' about the attractions of a *ménage à trois*, and the nauseating, sinister, anti-semitic but compelling 'If You Could See Her' danced with an organza-clad chimpanzee. Michael York co-starred as the young bisexual writer from Britain who fetches up in digs with Minnelli in Berlin, and through whose eyes the era is witnessed; Helmut Griem was the wealthy, irresponsible playboy with whom they both have affairs, and Marisa Berenson and Fritz Wepper a young Jewish department-store heiress and her sweetheart. It was dazzlingly photographed (in Technicolor) by Geoffrey Unsworth, with Ralph Burns in charge of the musical direction and orchestrations. Cy Feuer was responsible for the production. Other songs and musical numbers: *Maybe This Time* (Minnelli); *Sitting Pretty* (orchestra); *Tiller Girls* (Grey, girls); *Heiraten* (Greta Keller – voice only); *Tomorrow Belongs To Me* (boys' chorus).

1973

Academy Awards

Art Direction
NOMINATIONS INCLUDED: *Tom Sawyer* (Jacobs, Readers' Digest, United Artists) Phillip Jefferies; Robert de Vestel

Costume Design
NOMINATIONS INCLUDED: *Tom Sawyer* Donfeld

Music
Song
NOMINATIONS INCLUDED: 'Love' *Robin Hood* (Disney, Buena Vista) George Bruns *cm*; Floyd Huddleston *lyr*.

Best Scoring
Original Song Score and/or Adaptation
NOMINATIONS INCLUDED: *Jesus Christ Superstar* (Universal) Andre Previn, Herbert Spencer and Andrew Lloyd Webber. *Tom Sawyer* Richard M. Sherman and Robert B. Sherman and John Williams.

Honorary Award
To Groucho Marx in recognition of his brilliant creativity and for the unequalled achievements of the Marx Brothers in the art of motion picture comedy. (statuette)

The Annual Top Moneymaking Films
INCLUDED: *The Sound Of Music* (20th Century-Fox (re-issue). *Jesus Christ Superstar*. *Lady Sings The Blues* (Paramount). *Mary Poppins* (Disney, Buena Vista, re-issue).

Considering the generally mediocre quality of the latter-day Joseph Barbera and William Hanna cartoons, Paramount's **Charlotte's Web** – based on the celebrated children's classic by E.B. White which tells of a spider called Charlotte who unselfishly devotes her life to saving a piglet called Wilbur from the slaughterhouse – was a welcome surprise and an unexpected pleasure. Its charm was enhanced by the vocal participation of Debbie Reynolds as Charlotte and Henry Gibson as Wilbur, as well as Paul Lynde, Rex Allen, Martha Scott, Dave Madden, Danny Bonaduce, Agnes Moorehead and Pam Ferdin. The ubiquitous Sherman brothers provided the score, it was scripted by Earl Hamner Jr. and directed by Charles A. Nichols and Iwao Takamoto. Songs: *Charlotte's Web*; *A Veritable Smorgasbord*; *There Must Be Something More*; *I Can Talk*; *Chin Up*; *Mother Earth And Father Time*; *We've Got Lots In Common*; *Deep In The Dark*; *Zuckerman's Famous Pig*.

△

Another animated feature for youngsters everywhere, **Robin Hood** (see illustration), from the Disney stable, retold yet again the story of the bold adventurer who robbed the rich to give to the poor – but this time featured the birds and animals of Sherwood forest rather than its two-legged denizens. Hence Robin, in Larry Clemmons and Ken Anderson's new story and conception, became a wily fox, Little John a bear, Allan-a-Dale a rooster (who also served as the film's narrator), and evil Prince John a scrawny lion. Under the inventive direction of its producer Wolfgang Reitherman, and with vocal characterizations supplied by Brian Bedford (Robin), Andy Devine (Friar Tuck), Peter Ustinov (Prince John), Roger Miller (Allan-a-Dale), Phil Harris (Little John) and Pat Buttram (the Sheriff of Nottingham), the film was an unmitigated delight. (Technicolor). Songs: *Whistle Stop*; *Oo-de-Lolly*; *Not In Nottingham* Roger Miller; *Love* Floyd Huddleston, George Bruns; *Phoney King Of England* Johnny Mercer.

Probably the worst musical of the decade, Ross Hunter's tacky remake of Frank Capra's 1937 classic **Lost Horizon** (Columbia) lumbered its elephantine way on to the Panavision screen, trampling underfoot such talented performers as Peter Finch, Liv Ullman, Sally Kellerman, George Kennedy, Michael York, Charles Boyer and John Gielgud who not only couldn't sing and dance, but on this painful occasion, couldn't act either. Larry Kramer's screenplay, based on the novel by James Hilton (in which a group of plane passengers survive a crash in the Tibetan mountains, are rescued by an inscrutable Oxford graduate and led to the magical Shangri-La), borrowed liberally from Robert Riskin's 1937 screenplay, but ultimately choked itself on too much philosophizing. Charles Jarrott's direction was stodgy, Hermes Pan's choreography (number led by Bobby Van, illustrated) embarrassingly coy, Burt Bacharach and Hal David's score feeble, and Jerry Wunderlich's sets unimaginative. Also cast: Olivia Hussey, James Shigeta, Sian Phillips. Songs and musical numbers: *Lost Horizon*; *Share The Joy*; *The World Is A Circle*; *Living Together Growing Together*; *I Might Frighten Her Away*; *If I Could Go Back*; *Where Knowledge Ends*; *Question Me An Answer*.

△

Although there were some striking and innovative moments in producers Norman Jewison and Robert Stigwood's visually exciting cinematic version of Tim Rice and Andrew Lloyd Webber's **Jesus Christ Superstar** (Universal), it failed to repeat the success of the best-selling album of the same name, or the London version of the stage show based on the album. With a screenplay by Melvyn Bragg and Jewison that tacked a rather pretentious show-within-a-show format on to Rice's original book, direction (by Jewison) that displayed an imagination more frenzied than fertile, and performances that were mixed both in quality and in style – the film emerged as an eclectic hodge-podge with no discernible rhyme or reason for many of the visual images that accompanied the loud and plenteous score. Fortunately, many of those images were tellingly photographed in Technicolor by Douglas Slocombe (on location in Israel), and much of the score was stirringly conveyed under Andre Previn's direction. It was just that when all the diverse elements in the production merged, the overall effect was less than the sum of its parts. Ted Neeley (illustrated) was top-cast as Jesus, but lacked the charisma of co-star Carl Anderson as Judas; Yvonne Elliman (left) had her moments as Mary Magdalene, the best being her singing of 'I Don't Know How To Love Him' (one of the most durable songs to emerge from the show), with other roles going to an over-the-top Barry Dennen as Pontius Pilate, a swishy Joshua Mostel (son of Zero) who, as King Herod, couldn't quite manage to pull off the show-stopping 'Herod's Song'. Bob Bingham (Caiaphas), Larry T. Marshall (Simon Zealotes), Kurt Yaghjian (Annas) and Philip Toubus (Peter). Robert Iscove choreographed, often inventively. Musical highlights included 'What's The Buzz' (Neeley, Elliman and chorus) and 'Hosanna' (Neeley, Bingham and chorus). Other songs and musical numbers: *Heaven On Their Minds*; *Strange Thing, Mystifying*; *Then We Are Decided*; *Everything's Alright*; *This Jesus Must Die*; *Simon Zealotes*; *Poor Jerusalem*; *Pilate's Dream*; *The Temple*; *Damned For All Time*; *Blood Money*; *The Last Supper*; *Gethsemane (I Only Want To Say)*; *The Arrest*; *Peter's Denial*; *Pilate And Christ*; *Could We Start Again, Please*; *Judas's Death*; *Trial Before Pilate*; *Superstar*; *Crucifixion*; *John 1941*.

Jesus Christ was also the subject of **Godspell** (Columbia), a much more nimble-footed entertainment than *Jesus Christ Superstar*, in which Jesus was portrayed (androgynously) by Victor Garber as a clown-like flower child living (and dying) in Manhattan. As written by its director David Greene, and John-Michael Tebelak (based on Tebelak's off-Broadway production) **Godspell**, with its stunning Technicolor photography (by Richard G. Heimann), its exciting choreography (by Sammy Bayes, see illustration) and its tuneful razz-a-matazz approach to its subject, was more a glorification of show-business and of Manhattan than it was of the life of Christ. In essence the only religious thing about it was its dedication to and worship of Broadway razzle-dazzle. Everything it stood for was brilliantly encapsulated in a production number called 'All For The Best', performed by Garber and David Haskell (playing John the Baptist) as a soft-shoe shuffle in front of a Times Square advertising billboard composed entirely of pattern-making light bulbs. The other high spot in Stephen Schwartz's score was Robin Lamont's singing of the show's hit song 'Day By Day'. Edgar Lansbury produced, and his cast included Jerry Sroka, Lynne Thigpen, Katie Hanley, Gilmer McCormick, Joanne Jonas, Merrell Jackson and Jeffrey Mylett. Other songs and musical numbers: *O Bless The Lord My Soul*; *Prepare Ye The Way Of The Lord*; *Turn Back O Man*; *Beautiful City*; *Save The People*; *All Good Gifts*; *Light Of The World*; *Alas For You*; *On The Willows* Schwartz; *By My Side* Jay Hamburger, Peggy Gordon.

Produced by Arthur P. Jacobs for Readers' Digest, and released by United Artists, Mark Twain's **Tom Sawyer**, filmed on location in Missouri, was an engaging slice of mid-western Americana that suffered on occasion from some rather antiseptic direction (by Don Taylor), a self-conscious striving for wholesomeness and a tendency to cuteness. Its plus factors, however, were its De Luxe Color photography (by Frank Stanley), a pleasing score by the Sherman brothers (who also provided an imaginative screenplay) and the performances of Johnny Whitaker as Tom (illustrated 2nd left), Celeste Holm as Aunt Polly, Warren Oates as Muff Potter, newcomer Jeff East as Huck Finn (left) and Jodie Foster as Becky Thatcher. Musically, the best moments were Holm's singing of the title tune, and a number called 'Freebootin' (sung by Whitaker and East), dedicated to the art of doing nothing. A large-scale production number (choreographed by Danny Daniels) depicting the Hannibal, Mo. holiday picnic drenched the screen in nostalgia for a gone but not forgotten era (the 1840s) in American history. Completing the cast were Kunu Hank, Lucille Benson, Henry Jones, Noah Keen, Dub Taylor, Richard Eastham, Joshua Hill Lewis and Susan Joye. Other songs: *River Song* (the film's theme, sung by Charley Pride on soundtrack); *Gratifaction*; *A Man's Gotta Be (What He's Born To Be)*; *If'n I Was God*; *How Come? Hannibal Mo (Zouree)*; *Aunt Polly's Soliloquy*.

1974

Academy Awards

Music

Song

NOMINATIONS INCLUDED: 'Little Prince' *The Little Prince* (Paramount) Frederick Loewe

△ Presented by the American Film Theatre, **Lost In The Stars** (from the 1949 Maxwell Anderson-Kurt Weill musical of the same name fashioned from South African Alan Paton's powerful novel *Cry, The Beloved Country*) emerged as a dated melodrama. Daniel Mann's uneasy direction brought no conviction to the moving story of a black preacher's travels – and travails – through the shanty townships of Johannesburg in search of his son who has committed a murder and is hiding from the law. Mann failed completely to reconcile the 'stagey' Broadway feel of the property to the more naturalistic demands of the cinema, and the performances fell, likewise, uncomfortably short of conviction. Brock Peters (right) starred as the Reverend Kumalo, Clifton Davis was his fugitive son, Melba Moore (left) the son's girlfriend, and Paul Rogers a white bigot whose own son was the victim of the killing. Also cast: Raymond St Jacques, Paula Kelly (who staged the one dance sequence in the film), H.B. Barnum III, Jitu Cumbuka and Alan Weeks. It was written for the screen by Alfred Hayes, and was produced by Ely Landau. The one saving grace of this travesty was its superb score. Songs included: *Lost In The Stars*; *Cry The Beloved Country*; *Little Gray House*; *Trouble Man*; *Bird Of Paradise*; *Big Mole*; *Train Go Now To Johannesburg*.

When MGM decided to re-open its Ali Baba cave of treasures with a compilation-film of extracts from its musicals entitled **That's Entertainment**, box-office tills were set ringing everywhere. And no wonder! Although much of the linking, commentary (by such narrators as Fred Astaire, Gene Kelly, Bing Crosby, Peter Lawford, Liza Minnelli, Donald O'Connor, Debbie Reynolds, Mickey Rooney, Frank Sinatra, James Stewart and Elizabeth Taylor) was embarrassingly self-congratulatory and banal, and one might cavil at some of the films and stars included (or omitted), **That's Entertainment** fully lived up to its title, making the spectator feel like a child let

cm; Alan Jay Lerner *lyr*.

Scoring

Original Song Score and/or Adaptation

NOMINATIONS INCLUDED: *The Little Prince* Alan Jay Lerner, Frederick Loewe; Angela Morley and Douglas Gamley. *Phantom Of The Paradise* (20th Century-Fox) Paul Williams and George Aliceson Tipton.

The Annual Top Moneymaking Films

INCLUDED: *That's Entertainment* (MGM). *Robin Hood* (Disney, Buena Vista, re-issue)

loose in a toy factory. Here again – under the same roof, as it were – one could see the enormous wedding-cake number from *The Great Ziegfeld* (1936), a segment of the brilliant ballet from *An American In Paris* (1951), the joyous 'Atchison, Topeka and Santa Fe' number with Judy Garland and Ray Bolger from *The Harvey Girls* (1945), a couple of delirious water-ballets from *Bathing Beauty* (1944) and *Million Dollar Mermaid* (1952) (illustrated, with Esther Williams) and, of course, perhaps the single most enchanting moment of the whole genre, Gene Kelly 'singin' and dancin' in the rain'. There were some rarities too, such as the charming if inadequate rendering by Clark Gable of 'Puttin' On The Ritz' from *Idiot's Delight* (1939), The Gumm Sisters singing '*La Cucaracha*', and Cary Grant and Jean Harlow's duet 'Did I Remember' from *Suzy* (1936). But producer Jack Haley Jr (son of the Tin Man from *The Wizard Of Oz*, 1939) wisely judged that what audiences were looking for was a chance to wallow in a shared cinematic past, when both they and Hollywood were younger – the sort of movie, in fact, that sends you out singing – even in the rain. Haley wrote the narration, and the executive producer was Daniel Melnick.

▽

A really risible rock adaptation of Shakespeare's *Othello*, **Catch My Soul** (Cinerama) was burdened by an unintentionally hilarious screenplay by Jack Good, based on his stage show of the same name, in which the bard's immortal tragedy was transposed from Venice to the American South West, and in which the Moor became a black evangelist, Desdemona his flower-power wife and Iago the dyspeptic leader of a hippie commune with a Satan complex. Richie Havens (illustrated right) was Othello, Lance LeGault Iago and Season Hubley (left) Desdemona, with Tony Joe White (Cassio) and Susan Tyrrell (Emilia) in support. Good produced it with Richard Rosenbloom, and the director was Patrick McGoohan. Songs and musical numbers: *Othello*; *Working On A Building* Tony Joe White; *Wash Us Clean*; *Eat The Bread, Drink The Wine*; *Book Of Prophecy*; *Catch My Soul* White, Jack Good; *That's What God Said*; *Chug A Lug*; *I Found Jesus* Delaney Bramlett; *Looking Back* White, Bramlett; *Open Our Eyes* Leon Lumkins; *Lust Of The Blood*; *Put Out The Light* Ray Pohlman, Good; *Tickle His Fancy* Emil Dean Zoughby, Good; *Run Shaker Life* (traditional).

Unquestionably everybody's favourite aunt from modern fiction is – or should be – **Mame** (Warner Bros.) who began life in Patrick Dennis's best-selling novel *Auntie Mame*, later surfaced in a smash-hit Broadway play and an equally successful film, a Broadway musical and finally, the film version of the musical. A dazzling line-up of great ladies have incarnated, in one form or another, the flamboyant *grande dame*: Rosalind Russell, Angela Lansbury, Ginger Rogers, Bea Lillie, Constance Bennett, Eve Arden, Greer Garson, Sylvia Sidney and Juliet Prowse – and for the film musical Lucille Ball was chosen. Although possessing just as much pazazz as her predecessors, Lucy's infinite variety had been somewhat withered by age, notwithstanding the gallant efforts of photographer Philip Lathrop to envelop her in the softest of focuses, and those of choreographer Onna White to keep her on the sidelines of the more frenetic musical numbers. The rather mechanically regimented choreography,

in fact, proved an asset only in the catchy title number (illustrated, Ball centre), in which red-coated, black-toppered huntsmen energetically hopped, skipped and jumped around the slightly blurry star. Beatrice Arthur was splendidly decadent as Mame's actress friend Vera Charles (a role she played on Broadway); Robert Preston charming as her Southern beau, Jane Connell (also from Broadway) was marvellous as Agnes Gooch, and Bruce Davison, Kirby Furlong, Doria Cook, John McGiver and Joyce Van Patten gave solid support. It was written for the screen by Paul Zindel (from the musical by Jerome Lawrence, Robert E. Lee, and Jerry Herman, who composed the catchy score), directed by Gene Saks and produced (in Panavision) by Robert Fryer and James Cresson. Musical numbers: *Mame*; *If He Walked Into My Life*; *Bosom Buddies* (excised in GB); *It's Today*; *Loving You*; *My Best Girl*; *Gooch's Song (What Do I Do Now?)*; *Open A New Window*; *The Man In The Moon*; *We Need A Little Christmas Now*; *St Bridget*; *The Letter*.

Having succeeded the previous year with their *Tom Sawyer*, The Readers' Digest and producer Arthur P. Jacobs did the obvious and musicalized Mark Twain's **Huckleberry Finn** (United Artists). The results were disastrous. It bore no relation in mood and atmosphere to Twain's original, and the Sherman brothers' screenplay (they also wrote the instantly forgettable tunes) was cloying, and the film deadly dull. It was directed by J. Lee Thompson, who deserved a special Oscar for his under-achievement in turning a hitherto fool-proof property into a dud; and starred Jeff East (illustrated) – whose performance was nowhere near as effective as it had been in *Tom Sawyer* – as Huck, Paul Winfield as Jim, Arthur O'Connell as Colonel Grangerford, Natalie Trundy as Mrs Loftus and, best of all, Harvey Korman and David Wayne as the roguish King and Duke. At least they breathed some fresh air into a stale and stuffy entertainment. It was photographed in Panavision and Color De Luxe and choreographed by Marc Breaux. Songs and musical numbers: *Freedom*; *Huckleberry Finn*; *Someday Honey Darlin'*; *Cairo, Illinois*; *Rose In A Bible*; *Royalty*; *Royal Nonesuch*; *What's Right. What's Wrong*; *Rotten Luck*.

Loosely based on Gaston Leroux's classic chiller *The Phantom Of The Opera*, Brian De Palma's rock musical parody **Phantom Of The Paradise** (20th Century-Fox) concerned a disfigured musician whose song has been plagiarised by a sinister *entrepreneur*, and who takes his revenge by haunting the latter's 'Paradise' discothèque. Glittery and energetic, the film caught the disco craze as it was just starting and became something of a cult. Paul Williams (illustrated), who also wrote the score, played the impresario, William Finley the crazed Phantom and Jessica Harper the young singer desired by both. Also appearing were George Memmoli, Gerrit Graham and the singing group of Jeffrey Comanor, Archie Hahn and Harold Oblong. De Palma wrote his own screenplay, and the film was a Harbor Productions presentation produced (in Color De Luxe) by Edward R. Pressman. The undertaking provoked a lawsuit brought by Universal, the holders of the film rights to Leroux's original property. Songs and musical numbers: *Goodbye, Eddie, Goodbye*; *Faust*; *Upholstery*; *Special To Me*; *Old Souls*; *Somebody Super Like You*; *Life At Last*; *The Hell Of It*; *The Phantom's Theme (Beauty And The Beast)*.

1975

Academy Awards

Best Picture
NOMINATIONS INCLUDED: *Nashville* (ABC Entertainment-Weintraub-Altman. Paramount, produced by Robert Altman)

Supporting Actress
NOMINATIONS INCLUDED: Ronee Blakeley *Nashville* Lily Tomlin *Nashville*

Direction
NOMINATIONS INCLUDED: Robert Altman *Nashville*

Cinematography
NOMINATIONS INCLUDED: *Funny Lady* (Columbia) James Wong Howe

Costume Design
NOMINATIONS INCLUDED: *Funny Lady* Ray Aghayan and Bob Mackie

Sound
NOMINATIONS INCLUDED: *Funny Lady* Richard Portman, Don MacDougall, Curly Thirlwell and Jack Solomon

Music
Song
'I'm Easy' *Nashville* music and lyrics by Keith Carradine
NOMINATIONS INCLUDED: 'How Lucky Can You Get' *Funny Lady* music and lyrics by Fred Ebb and John Kander

Scoring
Original Song Score and/or Adaptation
NOMINATIONS INCLUDED: *Funny Lady* Peter Matz

The New York Film Critics Awards
Best Motion Picture
Nashville

Best Director
Robert Altman *Nashville*

Best Supporting Actress
Lily Tomlin *Nashville*

The New York Times Annual 'Ten Best'
INCLUDED: *Nashville*

The Annual Top Moneymaking Films
INCLUDED: *Funny Lady*

△

Funny Lady, a Ray Stark production for Columbia-Warner, took up the story of vaudevillian Fanny Brice where William Wyler's *Funny Girl* (1968) left off, proving that even in the lives of the greatest stars there wasn't always enough material for two biopics. It related how Brice, having finally worked gambler Nicky Arnstein (Omar Sharif reprising from the earlier movie) out of her system, meets up with showman Billy Rose (James Caan) during the tough Depression years and, somewhat on the rebound, marries him; subsequently, his infidelities and her professional commitments draw them apart. Barbra Streisand, needless to say, was once again perfectly cast as Brice: a star playing a star (illustrated). Director Herbert Ross, while unable to breathe life into the emotional episodes of Jay Presson Allen and Arnold Shulman's screenplay, managed to invest the backstage sequences with real glitter, even if the production numbers – particularly the Vincent Youmans-Edward Eliscu-Billy Rose Song, 'Great Day', which Streisand sang with writhing black girls at her feet – were often ponderously over-elaborate, Also cast (though, with Streisand around, it was a very dogged performer indeed who got his face in edgeways) were Roddy McDowall, Ben Vereen, Carole Wells, Larry Gates and Heidi O'Rourke. Betty Walberg choreographed, and the film was photographed in Eastmancolor by the great James Wong Howe. Other songs and musical numbers: *Blind Date*; *So Long, Honey Lamb*; *How Lucky Can You Get*; *Isn't This Better?*; *Let's Hear It For Me* (specially written for the film by John Kander, Fred Ebb); *More Than You Know* Youmans, Eliscu, Rose; *It's Only A Paper Moon* Harold Arlen, E.Y. Harburg, Rose with *I Like Him/I Like Her*, by Kander and Ebb, sung as a counter melody; *I Found A Million Dollar Baby In A Five And Ten Cent Store* Harry Warren, Mort Dixon, Rose; *Beautiful Face, Have A Heart* James V. Monaco, Fred Fisher, Rose; *If You Want The Rainbow, You Must Have The Rain* Oscar Levant, Dixon, Rose; *I Caught A Code In My Dose* Arthur Fields, Fred Hall, Rose; *Am I Blue?* Harry Akst, Grant Clarke, Rose; *Clap Hands, Here Comes Charley* Joseph Meyer, Ballard MacDonald, Rose; *Me And My Shadow* Al Jolson, Dave Dreyer, Rose; *If I Love Again* Jack Murray, Ben Oakland.

Though Peter Bogdanovich had gained both critical and commercial favour with earlier essays into movie nostalgia (*The Last Picture Show* (Columbia, 1971), *What's Up Doc* (Warner Bros. 1972) and *Paper Moon* (Paramount, 1973), he was to discover to his cost with **At Long Last Love** (20th Century-Fox) that the 30s could be a dangerous age. A pastiche of the Astaire-Rogers musicals, it was as lavishly mounted as one had a right to expect from its $6,000,000 budget and, filtered through Laszlo Kovacs's brilliant photography, its Long Island mansion, sparkling lawns and vintage automobiles looked exactly as *Top Hat* (RKO, 1935) or *The Gay Divorcée* (RKO 1934) might have done if shot in colour. There were 16 marvellous Cole Porter songs, some of them unfamiliar. And if the plot – the change-partners romancing of smooth playboy (Burt Reynolds, left), carefree deb (Cybill Shepherd, right), Broadway star (Madeline Kahn) and immigrant gambler (Duilio Del Prete) – was only workmanlike, it was no worse than those of
▽

innumerable well-loved and enduring Hollywood musicals. All that was lacking – but it proved to be everything – were Fred and Ginger themselves. Both Reynolds and Shepherd had charming screen presences, but their dancing was flat-footed in an embarrassingly literal sense, the wisecracks dreamt up by director-writer Bogdanovich for the secondary characters (played by such usually reliable foils as Eileen Brennan, Mildred Natwick and John Hillerman) were more cracked than wise, and the whole sorry spectacle was a resounding and deserved flop at the box office. Songs and musical numbers: *At Long Last Love*; *Just One Of Those Things*; *I Get A Kick Out Of You*; *You're The Top*; *It's De-Lovely*; *From Alpha To Omega*; *A Picture Of Me Without You*; *Well, Did You Evah?*; *Friendship*; *Find Me A Primitive Man*; *Let's Misbehave*; *But In The Morning, No*; *Most Gentlemen Don't Like Love*; *Which*; *I Loved Him (But He Didn't Love Me)* Porter; *Poor Young Millionaire* music Bogdanovich, Artie Butler, lyrics Porter.

Robert Altman's **Nashville** (Paramount) wove a rich tissue of narrative and musical strands as it traced the overlapping lives of 24 people in the Tennessee capital of country-and-western during the campaign of a Presidential candidate, whose assassination brings the film to a dramatic end. In spite of the dangers inherent in such an undertaking, it was a triumph for its director and his familiar repertory company of actors, many of whom themselves wrote the songs they sang. The film, by its very nature, boasted no star roles but, out of a huge cast, particularly noteworthy were Ronee Blakely as a singer on the verge of a breakdown, Gwen Welles as a starlet reduced to stripping at stag suppers, Shelley Duvall as a spaced-out groupie, Keith Carradine as a heartless Don Juan, Lily Tomlin as the mother of deaf-mute children, and Henry Gibson as the smooth *eminence grise* of country-and-western. Also to be seen were Ned Beatty, Karen Black, Allen Nichols (left), Barbara Harris (right), Michael Murphy, Keenan Wynn and, as Opal from the BBC, Geraldine Chaplin. It was
▽

scripted by Joan Tewkesbury (though, reportedly, everyone involved had a hand) and produced, in Panavision, by Altman, with Martin Starger and Jerry Weintraub as executive producers. Songs and musical numbers: *200 Years* Richard Baskin, Henry Gibson; *Yes, I Do* Baskin, Lily Tomlin; *Down To The River* Ronee Blakely; *Let Me Be The One* Baskin; *Sing A Song* Joe Raposo; *The Heart Of A Gentle Woman* Dave Peel; *Bluebird* Blakely; *The Day I Looked Jesus In The Eye* Baskin, Robert Altman; *Memphis*; *Rolling Stone*; *I Don't Know If I Found It In You* Karen Black; *For The Sake Of The Children* Baskin, Richard Reicheg; *Keep A' Goin'* Baskin, Gibson; *Swing Low Sweet Chariot* (arr. Millie Clements); *Tapedeck In His Tractor (The Cowboy Song)*; *My Idaho Home*; *Dues* Blakely; *I Never Get Enough* Baskin, Ben Raleigh; *Rose's Cafe* Allan Nicholls; *Old Man Mississippi* Juan Grizzle; *My Baby's Cookin' In Another Man's Pan* Jonnie Barnett; *One, I Love You* Baskin; *I'm Easy*; *Honey*; *It Don't Worry Me* Keith Carradine; *Since You've Gone* Gary Busey; *Trouble In The USA* Arlene Barnett.

Richard O'Brien's long-running stage musical *The Rocky Horror Show* was adapted and 'opened out' for the screen and called **The Rocky Horror Picture Show** (20th Century-Fox), a high camp blend of Gay Liberation and B-movie Gothick about an innocent young couple who stumble into the annual convention of transvestite aliens from the far-out (in both senses) planet of Transylvania. Tim Curry (left) reprised the role of Frank'n'Furter which he had created in the theatre, Susan Sarandon and Barry Bostwick were the 'straights', and O'Brien himself played the disconcerting butler Riff Raff. Also appearing were Jonathan Adams, Nell Campbell, Peter Hinwood (right), Charles Gray and Meatloaf. Director Jim Sharman also wrote it, and Michael White produced. Songs and musical numbers: *Science Fiction Double Feature*; *Wedding Song*; *Over At The Frankenstein Place*; *The Time Warp*; *Sweet Transvestite*; *The Sword Of Damocles*; *Charles Atlas Song*; *What Ever Happened To Saturday Night*; *Toucha Toucha, Touch Me*; *Eddie's Teddy*; *Planet Schmanet*; *It Was Great When It All Began*; *I'm Going Home*; *Super-Heroes* O'Brien.

With the combined talents of director Stanley Donen, composer Frederick Loewe, lyricist Alan Jay Lerner and choreographer Bob Fosse, Paramount's **The Little Prince** ought to have been a knockout. In the event, it was a leaden exercise in tweeness which, like aviator Richard Kiley's plane, never got off the ground. The basic problem was that Antoine de Saint-Exupéry's book – about a pilot grounded in the desert and his adventures among the stars with a space-travelling tot was – notwithstanding its status as a children's classic – a fragile little tale that failed to respond to Donen's tricksy optical effects or the relentless mugging of such performers as Gene Wilder, Joss Ackland, Clive Revill and Victor Spinetti. Nor was the Lerner-Loewe score – to put it mildly – one of their best and only Fosse (right) as the Snake scored in his 'Snake In The Grass' routine. The Little Prince was played by a six-year-old charmer called Steven Warner (left), with Graham Crowden and dancer Donna McKechnie also cast. Lerner wrote the screenplay and the film was produced (in Technicolor) by Donen, with A. Joseph Tandet as associate producer. Songs and musical numbers: *It's A Hat*; *I Need Air*; *I'm On Your Side*; *Be Happy*; *You're A Child*; *I Never Met A Rose*; *Why Is The Desert (Lovely To See)?*; *Closer And Closer And Closer*; *Little Prince (From Who Knows Where)*.
▽

1976

Academic Awards

Cinematography
NOMINATIONS INCLUDED: *A Star Is Born*
(First Artists, WB) Robert Surtees

Sound
NOMINATIONS INCLUDED: *A Star Is Born* Robert
Knudson, Dan Wallin, Robert Glass and
Tom Overton

Music
Song
'Evergreen' (Love Theme from *A Star Is
Born*) *A Star Is Born* Barbra Streisand *cm*;
Paul Williams *lyr*.

Original Song Score
and Its Adaptations or Best Adaptation Score
NOMINATIONS INCLUDED: *A Star Is Born* Roger
Kellaway

Folk-singer Leadbelly (real name Huddie Ledbetter) died at the age of 60 in 1949, after a violent life in which he served sentences on two chain gangs (one of them, in Texas, for murder), and spent a further year in prison in 1939 for stabbing a man. The singer's early life and hard times were the subject of Gordon Parks's good to look at, but ultimately synthetic and over prettified (photography by Bruce Surtees) biopic, called **Leadbelly** (Paramount). In keeping with Parks's glossy conception of the production was Roger E. Mosley's (right) somewhat passionless performance in the central role, though the vocals by HiTide Harris were first-class. Paul Benjamin was fine as Leadbelly's sharecropper father, with good work, too, from Madge Sinclair as a madame and Loretta Greene as the singer's serious love interest. Also cast: Albert P. Hall, Art Evans, James E. Broadhead and John Henry Faulk. It was written by Ernest Kinoy, and produced (in Eastmancolor) by Marc Merson, with David Frost as executive producer.

After William A. Wellman's straight version of 1937 and George Cukor's musical version of 1954 (Cukor's *What Price Hollywood*, made in 1932, also treated of the same material), it was almost inevitable that **A Star Is Born** (Warner Bros.) would be updated into the world of rock music. With a literate screenplay by John Gregory Dunne, Joan Didion and director Frank Pierson (based on the story by William Wellman and Robert Carson), the Barbra Streisand-Kris Kristofferson starrer succeeded surprisingly well in extracting viable dramatic mileage from the now rather too-familiar story of an ill-starred showbiz couple, her meteoric rise to fame a perfect mirror-image of his precipitous decline into failure and alcoholism. While in no way eclipsing the superlative Cukor version with Judy Garland and James Mason, it was a considerable achievement in an era of undistinguished disco musicals, and neither Streisand nor Kristofferson (illustrated) disgraced their prestigious predecessors – that it received a lambasting from the critics on its release was due more to Streisand's reputation for megalomania than to any crippling defects in the film, which grossed a very healthy $37,100,000. It was produced by Jon Peters for Barwood-First Artists and, in secondary roles, featured director Paul Mazursky, Gary Busey, Oliver Clarke, Vanetta Fields, Clydie King

and Martin Heflin. Songs and musical numbers: *Watch Closely Now*; *Spanish Lies*; *Hellacious Acres*; *Woman In The Moon*; *With One More Look At You* Paul Williams, Kenny Ascher; *Queen Bee* Rupert Holmes; *Everything* Holmes, Williams; *Lost Inside Of You* Leon Russell, Streisand; *Evergreen* Williams, Streisand; *I Believe In Love* Kenny Loggins, Alan Bergman, Marilyn Bergman; *Crippled Crow* Donna Weiss.

MGM's sequel to their hugely successful *That's Entertainment* (1974), **That's Entertainment, Part Two,** was originally announced as *That's Entertainment, Too*, and the decision of producers Saul Chaplin and Daniel Melnick to revert to the less jokey title perhaps reflects an avowal on their part that there was rather less entertainment on offer this time around. Not that there wasn't a great deal of pleasure to be derived from seeing or re-seeing clips from almost a hundred of the studio's most delightful movies, but audible above the familiar voices of the MGM stock company and the inimitably lush orchestrations was the distinct screech of a barrel being scraped. Rarities were, well, rare – and often, as with Arthur Freed's rendering of his own 'Wedding Of The Painted Doll', ludicrously truncated; and the montages of non-musical films were, in the context, quite misguided. Saddest of all however, were the witless linking passages which featured Gene Kelly and Fred Astaire. Better to recall the real highlights – Maurice Chevalier singing 'Girls Girls Girls' in *The Merry Widow* (1934), Garland (centre right) and Margaret O'Brien (centre left) in 'Have Yourself A Merry Little Christmas' from *Meet Me In St Louis* (1944) or Bobby Van's joyous hop dance 'Take Me To Broadway' from *Small Town Girl* (1953) – whose undimmed enchantment, coupled with the ineptitude of the film that framed them, only served the more forcibly to remind us that the MGM musical was, sadly, well and truly dead.

With a reportedly enormous budget (the Russian portion of which remains a mystery), one of Hollywood's most stylish directors, George Cukor, and three 'generations' of female stars – Ava Gardner, Elizabeth Taylor and Jane Fonda – the American-Soviet co-production of Maurice Maeterlinck's **The Blue Bird** must have seemed a wonderful idea. But, considering the meagre distribution it has had in the West, 20th Century-Fox (who had filmed a non-musical version of the play with Shirley Temple in 1941) no doubt learned, along with Mytyl and Tyltyl, the two infant protagonists of the movie, that the Blue Bird of Happiness (and profit) is to be found right there at home. Cukor was hamstrung by sub-standard studio facilities, and his customary taste and flair were totally absent from this grotesque hodge-podge of ballet (see illustration), cartoons, inadequate special effects and hideous decor. Edith Head decked out the female leads in amusingly garish costumes, but her years of experience had obviously not prepared her for 'clothing' the roles of Water, Bread, Milk, and other staple items called for by Maeterlinck's arch and irrevocably dated fantasy. The songs by Andrei Petrov and Irwin Kostal (English lyrics by Tony Harrison) were negligible, reaching a nadir of absurdity with Robert Morley in Heaven singing 'You're In The Hands Of Fate' to a group of yet-to-be-born children. The film was produced in colour by Paul Maslansky and also starred George Cole, Cicely Tyson, Mona Washbourne and Richard Pearson.

1977

Academy Awards

Best Actor
NOMINATIONS INCLUDED: John Travolta
Saturday Night Fever (Paramount)

Costume Design
NOMINATIONS INCLUDED: *A Little Night Music*
(Sascha-Wien/Elliot Kastner, New World
Pictures) Florence Klotz

Music
Song
NOMINATIONS INCLUDED: 'Candle On The
Water' *Pete's Dragon* (Disney, Buena Vista)
music and lyrics by Al Kasha and Joel
Hirschhorn. 'Someone's Waiting For You'
The Rescuers (Disney, Buena Vista) Sammy
Fain *cm*; Carol Connors and Ayn Robbins *lyr*.

Original Song Score
and Its Adaptation or Best Adaptation Score
A Little Night Music Jonathan Tunick
NOMINATIONS INCLUDED: *Pete's Dragon* Al
Kasha Joel Hirschhorn and Irwin Kostal.

The Annual Top Moneymaking Films
INCLUDED: *A Star Is Born* (First Artists, WB).
The Rescuers.

△

△
In **Outlaw Blues**, a Warner Bros. release of a
Fred Weintraub-Paul Heller Production, Peter
Fonda played a prison inmate determined to
track down the country-and-western star
(James Callahan) who plagiarized his blues
number and turned it into a hit. Totally undistinguished, and with songs so feeble one
imagined Fonda would have been delighted to
rid himself of them, it was directed by Richard T.
Heffron from a screenplay by B.W.L. Norton and
produced by Steve Tisch with a cast that also
included Susan Saint James (illustrated), as a
back-up singer employed by Callahan, but fired
after she refuses to comply with his advances,
Michael Lerner, Steve Fromholz, Richard Lock-
Miller and Matt Clarke. Songs: *Outlaw Blues*
John Oates; *Jailbirds Can't Fly* Harlan Sanders,
R.C. O'Leary; *Whisper In A Velvet Night* Lee
Clayton; *I Dream Of Highways*; *Beyond These
Walls*; *Water For My Horses* Hoyt Axton.

A brilliant but flawed pastiche of forties musicals, Martin Scorsese's **New York, New York**
(United Artists) traced the separate careers and
mutual marital difficulties of an embittered jazz
saxophonist (Robert De Niro, right) and a rising
singer (Liza Minnelli, left) against the background of the changeover from big bands to
bebop. Over ninety minutes were excised from
the original running time of four hours (including a full-scale production number 'Happy
Endings' by John Kander and Fred Ebb), some of
the cuts painfully unbalancing the narrative, and
Jazz purists objected to the numerous inaccuracies in style and chronology. Nevertheless, it
was an impressive directorial effort by Scorsese,
who managed to recapture the more seductive
textures of forties movies and, together, the two
principals were outstanding. In her rendering of
the catchy title number (by Kander and Ebb),
Minnelli's eerie resemblance to her mother, Judy
Garland, added yet more authenticity. Also
featured were Lionel Stander, Barry Primus,
Mary Kay Place, Diahnne Abbot and Georgie
Auld (who dubbed De Niro's saxophone play-
ing). The moody photography (in Panavision
and Technicolor) was the work of Laszlo Kovacs,
the film was written by Earl Mac Rauch and
Mardik Martin (from a story by Mac Rauch) and
produced by Irwin Winkler and Robert Chartoff.
Other songs and musical numbers: *There Goes
The Ball Game*; *But The World Goes Round*
Kander, Ebb; *Opus One* Sy Oliver; *You Brought A
New Kind Of Love To Me* Sammy Fain, Irving
Kahal, Pierre Norman; *Once In A While* Michael
Edwards, Bud Green; *You Are My Lucky Star*
Arthur Freed, Nacio Herb Brown; *It's A Wonder-
ful World* Jan Savitt, Johnny Watson, Harold
Adamson; *The Man I Love* George and Ira
Gershwin; *Just You, Just Me* Jesse Greer, Ray-
mond Klages; *Blue Moon* Richard Rodgers,
Lorenz Hart; *Honeysuckle Rose* Fats Waller, Andy
Razaf; *Don't Be That Way* Benny Goodman,
Edgar Sampson, Mitchell Parish; *Flip The Dip*;
Game Over Georgie Auld; *V-J Stomp*; *Hazoy*; *Once
Again Right Away*; *Bobby's Dream* Ralph Burns;
For All We Know J. Fred Coots, Sam M. Lewis;
Taking A Chance On Love Vernon Duke, John
Latouche, Ted Fetter.

The Rescuers (Buena Vista), Walt Disney's 22nd
animated feature was the captivating story
of two mice. One of them, Bianca, is a member of
the Mouse Rescue Aid Society whose organization operates from the basement of the United
Nations Building; the other, Bernard, the
society's shy caretaker who volunteers to rescue
Penny, an orphan girl, from an evil witch. The
adventure – structured by Larry Clemmons and
a team of writers from two stories by Margery
Sharp – was quintessential Disney with its
familiar combination of animal kingdom fantasy
and genuine terror – the swamp setting where
Penny is held captive was as scary as anything
ever perpetrated by the Disney animators. Five
songs and some really stunning animation,
notably in a magical sequence featuring a rather
goofy bird called Orville, and in the scenes
involving Evinrude, a helpful dragonfly, contributed to the film's success; so did the vocal
characterizations of Bob Newhart and Eva
Gabor as the two mice, Geraldine Page as the
wicked witch, Michelle Stacy as Penny, Jim
Jordan as Orville and James Macdonald as
Evinrude. Also: Joe Flynn, Jeanette Nolan, Pat
Buttram and John McIntire. It was produced in
Technicolor by Wolfgang Reitherman (executive producer Ron Miller), with Reitherman also
serving as co-director with John Lounsbery and
Art Stevens. Songs and musical numbers: *The
Journey*; *Rescue Aid Society*; *Tomorrow Is Another
Day* Carol Connors, Ayn Robbins; *Someone's
Waiting For You* Sammy Fain, Connors, Rob-
bins; *The US Air Force* Robert Crawford.
▽

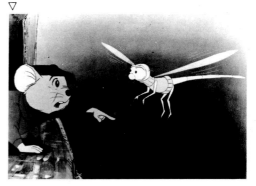

The main asset of Disney's live action plus animation fantasy **Pete's Dragon** (Buena Vista) was Elliott, the cartoon dragon itself (illustrated) – an endearingly clumsy, 12ft-tall creature with a mumbling voice (supplied by Charlie Callas, no relation to Maria) and the gift of instant invisibility. As soon as Elliott was off the screen, however, longueurs set in which not even such lively presences as Jim Dale, Mickey Rooney, Red Buttons and Shelley Winters could alleviate. Malcolm Marmorstein's screenplay (from a story by veteran Seton I. Miller and S.S. Field) concerned little orphan Pete (Sean Marshall) who flees his cruel foster family to find love and understanding from a sweet lighthouse keeper's daughter (played by pop singer Helen Reddy); and the setting in turn-of-the-century Maine gave Disney's draughtsmen plenty of opportunity to show their skills in the re-creation of a small New England town. But it was Elliott's show. The film was sluggishly directed by Don Chaffey, and produced by Ron Miller and Jerome Courtland with undistinguished choreography by Onna White and Martin Allen. Animator Ken Anderson was the creator of Elliott. Songs and musical numbers: *Candle On The Water*; *I Saw A Dragon*; *It's Not Easy*; *Every Little Piece*; *The Happiest Home In These Hills*; *Brazzle Dazzle Day*; *Boo Bop Bopbopbop (I Love You Too)*; *There's Room For Everyone*; *Passamashloddy*; *Bill Of Sale* Al Kasha and Joel Hirschhorn.

◁ **Saturday Night Fever** (Paramount) was a somewhat mechanical story about an inarticulate New York youth with a dead-end job who comes to life once a week at a local disco when he is acclaimed as a star. John Badham's flashily competent direction, the screenplay by Norman Wexler (from a story by Nik Cohn) with its accurate rendering of working-class speech patterns, and the complacent Dolby muzak of the Bee Gees all guaranteed that the Robert Stigwood-produced film would turn out to be a sleek and professional Hollywood package. That it also happened to become a phenomenal success at the box office and, more curiously, a genuinely moving depiction of the realities and aspirations of underprivileged youth, was entirely due to the presence of John Travolta (illustrated, with Karen Lynn Gorney), who became a star overnight. Both on and off the dance floor, Travolta exuded a charismatic sexuality that made him one of the key icons of the seventies, and even spectators unsympathetic to youth culture found themselves under his spell. Also cast were Barry Miller, Joseph Cali, Paul Pape and Bruce Ornstein. Kevin McKormick was the executive producer. Songs and musical numbers: *How Deep Is Your Love*; *Night Fever*; *Staying Alive*; *You Should Be Dancing*; *More Than A Woman*; *If I Can't Have You*; *Jive Talkin'* Barry, Robin and Maurice Gibb; *A Fifth Of Beethoven* adapted from Beethoven's Fifth Symphony by Walter Murphy; *Calypso Breakdown*; *Open Sesame* R. Bell, Kool and The Gang; *Boogie Shoes* H.W. Casey, R. Finch; *Disco Inferno* Leo Green, Ron Kersey; *Manhattan Skyline*; *Night On Disco Mountain* adapted from Mussorgsky's 'Night On The Bare Mountain', by David Shire; *Salsation*.

Four years after Universal's enormous success with *The Sting* (1973) the studio mounted a tribute to Scott Joplin, the composer whose ragtime music contributed greatly to the success of that film. Called, quite simply **Scott Joplin**, it starred Billy Dee Williams (illustrated) in the title role, with other parts in Don Hough's downbeat production going to Clifton Davis, Godfrey Cambridge, De Wayne Jessie, Mabel King, Taj Mahal, Spo-De-Odee, Eubie Blake, The Commodores, David Healy, Samuel Fuller and Art Carney. After a buoyant first half, Christopher Knopf's screenplay was plunged into gloom as it narrated Joplin's decline and eventual death, destitute and syphilitic, in 1917. The harrowing nature of the material was conveyed with great honesty (despite the meagre 20-day shooting schedule) in Jeremy Paul Keegan's atmospheric direction. With the exception of Harold Johnson's 'Hangover Blues', all the music featured was by Joplin.

With its impressive pedigree (an Ingmar Bergman film) and its refined operetta-like score by the talented Stephen Sondheim, **A Little Night Music** had been a critical success on Broadway and, somewhat surprisingly in view of its rather esoteric flavour, a resounding commercial hit too. Its transfer to the screen required uncommon delicacy, and the Sascha-Wien-New World production's choice of the original stage director Harold Prince probably seemed the safest guarantee of maintaining the show's charm and humour, and its wistfully mocking message of transience and human foolishness. But Prince and his producer, Elliott Kastner, made several fundamental errors, ejecting from the score memorable numbers ('Liaisons'; 'The Miller's Son') while retaining the lugubrious 'Soon' and 'Later' which slowed the film's pace to a halt in the early stages. Two of the best of the remaining numbers had their impact blunted by their staging: 'A Weekend In The Country' was weakened by choppy editing and interrupted choruses, and the show's hit song, the gorgeous 'Send In The Clowns' was sung by the heroine *across* a room to her lover. But there was still much to enjoy. What remained of Sondheim's score was lovely to listen to (especially in Jonathan Tunick's sublime orchestrations), the screenplay by Hugh Wheeler from his own libretto (which had been based on Bergman's 'Smiles of a Summer Night') was literate and ultimately moving. Arthur Ibbetson's colour photography captured the elegiac beauty of turn-of-the-century Viennese opulence and the leading players, Elizabeth Taylor (right) as the actress Desirée, Len Cariou (left) as the newly-married lawyer who rekindles their old affair, Lesley-Ann Down as his virginal wife, Diana Rigg as the haughty wife of Desirée's current lover, and Hermione Gingold as Desirée's mother, were all fine – though Taylor's singing of the film's big song only *just* got by. The film's musical highlight, in fact, turned out to be one of the lesser numbers, 'Every Day A Little Death', performed by Rigg and Down then reprised solo by Rigg. Two of the show's numbers were revised by Sondheim for the film: the duet 'The Glamorous Life' was re-written as a solo for Desirée's daughter (Chloe Franks) and the 'Night Waltz (The Sun Won't Set)' was given new lyrics, retitled 'Love Takes Time' and became the film's theme. Laurence Guittard, Christopher Guard, Heinz Marecek and Lesley Dunlop were also in key roles, and the choreography was by Patricia Birch. An entertainment of limited and perhaps rarefied appeal, it played so few engagements that many who would have found much to enjoy in it were, alas, never given the chance to find out. Other songs and musical numbers: *Now*; *You Must Meet My Wife*; *It Would Have Been Wonderful*.

1978

John Travolta consolidated his *Saturday Night Fever* (Paramount, 1977) success with **Grease** (Paramount), a Robert Stigwood-Allan Carr production of the long-running Broadway hit. Adapted by Carr from Jim Jacobs and Warren Casey's fifties-style book (screenplay by Bronte Woodard), it was designed specifically as a mammoth showcase for the good looks and sex appeal of its super-star lead and, as such, was a triumphant success. Though contemporary in its language and in its approach to its subject (high school romance) the film tapped a decided vein of nostalgia by virtue of its fifties setting, and the casting of such stalwarts as Eve Arden, Joan Blondell, Edd Byrnes, Sid Caesar, Alice Ghostley and Dody Goodman. Frankie Avalon was also in it (as part of a dream sequence) and there was a certain nostalgia about his token appearance as well. All about how Travolta's (right) summer romance with co-star Olivia Newton-John (left) sours when they find themselves attending the same high school, its infectious high spirits were the results of Patricia Birch's jet-propelled choreography, Woodard's racy (if somewhat loosely constructed) screenplay, an instantly accessible score by Jim Jacobs and Warren Casey (augmented by Barry Gibb, John Farrar, Louis St Louis and Scott J. Simon), and the attractive performances from a cast whose younger members included the marvellous Stockard Channing, Jeff Conaway, Barry Pearl, Michael Tucci, Kelly Ward and Didi Conn. It was stunningly photographed in Panavision and Metrocolor by Bill Butler. Songs and musical numbers: *Grease*; *Summer Nights*; *Hopelessly Devoted To You*; *You're The One That I Want*; *Sandy*; *Beauty School Dropout*; *Look At Me I'm Sandra Dee*; *Greased Lightnin'*; *It's Raining On Prom Night*; *Alone At A Drive-In Movie*; *Blue Moon*; *Rock'n Roll Is Here To Stay*; *Those Magic Changes*; *Hound Dog*; *Born To Hand-Jive*; *Tears On My Pillow*; *Mooning*; *Freddy My Love*; *Rock 'n' Roll Party Queen*; *There Are Worse Things I Could Do*; *We Go Together*; *Love Is A Many Splendoured Thing*.
▽

Paramount's **American Hot Wax**, an affectionate tribute to the rock'n'roll era, was marred by the too reverent treatment accorded its central character, the charismatic disc jockey Alan Freed. The movie glossed over his involvement in the payola racket, preferring to present him as the first martyr of youth culture. Otherwise, it all seemed pleasantly nostalgic (though, given the volume at which the incessant rock music was played, audiences may have felt the need of another kind of wax), with such guest stars as Buddy Holly, Chuck Berry, Jerry Lee Lewis (illustrated), Bobby Darin, Little Richard, The Everly Brothers, and Screamin' Jay Hawkins to confer 50s authenticity. Tim McIntire successfully impersonated Freed, and was supported by Fran Dreecher, Jay Leno and Laraine Newman. It was produced by Art Linson (in Metrocolor), and directed by Floyd Mutrux. Among some 40 songs featured were: *Hot Wax Theme* Kenny Vance, Paul Griffin, Ira Newborn; *Rock And Roll Is Here To Stay* David White; *Reelin' And Rockin'*; *Roll Over Beethoven*; *Sweet Little Sixteen* Chuck Berry; *Why Do Fools Fall In Love* Frank Lymon, Morris Levey; *That Is Rock And Roll* Jerry Leiber, Mike Stoller; *Whole Lotta Shakin' Goin' On* Dave Williams, Sunny David; *Great Balls Of Fire* Jack Hammer, Otis Blackwell.

△

The story of a 'creative' disc jockey battling with commercial pressures, **FM** (Universal) portrayed FM radio stations in a rather sentimentalized manner and offered, as musical support, the usual catchall soundtrack medley of rock numbers (in Dolby sound). Michael Brandon played the station Q-SKY Deejay, with Eileen Brennan, Cassie Yates (illustrated), Alex Karras, Cleavon Little and Martin Mull also featured. Photographer John A. Alonzo directed this Rand Holston production (in Technicolor) from a screenplay by Ezra Sacks. Over 30 songs were heard, including: *FM*; *Do It Again*; *FM Reprise* Walter Becker, Donald Fagen; *Livingston Saturday Night* Jimmy Buffett; *The Key To My Kingdom* Maxwell Davis, Claude Baum, Joe Josea; *Green Grass And High Tides* Hugh Thomasson; *Life In The Fast Lane* Joe Walsh, Don Henley, Glenn Frey; *Bad Man* J.D. Souther, Frey; *Tumbling Dice* Mick Jagger, Keith Richard; *Poor Poor Pitiful Me* Warren Zevon; *Love Me Tender* Elvis Presley Vera Matson; *Life's Been Good* Joe Walsh; *Cold As Ice* Mick Jones, Lew Gramus; *Feels Like The First Time* Jones; *Slow Ride* Dave Peverett; *Night Moves* Bob Seger; *Sentimental Lady* Bob Welch; *Fly Like An Eagle* Steve Miller; *Just The Way You Are* Billy Joel; *Lido Shuffle* Boz Scaggs; *Hollywood* Scaggs, Michael Omartin; *Your Smiling Face* James Taylor; *We Will Rock You* Brian May, Freddy Mercury; *More Than A Feeling* T. Scholz.

A fantasy fashioned around some 30 or so Beatles hits as performed, in the main, by Peter Frampton and The Bee Gees, **Sgt. Pepper's Lonely Hearts Club Band** (Universal) involved several somewhat bizarre characters in a plot to steal the musical instruments belonging to Sgt. Pepper's band, whose leader, in company with the Bee Gees, is Pepper's grandson, Bill Shears (Frampton, left). They don't succeed. End of plot (by Henry Edwards, who also scripted). A musical mish-mash overloaded with electronic visual effects, an insistent soundtrack and no sense of direction (by Michael Schultz), it also featured Frankie Howerd, Paul Nicholas, Donald Pleasence (as a Robert Stigwood-type music business genius), Dianne Steinberg (right), Sandy Farina, Alice Cooper, Stargard, Billy Preston, Earth, Wind and Fire and, as Mayor Kite, George Burns. The songs were by John Lennon, Paul McCartney and George Harrison, and the choreography by Patricia Birch. Among the numerous stars making 'guest' appearances were Peter Allen, Stephen Bishop, Keith Carradine, Carol Channing, Donovan, Jose Feliciano, Peter Noone, Helen Reddy, Chita Rivera, Johnny Rivers, Sha-Na-Na, Aerosmith, Del Shannon, and Connie Stevens. It was produced, in Technicolor, by Robert Stigwood. Songs and musical numbers: *Sgt. Pepper's Lonely Hearts Club Band* (Bee Gees, Nicholas); *With A Little Help From My Friends* (Peter Frampton, Bee Gees); *Fixing A Hole* (Burns); *Getting Better* (Frampton, Bee Gees); *Here Comes The Sun* (Farina); *I Want You (She's So Heavy)* (Bee Gees, Dianne Steinberg, Nicholas, Pleasence, Stargard); *Good Morning, Good Morning* (Nicholas, Frampton, Bee Gees); *Nowhere Man* (Bee Gees); *Polythene Pam* (Bee Gees); *She Came In Through The Bathroom Window* (Frampton, Bee Gees); *Sgt. Pepper's Lonely Hearts Club Band* (Reprise) (Frampton, Bee Gees); *Mean Mr Mustard* (Frankie Howerd); *She's Leaving Home* (Bee Gees, Jay MacIntosh, John Wheeler); *Lucy In The Sky With Diamonds* (Steinberg, Stargard); *Oh! Darling* (Robin Gibb); *Maxwell's Silver Hammer* (Steve Martin); *Because* (Alice Cooper, Bee Gees); *Strawberry Fields Forever* (Farina); *Being For The Benefit Of Mr Kite* (Maurice Gibb, Frampton, Bee Gees, Burns); *You Never Give Me Your Money* (Nicholas, Steinberg); *Got To Get You Into My Life* (Earth, Wind and Fire); *When I'm 64* (Farina); *Come Together* (Aerosmith); *Golden Slumbers* (Frampton); *Carry That Weight* (Bee Gees); *The Long And Winding Road* (Frampton); *A Day In The Life* (Barry Gibb, Bee Gees); *Get Back* (Preston); *Sgt. Pepper's Lonely Hearts Club Band* (Finale, full cast).

I Wanna Hold Your Hand (Universal) was a 'day in the life of . . .' film: in this case, a day in the life of four New Jersey teenagers bound for New York to catch the Beatles' debut on the Ed Sullivan Show in 1964. That the cinema audience was to be denied a glimpse of the four Liverpudlians was evident from the famous quartet's absence from the cast list, added to which tyro director Robert Zemeckis (a friend and protégé of Steven Spielberg) was more maladroit than amusing in his handling of dissociated shots of legs and shoulders intended to denote their charismatic presence. As a nostalgic celebration of Beatlemania, therefore, it failed to deliver the goods and, as a youth movie, one would be forgiven for supposing it had been made by characters just as dopey as those portrayed in the film by Nancy Allen, Wendy Jo Sperber, Susan Kendall Newman and Theresa Saldana (foreground). Bobby Di Cicco, Marc McClure and Eddie Deezen were also featured. It was scripted by Zemeckis and Bob Gale, and produced by Tamara Asseyev and Alex Rose (with Gale as associate producer and Spielberg as executive producer). Songs and musical numbers included: *I Want To Hold Your Hand*; *Please, Please Me*; *I Saw Her Standing There*; *Thank You Girl*; *Misery*; *Love Me Do*; *Do You Want To Know A Secret?*; *P.S. I Love You*; *From Me To You*; *There's A Place*; *She Loves You* John Lennon, Paul McCartney; *Boys* Carl Perkins; *Twist And Shout* Phil Medley, Bert Berns; *Till There Was You* Meredith Willson; *Money* Janie Bradford, Berry Gordy Jr; *Please Mr Postman* Brian Holland, Freddy C. Gorman.

The magic of Lassie was to be found in films like *Lassie Come Home* (MGM, 1943) and not in **The Magic Of Lassie** (International Picture Show), a heavy-handed throwback in which a crooked businessman steals the canine star from her young owner to force the boy's grandfather (James Stewart) to sell some prize-winning vineyards. Suitable for all children from eight to eight-and-a-half, its sole attraction for anyone outside that age group was the presence of Stewart, Mickey Rooney (illustrated right) and Alice Faye, each of whom sang one of Robert M. and Richard B. Sherman's sugary numbers, as does Lassie herself, whose celebrated coloratura voice was dubbed in by Debby Boone (Pat's daughter). Also featured were Pernell Roberts, Stephanie Zimbalist, Michael Sharrett and The Mike Curb Congregation. The ludicrous script was by Jean Holloway and the Sherman brothers. A Jack Wrather presentation, it was directed by Don Chaffey and produced by Bonita Granville Wrather and William Beaudine Jr. Songs: *A Rose Is Not A Rose* (sung by Alice Faye and, on a jukebox, the voice of Pat Boone); *That Hometown Feeling*; *Thanksgiving Prayer*; *When You're Loved*; *There'll Be Other Friday Nights*; *Brass Rings and Daydreams*; *Travelling' Music*; *Nobody's Property*; *I Can't Say Goodbye*; *Banjo Song*.

Bob Dylan (illustrated right, with Roger McGuinn) both directed and starred in **Renaldo And Clara** (Lombard Street Films), a long meandering, self-indulgent account of his 1975/76 tour with the Rolling Thunder Revue, intercut with fictional, semi-improvised scenes in which Dylan, his wife Sara, Joan Baez, Ronee Blakely, Ronnie Hawkins (playing 'Bob Dylan') and such luminaries of counterculture as Allen Ginsberg and Sam Shepard acted out the lyrics of the songs. For addicts only. Dylan also wrote the scenario (with additional dialogue by Shepard) and the film was produced by Mel Howard. Of the 47 songs featured, 22 were by Dylan. They included: *Isis I Want You*; *It Ain't Me Babe*; *Knockin' On Heaven's Door*; *Hurricane*; *Romance In Durango*; *One Too Many Mornings*; *One More Cup Of Coffee*; *Sara*; *Patty's Gone To Laredo*; *Just Like A Woman*; *A Hard Rain's A-Gonna Fall*; *Sad-Eyed Lady Of The Lowlands*; *When I Paint My Masterpiece*. Other songs included: *Chestnut Mare* Roger McGuinn; *Diamonds And Rust* Joan Baez; *Suzanne* Leonard Cohen; *Need A New Sun Rising* Ronee Blakely; *Salt Pork West Virginia* Jack Elliott; *Kaddish* Allen Ginsberg; *Cucurrucucu Paloma* Thomas Mendez; *Time Of The Preacher* Willie Nelson.

△

Buried somewhere under the rubble of Sidney Lumet's catastrophically misguided all-black remake of *The Wizard Of Oz* (MGM, 1939) – now abbreviated to **The Wiz** (Universal) – was author Frank Baum's reassuring message that, be it ever so humble, there's no place like home. The other underlying messages were that black is not always beautiful, and big is not always better. Though based on the hit Broadway musical of the same name, Joel Schumacher's screenplay transposed the action from Kansas to New York City, where Dorothy the heroine (Diana Ross) becomes a 24-year-old Harlem school teacher whose encounter with a snowstorm while chasing after her dog Toto, results in her disappearing into a vortex of snow crystals only to re-emerge in another part of Manhattan. Miss Ross's adventures in a Tony Walton-designed New York (the interiors were shot at the historic Astoria Studios and on location in and around Manhattan) more or less paralleled those young Judy Garland had in the earlier film, with only one thing missing: a sense of wonderment. Though no expense was spared in creating contemporary Oz out of New York City, Lumet's direction substituted noise and overblown spectacle for genuine creativity, succeeding only in making the least out of the most. But even more fatal was the casting of Diana Ross, who, as Dorothy (illustrated centre), was far too mature for Baum's innocent heroine, and lacked vulnerability. More happily, though by no means definitively, cast were Michael Jackson as Scarecrow (2nd left), Nipsey Russell as the Tin Man (right), and Ted Ross as the Cowardly Lion (left); Richard Pryor (under-used) was the Wiz himself and, best of all, Mabel King as the evil witch Evilene who, together with the Flying Monkeys employed in her Sweatshop, stopped the show with their galvanic 'Don't Bring Me No Bad News' number. Lena Horne appeared at the end of the film as Glinda the Good Witch, and gave her all to the black pride number 'Believe In Yourself'; with other roles in Rob Cohen's production (executive producer Ken Harper) going to Theresa Merritt (as Aunt Em), Thelma Carpenter, Stanley Greene and Clyde J. Barrett. The several large-scale production numbers were staged by Louis Johnson (and performed by the Louis Johnson Dance Theatre). It was photographed, by Oswald Morris, in Panavision and Technicolor. Other songs and musical numbers (all by Quincy Jones and Charlie Smalls): *Brand New Day; Home; He's The Wizard; The Feeling That We Have; Soon As I Get Home; You Can't Win; What Would I Do If I Could Feel; Slide Some Oil To Me; I'm A Mean Old Lion; Be A Lion; Ease On Down The Road; Emerald City; So You Wanted To See The Wizard* Charlie Smalls; *Liberation Agitato; The Wiz; Can I Go On?; March Of The Munchkins; Good Witch Glinda; Is This What Feeling Gets? (Dorothy's Theme); Now Watch Me Dance; Popper Girls; End Of The Yellow Brick Road; A Sorry Phoney* Quincy Jones.
▽

A very patent attempt to cash in on the phenomenal success of *Saturday Night Fever* (1977), **Thank God It's Friday** (Casablanca/Motown/Columbia) took place one Friday night in a Hollywood disco nightclub, aptly named The Zoo, and narrated the adventures, both professional and romantic, of its proprietors, performers and clients. Apart from a couple of amusing moments (the cod Gene Kelly dance performed by Chuck Vennera in a parking-lot, for example), it was totally forgettable teenage fodder. Written by Barry Armyan Bernstein and directed by Robert Klane, it starred Valerie Landsburg, Terri Nunn and Donna Summer, and also featured Phil Adams (illustrated centre), Ray Vitte, Mark Lonow, Andrea Howard and The Commodores. It was produced (in Metrocolor) by Rob Cohen, with Neil Bogart as executive producer. The plethora of songs and musical numbers included: *After Dark* Simon Soussan, Sabrina Soussan; *Find My Way* J. Melfi; *It's Serious* Gregory Johnson, Larry Blackman; *Let's Make A Deal* Michael Smith; *Romeo And Juliet* Alec Costadinos; *You're The Reason I Feel Like Dancing* H. Johnson; *From Here To Eternity* Giorgio Moroder, Pete Bellotte; *Dance All Night* Willie Hutch; *Love Masterpiece* H. Davis, J. Powell, A. Posey; *I'm Here Again* B. Sutton, M. Sutton, Kathy Wakefield; *Disco Queen* Paul Jabara; *Trapped In A Stairway* Jabara, Bob Esty; *Do You Want The Real Thing; You Can Always Tell A Lady By The Company She Keeps* Esty, D.C. LaRue; *Thank God It's Friday; You Are The Most Precious Thing In My Life* A.R. Costadinos; *I Wanna Dance* P. Bellotte; *Meco's Theme* Harold Wheeler; *Floyd's Theme* D. St Nicklaus; *Down To Lovetown* Don Daniels, Michael Sutton, Kathy Wakefield; *Lovin', Livin', And Givin'* Kenneth Stover, Pam Davis; *Sevilla Nights* N. Skorsky, J.M. Descarano, J. C. Petit; *Love To Love You Baby; Try With Your Love* Donna Summer, Moroder, Belotte; *Je t'àime* Serge Gainsbourg, arranged by Thor Baldursson.

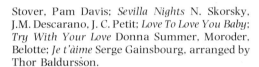

△

The odd omission of the singer's death in a plane crash in 1959 made **The Buddy Holly Story** (Innovasions – ECA) the kind of routine rags-to-riches show-biz narrative that had, in the past, served indiscriminately for musical comedy fiction, as well as film or opera star biopics. Robert Gittler's screenplay (based on the book *Buddy Holly, His Life And Music* by John Coldrosen) eschewed few of the genre's clichés, but the casting of Gary Busey (left) in the title role added immeasurably to the sense of authenticity – the gangling, buck-toothed actor not only resembled Holly physically but managed to recapture a voice and stage presence one had supposed inimitable. (Unusually for such films, Busey was not dubbed.) Co-stars were Don Stroud and Charles Martin Smith, with Conrad Janis, William Jordan and Maria Richwine (as Holly's wife) also featured. Steve Rash directed and Freddy Bauer produced (with associate producer Frances Avrut-Bauer and executive producers Edward H. Cohen and Fred T. Kuehnert). Songs and musical numbers: *Rock Around With Ollie Vee* Sonny Curtis; *That'll Be The Day; Peggy Sue* Jerry Allison, Holly, Norman Petty; *Rave On; Oh Boy* Sonny West, Bill Tilghman, Petty; *It's So Easy; Maybe Baby; True Love Ways* Holly, Petty; *Words Of Love* Holly; *Listen To Me* Charles Hardin, Petty; *Every Day I Have The Blues* Peter Chatman; *Well, All Right* Frances Faye, Don Raye, Dan Howell; *Chantilly Lace* J.P. Richardson; *Whole Lotta Shakin' Goin' On* Dave Williams, Sunny David; *You Send Me* L.C. Cooke.

△

412

A reverential biopic, heavily reminiscent of the fifties in style, which blinkered much of the truth and failed to ask some of the more provocative and probing questions concerning the rise and fall of its subject's staggeringly influential career, **Elvis** (Dick Clark Motion Pictures) was a superficial account of the life and times of Elvis Presley Super Star, which began and ended in Las Vegas in 1969 (the year of Presley's comeback performance in that city) and, in between, repeated certain well-documented facts about his impoverished hillbilly existence in Mississippi, his early professional struggles, his erratic movie career, his spell in the army, and his marriage to Priscilla Beaulifil which ended when he decided to make a theatrical comeback. Presley's life, and life-style, in the seventies were completely omitted. Doing as well as they could by producer Anthony Lawrence's superficial screenplay were Kurt Russell (illustrated) as Presley, Shelley Winters as his mother, Bing Russell as his father, Season Hubley as Priscilla, Pat Hingle as Colonel Parker, Abi Young as Natalie Wood, Felicia Fenske as Lisa Marie Presley, Randy Gray as the boy Elvis, and Charlie Hodge as himself. Russell's 'Presley' vocals were dubbed by Ronnie McDowell. It was photographed in Metrocolor and directed by Dick Clark. Songs included: *Mystery Train* Sam C. Phillips, Herman Parker Jr; *The Wonder Of You* Baker Knight; *That's Alright Mama* A. Crudup; *Blue Moon Of Kentucky* Bill Munroe; *Old Shep* R. Foley, E.M. Jones; *Heartbreak Hotel* Mae Boren Axton, Tommy Durden, Presley; *Rip It Up* Robert A. Blackwell, John Marascalco; *Love Me Tender* Presley, Vera Matson; *Are You Lonesome Tonight* Roy Turk, Lou Handman; *Crying In The Chapel* Artie Glenn; *Until It's Time For You To Go* Buffy Sainte-Marie; *Pledging My Love* Ferdinand Washington, Don D. Robey; *Suspicious Minds* Fred Zambon; *Burning Love* D. Linde; *Blue Suede Shoes* Carl Lee Perkins; *Finale: Dixie-Battle Hymn Of The Republic* Julia Ward Howe, music attributed to William Steffe; and a concert medley.

△

After the generation-gap comedy *Taking Off* (1971), and his version of a key novel of the sixties, Ken Kesey's *One Flew Over The Cuckoo's Nest* (1976), the choice of Czech director Milos Forman to bring the Galt MacDermot-Gerome Ragni-James Rado counter-culture musical hit **Hair** (United Artists) to the screen, was more logical than it first appeared. On to the heterogeneous sketches and vignettes that comprised the original, Michael Weller's screenplay grafted a slight but serviceable plotline concerning a young Oklahoma cowboy's arrival in New York to report to his army unit for service in Vietnam, and his involvement with a group of hippie dropouts; but it could not assuage the uneasy suspicion that it was either too soon or too late to revive this monument to Flower Power. Nevertheless, there was much to enjoy – Twyla Tharp's brilliant choreography sent the cast dancing through New York's Central Park (see illustration) with vigour, and Forman had plenty of striking visual ideas, such as the psychedelic church wedding and the lovely sequence when the horses of mounted policemen at a Central Park 'be-in' high-step to the music. John Savage played the young draftee and Beverly D'Angelo was a mixed-up deb, with other parts going to Treat Williams, Annie Golden, Melba Moore, Dorsey Wright, Don Dacus, Cheryl Barnes and the Twyla Tharp Dance Foundation. It was a CIP-Film-Productions feature produced (in Technicolor and Panavision) by Lester Persky and Michael Butler. Songs and musical numbers: *Aquarius; Colored Spade; Aint' Got No; Black Boys/White Boys; Electric Blues; Old-Fashioned Melody; The Flesh Failures; 3-5-0-0; Somebody To Hold; Sodomy; Donna; Hashish; Manchester; Abie Baby; Fourscore; I'm Black; Air; Party Music; My Conviction; I Got Life; Hair; LBJ; Hare Krishna; Where Do I Go; Walking In Space; Easy To Be Hard; Good Morning Starshine; What A Piece Of Work Is Man; Somebody To Love; Don't Put It Down; Let The Sunshine In* MacDermot, Ragni, Rado.

After their worldwide success on TV it was inevitable that the Muppets (illustrated) would transfer to the big screen, and the basic plotline of **The Muppet Movie** (ITC) – Kermit the Frog and Fozzie Bear journey across America, with various other members of the cloth menagerie hitching rides *en route* to Hollywood – appeared to offer a satisfactory peg on which to hang the usual ration of sketches, songs and guest appearances. Unfortunately, too many lugubrious songs held up the action; and of the guests – who included Edgar Bergen, Milton Berle, James Coburn, Dom DeLuise, Elliott Gould, Bob Hope, Madeline Kahn, Carol Kane, Cloris Leachman, Steve Martin, Richard Pryor, Telly Savalas, ▽

Orson Welles and Paul Williams – only Mel Brooks emerged with any honour (perhaps because he's something of a Muppet himself). The Jerry Juhl-Jack Burns screenplay, moreover, made certain elementary miscalculations, notably by allowing Kermit to requite Miss Piggy's affections, and the film was slackly directed by James Frawley. Jim Henson (the creator of the original TV series) produced, with Martin Starger as executive producer. Songs and musical numbers: *The Rainbow Connection*; *Frog's Legs So Fine*; *Movin' Right Along*; *Can You Picture That?*; *Never Before*; *Something Better*; *This Looks Familiar*; *I'm Going To Go Back There Some Day* Paul Williams, Kenny Ascher.

Bette Midler (illustrated) made an astonishing screen debut in **The Rose** (20th Century-Fox), a loosely disguised biopic of the late Janis Joplin. Set in the mid sixties against the background of an unpopular war and the radically changing social and personal values of American society, it charted the decline of Rose, a successful rock singer (Midler) whose small-town Florida background has failed to provide her with the emotional security she needs to cope with her public acclaim. A wild, undisciplined lady whose unconventional life-style renders permanent relationships impossible, Rose takes to drink to see her through her nights and, after ruining her chances of having what promises to be the most successful love affair of her life (with a professional soldier who has deserted after two tours in Vietnam), she overdoses herself with heroin and dies during a standing room only 'homecoming' concert in Florida. Frederic Forrest (excellent) played the soldier, and was billed third behind a rather morose and under-used Alan Bates as Midler's unsympathetic, fed-up-to-the-gills, commercially minded manager. Harry Dean Stanton, Barry Primus, David Keith and Sandra McCabe were also in it; so were female impersonators Michael Greer, Claude Sacha, Michael St Laurent, and Sylvester and Pearl White who, in one of the film's best scenes – set in a Greenwich Village nightclub – appear as Bette Midler (*à la* Rose), Barbra Streisand, Bette Davis, Mae West and Diana Ross, and invite Midler to join their act. Mark Rydell's pyrotechnic direction disguised the fact that the film, despite its raunchy dialogue (screenplay by Bill Kerby and Bo Goldman), was pretty old fashioned. So, of course, did Midler's courageous, no-holds-barred central performance. It was costumed by Theoni V. Aldredge, choreographed by Toni Basil, photographed by Vilmos Zsigmond in 70mm and Color De Luxe, and produced by Marvin Worth and Aaron Russo. Songs: *Let Me Call You Sweetheart* Leo Friedman, Beth Slater Whitson; *The Rose* Amanda McBroom; *Stay With Me* Jerry Ragavoy, George Weiss; *Camellia* Stephen Hunter; *The Night We Said Goodbye* Bill Elliott; *Evil Lies* Greg Prestopino, Carol Locatell; *Sold My Soul To Rock'n'Roll* Gene Pistilli; *Keep On Rockin'* Sammy Hagar, John Carter; *Fire Down Below* Bob Seger; *I've Written A Letter To Daddy* Larry Vincent, Henry Tobias, Mo Jaffe; *When A Man Loves A Woman* C. Lewis, A. Wright; *Midnight In Memphis* Tony Johnson; *Whose Side Are You On?* Kenny Hopkins, Charley Williams. ▽

Directed by Allan Arkush, **Rock'n'Roll High** ▷ **School** (New World) was a noisy throw-back to the fifties campus musical and something of an anachronism in 1979. Set in the Vince Lombardi High School and all about an avid fan of The Ramones pop group and her clash with a high school administration dedicated to stamping out rock'n'roll – it starred P.J. Soles as the fan (and an aspiring songwriter) and Vincent Van Patten as her secret admirer, with other roles going to May Woronov, Clint Howard, Dey Young and The Ramones (illustrated with Soles, centre), the latter performing several of their biggest hits. These included: 'Blitzkrieg Bop', 'Teenage Lobotomy', 'Pinhead', 'Sheena Is A Punk Rocker' and two new ones they wrote especially for the film, 'I Want You' and 'Rock'n'Roll High School'. In addition to those of The Ramones, the film featured nineteen other songs, including Paul McCartney's 'Did We Meet Somewhere Before?', Fleetwood Mac's 'Albatross' and 'Jigsaw Puzzle Blues', Alice Cooper's 'School's Out', Chuck Berry's 'School Days', Todd Rundgren's 'A Dream Goes Forever', MC5's 'High School', Eddie and the Hot Rods' 'Teenage Depression', The Paley Brothers' 'C'mon Let's Go' and 'You're The Best', Bent Fabric's 'Alley Cat', Devo's 'Come Back Jonee', Nick Lowe's 'So It Goes', Brian Eno's 'Spirits Drifting', 'Alternative 3', 'M386' and 'Energy Fools The Magician', The Velvet Underground's 'Rock'n'roll' and Brownsville Station's 'Smoking In The Boys' Room'. Siana Lee Hale was responsible for the choreography, it was written by Richard Whitley, Russ Dvonch and Joseph McBride from a story by Allan Arkush and Joe Dante. The film was produced by Michael Finnell (the executive producer was 'B' picture king Roger Corman).

△

All That Jazz (Columbia-20th Century-Fox) was the first musical whose subject was death. A self-indulgent though undeniably effective, often brilliant, examination of the life and death of its creator Bob Fosse (and a brutally unglamorous look at the tensions and pressures of life in the commercial theatre), it parted company from reality only in that director-choreographer Fosse, unlike his cinematic incarnation Joe Gideon, lived, after suffering a thrombosis, to tell the tale here told. Basically concerned with the period in Fosse's life (circa 1974) when he was overworking himself on the Broadway-bound musical *Chicago*, and the film *Lenny* (United Artists, 1974), it picked at the knots of the subject's life-style with unflinching honesty and candour. Special emphasis was laid on Fosse's insatiable sexual appetite, his treatment of people as mere objects, his quest for artistic perfection, and his obsessional avoidance of the conventional and ordinary. The choreographer's life (and death) was viewed as a massive production number – a device which cued in several typically Fosse routines, every one of them dazzling in both conception and execution. Fosse himself was convincingly played by Roy Scheider (illustrated), his wife (based on dancer Gwen Verdon, whose voice was heard in one of the numbers) by Leland Palmer, his young daughter by Erzsebet Foldi, and his then mistress by Ann Reinking. Cliff Gorman appeared as the star of Gideon's movie 'The Stand-Up' (actually *Lenny*), with Ben Vereen as an unctuous TV host and Jessica Lange (in the guise of a flirtatious showgirl) as Death herself. Robert Alan Aurthur produced (executive producer Daniel Melnick) in Panavision and Technicolor and, together with Fosse, wrote the screenplay. Songs and musical numbers: *On Broadway* B. Mann, C. Weill, Jerry Leiber, Mike Stoller; *Take Off With Us* Stan Lebowsky, F. Tobias; *Everything Old Is New Again* Peter Allen, Carol Bayer Sager; *South Mt Sinai Parade* Ralph Burns; *After You've Gone* Henry Creamer, J. Turner Layton; *There'll Be Some Changes Made* W.B. Overstreet, Billy Higgins; *Who's Sorry Now?* Ted Snyder, Burt Kalmar, Harry Ruby; *Some Of These Days* Shelton Brooks; *Going Home Now* Ralph Burns; *Bye Bye Love* Felice and Boudleux Bryant.

414

1980

Academy Awards

Original Score
NOMINATIONS INCLUDED: *Fame* (MGM) Michael Gore

Original Song
NOMINATIONS INCLUDED: 'Fame' *Fame* Michael Gore *cm*; Dean Pitchford *lyr*

Writing (Screenplay) – material written directly for the screen
NOMINATIONS INCLUDED: *Fame* Christopher Gore

Film Editing
NOMINATIONS INCLUDED: *Fame* Gerry Hambling

Set against the background of Manhattan's High School of the Performing Arts, director Alan Parker's **Fame** (MGM) couldn't quite make up its mind whether it wanted to be a traditional musical or a drama of social significance. The result was an unsatisfying melding of romanticism and realism, whose patchwork quilt of a screenplay (by Christopher Gore) traded in clichés as it itemised the hopes and dreams of eight young men and women over a period of four formative years. Most prominently featured were Irene Cara as an ambitious and gifted singer, Paul McCrane as a confused, vulnerable gay; Gene Ray (illustrated, foreground) as a rebellious, illiterate but stunning black dancer; Maureen Teefy as a mother-dominated young Brooklyn Jewess; Lee Carreri as a musician with a penchant for 'synthesized' music and, most talented of all, Barry Miller as a hip Puerto Rican who hides the truth of his squalid family background by lying about it. Also cast: Tresa Hughes (as the mother), Anne Meara, Laura Dean, Antonia Franceschi, Eddie Barth, Boyd Gaines and Albert Hague. Choreographed by Louis Falco whose two big numbers were, frankly, a mess; and the producers were David De Silva and Alan Marshall. Songs and musical numbers: *Red Light*; *Fame*; *I Sing the Body Electric* Michael Gore, Dean Pitchford; *Dogs In The Yard* Dominic Bugatti, Frank Musker; *Hot Lunch Jam* Gore, Robert F. Colesberry, Lesley Gore; *Out Here On My Own* Michael and Lesley Gore; *Is It Okay If I Call You Mine?* Paul McCrane.

▽

Unlike Al Jolson, Neil Diamond, who also made ▷ his movie debut playing a cantor's errant son, could hardly lay claim to being the world's greatest entertainer. Still, his performance as Jess Rabinovitch in **The Jazz Singer**, EMI's remake of Samson Raphaelson's famous play, was nothing to be ashamed of. Like Jolson, Diamond's personality is not exactly ingratiating, and although it strained at plausibility to ask audiences to believe in him as an assistant cantor, he projected a positive presence, both physically and vocally. Fortunately, not too much time is spent in the synagogue and, just as Jolson (and Danny Thomas in the 1953 Warner Bros. remake of the story) abandoned religion for the glitter of show business, much to poppa's disapproval, so Diamond takes off in search of a new life as a pop singer. He succeeds, and, in the end, even poppa joins in the standing ovation. Catlin Adams was cast as Diamond's wife, and Lucie Arnaz co-starred as the manager of a famous recording star (Paul Nicholas) and the woman Diamond leaves his wife for. As the aggrieved cantor Laurence Olivier (left, with Diamond) hammed it up in much the same way that Warner Oland did in the original 1927 version, with other roles in Jerry Leider's $15,000,000 production going to Franklyn Ajaye, Sully Boyar, Mike Kellin and Janet Brandt. It was written by Herbert Baker and Stephen H. Foreman (who, in one sequence, and true to the spirit of the original, had Diamond in blackface), and the director was Richard Fleischer. Songs: *You Baby Baby*; *Jerusalem*; *America* Neil Diamond; *Love On The Rocks*; *On The Robert E. Lee*; *Summer Love*; *Louise*; *Songs of Life* Diamond, Gilbert Becaud; *Hello Again* Diamond, Alan Lindgren; *Amazed And Confused* Diamond, Richard Bennett.

◁ A premeditated attempt on behalf of producer Allan Carr to recapture the lost innocence of MGM's youth-orientated musicals of the forties, **Can't Stop The Music** (EMI) updated the 'let's put on a show' formula, substituting a disco beat for swing, and Steve Guttenberg (as an aspiring composer) for Mickey Rooney. Valerie Perrine also appeared, as a top New York model, and Guttenberg's platonic best friend. The stars of the show, however, and its *raison d'être* were Village People (illustrated, with Perrine), who in the movie, are recruited by Perrine to help promote Guttenberg's music. In real life they are the creation of Jacques Morali who also wrote most of the film's music including (with lyricists Henry Belolo and Victor Willis) Village People's massive hit, 'Y.M.C.A.' The number was excitingly choreographed by Arlene Phillips, whose contribution to Carr's multi-million dollar box-office dud was its only saving grace. Nancy Walker, a veteran of three MGM musicals of the forties, directed a cast that included Tammy Grimes (wasted), Bruce Jenner, Paul Sand, Barbara Rush, Altovise Davis, June Havoc, The Ritchie Family, Hot Gossip, and Marilyn Sokol in the kind of ugly-duckling role so often played by Nancy Walker herself. It was written by Bronte Woodard and Allan Carr. Other songs and musical numbers: *Give Me a Break* Morali, Belolo, Ritchie Family; *The Sound of the City*; *Samantha*; *I'm A Singing Juggler*; *Sophistication* Morali, Belolo, Phil Hurtt; *Liberation*; *I Love You To Death*; *Can't Stop The Music* Morali, Belolo, Hurtt, Beauris Whitehead; *Magic Night*; *Milkshake* Morali, Belolo, Willis; *Macho Man* Morali, Belolo, Willis, Whitehead; *Danny Boy* Frederick E. Weatherly.

415

Eighties Musicals

Hal Ashby, Arthur Penn and Mike Nichols were ▷ all, at one time or another, set to direct **Popeye** (Paramount/Walt Disney), the live-action, all-singing, all-dancing version of the Famous E. C. Segar cartoon strip. And Dustin Hoffman and Lily Tomlin were tipped for the roles of the spinach-munching Popeye, and Olive Oyl. In the event, the director who finally saw the project through to completion was Robert Altman, and the stars were Robin Williams (right) and Shelley Duvall, both of whom did admirably in bringing their subjects to real life. The film itself – which had Popeye as a shipwrecked sailor arriving in the small harbour town of Sweethaven, saving Olive from marriage to Bluto, and finding both his long lost father and some hidden treasure – was less successful. While undoubtedly true in spirit and essence to the frantic knockabout style of the original cartoons, the overall effect when translated into live action was disquieting. And ear-pummellingly noisy. There were some nifty sight gags which every now and then bulldozed their way through the general tumult, but the movie might have been far more digestible had the Harry Nilsson songs been more tuneful. Ray Walston (left) appeared as Poopdeck Pappy and Paul Dooley as Wimpy, with other parts going to Richard Libertini, Donald Moffatt, MacIntyre Dixon, Roberta Maxwell and Donovan Scott. It was choreographed by Sahron Kinney, Lou Wills and Hovey Burgess, the latter responsible for Robin Williams' dances. Jules Feiffer scripted, and it was produced by Robert Evans. Songs and musical numbers: *I Yam What I Yam*; *He Needs Me*; *Swee' Pea's Lullaby*; *Sweethaven*; *Blow Me Down*; *Everything Is Food*; *Sailin'*; *It's Not Easy Being Me*; *He's Large*; *I'm Mean*; *Kids* Nilsson; *I'm Popeye The Sailor Man* Sam Lerner.

△
A great deal of hardware was sacrificed in the service of **The Blues Brothers** (Universal), a frenetic but entertaining musical farce which traced the violent misfortunes of the titular heroes (John Belushi, right, and Dan Aykroyd, left) as they attempt, after Belushi's release from jail, to re-establish their erstwhile musical combo by persuading its former members to jettison their present jobs and regroup themselves. It's anything but a smooth ride though, for the orgy of destruction unleashed by the Blues Boys wherever they go, puts them on practically every 'wanted' list in the state of Illinois. Messrs Belushi and Aykroyd (a sort of latter day Abbott and Costello), plus a supporting cast that included James Brown, Aretha Franklin, Kathleen Freeman, Carrie Fisher, John Candy, Henry Gibson, Steve Lawrence, Ray Charles, Twiggy, and Cab Calloway (singing his immortal 'Minnie The Moocher', which he wrote with Irving Mills) did wonders for Aykroyd and John Landis's knockabout screenplay. The storyline itself was straight out of the forties, but the language in

which it was couched belonged distinctly to the eighties; so did the zesty direction by Landis who, to judge from the number of cars that are destroyed in the film's 133 minutes, clearly bears a grudge against the motor industry. Carlton Johnson choreographed several lively but not particularly distinguished routines, and the producer was Robert K. Weiss. Songs and musical numbers: *She Caught The Katy* Taj Mahal, Yank Rachel; *Peter Gunn Theme* Henry Mancini; *Gimme Some Lovin'* Steve Winwood, Muff Winwood, Spencer Davis; *The Old Landmark* A.M. Brunner; *Quando, Quando, Quando* Tony Renis, A. Testa; *Boom Boom* John Lee Hooker; *Think* Aretha Franklin, Ted White; *Shake Your Tailfeathers* A and P and D and E Love, Z. Phillips, T. Judy; *Theme From Rawhide* Dimitri Tiomkin, Ned Washington; *Stand By Your Man* Tammy Wynette, Billy Sherill; *Can't Turn You Loose* Otis Redding; *Time Is Tight* Booker T; *Everybody Needs Somebody To Love* Jerry Wexler, Bert Berns, Solomon Burke; *Sweet Home Chicago* Woody Payne; *Jailhouse Rock* Jerry Leiber, Mike Stoller.

◁ Like *Can't Stop The Music*, **Xanadu** (Universal), which starred Olivia Newton-John (left) and Gene Kelly (centre), was a throwback to the Hollywood musical of the forties, its particular inspiration being Columbia's *Cover Girl* (1944), in which Kelly had also appeared. But with this casting duplication (in both films Kelly was called Danny McGuire) the similarities ended. Richard Christian Danus, Michael Kane and Marc Reid Rubel's mind-bogglingly inept fantasy also featured Michael Beck (right) as a frustrated artist who, while in the process of searching for a mysterious and beautiful muse (Newton-John) meets a wealthy but embittered clarinettist (Kelly – uneasy in the role) and persuades him to invest his money in a spectacular disco nightclub. With Gene on hand to appeal to the mums and dads, and Olivia to their children, **Xanadu's** producer Lawrence Gordon was clearly hedging his bets. The gamble, however, misfired (Olivia could hardly be called charismatic) and, apart from Kenny Ortega and Jerry ·Trent's lively staging of the musical numbers, the show was decidedly deficient in goodies. Sandra Katie Hanley, Fred McCarren and Ren Woods completed the cast (Coral Browne and Wilfrid Hyde-White's voices were heard in a fantasy sequence towards the end), and the director was Robert Greenwald. Songs and musical numbers: *I'm Alive*; *The Fall*; *Don't Walk Away*; *All Over The World* (sung by the Electric Light Orchestra) Jeff Lynne; *Xanadu* (Newton-John) Lynne; *Magic* (Newton-John); *Suddenly* (Newton-John, Cliff Richard); *Dancing* (Newton-John, The Tubes); *Suspended In Time* (Newton-John); *Whenever You're Away From Me* (Newton-John, Gene Kelly) John Farrar.

1981

Academy Awards

Writing (Screenplay) – adaptation
NOMINATIONS INCLUDED: *Pennies From Heaven*
(MGM) Dennis Potter

Costume Design
NOMINATIONS INCLUDED: *Pennies From Heaven*
Bob Mackie

Sound
NOMINATIONS INCLUDED: *Pennies From Heaven*
Michael J. Kohut, J.M. Harding, Richard
Tyler, Al Overton

△

Made in the UK, and not exactly a formula Hollywood musical, **The Great Muppet Caper** (ITC) nevertheless boasted the American creative talents of its successful predecessor, *The Muppet Movie* (ITC, 1979). The script (by Tom Patchett, Jay Tarses, Jerry Juhl and Jack Rose) placed Kermit the Frog, Fozzie Bear, and porcine superstar Miss Piggy in a Muppet extravaganza of jewel theft, grand passion and mistaken identity. Though enhanced by a series of droll movie parodies (notably an Esther Williams-style water ballet (illustrated) choreographed *à la* Busby Berkeley for Miss P), the narrative was sluggish, and few of the guest stars – who included Diana Rigg, Charles Grodin, John Cleese, Robert Morley, Peter Ustinov, Jack Warden and Peter Falk – managed to make much of an impression. Jim Henson, the original Muppeteer, directed competently if impersonally, the music and lyrics were by Joe Raposo, Anita Mann choreographed, and the film's producers were David Lazer and Frank Oz. Songs and musical numbers: *A Movie*; *The Big Bus*; *Happiness Hotel*; *Lady Holiday*; *Steppin' Out With A Star*; *The Apartment*; *Night Life*; *The First Time It Happens*; *Couldn't We Ride*; *Piggy's Fantasy ('Miss Piggy')*; *Homeward Bound*; *The Great Muppet Caper*; *a) The Heist b) The Muppet Fight Song c) Muppets To the Rescue*.
▽

A reworking by Dennis Potter of his successful British TV serial of the same name, **Pennies From Heaven** (MGM) switched locales from Britain to America but retained the period (the mid-thirties) of the original. All about a sheet-music salesman working in Depression-hit Chicago, the film took an extraordinarily bleak look at his dreary, workaday life and unsatisfactory marriage, and juxtaposed that bleakness with a fantasy existence – in which all the characters burst into song – inspired by the sunny lyrics he carried with him in his bag. It was a brilliant conception, brilliantly realised by director Herbert Ross, with the best moment of all occurring towards the end when the salesman, to escape the proliferating troubles that are befalling him (including a murder rap), slips into a cinema to see *Follow The Fleet* (RKO, 1936) and physically projects himself into the 'Let's Face The Music And Dance' (Irving Berlin) routine. The salesman was quite exceptionally well played by Steve Martin (centre), Jessica Harper was his love-shy wife, and Bernadette Peters the schoolteacher he meets on one of his trips, and with whom he has a serious affair. Also cast: Vernel Bagneris, John McMartin, John Karlen, Jay Garner, Robert Fitch, Tommy Rall and, in a special guest appearance, Christopher Walken, whose solo strip dance in a bar was one of the best things in this exciting and adult musical. It was produced by Herbert Ross and Nora Kaye, photographed by Gordon Willis, and choreographed with immense visual flair by Danny Daniels, who superimposed the actual songs of the period (sung by the artists who recorded them) over the action. Also contributing to the musical programme were Marvin Hamlisch, and Billy May who arranged and conducted most of the routines. As much a homage to the Hollywood musical as a salutary evocation of a grim period in America's history, **Pennies From Heaven** was sadly underrated on its release, played to poor business, and quickly disappeared from the circuits. Songs and musical numbers: *The Clouds Will Soon Roll By* Harry Woods, George Brown; *My Honey Says Yes* Con Conrad, Cliff Friend; *I'll Never Have To Dream Again* Isham Jones, Charles Newman; *Roll Along Prairie Moon* Ted Fiorito, Harry Macpherson, Albert Von Tilzer; *Did You Ever See A Dream Walking?* Mack Gordon, Harry Revel; *Pennies From Heaven* Johnny Burke, Albert Johnston; *It's The Girl* Abel Baer, Dave Oppenheim; *Love Is Good For Anything That Ails You* Cliff Friend, Matt Malneck; *Let's Put Out The Lights And Go To Sleep* Herman Hupfeld; *It's A Sin To Tell A Lie* Billy Mayhew; *I Want To Be Bad* Buddy De Sylva, Lew Brown, Ray Henderson; *Life Is Just A Bowl Of Cherries* Henderson, Brown; *Let's Misbehave* Cole Porter; *Serenade In The Night* Cesare A. Bixio, B. Cherubini, Jimmy Kennedy; *Fancy Our Meeting* Phil Charig, Joseph Meyer, Douglas Furber; *The Glory Of Love* Billy Hill.

1982

Academy Awards

Best Actress
NOMINATION: Julie Andrews *Victor/Victoria* (MGM)

Best Supporting Actress
NOMINATION: Lesley Ann Warren *Victor/Victoria*

Art Direction (Set Direction)
NOMINATION: Dale Hennesy; Marvin-March *Annie* (Columbia) Roger Maus, Tim Hutchinson and William Craig Smith; Harry Cordwell *Victor/Victoria*

Music (Song)
NOMINATION: John Williams, Alan and Marilyn Bergman 'If We Were In Love' *Yes, Giorgio* (MGM/UA)

Original Song Score And Its Adaptation or Adaptation Score
Leslie Bricusse and Henry Mancini *Victor/Victoria*
NOMINATION: Ralph Burns *Annie* (Rastar-Columbia)

Costume Design
NOMINATION: Patricia Norris *Victor/Victoria*

An anachronism redolent of the musicals assembled by *schmaltz* merchant Joe Pasternak for Mario Lanza in the fifties, **Yes, Giorgio** (MGM) was a major disaster. A vehicle for the overweight opera star Luciano Pavarotti (left), it was barely able to sustain its running time as it told the story of Giorgio Finzi, a world famous tenor who, while on a tour of the United States, falls in love with a beautiful throat specialist (Kathryn Harrold, right) after she treats him for a 'crisis of the voice'. Trouble is, she doesn't particularly like opera, and he's a married man with a family. A relationship of sorts does, however, develop (though not on a physical basis), but it is doomed, and the film ends unhappily with the lady doctor realising that Giorgio will never desert his family for another woman. It was such unadulterated piffle from start to finish, that even the operatic extracts failed to make it in any way palatable. Eddie Albert co-starred as Giorgio's manager, with other roles under Franklin J. Schaffner's blush-making direction going to Paola Borboni, James Hong, Beulah Quo, Norman Steinberg and Kathryn Fullen. Norman Steinberg wrote it (from a novel by Ann Piper) and Peter Fetterman produced. Songs and operatic arias: *If I Were In Love* Alan and Marilyn Bergman, John Williams; *Una Furtiva Lagrima* (from 'L'Elisir D'Amore') Donizetti; *La Donna E Mobile* (from 'Rigoletto') Verdi; *Cielo E Mar* (from 'La Gioconda') Ponchielli; *Donna Non Vidi Mai* (from 'Manon Lescaut') Puccini; *Nessun Dorma* (from 'Turandot') Puccini; *Ave Maria* Schubert; *O Sole Mio* Di Capua; *Santa Lucia* (traditional); *Mattinata* Leoncavallo; *Funiculi Funicula* Denza; *I Left My Heart In San Francisco* Douglass Cross, George Cory.

Rarely can a movie have been as misnamed as Francis Coppola's **One From the Heart** (American Zoetrope), a $30,000,000 *hommage* to the whole tradition of the musical. A huge and visually resplendent spectacle, it lacked for nothing except – like the Tin Man in *The Wizard Of Oz* (MGM, 1939) – a heart. Though the project originated from a wish on its director's part, after the budgetary and meteorological ordeal of his Vietnam War epic, *Apocalypse Now* (United Artists, 1979), to switch to a comedy-drama of modest dimensions, somewhere along the line its simple, over-familiar plot (a not-so-young estranged couple based in Las Vegas indulge in a little casual romancing on the side before their final reconciliation) got inflated out of existence. The four principals, played with varying degrees of charm by Frederic Forrest, Teri Garr, Raul Julia and Nastassia Kinski (illustrated), were lost in the vast expanses of Dean Tavoularis' admittedly stunning studio recreation of the gaudy Nevada resort; while Coppola seemed to have been too busy tinkering with all his wonderful new video technology (for which the movie was intended as a showcase) to bother with directing his actors. The dance numbers, reportedly supervised by Gene Kelly, were embarrassingly reminiscent of Peter Bogdanovich's *At Long Last Love* (20th Century-Fox, 1975), and the songs (by Tom Waits who, with Crystal Gale, also sang most of them), though intermittently tuneful, would more appropriately have graced a hotel lounge than a Hollywood musical. Armyan Bernstein was responsible for the story and screenplay, it was produced by Gray Frederickson and Fred Roos (executive producer Bernard Gersten), and featured Lainie Kazan and Harry Dean Stanton in support. All in all, the venture was a grossly squandered opportunity and an appalling waste of talent, whose failure was pounced upon by the critics and reflected at the box office where it registered as one of the most calamitous flops in screen history. Songs and musical numbers: *Once Upon A Town*; *The Wages Of Love*; *Is There Any Way Out Of This Dream?*; *Picking Up After You*; *Old Boyfriends*; *Broken Bicycles*; *I Beg Your Pardon*; *Little Boy Blue*; *The Tango* (instrumental); *Circus Girl* (instrumental); *You Can't Unring A Bell*; *This One's From The Heart*; *Take Me Home*; *Presents* (instrumental).

Eighties Musicals

Very much in the style of Ernst Lubitsch and Billy Wilder, Blake Edwards' **Victor/Victoria** (MGM/UA), a remake of a 1933 German UFA comedy called *Viktor Und Viktoria*, scintillated for all of its 133-minute running time. Set in Rodger Maus' sumptuous studio-bound Paris in 1934, it starred Julie Andrews as an impoverished chanteuse whose chance meeting in a bistro one snowy evening with an outrageously gay nightclub entertainer (Robert Preston), also down on his luck, soon leads to fame and fortune for them both. For Preston (centre left), having heard Miss Andrews audition at the very club from which he has recently been fired, has the brilliant notion of masquerading her as a man. Not just *any* man, but the world's greatest female impersonator. The ploy succeeds stunningly and, in no time at all, Miss Andrews alias Victor (centre right) becomes the toast of Gay Paree. There are problems, of course, and they come mainly in the shape of James Garner, a Chicago gangster who sees Miss Andrews' act and immediately falls in love with her, only to be shattered when he is assured that the 'she' is really a 'he'. Using this potentially farce-laden situation to maximum comic effect, Edwards'

breezy screenplay (conceived by Hans Hoemburg and originally scripted for the UFA version by Reinhold Schunzel) drew non-stop laughter and was especially remarkable in that most of the gags in it were repeated twice – and even three times – without the law of diminishing returns taking its toll. The film also carried a live-and-let-live message of sorts: that it is wrong to categorize people into sexual stereotypes. Paddy stone's dance routines did the Henry Mancini-Leslie Bricusse score proud, and were as witty as the screenplay into which they were skilfully sandwiched. Robert Preston's unrestrained performance as 'the old queen' was a joy, and there was a peach of a characterization from Lesley Ann Warren (whose number, 'Chicago Illinois' was one of the highspots) as Garner's sex-pot moll. Alex Karras was featured as Garner's bodyguard, and the rest of the cast included John Rhys-Davies, Peter Arne, Sherloque Tanney and Graham Stark. Blake Edwards and Tony Adams produced. Other songs and musical numbers: *Crazy World*; *You And Me*; *The Shady Dame From Seville*; *Alone In Paris* (instrumental); *King's Can-Can* (instrumental); *Le Jazz Hot*; *Cat And Mouse* (instrumental); *Gay Paree*. ▷

◁ The main trouble with **Annie** (Columbia) – 'the movie of Tomorrow' as its slogan proclaimed – was director John Huston's total inability to perceive the material in musical comedy terms. Daunted, no doubt, by the gargantuan $35 million budget allocated by producer Ray Stark, Huston had little choice but to deliver a 'big event', and the same kind of unwieldy, top-heavy elephantiasis that afflicted Sidney Lumet's *The Wiz* (Universal, 1978) was very much in evidence throughout this disappointing occasion. Also contributing to the film's leaden texture was the insensitive way in which the dance numbers were photographed and edited. The musical sequences were created by executive producer Joe Layton, but staged and choreographed by Arlene Phillips, so it was difficult to know precisely at whose feet to lay the blame. After a nationwide search of Scarlett O'Hara proportions, a 10-year-old girl named Aileen Quinn (right) from Pennsylvania was chosen to play the part of little orphan Annie, the other major roles going to a less comfortably cast Albert Finney (left) as Daddy Warbucks, and to the vivacious Carol Burnett as Miss Hannigan, a fool-proof part if ever there was one. Ann Reinking was wasted as billionaire Warbucks' secretary; nor was justice done to the talents of Tim Curry, Bernadette Peters and Geoffrey Holder. It was written by Carol Sobieski, who found places for four songs (music by Charles Strouse, lyrics by Martin Charnin) that were not in the original Broadway show. Songs and musical numbers included: *Maybe*; *It's A Hard-Knock Life*; *I Think I'm Gonna Like It Here*; *Tomorrow*; *Easy Street*; *You're Never Fully Dressed Without A Smile*; *Little Girls*; *I Don't Need Anything But You*.

When Paramount's 1977 hit *Grease*, took a mammoth $96 million at the box office to become one of the most successful musicals in Hollywood's history (and one of the ten top money-making films of all time) a sequel was inevitable. **Grease 2** was its title, and it in no way equalled the pulling power of its energetic predecessor. Not only was it five years too late, but leading players Maxwell Caulfield (right, from Britain) and Michelle Pfeiffer (left) lacked the box-office clout of John Travolta and Olivia Newton-John, the stars of the first version. Add to this a virtually plotless screenplay (in which Pfeiffer's predilection for leather-clad bikers forces new boy Caulfield to prove himself in this area) and the reasons for the public's lack of enthusiasm become apparent. The film's saving grace was director/choreographer Patricia Birch's lively dance routines, particularly the one set in a bowling alley. Adrian Zmed, Christopher McDonald, Peter Frechette, Leif Green and Lorna Luft (centre) were in it too; so were Tab Hunter, and old-timers Eve Arden, Sid Caesar and Dody Patterson. Ken Finkleman wrote it, and it was produced by Robert Stigwood and Allan Carr. Songs and musical numbers: *Back to School Again*; *Who's That Guy?*; *(Love Will) Turn Back The Hands Of Time* Louis St Louis, Howard Greenfield; *Charaders* St Louis, Michael Gibson; *Girl For All Seasons*; *Rock-A-Hula Luau (Summer Is Coming)* Dominic Bugatti, Frank Musker; *Score Tonight* Bugatti, Musker, St Louis; *Prowlin'* Bugatti, Musker, Christopher Cerf; *Brad* Cerf; *Reproduction*; *Cool Rider* Dennis Linde; *We'll Be Together* Bob Morrison, Johnny MacRae; *Do It For Our Country* Rob Hegel; *Our Day Will Come* Bob Hilliard, Mort Garson; *Rebel Walk* Duane Eddy, Lee Hazlewood.

▽

1983

Academy Awards

Cinematography
NOMINATION: Don Peterman *Flashdance*
(Paramount)

Art Direction (Set Decoration)
NOMINATION: Roy Walker and Leslie
Tomkins; Tessa Davies *Yentl* (MGM)

Music
Giorgio Moroder, Keith Forsey, Irene Cara
'Flashdance. . . . What a Feeling' *Flashdance*
NOMINATIONS: Michael Sembello, Dennis
Matkosky 'Maniac' *Flashdance* Michel
Legrand, Alan and Marilyn Bergman 'Papa
Can You Hear Me?' and 'The Way He Makes
Me Feel' *Yentl*

Original Song Score or Adaptation Score
NOMINATION: Michel Legrand, Alan and
Marilyn Bergman *Yentl*

Although more than just a filmed version of the
New York Shakespeare Festival production of
The Pirates Of Penzance (Universal), director
Wilford Leach's adaptation left audiences in no
doubt that the entertainment they were watch-
ing owed more to the stage than to the screen.
With the exception of Angela Lansbury (as
Ruth), Leach's principal players were the ones
he had assembled for the Broadway production
and included a boisterous Kevin Kline as the
Pirate King, Linda Ronstadt as Mabel, George
Rose as the very model of a Major-General, Rex
Smith as the love-struck Frederic, and the
gloriously eccentric, rubber-limbed Tony Azito
as the Sergeant. Leach, who also fashioned the
screenplay from Gilbert and Sullivan's peren-
nially popular D'Oyle Carte operetta, took a
delightfully irreverent approach to the work,
and, like set designer Elliott Scott and choreographer Graciela Daniele, knew just how far to
go without nudging the enterprise into dis-
respectful caricature. The music was adapted,
orchestrated and conducted by William Elliott,
it was filmed at Shepperton Studios in England
and the producer was Joseph Papp.

△

Barbra Streisand co-produced (with Rusty
Lemorande), co-wrote (with Jack Rosenthal),
directed and starred in **Yentl** (MGM/UA), a
labour of love set in Poland, 1904, and all about
the problems faced by a young Jewish woman
whose one desire in life is to become a Talmudic
scholar – an occupation practised only by males.
In order not to offend tradition she crops her
hair, dresses as a boy, and enters a Yeshiva. Her
deception cues the inevitable complications and
soon Yentl, now called Anschul, falls in love
with fellow student Avigdor (Mandy Patinkin),
who is engaged to Hadass (Amy Irving) and
unaware that Anschul is really a woman. When
Hadass decides to break off her engagement to
Avigdor she complicates the situation further by
falling in love with Yentl/Anschul. The story
(based on Isaac Bashevis Singer's *Yentl, The
Yeshiva Boy*) ends with Yentl deciding to take a
boat for America in order to continue her studies
in the New World. Streisand's dynamic central
performance made suspension of disbelief that
much easier, while Patinkin and Irving did the
best they could considering the movie was very
much a show-case for its star/director. In
supporting roles, though, Nehemiah Persoff (as
Yentl's father), Steven Hill, Allan Corduner,
Bernard Spear, Doreen Mantle, Lynda Baron,
Ruth Goring and David DeKeyser didn't stand a
chance. The film was shot on location in
Czechoslovakia (and at Lee International in
England) and photographed by David Watkin.
Most of the nine Michel Legrand-Alan and
Marilyn Bergman songs (all performed by Strei-
sand) were sung "internally" as voice-overs.
They were: *No Matter What Happens*; *A Piece Of
Sky*; *This Is One Of Those Moments*; *Tomorrow
Night*; *Where Is It Written*; *The Way He Makes Me
Feel*; *No Wonder*; *Pappa Can You Hear Me?*; *Will
Someone Ever Look At Me That Way?*

▽

An enormous money-maker, **Flashdance** (Paramount) cashed in on the aerobics-as-dance craze to tell the simple, if not simple-minded tale of a pretty young welder (the shapely Jennifer Beales) who works in a Pittsburgh mill, and who, by night can be found dancing erotically in a local workingmen's club. Though sexy pelvic thrusts are all very well, Beales wants to become a serious ballerina and her ambition is encouraged by her foreman boyfriend (Michael Nouri). After a few obligatory romantic misunderstandings Beales successfully auditions for a place in the ballet school – and even gets her man. It was written by Tom Hedley and Joe Esterhas (story by Hedley) whose undemanding screenplay furnished roles for Lila Skala, Sunny Johnson, Kyle T. Heffner, Lee Ving and Ron Karabatsos. Marine Jahan (uncredited) was Ms Beales's stand-in for most of the dance sequences, it was produced by Don Simpson and Jerry Bruckheimer, choreographed by Jeffrey Hornaday, and flashily directed by Adrian Lyne whose eye for a striking angle and the effective jump-cut helped imbue the film with a spurious sense of movement and excitement. Songs and musical extracts included: *Prélude À L'Après-Midi D'Un Faune* Claude Debussy; *Resolution* Jacques Noel; *Adagio For Strings* Albinoni; *Imagination* Michael Boddicker, Jerry Hey, Phil Ramone, Michael Sembello; *Gloria* Giancarlo Bigazzi, Umberto Tozzi, Trevor Veitch; *Flashdance . . . What a Feeling* Giorgio Moroder, Keith Forsey, Irene Cara; *I'll Be Here Where The Heart Is* Kim Carnes, Duane Hitchings; *Seduce Me Tonight, Lady, Lady, Lady,* Moroder, Forsey; and *Manhunt* Doug Cotler, Richard Gilbert.

At the insistence of director Sylvester Stallone, John Travolta underwent a crash course in body-building for his role as Tony Manero in **Staying Alive** (Paramount), a lustreless sequel to *Saturday Night Fever* (Paramount, 1977). Body-heat alas, wasn't enough to generate the kind of box-office heat the studio was hoping for six years after Travolta first strutted his stuff to the happy tune of $200 million. A backstage yarn concocted by Stallone and Norman Wexler (based on characters created by Nik Cohn) it was a yawnsome affair in which Travolta, having left the discos of Brooklyn, now finds himself in the chorus of a new Broadway musical called *Satan's Alley*. Talent, however, will out, and after the show's male lead proves incapable, Travolta auditions for the role and, against the wishes of leading lady Finola Hughes (with whom he has had a one-night stand) is successful. The show is a hit and climaxes with Travolta literally pushing Hughes aside and hogging the limelight in the big solo spot. Cynthia Rhodes provided the romantic interest despite the fact that the most conspicuous love affair on view was the one Travolta seemed to be having with his well-honed body. Steve Inwood, Julie Bovasso (as Mrs. Manero), Charles Ward, and Steve Bickford also appeared; it was produced by Stallone and Robert Stigwood and choreographed by Dennon Rawles and Sayhber Rawles. Songs included: *The Woman In You; I Love You Too Much, Breakout, Someone Belongs To Someone, Life Goes On, Stayin' Alive* Barry Gibb, Maurice Gibb, Robin Gibb; *Devils and Seducers* Gari Wright, Dori Wright; *Far From Over*, Frank Stallone, Vince DiCola; and *Finding Out The Hard Way* Frank Stallone, Roy Freeland.

1984

Academy Awards

Art Direction (Set Direction)
NOMINATION: Richard Sylbert, George Graines
The Cotton Club (Zoetrope/Orion)

Music (Song)
NOMINATION: Kenny Loggins, Dean Pitchford
'Footloose' *Footloose* (Paramount) Dean
Pitchford and Tom Snow 'Let's Hear It For
The Boy' *Footloose*

Original Song Score
NOMINATION: Jeffrey Moss *The Muppets Take
Manhattan* (Tri-Star) Kris Kristofferson
Songwriter (Tri-Star)

Writer Dean Pitchford went back about three
decades for **Footloose** (Paramount), a pleasant
enough trifle that took the industry by surprise
and grossed a walloping $34 million. Needing
the assistance of a strong magnifying glass, its
plot told of a young Chicagoan (Kevin Bacon,
top-starred) who moves to a small town in the
Mid-West and discovers that its fundamentalist
minister (John Lithgow, perfectly cast) won't
allow dancing in the town as he believes that it is
a pursuit of the devil and leads to all kinds of
unsavoury activities. How the enterprising
Bacon succeeds in rectifying the situation and,
in the process, gets the girl (Lori Singer) comprised the mirage-like content of Pitchford's
screenplay. It did, however, give the appealing
Mr. Bacon and some of the younger members of
the cast a marvellous excuse to dance it up
(choreography by Lynne Taylor-Corbett) – not
that they needed one as the movie was predi-
cated on nothing else. Dianne Wiest was in it
too; so were Christopher Penn, Sarah Jessica

Parker, John Laughlin, Elizabeth Gorcey and, as
Bacon's mother, Frances Lee McCain. It was
produced by Lewis J. Rachmil and Craig Zadan,
and breezily directed by Herbert Ross. Songs
included: *Footloose, I'm Free* Kenny Loggins,
Dean Pitchford; *Let's Hear It For The Boy,
Somebody's Eyes* Pitchford, Tom Snow; *The Girl
Gets Around* Pitchford, Sammy Hagar; *Dancing
In The Streets* Pitchford, Bill Wolfer; *Almost
Paradise* Pitchford, Eric Carmen; *Never* Pitchford,
Michael Gore; *Holding Out For A Hero* Pitchford,
Jim Steinman.

A triumph of stylization over content **Streets Of
Fire** (Universal), described by its director, Walter
Hill, as 'comic book in orientation, mock-epic in
structure, movie heroic in acting style, operatic
in visual style, and cowboy-cliche in dialogue'
was a rock'n'roll fable set in 'another time,
another place'. It was also a paper-thin concoction, redolent of the 1950s, whose sorry excuse
for a plot finds rock star Diane Lane kidnapped
while performing on stage by Raven (Willem
DaFoe) and a motorcycle gang called The
Bombers. Enter Lane's ex-boyfriend (Michael
Pare) and, for a sum of $10,000 offered by her
current beau (Rick Moranis), agrees to rescue
her. Accompanying him on his mission is Amy
Madigan, a hardened ex-soldier he has
befriended. An amalgam in mood and visual
style of *The Warriors* (Paramount, 1979), *Escape
From New York* (Avco, 1981), *Blade Runner*
(Warner Bros. 1982) and *One From The Heart*
(Zoetrope, 1982), the film looked great (it was
shot on Universal's backlot) but had nothing to
say that lifted it out of the realms of an expensive
rock video. It was produced by Lawrence Gordon
and Joel Silver, written by Hill and Larry Gross,
photographed by Andrew Laszlo (the real star of
the show) and choreographed by Jeffrey Hornaday. Also featured were Deborah Van Valken-
burgh, Richard Lawson, Rick Rossvich, Lee
Ving, and, briefly as a stripper, Marine Jahan,
who, uncredited, did Jennifer Beales's dancing in
Flashdance (Paramount, 1983). Diane Lane's
vocals were dubbed by Laurie Sargent. Songs
included: *Tonight Is What It Means To Be Young,
Nowhere Fast* Jim Steinman; *Get Out Of Denver*
Bob Seger; *Hold That Snake, You Got What You
Wanted* Ry Cooder, Jim Dickinson; *One Bad Stud*
Jerry Leiber, Mike Stoller; *Blue Shadows* Dave
Alvin; *Sorcerer* Stevie Nicks; *Never Be You* Tom
Petty, Benmont Tench; *First Love First Tears*
Duane Eddy, Lee Hazlewood.

It was no masterpiece, heaven knows, yet Francis Coppola's **The Cotton Club** (Zoetrope/Orion) was infinitely better than *One From The Heart* (Zoetrope/Columbia, 1982) his previous excursion into musical territory. Though its chequered and well-documented pre-production history could, in all probability, have furnished Coppola with a better story than the one he devised with William Kennedy and Mario Puzo (screenplay by Kennedy and Coppola, inspired by a pictorial history by James Haskins), what he finally settled on was a sprawling four-in-one tale that married New York's criminal under-world (circa 1928) to the jazz milieu of Harlem. Richard Gere shouldered the main burden of the plot as Dixie Dwayne, a cornet player whose career is given a boost when he saves a racketeer from a gunman's bullet. Turns out the grateful customer is none other than beer baron Dutch Schultz (James Remar), who shows his gratitude by entrusting his unfaithful girlfriend (an under-cast Diane Lane) to his care. He also hire's Gere's brother (Nicolas Cage) to be his bodyguard. In tandem with Gere's escalating fortunes is a plot

involving two black dancers (Gregory and Maurice Hines), one of whom (Gregory) has his eye on chorus girl Lonette McKee. But as the narrative threads become entangled even further, they choke much of the movie's dramatic impact. Still, as a homage to the gangster flicks of the 1930s (especially as purveyed by Warner Bros.) and as a nostalgic recreation of a golden-age in jazz, the film was not without quality. It did, however, suffer from the musical equivalent of *coitus interruptus*; i.e. Coppola's perverse refusal to allow the many production numbers to reach their climaxes. He was so busy cutting away from them in order to further the various plots, the impression conveyed was that his interest in the musical programme was perfunctory, to say the least. A pity, as the assembled song-and-dance talent was the film's most potent calling-card, two highlights being *Minnie The Moocher* (Cab Calloway, Irving Mills) sung by Larry Marshall as Calloway, and Ted Kohler and Harold Arlen's *Ill Wind* sung by Lonette McKee. Bob Hoskins played a nightclub owner and gangland peacemaker, with other roles going to

Allen Garfield, Gwen Verdon (in the small role of Gere's mother), Julian Beck, Larry Fishburne, Tom Waits, Wynonna Smith, Charles (Honi) Coles, Joe Dallesandro (as Lucky Luciano) and Woody Strode. Robert Evans produced, and the musical numbers were staged by Michael Smuin, Henry Le Tang, Gregory Hines, Claudia Asbury, George Faison, Arthur Mitchell, and Michael Meacham. Songs included: *Creole Love Call* Duke Ellington; *Bandana Babies* Dorothy Fields, Jimmy McHugh; *Lady With The Fan* Cab Calloway, Jeanne Burns, Al Brackman; *Jitterbug* Ed Swayze, Cab Calloway, Irving Mills; *Creole Rhapsody, Hot And Bothered, Black Beauty, Daybreak Express, Wall Street Wail, Slippery Horn, High Life* Duke Ellington; *Diga Diga Doo, Doin' the New Lowdown* Dorothy Fields, Jimmy McHugh; *Stormy Weather, Trickeration*, Ted Koehler, Harold Arlen; *Aint Misbehavin'*, Fats Waller, Andy Razaf, Harry Brooks; *Am I Blue?* Grant Clark, Harry Akst; *Mood Indigo*, Duke Ellington, Irving Mills, Albany 'Barney' Bigard; *Truckin'* Ted Kohler, Rube Bloom; *Copper Colored Gal* Benny Davis, J. Fred Coots.
▽

Grand Master Melle Mel and The Furious Five, Afrika Bambaata, Soul Sonic Force, Shango, Icy Ice, Cosmic Pop, Rock Steady Crew, Flip Rock, Buck Four and Fast Break were just a few of the groups featured in **Beat Street** (Orion), a rap and breakdance musical that exploited – in the most acceptable sense of the word – the current craze from the South Bronx. Words took second place to music on this jolly occasion, the screenplay by Andy Davis, David Gilbert and Paul Golding (story by Steve Hager) being a mere trifle about a rap disc jockey (Guy Davis, son of Ossie Davis and Ruby Dee), his dancer brother (Robert Taylor) and the college music major (Rae Dawn Chong, daughter of Tommy) who, for different reasons, takes an interest in both of them. A secondary plot involved the domestic tribulations of a Puerto Rican subway-train graffiti artist (Jon Chardiet) and his girlfriend Carmen (Saundra Santiago). The movie climaxed at the Roxy roller disco in downtown Manhattan and

was a joyous celebration of expression through dance. Though influenced by such youth-orientated successes as *Fame* (MGM, 1980) *Wild Style* (Independent, 1983), *Flashdance* (Paramount, 1983) and even *West Side Story* (United Artists, 1961), **Beat Street** had its own energy and was as much a sociological document as it was an entertainment. It was choreographed by Lester Wilson of the New York City Breakers, Michael Holman (Magnificent Force) and Julie Fraad, produced by David V. Picker and Harry Belafonte, and directed by Stan Lathan. Songs and musical numbers included: *Baptise The Beat* Michael Murphy, David Frank; *Beat Street Breakdown* Melvin Glover, Reggie Griffin; *Stranger In a Strange Land* Jack Holmes; *Beat Street Strut* Eumir Deodato, Alan Palanker, Milton G. Barnes, Katreese Barnes; *Us Girls* Ross Levinson, Debora Hooper; *This Could Be The Night* Arthur Baker, Tina B. Evan, Carl Sturken, Chris Lord-Alge, and *Breakers Revenge* Arthur Baker.
▷

Eighties Musicals

Made in a hurry to cash in on the breakdance ▷ craze (it began shooting in February and was released in May), **Breakin'** (G.B. **Breakdance**) (MGM/UA), written by Charles Parker, Allen DeBevoise and Gerald Scaife, relocated the craze from New York to Los Angeles, and, ignoring the fact that this form of expression belonged primarily to young, male, working-class blacks, chose a middle-class white heroine (Lucinda Dickey). She's a serious student of the dance who, when we first meet her, dislikes her lecherous dance-master (Ben Lokey) as well as her job as a waitress. The quality of her life changes, however, when a young gay friend (Phineas Newborn III) introduces her to two well-known L.A. street dancers (Michael 'Boogaloo Shrimp' Chambers and Adolfo 'Shabba-Doo' Quinones). She joins them, becomes a natural breakdancer, and ends up in a Broadway show. Though the influences of both *Flashdance* and *Staying Alive* (Paramount, 1983), were all too obvious, the film managed to stand, or rather dance, on its own feet most effectively, credit for which must go to its leading trio of performers and to choreographer Jaime Rogers. Allen DeBevoise and David Zito produced, Joel Silberg directed, and the songs and musical numbers included: *Tibetan Jam, Reckless* David Storrs, Tracey 'Ice-T' Morrow; *Heart Of The Beat* Dan Hartman, Charlie Midnight; *Breakin' . . . There's No Stoppin' Us, Street People* Ollie E. Brown, Jerry Night; *Showdown* Ollie E. Brown, Joe Curiale; *99½* Joe Footman, Maxie Anderson.

△

Little more than a tired reworking of such classic 'hey, kids, let's put on a show!' musicals such as *Babes in Arms* (MGM, 1939) and *Babes On Broadway* (MGM, 1941), **The Muppets Take Manhattan** (Tri-Star) was a disappointment that pleased neither the youngsters at whom it was aimed, nor, for that matter, their parents. The screenplay, devised by Frank Oz, Tom Patchett and Jay Tarses (story by Patchett and Tarses) found Kermit and the gang staging a show called 'Manhattan Melodies' at Danhurst College, the success of which convinces them that it is good enough to take to Broadway. Their attempts to reach The Great White Way provided the plot as well as cameo spots for Joan Rivers (as a Big Apple cosmetician), Liza Minnelli, Art Carney,

James Coco, Dabney Coleman, Gregory Hines, Linda Lavin, Elliot Gould, Brooke Shields, John Landis, Vincent Sardi, Francis Bergen and even Mayor Ed Koch. As usual Jim Henson was the voice of Kermit, Frank Oz vocalized for Miss Piggy/Fozzie/Animal, Dave Gould was Gonzo/Rat/Chester/Zoot, and Richard Hunt Scooter/Janice/Statler. Other roles went to Julianna Donald, Lonny Price and Louis Zorich. The rats' kitchen number was choreographed by Chris Chadman, Ralph Burns wrote the score, it was produced by David Lazar and directed by Frank Oz. Jeff Moss wrote the songs and they included *Together Again, You Can't Take No For An Answer, Saying Goodbye* and the nursery dream sequence *I'm Gonna Always Love You.*

Willie Nelson and Kris Kristofferson starred in and wrote the songs for **Songwriter** (Tri-Star) an amiable musical drama in which they played characters loosely based on themselves. Nelson (*sans* beard in the opening scenes) was top-billed as Doc Jenkins, the *numero uno* of Country music; while Kristofferson was Blackie Buck, a likeable rebel destined never to settle down but who comes to Nelson's rescue after he is fleeced by an opportunistic music publisher called Rodeo Rocky (Richard C. Sarafian). Melinda Dillon and Rhonda Dotson appeared as Nelson's estranged wife and daughter respectively. Rip Torn was in it too – as a music promoter – so was Lesley Ann Warren – as Gilda, one of Nelson's (alcoholic) singing discoveries. It was produced by Sydney Pollack, written by Bud Shrake and directed by Alan Rudolph. Songs included: *How Do You Feel About Foolin' Around, Songwriter, Who'll Buy My Memories, Write Your Own Songs, Nobody Said It Was Going To Be Easy* Willie Nelson; *Eye Of The Storm, Crossing The Border, Down To Her Socks, Under The Gun, Final Attraction* Kris Kristofferson.

The indecent haste in which *Breakin'* was made and released was echoed in the equally record-breaking time it took producer Menahem Golan and Yoram Globus to cash in on its popularity with a sequel **Breakin' 2: Electric Boogaloo** (G.B. **Breakdance 2-Electric Boogaloo**) (Cannon-Tri-Star). Though rooted very much in the contemporary world of street-dancing, Jan Ventura and Julia Reichert's screenplay (based on characters created by Charles Parker and Allen DeBevoise) went back to the 1930s for the storyline that underpinned the main business of the entertainment – i.e. its dancing. Carrying on where *Breakin'* ended, we learn that Messrs Adolfo 'Shabba-Doo' Quinones and Michael 'Boogaloo Shrimp' Chambers, in company with Lucinda Dickey did not take the Big Apple by storm and are back in Los Angeles. Dickey has returned to the bosom of her wealthy parents (Jo de Winter and John Christy Ewing) who would like her to study law at Princeton; while Chambers and Quinones are running a youth-club, called Miracles, in East Los Angeles. Complications intrude in the shape of a real-estate developer

(Peter MacLean) who plans to build a shopping mall on the site of the club unless $200,000 can be raised in 30 days. So, doing exactly what Judy Garland and Mickey Rooney would have done four decades earlier, the protagonists decide to turn all of East Los Angeles into a mammoth stage and put on a show. It's a success and all concerned live happily ever after – including Golan-Globus whose modest investment showed many happy returns. Aided by Bill Goodson's energetic, high-octane choreography, Quinones was terrific in an effective mating number as well as a routine high above the city. The film's Capra-esque message? That miracles really *can* happen. Sam Firstenberg directed, and the songs included: *Stylin'*, *Radiotron* Ollie E. Brown, Jerry Knight, Attala Z. Giles; *Electric Boogaloo* Brown, Giles, Russ Regan; *Spice* Brown, Knight; *Action* Brown, Knight, Giles; *Physical Clash* Brown, Johnny Burton; *Believe In The Beat* Layng Martine, Brown, Sylvester L. River; *Gotta Have The Money* Jimmy George; *When I.C.U.* Brown, Giles, Knight; *Go Off* David Storrs, Tracey 'Ice-T' Morrow. ▷

△
24 year-old rock-'n'-roll star Prince made his big screen debut in the misogynistic **Purple Rain** (Warner Bros.) playing a manic-depressive singer called The Kid. Set in Minneapolis, Minnesota, Albert Magnoli and William Blinn's screenplay (with its many semi-biographical touches *vis à vis* its star) tells of the twin rivalry between Prince's band – called The Revolution – and a group called The Time, lead by Morris Day; as well as the rivalry between Prince and Day for the love of a newcomer to the town (and would-be star) called Appolonia (Appolonia Kotero). Prince offers her his love and a rather sadistic temperament inherited from his drunken, failed

musician father (Clarence Williams III); Day promises her a job with his band. In the end Appolonia not only succeeds professionally, but after a brief liaison with the over-amorous Day finds romance with a reformed Prince, whose unpleasant father has, in the meantime, shot himself after a particularly violent domestic fracas. A coterie of Prince's real-life friends helped swell the cast, most of them retaining their own names. They included Jerome Benton, Billy Sparks, Jill Jones, Dez Dickerson, Charles Huntsberry, Brenda Bennett and Susan Moonsie. The concert sequences, stunningly photographed by Donald Thorin and strikingly lit by

LeRoy Bennett, gave the movie its special appeal and provided adequate compensation for the overall lack of humour in the enterprise – despite a version of Abbott and Costello's vintage 'Who's On First?' routine performed by Day and Benton. The producers were Robert Cavallo, Joseph Ruffalo and Steven Fargnoli. Albert Magnoli's streamlined direction kept the accent squarely on youth. Songs included: *Let's Go Crazy, Purple Rain, When Doves Cry*, Darling Nikki; *Would Die 4 U, Baby I'm A Star* Prince; *Sex Shooter* Appolonia and The Starr Company; *Jungle Love The Bird* Morris Day, Jess Johnson, *Modernaire* Dez Dickerson; *Father's Song* John L. Nelson.

1985

Academy Awards

Best Sound
NOMINATION: Donald C. Mitchell, Michael Minkler, Gerry Humphrey, Chris Newman *A Chorus Line* (EMI-Polygram)

Best Song
Lionel Ritchie 'Say You, Say Me' *White Nights* (Columbia)
NOMINATION: Stephen Bishop 'Separate Lives' *White Nights* Marvin Hamlish, Edward Kleban 'Surprise, Surprise' *A Chorus Line*

Best Film Editing
NOMINATION: John Bloom *A Chorus Line*

△

△

Too little, too late might be the most appropriate way to sum up **Fast Forward** (Columbia), yet another tired replay of MGM's *Strike Up The Band* (1940) in which a motley collection of talented youngsters fetch up in the Big Apple and, in a matter of a couple of weeks, find success. In John Patrick Vetch's insubstantial production, eight teenagers from a racially mixed high-school in Ohio decide to audition for a New York-based show called 'The Big Showdown'. After finding themselves stranded when their one contact dies, they resourcefully meet all the challenges New York flings their way and manage to give a teriffic account of themselves. Though the dancing was first-class, the acting wasn't; neither was Richard Wesley's cosy screenplay (story by Timothy March). It was wholesomely directed by Sidney Poitier – which was the best that could be said for it. Irene Worth had fun playing a veteran agent who emerges from the woodwork to help the group on its way and the rest of the unknown cast included John Scott Clough, Don Franklin, Tamara Mark, Tracy Silver, Gretchen F. Palmer, Monique Cintron and Debra Varnado. Songs included *Long As We Believe* Preston Glass, Narada Michael Warden, Walter Afanaisieff, Tom Bahler, Siedah Garrett; *Fast Forward* Brock Walsh, Bahler, John Van Tongeren, Bunny Hull; *How Do You Do?* Walsh, Mark Vieha; *Pretty Girl* Jeff Scott; *Mystery* Rusty Anderson; *Curves* Glass, Walden; *Showdown* Jellybean, Toni C., Stephen Bray; *Do You Want It Right Now?* China Burton, Nick Straker; *Taste* Swanson, Garrett.

Another bumper compendium of clips from (mainly) MGM's incomparable musical archives. **That's Dancing!** (MGM), concentrated, as its title suggested, on the terpsichorean achievements of a handful of Hollywood dancers and choreographers including Gene Kelly, Fred Astaire, Ginger Rogers, Eleanor Powell, Bill Robinson, Busby Berkeley, James Cagney, Carol Haney, Ann Miller, Shirley MacLaine, Mikhail Baryshnikov, Debbie Reynolds, Bob Fosse, Ray Bolger, Jacques D'Amboise – but not, alas, Gene Nelson. A rather banal commentary by director Jack Haley Jr was a small price to pay for some of the goodies on offer, and although by no means definitive, the survey, which was divided into several sections, sped by painlessly enough. Gene Kelly introduced The Berkeley Years and The Future, Sammy Davis talked about the Great Stylists, Ray Bolger was on hand to guide us through The Golden years of the Movie Musical, while Liza Minnelli introduced the best of Broadway. David Niven Jr and Haley co-produced, and the title song was by Henry Mancini, Larry Grossman and Ellen Fitzhugh. The many extracts included sequences from *Show Of Shows* (Warner Bros. 1929), *Flying High* (MGM, 1931), *42nd Street* (Warner Bros. 1933), *Dames* (Warner Bros. 1934), *Roberta* (RKO, 1935), *The Gay Divorcée* (RKO, 1934), *Broadway Melody of 1936* (MGM, 1935), *The Littlest Rebel* (20th Century-Fox, 1936), *Down Argentine Way* (20th Century-Fox, 1941), *The Wizard Of Oz* (MGM, 1939), *Honolulu* (MGM, 1938), *The Harvey Girls*

(MGM, 1945), *The Hollywood Revue of 1929* (MGM, 1929), *The Red Shoes* (London Films, 1948), *Carousel* (20th Century-Fox, 1956), *Royal Wedding* (MGM, 1951), *Singin' In The Rain* (MGM, 1952), *Invitation To The Dance* (MGM, 1954), *Yankee Doodle Dandy* (Warner Bros. 1942), *Silk Stockings* (MGM, 1957), *Kiss Me Kate* (MGM, 1953), and *Fame* (MGM, 1980).

Ballet dancer Mikhail Baryshnikov was given his first starring role in **White Nights** (Columbia), directed by Taylor Hackford. In this hokey but enjoyable entertainment, he played a Russian defector who, while on a dance tour of Europe, crash-lands in Siberia and finds himself back in the country he risked everything to flee. Naturally, the KGB are delighted and do their best to see that he remains. In order to achieve this, a KGB official (director Jerzy Skolimowski) has Baryshnikov billeted with an American tap-dancer (Gregory Hines) who defected behind the Iron Curtain during the Vietnam war, in the hope that the American will persuade the Russian not to leave the old country. But just the reverse happens and the two men, aided by Baryshnikov's former lover (Helen Mirren), plan an elaborate escape to the U.S.A. Just how this is achieved provided James Goldman and Eric Hughes' screenplay with its extremely far-fetched climax. Before the great escape, however, both Baryshnikov and Hines were given several opportunities to do what they do best and they did so (especially Baryshnikov in Roland Petit's 'Le Jeune Homme et la Mort') most effectively. Beautiful Isabella Rossellini was featured as Hines's wife, while Geraldine Page brought her usual authority to the role of Baryshnikov's aggressive agent. John Glover, Stefan Gryff, Shane Rimmer and William Hootkins were also featured. Twyla Tharp and Baryshnikov choreographed, and Hackford and William S. Gilmore produced. Songs included: *Say You Say Me* Lionel Richie; *Separate Lives* Stephen Bishop; *The Other Side Of The World* Michael Rutherford, B.A. Robertson; *People On A String* Michel Colombier, Kathy Wakefield; *My Love Is Chemical* Walt Aldridge; *Snake Charmer* John Hiatt; *Prove Me Wrong* James Newton Howard, David Pack; *There's A Boat That's Leavin' Soon For New York* George and Ira Gershwin from *Porgy And Bess*.
◁

There is a moment in Richard Attenborough's costly **A Chorus Line** (EMI-Polygram) when Zach (Michael Douglas), the director of a new Broadway musical, interrupts his audition to have an intense talk with Cassie (Alyson Reed), a former chorus girl who once walked out of an affair with him. Cassie almost made it in Hollywood, but not quite. She's back in New York now, desperate to work again, even if it means returning to the chorus. Zach, however, insists that the chorus is no longer the place for her; that she's outgrown it and is destined for better things. To prove his point he directs her attention to a stage-full of auditioning hopefuls. What, in fact, he is showing her, is a line-up of men and women with ugly, exaggerated expressions on their faces indulging in a grotesque parody of the Nazi goose-step. It is not an edifying sight and the point being made is that a chorus line is something all self-respecting dancers try to get *out of*, not into. This 'message' is Attenborough's brainchild (he used a similar effect in *Oh What a Lovely War* (Paramount, 1969) and it illustrated just how completely he ignored the fact that the Tony Award and Pulitzer prize-winning *A Chorus Line*, which had a record-breaking 5756 performance run on Broadway, is an affectionate tribute to those anonymous 'gypsies', as they are known in the profession, rather than a condemnation of them. The plot, such as it is, revolves around an open audition in which, out of hundreds of hopefuls, only eight dancers will be chosen. Zach puts them through a series of routines in the course of which he narrows the field to 16. He then talks to each of the possibles, drawing from them information about their backgrounds and private lives. In the end the lucky handful is chosen. Though Attenborough resisted the temptation to open out the show (as in the original stage version it all takes place in a Broadway theatre) he couldn't, however, resist tampering with several of the songs by adding an irritating disco beat to them. Worse, his inability to shoot or cut-together a musical number did irreparable damage to Jeffrey Hornaday's choreography, which, in any case, wasn't as good as Michael Bennett's original Broadway staging. As for the dancers assembled by Attenborough and Hornaday, their overall excellence made it all the sadder that this legendary back-stage look at an arduous profession emerged less a tribute to the courage and stamina of 'gypsies' everywhere than a condemnation of what Attenborough clearly saw as mindless

What Robert Getchell's otherwise trenchant and gritty screenplay for **Sweet Dreams** (Tri-Star) never really made clear was just *how* big a star his subject – the country and western singer Patsy Kline – really was. Gretchell and his director, Karel Reisz, seemed more interested in the private rather than the public side of Kline's life and in this respect they succeeded admirably. Jessica Lange starred as the heroine – arguably the finest female C & W singer of all time – and Ed Harris played her second husband, Charlie Dick. Despite (or maybe because of) the emotional intensity of their relationship, it was, in many respects, a marriage made in hell, largely due to Dick's heavy boozing and joblessness. Though he probably understood her music better than anyone else, his outbursts of wife-bashing and womanizing made domestic tranquillity impossible – which was especially hard for someone like Patsy. True to the Hollywood biopic, most of the highlights of Kline's career are charted. Hence we see her appearance on the career-enhancing

Arthur Godfrey Talent Search, the birth of her first child, her near-fatal car accident, her success at Nashville's Grand Ol' Opry and, climactically, the plane crash that robbed her and her entourage of their lives. Throughout, the movie was laced with a generous quota of Kline standards, all of which Ms Lange lip-synched brilliantly. Indeed, the performances could not be faulted, including Ann Wedgworth's as Patsy's caring mother. David Clennon was featured as Kline's manager Randy Hughes, with other roles going to James Staley, Gary Basaraba, John Goodman, P.J. Soles and Terri Gardner. The producer was Bernard Schwartz. Songs included: *San Antonio Rose* Bob Wills; *Blue Moon Of Kentucky* Bill Monroe; *You Send Me* Sam Cooke (performed by Cooke); *Walking After Midnight* Don Hecht, Alan Block; *Crazy* Willie Nelson; *I Fall To Pieces Each Time I See You* Hank Cochran, Harlan Howard; *Young At Heart* Richard Leigh (performed by Frank Sinatra); *Sweet Dreams* Don Gibson.

masochism. This heartbreaking miscalculation and lost opportunity was produced by Cy Feuer and Ernest H. Martin (whose own track records suggest they should have known better), and featured Michael Blevins, Yamil Borges, Sharon Brown, Gregg Burge, Cameron English, Tony Fields, Nicole Fosse, Vicki Frederick, Jan Gan Boyd, Michelle Johnston, Justin Ross, Blane Savage and Pat McNamara. Arnold Schulman

scripted from the James Kirkwood-Nicholas Dante stage play, and the music and lyrics were by Marvin Hamlisch and Edward Kleban respectively. They included: *What I Did For Love, Looks 10 Dance 3, I Can Do That, At The Ballet, I Hope I Get It, Nothing, The Music And The Mirror, And. . ., Hello Twelve Hello Thirteen, One.* A new song, *Let Me Dance For You,* was written by Hamlisch and Kleban especially for the film.

1986

Academy Awards

Best Actor
NOMINATION: Dexter Gordon 'Round Midnight
(Warner Bros.)

Best Song
NOMINATION: Howard Ashman, Alan Menken
'Mean Green Mother From Outer Space' *The
Little Shop Of Horrors* (Warner Bros.)

Best Visual Effects
NOMINATION: Lyle Conway, Bran Ferren,
Martin Guttridge *The Little Shop Of Horrors*

△

Rarely, if ever, have the creative processes involved in the performing of jazz been more excitingly captured than in **'Round Midnight** (Warner Bros.), Bertrand Tavernier's marvellous evocation of the jazz scene as it existed in Paris and New York at the end of the 1950s. Based on the last years of pianist Bud Powell and also inspired by the superb musicianship of Lester Young, the screenplay, fashioned by Tavernier and David Rayfiel, was about an alcoholic, ill, formerly drug addicted bepop tenor saxophonist called Dale Turner, who, while playing at the famous Blue Note jazz club in Paris, is befriended by an impoverished commercial artist called François Cluzet. Because of Cluzet's great admiration for Turner, he takes the musician under his wing and attempts, with a modest degree of success, to nurse him back to something resembling health. But his success is short-lived and, after a brief period of rehabilitation and a trip back to New York (accompanied by Cluzet), Turner succumbs to his previous self-destructive lifestyle and dies. Musician Dexter Gordon (all 6 foot 5 inches of him) was cast as the tortured, laconic saxophonist and brought to his characterization an extraordinary authenticity; while Francis Borier as the admiring Cluzet was no less impressive. What one remembers most about this affecting movie is their developing friendship and interdependence that underpinned the narrative. Most of the music was recorded live on the set, and most of the performers were real-life musicians who brought to the screenplay a verisimilitude rarely encountered in films about jazz and jazzmen. Gabrielle Haker played Cluzet's young daughter, with other roles going to Sandra Reaves-Phillips, Lonette McKee, Christine Pascal, Herbie Hancock, Bobby Hutcherson and Benoit Regent. The producer was Irwin Winkler. Songs included: *Round Midnight* Thelonious Monk, Cootie Williams, Bernie Hanighen; *As Time Goes By* Herman Hupfeld; *Society* Red Dexter, Gordon Fairweather, Kenny Dorham; *Now's The Time* Charlie Parker; *Autumn In New York* Vernon Duke; *Una Noche Con Francis* Bud Powell; *Body And Soul* Johnny Green, Edward Heyman, Robert Sour, Frank Eyton; *It's Only A Paper Moon* Billy Rose, E.Y. Harburg, Harold Arlen; *Tivoli* Dexter Gordon; *How Long Has This Been Going On?* George and Ira Gershwin; *Put It Right Here* Bessie Smith; *I Love Paris, What Is This Thing Called Love?* Cole Porter.   ▷

Based on Roger Corman's modest but successful 1960 black comedy, and adapted by Howard Ashman from his 1982 off-Broadway hit, **The Little Shop Of Horrors** (Warner Bros.) was the decade's most successful stage-to-screen transfer of a musical. Set in 1960 in Skid Row and all about a *nebbish* florist called Seymour Krelborn who buys an exotic-looking plant that thrives on blood and grows to be $12\frac{1}{2}$ feet high, it starred Rick Moranis as the florist, the delightfully idiosyncratic Ellen Greene as Audrey, the girl of his dreams, Steve Martin as Audrey's masochistic dentist boy-friend Orin Scrivello, and Vincent Gardenia as Mushnik, the owner of the florist shop. Though director Frank Oz retained the sense of over-the-top fun that kept New York's Orpheum Theatre playing to S.R.O., several changes were made for the movie version, the biggest being the ending. Instead of the behemoth plant (called Audrey 2, and constantly demanding to be fed) surviving to destroy the planet, it is itself destroyed by Seymour who realizes he has no choice but to blow the monster to smithereens. Several new Ashman-Alan Menken songs, including *Mean Green Mother from Outer Space*, *Some Fun Now* and *Your Day Begins Tonight* were added, while *Now, Ya Never Know*, *Mushnik And Son*, *Closed For Renovations* and *Call Back In the Morning* were dropped. Tichina Arnold, Tisha Campbell and Michelle Weeks played Crystal, Chiffon and Ronette, a kind of Greek chorus *à la* The Supremes, with other roles going to James Belushi, John Candy, Vincent Wong, Stanley Jones, Bertice Reading, Christopher Guest, and, as the voice of Audrey 2, Levi Stubbs. The marvellous special effects were by Lyle Conway, and it was choreographed by Pat Garrett. Other songs: *Downtown, Suddenly Seymour, Suppertime* and *Somewhere That's Green*.

1987

Academy Awards

Best Song
NOMINATION: Frankie Previte, John de Nicola, Donald Markowitz 'I've Had The Time Of My Life' *Dirty Dancing* (Vestron)

Richard Valenzuela, a teenage Mexican fruit-picker, had a dream and a recurring nightmare. In his dream he became a famous rock singer; in his nightmare he died in an air crash. Both would come true. Changing his name to Richie Valens, Valenzuela was the first Mexican to free himself from his slum environment and succeed in the gringo-dominated world of rock 'n' roll. How he achieved the seemingly impossible was told in **La Bamba** (Columbia), a captivating though-conventional Hollywood biopic that managed to reproduce the sound of an era. Though physically very different from the real-life Valens, and with his vocals dubbed by David Hidalgo of the Latin rock group Los Lobos, newcomer Lou Diamond Phillips was, nevertheless, utterly convincing as the 17 year-old who recorded three hits (*La Bamba*, which he arranged and adapted, *Come on Let's Go*, and *Donna*, which he wrote) in the eight months he enjoyed as a professional singer, before he, Buddy Holly and The Big Bopper were killed when their plane crashed in stormy weather on the way back from a gig. Esai Morales was cast as Richie's resentful brother Bob, Rosana DeSoto was his mother Connie, with other roles under writer Luis Valdez's heartfelt direction going to Elisabeth Pena, Joe Pantoliano, Danielle von Zerneck, Marshall Crenshaw (Buddy Holly), Stephen Lee (The Big Bopper) and Howard Huntsberry. This tribute was produced by Taylor Hackford and Bill Borden and choreographed by Miguel Delgardo. Other songs included: *Rip It Up* John Marascalo, Robert A. Blackwell; *Goodnight My Love* Marascalo, George Motola; *Oh Boy* Sunny West, Billy Tilghman, Norman Petty; *Framed* Jerry Leiber, Mike Stoller; *We Belong Together* S. Weiss, R. Carr, J. Mitchell; *Ooh! My Head*, *The Paddi Wack Song*, Valens; *Bakersfield Shuffle* Los Lobos; *Crying Waiting Hoping* Buddy Holly; *Who Do You Love* E. McDaniel.

In *Two Weeks With Love* (MGM, 1950), Jane Powell, in the company of her sister, Debbie Reynolds, and parents, Louis Calhern and Anne Harding, found true romance with Ricardo Montalban while on holiday in the Catskills. Thirty seven years later, the Catskills again played host to a family and their two daughters – this time in the much less innocent **Dirty Dancing** (Vestron), produced by Linda Gottlieb and slickly directed by Emile Ardolino. It is 1963 and the plot revolves around the deflowering of 17-year-old Frances 'Baby' Houseman (Jennifer Grey) who, resisting her parents' attempts to pair her off with the owner of their hotel's smarmy grandson (Lonny Price), finds the resort's resident dance instructor, Johnny Castle (Patrick Swayze), far more appealing. The plot takes off when Johnny's dance partner Penny (Cynthia Rhodes) discovers she is pregnant by an Ivy League medical student (Max Cantor) working as a waiter, and has to find $250 for an abortion. And that's just for starters! As Eleanor Bergstein's screenplay hits its stride, Swayze is not only assumed to be responsible for Rhodes' pregnancy, but wrongly accused of theft. It all ends happily, though, with Grey stepping in for the indisposed Rhodes in the resort's end of season show. Swayze and Grey (Joel's daughter) looked sexy together and danced up a storm (choreography by Kenny Ortega), the plot contrivances did no damage to the ultimate box-office returns (the film grossed a healthy $25 million) and the songs – especially *(I've Had) The Time Of My Life*, by Frankie Previte, Donald Markowitz and John de Nicola, and performed by Bill Medley and Jennifer Warnes – though rooted in the eighties rather than the sixties – proved popular with audiences globally. The songs included: *Be My Baby* Jeff Barry, Ellie Greenwich; *Big Girls Don't Cry* B. Gaudio, B. Crewe; *Merengue, Johnny's Mambo* Erich Bulling, John D'Andrea, Michael Lloyd, *Fox Trot, Waltz* D'Andrea, Lloyd; *Where Are You Tonight* Mark Scola; *Do You Love Me* Bery Gordy; *These Arms Of Mine* Otis Redding; *Stay* Morris Williams; *Wipe Out* The Surfaris.

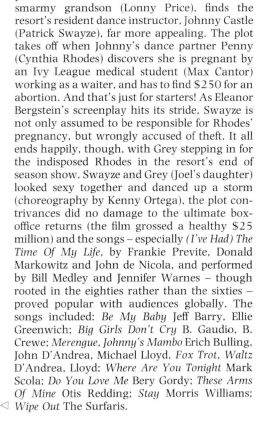

1988

Time was when the crude animation of the Disney Organization's **Oliver & Company** (Walt Disney-Silver Screen) would have been considered little more than a rough first draft and confined to the 'story board'. A contemporary reworking of Dickens's *Oliver Twist* and set in New York, the studio's 27th animated feature, with its ugly, angular lines and minimal attempt at characterization had no one asking for more. A few bracing sequences involving the hazards of life in the big city compensated for the two dimensionality of an over-cute Oliver (now an orphaned kitten), a routine Dodger (now a dog) and an unethnic Fagin (a human). It was written by Jim Cox, Timothy J. Disney and James Mangold with story contributions by Vance Gerry, Mike Gabriel, Joe Ranft, Jim Mitchell, Chris Bailey, Kirk Wise, Dave Michener, Roger Allers, Gary Trousdale, Kevin Lima, Michael Cedeno, Pete Young, and Leon Joosen, and had additional story material by Gerrit Graham, Samuel Graham, Chris Hubbell, Steve Hulett and Danny Mann. It was directed by George Scribner, and featured the voices of Joey Lawrence, Billy Joel, Cheech Marin, Richard Mulligan, Roscoe Lee Brown, Robert Loggia, Sheryl Lee Ralph, Dom DeLuise and Bette Midler. Songs included: *Once Upon A Time In New York* Howard Ashman; *Why Should I Worry?* Dan Hartman, Charlie Midnight; *Streets Of Gold* Dean Pitchford, Tom Snow; *Perfect Isn't Easy* Barry Manilow, Jack Feldman, Bruce Sussman; *Good Company* Rob Minkoff, Ron Rocha.

Bird (Warner Bros.) was a lengthy biopic of Charlie 'Yardbird' Parker, a 'jazz visionary who took the saxophone to new heights of expression' and who self-destructed, at the age of 34, on a diet of drugs and alcohol. In an attempt to avoid the hoary old clichés redolent of Hollywood biopics, producer-director Clint Eastwood deliberately imposed a confusing flashback/flashforward structure on the movie that concealed more than it revealed. Parker's childhood, for example, is dispensed with in two brief scenes sandwiched between the opening credits; his formative years and rise to fame are ignored; so is the development of the style that made him the most influential and imitated saxophonist of all time. Three of his four marriages aren't even mentioned, nor is his escalating dependence on drugs. If there were happy times in Parker's short life you would never know it from Eastwood and writer Joel Oliansky's preoccupation with the murkier aspects of their subject's existence. Apart from a sequence showing Parker's triumph in Paris, and a humorous one in the Deep South when white trumpeter Red Rodney (Michael Zeiniker) had to pretend to be an Albino to avoid a lynching, the film is a 2½ downer about the wastefulness of a drug-dependent life. And in order to capture the nocturnal world inhabited by jazz musicians everywhere Eastwood shot 95 per cent of the film in subterranean half-light. As Bird, Forest Whitaker brought a sweetness and likeability to a man whose thirst for life and women were hardly prerequisites for a stable relationship. His fourth wife Chan, a one-time dancer and a woman of fiercely independent spirit, must have been something of a saint to have endured her husband's dark moods and suicide attempts. As played by Diane Venora, Chan Parker emerged as a woman who was every bit as remarkable as the man she loved. With performances as secure as these it was a pity that the film's overall feeling of claustrophobia failed to allow the blazing light of Parker's genius to make itself truly felt. A Malpaso Production, it also featured Samuel E. Wright (Dizzy Gillespie), Keith David, Michael McGuire, James Handy, Damon Whitaker, Morgan Nagler and Sam Robards. Music and songs included: *Lester Leaps In* Lester Young; *I Can't Believe That You're In Love With Me* Clarence Gaskill, Jimmy McHugh; *All Of Me* Seymour Simon, Gerald Marks; *This Time The Dream's On Me* Harold Arlen, Johnny Mercer; *Reno Jam Session, One For the Road* Lennie Niehaus; *Why Do I Love You?* Jerome Kern, Oscar Hammerstein; *April In Paris* Vernon Duke, E.Y. Harburg; *Moose The Mooch, Now's The Time, Ko Ko* Charlie Parker.

Dedicated to the greater glory of its star, Michael Jackson, **Moonwalker** (Warner Bros.) was an accomplished ego trip – both visually and aurally that explored every facet of Jackson's personality in six separate sections. In Man In The Mirror its globally popular star is put in some sort of world perspective through concert footage and a montage of events. Retrospective offers a second montage, this time spanning Jackson's 24-year career – from childhood appearances with the Jackson 5 to contemporary mega-stardom. Badder is a remake of his Bad video, but with youngsters between the ages of eight and ten taking all the roles. Speed Demon mingles live action with animation to show Jackson, dressed as a cross between Bugs Bunny and the Road Runner giving a group of tourists visiting a film studio the slip. Leave Me Alone finds Jackson in a fairground rocket ship being hounded by journalists dressed as dogs. In Smooth Criminal he is joined by a trio of youngsters in a tale about a super-criminal called Mr. Big who plans to turn every kid into a junkie. The film ends with South Africa's Ladysmith Black Mambazo performing The Moon Is Walking. Smooth Criminal was written by David Newman (from a story by Jackson), directed by Colin Chilvers and produced by Dennis E. Jones; the anthology segments were by Jerry Kramer; Jackson and Vincent Paterson choreographed Smooth Criminal; Paterson did the dances for Speed Demon and Russell Clark for Badder. Songs included: *ABC, I Want You Back, The Love You Save*, The Corporation; *Dancing Machine* Hal Davis, Don Fletcher, Welson Parks; *2-4-6-8* Pamela Sawyer, Gloria Jones; *Who's Loving You* William Robinson Jr; *Beat it, Bad, Billie Jean, Dirty Diana, Smooth Criminal, Don't Stop Till You Get Enough, Leave Me Alone, Speed Demon, The Way You Make Me Feel* Michael Jackson; *Man In The Mirror* Siedah Garrett, Glen Ballard; *Come Together* John Lennon, Paul McCartney; *Ben* Don Black, Walter Scharf.

▽

Apart from a short zit-squeezing sequence, the ▷ bad-taste and devil-may-care approach director John Waters had hitherto adopted to bodily functions in such cult offerings as *Pink Flamingoes* (1974) and *Desperate Living* (1977) was nowhere in evidence in **Hairspray** (New Line) an inoffensive *hommage* to the sixties in general and fat girls and beehive hairdos in particular. Waters' idiosyncratic screenplay, set in Baltimore in 1962, was a mere trifle in which an oversized teenager, played with captivating unselfconsciousness by Ricki Lane, is, after a fair degree of speculation, crowned Miss Auto Show of 1963. A sub-plot involving a civil rights issue was treated as light-heartedly as everything else in this entertainingly irreverent spoof; so was Miss Pia Zadora's appearance as a pot-smoking bohemian. In his very last film, Divine, a Waters regular appeared as Lake's outrageous mother, with other roles in this sixties love-in going to Ruth Brown as Motormouth Maybelle, the owner of a rhythm-and-blues record store, Sonny Bono, Debbie Harry, Colleen Fitzpatrick, Jo Ann Havrilla, Ric Ocasek, Leslie Ann Powers, Clayton Prince, Mink Stole, and Michael St. Gerard. Rachel Talalay produced and the energetic choreography, especially the communal Bug (by Jerry Dallman, Milton Grant) was the work of Edward Love. Songs included: *Hairspray* Rachel Sweet, Anthony Battaglia; *You'll Lose A Good Thing* Barbara Lynn Ozen; *Mama Don't Lie* Curtis Mayfield; *Let's Twist Again, Dancin' Party, Gravy* Kal Mann, Dave Appel; *The Fly, You Don't Own Me* John Madera, David White; *Pony Time* Don Covay, John Barry; *Limbo Rock* John Sheldon, Billy Strange; *Waddle Waddle* Rudy Clark; *The Bird* Richard Parker, Leo Anstell.

△

Writer-director Spike Lee followed his successful first feature *She's Gotta Have It* (1986) with **School Daze** (Columbia) a free-wheeling, well-intentioned failure set in a black college in the South West and involving a clash of wills and personalities between Larry Fishburne, whose college faction is a revolutionary dark-skinned, politically motivated group called the Jigaboos, and Giancarlo Esposito, leader of the more conservative Gamma Phi Gamma fraternity or Wannabees (his followers wannabee light-skinned, straight-haired owners of BMW's and Brooks Brothers suits). Lee himself played 'Half Pint', Fishburne's cousin but a Wannabee at heart. The rivalry between Fishburne and Esposito shared centre-screen with a conflict involving the school's refusal to sever its invest-ments in South Africa. Though Lee raised several important racial issues, his film lacked the discipline to resolve them satisfactorily and the end result was a loosely structured, clumsily plotted free-for-all whose best musical number was a dance routine called *Straight 'n' Nappy*, choreographed by Otis Sallid, written by Bill Lee, and set in a hair salon. Spike Lee, Monty Ross and Loretha C. Jones produced and their cast included Tisha Campbell, Kyme, Joe Seneca, Ellen Holly, Art Evans, Paula Brown and Ossie Davis. Some of the songs were: *I'm Building Me A Home* Uzee Brown; *Be Alone Tonight* Raymond Jones; *I Can Only Be Me* Stevie Wonder; *Perfect Match* Lenny White, Tina Harris; *Be One, Wake Up Suite* Bill Lee; *We've Already Said Goodbye* Raymond Jones.

1989

Academic Awards

Best Original Score
Alan Menkin *The Little Mermaid* (Walt Disney Pictures)

Best Original Song
Howard Ashman, Alan Menkin 'Under The Sea' *The Little Mermaid*
NOMINATION: Howard Ashman, Alan Menkin 'Kiss The Girl' *The Little Mermaid*

The animation division of Walt Disney Pictures made a quite spectacular return to form with **The Little Mermaid** (Walt Disney Pictures), a feature-length cartoon (based on the Hans Christian Andersen fairytale) whose delightful set of seaworthy characterizations recalled the glories of the studio's golden past. All about a mermaid princess called Ariel whose passionate curiosity is always getting her into mischief on the ocean's surface (deemed out-of-bounds to her by her father, King Triton), and who risks life and 'limbs' to be part of the human world when she meets and falls in love with the prince of her dreams, it was rich in such typical Disney-esque creations as Flounder the Fish, Ursula the Sea Witch, Scuttle the misinformed seagull and Sebastian the crab – a kind of Jiminy Cricket whose job is to keep Ariel out of trouble. The set pieces, such as the Busby Berkeley-inspired *Under The Sea* and a sequence involving a temperamental French chef, were in the best tradition of *Pinocchio* (1940) and *Dumbo* (1941)

and made a welcome change after Disney's previous animated effort, the flat *Oliver And Company* (1988). The 28th full-length cartoon from the Disney Organization, it was written and directed by John Musker and Ron Clements produced by Clements and Musker, and featured the voices of Rene Auberjonois, Christopher Daniel Barnes, Jodi Benson, Pat Carroll, Paddi Edwards, Buddy Hackett, Jason Marin, Kenneth Mars, Ben Wright and Samuel E. Wright. The songs were by Howard Ashman and Alan Menken, and included: *Kiss The Girl, Part Of Your World, Poor Souls, Les Poissons, Fathom's Below, Daughters of Triton.*

In 1945, Betty Grable and June Haver starred in *The Dolly Sisters* (20th Century-Fox) as a pair of Hungarian entertainers whose lives were disrupted when Betty falls in love with a songwriter. **The Fabulous Baker Boys** (20th Century-Fox) loosely varied the theme by having a sexy chanteuse called Susie (Michelle Pfeiffer) upsetting the long-standing partnership between small-time cocktail pianists Jack and Frank Baker (Jeff and Beau Bridges). In a sequence not unlike the amateur rock contest in Milos Forman's *Taking Off* (Universal, 1971) and the cattle-call audition in Bob Fosse's *All That Jazz* (Columbia-20th Century-Fox, 1979), the Baker boys audition 36 prospective singers and can't believe their luck when sultry Susie, arriving late, sounds as good as she looks. She is hired to give their tired act a touch of sex appeal – and does just that. Predictably, romance intrudes and unleashes several attendant clichés: Susie succumbs to Jack's advances, Jack is troubled by the notion that he is far too serious a musician to be wasting his time on endless requests for *Feelings* (Louis Gaste, Morris Albert); while Frank, who has no illusions about his talent (or lack of it), would rather be at home with his wife and kids than on the road. Writer-director Steve Kloves' leisurely screenplay (too leisurely for so anorexic a plot line), camouflaged, with some astute characterization, what was, let's face it, little more than a trite, old-fashioned backstage triangle. Still, he accurately recreated the atmosphere of the quasi-glamorous world of chain-resort cocktail bars, and drew from his three stars exemplary performances. Pfeiffer was especially convincing, and her come-hither rendering of *Making Whoopee* (Walter Donaldson, Gus Kahn) a triumph. It was produced by Paula Weinstein, Mark Rosenberg and Bill Finnegan. Other songs included: *More Than You Know* Edward Eliscu, Billy Rose, Vincent Youmans; *Ten Cents A Dance* Richard Rodgers, Lorenz Hart; *Can't Take My Eyes Off You* Bob Crewe, Bob Gaudio; *The Look Of Love* Burt Bacharach, Hal David; *You're Sixteen, You're Beautiful, You're Mine* Robert Sherman, Richard Sherman; *The Pea Song* Richard Kloves; *My Funny Valentine* Rodgers, Hart.

Dennis Quaid starred as the self-destructive Jerry Lee Lewis in **Great Balls Of Fire** (Orion), an enjoyable if not particularly probing biopic of the popular rock 'n' roll star whose great hope was to dethrone Elvis Presley and wear the crown himself. Lewis's misguided marriage to his 13-year-old second cousin Myra (Winona Ryder) and his insistence that his child bride accompany him on a tour of Britain were, however, the beginning of the end of his short, (1956–1958) but spectacular career. Hounded by the British press, who also discovered he was a bigamist, the tour ended after five days. Lewis returned to the United States, and, with his career in ruins, took to drink and drugs prior to his long haul back to favour. Although director Jim McBride's screenplay, which he wrote with Jack Baran (based on a book by Myra Lewis and Murray Silver Jr.) handled this aspect of Lewis's life fairly convincingly, the complex Lewis psyche was glossed over. So too was the fact that he had two wives and a son before he married Myra. The singer's childhood was also misrepresented and bore all the familiar traces of a Hollywood biopic circa 1940. Lewis's preacher cousin, Jimmy Lee Swaggart (himself no stranger to notoriety) was played by a miscast Alec Baldwin, with other roles in producer Adam Fields' production going to John Doe (as Myra's father), Trey Wilson (as record-producer Sam Phillips, the man who discovered Presley, then let him go too soon), Steve Allen (as himself), Lisa Blount, Joshua Sheffield and Stephen Tobolowsky. Though Quaid was originally going to do his own singing, the songs were newly recorded by Lewis and lip-synched. They included: *Crazy Arms* Ralph Mooney, Charles Seals; *I'm Throwing Rice At The Girl I Love* Eddy Arnold, Edward Nelson, Steve Nelson; *Great Balls Of Fire* Otis Blackwell, Jack Hammer; *Breathless* Blackwell; *High School Confidential* Ron Hargrave, Jerry Lee Lewis; *I'm On Fire* Bob Feldman, Jerry Goldstein, Richard Gottehrer; *That Lucky Old Sun* Haven Gillespie, Beasley Smith; *Real Wild Child* Johnny O'Keefe, Johnny Greenan, Dave Owens; *Whole Lotta Shakin' Goin' On* David Williams, Sunny David.

▽

Any movie that celebrates the lost art of tap-dancing and features such elder statesmen of the genre as Harold Nicholas (of the immortal Nicholas Brothers), Sandman Sims and Steve Condos (of the Condos Brothers) had to have its heart in the right place. Add to the cast Sammy Davis Jr, hoofer Gregory Hines and a bright and talented youngster called Savion Glover, and you're cooking with gas. Or should have been. But it didn't work out that way. **Tap** (Columbia-Tri-Star) was a catalogue of lost opportunities. Lovingly and nostalgically conceived by writer-director Nick Castle, it was scuppered by a screenplay which focused on the reformation-through-dance of a small-time criminal (Hines) who decides he is better off apeing Fred Astaire than Al Capone. Frankly, it would have seemed old hat even in the thirties. Henry Le Tang was in charge of the 'improvography', and Hines the 'tap-tronics'. Gary Adelson and Richard Vane produced and the cast also included Suzanne Douglas (as the love interest), Joe Morton, Dick Anthony Williams, Bunny Briggs and Jimmy Slyde. The film featured extracts from the following 20th Century-Fox musicals: *Little Miss Broadway* (1938), *Orchestra Wives* (1942), *Wake Up And Live* (1937), *You're My Everything* (1949) and *Sun Valley Serenade* (1941). The songs: *All I Want Is Forever, Strong As Steel* Diane Warren; *Max's Theme, Lover's Intuition* Joe Ericksen, Barbara Rothstein, Dorothy Gazeley; *Baby What You Want Me To Do* Jimmy Reed; *Bad Boy* Dennis Matkosky, Matt Wilder; *Forget The Girl* Everton DeLuke McCalla; *Can't Escape The Rhythm* James Newton Howard, Glenn Ballard; *Free* Matosky, Wilder; *On The Sunny Side Of The Street* Dorothy Fields, Jimmy McHugh; *Stormy Monday* Aaron T. Walker; *Cheek To Cheek* Irving Berlin.

▽

◁ Yet another 'hey, kids, let's put on a show!' musical, **Sing** (Columbia-Tri-Star), told the predictable story of a handful of students who enter a song-and-dance competition at a Brooklyn school for no reason other than to express themselves and harness their energy to music. What this old-fashioned entertainment needed was, of course, Mickey Rooney and Judy Garland; what it got was Peter Dobson and Jessica Sweet. Dobson played a streetwise Italian who abandons petty crime after grudgingly allowing the showbiz bug to bite; Sweet is the single-minded student who steers him along the straight-and-narrow by dragooning him into choreographing their show. Naturally, they fall in love. Not only that, but Dobson even manages to appear in the finale when one of the kids accidentally knocks himself out – shades of Ruby Keeler going out a youngster and coming back a star in *42nd Street* (Warner Bros. 1933). It was produced by Craig Zadan, choreographed by Otis Sallid and John Carrafa, written by Dean Pitchford, and directed by Richard Baskin. Songs included: *Sing* Jonathan Cain, Martin Page, Dean Pitchford; *You Don't Have To Ask Me Twice* Pitchford, Tom Snow; *Birthday Suit* Pitchford, Rhett Lawrence; *Romance (Love Theme)* Pitchford, Patrick Leonard; *Total Concentration* Pitchford, Tom Kelly; *Somethin' To Believe In* Pitchford, Desmond Child, Diane Warren; *What's The Matter With Love?* Pitchford, Snow; *One More Time* Snow, Pitchford.

1990

By putting his racial anger on hold and entering the Hollywood main-stream, Spike Lee does the wrong thing in the disappointing **Mo'Better Blues** (Universal), which he wrote, produced and directed. He appeared in it too, modestly taking second billing to the charismatic Denzel Washington, who, as a self-obsessed jazz trumpeter called Bleek Gilliam, is the leader of a jazz quintet. Lee casts himself as Giant, the group's ineffectual manager-cum-compulsive gambler, and what little plot there is teeters precariously around Giant's feeble attempts to up the group's ante and extricate himself from his overwhelming gambling debts. Riding in tandem with his doomed efforts on both counts is the film's romantic interest – supplied by a soft-spoken school teacher called Indigo (Joie Lee) and a would-be nightclub singer called Clarke (Cynda Williams). Both women are in love with Bleek who beds them regularly on some kind of roster system. To neither does he conceal the fact that there is only 'grief, pain, tears and heartache' in

marrying a musician – and that the only true love of his life is his trumpet. Thus when Clarke bites his lip in a passionate moment of love-making, he rounds on her with a fury that leaves one in no doubt where his priorities lie. Visually Lee flexed his directorial muscle to excellent effect, but narratively speaking, all he offered was flab. The film's two obligatory whites (Jewish night-club owners) were grotesquely overdrawn, while, apart from Bleek, the boys in the band had no discernible personalities whatsoever. Even the musical sequences were dull. Looking like a black Toulouse-Lautrec, Lee continued to denigrate his physical appearance by playing an unattractive character, unable even to inspire contempt. After the high-energy quotient of his *Do The Right Thing* (1989), **Mo'Better Blues** lies there – and dies there. Also cast: Wesley Snipes, Giancarlo Esposito, Robin Harris, Bill Nunn, John Turturro, Dick Anthony Williams, Jeff 'Tain' Watts and Samuel J. Jackson. The original music score was by Spike's father Bill Lee. Songs included: *Mercy Mercy Mercy* Josef Zawinul; *Footprints* Wayne Shorter; *Mo'Better Blues*, *Again Never* Bill Lee; *Sing Soweto* Terence Blanchard; *Knocked Out The Box* B. Marsalis Steeplone; *Goodbye Pork Pie Hat* Charles Mingus; *Harlem Blues* W.C. Handy; *Lonely Woman* Ornette Coleman; *A Love Supreme* John Coltrane; *Jazz Thing* Lolis Eric Elie, Branford Marsalis, Christopher Martin, Keith Elam.

▽

Robert Lindsay, the award-winning star of the West End and Broadway's *Me And My Girl* made his movie debut in director Carl Reiner's **Bert Rigby You're A Fool** (Warner Bros.). The biggest fool, however, was Lindsay himself for not foreseeing the unavoidable disasters in this lamentable, jerry-built vehicle. He played an English coal miner with show-biz aspirations who, after entertaining the blokes down the pit with a rendition of *The Continental* (Con Conrad, Herb Magidson) wins a local talent contest and is proclaimed 'all time permanent greatest amateur' by the show's promoter (Robbie Coltrane). The nadir of this witless entertainment was reached when Lindsay and Coltrane (who becomes his manager) take off for Los Angeles in search of fame and fortune. A leaden tribute to the Hollywood musical, it compounded its ineptitude by featuring Anne Bancroft as an over-the-hill actress in what must surely be the most embarrassing performance by a star of stature ever to reach the screen. Lindsay was equally misguided, especially with his one-man *hommage* to *Singin' In The Rain* (MGM, 1952). Others taking part in producer George Shapiro's unmitigated disaster (dedicated to Gene Kelly, incidentally) were Corbin Bernsen, Cathryn Bradshaw, Jackie Gayle, Bruno Kirby, Liz Smith, Lila Kaye, Fanny Carby, Carmen Du Sautoy and Mike Grady. Larry Hyman choreographed and the songs included: *Whitegold Beer Commercial*, *They've Opened The Ritz Tonight*, *That's How I Turned Out To Be Mr. Elvis P.* Slaughterhouse Five, Earl Brown; *Isn't It Romantic?* Richard Rodgers, Lorenz Hart; *All Of You* Cole Porter; *I'll See You Again* Noel Coward; *Puttin' On The Ritz* Irving Berlin; *Dream A Little Dream Of Me* W. Schmidt, F. André, Gus Kahn; *My Little Ukelele* Jack Cottrell.

The Fifties were modestly, yet finger-snappingly evoked in **Cry Baby** (Imagine) written and directed by John Waters. An uninhibited throwback to such mindless rock 'n' roll jaunts of the period as *Untamed Youth* (Warner Bros. 1957) and *Bop Girl Goes Calypso* (United Artists, 1957), it was a non-stop, all-singing, all-dancing jamboree whose slender plot was little more than a clothes line on which to peg some two dozen or so songs. Though several characters – notably Kim McGuire's apparition-like Hatchet Face – offered a vague echo of Waters before he joined the Hollywood mainstream, the only sequence to carry this once controversial director's imprimatur involved several teenagers indulging in an orgy of French kissing. The plot was a mere footnote. The big Boo-Hoo, better known as Wade 'Cry Baby' Walker (Johnny Deep), a teenage 'hepcat' from the wrong side of the tracks, falls for a wealthy 'square' called Allison Vernon-Williams (Amy Locane) much to the disapproval of her formidible grandmother (Polly Bergen *à la* Gloria Swanson). It is a dangerous liaison to be sure and helps bring to a head the deadly rivalry between the 'squares' and the more colourful and delinquent 'drapes' – or, as Bergen defines them, 'boys with long hair who spit on the sidewalk and girls in tight pants.' Local gang rivalry, the infamous 'chicken run', the sight of Ms Locane collecting the tears she sheds over Depp, then drinking them, ducktail haircuts and a brief appearance by an unrecognizable Troy Donahue (welcome back, Troy!) payed tribute to 1954, the year in which it all takes place; so did Depp's characteristically physical way with a song. Waters never allowed his affection for the period to blur his sense of humour, thus ensuring that **Cry Baby** was as funny as it was tuneful. Rachel Talalay produced, Lori Eastside choreographed, and the cast included Susan Tyrrell, Iggy Pop, Ricki Lake, Traci Lords, Patty Hearst, Joe Dallesandro and Willem Dafoe. Songs included: *King Cry Baby* Doc Pomus, Dave Alvin; *Doin' Time For Bein' Young* John David Souther, Waddy Wachtel; *High School Hellcats* Alvin; *Cry Baby* Morgan C. Robinson, Lawrence Robinson; *Fingertips* Red Prysock; *Sh Boom* James Keyes, Claude Feaster, Carl Feaster, Floyd F. McRae, James Edwards; *A Teenage Prayer* Bix Reichner, Bernie Lowe; *Teardrops Are Falling* The Five Wings; *Bunny Hop* Ray Anthony, Leonard Auletti; *Mister Sandman* Pat Ballard; *Please Mister Jailer* Winona Carr.

△

The youth-orientated **House Party** (New Line), set in a middle-class black neighbourhood, was a simple-minded entertainment that revolved around incidents triggered off by a party given in the home of Play (Christopher Martin). One of the guests is a would-be rap artist called Kid (Christopher Reid) who is at the party against the wishes of his father (Robin Harris) and whose defection underpins the narrative. Also contributing to the so-called plot is Kid's flirtation with Sidney (Tisha Campbell) and Sharane (A.J. Johnson) and his involvement with an anti-social gang called Stab and Co. He even finds himself in jail facing the strong possibility of a homosexual gang rape (or, in this case, homosexual gang rap?). Director Reginald Hudlin's screenplay needed an interpreter for anyone not *au fait* with rap jargon, though there was a certain challenge in trying to work out who was saying what to whom, or why. An energetic (predominantly black) cast, including Martin Lawrence as a disc jockey, worked like blazes for Hudlin, whose brother Warrington produced. Songs included: *Why You Get Funky On Me*, *What A Feeling*, *Jive Time Sucker*, *House Party*, *I Can't Do Nothin' For You, Man*, *Fun House*, *To Da Break Of Dawn*, *Kid vs. Play*, *This Is Love*.

▽

Appendixes

The three appendixes were compiled because it was considered necessary at least to mention the films they contain if the book were to act as a comprehensive reference guide to the genre. In each case, the listing is chronological, and provides details of title, studio, director, stars, and a brief précis of content for each film. Appendixes 2 and 3 deal with specific areas of the musical and the inclusion of all the titles in them is not especially contentious. Appendix 1, however, covers what, for want of a better term, have been called 'fringe' musicals – films which, for one reason or another, were considered worthy of inclusion in the book, but not as main entries. The choice, as explained in the author's note on page 9, was necessarily subjective and, doubtless, arguments will rage among readers who may well not agree with all the distinctions made. It will be noticed that Elvis Presley's movies inhabit the main section of the book and not the pop appendix. This decision was taken because Presley was a unique phenomenon, both as a star, and in the number of main features in which he appeared. For the rest, the basic material of Appendix 2 was deemed to be of a different flavour to the rest of the main entries, as well as potentially offering a bulk of written material which would have caused the book as a whole to burst through any reasonable confines. The entries in Appendix 3 offer no elements in common with the body of the book, other than music and the use of celluloid.

Appendix 1 – Fringe Musicals – page 440

A chronological listing of films considered important for inclusion in the book, but not sufficiently 'musical' in their basic concept to merit a main entry. Wherever possible, relevant or notable musical information is provided.

Appendix 2 – Miscellaneous Pop Musicals – page 447

From 1956 a proliferation of youth-orientated 'pop' musicals flooded the market, reflecting the current trends of hit-parade music. Thus, there were Rock'n'Roll movies, Twist and Calypso movies, and what came to be known as 'Beach Party' movies. In style, convention and flavour they were radical departures from the Hollywood of, say, *42nd Street*, *Easter Parade* or *Funny Girl*. These pop movies, however, were (and are) undoubtedly part of the musical genre.

Appendix 3 – Documentaries – page 449

The fifties also saw the emergence of the documentary musical – the filming and recording of musical events at the time they were actually happening. Subject matter ranged over a wide spectrum, from international festivals of folk-dancing, through jazz at Newport, to fund-raising and 'protest' concerts. The artists captured for posterity included virtually every singer – male and female, black and white, and every group, who ever made an impact on the country-and-western, rock or soul music scenes over a period of twenty years or so. In style and presentation the documentaries ranged from poorly shot and badly edited exploitation movies (for example *Celebration At Big Sur*, 1971; *Janis*, 1975), to the superbly made and often inventive accounts of major musical events, such as *Jazz On A Summer's Day*, 1959, and *Woodstock*, 1970.

Indexes

In an attempt to make the searching of so extensive a list of references a little easier for the reader, this index has been divided into categories and becomes several indexes under the separate headings FILM TITLES, SONG AND MUSIC TITLES, PERFORMERS, COMPOSERS AND LYRICISTS and OTHER CREATIVE PERSONNEL. These cover material from the decade chapters only (that is, pages 18 to 415 inclusive); the introductory pages and the appendixes have not been indexed. Each index is alphabetically arranged in the usual way but, where a film or song title begins with an arabic numeral, for example *52nd Street*, it will be found under F, as if it were *Fifty-second Street*. Where appropriate, a few names appear in more than one index: Bob Fosse, for example, is listed both as a performer and under 'other creative personnel'.

Index 1 — Film Titles — page 451

All references to a specific film are listed. The page number which refers to that film's main entry is indicated by the use of bold type. If no bold page number is listed for a particular film, this denotes that it is merely mentioned in passing in another film's entry.

Index 2 — Song and Music Titles — page 453

The distinction between songs and music arises because of the many musical numbers without words (for example, 'The Frug' from *Sweet Charity*), and the featuring of instrumental music from the classical repertoire.

Index 3 — Performers — page 464

Where a performer is illustrated in the still which accompanies the account of a film, the relevant page number appears in italic type. It is perhaps appropriate to mention that many Hollywood actors and actresses used different spellings or presentations of their names at different times; we have opted for standardization based on majority usage.

Index 4 — Composers and Lyricists — page 472

Unfortunately, in certain cases, all research has failed to identify the composers of some musical numbers; such numbers are therefore mentioned without credits. This means that the page references listed for each composer or lyricist will not necessarily yield a comprehensive checklist of their output for the genre.

Index 5 — Other Creative Personnel — page 476

This is a mixed listing, and only reference to the entries themselves will provide the information as to the role the individual played. Included in this category are directors, producers (and associate producers), screenwriters, original story writers, editors, art directors, set and costume designers, cameramen, special effects men, sound recordists, choreographers and dance directors, and musical directors and orchestrators. This is not to suggest that the account of every film in the main text carries credits for photography, sound recording, special effects, or even design; such personnel have been mentioned only where their contribution to the film was especially noteworthy. On the other hand, every film is credited with a director and a writer, and most of them with a producer.

Index 6 — New Films, 1980 Onwards — page 479

This edition of the book contains a number of films that have been released since the first edition was published. These are not included in the above indexes but are indexed separately. This supplementary index contains *Popeye* (1980) and musicals released in 1981 and subsequently.

Fringe Musicals

1929

QUEEN OF THE NIGHTCLUBS (Warner Bros.)
The attempts of a successful nightclub entertainer (Texas Guinan) to prevent her jealous rivals from doing the dirty on her. Eddie Foy Jr, Jack Norworth, George Raft, Lila Lee; directed by Bryan Foy.

RED HOT RHYTHM (Pathe)
Songwriter (Alan Hale) of dubious reputation makes a living by fleecing other composers and publishing their works. Kathryn Crawford, Josephine Dunn; directed by Leo McCarey. (Technicolor sequences.) Songs included: *At Last I'm In Love* Robert Emmet Dolan, Walter O'Keefe.

THE BROADWAY HOOFER (GB: DANCING FEET) (Columbia)
A dancer (Marie Saxon) takes a sabbatical in a small country town and falls for the fourth-rate hoofer-manager (Jack Egan) of a burlesque show that is passing through. Directed by George Archainbaud.

1930

LOVE COMES ALONG (Radio Pictures)
Sailor falls in love with a stranded actress in Cuba. Bebe Daniels, Lloyd Hughes, Montague Love; directed by Rupert Julian. Songs included: *Until Love Comes Along*; *Night Winds* Oscar Levant, Sidney Clare.

MELODY MAN (Columbia)
Famous Viennese composer (John Sainpolis) flees to America with his daughter (Alice Day) after murdering his wife's lover in a jealous rage, and discovers jazz. Fifteen years later he returns to Europe to face trial. William Collier Jr; directed by Roy William Neill. Songs included: *Broken Dreams* Ballard McDonald, Arthur Johnston, Dave Dreyer.

MAN TROUBLE (Fox)
Tough cabaret owner (Milton Sills) falls in love with a girl (Dorothy Mackaill) who, in turn, falls in love with a crooning newspaper man (Roscoe Karns). Directed by Berthold Viertel. Songs included: *You Got Nobody to Love*; *Now I Ask You* James Hanley, Joseph McCarthy.

LILIES OF THE FIELD (Warner Bros.)
Corinne Griffith, after suffering an ugly divorce, becomes a gold digger and is arrested for vagrancy. Of interest for Roy Mack's staging of production numbers in a nightclub. Ralph Forbes; directed by Alexander Korda. Songs included: *I'd Like To Be A Gypsy* Herb Magidson, Ned Washington, Michael Cleary.

CHECK AND DOUBLE CHECK (RKO)
Amos 'n' Andy (as a couple of taxi drivers) spend a night in a haunted house and find a vital property deed without which young lovers Sue Carol and Charles Norton cannot marry. Freeman F. Gosden, Charles J. Correll; directed by Melville Brown. Songs included: *Three Little Words* Bert Kalmar, Harry Ruby; *Old Man Blues* Irving Mills, Duke Ellington.

1931

MEN OF THE SKY (Warner Bros./First National)
A French spy (Irene Delroy) in World War I, her aviator lover (Jack Whiting) and father (John Sainpolis), are discovered and shot; directed by Alfred E. Green. Songs included: *Every Little While*; *Boys March*; *Stolen Dreams*; *You Ought to See Sweet Marguerite* Jerome Kern, Otto Harbach.

JUNE MOON (Paramount)
Adaptation of a stage play by Ring Lardner and George Kaufman about a numbskull (Jack Oakie) with ambitions to become a Tin Pan Alley lyric writer. Frances Dee, June MacCloy; directed by Edward Sutherland. Songs included: *June Moon*; *Montana Moon* Lardner, Kaufman.

1932

DANCERS IN THE DARK (Paramount)
Bandleader Jack Oakie tries to save his pal from the clutches of a dancehall girl (Miriam Hopkins) but falls in love with her himself. William Collier Jr, George Raft; directed by David Burton. Songs included: *St. Louis Blues* W.C. Handy.

HORSE FEATHERS (Paramount)
The Marx Brothers' third feature film and the first to have an original screenplay (by Harry Ruby, Bert Kalmar and S.J. Perelman) abounded in visual and verbal non-sequiturs and featured Groucho as Wagstaff, the new president of Huxley College. Directed by Norman McLeod. Songs included: *I'm Against It*; *Everyone Says 'I Love You'* Kalmar, Ruby.

THE DEVIL'S BROTHER (GB: FRA DIAVOLO) (MGM)
Unsuccessful attempt to give Auber's romantic operetta the slapstick treatment. What remained of Auber's score was competently handled by Dennis King. Stan Laurel, Oliver Hardy, Thelma Todd; directed by Hal Roach and Charles Rogers.

NIGHT WORLD (Universal)
60 minute programmer, set in a New York nightclub, and involving an alcoholic customer (Lew Ayres), a friendly chorus girl (Mae Clarke) and the affair the owner's (Boris Karloff) wife (Dorothy Revier) is having with the cabaret's dance director (Russell Hopton). Hedda Hopper, George Raft; directed by Hobart Henley. The choreography (complete with overhead shots) was by Busby Berkeley.

BLONDE VENUS (Paramount)
Marlene Dietrich learns that husband Herbert Marshall needs $1500 to cure him of radium poisoning; she becomes a singer on the New York stage and, during her husband's absence abroad, has an affair with socialite Cary Grant. Marshall's unexpected return begins a melodramatic chain of events that leads to Dietrich's downfall and subsequent rehabilitation. Dickie Moore, Gene Morgan; directed by Josef von Sternberg. Musical numbers: *Hot Voodoo*; *You Little So And So* Sam Coslow, Ralph Rainger; *I Couldn't Be Annoyed* Leo Robin, Richard A. Whiting.

1933

CAVALCADE (Fox)
Screen version of Noël Coward's hit play chronicling the ups and downs of the Marryot family over a period of 33 years – from 1899 to 1932. Diana Wynyard, Clive Brook. Herbert Mundin, Una O'Connor, Ursula Jeans, Beryl Mercer; directed by Frank Lloyd. Songs included: *Twentieth Century Blues*.

DIPLOMANIACS (RKO)
Rhymed dialogue in song was the novelty in this Wheeler and Woolsey programmer in which Messrs W. and W. are handed a couple of million dollars by the Indians to journey to Geneva in an attempt to make the peace delegates stop fighting. Marjorie White, Phyllis Barry. Louis Calhern; directed by William Seiter. Songs included: *Sing To Me* Edward Eliscu, Harry Akst.

1934

KING KELLY OF THE USA (Monogram)
An American producer (Guy Robertson) falls for a princess (Irene Ware) aboard a Transatlantic ocean liner. Edgar Kennedy; directed by Leonard Fields. Songs included: *Right Next Door To Love*; *Believe Me* Bernie Grossman, Joe Sanders.

THE LOUDSPEAKER (GB: THE RADIO STAR) (Monogram)
A railway station express man (Ray Walker) yearns to become a radio star. Jacqueline Wells; directed by Joseph Santley. Songs included: *Who but You?*; *Doo Ah Doo Ah Doo Ah Know What I'm Doing?* Lew Brown, Harry Akst.

LOVETIME (Fox)
Sentimental story of the life and loves of composer Franz Schubert, with Nils Asther starring. Several Schubert melodies featured as background music. Pat Paterson, Herbert Mundin; directed by James Tinling.

BRIGHT EYES (Fox)
Shirley Temple's first starring vehicle, involving a custody battle over an orphan, contained the song that helped make her famous: *On The Good Ship Lollipop* by Sidney Clare and Richard Whiting. James Dunn, Lois Wilson; directed by David Butler.

FASHIONS OF 1934 (Warner Bros.)
A New York couturier (William Powell) pilfers the latest fashion designs from Paris, then passes them off as his own. Production number was directed by Busby Berkeley, and featured 50 girls draped in ostrich feathers being formed into a galleon 60ft long. They were also transformed into human harps. Bette Davis; directed by William Dieterle. Songs: *Spin A Little Web Of Dreams*; *Broken Melody* Irving Kahal, Sammy Fain.

COCKEYED CAVALIERS (RKO)
After appropriating the clothes of the King's inebriated physician and his assistant, Bert Wheeler and Robert Woolsey run amok in a routine mistaken identity plot. Noah Beery, Thelma Todd; directed by Mark Sandrich. Songs included: *And The Big Bad Wolf Was Dead*; *Dilly Dally* Val Burton, Will Jason.

STINGAREE (Radio Pictures)
Romantic tale, featuring operatic arias, based on a character created by E.W. Hornung, of an Australian Robin Hood who captures the heart of an opera singer (Irene Dunne). Richard Dix, Mary Boland; directed by William Wellman. Songs included: *Tonight Is Mine* Gus Kahn, W. Franke Harling; extracts from Gounod's *Faust* and Flotow's *Martha*.

ONE HOUR LATE (Paramount)
Trials and tribulations of a shipping clerk (Joe Morrison) whose naive stenographer sweetheart (Helen Twelvetrees) enjoys flirting innocently with her boss (Conrad Nagel). Arline Judge, Ray Walker; directed by Ralph Murphy. Songs included: *A Little Angel Told Me So*; *Last Roundup* Sam Coslow, Lewis Gensler, Leo Robin.

RAINBOW OVER BROADWAY (Chesterfield)
Unpopular stepmother (Grace Hayes) to a Kansas City family journeys to New York, with the family, to resume her career as a singer. Frank Albertson, Lucien Littlefield; directed by Richard Thorpe. Songs included: *I Must Be In Love With Love*; *Dance My Blues Away* Elizabeth Morgan, Harry Von Tilzer.

1935

THE NITWITS (Radio Pictures)
Confused whodunnit featuring Wheeler and Woolsey as a couple of cigar salesmen who find themselves involved in the murder of a music publisher. Fred Keating, Betty Grable; directed by George Stevens. Songs included: *Music In My Heart* Dorothy Fields, Jimmy McHugh; *You Opened My Eyes* L. Wolfe Gilbert, Felix Bernard.

THIS IS THE LIFE (Fox)
A vaudeville starlet (Jane Withers), dressed as a boy, runs away from her theatrical commitments and befriends a man (John McGuire) wanted by the police. Directed by Marshall Neilan. Songs included: *Gotta New Kind Of Rhythm*; *Sandy And Me* Sidney Clare, Sammy Stept.

KING SOLOMON OF BROADWAY (Universal)
Melodrama with nightclub background in which Edmund Lowe (as King Solomon), operates a nightclub for jailed gangster Edward Pawley, and loses the club while gambling with a trio of racketeers. Dorothy Page, Pinky Tomlin; directed by Alan Crosland. Songs included: *That's What You Think* Tomlin; *Flower In My Lapel* Con Conrad, Herb Magidson.

MANHATTAN MOON (GB: SING ME A LOVE SONG) (Universal)
Dorothy Page played a dual role: a temperamental entertainer, and the lookalike who deputizes for her at all social engagements. Ricardo Cortez supplied the romantic interest as a nightclub proprietor who falls for Page in her guise as a socialite; directed by Stuart Walker. Songs included: *Manhattan Moon*; *First Kiss* Arthur Morton, Betty Trivers.

THE MELODY LINGERS ON (United Artists)
Story of a concert pianist's (Josephine Hutchinson) self-sacrifice for her child (David Scott). George Houston; directed by David Burton. Music from Bizet's *Carmen*.

AFTER THE DANCE (Columbia)
Melodramatic programmer about an escaped convict (George Murphy) who befriends a cabaret girl, joins her act and becomes a sensation, but is two-timed by a rival dancer who tips off the police. Nancy Carroll; directed by Leo Bulgakov. Songs included: *Without You I'm Just Drifting*; *Tomorrow Night* Harry Akst.

THE LITTLE COLONEL (20th Century-Fox)
Little Shirley Temple is instrumental in reuniting her mother (Evelyn Venable) with her estranged grandfather (Lionel Barrymore). Directed by David Butler. Songs: *Love's Young Dream* Thomas Moore; *Stair Dance* (with Bill Robinson).

THE LITTLEST REBEL (20th Century-Fox)
Shirley Temple saves her father (John Boles) from a prison sentence during the Civil War by calling on President Lincoln. Directed by David Butler. Songs: *Believe Me If All Those Endearing Young Charms* Thomas Moore, Matthew Locke; *Polly Wolly Doodle* (with Bill Robinson).

HERE COMES COOKIE (GB: THE PLOT THICKENS) (Paramount)
Gracie Allen's father (George Barbier) temporarily places his considerable fortune at her disposal as a means of discouraging a male gold digger who is out to ensnare his other daughter. George Burns; directed by Norman McLeod. Songs included: *Lazy Moon* Bob Cole, J. Rosamond Johnson; *Vamp Of The Pampas* Leo Robin, Richard Whiting.

1936

POPPY (Paramount)
W.C. Fields's adopted daughter (Rochelle Hudson), after pretending to be a phony heiress, turns out to be a real one after all. Richard Cromwell, Lynne Overman; directed by Edward Sutherland. Songs included: *Poppy* Sam Coslow, Frederick Hollander; *A Rendezvous With A Dream* Leo Robin, Ralph Rainger.

DEVIL ON HORSEBACK (Grand National)
Crooning gaucho (Del Campo) with the soul of a Mexican Robin Hood vies with the son of a coffee millionaire (Fred Keating) for the affections of Lily Damita. Directed by Crane Wilbur. Songs included: *So Divine*; *Out Of The Hills*; *The Love Fiesta*; *Oh Bella Mia* Harry Tobias, Jack Stern.

1937

THE GIRL SAID NO (Grand National)
A bookie (Robert Armstrong) tries to become a producer to get even with a dance-hall hostess (Irene Hervey) who, one passionate evening, gave him the shakedown. He concocts a revenge scheme (involving some Gilbert and Sullivan players) that will land Hervey in showbusiness, by which ploy he hopes to retrieve the money he spent on her. Paula Stone, William Danforth; directed by Andrew L. Stone. Musical extracts from Gilbert and Sullivan's *The Mikado*; *Patience*; *Pirates Of Penzance*; *Ruddigore*.

BLONDE TROUBLE (Paramount)
Lyric writer Johnny Downs comes to Broadway via Schenectady to find fame and fortune, but after one of his songs becomes a radio hit, finds himself Hollywood-bound. Remake of Paramount's 1931 *June Moon*. Eleanore Whitney, Lynne Overman, Benny Baker, William Demarest; directed by George Archainbaud. Songs included: *It Was All In Fun* Burton Lane, Ralph Freed.

THANKS FOR LISTENING (Conn)
Pinky Tomlin starred as the innocent stooge for a gang of high class clip artists, headed by Aileen Pringle. Maxine Doyle, Claire Rochelle; directed by Marshall Neilan. Songs included: *The Love Bug Will Bite You*; *I Like To Make Music* Tomlin, Connie Lee.

HIGH FLYERS (RKO)
Wheeler and Woolsey pose as aviators, get tangled in a smuggling plot, and effect the capture of the culprits. Lupe Velez, Margaret Dumont, Jack Carson; directed by Edward Cline. Songs included: *Keep Your Head Above Water* Herman Ruby, Dave Dreyer.

HAWAIIAN BUCKAROO (20th Century-Fox)
Western with an Hawaiian setting in which Smith Bellew and sidekick Benny Burt, after finding employment with Evalyn Knapp on her ranch, save her from the machinations of a crooked foreman (George Regas). Directed by Ray Taylor. Songs included: *Hawaiian Memories*; *I Left Her On The Beach At Waikiki* Harry MacPherson, Albert von Tilzer, Eddie Grant.

THE KING AND THE CHORUS GIRL (Warner Bros.)
Fernand Gravet (making his American debut) falls head over heels for Folies Bergère chorus girl (Joan Blondell). Jane Wyman, Edward Everett Horton; directed by Mervyn LeRoy. Musical numbers staged by Bobby Connolly, including *For You*; *On The Rue De La Paix* Ted Koehler, Werner Heymann.

PICK A STAR (MGM)
Rowdy comedy with songs about two star-struck sisters (Patsy Kelly and Rosina Lawrence) in Hollywood. Laurel and Hardy appeared briefly in two sequences. Jack Haley, Mischa Auer, Lyda Roberti; directed by Edward Sedgwick. Musical numbers included: *Without Your Love* Johnny Lange, Fred Stryker.

WAY OUT WEST (MGM)
Western of sorts in which Laurel and Hardy help Rosina Lawrence to rescue her gold mine from villainous James Finlayson. Directed by James W. Horne. Songs included: *Commence To Dancing* J.L. Hill; *The Trail Of The Lonesome Pine* Harry Carroll, Ballard MacDonald.

WALLABY JIM OF THE ISLANDS (Grand National)
The adventures of the roistering skipper of a pearl-fishing brig in the South Seas. George Houston, Ruth Coleman; directed by Charles Lamont. Songs included: *Ia-O-Ra-Na*; *Hi-Ho-Hum* Felix Bernard, Irving Bibo.

SWING HIGH, SWING LOW (Paramount)
An adaptation of George M. Watters and Arthur Hopkins's play *Burlesque*, it charted the up-and-down career of a trumpet player (Fred MacMurray). Carole Lombard was the woman in his life. Charles Butterworth, Dorothy Lamour; directed by Mitchell Leisen. Songs included: *If It Isn't Pain Then It Isn't Love* Leo Robin, Ralph Rainger; *Panamania* Al Siegel, Sam Coslow.

1938

YOU AND ME (Paramount)
The story of a gangster (George Raft) who marries a girl (Sylvia Sidney) with a criminal past herself. An almost Brechtian hybrid of social drama, comedy and German Expressionism. Directed by Fritz Lang. Songs included: *You Can't Get Something For Nothing*; *The Right Guy For Me* Sam Coslow, Kurt Weill.

FOOLS FOR SCANDAL (Warner Bros.)
An impoverished French marquis (Fernand Gravet) instals himself as cook and butler to a film star (Carole Lombard) as a means of compromising her. Directed by Mervyn LeRoy. Rodgers and Hart provided the songs, most of which were removed from the final release print. Those that survived included: *There's A Big Boy In Harlem*; *How Can You Forget*.

STOLEN HEAVEN (Paramount)
Two jewel thieves (Olympe Bradna and Gene Raymond) are innocently harboured by an old, broken-down concert pianist (Lewis Stone) until they are ferreted out by the law. Glenda Farrell, Porter Hall; directed by Andrew L. Stone. Music by Wagner, Liszt, Moskowski, Chopin, Grieg and Strauss.

SWISS MISS (20th Century-Fox)
Laurel and Hardy, as a couple of waiters in an Alpine hotel, become involved with a composer (Walter Woolf King) who is trying to get away from his wife (Della Lind); directed by John G. Blystone.

THE GIRL FROM MEXICO (RKO)
Slapstick comedy with songs about an unknown Mexican singer (Lupe Velez) who is brought to New York by a radio executive (Donald Woods). Leon Errol; directed by Leslie Goodwins. Musical numbers included: *Negra Consentida* Joaquin Pardave; *Chiapanecas* Romero, Garuse, De Torre.

1939

SHE MARRIED A COP (Republic)
Film producers Jerome Cowan and Jean Parker fool Irish singing cop (Phil Regan) into falsely believing that he has landed the romantic lead in a new film. Regan marries Parker before she can reveal the deception. Directed by Sidney Salkow. Songs included:

ESCAPE TO PARADISE (RKO)
Bobby Breen, operating a motocycle taxi service in a South American seaport, guides Kent Taylor around the town and into romance with Maria Shelton, and then gets him into trouble by representing him as a buyer of maté leaves. Directed by Erle C. Kenton. Songs included: *Tra la La* Nilo Menendez, Eddie Cherkose.

1940

VILLAGE BARN DANCE (Republic)
Though singer Doris Day (not to be confused with the more famous Warner Bros. star) loves engineer Richard Cromwell, in order to save the merchants in her town from bankruptcy, she decides to marry wealthy industrialist Robert Baldwin. In the nick of time news reaches her that a radio show put on by the locals has been bought for sponsorship. George Barbier, Esther Dale, Andrew Tombes, radio personalities Lulubelle and Scotty, Barbara Allen (Vera Vague), Don Wilson and the Texas Wanderers; directed by Frank McDonald. Songs included: *What Are Little Girls Made Of* Scotty Wiseman, John Lair; *Howdy Neighbour* Eddie Cherkose.

GRAND OLE OPRY (Republic)
The Weaver family (Leon, Frank and June) starred in a familiar story of locals outwitting city slickers. The family manage to get Leon Weaver elected as governor after the usual difficulties encountered with crooked politicians. Roy Acuff's Smoky Mountain Boys, George Dewey Hay, and Uncle Dave Macon and Dorris supplied hillbilly music. Directed by Frank McDonald.

COMIN' ROUND THE MOUNTAIN (Paramount)
More Ozarkian humour, with Bob Burns returning to his backwoods Tennessee family after a brief sojourn in the city and being elected mayor of the town. Una Merkel, Jerry Colonna, Don Wilson; several tunes, purporting to be authentic music from the Tennessee hill country, were supplied by a hillbilly radio aggregate comprising Pat Barrett, Harold Peary, Bill Thompson, Cliff Arquette and Mirandy. Directed by George Archainbaud.

UP IN THE AIR (Monogram)
Frankie Darro, a radio station page boy, helps the cops discover who murdered singer Lorna Gray and cowboy Gordon Jones. Marjorie Reynolds, Mantan Moreland; directed by Howard Bretherton. Songs included: *By The Looks Of Things; Something Or Other* Edward Kay, Harry Tobias.

1941

ANDY HARDY'S PRIVATE SECRETARY (MGM)
Andy Hardy (Mickey Rooney) finally graduates from high school and finds himself with a new roadster and a secretary. Eighteen-year-old Kathryn Grayson, making her debut, played the secretary and, in the course of the film, sang a Cole Porter ballad, Strauss's 'Voices of Spring' and the mad scene from Donizetti's 'Lucia di Lammermoor'. Lewis Stone, Fay Holden, Ann Rutherford; directed by Howard B. Seitz.

VANISHING VIRGINIAN (MGM)
Kathryn Grayson, in her second feature, played authoress Rebecca Yancey whose Southern girlhood this family saga was all about. Frank Morgan (top starred), Spring Byington, Natalie Thompson, Douglass Newland; directed by Frank Borzage. Songs included: *The World Was Made For You; Evening By The Moonlight; Bill Bailey* (all sung by Grayson).

SMILIN' THROUGH (MGM)
Third version (the other two were in 1922 and 1932) of Jane Cowl and Jane Murfin's play in which a World War I Irish lassie (Jeanette MacDonald) finds her marriage to a young man (Gene Raymond) opposed by her elderly guardian (Brian Aherne) because of an incident in the past in which suitor Raymond's father slew guardian Aherne's bride. Ian Hunter, Frances Robinson; directed by Frank Borzage. (Technicolor). Songs included: *Drink To Me Only With Thine Eyes; A Little Love A Little Kiss* Leo Silesu, Adrian Ross; *Smilin' Through* Arthur Penn.

NEW WINE (United Artists)
Ilona Massey attempts to see that Franz Schubert (Alan Curtis) receives the recognition he deserves. Binnie Barnes, Albert Basserman (as Beethoven), Billy Gilbert, Sterling Holloway; directed by Reinhold Schunzel. The music included two songs (one *Ave Maria*) and extracts from symphonies by Schubert.

COUNTRY FAIR (Republic)
As soon as hillbilly June Clyde agrees to marry a fast-talking campaign manager (Eddie Foy Jr) for an aspirant governor (William Demarest), she sets out with a will to electioneer for his rival (Harold Peary). Harold Huber, Guinn Williams, Lulubelle Wiseman, The Vass Family, Simp Phonies; directed by Frank McDonald. Songs included: *Mornin' On The Farm* Jack Elliott.

HARD-BOILED CANARY (Paramount)
When the burlesque house in which little Susanna Foster is appearing as a singer of operatic arias is raided, she is spirited off by a pair of press agents (Allan Jones and Lynne Overman) to a summer music school in the mountains. Margaret Lindsay, Grace Bradley, William Collier Sr; directed by Andrew L. Stone. Extracts from Bizet's *Carmen* and Gounod's *Faust*.

LET'S GO COLLEGIATE (GB: FAREWELL TO FAME) (Monogram)
Frankie Darro and Jackie Moran, a couple of college kids, have promised their sweethearts that their boatcrew will be top-notch, but their ace crew member is drafted, so they pick a muscular truck driver (Frank Sully) off the street to impersonate the drafted boatman. Marcia Mae Jones, Keye Luke, Mantan Moreland, Gale Storm; directed by Jean Yarbrough. Songs included: *Look What You've Done To Me; Sweet Sixteen* Harry Tobias, Edward Kay.

ICE-CAPADES (Republic)
Backstage yarn involving a newsreel cameraman (James Ellison) who, after muffing an assignment at Lake Placid, fakes it with shots of the Central Park pond in New York. Jerry Colonna and skating stars Belita, Vera Hruba Ralston, Dorothy Lewis. Songs included: *Forever And Ever* Sol Meyer, George R. Brown, Jule Styne; *Sophisticated Lady* Duke Ellington.

IT STARTED WITH EVE (Universal)
A hat-check girl (Deanna Durbin) becomes the fiancée of a millionaire (Robert Cummings). Charles Laughton was a crusty old millionaire who is about to die in the opening scene, but actually lives on for the duration of the picture. Remade in 1964 as *I'd Rather Be Rich*. Directed by Henry Koster. Songs included: *Clavelitos* Valverde; *Going Home* Dvorak.

SING FOR YOUR SUPPER (Columbia)
The heartbreaks of a struggling bandleader (Charles 'Buddy' Rogers). Jinx Falkenburg; directed by Charles Barton. Songs included: *Why Is It So* Sammy Cahn, Saul Chaplin.

GLAMOUR BOY (Paramount)
Story of a once famous child star (Jackie Cooper), now a soda-jerk in a Hollywood drug store, who coaches the studio's newest child prodigy (Darryl Hickman) in a remake of one of his (Cooper's) early hits. Susanna Foster, Walter Abel; directed by Ralph Murphy. Songs included: *The Magic Of Magnolias; Love Is Such An Old-Fashioned Thing* Frank Loesser, Victor Schertzinger.

1942

CALL OUT THE MARINES (RKO)
Messrs. Victor McLaglen and Edmund Lowe join the Marines as sergeants and compete for the attentions of a café girl (Binnie Barnes), only to discover that she is an enemy agent. Directed by Frank Ryan and William Hamilton. Songs included: *Call Out The Marines; Light Of My Life* Mort Greene, Harry Revel.

THE YANKS ARE COMING (PRC)
Arrogant bandleader Henry King, who thinks any soldier without a commission is a chump, finds his band rebelling against his arrogance by enlisting *en masse*. Mary Healy, Little Jackie Helier, Maxie Rosenbloom, Parkyakarkus; directed by Alexis Thurn-Taxis. Songs included: *I Must Have Priorities On Your Love; Don't Fool Around With My Heart.*

1943

ALL BY MYSELF (Universal)
After being jilted by her lover (Neil Hamilton) who has fallen for a singer (Rosemary Lane), Evelyn Ankers blackmails a doctor (Patric Knowles) into posing as her fiancé. Also Tip, Tap and Toe and The Loumell Morgan Trio; directed by Felix Feist. Songs included: *All By Myself* Inez James, Buddy Pepper; *You're Priceless* Morey Amsterdam, T. Ramona.

THE GIRL FROM MONTEREY (PRC)
Programmer with a boxing background about a Mexican girl (Armida) and her romance with a light-heavyweight champion (Terry Frost). Edgar Kennedy, Veda Ann Borg; directed by Wallace Fox. Songs included: *Last Night's All Over; The Girl From Monterey* Louis Herscher.

THE AMAZING MRS HOLLIDAY (Universal)
War-time story in which Deanna Durbin played the spirited survivor of a small mission in China and foster mother to nine waifs of uncertain origin. Edmond O'Brien, Barry Fitzgerald; directed by Bruce Manning. Songs included: *Vissi d'Arte* (from Tosca) Puccini; *The Old Refrain.*

GET GOING (Universal)
Grace McDonald arrives in Washington from New England, lands Robert Paige, and uncovers the headquarters of a spy ring. Barbara Jo Allen (Vera Vague); directed by Jean Yarbrough. Songs included: *Got Love; Hold That Line* Everett Carter, Milton Rosen.

SO'S YOUR UNCLE (Universal)
Programmer with Jan Garber and Jack Teagarden and their orchestras, The Delta Rhythm Boys, Mary O'Brien and the Tailor Maids, lending musical support to a far-fetched yarn in which playwright Donald Woods finds himself impersonating his uncle. Musical interludes take place in a nightclub sequence. Billie Burke, Elyse Knox; directed by Jean Yarbrough. Songs included: *That's The Way It Goes* Everett Carter, Milton Rosen; *Don't Get Around Much Anymore* Duke Ellington, Bob Russell.

CHATTERBOX (Republic)
Joe E. Brown played a radio cowboy, Judy Canova the woman he marries in the last reel. Directed by Joseph Santley. Songs included: *Mad About Him, Sad About Him, How Can I Be Glad Without Him Blues* Larry Marks, Dick Charles; *Sweet Lucy Brown* Leon and Otis Rene.

IT AINT HAY (GB: MONEY FOR JAM) (Universal)
Remake of Damon Runyon's *Princess O'Hara* (Universal, 1935) as an Abbott and Costello vehicle in which the two comedians, by mistake, find themselves owners of a prize racehorse called Tea Biscuit. The usual complications ensue. Grace McDonald, Cecil Kellaway, Eugene Pallette; directed by Erle C. Kenton. Songs included: *Sunbeam Serenade, Hang Your Troubles On A Rainbow* Harry Revel, Paul Francis Webster.

SARONG GIRL (Monogram)
Burlesque queen (Ann Corio), an orphan, has to dredge up a mother if she is to remain out of jail when police close her show. Mary Gordon, Mantan Moreland, Irene Ryan, Johnny 'Scat' Davis; directed by Arthur Dreifuss. Songs included: *Woogie Hula* Louis Herscher, Andy Iola Long; *Darling Nellie Gray* Benjamin, Russell Hanby.

LADY OF BURLESQUE (GB: STRIPTEASE LADY) (United Artists)
Backstage melodrama involving murder and suicide. Based on Gypsy Rose Lee's novel *The G-String Murders*. Barbara Stanwyck, Michael O'Shea; directed by William Wellman. Songs included: *Take It Off The E String; So This Is You* Sammy Cahn, Harry Akst.

LAUGH YOUR BLUES AWAY (Columbia)
Ex-rich dowager (Isobel Elsom) tries to marry off her son (Douglas Drake) to the daughter (Phyllis Kennedy) of a wealthy Texas cattleman (Dick Elliott). Jinx Falkenburg (top-starred) and Bert Gordon appeared as a pair of jobless actors attempting to emulate a Russian count and countess. Directed by Charles Barton. Songs included: *Prairie Parade* Larry Marks, Dick Charles.

HI DIDDLE DIDDLE (United Artists)
Martha Scott and sailor Dennis O'Keefe find their 48-hour honeymoon fraught with frustrating interruptions. Adolphe Menjou (top-billed), Pola Negri, Billie Burke, June Havoc; directed by Andrew L. Stone. Songs included: *Loved Too Little Too Late; Big Sombrero* Foster Carling, Phil Boutelje.

HOOSIER HOLIDAY (Republic)
The Hoosier Hotshots, a hillbilly novelty band, appearing as the Baker Boys, find themselves opposed by the head of the draft board (Thurston Hall) when they decide to quit their farm and enlist. George D. Hay, Dale Evans, George Byron, Emma Dunn, The Music Maids, George 'Shug' Fisher; directed by Frank McDonald. Songs included: *Hoosier Holiday; Grandaddy Of Boogie Woogie* Johnny Marvin, Charles Henderson.

NEARLY EIGHTEEN (Monogram)
Aspiring singer (Gale Storm) attempts to find a niche for herself in show business, discovering, in the process, that she is too young to seek employment as a café singer, and too old to become a student in a noted music academy. Rick Vallin, Bill Henry, Luis Alberni; directed by Arthur Dreifuss. Songs included: *Smiles For Sale; Walking On Air.*

OH MY DARLING CLEMENTINE (Republic)
A group of itinerant hillbilly entertainers, managed by Frank Albertson, wind up in a snobby town in Dixie, and attempt to put on a show. Roy Acuff, Harry 'Pappy' Cheshire, Lorna Gray, Irene Ryan; directed by Frank McDonald. Music provided by Acuff and other hillbilly stars.

TRUE TO LIFE (Paramount)
Story of a writer (Dick Powell) of a family radio serial who moves in with an all-American family for inspiration. Mary Martin, Franchot Tone, Victor Moore; directed by George Marshall. Songs included: *There She Was*; *The Old Music Master* Hoagy Carmichael, Johnny Mercer.

CINDERALLA SWINGS IT (RKO)
All about Guy Kibbee's attempts to interest a Broadway producer in a small-town classical singer (Gloria Warren). Directed by Christy Cabanne. Songs included: *I Heard You Cry Last Night* Ted Grouya, Jerrie Kruger; *The Flag's Still There* George Jessel, Ben Oakland.

1944

LOUISIANA HAYRIDE (Columbia)
Judy Canova, movie-struck hick, outsmarts con-men Richard Lane and George McKay, and achieves her ambition to make it in pictures. Ross Hunter; directed by Charles Barton. Songs included: *Rainbow Road*; *You Gotta Go Where The Train Goes* Kim Gannon, Walter Kent.

A WAVE, A WAC AND A MARINE (Monogram)
Story of a Hollywood agent (Henny Youngman) who mistakenly signs a pair of under-studies (Elyse Knox and Anne Gillis) believing them to be the real stars of a Broadway show. Sally Eilers; directed by Phil Karlstein. Songs included: *Time Will Tell*; *Gee, I Love My G.I. Guy* Eddie Cherkose, Jacques Press, Freddie Rich.

GIRL RUSH (RKO)
Wally Brown and Alan Carney, comics in a San Francisco show *c*.1840, join the gold rush and wind up in the womanless town of Red Creek where they promise to recruit girls both as entertainers and as wives for the miners. Frances Langford; directed by Gordon Douglas. Songs included: *Rainbow Valley*; *If Mother Could Only See Us Now* Harry Harris, Lew Pollack.

SING NEIGHBOUR SING (Republic)
Young lothario (Brad Taylor) poses as a distinguished, elderly English psychologist in a small college town – until the real psychologist appears. Ruth Terry, Virginia Brissac, Roy Acuff and His Smoky Mountain Boys, Lulubelle and Scotty; directed by Frank McDonald. Songs included: *Blake Song*; *Phrenology* Jack Elliott, R. Dale Bates.

SONG OF RUSSIA (MGM)
Famous American conductor (Robert Taylor) tours Russia during World War II and falls in love with a young Russian pianist (Susan Peters) whom he marries. Directed by Gregory Ratoff. Music included a thematic serenade by Jerome Kern and E.Y. Harburg called *And Russia Is Her Name*.

HI BEAUTIFUL (GB: PASS TO ROMANCE) (Universal)
Remake of *Love In A Bungalow* (Universal, 1937). Romance between a caretaker of a model home (Martha O'Driscoll) and the soldier (Noah Beery Jr) she meets after he is unable to find accommodation in a hotel. Couple win a marital contest for the 'Happiest GI' pair but are, in fact, unmarried. Hattie McDaniel; directed by Leslie Goodwins. Songs included: *Don't Sweetheart Me* Charles Tobias, Cliff Friend; *Best Of All* Allie Wrubel.

ROSIE THE RIVETER (GB: IN ROSIE'S ROOM) (Republic)
Programmer about four wartime factory workers forced to live in one room because of the housing shortage; the men and women have to take turns. Jane Frazee, Frank Albertson, Vera Vague; directed by Joseph Santley. Songs included: *Rosie The Riveter* Redd Evans, John Jacob Loeb; *Why Can't I Sing A Love Song?* Harry Akst, Sol Meyer.

THREE LITTLE SISTERS (Republic)
A young soldier corresponds with his 'dream girl' whom he has never seen. In her letters, the girl describes her luxurious life in a family mansion with her two sisters. In reality, the sisters wash clothes for local villagers, and the girl is an invalid in a wheelchair. Mary Lee, Ruth Terry, Cheryl Walker; directed by Joseph Santley. Songs included: *Don't Forget The Little Girl Back Home*; *Sweet Dreams Sweetheart* Kim Gannon, Walter Kent.

MY BEST GAL (Republic)
A father (Frank Craven) tries to interest his daughter (Jane Withers) in the family's show-biz traditions; she tries to interest a backer in a musical written by Jimmy Lydon. Directed by Anthony Mann. Songs included: *Upsy Downsy*; *Where There's Love* Kim Gannon, Walter Kent.

EVER SINCE VENUS (Columbia)
A young man (Ross Hunter) invents a new kind of lipstick, sets out to market it and, in the process, falls in love with his secretary (Ann Savage). Ina Ray Hutton, Hugh Herbert; directed by Arthur Dreifuss. Songs included: *Wedding Of The Samba And The Boogie* Bernie Wayne, Ben Raleigh; *Glamour For Sale* Lester Lee, Harry Harris.

FOOTLIGHT GLAMOUR (Columbia)
Blondie and Dagwood Bumstead find themselves involved in the theatrical aspirations of a tool manufacturer's daughter (Ann Savage). Penny Singleton, Arthur Lake; directed by Frank Strayer. Songs included: *Bamboola*; *What's Under Your Mask, Madame?* Ray Evans, Jay Livingston.

JIVE JUNCTION (PRC)
To forget his grief after the death of his aviator father overseas, young Dickie Moore switches from classical to popular music and entertains the servicemen stationed nearby. Tina Thayer, Gerra Young; directed by Edward G. Ulmer. Songs included: *We're Just In Between*; Bell song from Delibes' *Lakme*.

MEN ON HER MIND (PRC)
An ambitious singer (Mary Beth Hughes) refuses to let love and marriage interfere with her career. Edward Norris, Ted North; directed by Wallace Fox. Songs included: *Heaven On Earth* Lee Zahler, Pat O'Dea.

NATIONAL BARN DANCE (Paramount)
When turned down by radio executive Robert Benchley for an audition, Charles Quigley and the National Barn Dance troupe pose as servants in Benchley's home and stage an impromptu show with positive results. Jean Heather, Mabel Paige, The Hoosier Hotshots, Lulubelle and Scotty, The Dinning Sisters; directed by Hugh Bennett. Songs included: *When Pa Was Courtin' Ma*; *Angels Never Leave Heaven*.

IN SOCIETY (Universal)
Bud Abbott and Lou Costello invade high society's horsey set with predictably chaotic results. Marion Hutton; directed by Jean Yarbrough. Songs included: *My Dreams Are Getting Better All The Time* Mann Curtis, Vic Mizzy; *What A Change In The Weather* Kim Gannon, Walter Kent.

LOST IN A HAREM (MGM)
In sets left over from *Kismet* (MGM, 1944), Abbott and Costello, as a pair of stranded magicians, find themselves up against wicked ruler Douglass Dumbrille and buxom Marilyn Maxwell; Jimmy Dorsey and His Band. Directed by Charles Riesner. Songs included: *What Does It Take?*; *It Is Written* Don Raye, Gene De Paul.

1945

THE BELLS OF ST MARY'S (RKO)
Bing Crosby, as Father O'Malley, comes to rescue the financially embarrassed parochial school run by Sister Ingrid Bergman. Henry Travers; directed by Leo McCarey. Songs included: *The Bells Of St Mary's* Douglas Ferber, A. Emmett Adams; *Adeste Fidelis*.

SWINGIN' ON A RAINBOW (Republic)
Songwriter Jane Frazee arrives in New York to seek vengeance on a bandleader who has stolen one of her songs, and falls in love with lyric writer Brad Taylor. Harry Langdon; directed by William Beaudine.

ABBOTT AND COSTELLO IN HOLLYWOOD (MGM)
Abbott and Costello, as a porter and a barber at a Hollywood studio, decide to enter the talent agency business. Frances Rafferty; directed by S. Sylvan Simon. Songs included: *I Hope The Band Keeps You Playing*; *Fun On The Wonderful Midway* Ralph Blane, Hugh Martin.

I LOVE A BANDLEADER (Columbia)
A housepainter (Phil Harris) suffers an amnesia attack and thinks he's a bandleader. Eddie (Rochester) Anderson; directed by Del Lord. Songs included: *Eager Beaver* Sammy Cahn, Jule Styne.

FRISCO SAL (Universal)
New England girl (Susanna Foster) finds employment in a Barbary Coast saloon while searching for the murderer of her brother. Turhan Bey; directed by George Waggner. Songs included: *Beloved* George Waggner, Edward Ward; *Good Little Bad Little Lady* Jack Brooks.

IT'S A PLEASURE (RKO)
Romantic tribulations of an exhibition skater (Sonja Henie) and an ice-hockey star (Michael O'Shea). (Technicolor). Directed by William A. Seiter. Songs included: *Romance* Walter Donaldson.

MASQUERADE IN MEXICO (Paramount)
Dorothy Lamour, a nightclub entertainer, finds herself suspected of a jewel theft in Mexico City. Arturo de Cordova, Patric Knowles; directed by Mitchell Leisen. Songs included: *Forever Mine* Bob Russell, Eddie Lisbona, Maria T. Lara; *Masquerade In Mexico* Ben Raleigh, Bernie Wayne.

EVE KNEW HER APPLES (Columbia)
Radio star (Ann Miller) is mistaken for a murderess, in the process of which she falls in love with a reporter (William Wright). Robert Williams, Ray Walker; directed by Will Jason. Songs included: *An Hour Never Passes*; *I've Waited A Lifetime*.

BECAUSE OF HIM (Universal)
Deanna Durbin has to convince actor Charles Laughton that she is an accomplished actress, capable of being his leading lady. Franchot Tone; directed by Richard Wallace. Songs included: *Lover* Richard Rodgers, Lorenz Hart; *Danny Boy*.

TAHITI NIGHTS (Columbia)
American bandleader (Dave O'Brien) arrives on a Tahitian island to discover that arrangements are underway for him to marry a princess (Jinx Falkenburg) of one of the tribes. Mary Treen, Florence Bates, The Vagabonds; directed by Will Jason. Songs included: *Let Me Love You Tonight* Mitchell Parish, René Touzet.

THE BIG SHOW-OFF (Republic)
Nightclub pianist Arthur Lake tries to score with singer Dale Evans by pretending that he is the unknown masked wrestler. Lionel Stander, George Meeker, Anson Weeks and His Orchestra; directed by Howard Bretherton. Songs included: *Cleo From Rio*; *Hoops My Dear* Dave Oppenheim, Roy Ingraham.

CRIMSON CANARY (Universal)
Five jazz bandsmen are about to depart from a smalltown night spot for San Francisco when the female vocalist is mysteriously murdered. Whodunnit? Noah Beery Jr, Lois Collier, John Litel; directed by John Hoffman. Songs included: *The Walls Of Jericho*; *One Meat Ball (And No Spaghetti)* Hy Zaret, Lou Singer.

1946

QUEEN OF BURLESQUE (PRC)
Murder mystery set against burlesque background. Evelyn Ankers, Carleton Young; directed by Sam Newfield. Songs included: *How Can I Tell You?*; *Flower Song* Gene Lucas, Al Stewart.

SPECTER OF THE ROSE (Republic)
Pretentious tale of ballerina Viola Essen's love for a mad and murderous dancing genius (Ivan Kirov). The several ballet sequences were choreographed by Tamara Geva. Judith Anderson. Michael Chekhov; directed by Ben Hecht.

I'VE ALWAYS LOVED YOU (GB: CONCERTO) (Republic)
Professional rivalry between a male chauvinist orchestral conductor (Philip Dorn) and a young pianist (Catherine McLeod) whose career he ruins by conducting his orchestra too loudly, thus drowning her efforts at the piano during Rachmaninov's *Piano Concerto No 2*. Directed by Frank Borzage. Music by Chopin, Beethoven, Mendelssohn, Wagner and Bach. Song: *I've Always Loved You* Aaron Goldmark, Ludwig Flato.

BETTY CO-ED (GB: THE MELTING POT) (Columbia)
After interrupting her career as a carnival singer to enrol as a student at Upton College, Jean Porter finds nothing but snobbery and hostility from the president (Shirley Mills) of the campus sorority. Directed by Arthur Dreifuss. Songs included: *Put The Blame On Mame*; *You Gotta Do What You Gotta Do* Doris Fisher, Allan Roberts.

MURDER IN THE MUSIC HALL (Republic)
During a performance of an ice revue, a former director of an ice show is found murdered. Vera Hruba Ralston and the show's conductor (William Marshall) attempt to solve the crime before the police inspector (William Gargan) does. Directed by John English. Songs included: *My Wonderful One*; *Mess Me Up*.

BREAKFAST IN HOLLYWOOD (GB: THE MAD HATTER) (United Artists)
Screen version of Tom Breneman's popular radio show with three separate stories interwoven into the narrative line, and all taking place on the same day. Bonita Granville; directed by Harold Schuster. Songs included: *It Is Better To Be Yourself* Nat King Cole; *If I Had A Wishing Ring* Marla Shelton, Louis Alter.

IDEA GIRL (Universal)
Songplugger Julie Bishop arranges amateur song contest and other stunts which, while helping to put the song publishers for whom she works on the map, also gives them problems. Jess Barker, George Dolenz, Alan Mowbray; directed by Will Jason. Songs included: *I Don't Care If I Never Dream Again*; *I Can't Get You Out Of My Mind* Jack Brooks, Edgar Fairchild.

IN OLD SACRAMENTO (Republic)
Romance between a music hall belle (Constance Moore) with rigid ethical standards, and a gentleman gambler who doubles as a notorious stagecoach robber (William Elliott). Hank Daniels, Ruth Donnelly, Eugene Pallette, Lionel Stander; directed by Joseph Kane. Songs included: *Speak To Me Of Love* Bruce Siever, Jean Lenoir; *The Man Who Broke The Bank At Monte Carlo* Fred Gilbert.

DING DONG WILLIAMS (RKO)
Studio music director (Felix Bressart) hires a clarinettist (Glenn Vernon) to compose a score for him, only to discover that Vernon cannot read or write a note of music. Marcy McGuire, Anne Jeffreys, 11-year-old pianist Richard Korbel, Bob Nolan and The Sons of The Pioneers; directed by William Berke. Songs included: *I Saw You First*; *Candlelight And Wine* Harold Adamson, Jimmy McHugh.

1947
IT HAPPENED ON FIFTH AVENUE (Monogram-Allied Artists)
A gentlemanly vagabond (Victor Moore) establishes residence in a millionaire's mansion each winter during the latter's absence, and surrounds himself with homeless war veterans. Don DeFore, Gale Storm. Ann Harding, Charlie Ruggles; directed by Roy Del Ruth. Songs included: *Speak My Heart*; *That's What Christmas Means To Me* Harry Revel.

WHEN A GIRL'S BEAUTIFUL (Columbia)
Young promotion man (Marc Platt) in a model agency submits a composite photograph of all a model's best features, then has to find a girl to fit the picture. Adele Jergens; directed by Frank McDonald. Songs included: *I'm Sorry I Didn't Say I'm Sorry*; *When A Girl's Beautiful* Allan Roberts, Lester Lee.

THE SECRET LIFE OF WALTER MITTY (Goldwyn-RKO)
Zany reworking of Thurber's story of a mother's boy (Danny Kaye) who, after spending most of his time day-dreaming of wild adventures from which he always emerges the hero, finds himself actually involved in just such an adventure. Songs: *Symphony For Unstrung Tongue (The Little Fiddle)*; *Anatole Of Paris* Sylvia Fine.

1948
A FOREIGN AFFAIR (Paramount)
Sparkling comedy with songs in which Jean Arthur is sent to investigate conditions in post-war Berlin, falls in love with John Lund and encounters a rival in Marlene Dietrich. Directed by Billy Wilder. Songs included: *Black Market*; *Ruins of Berlin*; *Iowa Corn Song* Frederick Hollander.

THE PALEFACE (Paramount)
Western send-up in which a dentist (Bob Hope) thanks to the help of Calamity Jane (Jane Russell) becomes a hero. Directed by Norman Z. McLeod. Songs included: *Buttons And Bows*; *Meetcha Round The Corner* Ray Evans, Jay Livingston.

VARIETY TIME (RKO)
An entertaining compendium of dance routines, musical numbers, short comedies and silent film clips. Jack Paar, Freddie Carle and His Orchestra, Edgar Kennedy, Pat Rooney, Jesse and James, Leon Errol, Lynn, Royce and Vanya, and Hans Conried. Directed by Hal Yates. Songs and musical numbers included: *Carle Boogie* Frankie Carle; *The Daughter Of Rosie O'Grady* Monte Brice, Walter Donaldson; *Babalu* Bob Russell, Marguerita Lecuona.

1949
MY FRIEND IRMA (Paramount)
Complications resulting from dim-witted Marie Wilson's decision to desert her layabout boyfriend (John Lund) for a singing orange juice stall-keeper (Dean Martin). Martin and Jerry Lewis's debut. Diana Lynn, Don DeFore; directed by George Marshall. Songs included: *Here's To Love*; *Just For Fun* Ray Evans, Jay Livingston.

THE SUN COMES UP (MGM)
Sentimental tale of bitter war widow Jeanette MacDonald (her last film) who finds life worth living again after she mothers orphan Claude Jarman Jr. Lloyd Nolan, Percy Kilbride, Lewis Stone, Margaret Hamilton, Lassie; directed by Richard Thorpe. Songs included: *Un Bel Di* from Puccini's 'Madame Butterfly'; *Songs My Mother Taught Me* Dvorak; *Romance* Anton Rubinstein, Paul Bourget.

1950
DOUBLE CROSSBONES (Universal)
Set in the colonial settlement of Charlestown in the Carolinas, the story involved the adventures of Donald O'Connor, as an apprentice shopkeeper, who is erroneously arrested for trafficking with pirates. Helena Carter; directed by Charles T. Barton. Songs included: *Percy Had A Heart*; *Song Of Adventure* Lester Lee, Dan Shapiro.

EVERYBODY'S DANCIN' (Lippert)
A phoney promoter with a heart of gold (Spade Cooley) tries to revive public interest in a behind-the-times dance-hall. Richard Lane, Barbara Woodall, Ginny Jackson and 10 musical groups. Directed by Will Jason.

FANCY PANTS (Paramount)
Echoing *Ruggles Of Red Gap* (Paramount, 1935), the story had Bob Hope playing an American actor playing an English butler (in the Wild West) to wealthy, status-seeking Lucille Ball. Bruce Cabot; directed by George Marshall. Songs included: *Home Cookin'*; *Fancy Pants* Ray Evans, Jay Livingston.

MY FRIEND IRMA GOES WEST (Paramount)
Marie Wilson and friends, on a trip to Hollywood in the company of Dean Martin and Jerry Lewis, stop over in Las Vegas to seek employment as entertainers. John Lund, Corinne Calvet, Diana Lynn; directed by Hal Walker. Songs included: *Baby Obey Me*; *Fiddle And Guitar Band*; *Querida Mia* Ray Evans, Jay Livingston.

LOVE HAPPY (United Artists)
The last film the Marx Brothers made as a team starred Harpo as a food thief who has unwittingly stolen a sardine-tin containing some valuable diamonds and Groucho as a detective out to catch him. Chico Marx, Ilona Massey, Vera-Ellen, Raymond Burr, Marion Hutton, Bruce Gordon and, in a brief appearance, Marilyn Monroe. Directed by David Miller. Songs included: *Willow Weep For Me*; *Mama Wants To Know*; *Love Happy* Ann Ronell.

1951
TWO GALS AND A GUY (United Artists)
Programmer that set out to spoof TV, but ended up as a routine backstage yarn chronicling the desperate efforts to find someone to take the place of the star female lead in a TV show. Robert Alda, Janis Paige, James Gleason, and The Three Suns instrumental trio; directed by Alfred E. Green. Songs included: *Laugh And Be Happy*; *So Long For Now* Hal David, Marty Nevins.

DOUBLE DYNAMITE (RKO)
Frank Sinatra as a shy bank clerk suspected of stealing $75,000. Low spot in the career of all concerned. Jane Russell, Groucho Marx; directed by Irving Cummings. Songs included: *It's Only Money*; *Kisses And Tears* Sammy Cahn, Jule Styne.

THE LEMON DROP KID (Paramount)
Bob Hope as a bookie whose incompetence lands him in trouble with a gangster. Marilyn Maxwell; directed by Sidney Lanfield. Songs included: *It Doesn't Cost A Dime To Dream*; *They Obviously Want Me To Sing* Ray Evans, Jay Livingston.

STRICTLY DISHONORABLE (MGM)
Opera star Ezio Pinza marries Janet Leigh for the sake of her reputation, after which the young wife, with the help of her husband's mother (Esther Minciotti), successfully attempts to put the marriage on a more conventional footing. Directed by Melvin Frank and Norman Panama (from the play by Preston Sturges). Songs included: *Everything I Have Is Yours* Harold Adamson, Burton Lane; *I'll See You In My Dreams* Gus Kahn, Isham Jones.

AT WAR WITH THE ARMY (Paramount)
Dean Martin played a sexually confident sergeant in pursuit of the girls, with Jerry Lewis as an incompetent private who spends most of his life on KP duty. Mike Kellin, Jimmy Dundee, Dick Stabile, Angela Green, Polly Bergen; directed by Hal Walker. Songs included: *The Navy Gets The Gravy And The Army Gets The Beans*; *You And Your Beautiful Eyes*; *Tanda Wanda Hoy* Mack David, Jerry Livingston.

THE MILKMAN (Universal)
Mindless tale about a milk delivery man (Jimmy Durante) whose firm gets him a job accompanying the idiot son (Donald O'Connor) of the director of a rival concern on his milk round. Joyce Holden, William Conrad, Piper Laurie, Henry O'Neill; directed by Charles T. Barton. Songs included: *Girls Don't Want My Money* Durante, Jack Barnett; *It's Bigger Than Both Of Us*; *Early Morning Song* Sammy Fain, Barnett; *That's My Boy* Durante, Barnett.

GI JANE (Lippert)
Tom Neal is an impresario about to go into the army who has a dream about the life ahead of him in which he populates a remote desert post with a platoon of WACS. Jean Porter, Iris Adrian, Jimmy Dodd, Jean Mahoney, Jimmy Lloyd; directed by Reginald Le Borg.

FOOTLIGHT VARIETIES (RKO)
Musical revue compiled from old and new footage, compered by Jack Parr and featuring Liberace, The Sportsmen, Grace Romanos, Buster West and Frankie Carle and His Orchestra; directed by Hal Yates. Songs and musical numbers included: *La Paloma* Sebastian Yradier; *Goodnight Ladies* E.P. Christy; *Liberace Boogie*.

YES SIR, MR BONES (Lippert)
A small boy wanders into a home for old minstrels, wants to know all about them, and via a flashback to an old river showboat, is shown how a group of minstrels prepared for a performance. Cotton and Chick Watts, Scatman Crothers, F.F. Miller, Billy Green, The Hobnobbers; directed by Ron Ormond. Songs included: *I Want To Be A Minstrel Man*; *Stay Out Of The Kitchen*; *Is Your Rent Paid Up In Heaven?*

1952

THE WAC FROM WALLA WALLA (GB: ARMY CAPERS) (Republic)
Judy Canova gets into the WACS by mistake and becomes a heroine when she corners some heavies who are trying to steal data on guided missiles. Stephen Dunne; directed by William Witney. Songs included: *Lovey*; *If Only Dreams Came True* Jack Elliott.

HAS ANYBODY SEEN MY GAL? (Universal)
Delightful comedy with songs, set in the twenties, in which millionaire Charles Coburn becomes a lodger in the home of a family descended from an erstwhile sweetheart of his. Family are unaware of his wealth. Piper Laurie, Gigi Perreau, Rock Hudson; directed by Douglas Sirk. (Technicolor) Songs included: *Gimme A Little Kiss*; *Will Ya Huh?* Roy Turk, Jack Smith, Maceo Pinkard; *When The Red Red Robin Comes Bob-Bob-Bobbin' Along* Harry M. Woods.

SAILOR BEWARE (Paramount)
Dean Martin and Jerry Lewis enter the armed forces with hilarious results. Leif Erickson, Marion Marshall, Don Wilson, Skip Homeier, an unbilled appearance by Betty Hutton, and guest star Corinne Calvet; directed by Hal Walker. Songs included: *Sailor's Polka*; *Today, Tomorrow, Forever*; *Never Before* Jerry Livingston, Mack David.

GLORY ALLEY (MGM)
Feeble psychological drama with music, set in a New Orleans Bourbon Street bar with Leslie Caron miscast as the loyal girlfriend of war-time 'coward' Ralph Meeker. Louis Armstrong's appearance was its only redeeming feature. Kurt Kasznar, Gilbert Roland; directed by Raoul Walsh. Songs included: *St Louis Blues* W.C. Handy; *Glory Alley* Mack David, Jerry Livingston.

SOUND OFF (Columbia)
Mickey Rooney plays a nightclub entertainer who suddenly finds himself in the army. Anne James; directed by Richard Quine. (Super Cinecolor). Songs included: *My Lady Love* Lester Lee, Bob Russell; *Blow Your Own Horn* Rooney.

BELLES ON THEIR TOES (20th Century-Fox)
Sequel to *Cheaper By The Dozen* (20th Century-Fox) recounting the further adventures of the Gilbreth family, but without papa Clifton Webb. Myrna Loy, Jeanne Crain, Debra Paget, Jeffrey Hunter; directed by Henry Levin. (Technicolor) Songs included: *Whispering* John Schonberger, Richard Coburn, Vincent Rose; *When You Wore A Tulip* Jack Mahoney, Percy Wenrich.

1953

TAKE ME TO TOWN (Universal)
Ann Sheridan is a lady with a past, who while hiding out from the Federals in a Northwest lumber town, takes advantage of an offer from three young boys who think she would make a good mother while their timberman father (Sterling Hayden) is away from home. Directed by Douglas Sirk. (Technicolor) Songs included: *Oh, You Red-Head* Frederick Herbert, Milton Rosen; *Take Me To Town* Lester Lee, Dan Shapiro.

LET'S DO IT AGAIN (Columbia)
Remake of the studio's 1937 comedy *The Awful Truth* about a philandering composer (Ray Milland) whose wife (Jane Wyman) decides to teach him a lesson by embarking on an affair. Tom Helmore, Don Ameche, Leon Ames, Karin Booth, Mary Treen; directed by

Alexander Hall. Songs included: *Call Of The Wild*; *Give Me A Man Who Makes Music* Lester Lee, Ned Washington.

LATIN LOVERS (MGM)
Tropical romance involving a millionairess (Lana Turner) who can't decide whether to settle for a man (John Lund) even richer than she is, or a poor but charming Brazilian (Ricardo Montalban). Directed by Mervyn LeRoy. (Technicolor) Songs included: *I Had To Kiss You*; *A Little More Of Your Amor* Nicholas Brodszky, Leo Robin.

GERALDINE (Republic)
John Carroll plays a musical instructor studying folk music at a western college, and Stan Freberg a top recording star who hears one of Carroll's musical discoveries and wants to record it. Mala Powers, Jim Backus, Kristine Miller; directed by R.G. Springsteen. Songs included: *Geraldine* Sidney Clare, Victor Young; *Wintertime Of Love* Edward Heyman, Young.

1954

THE COUNTRY GIRL (Paramount)
About an alcoholic actor (Bing Crosby) who is given a chance for a comeback by a young director (William Holden), and the mistaken belief that the actor's wife (Grace Kelly) is the reason behind his alcoholism. Directed by George Seaton. Songs: *The Pitchman*; *Live And Learn*; *The Search Is Through* Ira Gershwin, Harold Arlen.

KNOCK ON WOOD (Dena Productions, released Paramount)
Danny Kaye played a vaudeville ventriloquist whose dummy has been stuffed with secret documents, all of them vitally important to a nest of spies. Leon Askin, Abner Biberman, Steve Geray, Mai Zetterling, Diana Adams, Torin Thatcher; directed by Norman Panama and Melvin Frank. Songs and musical numbers: *Knock On Wood*; *All About You* Monohan O'Han.

1955

HOW TO BE VERY VERY POPULAR (20th Century-Fox)
Remake of *She Loves Me Not* (Paramount, 1934) in which Betty Grable and Sheree North flee from a San Francisco nightclub after the murder of a Chinese striptease artist and fetch up in an ivy-covered men's college. Robert Cummings, Charles Coburn; directed by Nunnally Johnson. (CinemaScope. Color by De Luxe). Songs included: *Shake, Rattle And Roll*; *Bristol Bell* Ken Darby, Lionel Newman; *How To Be Very, Very Popular* Jule Styne, Sammy Cahn.

1956

I'LL CRY TOMORROW (MGM)
Uncompromising account of singer Lillian Roth's 16-year battle with booze. Susan Hayward excellent in the lead; so was Jo Van Fleet as her pushy mother. Richard Conte, Eddie Albert; directed by Daniel Mann. Songs included: *Sing You Sinners* Sam Coslow, W. Frank Harling; *Happiness Is Just A Thing Called Joe* E.Y. Harburg, Harold Arlen.

THAT CERTAIN FEELING (Paramount)
About a cartoonist (Bob Hope) whose lack of confidence results in his hiring himself out as a 'ghost' to a comic-strip artist. Eva Marie Saint, George Sanders, Pearl Bailey; directed by Norman Panama and Melvin Frank. Songs included: *That Certain Feeling* George and Ira Gershwin; *Zing Went The Strings Of My Heart* James Hanley.

HE LAUGHED LAST (Columbia)
Gangster spoof of the twenties (told in flashback) about what happens when a singer-dancer (Lucy Marlow) inherits the money and the enterprises of an underworld czar (Alan Reed). Frankie Laine, Anthony Dexter; directed by Blake Edwards. (Technicolor) Songs included: *Strike Me Pink*; *Save Your Sorrows* Arthur Morton.

MAGIC FIRE (Republic)
Biopic of composer Richard Wagner, filmed on location

in Germany, with Alan Badel as Wagner. Yvonne de Carlo, Peter Cushing, Frederick Valk, Valentina Cortese; directed by William Dieterle. Music included abbreviated extracts from Wagner's music dramas.

PARDNERS (Paramount)
Dean Martin and Jerry Lewis spoof the traditional Western in a remake of Bing Crosby's 1936 *Rhythm On The River* (Paramount). Martin played a ranch foreman, Lewis a pampered millionaire from New York who becomes sheriff. Jeff Morrow and John Baragrey were the heavies; Lori Nelson and Jackie Loughery the female interest; directed by Norman Taurog. Songs included: *Me 'n' You 'n' The Moon*; *Buckskin Beauty* Sammy Cahn, Jimmy Van Heusen.

1959

SOME LIKE IT HOT (United Artists)
After witnessing a Chicago gangland slaying similar to the St Valentine's Day Massacre, musicians Tony Curtis and Jack Lemmon disguise themselves as a couple of broads and, for safety, join an all-girl band in Florida. Marilyn Monroe, George Raft, Pat O' Brien, Joe E. Brown; directed by Billy Wilder. Songs included: *I Wanna Be Loved By You* Bert Kalmar, Harry Ruby; *Runnin' Wild* Joe Grey, Leo Wood, A. Harrington Gibbs.

1960

CINDERFELLA (Paramount)
The familiar fairy tale, but with a switch of sex of the central character. Jerry Lewis, Ed Wynn, Judith Anderson, Anna Maria Alberghetti; directed by Frank Tashlin. (Technicolor) Songs included: *Somebody*; *Let Me Be A People* Harry Warren, Jack Brooks.

THE SUBTERRANEANS (MGM)
Film of Jack Kerouac's celebrated 'beatnik' novel. George Peppard as Olympic gold medallist Leo Percepied, Leslie Caron as the mixed-up girl he falls in love with while searching for a meaning to life in San Francisco's Bay area. Janice Rule, Roddy McDowell, Anne Seymour, Jim Hulton; music by André Previn, performed by, among others, Art Farmer, Shelly Manne, Red Mitchell, Dave Bailey. An Arthur Freed production; directed by Ranald MacDougall.

1961

WHERE THE BOYS ARE (MGM)
Youth-orientated melodrama with songs, set during Easter vacation in Fort Lauderdale, Florida, and involving four college girls in search of love and romance. George Hamilton, Dolores Hart, Paula Prentiss, Jim Hutton, Yvette Mimieux, Connie Francis; directed by Henry Levin. (Metrocolor, CinemaScope) Songs included: *Where The Boys Are*; *Turn On The Sunshine* Neil Sedaka, Howard Greenfield.

101 DALMATIONS (Buena Vista)
Full-length Disney cartoon about an English couple, their brood of dogs, and a lady 'dognapper' whose hobby is making coats out of Dalmatians' skins. Songs included: *Cruella De Ville*; *Dalmation Plantation* Mel Leven.

THE LADIES' MAN (Paramount)
Jerry Lewis played a houseboy in a Hollywood boarding house for girls run by Helen Traubel. Directed by Jerry Lewis. Songs included: *Don't Go To Paris* Harry Warren, Jack Brooks.

ALL HANDS ON DECK (20th Century-Fox)
Naval comedy with songs. Pat Boone, Buddy Hackett (as a wealthy and eccentric American Indian), Dennis O'Keefe (as the ship's commander), Gale Gordon, Barbara Eden; directed by Norman Taurog. (CinemaScope and Color Deluxe). Songs included: *All Hands On Deck*; *I've Got It Made* Jay Livingston, Ray Evans.

1964

THE LIVELY SET (Universal)
James Darren has to choose between hot-rod racing or college. Remake of *Johnny Dark* (Universal, 1954). Pamela Tiffin; directed by Jack Arnold. (Eastmancolor) Songs included: *If You Love Him*; *Casey Wake Up*.

I'D RATHER BE RICH (Universal)
Remake of Universal's 1941 release *It Started With Eve*. Sandra Dee has to find a fiancé to satisfy the last wish of her ailing grandfather (Maurice Chevalier). Robert Goulet, Andy Williams; directed by Jack Smight. (Eastmancolor) Songs included: *Almost There*; *Where Are You?* Harold Adamson, Jimmy McHugh.

THE PLEASURE SEEKERS (20th Century-Fox)
Three girls seek romance in Spain. Retread of *Three Coins In The Fountain* (20th Century-Fox, 1954). Carol Lynley, Ann-Margret, Pamela Tiffin, Tony Franciosa; directed by Jean Negulesco. (CinemaScope and Color by De Luxe) Songs included: *The Pleasure Seekers*; *Something To Think About* Sammy Cahn, Jimmy Van Heusen.

1966

MADE IN PARIS (MGM)
Fashion designer's assistant (Ann-Margret) goes to Paris and falls for couturier Louis Jourdan. Directed by Boris Sagal. Songs included: *Paris Lullaby* Sammy Fain, Paul Francis Webster; *Skol Sister* Quincy Jones.

1968

LIVE A LITTLE, LOVE A LITTLE (MGM).
Photographer Elvis Presley, working for conservative publisher Rudy Vallee as well as for a girlie magazine, expends a lot of energy trying to ensure that each of his respective bosses doesn't find out about the other. Michele Carey; directed by Douglas Laurence. (Panavision and Metrocolor) Songs included: *A Little Less Conversation* Billy Strange, Scott Davis; *Almost In Love* Randy Starr, Luiz Bonfa.

FOR SINGLES ONLY (Columbia)
Adventures of a group of young men and women in an apartment block restricted to unmarried people under thirty years of age. John Saxon, Mary Ann Mobley, Milton Berle; directed by Arthur Dreifuss. (Pathe Color) Songs included: *Kee Ka Roo* Walter Wanderley, Bobby Worth; *Take A Chance With Me* Wanderley.

1969

THE TROUBLE WITH GIRLS (MGM)
Presley's 30th film found him as the manager of a combination entertainment educational travelling show. Marilyn Mason; directed by Peter Tewksbury. (Panavision, Metrocolor) Songs included: *Clean Up Your Own Back Yard* Scott Davis, Billy Strange.

1970

NORWOOD (Paramount)
Glen Campbell, a Vietnam veteran, sets out from Texas to New York to find fame as a TV singer. *En route* he encounters, among several other people, a pregnant Kim Darby with whom he falls in love. Cass Daley, Jack Haley Sr. Directed by Jack Haley Jr. (Technicolor) Songs included: *Ol' Norwood's Comin' Home* Marie Mitchell Torok, Ramona Reed.

1972

SNOOPY COME HOME (National General)
Schulz's Snoopy leaves home to find Lila, his original owner, who writes from a hospital that she needs him. Featuring the voices of Bill Melendez (Snoopy), Johanna Baer (Lila), Chad Webber, Robin Kohn, Stephen Shea, David Carey; directed by Bill Melendez. Songs by Richard M. And Robert B. Sherman.

1976

BOUND FOR GLORY (United Artists)
Superbly evocative biography of folk singer Woody Guthrie (David Carradine) featuring Guthrie's own compositions. Ronny Cox, Melinda Dillon; directed by Hal Ashby. (Color) Songs included: *So Long It's Been Good To Know Yuh*; *This Land Is Your Land*; *Talking Dust Bowl Blues*; *Pastures Of Plenty*.

SPARKLE (Warner Bros.)
Story of a rock'n'roll sister act who determine to escape their Harlem background. Irene Cara, Lonette McKee, Dwan Smith, Mary Alice, Beatrice Winde, Philip M. Thomas, Dorian Harewood, Paul Lambert; directed by Sam O'Steen.

THE FIRST NUDIE MUSICAL (Paramount)
Second generation Hollywood producer (Stephen Nathan), after making a few flop porno flicks, decides to make a porno musical *à là* the 1930's. Cindy Williams, Bruce Kimmel, Leslie Ackerman; directed by Kimmel, who also wrote the score. (De Luxe Color).

1977

THE TURNING POINT (20th Century-Fox)
Dance-oriented drama about the effect a visit of a famous ballerina (Anne Bancroft) has on erstwhile friend (Shirley MacLaine), who has opted for domesticity rather than a dancing career, and regrets it. Bancroft fears old age and regrets not having had a family. Tom Skerritt, and ballet dancers Mikhail Baryshnikov, Leslie Browne, Antoinette Sibley; directed by Herb Ross. (Color by DeLuxe).

1978

GOIN' COCONUTS (Osmond Distribution Co.)
Extension of Donny and Marie Osmond's TV show, with a plot which finds Marie in possession of a necklace the show's baddies want. Herbert Edelman, Kenneth Mars, Ted Cassidy; directed by Howard Morris. (Color DeLuxe).

SEXTETTE (Crown International Pictures)
In this very poor movie, privately financed by a pair of her millionaire fans, Mae West (aged 87) starred as a beautiful movie star whose wedding night is interrupted by a summit conference being held in the same hotel. Timothy Dalton, Dom De Luise, Tony Curtis, George Hamilton, Walter Pidgeon, Rona Barret, Ringo Starr. Directed by Ken Hughes.

MOVIE MOVIE (Warner Bros.)
Second half of this 'double feature', called BAXTER'S BEAUTIES OF 1933, spoofs the Busby Berkeley backstage musical of the early thirties (with particular reference to *42nd STREET* (Warner Bros. 1933). Rebecca York was the Ruby Keeler character, Barry Bostwick, Dick Powell, and George C. Scott, Warner Baxter, Trish Van Devere, Barbara Harris; Michael Kidd choreographed; directed by Stanley Donen.

1979

A PERFECT COUPLE (20th Century-Fox)
On-off relationship between a wealthy, family-dominated Greek antique dealer (Paul Dooley), and a pop singer (Marta Heflin). Directed by Robert Altman. Songs included: *Hurricane* Tom Berg, Ted Neely, Allan Nichols; *Fantasy* Allan Nichols.

1980

THE COAL MINER'S DAUGHTER (Universal)
How coal miner's daughter Loretta Lynn (Sissy Spacek) made it from Butcher Holler to Nashville, with help from her husband Doolittle (Tommy Lee Jones) and folk singer Patsy Cline (Beverly D'Angelo); directed by Michael Apted. Songs included: *I'm A Honky Tonk Girl*; *You Ain't Woman Enough To Take My Man* Loretta Lynn.

TIMES SQUARE (Butterfly Valley)
A group of New York kids, including the daughter of Park Avenue parents and her lower-class lover, take to the street for destructive excitement. Music comes to their rescue – but not, alas, to the rescue of the paying customers. With Tim Curry, Trini Alvarado and Robin Johnson. Directed by Alan Moyle.

NIJINSKY (Paramount)
Disappointing biopic of the great Russian dancer with George De La Pena in the title role and a miscast Alan Bates as his lover Diaghilev. Leslie Ann Browne appeared as Romola, Nijinsky's wife, with other roles going to Alan Badel, Carla Fracci, Colin Blakeley, Janet Suzman and, as Stravinsky, Ronald Pickup. Herb Ross directed from a screenplay by Hugh Wheeler. Extracts from: *Le Sacre du Printemps*, *Petruschka* Stravinsky; *L'Après Midi D'Un Faune* Debussy; *Schéhérazade* Rimsky-Korsakov.

THE COMPETITION (Columbia)
A glorified soap-opera, set against the backdrop of a music competition in San Francisco, and involving the rivalry between Richard Dreyfuss and Amy Irving, two competitors. A Rastar-William Sackheim production, it also featured Sam Wanamaker and Vickie Kriegler, and was directed by debut-making Joel Oliansky.

HONEYSUCKLE ROSE a.k.a. **ON THE ROAD AGAIN** (Warner Bros.)
Wille Nelson starred as a country singer in this fine, semi-autobiographical drama about a man who has to choose between his family and his career. Dyan Cannon and Amy Irving co-starred and it was directed by Jerry Schatzberg.

1981

AMERICAN POP (Columbia)
An animated feature that unsuccessfully charted the history of popular American music from its beginnings in blues and jazz to rock 'n' roll and its discordant offspring – the kind of subject, in fact, that the Disney Organization would have taken in its imaginative stride. Ralph Bakshi directed.

1983

TENDER MERCIES (EMI)
Robert Duvall received an Oscar for his portrayal of a country singer on the skids in this downbeat drama for which he also supplied the songs. Tess Harper co-starred as a widow who helps Duvall reassemble his shattered life. Horton Foote also won an Oscar for his screenplay. The director was Bruce Beresford.

1984

AMADEUS (Orion)
Mediocrity clashed with genius in Peter Shaffer's compelling Oscar-winning screenplay (fashioned from his internationally successful play of the same name) and in which Oscar-winning F. Murray Abraham starred as Salieri, and Tom Hulce as Mozart. Oscar-winning Milos Forman directed this highly entertaining, Oscar-winning biopic.

1987

TRICK OR TREAT (De Laurentiis)
Heavy-metal rock featured prominently in this horror spoof whose story-line finds a recently deceased rock star (Tony Fields) coming back to life when his last unreleased record is played backwards. Nothing, however, brought the movie to life. Cast included Marc Price, Lisa Orgolini and Doug Savant. It was directed by Charles Martin Smith.

DANCERS (Canon)
Dreadful drama in which Mikhail Baryshnikov starred as a ballet dancer who, while rehearsing a movie version of *Giselle*, falls hopelessly in love with ballerina Leslie Browne. Herbert Ross directed.

Miscellaneous Pop Musicals

1956

ROCK AROUND THE CLOCK (Columbia)
First rock 'n' roll film, featuring Bill Haley and His Comets, involved efforts of a dance band manager (Johnny Johnstone) to promote them all. Directed by Fred Sears.

ROCK ROCK ROCK (Vanguard)
Twenty numbers tied to plot involving college girl's (Tuesday Weld) efforts to find money for new dress for Spring prom. Directed by Will Price.

1957

DON'T KNOCK THE ROCK (Columbia)
Group of rock exponents attempt to overcome small town's hostility to their music. Bill Haley and His Comets. Directed by Fred Sears.

CALYPSO HEAT WAVE (Columbia)
Juke box czar (Michael Granger) buys his way into record company to disapproval of partners (Johnny Desmond, Merry Anders). Directed by Fred Sears.

UNTAMED YOUTH (Warner Bros.)
Two sisters (Mamie Van Doren, Lori Nelson) are sent to a prison farm whose inmates are all rock 'n' roll addicts. Directed by Howard W. Koch.

MR ROCK 'N' ROLL (Paramount)
Disc jockey Alan Freed sets out to convince sceptical editor that rock 'n' roll is beneficial to its young adherents. Directed by Charles Dubin.

ROCK PRETTY BABY (Universal International)
High school music combo leader (John Saxon) has problems when parents refuse to lend him $300 for new guitar. Luana Patten, Edward C. Platt, Fay Wray, Rod McKuen. Directed by Richard Bartlett.

CALYPSO JOE (Allied Artists)
Romantic difficulties beset airline hostess (Angie Dickinson) and TV star (Edward Kemmer). Directed by Edward Dein.

SHAKE RATTLE AND ROCK (American International)
TV personality (Tom Connors) attempts to set up rock 'n' roll centre for underprivileged kids against opposition from reactionary reformers. Lisa Gaye, Sterling Holloway, Douglass Dumbrille, Margaret Dumont, Fats Domino. Directed by Edward L. Cahn.

BOP GIRL GOES CALYPSO (United Artists)
Rock singer (Judy Tyler) switches to Calypso at urging of shrink (Bobby Troup). Directed by Howard Koch.

JAMBOREE (GB: DISC JOCKEY JAMBOREE) (Warner Bros.)
Studio's first attempt to capture the youth market with story about a pair of singing sweethearts (Paul Carr, Freda Holloway) and their once married agents (Kay Medford, Robert Pastine). Directed by Roy Lockwood.

1958

THE BIG BEAT (Universal)
Classical recording company is taken over by the boss's son (William Reynolds), a rock fanatic. The Mills Brothers. Directed by Will Cowan.

KEEP IT COOL, also known as **LET'S ROCK** (Columbia)
Popular ballad singer (Julius La Rosa) loses favour with his fans when he refuses to board the rock bandwagon. Directed by Harry Foster.

SUMMER LOVE (Universal)
Tribulations of teenage love involving a young musician (John Saxon) whose affair with girlfriend Judy Meredith is threatened when he and his combo are given their first job away from home. John Wilder, Rod McKuen, Fay Wray, directed by Charles Haas.

SENIOR PROM (Columbia)
About a college girl (Jill Corey) and the two men in her life – snobby Tom Laughlin and pop singer Paul Hampton. Directed by David Lowell Rich.

1961

TEENAGE MILLIONAIRE (United Artists)
Teenage millionaire orphan (Jimmy Clanton) attempts to enter show biz against wishes of his aunt (ZaSu Pitts). Directed by Lawrence F. Doheny.

HEY LET'S TWIST (Paramount)
The successful efforts of brothers (Joey Dee, Teddy Randazzo) to turn father's ice-cream parlour into a haven for twist addicts. Directed by Greg Garrison.

1962

TWIST AROUND THE CLOCK (Columbia)
Unemployed agent (John Cronin) 'discovers', and attempts to promote, The Twist. Directed by Oscar Rudolph (remake of *Rock Around The Clock*).

TWIST ALL NIGHT (American International)
Louis Prima, Sam Butera and The Witnesses need money to pay rent on their nightspot after it is invaded by a group of teenagers. June Wilkinson, Ty Perry. Directed by William J. Hole.

DON'T KNOCK THE TWIST (Columbia)
About a TV producer (Gene Chandler) and his romantic entanglements with a dress designer (Mari Blanchard). Directed by Oscar Rudolph.

TWO TICKETS TO PARIS (Columbia)
On-off romance aboard liner between Joey Dee and Jeri Lynne Fraser. Directed by Greg Garrison.

1963

BEACH PARTY (American International)
Anthropologist Robert Cummings studies the sex habits of Malibu Beach *habitués*. Dorothy Malone, Frankie Avalon. Directed by William Asher.

1964

SURF PARTY (20th Century-Fox)
A trio of Arizona girls arrive at the coast in search of the brother of one of them. Directed by Maury Dexter.

BIKINI BEACH (American International)
Publisher Keenan Wynn's attempts to evict surfers from beach where he wants to build community for senior citizens. Directed by William Asher.

MUSCLE BEACH PARTY (American International)
Frankie Avalon heads group of surfers who clash head-on with muscle men. Directed by William Asher.

PAJAMA PARTY (American International)
A Martian (Tommy Kirk) is sent to earth to pave the way for forthcoming invasion, but falls in love with Annette Funicello instead. Elsa Lanchester, Harvey Lembeck, Jody McCrea, Jesse White, Buster Keaton, Dorothy Lamour, Rene Riano. Directed by Don Weiss.

1965

BEACH BLANKET BINGO (American International)
Pot-pourri of surfing, sky-diving and mermaids. Directed by William Asher.

A SWINGIN' SUMMER (United Screen Artists)
Three youngsters and local lifeguard help save a Californian dance pavilion threatened with closure. Directed by Robert Sparr.

THE GIRLS ON THE BEACH (Lebin Brothers Production, distributed by Paramount)
Adventures of three co-eds whose sorority beach house is in danger of closure through lack of funds. Directed by William Witney.

SKI PARTY (American International)
All about the rivalry between Frankie Avalon, Dwayne Hickman and Aron Kincaid for Yvonne Craig and Deborah Walley. Directed by Alan Rafkin.

WILD ON THE BEACH (Lippert Inc. Production, distributed by 20th Century-Fox)
Battle for possession of a beach house between Lee Sullivan and Frankie Randall. Directed by Maury Dexter.

HOW TO STUFF A WILD BIKINI (American International)
A mysterious redhead (Beverly Adams) appears from nowhere to fill a bikini floating aimlessly in mid-air. Frankie Avalon, Annette Funicello, Mickey Rooney, Buster Keaton, Harvey Lembeck, Dwayne Hickman, Brian Donlevy. Directed by William Asher.

1966

WILD WILD WINTER (Universal)
College heart-throb (Gary Clarke) finds himself competing in ski contest. Directed by Lennie Weinrib.

OUT OF SIGHT (Universal)
Butler (Jonathan Daly) to a rock 'n' roll star sets out to prevent a man with a hatred of rock music (John Lawrence) from sabotaging forthcoming music fair. Directed by Lennie Weinrib.

FIREBALL 500 (American International)
Frankie Avalon as a cocky racing driver competes with Fabian for the attentions of Annette Funicello. Directed by William Asher.

THE COOL ONES (Warner Bros.)
As a publicity stunt, impresario (Roddy McDowell) plays matchmaker to a rising pop singer (Debbie Watson) and a failing crooner (Gil Peterson). Directed by Gene Nelson.

1967

THE CATALINA CAPER (Crown International)
Last of the 'beach party' series in which Tommy Kirk helps a group of frugging teenyboppers on Catalina to nab a couple of gangs of art thieves. Directed by Lee Sholem. (Color).

1969

THAT TENNESSEE BEAT (20th Century-Fox))
A guitar-playing petty thief (Earl Richards) is rehabilitated and becomes a successful country musician on the Nashville theatre circuit. Sharon De Bord, Dolores Faith, Minnie Pearl, Merle Travis, Jim Reader. Directed by Richard Brill.

Documentaries

1954

THE WORLD DANCES (Festival Pictures)
70-minute film recording folk music and folk dancing groups from over twenty nations. Directed by Brooke L. Peters.

1956

SATCHMO THE GREAT (United Artists)
Louis Armstrong and His Band on tour in Europe and Equatorial Africa, with stopover dates in Stockholm, Paris, London and the Gold Coast. Climax at Lewisohn Stadium, New York, where band joined the Philharmonic Orchestra in a performance of W.C. Handy's 'St Louis Blues'. This footage originally shot for Ed Murrow's TV show, 'See It Now'.

ROCKIN' THE BLUES (Austin Productions)
A poorly produced melée of all-black acts (e.g. Flournoy Miller and Mantan Moreland, The Harptones, The Hurricanes, The Miller Sisters, Linda Hayes etc.) to exploit the then up-and-coming rock craze. Directed by Arthur Rosenblum.

1959

JAZZ ON A SUMMER'S DAY (Hillcrest)
A superbly photographed account of the July 1956 Newport, Rhode Island, Jazz Festival, capturing on celluloid artists of the calibre of Thelonius Monk, Anita O'Day, Dinah Washington, Gerry Mulligan, Chico Hamilton, Louis Armstrong, Jack Teagarden, Mahalia Jackson, Chuck Berry, George Shearing etc. Directed by Bert Stern.

1960

SING A SONG FOR HEAVEN'S SAKE (Marathon Pictures)
A musical revue by some fifty artists, performing some thirty songs, at a Gospel meeting in Nashville, Tennessee. Directed by Ulf Van Court.

1964

THE T.A.M.I. SHOW (American International Pictures)
A musical revue featuring such artists as The Beach Boys, Marvin Gaye, Lesley Gore, The Rolling Stones, Gerry and The Pacemakers, Billy J. Kramer and The Dakotas, The Supremes, at the Teenage Awards Music International. Staged at the Santa Monica Civic Auditorium in October, 1964. Directed by Steve Binder.

1966

THE BIG T.N.T. SHOW (American International)
Top artists performing their hit recordings at the Hollywood Moulin Rouge. The compere was David McCallum, the performers included Roger Miller, Joan Baez, Ray Charles, Donovan, Petula Clark, The Byrds, The Lovin' Spoonful, Ike and Tina Turner, The Ronettes, Bo Diddley etc. Directed by Larry Peerce.

MUSIC CITY USA (Gemini Pictures)
Disc Jockey T. Tommy and a group of his friends taking a look at music in Nashville, including the Record World Awards, and visiting a country and western nightclub where they hear, among many others, Webb Pierce, The Wilburn Brothers, Loretta Lynn, Dave Dudley, Jean Shepard, Warner Mack, Charlie Louvin and His Band, The Osborne Brothers, Lorene Mann, Hillous Butrum, Vincent Youmans Jr. Produced and directed by Preston Collins and James Dinet.

1967

SPREE (Producers Equity Corporation)
A poorly photographed and clumsily edited journalistic look at the Las Vegas casinos and some of their better known cabaret performers such as Vic Damone, Jayne Mansfield, Juliet Prowse, Mickey Hargitay, Constance Moore. Directed by Mitchell Leisen and Walon Green.

COUNTRY WESTERN HOEDOWN (Jam Art Pictures)
A musical revue consisting of country and western acts – e.g. Pee Wee King, Redd Stewart, Little Eller Long, Red Murphy, Neal Burris, Bonnie Sloan, Shorty Hayes etc – performing on barn dance stages throughout America, including at the Grand Ole Opry, Nashville. Directed by William R. Johnson.

FESTIVAL (Peppercorn-Wormser Inc.)
Footage (in black and white) of the Newport Folk Festivals of 1963-6, including interviews with performers and fans explaining the appeal of folk music. The plethora of artists on show included Joan Baez, Theodore Bikel, Mike Bloomfield, The Blue Ridge Mountain Dancers, Paul Butterfield Blues Band, Johnny Cash, Judy Collins, Cousin Emmy, Donovan, Bob Dylan, Mimi Farina, The Freedom Singers. Directed by Murray Lerner.

1968

YOU ARE WHAT YOU EAT (Commonwealth United)
A *pot-pourri* of scenes depicting America's contemporary youth revolution, with the major portion devoted to rock and folk performers such as Tiny Tim, Peter Yarrow, Barry McGuire, Super Spade, Harper's Bizarre, The Electric Flag, Carol Wayne, John Simon, The Family Dog, David Crosby etc. etc. Directed by Barry Feinstein.

1969

MONTEREY POP (Leacock Pennebaker Inc.)
A record of the 1967 Monterey International Pop Festival, emceed by Brian Jones of The Rolling Stones. A combination of heavy rock and the voguish serenity of 'flower children' which featured, among many others, Janis Joplin, The Mamas and The Papas, Canned Heat, Hugh Masekela, Jefferson Airplane, Grace Slick, Eric Burdon and The Animals, The Who, Country Joe and The Fish, Otis Redding, Simon and Garfunkel, Ravi Shankar, Jimi Hendrix. Directed by D.A. Pennebaker.

JOHNNY CASH! THE MAN, HIS WORLD, HIS MUSIC (Verite Productions)
Top country and western star Johnny Cash on a concert tour with his wife and other artists. Interviews and recording sessions with Carl Perkins and Bob Dylan featured. Directed by Robert Elfstrom.

1970

THE NASHVILLE SOUND (The Nashville Company/Aurora Publishers/Amram Nowak Associates)
Nearly 40 top country and western artists performing in Nashville, together with footage of interviews, the Country Music Association Disc Jockey Convention, and a young singer, Herbie Howell, embarking on his career. Some of those appearing included Archie Campbell, Johnny Cash, Skeeter Davis, Lester Flatt, Bubba Fowler, Loretta Lynn, Bill Monroe, Tracy Nelson and Mother Earth, Dolly Parton, Charley Pride, Del Reeves, Jeannie C. Riley, Tex Ritter, Earl Scruggs. Directed by Robert Elfstrom and David Hoffman.

ELVIS – THAT'S THE WAY IT IS (MGM)
Interviews, studio rehearsals, concert preparation and show numbers from live performances (mostly in Las Vegas) make up this creatively edited account of superstar Elvis Presley, and also features other artists such as Charley Hodge, Glen Hardin, Millie Kirkham, The Sweet Inspirations, The International Hotel Orchestra. Directed by Denis Sanders.

WOODSTOCK (Warner Bros.)
Superbly photographed and inventively edited account of the now legendary rock festival held near Bethel, N.Y., in 1969 and attended by 500,000 people. Raw footage includes interviews and candid coverage with and of the audience, local farmers, the army, the police. Drug sub-culture and anti-Vietnam sentiments well-caught, and perfectly blended with outstanding musical performances. Stunning montage of colours and images, and notable use of creative split-screen, multi-panel and variable-frame techniques. A milestone in rockumentary film making, the artists appearing included Richie Havens, Joan Baez, Crosby, Stills, Nash and Young, The Who, John Sebastien, Joe Cocker, Sha-Na-Na, Country Joe and The Fish, Arlo Guthrie, Santana, Sly and The Family Stone, Jimi Hendrix etc. Directed by Maurice Wadleigh.

GIMME SHELTER (Maysles Films)
Candid footage of the 1969 Rolling Stones American tour, which ended with the fatal stabbing of a black youth by a 'Hell's Angel' at Altmont. Among artists appearing with The Stones were The Jefferson Airplane and Grace Slick, The Flying Burrito Brothers, Ike and Tina Turner. Directed by David and Albert Maysles and Charlotte Zwerin.

GROUPIES (Maron Films)
A revealing but confused exposé, highlighting the drug-taking habits and sexual codes of the teenage girls (and boys) who camp-follow rock musicians – in this case Joe Cocker, Alvin Lee, Dry Creek Road, Terry Reid, Keith Webb, Peter Shelly, Spooky Tooth, Luther Grosvenor, Ten Years After – throughout America. Directed by Robert Dorfman and Peter Nevard.

IT'S YOUR THING (Paramount)
Straight, poorly photographed account of a marathon festival of commercial soul music, held at New York's Yankee Stadium in 1969. Among the performers appearing were Patty Austin, The Edwin Hawkins Singers, Jackie 'Moms' Mabley, Ike and Tina Turner, Brooklyn Bridge etc. Directed by Mike Garguilo.

JOAN – CARRY IT ON (Maron Films)
Folk singer Joan Baez and her non-violent activist husband, David Harris, featured in candid interviews (shot in black and white), preceding his three-year jail sentence for non-cooperation with the Draft Board; Baez, meanwhile, although pregnant, goes on a summer concert tour. Produced and directed by James Coyne, Robert C. Jones and Christopher Knight.

MAD DOGS AND ENGLISHMEN (MGM)
A nationwide American concert tour in 1970 by Joe Cocker and an entourage of 42 musicians, singers, their wives, girlfriends and children. Produced and directed by Pierre Adidge.

1971

PETE SEEGER . . . A SONG AND A STONE
(Theatre Exchange Activities)
A concert at Brandeis University, by the legendary folk singer Pete Seeger, intercut with sequences from TV shows and peace rallies, with Seeger explaining his views on politics, pollution and militarism. Other artists included Johnny Cash, Mike Seeger, Don McClean etc. Directed by Robert Elfstrom.

MEDICINE BALL CARAVAN (Warner Bros.)
A well-photographed chronicle of a cross-country bus junket by 150 youths, including artists B.B. King, Doug Kershaw, Alice Cooper, The Youngbloods, Delaney and Bonnie, Sal Valentino, Stoneground – who, to advertise alternative life-styles, staged small rock concerts along the way. Directed by Francois Reichenbach.

SOUL TO SOUL (Cinema Releasing Corporation)
Santana, Willie Bobo, Roberta Flack, Les McCann, Eddie Harris, The Staple Singers, Voices of East Harlem, Damas Choir, Amoa Azangio, Kumasi Drummers, Wilson Pickett, Ike and Tina Turner performing in rock, jazz and gospel concert held in Ghana in honour of the country's 14th anniversary. Directed by Denis Sanders.

SWEET TORONTO (Pennebaker Productions)
Cinema Verité filmization of selected performances from the 12-hour Toronto Rock 'n' Roll Festival held in September, 1969, where the performers included Bo Diddley, Jerry Lee Lewis, Chuck Berry, Little Richard, The Plastic Ono Band with John Lennon and Yoko Ono etc. Directed by D.A. Pennebaker.

CELEBRATION AT BIG SUR (20th Century-Fox)
Mediocre, and badly photographed, coverage of the 1969 Big Sur Folk Festival, where performers included Joan Baez, David Crosby, Mimi Farina, Joni Mitchell, Greg Reeves, Dallas Taylor, The Struggle Resistance Band etc. No director credited.

1972

THE CONCERT FOR BANGLADESH (20th Century-Fox)
A modest and well-photographed record of George Harrison's Madison Square Garden benefit concert for the Bangladesh refugees, where artists giving their services included Eric Clapton, Bob Dylan, Billy Preston, Leon Russell, Ravi Shankar, Ringo Starr, Badfinger, Jesse Davis, Claudia Linnear. Directed by Saul Swimmer.

FILLMORE (20th Century-Fox)
A nostalgic look at the Fillmore rock concerts from 1965 to 1972, and the final office closure of impresario Bill Graham who created them and spawned the now defunct 'San Francisco' sound. Among the featured artists were Santana, The Grateful Dead, Cold Blood, Hot Tuna, The Rowan Brothers, Quicksilver Messenger Service, The New Riders of the Purple Sage, It's A Beautiful Day. Directed by Richard T. Heffron.

1973

SAVE THE CHILDREN (Paramount)
122-minute record of a black rock show in the summer of 1972 at the Black Exposition in Chicago, sponsored by Operation PUSH. Much of the music interpolated into montages of contemporary black progress and urban living. Among the performers captured on film were The Temptations, The Main Ingredient, Isaac Hayes, Zulema, The Cannonball Adderly Quintet, Sammy Davis Jr. Roberta Flack, Quincy Jones and Nancy Wilson. Directed by Stan Lathan.

JIMI HENDRIX (Warner Bros.)
A homage to Jimi Hendrix who died from an overdose of drugs at the age of 27. Over twenty interviews, as well as footage from live performances at the Woodstock and Monterey Festivals etc., and participation by – among others – Pete Townshend, Eric Clapton, Paul Carusa, Dick Cavett, Al Hendrix, Little Richard, Edie Kramer, Mick Jagger, Jennifer Dean, Alan Douglas and Germaine Greer. Directed by Joe Boyd, John Head and Gary Weis.

LET THE GOOD TIMES ROLL (Columbia/Warner)
A compilation rock 'n' roll concert culled from several 1972 stage shows, as well as newsreel, feature film and television footage from the '50's. Artists included Chuck Berry, Fats Domino, Little Richard, Chubby Checker, Bo Diddley, The Shirelles, The Five Satins, Bill Haley and The Comets, Richard Nader. Directed by Sid Lewin and Robert Abel.

WATTSTAX (Columbia)
A benefit concert in aid of the coloured Californian community of Watts at the Los Angeles Memorial Coliseum. Sociological comment and interviews interpolated with music by black artists of the Stax record label such as Richard Pryor, Isaac Hayes, The Staple Singers, Luther Ingram, Johnny Taylor, The Emotions, Rufus Thomas, Reverend Jesse Jackson, Louise McCord, Debra Manning, Eric Mercury, Ernie Hines, Little Sonny etc. Directed by Mel Stuart.

ELVIS ON TOUR (MGM)
Elvis Presley's 1972 stage act, spliced with interviews, rehearsals, backstage banter and TV footage of the legendary star and his supporting artists. Produced and directed by Pierre Adidge and Robert Abel.

1974

LADIES AND GENTLEMEN, THE ROLLING STONES (Dragon Aire)
A 20-minute segment of film showing an audience filing into an auditorium precedes 15 deafening numbers, plus off-stage footage, culled from the Stones's 1972 American tour. Directed by Rollin' Binzer.

SING SING THANKSGIVING (Varied Directions)
A provocative filmed account of a rock concert held for the inmates of Sing Sing prison in November, 1972. As well as Joan Baez, Mimi Farina, B.B. King, Jimmy Walker, Joe Williams, The Voices of East Harlem, Tito Butler etc., several acts were performed by the prisoners themselves. Directed by David Hoffman and Harry Wiland.

1975

JANIS (Universal)
A slipshod assembly of footage from rock concerts in Woodstock, Monterey, Calgary and London, spliced with interviews, make up this homage to Janis Joplin who died of an overdose of drugs and alcohol in 1970. Directed by Howard Alk and Seaton Findlay.

1976

SALSA (Fania Records Inc.)
An account with additional footage, of a Latin American pop concert at the Yankee Stadium, New York, and part of another concert in San Juan, Puerto Rico. As well as a host of Latin American artists, including Celia Cruz and Jose Feliciano, film clips of Desi Arnaz, Al Jolson and Carmen Miranda were used. Directed by Jerry Masucci and Leon Gast.

VOLUNTEER JAM (Roger Grods Productions)
The Volunteer Jam concert held in October, 1975, at Middle Tennessee University. Backstage footage and a slow motion sequence of Charlie Daniels on horseback. Directed by Stanley Dorfman.

1977

THE GRATEFUL DEAD (Monarch/Noteworthy)
Concert footage and animated sequences, plus nostalgic examination of the West Coat music scene. Technically proficient rockumentary, featuring the veteran rock combo of the title. Jefferson Airplane, Janis Joplin, Quicksilver Messenger Service and Bill Graham also appeared.

1978

THE LAST WALTZ (United Artists)
An outstanding record of the farewell concert given by The Band on Thanksgiving Day, 1976, at Winterland, San Fransisco, after performing together, and as Bob Dylan's backing group, for 16 years. Among the personalities appearing were Rick Danko, Joni Mitchell, Neil Diamond, Emmylou Harris, Muddy Waters, Ringo Starr, Lawrence Ferlinghetti, Martin Scorsese etc. Directed by Martin Scorsese.

1979

THE LAST OF THE BLUE DEVILS (Cinegate)
Story of the music that emerged from Kansas City in the twenties and thirties when the Mid-Western watering-hole became the centre of an intense concentration of nightlife. Artists appearing included: Count Basie and his Orchestra, Bennie Motten and his Orchestra, Joe Turner, Jay McShann, Charlie Parker, The Oklahoma Blue Devils. Directed by Bruce Ricker.

1980

DIVINE MADNESS (Warner Bros.)
Filmed account of Bette Midler's dynamic stage show at the Pasadena Civic Auditorium, also featuring 'The Harlettes' – Jocelyn Brown, Ula Hedwig and Diva Gray; directed by Michael Ritchie. Songs included: *Sugar Me* Tom Waites; *I Shall Be Released* Bob Dylan; *Stay With Me* Jerry Ragovoy, George Weis.

1981

THIS IS ELVIS (Warner Bros.)
Film clips of the real Presley plus dramatic reconstructions of his life and times added up to an extremely suspect semi-biopic of the great Memphis innovator. With David Scott, Paul Boensch III, Johnny Hara. Directed by Malcolm Leo and Andrew Solt.

1982

LET'S SPEND THE NIGHT TOGETHER
(Raindrop Films)
In which three Rolling Stones concerts, given in the United States in 1981, have been edited together. For fans only. The band: Mick Jagger, Keith Richard, Charlie Watts, Ron Woods, Bill Wyman, Ian Stewart, Ian McLagan. Directed by Hal Ashby.

1987

CHUCK BERRY HAIL! HAIL! ROCK 'N' ROLL (Universal)
Two weeks before his sixtieth birthday concert on 16 October, 1986, at the Fox Theatre in St. Louis, a movie crew accompanies Chuck Berry to several locations that played an important part in his career. There are also interviews with Little Richard, Bo Diddley, Jerry Lee Lewis, Roy Orbison, The Everly Brothers and Bruce Springsteen. Terrific overview of the music of an era. Directed by Taylor Hackford.

Song and Music Titles

453

Performers

PERFORMERS

467

Composers and Lyricists

472

Other Creative Personnel